WARMAN'S
ANTIQUES
AND THEIR PRICES

22nd Edition

_____

*The Standard Price Reference for antiques
and collectibles, for collectors, dealers
and professionals in the trade.*

Edited by
Harry L. Rinker

_____

**Completely illustrated
and authenticated**

_____

Warman Publishing Co.,
Willow Grove, PA, 19090

ISBN: 0-911594-13-2
ISSN: 0196-2272
Library of Congress Catalog Card No. 82-643542
Printed in the United States of America

———

Additional copies of this book may be obtained from your bookstore or directly from the publisher, Warman Publishing Co., P.O. Box 1112, Dept. 22, Willow Grove, PA 19090. Enclose $11.95 plus $2.00 for postage and handling. Pennsylvania residents please add 72¢ state sales tax.

EDITORIAL STAFF, 22nd EDITION

HARRY L. RINKER
Editor

ELLEN L. SCHROY
Senior Editor

TERESE J. OSWALD
Associate Editor

STANLEY A. GREENE
Assistant Editor

JOHN AND ALICE AHLFELD, MIKE ANDERTON,
JERRY R. BAKER, DARRYL K. REILLY
Pattern Glass Advisory Board

BOARD OF ADVISORS

John and Alice Ahlfeld
2634 Royal Road
Lancaster, PA 17603
(717) 397-7313
Pattern Glass

Melvin and Barbara
Alpren
14 Carter Rd.
West Orange, NJ 07052
(201) 731-9427
Battersea Enamels;
Fairings and Trinket
Boxes; Russian
Enamels

Alan H. Altman
Golden Spike
Enterprises, Inc.
P. O. Box 422
Williamsville, NY 14221
(716) 689-9074
Railroad Items

Seymour and Violet
Altman
8970 Main St.
Clarence, NY 14031
(716) 634-4488
Buffalo Pottery

Mike Anderton
6619 52 St., NE
Marysville, WA 98270
(206) 334-1902
Pattern Glass

Mary Beth Appert
125 S. Main St.
Quakertown, PA 18951
(215) 538-0976
Belleek

David and Linda Arman
R. D. #1, Box 353A
Woodstock, CT 06281
(203) 928-5838
Staffordshire,
Historical

Susan and Al Bagdade
The Country Peasants
3136 Elder Ct.
Northbrook, IL 60062
(312) 498-1468
Quimper

Jerry R. Baker
P. O. Box 13081
St. Petersburg, FL 33733
(813) 323-5524
Pattern Glass

Phyllis Bess
14535 East 13th St.
Tulsa, OK 74108
(918) 437-7776
Frankoma Pottery

Paul and Paula Brenner
1215 Grand Ave.
Spencer, IA 51301
(712) 262-4113
Napkin Rings, Figural

Lissa L. Bryan-Smith
and Dick Smith
Holiday Antiques
Box 208, R. D. 1
Danville, PA 17821
(717) 275-7796
Christmas Items

Lee and Rally Dennis
The Game Preserve
Spring Road
Peterborough, NH 04458
(603) 924-6710
Games

Craig Dinner
P. O. Box 455
Valley Stream, NY
11582
(516) 825-0145
Doorstops

Robert A. Doyle
Doyle Auctioneers &
Appraisers
R. D. 3, Box 137
Osborn Hill Road
Fishkill, NY 12524
(914) 896-9492
Razors

Regis and Mary Ferson
122 Arden Road
Pittsburgh, PA 15216
(412)563-1964
Milk Glass

Mildred Fishman
37 Canaan Close
New Canaan, CT 06840
(203) 966-0748
*Goss and Crested
Wares*

Doug Flynn and Al
Bolton
Holloway House
P. O. Box 210
Lititz, PA 17543
(717) 627-4567
*British Royalty
Commemoratives*

Ron Fox
Fox-Terry Steins, Inc.
416 Throop St.
N. Babylon, NY 11704
(516) 669-7232
Mettlach, Steins

Walter Glenn
Geode Ltd.
3393 Peachtree Rd.
Atlanta, GA 30326
(404) 261-9346
Frankart

Dan Golden
5375-C Avenida Encinas
Carlsbad, CA 92008-
4362
(619) 438-8383
Telephones

Ted Hake
Hake's Americana &
Collectibles
P. O. Box 1444
York, PA 17405
(717) 848-1333
*Disneyana, Political
Items*

David and Betty Hallam
P. O. Box 175
Monmouth, IL 61462
(309) 734-4933
Old Sleepy Eye

Peg Harrison
Harrison's Antiques
2417 Edgewater Dr.
Orlando, FL 32804
(305) 425-6481
Haviland China

John High
415 E. 52nd St.
New York, NY 10022
(212) 758-1692
Stevengraphs

Alda Horner
Whitehall Shop
1215 E. Franklin St.
Chapel Hill, NC 27514
(919) 942-3179
Linens

Joan Hull
1376 Nevada
Huron, SD 57350
(605) 352-1685
Hull Pottery

David and Sue Irons
Irons Antiques
R. D. #4, Box 101
Northampton, PA 18067
(215) 262-9335
Irons

Judy Knauer
1224 Spring Valley Lane
West Chester, PA 19380
(215) 431-3477
Toothpicks

Glenn M. Kramer
20E Taylor Lane
Fishkill, NY 12524
(914) 896-6390
Musical Instruments

Edward W. Leach
381 Trenton Ave.
Paterson, NJ 07503
(201) 684-5398
Shaving Mugs

Ron Lieberman
The Family Album
R. D. #1, Box 42
Glen Rock, PA 17327
(717) 235-2134
Books, Americana

Elyce Litts
P. O. Box 394
Morris Plains, NJ 07950
(201) 361-4087
Geisha Girl

Elaine J. Luartes
Athena Antiques
100 Beta Drive
Franklin, TN 37064
(615) 377-3442
Jewelry

Clarence and Betty
Maier
The Burmese Cruet
P. O. Box 432
Montgomeryville, PA
18936
(215) 855-5388
*Burmese Glass, Crown
Milano, Royal Flemish*

James S. Maxwell, Jr.
P. O. Box 367
Lampeter, PA 17537
(717) 464-5573
Banks, Mechanical

Joan Collett Oates
5912 Kingsfield Dr.
W. Bloomfield, MI
48322
(313) 661-2335
Phoenix Bird Pattern

Evalene Pulati
National Valentine
Collectors Association
P. O. Box 1404
Santa Ana, CA 92702
Valentines

John D. Querry
R. D. 2, Box 137B
Martinsburg, PA 16662
(814) 793-3185
Gaudy Dutch

Richard and Joan
Randles
From The Cutter's
Wheel
P. O. Box 285
Webster, NY 14580
(716) 671-3760
Cut Glass

Darryl K. Reilly
Dendara's Antiques
P. O. Box 1203
Pepperel, MA 01463
(617) 433-8718
Pattern Glass

Ferill J. Rice
302 Pheasant Run
Kaukauna, WI 54130
(414) 766-9176
Fenton

Julie Rich
Tea Leaf Readings
9720 Whiskey Run
Laurel, MD 20707
(301) 490-7604
*Tea Leaf Ironstone
China*

Connie Rogers
1733 Chase St.
Cincinnati, OH 45223
Willow Ware

Daniel M. Snyder
43 Main St.
Leroy, NY 14482
(716) 768-6470
Salts, Open, Master

Mark Supnick
8524 NW 2nd St.
Coral Springs, FL 33071
(305) 755-3449
Shawnee Pottery

George Theofiles
Miscellaneous Man
Box 1776
New Freedom, PA 17349
(717) 235-4766
Posters

Margaret L. Tyrell
117 North 40th St.
Allentown, PA 18104
(215) 395-9364
Children's Books

Bill Wheeler
The Oarhouse
733 Edgwater Dr.
Dunedin, FL 34698
(813) 733-7447
*Nautical, Scrimshaw,
Whaling*

Kathy Wojciechowski
P. O. Box 230
Peotone, IL 60468
Nippon

INTRODUCTION

"Warman's Is The Key"

Warman's provides the keys needed by auctioneers, collectors, and dealers to open the doors to understanding and dealing with the complexities of the antiques market. A price list is only one of the many keys needed today. **Warman's** 22nd Edition contains many additional keys including histories, reference books, periodicals, collectors' clubs, and museums. Useful buying and collecting hints also are provided.

Warman's has been designed to be your first key to the exciting world of antiques. As you use the keys provided to advance beyond this book in specialized collecting areas, **Warman's** hopes you will remember with fondness where you received your start. When you encounter items outside your area of speciality, remember **Warman's** remains your key to unlocking the information you need, just as it has for over thirty-nine years.

ORGANIZATION

Listings: Objects are listed alphabetically by category, beginning with ABC Plates and ending with Zsolnay Pottery. If you have trouble identifying the category in which your object belongs, use the extensive index in the back of the book. It is designed to guide you to the proper category.

Until the 19th edition, Pattern Glass was listed as a separate section. It is now found alphabetically under the "P's." In addition to relocating Pattern Glass, we have combined our three previous sections [clear, colored, and opalescent] into one alphabetical listing of patterns. The new format gives a clearer and more concise listing of pattern glass and will be much easier to use. More than thirty pattern glass dealers have helped us in redesigning this section.

We have attempted to make the listings descriptive enough so that specific objects can be identified. We also have placed emphasis on those items which are actively being sold in the marketplace. Nevertheless, some harder-to-find objects are included in order to demonstrate the market spread.

Each year as the market changes, we carefully consider which categories to include, which to drop, and which to add. **Warman's** is a direct response to the developing trends in the marketplace. To further help collectors and dealers, **Warman** has published *Warman's Americana & Collectibles*, an excellent source for information and prices on 20th century collectibles and items of nostalgia.

History: Every collector should know something about the history of his object. We have presented a capsule background for each category. In many cases the background contains collecting hints or tips to spot reproductions.

References: Special references are listed for each category to help collectors learn more about their objects. Included are author, title, publisher [if published by a small firm or individual, we have indicated "published by author"], and date of publication or most recent edition.

Finding these books may present a problem. The antiques and collectibles field is blessed with a dedicated core of book dealers who stock these specialized publications. You will find them at flea markets, antiques shows, and advertised in leading publications in the field. Many dealers publish annual or semi-annual catalogs. Ask to be put on their mailing lists. Books go out-of-print quickly, yet many books printed over twenty-five years ago remain the standard work in a field. Used book dealers often can turn up many of these valuable reference materials.

Periodicals: Generally, the newsletter or bulletin of a collectors' club focuses on the specific publication needs within a category. However, there are other publications, not associated with collectors' clubs, of which the collector and dealer should be aware. These are covered under specific categories.

In addition, there are general interest newspapers and magazines which deserve to be brought to our user's attention. These are:

Antique Monthly, P.O. Drawer 2, Tuscaloosa, AL 35402
Antique Review, P. O. Box 538, Worthington, OH 43085
Antique Showcase, Amis Gibbs Publications, Ltd., Canfield, Ontario, Canada, N0A 1C0
Antique Trader Weekly, P. O. Box 1050, Dubuque, IA 52001
Antique Week - Tri-State Trader, P. O. Box 90, Knightstown, IN 46148
Antiques (The Magazine Antiques), 551 Fifth Avenue, New York, NY 10017
Collector News, Box 156, Grundy Center, IA 50638
Hobbies, 1006 S. Michigan Ave., Chicago, IL 60605
Maine Antique Digest, P. O. Box 358, Waldoboro, ME 04572
Southern Antiques, P. O. Box 1550, Lake City, FL 32055
West Coast Peddler, P. O. Box 5134, Whittier, CA 90607

It is impossible to list all the national and regional publications in the antiques and collectibles field. The above is merely a sampling. A check with your local library will bring many other publications to your attention.

Collectors' Clubs: The large number of collectors' clubs adds vitality to the antiques and collectibles fields. Their publications and conventions produce knowledge which often cannot be found anywhere else. Many of these clubs are short-lived; others are so strong that they have regional and local chapters.

Museums: The best way to study a specific field is to see as many documented examples as possible. For this reason, we have listed museums where significant collections in that category are on display. Special attention must be directed to the complex of museums which make up the Smithsonian Institution in Washington, D.C.

Reproductions: Reproductions are a major concern to all collectors and dealers. Most reproductions are unmarked; the newness of their appearance is often the best clue to uncovering them. Specific objects known to be reproduced are marked within the listings with an asterisk (*).

Index: A great deal of effort has been expended to make our index useful. Always try to find the most specific reference. For example, if you have a piece of china, look first for the maker's name and second for the type. The key is to ask the right questions of yourself.

Photographs: You may encounter a piece you cannot identify well enough to use the index. Consult the photographs and marks. If you own the last several editions of **Warman's**, you have assembled a valuable photographic reference to the antiques and collectibles field.

PRICE NOTES

In assigning prices we assume the object is in very good condition. If otherwise, we note this in our description. It would be ideal to suggest that mint, or unused, examples of all objects do exist. The reality is that objects from the past were used, whether they be glass, china, dolls, or toys. Because of this, some normal wear must be expected. In fact, if an object such as furniture does not show wear, its origins may be more suspect than if it does show wear.

Whenever possible, we have tried to provide a broad listing of prices within a category so you have a ''feel'' for the market. We emphasize the middle range of prices within a category, while also listing some objects of high and low value to show the market spread.

We do not use ranges because they tend to confuse rather than help the collector and dealer. How do you determine if your object is at the high or low end of the range? There is a high degree of flexibility in pricing in the antiques field. If you want to set ranges, add or subtract 10% from our prices.

One of the hardest variants with which to deal is the regional fluctuations of prices. Victorian furniture brings widely differing prices in New York, Chicago, New Orleans, or San Francisco. We have tried to strike a balance. Know your region and subject before investing heavily. If the best prices for cameo glass are in Montreal or Toronto, then be prepared to go there if you want to save money or add choice pieces to your collection. Research and patience are key factors to building a collection of merit.

Another factor that affects prices is a sale by a leading dealer or private collector. We have tempered both dealer and auction house figures.

PRICE RESEARCH

Everyone asks—where do we get our prices? They come from many sources.

First, we rely on auctions. Auction houses and auctioneers do not always command the highest prices. If they did, why do so many dealers buy from them?

The key to understanding auction prices is to know when a price is high or low in the range. We think we do this and do it well.

Second, we work closely with dealers. We screen our contacts to make certain they have a full knowledge of the market. Dealers make their living from selling antiques; they cannot afford to have a price guide which is not in touch with the market.

Over thirty antiques magazines, newspapers, and journals come into our office regularly. They are excellent barometers of what is moving and what is not. We don't hesitate to call an advertiser and ask if their listed merchandise sold.

When the editorial staff is doing field work, we identify ourselves. Our conversations with dealers and collectors around the country have enhanced this book. Teams from **Warman's** are in the field at antiques shows, flea markets, and auctions recording prices and taking photographs.

Collectors work closely with us. They are specialists whose devotion to research and accurate information is inspiring. Generally, they are not dealers. Whenever we have asked them for help, they have responded willingly and admirably.

BOARD OF ADVISORS

Our Board of Advisors are specialists, both dealers and collectors, who feel a commitment to accurate information. You'll find their names listed in the front of the book. Several have authored a major reference work on their subject.

Members of the Board of Advisors file lists of prices in their categories for which they are responsible. They help select and often supply the photographs used. If you wish to buy or sell an object in their field of expertise, drop them a note along with an SASE. If time or interest permits, they will respond.

BUYER'S GUIDE, NOT SELLER'S GUIDE

Warman's is designed to be a buyer's guide to what you would have to pay to purchase an object on the open market from a dealer or collector. **It is not a seller's guide to prices.** People frequently make this mistake. In doing so, they deceive themselves. If you have an object listed in this book and wish to sell it to a dealer, you should expect to receive approximately fifty percent (50%) of the listed value. If the object is not anticipated to be resold quickly, expect to receive even less.

A private collector may pay more, perhaps seventy to eighty percent of our list price. Your object will have to be something needed for his or her collection. If you have an extremely rare object or an object of exceptionally high value, these guidelines do not apply.

Examine your piece as objectively as possible. As an antiques appraiser, I spend a great deal of time telling people their treasures are not ''gold'' at all, but items readily available in the marketplace.

In respect to buying and selling, a simple philosophy is that a good purchase occurs when the buyer and seller are happy with the price. Don't look back.

Hindsight has little value in the antiques field. Given time, things tend to balance out.

COMMENTS INVITED

Warman's Antiques and Their Prices continues to be the leader in the antiques and collectibles price guide field because we listen to our readers. Readers are encouraged to send their comments and suggestions to our Editorial Office, P. O. Box 265, Zionsville, PA 18092.

ACKNOWLEDGEMENTS

This edition represents the combined efforts of a dedicated staff, a loyal Board of Advisors, and thoughtful individuals throughout the antiques and collectibles field who shared their knowledge so that the information, listings and prices are as accurate as possible.

The smooth, day to day functioning of the editorial office rests securely on the shoulders of Senior Editor Ellen Schroy. She is truly the glue that holds the place together. Jocelyn Butterer, an associate editor, unfortunately suffered an illness during the year; happily, she is recovering and we wish her well. We miss her enthusiasm.

Brenda Verderosa, an editorial assistant, has moved to Florida with her family and is monitoring the market there as our southern correspondent.

Teresa Oswald joined our staff during the year; her experience and knowledge are valuable ingredients to the research for this edition.

I dare not question the forebearance of my wife, Connie, whose staunch support has seen me through the past seven editions of *Warman's Antiques and Their Prices,* three editions of *Warman's Americana & Collectibles,* and numerous other books. Her encouragement gets me through the necessary details, and her company makes the enjoyable facets even better.

Finally, a general note of thanks to everyone who submitted price lists and letters of information to us, allowed their material to be photographed, and took the time to discuss the antiques business on the telephone and in the field.

Editorial Office   Harry L. Rinker
Warman Publishing Co., Inc.   Editor-in-Chief
P. O. Box 265
Zionsville, PA 18092
March, 1988

STATE OF THE MARKET

The 1987–88 antiques and collectibles market will be remembered as the "Sticker Shock" market. It was the period when prices for objects in the middle and low end of each collecting category began moving upward, adjusting to the ever increasing prices for the "masterpiece" objects at the top. Collecting antiques simply became increasingly more expensive. Examples of price increases were everywhere, from the admission price to an antiques show (several now over $5.00 admission per day) to the higher costs for auction catalogs, books, and periodicals.

During the past year, two dangerous trends appeared. The first is the reliance by many dealers and collectors upon age as the sole determining factor in placing a high value on objects, Have we forgotten that there was a great deal of non-aesthetic junk produced during the eighteenth and nineteenth centuries? Just because an object is old and has survived does not mean it should be worth a fortune. Garbage smells, no matter whether it was made in 1788, 1888, or 1988.

Of far greater concern is the entrance back into the market of the speculative investor. A decade has past since the speculation bubble of the mid-1970s; few seem to remember what happened. Speculators are buying second rate material at top market prices. They have forgotten that the final selling price of any antique and collectible involves profit for someone and that the liquidity of antiques and collectibles should not be taken lightly.

Overall the antiques and collectibles market is calm. Most dealers and serious collectors expect some reaction to the stock market crash of October 1987. No one is certain exactly what it will be. Nothing concrete, either positive or negative, has occurred as of March 1988. As a result, the calm is an uneasy one.

A number of shifts in collecting emphasis have solidified and surfaced during the past year. Increased emphasis on the streamlined modernistic products, heralded at the 1939 New York World's Fair, was evident at all levels. At the moment the field seems to be having trouble labeling the new trend. We cannot define "modernism," "art retro," or "belle epoque" with the same precision as we do "Queen Anne" or "Chippendale." Why not simply call it the "streamlined" era?

Many of us laughed during *The Graduate* when Dustin Hoffman's character was given the magic word, "plastics." The collectors who followed that advice are enjoying the last laugh now. 1950s plastic and other items associated with that decade, from blond kidney tables to poodle skirts, are highly collectible. As the decades of the 1990s approaches, the decade of the the 1950s is distant enough to attract attention.

In fact, we have reached a point where anything predating World War II is rapidly being viewed as an antique rather than a collectible, reflected in great measure by the increased prices being asked for pre-1940 material. Nothing illustrates this more than many traditional antiques dealers showing factory-made furniture from the 1900 to 1940 period. In one such shop, I saw a Queen Anne style highboy from the 1930s priced at well over $4,000.00.

There is a renewed interest in art glass and art pottery, especially in Lalique. However, this should not be interpreted as an Art Nouveau revival. Instead, emphasis is on pieces stressing simplicity of form and modernistic design.

The vast majority of collecting categories in the antiques and collectibles field enjoy a stable pricing structure, i.e., prices do not rise or fall more than five percent from the norm. However, there always are areas gaining and declining in value. You may not agree with my conclusions, but you would be well advised to think seriously about them.

Gaining	*Declining*
American Furniture, Colonial Revival styles	Arts and Crafts Movement
Clocks	Bakelite Jewelry
Chase Brass and Chrome	Base Metals, especially brass and copper items
Children's Books, especially pop-up books	
Fisher Price Toys	Doorstops
Glass, Early American	Hooked Rugs
Judaica	Indian Artifacts
Plastic from the 1940s and 1950s	Perfume and Cologne Bottles
Post-1900 Quilts	
Sewing Items	Samplers
Shaker	Steuben
Silver Plate	Tiles

English and French "container" goods experienced a significant decline in value, especially the bleached pine pieces. Collectors lost interest in stylistic reproductions of the Edwardian era and newly assembled furniture from the twentieth century. On the other hand, quality period furniture remained exceptionally strong. The declining value of the dollar has forced many foreign dealers to stress the retail as opposed to the wholesale side of their business. The flow of English and Continental goods will be reversed. European buyers will come to the United States to buy their country's products and take them back home. This already is happening in the pottery and porcelain areas.

The role of the antique and collectible in the average household decorative environment is shifting. Few individuals are stressing period room settings. Instead, objects are becoming "accent" pieces. As a result, a new value, the "pizzazz" value, has to be considered in determining the price of an object. This value is trendy and stylistic. It is above the object's intrinsic antique or collectible value. When styles shift, this portion of an object's value may decline.

In the last edition I commented on the investigation into pooling practices. In

1987 and 1988 a number of auctioneers, collectors, and dealers pleaded guilty to this practice. Punishment ranged from fines (up to $50,000.00) to jail sentences. The United States Justice Department has made it clear that it intends to continue its investigation. Cracking down on pools is an important first step. Now, if the Justice Department would prosecute the individuals selling reproductions and fakes as period antiques and collectibles, something positive would really be accomplished.

AUCTION HOUSES

The following auction houses cooperated with Warman Publishing Co. by providing catalogs of their auctions and price lists. This effort is most appreciated.

W. Graham Arader III
1000 Boxwood Court
King of Prussia, PA
19406
(215) 825-6570

Ark Antiques
Box 3133
New Haven, CT 06515
(203) 387-3754

Arman Absentee
Auctions
RR 1 Box 353A
Woodstock, CT 06281
(203) 928-5838

Robert F. Batchelder
1 West Butler Avenue
Ambler, PA 19002
(215) 643-1430

Richard A. Bourne Co.,
Inc.
Corporation St.
P. O. Box 141
Hyannis, MA 02647
(617) 775-0797

Butterfield's
1244 Sutter Street
San Francisco, CA
94109
(415) 673-1362

Christie's
502 Park Avenue
New York, NY 10022
(212) 546-1000

Christie's East
219 E. 67th Street
New York, NY 10021
(212) 546-1000

Marvin Cohen Auctions
Box 425, Routes 20 &
22
New Lebanon, NY
12125
(518) 794-7477

Robert A. Doyle
Doyle Auctioneers &
Appraisers
R. D. 3, Box 137
Fishkill, NY 12524
(914) 896-9492

William Doyle Galleries,
Inc.
175 E. 87th Street
New York, NY 10028
(212) 427-2730

Early Auction Co.
123 Main Street
Milford, OH 45150
(513) 831-4833

Fine Arts Co. of
Philadelphia, Inc.
2317 Chestnut Street
Philadelphia, PA 19103
(215) 564-3644

Ron Fox
F. T. S. Inc.
416 Throop Street
N. Babylon, NY 11704
(516) 669-7232

Garth's Auction, Inc.
2690 Stratford Road
P. O. Box 369
Delaware, OH 43015
(614) 362-4771 or 369-
5085

Guerney's
Tuxedo Park, NY 10987
(212) 794-2280

Hake's Americana and
Collectibles
P. O. Box 1444
York, PA 17405
(717) 848-1333

Harris Auction Galleries,
Inc.
873-875 N. Howard
Street
Baltimore, MD 21201
(301) 728-7040

Leslie Hindman, Inc.
215 West Ohio Street
Chicago, IL 60610
(312) 670-0010

Milwaukee Auction
Galleries
4747 West Bradley Road
Milwaukee, WI 53223
(414) 355-5054

Neal Alford Company
4139 Magazine Street
New Orleans, LA 70115
(504) 899-5329

New England Auction
Gallery
Box 8087
East Lynn, MA 01904
(617) 581-5366

Phillips
876 Madison Avenue
New York, NY 10021
(212) 570-4830

Lloyd Ralston Toys
447 Stratfield Road
Fairfield, CT 06432
(203) 366-3399 or 335-
4054

R. Niel & Elaine
Reynolds
Box 133
Waterford, VA 22190
(703) 882-3574

Roan Bros. Auction
Gallery
R.D. 3, Box 118
Cogan Station, PA 17728
(717) 494-0170

Robert W. Skinner Inc.
Bolton Gallery
Route 117
Bolton, MA 01740
(617) 779-5528

Sotheby's
1334 York Avenue
New York, NY 10021
(212) 472-8424

Swann Galleries, Inc.
104 E. 25th Street
New York, NY 10010
(212) 254-4710

Don Treadway
P.O. Box 8924
Cincinnati, OH 45208
(513) 321-6720

Waverlys Auctions
7649 Old Georgetown
Road
Bethesda, MD 20814
(301) 951-0919

Wolf's Auction Gallery
13015 Larchmere Blvd.
Shaker Heights, OH
44120
(216) 231-3888

Woody Auction
Douglass, KS 67039
(316) 746-2694

ABBREVIATIONS

The following are standard abbreviations which we have used throughout this edition of **Warman's**.

C =	century	ls =	low standard
c =	circa	MIB =	mint in box
circ =	circular	mkd =	marked
cov =	cover	MOP =	mother of pearl
d =	diameter or depth	NE =	New England
dec =	decorated	No. =	number
emb =	embossed	opal =	opalescent
ext. =	exterior	orig =	original
FE =	first edition	os =	orig stopper
ftd =	footed	pat =	patent
ground =	background	pcs =	pieces
h =	height	pr =	pair
hp =	hand painted	rect =	rectangular
hs =	high standard	sgd =	signed
imp =	impressed	sngl =	single
int. =	interior	SP =	silver plated
irid =	iridescent	SS =	Sterling silver
IVT =	inverted thumbprint	sq =	square
j =	jewels	w =	width
K =	karat	yg =	yellow gold
l =	length	# =	numbered
litho =	lithograph		

ABC PLATES

History: The majority of early ABC plates were manufactured in England, imported into the United States, and achieved their greatest popularity from 1780 to 1860. Since a formal education was limited in the early 19th century, the ABC plate was a method of educating the poor for a few pennies.

ABC plates are found in glass, pewter, porcelain, pottery, and tin. Porcelain plates range in diameter from 4⅜ to slightly over 9½ inches. The rim usually contains the alphabet and/or numbers; the center features animals, great men, maxims, or nursery rhymes.

Reference: Susan and Al Bagdade, *Warman's English & Continental Pottery & Porcelain, 1st Edition,* Warman Publishing Co., Inc., 1987; Mildred L. and Joseph P. Chalala, *A Collector's Guide to ABC Plates, Mugs and Things.* Pridemark Press, 1980.

Plate, 7¼", brown alphabet, green transfer, marked "Tunstall, England," $55.00.

GLASS

American Flag center, clear	75.00
Clock, 7", blue	35.00
Dog's Head, 6", blue	45.00
Ducks, 6", amber	45.00
Elephant, howdah, 3 figures on howdah waving flag, 6", sgd R & C (Ripley & Co.) on howdah	150.00
Emma, girl's head center, beaded rim, Higbee	85.00
Floral Bouquet with bow, clear	50.00
Garfield, 6", clear	65.00
Hen and Chicks, 6", clear	40.00
Rabbit running, 6" frosted	50.00
Sancho Panza and Dabble, frosted center, clear border	52.50

Santa on Chimney, "Christmas Eve," 6", clear	65.00
Star Medallion, 6", clear	40.00
Stork, carnival	65.00
Stork, frosted, Iowa City	95.00

PORCELAIN OR POTTERY

Aesop's Fables, The Fox and the Grapes, 7¼", transfer, Brownhills Pottery Co, Tunstall, 1875	55.00
American Sports, Baseball, Out on the Third Base, 7⅛", black transfer, Staffordshire	60.00
Baby Bunting and Little Dog Bunch	55.00
Boy, fishing, 6", Staffordshire	35.00
Campbell Kid	50.00
Christmas, snowman, children	55.00
Deaf and Dumb, sign language, 6½", pink transfer, hands making signs of alphabet on inner rim, 2 elegantly dressed cats in center, H. Aynsley & Co., London, England, c1904	150.00
Dog and Bird, 7⅝", black transfer, Staffordshire	60.00
Elephant, fishing, 2 little girls, pink transfer, Staffordshire	85.00
Franklin Maxim	
Dost Thou Love Life, Then Do Not Squander Time, brown transfer, polychrome enameling	67.50
Like Rest Consumes Faster Than Labor While the Used Key is Always Bright	80.00
Goat Herd Boy, horn, dog and goat center, 5", emb border	75.00
Going to Market, chromolithograph, c1840	60.00
Harvest Home, hay wagon, 5½", emb border, J.G. Meakin, c1870	75.00
Men Fighting on Donkeys, 7"	65.00
Nursery Rhyme, 7¼", D.E. McNicol	24.00
Organ Grinder, 8¼", Staffordshire	40.00
Punch and Judy, 7", Ironstone, blue transfer, mkd Allertons, England	75.00
Robinson Crusoe at Work, 7¼", transfer, printed alphabet border, Brownhills Pottery Co., Tunstall, c1875	55.00
Shepherd Boy, horn, dog, goat, 5¼"	75.00
Sly Old Fox	65.00
Stag's Head, 6"	25.00
Washington, 7¼", Staffordshire	90.00
World's Fair, 1893, "Machinery Hall"	85.00
Zebra Hunt, 8", emb border	65.00

TIN

Alphabet, 6½", emb overall	48.00
Animals and bird, 8"	40.00

1

Bear and children border, sea horse center, 8", hp	**25.00**
Cat with yarn, 4"	**35.00**
Children center, alphabet rim, 2"	**65.00**
Girl on swing, 3½"	**40.00**
Hey Diddle Diddle, 8"	**55.00**
Jumbo the Elephant, 6"	**90.00**
Mary had a Little Lamb, 8" d	**90.00**
Victoria and Albert, 5½"	**45.00**

ADAMS ROSE

History: Adams Rose, made c1820–40 by Adams and Son in the Staffordshire district of England, is decorated with brilliant red roses and green leaves on a white ground.

G. Jones and Son, England, made a variant known as "Late Adams Rose." The colors are not as brilliant and the ground is a "dirty" white. It commands less than the price of the early pattern.

Reference: Susan and Al Bagdade, *Warman's English & Continental Pottery & Porcelain, 1st Edition,* Warman Publishing Co., Inc., 1987.

Cup and Saucer, late, 6" d saucer, $75.00.

Bowl	
5½", late	**75.00**
8¾", early	**600.00**
Creamer, late	**95.00**
Cup and Saucer, handleless, late	**65.00**
Cup Plate, 4¼"	**48.00**
Milk Pitcher	
4⅞", c1840	**75.00**
6¾", bulbous, emb	**130.00**
Plate	
7¼", early	**145.00**
7½", late	**35.00**
8½", late	**45.00**

8¾", late	**50.00**
9¼", early	**175.00**
9½", late	**65.00**
Platter, 15", oval, early, c1820	**300.00**
Soup, flange rim, late	**75.00**
Sugar, cov, late	**150.00**
Teapot	
Early	**600.00**
Late	**210.00**
Vegetable Dish, cov, 12⅝", c1850	**500.00**
Wash Bowl and Pitcher, early	**1,000.00**

ADVERTISING

History: Before the days of mass media, advertisers relied on colorful product labels and advertising giveaways to promote their products. Containers were made to appeal to the buyer by the use of stylish lithographs and bright colors. Many of the illustrations used the product in the advertisement so that even an illiterate buyer could identify a product.

Advertisements were put on almost every household object imaginable and were constant reminders to use the product or visit a certain establishment.

References: Jim Cope, *Old Advertising*, Great American Publishing Co., 1980; Ray Klug, *Antique Advertising Encyclopedia*, Vol. 1 (1978) and Vol. 2 (1985), L-W Promotions; Ralph and Terry Kovel, *Kovels' Advertising Collectibles Price List*, Crown Publishers Inc., 1986; Joleen Robison and Kay Sellers, *Advertising Dolls: Identification and Value Guide*, Collector Books, 1980; Robert W. and Harriet Swedberg, *Tins "n" Bins*, Wallace-Homestead, 1985.

Collectors' Clubs: The Ephemera Society of America, 124 Elm Street, Bennington, VT 05021. Dues: $20.00; National Association of Paper and Advertising Collectibles, P. O. Box 500, Mount Joy, PA 17552. Dues: $10.00; Tin Container Collectors Association, 11650 Riverside Drive, North Hollywood, CA 91602. Dues: $20.00.

Additional Listings: See *Warman's Americana & Collectibles* for more examples.

Airplane, Lindy Brand Bread, paper	**10.00**
Ashtray	
Fatima Cigarettes, orig pack of cigarettes, marked "Made in Austria"	**75.00**
Providence Ins. Co., brass	**15.00**
Bank, Log Cabin Syrup, glass	**30.00**
Basket, "Kool-Aid–2 cents" painted on top, picnic type	**35.00**
Blotter	
Mazda, cardboard, full color illus, 3½ x 6", 1912 copyright by General Electric Co, unused	**5.00**
Morton's Salt, full color illus pair of animals headed under ark under torrential rain as salt continues to pour, 4 x 9", c1930, unused	**15.00**

Box, Baby Doll Toilet Soap, 2½ x 4 x 1½", Proctor & Gamble, $10.00.

Bookmark, Cracker Jack, black, white, and tan litho, tin Scotty dec	20.00
Bottle, Jewel Tea Extract	35.00
Brush, Crescent Ice Cream	15.00

Button

Acme Advertising Novelty Co, light green ground, red lettering, globe, 1½", c1900	25.00
Mulford's Septic Shield, arm patch, paper adv reverse, ⅞", c1900	25.00
Weilands Pork Products, multicolored "Willie," blue ground, 1¼", c1930s	15.00

Calendar

Deering Harvesters, 1906, lady seated on farm wall eating cherries, metal band top, 13 x 20"	150.00
Selz Shoes, beautiful lady, red dress, white feather fan, wood frame, 36 x 11½"	135.00
Calendar Plate, 1909, Foran Furniture Co. New London, Conn, calendars on outer rim, bird holding ribbon in beak	55.00
Can, A&P Baking Powder, litho tin, grandmother Ginna, 1800s	100.00

Candy Box

Clark, stork on back	10.00
Powerhouse, picture of boy	20.00
Zagnut	15.00
Candy Pail, Lovell & Kovell, historical scene	350.00

Cigarette Lighter

Dow Oven Cleaner, can shape top	10.00
Zarkin Machines, chrome, black glass	15.00
Cheese Box, Kraft, wood	8.00
Clicker, Pez, U.S. Zone Germany	65.00
Clipboard, Indianapolis Lumber Insurance Agency, metal, 5¢ tablet	15.00
Clock, "Let Us Bake Your Calumet Cake," wall type, calendar, 39" h	675.00
Coffee Grinder, None-Such Mincemeat, tin	135.00

Cookie Cutter, Winnie Winkle, Pillsbury, comic, 1937, boxed	25.00

Crock

Heinz, orig label, "Preserved Red Raspberries"	450.00
Wesson Oil	70.00
Cup and Saucer, Vah Dole's Hot Chocolate, green and purple irid porcelain, c1930, marked "Made in Japan"	15.00
Demitasse Spoon, Log Cabin Syrup	15.00
Dispenser, Gold Medal Products, Cincinnati, pink	60.00

Display, Counter

Pall Mall Herbert Tareyton, wood case, plastic front, black, gold lettering, 10½ x 6 x 9½", orig paper label, "Duranol"	20.00
Vellastic Underwear, oval frame, Art Deco litho, brown stand, shows family in underwear, 10 x 7", orig paper label dated 1918	165.00
Display Dispenser, Clarke's Teaberry Gum, vaseline glass, counter top	80.00
Doll House, Dunham Coconut	300.00

Door Push

Junge's Bread, porcelain over steel, gray lettering, yellow ground, 9 x 4"	30.00
Vicks, porcelain	100.00

Fan

Schlitz Beer, early 1900s	10.00
Wacker Brewing Co, diecut, cardboard, full color illus, 7½ x 9", 1930s	25.00
Flour Sifter, Calumet	15.00
Fly Swatter, Schell's Beer, wood and screen	30.00
Glass, 7-Up, set of 4	40.00
Globe, Mobil Oil Gargoyle, one piece	450.00
Horseshoe, raised "Take Simmons Liver Regulator," 6" h, 6" w	40.00

Jar

National Biscuit Company, emb clear glass, red metal top, 10 x 11"	100.00
Planters Peanut, football shape	185.00

Key Holder

American-Maid Bread, brass, figural, loaf of bread design,	10.00
Dr. Pepper, 1930	5.00
Lamp, John Anderson Co, cast white metal, brass finish, newsboy by street lamp, cigar cutter in base, white globe, 21¾" h	650.00
Lapel Pin, Top-Round Shoes, three cherubs carrying shoes up a ladder to the top of the world, ⅞", c1900	25.00
Letterhead, matching envelope, Pond's Bitters Co.	20.00
Letter Opener, Boyertown Burial Casket Co., dark finish brass, raised illus of a casket on both sides of handle, 10½", early 1900s	25.00
Mannequin, Jordan Marsh Store, Boston, figure of Thomas Jefferson, 50"	

h, 1876 one hundredth anniversary window display 1,350.00
Measuring Cup, Kellogg's, glass, green 15.00
Menu Holder, Borden's Ice Cream, pictures Elsie 50.00

Paperweight, Hotel Griswold Barber Shop, 4 x 2½ x¾", $20.00.

Pill Holder, Phillips Milk of Magnesia, cylinder type, patent date April 15, 1902, belt type 35.00
Playing Cards, Sealy Orthopedic, double deck, mattress shape box 25.00
Punchboard, Planters Cocktail Peanuts, full color peanut can, unused, punching tool still sealed under paper label, 7½ x 8 x ¾" 75.00
Puzzle, Heinz 57 Varieties, diecut, numerals, 1940s juvenile grocery store setting, 10 x 12", orig mailing envelope 50.00
Rolling Pin, Crockery, Sheldahl, Iowa . 150.00

Mirror, The Invincible Junior (vacuum cleaner), celluloid, 1¾ x 2¾", $25.00.

Mirror
  Angelus Marshmallows, oval, pocket type 45.00
  Gilford-Strauss, Chicago 35.00
  KoKo Tulu Chewing Gum, wood frame, beveled glass, white lettering, 11 x 7½" 60.00
  Silverman Bros, Chicago, Wool Commission Merchants, sheep, bright green colored grass, red and black lettering 75.00
Mold, Hershey Chocolate 100.00
Mug
  Hamm's Krug Klub, set of 6, marked "Red Wing" 325.00
  Hire's Root Beer, stoneware, branch handle, ornate 250.00
Needle Holder, Hires Condensed Milk, cardboard, full color illus, 1½ x 2½", 1899 copyright 15.00
Needle Threader, Prudential Insurance 10.00
Notebook, Hunt's Supreme Quality Sliced Lemon Cling Peaches, diecut, can shape, celluloid cov, yellow peaches, blue and gold bowl, bright red ground, 1915 calendar, brass rings 25.00
Paperweight, Libby, McNeil & Libby, Chicago, Canned Meats, figural, steer standing on platform, orig gold paint, 3 x 3¼" 25.00
Pen, Eagle Pencil Co, black wood handle, engraved eagle on nib front, marked in silver "Just for Fun" 5.00
Pencil, Ace Pencil Co, USA, yellow, 62" 100.00

Sign, Buster Brown Health Shoes, reverse painting on glass, framed, 9½ x 9¾", $200.00.

Sign
  Bartle's Beer, round, blue and white 125.00
  Coca-Cola Golf Tournament, cast iron pole 250.00
  Drivers Hardware Store, wood, mus-

tard yellow, red, and black, 33 x 99¾" **200.00**
Fisk Tires, boy with tire **2,000.00**
Portage Rubber Co, tin, Portage tire rolling down a dirt country road, sheep in background, sgd by R.J. Kennedy, 38 x 25½", 3" frame ... **575.00**
National Tobacco Co, emb, 40 x 30" **35.00**
Nu Grape Soda, porcelain on steel, blue lettering, yellow ground **30.00**
Tasty Dixie Milk, neon, 22" **350.00**
The Wadsworth Watch Case Co, tin, factory scene, city and river background, reddish brown frame, 22½ x 28½", sgd Patent Oct. 10, 1905, marked "The H.D. Beach Co. Coshocton, OH" **1,000.00**
T. R. Havana Cigars, tin, cardboard backed, royal blue ground, gold trim and bottom lettering, full color picture of Teddy Roosevelt in center, gold and orange frame, 30 x 20" **450.00**
White Rock Mineral Water, white lettering, blue ground, 4 x 10" **20.00**
Spinner, Gold Dust Washing Powder, celluloid, white, brown, and yellow, two black boys in a washtub filled with soap bubbles, early 1900s **75.00**
Spittoon, Redskin Cut Plug Chewing Tobacco, brass **110.00**
Spool Cabinet, Clark's, two drawer, oak **350.00**
Tape Dispenser, Karo Syrup, porcelain, white **40.00**
Tape Measure, Colgate's Fab, celluloid, 1930s laundry product, inscribed bottom **12.00**
Tart Pan, Parkersburg Iron & Steel Co, WV **15.00**
Thermometer
Hills Brothers Coffee, porcelain **300.00**
Prestone Anti-Freeze, off-white ground, blue square at top, red oval at bottom, white lettering, 35" ... **65.00**
Old Brown Forman's King Whiskey . **250.00**
Tin
Beechnut, litho, five factory scenes, 6 x 12" **45.00**
Blanke's Coffee, 2 lb, dome type canister, woman on horse **150.00**
Frontenag Brand Peanut Butter, red and blue lettering trimmed in gold, white ground, 4 x 3" **35.00**
Half & Half **80.00**
Hancock Old Black Joe Axle Grease, orig contents, picture of Old Black Joe on front and back, cane on either side, 4½ x 3" **45.00**
Jarvina Coffee, black and red lettering, silver trim, red ground, 6 x 4" **35.00**
Monarch Tea **40.00**
Mt. Cross Coffee, 10 lb., litho, re-

cessed lid, bail, marked "Product of Denver, Colo" **85.00**
Pennzoil United Air Lines Motor Oil, pictures air liner, owls, and Liberty Bell **45.00**

Tin, La Espana Chocolates y Dulces, lithographed tin, wood grain ground, 10¼ x 6¾ x 2¼", $65.00.

Rexall Drugs Foot Powder, dome top **25.00**
Universal Buck Powder, pictures black and white Kewpies, "For White & Colored Kids" **75.00**
Tip Tray
Ben Franklin Insurance, Springfield, Ill **25.00**
Hopski Soda, litho, frog pouring drinks **50.00**
Moxie, purple flowers and lady **150.00**
Token, Evans Dairy, Davenport, IA ... **5.00**
Tray
Hamm Brewing Co. **275.00**
H. Miller Liquors, Germantown, PA . **85.00**
Miller High Life, girl sitting on moon . **25.00**
Old Reading Beer, red border, white lettering, blue ground **50.00**
Peerless Ice Cream **85.00**
Umbrella, Buick **35.00**
Watch Fob
Broderick & Bascom Rope Co **45.00**
Keystone Steel and Wire Company, Peoria, Ill, brass, silvered, red porcelain bale of wire fence with three columns numbered 1-2-3 superimposed on front **95.00**
Paul Revere Insurance **15.00**
Whistle
Buster Brown Shoes, Buster holding shoe, "First Because Of The Last," 1¼", c1910 .... **75.00**
Red Goose Shoes, yellow and red litho, 1½", 1930s **15.00**
The Farmer's Agency, wood, carved **15.00**

ADVERTISING TRADE CARDS

History: Advertising trade cards are small, thin cardboard cards made to advertise the merits of a product and usually bear the name and address of a merchant.

With the invention of lithography, colorful trade cards became a popular advertising media in the late 19th and early 20th centuries. They were made especially to appeal to children. Young and old alike collected and treasured them in albums and scrapbooks. Very few are dated; 1880 to 1893 were the prime years for trade cards; 1810 to 1850 cards can be found, but rarely. By 1900 trade cards were rapidly lossing their popularity. By 1910 they had all but vanished.

References: Kit Barry, *The Advertising Trade Card*, Book 1, Iris Publishing Co., 1981; John and Margaret Kaduck, *Advertising Trade Cards*, privately printed; Jim and Cathy McQuary, *Collectors Guide To Advertising Cards*, L-W Promotions, 1975; Murray Card (International) Ltd., *Catalogue of Cigarette & Other Trade Cards 5th Edition*, 1983.

Periodical: *Trade Card Journal*, 86 High Street, Brattleboro, VT 05301. Quarterly. Subscription: $18.00.

Additional Listings: See *Warman's Americana & Collectibles* for more examples.

Stove Polish, Dixon's Stove Polish, Dixon Crucible Co., Jersey City, NJ, multicolored, printed by Major & Knapp, NY, $7.50.

CLOTHING

Ball's Health Preserving Corsets, woman wearing corset stands at table, guarantee unfolds onto floor, adv on back, Shober & Carqueville, Chicago, 3¼ x 4⅝″ **4.00**
Bonner & Co, NYC, ext. and int. views of store, adv on back for clothing department with directions for ordering by mail, Sackett, Wilhelms & Betzig, NY, 5¾ x 3⅝″ **7.50**
Celluloid Waterproof Collars, Cuffs, and Shirt Bosoms, Oriental dressed child smoking pipe, dealer's name on back, 2⅞ x 4¾″ **3.00**
Duplex Corset, The Secret Out At Last/ Why Mrs. Brown Has Such A Perfect Figure, adv on back, c1890, 3½ x 5½″   **10.00**
Kline & Bros, Hatter, Allentown, PA, man before mirror trying on derby, Ketterlinus, Philadephia, 2¾ x 4¼″ **2.50**

COFFEE

Flint's Ground Golden Rio Coffee, white vase, open pink rose, foliage, pink rose bud, grapes, adv on back **2.00**
Great Atlantic & Pacific Tea Company, black landlord and renter discussing A & P teas and coffees, adv on back, 1884, 8 x 9″ **35.00**
McLaughlin's XXXX Coffee, jungle scene, brown bear fighting lion **5.00**

FARM MACHINERY

Columbus Buggy Co, mechanical, horse and buggy, wheels turn **15.00**
DeLaval Cream Separators, diecut, litho, Jersey cow, adv on back, c1900, 3 x 5″ **25.00**
Eclipse Halter, multicolored, tethered black and white cow in stall, adv on back for Montrose, PA harness dealer, 1884, 3x 5″ **5.00**
Wm. Deering & Company, Agricultural Equipment Manufacturer, two young girls and dog transform into sockets of skull, adv on back, c1890, 4 x 6½″   **20.00**

FOOD

American Breakfast Cereals, multicolored, hummingbird seated on wheat shafts, ears of corn in background, adv on back, c1880, 3½ x 5¾″ **6.00**
Anheuser Busch, Christopher Columbus bust, girl with flag, large beer cask, Columbian Expo **18.00**
Calumet Baking Powder Co, young boy in soldier suit saluting photograph of soldier, mother in pink gown, infant in white wicker basket, 1918 . . . .   **4.00**
Hire's Root Beer, diecut, boy holding glass standing in front of bicycle, c1897, 3 x 5″ **15.00**
Jell-O Ice Cream Powder, blonde girl serving older lady molded ice cream

with strawberries, directions on reverse 3.00

Mellin's Food, diecut of baby in high chair, white dress, pink bow, adv on back, c1915, 4 x 5½" 8.00

Sanford's Ginger, black girl rocking baby 75.00

Windisch-Mulhauser Brewing Co, Cincinnati, mechanical, rotating fortune telling wheel, 4½ x 7" 35.00

Woolson Spice co, multicolored, Christmas scene with Santa carrying large sack over shoulder, title The Woolson Spice Co. Wishes You A Merry Christmas and A Happy New Year, adv on back for Lion Coffee in black and white, 5" sq 45.00

MEDICINE

Brown's Iron Bitters, Knapp, c1891, hold to the light type 8.00

Dr. Wm. Hall's Balsam For The Lungs, diecut, young girl on ladder with dog at feet, adv on back, 1883, 4 x 14" . 20.00

Dr. Seth Arnold's Cough Killer, girl holding puppy, "It Works Like Magic" ... 5.00

German Corn Remover, man dancing, c1890, 3" sq closed, 3 x 5" open ... 10.00

Henry's Carbolic Salve, Alphonso gaining Imogene's favors, c1890, 3" sq closed, 3 x 5" open 10.00

Lutted's Cough Drops, man and woman snowshoeing, Gies 5.00

Kendall's Spavin Cure, black jockey and race horse, testimonials on back, c1890, 4 x 6" 8.00

Mrs. Dinsmore's Cough & Croup Balsam, man sitting at desk, shadow of a fox, black and white, Bufford 4.00

Warner's Safe Yeast, woman before window, logo at right, factory in shield cut at bottom left, title "Up With The Sun," Mensing & Stecher, NY, 3⅞ x 5½" 7.50

Williams' Blood Purifier, pictures woman sitting in a chair before taking, and woman sweeping room after taking, black on white 5.00

MISCELLANEOUS

Austens Forest Flower Cologne, Oswego, NY, multicolored, diecut, young boy and girl picking flowers, adv on back for cologne and Oswego Bitters, 7 x 10" 45.00

Forepaugh Wild West Show, mulitcolored, scenes of Battle Of The Little Big Horn/Death Of Custer, adv on back, c1890, 4 x 5" 20.00

Frank Miller & Sons, diecut, shoe

shape, woman and children in shoe, "Will Not Injure The Finest Leather" 10.00

Lehigh Lumber Scale, cello, double faced, mechanical, inner spinner wheels to measure lumber and proportions for mixing cement and concrete, c1930, 2½ x 4½" 20.00

National Cash Register, mechanical .. 45.00

Solon Palmer Perfumer, New York, diecut, paint pallet shape, side view bust of a young girl, flowers 6.00

Schubert Piano Co, mechanical, when card is opened woman's arms drop to piano, patented 1892, 1898 .... 10.00

SOAP AND CLEANERS

Babbitt's Soap, colonial man offers bar of soap to lady, "1776 Powder," Hatch Litho Co, NY, adv on back, 6⅛ x 4" . 5.00

Bell Soap, white buffalo pulling children in soap box, adv on back 4.00

Pears' Soap, child in tin basin reaching for soap, title "He Won't Be Happy, Till He Gets It," 4¾ x 4¼" 10.00

Thread, Clark's O.N.T. Cotton Thread, multicolored, $2.50.

THREAD AND SEWING

Clark's Mile-End, goose pulling cart, spools of thread are wheels, Donaldson 5.00

James Chadwick & Bros, girl sitting on spool of thread holding a small chalkboard, reverse looks like a school chalk board, Stahl & Jaeger, 1887 .. 7.00

New Home Sewing Machine Co, multicolored, diecut, mother holding bouquet of flowers with daughter and doll seated next to sewing machine, c1890, 7 x 9" 20.00

TOBACCO

Fragrant Vanity Fair Cigarettes, multi-colored, young girl in bonnet, blank back, c1882 .... 4.00
Mail Pouch, oval cut out on front opens to show baby slipping hand under diaper, title Just Found His Mail Pouch, adv on back, 1938, 3½ x 5" 15.00

TRANSPORTATION

Frank Matthews Sale & Exchange Stable, NYC, blue, white, and black, carriage with two horses, c1840 .... 25.00
Pittsburgh Locomotive Works, three trains, steel engraving, Western Bank Note Co, Chicago, 1884 .... 25.00
Ryders Excursion, Thompsonville to Rockaway Beach, shows paddlewheel, 1881 .... 20.00

AGATA GLASS

History: Agata glass was invented in 1887 by Joseph Locke of the New England Glass Company, Cambridge, Massachusetts.

Agata glass was produced by using a piece of peachblow glass, coating it with metallic stain, spattering the surface with alcohol, and firing. The result was a high gloss, mottled appearance of oil droplets floating on a watery surface. Shading usually ranged from opaque pink to dark rose. Pieces are known in a pastel opaque green. A few pieces have been found in a satin finish.

Fingerbowl, 5¼" d, 2⅝" h, ruffled top edge, raspberry to creamy pink with all over gold oily mottling, blue mottling highlights, $1,250.00.

Bowl, 5⅜" d, crimped rim 600.00
Celery Vase, 6½" h, scalloped rim ... 1,300.00
Creamer 1,200.00
Finger Bowl, 5¼" d, 2⅝" h, crushed raspberry shading to creamy pink, all over gold mottling with bits of blue mottling 1,250.00
Juice Glass, 3¾" h 825.00

Pitcher, 6⅜" h, crimped rim 1,650.00
Spooner, 4½" h, green opaque, gold band and mottling 650.00
Toothpick, 2¾", cylindrical 550.00
Tumbler, 3¾" h, wild rose color fading to cream at base, profuse mottling . 545.00
Vase, 4½" h, sq, pinched sides, ruffled 4 scalloped rim 550.00
Whiskey Taster, 2⅝" 575.00

AMBERINA GLASS

History: Joseph Locke developed Amberina glass in 1883 for the New England Glass Works. "Amberina," a trade name, describes a transparent glass which shades from deep ruby to amber color. It was made by adding powdered gold to the ingredients for an amber glass batch. A portion of the glass was reheated later to produce the shading effect. Usually it was the bottom which was reheated to form the deep red; however, reverse examples have been found.

Most early Amberina is of flint quality glass, blown or pattern molded. Patterns include Diamond Quilted, Daisy and Button, Venetian Diamond, Diamond and Star, and Thumbprint.

In addition to the New England Glass Works, the Mt. Washington Glass Company of New Bedford, Massachusetts, copied the glass in the 1880s and sold it at first under the Amberina trade name and later as "Rose Amber." It is difficult to distinguish pieces from these two New England factories. Boston and Sandwich Glass Works never produced the glass.

Amberina glass also was made in the 1890s by several Midwest factories, among which was Hobbs, Brockunier & Co. Trade names included "Ruby Amber Ware" and "Watermelon." The Midwest glass shaded from cranberry to amber and resulted from a thin flashing of cranberry applied to the reheated portion. This created a sharp demarkation between the two colors. This less expensive version caused the death knell for the New England variety.

In 1884 Edward D. Libbey was assigned the trade name "Amberina" by the New England Glass Works. Production occured in 1900, but ceased shortly thereafter. In the 1920s Edward Libbey renewed production at his Toledo, Ohio, plant for a short period. The glass was of high quality. Amberina from this era is marked "Libbey" in script on the pontil.

Reproduction Alert: Reproductions abound.

NEW ENGLAND

Bowl
5¾" h, 10" d, IVT, 3 applied amber feet, 3 way top, fancy amber ap-

plied edging, heavy gold flowers and leaves dec 400.00
7", bulbous, 4 feet, blown, melon ribbed 325.00
9" sq, berry, Daisy & Button 230.00
Butter Tub, cov, Daisy & Button, amberina, cov lid has flakes 475.00

Tumbler, 3⅞" h, vertical leaf-stem pattern, possibly European, $125.00.

Celery
5¾", scalloped sq top, pinched paneled sides 120.00
6½", scalloped rim, Venetian Diamond 425.00
7", scalloped top, DQ 375.00
Champagne, 4" hollow stem 200.00
Cruet
6", amber stopper, applied amber handle 200.00
6¾", 3" d, amber cut faceted orig stopper, amber applied handle ... 225.00
Curtain Tiebacks, pr, orig shanks 150.00
Cuspidor, 9 x 5", hourglass shape, ruffled rim, Swirl, gold trim 375.00
Finger Bowl, 5½", ruffled rim, slightly paneled 125.00
Ice Cream Plate, 5⅝" sq, Daisy & Button 110.00
Lemonade Glass, 5¼", swirled, gold dec, applied handle 225.00
Parfait, 6½", ftd, swirled, gold leaf and bud dec 275.00
Pickle Jar
5½", pewter cov, wavy lines and thumbprints, silver and gold bowl of fruit dec 400.00
6¾", pewter cov, IVT, enameled floral dec, Mt. Washington 225.00
Pitcher
5¾", bulbous, IVT, applied amber reeded handle, Mt. Washington .. 160.00
8½", triangular top, IVT, amber

reeded applied handle, Mt. Washington 225.00
Punch Cup, DQ, applied reeded handle, Libbey 100.00
Ramekin' underplate, 2¼" h, 4¼" d, slightly ribbed, New England Glass Works 200.00
Salt Shaker, 3½", baby IVT, enamel floral dec, Mt. Washington 165.00
Spoon Holder, 5", pinched scalloped top, DQ 135.00
Syrup, orig pewter top, IVT, New England Glass Works 325.00
Toothpick
2½", baby DQ, New England Glass Co. label, Pat July 24, 1881 .... 375.00
2¾", ftd, Daisy & Button 250.00
Barrel Shape, straight collar, baby DQ 225.00
Candy ribbon pleated top 250.00
Tumbler, Venetian Diamond, New England Glass Works 90.00
Vase
5⅛", lily, orig Libbey label 325.00
5¾", fold over rim, IVT, 5 applied feet, Mt. Washington 125.00
6", trumpet 250.00
Whiskey Glass, 2½", DQ 120.00
Wine, 4¾" h, ribbed, c1895 .... 150.00

MID-WESTERN

Bowl, 4½" sq, Hobnail 120.00
Carafe, 7⅛", IVT, reversed color, swirled neck 150.00
Celery, 16", Inverted Coinspot 65.00
Creamer, 4½", Hobnail, clear reeded handle 175.00
Cruet, 6", IVT, orig amber stopper ... 225.00
Dish, 5" sq, Daisy & Button 120.00
Lamp, hand, 10¾" h overall, 5" base, Baby Hobnail, 6 applied shell feet, 5 amber leaf-like extensions rising to middle of lamp, applied amber branch handle 475.00
Mug, IVT, enameled flowers 95.00
Pitcher
6½", Coin Spot Opalescent 220.00
6¾", Hobnail, Hobbs, Brockunier & Co. 165.00
7", 5½" d, bulbous, round mouth, IVT, applied amber handle 175.00
7⅝", bulbous crackle, amber reeded applied handle 175.00
Punch Cup, DQ, applied reeded handle 85.00
Sauce Dish, 5½" sq, Daisy & Button, Hobbs, Brockunier & Co 200.00
Toothpick, 2¼", cylindrical, baby IVT, floral dec 175.00
Tumble-Up, 7" h, 4⅛" d, Optic on carafe and tumbler 195.00
Vase, 5½" h, 4⅛" d, bulbous, IVT, applied amber leaf feet 145.00

AMBERINA GLASS—PLATED

History: The New England Glass Company, Cambridge, Massachusetts, first made Plated Amberina in 1886; Edward Libbey patented the process for the company in 1889.

Plated Amberina was made by taking a gather of chartreuse or cream opalescent glass, dipping it in Amberina and working the two, often utilizing a mold. The finished product had a deep amber to deep ruby red shading, a fiery opalescent lining, and often vertical ribbing for enhancement. Designs ranged from simple forms to complex pieces with collars, feet, gilding, and etching.

A cased Wheeling glass of similar appearance had an opaque white lining, but is not opalescent and the body is not ribbed.

Vase, bulbous base, ribbed motif, $2,500.00.

Bowl, 5¼", ruffled rim, cream int.	1,900.00
Celery	2,600.00
Cruet, 6¾" h, faceted amber stopper .	3,200.00
Parfait, applied amber handle, c1886 .	1,250.00
Pitcher, milk, applied amber handle, orig "Aurora" label	7,000.00
Punch Cup, vertical ribs, applied handle	1,500.00
Salt Shaker, orig top	1,000.00
Syrup Pitcher, orig top, applied handle	5,500.00
Tumbler, 3¾", vertical ribs	2,250.00
Vase, 9¾", lily shape	5,500.00

AMPHORA

History: The Amphora Porcelain Works was one of several pottery companies located in the Teplitz-Turn region of Bohemia in the late 19th and early 20th centuries. It is best known for art pottery, especially Art Nouveau and Art Deco pieces.

Several markings were used, including the name and location of the pottery and the Imperial mark which included a crown. Prior to WWI Bohemia was part of the Austro-Hungarian Empire so the word "Austria" may appear as part of the mark; after WWI the word "Czechoslovakia" may be part of the mark.

Reference: Susan and Al Bagdade, *Warman's English & Continental Pottery & Porcelain, 1st Edition,* Warman Publishing Co., Inc., 1987.

Additional Listings: Teplitz.

Basket
    7 x 11", floral and cupid dec, sgd "Amphora" with crown **200.00**
    9 x 8", cobalt, reserves of portraits, buildings, and steeples **175.00**
Bowl
    2¾ x 3¾", matte ground, enamel sailboat **50.00**
    9 x 8", four handles, gray, enameled poppies, sgd **275.00**
Ewer, 9½", handles, spout, oval reserve of gladiator **125.00**
Figurine
    8", girl selling roses, mkd "Amphora-Teplitz" **150.00**

Figurine, Arab warrior and horse, 10" h, oval base impressed "8251" over "38," Amphora Teplitz, $425.00.

    10 x 5", lion stalking over rocky cliff formation **275.00**
    12", full figured lady holding bowl . . **400.00**
    19½", woman holding a child, polychrome, black oval base **350.00**
Rose Bowl, 4¾", enamel poppies dec, pebble finish **100.00**
Vase
    5½", Art Deco bird **150.00**
    6¾ x 4", satin tan ground, parrots and

flowers dec, glossy navy bands top and bottom, small handles, mkd, sgd "Campina" **165.00**

7", beige with purple and red gooseberries, sgd **150.00**

7", four handles, yellow roses **150.00**

8½", bulbous, long neck, ivory crackle glaze, oxblood streaks **200.00**

9¼ x 6¼", satin gray ground, glossy navy top bands, raised navy dots with big multicolored flowers around bands, Deco style, mkd . . **175.00**

10½", stylized polychrome bird **150.00**

11", four handles, enamel dec, stamped Amphora **300.00**

11½", stylized floral dec, polychrome, sgd "Amphora, Austria" **215.00**

17", shouldered ovoid, painted floral sprigs and buds, gilt molded and stippled ground, imp "Amphora 122," orig paper label **275.00**

ARCHITECTURAL ELEMENTS

History: Architectural elements are those items which have been removed or salvaged from buildings, ships, or gardens. Many are hand crafted. Frequently they are carved in stone or exotic woods. Part of their desirability is due to the fact that it would be almost impossible to duplicate the items today.

The current trend of preservation and recycling architectural elements has lead to the establishment and growth of organized salvage operations who specialize in removal and resale of elements. Special auctions are now held to sell architectural elements from churches, mansions, office buildings, etc. Today's decorators often design an entire room around one architectural element, such as a Victorian marble bar or mural, or use several as key accent pieces.

Additional Listings: Stained Glass.

Aviary, 60 x 144", iron and wirework, faceted onion dome top, rect vertical cage, arched sides, radiating spandrels, painted white, French **4,500.00**

Baluster, 18½", walnut and inlaid ivory, late Georgian, early 19th C **100.00**

Barber Pole, 77" h, turned wood, worn red, white, and blue paint, repainted finial **475.00**

Birdbath

28½ x 41", cast iron, figural, three putto, one seated on dolphin, lobed circular basin, raised circular base, painted red, French **1,500.00**

43 x 84", cast iron, figural, two sections, putto with upraised arms supporting shell, octagonal basin on acanthus and cabochon cast baluster standard, painted green, inscribed "Salin Fondeur" **3,500.00**

Bracket, 21 x 25", cast iron, scrolled foliage dec, worn black paint, set of 4 **520.00**

Capital, 13½ x 12", white marble, carved scrolls above acanthus panels, weathered, Roman style . . **125.00**

Cistern, 21", lead, inswept lobed trefoil form, relief dec of swirling foliage and flowers, English, c1815, pr **875.00**

Conservatory Gazebo, 92" h, rattan, semicircular latticed domed top, four supports, circular base inset with woven rush seat platform, Chinese style **500.00**

Corbel, 16 x 8", polychromed wood, three cherub faces, gilt, brown and flesh tones, carved brown painted scrollwork, Spanish Baroque style, 19th C **500.00**

Door

24 x 98", bi-fold, pine, paneled, double hinges, French, pr **275.00**

70 x 112", walnut, rect panels carved with three registers of trapezoidal, scrolling strapwork and star motif, ivory inlay, Near East, 17th C, pr . **6,000.00**

Doorway

64 x 93", interior, pine, four paneled pilasters, leaf tip and beaded capitals, matching cornices, Greek Revival, Washington Sq area, New York City, c1830, pr **1,565.00**

82½ x 128", exterior, pine, pitched projecting cornice with dentil molding and carving, mullioned and glazed fan light, fluted pilasters with rosettes, painted, Federal, Maryland, c1800, snapshots of door in orig location and 1928 measured drawing **12,650.00**

126", exterior, pine, pitched projected cornice, fan light with incised dec, reeded pilasters, painted, Federal, Trenton, NJ, c1800, 1928 measured drawing **6,000.00**

126½" h, exterior, pine, pitched projected cornice with dentil molding, arched fan light, molded sides, carved fluted pilasters, Federal, Bristol, RI, c1800, 1930 measured drawing **10,000.00**

Fanlight, 52 x 22", hinged, wooden fan shaped frame, mullioned glazed panels, beaded swags dec, Federal, New England, c1810 . . . . **3,200.00**

Fencing, 28" h, 64 linear feet, 18 sections, two gates, bronze, open work rect panel quartered and cast with scrolled acanthus leaves, vacant cartouche on gates, molded plinth base, dark green-brown patina, late 19th C **3,575.00**

Fire Board, 34½ x 38¾″, pine, orig bird's eye and curly maple imitation graining, colored striping, beaded edge tongue and groove boards, batten back **100.00**

Fireplace, 40¾ x 39¼″, brown marble, shaped shelf and apron, oval central cartouche, angled fluted stiles, orig brickwork, Napoleon III, c1870 . . . . **1,320.00**

Fountain, 33 x 63″, metal, two graduated basins cast with shells and repousse, triform standard cast with three herons, circular base, painted . **1,450.00**

Garden Bench
48″ l, cast iron, fern back, pierced seat, splayed legs, late 19th C . . . **500.00**

52″ x 18″, composition, curved, ovolo molded edges, lyre form double console end standards **450.00**

58″, cast iron, reeded scroll ends, grotesque masks, animal leg form supports, painted, Regency **400.00**

74″, metal, arched back, hexagonal lattice work feet, painted green, Gothic Revival **825.00**

Garden Figure
15″ l, composition stone, cat, crouching position, head tilted **65.00**

21½″, lead, seated hound, face raised **450.00**

23″, terra cotta, dogs, standing stance, c1900, pr **500.00**

60″, bronze, cranes, long slender legs, one with head raised, other preening, brown patina, pr **2,750.00**

Gate
34¾ x 82½″, wrought iron, arched, tall tree with sprays of leafy branches, flowers, and tendrils, Continental, 19th C **700.00**

39 x 82″ door, 24 x 69″ side panel, gilt bronze mounted wrought iron, tabular central section, reeded frame, stylized palmette finial, gilt bronze central figure of Diana and deer amid lacy foliage, stylized flowers, conforming rect side panels, painted gray, designed by Edgar Brandt, c1925 . . . . **80,000.00**

68 x 70″, double, wrought iron, center urn on each panel, parcel gilt dec, Neoclassical, Continental **2,750.00**

Gatepost Finial
17½″, stone, cannon ball, coved socles, sq base, 19th C, pr **450.00**

21″, composition, bud form, faceted inverted baluster **115.00**

Grill, 22 x 33¾″, cast and wrought iron, rect frame, classical detail, rayed spears **100.00**

Hardware
Hinges, 41½″ l, wrought iron, strap, pr **20.00**

Latch, wrought iron, thumb latch type **85.00**

Lock Plate, 23½ x 10″, hammered brass, Art Nouveau, c1900, pr . . . **175.00**

Mail Box
29 x 70″, bronze, architectural form, cast medallions and foliate borders, slightly arched pediments, paneled sides, labeled "U. S. Mail, Cutler Manufacturing Company, Rochester, NY" **800.00**

44″ h, painted metal, pagoda form, front and sides molded in relief of equestrian postmen, foliage cast baluster pedestal, rect base, painted dark green, Victorian **675.00**

Mantel
58¾ x 39″, gray veined white marble, rect shelf, plain frieze, molded jambs with gilt bronze ribbon tied husk pendants, Neoclassical style **1,000.00**

59 x 42¼″, veined white marble, serpentine shelf, molded edge, scalloped front, gilt bronze shell flanked by acanthus scrolls, and floral sprigs, scrolled jambs mounted with floral sprig pendants, Louis XV style, c1900 . . . . **6,500.00**

68¼ x 57¾″, poplar, molded and circle details, old white paint, Federal **325.00**

75½ x 58″, black veined marble, rect top, two carved Ionic capitals, columnar supports, Empire, New York, c1830 . . . . **2,225.00**

78½ x 56″, pine, molded rect top, frieze dec with central allegorical figures, garlands, and urns, twisted ribbons on pilasters, inset marbleized wooden panels, painted, Federal, Boston, MA, c1800 . . . . **4,300.00**

Niche, 41 x 92″, polychrome and parcel gilt, arched shell carved opening flanked by disengaged columns supporting paneled entablature, applied drapery swags, semicircular cresting, vacant cartouche, Italian Baroque, 18th C **3,000.00**

Pedestal
8½ x 58½″, simulated porphyry, Doric, raised sq plinth, pr **635.00**

24″, composition, stone, paneled sq shaft, sq base **225.00**

28½″, composition stone, baluster form, 19th C **150.00**

Planter, 66 x 32″, wirework, looped sides over diamond braced ends, tier supporting three divisions, French, 19th C **600.00**

Screen Door, 32 x 81½″, wood, rustic, relief carved leaf, flower, and geometric designs on stiles and rails . . **50.00**

Sun Dial, 12″, bronze, composition

stone pedestal, inscribed "Thomas Grice 1705," **200.00**
Trough, 18″ sq, stone, central drain, York **275.00**
Urn
17 x 22¼″, cast iron, circular thumb grooved rim, fluted and lobed tapering body, stepped plinth base, Neoclassical, Continental, pr **600.00**
19″, composition, terra cotta finish, circular, leaf molded everted rim, lobed body, sq base, Neoclassical, pr **250.00**
19 x 21″, terra cotta, lobed lower section, coved socle, sq base, 19th C **225.00**
Window, 39 x 66″, oak, three rect sashes, middle hinged, diamond shaped leaded glass, oak reinforcing rods, 17th C style, 1924 .... **100.00**
Window Basket, 36″, wrought iron, rect, repeating alternating flowerheads and tulips, Victorian **250.00**

ART DECO

History: The Art Deco period was named for an exhibition, "L'Exposition Internationale des Arts Decoratifs," held in Paris in 1927. It is a later period than Art Nouveau, but sometimes the two styles overlap since they were closely related in time.

Art Deco designs are angular and of simple lines. This was the period of skyscrapers, movie idols, and the cubists works of Picasso and Legras. It was used for every conceivable object being produced in the 1920s and 1930s, including ceramics, furniture, glass, and metals, not only in Europe, but in America as well.

References: Victor Arwas, *Glass: Art Nouveau To Art Deco*, Rizzoli, 1977; Lillian Baker, *Art Nouveau & Art Deco Jewelry: An Identification & Value Guide*, Collector Books, 1981; Bryan Catley, *Art Deco And Other Figures*, Antique Collectors' Club; Katherine Morrison McClinton, *Art Deco: A Guide For Collectors*, reprint, Clarkson N. Potter, 1986.

Additional Listings: Furniture and Jewelry. Also check glass, pottery, and metal categories.

Ashtray, 4″ d, three rearing malachite green horses form legs, heavy glass dish, Czechoslovakian **150.00**
Biscuit Jar, 6 x 5⅜″, pottery, nasturtium pattern, orange and yellow flowers, green leaves, brown spatter trim, yellow and orange bands on lid, orig wicker handle, marked "Clarice Cliff Bizarre" **275.00**
Bookends, metal, bronze finish, figural, race horse and jockey, pr **75.00**
Bowl, Ziggaurat handles, Cafe Au Lait semi-gloss glaze, chocolate brown rim **50.00**

Planter, 4½ x 8¼ x 10″, pale green, drilled as a lamp base, $95.00.

Candelabras, 28″, twelve light, gilt bronze, each surmounted by exotic woman holding orbs in each hand, polygonal base, masks supporting candle arms, pr **1,500.00**
Cigarette Case, 3¼″, cushioned rect, monogrammed, shagreen, French, c1925 .... **125.00**
Clock, 60″, composition lighted face, alabaster sides and back, zodiac dec, reticulated wrought iron base, French, c1925 .... **2,800.00**
Cologne Bottle, acid treated glass, enameled cobalt blue and yellow stylized flowers, large mushroom stopper **175.00**
Compact
2¼″, octagonal, monogrammed, silver, green and gold enamel, brass scalework and fleur-de-lis, beveled mirror, Austrian, c1925 .... **100.00**
2½″, rect, monogrammed, shagreen, beveled mirror, divided compartment, jade bead and jet strap, French, 1925 .... **175.00**
Doorstop, 7 x 9″, bronze, woman, standing, holding out skirt of clinging gown **150.00**
Figure
9½″, bisque, harem dancer, ivory, gold trim, artist sgd **125.00**
9¾″, bronze, nude astride snarling, prancing tiger, brown patina, high ochre marble rect plinth base, inscribed "P. Philippe," imp circular foundry seal for F. P. Samson Succr, Hamburg, c1920 .... **675.00**
14⅛″, bronze, young woman, standing on toes, arms extended high at her sides, enameled jewel dec band on forehead, brown enameled traces on hair, gray and red marble plinth base, inscribed "Grundmann," Germany, c1925 .. **500.00**
Furniture
Bed, 60″ w, Ebene De Macassar and

burl wood, ebony stringing, MOP
inlay, French, c1925 . . . . 2,000.00

Chair
Deck, painted wood, orig cushions,
monogram, designed for *S. S.
Normandie*, c1934, pr 1,150.00
Dining, armchair, Aubusson upholstery, *S. S. Normandie* first
class section, set of 4 . . . . 7,750.00
Chest of Drawers, 44½ x 35", parchment covered, rect top, three tapering drawers, pyramidal mirrored
stiles, bracket feet, back branded
"Quigley," French, c1925 . . . . 2,750.00
Liquor Cabinet, 28½ x 45", mahog-
any, rect mirrored top, pair of cupboard doors, gilt bronze handles
cast as stylized dancing nude
maidens, mirrored int., two glass
shelves, raised tapering cylindrical
feet, French, c1925 . . . . 600.00
Magazine Stand, 15" h, bronze, two
centaurs 200.00
Screen, 94" h, 22" wide panels, mir-
rored, beveled edge plate mirrors,
framed by alternating sq and rect
beveled mirror pcs, four fold 1,650.00
Vanity, 43 x 23¾", rect top, two drawers, cupboard doors flanking recessed door, mirrored glass panels 425.00
Vitrine, 72", walnut, glazed upper section, two side doors, German 650.00

Jewelry
Belt Buckle, red rhinestones 20.00
Bracelet, SS, flowered links, Georg
Jensen 65.00
Choker Necklace, black glass beads,
velvet ribbon tie 36.00

Lamp, table, bronze, figural, white
striated black marble base
14¼", young woman kneeling on one
knee, balancing globular frosted
crackled glass light on other, stylized drape streaming back from
right shoulder, brown-black patina,
rect base, inscribed "Geo. Maxim" 385.00
17¾", stylized female figure, short tunic dress, descending stepped platform, flanked by two small frosted
crackled glass shades, shaped rect
base inset with mirror, green patina,
French 360.00
19¾", stylized young nude woman,
drape suspended from waist, walking on toes, holding rouge frosted
glass fan-shaped shade with both
hands behind her head, skirt and
shade molded with cubist style floral motif, green patina, stepped rect
plinth base, pr 1,450.00
26", stylized nude woman, tip-toe,
arched back arms outstretched
holding frosted crackled glass
spherical shade, green patina, octagonal stepped base, factory mark
inscribed "LeVerriere," pr 1,320.00

**Tin, 7½" d, Gloria Swanson by Henrx
Clir, marked "Beautebox/Canco,"
$60.00.**

Pedestal, 18¼ x 42", mirrored, beveled
edges, shaped sq top, four recessed
sides, projecting canted corners, pr . 850.00
Perfume Bottle, 3¼ x 6½", cranberry
glass, cased, deep cut opposing triangles, high matching stopper 115.00
Picture Frame, 11½", bronze, girl standing on one side of frame reaching up
to flowers on top, scrolled, green-
brown finish 100.00
Plaque, 16" d, Bursley Ware, tropical

**Light, 12½" h, chrome, white milk glass
shades, $90.00.**

dec, multicolored, sgd "Charlotte
Rhead" **175.00**
Powder Box, 5½", black glass base, SP
cov, wolf hound finial **60.00**
Teapot, 6", SS, shaded harp shape, ne-
phrite handle **350.00**
Tray, 15" l, chrome, four cobalt blue
glass inserts **60.00**
Wall Sconce, 13½" h, gilt bronze flaring
stem cast with overlapping stylized
palm leaves, frosted glass shade, pr **575.00**

ART NOUVEAU

History: Art Nouveau is the French term for the
"new art" which had its beginning in the early
1890s and continued for the next 40 years. The
flowing and sensuous female forms used in this
period were popular in Europe and America.
Among the most recognized artists of this period
were Galle, Lalique, and Tiffany.

Art Nouveau can be identified by its flowing,
sensuous lines, floral forms, insects, and the fem-
inine form. These designs were incorporated on
almost everything produced at that time, from art
glass to furniture, silver, and personal objects.

References: Victor Arwas, *Glass: Art Nouveau
To Art Deco*, Rizzoli, 1977; Lillian Baker, *Art Nou-
veau & Art Deco Jewelry: An Identification & Value
Guide*, Collector Books, 1981; Don Fredgant, *Col-
lecting Art Nouveau: Identification And Values*,
Books Americana, 1982; Albert Christian Revi,
American Art Nouveau Glass, reprint, Schiffer
Publishing, 1981.

Additional Listings: Furniture and Jewelry.
Also check glass, pottery, and metal categories.

Asparagus Tray, SS, 12½" l, curved
sides, chased flowers and foliage,
script monogram, pierced mazarine,
hinged bracket handles, marked
"Reed & Barton," c1900 . . . . **1,000.00**
Basket, 9½" l, SS, monogram, marked
"Frank W. Smith Silver Co., Inc. for
Bailey, Banks, and Biddle Co" **350.00**
Billiard Table, 121 x 66 x 32", walnut,
leather playing surface, six leather
pockets with rosewood borders, six
flared sq form legs, geometric patterns of ebony and MOP, Brunswick,
c1916 . . . . **8,250.00**
Bust, 5¼", bronze, brown patina, sleep-
ing sprite, head inclined to one side,
flowing hair with poppies, after Hans
Muller, late 19th C, Austria **400.00**
Clock, 7¼", gilt bronze, enameled dial,
tapering tall case, trailing fruiting
vines repouse, marked "Susse
Freres, Paris," c1900 . . . . **565.00**
Creamer, 6¼" h, SS, iris dec, marked
"Shreve & Co" **250.00**

Bookends, 7½" h, 7½" w, cast metal,
bronze figures, green finish on seats,
$200.00.

Dresser Set, SS
5 pcs, repousse figural and iris dec,
two hair brushes, clothes brush,
hand mirror, and comb **450.00**
15 pcs, repousse floral, mono-
grammed, four hair brushes,
clothes brush, hand mirror, shoe
horn, nail file, pin tray, two cut glass
powder jars with matching lids,
powder puff with matching handle,
three cut glass cosmetic jars with
matching lids **900.00**
Figure
6", bronze, one arm over head, other
bent at waist, long flowing hair, dol-
phin base **100.00**
9½", gilt bronze, nymph skipping
rope, rouge marble circular base,
inscribed "A Marionnet," French,
c1910 . . . . **385.00**
12", silvered spelter, dancing classical
maiden, fruiting vines in hair, playing ivory double flute, rect straited
red marble base, inscribed "Dan-
seuse aux Flutes," c1900 . . . . . . **300.00**
Flatware Service, SS, dinner knives,
teaspoons, luncheon forks, cream
soup spoons, bouillon spoons, demitasse spoons, flat butter spreaders,
scoops, cocktail forks, serving pieces,
120 pcs **1,400.00**
Furniture
Armoire, 84" h, carved mahogany,
burl walnut, gilt bronze mounts,
Louis Marjorelle style, glazed central door, marquetry panels with
elaborate leafage **2,500.00**
Bed
51 x 66", mahogany, high headboard with V shaped top, slightly
arched paneled foot board,
shaped side rails, c1910 . . . . . **350.00**

52", twin, carved fruitwood, cartouche form headrest, floral surmount, carved game among rushes, Ecole de Nancy, pr . . . **2,500.00**

Cabinet, 40" h, bedside, carved mahogany, burl walnut, gilt bronze mounts, Louis Marjorelle style, single drawer and door, blossom pulls, marble inset int., black glass top, applied retailer's label, "Epaux, Paris" **400.00**

Chaise Lounge, 72" l, oak, scrolled, foliate carved support, molded seat rail, bracket feet, French, c1900 . . **700.00**

Dressing Table, 38 x 21 x 50", walnut, arched and molded mirror back, carved leaf and vine dec, two carved drawers, carved legs, stretchers, lower shelf, splayed club feet, c1900 . . . . **500.00**

Firescreen
33½", gilt bronze mounted wrought iron, central section of dancing classical figure, imp signature of designer, Edgar Brandt, c1925 . **6,570.00**
35 x 27", tooled leather, girl's head, c1900 . . . . **150.00**

Mirror, 28¼", table, matte glazed painted pottery, figural, youth with arms raised above his head holding crescent fitted with circular mirror, nymph holding a drape partially covering him, both standing at water's edge, shaped oval dish at feet, shaded green and amber, back inscribed "Schoop" **385.00**

Music Stand, 26 x 56", mahogany, adjustable, center carved lyre, pierced meandering flowering vines carved rest and crest, carved baluster standard, three leafy-vine carved cabriole legs **500.00**

Screen, 68" h, three panels, upholstered, tapestry type **750.00**

Table
Dining, 52 x 29", walnut, shaped rect top, rounded corners, molded edge, foliate carved legs, leaf carved X-form arched stretcher, two later unfinished leaves, French, c1900 . . . . **890.00**
Nest of four, 23⅞ x 15⅜ x 29", fruitwood, marquetry, rect top inlaid with daffodils and butterflies, stork at shore, autumn leaves, trestle legs, shaped pierced stretchers, signed in marquetry "Emile Galle," c1900 . . . . **2,000.00**

Hardware, lock plate, 23½ x 10", hammered brass, c1900, pr **175.00**

Inkwell
8½", gilt bronze, pale copper patina,

oval, cast spray of daffodils on swirled border, French **200.00**
14", pottery, woman with glazed cap, marked "Charenton" **185.00**

Jewelry Box
9½", SS, chased, floral strapwork . . **1,400.00**
10 x 8 x 7", ormolu, raised figural and floral dec, plaque dated 1903 . . . **225.00**

Lamp
Desk, 13", bronze, petaled amber frosted glass floriform shade, foliate cast C-scroll stem, scallop shell base, brown patina, French, pr . . **200.00**

Table
16" h, carved alabaster, bust of young girl, head tilted to side, wearing close fitting cap, gazing at oncoming wave, leaf incised rect base, Italian, c1900 . . . . . . **675.00**
17½" h, painted bronze, figural, Arabs at tea, inscribed "Chotka," attributed to Franz Bergman, Austria **2,000.00**

Magazine Cover, 13¼ x 10½", L'Habitation Pratique, Paris, 1910, photo relief engraving, dark blue ink on blue wove paper, artist sgd "Alphonse Marie Mucha," framed **450.00**

Match Holder, 5" h, painted bronze, figural, imp marks, Franz Bergman, c1910 . . . . **475.00**

Mirror, 21", bronze **100.00**

Plaque
10 x 8", oval, pietre dure, elderly couple with a child, gilt wood frame . . **1,000.00**
10 x 13", oval, bronze, bust of lady in flowing blue gown, marked "Bradley & Hubbard" **385.00**
15½", rect, lead, lily pad, flowers, and lizard **200.00**

Plate, 14¾", pottery, black feathering, geometric motifs, translucent blue glaze, Islamic taste, inscribed "Carl Walters," two monograms, c1924 . . **500.00**

Razor, straight, woman with long hair . **20.00**

Scale, 4¼" h, desk, postal, SS, cased, monogram, marked "Shreve & Co," c1900 . . . . **250.00**

Torchere, 56", wrought iron, prancing horse, adjustable standard, attributed to Hunt Diederich, c1925 . . . . **900.00**

Trophy, 24", SS, three handles, female figural lid, pedestal base, applied dec, inscribed as prize for Uniform Rank–Knights of Pythias, marked "Shreve & Co," c1902 . . . . **1,320.00**

Vase
8½", SS mounts, engraved glass, poppy dec **450.00**
9⅛", gold luster, threaded, applied dec, feather design, bogus Tiffany signature **1,200.00**

10", lustered mottled green ground, inlaid blue flowers and veining, Austrian **100.00**
14½", jack in the pulpit shape, amethyst and gold lustre, feather veining **200.00**
24½", patinated metal, floriform, slender cylindrical neck tapering to bulbous body, molded circular foot, molded water lilies, entwined leaves, green and white, gilt edges, large crimson cymbidium orchid on neck, brown ground, French, c1900 **575.00**
29", pewter and engraved glass, modeled with couple amidst wave motifs, French, pr **1,200.00**

ART PEWTER

History: Pewter objects produced during the Art Nouveau, Arts and Crafts, and Art Deco periods are gaining in popularity. These mostly utilitarian objects, e.g., tea sets, trays, and bowls, were elaborately decorated and produced in the Jugendstil manner by German firms, such as Kayserzinn, and Austrian companies, such as Orivit. In England, Liberty and Company marketed Tudric Pewter, which often had a hammered surface and was embellished with enameling or semi-precious stones. Most pieces of art pewter contain the maker's mark.

EDELZINN

Sugar Box, cov, 5½" h, sq, fitted pyramidal cov, emb with curvilinear motif, marked "Edelzinn, F Hueck," 1930 **825.00**

FIEN ZINN

Bow,, 9½", large open rim handles, marked "S Rothhan, Fien Zinn" . . . **50.00**
Pitcher, 12", marked "Wien, Fien Zinn" **85.00**

Kayserzinn, candy dish, marked "4065," $100.00.

KAYSERZINN

Bowl, 10", #4104 . . . . **100.00**
Candy Dish, #4065 . . . . **100.00**
Chamberstick, Art Nouveau floral dec . **75.00**
Pitcher, Mephistopheles, sgd and numbered **185.00**
Punch Bowl, cov, cherub on top, ball and claw feet **575.00**
Sugar Bowl, 7" h, cov, oval, cast wave motif, two snail shells, imp oval factory mark and "Kayserzinn/4135" . . **185.00**
Tray, 13", rect, low relief, poppy dec in opposing corners, scrolling stems form handles **200.00**
Vase, 7¾", wheat and butterflies, #4310 . . . . **125.00**

ORVIT

Creamer, individual, floral design **25.00**
Pitcher, claret type, green glass insert, Art Nouveau vines and floral dec . . **125.00**
Vase, 7", Art Nouveau florals and vines **80.00**
Wine Cooler, 8 x 10½", floral dec **275.00**

TUDRIC

Basket, 6" h, handle, hammered finish **75.00**
Candlesticks, 9¼", hand hammered, three part pedestal, marked "Liberty Tudric," pr **400.00**
Compote, 10½ x 10", hand hammered, three part pedestal, c1900 . . . . **375.00**
Teapot, wooden handle, hammered finish, marked "Libery and Co" **85.00**

ART POTTERY (GENERAL)

History: The period of art pottery reached its zenith in the late 19th and early 20th century. Over a hundred companies produced individually designed and often decorated wares which served a utilitarian as well as a aesthetic purpose. Artists moved about from company to company, some forming their own firms.

Quality of design, beauty in glazes, and condition are the keys in buying art pottery. This category covers companies not found elsewhere in the guide.

References: Paul Evans, *Art Pottery of the United States,* Everybodys Press, Inc., 1974; Lucile Henzke, *Art Pottery of America,* Schiffer Publishing; Ralph and Terry Kovel, *The Kovels' Collector's Guide to American Art Pottery,* Crown Publishers, Inc., 1974.

Additional Listings: See Cambridge, Clewell, Clifton, Cowan, Dedham, Fulper, Grueby, Jugtown, Marblehead, Moorcroft, Newcomb, North Dakota School of Mines, Ohr, Owens, Paul Revere, Peters and Reed, Rookwood, Roeville, Van Briggle, Weller, and Zanesville.

Arc-En-Ciel, (1903–05), Zanesville, OH
Vase
    10″, waisted, poppy relief, gold irid   **250.00**
    10½″, tree bark body, purple and
      gold irid luster **200.00**
Arequipa, (1911 to 1918), Fairfax, CA
Bowl
    1½ x 4¾″, octagonal, gray matte,
      die mark **125.00**
    9 x 4¾″, flower and leaf mold, black
      and white **150.00**
Vase
    3¼″, carved leaf and berries, purple
      matte, imp mark **380.00**
    5⅝″, irregular green matte glaze .   **240.00**

Brush-McCoy, vase, 4″, Zuni, unfired tan ground, enameled diamonds and swastikas, hp blue, brown, green, and brown lines, unmarked, $135.00.

Brush-McCoy (1911–25), Zanesville, OH
    Bowl, 6″, Zuniart **50.00**
    Candlesticks, 10¼″, Jetwood, pr . . .   **185.00**
    Umbrella Stand, 22½″, Onyx **145.00**
    Vase, 8½″, Navarre, white Art Nou-
      veau lady, green ground, handles   **250.00**
California Faience
    Bookends, pr, eagle, blue matte . . .   **675.00**
    Bowl, 10½″, black matte, turquoise
      int., frog, pedestal base **150.00**
    Box, 1½ x 4½ x 3½″, raspberry tile
      top, cloisonne dec **100.00**
    Potpourri Jar, 4½″ h, Oriental shape,
      yellow matte, incised mark **225.00**
Vase
    6½″, red glossy glaze, large styl-
      ized carved leaves **180.00**

    10″, baluster, salmon ground, tan
      drip dec **200.00**
Chelsea Keramic Art Works (1872–89), Chelsea, MA
    Pitcher, 8″, geometric rim and handle
      motif, hp birds, three line mark . .   **285.00**
    Vase, 4½″, octagonal, elephant head
      handles, brown flambe **375.00**
Kenton Hills ((1939–42), Erlanger, KY
    Ashtray, 7 x 6½″, stylized horse head
      shape, turquoise glossy glace,
      marked **42.00**
    Bowl, 3½″, olive glossy glaze **100.00**
    Vase, 7 x 6″, brown irid glaze **115.00**
Merrimac Ceramic Co. (1897–1908), Newburyport, MA
    Bowl, 8 x 3″, green matte, red and
      orange glossy int., thrown and
      modeled **180.00**
    Vase, 8″, red and orange glossy
      glaze, handles, imp mark **175.00**
Pewabic Pottery (1903–61), Detroit, MI
    Plate, 9″, hp, cottage scene border .   **150.00**
    Tile, 2¾″, floral nosegay dec, blue
      luster, matte white ground **65.00**
    Vase, 5 x 4″, high glaze, purple and
      turquoise, orig paper label **265.00**
Pisgah Forest (1913–present), Mt. Pis-gah, NC
    Creamer, blue, pink int. **15.00**
    Cup and Saucer, yellow and pink . .   **25.00**
    Pitcher
      6½″, green **55.00**
      9″, yellow and pink, 1956 . . . . . .   **120.00**
    Urn, 4¼″, white crackle, pink int.,
      1936 . . . .   **35.00**
    Vase
      7″, turquoise, 1949 . . . .   **85.00**
      10″, bulbous, green mottled glaze,
      1928 . . . .   **128.00**

Swastika Keramics, pitcher, 10¼″, copper luster, green leaves, $375.00.

Swastika Keramics (1902–04), Owens
China Co., Minerva, OH
Ewer, 11", green grapes, copper
leaves, gold ground, wide base . . **200.00**
Vase, 7½", round body, cone top,
large red luster flower, gold ground **180.00**
Teco (1886–30), Terra Cotta, IL
Ash Bowl, frog overlooking 4½" bowl,
cream matte finish, sgd **200.00**
Vase
7", gourd shape **500.00**
13", tower shape **650.00**
Wall Pocket, 14½", green, deep gray
spatter, marked **175.00**
Vance/Avon Pottery (1892–1908), Til-
tonville, OH and Wheeling, WV
Basket, 6½", gourd shape, vine han-
dle, sgd "R Lorber" **65.00**
Pitcher, 10¼", tankard shape, multi-
colored troubadour dec, marked
"Wheeling" **100.00**
Volkmar Pottery (1882–1903), Tremont,
NY
Charger, 12" d, Washington's Head-
quarters, Newburgh, emb sgd . . . **100.00**
Tile, 9 x 5", hp, Yale College scene,
set of 2 . . . . **200.00**
Vase, 8 12", thickly textured varie-
gated green glaze, medium green
underglaze, thick matte gunmetal
gray spots, marked **300.00**
Walrath Pottery (1900–1920), Roches-
ter, NY
Bowl, 4¾", green florals, brown
ground **225.00**
Figure, 6", lion, seated, one paw
lifted, 1913 . . . . **250.00**
Mug, 6", brown florals, green matte
ground, sgd "RB," incised mark . . **250.00**
Pitcher, 10", two colored stylized floral
band, marked **250.00**
Vase, 4¾", cylindrical, hp buds and
leaves, green ground **750.00**

ARTS AND CRAFTS MOVEMENT

History: The Arts and Crafts Movement in
American decorative arts took place between 1895
and 1920. Leading proponents of the movement
were Elbert Hubbard and his Roycrofters, the
brothers Stickley, Frank Lloyd Wright, Charles and
Henry Greene, George Niedecken, and Lucia and
Arthur Mathews.

The movement was marked by individualistic
design (although the movement was national in
scope) and re-emphasis on handcraftsmanship
and appearance. A reform of industrial society was
part of the long range goal. Most pieces of furniture
favored a rectilinear approach and were made of
oak.

References: David M. Cathers, *Furniture Of
The American Arts and Crafts Movement,* New
American Library, c1981; David A. Hanks, *The
Decorative Designs Of Frank Lloyd Wright,* E. P.
Dutton, 1979; Coy L. Ludwig. *The Arts and Crafts
Movement In New York State, 1890s–1920s,* Gal-
lery Association of New York State, 1983.
Periodical: *Tiller,* c/o Artsman, P. O. Box 508,
Bryn Mawr, PA 19010. Subscription: $125.00 (bi-
monthly).
Museum: Museum of Modern Art, New York,
NY.
Additional Listings: Roycroft Items, Stickleys,
and art pottery categories.

Ashtray, 6¼", hammered copper, round,
puffed out rim areas, aged patina,
marked "Benedict Studio" **165.00**
Basket, 8½", SS, glass, marked "Whit-
ing and Lebolt" **350.00**
Bookends, pr, 4½ x 4", heavy brass, buff
colored bisque Batchelder tiles,
greenish white glaze, stylized lovebirds, marked "Potter Studio" **225.00**
Bowl
8½", SS **230.00**
10", SS, ftd, lobed, marked "The Kalo
Shops" **275.00**
Brooch, 2½ x 1¼", oval, German silver,
sunburst lines radiating from simulated amethyst, marked "Forest Craft
Guild" **45.00**
Candlesticks, pr, 15", copper and white
metal, cobalt flowers, rust and green
enamel accents, marked "Arts and
Crafts Shop" **185.00**
Chafing Dish, 19" l, copper, silver
mounts, three rabbits on scrolling
supports **800.00**
Cigarette Set, cigarette box, four match
holders, 20" l tray, hammered SS,
marked "Tray Shreve and Co" **700.00**
Easel, 72", ebonized wood **600.00**
Flatware Service, SS, knives, tea-
spoons, tablespoons, soup spoons,
luncheon forks, dinner forks, fish
forks, salad forks, cocktail forks,
demitasse spoons, butter spreaders,
fish knives, serving fork and spoon,
fruit knives, marked "Shreve, Crump
& Low Co," partial service for 12, 138
pcs **1,200.00**
Furniture
Cabinet, 20½ x 88½", mahogany,
arched superstructure inlaid with
large floral sprigs, shaped mirror
flanked by circular platforms, rect
lower section top, panel inlaid with
fully rigged ship at sea, glazed
doors, pierced floral sprig carved
apron, sq legs, flared sq feet, En-
glish **1,200.00**

Foot Stool, 10 x 15″, leather cover, marked "Roycroft," $200.00.

Campaign Chest, 38 x 18 x 40″, oak, three long drawers, one deep drawer, cupboard, brass mounts, c1910 .... 650.00
Chair, hall, 36 x 25 x 55″, oak, upholstered back, columns with carved leaf finials, rect arms, drop-in seat, paneled front and sides, c1900 .. 325.00
Desk, 48 x 30 x 30″, oak, rect top, one drawer, open bookshelf sides, sq legs, c1910 .... 300.00
Music Stand, 41″ h, c1910 .... 100.00
Server, 50¼ x 50¼″, oak, rect top, mirrored backboard, two short drawers, one long drawer over pair of cupboard doors, hammered metal pulls, plain stiles continue to form feet, c1910 .... 1,200.00
Lamp, table, 14⅝″ d shade, 15½″ h, bulbous ovoid base, hammered copper shade with top concave circular disc riveted with four slender cylindrical curving arms, four panel copper frame with four mica panels, orig fittings, imp windmill mark above closed box enclosing "D'Arcy/Dirk Van Erp," c1910 .... 11,000.00
Loving Cup, hammered copper, three handles 100.00
Plate, 12″, copper, service, wide border, stylized block monogram, imp windmill mark above an open box enclosing "Dirk Van Erp/San Francisco" .. 100.00
Tea Kettle, 12¼″ h, planished silver, beehive form, pierced and wicker bound loop handle, stand with burner, Christopher Dresser style, English, c1900–10 .... 200.00
Tray
5¾″, copper, applied enamel dec, stylized cobalt and green flowers, marked "Art Crafts Shop, Buttalo," c1905 .... 90.00
23½″, rect, hammered copper, carp dec, emb initials in corner, attrib-

uted to Charles Rene Mackintosh, c1900 .... 150.00
Trophy, 10″, 34 ounces, SS, marked "Lebolt" 450.00
Umbrella Stand, 20″ h, brass, applied copper leaves, fluted sections, brass rivets, tin liner 115.00
Vase
4⅛″, bronze, applied SS full length pussy willow stems, dark patina, marked "Heinz Art Metal" 75.00
9¾″, green matte, four open wing handles, incised dec, relief leaves at neck, marked "Radura/013," Radford Pottery 265.00

AUSTRIAN WARE

History: Over a hundred potteries were located in the Austro-Hungarian Empire in the late 19th and early 20th centuries. Although Carlsbad was the center of the industry, the factories spread as far as modern day Czechoslovakia.

Many of the factories were either owned or supported by Americans; hence, their wares were produced mainly for export to the United States. Responding to the 1891 law that imported products must be marked as to country of origin, many wares do not have a factory mark, but only the word "Austrian."

Reference: Susan and Al Bagdade, *Warman's English & Continental Pottery & Porcelain, 1st Edition,* Warman Publishing Co., Inc., 1987.

Additional Listings: Amphora, Carlsbad, Royal Dux, and Royal Vienna.

Ashtray, Fatima Cigarettes 75.00
Berry Set, 7 pcs, 8¾″ bowl, six 4½″ dishes, seascape scenes, gold scalloped edges, artist sgd 100.00
Candlesticks, pr, 8½″, hp dark green and blue flowers 65.00
Celery Tray, 12″, scalloped border, pink roses, green leaves, gold trim 45.00
Compote, 9″ d, irid, metal mounts 175.00
Decanter, 19¼″ h, glass, cranberry, gold dec, applied porcelain flowers, steeple stopper, pr 275.00
Ewer
8¾″, glass, cranberry, heavy gold and floral dec 90.00
9″, handle reserve with cherubs, rust ground, marked "Victoria" 175.00
10¾″, gold and floral dec, cobalt blue ground 75.00
Ferner, hp, roses, marked "MZ Austria" 68.00
Pitcher
5½″, floral 15.00
13½″, hp floral dec, gold dragon handle, marked "Hapsburg Austria" .. 225.00

Cake plate, 11½″ d, multicolored daisies, white ground, Carlsbad, $90.00.

Plate
- 8″, purple edge, gold trim, floral rim dec, gold floral center, marked "OE & G," "Royal" in wreath, set of 6 . . **50.00**
- 9¼″, game bird, pearl lustre border, marked "MZ Austria", set of 6 . . . **75.00**
- 9½″, pink and yellow roses, green leaves in center and border, gold scalloped rim, marked "MZ Austria", set of 6 . . . . **75.00**

Powder Box, 3 x 4″, yellow flowers, green leaves, white ground, marked "O & E G" **35.00**

Relish Dish, 9 x 6″, oval, pink flowers, white ground, gold trim, marked "MZ Austria" **65.00**

Sardine Box, sardine finial on cov, marked "Victoria, Austria" **50.00**

Stamp Box, 4¼ x 3⅛″, cov, ftd, 2 compartments, hp roses, gold trim **35.00**

Sugar Shaker, yellow flowers, green leaves, pale yellow ground, gold metal top **40.00**

Tureen, cov, floral dec, marked "O & E G" **60.00**

Vase
- 5¾″, irid, purple, blue and gold, pinched in sides **65.00**
- 6″, handles, woman in portrait medallion **60.00**
- 7″, enamel, bulbous, four handled, Art Deco type poppy dec, matte ground **65.00**
- 8½″, irid, waisted with four dimpled sides, blue striations dec **625.00**
- 9″, irid, amber, amphora form **425.00**
- 14″, gold and green, transfer scene of classical ladies, beehive mark . **125.00**

Wine Glass, cranberry glass bowl, opaque white standard **20.00**

AUTOGRAPHS

History: Autographs occur in a wide variety of formats—letters, documents, photographs, books, and cards, etc. Most collectors focus on a particular person, country, or category, e.g. signers of the Declaration of Independence.

The condition and content of letters and documents bears significantly on value. Collectors should know their source since forgeries abound, and copy machines compound the problem. Further, some signatures of recent presidents and movie stars are done by machine rather than by the persons themselves. A good dealer or advanced collector can help one spot the differences.

The leading auction sources for autographs are Swann Galleries, Sotheby's, Christie's, and Phillips, all located in New York City.

References: Mary A. Benjamin, *Autographs: A Key To Collecting*, reprint, Dover, 1986; Bob Bennett, *A Collector's Guide To Autographs With Prices*, Wallace-Homestead, 1986; Charles Hamilton, *American Autographs*, University of Oklahoma Press, 1983.

Collectors' Club: Universal Autograph Collectors Club, P. O. Box 467 Rockville Center, NY 11571.

Additional Listings: See *Warman's Americana & Collectibles* for more examples.

The following abbreviations denote type of autograph material and their sizes.

ADS	Autograph Document Signed
ALS	Autograph Letter Signed
AQS	Autograph Quotation Signed
CS	Card Signed
DS	Document Signed
LS	Letter Signed
PS	Photograph Signed
TLS	Typed Letter Signed

Sizes (approximate):

Folio	12 x 16 inches
4to	8 x 10 inches
8vo	5 x 7 inches
12mo	3 x 5 inches

COLONIAL AMERICA

Carroll, Charles, signer of Declaration, check, completed and signed, January 10, 1824 . . . . **435.00**

Ellsworth, Oliver, pay order to Capt. William Coit, "for his company last year in the Colony's service and for losses of clothing and arms they sustained in action at Bunker Hill" sgd August 7, 1776 . . . . **950.00**

Gridley, Richard, Revolutionary War General, order to James Fitter, Pay Office, Horse Guards, for payment of 42 sterling to Jonathan and John Amory, sgd Boston, June 25, 1771 . **450.00**

Hart, John, signer of Declaration, DS, attesting to the value of goods in the estate of Joseph Stout, inventory on the reverse side which includes a list of slaves, sgd April 14, 1767 . . . . . . **495.00**

Ingersoll, Jared, signer of Constitution, ALS, regarding disposition of Mr. Taylor's claim against Callender's estate, Philadelphia, October 13, 1788 . . . . **875.00**

King, Rufus, DS, 1818, 5 pgs, 8 x 12, mortgage indenture for property in NYC, seal with ribbons **130.00**

Otis, James, orator and patriot, DS, appointing James Warren as sheriff of Plymouth County, over 100 words . . **325.00**

EUROPEAN

De Gaulle, Charles, French general, PS, entitled "General Charles De Gaulle, President of the French Republic and of the Community," inscribed lower margin: "Pour Sidney/ affectueuse-ment/C. de Gaulle" . . . **350.00**

Duke of Wellington, DS, appointing Samuel Paul Baghott a Lieutenant in the 80th Regiment of Foot for Staffordshire Volunteers, October 9, 1821 **675.00**

George III, King of England, appointment of Robert Gordon As Lieutenant Colonel of Foot in the Army, dated January 18, 1762 . . . . **650.00**

Hugo, Victor, French poet, ALS, expressing regrets that he is too busy to help Madame Reynaud but expressing the hope that General Lamoriciere will grant her request, written and sgd September 13, 1848 . . **265.00**

Louis XV, King of France, military commission appointing d'Bellisle de Vieleastel a Captain in the "Regiment Dauphine," August 1, 1743 . . . . **385.00**

Napoleon Bonaparte, DS, names Jean C. Lorine a Knight of the Empire, seal attached, rolled in a tin sleeve, April 2, 1812 . . . . **2,875.00**

Queen Victoria, ALS, written on her gold emb stationery to the Marquis Wellesley thanking him for his "very valuable and interesting presents," April 14, 1842 . . . . **385.00**

Rodin, Auguste, French sculptor, ALS, Rue de l'Universite stationery to Morice regarding concern for his convalescence and hoping he will draw some pages to "The Cathedrals," dated April 28, 1911 . . . . **985.00**

GENERAL

Anthony, Susan B., Suffragette, ALS, 6 x 5″ tan sheet, refers to book from which it was cut, 1850 . . . . **495.00**

Barnum, P. T., check, payable to S. H. Hurd for $500, October 17, 1865 . . . **390.00**

Clark, William, DS, indenture transferring property from Jeduthan Kendall to Clark, November 5, 1811 . . . . . . **1,450.00**

Edison, Thomas, check, to Walter N. Archer, January 16, 1929 . . . . **425.00**

Guillotine, Joseph I., DS, freemason certificate, "a la Gloire du Grand Architecte de l'Univers," December 20, 1777 . . . . **750.00**

Hopkinson, Joseph, ANS, to the Mayor of Philadelphia John Scott, introducing J. W. Audubon, September 30, 1833 . . . . **390.00**

Montezuma, Carlos, PS, sgd on back with an attached signature of the front **175.00**

Pasteur, Louis, ALS, expressing his gratitude, pays tribute to late statesman Adolphe Thiers, October 26, 1877 . . . . **1,400.00**

Patton, George, ALS, to Lt. Gen. John C. H. Lee, remarks "I had the honor of being among the first people to cross over the Mainz railway bridge," also recommends Col. Harry Hulen for the Legion of Merit or a DSM, April 15, 1945 . . . . **1,175.00**

Peary, Robert E., check, Lincoln National Bank of New York City to Robert Stafford, January 28, 1910 . . . . . **275.00**

Picasso, Pablo, Spanish artist, ALS, to Edgar M. Jaeger, Director for U.S.C. in France, concerning the anticipated closing of a convalescent home in Meillin, March 11, 1948 . . . . **1,950.00**

Pope Pius X, PS, silver print photograph showing him seated, also sgd by Archbishop of Balisa and the Bishop of Sao Paulo, 1906 . . . . **1,275.00**

Rockwell, Norman, ALS, to John D. Lippy Jr., answering a request for assistance in locating a Rockwell picture, envelope **360.00**

Thornton, William, DS, deed for the purchase in 1823 of a slave boy for $300, witness for transaction between Charles Wharton and Henry Waring **675.00**

Washington, Booker T., ALS, to the Editor, The Boston Courant, soliciting publication of material designed to publicize the organization of a National Negro Business League, July 14, 1900 . . . . **285.00**

LITERATURE

Burroughs, Edgar Rice, ALS, concerning E. C. Hettel's request for Burroughs' autograph on personal stationery, sgd June 1, 1931 .... 235.00

Cooper, James Fenimore, check, #316, Cooperstown, filled in and sgd, November 19th, 1839 .... 260.00

Dickens, Charles, check, London, Messrs. Coutts and Company, to the Jullen Fund, dated March 15, 1860 . 590.00

Grey, Zane, State of Oregon hunting license, dated September 2, 1925, signed in three places 890.00

Keller, Helen, ALS, 4to, personal stationery, 1958, to Mr. Konigsmark, re: Am foundation for the Blind, giving details of the work it does and asking for money, pencil signature at conclusion, envelope 150.00

Greeley, Horace, ALS, 8vo, 1 pg, Nov. 28, 1872, responding to request for autograph, $65.00.

Longfellow, Henry Wadsworth, ALS, to Cary & Hart, Philadelphia, concerning the details of publication of various of his works, dated December 3, 1844 475.00

Reed, John, ALS, written in haste to Jack Carvey while in court awaiting a verdict from the jury 2,500.00

Torrence, Ridgley, ALS, 8vo, 1922, mentions "fortunate experience" in Miami, etc 35.00

Woolf, Virginia, ALS, typed on Monk's House stationery refusing a request, sgd January 3, 1928 .... 485.00

Wyeth, Jamie, 1st printing *Jamie Wyeth*, sketched on middle blank area of title page, happy-faced pig, signature beneath sketch 550.00

MUSIC

Callas, Maria, opera singer, first day cover sgd, 1970 .... 450.00

Carmichael, Hoagy, AQS, 8vo, 1 pg, no date, three bars from "Stardust" ... 150.00

Eddy, Nelson, DS, 7 x 9", publicity release form, 1949 .... 35.00

Farrar, Geraldine, PS, 4to, sepia 50.00

Miller, Glenn, PS, 8 vo, pictured in suit playing trombone 195.00

Piatigorsky, Gregor, CS, black in signature, dated "1950," one bar of music 25.00

Presley, Elvis, PS, 4to, bust pose in white sequined costume holding microphone performing last time in Las Vegas, signed 500.00

Sousa, John Philip, sgd on the first page of *Marching Along, Recollections of Men, Women, and Music,*, 1928 ... 350.00

Strauss, Richard, AQS, signature and 2 bars of music on approx 6 x 5" blank side of Excelsior Hotel-Italie Florence 1,000.00

PRESIDENTIAL, AMERICAN

Adams, John Quincy, DS, passport issued to Henry Hill, October 28, 1815 775.00

Buchanan, James, four language ship's paper, for Francis E. Strawburg, master of the ship "Congress" bound for the Pacific Ocean, sgd August 2, 1858 .... 1,275.00

Eisenhower, Dwight D., ALS, White House letterhead to the Overseas Press Club of America, March 25, 1958 .... 685.00

Grant, U. S., warrant for pardon of Francis E. Dickerson, February 4, 1870 . 675.00

Hayes, Rutherford B., ALS, Executive Mansion stationery, dated March 25, 1880, gives the closing paragraphs of his recent message on the canal across the American Isthmus 375.00

Jefferson, Thomas, ALS, written to Mrs. Eleanor Worthington acknowledging the receipt of the seeds of the Serpentine Cucumber and the debts of an old friendship, April 22, 1826 ... 2,950.00

Johnson, Andrew, appointment of Frederick T. Dent as Brigadier General of Volunteers from the fifth day of April, 1865, sgd March 10, 1866 ...... 975.00

Lincoln, Abraham, DS, for Captain Abner R. Benedict in the Fourth Regiment of Infantry, July 1, 1864 ..... 3,900.00

Madison, James, check, Office of Pay

and Deposite of the Bank of Columbia, Washington, filled in and sgd, March 27, 1816 . . . . 1,585.00

Monroe, James, DS, 13 x 8″, 1819, land grant "Chillicothe" with seal intact . . 395.00

Pierce, Franklin, appointment of Edwin C. Bailey as Deputy Postmaster at Boston, September 23, 1853, seal attached 650.00

Roosevelt, Theodore, PS, 4to, inscribed for Felix Maguire with the best wishes of Theodore Roosevelt 650.00

Taft, William, H. ALS, appointing Rear Admiral Charles F. Stokes a member and vice-chairman of the War Relief Board of the American National Red Cross, dated December 11, 1912 . . 450.00

Truman, Harry S., check, City Bank of Kansas City, filled in and sgd, July 21, 1925 . . . . 750.00

SHOW BUSINESS

Bogart, Humphrey, DS, 4to, 1943, giving permission for Red Skelton to use Bogart's name in photoplay 1,500.00

Garbo, Greta, check, Chase Manhattan Bank, filled in and signed, envelope 2,500.00

Hart, William S., SP, sepia, 7 x 8″, full pose, large sentiment and full signature in lower right corner 200.00

Karloff, Boris, PS, 4to, close-up of sinister face, blue ink "Sincerely, Boris Karloff" 500.00

Monroe, Marilyn, and Joe DiMaggio, menu, cut to 4 x 3″, matted, 9 x 7″ black and white glossy photo, sgd "Warmest Regards/Marilyn Monroe &," his signed full name underneath, dated Saturday, May 16, 1953 . . . . 2,000.00

Novarro, Ramon, PS, 10 x 13″, silent film star, close-up bust portrait 250.00

Sellers, Peter, program, 4 pgs, 9 x 12″, "The Pink Panther Strikes Again," black ink signature in lower white blank area 125.00

SPORTS

Baseball, autographed by 10 players who hit 500 or more home runs, Mantle, Williams, Mathew, Jackson, McCovey, Aaron, Robinson, Killebrew, Mays, and Banks, display holder 175.00

Dempsey, Jack, SP, sepia, 4to, full length pose in boxing stance, sgd "Best regards/Jack Dempsey/Nov. 22, '27" 75.00

Ruth, Babe, 1939 Commemorative U. S. Postage Stamp, The Centennial of Baseball 375.00

STATESMEN, AMERICAN

Carroll, William, grant of 160 acres of land to John Davis, John C. McLemond, and George M. Campbell, in Humphrey County, sgd June 22, 1822 185.00

Clinton, De Witt, DS, appointment of Elisha Waters as an Ensign in the 24th Regiment of Infantry, March 27, 1819 . . . . 95.00

Davis, Jefferson, ALS, endorsement on a letter concerning the Allegheny Valley R. R. Co., April 28, 1853 . . . . . 485.00

Ellsworth, Oliver, pay order, Lt. Elnathan Nichols, August 5, 1777 . . . . 250.00

Hall, A. Oakley, Mayor of NYC, ALS, 8vo, 4pp, Executive Depart., City Hall, response to inquiry re: "the new charter," envelope included 300.00

Henry, Patrick, land grant to William Gehee for 400 acres in Washington County, Virginia, sgd as Governor, March 20, 1785 . . . . 950.00

Holmes, Oliver Wendell, calling card, February 13, 1913 . . . . 490.00

Houston, Sam, postal envelope addressed to John Burt, Esq., written by Houston: "Free/Sam Houston," sgd during second term as US Senator . 1,375.00

Jay, John, DS, appointing Henry Saltsman Pay Master of the Regiment of Militia in the county of Montgomery, April 18, 1800 . . . . 790.00

Webster, Daniel, ALS, to W. H. Morell, Esq., concerning forwarding dispatch bags to the Department, February 17, 1852 . . . . 350.00

AUTOMOBILES

History: Automobiles can be classified into several categories. In 1947 the Antique Automobile Club of America devised a system whereby any motor vehicle (car, bus, motorcycle, etc.) made prior to 1930 is an "antique" car. The Classic Car Club of America expanded the list focusing on luxury models from 1925 to 1948. The Milestone Car Society developed a list for cars in the 1948 to 1964 period.

Some states, such as Pennsylvania, have devised a dual registration system for older cars—antique and classic. Models from the 1960s and 1970s, especially convertibles and limited production models, fall into the "classic" designation depending how they are used.

References: Quentin Craft, *Classic Old Car Value Guide, 21st Edition*, published by authors, 1987; Beverly Rae Kimes, *Standard Catalog of American Cars, 1805-1942*, Krause Publications, 1985; *The Official Price Guide To Collector Cars, 7th Edition*, House of Collectibles, 1986.

Periodicals: *Hemmings Motor News,* Box 100, Bennington, VT 05201. Subscription: $17.95; *Old Cars Price Guide,* 700 E. State Street, Iola, WI 54990. Subscription: $11.95; *Old Cars Weekly,* 700 E. State Street, Iola, WI 54990. Subscription: $24.95.

Collectors' Clubs: Antique Automobile Club of America, 501 W. Governor Road, Hershey, PA 17033; Classic Car Club of America, P. O. Box 443, Madison, NJ 07940; Milestone Car Society, P. O. Box 50850, Indianapolis, IN 46250.

Note: The prices below are based upon a car in running condition, with a high percentage of original parts, and somewhere between 60 and 80% restored. *Prices can vary by as much as 30% in either direction.*

Many older cars, especially if restored, now exceed $15,000.00. Their limited availability makes them difficult to price. Auctions, more than any other source, are the true determinant of value at this level. Especially helpful are the catalogs and sale bills of Kruse Auctioneers, Inc., Auburn, Indiana, 46706.

AUTOMOBILES

Abingdon, 1902, Meredith, 2 cyl.	5,000.00
Allen, 1914, Touring, 4 cyl.	5,000.00
Auburn, 1915, Model 4-36, Touring, 4 cyl.	17,000.00
Auburn, 1935, Model 653, Sedan, 6 cyl.	8,500.00
Austin-Healy, 1964, Model 3000 MK II, Convertible, 6 cyl.	7,500.00
Bentley, 1953, Park Ward, Convertible, 4.6 Litre	28,000.00
Brewster, 1914, Town Car, Limousine, 4 cyl.	22,000.00
Bricklin, 1975, Model SV-1, Gullwing Coupe	8,000.00
Bugatti, 1932, Type 46, Sedan, 8 cyl., 5 Litre	32,000.00

Chevrolet, 1964, Corvair Spider, convertible, two door, $3,250.00.

Buick, 1941, Roadmaster, Sedan, 8 cyl.	15,000.00
Buick, 1967, Riviera GS, Coupe, 8 cyl.	25,000.00
Buick, 1970, Wildcat, Convertible, 8 cyl.	3,000.00

Cadillac, 1931, Model 370, Cabriolet, V-12	42,000.00
Cadillac, 1942, Model 62, Fast Back, V-8	8,000.00
Cadillac, 1962, 62 Park Avenue, Short Sedan, V-8	2,500.00
Cadillac, 1968, Calais, 2 door, V-8	3,500.00
Chandler, 1927, Big Six, Sedan, 6 cyl.	4,800.00
Chevrolet, 1912, Classic Six, Touring, 6 cyl.	8,800.00
Chevrolet, 1921, Model 490, Coupe, 4 cyl.	5,000.00
Chevrolet, 1933, Eagle, Rumble Seat Coupe, 6 cyl.	6,000.00
Chevrolet, 1958, Corvette, Roadster, V-8	15,000.00
Chevrolet, 1965, Corvair, Convertible, 6 cyl.	4,000.00
Chrysler, 1928, Imperial, Sedan, 6 cyl.	9,000.00
Chrysler, 1932, Royal CT, Sedan, 8 cyl.	10,000.00
Chrysler, 1941, Newport, Dual Cowl Phaeton, 8 cyl.	125,000.00
Chrysler, 1959, Saratoga, Sedan, V-8	3,000.00
Columbia, 1925, Six, Sedan, 6 cyl.	8,000.00
Cord, 1968, Warrior, Roadster Convertible, V-8	6,800.00
Cunningham, 1929, Model V9, Roadster, 6 cyl.	20,000.00
Daniels, 1920, Submarine, Speedster, V-8	24,500.00
Dayton, 1913, Tandem, Cycle, 2 cyl.	3,000.00
Delahaye, 1935, Superlux, Roadster, 6 cyl.	12,000.00
DeSoto, 1913, Model 55, Touring, 6 cyl.	5,000.00
DeSoto, 1931, Model 31, Rumble Seat Coupe, 6 cyl.	4,200.00
DeSoto, 1952, Firedome, Convertible Coupe, V-8	6,000.00
DeSoto, 1961, Adventurer, 2 door hardtop, V-8	2,000.00
Dodge, 1914, Model Four, Touring, 4 cyl.	5,000.00
Dodge, 1921, Model 21, Touring, 4 cyl.	3,500.00
Dodge, 1949, Wayfarer, Roadster, 6 cyl.	4,000.00
Dodge, 1966, Charger, Coupe, V-8	2,200.00
Dort, 1915, Model 5, Touring, 4 cyl.	5,000.00
Dort, 1924, Model 27, Touring, 6 cyl.	4,000.00
Dragon, 1906, Model 25, Touring, 4 cyl.	5,500.00
Drexel, 1916, Model 7-60, 7 passenger touring, 4 cyl.	5,000.00
Drummond, 1915, Town, 4 cyl.	4,200.00
Duesenberg, 1931, LeBaron-J, Convertible Berline, 8 cyl.	125,000.00
Durant, 1928, Model M, Sedan, 4 cyl.	4,800.00
Durant, 1930, Model 617, Roadster, 6 cyl.	10,000.00
Edsel, 1958, Ranger, 2 door hardtop, V-8	2,400.00
Eureka, 1899, High-Wheel, Surrey, 3 cyl.	5,000.00
Excalibur SS, 1973, Model SSK, Roadster, V-8	11,500.00

Ford, 1956, Thunderbird, $11,000.00.

Falcon, 1922, Touring, 4 cyl. 5,000.00
Ferrari, 1956, Tipo 375, Touring, V-12 27,000.00
Ford, 1903, Model A, Runabout, 2 cyl. 11,500.00
Ford, 1926, Model T, Coupe, 4 cyl. . . . 2,800.00
Ford, 1940, Deluxe, Sedan Delivery, V-
8 . . . . 6,800.00
Ford, 1958, Thunderbird, Hardtop, V-8 3,500.00
Ford, 1960, Galaxie, Victoria, V-8 . . . . 3,000.00
Ford, 1965, Shelby GT 350, Fastback,
V-8 . . . . 6,800.00
Ford, 1966, Mustang, Convertible, 6 cyl. 6,000.00
Fox, 1921, Model A, Sedan, 6 cyl. . . . 5,000.00
Franklin, 1930, Model 14, Convertible
Sedan, 6 cyl. 20,000.00
Franklin, 1933, Olympic, Cabriolet, 6
cyl. 7,000.00
Frazer, 1951, Manhattan, Convertible, 8
cyl. 5,000.00
Fritchle, 1916, Touring, 4 cyl. 5,000.00
Fuller, 1907, Model 60, Touring, 6 cyl. 15,000.00
Gardner, 1929, Model 130, Roadster, 8
cyl. 12,000.00
Graham-Paige, 1935, Crusader, Sedan,
6 cyl. 3,500.00
Graham-Paige, 1941, Hollywood, Con-
vertible Coupe, 6 cyl. 10,000.00
Grant, 1921, Model HZ, Sedan, 6 cyl. . 4,500.00
Grout, 1899, Runabout, Steam 10,000.00
Haynes, 1923, Special, Speedster, 6
cyl. 10,000.00
Hillman, 1967, Huskey, Station Wagon,
1.7 Litre 1,200.00
Hudson, 1948, Super 6, Convertible
Coupe, 6 cyl. 5,000.00
Hupmobile, 1940, Skylark, 4 door Se-
dan, 6 cyl. 4,800.00
Jaguar, 1951, Mark VII, Sedan, 6 cyl. . 3,600.00
Jaguar, 1966, XKE, Sport Racing, 4.2
Litre 6,500.00
Jeep, 1968, Jeepster, Convertible, V-6 3,000.00
Jordan, 1920, Playboy, Roadster, 6 cyl. 12,000.00
Julian, 1922, Model 60, Coupe, 8 cyl. . 10,000.00
Kissel, 1925, Gold Bug, Speedster, 6
cyl. 18,000.00
Lambert, 1909, Roadster, 6 cyl. 8,000.00

LaSalle, 1932, Model 345B, Victoria
Coupe, 8 cyl. 9,500.00
LaSalle, 1940, Model 52, Club Coupe,
V-8 . . . . 5,000.00
Lexington, 1915, Minute Man, Roadster,
6 cyl. 12,000.00
Lincoln, 1935, Dietrich, Convertible
Coupe, V-12 . . . . 28,000.00
Lincoln, 1954, Capri, 2 door hardtop, V-
8 . . . . 2,000.00
Lotus, 1966, Mark 46 Europa, Coupe,
1.5 Litre 2,000.00
Marmon, 1917, Cloverleaf, Roadster . . 14,000.00
Mercedes-Benz, 1935, Model 170-V,
Limousine 15,000.00
Mercedes-Benz, 1956, Model 190SL,
Convertible, 4 cyl. 9,000.00
Mercury, 1940, Series 09A, Convertible,
8 cyl. 10,000.00
Mercury, 1955, Monterey, Sedan 1,500.00
Mercury, 1963, Comet S-22, Converti-
ble, 8 cyl. 2,400.00
Metropolitan, (Hudson), 1956, Series
1500, Hardtop, 4 cyl. 1,500.00
MG, 1961, MGA, 1600 Coupe, 4 cyl. . 4,000.00
Nash, 1954, Ambassador, 2 door hard-
top, 8 cyl. 1,200.00
Nash, 1962, Metropolitan, Convertible,
4 cyl. 2,300.00
Oldsmobile, 1942, Model 66, Station
Wagon, 6 cyl. 4,000.00
Oldsmobile, 1949, Futuramic, Coupe,
V-8 . . . . 2,000.00
Oldsmobile, 1966, Toronado, Coupe, V-
8 . . . . 3,000.00
Opel, 1926, Laubfrosch, Sedan, 4 cyl. . 1,800.00
Opel, 1938, Admiral, Drophead Coupe,
3.6 Litre 1,700.00
Packard, 1901, Model C, Runabout, 1
cyl. 25,000.00
Packard, 1928, Model 426, Roadster, 6
cyl. 14,000.00
Packard, 1940, Darrin, Convertible Vic-
toria, 8 cyl. 25,000.00
Packard, 1956, Clipper, Coupe, V-8 . . 1,600.00
Peugeot, 1939, Darl mat, Coupe, 2.1
Litre 1,200.00
Peugeot, 1964, Model 505, Sedan, 1.5
Litre 900.00
Pilot, 1922, Model 50, Touring, 6 cyl. . 8,000.00
Pittsburgh, 1911, 7 Passenger Touring,
6 cyl. 6,500.00
Plymouth, 1928, Model Q, Sport Roads-
ter, 4 cyl. 8,500.00
Plymouth, 1942, Model P145, Sedan, 6
cyl. 2,500.00
Plymouth, 1957, Fury, Convertible, V-8 4,000.00
Pontiac, 1950, Silver Streak, Converti-
ble Coupe, 8 cyl 6,800.00
Pontiac, 1958, Bonneville, 2 door hard-
top, V-8 . . . . 2,800.00
Pontiac, 1966, GTO, Convertible, V-8 . 5,200.00

Porsche, 1948, Type 356, Roadster, 4
cyl. 8,500.00
Porsche, 1969, Model 911 T, Coupe, 4
cyl. 6,800.00
Premier, 1911, Model 440, 5 passenger
touring, 6 cyl. 8,000.00
Renault, 1955, Fregate, Convertible, 2
Litre 2,000.00
REO, 1923, Model T6, Sport Touring, 6
cyl. 9,500.00
Rolls Royce, 1929, Pall Mall, touring, 6
cyl. 60,000.00
Rolls Royce, 1946, Sedan, 6 cyl. 15,000.00
Rolls Royce, 1952, Silver Dawn, Tour-
ing Limousine, 6 cyl. 18,000.00
Stanley, 1905, Large Model, Runabout,
Steam 15,000.00
Studebaker, 1933, President, Converti-
ble, 8 cyl. 10,000.00
Studebaker, 1949, Champion, Convert-
ible, 6 cyl. 4,800.00
Studebaker, 1963, Avanti, Coupe, V-8 . 5,000.00
Stutz, 1914, Bearcat, Roadster, 6 cyl. . 45,000.00
Stutz, 1927, Black Hawk, Speedster, 8
cyl. 8,000.00
Sun, 1924, Touring, 4 cyl. 4,200.00
Sunbeam, 1958, Alpine, Sport, 4 cyl. . 2,800.00
Triumph, 1949, Model 2000, Roadster,
2 Litre 4,500.00
Volvo, 1965, Model 544, 2 Door Sedan,
4 cyl. 1,000.00

MISCELLANEOUS

Fire Engine
Autocar, 1941, pumper, Hale pump . 3,500.00
Diamond T, 1947, pumper 2,500.00
Dodge, 1932, pumper 3,500.00
Dodge, 1945, pumper, 6 cyl., Ameri-
can LaFrance 2,500.00
Ford, 1925, Model TT 7,000.00
Ford, 1929, Model AA 4,800.00
Ford, 1940, pumper, flat V-8 . . . . . . 6,500.00
Mack, 1936, pumper, Hale pump . . . 4,000.00
Motorcycle
AJS, 1916, Model V Twin 4,500.00
BMW, 1966, Thumper R27 . . . . 1,800.00
BSA, 1943, Military 3,800.00
Harley-Davidson, 1952, Model K . . . 1,800.00
Harley-Davidson, 1961, DuoGlide . . 4,500.00
Henderson, 1929, KJ Streamline . . . 2,500.00
Indian, 1948, Flathead 3,200.00
Triumph, 1921, Baby 1,500.00
Triumph, 1949, Springfield Scout . . 4,200.00
Vincent, 1942, Comet, Series C . . . 6,800.00
Vincent, 1948, Model B Rapide 7,500.00
Truck
Chevrolet, 1928, Pickup, 1 Ton, V-8 2,300.00
Chevrolet, 1940, Carryall, Closed
Back, V-6 . . . . 2,500.00
Chevrolet, 1957, Pickup, ½ Ton,
Short Bed, V-6 . . . . 2,300.00

Dodge, 1937, Pickup, ¾ Ton, Slant 6 **2,000.00**
Dodge, 1957, Sweptside, ½ Ton, V-8 **800.00**
Ford, 1920, Model A, Custom Cab, 4
cyl. **4,500.00**
Ford, 1941, F-1 Stake, 8 Foot Bed,
V-8 Lemi **2,500.00**
Ford, 1956, F-100, Custom Cab, V-8 **2,500.00**
Ford, 1966, Pickup, Short Bed, De-
luxe Package, V-8 352 . . . . **2,600.00**
G.M.C., 1942, Stake, 1½ Ton, V-8 . **1,500.00**
G.M.C., 1956, Pickup, Fiberglass
Bed, V-8, 3-Speed **1,800.00**
Plymouth, 1938, Pickup, High Side,
Slant 6 . . . . **2,400.00**
Stewart, Pickup, 1 Ton, 4 cyl. **3,200.00**
VW, Pickup, Short Bed, 1600 cc . . . **1,400.00**
Willys
1902, Runabout, 2 cyl. **3,000.00**
1928, Model 70, Sedan, 6 cyl. **1,800.00**
1941, Americar, Sedan, 4 cyl. **1,800.00**
1960, Maverick Special, Station Wa-
gon, 4 cyl. **1,500.00**

AUTOMOBILIA

History: The amount of items related to the
automobile is endless. Collectors seem to fit into
three groups—those collecting parts to restore a
car, those collecting information about a company
or certain model for research purposes, and those
trying to use automobile items for decorative purposes. Most material changes hands at the hundreds of swap meets and auto shows around the
country.
Periodical: *Hemmings Motor News,* Box 100,
Bennington, VT 05201. Subscription: $17.95.

Advertising
Ashtray
American Motor Club, enameled
brass **15.00**
Evergreen Tubes, green glazed
Weller pottery insert, tire shape **40.00**
Goodrich Silvertowns, rubber tire
shape, glass insert **15.00**
Kaiser—Frazer, aluminum, car in re-
lief **55.00**
Paperweight
Goodyear Rubber Co., celluloid tur-
tle, cast iron base **25.00**
Yellow Taxicab Service, 3″, round **30.00**
Sign
Dunlop Tires, 60 x 13½″, tin, verti-
cal **28.00**
Ford Parts, porcelain, c1924 . . . . **90.00**
Invincible Motor Insurance, tin,
1928 . . . . **50.00**
Mobil Gas, 12 x 12″, shield with
flying horse, porcelain **45.00**
Thermometer, Ford Auto, 24 x 6″, tin **45.00**

Carburetor
Buick, 1931 . . . . 90.00
Oakland, 1926 . . . . 75.00
Engine
Overland, 1916, 6 cyl., carb., and
mag. 325.00
Ford, 1938, 21 stud engine 275.00
Grille
Ford, 1931, painted red 125.00
Nash, 1937, LaFayette 400 . . . . 145.00
Plymouth, 1950 . . . . 50.00

**Clipboard, 6⅛ x 7⅛", aluminum, Print
Line, NY, $25.00.**

Headlights, pr
Chevrolet, 1934 . . . . 85.00
Franklin, 1928 . . . . 230.00
Horn
Autolite, H-1001 . . . . 45.00
Spartonet, non-electric, push down
handle 60.00
Trojan United, electric 50.00
Yoders Super Goose, chrome, bulb
type 35.00
Hood Ornament, Hudson, 1936 . . . . . 50.00
Hubcap
Durant, 6½" 60.00
Edsel, spinner type 35.00
Jack
Hudson, 1930 . . . . 25.00
Jaguar 30.00
Lamp
Gray–Davis, 7" face, side, early Cad-
illac 125.00
Neverout, No. 67, headlamp with fork 200.00
Literature
Brochure
Buick for 1930 . . . . 45.00
Chevrolet & GMC Trucks, 1948, 8
pgs 8.00
Oldsmobile, 1948, 8 pgs 8.00
Standard Oil, Walt Disney illus . . . 30.00
Studebaker, 1934 . . . . 48.00

Catalog
DeVilbiss Automotive, 60 pgs . . . 18.00
Oldsmobile, 1946, 24 pgs 20.00
Western Auto, Ford Supply Co.,
1929 . . . . 25.00
Owner's Manual
American Motors, Rambler, 1958 . 20.00
Chevrolet, 1942 . . . . 18.00
Magneto
Cadillac, 1904 . . . . 500.00
Liberty, 1940, 12 cyl. 750.00
Radiator Ornament
Jewell, 1923 . . . . 125.00
Packard, 1938 . . . . 50.00
Radio, Lincoln Town and Country, 1957 75.00
Temperature Gauge
Chevrolet, 1933 . . . . 42.00
Oldsmobile, 1936 . . . . 25.00

BACCARAT GLASS

History: The Sainte-Anne glassworks at Baccarat in the Voges, France, was founded in 1764
and produced utilitarian soda glass. In 1816 Aime-
Gabriel d'Artigues purchased the glassworks, and
a Royal Warrant was issued in 1817 for the opening of Verrerie de Vonĉche á Baccarat. The firm
concentrated on lead crystal glass products. In
1824 a limited company was created.

From 1823 to 1857 Baccarat and Saint-Louis
glassworks had a commercial agreement and
used the same outlets. No merger occurred. Baccarat began the production of paperweights in
1846. In the late 19th century the firm achieved an
international reputation for cut glass table services,
chandeliers, display vases and centerpieces, and
sculptures. Products eventually included all forms
of glass ware. The firm still is active today.
Additional Listing: Paperweights.

Atomizer, Rose Tiente 75.00
Ashtray, 4½" d, Pinwheel, sgd 85.00
Biscuit Jar, vaseline, shaded frosted to
clear, swirling flowers, sgd 200.00
Bowl, 8", Rose Tiente, scalloped, ftd,
sgd 100.00
Box, cov, 4" sq, crystal, geometric de-
signs 125.00
Candlestick
9¾", triple cut overlay, deep blue cut
to white to clear 150.00
10¾", Eiffel Tower pattern, Rose
Tiente, pr 225.00

Water Bottle, 7″ h, light red shading to amber, $75.00.

Castor Set, 5-bottles, Rose Tiente, SP
frame 175.00
Celery, 3½ x 9½″, Rose Tiente 50.00
Cologne Bottle
  5½″ h, Rose Tiente, Diamond Point
    Swirl, orig stopper 75.00
  6¾″, overlay, white cut to cobalt blue,
    gold striping, orig stopper 100.00
Compote, 4½ x 3¾″, Rose Tiente, Swirl
  pattern 60.00
Decanter, 9¾″, Rose Tiente, orig stopper 115.00
Dresser Jar, 5⅜″ d, round, double cut
  overlay, pink cut to clear over opaque
  white, cut vertical panels, gold dec . 125.00
Epergne, 15″ h, scalloped edges, Rose
  Tiente, 3 pcs 450.00
Fairy Lamp
  3⅞″ h, shaded white to clear 275.00
  5¼ x 4″, Rose Tiente, emb Sunburst
    pattern, matching saucer base ... 235.00
Finger Bowl
  4¾″ d bowl, 6¼″ d underplate, ruby,
    medallions and flowers gold dec . 325.00
  5″, Rose Tiente, Swirl pattern 115.00
Goblet
  Perfection pattern 36.00
  Vintage pattern, cone shaped amber
    bowl, etched grape design, cut
    stem and base, set of 6 .... 100.00
Jar, cov
  3 x 5″, Rose Tiente, Swirl pattern .. 75.00
  7″, cameo glass, gilt metal mounts,
    imp "Baccarat" 350.00
Jewelry Box, 4″ d, 2¾″ h, hinged lid,
  Button and Bow pattern, sapphire
  blue, brass fittings 125.00
Lamp
  Fluid, crystal and gilt metal, electrified 800.00
  Table, crystal and gilt metal
    Column form, pr 3,200.00
    Urn form, pr 3,000.00

Pitcher, 9¼″, Rose Tiente, Helical Twist
  pattern 275.00
Rose Bowl, 3″ h, cranberry, lacy enamel
  dec 150.00
Sweetmeat Jar, cranberry strawberries,
  blossoms, and leaves, cut back to
  clear ground of ferns, SP cov and
  handle, sgd 350.00
Toothpick Holder, 2½″, scalloped, Rose
  Tiente 100.00
Tray, 11¼″ d, scalloped, Rose Tiente . 85.00
Tumble-Up, Rose Tiente, Swirl pattern,
  carafe and tumbler 200.00
Tumbler, Rose Tiente, Swirl pattern .. 40.00
Vase
  8¼″, bamboo stalk form, relief molded
    leaf sprig at side, coiled snake
    around base, enameled and gilt in-
    sects, early 20th C, sgd 500.00
  15″ h, Rose Tiente, emb Swirl pattern,
    attached ormolu base 225.00
Wine Glass, tall, cut crystal, cranberry
  bowl, heavy gold scroll and shell dec,
  set of 8 .... 275.00

BANKS, MECHANICAL

History: Banks which display some form of action while utilizing a coin are considered mechanical banks. Although mechanical banks are known
which date back to ancient Greece and Rome, the
majority of collectors center their interests in those
made between 1867 and 1928 in Germany, England, and the United States. Recently there has
been an upsurge of interest in later types, some
of which date into the 1970s.

Initial research suggested that approximately
250 to 300 different or variant designs of banks
were made in the early period. Today that number
has been revised to 2,000–3,000 types and varieties. The field remains ripe for discovery and research.

Over 80% of all cast iron mechanical banks produced between 1869 and 1928 were made by J.E.
Stevens Co., Cromwell, Connecticut. Tin banks
tend to be German in origin.

While rarity is a factor in value, appeal of design,
action, quality of manufacture, country of origin,
and history of collector interest also are important.
Radical price fluctuations may occur with an im-
balance of these factors. Rare banks may sell for
a few hundred dollars while one of more common
design with greater appeal will sell in the thousands.

The prices on our list represent fairly what a
bank sells for in the specialized collectors market.
Some banks are hard to find and establishing a
price outside auction is difficult.

The prices listed are for original old mechanical
banks with no repaired, missing, or replaced parts,

in sound operating condition, and with the vast majority of the original paint intact.

Reference: Bill Norman, *The Bank Book: The Encyclopedia of Mechanical Bank Collecting,* Collectors' Showcase, 1984.

Reproduction Alert: Reproductions, fakes, and forgeries exist for many banks. Forgeries of some mechanical banks were made as early as 1937, so age alone is not a guarantee of authenticity. In our listing two asterisks indicate banks for which serious forgeries exist and one asterisk indicates banks for which casual reproductions have been made.

Advisor: James S. Maxwell, Jr.

Uncle Sam, iron, standing figure, $1,000.00.

**	Acrobats, iron	950.00
	African Bank	1,250.00
	Alligator, grabs coin in mouth, tin	1,150.00
**	American Sewing Machine, iron	2,000.00
*	Artillery, four-sided block house	550.00
	Atlas, lead and wood	1,150.00
	Australian William Tell, brass, wood, and tin	1,200.00
	Automatic Coin Savings, tin, strong man in leopard skin holding man by hair	2,000.00
*	Bad Accident, iron	950.00
	Bank of Education & Economy	550.00
	Barking Dog, wood and steel	1,400.00
**	Bear, standing, iron	350.00
**	Billy Goat, iron	1,000.00
**	Bismark, iron	2,350.00
	Bonzo, tin	650.00
	Bowing Man in Cupola, iron	3,000.00
**	Boy & Bull Dog, iron	550.00
**	Boy on Trapeze, iron	875.00
*	Boy Scout Camp, iron	2,000.00
**	Boys Stealing Watermelons, iron	850.00
	British Lion, tin	850.00
**	Bull & Bear, iron	12,000.00
*	Bull Dog, iron, coin on nose	650.00

	Bull Dog Savings, iron, key wind	2,000.00
	Bull Tosses Boy in Well, brass	2,200.00
	Bureau, Freedman's, wood	650.00
	Bureau, tin, ideal	475.00
	Bureau, wood, Serrill Pat. Appld. For	400.00
	Bureau, wood, stenciling on front	350.00
**	Butting Buffalo, iron	950.00
	Butting Ram, man thumbs nose	1,700.00
**	Calamity, iron	4,500.00
**	Called Out, orig unpainted iron	10,000.00
	Called Out, lead master pattern	12,000.00
	Calumet with Calumet Kid, tin can	150.00
	Calumet with Soldier, tin can	1,000.00
	Calumet with Sailor, tin can	1,2000.00
**	Cannon, U.S. & Spain	1,850.00
	Cat & Mouse, iron and brass, cat standing upright	12,000.00
	Cat Chasing Mouse in Building, tin	2,400.00
	Chandlers, iron	250.00
	Child's Bank, Clark Thread	350.00
**	Chimpanzee, iron and tin	1,150.00
	Chinaman, iron, reclining	1,650.00
	Chocolat Menier, tin	75.00
**	Circus Ticket Collector, man at barrel	800.00
	Clown & Dog, tin	850.00
	Clown, tin, black face	250.00
**	Clown, Harlequin, Columbine, iron	14,500.00
**	Clown on Globe, iron	775.00
	Coin Registering, iron, domed building	300.00
	Confectionery, iron	2,800.00
	Crescent Cash Register, iron	125.00
	Crowing Rooster, tin	275.00
	Dapper Dan, tin	450.00
	Darky Bust, tin	450.00
**	Dentist, iron	2,200.00
	Dinah, aluminum	125.00
	Dog Goes Into House, lead and brass	3,800.00
	Dog, pot metal, spring jawed	275.00
**	Dog With Tray, iron, oval base	1,000.00
	Ducks, lead, two	650.00
	Electric Safe, steel	150.00
	Elephant Baby, lead, with clown at table	3,700.00
**	Elephant With Howdah, iron, man pops out	375.00
**	Elephant With Locked Howdah, iron, oval base	600.00
**	Elephant, iron, "Light of Asia" on wheels	675.00
	Elephant, tin, Royal Trick	850.00
**	Elephant On Wheels, iron, trunk moves	700.00
**	Elephant, iron, trunk moves, raised coin slot	120.00
	Face, wood	875.00
**	Feed the Kitty, iron	400.00
**	Ferris Wheel, iron and tin, marked "Bowen's Pat."	1,400.00
	Fire Alarm, tin	1,250.00
	Flip The Frog, tin	950.00
	Football, iron, black man and watermelon	14,000.00
	Fortune Teller Safe, iron	450.00
	Freedman (man at desk)	38,500.00

**	Forty-Niner, iron	400.00
	Frog On Arched Track, tin	2,000.00
	Frog on Rock, iron	350.00
	Fun Producing Savings, tin	275.00
	Germania Exchange, iron, tin and lead	2,800.00
**	Giant Standing, iron	6,800.00
**	Girl in Victorian Chair, iron	2,350.00
	Give Me A Penny, wood	700.00
**	Glutton, brass, lifts turkey	425.00
	Golden Gate Key, aluminum	125.00
	Grasshopper, tin, wind-up	5,000.00
	Guessing, lead and iron, man's figure	2,000.00
	Hall's Excelsior, iron and wood, police-man figure	1,400.00
	Hall's Lilliput, Type II	250.00
	Hall's Yankee Notion, brass	850.00
	Harold Lloyd, tin	950.00
	Hillman Coin Bank, wood, iron, and glass	3,200.00
**	Hold The Fort, iron, five holes	1,400.00
	Home, iron	375.00
	Home With Dormer Windows, iron	475.00
**	Horse Race, iron, tin horses, flanged base	2,000.00
**	Humpty Dumpty, iron	425.00
	I Always Did 'Spize a Mule, black, sitting on bench	575.00
	Huntley And Palmers Readings	250.00
*	Indian And Bear, iron, white bear	750.00
**	Initiating First Degree, iron	2,800.00
	Jack on Roof, tin	300.00
	Joe Socko, tin	275.00
	John R. Jennings Money Box, wood	2,800.00
	Jolly Joe Clown, tin	400.00
**	Jolly Nigger, aluminum, moves ears	100.00
**	Jolly Nigger, aluminum, string tie	100.00
**	Jolly Nigger, iron	150.00
	Jolly Nigger, iron, high hat	250.00
	Jonah And Whale, iron, ftd base	12,500.00
	Key, iron, World's Fair	300.00
	Kick Inn, paper on wood	275.00

Lighthouse, pot metal, $600.00.

**	Leap Frog, iron	1,250.00
**	Lighthouse, iron	600.00
	Lion Hunter, iron	1,650.00
	Little High Hat, iron	500.00
	Little Jocko Musical, tin	900.00
	Little Moe, tin, tip hat	450.00
	Long May It Wave, iron and wood	400.00
	Lucky Wheel Money Box, tin	150.00
**	Magic Safe, iron	175.00
**	Magician, iron	1,650.00
**	Mama Katzenjammer, iron, 1930s	550.00
	Mama Katzenjammer, iron, 1905–08, low cut dress with white fringe	3,700.00
	Man on Chimney	550.00
**	Mason, iron	1,450.00
	Merry-Go-Round, mechanical	4,500.00
	Metropolitan, iron	150.00
	Mikado, iron	7,500.00
	Minstrel, tin	450.00
	Model Railroad Stamp Dispenser, tin	650.00
	Model Railroad Sweet Dispenser	650.00
	Model Savings, tin	500.00
*	Monkey & Coconut, iron	750.00
	Monkey & Parrot, tin	200.00
	Monkey With Tray, tin	350.00
	Moonface, iron	20,000.00
	Mosque, iron	450.00
*	Mule Entering Barn, iron	650.00
	Musical Church, wood, rotating tower	2,500.00
	Musical Savings, tin	800.00
	Musical Savings, wood house	1,200.00
	New, iron, lever in center	450.00
	New Creedmoor Bank, iron	450.00
**	Novelty, iron	400.00
	Octagonal Fort, iron	1,500.00
*	Organ, iron, cat and dog	475.00
**	Organ, iron, miniature	450.00
**	Organ Grinder With Performing Bear, iron	1,600.00
	Owl, iron, slot in head	250.00
	Owl, turns head, iron	225.00
*	Paddy & Pig, iron	875.00
	Pascal Savings, tin	250.00
**	Peg Leg Begger, iron	600.00
**	Pelican With Mammy, iron	600.00
**	Pelican With Rabbit, iron	700.00
**	Piano, iron, old conversion to musical	2,200.00
	Pig In High Chair, iron	450.00
	Pistol, stamped metal	325.00
	Postman, tin, English	250.00
	Presto, iron, penny changes to quarter	3,700.00
	Presto, paper on wood, mouse on roof	3,500.00
	Pump & Bucket, iron	425.00
*	Punch & Judy, iron	750.00
	Punch & Judy, tin	1,500.00
	Queen Victoria Bust, iron	5,000.00
**	Rabbit, iron, large	275.00
	Rabbit In Cabbage	250.00
**	Red Riding Hood, iron	5,500.00
	Rival, iron	5,000.00
	Rollerskating, iron	4,000.00
	Safety Locomotive, iron	250.00

Saluting Sailor, tin	500.00
Sam Segal's Aim to Save Target, iron	4,500.00
Savo, tin, round drum	125.00
Savo, tin, rect, children	200.00
Savo, tin, round, children	125.00
Scotchman, tin	375.00
Sentry, tin, raises rifle	550.00
Sentry, wood, c1910	450.00
Shoot The Hat, brass	2,500.00
Signal Cabin, tin	150.00
Snake & Frog In Pond, tin	1,200.00
* Speaking Dog, iron	750.00
Sportsman, iron, fowler	4,500.00
** Squirrel & Tree Stump, iron	800.00
Stollwerk, tin, Victoria	250.00
Sweet Thrift, tin	150.00
* Tammany, iron	275.00
* Tank & Cannon, aluminum	200.00
Target, iron, fort and cannon	2,750.00
Ten Cent Adding Bank, iron	400.00
Thrifty Tom's Jigger, tin	400.00
Tiger, tin	950.00
Time Lock Savings, iron	1,100.00
Toboggan, SP Britannia metal	850.00
Treasure Chest Music, pot metal	375.00
** Trick Dog, iron, solid base	450.00
* Trick Pony, iron	675.00
Trick Savings, wood, front drawer	125.00
Try Your Weight Scale, tin	250.00
** Uncle Remus, iron	1,650.00
** Uncle Sam Bust, iron	475.00
Uncle Tom, iron, star base	250.00
United States Bank, iron, picture pops up	875.00
Viennese soldier, lead	1,800.00
Volunteer, iron	450.00
Watch Dog Safe, iron	250.00
Weeden's Plantation, tin, wind-up	650.00
Wimbledon, iron	1,600.00
Wishbone, brass	6,000.00
Woodpecker, iron, 1920s	850.00
World's Banker, tin	950.00
** Zoo, iron	850.00

BANKS, STILL

History: Banks with no mechanical action are known as still banks. The first still banks were made of wood, pottery, or from gourds. Redware and stoneware banks, made by America's early potters, are prized possessions of today's collectors.

Still banks reached a "golden age" with the arrival of the cast iron bank. Leading manufacturing companies include Arcade Mfg. Co., J. Chein & Co., Hubley, J. & E. Stevens and A. C. Williams. The banks often were ornately painted to enhance their appeal. During the cast iron era, banks and other businesses used the still bank as a form of advertising for attracting customers.

The tin lithograph bank, again frequently with advertising, did not reach its zenith until the 1930 to 1955 period. The tin bank was an important premium, whether it be a Pabst Blue Ribbon beer can bank or a Gerber's Orange Juice bank. Most tin advertising banks resembled the packaging shape of the product.

Almost every substance has been used to make a still bank—diecast white metal, aluminum, brass, plastic, glass, etc. Many of the early glass candy containers also converted to a bank when the candy was eaten. Thousands of varieties of still banks were made, and hundreds of new varieties appear on the market each year.

References: Earnest Ida and Jane Pitman, *Dictionary of Still Banks*, Long's Americana, 1980; Andy and Susan Moore, *Penny Bank Book, Collecting Still Banks*, Schiffer Publishing, Ltd., 1984; Hubert B. Whiting, *Old Iron Still Banks*, Forward's Color Productions, Inc. 1968, out of print.

Collectors' Club: Still Bank Collectors Club of America, P. O. Box 356, Bradford, VT 05033. *Penny Bank Post.*

Museum: Perelman Antique Toy Museum, Philadelphia, PA; Margaret Woodbury Strong Museum, Rochester, NY.

GLASS

Baseball, camphor glass	18.50
Charlie Chaplin, 3¾" h, pressed glass with polychrome	135.00
Dog, 3¼" barrel	75.00
House	
3¼", Save With Pittsburgh Paints, clear, pressed	25.00
4", brick, orig brown piant, milk glass, orig mustard label on bottom	40.00
Kewpie, 3⅛" h, pressed glass with polychrome	75.00
Liberty Bell, dated 1919	20.00
Log Cabin, 4", milk glass	20.00
Mason Jar, 3⅝" h, Atlas, pressed, zinc lid	25.00
Milk Bottle, 4½", Elsie The Borden Cow	25.00
Monkey, 5"	35.00
Owl, 7", carnival glass, marigold	25.00
Rabbit, amber	22.50

METAL Cast Iron unless otherwise stated.

Animal	
Bear, 5⅜" h, brass, holding pig	35.00
Bird Dog, 3½"	45.00
Boston Bull, 4⅜" h, seated, polychrome	85.00
Camel, 7¼" l, gold, red and orange	215.00
Cat with ball, 5⅝" l, gray, gold ball	150.00
* Dog with pack, 5½"	58.00
Donkey, 6¾"	100.00
Elephant	
3⅞", Circus, Hubley Mfg	85.00
4", gold trim	115.00

Metal, Crown Savings Bank, handle, patent Chicago, IL, USA, complete with key, $20.00.

Frog, 3¼″ h, Professor Pug, green and gold **200.00**
Goats, 4½″, two black kids on green stump **650.00**
Goose, 3¾″, "Red Goose School Shoes" **100.00**
Hippopotamus, 5″ l, black **200.00**
Newfoundland, 3⅝″ h, black **40.00**
Pig
2½″, "Decker's Iowana," gold . . . **65.00**
7″, emb "A Christmas Roast," nickel plated **90.00**
Possum, 2 1/12″, gold or silver **165.00**
Scottie, 3 5/16″, black **70.00**
Seal, 3⅜″ h, gold **240.00**
* Sheep, 5¼″, gold **65.00**
Spitz, 5″ l, gold **210.00**
St. Bernard with pack, 7¾″ l, black and gold repaint **25.00**

Other
Alarm Clock, 6″ h, white, gold finish . **45.00**
Barrel, 2¾″, black **70.00**
Baseball Player, 5¾″, gold or blue . . **75.00**
Battleship, "Maine", 4½″, japan finish **300.00**
Bicentennial, 1776–1976, 6 x 6″ . . . **40.00**
"Billiken, good luck," 4⅛″ h, gold . . . **50.00**
Boy Scout, 5¾″, gold **65.00**
Building
5¾″, "Flat Iron" **60.00**
7″, "Columbia," nickel finish **80.00**
Bungalow, 3¾″ h, polychrome, porch **175.00**
Campbell Kids, 3¼″, gold **125.00**
Castle, 3″ h, brown japanning, gold trim **250.00**
Clock, "Time Is Money," 3 3/16″, black **55.00**
Colonial House, 3″ h, gold and green **95.00**
Devil, 4¼″, two faced, red **285.00**
Dutch Girl, 5¼″, flowers **35.00**
Football Player, 5½″ h, gold **280.00**
Frowning Face, 5¾″ h, unpainted . . **485.00**
Garage, 2½″ h, aluminum, two car, red **135.00**

German Helmet, 4⅞″ l, lead, olive drab, key trap **175.00**
Gingerbread House, 2½″, tin, German **35.00**
Gothic Bank, 4⅜″, early tin, American **40.00**
Globe, 5¾″, on stand, eagle finial, red **90.00**
Golliwog, 6¼″, English **115.00**
Goodyear Zeppelin Hanger, 2 5/16″, aluminum **130.00**
High Rise, 5½″ h, silver, gold trim . . **65.00**
Hot Water Heater, Rex, 7¾″ h, green litho finish **20.00**

Metal, Battleship Maine, cast iron, 4½″, $300.00.

* Ice Cream Freezer, 4″, nickel finish . **200.00**
Indian Head, 4½″, white metal, made in Japan **35.00**
* Junior Cash Register, 5¼″, nickel finish **75.00**
Mary, 4⅜″, lamb **190.00**
Mutt and Jeff, 5⅛″ h, gold **85.00**
Pass Around The Hat, 2⅜″, black . . **60.00**
Plymouth Rock, 3⅞″, dated "1620," white metal **20.00**
Porky Pig, 4 7/16″, tree trunk, white metal **60.00**
Radio, 4½″, "Majestic," steel back . . **45.00**
Rose Window, 2¼″ h, brown japanning **145.00**
Safe, 4″, "Mascot," tin **25.00**
Statue of Liberty, 6⅜″, silver **75.00**
Stop Sign, 4½″, painted **140.00**
Stove, 5⅜″, "Gas Stove Bank," black **80.00**
Taxi, 4″, "Yellow Cab," Arcade **240.00**
Teddy Roosevelt, 5″ h, gold, red and silver trim **145.00**
U.S. Mailbox, 4¾″, silver **30.00**
"White City Puzzle Pail," 3⅛″, nickel finish **45.00**
Woolworth Building, lead, 4″ h, silver **30.00**
Wringer Washing Machine, 4⅝″ h, gray, key trap **175.00**

Pottery, Die, 2¾″ sq, ochre, $35.00.

POTTERY

Acorn, 3½″, Rockingham glaze	**50.00**
Apple, 2½″, redware	**80.00**
Bear	**22.50**
Cat	
4″, sitting, tail wrapped around ball .	**40.00**
5½″, sitting in basket, blue and green	**35.00**
Dog, 5¼″, spaniel, yellowware, brown	
splashes, translucent green glaze on	
base rim	**200.00**
Duck, 2¾″, blue and white spongeware	**65.00**
Elephant	**25.00**
Fish, brown glaze	**45.00**
Frog, 4″	**40.00**
Mail Box, 3¾″, U.S. Mail, red, white, and	
blue	**40.00**
Owl, 6¾″, brown glaze, yellow eyes ..	**70.00**
Peacock, 5″, multicolored glaze	**75.00**
Pig	
6 x 2¾″, Bennington-type, dark brown	
sewer pipe, tooled eyelashes ..	**125.00**
10″, sewer pipe, tooled eyelashes ..	**400.00**
Porky Pig, bisque	**70.00**
Shoe, 5″, high button, tan	**80.00**
Walrus, Rockingham glaze	**75.00**
Watermelon Slice, 4 x 9½″, hanging ..	**75.00**

BARBER BOTTLES

History: Barber bottles, colorful glass bottles found on the shelves and counters in barber shops, held the liquids barbers used daily. A specific liquid was kept in a specific bottle which the barber knew by color, design, or lettering. The bulk liquids were kept in utilitarian containers under the counter or in a storage room. The attractive bottles held the place of honor.

Barber bottles are found in many types of glass: art glass with varied decoration, pattern glass, and commercially prepared and labeled bottles.

References: Richard Holiner, *Collecting Barber Bottles*, Collector Books, 1986; Ralph & Terry Kovel, *The Kovels' Bottle Price List*, Crown Publishers, Inc. 1984, 7th ed.

Note: Prices are for bottles without original stoppers unless otherwise noted.

Amethyst, 8″ h, light green, white, and red enamel, raised floral design, rolled lip exposed pontil	**100.00**
Aqua, 6″ h, handblown, exposed pontils, emb lettering, "TRICOPHEROUS FOR THE SKIN & HAIR," pr	**50.00**
Blue, 8″ h, horizontal brown band design, applied white enamel floral pattern above and below the band, sheared lip, exposed pontil	**100.00**
Clambroth, 8″ h, emb "WATER" in red across front, porcelain stoppers ...	**35.00**
Clear Glass	
6½″ h, ribbed style, decorated band around center, gold trim, raised enamel dot pattern, pontil	**50.00**
7″ h, recessed underglass label ...	**25.00**
Cobalt Blue, 8½″ h, bell shape, raised white and orange flowers, sheared lip, exposed pontil	**50.00**
Cranberry	
7″, melon base, fern pattern, white design, rolled lip, pr	**250.00**
Frosted, 8″ h, raised floral enamel design, pontil ground, pr	**75.00**
Handpainted	
7½″ h, red, frosted oval areas, purple and white flowers, green leaves, pontil, pr	**200.00**
11″ h, frosted glass, gold medallion, raised enamel around it, blue highlight, gold lip, pontil	**25.00**
Hobnail	
Blue, 7¼″ h, four neck rings, uneven rolled lip, pontil	**40.00**
Cranberry, 7½″ h, three neck rings, rolled lip, pontil	**30.00**

Cranberry, opalescent stripes, 7¼″ h, $150.00.

Irid Art Deco, 7½" h, greenish coating
over cobalt blue, pontil ground 200.00
Mary Gregory, 8" h, cobalt blue, one
with woman holding a bird, other
hunter with bird on hand, gold
trimmed lips, pr 300.00
Milk Glass, 9" h, hp, "BAY RUM," pink
and white flowers, green leaves, pas-
tel ground, rolled lip, pontil 125.00
Opalescent
Blue
7", stars and stripes pattern, pontil   200.00
7½" h, melon base, daisy and fern
trim, rolled lip, pontil 120.00
Cranberry, 7½" h, melon based, ver-
tical stripes, rolled lip, pontil 150.00
Light Blue, 7½", striped pattern, rolled
lip 75.00
White, 8½" h, fern pattern, rolled lip,
sq base 55.00
Yellow, blown three mold, fern and
flower pattern, rolled lip, melon
sided, pr 125.00
Porcelain, 9" h, flowers decorated on
three sides, one is emb "TONIC" in
black, other is "WITCH HAZEL," pr .   200.00
Spatter glass, 8¼", red and white 150.00
Teal Blue, 8½" h, white and orange
enamel dot pattern, rolled lip, ex-
posed pontil 75.00

BAROMETERS

History: A barometer is an instrument which
measures atmospheric pressure which, in turn,
aids weather forecasting. Low pressure indicates
the coming of rain, snow, or storm; high pressure
signifies fair weather.

Most barometers use an evacuated and graduated glass tube which contains a column of mercury and are classified by the shape of the case.
An aneroid barometer has no liquid and works by
a needle connected to the top of a metal box in
which a partial vacuum is maintained. The movement of the top moves the needle.

Aneroid, 7¼", Boston Brand, highly po-
lished brass case 225.00
Banjo
38" h, George III, mahogany, broken
arch pediment, convex mirror, sgd
"P Salvade Liverpool," early 19th C   425.00
38½", Hepplewhite, mahogany, line
inlay, inlaid shells and flowers, engraved silvered brass dial marked
"C.A. Cantil, Warranted" 1,200.00
38½", mahogany case, hygrometer,
thermometer, balancing level,
marked "A & V Cattania, York, Eng-
land" 450.00

Banjo, 33½" h, mahogany, marked
"Short & Mason, London, TYCOS
#2468," $1,300.00.

39", George III, inlaid mahogany,
molded broken arch pediment,
brass finial, sgd "Jas Galty, No. 132
Holborn, London," early 19th C . .   475.00
39¼", Regency, mahogany, sgd "A
Intross & Co. Chaltham," early
19th C 450.00
44", George III, inlaid mahogany, dry/
damp dial in cresting oblong thermometer, circular dial, level gauge
inscribed "C. Masper, Manchester,"
early 19th C 1,000.00
Desk
4", brass dial, English 75.00
Weather House, tin, paint dec, chalk
man and lady, sgd "Alvan Lovejoy,
Boston," label on back 150.00
Pocket
2¾", Negretti and Zambra, back inscribed "G.P.R.B." from H.L.B.
1886," orig leather case 150.00
3¼" d, brass case shaped like pocket
watch, worn wooden case, marked
"Eugene Dietzgen, Co. NY - Chi-
cago, Made In England" 65.00
Stick
35", George III, rosewood, ivory vernier scale and thermometer, brass
counterbalance and gimble,
marked "J. Bruce, Liverpool,"
c1801 . . . .   2,000.00
36", Admiral Fitzroy's, printed instruc-
tion panel, thermometer marked
"Dublin" and atmospheric chart,
mid 19th C 400.00
36", Irish, rosewood, ivory scales,
fruitwood caps, marked "Wallace
Limerick," early 19th C 1,200.00

37", George IV, mahogany, glass
panels, silvered thermometer
scale, brass vernier scale inscribed
"Lilley, London," brass gimble
mount, early 19th C **2,500.00**
38", walnut case, Woodruff's patent,
June 5, 1860, Charles Wilder, Peterborough, NH, minor loss to case
moldings **400.00**
40¼", rosewood, three beveled glass
panels, ivory vernier scales, mercury cistern, brass gimble, marked
"Dillon and Tuttle, NY," early
19th C **2,500.00**
Wheel
38½", inlaid mahogany, marked "Do-
negan & Co, London," 19th C ... **400.00**
39 d", shell inlaid mahogany, marked
"Jennings, Ipswich, England," mid
19th C **450.00**
40", French, gilt wood, frame carved
with garlands and pairs of doves,
late 18th C **500.00**

BASKETS

History: Baskets were invented when man first
required containers to gather, store, and transport
goods. Today's collector, influenced by the country
look, focuses on baskets made of splint, rye straw,
or willow. Emphasis is placed on handmade examples. Nails or staples, wide splints which are
thin and evenly cut, and a wire bail handle denote
factory construction which can date back to the
mid-19th century. Painted or woven decorated
baskets rarely are handmade, unless American
Indian.

Baskets are collected by (a) type–berry, egg, or
field, (b) region–Nantucket or Shaker, and (c) composition–splint, rye, or willow. Stick to examples in
very good condition; damaged baskets are a poor
investment even at a low price.

References: Don and Carol Raycraft, *Country
Baskets,* Wallace-Homestead; Don and Carol
Raycraft, *The Basket Book,* Collector Books,
1981; Christoph Will, *International Basketry For
Weavers and Collectors,* Schiffer Publishing,
1985; Frances Thompson, *Antique Baskets and
Basketry,* Wallace-Homestead, 1985; Frances
Thompson, *Wallace-Homestead Price Guide To
Baskets,* Wallace-Homestead, 1987; Martha
Wetherbee and Nathan Taylor, *Legend of the
Bushwhacker Basket,* privately printed, 1986.

Reproduction Alert: Modern reproductions
abound, made by diverse groups ranging from
craft revivalists to foreign manufacturers.

Berry
8 x 9½ x 5", splint and red, melon rib,
old red paint **200.00**
10 x 10½ x 6", plus wooden handle,

Splint, center rib, $125.00.

woven splint, buttocks, good age
and color **80.00**
10¾ x 11½ x 5½", plus wooden han-
dle, woven splint, buttocks **125.00**
Drying, 11 x 15 x 6¼", woven splint,
open work bottom, open rim handles **48.00**
Egg
10½ x 12 x 6", plus bentwood handle,
woven splint, radiating ribs, old varnish finish **60.00**
11 x 11 x 6", splint, finely woven,
bentwood handle **140.00**
12 x 12 x 7", splint, eye of God design, bentwood handle, worn pink
paint **50.00**
12 x 15 x 7", splint, handle **100.00**
13 x 14 x 7½", splint, radiating ribs
design, bentwood handle **100.00**
14 x 18 x 8", woven splint, radiating
ribs, bentwood handle **75.00**
Gathering
10 x 10½ x 6", reed, splint melon ribs,
bentwood handle, "H.P." carved
into handle **100.00**
14 x 25", woven splint, bentwood handle mkd "Lookout Mt" **30.00**
17 x 23 x 7¾", woven splint, oblong,
built up rim handles, good age and
color, minor rim wear **70.00**
18 x 9 x 13", woven splint, well
shaped bentwood handles, faded
red and blue design **75.00**
19 x 27", splint, oval, plaited rim, bentwood handles **120.00**
Kitchen, 12 x 14 x 6½", plus handle,
woven splint, buttocks, woven in 3
shades of splint **150.00**
Laundry, 19 x 31 x 13½", Shaker, woven
splint, bentwood rim handles **100.00**
Market, 13½ x 19 x 8½", splint and
cane, bentwood carved handle **80.00**
Miniature
3" d, 4½" h, splint, fixed handle,
painted olive green **300.00**

3¾" d, 2¼" h, splint, cylindrical, plain plaiting, double handles, wrapped rim with blue paint **150.00**
5 x 6 x 3", splint, buttocks **140.00**
Nantucket
6½ x 9⅛ x 4", plus wooden handle, tightly woven, stationary handle, oval **400.00**
10 x 8 x 7", hinged top, carved ra-coons mounted on rosewood, sgd "Jose Formoco Reyes, 1954" . . . **800.00**
Picnic, 7¾ x 15 x 6", splint, double hinged lid, int. with pattern of green and natural, faded ext., bentwood handle **100.00**
Sewing, 8¼ x 8½ x 3¼", plus handle, finely woven splint, bands of curlicues and woven grass, attached small oval basket and pincushion **45.00**
Sower's
12 x 14½ x 7", plus wooden handle, woven splint **50.00**
12 x 16½ x 8", plus wooden handle, woven splint **60.00**
Storage
10" h, rye straw, oval shape **50.00**
11½" h, woven splint, bentwood rim handles **65.00**
21" h, woven splint, lid **80.00**

BATTERSEA ENAMELS

History: Battersea enamel is a generic term for English enamel-on-copper objects of the 18th century.

In 1753 Stephen Theodore Janssen established a factory to produce "Trinkets and Curiosities Enamelled on Copper" at York House, Battersea, London. Here the new invention of transfer printing developed a high degree of excellence, and the resulting trifles delighted fashionable Georgian society.

Recent research has shown that enamels actually were being produced in London and the Midlands several years before York House was established. However, most enamel trinkets still are referred to as "Battersea Enamels," even though they were probably made in other workshops in London, Birmingham, Bilston, Wednesbury, or Liverpool.

All manner of charming items were made, including snuff and patch boxes bearing mottos and memory gems. (By adding a mirror inside the lid, a snuff box became patch box.) Many figural whimsies, called "toys," were created to amuse a gay and fashionable world. Many other elaborate articles, e.g., candlesticks, salts, tea caddies, and bonbonnieres, were made for the tables of the newly rich middle classes.

Reference: Susan Benjamin, *English Enamel Boxes*, Merrimack Publishers Circle, 1978.
Advisors: Barbara and Melvin Alpren.

Bird, blue specked head, rose breast, green, purple, red, black, yellow and green wings, dec on base with bird, dandelion, hallmarked, 2½ x 1½ x 2½", $3,750.00.

Bonbonniere
1⅛" h, miniature apple shaped box, painted in natural colors, Bilston, c1770 . . . . **1,450.00**
2¼", finch, realistically painted, lid with bird on branch, Bilston, c1770 **1,800.00**
Bougie Box, (wax jack container), 1¼" d, 2" h, turquoise, raised all-over flowers, Bilston, c1770 . . . . **950.00**
Box, 1¾ x 1½ x 1", "A Trifle from Mother," black lettering, gold, white, and blue **575.00**
Candlesticks, pr, 11" h, white ground, cobalt reserves, all-over spring flower dec, Bilston, c1780 . . . . **3,500.00**
Cloak Hooks, pr, 1¼" d, pastoral scenes, Battersea, c1770 . . . . **500.00**
Patch Box
1¼" l, oval
"A am all Thine," small slip on cover with motto, Bilston, c1770 **350.00**
"A Pleasing Gift" inscribed with bowknots, pink ground, Bilston, c1780 . . . . **600.00**
"Esteem the Giver" inscribed within large heart surrounded by garlands of flowers and lovebirds, Bilston, c1780 . . . . **500.00**
1¼", round, white ground, realistic roses on top and sides, Birmingham style, c1790 . . . . **600.00**
1⅞" l, oval, historical, "A Trifle from Bath, North Parade," natural colors, pink base, Bilston, c1770 . . . . . . **500.00**
2", oval, "Remember Me, When This You See," lovers, ship, and wreath

on lid, green base, South Stafford-
shire, c1780 . . . . 600.00
Scent Bottle Holder, ½ x 1¼ x 2¼",
white ground, purple dec, green
leaves, rose and blue flowers, bow
and arrow sheaf on reverse 400.00
Scent Flask, 2⅜" h, hinged cov, orig
glass scent bottle inside, white
ground, blue and green trellis work,
Birmingham, c1770 . . . . 1,000.00
Snuff Box, 2 x 1½", rect, yellow, painted
cabbage rose, rare color, South Staffordshire, c1780 . . . . 1,000.00
Table Snuff, 2" l, rect, painted fruits and
birds (in style of Hancock) on lid, Bilston, c1780 . . . . 900.00
Toy Watch, 1¼" d, hinged snuff box,
lavender ground, posy sprays, Bil-
ston, c1790 . . . . 1,250.00

BAVARIAN CHINA

History: Bavaria, Germany, was an important
porcelain production center, similar to the Staffordshire district in England. The name Bavarian China
refers to companies operating in Bavaria, among
which were Hutschenreuther, Thomas, and Zeh,
Scherzer & Co. (Z. S. & Co.). Very little of the
production from this area was imported into the
United States prior to 1870.

Reference: Susan and Al Bagdade, *Warman's
English & Continental Pottery & Porcelain, 1st Edition,* Warman Publishing Co., Inc., 1987.

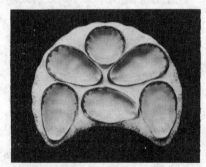

Oyster Plate, 9", shaded blue, gold border, $75.00.

Biscuit Jar, cream and gold, large peach
blossoms, R W mark 75.00
Bowl, 9½", hp strawberries, flowers, and
leaves on green ground, artist sgd . 45.00
Celery Tray, 11" l, basket of fruit in center, lustered edge, c1900 . . . . 35.00

Charger, scalloped rim, game bird in
woodland scene, bunches of pink and
yellow roses, connecting garlands . . 75.00
Chocolate Set, chocolate pot, cov, 6
cups and saucers, shaded blue to
white, large white leaves, pink, red,
and white roses, crown mark 235.00
Cup and Saucer, roses and foliage, gold
handle 20.00
Figurine, 10½" h, dark blue and pale
orange marabou standing beside tan
and navy cactus, marked "Hutschenreuther Selb-Bavaria, K. Tutter" . . . 250.00
Hair Receiver, 3½ x 2½", apple blossom
dec, T. S. & Co 45.00
Pitcher, 9" bulbous, blackberry dec,
shaded ground, burnished gold lizard
handle, sgd "D. Churchill" 110.00
Plate
7", reticulated rim, Dresden type floral
dec, artist sgd "Schumann" 75.00
8", fruit decal 18.00
8½", hp, poinsettia dec 45.00
9", portrait, side view of lady, sgd "L.
B. Chaffee, R. C. Bavarian" 70.00
10", violets, gold handle, sgd "L.
Leonhard" 45.00
Platter, 16", Dresden flowers 85.00
Punch Bowl, hp roses int. and ext., gold
pedestal base, marked "H & C" . . . 250.00
Ramekin, underplate, ruffled, small red
roses with green foliage, gold rim . . 40.00
Salt and Pepper Shakers, pink apple
blossom sprays, white ground, reticulated gold tops, pr 25.00
Shaving Mug, pink carnations, marked
"Royal Bavarian" 45.00
Sugar, cov, white, green grapes dec . . 30.00
Sugar Shaker, hp, pastel pansies 45.00
Tray, 14", 2 handles, portrait center,
gold rim, artist sgd 145.00
Vase
9", 2 handles, brush gold dec top and
bottom, cream ground, pink pan-
sies and daisies 40.00
14", shaded green ground, red roses,
green leaves, gold trim 150.00

BELLEEK

History: Belleek, a thin, ivory colored, almost
iridescent-type porcelain, was first made in 1857
in county Ferman, Ireland. Production continued
until World War I, was discontinued for a period of
time, and then resumed. The Shamrock pattern is

most familiar, but many patterns were made, including, Limpet, Tridacna, and Grasses.

Irish Belleek has several identifying marks, e.g., the Harp and Hound (1865–80) and Harp, Hound, and Castle (1863–91). After 1891 the word "Ireland" or "Erie" was added. Some pieces are marked "Belleek Co., Fermanagh."

There is an Irish saying: If a newly married couple receives a gift of Belleek, their marriage will be blessed with lasting happiness.

Several American firms made a Belleek-type porcelain. The first was Ott and Brewer Co. Trenton, New Jersey, in 1884, followed by Willets. Other firms included The Ceramic Art Co. (1889), American Art China Works (1892), Columbian Art Co. (1893), and Lenox, Inc. (1904).

Reference: Mary Frank Aston, *American Belleek*, Collector Books, 1984.

Additional Listings: Lenox.

Abbreviations: 1BM = 1st Black Mark; 2BM = 2nd Black Mark; 3BM = 3rd Black Mark; 4GM = 4th Green Mark; 5GM = 5th Green Mark.

Advisor: MaryBeth Appert.

AMERICAN

Bowl
  6¼" l, Wavecrest, Roses pattern, Lenox green wreath mark **75.00**
  9" l, Wavecrest, green, heavy gold trim, white curled handle, Lenox green wreath mark **90.00**
Cup, demitasse liner, gold band border, SS holder with saucer, Lenox green wreath mark **55.00**
Cup and Saucer, 6" h, square pedestal base, undecorated, Willets brown mark **35.00**
Dresser set, cov powder box, pin tray, buffer and container, nail brush, pin cushion, hp violets, artist sgd "M.R.", Willets brown mark, 6 pcs **550.00**
Figure
  4"
    Elephant, white, Lenox green wreath mark **315.00**
    Swan
      Green, Lenox green wreath mark   **65.00**
      Pink, Lenox green wreath mark   **50.00**
  5½", rabbit, perfumers, white, Lenox green wreath mark,pr **525.00**
Loving Cup, three handles, wine keeper in wine cellar, artist sgd, SS repousse collar, CAC mark **185.00**
Mask, 7½", lady's face, black, Lenox green wreath mark **175.00**
Mug
  5"
    Green and red grape bunches, artist sgd "ABJ," CAC mark **85.00**
    Monk drinking, Lenox green wreath mark **125.00**

7", William Penn, Lenox green wreath mark **175.00**
7½", grapevines and olive green grapes, SS overlay, CAC mark . .   **225.00**
Pitcher, 5½", body indentation, tree branch shaped handle, gold paste floral dec, Willets brown mark **375.00**
Powder Box, 4 x 6"
  Pink, gold wheat on lid, Lenox green wreath mark **40.00**
  White, hp, portrait of dog on lid, artist sgd "Nosek" **600.00**
Salt
  1"
    Gold rim, Willets brown mark **12.00**
    Pink roses, gold rim, CAC mark . .   **16.00**
  2", gold ftd, green ground, pink rose ext., single pink rose int., gold rim, CAC mark **25.00**
Salt and Pepper Shakers, 1" d salt, 2" h egg shape pepper, pink roses, Lenox green palette mark, pr **35.00**
Vase
  8½", bulbous shape, pine cone and branches decor, Lenox green wreath mark **55.00**
  9", fluted lily shape, sq pedestal base, Roses pattern, Lenox green wreath mark, pr **225.00**
  12" h, 8½" d, applied handles, floral ground, artist sgd, CAC mark . . .   **475.00**
  Art Deco, SS overlay, white porcelain, three openings for flowers, Lenox green wreath mark **150.00**

Irish, vase, 6¼" h, 4½" w, tree trunk, green clover dec, 3rd black mark, $170.00.

IRISH

Ashtray, 4½", shamrock horseshoe, 4GM **45.00**
Basket
  9" d, Sydenham **450.00**

Oval, cov pearl, 2BM	1,715.00
Rathbone, pearl	2,110.00
Butter Plate, leaf, No. 1, 5GM	20.00
Cup and Saucer, 6″ d, 2″ h, Shamrock pattern, 2BM	200.00

Cake Plate

Limpet pattern, 2BM	175.00
Shamrock pattern, 3BM	125.00
Creamer, Lotus pattern, green handle, 2BM	75.00

Creamer and Sugar

Lily pattern, 5GM	45.00
Lotus pattern, 5GM	45.00
Toy, Shamrock pattern, 3BM	105.00
Tridacna, green rim, 3BM	115.00
Dish, 6½″, heart shape, 3BM	95.00

Figure

3½″, Terrier, 4GM	35.00
4½″, Swan, 3BM	65.00

14⅝″

Affection, multicolored, 1BM	2,500.00
Meditation, multicolored, 1BM	2,500.00
Flower Holder, 3½″ h, Seahorse, one with white head, other with brown, 1BM, pr	1,200.00
Salt, boat, 5GM	30.00
Sandwich Tray, Mask pattern, 2BM	275.00

Sugar

Cleary pattern, 3BM	60.00
Shamrock pattern, cov, 3BM	65.00
Tea and Dessert Service, Eugene Sheran, partially decorated, c1887, 32 pcs	7,900.00

Tea Set

Limpet pattern, 7″ teapot, 3¼″ creamer, 4½″ covered sugar, 3BM, 3 pcs	350.00
Neptune pattern, teapot, creamer, sugar, six cups and saucers, and six dessert plates, 15 pcs, 2BM	1,500.00

Vase

5½″, Shamrock spill, 4GM	35.00
5⅜″, ftd, flower spill, applied flowers, 3BM	325.00
6¼″, Shamrock tree trunk 2BM	145.00
5GM	40.00
6½″, Harp, Shamrock pattern, 5GM	40.00
7¾″, rock spill, 5GM	90.00
7⅞″, Panel, shamrocks with yellow gilt, 6GM	65.00
Tub, 3¼″ d, Shamrock pattern, 3BM	55.00

BELLS

History: Bells have been used for centuries for many different purposes. They have been traced as far back as 2697 B.C., though at that time they did not have any true tone. One of the oldest bells is the "crotal," a tiny sphere with small holes and a ball or stone or metal inside. This type now appears as sleigh bells.

True bell making began when bronze, the mixing of tin and copper, was discovered. There are now many types of materials of which bells are made—almost as many materials as there are uses for them.

Bells of the late 19th century show a high degree of workmanship and artistic style. Glass bells from this period are sometimes an example of the glass blower's talent and the glass manufacturer's product.

Additional Listings: See *Warman's Americana & Collectibles* for more examples.

Cigar Counter Bell, brass, cast iron base, 8 x 7″, marked "Russel & Erwin Mfg Co., New Britain, CT, USA, Pat'd Aug 1, 96, Rd. No. 269895," $245.00.

Animal

Camel, second bell as clapper	85.00
Cow, brass, iron clapper, 7″	35.00
Donkey, brass, ten bells on leather strap	145.00
Horse, brass, swing type, red and brown horsehair cockade, mounted on wood base, 10¾″	150.00
Sheep, sheet iron, orig label "Holstein Sheep Bell No. 6," 3½″	15.00

China

Dresden, floral dec, gold handle	60.00
Limoges, cow shape, pale blue, pink roses, gilded handle, 4″	38.00

Staffordshire, figural, girl

5¼″, full skirt	65.00
6″, blue, white, and gold	85.00
Church Steeple, cast iron, Hollsboro, OH, 1886, N2 yoke	220.00

Desk

Brass, face in top center of fancywork, operating gonger on each side, 7″	120.00
Bronze, white marble base, side tap	40.00
Silverplate, open filagree skirt, windup, top knob	85.00

Glass

Amethyst, applied threading, 12″	375.00

Bohemian, ruby flashed, Deer & Castle, clear handle and clapper, 4½"	80.00
Bristol, wedding bell, Swirl pattern, red barrel, clear swirl handle, four ball finial, clapper, 13¼"	130.00
Burmese, shaded deep pink to ivory, satin finish, 6¼"	70.00
Carnival, figural, Southern Belle, white imperial	38.00
Custard, souvenir, "Alamo - Built 1718, San Antonio, TX," gilt band	90.00
Cut	
Clear, pinwheels, notched handle, Brilliant Period	285.00
Kalana Lily, etched, Dorflinger, 6"	85.00
Heisey, frosted, Victorian Belle	125.00
Milk, smocking, mkd "Akeo, Made in USA"	22.00
Venetian, latticino, 4¼"	150.00
Hand, brass, figural	
Fish handle, 5"	42.00
Dickens man with pipe, 3⅞"	65.00
Gourd and leaf, ftd, base with man holding bracket and striker	25.00
Lady, bust, quilted pattern on bell, 3⅝"	35.00
Monk, carries umbrella and basket, 5"	75.00
Old Woman carrying pot, feet form clapper, 5"	70.00
Suffragette, "Votes for Women, Thou Shall Have A Vote," marked "Arcadian Junus"	175.00
Turtle, bell bracket and striker on shell	30.00
Liberty, nickel steel base, green, 4⅜"	70.00
Locomotive, brass, emb "E.M.D.", cast iron ball clapper, mounted in steel tripod, 12" d	270.00
Plantation, cast iron, rocker arm, 13 x 10"	380.00
School, metal, turned handle, 8"	28.00
Silver, German, florentine, emb figures, 2¾"	75.00
Sleigh, brass	
Four, 15½" leather strap	60.00
Twenty, 36" pigskin strap	75.00
Twenty-five, acorn shape, leather strap	85.00
Thirty-six, crotal type, 89" leather strap	180.00

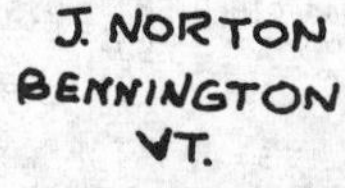

BENNINGTON AND BENNINGTON-TYPE POTTERY

History: In 1845 Christopher Webber Fenton joined Julius Norton, his brother-in-law, in the manufacturing of stoneware pottery in Bennington, Vermont. Fenton sought to expand the company's products and glazes; Norton wanted to concentrate solely on stoneware. In 1847 Fenton broke away and established his own factory.

Fenton introduced the famous Rockingham glaze, developed in England and named after the Marquis of Rockingham, to America. In 1849 he patented a flint enamel glaze, "Fenton's Enamel," which added flecks, spots, or streaks of color (usually blues, greens, yellows, and oranges) to the brown Rockingham glaze. Forms included candlesticks, coachman bottles, cow creamers, poodles, sugar bowls, and toby pitchers.

Fenton produced the little known scroddled ware, commonly called lava or agate ware. Scroddled ware is composed of different colored clays, mixed with cream colored clay, molded, turned on a potter's wheel, coated with feldspar and flint, and fired. It was not produced in quantity, as there was little demand for it.

Fenton also introduced Parian ware to America. Parian was developed in England in 1842 and known as "Statuary ware." Parian is a translucent porcelain which has no glaze and resembles marble. Bennington made the blue and white variety in the form of vases, cologne bottles, and trinkets.

Five different marks were used, with many variations. Only about twenty percent of the pieces carried any mark; some forms were almost always marked, others never. Marks: (a) 1849 mark (4 variations) for flint enamel and Rockingham; (b) E. Fenton's Works, 1845–47, on Parian and occasionally on scroddled ware; (c) U. S. Pottery Co., ribbon mark, 1852–58, on Parian and blue and white porcelain; (d) U. S. Pottery Co., lozenge mark, 1852–58, on Parian; and (e) U. S. Pottery, oval mark, 1853–58, mainly on scroddled ware.

The hound handled pitcher is probably the best known Bennington piece. Hound handled pitchers also were made by some 30 potteries in over 55 different variations. Rockingham glaze was used by over 150 potteries in 11 states, mainly the Mid-West, between 1830 and 1900.

References: Richard Carter Barret, *How To Identify Bennington Pottery*, Stephen Greene Press, 1964; Laura Woodside Watkins, *Early New England Potters And Their Wares*, Harvard University Press, 1950.

Museums: Bennington Museum, Bennington, VT; East Liverpool Museum of Ceramics, East Liverpool, OH.

Additional Listings: Stoneware.

BENNINGTON POTTERY

Book Flask	
5½"	
"Departed Spirits," flint enamel, dark brown and cream glaze, splotches of blue and yellow	450.00
"Departed Spirits, G," flint enamel,	

Bennington, Toby jug, 5⅞" h, Fenton, $525.00.

flowing brown, amber, blue and cream glaze, minor maker's irregularities 450.00

7½", "Ladies Companion," flint enamel, dark brown, amber, blue and green glaze, two quart 1,000.00

7¾", untitled, flint enamel, dark brown, amber, blue and cream glaze, two quart 500.00

8", "Departed Spirits," flint enamel, light cream glaze with flecks of blue and amber, two quart 1,000.00

10¾", "Bennington Companion," flint enamel, dark brown, amber, blue, and green glaze, four quart, professional repairs in three areas 700.00

Bottle, 10⅜" h, coachman, Rockingham glaze, 1849 mark on bottom, professional restoration to hat 200.00

Candlestick

6¾", columnar, flint enamel, yellow-brown, blue glaze 400.00

7⅞" h, Rockingham glaze, pr 850.00

Chamber Pot, flint enamel, Scalloped Rib pattern, olive green, amber, and yellow glaze, 1849 mark on bottom . 400.00

Coffeepot, 12¾" h, flint enamel, olive and mottled amber glaze, fluted finial, c1849–58, one tiny nick to top of spout 1,700.00

Creamer, 5½" h, cow, Rockingham glaze, imp "N," two small chips under foot rim 300.00

Curtain Tiebacks, pr, 3¾", flint enamel, dark brown, cream and brown glaze, unmarked 150.00

Dish, 9¼", deep, flint enamel, Fenton Co. mark, 1849 .... 400.00

Ewer, 10¼", Parian, blue and white, applied grapes and leaves dec, c1850 225.00

Foot Bath, flint enamel, Scalloped Rib pattern, c1849–58

19½" l, brown and cream mottled glaze, blue and amber highlights, chemical deposit int., slight wear, 4" vertical crack beside one handle . 700.00

20" l, dark brown and cream vertically mottled pattern, splashes of green, blue, and amber, 1849 mark on bottom, undamaged 1,750.00

Frame, 9½ x 8½", oval, flint enamel, c1849–55 .... 675.00

Goblet, 4½" h, Rockingham glaze 275.00

Mantel Ornament

Lion, 11¼ x 9¼", Rockingham glaze, 1849 signature under base, repaired 1,750.00

Poodle, 9½ x 8½", Rockingham glaze, holding basket of colored fruit in mouth, applied coleslaw, c1849–55 .... 3,600.00

Pitcher

8", Parian, white, tulip and sunflower pattern, c1852 .... 225.00

9½"

Parian, blue and white, applied charter oak dec, USP ribbon mark, c1852 .... 500.00

Rockingham glaze, small glaze imperfection caused in the making 1,000.00

Slop Jar, 14¼" h, flint enamel, Scalloped Rib pattern, marked, c1849–58, upper rim professionally repaired for glaze ware 450.00

Snuff Jar, 4", Rockingham glaze, toby hat, Fenton, 1849 mark 400.00

Soap Dish

Covered, flint enamel, mottled dark brown, green, and cream, 1849 mark 600.00

Open, 5¼", flint enamel, olive brown and cream, flecks of green in glaze, 1849 mark on bottom 125.00

Sugar, cov, flint enamel, mottled olive green and cream glaze, blue and amber highlights, 1948 mark, two minor glaze flakes on upper rim 700.00

Teapot, 7⅜" h, flint enamel, Alternate Rib pattern, marked 500.00

Toby Jug, 6⅜", seated, Rockingham glaze, 1849 mark 325.00

Vase, 9", tulip, flint enamel, c1849–55 . 475.00

BENNINGTON-TYPE

Bank, 3¼", ewe, oval base, Rockingham glaze 100.00

Book Flask, 5½", "History of Holland," blue glaze 215.00

Bottle, 6", figural, pair of high button shoes, Rockingham glaze 175.00

Bennington Type, pitcher, tulip, New Jersey, medium brown glaze, 5″, $165.00.

Pitcher, 10½″, Rockingham glaze,
  paneled, c1850 .... **225.00**
Toby, 6″, Rockingham glaze **325.00**

BISCUIT JARS

History: The biscuit or cracker jar was the forerunner of the cookie jar. They were made of various materials by leading glassworks and potteries of the late 19th and early 20th centuries.

Note: All items listed have silver plated mountings unless otherwise noted.

Wavecrest, 7½″ h, unsigned, $200.00.

Art Deco, 6 x 5⅜″, pottery, nasturtium
  pattern, orange and yellow flowers,
  green leaves, brown spatter trim, yellow and orange bands on lid, orig
  wicker handle, marked "Clarice Cliff
  Bizarre" **275.00**
Jasperware, 5⅜ x 6¾″, deep blue, white

classical ladies with cupid, SP rim, lid,
  handle, and ball feet, marked "Wedgwood" only **150.00**
Nippon, 4½ x 7¼″, sq, white, multicolored floral bands, gold outlines and
  trim, marked "E. E." **85.00**
Pairpoint, 9½″, burnt orange, large floral
  dec, blown-out floral base, sgd **325.00**
Royal Bonn, 6 x 7½″, beige and cream
  ground, pink, blue, rose, and orange
  flowers, gold outlines, emb swirls, SP
  rim, lid, and handle, marked **125.00**
Satin Glass
  7¼″, pink, shell pattern base, enameled floral dec, SP lid and handle **300.00**
  9 x 5″, flared base, rainbow, DQ,
  MOP, shiny finish, SP cov, and handle, marked "Patent" **950.00**
Schlegelmilch, R. S. Prussia, pearlized
  luster, lily of the valley dec, ftd scalloped base, red mark **285.00**
Silverplated, 8 x 8″, round, hinged lid,
  bright cut floral dec, pierced ftd base,
  late 19th C **165.00**
Smith Bros. sq, swirled rib, daisy spray
  dec, SP lid and handle, rampant lion
  mark **700.00**
Stevens and Williams, 5½ x 7¾″, amber
  and green applied leaves, cream
  opaque ext., deep pink int., SP rim,
  lid, and handle **275.00**
Tuncliffe, 5 x 7¼″, tapestry, beige
  ground, lavender and white flowers,
  green leaves, emb swirl pattern, emb
  leaves at base, SP rim, lid, and handle, marked **125.00**
Wave Crest
  5½ x 9″, long stemmed yellow roses,
  molded multicolored Helmschmied
  swirls ground, incised floral and
  leaf dec on lid, marked "Quadruple
  Plate" **385.00**
  6 x 9½″, puffy egg crate shape, poppies dec, marked "C F Monroe" . **250.00**
Wedgwood, 7½″, dark green, light green
  Washington, Franklin, and Lafayette
  medallions, acorn finial **480.00**

BISQUE

History: Bisque or biscuit china is the name given to wares that have been fired once and are not glazed.

Bisque figurines and busts were popular during the Victorian era, being used on fireplace mantels, dining room buffets, and end tables. Manufacturing was centered in the United States and Europe. By the mid-20th century the Japanese were the principal source of bisque items, especially character related items.

Reference: Susan and Al Bagdade, *Warman's English & Continental Pottery & Porcelain, 1st Edition,* Warman Publishing Co., Inc., 1987.

Figure, 4¾" h, pot reads "Scratch my back," $60.00.

Animal Dish, cov, 9 x 6½ x 5½", brown and white dog, green blanket, white and gilt basketweave base	500.00
Basket, 8", barefoot boy with wide brimmed hat seated on rim, marked "Germany"	48.00
Bust, 10", blonde boy and girl, floral shirts, pleated collars, marked "Germany," pr	325.00
Cigar Holder, 6" h, figural, French soldiers, match holder, French	150.00

Figure

Bathing Beauty, 5" l, lying on stomach, green bathing suit, red floppy hat, marked "Germany"	125.00
Bonnie Prince Charlie, 8", French . .	30.00
Girl, 3¼ x 2¼ x 6½", dancing, green dress, white collar, pink bow, marked "Heubach"	75.00
Hanging type, two children on swing, 5⅝"	45.00
Man offering lady a rose, pr, 20¾" h, Victorian costumes, polychrome, German, late 19th C	300.00
Flower Pot, carriage, four wheels, royal markings, pale blue and pink, white ground, gold dots, blank back	135.00
Night Light, owl head, 3½", 2⅞", gray, brown glass eyes, blue bow around neck	175.00
Nodder, 2½ x 3½", seated jester, holding pipe, pastel peach and white, gold trim	75.00

Piano Baby

5", black boy, polka dot rompers, marked "Heubach"	800.00
7", seated, holding gold watch to ear, fancy gown, German	150.00
7¼", seated, hands on one foot, white gown, blue trim, marked "Heubach"	275.00
8", boy, seated, blue hat, holding drum, marked "Royal Rudolstadt, Germany"	350.00
Tobacco Jar, 4⅞", figural, boy's head .	150.00
Toothpick, kitten playing with mouse .	35.00
Vase, 1⅞ x 3½", figural, googly eyed girl, blonde hair, blue skirt, orange blouse, white apron and hat, small brown teddy bear, marked "Shafer & Vater"	75.00

BITTERS BOTTLES

History: Bitters, a "remedy" made from natural herbs and other mixtures with an alcohol base, often was viewed as the universal cure-all. The names given to various bitter mixtures were imaginative, though the bitters seldom cured what their makers claimed.

The manufacturers of bitters needed a way to sell and advertise their products. They designed bottles in many shapes, sizes, and colors to attract the buyer. Many forms of advertising, including trade cards, billboards, signs, almanacs, and novelties proclaimed the virtues of a specific bitter.

During the Civil War a tax was levied on alcoholic beverages. Since bitters were identified as medicines, they were exempt from this tax. The alcohol content was never mentioned. In 1907 when the Pure Foods Regulations went into effect, "an honest statement of content on every label" put most of the manufacturers out of business.

References: Carlyn Ring, *For Bitters Only,* 1980; J. H. Thompson, *Bitters Bottles,* Century House, 1947; Richard Watson, *Bitters Bottles,* Thomas Nelson and Sons, 1965.

Periodical: *Old Bottle Magazine,* Maverick Publications, P. O. Box 243, Bend, OR 97701. Subscription: $10.00

Amazon Bitters, sq, amber	105.00
Angostura Bark Bitters, amber, 7"	90.00
Atwood's Quinine Tonic, aqua	35.00
Barto's Great Gun Bitters, "Reading, Pa." in center circle, cannon shop bottle, olive amber, 11 x 3¼"	785.00
Brady's Family Bitters, olive amber . . .	65.00
Brown's Celebrated Indian Herb Bitters, Indian queen, yellow, rolled mouth, 12"	750.00
Bryant's Stomach Bitters, eight sided, pontil, olive, 11¾"	125.00
Callendar, Dr., & Son Liver Bitters, "Celebrated Liver Bitters," light amber . .	78.00
Capp's, Dr., White Mountain Bitters, aqua	75.00
Catawba Wine Bitters, cluster of grapes in front and back, green, 9"	65.00

Clarke's Vegetable Sherry Wine, aqua, 11½" **50.00**

Clayton's & Russell's Bitters, "Celebrated Stomach Bitters," sq **68.00**

Climax Bitters, pale gold amber **75.00**

Constitution Bitters, deep amethyst, sloping collared mouth, 9⅛" **725.00**

Damiana Bitters, round, Baja, CA, aqua **100.00**

Dandelion Bitters, rect bottle, clear, amber, tapered top, 8" **32.00**

Doyle's Hop Bitters, amber, sloping collared mouth, 9⅜" **25.00**

East Indian Root Bitters, Boston, MA, amber **250.00**

Emerson Excelsior Botanic Bitters, "E.H. Burns, Augusta, ME," amber, 9" **75.00**

English Femal Bitters, clear **70.00**

Abbotts Bitters, 9" h, pewter top, raised letters, $125.00.

Fish Bitters, W.H. Ware Pat 1866, fish, amber, 11¾" **125.00**

Globe, The, Tonic Bitters, amber, sloping collared mouth, 10" **65.00**

Goff's Bitters, H on bottom, clear and amber, 5¾" **25.00**

Hardy, Dr. Manley, aqua, tooled mouth, 7¼" **75.00**

Holtzermann's Patent Stomach Bitters, rect cabin, yellow amber, sloping collared mouth, 9½" **425.00**

Hartnig's Celebrated Alpine Bitters, "St Joseph, MO," sq **75.00**

Hart's Star Bitters, Philadelphia, PA .. **175.00**

Hostetter's Dr. J, Stomach Bitters, dark olive green, 9½" **70.00**

Hutching's Dispepsia Bitters, aqua, sloping collared mouth, 8⅜" **75.00**

Jones Indian Specific Herb Bitters, amber "Patent" **185.00**

Kimball's Jaundice Bitters, golden amber, sloping collared mouth, iron pontil, 7" **150.00**

King Solomon's Bitters, amber **150.00**

Lorimer's Juniper Bitters, sq, blue green, 9½" **60.00**

McKeever's Army Bitters, on shoulder, drum shaped bottom, cannonballs stacked on top, tapered top, amber, 10¼" **600.00**

Moffit, John, NY, Phoenix Bitters, olive amber, eight-sided, round collar pontil, 6⅜" **2,500.00**

Niagara Star Bitters, sq, yellow amber, sloping collared mouth, 10" **200.00**

Old Homestead Wild Cherry Bitters, sq cabin, deep golden amber, sloping collared mouth, 9½" **150.00**

Oregon Grape Root Bitters, round, clear, 9¾" **48.00**

Pendleton Pineapple Bitters, amber .. **65.00**

Phoenix Bitters, olive amber, rolled mouth, 5⅛" **250.00**

Porter's, Dr., Medicated Stomach Bitters **70.00**

Reed's Bitters, lady's leg, golden amber, sloping collared mouth, 12⅜" **250.00**

Rothenberg, S.B., Sole Agent, U.S., gin shape, milk glass, applied collared mouth, 9" **100.00**

Sanborn Kidney & Liver Vegetable Laxative Bitters, amber **65.00**

Sazerac Aromatic Bitters, lady's leg, milk glass, applied mouth, 12¼" ... **275.00**

Simon's Centennial Bitters, bust of George Washington, golden amber, collar mouth, 10" **825.00**

Suffolk Bitters, pig, yellow amber, double collared mouth, 10" **325.00**

Sunny Castle Stomach Bitters, light amber **60.00**

Tippecanoe Bitters, round, deep golden yellow, mushroom mouth, 9" **75.00**

Toneco Stomach Bitters, "Appetizer & Tonic," clear, sq **60.00**

Traveller's Bitters, man standing with cane, oval, amber, 1834–1870, 10½" **260.00**

Zingari Bitters, round, lady's leg neck, amber, 11¾" **185.00**

BLOWN THREE MOLD

History: The Jamestown colony in Virginia introduced glass making into America. The artisans used a "free blown" method.

Blowing molten glass into molds was not introduced into America until the early 1800s. Blown three mold glass used a pre-designed mold that consisted of two, three, or more hinged parts. The glass maker placed a quantity of molten glass on the tip of a rod or tube, inserted it into the mold, blew air into the tube, waited until the glass cooled, and removed the finish product. The three part mold is the most common and lends its name to this entire category.

The impressed decorations on blown mold glass usually are reversed, i.e., what is raised or convex on the outside will be concave on the inside. This is useful in identifying the blown form.

By 1850 American made glassware was in relatively common usage. The increased demand led to large factories and the creation of a technology which eliminated the smaller companies.

In 1986–87 Richard A. Bourne Co., Inc., sold the William J. Elsholz collection of Early American glass in a three catalog sale. Blown three mold did very well with a dark amber lidded sugar bowl, attributed to the White Glass Works of Zanesville, Ohio, bringing $13,500.00.

Reference: George S. and Helen McKearin, *American Glass,* reprint, Crown Publishers, 1941, 1948.

Basket, clear, possibly Boston and Sandwich Glass Company, McKearin GV-24, ex-Culbertson collection ... **180.00**
Bottle
  Aquamarine, 7¾″ h, eight sided, geometric, McKearin GI-18 .... **1,550.00**
  Deep olive green, 8½″ h, quart, barrel shape, attributed to Keene Glass Works, McKearin GII-7, ex-William Elsholz and James H. Rose collections **1,750.00**
  Light Green, sq, orig ribbed ball stopper, McKearin GII-28, stopper type 20, ex-William Elsholz collection . **2,000.00**

Bowl, 5″ d, 1⅞ " h, clear, rayed base, McKearin GIII–21, $300.00.

Bowl, clear, 5⅝″ d, 1³⁄₁₆″ h, folded rim, pontil, twelve diamond base, McKearin GII-6 .... **85.00**
Carafe, deep green, flanged mouth, rayed base, geometric, qt, McKearin GI-29 .... **1,800.00**
Cologne, paneled, sapphire blue, 6″, smooth plain base **160.00**
Cordial, clear, 2⅞″ h, ringed base-pontil, somewhat hollow stem, flat heavy circular foot, blown into small whiskey

glass mold and formed free hand, McKearin GII-16 .... **450.00**
Creamer
  Clear, bold flaring rim, pouring spout, applied solid handle with fine curled end, McKearin GI-29 .... **550.00**
  Purple-Blue (deep), 3½″, applied handle, McKearin GII-11, ex-William Elsholz collection **1,750.00**
Cruet
  Cobalt Blue (deep), 7¾″ h, scroll scale pattern, ribbed base-pontil, applied handle, French **250.00**
  Sapphire Blue (deep), 6¾″ h, solid "Tam" stopper, pontil, McKearin GI-7, type 2 .... **220.00**
Decanter
  Clear
    Half Pint, pressed ball stopper, partially rayed base-pontil, McKearin GIII-4, unlisted as a decanter, ex-McKearin and Culbertson collections **75.00**
    Pint, 8½″, period sunburst stopper which may be original, possibly Irish, McKearin GII-7 .... **140.00**
    Quart, 10½″ h, 3½″ d, prior to expansion in the tree mold, piece was molded in sixteen vertical rib mold, applied spiral threading around neck, flanged neck-pontil, McKearin GIII-5, ½″ piece of applied threading flaked off, stopper McKearin GII-18, ex-McKearin, Guggenheim, Logan, and Gotjen collections **1,500.00**
  Olive Amber
    Pint, 5⅝″ h, 3¼″ d, diamond sunbursts between swirled flutes, flanged neck-pontil, product of Mount Vernon Glass Co., McKearin GIII-2, type 1, minute shallow pinpoint flake on underside of flange, ex-Gotjen collection **1,400.00**
    Quart, Keene, NH, McKearin GIII-19, unusual in that this has flanged lip as opposed to funnel shaped mouth, slight int. stain . **850.00**
  Olive Green, 7″ h, geometric, no stopper, McKearin GIII-16 .... **325.00**
  Purple Blue, miniature, half pint, fitted with vinegar bottle stopper which is not original, McKearin GI-29 .... **500.00**
Dish
  Deep, clear, 8″ d, New England, McKearin GII-18 with McKearin base #21 .... **120.00**
  Shallow, clear, 7¼″ d, 1⅜″ h, folded rim, diamond base-pontil, McKearin GII-21, ex-Culbertson collection **100.00**

Flask

Clear, 5¼" h, pattern of arches, then diamonds within diamonds, then inverted arches resting upon small dots, sheared mouth-pontil, Continental, slight interior haze **300.00**

Clear with light yellow tint, one-half pint, 4½" h, 3⅞" w, chestnut shape, sheared mouth-pontil, McKearin GII-24, mouth roughness (two tiny shallow flakes on top of mouth rim), 1 x ½" oval shallow sliver/smooth broken bubble off underside of base (in making), ex-Tiffany and Gotjen collections **1,100.00**

Deep yellow-green, 7¼", pint, plain base, slight wear, slight chemical deposit on one rib, McKearin GI-22, ex-William Elsholz and George S. McKearin collections **1,250.00**

Pale Blue, 5⅜", three quarter pint, Type VI rayed base, McKearin GIII-24, ex-William Elsholz, Crawford Wettlaufer, and Richard H. Wood collections **3,750.00**

Flip, clear

4¾" h, plain base pontil, McKearin GIII-22 .... **150.00**

5⅛" h, 4½" d, sixteen diamond base-pontil, McKearin GII-18 .... **150.00**

6", barrel shaped, eighteen diamond base, McKearin GII-18, ex-Culbertson collection **220.00**

Fountain, bird cage, clear, 3" w across bottom and front, 5⅞" h, applied bird finial, opening for front has never been opened, Boston and Sandwich Glass Co., McKearin GI-12, ex-Gotjen collection **375.00**

Glass, clear, 3¼" h, plain base pontil, McKearin GI-24 .... **65.00**

Hat, Beaver

Clear, rayed pontiled base, McKearin GIII-3 .... **100.00**

Cobalt Blue, 2⁷⁄₁₆" h, McKearin GIII-4, ex-William Elsholz collection **1,100.00**

Sapphire Blue (deep), 2³⁄₁₆" h, McKearin GIII-25, ex-William Elsholz collection **600.00**

Inkwell

Olive amber, dark, 2" h, 2⅛" d, open pontil, geometric, McKearin GII-18F **125.00**

Olive amber, 1¾" h, 2¾" d, ringed base-pontil, flat collar, McKearin GII-18E **65.00**

Sapphire blue, 1⅝" h, 2" d, smooth base, short ground neck, possibly Boston and Sandwich Glass Company, McKearin GI-7, tiny open bubble on one rib, ex-Tiffany and Gotjen collections **300.00**

Lamp

Font, clear, 4⅞" h, pressed sq stepped lacy base, conical shape ending in a melon knop, McKearin GI-7, type 1, small chip in one corner of pressed base, slight residue inside font **650.00**

Peg, clear, 3⅞" h, 3⅛" w, ball shaped, short sheared neck and solid applied peg, McKearin GII-21, ex-Tiffany and Gotjen collections **1,400.00**

Sparking, clear, 2⅛" h, blown in stopper mold, applied sheared handle with tiny flake, iron pontil, drop burner, stopper illustrated in McKearin 114-6 .... **800.00**

Sparking ink, sapphire blue, waisted, hour glass form, sheared short neck-pontil, Boston and Sandwich Glass Co., McKearin GIII-23, ex-Fish, Gest, Rolfing, and Gotjen collections **4,200.00**

Mustard, clear, 4¼"h, pontil, cork stopper, orig paper label, "SWEET SPIRIT OF NITRATE..../H M Baldwin and Son/West Stockbridge, Mass.," McKearin GI-15 .... **40.00**

Pitcher

Clear, 6¼" h, Baroque pattern, hollow applied handle, McKearin GV-6, ex-William Elsholz and James H. Rose collections **600.00**

Clear, 8⅛", Horn of Plenty pattern, applied hollow blownhandle, McKearin GV-17, ex-William Elsholz and George S. McKearin collections **2,400.00**

Light Aquamarine, 7¼" h, quart, Mt. Vernon Glass Co., McKearin GIII-2, Type 1, ex-William Elsholz, George S. McKearin, and Crawford Wettlaufer collections **7,500.00**

Punch Bowl, clear, 8¾" d bowl, 5¼" d foot, 7⅜" h, McKearin GII-18, foot pattern GIII-21, ex-William Elsholz collection **4,000.00**

Salt

Clear, 2⁹⁄₁₆" h, made from tumbler mold, hollow foot, McKearin GII-9 **110.00**

Cobalt blue, 2½" h, galleried, fifteen diamond base, McKearin GII-18 .. **550.00**

Purple Blue, 2¹⁄₁₆" h, rayed base-pontil, McKearin GIII-3, top portion of pattern indistinct, rim ground **50.00**

Sapphire Blue, 1¹¹⁄₁₆" h, deep color, low ftd, flaring rim, McKearin GIII-25, ex-William Elsholz and George S. McKearin collections **500.00**

White (opaque), rayed foot, smooth base, McKearin GV-24, ex-McKearin and Culbertson collections **210.00**

Sauce Dish, deep purple-blue, 4⁹⁄₁₆",

McKearin GIII-23, ex-William Elsholz and Crawford Wettlaufer collections . **3,250.00**
Sugar Bowl, cov, 5¾", clear, galleried rim, McKearin GII-18, ex-William Elsholz collection **3,000.00**
Toilet Bottle
  Blue-purple (deep), plain base-pontil, McKearin GI-7, type II **400.00**
  Light yellow-green, 5⅞", orig stopper, McKearin GI-3, Type 2, ex-William Elsholz collection **700.00**
Tumbler, clear, 3½" h, barrel shaped, sixteen diamond base, McKearin GII-33 . . . . **90.00**
Vase, clear, 6⅝" h, patterned from pint decanter mold, McKearin GII-18, ex-William Elsholz collection **2,000.00**
Vinegar Bottle, cobalt blue, period stopper, McKearin GI-VII-4 . . . . **275.00**
Whiskey Tumbler
  Amber (deep), 2⅞" h, 2⅞" d, pontil diamond base, McKearin GII-18, ex-McKearin collection, illus plate #8, Girl Scout Loan Exhibition Catalog, 1929 . . . . **2,700.00**
  Clear, 2⅞" h, pontil, smooth base with three tiny raised dots, McKearin GII-21, slight hint of cloudiness . . **95.00**
Wine, clear, 4⅛" h, knop stem on flat base, McKearin GII-19, base rim slightly ground **235.00**

BOHEMIAN GLASS

History: The once independent country of Bohemia, now a part of Czechoslovakia, produced a variety of fine glassware: etched, cut, overlay, and colored. Their glassware was first imported into America in the early 1820s and continues today.

Bohemia is known for its "flashed" glass that was produced in the familiar ruby color, and also in amber, green, blue, and black. Common patterns include "Deer and Castle," "Deer and Pine Tree," and "Vintage."

Most of the Bohemian glass encountered in today's market is of the 1875–1900 period. A Bohemian type glass also was made in England, Switzerland, and Germany.

Reproduction Alert.

Basket, 5¼", double cut overlay, pale red cut to clear, fans, stars, and thumb cutting, clear molded cut handle **75.00**
Beaker
  4³⁄₁₆", clear, cut and engraved, initialed, dated 1836 . . . . **80.00**
  5½", amber flashed, engraved, animals and building, C scroll panels, flared foot, c1860 . . . . **75.00**
Bell, 4½", blue, clear and frosted **85.00**

Bowl
  8", ruby flashed, Deer and Castle, clear and frosted **65.00**
  12½", double cut overlay, cobalt blue cut to clear **250.00**
Box
  3½", domed lid, ruby flashed, Vintage, engraved clear and frosted grape clusters and vines, gilt brass fittings **125.00**
  3¾", domed hinged lid, ruby flashed, engraved clear and frosted buildings, scrolling foliate bands, brass fittings **85.00**
Candlestick, 3½", amber, enameled heron and floral dec **60.00**
Candy Dish, cov, ruby flashed, Deer and Castle, clear and frosted **85.00**
Celery Dish, ruby flashed, Deer and Castle, clear and frosted **80.00**
Cologne Bottle, 3¾ x 7¼", double cut overlay, ruby to clear, clear frosted base, ruby stopper **115.00**
Compote
  7" d, amber flashed, cut leaf and floral dec, green band at top, pedestal base **100.00**
  9½ x 6½", amber flashed, Deer and Castle, engraved clear and frosted animals, castle, and trees **150.00**
Cordial Set, decanter, six wine glasses, blue, clear, etched Vintage pattern . **300.00**

Decanter, 15" h, Vintage pattern, ruby, hollow teardrop stopper, $100.00.

Decanter
  14⅜", ruby flashed, engraved band of grapevines around center, orig stopper **65.00**
  14¾"
    Crystal, octagonal, greenish tint,

engraved forest and deer scene, orig stopper **80.00**

Ruby flashed, engraved deer, birds, buildings, and rococo designs, replacement stopper **50.00**

Flip Glass, 6 x 6″, clear, cut, engraved forest scene with fox and birds **100.00**

Goblet

6″, amethyst, gilt lip, etched blossoms, late 19th C **85.00**

7″, crystal, octagonal, etched, two deer, woodland scene **145.00**

11″, ruby flashed, gilt dec, scalloped scent bottle top **175.00**

Mantel Luster, ruby flashed, Deer and Castle, clear and frosted, long prisms, pr **325.00**

Mug

2¼″, ruby flashed, engraved dog, grass, and trees **45.00**

6″, ruby flashed, engraved castle and trees, applied clear handle, sgd "Volmer, 1893" **80.00**

Perfume Bottle

7″, ruby flashed, Deer and Castle, clear and frosted, gold dec **85.00**

8″, amber flashed, etched flowers . . **100.00**

Pickle Jar, cov, 6″, ruby flashed, Deer and Castle, clear and frosted **50.00**

Powder Box, 4¼″ d, round, straight sides, flat top, ruby flashed, etched cov with leaping stag, forest setting, landscape and birds on sides, clear base **100.00**

Rose Bowl, 8½″ d, ruby flashed, Deer and Castle, clear and frosted **225.00**

Stein

2¾ x 4½″, ruby flashed, engraved dog and deer in forest, "Souvenir de Luchon" on front, pewter mounts **225.00**

3 x 6½″, ruby flashed, engraved cathedral panel, leaves, and scrolls, pewter mounts, ruby inset lid **300.00**

Sugar Shaker, ruby flashed, Bird and Castle, clear and frosted **65.00**

Teapot, 11″ w, cranberry cut to clear, panels of flowers, gilt spout and handle **185.00**

Tumbler

4″, ruby flashed, cut design, gold dec, set of 4 . . . . **125.00**

4¼″, engraved scene, early 19th C . **150.00**

Vase

5″, flared, double cut, cranberry to clear, Diamond and Oval pattern . **145.00**

7⅜″, ruby flashed, finely engraved and frosted rim band of flowers, paneled and flattened diamond point cutting on center and foot band **200.00**

9¼″, double cut, ruby cut to clear,

pale amber cut foot, band of cut and frosted roses, panel and diamond point cutting bands **175.00**

12″, double cut overlay, green cut to clear, starbursts, fans, and crosshatched diamonds **500.00**

16″, elongated floriform, double cut, white cut to clear, gilt overlay, cut lappets dec, pr **750.00**

Whiskey Glass, 3¼″, engraved, clear, early 19th C, pr **225.00**

Whiskey Set, green overlay cut to clear, decanter, four shot glasses **125.00**

BOOKS, AMERICANA

History: America's fascination with local, regional, state, and national history owes its origin to the nation's centennial in 1876. The next thirty years witnessed a proliferation of histories, atlases, genealogies, and photographic studies. Historical groups organized and published pamphlets or annual studies. A renewal of interest in local history occurred with the historic preservation movement of the 1950s forward. As communities and states celebrated the 50th, 75th, 100th, 150th, 200th, and more anniversary of their establishment, committees organized celebrations, one byproduct of which was a local history publication.

The number of books and pamphlets range in the hundreds of thousands. Pennsylvania has been chosen as a typical example. Readers are asked to compare what they have to the items cited. The prices are approximately the same nationally for the identical type of material. More recent publications, i.e., those published within the last twenty-five years, rarely are valued above their initial selling price.

On October 9 and 10, 1984, Sotheby's in New York held a major sale of over 1,000 early cookbooks. One buyer was primarily responsible for driving up prices from 5 to 70 times above catalog estimates. Cookbooks caught fire and are now among the hottest items in the antique book market.

Please remember that condition is perhaps the greatest factor in properly pricing a book. Also, local and region books will bring slightly higher prices in the areas to which their subjects relate.

See *Warman's Americana & Collectibles* for additional listings in the Books: Limited Edition Club, Cookbooks, Paperback Books, and Pulp Magazine categories.

Advisor: Ron Lieberman

PENNSYLVANIANA

Atlas of the City of Harrisburg, Roe, Philadelphia, 1889, 91 pgs, colored plates, spine taped **85.00**

Baldwin Locomotive Works, Illustrated

Catalogue, M. Baird & Co, Philadelphia, c1872, 134 pgs, illus 500.00

Bates, Samual P., *The Battle of Gettysburg*, Philadelphia, 1875, 336 pgs, engraved portraits after photos by Brady, disbound 55.00

Birmingham Friends, *250 Years of Quakerism at Birmingham, Chester County, PA, 1690–1940*, West Chester, 1940, 128 pgs, illus 20.00

Browning, Charles H., *Welsh Settlement of Pennsylvania*, Philadelphia, 1912, 631 pgs, illus, library binding 32.00

Callender, James, *The Political Progress of Britain...Tending to Prove the Ruinous Consequences of the Popular System of Taxation, War, & Conquest*, 1st Pt. Folwell, Philadelphia, 1795, 120 pgs, later marbled wraps 70.00

Carmer, Carl, *The Susquehanna*, Rivers of America Series, NY, 1955, 493 pgs, illus, DJ, sgd by author 35.00

Colby, George, *The Horseman's Friend*, Wible, Gettysburg, 1868, 31 pgs, advertisements, 24 mo 40.00

Companion To Mitchell's Traveler's Guide Through The U. S. The Principal Stage, Steam Boat, & Canal Routes in the U. S., Mitchell & Hinman, Philadelphia, 1835, 96 pgs, 32mo, orig wraps and paper label . . 30.00

Cumberland And Adams Counties, PA, Chicago, 1886, illus and maps 120.00

Dahlinger, Charles W., *Pittsburgh: A Sketch of Its Early Social Life*, Zadok Cramer, publisher, 1916, 216 pgs . . 30.00

East Stroudsburg Centennial, 1870–1970, 200 pgs, wraps, 4to 10.00

Eshleman, H. Frank, *Lancaster County Indians, Annals of the Susquehannocks and Other Indian Tribes of the Susquehanna Territory from 1500–1763, the Date of their Extinction*, Lancaster, 1908, 415 pgs, new wraps, limited to 550 copies 60.00

Gibson, John, *History of York County, PA...*, Chicago, 1886, 979 pgs, litho plates, thick 4to, ½ morocco binding 160.00

Hain, H. H., *History of Perry County, PA*, Harrisburg, 1922, 1088 pgs, illus . . . 130.00

Jones, Charles H., *History Of The Campaign For The Conquest Of Canada In 1776*, Philadelphia, 1882, 234 pgs, illus, detailed study of PA regiments 35.00

King, Moses, *Philadelphia & Notable Philadelphians*, bound with *King's Views of Phila.*, Philadelphia, 1902, 218 pgs, portraits and views, folio, full morocco 50.00

Lewis, John F., *Redemption Of The Lower Schuylkill...*, Philadelphia, 1924, 171 pgs, illus, sgd by author . 16.00

Masterpieces Of The Centennial Exhibition Illustrated, edited by sections by Edward Strahan, Walter Smith, and Joseph W Wilson, Gebbie & Barrie, Philadelphia, 1876, three volumes, 1260 pgs, illus, steel engravings and woodcuts, crimson cloth binding 140.00

McKeesport, PA, The First 100 Years, Abbott & Harrison, McKeesport, 1894, 178 pgs, illus 30.00

Nutting, Wallace, *Pennsylvania Beautiful*, Garden City, NY, 1935, 296 pgs, dj 25.00

Pearse, John B., *A Concise History Of The Iron Manufacture Of The American Colonies Up To The Revolution, and of Pennsylvania Until The Present Time*, Philadelphia, 1876, 282 pgs, illus, orig cloth, first edition . . . 65.00

Pennypacker, Samuel Whitaker, *Annals of Phoenixville & Its Vicinity...*, Philadelphia, 1872, 295 pgs, illus, orig morocco cloth, military history of Chester and Montgomery counties . 85.00

Punkin, Jonathan, (Pseud.), *Downfall of Freemasonry...& The Origin & Increase of Abolition*, Philadelphia, 1838, 48 pgs, caricature plates, ds . 40.00

Report of the National Sesquicentennial Exhibition Commission, Philadelphia, 1927, 536 pgs 15.00

Roberts, Elwood, *Biographical Annals of Montgomery County, PA*, New York, 1904, two volumes, 1068 pgs, illus, 4to, spines taped 120.00

Rupp, Israel Daniel, *History Of The Counties of Berks And Lebanon: Containing a Brief Account of the Indians*, Lancaster, 1844, 513 pgs, plates, full leather binding 100.00

Sellers, Charles Coleman, *Benjamin Franklin In Portraiture*, Yale, New Haven, 1962, 254 pgs, 45 pgs illus . . . 40.00

Sewel, William, *The History of the Rise, Increase & Progress of the Christian People Called Quakers...*, 3rd ed, corrected, Issac Collins, Trenton, 1774, 828 pgs, folio, worn orig leather 275.00

Sutton, George M., *Birds of Pennsylvania*, Harrisburg, 1928, 168 pgs, illus, dj 10.00

Swope, *History of the Families of McKinney-Brady-Quigley*, Chambersburg, 1905, 326 pgs, illus, colored coat of arms 35.00

Thayer, William M., *The Printer Boy. How Benjamin Franklin Made His Mark...,"* London, 1860, 264 pgs, illus, hand colored 15.00

Venango County: Centennial Celebration of the Bench & Bar, Franklin, 1905, 169 pgs, illus 20.00

Walker, J. H., Rafting Days In Pennsylvania, Altoona, 1922, 122 pgs, illus . 40.00

Warren, B. H., Report on the Birds of Pennsylvania, 434 pgs, 100 chromolitho plates, expanded 2nd ed 85.00

Weaver Organ & Piano Co., New Improved Method For The Organ, York, 1892, oblong 4to, chromolitho Weaver trade cards 25.00

York County Atlas, Beach Nichols, Philadelphia, 1876, 81 pgs, colored maps, litho plates 175.00

COOKBOOKS

Barry, Edward, Observations Historical, Critical, and Medical, on the Wines of the Ancients, 4to, London, 1775 . 225.00

Bitting, A. W., Appetizing; or, The Art of Canning: its History and Development, 4to, 1st ed, cloth, San Francisco, 1937 . . . . 95.00

Bitting, Katherine Golden, Gastronomic Bibliography, illus, 4to, 1st ed, San Francisco, 1939 . . . . 200.00

Bradley, Martha, The British Housewife: or, the Cook, Housekeeper's, and Gardiner's Companion, 2 volumes, London, c1790 . . . . 200.00

Brillat-Savarin, J. A., The Physiology of Taste; or, Meditations on Transcendental Gastronomy, 4to, Garden City, 1926, one of 500 numbered copies . 40.00

Brown, Eleanor and Bob, Culinary Americana: Cookbooks published during the Years from 1860 through 1960, 8vo, 1st ed, dj, New York, 1961 65.00

Butler, Frank H., Wine and the Wine Lands of the World, 8vo, 1st ed, London, 1926 . . . . 40.00

Dumas, Alexandre, Grand Dictionnaire de Cuisine, 8vo, 1st ed, Paris, 1873 200.00

Edwords, Clarence E., Bohemian San Francisco: its Restaurants and their most Famous Recipes, 8vo, cloth, dj, San Francisco, 1914 . . . . 35.00

Escoffier, Auguste, Le Guide Culinaire, 8vo, Paris, 1907 . . . . 100.00

Eustis, Celestine, Cooking in Old Creole Days, 8vo, New York, 1904 . . . . . 95.00

Francatelli, Charles, The Modern Cook, large 8vo, Philadelphia, c1850 . . . . 40.00

Glasse, Hannah, The Art of Cookery, Made Plain and Easy, 4to, 5th ed, London, 1755 . . . . 150.00

Graham, Thomas John, Sure Methods of Improving Health, and Prolonging Life, 12 mo, straight-grain morocco gilt, London, 1827 . . . . 80.00

Hammond, Ericsson, Swedish French American Cook Book, 8vo, New York, 1918 . . . . 25.00

Haraszthy, Agoston, Grape Culture, Wines, and Wine-Making,with Notes upon Agriculture and Horticulture, 8vo, New York, 1862 . . . . 300.00

Henderson, William Augustus, The Housekeeper's Instructor; or, Universal Family Cook, 8vo, London, c1790 125.00

Kitchiner, William, The Cook's Oracle, 12 mo, New York, 1825, dedication page sgd by author 60.00

Lawlor, C. F., The Mixicologist; or, How to mix All Kinds of Fancy Drinks, 12mo, orig wrappers, Cincinnati, 1899 . . . . 50.00

Packman, Ana, Early California Hospitality: The Cookery Customs of Spanish California, 8vo, Glendale: Arthur Clark, 1938 . . . . 85.00

Pennell, Elizabeth Robins
My Cookery Books, 8vo, Boston, 1903, one of 330 numbered copies 95.00
The Delights of Delicate Eating, 4to, New York, 1901 . . . . 75.00

Quennell, Nancy, The Epicure's Anthology, with an Essay by A. J. A. Symons, illus by Osbert Lancaster, 8vo, Golden Cockerel Press, London, 1936, one of 150 numbered copies sgd by illus 50.00

Redding, Cyrus, A History and Description of Modern Wines, 8vo, London, 1836 . . . . 80.00

Reynolds, Bruce, A Cocktail Continentale: Concocted in 24 Countries, Served in 38 Sips, and a Kick Guaranteed; A Travel Tale That Reads Like Lightening, , 8vo, 12 Art Deco illus, 1st ed, New York, 1926 . . . . . 90.00

Richardson, A. E., and Eberlein, H.D., The English Inn Past and Present, 8vo, 1st ed, London, 1925 . . . . 25.00

Rundell, Maria Eliza, A New System of Domestic Cookery, 12mo, New York, 1814 . . . . 75.00

Seldes, Gilbert, The Future of Drinking, 8vo, 1st ed, Boston, 1930 . . . . 25.00

Wayland, Virginia and Harold, Of Carving, Cards, and Cookery, 8vo, Raccoon Press, Arcadia, California, 1962, one of 275 numbered copies . 70.00

Wells, J. R. The Family Companion, 12mo, Boston, 1846 . . . . 50.00

Williams, W. Mattieu, The Chemistry of Cookery, 8vo, New York, 1885 . . . . 50.00

Young, H. M., Domestic Cookery, with Special Reference to Cooking by Gas, 12mo, London, 1886 . . . . 25.00

BOOTJACKS

History: Bootjacks are metal or wooden devices that facilitate the removal of boots. Bootjacks are used by placing the heel of the boot in the "U" shaped opening, putting a foot on the back of the bootjack, and pulling the front boot off the foot.

**Cast iron, eagle top, lyre base, 11½",
$90.00.**

Cast Iron
American Bulldog, 8¼" l pistol shape, folding	80.00
Beetle, black paint, 9¼"	35.00
Cricket, emb lacy design, 11¾"	25.00
Lyre shaped, 10¼" l	50.00
Mule's head	40.00
Naught Nelly, old worn polychrome repaint, 9¾" l	45.00
Tree center, two footed, 12" l	30.00
Vine design, 12" l	35.00
Wishbone, curling ends on arched feet	130.00

Wood
Birch, folding, hinged	30.00
Hewn, tree shape, pierced for hanging, 22"	35.00
Pine, oval ends, sq nails, 25"	28.00
Tiger Stripe Maple, 4 x 10"	20.00
Walnut, plain, refinished	22.50

BOTTLES, GENERAL

History: Cosmetic bottles held special creams, oils, and cosmetics, designed to enhance the beauty of the user. Some also claimed, especially on their colorful labels, to cure or provide relief from common ailments.

A number of household items, e.g., cleaning fluids and polishes, required glass storage containers. Many are collected for their fine lithograph labels.

Mineral water bottles contained water from a natural spring. Spring water was favored by health conscious people between the 1850s and 1900s.

Nursing bottles, used to feed the young and sickly, were a great help to the housewife because of graduated measures, replaceable nipples, ease of cleaning, sterilizing, and reuse.

References: Ralph & Terry Kovel, *The Kovels' Bottle Price List*, Crown Publishers, Inc., 1984, 7th ed.; Carlo & Dot Sellari, *The Illustrated Price Guide To Antique Bottles*, Country Beautiful Corp, 1975.

Periodicals: *Antique Bottle World*, 5003 West Berwyn, Chicago, IL 60630; *Old Bottle Magazine*, P. O. Box 243, Bend, OR 97701. Subscription: $10.00.

Additional Listings: Barber Bottles, Bitter Bottles, Figural Bottles, Food Bottles, Ink Bottles, Medicine Bottles, Poison Bottles, Sarsaparilla Bottles and Snuff Bottles. Also see the bottle categories in *Warman's Americana & Collectibles* for more examples.

COSMETICS

California Perfume Co, rect, fruit flavors on front panel, amethyst, 5½"	15.00
Hyacinthia Toilet Hair Dressing, rect, crude applied lip, open pontil, aqua, 6"	22.00
Mineralava Face Finish, NY, Scotts Face Finish on back, clear, 5¼"	6.00
Pompeian Massage Cream, amethyst, 2¾"	4.00
Violet Dulce Vanishing Cream, eight panels, 2½"	5.00

HOUSEHOLD

Caulk's Petroid Cement, clear, 2¼"	2.00
Gordon's Chafola Furniture Polish, emb, open pontil	150.00
Osborn's Liquid Polish, round, open pontil, amber	325.00
Sapo Elixir Dry Cleaner, clear, 6"	3.00
Seabury Laundry Blueing, open pontil, light green, 4"	85.00

MINERAL OR SPRING WATER

Avon Spring Water, G.H. Nowlen, NY, sapphire blue, 7½"	380.00
Crystal Spring Water, Saratoga, NY, horseshoe shape, green, qt, 9½"	85.00
Geyser Springs, emerald green, 7⅝"	550.00
Lynch & Clark, New York Mineral Water, tapered top, ring pontil, olive amber, pt	100.00
Round Lake Mineral Water, red-amber, 9¼"	750.00
Rutherford's Premium Mineral Water, ground pontil, dark olive, 7½"	60.00

Mineral Water, Superior Mineral Water, Graphite Bottle, Twitchel, Philadelphia, 7⅛", $40.00.

San Francisco Glass Works, tapered neck, blob top, sea green, 6⅞" 15.00
Vichy Water Cullums Spring, Choctaw Co, AL, dark olive, 7¼" 35.00
Syracuse Springs Excelsior, golden yellow, 9¾" 340.00
Washington Spring Co, bust of George Washington, emerald green 300.00
Witter Medical Spring Co, amber, 9½" 8.00
Zarembo Mineral Spring Co, Seattle, WA, tapered top, blue, 7½" 18.00

NURSING

Handy Nurser, emb, pear shape, clear, 6 oz 22.00
Marguerite Feeding Bottle, inside screw, daisy on top 32.00
Mother's Comfort, turtle type, clear ... 20.00
Teddy Bear, emb, clear, c1915 ...... 45.00
Tube Feeder, emb crystal, 18 star shield, aqua 70.00

BRASS

History: Brass is a durable, malleable, and ductile metal alloy consisting mainly of copper and zinc. It achieved its greatest popularity as utilitarian and decorative art items in the eighteenth and nineteenth centuries.

Reference: Mary Frank Gaston, *Antique Brass: Identification and Values*, Collector Books, 1985; Peter, Nancy, and Herbert Schiffer, *The Brass Book*, Schiffer Publishing, Ltd, 1978.

Additional Listings: Bells, Candlesticks, Fireplace Equipment, and Scientific Instruments.

Reproduction Alert: Many modern reproductions are being made of earlier brass forms, es-

pecially in the areas of buckets, fireplace equipment, and kettles.

Andirons, 20", faceted finials, ring turned shafts, scrolled legs, pr 275.00
Bed Warmer, 40", circular cov, incised stylized floral and foliate motif, turned wooden handle, late 18th C 225.00
Bleeding Dish, 5", scalloped handle, molded rim, early 18th C 200.00
Bucket, 10¼", cylindrical, bail handle, 19th C 120.00
Button, 1", uniform, Richmond Fire Association 48.00
Candlestick
　6½", Queen Anne, drinking glass bases, English, c1710, pr 575.00
　7⅞", Victorian with pushups, beehive and diamond quilted detail, pr ... 150.00
　7¼", Dutch Heemskerk, tulip socket, acorn knop, c1700 .... 400.00
　11", beaded rim on bobeche, twisted baluster shape with acanthus leaf, raised round foot with bead and leaf detail, French, 18th C, pr ... 500.00
Chandelier, 11", baluster shaped standard, wrought iron chain, three scrolled supports ending in shaped candlecups with drip pans, 18th C .. 1,100.00
Chestnut Roaster
　18", brass handles 130.00
　22", cast coat of arms on handle, English 90.00
Coal Bucket, helmet shape, hinged turned handle, English, 19th C 325.00
Coat Rack, 73", columnar standard, four hooks, four high legs, ball finial, C1900 .... 80.00
Compass and Sundial, 2⅜", brass case, English, 18th C 350.00

Vase, 8⅜" h, triangular shape, flared, three handles, $60.00.

Cup, 4¼" h, rabbit at top of handles, grapes and leaves in heavy relief .. 90.00
Door Bell, 7" d top, cast iron, scrolled back, Pat 1872 .... 125.00
Door Handles, pr, 9¼" h, shaped plate, molded D-shaped handle, oval thumb grip, English, 18th C 175.00
Dresser Box, 6" l, shaped, emb, oval porcelain inset in lid with bust of 18th C lady 125.00
Fireplace Fender
36" l, pierced, urn finials on paw feet, Regency, 19th C 425.00
51" l, 14½" h, arched with serpentine front, three brass finials, wire work screen with scrolled tracery, c1800 2,000.00
Fireplace Screen, 27½ x 27½", sq, tavern scene, ftd 165.00
Frame, 10¾ x 6½", 4 x 2¾" opening, winged cupid, nude nymph, griffin heads, garlands, scroll footing, easel arm 85.00
Grain Scoop, 5¼ x 8¾", c1870 ..... 70.00
Horse, figural, 7¼" h, Middle Eastern . 42.00
Jam Hook, 6" h, 19th C 50.00
Jardiniere
4½" h, sq, cast, foliage, ringed standard on sq black base 185.00
8½" l, oval, repousse, repeating scene of maiden and gentleman in landscape setting, foliate scroll feet, 18th C 100.00
10" h, three lion head handles, three ball feet 65.00
Kettle, two qt, long iron handle, c1850 185.00
Lamp
15", desk, lily pad, cranberry and opalescent hobnail shade 75.00
19", table, yellow globular shade, emb brass font, wrought iron standard 50.00
32", banquet, figural standard 150.00
Lantern
13", whale oil lamp, brass globe ... 165.00
16¾", railroad, chimney engraved "B. Smith," within wreath 125.00
Magazine Rack, 16¾" h, cast, Art Deco, figure of Peter Pan with pipe 65.00
Match Holder, 2½" h, barrel shape ... 65.00
Pail, 7½" h, iron bale handle, stamped label "Hayden's patent, Ansonia Brass Co." 40.00
Pan, sauce, 8" d, heavy, copper rivets, wrought iron handle 175.00
Plant Stand, 33" h, gilded detail, colored marble inserts 85.00
Pepper Mill, 9", cylindrical, jointed crank handle, 18th C 85.00
Rim Lock, 7¾ x 5⅛", ogee molded edge, ball turned knob, smaller knob and two turned pins, English, 18th C 150.00
Scales, set, butcher, 22", ringed

stepped standard, bull's head finial with beam balance, smaller balance behind, shaped base fitted with eight weights 220.00
Servant's Bell, 13" l, wall type, c1780 . 140.00
Spittoon
6½" d, ribbed, weighted base 30.00
7" d, 5" h, hammered border 45.00
Standish, rect base, shaped skirt supporting three cannisters, columnar feet 400.00
Sugar Shaker, 4½", applied handle, molded base 145.00
Trivet
4" l, rect, paw feet, reticulated top with engraved slip, English 50.00
7" l, triangular, cut out deer and tree 100.00
Umbrella Stand, 23", hammered finish, two lion head handles 60.00
Utensils, Dipper and Skimmer, 20½" l, wrought iron handles 75.00
Wick Trimmer Scissors, 6½" l, engraved, 9⅝" emb tray 85.00
Wine Cooler, 8" d, 10" h, circular, pedestal base, applied lion's head and ring handles, mid 20th C 40.00

BREAD PLATES

History: Beginning in the mid-1880s, special trays or platters were made for serving bread and rolls. Designated by collectors as "bread plates," these small trays or platters can be found in porcelain, glass (especially pattern glass), and metals.

Bread plates often were part of a china or glass set. However, many glass companies made special plates which honored national heroes, commemorated historical or special events, offered a moral maxim, or supported a religious attitude. The theme on the plate can be either in a horizontal or vertical format. The favorite shape for these plates is oval, with a common length being ten inches.

Reference: Anna Maude Stuart, *Bread Plates And Platters,* published by author, 1965.

Additional Listings: Pattern Glass.

Brass, 14", Art Deco style, engraved . 47.50
China
Meissen, 14¼ x 8¼", double handles, 24K borders, floral center, 19th C, X-swords mark 275.00
Noritake, 10", gold handled, hp scene in center, wide border, hp stylized flowers, maroon wreath 65.00
Red Wing, Bobwhite, long, narrow . 75.00
Silhouette, Crooksville 80.00
Pattern Glass
Actress, 7 x 12", HMS Pinafore 90.00

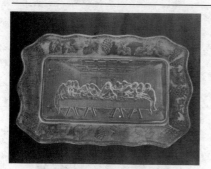

Last Supper, clear glass, frosted grape leaf border, 10⅞ x 7", $65.00.

Aurora, 10" round, large star in center, ruby stained	35.00
Baltimore, 12½"	70.00
Be Industrious, 12 x 8¼", oval, clear, handled	50.00
Butterfly & Fan, clear	40.00
Canadian, 10", clear	45.00
Chain with star, 11", handled	35.00
Cupid and Venus, amber	75.00
Daisy and Button, 13", apple green	60.00
Deer and Pine Tree, blue	100.00
Egyptian, Mormon Temple	300.00
Frosted Stork, oval	50.00
Garfield Drape, Memorial, portrait of Garfield	65.00
Grace	60.00
Horseshoe, 14 x 10", double horseshoe handles	65.00
Iowa, motto	80.00
Kokomo, clear	30.00
Lion, 12", frosted, including lion handles, GUTDODB	125.00
Moon and Star, rect, clear	45.00
One Hundred One, 11", farm implement center	75.00
Palmette, 9", handled	30.00
Polar Bear, frosted	150.00
Queen Anne	50.00
Rosette, 9", handled	25.00
Scalloped Tape, oval, "Bread Is The Staff of Life"	45.00
Shell and Tassel, round	55.00
Tennessee, colored jewels	75.00
Three Presidents, frosted center	85.00

BRIDE'S BASKETS

History: A ruffled edge, glass bowl in a metal holder was a popular wedding gift in the 1880–1910 era, hence, the name of "bride's basket." The glass bowls can be found in most glass types of the period. The metal holder was generally silver plated with a bail handle, thus enhancing the basket image.

Over the years bowls and bases became separated, and married pieces resulted. When the base has been lost, the bowl is sold separately.

Reference: John Mebane, *Collecting Bride's Baskets And Other Glass Fancies*, Wallace-Homestead, 1976.

Reproduction Alert: The glass bowls have been reproduced.

Note: Items listed have silver plated holder unless otherwise noted.

11¼" d, 11" h, cased glass, white exterior, shaded pink interior, stand marked "Middletown Plate, Quad Plate," $175.00.

Burmese, 4½ x 8", enamel chrysanthemum dec, acid finish, SP holder	1,375.00
Cameo, 8" sq, pink cut to white, floral sprays, Mt Washington, period SP holder, minor damage	175.00
Cased	
8¾ x 10½", deep pink int., enameled gray and white bird center, flowers and leaves, white ext., folded over ruffled rim, amber edging, ormolu frame, applied foliage and bow	275.00
10 x 14¼", white int., cobalt blue ext., enameled gold flowers and leaves, ruffled rim, SP frame, emb leaves	400.00
Cranberry, 9 x 4", custard glass overlay, ruffled, SP holder	175.00
Custard, 10" sq, melon ribbed bowl, enameled daisies, applied rubena crystal rim, twisted and beaded handle, ftd emb SP frame, marked "Wilcox"	425.00
Hobnail, 10½", pink, enameled flowers, ruffled rim, reticulated SP frame	225.00
Loetz, 8 x 10½", irid gold, blue, and purple, recessed indentations, ruffled, ground pontil, ftd metal stand	300.00

Opalescent, 9¼", blue, crimped rim, reticulated SP holder marked "Wallingford, Biggins & Rodgers Co" 165.00

Peachblow, 9½ x 7", cased, pink shading to white, enameled white frilly hearts, satin finish 800.00

Satin

  8 x 10¾", blue, period SP holder . . . 175.00

  10½", butterscotch fluted, ruffled bowl, ornate SP pedestal holder with four floral arms 375.00

  11 x 15½", deep rose, enamel dec, swan surrounded by flowers, heavy bronze holder with birds perched on top 400.00

  11¼", emerald green, shaded light to dark bowl, enameled dec, ornate ftd SP frame 265.00

  11½ x 10½", cased bowl, white int., shaded pink MOP DQ ext., ruffled rim, frosted edging, SP frame with applied leaves, marked "Manhattan" 800.00

Spangled, 10⅜", multicolored, ruby, cranberry, and green, ivory and yellow base, silver flecks 100.00

Spatter, yellow, brown, and purple, ruffled and crimped, SP holder 235.00

Stevens and Williams, triangular, pink enameled ext., white cased int. amber glass trim, ribbon candy edge 375.00

BRISTOL GLASS

History: Bristol glass is a designation given to a semi-opaque glass, usually decorated with enamel and cased with another color. Initially the term referred only to glass made in Bristol, England, in the 17th and 18th centuries. By the Victorian era firms on the Continent and in America were copying the glass and its forms.

Biscuit Jar

  5 x 6½", pink, enameled yellow and blue flowers, green leaves, SP rim, lid, and bail handle 165.00

  5 x 7½", green, enameled pink flowers, green and yellow leaves, white, pink, and tan heron, brass rim, cov, and base, strawberry finial, bail handle 150.00

Box, 1½", round, Victorian lady and gentleman dec, brass trim 48.00

Cake Plate, 11½" d, enameled bird and flower dec 75.00

Cake Stand, celadon green, enameled herons in flight, gold trim 125.00

Candlestick, 7" h, soft green, gold band, pr 60.00

Castor Set, 3-bottle, cream opaque,

Vase, 12¼" h, cream ground, bird and water scene, greens, yellows, and blues, $100.00.

enameled leaves and fruit dec, SP frame 115.00

Cologne Bottle, 2⅛ x 5¼", green, pink roses, blue, and white flowers, white scrolls and gold trim, matching ball shaped stopper 75.00

Cruet, 2¼ x 4¾", blue, white flowers, gold leaves, applied blue handle, matching ball stopper 90.00

Decanter, 8", blue, matching stopper . . 75.00

Dresser Set, two cologne bottles, cov powder jar, white, gilt butterflies dec, clear stoppers 50.00

Ewer, 17", white, enameled cupid scene 80.00

Fairy Lamp, 4 x 4½", opaque white shade, blue shading to yellow and pink, clear marked "Clarke" base . . 140.00

Hatpin Holder, 6⅛", ftd, blue, enameled jewels, gold dec 100.00

Mantel Luster, 11½", cased, pink, flower dec, prisms, pr 250.00

Perfume Bottle, 3¼", squat, blue, gold band, white enameled flowers and leaves, matching stopper 100.00

Pickle Castor, pink, flower dec 300.00

Rose Bowl, 3½", shaded blue, crimped edge 60.00

Sugar Shaker, 4¾", white, hp flowers . 60.00

Sweetmeat Jar

  3 x 5½", deep pink, enameled flying duck, leaves, blue flower dec, white lining, SP rim, lid, and bail handle 100.00

  5¾ x 4½", green, enameled garlands of pink, white, yellow, blue, and green flowers, four butterflies, SP rim, lid, and bail handle 120.00

Vase

  8", bud, blue, hp, pr 65.00

10½", white, satin finish, gold and
jewel dec, pr **75.00**
12½", white, gold dec, one marked
"Remember Me," other marked
"Forget Me Not," pr **85.00**

BRITISH ROYALTY COMMEMORATIVES

History: British commemorative china, souvenirs to commemorate coronations and other royal events, dates from the 1600s, with the early pieces being rather crude in design and form. The development of transfer printing, c1780, led to a much closer likeness of the reigning monarch on the ware.

King George IV's coronation was the first royal occasion at which children received municipal gifts. Victoria's Jubilee expanded the practice. The Royal Wedding of Prince Charles to Lady Diana Spencer and the subsequent births of their sons, Prince William Philip Louis [heir to the throne] and Prince Henry Charles Albert David, heralded a new wave of commemoratives.

Some British Royalty commemoratives are easily recognized by their portraits of past or present monarchs. Some may be in silhouette profile. Other royal symbols include crowns, dragons, royal coats of arms, national flowers, swords, sceptres, dates, messages, and initials.

On August 25, 1984, Phillips in New York conducted the first American auction to feature a majority of British Royalty commemoratives.

References: John May, *Victoria Remembered, A Royal History 1817–1861*, London, 1983: John and Jennifer May, *Commemorative Pottery 1780–1900, A Guide for Collectors*, Charles Scribner's Sons, 1972; Josephine Jackson, *Fired For Royalty*, Heaton Moor, 1977; David Rogers, *Coronation Souvenirs and Commemoratives*, Latimer New Dimensions, Ltd., 1975; Sussex Commemorative Ware Centre, *200 Commemoratives*, Metra Print Enterprises, 1979; Geoffrey Warren, *Royal Souvenirs*, Orbis, 1977; Audrey B. Zeder, *British Royal Commemoratives*, Wallace-Homestead, 1986.

Additional Listings: See *Warman's Americana & Collectibles* for more examples.

Advisor: Doug Flynn and Al Bolton.

Beaker
Edward VII/Alexandra, 1902 Coronation, 4" h, Royal Doulton **55.00**
Elizabeth II, 1953 Coronation, 4" h, official design **12.00**
Elizabeth II, 60th Birthday, 4½" h, Sutherland, limited edition 250 . . .   **45.00**
George VI/Elizabeth, 1937 Coronation, 4½" h, Wedgwood & Co. Ltd   **55.00**
George/Mary, 1911 Coronation, 3¾" h, Foley **65.00**

Plate, Victoria, 1897 Jubilee, color portrait, serviceman, ships, 8" d, $165.00.

Bowl
Elizabeth II, 1953 Coronation, 4¾" h, pressed glass **60.00**
George VI/Elizabeth, 1937 Coronation, sepia Marcus Adams portrait, color dec, 6" sq, J & G Meakin . .   **39.00**
Edward VIII, 1937 Coronation, profile in well, 10" d, pressed glass **65.00**
Victoria, 1897 Jubilee, 19¼" d, pressed glass, amber **65.00**
Box
Elizabeth II, 25th Anniversary of Coronation, 4¼" d, Coalport **40.00**
Elizabeth, The Queen Mother, 80th Birthday, color portrait, 4" d, Crown Staffordshire **65.00**
Cup and Saucer
Charles/Diana, 1981 Wedding, Royal Albert **26.00**
Charles, 1969 Investiture as Prince of Wales, Duchess **47.00**
George/Mary, 1911 Coronation, color portraits, no mark **55.00**
Edward VII/Alexandra, 1902 Coronation, Foley **45.00**
Jug
Edward VII, In Memoriam, brown and green, relief portrait, 6¼" h **65.00**
Edward VIII, character, 8" h, Bretby .   **125.00**
Elizabeth II, 1953 Coronation, color portrait, 3¾" h, Royal Stafford . . .   **60.00**
Lithophane
Alexandra, 1902, cup, crown, and cypher, 2¾" h **175.00**
Edward VII, 1902, mug, crown, and cypher, 2¾" h **85.00**
George V, 1911, mug, crown, and cypher, 2¾" h **140.00**
Mary, 1911, cup, crown, and cypher, 2¾" h **250.00**
Loving Cup
Charles/Diana, 1981 Wedding, brown on white portraits, Royal Doulton, limited edition 5,000 . . . .   **85.00**

Elizabeth II, 1972 Silver Wedding Anniversary, 3″ h, Paragon 147.00
Elizabeth, The Queen Mother, 80th Birthday, gold profile, 3″ h, Royal Crown Derby, limited edition 500 . 235.00
Victoria, 1897 Jubilee, brown portrait, 4″ h, Victoria 175.00
William, 1982 Birth, 3″ h, paragon . . 105.00

Mug, Victoria, 150th Anniversary of Coronation, 3⅝″ h, marked "Caverswall," $35.00.

Mug
Andrew/Sarah, 1986 Wedding, color portraits, 3¾″ h, Calclough 22.00
Duke/Duchess of Windsor, In Memoriam, black and white portraits; birth, marriage, accession, abdication, death dates, 3⅜″ h, Dorincourt 50.00
Edward VII/Alexandra, 1902 Coronation, 3″ h, Johnson Brothers 55.00
Edward VIII, 1937 Coronation, sepia portrait, 3½″ h, Empire 40.00
Elizabeth II, 60th Birthday, color portrait, 3½″ h, Coronet 20.00
Henry, 1984 Birth, blue design, silver trim, 4¼″ h, R. Guyatt design, Wedgwood, limited edition 1,000 . 65.00
Victoria, 1887 Jubilee, black and white portrait, 3″ h, CTM 95.00
Victoria, 150th Anniversary of Coronation, 3⅝″ h, Caverswall 35.00
William 3rd Birthday, Henry 1st Birthday, black and white portraits, 2⅝″ h, Dorincourt, limited edition 150 . 50.00
Paperweight
Edward VIII, 1937 Coronation, black and white portrait, 4¼ x 1⅛″ 25.00
George VI/Elizabeth, 1937 Coronation, black and white Marcus Adams portrait, 2½″ d 35.00
Victoria/Albert, black and white portraits, color and glitter, 2⅞″ 30.00
Pin Tray
Edward VII/Alexandra, 1902 Coronation, sepia portraits, 4″ d 35.00

Edward VIII, 1937 Coronation, 4⅞ x 3¾″, Hammersley 47.00
Elizabeth II, 1959 Canada visit, sepia photograph, 4¼″ sq 28.00
Victoria, 1897 Jubilee, sepia portrait, 5″ d 39.00
Pitcher
Elizabeth II, 1953 Coronation, brown portrait, 6¼″ h, Royal Doulton . . . 175.00
Victoria, 1887 Jubilee, black and white portrait, 5″ h 120.00

Plate, Edward VII/Alexandra, 1902 Coronation, 7″ d, marked "Royal Copenhagen," $185.00.

Plate
Andrew/Sarah, 1986 Wedding, silhouette portraits, 8½″ d, Caverswall, limited edition 1,500 . . . . . . 45.00
Charles, 1969 Investiture as Prince of Wales, sepia portrait, 8″ d, Coronet 65.00
Edward VII/Alexandra, 1902 Coronation, blue and white portraits, 10¼″ d 165.00
Edward VII/Alexandra, 1902 Coronation, 7″ d, Royal Copenhagen . . . 185.00
Elizabeth II, 60th Birthday, large color portrait, 10½″ d, Coalport, limited edition 20,000 . . . . 80.00
George/Mary, 1911 Coronation, 8½″ d, C.T. Maling 65.00
George VI/Elizabeth, 1937 Coronation, sepia portraits, 9½ x 8¼″, Shelley 75.00
Victoria, 1887 Jubilee, orange and white portrait, 10½″ d, Royal Worcester 125.00
Victoria, 1897 Jubilee, color dec, 7¼″ d, Foley 39.00
Victoria, 1897 Jubilee, color portrait, servicemen, ships, 8″ d 165.00
Victoria, 150th Anniversary of Coro-

nation, gold portrait, 10½" d, Caverswall, limited edition 150 ..... **135.00**

Playing Cards

Edward VIII, 1919 Canada visit, color portrait, single deck, C. Goodall & Co **75.00**

Elizabeth II, 1977 Jubilee, sepia portrait, single deck, Waddingtons ... **25.00**

George/Mary, 1911 Coronation, color portraits, double deck **75.00**

George VI/Elizabeth, 1937 Coronation, color portrait, double deck, Canadian Playing Card Co **65.00**

Shaving Mug

Edward VII/Alexandra, 1902 Coronation, color portraits, 3¾" h **100.00**

Edward VII, 1937 Coronation, sepia portrait, 4" h, no mark **85.00**

Elizabeth II, 1953 Coronation, color portrait, 4" h **65.00**

George VI/Elizabeth, 1937 Coronation, sepia portraits, 4½" h, Shelley **95.00**

Teapot

Charlotte, In Memoriam, black and white dec, 6" h **250.00**

Edward VII/Alexandra, 1902 Coronation, color portraits, 4¾" h, no mark **65.00**

Elizabeth II, 1953 Coronation, relief portraits, white on royal blue Jasperware, 5" h, Wedgwood **225.00**

George/Mary, 1911 Coronation, color portraits, 6" h, bone china, no mark **245.00**

Victoria, 1897 Jubilee, color portraits, 4" h **130.00**

Victoria, 1897 Jubilee, color coat of arms, 6" h, Aynsley **220.00**

Tea Set, Elizabeth II, 1953 Coronation, teapot, creamer, and sugar, relief portraits, light blue on white Queensware, Wedgwood **275.00**

Tin

Andrew/Sarah, 1986 Wedding, color portraits, 8" d **20.00**

Edward VII/Alexandra, 1902 Coronation, color portraits, hinged, 4¼ x 5½" **65.00**

Edward VII/Alexandra, 1907 Cardiff visit, color portraits, 6 x 3½", J. S. Fry & Sons **46.00**

Edward VIII, 1937 Coronation, color portrait, hinged lid, 5¾ x 3¾", Riley's Toffee **45.00**

Elizabeth II, 1953 Coronation, color portrait, 10 x 7", E. Sharp **29.00**

George/Mary, 1935 Jubilee, color portrait, 6¾ x 4½" **45.00**

George VI/Elizabeth, 1937 Coronation, gold portraits, 3" h, Oxo **18.00**

George VI/Elizabeth, 1936–37, Accession and Coronation, color portraits, 5½ x 3¼" **45.00**

Victoria, 1897 Jubilee, color portraits

(young, mature), hinged lid, 3¼ x 3" **95.00**

Victoria, color portrait on hinged lid, 6¾ x 4½ x 3¼" **75.00**

BRONZE

History Bronze is an alloy of copper, tin, and traces of other metals. It has been used since Biblical times not only for art objects, but also for utilitarian purposes. After a slump in the Middle Ages, bronze was revived in the 17th century and continued in popularity until the early 20th century.

Reference: Anita Jacobsen (ed.), *Jacobsen's Painting and Bronze Price Guide,* published by author.

Notes: Do not confuse a "bronzed" object with a true bronze. A bronzed object usually is made of white metal and then coated with a reddish-brown material to give it a bronze appearance.

A signed bronze commands a higher market price than an unsigned one. There also are "signed" reproductions in the market. It is very important to know the history of the mold and the background of the foundry.

Andirons, 36" h, gilt, figural, Renaissance style, pr **2,400.00**

Animal

Buddhist Lion, 2¾" h, looking backwards, standing on shaped plinth, gilt, Chinese, Ming Dynasty **700.00**

Flamingos, pr, marble base **250.00**

Moose, 14" l, marble base **200.00**

Bookends, 7", figural, scotties, brown patina, inscribed "model by Edith B Parsons," foundry mark, Gorham Co, early 20th C, pr **1,000.00**

Bust, 10" h, statesman, brown patina, inscribed foundry marks for Barbedienne, early 20th C **225.00**

Plaque, Marat, 8½", $275.00.

Candelabra, pr
   7", twin paneled baluster form nozzles, snuffer tray, stepped base, Regency style 600.00
   10", gilt, satyr and satyress, holding twin cornucopias, kneeling amidst foliage, Louis XV, mid 18th C 4,000.00
   15½", gilt, scrolling swan form arm supports, engine turned columns with wreaths of flowers, Empire, c1825 .... 1,600.00
   17½", gilt and patinated bronze, trumpeting putto, horns terminating in candle nozzles, green veined marble socle, Louis XVI 2,000.00

Candlesticks, pr
   9½", parcel gilt, Empire Revival 275.00
   10½", gilt, turned standard, molded stepped base, Louis XVI style ... 850.00
   12½", gilt and patinated bronze, putto holding scrolling cornucopia ending in candle nozzle, oval socle with bas relief panels of rams, Louis XVI, c1775 .... 2,000.00

Centerpiece, 10½" d, 11½" h, gilt, reticulated everted bowl, two spring maidens, cylindrical base, bas relief putti trailing garlands, sgd "Thomire a Paris," Empire, early 19th C 5,500.00

Chandelier
   26" h, gilt and patinated bronze, circular reservoir border, lion mask handles, dished base, six projecting candle arms, mask and anthemia dec, engine turned canopy, Empire, early 19th C 3,200.00
   29", gilt and patinated bronze, molded corona with cast chains, dished reservoir, ten scrolling candle branches, Empire 7,500.00
   34" h, gilt, baluster form standard, pendant crystal beadwork swags, nine scrolling candle arms, turned nozzles, ruffled bobeches, faceted prisms, Rococo Revival, mid 19th C 2,500.00
   48" h, gilt, basket form, central crystal baluster, pyriform pendants, sixteen scrolling candle arms, beaded columnar nozzles, faceted crystal pendants, Louis XVI 9,000.00

Clock
   Carriage, 8", gilt, circular enamel dial, molded bezel, sq case, snake handle, Louis XVI 850.00
   Mantel
      13½", gilt and patinated bronze, circular enameled dial sgd "Charles Aine Orleans," molded bezel, oil lamp form case, playful child testing flame with butterfly, gad-

rooned and molded base, bun feet, Louis XVI, late 18th C ... 600.00
      18", gilt and patinated bronze, "Le Jardinier Fatigue" figure holding water sack and tools, steadying Versailles pot with enamel dial and movement, molded base, Empire, early 19th C 1,600.00
      18½", gilt, allegorical, circular enamel dial sgd "Imbert l'aine," movement for days of the week, drum form case surrounded by paste brilliants and emblems of war, tableau of grieving lovers and gendarmes, Paris, late 18th C 7,750.00

Compote, 13", gilt, figural, Napoleon III 450.00

Figure
   10", gilt and patinated bronze, playful infants, seated on pillow, one holding empty cage, other clutching dove and offering seed, molded guilloche ornamented base, Louis XVI, pr 6,250.00
   13½", hunter and hound, brown patina, inscribed "O Hertel," Continental, c1900 .... 275.00
   17", woman, seated, elaborate dress, brown patina, inscribed "B Ulcek, 10/7," foundry marks and "F. Bartak," Czechoslovakian, c1909 ... 600.00
   18", Cleopatra, brown patina, shaped red marble plinth, gilt bronze feet, after antique model in Vatican, French, late 19th C 1,000.00
   19", fisherboy, brown patina, imp foundry mark, inscribed "Lavergne," French, c1900 .... 500.00
   21", nymph, rich brown patina, marble plinth, inscribed "C Stotz, 1898," Continental 600.00
   29", equestrian group, parcel gilt, Cossack warrior on rearing horse, brown-black patina, ebonized wood plinth, Russian, late 19th C, pr ... 12,000.00

Fire Tools
   28" h, chased, brush, tongs, shovel, and poker, matching stand, Louis XVI style, 19th C 500.00
   34" h, gilt, mounted iron, matching stand, Renaissance style 1,150.00

Fireplace Fender, 29" l, gilt and patinated, two Neoclassical figures kneeling to hearth, paneled base, chiseled leaf tips and Apollo masks, Empire, early 19th C 13,000.00

Furniture
   Mirror, dressing, 21½", circular, palmette ornamented frame, supported by cherub resting on orb, three drawer case, cut glass sides,

bronze pulls, swan form feet, Empire, early 19th C **1,500.00**

Stand, 15½″ d, 56″ h, gilt and patinated bronze, four circular verde antico marble surfaces, swan form supports, molded incurvate triangular base, Empire, mid 19th C . . **9,000.00**

Table, center

42″ d, circular marble top, three scrolling gilt bronze supports, paw feet, Louis XVI style, late 19th C **4,500.00**

42 x 28 x 32½″, rect patinated top, cast water leaf border, plain frieze, cast oak leaves and acorns, tapering fluted legs, sunk panels with bas relief profiles of goddesses, paw feet, c1810 . . . **42,000.00**

Garden Urn, 21″ d, 36″ h, patinated, baluster form, beaded edge, leaf tip rim, molded border of shells and acorns, boar's head masks, paneled arms with Janus head terminals, Greek key band, fluted standard, sq base, 19th C **13,000.00**

Garnitures, 5½ x 8½″, gilt, compressed urn, spirally engine turned column, sq base, Empire, early 19th C, pr **1,800.00**

Girandoles, crystal pendants, Louis XVI, pr **700.00**

Inkstand, 10″ l, figural, classical figure beside basket, French, c1900 . . . . . **750.00**

Jardiniere, 15″, cachepot, bamboo style base, marked "Susse Freres," early 20th C **400.00**

Jewelry Box, 11″ l, gilt, Renaissance style **600.00**

Lamp

15½″, gilt and patinated bronze, figural, victorious soldier holding olive branches, Empire, early 19th C **1,400.00**

17″, figural, peacock, spread wings, beadwork dec, pr **1,000.00**

Lantern, 22″, hall, gilt, inverted acorn form, etched glass shade, basal finial suspended by three chains, fitted saucer shaped smoke bell, Louis Philippe, c1835 . . . . **800.00**

Lusters, 21½″, lyre form, three scrolling candle arms, turned nozzles, molded incurvate triangular base, cabochon faceted pyriform and floriform brilliants, Neoclassical, pr **1,200.00**

Music Box, 4″, gilt, filigree dec, German **425.00**

Seal, 4″ h, drum form, mandarin duck standing on lotus base, characters on underside, gilt, Chinese, Sui Dynasty **3,000.00**

Sconces, pr

23″, figural, Roman soldier figure backplate, naturally modeled branches ending in candle nozzles, Louis XVI style, 19th C **3,800.00**

41″, gilt, quiver of arrows backplate, bowknot and ribbon holding five scrolling candle arms, husk ornamented nozzles, Louis XVI style, 19th C **4,250.00**

Spigot, 6″, Sythian lion head, Renaissance, 17th C **300.00**

Spoon Mold, 8¼″ l, to make pewter tablespoons **275.00**

Urn

11½″, gilt and patinated bronze, engine turned lip, reeded body and columnar base, Empire, early 19th C, pr **2,250.00**

14″, cov, pine cone finial, ram's head handles, pierced and molded balustrade, Louis XVI, c1775, pr . . . **2,000.00**

Vase

10″, bottle form, two lively dragons on shoulders, fitted base, Chinese, 18th C **500.00**

12″, inverted bell form, modeled with three nudes grasping laurel festoons, domed foot, inscribed "Cast from model by Mable Conkling," American Art Foundry marks, early 20th C **1,600.00**

Wall Lights, 18″ h, gilt, scrolling wall plate, foliage and asymmetrical branches ending in spirally twisted foliate nozzles, crowned "C" mark, Louis XV, mid 18th C, pr **12,000.00**

BUFFALO POTTERY

History: Buffalo Pottery Co., Buffalo, New York, was chartered in 1901. The first kiln was fired in October 1903. Larkin Soap Company conceived Buffalo Pottery to produce premiums for its extensive mail order business. Wares also were sold to the public by better department and jewelry stores. Elbert Hubbard and Frank L. Wright, who designed the Larkin Administration Building in Buffalo in 1904, were two prominent names associated with the Larkin Company.

Early production consisted mainly of dinner sets of semi-vitreous china. Buffalo was the first pottery in the United States to produce successfully the

Blue Willow pattern, marked "First Old Willow Ware Mfg. in America." Buffalo also made a line of hand decorated, multicolored willow ware, called Gaudy Willow. Other early items include a series of game, fowl, and fish sets, pitchers, jugs, and a line of commemorative, historical, and advertising plates and mugs.

In 1908–09 and 1921–23, Buffalo Pottery produced the line for which it is most famous, Deldare Ware, The earliest of this olive green, semi-vitreous china depicts hand decorated scenes from the English artist Cecil Aldin's *Fallowfield Hunt.* Hunt scenes only were done in 1908–09. English village scenes also were characteristic and found throughout the series. Most are artist signed.

In 1911 Buffalo Pottery produced Emerald Deldare, which used scenes from Goldsmith's *The Three Tours of Dr. Syntax* and an Art Nouveau type border. Completely decorated Art Nouveau pieces also were made.

In 1912 Abino was born. Abino was done on Deldare bodies and showed sailing, windmill, and seascape scenes. The main color was rust. All pieces are artist signed and numbered.

In 1915 the pottery was modernized, giving it the ability to produce vitrified china. Consequently, hotel and institutional ware became their main production, with hand decorated ware de-emphasized. Buffalo china became a leader in producing and designing the most famous railroad, hotel, and restaurant patterns. These wares, especially railroad items, are eagerly sought by collectors.

In the early 1920s fine china was made for home use, e.g., the Bluebird pattern. In 1950 Buffalo made their first Christmas plate. They were given away to customers and employees from 1950–60. Hample Equipment Co. ordered some in 1962. The Christmas plates are very scarce.

The Buffalo China Company made "Buffalo Pottery" and "Buffalo China," the difference being one is semi-vitreous ware and the other vitrified. In 1956 the company was reorganized, and Buffalo China became the corporate name. Today Buffalo China is owned by Oneida Silver Company. The Larkin family no longer is involved.

Reference: Seymour and Violet Altman, *The Book of Buffalo Pottery,* reprint, Schiffer Publishing, 1987.

Note: Numbers in parenthesis refer to plates in the Altman's book.

Advisor: Seymour & Violet Altman.

ABINO WARE

Plaque
12″, desert scene (239)	1,750.00
12¼″, sailing ships (241)	1,000.00
13½″, pasture scene (244)	2,500.00
Plate, 6½″, windmill scene with ships (243)	275.00
Sugar, cov, nautical scene (249)	565.00

Blue Willow, gravy boat, blue mark, dated 1911, $45.00.

BLUE AND GAUDY WILLOW

Blue Willow
Chicago Jug, 1 pint (103)	125.00
Creamer, double lip (30)	15.00
Cup and Saucer (26)	40.00
Plate, 9¼″ (75)	25.00

CHRISTMAS PLATES

1951 (261)	50.00
1956 (266)	48.00
1960 (270)	50.00

COMMERCIAL SERVICES

Cup and Saucer, Genesee Hotel (302)	55.00
Plate	
7½″, Jack Dempsey's Restaurant (289)	100.00
9½″, Barclay Hotel (292)	100.00
10½″, Mont Clair Hotel (293)	100.00
11″, Hotel Pere Marquette (297)	150.00

DELDARE WARE

Bowl, 9″, The Fallowfield Hunt, The Death (125)	480.00
Cake Plate, 10″, Ye Village Gossips (148)	375.00
Calling Card Tray, Ye Lion Inn (173)	300.00
Chocolate Pot, 9″ (163)	1,500.00
Cup and Saucer, chocolate (163)	250.00
Hair Receiver, cov, Ye Village Street (143)	300.00
Humidor, 7″, octagonal, Ye Lion Inn (174)	675.00
Mug, 4¼″, At The Three Pigeons (122)	250.00
Nut Bowl, 8″, Ye Lion Inn (175)	475.00
Pitcher, 6″, Their Manner of Telling Stories (165)	415.00

Plate

8½", Fallowfield Hunt, The Death (123)	135.00
14", Fallowfield Hunt, The Start	565.00
Powder Jar, cov, Ye Village Street (143)	300.00
Punch Bowl, 14¾ x 9¼", Fallowfield Hunt scenes	5,000.00
Relish Tray, Ye Olden Times (151) ...	365.00
Tea Tile, 6", Traveling In Ye Olden Days (140)	300.00
Teapot, 5¼", Scenes of Village Life In Ye Olden Days	375.00
Vase, 8", untitled, fashionable men and women (162)	675.00
Wall Plaque, 12", Fallowfield Hunt, Breakfast At The Three Pigeons (120)	500.00

DELDARE WARE, MISC

Mug, 4½", Indian scene (231)	500.00
Plaque, 13½", Lost, sheep in winter scene (220)	2,000.00

Emerald Deldare, plate, 7" d, "Dr Syntax Robbed of His Property," $575.00.

EMERALD DELDARE

Candlestick, 9", bayberry motif (192) .	800.00
Fern Dish, 8", butterflies and flowers (186)	700.00
Fruit Bowl, octagonal, matching underplate, Art Nouveau dec (183)	3,550.00
Inkwell, Art Nouveau dec (196)	5,000.00
Plaque, 16½", The Garden Trio (211) .	3,500.00
Vase, 8", kingfisher, dragonflies, iris, and waterlilies (188)	875.00

GAME SET

Plaque, 9", The Gunner (70)	80.00
Plate, 9"	
Fish	
Rainbow Trout (59)	60.00
Striped Bass (60)	65.00

Fowl

American Woodcock (65)	70.00
Mallard Duck, (63)	70.00
Platter, 11 x 14", The Buffalo Hunt ...	200.00

HISTORICAL, COMMEMORATIVE, AND ADVERTISING WARE

Jug, George Washington	325.00
Mug, 4½", Masonic (110)	75.00
Plate	
7½", Erie Tribe, Improved Order of Redman (91)	75.00
8", Theodore Roosevelt (87)	200.00
10", Independence Hall, Philadelphia, PA (82)	75.00
Saucer, 4⅜", Wanamaker Store Jubilee Year, 1861–1911, green and white, buffalo mark	60.00

MISCELLANEOUS

Child's Feeding Dish, bluebird (321) ..	40.00
Cowboy Hat (354)	30.00
Dinner Set, 100 pcs, Kenmore (315) ..	500.00
Jug, Landing of Roger Williams (36) ..	550.00
Pitcher, nautical scene (34)	500.00
Tea Rose (314)	400.00
Teapot, matching teaball, Argyle (336)	185.00
Vase, Portland, 1946 series (341)	625.00

BURMESE GLASS

History: Burmese glass is a translucent art glass originated by Frederick Shirley and manufactured by the Mt. Washington Glass Co., New Bedford, Massachusetts, from 1885 to c1891. Burmese glass shades from a soft lemon to a salmon pink. Uranium was used to attain the yellow color and gold was added to the batch so that on reheating one end turned pink. Upon reheating again, the edges would revert to the yellow coloring. The blending of the colors was so gradual that it was difficult to determine where one color ended and the other began.

Although some of the glass has a surface that is glossy, most of it is acid finished. The majority of the items were free blown, but some were blown molded in a ribbed, hobnail, or diamond quilted design.

American-made Burmese is quite thin, fragile, and brittle. The only factory licensed to make Burmese was Thos. Webb & Sons in England. Out of deference to Queen Victoria, they called their wares "Queen's Burmese."

Reproduction Alert: Reproductions abound in almost every form. Since uranium can no longer be used, some of the reproductions are easy to spot. In the 1950s Gunderson produced many pieces in imitation of Burmese.

MW = Mount Washington
Wb = Webb
a.f. = acid finish
s.f. = shiny finish
Advisor: Clarence and Betty Maier.

Bowl
2½″ d, Wb, a.f., crimped top, acorn dec, sgd 350.00
5″ d, 7″ h, MW, a.f., ball shape, top with four fold-down edges, four applied feet, berry pontil 450.00
6½″ l, 2½″ h, MW, a.f., undecorated, applied rigaree dec on edges of fold-down sides 345.00
Condiment, MW, a.f.
Cylindrical ribbed salt and pepper shakers and mustard, sgd Pairpoint holder 365.00
Twin undecorated melon ribbed cruets, molded faceted stoppers, two cylindrical ribbed salt and pepper shakers, sgd SP Pairpoint holder 1,500.00

Vase, 6¾″ h, autumn leaves dec, blue berries, $485.00.

Creamer and Sugar, 2¾″ h, MW, a.f., single applied handle on creamer, two applied handles on sugar bowl, pr .. 785.00
Cruet, MW, a.f., melon ribbed, superb enamel dec 2,450.00
Epergne, 9½″ h, Wb, a.f., two undecorated fairy lamps with sgd Clarke bases, twin bud vases, centered metal standard holding upright vase, SP stand 1,400.00
Fairy Lamp, Wb, a.f.
Dome shaped shade, urn shaped base, double prunus blossoms dec,

sgd Clarke candle cup and candle cup holder, 9½″ 945.00
Twin undecorated fairy lamps, clear sgd Clarke glass candle cups, brass stand, centered brass dolphin 750.00
Undecorated dome shaped shade, clear sgd Clarke glass base 200.00
Hat, 1¼″ h, Pairpoint Corp., s.f., c1930 450.00
Lamp Shade, 5″, gaslight
MW, a.f. 225.00
MW, s.f. 285.00
Plaque, 11¾″, MW, a.f., cottage, birds and daisies dec 750.00
Pitcher
2½″ h, Wb, a.f., prunus blossom dec 535.00
9″ h, MW, a.f., tankard, Queen's design dec 2,000.00
9″ h, MW, a.f., tankard, rural scene, florals, Longfellow verse 3,250.00
Rose Bowl, 3″ d, Wb, a.f., prunus blossom dec 365.00
Rose Jar, 5¼″ h, MW, cov, floral dec .. 400.00
Salt, Wb, a.f., 2¾″ d,¾″ h, bittersweet colored blossoms, shiny gold branches 445.00
Sweetmeat, 7″ h, Wb, a.f., cylindrical, bittersweets and shiny gold foliage, sgd, SP collar, lid, and bail handle .. 450.00
Syrup Pitcher, MW, a.f., elaborate raised enamel floral dec, SP fittings 3,500.00
Toothpick Holder, MW
2″, a.f., fig shape, floral dec (Heacock #2) 465.00
2½″, a.f., cylindrical, trefoil top, floral dec, optic diamond quilting (Heacock #4) 415.00
2¾″, a.f., cylindrical
Crimped top, undecorated, optic diamond quilting, paper label (Heacock #44) 485.00
Square top, floral dec (Heacock #28) 465.00
Tumbler, MW
a.f., undecorated 185.00
s.f., undecorated 285.00
Vase
6″, Wb, a.f., elongated tubular shape, wafer base, exquisite prunus blossom dec 900.00
7″, MW, a.f.
Classic urn shape, floral dec, two applied handles 1,100.00
Flower form, undecorated, metal holder, putti holding vase in upraised arms, Pairpoint mark . 485.00
8″, MW, a.f., gourd shape, Queen's design dec, orig paper label 2,200.00
9″, MW, a.f., petticoat shape, long neck, trefoil top, undecorated 585.00
10″, Gunderson, a.f., lily shape, undecorated, c1955 .... 175.00

10½", Pairpoint, s.f., urn shape, pedestal base, c1930 .... **665.00**
12", MW, a.f.
  Bulbous shape, stylized oak leaves dec **1,250.00**
  Chinese manner dec, florals, geometrics, and two dragons, two applied handles **1,750.00**
  Classic shape, trefoil top **685.00**
12½", Wb, a.f., jack-in-the-pulpit, prunus blossom dec **1,250.00**

BUSTS

History: The portrait bust has its origins in pagan and Christian tradition. Greek and Roman heroes, and later images of Christian saints, dominate the early examples. Busts of the "ordinary man" first appeared in the Renaissance.

Busts of the nobility, poets, and other notable persons dominated the 18th and 19th centuries, especially those designed for use in a home library. Because of the large number of these library busts, excellent examples can be found at reasonable prices, depending on artist, subject, and material.

Reference: Anita Jacobsen (ed.), *Jacobsen's Painting and Bronze Price Guide,* published by author.

Additional Listings: Ivory, Parian Ware, Soapstone, and Wedgwood.

Jesus Christ, parian ware, 9" h, $125.00.

Alabaster and Marble, Ispirazione, maiden gazing heavenward, laurel band on head, Italian, late 19th C, 13 1/2" **475.00**
Bisque
  Girl and Boy, gilt metal waisted socle, inscribed "B. Hierli", 12" **150.00**

Woman, voluptuous, blue gown, blonde curls, emerging from center of yellow flower, waisted socle, fluted column base, German, late 19th C, 30 3/4" **1,300.00**
Bronze
  Art Nouveau, woman wearing tiara, cast from model by Emmanuel Villanis, executed by Solciete des Bronzes de Paris, cast title "Favorite," inscribed "E. Villanis," foundry mark, c1900, 22" **625.00**
  Roman Military Officer, armorial breast plate depicting tasks of Hercules, black patina, white marble plinth, 24" **900.00**
Earthenware, Dutch girl, Art Nouveau, polychrome, buff and gilt, incised signature "A. Nelson", 20" h **250.00**
Lead, goddess Hera, diadem in parted hair, loose tunic tied at shoulders, 18th C, 28" **1,150.00**
Majolica, Charles V, short hair, full beard, intaglio dec, scrolling foliage, Order of the Golden Fleece around neck, mustard, rust, and green edged epaulets, 16th C, 29 1/2" **2,500.00**
Marble
  Athlete, head inclined to left, circular socle, 17 3/4" **400.00**
  Emperor Augustus, short curly hair, open eyes, slightly parted lips, mantle secured with disc brooch, white marble socle, 18th C, 37" .. **9,000.00**
  Napoleon, marble socle, Continental, late 19th C, 20 1/2" **500.00**
Painted Metal, Arab, titled "Jeweled," inscribed "Waagen," French, c1900, 21" **600.00**
Plaster, patinated, young woman, curly upswept hair, imp PARJB, white plaster socle, French, 19th C, 20" **800.00**
Terra Cotta
  Child, crying, canvas newspaper hat, fly on nose, inscribed "G.D. Paris Depose," 6" **85.00**
  Girl, Art Nouveau, lily pad form base, green tone, incised signature, 21" **225.00**
Wood, Benjamin Franklin, oak, old brown alligatored finish, "Harris" carved in back, 15" **725.00**

BUTTER PRINTS

History: Butter prints divide into two categories: butter molds and butter stamps. Butter molds are generally of three piece construction—the design, the screw-in handle, and the case. Molds both mold and stamp the butter at the same time. Butter stamps are of one piece construction, sometimes two pieces if the handle is from a separate piece of wood. Stamps decorate the top of butter after it is molded.

The earliest prints were one piece and hand carved, often thick and deeply carved. Later prints were factory made with the design forced into the wood by a metal die.

Some of the most common designs are sheaves of wheat, leaves, flowers, and pineapples. Animal designs and Germanic tulips are difficult to find. Rare prints include unusual shapes, such as half-rounded and lollipop, and those with designs on both sides.

Reference: Paul E. Kindig, *Butter Prints And Molds*, Schiffer Publishing, 1986.

MOLD

Lily of the Valley, wood, hand carved, oblong case, 2 lb	**185.00**
Peacock, copper, round, 4¼″	**100.00**
Pineapple, "Patd Apr. 17, 1866," 5″	**80.00**
Rooster, wood, hand carved, round	**75.00**
Sheaf of Wheat, tin and copper, 4¼ x 6 x 7″	**90.00**
Swan, wood, hand carved	**100.00**

Stamp, stylized thistle carving, semi-circular, 3¼ x 7″ d, $75.00.

STAMP

Eagle, star, and foliage, round, 4″	**300.00**
Heart, turned handle, 3⅞″	**90.00**
Pineapple and Foliage, turned inserted handle, semicircular, 6⅞″ l	**275.00**
Rising Sun, lollipop shape, 6¼″ l	**325.00**
Rose, turned handle, varnished, 3¾″	**50.00**
Scallop, wood, fan center, crimped edge, 3½″ d, 2⅝″ h	**80.00**
Starflower, hearts, tulips, flowers, wooden, hand carved, rope carved edge, turned wood handle, 4⅝″	**275.00**
Sunflower, wood, hand carved, round	**48.00**
Tulip, lollipop, wood, hand carved, scrubbed finish, 8¾″	**425.00**
Wheel, carved acorns, 7″ l	**75.00**

CALENDAR PLATES

History: Calendar plates were first made in England in the late 1880s. They became popular in the United States after 1900, the peak years being 1909 to 1915. The majority of the advertising plates were made of porcelain or pottery with a calendar, the name of a store or business, and either a scene, portrait, animal, or flowers. Some also were made of glass or tin.

Additional Listings: See *Warman's Americana & Collectibles* for more examples.

1911, couple, "Should Auld Acquaintance Be Forgot," $25.00.

1907, Christmas snow scene	50.00
1908, 9″, purple violets	40.00
1908, 9½″, two monks drinking wine	65.00
1908, 9¾″, hunting dog, Pittston, PA	35.00
1909, 7½″, Santa in zeppelin dropping presents to children	50.00
1909, 8¼″, flowers	18.00
1909, 9″, woman and man in patio garden	22.00
1910, 8″, The Old Swimming Hole	45.00
1910, 9″, cherubs ringing in New Year	30.00
1910, ships and windmills	20.00
1911, 8¼″, hunting scene, W.A. Craft, Roslyn, NY	25.00
1912, 7½″, bowl of pink roses	30.00
1912, 9¼″, Martha Washington	35.00
1913, 7½″, early biplane in flight	40.00
1914, 6¾″, Point Arena, CA	25.00
1915, 7½″, compliments of Hobbs, Rawlins, WY	28.00
1915, 9″, black boy eating watermelon	32.00
1916, 8¼″, eagle with shield and American flag	32.00
1917, basket of flowers, gold trim	25.00
1920, "The Great War," MO	25.00
1921, 9″, bluebirds and fruit	25.00
1922, dog watching rabbit	30.00
1924, 9″, steeplechase scene	28.00

1929, 6¼", flowers, Valentine, NE **25.00**
1929, 9", boy with dog **30.00**

CALLING CARD CASES AND RECEIVERS

History: Calling cards, usually carried in specially designed cases, played an important social role in the United States from the period of the Civil War until the end of World War I. When making a formal visit, a caller left their card in a receiver (card dish) in the front hall. Strict rules of etiquette developed. For example, the lady in a family was expected to make calls of congratulations, visits to the ill, and condolence.

The cards themselves were small, embossed or engraved with the caller's name, and often carried a floral design. Many hand done examples, especially in Spencerian script, can be found. The cards themselves are considered collectible and range in price from a few cents to several dollars.

Note: Don't confuse a calling card case with a match safe.

Sterling Silver, English, 2½ x 3⁷⁄₁₆", marked "18" and "WGH," chain, $60.00.

CALLING CARD CASES

Ivory
  2¾ x 4¼", carved intricate undercutting **65.00**
  3¼", deeply carved scene of tale of William Tell, German **185.00**
  3¼ x 2", inlaid with silver and malachite geometric quilted design **60.00**
Mother of Pearl, 4 x 2¾" **35.00**
Paper, 3", Mrs. L. Sherrard's Confectionery Store, Phila, cream, pink, and red carnations **20.00**

Silver
  Coin, 3", engraved bird, orig hinged box, A. Cole, NY **100.00**
  Sterling
    2½ x 3½", rect, rounded corners, hinged lid, repousse and chased, cathedral against punched ground, reverse with fortress in landscape, marked "Leonard & Wilson, Phila.," c1845 .... **200.00**
    3" h, Unger Bros, rect, each side chased, scene of bathing maiden **75.00**

CALLING CARD RECEIVERS

Carnival Glass, Grape & Cable, purple, sgd "Northwood" **135.00**
Cast Metal, figural lady, painted green, Art Deco **85.00**
China, hp, 10", roses, gold handles .. **30.00**
Crystal, blown out flowers, pedestal base **35.00**
Nippon, creamy white ground, gold center handle, gold rim, scene of pagoda on hillside, bird in flight, sailing ship edged in black, burnished gold **45.00**
Silver Plated
  Cherub pushing holder, rect base .. **60.00**
  Ornate, upright, marked "Wilcox" .. **75.00**
Sterling Silver, American, marked "S Kirk & Sons," 1880 .... **125.00**

CAMBRIDGE GLASS

History: Cambridge Glass Company, Cambridge, Ohio, was incorporated in 1901. Initially the company made clear tableware, later expanding into colored, etched, and engraved glass. Over 40 different hues were produced in blown and pressed glass.

Five different marks were employed during the production years, but not every piece was marked.

The plant closed in 1954. Some of the molds were later sold to the Imperial Glass Company, Bellaire, Ohio.

References: National Cambridge Collectors, Inc., *The Cambridge Glass Co., Cambridge, Ohio* (reprint of 1930 catalog and supplements through 1934), Collector Books, 1976; National Cambridge Collectors, Inc., *The Cambridge Glass Co., Cambridge, Ohio, 1949 Thru 1953* (catalog reprint), Collector Books, 1976; National Cambridge Collectors, Inc., *Colors In Cambridge Glass*, Collector Books, 1984; Mark Nye, *Cambridge Stemware*, published by author, 1985.

Collectors' Club: National Cambridge Collectors, Inc., P. O. Box 416, Cambridge, OH 43725. Dues: $13.00. *Crystal Ball* (monthly).

Ashtray, Caprice, crystal, 2¾" 4.50
Basket
  Caprice, crystal, ftd, handle 20.00
  Decagon, light blue, 6" 20.00
Bonbon
  Apple Blossom, yellow, 5½" 22.00
  Caprice, crystal, 6", handle 7.00
  Cleo, blue-green, 6", dec 18.00
  Gloria, amber 22.00
Bottle, dressing
  Diane, crystal, "French Dressing" . . 200.00
  Wildflower, "Oil" 90.00
Bowl
  Apple Blossom, amber, 5½", fruit,
   liner 15.00
  Caprice
   10", pink, ftd 65.00
   12½", crystal, bell form 30.00
  Cleo, blue-green, 12", flared 30.00
  Crown Tuscan, 8", oval, ftd 30.00
  Decagon, light blue
   3¾", cranberry 18.00
   6½", cereal, wide rim 18.50
   10", two handles 40.00
  Diane, 11" 22.50
  Tally Ho, dark green, 13" 25.00
Butter, cov, Rosepoint, 5" 155.00
Cake Plate, Wildflower, 13", ftd, Martha
  blank 100.00
Candlesticks, pr
  Alpine, crystal and frosted, triple . . . 38.00
  Caprice
   Blue, 7", prisms 75.00
   Crystal, 2½" 20.00
Candy Box
  Chantilly, crystal, round 32.00
  Wildflower 65.00
Candy Dish, cov, Caprice, pink 110.00
Celery
  Caprice, blue 160.00
  Portia, crystal, 11" 25.00
  Rosepoint, 11" 60.00
Champagne, Carmen, nude stem 125.00
Cheese Stand, Rosepoint 25.00
Claret, Carmen, nude stem 125.00
Coaster, Caprice, crystal, 3½" 7.00
Cocktail
  Carmen, nude stem 85.00
  Cascade, crystal 14.00
  Mt Vernon, crystal, 3½ oz 13.00
  Rosepoint 30.00
  Tally Ho, amber, 3 oz 9.00
Cocktail Shaker, Chantilly, crystal, 32
  oz, SS ball top 110.00
Compote, Caprice
  Blue, 7", low standard 30.00
  Crystal, 8", low standard 18.00
Console Bowl
  Avocado 35.00
  Jade, silver overlay 45.00
Cordial
  Mt Vernon, crystal 7.00

Regency, forest green 40.00
Cordial Set, decanter, eight stemmed
  emerald green cordials, basket type
  handled Farber tray, 9 pc 165.00
Creamer and Sugar
  Caprice
   Blue, individual size 32.00
   Crystal, table size 18.00
  Decagon, blue 22.00
  Everglades, amber 40.00
  Rosepoint, individual size 42.00
Cup
  Caprice, crystal, ftd 9.00
  Daisy, marked "Nearcut" 6.00
  Wild Rose 12.00
Cup and Saucer
  Caprice, blue 35.00
  Cascade, crystal 17.00
  Decagon
   Amber 7.50
   Blue 12.50
   Pink 5.00
Epergne, two vases, three lites, Ca-
  price, crystal 80.00
Finger Bowl, Alpine, blue 45.00
Flower Frog
  Bashful Charlotte, green, 13" 200.00
  Sea Gull, crystal 50.00
Fruit Cocktail, Cleo, green, 3 pc 65.00
Goblet
  Caprice, crystal, 9 oz 14.00
  Carmen, nude stem 150.00
  Diane, crystal, 9 oz 20.00
  Mt Vernon, crystal, 10 oz 14.00
  Portia, crystal, 9 oz 18.00
  Rosepoint, 10 oz 24.00
  Wildflower, crystal, gold rim, 10 oz . 20.00
Hurricane Lamp, Rosepoint, all-over
  etching, bowl base, 10" 425.00
Hurricane Shade, Wildflower, 10" 100.00
Ice Bucket
  Cleo, dark green 45.00
  Diane 60.00
Jelly, Caprice
  Blue, 7", crimped 45.00
  Crystal, 4", sq, two handles 12.00
Juice Tumbler
  Rosepoint 22.50
  Wildflower, ftd 12.00
Ladle, punch bowl, Tally Ho, red 100.00
Lemon Plate, Caprice, crystal, 5" 7.00
Marmalade, Rosepoint 175.00
Mayonnaise
  Cleo, blue 35.00
  Diane, crystal, SS holder, 2 pt 25.00
Nut Dish, Caprice, blue, individual size 65.00
Pickle Dish
  Caprice, crystal, 9" 2.00
  Gloria, yellow, 9" 35.00
Pitcher
  Etched, #937, pink 24.00
  Rosepoint, Poulton 255.00

Plate
Alpine, 8″, light blue 30.00
Caprice
7½″, salad, crystal 7.00
8½″, luncheon, blue 18.00
14″, carabet, crystal 26.00
Cleo, blue
6″ 10.00
8¾″ 12.00
Decagon
6″, bread and butter, amber 3.50
7½″, salad, pink 5.00
7¾″, blue 6.50
9½″, dinner, light blue 26.00
Diane, crystal, 8″ 14.00
Etch #739, light blue, 8⅜″ 8.00
Lorna, pink, 8⅜″, #597 dec 6.00
Wildflower, crystal, gold rim, 7½″ . . . 9.00
Platter, Decagon, light blue, 12½″ . . . 42.00
Relish
Diane, five parts, amber 35.00
Rosepoint, three parts 42.00
Wildflower, five parts 35.00
Rose Bowl, Caprice, blue, 5″ 90.00
Sandwich Server, Decagon, blue 32.00
Salt and Pepper Shakers, pr
Chantilly, crystal 20.00
Rosepoint 80.00

Crown Tuscan, sherbet, $42.00.

Sherbet
Caprice, crystal 7.00
Elaine, crystal 16.00
Rosepoint 18.00
Tally Ho, cobalt blue, 4⅞″ 20.00
Wildflower, crystal, gold rim, low . . . 15.00
Torte Plate, Diane, crystal 40.00
Tray, Caprice, blue, 9″, oval, handles . 35.00
Tumbler
Caprice, crystal, 9 oz, ftd 15.00
Cascade, crystal, 12 oz 16.50
Decagon, blue, 5 oz 8.00

Elaine, crystal, 10 oz, ftd 18.00
Imperial Hunt Scene, pink and green,
5 oz, ftd 18.00
Rosepoint, 10 oz, ftd 23.00
Vase
Caprice, blue, 3½″ 110.00
Rosepoint
6″, flared 45.00
12″, keyhole base 110.00
Wildflower, 10″ bud vase 30.00
Wine
Caprice, crystal 20.00
Decagon, light blue 30.00
Mt Vernon, crystal, 1 oz 6.50

CAMBRIDGE

CAMBRIDGE POTTERY

History: The Cambridge Art Pottery was incorporated in Ohio in 1900. Between 1901 and 1909 the firm produced the usual line of jardinieres, tankards, and vases with underglazed slip decorations and glazes similar to other Ohio potteries. Line names included Terrhea, Oakwood, Otoe, and others.

In 1904 the company introduced Guernsey kitchenware. It was so well received that it became the plant's primary product. In 1909 the company's name was changed to Guernsey Earthenware Company.

All wares were marked.

Vase, 6½″ h, green, acorn mark, $90.00.

Bank, 6 x 3¼", pig shape, dark glaze . 90.00
Bowl
8", floral motif, brown glaze, Terrhea 250.00
8½" d, 5¾" h, matte green glaze, ftd,
four imp signed acorn marks 100.00
Custard Cup, Guernsey mark 30.00
Pitcher
5", ewer shape, marbleized effect,
green, brown, and yellow, Oakwood 80.00
16½", tankard, two ears of corn, incised signature, mold #263 ..... 650.00
Plate, 8", royal blue 45.00
Tile, 6" sq, majolica type glaze, high
relief florals 85.00
Vase
5½", ovoid, grapes and leaves, artist
sgd 125.00
6½", tapering sides, inward flaring
collar, raised sq motif with raised
circles, green matte finish, acorn
mark 90.00
6¾", pear shape, waisted, flaring
neck, mottled yellow to green to
brown, Oakwood 100.00
8", saucer base, extended body, applied shaped handles, high glaze,
yellow, green, and brown, Oakwood, mold #235 .... 150.00

CAMEO GLASS

History: Cameo glass is a form of cased glass.
A shell of glass was prepared; then one or more
layers of glass of a different color(s) was faced to
the first. A design was then cut through the outer
layer(s) leaving the inner layer(s) exposed.

This type of art glass originated in Alexandria,
Egypt, 100-200 A.D. The oldest and most famous
example of cameo glass is the Barberini or Portland vase which was found near Rome in 1582. It
contained the ashes of Emperor Alexander Server-
erus who was assassinated in 235 A.D.

Emile Gallé is probably one of the best known
artists of cameo glass. He established a factory at
Nancy, France, in 1884. Although much of the
glass bears his signature, he was primarily the
designer. On many pieces assistants did the actual
work, even to signing his name. Glass made after
his death in 1904 has a star before the name Gallé.
Other makers of French cameo glass include D'Argental, Daum Nancy, LeGras and Delatte.

English cameo does not have as many layers
of glass (colors) and cuttings as do French pieces.
The outer layer is usually white, and cuttings are
very fine and delicate. Most pieces are not signed.
The best known makers are Thomas Webb & Sons
and Stevens and Williams.

Reference: Victor Arwas, *Glass Art Nouveau to
Art Deco*, Rizzoli International Publications, Inc.,
1977; Ray and Lee Grover, *English Cameo Glass*,
Crown Publishers, Inc., 1980; Albert C. Revi, *Nineteenth Century Glass*, reprint, Schiffer Publishing,
1981.

AMERICAN

Mt Washington
Vase, 9", pink and white, winged Grif-
fins and shields 800.00
New England Glass Co
Lamp, fluid, base, 10¾" h, 8" d, pink
birds and flowers, white ground,
iron base, brass font 300.00
Tiffany
Vase, 8½", ovoid, white calla lilies,
lime green leaves, and insects,
pearly irid body, inscribed "L. C. T.,
X1175," c1892–1928 .... 5,650.00

ENGLISH

Geo. Woodall
Vase, 14", white Grecian woman with
urn, dark blue ground, sgd 25,000.00
Stevens & Williams
Lamp, 8", red fuchsias and leaves,
yellow ground, sgd 2,500.00
Vase
8", white florals, blue ground, ruffled top, sgd 950.00
Unknown Maker
Basket, 6" d, multicolored wreath of
leaves, opaque white ground, three
frosted feet, ruffled edge, satin finish, SS handle 400.00
Perfume Bottle, 5¾", round, white
flowers and butterfly, raisin brown
ground, SS top 1,400.00
Vase
6¼", Chinese red palm fronds and
butterfly, Mandarin yellow
ground, top layer fire polished . 1,500.00
7", white flowers, frosty blue ground 825.00
Thomas Webb & Sons
Bowl, 4⅞", white morning glories,
deep raspberry red ground 850.00
Compote, 10 x 4", blue, pink, and
white florals, sgd 1,850.00
Fairy Lamp, 5½", blue peach blossoms and leaves, white ground,
sgd "Thomas Webb & Sons" 2,250.00
Inkwell, 3½ x 4", bluish-white flowers,
frosted amber ground, SS hinged
top, sgd 950.00
Lamp, 4½ x 4", fluid, three frosted
feet, white flowering vine, blue
ground, sp collar, sgd 450.00
Perfume Bottle, 2¼", round, pink and
white roses, frosty white ground,
SS collar and repousse stopper,
sgd 600.00

Pitcher, 6", white dogwood blossoms, raspberry red ground, acid cut ground with pattern of flowers and vines, heat check on upper handle ... 600.00

Rose Bowl, 4", white honeysuckle, raspberry red ground 600.00

Scent Bottle

3⅞", teardrop shape, white flowers, frosted raspberry ground, SS collar and hinged top, sgd 500.00

6⅝", white flowers, butterfly and dragonfly, raspberry red ground, SS screw top, sgd 700.00

Vase

5¾", blue berry bushes, white to frosty light blue ground 700.00

8", white florals, vines, and leaves, raspberry red ground, sgd "Webb & Sons" 1,800.00

9½", ovoid, white dogwood blossoms and leaves, raspberry red ground 600.00

FRENCH

Arsall

Vase, 6", flowers and leaves, light green, dark green, and black, pink ground, c1900 .... 600.00

D'Argental, pieces sgd "D'Argental" in cameo

Bowl, 5 x 3½", brown flowers and leaves, yellow to white frosted ground, sgd 425.00

Flask, 6", pink bleeding hearts 400.00

Vase, 6½", clear leaves and berries, frosted blue ground, sgd 450.00

Daum Nancy, pieces sgd "Daum Nancy" in gilt intaglio

Biscuit Jar, 6½", Clair de Lune, ornate silver lid and bail handle, sgd ... 650.00

Bowl

1⅝ x 1 x 2¼", oval, barren forest landscape, snow on branches and ground, mottled gold frosted ground, sgd 575.00

9 x 3½", blue winter plants, mottled frost ground, crimped top 950.00

9 x 4", brown Chinese Junk scene, yellow, orange and tan mottled ground 1,200.00

Creamer, 4¼", colorful enameled tulips, mottled green and peach ground, cameo cut handle, sgd .. 325.00

Decanter, 10", red berries, green leaves, frosted ground, sgd 750.00

Jar, 3¼", red flower buds, green leaves, lavender and opalescent ground, sgd 200.00

Lamp, 22", winter scene, orange ground, sgd 3,600.00

Perfume Bottle

8", winter scene, orange frosted ground, sgd 725.00

10", iris, gold enamel highlights, green ground, incised label "Parfum de Vertus," sgd 325.00

Pitcher, 5", mottled rusty-orange base shading to lemon yellow, applied handle, body overlaid with clear glass, bellflower blossoms, buds, and foliage, naturalistic enamel coloration, gold brushed lip, name sgd in gold with Cross of Lorraine logo 985.00

Rose Bowl, 3", sailboat scene, sgd . 750.00

Salt

2", blackbirds in snow, sgd 225.00

2¼", opal green leaves, frosted ground, sgd 175.00

Toothpick, 2 x 1¼", acid etched and enameled violets, leaves, and stems, mottled ground shading from white to deep violet, sgd ... 300.00

Tumbler, 3½", spring scene, sgd ... 275.00

Vase

3½", red flowers, tan ground, sgd 275.00

4", winter scene, sgd 345.00

11", sunrise scene, swallows 1,750.00

12", blue cornflowers, pale yellow ground, small handles at top .. 1,250.00

16", blown out forest scene, reds and browns, sgd 5,575.00

de Vez, pieces sgd "de Vez" in cameo, c1920

Vase

7½", gourd shape, deep blue and brown pattern of flowers, leaves, insects, and birds, peach and opaque ground, sgd 400.00

9¾", Clair de Lune blank, poppies, green and red, three cuttings .. 950.00

10", green leafless trees, frosty white sky, sgd 265.00

Galle, pieces sgd "Galle" in cameo

Bowl, 7 x 3", blue passion flowers, frosted ground 775.00

Box, 4 1 2 x 2½", pink peach blossoms, white frosted ground 750.00

Dish, 9", rolled leaf shape, light green leaves, frosted ground, sgd 800.00

Flask

5½", red gooseberries, frosted white ground shading to gold at top and bottom, two applied handles, sgd 600.00

6¾", green grapes and leaves, frosted clear ground 675.00

Lamp

19", blue mountain scene, birds on shade, sgd 4,000.00

23", dark blue and yellow butterflies, light blue ground, sgd ... 7,200.00

Galle, vase, 4¼″, frosted, gold poppies, partial paper label "Nancy...," $625.00.

Lamp Base, 14½″, amethyst flowering vines and leaves, fiery opal ground, sgd 800.00
Perfume Bottle, 7½″, red fuchsias, yellow frosted ground, sgd 750.00
Tumbler, 3″, topaz thistles, frosted ground, sgd 325.00
Vase
   3½″, green leaves, frosted deep reddish-brown ground, brass rim, branches and leaves ornamentation, sgd 535.00
   3¾″, green leaves, pink vines and flowers, frosted clear ground, sgd 250.00
   5½″, amber flowers, frosted ground 275.00
   8″, shaded maroon leaves swirling at top, frosted peach ground, sgd 750.00
   11″, Chinese red carved irises, creamy lemon ground, sgd 3,000.00
   12″, dark green leaves and flowers, light green ground, sgd 950.00
   13¼″, stick, dark brown grapes and vines, frosty white and peach ground, sunset shading, sgd .. 650.00
Le Gras
  Rose Bowl
   3″, enameled forest scene 300.00
   7½″, winter sunset scene, snow on ground, sgd near base 250.00
  Vase
   5½″, red flowers 300.00
   7½″, peach and beige boat scene, two fisherman, enamel dec, brown ground, sgd 750.00
   15¾″, sq, tapered, green leaves, yellow flowers, sgd 425.00
Le Verre Francasis
  Compote, 11 x 6″, orange florals, blue scrolls, yellow ground, sgd 350.00

Ewer, 12″, orange geometric design, white ground, blue handle and rim, sgd 450.00
Lamp, 15″, white, orange, and blue fuchsias 900.00
Night Light, horse chestnut shape shade, mottled brown horse chestnuts, sunset colored ground, sgd on shade, made-up base 250.00
Pitcher, 11¼″, ovoid, lavender and amethyst flowers and leaves, applied amethyst handle, sgd 850.00
Richard
  Box, 3½ x 2½″, blue-green flowers, yellow ground 275.00
  Vase
   3″, purple flowers, frosted ground, sgd 200.00
   4⅜″, black holly leaves and berries, tomato red ground, sgd 300.00
St. Louis
  Atomizer, 7¼″, chartreuse flowers, frosted cut window pane ground, gold washed atomizer, sgd 325.00
  Box, 5 x 2¾″, cranberry flowers, green ground 350.00
  Ice Bucket, 5¾ x 5¾″, red poppies, vaseline ground, gold highlights, brass handle and mountings, sgd 500.00
  Vase, 10″, green branches, peach fleurettes, opaque pink ground, sgd 425.00
Vallerystahl
  Box, 5 x 3″, dark green, applied and cut dec, sgd 950.00
  Cologne Bottle, 6¾″, fuchsia flowers and leaves, frosted cranberry ground, gold colored collar and screw stopper, sgd "Cristaherie Le Gantin" 475.00
  Vase
   9½″, purple tulips, frosted ground, sgd 500.00
   12″, amberina, gold daffodils, sgd 3,500.00
   14″, insects and flowers, cut and enameled, sgd 5,000.00

LeGras, vase, 5 x 3½ x 4¾″, sunset, rust to orange to gray to green, black scene, $500.00.

CAMERAS

History: The collecting of cameras, except in isolated instances, started about 1970. Although photography generally is considered to have had its beginning in 1839, it is very unusual to find a camera made before 1880. These cameras and others made before 1925 are considered to be antique cameras. Most cameras made after 1925 that are no longer in production are considered to be classic cameras. American, German, and Japanese cameras are found most often.

Value of cameras is affected by both exterior and mechanical conditions. Particular attention must be given to the condition of the bellows if cameras have them.

References: John F. Maloney, *An Identification And Value Guide To Vintage Cameras And Images*, Books Americana, 1981; J. M. and J. C. McKeown, *Official Dealer Blue Book of Cameras*, Centennial Photo Service, 1982, 1st edition; J. M. and J. C. McKeown, *Price Guide To Antique and Classic Still Cameras*, Centennial Photo Service, 1983, 4th edition; David Sharbrough, *American Premium Guide To Olde Cameras*, Books Americana, 1983; M. Wolf, *Blue Book Illustrated Price Guide to Collectible Cameras*, Photographic Memorabilia, 1983.

Collectors' Clubs: American Photographic Historical Society, P. O. Box 1775, Grand Central Station, New York, NY 10163. Dues: $22.50. *Photographica*; Leica Historical Society of America, 2314 W. 53rd Street., Minneapolis, MN 55410. Dues: $20.00; National Steroscopic Association, P. O. Box 14801, Columbus, OH 43214. Dues: $20.00. *Stereo World* (bimonthly).

Museum: George Eastman Museum, Rochester, NY; Smithsonian Institution, Washington, DC.

Additional Listings: See *Warman's Americana & Collectibles* for more examples.

Aires, Model 35V, 35 mm, f1.5/45mm coated lens, c1957, (Japan)	60.00
Argus, Model A, 35 mm, f4.5/50mm fixed focus anastigmat lens, c1936–1941, (Ann Arbor, MI)	20.00
Baldinette, folding 35mm, f2.9/50, Schneider Radionar, Balda-Werke, 1950, (Dresden, Germany)	48.00
Bell & Howell, Filmo Turret Movie Camera, 8 mm, triple lens holder, variable speeds, 16–64 frames, c1938, (Chicago, IL)	15.00
Busch, Verascope F-40, f3.5/40 Berthiot lens, guillotine shutter to 250, RF, 1950s, (Chicago, IL)	375.00
Canon, Canonflex 2000, Canomatic lenses, 1960–62, (Tokyo, Japan)	100.00
Ciro, Ciroflex B, c1948, (Delaware, OH)	15.00
Coronet, midget, bakelite, black, 15 mm roll film, c1935, (Birmingham, England)	35.00

Devry, 16 mm movie camera, c1932, (Chicago, IL)	25.00
Dubroni, Le Photographe de Poche, wooden box, porcelain int. for in-camera processing, cl860, (Maison Dubroni, Paris)	3,000.00
Eastman Kodak (Rochester, NY)	
Automatic Kodak Junior, No. 2C, c1916–27	15.00
Baby Brownie Special, c1939	5.00
50th Anniversary Box Camera, brown with silver seal, c1938	25.00
No. 2, Folding Pocket, 101 roll film, 3½ x 3½", 1899–1903	15.00
No. 4 Bullet, box, c1896	45.00
Pocket Kodak Special, No. 1, 1926–29	15.00

Century, Grand, 5 x 7″ folding plate, top of the line, Planatic Series III triple convertible lens, 24″ red triple extension bellows, front double sliding rack and pinion, back swings, dovetailed construction, black cowhide covering, 6½ x 8½″, c1902, $135.00.

Foth, Derby 11, folding, (Berlin, Germany)	40.00
Genie, brass magazine-box, string-set shutter, push-pull action changes plates and actuates exposure counter, c1892, (Philadelphia, PA)	450.00
Ingento, 3A Folding, Burke & James, (Chicago, IL)	35.00
Kalimar A, 35 mm, non-RF, f3.5/45mm Terionar lens, c1950, (Japan)	25.00
Leitz (Wetzier, Germany)	
Leica E (Standard), black, c1932–46	275.00
Leica M2, black, c1950	400.00
Nikon, Nikon F Photomatic, 35 mm, c1965, (Tokyo, Japan)	150.00
Revere, Ranger Model 81, 8 mm movie camera, c1947, (Chicago, IL)	10.00
Seneca, Busy Bee, box, c1903, (Rochester, NY)	70.00
Tom Thumb Camera Radio, Automatic Radio Mfg Co, 1948, (Boston, MA)	110.00

Tynar, 10 x 14mm exposures on specially loaded 16mm cassettes, single speed guillotine shutter, c1950, (Los Angeles, CA) **40.00**
Universal Camera Corp (New York, NY)
　Buccaneer, 35mm, Tricor lens, Chronomatic shutter 10-300, c1945 **18.00**
　Roamer 63, 100 mm f6.3 lens, 120 roll film **10.00**
　Univex AF, compact, collapsing for Number 00 roll film, cast metal body, 1930s **15.00**
　Vitar 35 mm, Flash Chronomatic shutter **15.00**
Vidmar, Vidax, folding, 120 roll film, c1951, (USA) **250.00**
Wing, New Gem, 15 exposures on 5 x 7″ plates, sliding front lens panel, c1901, (Charleston, MA) **750.00**

CAMPHOR GLASS

History: Camphor glass derives its name from its color. Most pieces have a cloudy white appearance, similar to gum camphor; the remainder has a pale colored tint. Camphor glass is made by treating the glass with hydrofluoric acid vapors.

Powder Jar, 4½″ h, 4½″ w, green, dog finial, $30.00.

Basket, 3½″ w, flared rim, pink, applied braided handle **18.00**
Bookends, pr, Grecian columns **100.00**
Bowl, 10″, fluted rim, polished pontil .. **125.00**
Cologne Bottle, 7¾″, bulbous, long thin neck, gold trim, orig stopper **45.00**
Creamer, 3¾″ **20.00**
Cruet, hp, enameled roses, orig stopper **30.00**
Miniature Lamp, 4½″, hp, violets **75.00**
Perfume Bottle, 8½″, pinched shape, mushroom stopper **50.00**
Place Card Holder, 3¾″, ftd **35.00**
Plate, 7¼″, owl dec **30.00**
Powder Jar, cov, 4½″, pink-salmon, emb flowers on lid, figural love birds finial **48.00**

Ring Tree, 4½″ **18.00**
Salt and Pepper Shakers, blue, Swirl pattern, orig tops, pr **40.00**
Sugar Shaker, 3½″, yellow, pressed leaf dec, SP top **50.00**
Toothpick Holder
　Boot, 2½″ **25.00**
　Bucket **25.00**
Vase
　8″, fan shape, clear leaf design and trim **80.00**
　8½″, Art Deco, nude dec **35.00**

CANDLESTICKS

History: The domestic use of candlesticks is traced to the 14th century. The earliest was a picket type, named for the sharp point to hold the candle. The socket type was established by the mid-1660s.

From 1700 to the present, candlestick design mirrored furniture design. By the late 17th century, a baluster stem was introduced, replacing the earlier Doric or clustered column stem. After 1730 candlesticks reflected rococo ornateness. Neoclassic styles followed in the 1760s. Each new era produced a new grouping of candlesticks.

However, some styles became universal and remained in production for centuries. For this reason, it is important to examine the manufacturing techniques of the piece when attempting to date a candlestick.

Reference: Margaret and Douglas Archer, *The Collector's Encyclopedia Of Glass Candlesticks,* Collector Books, 1983.

Brass
　5⅜″, capstan base, Spanish, c1600 . **450.00**
　5½″, sq footed base, Spanish, c1600–50 .... **250.00**
　8¼″ h, shell pattern, English, 18th C, pr **2,000.00**
　8½″ h, mid drip, Heemskerk, c1650 . **700.00**
　14½″ h, columnar, raised dec of grapes and vines **150.00**
Glass
　Cut, 10″ h, hollow center, frosted butterfly and flowers **85.00**
　Imperial, 7½″, pressed, crystal, orig stickers **30.00**
　Opalescent, 6″ h, rose dec, pr **50.00**
　Rose Point, ram's head, Cambridge **195.00**
　Sandwich, flint, clear dolphin, petal sockets, pr **450.00**
　Shrimp Shell, pr **125.00**
　Steuben, 8¾″, clear glass, tear drop, baluster form, model #7792, inscribed **600.00**
　Venetian, 3¾″, flower form, aqua, opalescent and clear glass touched with gold **75.00**

Bennington, brown glaze, 8¼" h, $125.00.

Pewter
6½" h, snuffer provision, weighted base, c1700	225.00
8¾" h, pushup ejectors, English, c1800–25	375.00
9" h, pushups, pr	450.00
9⅞" h, trumpet shape, Henry Hopper, New York, 1842–47	300.00

Sterling Silver
3", weighted base, floral design, Kirk	210.00
4½", circular, gadrooned mouth and base, Empire	55.00
9", baluster shafts surmounted by urns, beaded base, drip pan, Goodnow & Jenks	220.00
17¾", weighted and monogrammed base, Gorham	700.00

Tin
4 x 5½", saucer base with lift, ring handle, c1840	60.00

Wood
4¾" h, turned base, pewter socket	65.00
25", baroque style, tapering shaft carved with spiralling berried foliage, carved acanthus and cartouches triform base	440.00

CANDY CONTAINERS

History: In 1876 Croft, Wilbur and Co. filled a small glass Liberty Bell with candy and sold it at the Centennial Exposition in Philadelphia. From that date until the 1960s glass candy containers remained popular and served to outline American and American transportation history.

Jeannette, Pennsylvania, a center for the packaging of candy in containers, was home for J. C. Crosetti, J. H. Millstein, T. H. Stough, and Victory Glass. Other early manufacturers included: George Borgfeldt, New York, New York; Cambridge Glass, Cambridge, Ohio; Eagle Glass, Wheeling, West Virginia; L. E. Smith, Mt. Pleasant, Pennsylvania; and, West Brothers, Grapeville, Pennsylvania.

Candy containers with original paint, candy, and closures command a high premium, but be aware of reproduced parts and repainting. The closure is a critical part of each container; its loss detracts significantly from the value.

Small figural perfumes and other miniatures often are sold as candy containers.

References: George Eikelberner and Serge Agadjanian, *The Compleat American Glass Candy Containers Handbook*, revised and published by Adele L. Bowden, 1986; Jennie Long, *An Album Of Candy Containers*, published by author, Volume I: 1978, Volume II: 1983.

Collectors' Club: Candy Container Collectors Of America, P.O. Box 1088, Washington, PA 15301. Dues: $18.00. *The Candy Gram* (bimonthly).

Museums: Cambridge Glass Museum, Cambridge, OH; L. E. Smith Glass, Mt. Pleasant, PA.

Additional Listings: See *Warman's Americana & Collectibles* for more examples.

Apothecary Jar, 5¼" h, clear, graduated hobnail bands, hollow stopper with 8-point star, "Old Fashioned–Apothecary Candy Jar" printed on front, T. H. Stough, Jeannette, PA	50.00

Automobile
Coupe, 5¼" l, 3" h, clear, pressed, long hood, snap on tin closure	75.00
Limousine, 4⅛ x 1¹⁵⁄₁₆ x 2½", clear, pressed, black painted tin wheels, open top, c1912–1914	70.00

Man, plaid jacket, clear glass, black plastic hat, 3⅜" h, $30.00.

Baseball, 3¼" h, 2" d, clear, raised stitching, tin and plastic mount **30.00**

Bath Tub, 4¾" l, 1⅞" h, clear, pressed, open top, traces of white paint, "Dolly's Bath Tub" marked on sides, Victory Glass Co, Jeannette, PA, USA . **2,200.00**

Boat

Battleship, 5½", cardboard closure, Victory Glass **30.00**

S. S. Colorado, 6½" **325.00**

Bureau, clear, pressed, inserted mirror, painted gold and black trim, tin slide-on closure **125.00**

Bus, Victory Lines Special, gray paint, cardboard closure **50.00**

Candlestick, clear, pressed, handled, candle socket, tin screw-on cap ... **150.00**

Cash Register, 3 x 1½ x 2⅝", clear, pressed, gold paint, tin slide closure, Dugan Glass Co, Indiana, PA **325.00**

Clock, 3¼ x 2½ x 1¾", opaque milk white, pressed, painted gilt scrolls, pink rose and green leaf spray, tin slide closure **150.00**

Dice, 3⅜" sq, 3¼" h, clear, pressed, traces of green paint, slightly concave, self closure lid, "Bristol–Diced–Mints" on lid, Brandel & Smith Co, Phila, USA **20.00**

Dog, 3½" h, begging, clear, pressed, round open base **150.00**

Elephant, 2¾", G.O.P. **110.00**

Felix, 3¼" h, 2⅛" d, pedestal base with block letters, painted black body, white eyes, smiling mouth, metal screw cap **2,200.00**

Fish, 5", papier mache **90.00**

Girl, 5¾" h, clear, pressed, two geese, oval base, c1950 .... **20.00**

Goblin, head, 3⅝" h, clear, pressed, orange face, green with orange splash raised leaves, white bulging eyes, white incised teeth, gold tin screw lid **350.00**

Gun, 3⅝" l, 2" h, clear, molded, cream enamel screw cap, waffle type pattern grip **12.00**

Hat, clear, opaque white and stained colors, screw-on tin brim **60.00**

Horn, musical, tin whistle, cardboard tube

Clarinet **30.00**

Piccolo **45.00**

Kettle, 2" h, 2¼" d, clear, pressed, three feet, cardboard closure, T.H. Stough Co **45.00**

Lantern, glass barn type frame, tin bottom, friction closure **50.00**

Man on motorcycle, side car, clear, pressed, painted, red tin snap closure, Victory Glass Co, Jeannette, PA **350.00**

Mailbox, 3¼" **50.00**

Nursing Bottle, clear, pressed, natural

wood nipple closure, T. H. Stough Co, c1940–45 .... **15.00**

Opera Glasses, 3⅝", swirl rib **45.00**

Owl, 4⅜" h, clear, pressed, stylized feathers, gold tin screw cap **80.00**

Phonograph, clear, pressed, gold tin horn, molded arm, black painted glass record disc, gold slide closure **225.00**

Pumpkin Man, 5½", papier mache ... **75.00**

Purse, 4⅛ x 2½ x 3⅝", clear, pressed, light emerald, alligator leather design, gilded metal parts, gold souvenir panel, aluminum closure **275.00**

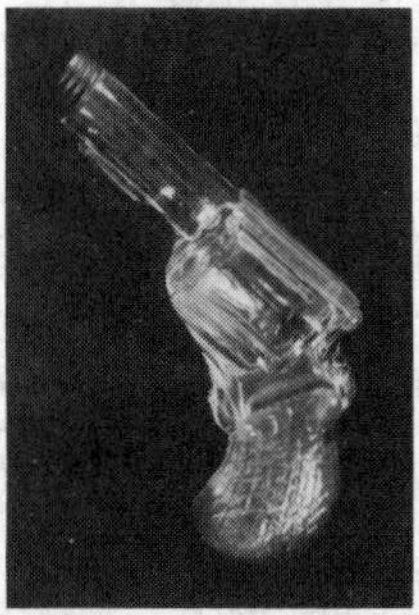

Revolver, emb grip handle, clear glass, screw cap, 8" l, $45.00.

Rabbit

3¾", crouching **50.00**

4¾", papier mache, glass eyes, top hat **45.00**

Radio, emb tune-in, tin closure, V.G. Co. **85.00**

Refrigerator, clear, pressed, painted white, gilded hinges, handles, and latches, four legs, USA–V.G. Co.–Jeannette, PA **1,000.00**

Santa, 12", crepe paper, cotton, white, gold snowflakes, painted plaster feet, face, German **225.00**

Soldier, 5⅛" h, molded, holding sword, painted, stepped plinth type base, tin slide closure **800.00**

Squirrel on stump, 5" h, clear, pressed, sitting upright holding nut, emb leaves, twig, and acorn design, tree bark ground, metal screw cap **1,200.00**

Statue of Liberty, 5¾" h, lead top, clear glass bottom **1,100.00**

Suitcase, 3⅝", emb straps, tin closure, wire handle **35.00**

Telephone, desk, French, Crosetti ... **20.00**

Traffic Sign, 4½", "Don't Park Here" .. **60.00**

Turkey, 3¾", papier mache, lead feet .. **15.00**

Wheelbarrow, red tin wheels, tin closure, V. G. Co. **50.00**

Windmill, orig blades and closure, Play
Toy Co. 60.00

CANES

History: Canes and walking sticks were important accessories in a gentleman's wardrobe in the
18th and 19th centuries. They often served both
a decorative and utilitarian function. Collectors frequently view carved canes in wood and ivory as
folk art and pay higher prices for them. Glass
canes and walking sticks were glass makers'
whimsies, ornamental rather than practical.

Reference: Catherine Dike, *Cane Curiosa*, published by author, 1983.

Ivory handle, ebony, 35″ l, $50.00.

CANES

Ebony, 36″, gold ferrule, crouching lion
handle, horn tip 250.00
Glass
Aqua, 59″, twisted handle, straight rib 90.00
Clear, 46⅜″, int. twist, red, white, and
blue 75.00
Ivory, 40″, whale, dove of peace carved
handle, wings outlined in incising,
perched atop knob and shaft, c1860 4,200.00
Scrimshaw
29¾″, rosewood shaft, whale ivory
knob set with 1857 dime 175.00
31″, lady's, whalebone, carved walrus, ivory dog's head handle 150.00
36″, Lady's, whalebone with whalebone ivory knob, baleen and shell
inlays, c1850 . . . . 375.00
Sword, 35″, horn handle in shape of
dog's head 150.00

Wood
Birch, 35½″, light shade, inlaid handle
of torsia floral and leaves 115.00
Walnut, 35½″, horse's head handle of
carved ram's horn, amber ferrule,
horn tip 250.00

WALKING STICKS

Bamboo, 36½″, carved, engraved silver
head 25.00
Bone, 35½″, tapered fluted to round
shaft, carved ivory fist 500.00
Curly Maple, 35¾″, tapered octagonal
shaft 55.00
Ebony, 25½″, ivory head, short stiletto
sword 125.00
Folk Art, 38″, carved snake, wood
burned and red and black ink detail . 80.00
Glass
Clear, 42½″, swirled 75.00
Nailsea type, 63″, clear with swirls of
blue, red, white, and pale green . . 200.00
Wood, 33″, Mahogany, ivory tip,
paneled, bulbous knob 250.00

HANDLES

Celluloid, carved, dog's head, glass
eyes 30.00
Gold, 14K, plain 85.00

CANTON CHINA

History: Canton china is a type of oriental porcelain made in the Canton region of China from
the late 18th century and early 19th century to the
present and produced largely for export. Canton
china is hand decorated in light to dark blue underglaze on white. Design motifs include houses,
mountains, trees, boats, and a bridge. A design
similar to "willow china" is the most common.

Borders on early Canton feature a rain and
cloud motif (a thick band of diagonal lines with a
scalloped bottom). Later pieces usually have a
straight line border. The markings "Made in China"
and "China" indicate wares which date after 1891.

Reproduction Alert: Several museum gift
shops and private manufacturers are issuing reproductions of Canton china.

Reference: Sandra Andacht, *Oriental Antiques
& Art: An Identification And Value Guide,* Wallace-
Homestead, 1987.

Basin, 15½″, pagoda scene, floral and
trellis border 750.00
Bottle, 10″, bulbous 400.00
Bowl
3″, Famille Rose dec, bird and butterfly reserves, dense foliate tendril
ground 100.00

Platter, 13 x 16¼", oval, wall and tree design, $450.00.

5¾", enamel, continuous scene of scholars conversing in garden, floral borders, plain int., 18th C 665.00
8⅛", round, shallow, 19th C 225.00
9¾" d, landscape, 19th C 375.00
10¼", shallow, scalloped rim, pagoda scene, 19th C 425.00
Butter Pat, 3" d, blue and white, 19th C 60.00
Candlestick, 7½", cylindrical, tapered, scenic, 19th C 500.00
Charger, 15", scenic, boat and bridge . 375.00
Coffeepot, 9½", dome top, scenic 850.00
Cream Pot, 4¾" h, dark blue, scenic, trees and flowers, intertwined strap handle, lid missing, late 18th C 150.00
Creamer, 5¾", scenic, 19th C 275.00
Cup and Saucer, coffee, loop handle, pagoda scene, c1900 .... 65.00
Dish
10" l, shell shape, river landscape, pagoda, early 19th C 150.00
11" l, cov, serving, diamond shape, scalloped edge, pinecone knob, early river landscape, pagoda, 19th C 250.00
Garden Seat, 18½", octagonal, blue and white, figural reserves 1,350.00
Ginger Jar, 10" h, 8" d, pagoda scene . 400.00
Hot Water Plate, 8¾" d, octagonal, blue and white, scenic, 19th C 250.00
Jardiniere, 4½ x 10", rect, turquoise with cobalt blue and red dec, c1890 .... 500.00
Mug, 4", scenic, twisted handle, 19th C 250.00
Pitcher, 9½", cov, barrel shape, pagoda scenes, twisted handle, early 19th C 600.00
Plaque, 12½", mountain, trees, underglaze blue signature 175.00
Plate
8½", Willow pattern 75.00
10", scallop and slash border, landscape with pagoda, early 19th C . 120.00

Platter, 17½" l, blue and white, river landscape scene 500.00
Punch Bowl, 15" d, polychrome enamel, birds, flowers, and court ladies 1,250.00
Rice Bowl, 4½", ext. with eight figures in various scenes, int. with band with birds and flowers 75.00
Sauce Boat, ovoid, double spout, twig handle, matching liner, landscape scenes, early 19th C 120.00
Spoon Dish, 3¾", oval, scenic, 19th C 150.00
Tea Bowl and Saucer, women in garden, Famille Rose style, c1829 .... 270.00
Tea Caddy, 4⅜" h, dark blue, scenic gold stripe on shoulder, orig cov, late 18th C 150.00
Tea Tile, hexagonal, tea house scene 200.00
Teapot, 5⅛", drum shape, scenic, sq handle, berry finial, late 18th C ... 300.00
Tray, 8½", oblong, pagoda, lake, 19th C 165.00
Tureen, cov
8½" l, undertray, twig handles, landscape scenes, early 19th C 400.00
13 x 7½", ovoid, blue and white, ox head handles, curled knobs, painted sampans in river landscapes, pagodas on banks, early 19th C, pr 1,300.00
Umbrella Stands, 23½", cylindrical, Famille Rose dec, flower ground, panels of figures, base with double grooved bands, pr 2,400.00
Vase
9½", white, blue floral and leaf dec . 200.00
23½", crackle, ivory, figures and floral dec 700.00
Vegetable Dish, cov
8", oblong, scenic, berry finial, late 18th C 225.00
9½", oblong, berry finial, late 18th C 375.00

CAPO-DI-MONTE

History: In 1743 King Charles of Naples established a soft paste porcelain factory near Naples which made figures and dinnerware. In 1760 many of the workmen and most of the molds were taken to Buen Retiro, near Madrid, Spain. A new factory opened in Naples in 1771 and added hard paste porcelains. In 1834 the Doccia factory in Florence purchased the molds and continued their production in Italy.

Capo-di-Monte was copied heavily by factories in Hungary, Germany, France, and Italy. Many of the pieces in today's market are of recent vintage. Do not be fooled by the crown over the "N" mark; it also was copied.

Reference: Susan and Al Bagdade, *Warman's*

English & Continental Pottery & Porcelain, 1st Edition, Warman Publishing Co., Inc., 1987.

**Plaque, Neptunes Maidens, 11 x 16¾",
black painted frame, 18th C, $285.00.**

Basket, 13" h, filled with roses, scroll
  feet, pr **225.00**
Bowl, cov, multicolored allegorical
  scene, goddesses in relief **125.00**
Box, hinged lid
  5 x 4 x 2½", children sitting in garden
    eating fruit, gold int. sgd, blue N
    and crown under glaze, c1830 . . .   **225.00**
  6", relief molded and enameled
    cherub scenes, ormolu fittings . . .   **300.00**
Candleholder, 3", raised flowers and
  nude figures **95.00**
Compote, cov, 9", oval, relief molded
  cherubs on sides, cherub finial and
  handles **225.00**
Cup and Saucer, florals, hp, sgd **40.00**
Demitasse Set, 17 pcs, pot, cov, crea-
  mer, sugar, 6 ftd cups and saucers,
  large round ftd tray, artist sgd **250.00**
Ewer, 14", semi-nude maiden in relief .   **110.00**
Ferner, 11", oval, relief molded and
  enameled allegorical figures, full relief
  female mask at each end **100.00**
Figurine
  Flower Girl, 9", c1880 . . . .   **325.00**
  Soldier on horseback, 9 x 8", dated
    1840 . . . .   **350.00**
Jewel Box, 9¾", oval, relief molded and
  brightly painted frieze of drunken
  cherub being carried away by baby
  satyrs, domed cov with Venus, entwined rose garland and feather bor-
  ders, 19th C **350.00**
Perfume, 3", cherub in garden, blue
  crown mark **65.00**
Plaque, 22½ x 16½", harvest scene,
  high relief, velvet covered molded
  frame **290.00**
Plate, semi-nudes bathing beside brook
  relief, floral festoon border **95.00**
Snuff Box, 3¼", hinged lid, cartouche

shape, molded basketweave and
  flowerhead ext., painted int. with court
  lady and page examining portrait of
  gentleman, gold mountings, c1740,
  minor restoration **1,650.00**
Stein, garden scene, adults and chil-
  dren, lion on cov, sgd **120.00**
Urn, 12¾", ovoid, circular foot, floral
  sprig, molded festoons of fruit and floral garlands, applied mermaid and
  putto, grotesque mask, 4 eagles circle
  base, crowned N in under glaze blue,
  c1850 . . . .   **180.00**
Vase, 12½", white and gold ruffled rim,
  figures with urns, high relief **130.00**

CARLSBAD CHINA

History: Because of changing European boundaries, German-speaking Carlsbad found itself located in the last hundred years first in the Austro-
Hungarian Empire, next in Germany, and currently
in Czechoslovakia. Carlsbad was one of the leading pottery manufacturing centers in Bohemia.

Wares from the numerous Carlsbad potteries
are lumped together under the term "Carlsbad
China." Most pieces on the market are post-1891,
although several potteries date to the early 19th
century.

Reference: Susan and Al Bagdade, *Warman's
English & Continental Pottery & Porcelain, 1st Edition,* Warman Publishing Co., Inc., 1987.

Biscuit Jar, 6½" h, 5" d, cream, pink
  flowers, yellow centers, green leaves
  and stems, marked "Victoria Carls-
  bad" **45.00**

**Vegetable Dish, cov, 6½ x 8½", blue
bachelor button and light brown floral
motif, white ground, 6½ x 8½", $25.00.**

Bowl
  8", fluted, white, yellow roses, green
    leaves 40.00
  10", portrait, green border, gold trac-
    ings, sgd "Boucher, Victoria Carls-
    bad, Austria" 60.00
Box, 6½", floral, gold scroll trim 80.00
Butter Pat, 2", round, white, blue floral
    dec 10.00
Cake Plate
  10", open handled, irregular edge, 2
    women, cherub, soft cream, dark
    green band, gold tracery, sgd
    "Kauffman, Victoria Carlsbad" . . . 75.00
  12", blue floral, gold trim and edge,
    marked "L. S. & S., Carlsbad" . . . 55.00
Chocolate Pot, 10", blue, scenic portrait,
    marked "Carlsbad Victoria" 110.00
Creamer and Sugar, Bluebird pattern,
    marked "Victoria Carlsbad" 55.00
Cup and Saucer, rosebuds, vines, and
    leaves, c1875, set of 6 . . . . 125.00
Ewer
  6", cream, pastel pink, gold, floral dec 75.00
  14", handles, light green, floral dec,
    gold trim, marked "Carlsbad, Vic-
    toria" 80.00
Hair Receiver, 4" d, white, cobalt blue
    flowers, gold trim, emb basketweave
    at top 30.00
Oyster Plates, set of 10, 8¾", white, lav-
    ender flowers, gold outlining 95.00

Pin Tray, 8½", irregular scalloped
    shape, white, bunches of small roses,
    green leaves, marked "Victoria,
    Carlsbad, Austria" 30.00
Pitcher, 8", ornate handle, soft cream,
    gold floral dec 60.00
Plate
  7", white, fancy reticulated border,
    c1860 . . . . 15.00
  9", cherries, hp, sgd 25.00
Portrait Plate, 8½", Melle La Vallerie,
    blue mark L.S.& S./Carlsbad/Austria 35.00
Powder Box, cov, 5" d, Bluebird pattern,
    Victoria, Carlsbad 45.00
Soup Tureen, cov, large white, deep
    pink and yellow roses, green leaves,
    gold trim buckle handles and finial,
    imp mark 65.00
Sugar Shaker, 5½", egg shape, floral
    dec 60.00
Vase
  7¾", squat, Art Nouveau, lustered
    blue, lavender, and green body,
    gold reticulated plant form neck . . 250.00
  9½"
  Handled, green, applied roses and
    birds, marked "Carlsbad, Victo-
    ria" 65.00
  Portrait, deep pink, gold trim, artist
    sgd "Fr. Stahl," marked "Victoria,
    Carlsbad, Austria" 85.00

CARNIVAL GLASS

History: Carnival glass, an American invention, is colored pressed glass with a fired on iridescent finish. It was first manufactured about 1905 and was immensely popular both in America and abroad. Over 1,000 different patterns have been identified. Production of old carnival glass patterns ended in 1930.

Most of the popular patterns of carnival glass were produced by five companies—Dugan, Fenton, Imperial, Millersburg, and Northwood. Northwood patterns frequently are found with the "N" trademark. Dugan used a diamond trademark on several patterns.

In carnival glass color is the most important factor in pricing. The color of a piece is determined by holding the piece to the light and looking through it.

The listing below combines the variety of colors into three basic color units: Marigold, dark (blue, green, or purple), and pastel (white, light blue or green, and vaseline).

References: Bill Edwards, *The Standard Encyclopedia of Carnival Glass, Sixth Edition,* Collector Books, 1987; Marion T. Hartung, *First Book of Carnival Glass to Tenth Book of Carnival Glass* [series of 10 books], published by author, 1968 to 1982; Thomas E. Sprain, *Carnival Glass Tumblers,* New and Reproduced, published by author, 1984.

Collectors' Clubs: American Carnival Glass Association, Box 3514, Plymouth, MA 02360. Dues: $10.00. *American Carnival Glass News,* quarterly; Heart of America Carnival Glass Association, 3048 Tamarak Drive, Manhatten, KS 66502. Dues: $20.00 *HOCGA,* monthly; International Carnival Glass Association, Inc., R.D. #1, Box 14, Mentone, IN 46539. Dues: $10.00. *The Carnival Pump,* quarterly.

	Marigold	Dark	Pastel
APPLE TREE (FENTON)			
Pitcher, water.	165.00	350.00	900.00
Tumbler	45.00	65.00	80.00

	Marigold	Dark	Pastel
BLACKBERRY BLOCK (FENTON)			
Pitcher, water.	250.00	900.00	1,200.00
Tumbler	50.00	65.00	150.00
BO PEEP (WESTMORLAND)			
ABC Plate	400.00	—	—
Mug	200.00	—	—
CHERRY (MILLERSBURG)			
Bowl			
4"	30.00	50.00	365.00
5", hobnail ext.	—	—	800.00
7"	65.00	80.00	—
10", ice cream	115.00	150.00	—
Butter, cov	125.00	165.00	—
Compote, large	800.00	850.00	—
Creamer	75.00	100.00	—
Pitcher, milk.	650.00	550.00	—
Plate, 6"	400.00	—	—
Spooner	75.00	100.00	—
Sugar, cov.	90.00	110.00	—
Tumbler	250.00	450.00	—
COSMOS AND CANE			
Bowl			
5"	50.00	—	75.00
10"	60.00	—	125.00
Butter, cov.	175.00	—	300.00
Compote	165.00	—	225.00
Creamer	125.00	—	230.00
Pitcher	650.00	—	1,300.00
Plate, chop	375.00	—	475.00
Rose Bowl.	100.00	—	175.00
Spittoon	3,250.00	—	500.00
Spooner	125.00	—	235.00
Sugar, cov.	130.00	—	250.00
Tumbler	75.00	—	150.00
CRAB CLAW (IMPERIAL)			
Bowl			
5"	25.00	35.00	—
10"	45.00	50.00	—
Pitcher	200.00	—	—
Tumbler	45.00	—	—
DAHLIA (DUGAN)			
Berry Set, master bowl, 5 sauces	300.00	275.00	775.00
Bowl, 10", ftd.	100.00	150.00	200.00
Butter, cov.	115.00	150.00	400.00
Creamer	75.00	100.00	200.00
Pitcher	300.00	750.00	475.00
Sauce	50.00	55.00	100.00
Spooner	75.00	100.00	200.00
Sugar, cov.	85.00	100.00	225.00
Tumbler	85.00	95.00	165.00

	Marigold	Dark	Pastel
DRAGON & LOTUS (FENTON)			
Bowl			
7", 3 ftd	45.00	50.00	150.00
8", flat, collared base	50.00	60.00	150.00
8", 3 ftd	48.00	65.00	165.00
10", ice cream	65.00	45.00	175.00
FASHION (IMPERIAL)			
Bowl, 9"	20.00	75.00	125.00
Compote	60.00	85.00	150.00
Creamer	40.00	90.00	50.00
Pitcher, water	150.00	750.00	350.00
Punch Bowl and base	75.00	250.00	—
Punch Cup	15.00	35.00	32.00
Rose Bowl	45.00	150.00	—
Sugar, cov	20.00	100.00	90.00
Tumbler	25.00	75.00	80.00
FLORAL & GRAPE (DUGAN)			
Hat	45.00	—	—
Pitcher, water	100.00	575.00	850.00
Tumbler	30.00	45.00	65.00
FRUIT SALAD (WESTMORELAND)			
Punch Bowl, base	650.00	800.00	2,800.00
Punch Cup	35.00	40.00	45.00
GRAPE AND CABLE (NORTHWOOD)			
Banana Boat	175.00	200.00	400.00
Bonbon	45.00	50.00	60.00
Bowl			
7½"	30.00	45.00	60.00
9", ruffled	45.00	65.00	—
10½", ice cream	110.00	225.00	275.00
Butter Dish, cov	150.00	180.00	200.00
Candlestick	75.00	115.00	185.00
Cologne Bottle	150.00	200.00	—
Compote, cov	250.00	400.00	425.00
Cookie Jar	155.00	150.00	1,250.00
Creamer	75.00	125.00	150.00
Dresser Tray	125.00	200.00	375.00
Hat	35.00	50.00	85.00
Hatpin Holder	150.00	185.00	350.00
Nappy	55.00	90.00	85.00
Orange Bowl, ftd	125.00	400.00	750.00
Perfume Bottle	385.00	285.00	—
Pitcher, water	200.00	90.00	2,500.00
Plate, 9"	75.00	100.00	110.00
Powder Jar	75.00	600.00	—
Punch Bowl	150.00	35.00	950.00
Punch Cup	20.00	175.00	65.00
Sauce	20.00	25.00	50.00
Sherbet	35.00	45.00	—
Spooner	65.00	90.00	125.00
Sugar, cov	75.00	110.00	175.00
Sweetmeat, cov	250.00	400.00	425.00

Left, Fashion, creamer, dark, $90.00; center, Floral and Grape, tumbler, dark, $45.00; right, Persian Garden, bowl, 11″, pastel, $225.00.

	Marigold	Dark	Pastel
Tumbler	35.00	35.00	125.00
Whiskey, shot glass	150.00	175.00	—

HOBSTAR (IMPERIAL)

Bowl

	Marigold	Dark	Pastel
5″	25.00	—	40.00
10″	35.00	—	45.00
12″	40.00	—	48.00
Bride's Basket	75.00	—	—
Butter, cov	65.00	—	80.00
Compote	50.00	—	55.00
Cookie Jar	65.00	—	—
Creamer	40.00	—	45.00
Pickle Castor	375.00	—	—
Spooner	40.00	—	80.00
Sugar, cov	45.00	—	65.00

HOBSTAR & ARCHES (IMPERIAL)

	Marigold	Dark	Pastel
Bowl, 9″	50.00	65.00	55.00
Fruit Bowl, base	60.00	70.00	—

INVERTED STRAWBERRY (CAMBRIDGE)

	Marigold	Dark	Pastel
Bowl, 8″	75.00	150.00	—
Candlesticks, pr, 7″	375.00	400.00	—
Celery Vase (Aqua)	—	—	275.00
Compote	100.00	250.00	—
Creamer	90.00	85.00	—
Pitcher, tankard	850.00	800.00	—
Powder Jar, cov	100.00	110.00	—
Spittoon	500.00	600.00	—
Spooner	90.00	75.00	—
Sugar, cov	100.00	100.00	—
Tumbler	250.00	215.00	—

NIPPON (NORTHWOOD)

	Marigold	Dark	Pastel
Bowl, 8½″	50.00	60.00	125.00
Plate, 9″	100.00	175.00	275.00

	Marigold	Dark	Pastel
OKLAHOMA (IMPERIAL)			
Lamp Shade....................	—	—	100.00
Pitcher........................	500.00	—	—
Tumble-up	175.00	—	—
OPEN ROSE (IMPERIAL)			
Bowl			
5½"............................	25.00	30.00	60.00
7".............................	40.00	65.00	70.00
9", ftd........................	45.00	50.00	90.00
12", ftd.......................	50.00	55.00	110.00
Plate, 9"......................	70.00	90.00	100.00
PANSY (IMPERIAL)			
Bowl, 8¾"......................	35.00	50.00	60.00
Creamer........................	25.00	40.00	50.00
Dresser Tray...................	60.00	90.00	110.00
Nappy	20.00	—	—
Pickle, oval...................	30.00	50.00	75.00
Plate, ruffled.................	75.00	95.00	100.00
Sugar..........................	35.00	50.00	65.00
PANTHER (FENTON)			
Bowl			
5", ftd........................	60.00	100.00	—
10", ftd.......................	100.00	175.00	—
10½"...........................	—	900.00	—
PERSIAN GARDEN (DUGAN)			
Bowl, berry			
5".............................	45.00	—	65.00
10"............................	150.00	—	185.00
Bowl, ice cream			
6½"............................	65.00	75.00	80.00
11"............................	150.00	200.00	225.00
Fruit Bowl, base	115.00	—	225.00

Left, Persian Medallion, bowl 8½", dark, $50.00; center, Wishbone, bowl, 8", ftd, marigold, $75.00; right, Diamond and Rib, vase, 7⅛" h, marigold, $28.00.

	Marigold	Dark	Pastel
Plate			
6″	55.00	95.00	110.00
12″, chop	—	2,550.00	2,000.00

PERSIAN MEDALLION (FENTON)

	Marigold	Dark	Pastel
Bonbon	20.00	40.00	85.00
Bowl			
8½″	45.00	50.00	90.00
10″	50.00	60.00	—
Compote	45.00	60.00	90.00
Hair Receiver	35.00	50.00	95.00
Nappy	—	30.00	—
Plate, 9″	95.00	125.00	275.00
Rose Bowl	50.00	45.00	135.00

PILLOW & SUNBURST (WESTMORELAND)

	Marigold	Dark	Pastel
Bowl			
7½″	55.00	60.00	—
9″	60.00	65.00	—

RAMBLER ROSE (DUGAN)

	Marigold	Dark	Pastel
Pitcher	125.00	200.00	—
Tumbler	40.00	50.00	—

RANGER (IMPERIAL)

	Marigold	Dark	Pastel
Butter, cov	100.00	—	—
Creamer	45.00	—	—
Pitcher, milk	175.00	—	—
Sugar, cov	150.00	—	—
Tumbler	275.00	—	—

SILVER QUEEN (FENTON)

	Marigold	Dark	Pastel
Pitcher	175.00	—	—
Tumbler	50.00	—	—

STAR & FILE (IMPERIAL)

	Marigold	Dark	Pastel
Bonbon	30.00	—	—
Bowl			
7″	30.00	—	35.00
9″	35.00	—	40.00
Compote	40.00	—	55.00
Creamer	30.00	—	—
Custard Cup	25.00	—	—
Decanter, stopper	125.00	—	—
Goblet	45.00	—	60.00
Pickle Dish	40.00	—	50.00
Pitcher	175.00	—	—
Plate, 6″	65.00	—	—
Rose Bowl	75.00	—	—
Spooner	45.00	—	—
Sugar	30.00	—	—
Tumbler	90.00	—	—
Vase, handle	50.00	—	45.00
Wine	45.00	—	—

	Marigold	Dark	Pastel
STORK & RUSHES (DUGAN)			
Bowl			
5″	25.00	30.00	—
10″	45.00	50.00	—
Butter, cov	150.00	175.00	—
Basket	50.00	—	—
Creamer	80.00	100.00	—
Hat	20.00	30.00	—
Mug	40.00	85.00	—
Pitcher	250.00	450.00	—
Punch Bowl	200.00	275.00	—
Punch Cup	25.00	35.00	—
Spooner	80.00	100.00	—
Sugar	90.00	110.00	—
Tumbler	35.00	45.00	—
STREAM OF HEARTS (FENTON)			
Bowl, 10″, ftd	60.00	75.00	—
Compote	50.00	—	75.00
TREE BARK (IMPERIAL)			
Bowl, 7½″	20.00	—	—
Candlesticks, pr, 4½″	35.00	—	—
Candy Jar	30.00	—	—
Pickle Jar	35.00	—	—
Pitcher, tankard	75.00	—	—
Sauce, 4″	10.00	—	—
Tumbler	25.00	—	—
WATERLILY & CATTAILS (FENTON)			
Bonbon	65.00	75.00	
Bowl			
5″	35.00	50.00	—
7″	40.00	—	—
9″	45.00	—	—
Butter, cov	150.00	—	—
Creamer	80.00	—	—
Pitcher	300.00	—	—
Spittoon	1,250.00	—	—
Spooner	80.00	—	—
Sugar	100.00	—	—
Toothpick	55.00	—	—
Tumbler	100.00	—	—
WISHBONE (NORTHWOOD)			
Bowl			
8″, ftd	75.00	80.00	750.00
10½″	85.00	90.00	800.00
Epergne	175.00	210.00	425.00
Plate			
9″, ftd	—	325.00	—
10″	—	425.00	—

MISCELLANEOUS

Age Herald (Fenton), plate, 10″, aqua .	**950.00**
Blackberry Spray (Fenton), hat, red . . .	**250.00**
Cleveland Memorial (Millersburg), ashtray, marigold, ...	**1,800.00**
Crucifix (Imperial), candlesticks, pr, marigold.	**400.00**
Elks (Fenton), bell, Atlantic City, 1911, blue	**850.00**

Near Cut (Cambridge), decanter, stopper, green.	**2,225.00**
Poinsettia (Imperial), milk pitcher, aqua	**850.00**
S-Repeat (Dugan), punch bowl, base, aqua	**1,500.00**
Wistera (Northwood), bank, pastel	**800.00**

CAROUSEL FIGURES

History: By the late 17th century carousels were found in most capital cities of Europe. In 1867 Gustav Dentzel carved America's first carousel. Other leading American manufacturers include Charles I. D. Looff, Allan Herschell, Charles Parker, and William F. Mangels.

Original paint is not critical, since figures were repainted annually. Park paint indicates layers of accumulated paint; stripped means paint removed to show carving; restored involves stripping and repainting in the original colors.

References: Charlotte Dinger, *Art Of The Carousel*, Carousel Art, Inc., 1983; Tobin Fraley, *The Carousel Animal*, Tobin Fraley Studios, 1983; Frederick Fried, *The Pictorial History Of The Carrousel*, Vestal Press, 1964; William Manns, Peggy Shank, and Marianne Stevens, *Painted Ponies: American Carousel Art*, Zon International Publishing, 1986.

Periodical: *Carrousel Art*, P.O. Box 992, Garden Grove, CA 92642.

Collectors' Clubs: The American Carousel Society, 470 South Pleasant Avenue, Ridgewood, NJ 07450; National Carousel Association, 7266 West Stanley Road, Flushing, MI 48433.

Cat, row two, fish in mouth, park paint, Dentzel	**16,000.00**
Chicken, old paint, needs some repair, Herschell/Spillman, c1910	**4,000.00**
Donkey, jumper, stripped, restored, Dentzel, c1908	**10,000.00**
Giraffe, ornate carving, Phila Toboggan Co	**24,000.00**
Horse	
Bucking, park paint, Herschell/Spillman	**7,000.00**
Galloping, black, horsehair tail, leather harness, wood, carved, orig paint, mounted on spiral brass pole, 59″ l, 57″ h, Phila Toboggan Co	**4,500.00**
Jumper	
Outer row, park paint, raised head, jeweled trappings, Carmel, c1911	**13,000.00**

Row two, head down, stripped to bare wood, Dentzel	**6,250.00**
Prancer	
Inner row, head down, park paint, Dentzel	**4,500.00**
Outer row, park paint, Looff	**6,750.00**
Standing	
Outer row, Muller style, figural on side, Dentzel, c1890–1903	**15,000.00**
Track machine style, American flag on side, restored, primer paint, Armitage/Herschell, c1900	**2,500.00**
Mirror, three 18th C figures and flowers dec, 37″ w, 42½″ h, Ralph Cahoon dec	**600.00**
Mule, galloping, left ear forward, right ear back, wood, carved, orig paint, mounted on spiral brass pole, 53″ l, 54½″ h, Phila Toboggan Co	**5,000.00**
Shield, clown face, park paint, needs repair, Herschell	**500.00**
Tiger, stander, outer row, side cherub figurals being persuaded by another figure, Phila Toboggan Co	**18,500.00**
Zebra, old paint, Herschell/Spillman, c1910	**3,000.00**

CASTLEFORD

History: Castleford is a soft paste porcelain made in Yorkshire, England, in the 1800s for the American trade. The ware was warm, white ground, scalloped rims (resembling castle tops), and is trimmed in deep blue. Occasionally pieces are decorated further with a coat of arms, eagles, or Liberty.

Creamer, 4¼″, white, parian, deep blue striping, emb classical scenes of cherubs	**100.00**
Milk Jug, 4¾″ h, oval, relief of American Eagle on one side, Liberty and cap on reverse, acanthus leaf border . . .	**175.00**
Sugar, cov, relief of classical figure leaning on urn, acanthus leaf panel, blue enamel border, scalloped edge, three enamel bands on cov	**245.00**
Teapot, 7″ h, emb dec, American eagle,	

Milk Jug, 4¾" h, oval shape, American eagle on one side, Liberty and Cap on other, acanthus leaf decor, $175.00.

dark brown edge stripe, professional
repairs **275.00**

CASTOR SETS

History: A castor set consists of matched condiment bottles within a frame or holder. The bottles are for condiments such as salt, pepper, oil, vinegar, and mustard. The most commonly found castor set consists of three to five glass bottles in a silver plated frame.

Although castor sets were known as early as the 1700s, most of the sets encountered today date from the 1870 to 1915 period when they enjoyed great popularity.

2-bottles, mirror luster cruets with amethyst cut stoppers, applied handles, sp frame marked "James J Tufts," 8¾" h **150.00**
3-bottles, clear, American Shield pattern, pewter stand, child size **100.00**

6-bottles, cut and etched bottles, silverplated holder, 14" h, $140.00.

3-bottles, clear, Daisy and Button bottles, toothpick holder in center, matching glass holder **100.00**
3-bottles, clear, Ribbed Palm pattern, pewter tops and stand **165.00**
3-bottles, cranberry glass, SP crescent moon shaped stand, orig spoon ... **175.00**
4-bottles, clear, bulbous, floral etching, cut honeycomb and circles dec, shaker, two cruets, mustard, SP frame, ladies' heads on base and handle, cherub holding up handle, sgd "Rogers Bros" **150.00**
4-bottles, clear, King's Crown pattern bottles, matching glass stand, metal center handle **100.00**
4-bottles, cranberry glass, IVT pattern bottles, enameled floral dec, SP stand, marked "Meriden" **100.00**
4-bottles, green cut to clear, sq bottles, sq SP stand **335.00**
5-bottles, amberina glass bottles, engraved leaf pattern on each bottle, two orig honeycomb cut amberina stoppers, three with SP tops, orig tripled silver plated holder marked "Aurora Manufacturing Co," presentation engraving "Mrs. W L Smith from Hank & May, Christmas 84" **2,400.00**
5-bottles, china, Willoware pattern, matching china stand **115.00**
5-bottles, clear, cut, all over lunar and geometric cutting, SS mounts and stand, Warwick form, shell shaped foot, English hallmarks, c1750, 8½" h **600.00**
5-bottles, clear, cut, Honeycomb pattern and etched floral bottles, SP stand, marked "Tufts" **185.00**
5-bottles, cut, three ball and claw feet, open cartouche circular handle, SS stand, English hallmarks, c1861 ... **375.00**
5-bottles, clear, etched glass bottles, revolving SP stand, 16" **125.00**
5-bottles, ruby cut to clear glass bottles, SP stand **185.00**
6-bottles, clear, fluted glass, SS stand, circular, vertical fluted border, central ring of cast anthemion and ivy leaf dec, sgd "Tiffany & Co, NY," c1865, 11" h **1,250.00**
6-bottles, clear, cut glass, three SS mounts, oblong boat shaped SS stand, wooden base, winged paw feet, central stem with open wreath handle, George III, London, 1815, 7"l **600.00**

CATALOGS

History: The first American mail order catalog was issued by Benjamin Franklin in 1744. This popular advertising tool helped to spread inventions, innovations, fashions, and other necessities of life to rural America. Catalogs were profusely illustrated and are studied today to date an object, identify its manufacturer, study its distribution, and determine its historical importance.

Reference: Don Fredgant, *American Trade Catalogs: Identification and Value Guide,* Collector Books, 1984; Lawrence B. Romaine, *A Guide To American Trade Catalogs 1744–1900,* R. R. Bowker, 1960.

Additional Listings: See *Warman's Americana & Collectibles* for more examples.

Abbey & Imbrie Fishing Catalog, 1911, orig envelope 70.00
American Flyer Trains, color, 52 pgs, 8½ x 11", 1929–30 . . . . 50.00
Arcade Cast Iron Toys, 12 pgs, 5 x 7¼", 1927 . . . . 65.00
Ario's Cowboy Catalog, 66 pgs, 1942 . 15.00
Autos Chalmers, Deluxe, color, 32 pgs, 7¼ x 9¼", 1914 . . . . 50.00

Starrett Precision Tools, L. S. Starrett Company, Athol, MA, Catalog #26, copyright 1938, 4⅞ x 7", $20.00.

Bannermann Military Goods, 1931 . . . 140.00
C. Fischer, 120 pgs, 9½ x 12½", 1902 95.00
Chandler and Barber Metal Working Tools, 1907 . . . . 15.00
Chicago Engineer Supply Co, hard cover, 528 pgs, 1915 . . . . 25.00
Colt, 1909 . . . . 30.00
Crane Co., Valves, Fittings, 743 pgs, 1923 . . . . 15.00
DuPont, American Game Birds, Lynn Bogue Hunt 30.00
FAO Schwartz Christmas, 151 pgs, 1965 . . . . 20.00
Fenestra Windows, c1920 . . . . 15.00
George Gibson, Belfast, Irish linens, 22 pgs, 1930 . . . . 20.00

Heywood Wakefield Furniture, c1927 . 55.00
International Trucks, Model SL, 8 pgs, 9 x 12" 20.00
John Plain Co., fine jewelry and watches, 97 pgs, 1925 . . . . 25.00
Kewannee Book of Laboratory, Vocational, Home Economics, Furniture, 391 pgs, 1937 . . . . 35.00
Laboratory Supply, hard cover, 1,000 pgs, 1938 . . . . 25.00
Lincraft Rustic Furniture, Fences, c1920 15.00
Lloyd's Cane Furniture, 1925 . . . . 75.00
Marlin, 1915 . . . . 65.00
Mitchell Motion Picture Cameras, 44 pgs, 9 x 11½", 1937 . . . . 35.00
Montgomery Ward, 1925 . . . . 30.00
Oliver (Hart-Parr) Tractor and 36 H.P. Engines, 144 pgs, 1929 . . . . 20.00
Olson Rugs, color, 1931 . . . . 10.00
Phillip Bernard Co. Farm Equipment #7 15.00
Remington, pocket type, 1935 . . . . . . 25.00
Restaurant Supplies, 1923 . . . . 25.00
Rubber Swim Caps, color, c1920 . . . . 18.00
Snap-On Tool, 1941 . . . . 15.00
Stanley Tool, 1948 . . . . 40.00
Stevens, 1907 . . . . 65.00
Stromber, Carburetors, 1939 . . . . 50.00
The Mershow Co. Firearm Accessories and Police Equipment, 1940 . . . . . . 20.00
The Winton Six, hard cover, 54 pgs, 5¼ x 8", 1913 . . . . 50.00
Thomas Register of American Manufacturers, 5,200 pgs, 1937 . . . . 145.00
Victor Red Seal Records, 1924 . . . . . 20.00
Waukesha 6 Cycle Engines and Trucks, 1st ed, 80 pgs, 1928 . . . . 20.00
White Trucks, 225 pgs, 9 x 12", 1917 . 125.00
Wurlitzer Musical Instruments, No #80 150.00

CELADON

History: The term celadon, meaning a pale grayish green color, derives from a theatrical character Celadon, who wore costumes of varying shades of grayish green, in Honore d'Urfe's 17th century pastoral romance, "L'Astree." French Jesuits living in China applied it to a specific type of Chinese porcelain.

Celadon divides into two types. Northern celadon, made during the Sung Dynasty up to the 1120s, has a gray to brownish body, relief decoration, and monochrome olive green glaze.

Southern (Lung-ch'uan) celadon, made during the Sung Dynasty and much later, is paint decorated with floral and other scenic designs and found in forms which would appeal to the European and American export market. Many of the Southern pieces date from 1825 to 1885. A blue square with Chinese or pseudo-Chinese characters appears on pieces after 1850. Later pieces also have a larger and sparser decorative patterning.

Reproduction Alert.

Bowl, 7″ d, footed, shallow, pale green ground, pink floral dec, peacock in center, c1810, $350.00.

Bottle, 10½″, tapered, flat shoulder, waisted neck, everted rim, shaded pale sea green crackle glaze, Koryu period 575.00
Bowl, 8½″, blue and white dragon in center 65.00
Brush Bowl, 2¼ x 2″, slightly bulbous, crackle 100.00
Cake Stand, 10½ x 4½″, Canton, 19th C 300.00
Censer, 3¾″, lobed body, short neck, outturned rim, ruyi scroll work, key fret neck band, two rope twisted handles, three burnt orange flared feet 275.00
Charger, 14¼ x 10¾″, octagonal, peacock, flowers 175.00
Dish, 6¼″, pale, incised single floral spray in center 200.00
Fish Bowl, 8⁷⁄₁₆″, flattened rim, carved petals, int. with two small fish swimming left and right, luminous glaze . . 350.00
Ginger Jar, 6″, bulbous, multicolored relief floral dec, dark green leaves, gold trim 125.00
Jar, 14″, ovoid, underglaze blue dec, large phoenix, flowering and fruiting plants, inset lid, knob finial 100.00
Jardiniere, 12″, circular, pale green glaze, molded as alternating shaped medallions with stags and owls, bird and floral border, pr 475.00
Lamp
12″, bottle shape vase base, crackle glaze, relief scrolling vines, gourd handles, Tao Quan 275.00

25″, baluster shape vase base, white relief dec, prunus, chrysanthemum, and lotus, Ch'ien Lung, pr 825.00
Libation Cup, 3¾″, steep tapering sides, foliate rim, dragon and clouds, blue-green glaze, 19th C 65.00
Plate, 6″, birds, butterflies and roses dec 85.00
Planter
5″, spherical, incised peony blossoms, foliate tendrils, glazed white int., pr 150.00
7½″, cylindrical body, molded, bundle of bamboo stalks tied together with blue and white ribbon, stylized calligraphy, glazed deep celadon . . . 200.00
Vase
5¾″, ovoid, pale blue, slender neck flanked by molded elephant head handles, body carved with band of petals, Yongle mark, 19th C 250.00
9″, double gourd shape, Chinese crackle, Louis XVI style, dore bronze mounts with ram's head motif 600.00
14″, ovoid, slender neck, handles formed by standing children, another child resting on shoulder, reaching down towards others, pale celadon glaze 200.00
23¼″, ovoid, stick neck, high relief pattern of fruiting trees, pale green glaze 450.00

CELLULOID ITEMS

History: In 1869 brothers J. W. Hyatt and I. S. Hyatt developed celluloid, the world's first synthetic plastic, as an ivory substitute because elephant herds were being slaughtered for their ivory tusks.

Known as "Ivorine" or "French Ivory," celluloid was made of nitrocellulose and camphor. Early pieces have a creamy color with stripes and grooves to imitate the texture of ivory or bone. The 1897 Sears catalog featured celluloid items. Celluloid was used widely until synthetics replaced it in the early 1950s. Celluloid often is used as a generic term for all early plastics.

Animal
Cat, 12″, orig paint 45.00
Lion, 2½″ h 22.00
Peacock on pedestal, 5½″ h 25.00
Baby's Set, brush, comb, jar, cov, and rattle, orig box 35.00
Bookmark, figural, teddy bear, 1½″ x 3″, adv "Buckwalter Stove Co., Royersford, PA" 15.00
Candlestick, 5″, creamy ivory 10.00

Cane Handle, carved dog's head, glass eyes	30.00
Collar Box, white chrysanthemums and green leaves on cov, velvet lined	45.00
Comb, lady's, creamy ivory	18.00
Doll, 10", French, elaborate costume, marked "270"	50.00
Door Knob, creamy ivory	35.00
Dresser Set, 10 pcs, amber, black and gold overlay, beveled edge mirror	90.00

Perfume Bottle Holder, orig bottle and stopper, $20.00.

Figure
Felix, black, hands behind back, c1930	50.00
Soldier carrying gun	18.00
Frame, 4 x 3", easel back, creamy ivory, reticulated border	25.00
Glove box, hp floral dec on cov, pink lining, dated 1869	35.00
Jewelry Box, creamy ivory, red roses on cov	30.00
Nail File, folding, emb floral dec	12.00
Napkin Ring, creamy ivory	10.00
Necktie Box, 2½ x 3 x 4", creamy ivory, gold and floral dec on cov	42.00
Pencil Box, Red Goose Shoes adv	75.00
Rattle, blue and white, c1930	12.00
Roly Poly, chicken	10.00
Scissors, manicure, 4", creamy ivory handle	12.00
Stick Pin, color portrait of woman, yellow and green ribbons, "Welcome to Eugene, Oregon"	25.00
Toy, wind-up	
Betty Boop, 7", orig box	150.00
Clown, 7½", marked "Occupied Japan"	60.00
Penguin, 3", marked "Made In Japan"	30.00
Rabbit, marked "Irwin"	19.00
Wall Plaque with hanging cord, 9", masted schooner, colored, orig label, "P.N.Co. Art Plaque," c1920	20.00

CHALKWARE

History: William Hutchinson, an Englishman, invented chalkware in 1848. It was a substance used by sculptors to imitate marble. It also was used to harden plaster of paris, creating a confusion between the two products.

Chalkware often copied many of the popular Staffordshire items of the 1820 to 1870 period. It was cheap, gayly decorated, and sold by vendors. The Pennsylvania German "folk art" pieces are from this period.

Carnivals, circuses, fairs, and amusement parks used chalkware pieces as prizes during the late 19th and 20th centuries. They often were poorly made and gaudy. Don't confuse them with the earlier pieces. Prices for these chalkware items range from five to forty dollars.

References: Thomas G. Morris, *Carnival Chalk Prize*, Prize Publishers, 1985; Ted Soufe, *Midway Mania: A Collectors Guide To Carnival Plaster Figurines, Prizes, and Equipment 1900–1950*, L-W, Inc., 1985.

Additional Listings: See Carnival Chalkware in *Warman's Americana & Collectibles*.

Figure, ewe and lamb, 4" x 8⅝", 7¼" h, $350.00.

Bank
Boston Bulldog, reclining	65.00
Cat, 10", smoking pipe, 19th C	100.00
Santa asleep in arm chair, large	60.00
Bookends, pr, boy and girl, seated, reading	65.00
Bust, Hiawatha, 20", 1890s	115.00
Church, 9½ x 18", molded, white, pierced with decorative holes, colored glass insert window, PA, 19th C	1,050.00
Figure	
Cat, 16", seated, black paint, white eyes, pink ears, and mouth, oval base	400.00

Easter Rabbit, 6½", coming out of
egg, red with yellow, black, and orange **45.00**
Ewe and Lamb, 6", green-gold with
red, black, and yellow features .. **350.00**
Frog, 3½ x 4 x 5", dark green, yellow
splotches **130.00**
Lamb, 5¼", standing, white with red
and yellow face, green base **240.00**
Rooster, 4¾", gold with black and red
paint **240.00**
Snake, curled, c1910 **15.00**
Squirrel, 7", holding nut, orig white,
yellow, red, black, and brown paint **285.00**
Stag, reclining, 5⅜", orig olive amber
with black stripes, red and black
features, oblong base **300.00**
Garniture, fruit basket with pair of love
birds, 7¾", yellow, red, and black .. **400.00**
Match Holder, 6", figural, man with long
nose and beard, adv "Northwestern
National Insurance Co.," c1890 .... **95.00**
Nodder, cat, 6", orig red and black dec **325.00**
Penny Toss, clown, toss penny in
mouth, buttons light up **150.00**

CHARACTER AND
PERSONALITY ITEMS

History: The use of the "star" product endorser
began in the late 19th and early 20th centuries.
By the 1930s the system was entrenched.

Two groups evolved. The first was the characters found in cartoons or portrayed on radio, in the
movies, or on television by actors. Some characters, e.g., Tony The Tiger, were created by the
advertising industry solely for advertising use.

The second group consists of "real" people,
e.g., actors, sports personalities, heroes, or political figures. The 1960s and 70s witnessed the pinnacle of star endorsed products.

References: David Longest, *Character Toys
and Collectibles,* Collector Books, 1984; David
Longest, *Character Toys And Collectibles, Second Series,* Collector Books, 1987.

Additional Listings: See *Warman's Americana
& Collectibles* for expanded listings in Cartoon
Characters, Cowboy Collectibles, Movie Person-
alities and Memorabilia, Shirley Temple, and
Space Adventurers.

CHARACTERS

Jack Armstrong
Ring, dragon's eye, crocodile design,
green stone **300.00**
Telescope **10.00**
Betty Boop
Handkerchief, 8½" sq, white cotton,
black, white, and light green illus

on each corner, detail closeup on
one corner, 1930s **30.00**
Pin, gold colored metal with attached
link chain to Scotty dog, Fleisher
Studios copyright, 1930s, attached
to orig sample retail card **150.00**
Tea Set, 3½" h teapot, 2" d cup, and
4" d saucer, china, beige, color picture on side, Betty playing tennis
and Betty and Koko singing from
sheet music, 1930s **100.00**

Buster Brown, clicker, $10.00.

Buster Brown
Card Game, set of 40, instruction
sheet, different full color scene of
circus on each card with brief de-
scriptive caption line, published by
Selchow & Righter, early 1900s .. **75.00**
Clicker, 1¾" litho metal, "Brown Shoe
Co." inscription, c1930 .... **10.00**
Drawing Book, 8 pgs, thin film tracing
sheets between each illus page, six
neatly traced sheets, issued by
Emerson Piano Co **45.00**
Pitcher, 4" h, white, china, full color
illus, early 1900s **75.00**
Campbell Kids
Child's knife, fork, and spoon, SP .. **50.00**
Reverse Painting on Glass, 7½ x
9½", kids loading baskets in a veg-
etable patch, "C" on shirt, 11 x
12½" gray wood frame, c1970 ... **60.00**
Salt and Pepper Shakers, 4½" h,
plastic, kids in red and white outfits
holding kitchen utensils, "Campbell
Soup Co." authorization on each,
c1950, pr **20.00**
Thermometer, tin, figural, adv **35.00**
Cracker Jack
Christmas Sign, 9½ x 12", diecut,
cardboard, punched hole at top for
suspension from store ceiling,
c1920 .... **150.00**
Whistle, 2¼" l, inscribed on bottom . **15.00**

Dennis The Menace
  Mug, 4″ h, plastic, picturing Dennis,
    1950s 15.00
  Spoon, 6″ l, SP, emb figure at top of
    handle, name vertically on handle,
    1950s 25.00
Dick Tracy
  Book, *Dick Tracy and The Stolen
    Bonds*, Whitman Big Little Book,
    #1105, 1934 .... 30.00
  Game, Dick Tracy Electronic Target
    Game, battery operated, silent ray
    gun, shoots a beam of light at a
    revolving cardboard drum, elec-
    tronic photocell bullseye, automatic
    scorekeeper, 11″ black plastic pis-
    tol, instruction sheet, American Doll
    & Toy Corp, 1961 copyright, un-
    used 100.00
  Pistol, 4½″ l, glossy black enamel,
    green, red, white, and yellow decal,
    clicker sound, boxed, c1936 .... 125.00
Elsie The Cow
  Bank, 5 x 6 x 7″, white, metal, three
    dimensional, row of yellow daisies
    around neck, c1950 .... 60.00
  Button, 2¼″, emb brass, raised head,
    c1940 .... 25.00
  Ring, plastic, green, color inset pic-
    ture, Borden Company copyright,
    c1950 .... 50.00
Felix The Cat
  Place Card Holder, celluloid 1¾″ Felix
    figure, ½″ h arched back black cat,
    base, glossy black holder, Japa-
    nese, 1930s 80.00
  Teacup, white china, Felix strolling by
    a fluffy white female kitty, dog nips
    at his heels, inscription "Now Felix
    Keep On Walking," Pat Sullivan
    copyright, c1920–30 .... 30.00
  Valentine, diecut, jointed cardboard,
    full color, valentine pictured on his
    tail, "Purr Around If You Want To
    Be My Valentine" inscription, Pat
    Sullivan copyright, c1920 .... 15.00
  Yarn Holder, 6½ x 6½″, diecut wood,
    black images, inscription "Felix
    Keeps On Knitting," "Pathe Pre-
    sents" symbol in center, c1920–30 35.00
Hopalong Cassidy
  Badge, silver metal, star shape,
    raised portrait at center, c1950 ... 20.00
  Ring, adjustable, silvered brass, por-
    trait on top with initials and the Bar
    20 symbol, c1950 .... 30.00
  Shirt, button, red trim slit pocket and
    collar, six different images, red in-
    scription, "Little Champ Of Holly-
    wood" label, size 12, early 1950s 150.00
  Tablet, 8 x 10″, color photo cov, fac-

simile signature, unused, early
    1950s 20.00
  Watch, ¾″, silvered metal case, re-
    verse "Good Luck From Hoppy,"
    black and white dial face, illus on
    gray background, red hands and
    numerals, silvered metal expansion
    band 25.00
Howdy Doody
  Cookbook, 36 pgs, Welch Grape
    Juice Co, full color cov, Howdy and
    friends, 1952 copyright 50.00
  Marionette, 16″ h, wood and stuffed
    cloth, composition hands, movable
    lower mouth, plastic jiggle eyes,
    fully strung, hand control board,
    printed instructions 200.00
  Record Spindle Spinner, 4″ h plastic
    figure, movable mouth, figure
    mounted on 3″ d plastic base, cen-
    ter hole for placement over record
    player spindle, inscription "Hi Ya
    Kids/Watch Me Go Round On Your
    Record" on base, Kagran copy-
    right, 1951–56 .... 50.00
  Wall Light Shade, parchment-like
    heavy paper, plastic edge lacing,
    soft blue, red, and yellow illus, off
    white background, Kagran copy-
    right c1951–56, orig wall mount .. 75.00
Sonja Henie, pinback button, 1¼″, pink
    and brown, "Skate for Pleasure,"
    1937 .... 15.00
Little Orphan Annie
  Ashtray, 4 x 3½ x 3″, china, luster,
    orange dress, blonde hair, black
    shoes, yellow pearl tone Sandy,
    copyright, c1930 .... 65.00
  Gravy Boat, lusterware, white, or-
    ange, yellow, and black 175.00
  Nodder, 3½″ h, painted bisque,
    stamped on back "Orphan Annie,"
    1930s 150.00
  Pastry Set, miniature baking utensils,
    two aluminum mixing spoons,
    wood pestle shape rolling pin, flour
    cup, and 6 x 8″ rolling board,
    boxed, Transogram "Gold Medal"
    Toy, 1930s 75.00
  Sheet Music, "Little Orphan Annies
    Song," 4 pgs, Ovaltine premium,
    1931 copyright 15.00
Lone Ranger
  Handkerchief and Tie Set, 8″ sq
    handkerchief, 48″ l necktie, dark
    blue cotton, Lone Ranger depiction
    on silver, Lone Ranger copyright,
    orig card, c1940 .... 100.00
  Holster, 9″ stiff cardboard, colored to
    resemble tan leather, steer design,
    brand initials "GA", inscription in
    rope script, khaki web army style

belt, includes a 7" l aluminum single shot cap pistol with white plastic grips, boxed, 1942 copyright **75.00**

Pencil Case, 1 x 4 x 8¼", textured stiff cardboard, gold cov design is lightly emb, dark blue background, American Lead Pencil Co, Lone Ranger copyright, 1930s **40.00**

Rifle, 24" l, plastic, simulated metal and wood parts, gold script inscription, emb Indian head and bear in woods on sides of stock, clicking sound, sighting scope, c1960 ... **25.00**

Mr. McGoo, puzzle, 11½ x 14½", full color frame tray, Whitman, 1965 copyright **25.00**

Mr. Peanut

Bank, 8½" h, molded tan plastic, coin slot in top of hat, inscription on hat brim, c1950 .... **40.00**

Pencil, mechanical, 5¼", red and white plastic, cylinder at top contains miniature tan figure, inscription on side, c1940–50 .... **15.00**

Annie Oakley

Coloring Book, 11 x 14", Whitman, soft color, 1955, unused **18.00**

Suspenders, 4½ x 12", card, multicolored, elastic, Annie Oakley on one, Tagg on other, c1960 ..... **15.00**

Popeye

Book, *Popeye Funny Films,* three full color filmstrips and viewer, Saalfield, 1934 .... **55.00**

Lamp, figural, 16" h, dark maroon with gold accent striped shade, gray metal base with 8" h figure, arms around brown lamp pole **150.00**

Sand Pail and Shovel, 4" h litho metal pail, full color continuous scene around sides, 6" red metal shovel **75.00**

Watch, 1¼", silver colored metal case, dial pictures Popeye holding spinach can, gray leather bands, c1960 .... **50.00**

Red Ryder

Book, *Red Ryder and Circus Luck,* Whitman Better Little Book #1466, 1949 .... **25.00**

Glove Case, black enameled metal and cardboard, illus on lid, leather carrying handle, elastic straps for holding supplies, silvered metal spring clip fasteners, 1951 salesman program, Wells-Lamont Glove Company **150.00**

Reddy Kilowatt

Pin, 1" h, brass, red accent enameling, cardboard 4 page folder, 1948 copyright **25.00**

Soap, three 1½ x 2½ x ½" bars, white

imprinted in red and blue, unused, orig marked box, c1950 .... **20.00**

Skippy, ice cream sign, 24 x 36", diecut cardboard, "Fro-joy" ice cream container, color, 1930s **200.00**

Straight Shooter, (Tom Mix)

Coloring Book, 8½ x 11", health and hygiene, Ralston premium, unused **75.00**

Ring, brass, checkerboard logo on top with steer head and gun design on sides, 1935 .... **50.00**

Yellow Kid

Cigar Box, 3½ x 4¼ x 9", wood, illus and name inscription in bright gold, brass hinges, label inside "Smoke Yellow Kid Cigars/Manuf'd By B. R. Fleming, Curwesville, Pa." tax label strips on back, c1896 .... **200.00**

Postcard, 3¾ x 6", full color illus for month of October, issued as reminder from Ohio hardware company, 1911 post mark **40.00**

Soap, 4" h, tan, molded figure, tiny insert eyes, printed on front of night shirt "Dis Sope Is Grate See!", imprinted on back is "D.S. Brown & Co," orig yellow box, 1896 copyright **100.00**

PERSONALITIES

Jimmie Allen

Member Card, 2¾ x 4¾", yellow and blue, sponsored by Richfield Oil, c1934 .... **30.00**

Pocket Knife, two bladed, simulated bone grips, set in silver wing bearing name on one side, inscribed "Official Jimmie Allen Knife" on largest blade, Robeson Cutlery .. **80.00**

Amos and Andy

Record, 78 rpm, "The Presidential Election," Victor, Brunswick Record dust cov **30.00**

Sheet Music, 6 pgs, "Three Little Words," from movie "Check and Double Check," 1930 copyright ... **25.00**

Gene Autry

Cap Pistol, 6½", silver, cast iron, bright red plastic grips, "Gene Autry" script on each side, uses roll caps, 1940s **75.00**

Wallet, 4 x 4½", brown, leather, zippered, "Gene Autry" in script on front and back, 1940s **25.00**

Edgar Bergen

Lobby Card, 10½ x 14", yellow, blue tone caricature sketches, from 1942 movie "Here We Go Again" **15.00**

Pinback Button, ¾", celluloid, black and white portrait of Charlie, c1930 **65.00**

Notepad, 5½ x 9″, black, white, and
green, lined paper, 1938 . . . .   **20.00**
Eddie Cantor, tin, brass, diecut, depicts
Cantor in large red top hat, 1930s . .   **25.00**
Charlie Chaplin
  Coloring Book, 11 x 15″, Saalfield, 52
    pgs, 1941 . . . .   **30.00**
  Pennant, felt, 1¼ x 2″, dark plum with
    a pink tinted black and white photo,
    tan lettering and design, c1915–20   **40.00**

**Bing Crosby, record duster, yellow
ground, 3½″ d, $7.50.**

Bing Crosby, script, 9 x 11″, hardcover,
dated April 12, 1939, Paramount
movie "The Star Maker," title page
autographed **75.00**
Joe DiMaggio, glass, 4″ h, clear glass
from DiMaggio's San Fransico restaurant, bright blue illus and text on
one side, 1950s **25.00**
Dionne Quintuplets
  Ink Blotter, 4 x 9″, color photo of two-
    year old quints, birth date and
    weights at birth, unused, 1936 . . .   **25.00**
  Fan, 8 x 9″, diecut cardboard, wood
    handle, Elvgren illus celebrating
    their fifth birthday **8.00**
  Thermometer, 3⅞″ x 6″, cardboard,
    multicolored, Cupp's Dairy **25.00**
Gabby Hayes, target set, 18″ sq card-
board target, 6½″ l plastic dart pistol,
two rubber cup plastic darts, orig box,
Haecker Industries, c1950 . . . .   **100.00**
Charles Lindbergh
  Belt, 1½″ w, 35″ l, leather, gray, emb,
    silvered brass buckle **60.00**
  Book, *Trophies and Decorations*, 8 x
    11″, soft cov, 64 pgs, black and
    white photos, Missouri Historical
    Society, 1933 copyright **40.00**
  Bunting, 1¼″, "Lucky Lindy," red
    white and blue, gold horseshoe,
    black and white photo **40.00**
Willie Mays, photo, 2″ black and white,
Willie in New York Giants cap, red,

white, and blue ribbon, green plastic
bat, and white ball attached below,
c1961 . . . .   **50.00**
Roy Rogers
  Nodder, 6½″ h, composition figure,
    head mounted on neck spring, sig-
    nature decal on base, 1962 copy-
    right and "Japan" stamped on bot-
    tom **40.00**
  Watch, 1 x 1¼″ dial face illus in
    brown, red, black, and white, sig-
    nature in black, red numerals, sil-
    vered metal with floral pattern
    edges on case, stainless steel ex-
    pansion band, 1940s **100.00**
Babe Ruth
  Figure, 8″ h, realistically detailed,
    white uniform with dark blue
    sleeves, insignia, outer stockings
    and cap, removable bat in orange
    tone, Hartland **150.00**
  Score Counter, playing diamond and
    disc wheels are turned to record
    runs, strikes, balls, on one side,
    other side 1¾″ black and white
    photo, 1920–30 . . . .   **60.00**
Shirley Temple
  Bank, 4 x 2 x 6″, metal, gold paint,
    saluting, c1930 . . . .   **75.00**
  Paper Doll, #1782 Saalfield book, 14″
    punchout doll, 8 pgs, uncut cloth-
    ing, 1939 . . . .   **150.00**
  Pin, 1⅛″, diecut, brass, white, blue,
    and red enameling **125.00**
  Postcard, 3½ x 5½″, full color, titled
    "Home of Shirley Temple," c1940,
    unused **5.00**

CHELSEA

History: Chelsea is a fine English porcelain designed to compete with Meissen. The factory began operating in the Chelsea area of London, England, in the 1740s. Chelsea products are divided
into four periods: (1) Early period, 1740s, with incised triangle and raised anchor mark; (2) The
1750s, with red raised anchor mark; (3) The
1760s, the gold anchor period; and (4) The Derby
period from 1770–1783. In 1924 a large number
of the molds and models of figurines were found
at the Spode-Copeland Works, and many items
were brought back into circulation.

Reference: Susan and Al Bagdade, *Warman's
English & Continental Pottery & Porcelain, 1st Edition,* Warman Publishing Co., Inc., 1987.

Basket, 11″ l, pierced basketweave rim
with purple and green scrolls, hp fruit

Figure, 6½" h, seated couple, multicolored, $500.00.

inside, double shell handles, gold anchor mark, c1760 . . . . **700.00**
Beaker, 2⅝", octagonal, iron red, oriental floral sprays, rose, green, blue, and yellow, red anchor mark, c1750 **1,400.00**
Bonbonniere, 2⅛", boy wearing green hat, puce jacket, turquoise breeches, fur satchel over shoulder, inscription on strap, kneeling on green mound with colorful molded flowers and green leaves, shearing the mane of brown-gray boar, int. painted with three iron-red, yellow, and puce flower sprigs, shaded green leaf border, hinged gold mount at rim, white cov painted with flower sprigs, red anchor mark **2,000.00**
Cup and Saucer, white, multicolored exotic birds, gold anchor, c1765 . . . . . **750.00**
Dish
6³⁄₁₆", pr, silver form molded edge, sprays of flowers and leaves, red anchor mark, c1755 . . . . **350.00**
6½", 10 sided, Flying Dog, Kakiemon style, red anchor mark, c1755 . . . **1,250.00**
Figure
Bird, 4¼" h, 3¾" w, perched on double stump, green leaves, acorn, gold anchor mark, c1760 . . . . **125.00**
Gentleman, 2", miniature, long pink jacket, white and gold waistcoat, white pants with gold and red spots, black shoes, green tricorn hat, gold anchor, c1760 . . . . **275.00**
Plate, 8", botanical center, large flowering branch, insects, flower spray, brown rim, red anchor mark, c1775, Hans Sloane **1,350.00**
Scent Bottle, 2½", figural, cauliflower head, pink ribbed green leaves, thick

olive green stem, white florette stopper, gold mounts, red anchor, c1756 **3,400.00**
Seal, cupid, 1¼", cupid disguised as a barrister, set with a sardonyx intaglio, inscribed "Je Plait Pour Ma Belle," c1760 . . . . **450.00**
Soup Plate, 9⅜", octagonal, center painted with iron-red and gold phoenix in flight, yellow breasted blue and iron-red pheasant, turquoise rock, iron-red, blue, turquoise, and gold flowering tree, ridged rim, iron-red floral border, red anchor, c1753 . . . . . **2,000.00**
Teabowl and Saucer, scalloped gilt edge, painted with foliate sprays, c1754 . . . . **1,135.00**
Toy Figure, lady with a muff, 1⅛" h, c1765 . . . . **225.00**

"CHELSEA" GRANDMOTHER'S WARE

History: "Chelsea" Grandmother's ware identifies a group of tableware with raised reliefs of either grapes, sprigs of flowers, or thistles on a white ground. Some examples are lustered.

The ware was made in the first half of the 19th century in England's Staffordshire district by a large number of manufacturers. The "Chelsea" label is a misnomer, but commonly accepted in the antiques field.

Egg Cup, grape pattern, marked "Royal Adderley/Blue Chelsea/Ridway Potters Ltd," $25.00.

Bowl, 3½ x 6", Grape	**28.00**
Butter Pat, Grape	**5.00**
Cake Plate, 10", Grape	**40.00**
Creamer, Sprig	**50.00**
Coffeepot, cov, Grape	**145.00**

Cup and Saucer, Sprig	**25.00**
Egg Cup, Grape	**25.00**
Pitcher, milk, Sprig	**50.00**
Plate	
8", Grape	**20.00**
9", Sprig	**30.00**
Ramekin, underplate, Sprigs, blue . . .	**12.00**
Sauce Dish, Sprig	**5.00**
Sugar, cov, 7½", Sprig	**110.00**
Tea Set, cov teapot, creamer, cov sugar, Grape, 5 pcs	**200.00**
Tureen, cov, applied handles, Grape, c1840	**75.00**
Vegetable Bowl, oval, Grape	**25.00**

Carroll, Lewis, *Alice's Adventure in Wonderland,* Willy Pogany, illus, Dutton, 1929, 192 pgs, 1st ed	**40.00**
Chapin, Anna, *True Story of Humpty Dumpty,* Ethel Betts, illus, Dodd, 1905, 206 pgs, 1st ed	**95.00**
Chubb, Ida, M., *Little Pickaninnies,* Whitman, 1929, unp, wraps	**60.00**
Collodi, C., *Pinocchio,* Maria Kirk, illus, Lippincott, 1916, 234 pgs, 1st ed . .	**40.00**
Disney, Walt, *Dance of the Hours from Fantasia,*, Harper, 1940, unp, 1st ed	**40.00**
Dr. Seuss, *Bartholomew and the Oobleck,* Random House, 1949, unp, 1st ed, sgd	**75.00**

CHILDREN'S BOOKS

History: Because there is a bit of the child in all of us, collectors always have been attracted to children's books. In the 19th century books were popular gifts for children, with most of the children's classics written and published during this time. These books were treasured and often kept throughout a lifetime.

Developments in printing made it possible to include more attractive black and white illustrations and color plates. The work of these artists and illustrators has added value beyond the text itself.

References: Barbara Bader, *American Picture Books From Noah's Ark To The Beast Within*, Macmillan, 1976; Virginia Haviland, *Children's Literature, A Guide To Reference Sources*, Library Of Congress, 1966, first supplement, 1972, second supplement, 1977, third supplement, 1982.

Libraries: Free Library Of Philadelphia, PA; Library Of Congress, Washington, D.C.; Pierpont Morgan Library, New York, NY; Toronto Public Library, Toronto, Ontario, Canada.

Additional Listings: See *Warman's Americana & Collectibles* for more examples and an extensive listing of collectors' clubs.

Note: dj = dust jacket; wraps = paper covers; pgs = pages; unp = unpaged; n.d. = no date; teg = top edges gilt

Advisor: Margaret L. Tyrrell.

Alcott, Louisa M., *A Garland for Girls,* Roberts Bros, 1888, 258 pgs, 1st ed	**80.00**
Barrie, J. M., *The Picture Story Book of Peter Pan,* Roy Best, illus, Whitman, 1931, unp, 1st ed, dj	**60.00**
Barrows, Marjorie, *Muggins Mouse,* Deith Ward, illus, Reilly & Lee, 1932, 60 pgs	**50.00**
Buck, Pearl S., *Johnny Jack and His Beginnings,* Werth, illus, John Day, 1954, 47 pgs, 1st ed, dj	**30.00**
Burnett, Frances, Hodgson, *Sara Crewe or What Happened at Miss Minchin's,* Reginald Birch, illus Scribner's, 1888, 83 pgs, 1st ed	**75.00**

***Aladdin And The Wonderful Lamp,* Charles E. Graham & Co., NY, #0499, Good Story Series, $7.50.**

Field, Rachel, *Hitty: Her First Hundred Years,* Dorothy Lathrop, illus, Macmillan, 1929, 207 pgs, 1st ed, sgd by Lathrop	**70.00**
Garer, Elvira, *Ezekiel,* Holt, 1937, unp, 1st ed, dj	**35.00**
Greenaway, Kate, *Almanac for 1889,* Routledge, n.d. unp. teg	**100.00**
Habberton, John, *Helen's Babies,* Loring, 1876, 206 pgs, 1st ed	**75.00**
Harris, Joel Chandler, *The Tar Baby and other Rhymes of Uncle Remus,* A. B. Frost & E. W. Kemple, illus, D. Appleton, 1904 190 pgs, 1st ed . . .	**70.00**
Hoffmann, Heinrich, *Slovenly Peter,* Fritz Dredel, illus, German to English by Mark Twain, limited edition club, 1935, 34 pgs, numbered ed in box .	**135.00**
Kipling, Rudyard, *Just So Stories,* Macmillan, 1902, 249 pgs, 1st ed	**125.00**
Lenski, Lois, *The Easter Rabbit's Parade,* Oxford, 1936, 32 pgs, 1st ed .	**45.00**

Mariana, *Miss Flora McFlimsey and Little Laughing Water,* Lothrop, Lee, & Shepard, c1954, dj 20.00

May, Robert L., *Rudolph the Red Nosed Reindeer,* Denver Gillen, illus, Montgomery Ward, 1939, unp, 1st ed 75.00

McCready, T.L., *Biggity Bantam,* Tasha Tudor, illus, Ariel/Farrar, Straus, Young, 1954, unp, 1st ed, dj 55.00

Moore, Clement, *The Night Before Christmas,* Elizabeth MacKinstry, illus, Dutton, 1928, unp, 1st ed 65.00

Newberry, Clare, *Babette,* Harper, 1937, 30 pgs, 1st ed, dj 43.00

Nura, *Nura's Garden of Betty & Booth,* Morrow, 1935, 41 pgs, 1st ed 50.00

Owen, Dora, *The Book of Fairy Poetry,* Warwide Goble, illus, Longmans, 1920, 129 pgs, 1st ed 95.00

Phillpotts, Eden, *The Girl and the Fawn,* Frank Branquyn, illus, London, 1916, 78 pgs, dj 125.00

Pyle, Howard, *The Garden Behind the Moon,* Scribner's, 1895, 192 pgs, 1st ed 115.00

Sarg, Tony, *Where is Tommy?* Greenberg, 1932, unp, 1st ed 55.00

Southwold, Stephen, *The Book of Animal Tales,* Honor/C. Appleton, illus, Crowell, n.d. c1930, 286 pgs 50.00

Stevenson, Robert Louis, *A Child's Garden of Verses,* Toni Frissell, photographs, U. S. Camera Book, 1944, 95 pgs, 1st ed, dj 50.00

Tarcov, Edith, *Rumpelstiltskin,* Edward Gorey, illus, Four Winds, 1974, 46 pgs, 1st ed, dj 45.00

Tate, Sally Jane, *Sally's ABC Sewed in a Sampler in 1795,* Dugald Stewart Walker, illus, Harcourt, Brace, 1929, unp, 1st ed 65.00

Thompson, Kay, *Eloise,* Hilary Knight, illus, Simon and Schuster, 1955, 65 pgs, 1st ed, dj 50.00

Upton, Bertha, *The Golliwogg's Desert Island,* Florence K. Upton, illus, Longmans and Green, 1906, unp, 1st ed 100.00

West, Paul, *The Pearl and the Pumpkin,,* W. W. Denslow, illus, Donohue, 1904, 239 pgs 175.00

Wiggin, Kate Douglas, *Rebecca of Sunnybrook Farm,* Houghton-Mifflin, 1903, 327 pgs, 1st ed 90.00

CHILDREN'S FEEDING DISHES

History: Unlike toy dishes meant for play, children's feeding dishes are the items actually used in the feeding of a child. Their colorful designs of animals, nursery rhymes, and children's activities are meant to appeal to the child and make meal times fun. Many plates have a unit to hold hot water, thus keeping the food warm.

Although glass and porcelain examples from the late 19th and early 20th centuries are most popular, collectors are beginning to seek some of the plastic examples from the 1920s to 40s, especially those with Disney designs on them.

References: Doris Anderson Lechler, *Children's Glass Dishes, China and Furniture,* Collector Books, 1983; Doris Anderson Lechler, *Children's Glass Dishes, China, Furniture, Series II,* Collector Books, 1986; Lorraine May Punchard, *Child's Play,* published by author, 1982; Margaret & Kenn Whitmyer, *Children's Dishes,* Collector Books, 1984.

Donald Duck, pink, base holds hot water, 6¾ x 8", $40.00.

Baby Dish, warming type
  Campbell Kids, marked "Buffalo Pottery" 85.00
  Circus, 8" red decals, white ground, divided, marked "Hazel Atlas" ... 8.00
  Elsie, The Borden Cow, 9⅛", divided, hot water reservoir, decals of Elsie, Elmer and Beulah 30.00
Bowl
  5", SS, marked "Gorham" 100.00
  6", Mickey Mouse, red beetleware .. 25.00
  6¾", Beach Baby, marked P. K. Unity, Germany" 42.00
  9", Sing A Song of Sixpence 40.00
Breakfast Set, plate, bowl, and creamer, white, blue design of children playing 75.00
Creamer
  Bunnykins, marked "Royal Doulton" 40.00
  Buster Brown 50.00
Cup and Saucer
  Century of Progress, nursery rhyme dec, marked "Shenango," 1933 .. 48.00
  Old Mother Hubbard, marked "Royal Doulton" 50.00
  Sand Baby, marked "Royal Bayreuth" 75.00

Strawberry, figural, red cup, green
leaf saucer, porcelain **25.00**
Mug
China
2¾", portraits of boy and girl,
marked "Germany" **35.00**
3½", Little Bo Peep, transfer print
of scene and rhyme, marked
"England" **70.00**
Glass, Dog and Bird, beaded handle **35.00**
Silver
Silverplated, Tom the Piper's Son,
reeded handle, monogram, nurs-
ery rhyme engraved on side . . . **65.00**
Sterling, christening, hallmarked,
"R. Redgrave, R. A.," London,
c1865 . . . . **500.00**
Plate
4½", children playing, Kate Greena-
way illus **72.00**
6½", Sunbonnet Babies, babies sew-
ing, marked "Royal Bayreuth" . . . **165.00**
7½", hexagon, emb floral border,
green transfer of child and cat,
marked "Davenport" **85.00**
8½", Fancy Cat, divided **200.00**

CHILDREN'S NURSERY ITEMS

History: The nursery is a place where children
live in a miniature world. Things come in two sizes.
Child scale designates items actually used for the
care, housing, and feeding of the child. Toy or doll
scale denotes items used by the child in play and
for creating a fantasy environment which copies
that of an adult or his own.

Cheap labor and building costs during the Victorian era enabled the nursery to reach a high level
of popularity. Most collectors focus on items from
the 1880 to 1930 period.

References: Doris Anderson Lechler, *Children's Glass Dishes, China, and Furniture*, Collector Books, 1983; Doris Anderson Lechler, *Children's Glass Dishes, China, Furniture, Series II*,
Collector Books, 1986; Lorraine May Punchard,
Child's Play, published by author, 1982.

Additional Listings: Children's Books, Children's Feeding Dishes, Children's Toy Dishes,
Dolls, Games, Miniatures, and Toys.

Alphabet Scroll, 7 x 7", multicolored litho
scenes for each letter, mounted in
wooden box **35.00**
Baby Rattle, SS, attached bell and coral
teething ring **350.00**
Bride's Basket, miniature, 5¾ x 5½",
ruffled cranberry bowl, SP holder
marked "Reliance Quadruplate Sil-
ver" **200.00**
Carriage, 52" l, open, push type,
wooden wheels, wooden and iron

frame, bentwood handle, adjustable
fringed top, cast iron frame, orig worn
brown and black paint and striping . **275.00**
Chamber Set, wash bowl, pitcher,
chamber pot, cov soap, toothbrush
and comb holder, slop bucket, hp, flo-
ral dec, 8 pcs **175.00**

Doll high chair, 19¼" h to top of seat,
36" h overall, 10¼" w, spool turnings,
$225.00.

Furniture
Bed, baby, turned posts and legs, four
rails with lattice slats, solid board
bottom, old green paint over red,
29 x 48 x 30½" **75.00**
Chair
Arrowback, armchair, old red paint
beneath green paint, 18½" h . . **175.00**
Chippendale, mahogany, armchair,
salmon colored linen upholstered
slip seat, 24" **800.00**
Hepplewhite, Martha Washington
style, armchair, upholstered back
and seat, 30" **650.00**
Chest of Drawers, Georgian style,
burl walnut, band inlay, 15½ x 8¼
x 16⅜" **700.00**
Cradle
Walnut, 37" l, dovetailed, cut out
rockers, shaped sides, hand
holds **225.00**
Wicker, ornate basket suspended
between two supports, swings,
ornate shelf, high crown mount-
ing at head end to hold netting . **2,000.00**
Cupboard, pine, orig dark brown finish, stenciled gold and silver dec,
decoupage, top with double doors,
glass pane in each, drawers and
doors in base, late wire nail construction, 17 x 12½ x 30¾" **200.00**

Highchair, oak, pressed back, cane
  seat, Victorian, converts to stroller   **400.00**
Rocker, ladder back, turned arms,
  three slats, turned finials, old dark
  finish, 26" h **150.00**
Mug
  China
    Copper Luster, putty colored band,
      "Eliza," 2½" **50.00-**
    Staffordshire, purple transfer, poly-
      chrome enamel dec, children
      playing, 2½" h **75.00**
  Glass, complete raised alphabet,
    raised scene of little girl looking at
    Christmas tree and boy at desk . .   **125.00**
Quilt
  Child size, 40 x 58", nursery rhyme
    characters, embroidered names . .   **100.00**
  Crib
    Appliqued, 30 x 35", red and green
      calico patches, snowflakes, stars
      and floral motifs, bunches of
      grapes and cherries with em-
      broidered stems, center of large
      appliqued wreath with inscription
      "Presented to J Miller Merritt/
      February 8, 1860," sawtooth bor-
      der **1,450.00**
    Crazy pattern, patchwork and ap-
      plique, velvet, satin, and cotton
      patches, elaborate embroidery .   **450.00**
Rocking Horse, 34" l, 40" h, 58" l
  wooden rockers, wooden head and
  legs, red burlap cov, straw filled, red
  paint, red felt and leather saddle, hair
  mane, marked "Cebasco, Made in
  Germany" **975.00**
Sled, Victorian, stenciled "No. 52, Paris
  Mfg Co., So. Paris, Maine," maple
  and steamed oak, center board red
  with stenciled flowers and transfer
  portrait of Indian, 27½" **1,000.00**
Tea Set, ironstone, red transfer of
  Punch and Judy, three 5¾" d plates,
  5⅜" h teapot, 3¾" d waste bowl,
  sugar, four cups and saucers, minor
  stains **165.00**
Teether, 5¼", SS, Father Christmas,
  bag of toys emb on back, MOP
  teether, English **275.00**
Tricycle, wooden frame and wheels,
  orig red paint, black striping **500.00**
Tumble-Up, 4¼" h, blue glass, tiny white
  and orange flowers **155.00**
Wagon, wooden, "Blue Blazer" **200.00**

CHILDREN'S TOY DISHES

History: Dishes made for children often served
a dual purpose—play things and a means of learn-
ing social graces. Dish sets came in two sizes.

The first was for actual use by the child when
entertaining her friends. The second, a smaller
size than the first, was for use with dolls.

Children's dish sets often were made as a side
line to a major manufacturing line either as a com-
plement to the family service or as a way to use
up the last of the day's batch of materials. The
artwork of famous illustrators, such as Palmer Cox,
Kate Greenaway, and Rose O'Neill, can be found
on porcelain sets.

References: Doris Anderson Lechler, *Chil-
dren's Glass Dishes, China and Furniture,* Collec-
tor Books, 1983; Doris Anderson Lechler, *Chil-
dren's Glass Dishes, China, Furniture, Series II*
Collector Books, 1986; Lorraine May Punchard,
Child's Play, published by author, 1982; Margaret
& Kenn Whitmyer, *Children's Dishes,* Collector
Books, 1984.

Akro Agate
  Creamer and Sugar, Stacked Disc,
    green **15.00**
  Cup and Saucer, Concentric Ring,
    yellow **5.50**
  Plate, 3¼"
    Azure Trans-Optic **8.50**
    Oxblood and Lemonade, octagonal   **12.00**
  Set, Chiquita, green, service for six,
    MIB **75.00**
  Teapot, Plain Jane, fired on blue . . .   **5.00**
  Tumbler, Interior Panel, transparent
    blue **8.00**
  Water Set, Stacked Disc, 7 pcs, MIB   **45.00**
Bohemian Glass, decanter and glasses,
  ruby flashed, Vintage dec, 5 pcs . . .   **125.00**
China
  Creamer, Sunbonnet Babies, babies
    sewing, bulbous **140.00**
  Cup, Willow Ware, blue, 1 x 1¾",
    marked "Occupied Japan" **6.00**
  Dinner Set
    22 pcs, blue, gold band, marked
      "Copeland" **200.00**
    23 pcs, Moss Rose **85.00**
    25 pcs, Blue Willow **145.00**
  Mug, Sunbonnet Babies, babies sew-
    ing, marked "Royal Bayreuth" . . .   **150.00**
  Tea Set
    Noritake, gold band, four cups and
      saucers, creamer, cov sugar, tea-
      pot, 13 pcs **150.00**
    Ridgway, marked "Ridgway, Stoke
      on Trent," c1882, 24 pcs **265.00**
  Tureen, attached tray, marked "Por-
    celaine Empire" **8.50**
Depression Glass
  Creamer, Moderntone **2.50**
  Cup, Moderntone **2.50**
Milk Glass
  Butter, cov, Wild Rose **70.00**
  Creamer, Wild Rose **65.00**
  Cup, Nursery Rhyme **20.00**

Depression Glass, Doric and Pansy, open sugar, 3¼" d, 2½" h, $35.00.

Punch Cup, Wild Rose, hp blue dec	**15.00**
Sugar, Wild Rose	**65.00**
Pattern Glass	
Berry Set, Flute, Higbee, 5 pc	**45.00**
Butter, cov	
Beaded Swirl	**45.00**
Menagerie, turtle	**275.00**
Cake Stand	
Fine Cup and Fan	**35.00**
Palm Leaf Fan	**30.00**
Rexford	**25.00**
Candlesticks, Moonlight Blue, pr	**20.00**
Condiment Set, Hickman, open salt, pepper shaker, cruet, and leaf shaped tray	**60.00**
Creamer	
Hobnail, thumbprint base, blue	**25.00**
Michigan	**35.00**
Nursery Rhymes	**50.00**
Tappan, Virginia Blue	**12.50**
Tulip and Honeycomb	**20.00**
Cup, Tulip and Honeycomb	**7.00**
Mug	
Begging Dog	**40.00**
Drum	**15.00**
Grapevine	**20.00**
Pitcher, Galloway	**24.00**
Punch Cup, Lion	**35.00**
Rose Bowl, Star, 2½"	**25.00**
Spooner	
Amazon	**20.00**
Hawaiian Lei	**20.00**
Mardi Gras, Duncan & Miller 42	**35.00**
Nursery Rhymes	**40.00**
Tulip and Honeycomb	**26.00**
Sugar	
Beaded Swirl	**35.00**
Drum	**60.00**
Menagerie, bear, blue	**225.00**
Tulip and Honeycomb	**25.00**
Tray, Doyle 500, blue	**35.00**
Vegetable Dish, cov, Tulip and Honeycomb, oval, 3¾"	**65.00**

Tin

Dinner Set, four dinner plates, dessert plates, cups, and saucers, strawberry dec, white ground, marked "J. Chein," 16 pcs	**30.00**
Tea Set, teapot, creamer, sugar, tray, four plates, cups and saucers, fairies, flowers, bright yellow moon, blue ground, marked "Ohio Art," 7 pcs	**35.00**

CHRISTMAS ITEMS

History: The celebration of Christmas dates back to Roman times. Several customs associated with modern Christmas celebrations date back to the early pagan rituals.

Father Christmas, believed to have evolved in Europe in the 7th Century, was a combination of the pagan god Thor, who judged both the good and punished the bad, and St. Nicholas, the generous Bishop of Myra. Kris Kringle originated in Germany and was brought to America by the Germans and Swiss who settled in Pennsylvania in the late 18th Century.

In 1822 Clement C. Moore wrote "A Visit From St. Nicholas" and developed the character of Santa Claus into what we know today. Thomas Nast did a series of drawings for *Harper's Weekly* from 1863 until 1886 and further solidified the character and appearance of Santa Claus.

Reference: Robert Brenner, *Christmas Past*, Schiffer Publishing, 1986; Francine Kirsch, *Christmas Collectibles*, Wallace-Homestead, 1985; Maggie Rogers and Peter R. Hallinan, *The Santa Claus Picture Book: An Appraisal Guide*, Dutton 1984; Maggie Rogers and Judith Hawkins, *The Glass Christmas Ornament, Old and New*, Timber Press, 1979; Nancy Schiffer, *Christmas Ornaments: A Festive Study*, Schiffer Publishing, 1984; Clara Johnson Scroggins, *Hallmark Keepsake Ornaments: A Collector's Guide, Second Edition*, Wallace-Homestead, 1985; Phillip V. Snyder, *The Christmas Tree Book*, Penguin Books, 1985.

Additional Listings: See *Warman's Americana & Collectibles* for more examples.

Advisor: Lissa L. Bryan-Smith.

Candy Container	
Santa, cardboard, red glass bead coat, pointed hat, separates at waist, nodder head, marked "Germany"	**38.00**
Snowman, papier mache, black broom and hat, 7" h	**18.00**
Christmas Fence	
Cast Iron, silver and gold gilding, 18 sections and gate	**150.00**
Metal and wire, green and red, 8 sections, orig box	**100.00**

Candy Container, Santa sitting in chenille basket, composition face and beard, red cloth suit, $125.00.

Wooden
Folding, red and green	40.00
Lighted, red, 6 sections and gate .	65.00

Church, musical, wind-up, plays "Silent Night," mica covered, wood 28.00

Deer
3" h, composition, wood legs, metal
   antlers, German 35.00
5" h, metal, brown, marked "Germany" 35.00
6" h
   Celluloid, red glass eyes, Japanese 15.00
   Glass, silvered, blown glass base, German 40.00

Display Box, Fairy Soap, litho picture of Christmas fairy 110.00
Doll House, two story, wooden, homemade, furnished 365.00

Light Bulb
Japanese Lantern	10.00
Kewpie	35.00
Moon Mullins	40.00
Orphan Annie	35.00
Red Riding Hood	40.00
Santa, with tree	20.00
Star	8.00
Teddy Bear	30.00

Lights, bubble, one string, orig box . . . 20.00

Ornament
Chromolithograph
   Angels, group of three, cellophane and tinsel 22.00
   Child, sleeping, surrounded by toys, tinsel 28.00
   Father Christmas, blue coat, head and shoulders, tinsel 40.00
   Father Christmas, red coat, standing, toys attached to belt 35.00
   Young Couple, arms linked, tinsel 20.00

Cotton Batting
Baby, composition face, skis with
   poles, 3½" h, Japan 70.00
Dog, standing on back legs 20.00
Girl, composition face, skis with
   poles, 5½" h, Japan 110.00
Peach, rose blush 12.00
Santa, composition face, faded red
   coat, black legs 100.00

Ornament, doghouse, 2¾" h, red mercury glass, white dog, gold dec, $60.00.

Dresden
Crescent Moon, gold, 3" h 20.00
Fish, silver, two sided 150.00
Owl, on branch, three dimensional,
   realistic coloring 300.00
Star, gold, 2" h 15.00
Washtub, gold, chromolithograph
   children, 4" h 100.00

Glass
Accordion	18.00
Airplane, spun glass wings	175.00
Angel, head	75.00
Bell, red, white, and blue	25.00
Cat in Shoe	95.00
Champagne Bottle	28.00
Crown, gold	16.00
Deer, silvered, glass hook	40.00
Devil, head and neck	130.00
Graf Zeppelin	250.00
Los Angeles Zeppelin	275.00
Punch and Judy, stage	155.00

Santa
   Clip on 40.00
   Gold coat 40.00
   Red suit, green tree 35.00
Stork, clip 42.00
Sugar Bowl 22.00
Teapot 23.00
Urn 25.00

Kugels
 2" h, oval, ribbed **22.00**
 4" d, round, blue **60.00**
Wax, early, angel
 Large **75.00**
 Small **40.00**
Pinback Button, "Christmas at Butlers" **25.00**
Putz Animal
 Camel
 3" h, celluloid **8.00**
 5" h, composition, Japanese **12.00**
 7" h, composition body, hide covering, wood legs **50.00**
 Cow
 3" h, celluoid **8.00**
 4" h, composition, Japanese **7.00**
 6" h, composition body, cloth cov,
 wood legs **40.00**
 Ram, 4" h, celluloid **10.00**
 Sheep
 1½" h, composition, Japanese ... **5.00**
 2" h, composition on stuffed body,
 cotton covering, wood legs **25.00**
 8" h, composition on stuffed body,
 cotton covering, wood legs **85.00**
Santa
 1¼" h, bisque, green pack, Japanese **18.00**
 2" h, 4" l, celluloid, driving station wagon, one piece, Japanese **30.00**
 2½" h, chenille, red, composition
 face, Japanese **22.00**
 4½" h
 Father Christmas, white mica coat,
 holding feather tree **400.00**
 Santa, celluloid, metal skis, wood
 poles, Japanese **42.00**
Sheet Music, "Silver Bells," E. T. Paul **25.00**
Toy
 Pop-Up Santa, litho cov cardboard,
 chimney, top opens, cloth cov
 Santa, composition face, c1910,
 German **110.00**
 Wilson Walkie, Santa, red, orig box . **40.00**
Tree
 2" h, brush, green, snow, Japanese . **2.00**
 6" h, brush, red, snow, glass balls,
 Japanese **8.00**
 12" h, brush, green, snow, Japanese **9.00**
 24" h, feather, white, sq red base,
 West Germany **85.00**
 36" h, feather, green, round white
 base, candle clips, Germany **300.00**

CIGAR CUTTERS

History: Counter and pocket cigar cutters were used at the end of the 19th and the beginning of the 20th centuries. They were a popular form of advertising. Pocket-type cigar cutters often were a fine piece of jewelry that was attached to a watch chain.

CIGAR CUTTERS

Advertising
 Arrow-Cupples Co, cast iron, counter
 type **40.00**
 Betsy Ross 5¢ Cigars, cast iron, pic-
 ture **375.00**
 Blackstone Cigars, cast iron, keywind
 spring cutter **350.00**
 Gentlemen's Preference, El Santo,
 glass base **115.00**
 Great Ohio 5'ct Cigar, cast iron, pig
 shape **425.00**
 Strauss & Hamburger, Chicago, oak,
 match holder, lighter, cigar cutter,
 and container, 7½" x 11" **100.00**
Figural
 Boy sitting on ornate rock, metal, 7" **400.00**
 Bulldog, cast iron, desk type **40.00**
 Horse's head, bridle, flowing mane,
 SP, 5¾" **100.00**
 Mariner's wheel, brass and wood,
 6½" **125.00**

Pocket, scissors type, silverplated, $150.00.

POCKET

Advertising
 5th Ave Cigar, keywind **25.00**
 Lord Closter Cigars, pipe tamper,
 metal **20.00**
 New Bachelor, brass **20.00**
 Swift & Co, watch chain **45.00**
Knife Type
 Brass
 Bottle **40.00**
 Girl on potty **90.00**
 Revolver, black onyx handle, 3½" **150.00**
 Trumpet **50.00**
 Ivory, boar tusk, SS mount **200.00**
 Silverplated, arrowhead, enamel dec **125.00**

Silver, Sterling, Art Nouveau, nude on
waves, repousse, ring at end **50.00**

CIGAR STORE FIGURES

History: Cigar store figures were familiar sights
in front of cigar stores and tobacco shops from
about 1840. Figural themes included Sir Walter
Raleigh, sailors, Punch figures, ladies, and Indians, the most popular.

Most figures were carved in wood, although figures also were made in metal and papier mache
for a short time. Most carvings were life size or
slightly smaller and brightly painted. A coating of
tar acted as a preservative against the weather.
Of the few surviving figures, only a small number
have their original bases. Most replacements are
due to years of wear and usage by dogs.

Use of figures declined when local ordinances
were passed requiring shop keepers to move the
figures inside at night. This soon became too much
trouble, and other forms of advertising developed.

Reference: A.W. Pendergast and W. Porter
Ware, *Cigar Store Figures*, The Lightner Publishing Corp., 1953.

**Warrior, polychrome, 108″ h,
$11,000.00.**

Dromedary, 34″ l, 48″ h, pine, carved full
figure, double hump, brown paint,
brass studded leather saddle, black
velvet saddle blanket, molded wood,
painted brown base, tail missing, late
19th C **1,200.00**
Indian
Brave, 67″, carved and painted wood,

full length, feathered headdress
and costume, holding block of tobacco in one hand, bunch of cigars
in other, green painted composition
base, c1880 . . . . **7,000.00**
Maiden, 70″, full length, carved in full
round, headdress of red, blue, and
yellow flowers, red cloak with green
fringe, blue dress, dagger in right
hand, bunch of cigars in other, S.A.
Robb, NY, late 19th C **6,250.00**
Princess
56½″, yellow dress, blue feathers,
red band, 16″ h green base . . . **3,200.00**
68″, carved in full round, feathered
headdress, fringed shawl, dress,
and pants, holding cigars in
raised right hand, brown painted
sq tapered base, "CIGARS," late
19th C **4,500.00**
Lincoln, Abraham, 63″, carved pine,
holding rolled document in left hand,
standing on box, platform base, 20th
C **2,250.00**
Punch
48¼″ h, carved and painted pine,
dressed as gent, gray and yellow
with red tassel stocking cap, holding bunch of cigars in right hand,
mounted on black painted wood
and composition base, 1870–80 . **80,000.00**
82″ h, carved and painted, holding
bunch of cigars in left hand, polychrome and gilt highlights, rect
base on casters **25,000.00**
Scotsman, 67½″, carved in full round,
kilt, epaulettes, plaid hat and socks,
bow-tied shoes, holding pipe in left
hand, rect base, American, late 19th
C **1,750.00**

CINNABAR

History: Cinnabar is a ware made of numerous
layers of a heavy mercuric sulfide and often referred to as vermillion, the red hue in which it is
most commonly found. It was carved into boxes,
buttons, snuff bottles, and vases. The best examples were made in China.

Reference: Sandra Andacht, *Oriental Antiques
& Art: An Identification And Value Guide,* Wallace-
Homestead, 1987.

**Bracelet, 7½″ l, plus clasp, marked
"China," $100.00.**

Bookends, 5″ h, 3½″ w, carved flowers and leaves, pr **175.00**
Bowl, 8″ d, 2¾″ h, garden scene, blue enamel int. **225.00**
Box
  5¾ x 4 x 2½″, intricate carving, reserved on lid of birds and florals, Greek key border, sgd in Oriental script on brass base **65.00**
  11 x 10″, camel shape, carved figural scene **225.00**
Cigarette Case, 6⅛″ l, rect hinged top, cinnabar lacquer and ivory, carved courtly scene, key fret band border . **350.00**
Ginger Jar, 9″, ivory, marked "China," pr **650.00**
Plate, 7″, carved village scene **185.00**
Snuff Bottle, 3½″, carved scene, figures in garden, carved matching stopper, c1825 . . . . **250.00**
Table Screen, 22¼″, figural scene with monk rowing boat, reverse with 3 dragons above rock, flower scroll border, stand **300.00**
Tray, 8 x 12″, carved garden scene . . **225.00**
Vase
  10″, landscape, eight people in garden **250.00**
  12¼″, six lobed pear shape, carved with flowering plants, flower scrolls at neck, 19th C **200.00**
Walking Stick, 39½″, figural and flower scroll, black and green **100.00**

CLAMBROTH GLASS

History: Clambroth glass is a semi-opaque, grayish-white glass which resembles the color of the broth from clams. Pieces are found in both a smooth finish and a rough sandy finish. Sandwich Glass Co. and other manufacturers made clambroth glass.

Candlesticks
  7¼″, hexagonal petal top, Sandwich, pr **225.00**
  8¾″, reeded, scalloped base, pr . . . **100.00**
  10¼″, dolphin, floral dec on single step base, gold highlighting, translucent blue candle cup **350.00**
Ladle, 9½″ **30.00**
Lamp Shades, sgd "Northwood," pr . . **42.00**
Mug, Lacy Medallion, souvenir **35.00**
Plate, 8½″ **35.00**
Pomade Jar, 3¾″ h, bear, made for F. B. Strouse, NY **375.00**
Salt, master, Sawtooth, Sandwich, c1850 . . . . **50.00**
Soap Dish, cov, orig insert, robin and Wheat pattern **100.00**

Barber Bottle, 7″, Witch Hazel in gold lettering, marked "M. A. Co.," $30.00.

Talcum Shaker **20.00**
Urn, 3⅞″ h, ftd, pr **75.00**

CLEWELL POTTERY

History: Charles Walter Clewell was first a metal worker and second a potter. In the early 1900s he opened a small shop in Canton, Ohio, to produce metal overlay pottery.

Metal on pottery was not a new idea, but Clewell was perhaps the first to completely mask the ceramic body with copper, brass, "silvered" and "bronzed" metals. One result was a product whose patina added to the character of the piece over time.

Most of the wares are marked with a simple incised "CLEWELL" along with a code number. Because Clewell used pottery blanks from other firms, the names "Owens" or "Weller" are sometimes found.

Since Clewell operated on a small scale with little outside assistance, only a limited quantity of his art work exists. He retired at the age of 79 in 1955, choosing not to reveal his technique to anyone else.

References: Paul Evans, *Art Pottery of the United States*, Everybodys Press, Inc., 1974; Ralph and Terry Kovel, *The Kovels' Collector's Guide To American Art Pottery*, Crown Publishers, Inc., 1974.

Bowl, 7 x 2¾″, copper clad, green-blue patina, marked **175.00**
Box, round, riveted, imp "Clewell, Canton, OH" **275.00**
Mug, 5″, riveted design **125.00**
Pitcher, 5¾″, copper clad Owens blank, green patina **150.00**

Ashtray, copper, 3¾" d, 1¼" h, 1922, imp mark in circle, Clewell, Canton, Ohio, $200.00.

Vase

4¾", marked "2/Owens/120"	400.00
5¾", green patina	150.00
6¼", leaf dec, dark patina, marked .	175.00
11" h, gourd shape, green patina, marked and numbered	250.00

CLIFTON

CLIFTON POTTERY

History: The Clifton Art Pottery, Newark, New Jersey, was established by William A. Long, once associated with Londhuna Pottery, and Fred Tschirner, a chemist.

Production consisted of two major lines: Crystal Patina, which resembled true porcelain with a subdued crystal-like glaze, and Indian Ware or Western Influence, an adaptation of the American Indians' unglazed and decorated pottery with a high glazed black interior. Other lines included Robin's Egg Blue and Tirrube. Robin's Egg Blue is a variation of the crystal patina line but in blue-green instead of straw colored hues and with a less prominent "crushed crystal" effect in the glaze. Tirrube is on a terra cotta ground, features brightly colored, slip decorated flowers, and is often artist signed.

Marks are incised or impressed. Early pieces may be dated and shape numbers impressed. Indian wares are identified by tribes.

References: Paul Evans, *Art Pottery Of The United States,* Everbodys Press, Inc., 1974; Ralph and Terry Kovel, *The Kovels' Collector's Guide To American Art Pottery,* Crown Publishers, Inc., 1974.

Bowl

3½", Indian Ware, red clay body, feather design, glazed black int., c1906	250.00
8", Indian Ware	90.00
Candleholder, 7 x 4", two handles . . .	115.00
Coffeepot, cov, Indian Ware	75.00
Humidor, 4½ x 4¼", Indian Ware, brown	50.00
Teapot, cov, 7", Indian Ware	65.00

Vase

2", crystal patina luminous medium green, dated 1906, marked	65.00
4¾", bulbous, heavy green crystaline glaze, 1903	100.00
5", crushed crystaline glaze, 1903 . .	120.00
5", bulbous gourd shape, 1906	100.00
9", crystal patina glaze, pale green, 1906	145.00

Bowl, 3½" d, 2½" h, Indian Ware, red clay body, feather design, glazed black interior, c1906, $250.00.

CLOCKS

History: The sundial was the first man-made device for measuring time. Its basic disadvantage is well expressed in the saying: "Do like the sundial, count only the sunny days."

With need for greater dependability, man developed the water clock, oil clock, and the sand clock respectively. All these clocks worked on the same principle—time was measured by the amount of material passing from one container to another.

The wheel clock was the next major step. These clocks can be traced back to the 13th century. Many improvements on the basic wheel clock were made and continue to be made. In 1934 the quartz crystal movement was introduced.

Recently an atomic clock has been invented that measures time by the frequency of radiation and only varies one second in a thousand years.

Identifying the proper model name for a clock is critical in establishing price. Condition of works also is a critical factor. Examine the works to see how many original parts remain. If repairs are needed, try to include this in your estimate of purchase price. Few clocks are purchased purely for decorative value.

References: Roy Ehrhardt, *Clock Identification And Price Guide: Book I*, rev. ed., Heart of America Press, 1979; Roy Ehrhardt, *Clock Identification And Price Guide: Book II*, Heart of America Press, 1979; Roy Ehrhardt, ed., *The Official Price Guide To Antique Clocks*, House of Collectibles, Third Edition, 1985; Tran Duy Ly, *Clocks: A Guide To Identification and Prices*, Arlington Book Company, 1984; Alan and Rita Shenton, *The Price Guide To Clocks, 1840-1940*, Antique Collectors' Club, 1977.

Collectors' Club: National Association of Watch and Clock Collectors, Inc., P. O. Box 33, Columbia, PA 17512. Dues: $20.00. *Bulletin* (bimonthly).

Museum: American Clock & Watch Museum, Bristol, CT; Museum of National Association of Watch and Clock Collectors, Columbia, PA.

MISCELLANEOUS

Advertising
C. F. Chauffet, Jeweler, Buffalo, NY, 1901, shaped like frying pan to advertise the Pan American Exposition, inscribed, 30 hour balance wheel movement, brass hands, 11½" **75.00**
Chelsea Exchange Bank, New York City, mantel, brass and metal, New Haven Clock Co. **50.00**
Foster & Co., Beloit, WI, USA, 1910, The World's Best Shoes For Men, pocket watch shape, nickel plated, dial inscribed, back of case opens, 30 hour spring driven balance wheel movement, 10¼" **150.00**
Hollow Tile Fire Proofing, Henry Maurer & Son, 420 E. 23rd St., New York, nickel case, 30 hour time movement, sgd on dial, German, 1940, 4" **35.00**
Old Mr. Boston, Gilbert Clock Co., Winstead, CT, 1900, replica of bottle, painted sheet iron, 8 day balance wheel movement, maker's signature on dial, 21½" **275.00**
The Blade, Keen Sharp, Toledo, Ohio, Baird Clock Co., Plattsburg, NY, 1875, case painted pale red, white letters, paper on zinc dial inscribed by maker, 8 day time movement, 30¾", case repainted and refinished, label missing **2,300.00**
Alarm
Ansonia Clock Co., Ansonia, CT
Nickel plated case, black and gold

dial, pressed brass dial surround with image of Father Time, 30 hour time and alarm movement striking bell in bottom of case, trademark on dial and back of case, patent 3/27/77, 8" **100.00**
Oriole, musical, brass case, painted zinc panels, 30 hour time movement plays musical tune when alarm is triggered, maker's signature on dial, patent 1878, 8¼" **125.00**
Boat Clock, used on Erie Canal, 1900, American oak case, conical dial, 30 hour time and alarm movement, 6¾" **125.00**
Kroeber Clock Co., New York City, 1890, "Brass Plaque #4," gilted pressed tin front, 4 inset colored glass prisms, clock face with red velvet background, applied porcelain numerals, 30 hour time and alarm movement, brass hands, 12" **100.00**
Lux Clock Mfg. Co., Waterbury, CT, 1930, animated, dial with scene of man and woman at home, woman at work at spinning wheel, wheel turns in conjunction with movement escapement, colorful dial with dog in front of fireplace, painted black tin case, 30 hour time and alarm movement, maker's signature on dial, 4½" **125.00**
Rolling Bell, c1800, nickel plated case with bell on top which swings back and forth when alarm is triggered, blue velvet panels, 10½" **150.00**
Candlestand, Seth Thomas Sons & Co., New York City, 1890, painted and gilted stand, porcelain dial, 8 day movement, maker's signature on movement, under orig glass dome, 10¾" **550.00**
Desk
Ansonia Clock Co., New York, patent 1878, white metal case in shape of front of train, including engineers, amber reflector, and numerals "45," 30 hour balance wheel movement, paper dial, gilt highlights, maker's signature on dial, 8" **600.00**
Lux Clock Mfg. Co., Waterbury, CT, 1930, animated, painted scene of Church on dial, bell in tower moves with escapement, 30 hour movement, maker's signature on dial, 4" **75.00**
Octavia Clock Co., Switzerland, 1900, gold plated, engraved, 15 jewel watch movement, porcelain dial with seconds bit, maker's signature on movement, 4" **100.00**

Gaslight, Waltham, opaque glass dial, balance wheel movement, 5½″ **165.00**

Novelty

Ansonia Clock Co., New York

Armor #25, 1900, pressed nickel plated case, orig leather belt for hanging, case includes removable helmet and two spears, 30 hour time balance wheel movement, 11″ **275.00**

Cherub, 1890, two cast white metal figures supporting 30 hour time balance wheel movement, unusual winding mechanism, porcelain dial, hairline crack in dial, gilting removed, 4¼″ **80.00**

Lux Clock Mfg. Co., Waterbury, CT, 1890, figural, town hall, painted, 30 hour weight driven movement that strikes on hour and half hour, as clock strikes, bell in steeple rocks back and forth, 12″ **475.00**

New Haven Clock Co., New Haven, CT, 1900, banjo shape, detailed white metal case, 30 hour balance wheel movement in lower section, sgd on dial, 10½″ **200.00**

Parker Clock Co., Meriden, CT

Model #11, brass case with chains supporting works, 30 hour balance wheel movement with calendar mechanism, patent Nov 28, 1876 on rear of case, maker's signature on back plate, dial faded, 9½″ **400.00**

Travel type, carrying handle, brass case, 30 hour balance wheel movement, beveled glass over dial, sgd on back of case, 1890, 7″ **250.00**

Seth Thomas, Plymouth Hollow, CT, 1860, alarm mechanism by G. K. Proctor & Co., Beverly, MA, rosewood veneered case, 30 hour time and alarm movement, painted zinc dial, mirror tablet, orig "S T" hands, mechanism at top ignites a small lamp at the moment the alarm strikes, maker's signature on label on back, veneer missing from base, minor paint loss on dial, 11½″ ... **650.00**

Unidentified Maker, Connecticut, 1860, "Topsy," eyes move with escapement of movement, 30 hour time, unsigned, dial repainted, 16½″ **1,600.00**

Welch, E. N., Bristol, CT, 1860, Briggs rotary patent, rotary escapement mounted on turned wood base, cast feet, orig glass dome, unsigned, base repainted, 8″ **375.00**

SHELF CLOCKS

Acorn, J. C. Brown, Bristol, CT, laminated case, rosewood facings, 8 day brass time and strike movement with fusees, orig paper label, "Forestville Mfg. Co." sgd on dial, 19⅛″ **3,000.00**

Balloon, Gilbert Clock Co., Winstead, CT, c1900, mahogany case, pattern inlay around edge, porcelain dial, 8 day movement with lever escapement, 9″ **150.00**

Beehive

Brewster & Ingraham, Bristol, CT, 1850, rosewood veneered case, orig painted tablet, painted zinc dial, 8 day time and strike movement with strike advance method of raising the strike hammer, maker's signature on label, movement, and dial, case refinished, 18¾″ **400.00**

Jennings Bros., Brush Brass Novelty No. B5437, filigree panel beneath face, 5″ **90.00**

New Haven Clock Co.

Mahogany and rosewood veneered case, 1865, orig painted tablet, painted zinc dial, 30 hour time, strike, and alarm movement, maker's signature on paper label, columns reveneered, 19½″ **200.00**

Rosewood veneered case, 1860, painted beehive tablet, painted zinc dial, 8 day time and alarm movement, maker's signature on paper label, some veneer loss, tablet replaced, 19″ **175.00**

Seth Thomas, stenciled mahogany and rosewood veneered case, black and gold tablet, painted zinc dial, 8 day time, strike, and alarm Seth Thomas movement (not orig to case), sgd "Chauncey Jerome" on label on case, 19″ **225.00**

Box or Cottage

Ansonia Clock Co., c1910, veneered, 8 day time and strike movement, 9½″ **150.00**

Gilbert, William L. Clock Co., "Rose Cottage Time," gilt rose dec, 30 hour, 9⅞ x 7¾″ **125.00**

Terry, S. B., Plymouth, CT, 1860, mahogany and pine case, door with orig stenciled tablet, painted wood dial, 30 hour ladder movement with alarm, unsigned, 11½″ **325.00**

Waterbury Clock Co., c1858, painted green wood case, 30 hour brass spring movement and alarm, 12″ . **175.00**

Bracket

Bosley, Joseph, London, c1750, George II, mahogany and gilt

bronze bell topped case, pineapple finials, crown wheel escapement, musical, 21¼" **3,850.00**

Dent, London, George II, gilt metal and bronze mounted red japanned, 2nd half 18th C, 17", 5¾" d pewter dial, black-painted Roman numerals, movement gong striking on hour, strike silent mechanism in cresting, lantern-form case, dec allover with chinoiseries in gold, tones on a vermilion ground, various gilt enrichments **2,475.00**

European, 1880, brass case, cast with pierced frets and ornamentation, replaced red velvet backing, silver engraved dial, 8 day time and strike fusee movement striking on hour and half hour, opens in rear, 14 x 27½" **1,000.00**

Japanese, 1800, rosewood or teakwood case, mother of pearl and brass inlay, brass finials, early 8 day time and strike fusee movement with crown wheel escapement, engraved brass dial with animals of the zodiac, sweep second hand, some veneer loss, modern reproduction dial, hands do not match, 18½" **500.00**

Payne, London, c1810, Regency, gilt bronze mounted burr yew wood, acanthus chased bail handle, anchor escapement, glazed on all sides, fluted border at top, ogee molded base, four gilt ball feet, 10" **2,125.00**

Calendar

Ansonia, Banker's Inkstand, bronze, nickel finish, Egyptian motif, 1 day, 12" **375.00**

Feishtinger, C. W., Fritztown, PA, 1895, walnut case, door with orig glass tablet with silver dec, two painted zinc dials, 8 day time and strike movement, day indicator roller in base, lower dial with pointers to indicate date and month, pendulum seen through small aperture in bottom of calendar dial, orig instruction label on back, case refinished, tablet cracked, 22" . . . **350.00**

Ithaca Calendar Clock Co.

Oak, 1880, No 17 Mantel Index, solid oak case with carved dec, door opens to two paper on zinc discs, 8 day time and strike spring driven movement sgd E. N. Welch, calendar mechanism showing day of week, date, and month, maker's label on back, sgd on calendar dial, case refinished, 28¾" **500.00**

Walnut case, octagonal top, glass door, double paper dial with pendulum opening, 8 day time and strike spring driven movement marked "E. N. Welch, Ithaca Calendar Mechanism," days and months printed in Spanish, 21" . . **400.00**

Southern Calendar Clock Co., St. Louis, Missouri, 1879, Fashion Model #3, solid walnut case, moldings, columns, and finials, glass door with orig gold leaf inscription, 8 day time and strike Seth Thomas movement, separate calendar mechanism and dial, black paper label in back of case, 32" **1,700.00**

Waterbury, Office Calendar, Double Dial No. 40, walnut case, time, strike, and alarm movements, 24" **625.00**

Welch, E. N., Forestville, CT, 1875, Aditi Model, D. J. Gale's patent perpetual calendar, walnut case, two paper on zinc dials, lower with day and month indicators, 8 day time and strike movement, maker's signature on paper label on back, cast int. label, and movement, case refinished, upper dial faded, 27½" . . **700.00**

Carriage, French, brass, four beveled glass panels, 2½ x 3¼ x 4½", $500.00.

Carriage

Black Starr & Forest, c1900, champleve enamel, platform lever movement, porcelain dial, multicolored, 5½" **1,200.00**

French, 1875, elaborate bracket handle, porcelain dial with time and alarm indicators, 8 day time, strike, and alarm movement, 6¼" **300.00**

Le Roy et Fils, c1900, gilt metal, detached lever movement, alarm, patented bottom wind, fitted leather case, 5¼" **1,425.00**

Limoges, 1898, Grande Sonnerie, gilt metal, platform lever movements, repeating, alarm, case with four free standing columns with Corinthian capitals and acanthus chased urn finials, inset with enamel panels painted with classical women holding a jewel box, basket of flowers, gilt highlights, maroon ground, fitted leather case with key, 6¾" . . . **10,000.00**

Seikosha, Tokyo, Japan, 1900, pressed brass case, porcelain dial with date and day indicators, 8 day balance wheel movement, 7" **175.00**

Voak, London, c1840, gilt metal, engraved, diamond endstone, lever movement mounted on back, 43¾" **1,225.00**

Waterbury, 1890, porcelain dial, jeweled movement with hour and half hour strike and repeat mechanism, sgd on dial and movement, 6" . . . **175.00**

Crystal Regulator

Ansonia Clock Co., 1880, brass case, beveled glass panels, porcelain dial, 8 day time and strike movement, visible Brocot escapement, 2-jar simulated mercury pendulum, 9¾" **275.00**

French, 1860, painted case, elliptic front, 8 day time and strike movement, orig mercury filled pendulum, 10½" **750.00**

Gilbert, W. L., Tunis, 8 day, half hour strike **675.00**

Seth Thomas, 1890, brass case, beveled glass panels, porcelain dial inscribed "Mitchell Vance & Co., NY," 8 day time and strike movement inscribed "R. Kaiser, Seth Thomas," 11" **225.00**

Waterbury, Bordeau, gold plated, 8 day, half hour strike **850.00**

Figural

Ansonia Clock Co.

Cupid, 1880, gold plated ormolu, 30 hour time movement, porcelain dial, maker's signature on dial, quiver of arrows finial, 8¼" **250.00**

Swinging Doll, 1890, brass cased alarm clock and support with ceramic figure of boy which swings with the movement, 30 hour time movement, paper dial with maker's name and trademark, 11½" **400.00**

German, 1890, Diana, cast white metal figure supports watch movement which swings its own pendulum, 30 hour time movement, maker's signature on back of movement, "Made In Germany," 13½" **350.00**

Gilbert Clock Co., chariot, gold plated ormolu, 30 hour time movement, paper dial, patent 1891, 6½" **225.00**

Kennedy, T., CT, 1860, John Bull, blinking eyes, 30 hour time only balance wheel movement, "T. Kennedy, Patent applied for 1856" stamped on base, dial repainted, 16½" **1,200.00**

Unknown Maker, violin, mahogany case shaped like violin on base, paper on zinc dial, 8 day time and strike movement, black and gold glass, some restoration, 28" **500.00**

Gingerbread (Kitchen)

Ansonia, c1890, Kentucky, ash, rosewood trim, 6" dial, 8 day strike, spring wound, 22" **215.00**

Gilbert, William L., Clock Co., 1899, Excelsior No. 2, oak, 8 day half hour strike, 16½" **200.00**

Ingraham, 1905, Cayuga, solid oak, emb, 8 day half hour strike, 22" . . **225.00**

New Haven Clock Co., pressed oak case, door glass with gold design, 8 day time, strike, and alarm movements, paper label on back "Our Pride 8 day Striking Alarm," sgd on movement and paper label, case refinished, 25" **175.00**

Waterbury, Ideal O, black walnut, 8 day, cathedral gong, wire bell . . . **300.00**

Welch, E. N., 1880, walnut, white dial, brass alarm bell, 8 day, 23⅜ x 14½ x 15⅛" **265.00**

Mantel

Brush Brass, B5436, Waterbury movements, 5½" **60.00**

Chelsea Clock Co., E. A. Brown, Boston, MA, c1910, fruitwood case, 8 day movement **80.00**

Gilbert Clock Co., 1890, marbleized wood case, gilted white metal feet and bell mount, 8 day time and strike movement striking hours and half hours on gold painted bell mounted on top, paper dial inscribed by maker, 17½ x 17¼" . . **150.00**

Kroeber Clock Co., 1875, solid walnut, moldings, 8 day time and strike movement, maker's signature on paper label, case refinished, 14½" **225.00**

New Haven Clock Co., 1910, tambour, mahogany case, porcelain dial, 30 hour time movement, maker's signature on dial, 6¾" **50.00**

Sessions Clock Co., 1920, inlaid ma-

Mantel, Louis Majorelle, rosewood, iron metal work, bronze patina, 8″ h, $1,500.00.

hogany case, porcelain dial, 30 hour time movement, maker's signature on dial, one ball foot missing, 8¼″ **80.00**

Seth Thomas

Brass and glass, 1900, fancy case, copper plated white metal base and top, porcelain dial, 8 day time and strike movement, maker's signature on dial and movement, 12″ **250.00**

Wood, 1875, solid walnut case, painted gold tablet, orig paper dial, 8 day time and alarm movement which sounds with two hammers on a gong and bell, maker's signature on label and dial, case refinished, 21¾″ **275.00**

Waltham Watch Co., 1920, hardwood tambour case, 8 day movement adjusted with 15 jewels, removable front bezel, sgd on dial and movement, 5¾″ **100.00**

Marble, French, 1885, black marble case, gold dec, porcelain dial, 8 day time and strike movement with Brocot visible escapement, 14 x 10″ **175.00**

Massachusetts Shelf

Boston Clock Co., Chelsea, MA, 1888, Empire style painted black wood case, four columns with brass capitals, brass dec on op and bottom of case, etched and cut glass tablet with flaming leaf motif, emb brass rim surround on paper dial, one year, torsion escapement patented by Aaron Crane, fusee powered, tin and strike, orig label, minor stains on dial, one fusee cord broken, possible brown spring on strike side, 21″ **2,500.00**

Hubbard, Daniel, Medfield, MA, c1820, Federal, mahogany and eglomise, shaped crest, urn and foliate form finial, rect eglomise door dec with lyres and foliate motifs, gold painted dished dial, hinged eglomise door with mill and waterfall scene, molded base, giltwood ball feet, 36″ **42,000.00**

Unknown Maker, miniature, iron case, mother of pearl inlay, painted gold dec, orig dial, 30 hour time only movement, with S. B. Terry patent torsion balance, marked "Oct 5th, 1852," 8½″ **1,500.00**

Willard, Aaron, Boston, c1820, Federal, mahogany and eglomise, shaped crest, brass eagle finial, door dec with polychrome foliate and lyre motifs, white painted dished dial above eglomise panel painted with corner lyre motifs, oval mirror, brass ball feet, 34½″ **9,500.00**

Metal

Brass, cast, 1900, figural, Liberty, paper dial, 30 hour movement, 14″ . **75.00**

Bronze

Ansonia, figural, MacBeth, seated in ornate chair, 8 day, half hour strike, sounding board, patent regulators, white 5″ dial, 11½″ . **250.00**

Du Buc, Paris, c1805, gilt bronze, surmounted by spread winged American eagle, shield, arrows and olive branch on top of a globe and plinth inscribed "E Pluribus Unum," white enameled dial centering inscription "Du Buc, Rue Michel-le-Comte No. 33, A Paris," and "Washington, the first in war, first in peace, and in his countrymen's hearts," flanking standing figure of Washington holding scroll in right hand, sword and gloves in left hand, lower section with giltmetal mount centering female's head, chased flattened ball feet **25,300.00**

Jennings Bros, 1906, gold finish, 2″ ivory dial, 1 day time, 4⅝″ **65.00**

Seth Thomas, Duchess, cottage style, emb flowers, foliage, and scrolls, 4½ dial, 9¾″ **185.00**

Copper, New Haven, CT, 1885, hammered ground, SS ornaments of lily and lily pad, fold over corners, easel back, 1 day time, 8½″ **165.00**

Iron

Ansonia Clock Co., 1890, porcelain dial, 30 hour balance wheel time movement, musical mechanism in bottom of gold painted case, busts of Beethoven and Wagner, musical motifs, sgd on dial, 10¾" **125.00**

New Haven Clock Co., 1890, cast iron, gilted white metal ornamentation, mother of pearl inlay, painted dec, 8 day time and strike movement, unsigned, 8" . **200.00**

Muller, Nicholas, 1886, figural, boy pushing wheelbarrow containing clock, 1 day time, small movement, 6½" **165.00**

Noah Pomeroy & Co., 1860, mother of pearl inlay and painted dec, 30 hour balance wheel movement with nickel plated balance wheel that shows through opening in dial, maker's signature on movement, 10" **600.00**

Terry Clock Co., 1875, round top, zinc dial with applied paper, 8 day time and strike movement with fixed pendulum, maker's label on case, case repainted black, 9" **100.00**

Unidentified American Maker, 1890, circular clock, pedestal on rect base, porcelain dial, 30 hour balance wheel movement, 12" . **75.00**

Waterbury Clock Co., 1860, case marked "Muller, NY," 30 hour time and strike movement and pendulum opening to lower part of case, maker's signature on paper label and case, 16¾" **100.00**

Nickel Plated Brass, Seth Thomas Clock Co., Thomaston, CT, 1900, kite shape, pressed front with floral designs and inscription "Time Flies," three feet form stand, maker's signature on dial, 8" **200.00**

Pot Metal

Unidentified Maker, 1910, gilted metal case supported by pressed glass columns, 30 hour balance wheel movement, case repainted, 16¼" **50.00**

Westclox, 1918, gray silver finish, emb Dutch figures, 1 day movement, 4½" **60.00**

Mirror Side

Ansonia, Triumph, silvered cupids, bronze ornaments, 8 day movement, 24½" **325.00**

New Haven, Occidental, walnut, gilt ornaments, 8 day strike, 24" **375.00**

Ogee

Ansonia, 1891, central panel of petit point etching with cupid holding basket of flowers, 1 day, strike, and alarm movements, 26" **225.00**

Brewster, E. C., Bristol, CT, 1840, mahogany veneered case, repainted tablet, heavy painted zinc dial, spring driven movement with cast iron back plate, maker's label, 26" **200.00**

Forestville Manufacturing Co., Bristol, CT, 1850, mahogany case with choice figured veneers, double door, painted floral tablet in lower door, painted zinc dial inscribed with maker's name, 8 day time and strike movement, 31" **275.00**

Gilbert, Wm. L., c1870, goldfinch dec, 30 hour weight, strike, 25⅞" **175.00**

Hills, George, Plainville, CT, inverted ogee mahogany veneer, mirror, 30 hour brass time only movement, replaced dial, 36½" **450.00**

Hunt, John, Farmington, CT, 1835, mahogany and rosewood veneered case, four orig feet, glazed door, orig wood dial, replaced glass tablet, brass 8 day time and strike movement retaining orig weights, partial paper label, minor veneer loss, 30¼" **300.00**

New Haven Clock Co., 1880, zebra case, etched lyre and foliage dec, 1 day strike, orig weights, 26" . . . **225.00**

Jerome & Co., New Haven, CT, 1860, mahogany veneered case, double doors, lower with frosted design, painted zinc dial, 8 day time and strike weight driven movement, maker's label, 30" **275.00**

Walton, Hiram, Terryville, CT, 1850, mahogany veneered case, wood painted dial, orig painted glass tablet with floral motif, vertical oval center, 30 hour time and strike brass weight driven movement, orig weights, paper label, some flaking to tablet, 26" **235.00**

Pillar and Scroll

Clark, Herman, Plymouth, CT, 1820, mahogany and veneered case, painted iron dial sgd "H Clark, Plymouth," painted glass tablet with harbor scene of boats, leaf like surround, 8 day brass weight driven time and strike movement, orig paper label, right ear piece out, tablet restored, 3 contemporary finials, 20¼" **5,600.00**

Hoadley, S., Plymouth, CT, 1825, mahogany case, scrolled ears, turned columns, cut out feet, orig painted wood dial, orig painted tablet, orig upper glass, ivory brushed 30 hour

Pillar and Scroll, Eli Terry & Sons, 8 day, brass finials, French feet, Plymouth, CT, $875.00.

wood upside down movement, orig weights, maker's label with picture of Benjamin Franklin and motto "Time is Money," finials missing, 28¾" **2,500.00**

Ives, Joseph, Bristol, CT, 1820, tiger maple pillar with reeded back columns, brass plates, iron posts, tin keystone, 8 day movement, single winding arbor, time, and strike, bell strikes hourly, 29¾" **6,500.00**

Leavenworth & Son, Mark, Waterbury, CT, 1820, mahogany case, painted wood dial, orig glass with landscape of mansion and lake, 30 hour wood time and strike, orig paper label, orig brass urn finials, 28½" **2,125.00**

North, Norris, Torrington, CT, c1820, 30 hour wood time and strike movement (east-west), orig dial and finials, paper label, 29¾" **2,000.00**

Seth Thomas, 1820, mahogany case, turned columns, scrolled feet and crest, glazed door with replaced painted tablet, enameled wood dial and maker's label, 30 hour time and strike movement with iron weights, finials replaced, 31" **850.00**

Terry, Eli, Plymouth, CT, 1817, tiger maple and mahogany case, dial dec with eagle and crossed flags, 30 hour movement, outside escapement, time, and strike, 30½" . **10,000.00**

Unidentified Maker, CT, 1825, mahogany case, painted wood dial and glass tablet, 30 hour time and strike weight driven wood movement, door reveneered, label done, glass repainted, 16½ x 28¾" **500.00**

Porcelain or China Case

Ansonia, 1901, Royal Bonn, Romance, rococo sash, 5" cream porcelain escapement dial, Roman numerals, 8 day, half hour cathedral gong, multicolored shell and floral motif, 11" **375.00**

Germany, 1880, off white and pale green china case, paper dial and brass rim, 8 day time wheel balance movement supported by two columns, 16" **75.00**

Gilbert, Wm. L., 1900, Cameo, white landscape and florals, green ground, 2" dial, 1 day time, 6¼" .. **80.00**

Kroeber, F., NY, 1888, lever movement, urn shape, gilt foliate handles and finial **225.00**

Waterbury, 1903, boudoir, clover dec, pastel ground, 2" dial with beveled glass, 1 day lever time, 5⅝" **85.00**

Shelf, E. N. Welch, teardrop, 22½" h, walnut, 8 day movement, $300.00.

Shelf

Atkins & Porter, Bristol, CT, 1850, mahogany and rosewood veneered case, orig painted tablet and zinc dial, 30 hour time and strike weight driven movement, maker's label on case int., case refinished, 24½" .. **250.00**

Birge & Peck, Bristol, CT, 1850, mahogany veneered case with gilted and painted dec split columns and splat, painted tablet in lower door, mirror in center section, orig dial and paper label in top section, 8 day weight driven time and strike movement with rolling pinions, case refinished, 35½″ **475.00**

Birge, Mallory & Co., 1840, choice mahogany case, carved crest, turned columns, ball feet, orig painted tablet in lower door, two clear glasses in upper door, orig painted wood dial, maker's label, and large strap brass 8 day weight driven time and strike sgd movement, case refinished, tablets cracked, 38½″ **800.00**

Boardman & Wells, Bristol, CT, 1830, mahogany case with gilted split columns, stenciled splat with maker's name, painted tablet with naval battle scene, 30 hour time and strike wood movement, orig weights, black and gold wood dial, paper label, 32¾″ **275.00**

Brewster & Ingraham, 1850, round laminated and turned mahogany case, convex glass, painted zinc dial, 8 day horizontal movement, sgd on dial, case refinished, 11¼″ **500.00**

Clark & Morse, Plymouth, CT, 1825, mahogany veneered case with four columns flanking two doors, lower with orig painted tablet, upper with orig glass, painted iron dial inscribed by maker, high quality 8 day brass weight driven Salem Bridge movement with orig weight, scrolled crest and three brass finials, 30¾″ **2,800.00**

E. Ingraham & Co.

Grecian Model, 1870, walnut case, turned and laminated bezel, applied paper face on zinc dial, 8 day time, strike, and alarm movement, sgd on paper label, case refinished, 14¾″ **250.00**

Venetian, rosewood veneered case with turned split columns, painted tablet inscribed "E Pluribus Unum" with eagle and American shield, Joseph Ives 8 day time and strike tin plate movement with squirrel cage roller escapement and rolling pinions, maker's signature on label, case refinished, one hand replaced, 18″ **2,100.00**

Venetian #2 (Candy Striper), 1875, mosaic front, alternating light and dark woods, orig table, paper on zinc dial, unsigned, 18″ **225.00**

French, 1850, walnut inlaid case, painted dial, 8 day spring driven time movement with fixed pendulum, maker's instruction label on case int. and label of "Jesse Smith, 262 Essex St., Salem," 8″ **130.00**

Hotchkiss & Benedict, Auburn, NY, 1820, mahogany case with choice veneers, columns with carved capitals, upper door opens to painted wood dial, lower door with mirror and orig paper label, detailed inscription of maker, shaped crest, 8 day time and strike movement with orig lead weights, second hand shaped like human hand with finger pointing, sgd on dial and label, patent by Asa Munger, 38″ **1,150.00**

Jerome & Co., 1870, rosewood veneered case, door with gutta percha pressed and gilted design, painted zinc dial, 8 day time, strike, and alarm movement, blue paper maker's label, 14¾″ **225.00**

Jerome, Gilbert & Grant, 1840, mahogany case with rounded sides, two painted tablets, painted zinc dial, 30 hour time and strike weight driven movement, maker's label, 22¼″ **275.00**

Marsh, George, Bristol, CT, 1830, Empire mahogany case, carved crest, columns, and feet, door with mirror and painted tablet, repainted wood dial, paper maker's label, unusual time and strike wood movement with very small winding drums and ivory bushings, old lead weights, minor veneer damage, finials missing, movement not orig to case, 38″ **450.00**

Mills, J. R. & Co., NY, c1845, mahogany veneered case with grained columns, gilt capitals, painted glass dial with pressed brass surround, 30 day weight driven time and strike movement with A. D. Crane's Patent torsion escapement and three ball pendulum, paper label, door, glass dial, weights, and suspension spring replaced, 22″ **1,600.00**

Mitchell, George, Bristol, CT, 1830, mahogany case with stenciled columns and crest, door with replaced mirror tablet, enameled wood dial, paper label, 30 hour time and strike weight driven wood movement, period weights, 35″ **250.00**

Munger, Asa, Auburn, NY, 1830, mahogany and walnut case, molded cornice and base, carved columns on door, orig dec metal plate around dial, mirror, 8 day time and strike weight driven movement with exceptional brass hands, period iron weights and orig eagle pendulum, case refinished, 38¼″ **2,225.00**

Roberts, Titus, Bristol, CT, 1840, mahogany veneered case, paint dec and gilted columns, painted wood dial, black and gold tablet, 30 hour time and strike weight driven wood movement, maker's signature on paper label with inscription "For Henry Hart," gilted ball feet, 32¾″ **375.00**

Seth Thomas

Club Foot Model, 1870, choice walnut veneers and moldings, painted zinc dial, 8 day time, strike, and alarm movement, 15½″ **175.00**

Round Top, 1875, rosewood veneered case, painted zinc dial, paper label, 8 day time and strike movement, maker's signature on label and dial, 15″ **175.00**

Sleigh Front, 1865, rosewood veneered case with gilted and paint dec columns, two painted tablets, painted zinc dial, 8 day time and strike weight driven movement, maker's label, 32½″ **1,650.00**

Stratton, Charles, Worcester, MA, 1860, mahogany veneered reverse ogee case, mirror tablet, painted zinc dial, 30 hour time and strike weight driven movement with orig weights, over pasted maker's label, 23½″ **225.00**

Terry & Andrews, Ansonia, CT, rose-

Shelf, Eli Terry & Sons, 8 day, stencil dec, claw feet, Plymouth, CT, $450.00.

wood veneered case with painted dec, two painted tablets, painted zinc dial, 8 day time and strike lyre movement, blue paper maker's label, 15½″ **700.00**

Terry, Eli & Sons, Plymouth, CT, 1830, mahogany case with orig gold stenciling on splat and quarter columns, replaced painted tablet, painted wood dial, 30 hour time and strike weight driven wood movement, maker's signature on paper label, 29¾″ **350.00**

Terry, Henry, & Co., Plymouth, CT, 1830, mahogany case with split columns, carved pineapples, carved crest, black and gold painted wood dial, 30 hour time and strike wood movement with orig weights, maker's label, bottom door glass missing, 33¾″ **225.00**

Terry, Silas B., choice mahogany case, black and gold painted wood dial, orig mirror tablet, round movement, sgd on label, labeled and sold by Williams, Orton, Prestons & Co., Farmington, CT, 1840, ivory escutcheons missing, 32¾″ **350.00**

Waterbury Clock Co., 1875

Rosewood veneered case with applied rippled molding, painted zinc dial with seconds indicator, 30 hour time and strike balance wheel movement, maker's signature on movement, case refinished, 11¾″ **250.00**

Rosewood veneered case with mirror, painted zinc dial, 8 day time, strike, and alarm movement, maker's label, 17″ **275.00**

Whiting, Riley, Winchester, CT, 1830, mahogany case with carved eagle crest and columns, replaced mirror tablet, black and gold painted wood dial, 30 hour time and strike movement, orig weights, maker's label, 35¼″ **475.00**

Skeleton

Terry Clock Co., 1875, miniature, porcelain dial, pressed brass ornamentation including maker's name, 8 day double wind time movement, base with painted dec and marbleization, maker's signature on plate above dial, under dome, 8¾″ **1,150.00**

Unidentified Maker, CT, 1850, mounted on walnut base, cov with glass dome, painted zinc dial, 30 hour time movement with S. N. Botsford Patent escapement with horizontal balance wheel, some marriage of parts, 12¾″ **175.00**

Solar

Arkell, James & A. G. Richmond, Canjohaire, NY, 1880, patented by Lewis Paul Juvet, Glens Falls, NY, globe on solid cast base, globe with paper covering rotates once every 24 hours, beveled glass time dial with reverse gold leaf numerals, 30 hour movement, compass hangs from base of the pole, maker's signature on globe, 12" d globe, 48" h **4,250.00**

Whiting, Dr. Lewis, Saratoga, NY, 1863, patent by Thedore Timby, Baldwinsville, NY, walnut case, 8 day movement, globe made and installed by Gilman Joslin, Boston, MA, 12 hour dial above globe and minute dial below, believed to be one of only 600 made, lower dial, lower door, and one drop acorn replaced, 27" **2,600.00**

Steeple

Boardman, Chauncey, patent 1847, mahogany veneered case, painted tablet with Windsor Castle, painted zinc dial, 30 hour time and strike fusee movement, maker's signature on movement and paper label, 20" **475.00**

Brewster & Ingraham, Bristol, CT, 1845, Gothic, round, twin steeples, rosewood veneered case, cut glass tablet, painted zinc dial, maker's label and rare repeating 8 day time and strike movement with strike snail and retaining both brass springs, maker's signature on label and movement, case refinished, base reveneered, two finials missing, 20" **800.00**

Roswell Kimberly, 1850, standard 8 day time and strike movement, silver and black painted tablet of an eagle, inscription on top of case "Patented Oct 11th 1850 by R. Kimberly, Ansonia, Ct," case refinished, 20½" **700.00**

Smith & Goodrich, Bristol, CT, 1850, mahogany veneered case with turned finials, painted tablet, painted zinc dial, 30 hour time and strike fusee movement, maker's label, case and dial refinished, 19¾" **275.00**

Terry & Andrews, Bristol, CT, 1850, rosewood veneered case, orig painted tablet, painted zinc dial, 8 day time and strike lyre sgd movement with orig brass springs, blue paper maker's label, minor veneer repair, case refinished, hands replaced, 20" **475.00**

Terry, Silas Burnham, Terryville, CT,

1845, mahogany and rosewood case, painted scene in door, painted wood dial with seconds aperature, heavy strap brass movement, 30 hour time and strike with two large wooden fusee cones, minor veneer loss, old replaced tablet, 24¾" **3,750.00**

TALL CASE CLOCKS

Blasdel, David, Amesbury, MA, 1775, 81¾", flat top case with strong top molding, arched door, brass and pewter dial inscribed in arch "Made by/ David Blasdel/in Amesbury/ MDCCLV," long wide waist, molded base, grain painted, 8 day movement, calendar mechanism, waist door and two flanking boards not orig to clock **3,500.00**

Burnap, Daniel, East Windsor, CT, c1780, 88", Chippendale carved cherrywood, molded hood surmounted by a pierced cresting centering three ball and spirally twisted finials above glazed door opening, engraved brass dial, inscription "Daniel Burnap, East Windsor," minute and date registers, waisted case with hinged shaped door flanked by fluted quarter columns, molded base **13,200.00**

Effingham Embree, New York, c1800, 94¾", Federal inlaid mahogany, molded hood centering and eagle inlaid tympanum above arched door opening, white painted dial with minute and date registers, painted bucolic scene above inscription "EFFINGHAM EMBREE, NEW YORK," waisted case with bookend inlaid frieze and fan inlaid door, fluted quarter columns, fan inlaid base on bracket feet, restored hood molding **22,000.00**

Garrett, Philip, Philadelphia, PA, c1775, 100¾", Chippendale carved mahogany, bonnet with swan's neck pediment ending in carved rosettes, three urn and flame finials, arched glazed door, painted face with minute and date registers, painted arch panel of sporting scene, maker's name and location below date register, waisted case with shaped and recessed oval panel door, fluted quarter columns, 8 day, scalloped recessed panel in base flanked by fluted quarter columns, ogee bracket feet, rear feet replaced **14,500.00**

Harland, Thomas, Norwich, CT, 1785, 91", Chippendale cherry case, molded arched bonnet with three flame finials, and whale's tail fret, fluted columns with brass capitals flank glazed door, silvered brass dial, inscribed "Thomas Harland, Norwich" in arch, seconds bitt, calendar aperture, 8 day, brass time and strike movement, orig weights, wood pendulum rod, and brass bob, waisted case with tombstone door, molded base with scroll pattern applied to top and side panels, double molded base, ogee bracket feet, hardware on door not orig, old replacement in fret, two finial replacements **20,000.00**

Hill, Samuel, Harrisburg, PA, c1780, 103½", Chippendale carved mahogany, bonnet with molded broken arch pediment ending in carved rosettes and centering three carved urn and pierced flame finials, arched glazed door, white painted dial with floral spandrels and birds in fountain in arch, minute and date registers, "SAML HILL" at base of number, "VI," fluted columns flanking bonnet door, waisted case, molded shaped hinged door, fluted quarter columns in waist and base, molded shaped panel on base, ogee bracket feet **14,500.00**

Kepplinger, Samuel, Baltimore, MD, c1810, 106", carved and inlaid satinwood and plum pudding mahogany, bonnet with molded swan's neck cresting ending in inlaid roundels, acorn wood center finial, arched glazed door, white painted dial, moon phases, 8 day, minute and date registers, inscription "Samuel Kepplinger BALTIMORE" between registers, waisted case, rect cock beaded door, satinwood inlaid frieze, line inlaid quarter columns, line inlaid base with plum pudding mahogany panel, ogee bracket feet **8,000.00**

Pratt, John, Washington, NJ, 1824, Federal carved curly maple, hood with swan's neck crest above a carved teardrop relief and hinged glazed door opening, white painted dial with moon phases, minute and date registers, inscription "John Nicholl," waisted case with shell carved hinged door flanked by canted corners, molded base with shaped skirt, turned feet, case sgd, "January 25th, 1824, made by John S. Pratt, Washington," moon phases repainted, slight repair to crest **7,150.00**

Rogers, Paul, Berwick, ME, c1800, 85", flat top, pine case, long slender arched waist door and upper glazed door, 8 day, double molded base, brass gears and iron plates, engraved brass dial inscribed "Paul Rogers, Berwick" **4,000.00**

Rota, Jacob, Berks County, PA, c1770, 94½", Chippendale, carved, inlaid, and turned walnut, molded swan's neck cresting bearing initials "MF," ending in floral carved rosettes, centered by three turned finials above arched white painted dial, dec with bird and flowers, turned colonettes flanking, case with arched and hooded door flanked by fluted quarter-columns, base with molded rect panel, molded base and ogee bracket feet, orig printed operating instructions, six month warranty printed in Germany by J. Ritter & Co., Reading to clock maker, Jacob Rota **19,250.00**

Spaulding, Edward, Providence, RI, c1760, Chippendale, mahogany, block and shell carved, bonnet with arched molded cornice, three fluted urn and flame carved finials, arched glazed door, brass engraved dial, "Edward Spaulding/Providence" in arch, brass spandrels, 8 day, calendar aperture and second dial, four fluted columns, waist with arched door centering a block figured mahogany panel and carved shell, molded base with figured front, ogee bracket feet, refinished, numerous minor repairs **27,500.00**

Willard, Aaron, Boston, MA, c1800, 88", Federal inlaid mahogany, hood with pierced shaped crest centering three brass finials above line inlaid glazed hinged door opening, white painted dial with moon phases, minute and date registers, painted wing spread eagle above inscription "Aaron Willard Boston," brass stop-fluted quarter columns flanking fan inlaid base centering satinwood conch inlaid oval reserve, ogee bracket feet, slight repair to pierced crest, reduced feet . . **46,750.00**

Unknown, European, 1775, 90½", carved solid oak case, painted black, inscription "M. 1676 S." on upper door, 8 day time and strike, silvered engraved brass dial with attached spandrels, iron weights and period pendulum, case needs regluing, back board replacement, missing feet . . . **3,000.00**

Unknown, New Jersey, c1815, 92¼", mahogany case with choice veneers, broken arch hood, inlaid panel in door and in base, strike movement with period weights and pendulum, painted iron dial with moon phases, 8 day time, ear on hood reattached, one molding missing, veneer damage and repair **6,500.00**

Unknown, New York, c1800, satinwood inlaid mahogany, hood with molded swan's neck pediment ending in wavy star inlaid rosettes centering three brass finials above arched glazed door opening, white painted metal dial with moon phases, second, minute, and date registers, fluted colonettes flanking waisted case, fluted quarter columns and arched hinged inlaid door flanked by two satinwood inlaid urns, scalloped skirt, flared bracket feet **11,000.00**

Unknown, New York or New Jersey, c1800, 101½", Federal inlaid mahogany, molded swan's neck crest centering three brass finials hinged glazed door opening, white painted dial, oval inlaid door on waisted case, inlaid base, shaped feet, restored base and crest **4,675.00**

Unknown, Pennsylvania, 1825, 92½", cherry case, broken arch hood, turned feet, 30 hour pull up movement, dial and period pendulum, hood surmounted by carved finial from a lyre or banjo clock, ears pieced out on hood, minor paint loss on dial, finial not original, minor repairs **1,700.00**

Banjo, Howard & Davis, Boston, MA, rosewood grained case, 32", $2,100.00.

WALL

Banjo
Curtis & Dunning, Burlington, VT, c1815, 32¾", mahogany, giltwood

case, foliate waist, brass fillets, naval battle **7,000.00**

Derry Manufacturing Co., Derry, NY, c1895–1900, 35", mahogany case, eagle finial, 8 day, reproduction of Willard Clock **1,000.00**

Howard-type, MA, 1820, 36½", mahogany case, drop on bottom, two black and gold glasses in hinged frames, 8 day time movement with period lead weight and pendulum, turned wood finial and bezel, unsigned, pendulum rod repaired, finial not original, minor veneer damage, replaced bracket **850.00**

Howard-type, MA, 1840, 29", softwood case, two black and gold painted tablets, painted zinc dial, turned wood bezel, 8 day time movement, old weight and pendulum, unsigned, restoration to glass, refinished case, replaced weight pan **700.00**

Low, John J. & Co., Boston, MA, c1828, 39½", Empire, painted stenciled case, landscape scene, eagle on ball finial **3,000.00**

Seward, J., Boston, MA, 1835, 29½", gold front, painted tablets, brass side arms and bezel, painted iron dial inscribed "Seward," acorn finial, 8 day time movement with orig weight, cracked throat tablet, finial not original, gilted rope missing .. **1,600.00**

Unknown, MA, 1820, 32", mahogany case with two painted tablets one "Girard's Bank," painted iron dial inscribed "Zacheus Gates," 8 day time movement with period cast iron weight, brass side arms, bezel and eagle finial, replacements, minor veneer damage **900.00**

Waltham, No. 1540, 40½", walnut case, foliate waist, brass fillets, eagle finial, rural village scene **1,250.00**

Willard, S., MA, c1820, 11½" w, 37½" h, Federal, mahogany and eglomise, giltwood acorn finial, circular glazed door opening to white painted dial, eglomise throat panel depicting female figure of Justice flanked by brass side arms, hinged door centering eglomise panel depicting Neptune and Father Time with inscription "S. Willard's Patent," eglomise panels restored ... **2,250.00**

Willard School, Boston, 1810, 29½", mahogany case with dovetailed bottom, cross banded frames, 4" movement, painted iron dial, brass bezel and side arms, gilted acorn finial, two painted tablets, period lead weight, dial inscribed "A. Willard," movement inscribed, "Cleaned by E. Taber, 1834," replaced finial, wheel, and glass, minor veneer damage **1,000.00**

Williams, David, Rhode Island, 1820, 34", mahogany case, two modern tablets, painted iron dial, 8 day "A frame" movement, brass finial, sidearms, bezel, sgd repainted dial, replacements, repainted, and reveneered **900.00**

Calendar

Ansonia Brass & Copper Co., Ansonia, CT, 1875, 26", round drop, rosewood veneer case, turned wood bezel, dial inscribed by maker and "Terry's Patent," black and gold tablet, turned finials, 8 day time and strike movement, attached calendar mechanism, one finial replacement, reveneered lower door **900.00**

Gilbert, Wm. L., c1861, 24½", oak, octagonal, 8 day strike, marked "Patented by Galusha Maranville, March 5, 1861" **1,500.00**

Ithaca Calendar Clock Co., Ithaca, NY, 1881, 33", walnut case with bracket, molding, carved crest, 8 day time and strike movement, calendar dial and mechanism, 5" time dial, 7" calendar dial, orig paper instruction label, sgd label and calendar dial, replacements, loose hood molding **1,000.00**

New Haven, 29½", Ionie figure, double dial, 8 day **1,200.00**

Prentise, Empire, walnut, 60 day, two springs **1,875.00**

Waterbury Clock Co., Waterbury, CT, 39½", oak case, pressed and reeded dec, turned finials, two painted zinc dials inscribed, "Pat. July 30th 1889" on calendar dial, paper label, 8 day time and strike movement with large brass bob . . **950.00**

Cuckoo

American Clock Co., Philadelphia, PA, c1930, 17 x 14 x 7½", Victorian, carved wood case, carved spread eagle at top, red, blue, and black painted cuckoo, 8 day brass movement **150.00**

Keebler Clock Co., Philadelphia, PA, 1920, 5 x 4 x 1¾", pressed log design, leaves, flowers, nest of birds, brass spring pendulum **75.00**

Kroeber, F., c1888, 18", walnut case, brass movement, two weights, pendulum **250.00**

Gallery

Ingraham, 12", chestnut, 8 day **250.00**

Sempire, No 8, 21⅛", electric, oak . **265.00**

Seth Thomas, Wardroom, c1905, 5½" d **225.00**

Girandole, Lemuel Curtis, 1815, 13½" w, 46" h, Federal, eglomise and giltwood mahogany, giltwood spread wing eagle finial above metal circular hinged door mounted with spherules, opening to gilt and white painted dial with inscription "L. Curtis, Patent," eglomise throat panel dec with standing female figure above spread wing American eagle, shield, and flag above tomb inscription "Washington, Lawrence, Ludlow, Durrows," gilt metal sidearms flanking, circular eglomise panel below dec with allegorical scene of female figure on boat with gentleman in background, giltwood acanthus form pendant below, slight repair to pendant, lower eglomise panel repainted **19,800.00**

Lantern, W. Tonnley, Bourton, English, c17th C, 16¼", brass short pendulum, name on dial **2,750.00**

Lyre

Ives, Joseph, c1840, 38¼", elaborately carved and gilted Lyre front, gilted dial with raised dec panel, entire clock is very ornate, brass 8 day time and strike movement, dial replaced, upper glass replaced, lower door hinge replaced **5,000.00**

Sawin, John, Boston, MA, 1830, 36½", carved mahogany case, brass bezel, painted iron dial inscribed "Sawin," eagle finial, painted tablet, 8 day weight driven time movement, replaced finial and plinth, refinished and reglued, some replacements **1,000.00**

Mirror

Dewey, I, Chesea, VT, c1830, 44¾", wood case, scroll crest, three urn finials, 8 day **2,500.00**

Ives, Joseph, 36½", wood case, pineapple finials, carved capitals with fluted columns, scenic panel below mirror, wood movement **1,500.00**

Unsigned, NH, 1820, 30", half round gilted and black painted columns, brass rosettes in corners, mirror in lowers section, primitive tablet of rose and trefoil leaf motif, 8 day time and strike brass weight driven movement, rat trap striking mechanism, orig dial, dovetailed case . **3,750.00**

Miscellaneous

Jerome, C., New Haven, CT, 1860, 21¾", rosewood veneered case, rippled molding, carved dec, brass pendulum, painted zinc dial, 8 day time fusee movement, blue paper maker's label, case needs regluing, veneer loss and damage, paint touch-up on dial **900.00**

New Haven Clock Co., New Haven, CT, 1875, 35¼", Winnipeg model, Victorian, walnut case, turned finials, 8 day time and strike movement, painted zinc dial, brass pendulum bob, orig maker's label on back of case, orig glass on door with painted dec **650.00**

Regulator

Ansonia Clock Co., CT, 1880, 49¼", walnut case, carved and reeded dec, porcelain dial with maker's trademark, brass pendulum and regulator gauge, 2-weight time movement, two period brass weights, replacements, refinished case **800.00**

French, 1860, 10½", crystal, painted case, elliptic front, 8 day time and strike movement, orig mercury filled pendulum **750.00**

Freres, Japy, Paris, early 20th C, 12⅛", gilt bronze, hour glass, bezel and pendulum set with pastes, colonnaded case **385.00**

Howard, E., #70, oak, 8 day, weight, time only **1,250.00**

New Haven, Prussian Oak, 51½", 90 day **600.00**

Terry, S. B., Plymouth, CT, 1835, 34½", mahogany case, turned wood bezel opens to painted wood dial, crotch mahogany panel lower door opens to paper label, 8 day weight driven time movement, round front plate, sgd label, replaced weight, replaced upper glass, minor veneer damage **3,500.00**

Seth Thomas, Regulator No 60, 58½", oak, weight, 8 day, Graham escapement **3,250.00**

Waterbury, Regulator B24, 83", 8 day, Swiss movement, weight **3,750.00**

Willard, Jr., A., Boston, MA, 1830, mahogany case with applied rippled moldings, turned laminated bezel, painted zinc dial, 8 day banjo type movement, orig lead weight, sq pendulum rod, replaced weight pan, minor touch-up on dial **1,400.00**

School House

Atkins Clock Co., Bristol, CT, 1855, 25"h, 17" w, rosewood veneer case, octagonal shape top, rippled molding around edge, lower door with black and gold glass, 30 day fusee

time and strike movement, orig label, missing ivory knob on lower door **2,000.00**

Gilbert, Wm. L., 26¾", Standard Admiral, oak case, 8 day strike **325.00**

Imperial, Regulator No 4T120E, 34½", electric, oak finish **425.00**

New Haven, 24", 12" Mosaic Drop, octagon top, 8 day **250.00**

Seth Thomas, Litchfield, 31", mahogany finish, 30 day, spring Graham dead beat escapement **525.00**

Waterbury, 27¾", English Drop No 2, calendar, veneered oak case **450.00**

Wag on Wall

Dutch, 19th C, oak case, removable hood, arched glazed door, painted iron dial, 30-hour movement, pendulum, three pressed brass paint dec finials, case needs regluing, window broken, missing pendulum, weights, hands, brass mount and side windows **750.00**

Terri, Eli, CT, c1790, 16 x 11", Federal, wooden works, tin weight, painted dial with ship and flower sprigs **675.00**

CLOISONNÉ

History: Cloisonné is the art of enameling on metal. The design is drawn on the metal body; wires, which follow the design, then are glued or soldered on the body. The cells thus created are packed with enamel and fired; this step is repeated several times until the level of enamel is higher than the wires. A buffing and polishing process brings the level of enamels flush to the surface of the wires.

This art form has been practiced in various countries since 1300 B.C. and in the Orient since the early 15th century. Most cloisonné found today is from the late Victorian era, 1870–1900, and was made in China and Japan.

Animal

Camel, 6½" l, 2 removable humps, rust, multicolored bird, swirls **300.00**

Crane, 7" h, light blue, multicolored design **125.00**

Foo Dog, 5" h, gold curls on head, back, and tail, dark blue, multicolored design **450.00**

Bowl

2½ x 8", yellow dragons, flaming pearl around rim and int. black ground, brass stand **125.00**

12" d, 3½" h, turned in rim, marine blue, variety of large lotus blossoms, clusters of small circle cloisonnes, cobalt border with silkworm cloisonnes, overlapping pomegranates on bottom, unmarked Chinese **400.00**

Box, 2½" h, 3¼" d, black, cloud cloisonnes, blue dec, dragon on lid ... **115.00**

Brush Pot, 5", asters and butterfly dec, light blue ground, sgd "Takeuchi," Japanese, c1875 .... **200.00**

Button, black and white flying birds, red ground, brass base **65.00**

Charger, 10¾", geometric border, red roses, pink daisies, blue flowers and butterflies, green leaves, turquoise ground **335.00**

Cigarette Case, green, three dragons, multicolored, Chinese **125.00**

Figure, 22¾", horse, enameled body, multicolored, turquoise ground, molded collar, gilt metal mane, removable saddle and blanket, standing on stylized wood base, pr **1,250.00**

Powder Jar, 3¾" d, yellow ground, $90.00.

Humidor, 5¾ x 8", cov, multicolored flowers, brick red ground, light blue border, double "T" fret cloissones, figural brass Foo dog finial, ornate teakwood base **225.00**

Incense Burner, multicolored floral dec, cobalt blue ground, three cobalt blue round feet, cut out butterflies on brass lid **225.00**

Jardiniere, 12½", turquoise, flowering branches, butterflies, birds, gilt rim, Chinese, early 19th C **250.00**

Libation Cup, 5½" l, figural ram's head, blue, multicolored swirl and dragon design **225.00**

Plate, 9¾", marine blue, 2 white cranes in scenic terrain, peonies, foliage, etc, unmarked, Japanese **300.00**

Potpourri Jar, cov, 4¼", 4⅛", panels around top, multicolored with flowers and butterflies, black, gold, and blue below with flowers, Japanese **265.00**

Sauceboat, green handle, turquoise artichoke dec, marked "China" **115.00**

Stamp Box, 4¼" l, green, multicolored flowering branch **25.00**

Sugar, 4½", handle, black, multicolored, yellow dragons **85.00**

Tea Jar, 4⅝", bulbous, Totai, cobalt, multicolored flowers, large reserves of flowers, butterfly and bird, sgd, c1870, 3 pcs **300.00**

Teapot, cov, 4½" h, 4½" w, tree bark ground, dragon, artist sgd, Japanese **365.00**

Temple Jar, cov, 13" h, 24" d, black ground, 2 yellow five-toed dragons fighting over flaming pearl, blue, red, white, and pink **400.00**

Tile, 5¾" h, 4¼" w, Totai, cobalt, multicolored, bird, flower, diapering, sgd Kinzozan, imp, c1870 .... **225.00**

Vase

3½", multicolored peacock, white foil ground, silver wire flowers at base, Japanese **650.00**

3¾", bulbous, goldstone, floral and scrolled leaf, reserves of butterflies, floral, Japanese, unmarked **110.00**

5", blue ground, Japanese lady among butterflies and leaves, Japanese, 19th C **475.00**

9¾", shield shape panels, exotic dragons, blue ground, green and goldstone dec, small butterflies around top, Japanese **400.00**

40½" h, cov, double gourd shape, aubergine, green, yellow, and white leafy vines with double gourds, white and aubergine flowers, redbrown ground, conforming cov, applied gilt bronze stalks, Chinese, 19th C, pr **8,800.00**

CLOTHING

History: While museums and a few private individuals have collected clothing for decades, it is only recently that collecting clothing has achieved a widespread popularity. Clothing reflects the social attitudes of an historical period.

Christening and wedding gowns abound and, hence are not in large demand. Among the hardest items to find are men's clothing from the 19th and early 20th centuries. The most sought after clothing is by designers, such as Fortuny, Poirret, and Vionnet.

Note: Condition, size' age, and completeness are critical factors in purchasing clothing. Collectors divide into two groups: those collecting for aesthetic and historic value and those desiring to wear the garment. Prices are higher on the west coast; major auction houses focus on designer clothes and high fashion items.

References: Maryanne Dolan, *Vintage Clothing 1880–1960*, Second Edition, Books Americana, 1987; Tina Irick-Nauer, *The First Price Guide to Antique and Vintage Clothes*, E.P. Dutton, 1983; Sheila Malouff, *Clothing With Prices*, Wallace-Homestead, 1983.

Periodical: *Vintage Clothing Newsletter*, P.O. Box 1422, Corvallis, OR 97339. Subscription: $12.00.

Collectors' Club: The Costume Society of America, P.O. Box 761, Englishtown, NJ 07726. Dues: $40.00.

Museums: Los Angeles County Museum (Costume and Textile Dept.), Los Angeles, CA; Metropolitan Museum of Art, New York, NY; Museum of Costume, Bath, England; Philadelphia Museum of Art, Philadelphia, PA; Smithsonian Institution (Inaugural Gown Collection), Washington, D.C.

Additional Listings: See *Warman's Americana & Collectibles* for more examples.

Bed Jacket, satin crepe, peach, three pearl buttons, 1940s, $25.00.

Blouse
   Battenberg lace, handmade, 1900 ..   **325.00**
   Cotton, batiste, white, lace and tuck insert in front and at top of sleeves, outlined in net ruffle, boned lace collar, snap-fasten back, 1870 ...   **60.00**
   Silk, brocade, embroidered, Chinese kimono style **100.00**
   Silk, taffeta, pale green, handmade bobbin lace trim, 1900 . . . .   **400.00**
Cape
   Brocade, black, 3″ jet beaded neck band, 2″ tassels at hem **75.00**
   Gauze, black, stenciled foliate scrolls, tied at shoulders, hem threaded with striped Venetian glass beads, Fortuny, 36″ l **400.00**
   Satin, evening, semi-circular, hip length, ivory, brocade poppies, pink

satin lining, ruffled pink and ivory silk organdy trim, ivory ostrich feather neck dec **200.00**
Silk, black, full length, hood and shawl lined in black velvet, c1880   **150.00**
Chemise, silk, cream, Valenciennes lace trim, garlands of flowers embroidered in French knots, V neck, pale yellow ribbon **275.00**
Christening Dress, cotton, white, eyelet inset and trim, 1920–30 . . . .   **40.00**
Coat
  Lady's
    Battenberg lace, black, midcalf length, neckline and back draped with black macrame silk cord trimmed with jet beads and sequins, 1890 . . . .   **400.00**
    Brocade, evening, bat-wing shape, gold leaf and flower design, collared V neck, appliqued scroll embroidered closures, c1915 ..   **200.00**
    Gabardine, lavender-gray, flaring form, panels of blue and gray silk, floral embroidery, gray rabbit fur collar **120.00**
    Irish linen, lavish embroidery, lace inserts on front, back, and on French cuffs, 1885 . . . .   **175.00**
    Leather, wrap style, lavender, long, tie belt, cuffed dolman sleeves, slash pockets, irid taffeta lining .   **125.00**
    Wool, green, full-length, black mouton trim, bustle, and leg-of-mutton sleeves, c1900 . . . .   **275.00**
Dress
  Day
    Cotton, plaid, portrait buttons of Jennie Lind, c1860 . . . .   **80.00**
    Cotton, turquoise, high neck, lace inserts, ruffled sleeves, 1895 ..   **200.00**
    Cotton, white and pink striped, carved jet buttons, black braid trim, handmade, 18601865 . . . .   **200.00**
    Rayon, pink, blue piping, padded shoulders, 1935–45 . . . .   **35.00**
    Silk, irid green, lace trim, handmade, 1890–1900 . . . .   **225.00**
  Evening
    Chiffon, brown and beige, velvet and rhinestone appliques, matching scarf, 1925–30 . . . . .   **85.00**
    Gabardine, royal blue, net and silk satin, self-colored piping, white lace, black velvet trim, 1890–1900 . . . .   **225.00**
    Lace, silk, 2 piece, nile green, long waisted, snug fitting bodice, layered rows of ruffled skirt, hip length jacket, 1928 . . . .   **50.00**
    Organdy, white, bias cut, layered

ruffled sleeves, high scoop neck, c1930 .... 50.00

Silk, chiffon, gray, multicolored floral, dropped waist, variegated ribbon belt, 8″ lace insert, cape collar, size 8-10, c1923 ...... 50.00

Silk, pleated, black, dolman sleeves, V neck, black, white, and blue Venetain glass beads, Fortuny, 57″ l 2,000.00

Taffeta, black, sequin flowers, label "Jeanne Lanvin, Paris Hiver," 1938–39 .... 325.00

Taffeta, blue, white lace sleeves, side zipper, 1936–40 .... 60.00

Jacket

Cotton, calico print, brown and white, pearl buttons, 1900 .... 40.00

Fur, brown fox, label "Henry Marshall, Brooklyn," 1940–50 .... 250.00

Silk, irid blue moire, full-length sleeves and cording, c1855 ..... 70.00

Wool, pinstripe, black and white, silk lined, 1910–20 .... 55.00

Robe

Gauze, black, gilt foliate scrolls and medallions, Fortuny, 44″ l 1,000.00

Silk, blue ground, eight couched gold dragons chasing flaming pearls, stylized clouds and bats, boashan haishui band at hem, Chinese, mid 19th C 1,700.00

Skirt

Cotton, cord, white, Victorian 40.00

Felt, gray, velvet embroidered border, c1880 .... 40.00

Satin, red, peasant-type, black velvet stripes, braiding, lace apron, 1906 100.00

Smoking Jacket, velvet, brown, silk quilted collar, cuffs, and pockets, silk lined, 1900–10 .... 75.00

Suit, lady's

Gabardine, red, padded shoulders, 1940 .... 50.00

Rayon, white and black print, padded shoulders, peplum, 1935 .... 65.00

Sweater

Cashmere, black, fox collar, 1960–70 80.00

Knit, cream, pastel floral embroidery and beads, 1960–65 .... 45.00

Orlon, white, rabbit collar, 1960–70 . 60.00

Tuxedo, wool, black, cutaway coat, pants button in front, 1900–10 .... 100.00

Wedding Gown

Lacy, white, hoop skirt, beaded crown veil, slip, 1942 .... 125.00

Chiffon, white, satin appliques, 1930–40 .... 85.00

Satin, ivory, heavily embroidered pastes, crystal beads in geometric pattern, petaled long embroidered

train, silver gilt edge slip, 36″ waist, c1920 .... 175.00

CLOTHING ACCESSORIES

References: Evelyn Haetig, *Antique Combs & Purses,* Gallery Graphics Press, 1983; Richard and Teresa Holiner, *Antique Purses,* Second Edition, Collector Books, 1987.

Additional Listings: See *Warman's Americana & Collectibles* for more examples.

Spats, brown felt, $20.00.

Apron, blue and white, 3 panels, white embroidery, 37″ l 45.00

Bonnet

Shaker, winter, faded black silk, embroidered floral design, blue polished linen lining 60.00

Sun, woven check material, green and white, machine sewn 45.00

Boots, lace up, beaver fur, black 30.00

Cigarette Case, metal, white, thumbpiece ornament of faux sapphires, set in gold, black suede handled folder, c1920 .... 650.00

Collar, Swiss muslin, lace insertion, lace fichu, c1871 .... 30.00

Comb

Celluloid, yellow, blue rhinestones, hand carved, c1900 .... 45.00

Tortoiseshell, 18K gold overlay, c1880 .... 125.00

Cummberbund, black and plaid satin, c1940 .... 10.00

Fan

Celluloid, white, airbrushed flowers, 1935–45 .... 20.00

Linen, white, hand painted pastel flowers, 1900 .... 45.00

Peacock feathers, hand-carved teakwood sticks, 1910 .... 75.00

Gloves
    Silk, black, shirred, c1940 . . . . **15.00**
    Wool, Art Deco style, c1920 . . . . . . **20.00**
Handbag
    Beaded
        Jeweled frame, multicolored scene
            of boy and girl at fountain, trees,
            7½" **175.00**
        Rhinestone ball closure, navy, irid,
            clutch style **50.00**
    Chiffon, white beads, embroidered
        flowers **30.00**
    Mesh
        Blue, diamond design, marked
            "Whiting & Davis," 7" l **75.00**
        Portrait of man, marked "Whiting &
            Davis," 6¼" l **250.00**
    Silk, sequins, beaded loop fringe . . . **20.00**
    Tapestry, scene of courting couple
        and sheep, jeweled frame, 8¼" l . **200.00**

**Hat, man's, straw, navy and red striped
band, size 7, Cosmopolitan label, 1911,
$35.00.**

Hat
    Felt, black, rhinestone clip in front,
        1938 . . . . **25.00**
    Fur, red, matching feathers worked
        into scroll design, 1933 . . . . **90.00**
    Straw, wide basketweave, grosgrain
        ribbon and buttons, 1936 . . . . **40.00**
Leggins, wool, black, knee length, 1900 **20.00**
Parasol, silk, black, 14K gold handle,
    mother-of-pearl inlay, 1880–1900 . . **90.00**
Shawl
    Paisley, woven, rect, shades of gray
        and black **125.00**
    Silk, orange, deep fringe, multico-
        lored embroidery, 1926 . . . . **125.00**
    Wool, black, hand embroidered, hand
        tied fringe, c1900 . . . . **85.00**
Shoes
    Lady's, leather, navy, mesh insert,
        1940 . . . . **45.00**
    Man's, canvas, white, button **25.00**

Sunglasses, plastic, black, red, and
    white striped, dark green lenses,
    stamped "Claire McCardell," c1950 . **145.00**

COALPORT

History: In the mid-1750s Ambrose Gallimore
established a pottery at Caughley in the Severn
Gorge, Shropshire, England. Several other potteries, e.g., Jackfield, developed in the area.

About 1795 John Rose and Edward Blakeway
built a pottery at Coalport, a new town founded
along the right-of-way of the Shropshire Canal.
Other potteries located adjacent to the canal were
those of Walter Bradley and Anstice, Horton, and
Rose. In 1799 Rose and Blakeway bought the
"Royal Salopian China Manufactory" at Caughley.
In 1814 this operation was moved to Coalport.

A bankruptcy in 1803 led to refinancing and a
new name, John Rose and Company. In 1814
Anstice, Horton, and Rose was acquired. The
South Wales potteries at Swansea and Nantgarw
were added. The expanded firm made fine quality,
highly decorated ware. The plant enjoyed a renaissance in the 1888 to 1900 period.

World War I, decline in trade, and shift of the
pottery industry away from the Severn Gorge
brought hard times to Coalport. In 1926 the firm,
now owned by Cauldon Potteries, moved from
Coalport to Shelton. Later owners included Crescent Potteries, Brain & Co., Ltd., and finally, in
1967, Wedgwood.

Reference: Susan and Al Bagdade, *Warman's
English & Continental Pottery & Porcelain, 1st Edition,* Warman Publishing Co., Inc., 1987.

Additional Listings: Indian Tree Pattern.

Basket, 11½" w, shaped rim, pink and
    gilt, floral bouquets, peach panels, gilt
    entwined strap handle, c1830 . . . . . **275.00**
Bough Pot, 11½" h, yellow ground, hp
    landscape scene with two British sol-
    diers, gilt floral dec, c1809 . . . . **350.00**
Compote, 12" d, round, pedestal on sq
    ft, red ground, gilt scroll molded rim,
    flower sprays within, gilt and foliage
    surrounds, c1830 . . . . **450.00**
Cooler, 10¾" h, cov, liner, blue and gilt
    all-over flowering chrysanthemums
    and foliage pattern, gilt finials and
    handles, c1800, pr **1,400.00**
Cup and Saucer, Harebell pattern **25.00**
Dessert Service, fourteen plates, two ftd
    dishes, botanical green pattern
    #5451, flower specimen on each, gilt

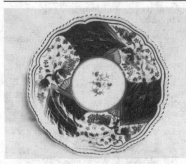

Plate, 10", crimped edge, shallow well, gold trim, Indian tobacco leaf design, unmarked, $150.00.

shaped rims with stylized flower head, c1840, 16 pcs	**1,250.00**
Dish, leaf shape, apple green, garden flower bouquet, gilt foliage, c1820 . .	**90.00**
Figure, Judith Anne, 7", plum dress, blue hat, muff, shawl, and necklace, 1920–45 mark	**75.00**
Ginger Jar, cov, Blue Willow pattern . .	**65.00**
Plate, 9", pink roses, green garlands, heavy gold, artist sgd, made for Davis Collamore, NY	**85.00**
Soup Plate, 10" d, gilt scalloped rim, burgundy band, flowering branch centering oval reserve	**20.00**
Spill Vase, 5", flared rim, sq base, pink, band of garden flowers, gilt scroll bands, bird's head handles with gilt rings, c1830, set of three	**875.00**
Tureen, 12½", cov, handles, iron red, yellow and gilt scattered flower sprays, gilt handles, flowerhead finial, c1850	**400.00**

COCA-COLA ITEMS

History: The originator of Coca-Cola was John Pemberton, a pharmacist from Atlanta, Georgia. In 1886 Dr. Pemberton introduced a patent medicine to relieve headaches, stomach disorders, and other minor maladies. Unfortunately, his failing health and meager finances forced him to sell his interest.

In 1888 Asa G. Candler became the sole owner of Coca-Cola. Candler improved the formula, increased the advertising budget, and widened the distribution. Accidentally, a "patient" was given a dose of the syrup mixed with carbonated water instead of still water. The result was a tastier, more refreshing drink.

As sales increased in the 1890s, Candler recognized that the product was more suitable for the soft drink market and began advertising it as such. From these beginnings a myriad of advertising items have been issued to invite all to "Drink Coca-Cola."

Dates of interest: "Coke" was first used in advertising in 1941. The distinctive shaped bottle was registered as a trademark on April 12, 1960.

References: Deborah Goldstein Hill, *Wallace-Homestead Price Guide to Coca-Cola Collectibles,* Wallace Homestead, 1983; Shelly and Helen Goldstein, *Coca-Cola Collectibles* (four volumes, plus index), published by author, 1970s; Allan Petretti and Cecil Munsey, *Official Coca-Cola Collectibles Price Guide,* Nostalgia Publishing Co., 1982; Al Wilson, *Collectors Guide To Coca-Cola Items, Volume I,* (revised: 1987) and *Volume II,* (1987), L-W Book Sales.

Collectors' Club: The Cola Clan, 2084 Continental Drive N.E., Atlanta, GA 30345. Dues: $15.00.

Additional Listings: See *Warman's Americana & Collectibles* for more examples.

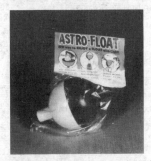

Astro-Float, plastic, red and white, orig packaging, $7.50.

Ashtray, red, silver letters, 1963	**5.00**
Bandana, 21 x 23", premium, Bill Williams-Kit Carson TV show	**25.00**
Bank, 5½", metal, figural vending machine, red paint	**70.00**
Bingo Game, 7 x 14" box, red and white, c1940	**25.00**
Bookmark, Lillian Russell, 1904	**70.00**
Bottle Carrier, 6 unused bottles, removable lucite protector, 1929	**110.00**
Bottle Opener, sword shape, emb "Drink Bottled Coca-Cola"	**18.00**
Calendar	
1913, 13½ x 22½", Hamilton King illus	**850.00**
1921, 12 x 31", "Girl in Garden" . . .	**250.00**
1933, 12 x 30", "The Village Blacksmith"	**175.00**

Cigarette Box, glass, frosted, 50th Anniversary, 1936 .... **210.00**
Clock, 16 x 16", wood frame, sq, 1939 **90.00**
Coupon, cardboard, black and white, 1900 .... **120.00**
Doll, Santa Claus, 15", vinyl, 1958 ... **40.00**
Door Handle, 8" l, plastic, 3 dimensional **28.00**
Fan, cardboard, wood handle, "Save With Ice," 1915 .... **65.00**
Glass, 6 oz, acid etched, 1935 ...... **15.00**
Hat, Soda Jerk, cloth, c1920 .... **10.00**
Ink Blotter, 4 x 9", cardboard, red and white, c1930 .... **12.00**
Jump Rope, 4" wood handles, inscribed "Drink Coca-Cola in Bottles, Pure as Sunlight," c1930 .... **20.00**
Knife, pocket, Chicago World's Fair, 1933 .... **30.00**
Lapel Pin, 5 year service, 10K gold .. **60.00**
Menu Board, wood and masonite, 1939 **90.00**
Mirror, 1¾ x 2¾", celluloid, aqua blue ground, black letters, red "Icy-O" logo, black soda dispenser, red and white Coca-Cola bottle, made by Parisian Novelty, Chicago **500.00**
Notebook, 3 ring, Sales Management Conference, 1958 .... **15.00**
Pillow, figural Coke bottle, c1940 .... **15.00**
Pocket Mirror, oval, Elaine, 1916 .... **100.00**
Postcard, Bottling Plant, 1910 ...... **40.00**
Pretzel Dish, 8" d, aluminum, three aluminum 4" h Coke bottles around sides, 50th Anniversary, Brunhoff Mfg Co, 1936 .... **75.00**
Radio
  8", bottle shaped, plastic case, made in Hong Kong **30.00**
  Ice Chest Shape **140.00**
Record, Bill Cosby Show, 45 RPM ... **20.00**
Ruler, wood, "Compliments The Coca-

Tray, 1934, 13 x 10", Johnny Weissmuller and Maureen O'Sullivan, $325.00.

Cola Bottling Company," reverse side "The Golden Rule," 1940 .... **5.00**
Sign
  Bottle, 35", figural, tin, 1923 ...... **85.00**
  Cheerleader, 15 x 27", cardboard frame, 1944 .... **80.00**
  Triangle, advertisement on 2 sides, porcelain, 1935 .... **300.00**
Thermometer, 30", tin, bottle shape, 1958 .... **30.00**
Tie Clip, metal, enamel, "All Star Dealer Campaign Award," 1950s **30.00**
Thimble, aluminum, "Drink Coca-Cola in Bottles" **25.00**
Tray
  1907, Relieves Fatigue, change ... **325.00**
  1912, Delicious & Refreshing, oval, change **120.00**
  1914, Betty, 10½ x 13¼" **350.00**
  1921, Autumn Girl, 10½ x 13¼" ... **425.00**
  1934, Johnny Weissmuller and Maureen O'Sullivan **325.00**
  1939, Spring Board Girl, Sunblom, artist, 14 x 10" **50.00**
  1958, picnic cart, 13½ x 19" **15.00**
Wallet, leather, bottle emb on cov **25.00**
Watch Fob, Coca-Cola, two bulldogs, adv on back, lead **80.00**

COFFEE MILLS

History: Coffee mills or grinders are utilitarian objects designed to grind fresh coffee beans. Before the advent of stay-fresh packaging, coffee mills were a necessity.

The first home size coffee grinders were introduced about 1890 The large commercial grinders designed for use in stores, restaurants, and hotels often bear an earlier patent date.

Reference: Terry Friend, *Coffee Mills,* Collector Books, 1982.

COUNTERTOP (COMMERCIAL)

Enterprise No 7, cast iron, 2 wheel, Pat 1873, 17" d wheels **550.00**
Landers, Frary, Clark, New Britain, CT, 1901, 12" h **450.00**
Woodruff and Edwards Co, cast iron, adv, "Elgin National Coffee," 14⅞" wheel, 24" h **325.00**

FLOOR MODELS (COMMERCIAL)

Crescent, Rutland, VT, 2 wheel, cast iron, 60" **1,200.00**
Star Mill, cast iron, 2 wheel, ornamental base, painted rim, gilt trim, cast inscription on each wheel, "Star Mill, Philadelphia, stenciled Henry Troem-

Landers, Frary and Clark, New Britain, CT, No. 2, 12″ h, 6½″ sq base, two wheels, cast iron, $450.00.

ner, Maker, Philadelphia," c1885,
61″ h **900.00**

LAP (DOMESTIC)

Arcade, oak base, dovetailed drawer, cast iron hopper and handle, emb imperial **75.00**
Delmew, Simons Hardware, St. Louis . **75.00**
Kendrick, cast iron, brass name plate, porcelain lined cup, iron drawer ... **75.00**
Universal 109, tin, Pat Feb 14, 1905, Landers, Frary, Clark **50.00**

TABLE (DOMESTIC)

Challenge Fast Grinder, wooden base, drawer, cast iron hopper, crank, and handle, wooden knob, 6½ x 6½ x 7½″ **80.00**
Grand Union Tea Co, cast iron **175.00**
Hobart, aluminum hopper, electric ... **150.00**
L F & Co, New Britain, CT **200.00**
Wrights Hardware Co, black and gold decal "Brighton Coffee Mill; Manufactured by Wrights Hardware Company," base and top 6½ x 6½″, box 5¾ x 5¾ x 5½″, grinding mechanism by Logan & Strobridge **60.00**

WALL (DOMESTIC)

Aroma, #9, tin and cast iron, red and black **75.00**
Golden Rule Coffee the Finest Blend in the World, cast iron, wood and tin, 17″ h **175.00**
Grand Union Tea, red tin, adv, gold trim, cast iron grinder **90.00**
Mystic, tin "V" shaped hopper, cast iron grinder **25.00**

National Specialty Co, Philadelphia, cast iron, orig red scroll, gilt dec ... **85.00**
Telephone Mill, Arcade Mfg Co, cast iron and wood, Pat 1893, 13″ h **300.00**

COIN OPERATED ITEMS

History: Coin operated items include amusement games, pinball, jukeboxes, slot machines, vending machines, cash registers and other items operated by coins.

The first jukebox was developed about 1934 and played 78 RPM records. Jukeboxes were important parts of teenage life before the advent of portable radios and television.

The first pinball machine was introduced in 1931 by Gottlieb. Pinball machines continued to be popular until the advent of solid state games in 1977 and advanced electronic video games.

The first three-reel slot machine, the Liberty Bell, was invented in 1905 by Charles Fey in San Francisco. In 1910, Mills Novelty Company copyrighted the classic fruit symbols. Improvements and advancements have lead to the sophisticated machines of today.

Vending machines for candy, gum, and peanuts, were popular from 1910 until 1940 and can be found in a wide range of sizes and shapes.

Because of the heavy usage these coin operated items received, many are restored and at the very least have been repainted by either the operator or manufacturer. Using reproduced mechanisms to restore pieces is acceptable in many cases, especially when the restoration will be able to perform as originally intended.

References: Jerry Ayliffe, *American Premium Guide To Coin Operated Machines,* Books Americana, 1981; Rick Botts, *1983 Jukebox Collectors Directory,* published by author, 1983; Richard Bueschel, *An Illustrated Guide To 100 Collectible Pinballs,* Coin Slot Books, 2 volumes, 1983 and 1984; Roger Pribbenow, *Gumball Guide,* published by author; Richard D. and Barbara Reddock, *Price Guide To Antique Slot Machines,* Wallace-Homestead, 1981.

Periodicals: *Gumball Gazette,* P. O. Box 272, Sun Prairie, WI 53590. Subscription: $21.00; *Jukebox Collector Newsletter,* 2545 SE 60th Street, Des Moines, IA 50317. Subscription: $20.00.

Additional Listings: See *Warman's Americana & Collectibles* for separate categories for Jukeboxes, Pinball Machines, Slot Machines, and Vending Machines.

GAME

Baffel Ball, Gottlieb, countertop, pinball, c1931 .... **600.00**
Bally Hoo, amusement, tilted wood case, glass top, plunger at front, 31″ l **75.00**

Foxhunt, pinball, 5¢, 65 x 21 x 51", Pat 1936, orig instruction card, 1940 . . . **175.00**
Kiss-o-Meter, 5¢, Exhibit Supply Co, c1930 . . . . **450.00**
Play Football, arcade, Chester Pollard Amusement Co, c1924 . . . . **800.00**
Select-Em, dice game, Exhibit Supply Co, Chicago **275.00**
Uncle Sam Grip Test, Caille, 1¢, 1910, restored **3,200.00**
Wow Mills, 5¢, pinball, table top, 32 x 18", 1932 . . . . **150.00**

JUKEBOX

Seeburg
Model P148, light up side columns, top changes colors with revolving lights, blue glass mirrored tile front, 5 plays for a quarter, 1948 . . . . . **1,450.00**
Symphonola Regal, veneered wood case framed by orange plastic panels, 20 selections, 55", c1940 . **1,200.00**
Wurlitzer
Model 81, countertop, walnut case, yellow and red marbleized plastic panels containing 12 selectors, 78 RPM mechanism, 23", c1940, restored **2,800.00**
Model 1015, bubble tubes framing glazed front, veneered wood case, 50" h, c1947 . . . . **2,700.00**
Model 1650, 48 selections, 55" h, light up side columns, 1954 . . . . **500.00**

SLOT MACHINE

Groetchen's, Columbia, countertop, 10¢ **1,000.00**
Indian, life size, carved wood with headdress, holding Bursting Cherry slot machine, 3 reels, restored **2,500.00**
Jennings, Silver Moon, 5, countertop, 1941, restored **1,200.00**
Jubilee, 1, 3 reels, blue, wood sides, diamond dec on right side **500.00**
Mills
Horsehead Bonus, 5¢, countertop, 3 reels, black and yellow paint, 1937, restored **1,450.00**
The Owl, 5¢, one wheel upright, oak cabinet carved with owl and foliage below color wheel, 5 way cast metal coin head, 64", c1905, restored **7,000.00**
War Eagle, 5¢, 3 reel, double jackpot, unrestored, c 1931 . . . . **1,800.00**
Pace, Comet Deluxe, 3 reel, twin jackpots, restored, c1939 . . . . **1,500.00**
Wattling, Blue Seal, 5¢, 3 reel, double jackpots, 24", c1932, restored **1,500.00**

Vending Machine, Ajax 5¢ Nut, three units, aluminum, Newark, NJ, $120.00.

VENDING

Ace, 1¢, peanuts, aluminum, 8 sided base, c1930 . . . . **125.00**
Adams, 1¢, gum, 10 x 4 x 22½", Art Deco lady on label **100.00**
Columbus, 1¢, Gumball Machine, 15" h, 8" d, cast iron, porcelain paint, light and dark green, orig key **300.00**
Hawkeye, 1¢, gum, cast metal, 6 sided, red paint, c1931 . . . . **120.00**
Lucky Strike Cigarettes, 1¢, Wilson Mfg **800.00**
Mansfield, 5¢, gum, 12" h, 10½" sq, etched glass front, glass sides **400.00**
Master, 1¢, peanuts, 16" h, 8" sq, cast metal, red and black paint, complete with orig keys, c1930s **120.00**
Nut Jewel, 5¢, 2 columns, peanuts, Lawrence Mfg Co **100.00**
Pulver Yellow Kid, 1¢, gum, clockwork movement of Yellow Kid with insertion of penny **550.00**
Stuart & Maguire, 1¢, Art Deco style, restored **175.00**
Yu Chu Co, gumball, 45" h, glass globe, cast iron pedestal, base marked "Reliable Peanut Co, New York" **85.00**

MISCELLANEOUS

Black Jack, 5¢, trade simulator type . . **325.00**
Cash Register
McCaskey, 23 x 23 x 27", oak, orig decal of manufacturer, metal account files, 2 drawers below, refinished **150.00**
National, brass
Model 421, keys up to $9.99, receipt machine at side, crank operated, oak cash drawer, 23" h . **650.00**

Model 542, keys up to $99.99, receipt machine at side, running totals at other side, crank operated, brass cash drawer, 24" h . **600.00**

Fare Box, Jonson, hand crank, patent 1914, restored **225.00**

Hotel Radio, "25 for 2 hours," 14 x 8 x 7½", gray metal case, Corado, c1940 **65.00**

Piano, Seeburg style A, mandolin attachment, oak case with art glass panel **6,750.00**

Stamp, Shermach, Detroit, 13 x 10 x 5", glass sides, 2¢ stamp on left, 4¢ stamp on right, 2 cranks in front . . . **175.00**

CONTINENTAL CHINA AND PORCELAIN (GENERAL)

History: By 1700 porcelain factories existed in large numbers throughout Europe. In the mid-18th century the German factories at Meissen and Nymphenburg were dominant. As the century ended, French potteries assumed the leadership role. The "golden age" of Continental china and porcelains was from the 1740s to the 1840s.

Americans living in the last half of the 19th century eagerly sought the masterpieces of the European porcelain factories. In the early 20th century this style of china and porcelain was a "blue chip" among the antiques collectors.

References: Susan and Al Bagdade, *Warman's English & Continental Pottery & Porcelain, 1st Edition,* Warman Publishing Co, Inc, 1987.

Additional Listings: France—Haviland, Limoges, Old Paris, Sarreguemines, and Sevres; German—Austrian Ware, Bavarian China, Carlsbad China, Dresden/Meissen, Rosenthal, Royal Bayreuth, Royal Bonn, Royal Rudolstadt, Royal Vienna, Schlegelmilch, and Villeroy and Boch; Italy—Capo-di-Monte.

FRENCH

Chantilly
Cuspidor, 5¼", kakiemon palette, c1735 . . . . **665.00**
Dish, 8½", kakiemon palette, c1735 . **400.00**
Snuffbox, 3¼", heart shape, butterfly on lid, modern gold mounts **250.00**
Teabowl and Saucer, kakiemon palette, c1735 . . . . **250.00**

Faience
Box, cov, 7½" d, cabbage form, natural colors, purple flower handle, late 19th C **75.00**
Figure, 21", bisque, nymph, standing, polychrome, curled pale brown hair, wreath of fruiting sprigs, blue sash, floral print drape, tree trunk, mound base, c1900, imp factory mark . . . **1,000.00**
Jardiniere, 22½" d, scalloped rim,

painted chrysanthemums, yellow, green, and blue **470.00**

Jacob Petit
Clock Case, 15¾", portrait of French courtesan, sgd, c1840, chips **1,000.00**
Cornucopia, 12⅜" h, tapering octagonal body, green, white, and maroon panels, floral sprigs, gilt foliate scrolls, petal molded rim, gilt bronze ram's head terminal, rect white marble plinth, foliate and shell cast gilt bronze feet, mid 19th C, pr **1,200.00**
Vase, 17¾" h, floral encrusted, baluster form, perched birds and leafy branches, white flowers with blue edges, domed cover with large floral spray, gilt circular foot, late 19th C, underglaze blue mark "JP," pseudo blue crossed swords mark, pr **2,500.00**

Mennency
Figure
6¾", group, white, two musicians, mid 18th C **625.00**
9", seated lady, polychrome and gilt dec, c1755, minor damage **3,300.00**
Gravy Boat, 9", 18th C, marked "DVA" **950.00**

St. Cloud
Bonbonniere and cov, cat form, SS mountings, late 19th C **225.00**
Cup and Saucer, trembleuse, c1750, pr **600.00**
Toilet Pot, cov, 4½", SS mountings, c1740 . . . . **1,200.00**

Samson
Jar, cov
12¼" h, Chinese Export armorial porcelain, fitted as lamps, pr . . **1,000.00**
19", globular body, cap form lid, famille verte dec Chinese Export porcelain, brilliant green, pale yellow, iron red, and blue enamel, scrolling gilt bronze mounts with leaves and flower head ornament, late 19th C, pr . **6,500.00**
Jardiniere, bisque, tapering cylindrical body, relief molded continuous frieze of dancing putti holding floral garland, white foliate scroll border on blue ground, gilt ram's heads, late 19th C, pseudo interlaced L's enclosing AA mark, pr **6,000.00**
Milk Pail, 16 x 15¼", sides molded with vertical slats, gilt outlines, rope molded bands, and ram's head handle, late 19th C, pseudo interlaced L's enclosing AA mark **2,000.00**
Plate, 9", octagonal, Chinese Export porcelain, armorial center, floral dec cavetto, gilded rim, late 19th C, set of 8 . . . . **1,700.00**

Sauce Tureen, cov, 8½″, Chinese Export armorial porcelain **1,600.00**

Vieux Paris

Clock, 13″ h vase form, yellow ground, minor chips, c1820 ..... **950.00**

Tea and Coffee Service, polychrome and gilt landscape dec, c1820, 21 pcs **600.00**

Tray, 13½″, sq, mythological dec, c1800, iron red factory mark, Duc d'Angouleme factory **450.00**

Vase, 14¾″, lavender ground, floral medallion, handles, sq marble plinth base, mounted as lamp, c1815, pr **3,125.00**

Frankenthal, teapot, 6¼″ h, multicolored harbor scene, dark brown surround, powdered lilac ground, c1770, blue crowned "CT" mark, $4,265.00.

GERMAN

Ansbach

Cup and Saucer, painted interlaced floral "MGT," floral garland, entwined handles, c1765, blue "A" mark **440.00**

Soup Plate, 10″, "Berliner Mustger" green ground border, c1770, underglaze mark "A" **1,175.00**

Frankenthal

Figure

4″, girl holding doll in swaddling clothes, c1756, blue rampant lion mark, monogrammed "PH" (Paul Hannong,) slight chips **1,220.00**

5¼″, harvester, modeled by J W Lanz, c1762, crown and "CT," incised "M" mark, minor damage **1,275.00**

Tea Service, teapot, milk jug, four teacups and saucers, polychrome dec of two lovers, rococo garden

ornament, floral sprays, c1762–95, underglaze blue crowned monogram, modeler's, gilder's, and artist's marks **3,200.00**

Furstenberg

Figure, 6″, woman, modeled by J Ch Rombrich, c1774, underglaze blue "F", restoration to right arm **1,000.00**

Plate, 9½″ d, painted by C G Albert, c1770, underglaze blue script "F" mark, pr **1,200.00**

Tea and Coffee Service, molded figures dec, c1800, underglaze blue "F" mark, 8 pcs **725.00**

Tea Cup and Saucer, purple dec, c1765, underglaze blue "F" mark . **500.00**

Hochst

Breakfast Service, teapot, creamer, sugar, cup and saucer, tray, gilt and enamel dec, c1765–74, wheel marks and underglaze blue crown **8,000.00**

Figure

3½″, The Bowing Chinaman, modeled by the "Master of the Turkish Emperors," c1750, imp "I" and "IH", painter's monogram for Adam Ludwig, minor restoration **1,325.00**

11″, group of lowers, rococo arbor entwined with grapes, c1765, underglaze wheel mark, incised triangle, minor restoration **9,250.00**

Tea Cup and Saucer, fruit dec, c1765–70 .... **200.00**

Hutschenreuther

Portrait Plate, 9⅝″ d, c1900, imp factory mark, blue "lamb Dresden 135.K," black title

Lady Anna Bingham, white brimmed hat, curled brown hair, blue eyes, buttoned white dress and shawl, blue sky ground, green scrolled border, gilt floral sprays, scrolls and flower filled urns **700.00**

Princess de Lamballe, yellow roses and pink ribbons in hair, white ruffled dress, gray ground, artist sgd "Vorberger" **800.00**

Queen Louise, curled blond hair, gilt tiara, white scarf, pearl necklace, maroon dress, white sleeves, pale blue ground, green scrolled border with gilt scrolls, floral sprays and flower filled urns, artist sgd "Vorberger" ... **825.00**

Kloster Veilsdorf

Coffee Service, iron-red travelers in landscapes, c1770, underglaze mark "CV", painter's mark, 17 pcs **3,700.00**

Plate, 10″, painted bouquets, foliage garland borders, puce ribbons, c1775, blue interlaced "CV" mark **265.00**

Ludwigsburg
 Coffee Cup, putto dec, c1770, underglaze blue crowned interlaced C's   **125.00**
 Figure
  4¼", sportsman, repaired, c1770 .   **430.00**
  5", peasant, modeled by Pierre
   Francois Lejeune, painted by D
   Chr Sausenhofer, c1768, underglaze blue interlaced C's be-
   neath crown mark, restored . . . **1,550.00**
 Teapot, cov, 3½", painted green,
  brown, blue, and iron-red, c1765,
  underglaze blue crowned inter-
  laced C's **1,100.00**
Nymphenburg
 Cup and Saucer, painted large bouquet and scattered sprays, brown
  rims, c1765, imp shield mark **200.00**
 Soup Plate, 9⅞" d, green and purple
  landscape, c1760, imp shield mark   **750.00**
Saxony
 Vase, cov, 21½", polychrome floral
  dec, applied flowers, and putti, gilt
  dec, massive floral finial, 19th C,
  blue mark, slight damage, pr **1,250.00**
Scnheeballen
 Vase, cov, 21¾", polychrome floral
  dec, applied flowers and foliate,
  domed cov, minor losses and repairs, underglaze blue pseudo
  crossed swords and stars marks, pr **2,000.00**
Unknown Manufacturer
 Bust, 31" h, maiden, bisque, diaphanous pale blue gown, wavy blond
  hair, blue eyes, yellow flowerhead
  base, waisted socle, fluted colum-
  nar base, late 19th C **950.00**
 Plaque, 4 x 5¼", oval, portrait of
  cupid, tousled brown hair, blue
  eyes, pale blue clouds, gilt foliate
  frame, c1900, imp "12" **275.00**
 Torcheres, figural, polychrome and
  parcel gilt dec, standing bacchant
  holding cornucopia, playful putto
  dancing, rockwork base, Baroque,
  southern, late 17th or early 18th C,
  pr **25,000.00**
Wallendorf
 Figure, 13", Adam and Eve, white,
  holding forbidden fruit, standing before tree stump, molded base,
  c1775, blue "W" mark, pr **525.00**
 Tea and Coffee Service, cornucopia
  dec, c1780, underglaze slate blue
  "W" mark, 27 pcs **2,000.00**

ITALIAN

Naples
 Vase, 13½", portraits of Francis I of
  Bourbon and his consort, rubbed

 gilding, sgd "Raffaele Giovine,
  1823," pr **6,000.00**
Unknown Manufacturer, figures, pr, 16¼
 and 17", masked ball attendants,
 maiden with black tricorn, gilt rim,
 white mask to side, black lace shawl,
 purple cape, gilt floral brocade trim,
 floral sprig dec yellow overdress, lace
 trim, open fan in crossed hands, gentleman resting against Louis XV
 chaise, black tricorn, black lace
 shawl, red cape, green coat with gilt
 foliate dec, brown breeches, white
 stockings, black shoes, putto beneath
 chair, scrolled molded base, imp "D,
 Fabris," late 19th C, gold anchor mark **1,325.00**

COPELAND AND SPODE

History: In 1749 Josiah Spode apprenticed to
Thomas Whieldon and in 1754 worked for William
Banks in Stoke-on-Trent. In the early 1760s Spode
started his own pottery, making cream colored earthenware and blue printed whiteware. In 1770 he
returned to Banks' factory as master, purchasing
it in 1776.

Spode pioneered the use of steam powered pottery making machinery and mastered the art of
transfer printing from copper plates. Spode
opened a London shop in 1778 and sent William
Copeland there about 1784. A number of larger
London locations followed. At the turn of the century Spode introduced bone china. In 1805 Josiah
Spode II and William Copeland entered into partnership for the London business. A series of partnerships between Josiah Spode II, Josiah Spode
III, and William Taylor Copeland resulted.

In 1833 Copeland acquired Spode's London operations and the Stoke plants seven years later.
William Taylor Copeland managed the business
until his death in 1868. The business remained in
the hands of Copeland heirs. In 1923 the plant
was electrified; other modernizations followed.

In 1976 Spode merged with Worcester Royal
Porcelain to become Royal Worcester Spode, Ltd.

References: Susan and Al Bagdade, *Warman's
English & Continental Pottery & Porcelain, 1st Edi-
tion,* Warman Publishing, 1987; D. Drakard & P.
Holdway, *Spode Printed Wares,* Longmans, 1983;

L. Whiter, *Spode: A History Of The Family, Factory, And Wares, 1733–1833*, Barrie & Jenkins, 1970.

Basket, 4⅞″, round, pierced cov, overhead loop handle, gilt ground, multicolored scrolling garden flowers, Spode, 1815 .... 425.00

Bowl, 10″, Copeland's Ruins, flow blue .. 45.00

Butter Dish, cov, Spode's Tower, blue, Copeland Spode 60.00

Butter Pat, hunt scene, blue transfer .. 20.00

Compote, 8½″ d, Indian Tree, orange and brown lustre, Copeland mark .. 40.00

Creamer, 4″, Spode's Tower, blue transfer 48.00

Cup and Saucer, Chelsea Garden ... 45.00

Dessert Set, botanical, yellow ground, painted and printed with flowers specimen, name on reverse, puce Spode and Pat #1569, c1795 .... 3,000.00

Dinner Set
Felspar, royal blue border outlined with gilt, puce printed Spode Felspar marks, iron-red Pat #3951, c1810, 95 pcs 1,600.00
Indian Tree, service for eight, 51 pcs, cov butter dish, vegetable bowl, 12″ pedestal cake plate, Spode 375.00

Dish, 11½″ w, 2 handled, mushroom ground, gilt foliage, gilt scroll molded handles, puce Spode Felspar mark, c1800 .... 125.00

Figure, Spaniel, 7¾″ l, recumbent on green cushion with gilt tassels, molded, brown and white hair markings, Copeland, green mark, c1833–47 .... 1,000.00

Fruit Cooler, 9¼ x 7¾″, handles, three pcs, underglaze blue, hp, florals, leaves, gilt highlights, heart shape knops, c1820, pr 1,250.00

Jar, cov, 10″, globular, handled, Oriental style, apple green, birds on flowering peony branches, iron-red, pink, and gilt, gilt knob finial, Spode mark, Pat #3086, c1820 .... 700.00

Jardiniere and Stand, 10½″ d, flared, 3 paw feet, iron-red and seeded gilt ground, panels of trailing flowers, rim with gilt foliage on orange ground, gilt mast handles, Spode, c1800 ...... 1,000.00

Jug, 6½″ dia, 8¼″ h, bright blue ground, raised ivory figures on front and back, raised leaf trim around top, Copeland, made for Columbian Expo, 1893 ... 200.00

Pitcher, 6¼″, pear shape, gilt ground, scrolling garden flowers, Spode, c1810 .... 325.00

Plaque, 5″ w, turquoise, printed multicolored sporting trophy, gilt scroll and foliage surround, green Copeland mark, late 19th C 30.00

Plate, 10¼″ d, Marathon, white center, cream border, blue floral dec, gold trim, $25.00.

Plate
6″, bird among flowers and foliage, heavy gold trim, Spode 100.00
8¾″, creamware, pink shell motif, gilt flowering foliage, brown net pattern ground, gilt rim, imp Spode mark, c1820 .... 80.00
9½″, bird perched on snowy branch, holly leaves and berries 100.00
10″, Egyptian tombs center, elephant and wild animal border, light blue transfer, Spode, pr 130.00

Platter
9½″, oval, birds on gnarled tree trunk issuing oriental flowers, peonies, chrysanthemums, and foliage border, imp Copeland Spode oval mark, pat #4639, 19th C 100.00
10½″ l, oval, creamware, pierced rim, Spode, mkd, c1820 .... 75.00

Potpourri Jar, 10″, pierced cov, flared rim and foot, Imari style, flowering plants, gilt knop finial, Spode mark, Pat #967, c1810 .... 600.00

Soup Plate, black transfer printed, multicolored insert and flowering plants, scrolling floral foliage borders, Spode mark, pattern #2148, c1810, set of 12 .... 450.00

Spill Vase, 4¾″, flared rims, pale lilac, gilt octagonal panels with portrait of bearded man, band of pearls on rims and bases, Spode, c1820, pr 400.00

Tray, 11½″, sq, rose spray center, floral bouquet in corners, blue ground with

gilt scale pattern, Pat #1163, iron-red
Spode, c1800 . . . .   350.00
Tureen, 17", cov, stand, stoneware, Japan pattern, iron-red, cobalt blue, and
gilt stylized flower filled urns and
scrolling foliage and blossoms, twig
shaped handles, leaf terminals,
c1820 . . . .   1,150.00
Waste Bowl, orange, reserved flower-
heads and gilt foliage, Spode mark,
Pat #8079, c1810 . . . .   90.00

COPPER

History: Copper objects, such as kettles, tea
kettles, warming pans, measures, etc., played an
important part in the 19th century household. Outdoors, the apple butter kettle and still were the two
principal copper items. Copper culinary objects
were lined with a thin protective coating of tin to
prevent poisoning. They were relined as needed.

Great emphasis is placed by collectors on
signed pieces, especially those by American
craftsmen. Since copper objects were made
abroad as well, it is hard to identify unsigned examples. Many modern reproductions also exist.

References: Mary Frank Gaston, *Antique Cop-
per*, Collector Books, 1985; Henry J. Kauffman,
Early American Copper, Tin, and Brass, Medill
McBride Co., 1950.

Additional Listings: Arts and Crafts Movement
and Roycroft.

Sauce Pan, iron handle, $75.00.

Baking Pan, 22 x 14½", dovetailed,
wrought iron handles each end 50.00
Basin, 14½" d, 4" h, marked "C.M.M. &
Sons 1924 . . . .   40.00
Bed Warmer, 41", polished, floral en-
graved cov, turned wooden handle .   250.00
Candle Snuffer, polished, wrought iron
handle 100.00
Candlesticks, 6", circular, capstan
bases, spiral twist stems, pr 35.00
Candy Kettle, 12" d, 6" h, loop handles   70.00
Cauldron, 18½" d, tapering cylindrical

body, wrought iron bail handle and 3
legs with disc feet, early 19th C . . .   250.00
Chafing Dish, 2 qt, copper pan, brass
holder, wooden handle, c1900 . . . .   125.00
Coffeepot, 10", lacquered 75.00
Colander, 13" d, hand wrought, brass
loop handle 75.00
Compote, pierced open-work dec 80.00
Cookie Board, 4½ x 7½", each of 12
emb squares shows a different oc-
cupation, wooden back 275.00
Cuspidor, 10½" w, 4" h 140.00
Figure, classical maiden, 16", flowing
robes, cape over shoulders, standing
by tree stump, gilded shaped onyx
base, c1850 . . . .   300.00
Funnel, 3½", brass handle 35.00
Haystack Measure, 8¼", dovetailed
construction, marked "2-Imperial,"
emb seal 135.00
Hot Water Bottle, 11", oval 65.00
Jardiniere, large, dovetail construction,
hammered 150.00
Megaphone, 36", nautical 100.00
Milk Pail, 6¼" h, wire bail handle 90.00
Pitcher, 8" d, 5" h, wide open mouth . .   32.50
Punch Bowl, 9¾" d, 7¾" h, pedestal
base, hammered, emb lion's head
handles, rim has 4 English copper
"1806" pennies with bust of George
III 200.00
Roaster, 5 x 10¼" x 14", open 100.00
Sap Bucket, wrought iron handles . . .   225.00
Sauce Pan, 8½", dovetailed with cast
iron handle 75.00
Sausage Stuffer 45.00
Shot Flask, 6½" l, emb cannon, eagle,
flags, brass fittings 100.00
Skillet, 8" d, cast iron handle 55.00
Taster Spoon, 9¼", wrought iron handle   125.00
Tea Kettle, 13" h, cylindrical, serpentine
spout, tubular handle, stepped dome
cov with acorn finial, c1910 . . . . . .   250.00
Teapot, brass handle, marked "MK
Majestic" in large letters 200.00
Wash Boiler, tin lid, wooden side han-
dles 65.00

CORALENE

History: Coralene is a glass or china object
which has the design painted on the surface of the
piece and tiny glass colorless beads applied with
a fixative. The piece is placed in a muffle which
fixes the enamel and sets the beads.

Several American and English companies made
glass coralene in the 1880s. Seaweed or coral was
the most common design. Other motifs were
"Wheat Sheaf" and "Fleur-de-Lis." Most of the
base glass was satin finished.

China and pottery coralene, made from the late 1890s to the post WW II era, is referred to as Japanese coralene. The beading is opaque and inserted into the soft clay. Hence, it is only half to three-quarters visible.

Reproduction Alert: Reproductions are on the market, some using an old glass base. The beaded decoration on new coralene has been glued and can be scraped off.

CHINA

Biscuit Jar, 6", matte finish, blue beading, gold foliage, SS bail and lid . . . 350.00
Pitcher, 4½", 1909 pattern, red and brown ground, beaded yellow daffodil dec 950.00
Vase
6⅝", handles, Daisy and Leaf pattern, shaded brown to green ground . . 400.00
7 x 7", two handles, pedestal, bulbous body, narrow neck, ornate scalloped collar, green, brown, and rust flowers and leaves, red patent applied form mark, Japanese 200.00
8½", pinched body, shaped green and purple flowers and leaves, green beading 185.00

Tumbler, satin glass, elongated thumbprint pattern, MOP, shaded orange-apricot to white, cased white interior, triangular mouth, yellow sheaves of wheat dec, 3¾", $250.00.

GLASS

Cup and Saucer, blue ground, beaded pink dragon, MOP int. 50.00
Pitcher, 6¼", Seaweed pattern, shaded yellow, white int. 350.00
Tumbler, 3¾", gold coral dec, satin glass, medium to light pink, white int., gold rim 225.00

Vase
4 x 5⅛", shaded rose DQ MOP satin finish, white int., yellow beaded Star pattern at intersection of diamonds 425.00
5½", deep peachblow, satin finish, coral coralene dec 300.00
5½ x 6¾", flattened oval shape, shaded deep pink to white satin overlay, white int., all over yellow Wheat pattern dec 450.00
6¾", peachblow, satin finish, fleur-de-lis coralene 250.00

CORKSCREWS

History: The corkscrew is composed of three parts: (1) handle, (2) shaft, and (3) worm or screw. The earliest known reference to "a Steele Worme used for drawing corks out of bottles" is 1681. Samuel Henshall, an Englishman, was granted the first patent in 1795.

Elaborate mechanisms were invented and patented from the early 1800s onward, especially in England. However, three basic types emerged: "T" handle (the most basic, simple form), lever, and mechanism. Variations on these three types run into the hundreds. Miniature corkscrews, employed for drawing corks from perfume and medicinal bottles between 1750 and 1920, are among the most eagerly sought by collectors.

Nationalistic preferences were found in corkscrews. The English favored the helix worm and tended to coppertone their steel products. By the mid-18th century English and Irish silversmiths were making handles noted for their clean lines and practicality. Most English silver handles were hallmarked.

The Germans preferred the center worm and nickel plate. The Italians used massive chrome plate or massive solid brass. In the early 1800s the Dutch and French developed elaborately artistic silver handles.

Americans did not begin to manufacture quality corkscrews until the late 19th century. They favored the center worm and specialized in silver mounted tusks and carved staghorn for handles.

LEVER

Brass, Italian, double, rack and pinion type, steel shaft with center worm, cap lifter in handle, c1920 . . . . 30.00
Chrome plated steel, Italian (Vogliotti-Torino), double, wire helix, marked "Japan" and "Christian-Brothers–San Francisco 1908" 125.00
Nickel plated steel, helical worm, stamped "Patent, Weir's Patent 1280425 Septr, 1884/J. Helley & Son Maker" 75.00

Steel, hinged, retractable, scalloped casing, nickel plated corkscrew, marked "The Handy" and "Patented Feb 24, 1891," round shaft with center worm **35.00**

MECHANISM

Copper finish metal open-framed corkscrew stamped "The Victor," butterfly handle and double-fly spinner, steel bladed worm, English **75.00**
Bone handle, polished, English rack and pinion corkscrew (King's Screw), brush and hanging ring, four plain post open barrel, narrow rack, long wire helix, side handle, sgd Verinder, c1800 .... **400.00**
Brass, solid, 4 triangular posts, open cage, uncyphered solid cutworm, probably Italian, c1890 .... **220.00**
Nickel plated steel, open cage, swivel over collar on handle to raise shaft, hanging ring, cyphered center worm, German Pat 1892 .... **40.00**
Wood barrel handle enclosed by metal caps, thick steel cylindrical sheath leading to metal rim stamped "Magic Cork Extractor Pat March 4–79, May 10–92," Mumford **300.00**

MINIATURE

Bone handle, turned tapered steel shaft, wire helix, early 19th C **85.00**
Brass, figural elephant, 2", tail is corkscrew, marked "Perage England, c1930" **30.00**
Meissen, porcelain head of Johann Von Schiller (1759–1805), poet and philosopher, uncyphered center worm, head marked with crossed swords under glaze, c1870 .... **385.00**
Nickel plated cut steel, 3" peg and worm, fluted wire helix, mid 18th C . **80.00**

NOVELTY

Brass
Dolphin catching a ball, figural, helical worm **40.00**
"Old Snifter," Senator Volstead depicted standing, corkscrew and bottle opener, helical worm, fixed hat **200.00**
White Celluloid, lady, figural, folding, helical worm, stamped "Ges. Gech," Germany **525.00**
Wood, horse, 5" l, tail is wire helix, c1925 .... **20.00**

T-HANDLE

Bone handle, Henshall-type, radially incised button, helical worm, lacks brush, c1820 .... **125.00**
Staghorn handle, 5½", figural, carved horsehead with flowing mane and spirited glass eyes, tapered shaft, center worm with point, c1880 .... **250.00**
Wood
Oak handle, serrated button, plain shaft with pointed center worm, probably by Murphy, c1890 ..... **25.00**
Turned mahogany handle, Henshall-type tapered shaft, fluted button, helical worm, lacks brush, 19th C . **60.00**

COSMOS GLASS

History: Cosmos glass is a milk glass pattern made by the Consolidated Lamp and Glass Company, c1900.

Cosmos glass is identified by its distinctive pattern. The ground is a molded cross-cut design. Relief molded flowers are painted in pink, blue, and yellow. Cosmos glass comes in an extended tableware line which includes several sizes and shapes of lamps.

Castor Set, salt and pepper shakers, mustard container, orig matching undertray, $225.00.

Butter Dish, cov, pink band **235.00**
Condiment Set, salt, pepper,and mustard, orig handled Cosmos pattern frame, pink band **300.00**
Creamer and Sugar, cov **315.00**
Miniature Lamp, 7½" h **290.00**
Pickle Castor, pink band, ftd SP frame **400.00**
Pitcher, water, 9", pink band **225.00**
Powder Box, cov **200.00**

Salt and Pepper Shakers, tall, pink band, orig tops, pr	**150.00**
Spooner	**120.00**
Syrup, orig top, pink band	**190.00**
Tumbler, 3¾", pink band	**85.00**
Vase, 7½" h, pink band	**125.00**

COWAN POTTERY

History: R. Guy Cowan founded the Cowan Pottery in 1913 in Cleveland, Ohio. The establishment remained in almost continuous operation until 1931 when financial difficulties forced closure.

Early production was redware pottery. Later a porcelain-like finish was perfected with special emphasis placed on glazes. Lustreware is one of the most common types. Commercial wares marked "Lakeware" were produced from 1927 to 1931.

Early marks include an incised "Cowan Pottery" on the redware (1913–17), an impressed "Cowan," and an impressed "Lakewood". The imprinted stylized semicircle with or without the initials R. G. was later.

References: Paul Evans, *Art Pottery of the United States,* Everybodys Press, Inc., 1974; Ralph and Terry Kovel, *The Kovels' Collector's Guide to American Art Pottery,* Crown Publishers, Inc., 1974.

Ashtray, figural, bird, pink	**40.00**
Bookends, Sunbonnet Girl, white glaze, pr	**375.00**

Vase, 7⅞" h, orange luster, sea horse standard, stamped mark, $70.00.

Bowl, 7¼ x 2¼", blue luster	**38.00**
Candlesticks, pr	
4", pink	**20.00**
8", triple light, ivory glaze	**75.00**
Charger, 11", bottle green glaze, pierced for hanging, sgd	**45.00**
Cigarette Holder, seahorse, ivory	**30.00**
Figure, 9", man, blue, irid gold, and maroon	**45.00**
Flower Frog	
5", mushroom, wide cap in center, small mushrooms clustered underneath, semi-gloss ivory glaze, sgd	**65.00**
7½", nude, high gloss glaze	**150.00**
Soap Dish, 4", seahorse, blue	**35.00**
Teapot, 7¼", white glaze	**75.00**
Trivet, 6½", scalloped rim, bust of young girl framed by flower, sgd	**250.00**
Vase	
4½ x 4¾", green and pink spots shading to pink	**75.00**
7¼", , seahorse standard, green glaze, imp mark	**50.00**
9", hp, dragonfly and cattails	**80.00**
9½", trumpet, ribbed, irid, lavender glaze over beige	**100.00**
12", speckled gray glaze, rose-brown ground, sgd	**100.00**

CRANBERRY GLASS

History: Cranberry glass is transparent and named for its color, achieved by adding powdered gold to a molten batch of amber glass which then is reheated at a low temperature to develop the cranberry or ruby color. The glass color first appeared in the last half of the 17th century, but was not made in American glass factories until the last half of the 19th century.

Cranberry glass was blown, mold blown, or pressed. Examples often are decorated with gold or enamel. Less expensive cranberry glass was made by substituting copper for gold and can be identified by its bluish-purple tint.

Reference: William Heacock and William Gamble, *Encyclopedia Of Victorian Colored Pattern Glass: Book 9, Cranberry Opalescent from A to Z,* Antique Publications, 1987.

Additional Listings: See specific categories, such as Bride's Baskets, Cruets, Jack-in-the-Pulpit Vases, etc.

Reproduction Alert: Reproductions abound. These pieces are heavier, off-color, and lack the quality of older examples.

Basket, 6", clear crimped rim, clear thorn handle	**150.00**
Bell, 6½", bell jar shape, clear crystal stopper and flat finial	**125.00**
Bonbon Dish, 6¼ x 6", applied clear shell trim, SP basket	**125.00**

Bowl
3⅞ x 3¾″, three crystal star shape appliques with berry centers, heavy foil pcs in glass, three crystal scroll applied feet, berry pontil 150.00
7¾″, paneled, flower dec, brass standard, mirrored base 100.00
Box, 4½ x 2⅝″, round, hinged, enameled colonial girl, white wig, black and white dress, basket of flowers 135.00
Butter Dish, cov, round, Hobnail pattern 100.00
Celery Vase, Swirl pattern, satin finish 100.00
Christmas Salt, orig top and breaker . . 300.00
Cocktail Shaker, 10″, paneled, nickel plated lid and pouring spout, applied clear glass handle 150.00
Cologne Bottle, 3 x 7″, dainty blue, white, and yellow flowers, green leaves, gold outlines and trim, orig clear ball stopper 180.00
Creamer, 2⅞″, blue, white, and coral flowers, lacy gold foliage, applied clear handle 125.00

Vase, 5½″ h, hobnail, $55.00.

Cruet
5″, bulbous, IVT, flower dec, pontil, applied clear ribbed handle, clear stopper 65.00
9½″, engraved flowers and leaves, applied clear handle, clear wafer foot, clear cut stopper 160.00
Cup and Saucer, 2⅟x 4⅛″, gold bands, enameled purple and white violets, gold handle 125.00
Decanter
16¾″, double cut overlay, cranberry cut to clear, orig matching stopper, applied clear handle, clear ftd base 100.00
19¼″ h, gold dec, applied raised porcelain flowers, steeple stopper, Austrian, pr 275.00
Dresser Jar, 4¼″ d, round, hinged lid, medallion of young girl in white playing lyre, yellow foliate dec 150.00
Epergne, 10⅛ x 22¼″ h, ruffled base, three large lilies, irregular petal tops, applied crystal spiral trim 350.00
Ewer, 8¾″ h, heavy gold and enamel dec, Austrian 90.00
Finger Bowl, scalloped, matching underplate, attributed to New England Glass Co 125.00
Jam Dish, 4½″ d, applied clear rim, SP holder 100.00
Lemonade Glass, 4½″, multicolored insects, leaves, and raised acorns . . . 175.00
Miniature Lamp
8¼″, bulbous, swirled, hobnail dec . 300.00
10½″, cylindrical, flared out shade, opal stripes 625.00
Mug, 1⅜ x 1¾″, applied clear handle, enameled blue and white flowers, blue and green leaves 30.00
Perfume Bottles, 5½″ h, pr, enameled, beveled glass house shaped casket, gilt brass fittings 335.00
Pin Dish, 3¾ x 3″ h, enameled white daisies and flowers, ftd ormolu holder 85.00
Pickle Castor, 3¼ x 10⅛″, enameled white band of flowers and leaves, gold trim, SP frame, lid, and tongs . 235.00
Pitcher
5¼″, Hobnail, applied clear handle . 75.00
6″, Coin Spot, white int. 225.00
7″, tankard, applied clear handle, adv "Daniel Crawford Scotch Whiskey" 150.00
10″, bulbous, long neck, applied amber handle, enameled flowers and leaves 315.00
Rose Bowl
3½″, melon ribbed 125.00
4¾″, egg shape, applied clear swags, scroll feet, berry pontil 250.00
Salt, master
2¾ x 1¾″, cut to crystal on sides, star design on base 70.00
2⅞ x 1¾″, gold band, enameled blue and white flowers, green leaves . . 55.00
3½ x 1½″, SP holder, lion's mask and claw feet 75.00
3½ x 2⅛″, four applied clear shell feet, applied clear shells trim 70.00
Shrimp Dish, 4⅛ x 3¾″, intaglio cut to clear, attached clear underplate . . . 100.00
Sugar Shaker
6″, Spanish Lace, opalescent pattern, nickel plated top 125.00
6¼″, Venetian Diamond pattern 100.00
6½″, Drape pattern, SS hallmarked top 85.00
Sweetmeat Dish, 5¾″, fluted, applied clear shell trim, SP basket holder . . 90.00
Syrup Pitcher, ribbed base, SP handle,

neck, and cov, marked "James W Tufts, Boston Warranted Quadruple Plate," c1885 .... **485.00**
Toothpick, 3½", IVT, applied clear base **50.00**
Tumbler
  3¾", all over multicolored enameling, gold trim **55.00**
  4", IVT, enameled white daisy, blue forget-me-not, and white lily-of-the-valley dec **35.00**
Urn, 5 x 12½", cov, deep all over cutting, raised diamonds, bands of bull's eyes, cut clear glass stem, sq pedestal base, cut dome cov, clear acorn finial **275.00**
Vase
  3½", enameled dainty pink and blue flowers, green leaves, gold all over dec **70.00**
  3¾", gold stars and crescent dec, enameled blue flowers **60.00**
  5", sq bulbous shape, sq tops, enameled cream and gold flowers and leaves, pr **120.00**
  6¾", IVT, bulbous, long neck, sq top **175.00**
  8", enameled blue and white flower sprays, gold trim **100.00**
  8½", applied clear ruffle around top, clear wafer foot **160.00**
  11", gold foliage, enameled white, pink, and blue flowers, gold trim, facing pr **375.00**
  12⅛", applied clear rigaree top edge, heavy gold dec, enameled white and blue flowers, gold trim, three applied clear feet, pr **600.00**
Water Set, 5½ x 10" pitcher, six 2⅞ x 4" tumblers, pressed, spade between flowers, band of emb flowers, gold trim, applied clear handle **225.00**
Wine Glass, cranberry bowl, opaque white standard, Austrian **20.00**

CROWN MILANO

History: Crown Milano is an American art glass produced by the Mt. Washington Glass Works, New Bedford, Massachusetts. The original patent was issued in 1886 to Frederick Shirley and Albert Steffin.

Normally it is an opaque white satin glass finished with light beige or ivory color ground embellished with fancy florals, decorations, and elaborate heavy raised gold. When marked, pieces carry an entwined CM with crown in purple enamel on the base. Sometimes paper labels were used.

The silver plated mounts often have "MW" impressed or a Pairpoint mark as both Mount Washington and Pairpoint supplied mountings.

Advisors: Clarence and Betty Maier.

Sweetmeat, 4" h, 6" d, white emb ground, heavy emb gold medallion, white and red enamel dec, pink floral shadows, emb SP fittings, twisted bail handle, $785.00.

Biscuit Jar
  8" h, sq shape, gold swirls and pink tulips, outlined in raised gold, SP lid and bail, sgd **800.00**
  9" h, jeweled starfish, molded stars background, sgd M.W. in SP lid .. **1,450.00**
Creamer and Sugar, sq shape, jeweled flowers, gold and green leaves outlined in raised gold, gold ribbed handles, pr **700.00**
Ewer
  9¾" h, autumn colored oak leaves and acorns, outlined in heavy gold, turquoise twisted handle extending around neck, sgd **1,750.00**
  13" h, flowers and trailing vines, heavy raised gold, gold shadow scrolling, trefoil fold-down top, unsigned **900.00**
Sweetmeat, 5½" h, petticoat shape, raised diamond design, glossy ground, green leaves and scrolls, raised enamel lily-of-the-valley dec, fancy bail and lid, lid sgd M.W. **600.00**
Tumbler, 3⅞" h, shiny finish, gold swag and ribbon dec, sgd **460.00**
Vase
  5" h, ball shape, molded in swirls, trefoil top, floral dec **800.00**
  8" h, sq, rounded corners, dragon's head medallions and floral dec in gold, ivory ground, two delicate applied handles **900.00**
  8¼" h, enameled chrysanthemum and thistle dec, raised gold borders, sgd **2,200.00**

9" h, shiny finish, applied scroll handles, large flowers dec, heavy gold highlighting, Albertine, (early Crown Milano) signature **1,000.00**

9¼" h, two heavy encrusted gold panels with cherubs, shadow floral background, unsigned **1,250.00**

10¼" h, 7" d, squat body, tall slender neck, applied serpent, overall dec of fierce dragon, unsigned **1,500.00**

CRUETS

History: Cruets are small glass bottles, used to hold oil, vinegar, wine, etc., for the table. The high point of cruet use was during the Victorian era when a myriad of glass manufacturers made cruets in a wide assortment of patterns, colors, and sizes. All cruets had stoppers; most had handles.

Reference: Dean L Murray, *More Cruets Only*, Killgore Graphics, Inc., 1973; William Heacock, *Encyclopedia of Victorian Colored Pattern Glass: Book 6, Oil Cruets From A To Z*, Antique Publications, 1981.

Additional Listings: Pattern Glass and specific glass categories such as Amberina, Cranberry and Satin.

Bubble Lattice pattern, blue opalescent design, applied clear handle, 5¾" h, $225.00.

Amber

5½", applied blue handle, white enamel dec, orig blue stopper . . .   **50.00**

10¾", applied blue spun rope handle, electric blue bubble stopper, berry prunt, blue pedestal foot **100.00**

13½", salamander applied to front, applied blue rings, applied blue handle, faceted blue stopper **175.00**

Amberina, 5¾", IVT, applied amber handle, amber stopper, Mt Washington .   **325.00**

Blue, hobnail, applied amber handle, amber stopper **70.00**

Cranberry, double cut overlay, cranberry to clear **80.00**

Custard, Argonaut Shell **425.00**

Emerald Green

Beaded Ovals In Sand, dec, orig stopper **135.00**

Esther, 5¾", gold dec, orig stopper .   **150.00**

Opalescent, Intaglio, blue and white . .   **125.00**

Peachblow, 7", enameled fish, water lilies, and cattails, gold outlines, acid finish, applied amber handle, orig faceted amber stopper **1,100.00**

Satin, 7", yellow, DQ, applied frosted handle, faceted clear stopper **250.00**

Spatter, 4½" h, red and white, tricorn top, applied clear handle **135.00**

Vaseline

Dewey, orig stopper, Greentown . . .   **135.00**

Hobnail, matching stopper **65.00**

CUP PLATES

History: Many early cups and saucers were handless, with deep saucers. The hot liquid was poured into the saucer and sipped from it. This necessitated another plate for the cup, the "cup plate."

The first cup plates made of pottery were of the Staffordshire variety. In the mid-1830s to 40s, glass cup plates were favored. Boston and Sandwich Glass Company was one of the main contributors to the lacy glass type.

It is extremely difficult to find glass cup plates in outstanding (mint) condition. Collectors expect some marks of usage, such as slight rim roughness, minor chipping [best if under rim], and in rarer paterns a portion of a scallop missing.

Reference: Ruth Webb Lee and Robert Rose, *American Glass Cup Plates*, published by author, 1948/reprinted by Charles E. Tuttle Co., Inc. in 1985.

Notes: The numbers used are from the Lee-Rose book in which all plates are illustrated.

Prices are based on plates in "average" condition.

LR 1, light green, 3¼", blown, ex-William Elsholz collection **60.00**

LR 3, clear, 3⅞", blown three mold, attributed to Boston and Sandwich Glass Co **175.00**

LR 4-A, 4⅛", clear, swirled red and white latticino, gold flecks in rim, attributed to Nicholas Lutz, ex-William Elsholz collection **150**

LR 11, 2¹³⁄₁₆", clear, New England origin, small shallow rim chips and roughage   **60.00**

LR 15, $3\frac{7}{16}$″, clear, pontil, New England origin, seven shallow rim chips, edge roughage . . . 75.00

LR 22-B, $3\frac{7}{16}$″, clear, pontil, New England origin, slight roughage . . . 80.00

LR 26, $3\frac{9}{16}$″, clear, attributed to Sandwich or New England Glass Co . . . 150.00

LR 37, $3\frac{1}{4}$″, opalescent, attributed to Sandwich or New England Glass Co, two heat checks in rim, light roughage 150.00

LR 44, $3\frac{1}{4}$″, clear, attributed to Sandwich or New England Glass Co, very slight rim roughage . . . 100.00

LR 45, $3\frac{9}{16}$″, pale opalescent, attributed to Sandwich or New England Glass Co, mold overfill, slag deposit near center . . . 100.00

LR 51, $3\frac{3}{4}$″, clear, pontil, eastern origin, moderate rim roughage, few shallow flakes . . . 175.00

LR 58, $3\frac{3}{8}$″, clambroth, unlisted, eastern origin, ex-William Elsholz collection . 275.00

LR 61, $3\frac{3}{8}$″, opalescent, attributed to New England Glass Co . . . 250.00

LR 64-A, opaque white, known as Parker White cup plate, ex-William Elsholz and James H. Rose collections, five small shallow flakes on upper rim 3,250.00

LR 75-A, $3\frac{13}{16}$″, clear, attributed to New England Glass Co, one tiny rim flake 70.00

LR 80, $3\frac{3}{4}$″, opalescent, New England origin, ex-William Elsholz, Harry S. High, James H. Rose collections . . . 250.00

LR 81, $3\frac{3}{4}$″, fiery red opalescent, New England origin, ex-William Elsholz, Louise S. Esterly, James H. Rose collections . . . 350.00

LR 88, $3\frac{11}{16}$″, deep opalescent opaque, attributed to Sandwich or New England Glass Co, two minute under-rim flakes . . . 175.00

LR 95, $3\frac{5}{8}$″, opalescent opaque, attributed to New England, tiny under rim nick . . . 150.00

LR 100, $3\frac{1}{4}$″, clear, attributed to Philadelphia area, unseen flake under rim, normal mold roughness . . . 75.00

LR 107, $3\frac{3}{8}$″, clear, lacy, attributed to Philadelphia area, very slight rim roughage . . . 50.00

LR 121, $3\frac{1}{16}$″, clear, lacy, midwestern, slight rim roughage, two minor nicks, mold overfill . . . 100.00

LR 242-A, $3\frac{1}{2}$″, black amethyst, lacy, eastern origin, mold underfill and overfill . . . 650.00

LR 247, $3\frac{7}{16}$″, emerald green, lacy, attributed to Sandwich or New England Glass Co, small chip on one scallop 750.00

LR 253, $3\frac{9}{16}$″, bluish-green, Roman Rosette, midwestern origin, two very small rim nicks . . . 300.00

LR 259, $3\frac{7}{16}$″, clear, eastern origin, small chip on one point and one scallop, normal mold roughness . . . 85.00

LR 276, $3\frac{7}{16}$″, blue, lacy, Boston and Sandwich Glass Co., slight opalescenct bloom . . . 325.00

LR 279, $2\frac{7}{8}$″, light green, lacy, eastern origin, two chipped scallops . . . 250.00

LR 291, 3″, amethyst, ex-William Elsholz collection . . . 300.00

LR 319, $3\frac{5}{16}$″, clear, one scallop missing, five have small flakes, normal mold roughness . . . 100.00

LR 399, $3\frac{5}{16}$″, clear, eastern origin, normal mold roughness . . . 60.00

LR 433, $4\frac{1}{8}$″, clear, two chips, mold roughness . . . 75.00

LR 440-B, $3\frac{1}{2}$″, gray-blue, attributed to Sandwich, nine scallops flaked, one missing . . . 100.00

LR 445, $3\frac{7}{16}$″, cloudy, midwestern origin, four bull's eyes missing, five chips, mold roughness . . . 265.00

LR 516, $3\frac{1}{4}$″, amethyst, attributed to Sandwich, rim chip on underside, surface spalls, and rim roughage . . . 425.00

GLASS, HISTORICAL

LR 564, $3\frac{5}{8}$″, medium blue, floral rim, Henry Clay int., attributed to Sandwich, discolored air bubble at rim . . 75.00

LR 568, $3\frac{7}{16}$″, clear, attributed to Sandwich, one scallop tipped, mold roughness . . . 50.00

LR 580-B, $3\frac{3}{4}$″, clear, English origin, underfill covering $1\frac{1}{2}$ of rim . . . 275.00

LR 586-B, clear, Ringgold, Palo Alto, stippled ground, small letters, Philadelphia area, 1847–48, trace of mold roughness . . . 650.00

LR 595, $3\frac{1}{4}$″, amber, attributed to Sandwich, three small mold spalls, one scallop missing, six scallops tipped, one spall on underside, average mold roughness . . . 265.00

LR 615-A, $3\frac{3}{8}$″, clear, unknown origin, Constitution . . . 650.00

LR 691-A, $3\frac{3}{16}$″, clear, midwestern origin, normal mold roughness . . . 450.00

LR 695, 3″, clear, midwestern origin two scallops tipped, normal mold roughness . . . 125.00

LR 699, $3\frac{1}{4}$″, clear, leaf rim, dot int., unknown origin, eight points and scallops tipped . . . 75.00

PORCELAIN OR POTTERY

Gaudy Dutch, Butterfly pattern . . . 750.00

Leeds, $3\frac{3}{4}$″, softpaste, gaudy blue and

Porcelain, Staffordshire, "Woodlands near Philadelphia," Stubbs, dark blue, 3⅛", $325.00.

white floral dec,very minor pinpoint edge flakes	240.00
Staffordshire, Historical	
Armitage Park, 4¾", grapevine border series, dark blue, Wood	50.00
Franklin Tomb (so-called), 3½", dark blue, Wood, faint hairline	600.00
Landing of Lafayette, 4⅜", dark blue, full border, Clews	425.00
The Tyrants Foe...Lovejoy, 4", light blue, unknown maker, minute pinpoint on foot rim	275.00
Unidentified View of Country Estate, 4⅝", grapevine border series, dark blue, Wood	60.00
Washington-Lafayette, 3⅝", carmine transfer, carmine line border, Wood	165.00
Staffordshire, Romantic	
Balantyre, twelve sided, J Alcock	50.00
Garden Scenery, twelve sided, pink, Mayer	30.00
Oriental, Ridgway, c1830–34	60.00

CUSTARD GLASS

History: Custard glass was developed in England in the early 1880s. Harry Northwood made the first American custard glass at his Indiana, Pennsylvania, factory in 1898.

From 1898 until 1915, many manufacturers produced custard glass patterns, e.g., Dugan Glass, Fenton, A. H. Heisey Glass Co., Jefferson Glass, Northwood, Tarentum Glass, and U.S. Glass. Cambridge and McKee continued the production of custard glass into the Depression.

The ivory or creamy yellow custard color is achieved by adding uranium salts to the molten hot glass. The chemical content makes the glass glow when held under a black light. The higher the amount of uranium, the more luminous the color. Northwood's custard glass has the smallest amount of uranium, creating an ivory color; Heisey used more, creating a deep yellow color.

Custard glass was made in patterned tableware pieces. It also was made as souvenir items and novelty pieces. Souvenir pieces are marked with place names or hand painted decorations, e.g., flowers. Patterns of custard glass often were highlighted in gold, enamel colors, and stains.

Reference: William Heacock, *Encyclopedia Of Victorian Colored Pattern Glass, Book IV: Custard Glass From A to Z,* Peacock Publications, 1980.

Reproduction Alert: L. G. Wright Glass Co. has reproduced pieces in the Argonaut Shell and Grape and Cable patterns. It also introduced new patterns, such as Floral and Grape and Vintage Band. Moser reproduced toothpicks in Argonaut Shell, Chrysanthemum Sprig, and Inverted Fan & Feather.

Additional Listings: Pattern Glass.

Banana Boat, Louis XV	115.00
Berry Bowl	
Argonaut Shell	42.00
Cherry Scale, master	100.00
Inverted Fan and Feather, master	225.00
Maple Leaf, master, pedestal, gold and enamel dec	200.00
Butter, cov	
Argonaut Shell	215.00
Chrysanthemum Sprig, 6" h	275.00
Intaglio	175.00
Victoria	280.00
Celery	
Georgia Gem	175.00
Ring Band	300.00
Cologne Bottle, Grape, nutmeg stain, orig stopper, marked "N"	400.00
Compote, jelly	
Argonaut Shell	160.00
Beaded Circle	350.00
Intaglio, green trim	100.00
Condiment Set, Creased Bale, 4 pcs	180.00
Creamer	
Grape, nutmeg stain	100.00
Heart with Thumbprint	80.00
Cruet	
Argonaut Shell, orig stopper	425.00
Chrysanthemum Sprig, clear stopper, goofus dec	60.00
Intaglio, green dec	400.00
Ribbed Drape	350.00
Custard Cup, Winged Scroll	50.00
Dresser Tray, Winged Scroll, hp dec	165.00
Goblet, Grape and Gothic Arches, nutmeg stain	65.00
Hair Receiver, Winged Scroll	125.00
Humidor, Winged Scroll	175.00
Ice Cream Set, Fan, 7 pcs	500.00
Nappy	
Northwood Grape	50.00
Prayer Rug, 6" d	50.00
Pickle Dish, Beaded Swag	250.00

Pin Tray, Chrysanthemum Sprig	50.00
Pitcher, water, Argonaut Shell	300.00
Plate, 7½" d	
Prayer Rug	20.00
Three Fruits	22.00
Punch Cup	
Inverted Fan and Feather	250.00
Northwood Grape	48.00
Rose Bowl, Grape and Gothic Arches .	75.00
Salt and Pepper Shakers, pr	
Chrysanthemum Sprig	150.00
Heart	60.00
Punty Band	85.00
Vine with Flowers	50.00
Sauce	
Cane Insert	30.00
Intaglio	35.00
Jefferson Optic, dec	15.00

Grape and Gothic Arches, gold, carnival finish	55.00
Inverted Fan and Feather	100.00
Ring Band	65.00
Wild Bouquet	25.00
Vase	
Diamond Peg, 8" h	100.00
Grape Arbor, nutmeg stain	65.00
Water Set, 7 pcs	
Fan	700.00
Louis XV	500.00
Wine	
Beaded Swag	75.00
Punty Band	65.00

CUT GLASS, AMERICAN

History: Glass is cut by the process of grinding decoration into the glass by means of abrasive-carrying metal wheels or stone wheels. A very ancient craft, it was revived in 1600 by Bohemians and spread through Europe, to Great Britain, and to America.

American cut glass came of age at the Centennial Exposition in 1876 and the World Columbian Exposition in 1893. The American public recognized American cut glass to be exceptional in quality and workmanship. America's most significant output of this high quality glass occurred from 1880 to 1917, a period now known as the "Brilliant Period."

About the 1890s some companies began adding an acid-etched "signature" to their glass. This signature may be the actual company name, its logo, or chosen symbol. Today, signed pieces can command a premium over unsigned pieces since the signature clearly establishes the origin.

However, caution should be exercised in regard to signature identification. Objects with forged signatures have been in existence for some time. To check for authenticity, run your finger tip or finger nail lightly over the area with the signature. As a general rule, a genuine signature cannot be felt; a forged signature exhibits a raised surface.

Many companies never used the acid-etched signature on the glass and may or may not have affixed paper labels to the items originally. Dorflinger Glass and the Meriden Glass Co. made cut glass of the highest quality, yet never acid-etched a signature on the glass. Furthermore, cut glass made before the 1890s was not signed. Many of these wood polished items, cut on blown blanks, were of excellent quality and often won awards at exhibitions.

Consequently, if collectors restrict themselves to signed pieces only, many beautiful pieces of the highest quality glass and workmanship will be missed.

References: E. S. Farrar & J. S. Spillman, *The Complete Cut & Engraved Glass Of Corning,*

Spooner, 4¼" h, Wild Bouquet pattern, Northwood, $85.00.

Spooner	
Chrysanthemum Sprig, blue, gold trim	220.00
Geneva	50.00
Sugar	
Everglades	150.00
Fluted Scrolls	150.00
Heart and Thumbprint, individual . . .	75.00
Victoria	175.00
Syrup	
Ring Band	300.00
Winged Scroll	350.00
Table Set, cov butter, creamer, spooner, and cov sugar	
Cane Insert	425.00
Chrysanthemum Sprig	550.00
Louis XV	225.00
Toothpick	
Argonaut Shell	275.00
Chrysanthemum Sprig, blue	300.00
Maple Leaf	550.00
Ribbed Drape	150.00
Tumbler	
Cherry Scale	40.00
Geneva, red and green enamel dec	50.00

Crown Publishers [Corning Museum of Glass monograph],1979; J. Michael Pearson, *Encyclopedia Of American Cut & Engraved Glass,* Volumes I to III, published by author, 1975; Albert C. Revi, *American Cut & Engraved Glass,* Thomas Nelson, Inc., 1965; Martha Louise Swan, *American and Engraved Glass,* Wallace-Homestead, 1986; H. Weiner & F. Lipkowitz, *Rarities In American Cut Glass,* Collectors House of Books, 1975.

Collectors' Club: American Cut Glass Association, 1603 SE 19th, Suite 112, Edmond Professional Bldg., Edmond, OK 73013. Dues: $20.00. *Hobstar* (10 times a year).

Museums: The Corning Museum of Glass, Corning, NY; High Museum of Art, Atlanta, GA; Huntington Galleries, Huntington, WV; Lightner Museum, St. Augustine, FL; Toledo Museum Of Art, Toledo, OH.

Advisors: Richard and Joan Randles.

Basket
5½ x 6 x 4½" h, handled, hobstars, strawberry diamond, and fans . . .	255.00
5½ x 9½ x 14" h, hobstar base, notched handle, honeycomb near base, hobstars and cane filled vesicas	1,000.00
8 x 11", Harvard, hobstars, and prism cut	475.00

Bell
4½" h, hobstars and fans	220.00
5¾" h, dinner size, hobstars, fans, strawberry diamond	255.00
6¾" h, strawberry diamond and fan sharply cut, pattern on knob at end of stem as well	550.00

Bowl
7 x 2"	
Figured blank, hobstars and fans .	75.00
"Grecian," sgd Hawkes	625.00
8 x 2", cross-cut diamond and fan . .	60.00
8 x 3", "Iris," sgd Hawkes Gravic . . .	250.00
8 x 4", "Ellsmere," sgd Libbey	600.00
9"	
"Palm," five sided, Taylor Bros . .	450.00
Russian, cane, feather, and hobstars	140.00
9 x 4", "Prima Donna," sgd Clark . .	375.00
9¾ x 6¾ x 3¾", orange, hobstars and strawberry diamond	180.00
10", "Kohinoor," blown-out type blank, swirled pattern design, sgd Hawkes	1,250.00
10 x 4", "Nautilus," blown blank, Hawkes	2,400.00
10 x 4½"	
"Chrysanthemum," wood polished, Hawkes	650.00
"Venetian," wood polished, Hawkes	500.00
10 x 8", "Sultana," folded-in sides, Dorflinger	525.00

Box
4 x 11", glove, hinged lid, silver fittings, Harvard border around intaglio cut floral	750.00
5 x 3", intaglio pears and cherries, sgd Heisey	110.00
6 x 5", round, green cased to clear, SS repousse lid, hobstar base, vertical punties and prism columns . .	500.00
8" d, hinged, round, Florence hobstar lid, miter cut sides	320.00

Bread Tray, 11 x 5", hobstars, sgd Clark — **275.00**

Butter, cov, 5" h
7" d plate, Russian and floral	385.00
8" d plate	
Hobstar chain cut on figured blank	325.00
Hobstars and fans, sgd Libbey . .	425.00

Butter Pat
Pair, "Cypress," Laurel, each	32.00
Set of 4, sgd Hawkes, each	20.00
Set of 6, well cut hobstars, each . . .	30.00

Candlestick
8" h	
Hollow teardrop stems, rayed bases, hobstars, hobnail, and diamonds, pr	975.00
Teardrop stems, floral and Harvard, pr	250.00
9½" h, teardrop stem, hobstar base, hobstars	230.00
11" h, teardrop stem, notched prisms, 24 pt hobstar base, pr	600.00
12" h, "Adelaide," amber, Pairpoint, pr	250.00
14" h, teardrop stems, cut and engraved, sgd Sinclaire, pr	325.00

Canoe
11" l, Harvard	240.00
13½ x 4½", floral and leaves	75.00

Carafe
Clear button Russian	325.00
Harvard	160.00
Hobstars and notched prisms	110.00
"Wedgemere," 9" h, Libbey	1,000.00

Casserole, cov, 8½ x 7" h, "Palm," sgd Taylor Bros **1,300.00**

Celery
11", hobstars, double miters, strawberry diamond on blown blank . . .	150.00
11½ x 5", hobstars, cross hatch, and notched prisms on figured blank .	60.00
12", hobstars, flashed double vesicas, sgd Alford	250.00

Champagne Bucket, 7 x 7", sgd Hoare — **350.00**

Cheese and Cracker Dish, "Double Lozenge" **275.00**

Cheese Dish, cov
9½" d plate, hobstars, prisms, clear tusks	550.00
"Encore," Straus	375.00
Hobstars, deep miters, cane	450.00

Cigar Jar
7½", "Middlesex," Dorflinger, hollow stopper, lid to hold sponge	475.00

9"

"Monarch," Hoare, pattern cut lid
hollow for sponge, hobstar base ... **625.00**
Pattern cut lid hollow for sponge,
hobstars, beaded split vesicas,
hobstar base **550.00**

Cigarette Holder, 4" l, ¾" w, nailhead
diamond, strawberry diamond, fans,
and honeycomb **630.00**

Cocktail Shaker, strawberry diamond
and fan, SS top, sgd Hawkes **275.00**

Cologne

5", bulbous, strawberry diamond, fans
and hobstars **150.00**
6" h, green cased to clear, "Hob and
Lace," Dorflinger, pattern cut stop-
per **600.00**
7½ x 2¾", "Parisian, Dorflinger, "sq
shape, pr **620.00**
Ruby cased to clear, all over cane . . **250.00**

Compote

5" h, 7" d, hobstars, rayed foot, sgd
Maple City **150.00**
7" h, 8½" d, two notch cut handles,
hobstar base, teardrop stem, hob-
stars **400.00**
8" h, daisies and leaves **80.00**
9"h, 6" d, "Ribbon Star," rayed foot . **275.00**
9 x 9", teardrop stem, hobstars and
diamonds **275.00**
9¾" h, cov, "Arcadia," Bergen . . . **1,850.00**
14 x 10", "Design #100," Elmira,
notch cut teardrop stems, hobstar
base, pr **2,700.00**

Console Center Set, "Victoria," pedestal
bowl, pair candlesticks, 3 pc **325.00**

Cookie Jar

6½" h, hobstars, fans, double "X" cut
vesicas, strawberry diamond,
curved-in sides, matching pattern
cut glass lid rests into SS rim . . . **800.00**
Hobstars, strawberry diamond, cane
and fans, pattern cut glass lid . . . **900.00**

Cordial Set, green cased to clear,
"Flute," Dorflinger, 9" h handled decanter with ringed neck and matching
colored stopper, set of 8 cordials . . . **875.00**

Creamer, 4", prism and punties **65.00**

Creamer and Sugar

Clear button Russian, hobstar bases,
cut creamer handle, cov sugar with
wafer foot, pattern cut lid **800.00**
Hobstar clusters, blown blanks, El-
mira **275.00**
Hobstars and fans, figured blanks,
plain handles **90.00**
Hobstars, fans, and strawberry dia-
monds, notched handles **145.00**
Intaglio fruit and geometric cutting . . **75.00**
Pedestal, 7" h cov sugar, pinwheel,
hobstar, fans, rayed bases **975.00**

Cruet

6" h, "Chrysanthemum," Hawkes, tri-
pour spout, cut handle and stopper **350.00**
7", "Butterfly and Daisy," Pairpoint . . **85.00**
9½" h, "Alhambra," honeycomb han-
dle, tall pyramidal shape **675.00**
Ship's cruet, wide bottomed, tri-pour **145.00**
Squat oil, hobstars and cross-cut dia-
monds **95.00**

Decanter

7" h, "Lotus," Egginton, ship's, pattern
cut stopper **380.00**
10" h, bulbous, hobstars and straw-
berry diamonds **275.00**
11" h
"Argand," Hoare, SS flip-top lid and
handle **700.00**
Stopper cut in matching geometric
pattern, sgd Hawkes **525.00**
12" h, "Russian and Pillar," pattern cut
stopper **1,100.00**
13½" h, "Brazilian," Hawkes, heavy
blank, bulbous, wood polished . . . **650.00**

Dish, 10 x 7", hobstar button Russian,
heart shape **220.00**

Door Knob, facet cut **25.00**

Fernery

8" d, hobstar and fan, three ftd **80.00**
"Expanding Star," three ftd **325.00**
"Royal," Hunt, three ftd **195.00**

Finger Bowl

5" d, cross-cut diamond and fan, pr . **70.00**
"Glenwood," Bergen **60.00**
Strawberry diamond and fan, set of 4 **175.00**

Flask, ladies, 6 x 3½", SS lid, cross-cut
diamond, strawberry diamond and
fan **180.00**

Flower Center

6" d, 5" h, flat-bottomed, hobstars,
flashed fans, hobstar chain and
base **300.00**
10" d, 7½" h, hobstars in diamond
shape fields, fans, strawberry diamond, honeycomb neck **775.00**

Flower Pot, 6 x 6", hobstars and ffans,
pyramidal starred fields **775.00**

Hair Reciever

4" d, 3" h, engraved SS top, floral and
leaves, rayed base **75.00**

**Creamer and Sugar, "Heart," hobstar
base, notched handles, $175.00.**

5″ d, 3½″ h, "Harvard" **150.00**

Humidor

  6¾″ h, all over notched prism, glass

    lid **350.00**

  8″ h, "Monarch," SS repousse lid . .   **650.00**

Hanging Globe, 12″ d, cross-cut dia-

  mond and fan, 20″ to top of brass

  finial, orig brass chain and mounting

  fixture **475.00**

Ice Bucket

  6″ d, "Jewel," Clark, hobstar bases,

    two handles, 8½″ d underplate . . .   **525.00**

  6″ d, 6″ h, hobstar and cross-cut

    panels, tab handles **350.00**

  7″ d, 5½″ h, "Harvard," tab handles .   **440.00**

Ice Cream Set, 13 x 8″ tray with curved

  ends, six 5″ sq bowls, rayed button

  Russian, 7 pc **1,100.00**

Ice Cream Tray

  12 x 9″, hobstars, cane, single stars,

    strawberry diamonds **335.00**

  14 x 7½″, hobstar and Russian panels   **290.00**

  14″ x 10″, rect, "Devonshire," sgd

    Hawkes **925.00**

Jar

  4″ h, 5″ d, glass lid, sgd Libbey **260.00**

  6″ h, "Holland," hobstar lid, sgd

    Hawkes **300.00**

  1¾″ sq

    Prism and cane, rayed base, SS

      repousse lid, marked Unger Bros   **75.00**

    Rouge, cut panels, engraved SS

      tops, pr **75.00**

Kerosene Lamp, 7″ h to top of chimney,

  geometric pattern **425.00**

Ketchup Bottle

  6½″ h, "Ramona," Pairpoint **450.00**

  8½″ h, hobstars **240.00**

**Knife Rest, 5″ l, master size, pinwheel
cut ball ends, $75.00.**

Knife Rest

  3″, facet cut **50.00**

  4″, facet panel cut, orig box, pr **100.00**

  4½″, all over strawberry diamond and

    miter **75.00**

  4¾″, nailhead diamonds and straw-

    berry diamonds **85.00**

Ladle

  11½″ l, SP emb shell, cut and notched

    prism handle **145.00**

  15″, hobstars, strawberry diamond,

and fans in teardrop handle, sgd

  Bergen **400.00**

  17″ l, double pouring spout, hobstars

    and notched prisms, sgd Meriden   **500.00**

Lamp

  13″ h, 6½″ d, mushroom shade, St.

    Louis Diamond neck, notched

    prism and hobstars, flashed fans .   **400.00**

  18″ h, mushroom shade, hobstars,

    cane vesicas, fans, pr **4,300.00**

  21″ h, 12″ shade, "La Rabida,"

    Straus, double light **3,200.00**

  22″ h, 10″ d, mushroom shade, hob-

    stars, cane vesicas, fans, double

    light **2,500.00**

  22½″ h, Sultan's hat shade, Harvard

    and late floral **500.00**

  23″ h, 2″ shade, hobstars, beaded

    double miters, fans, double light .   **2,800.00**

  27″ h, pointed top, Harvard, hobstars   **2,750.00**

  32″ h banquet, 37″ h to top of chim-

    ney, all over St. Louis Diamond,

    rare **4,500.00**

Light Shade, 7½″ h, 7″ w, hobstar button

  Russian **225.00**

Loving Cup, 5½″ h, SS rim, mono-

  grammed, dated 1900 . . . .   **400.00**

Mayonnaise Set, two pc

  Bowl and matching underplate, pun-

    ties, flashed pinwheel **135.00**

  Hobstars, cane, and strawberry dia-

    mond on blown blanks **275.00**

  Prism and hobstars **190.00**

Medicine Bottle, globe shape, clear but-

  ton Russian, pattern cut top **625.00**

Mug, 4″ h, "Tyrone," Pairpoint, handled   **235.00**

Mustard

  2¾″ h, "Sultana," Dorflinger, SS lid,

    blown blank **165.00**

  Hobstars and notched prisms, figured

    blank, cov **60.00**

  "Renaissance," cov, underplate **135.00**

  Silverplate hinged lid and handle,

    strawberry and fan **60.00**

Napkin Ring, hobstars and bow tie fans   **85.00**

Nappy

  5″ d, hobstars and cross-cut diamond,

    handle **35.00**

  6″ d

    Cane, strawberry diamond, hobstar

      chain, handled **65.00**

    Cane and cross hatching, two han-

      dles **125.00**

    Divided, cane, hobstars, and cross

      hatching, handled **120.00**

    Figured blank, hobstar cluster, no

      handle **50.00**

    "Good Wishes," Harvard, en-

      graved, handled **200.00**

Paste Pot, vertical notched prisms,

  crossing miters **170.00**

Perfume

4″ h, 2½″ sq, atomizer, gold washed
top, Harvard **125.00**
5¾″ h, three panels Harvard and
three panels floral **125.00**
3½″ l, pistol shape, SS fittings **230.00**
5¾″ l, lay-down, SS fittings, Russian **125.00**
Picture Frame, 4¾ x 6¾″, heavy cut
corners with florals on each panel, pr **250.00**
Pitcher

6″, milk, hobstars and fans **200.00**
8″, tankard, sunburst, hobstar bands,
rayed base, sgd Libbey **275.00**
8½″, tankard, "Brunswick," sgd
Hawkes **500.00**
9″, tankard, "Orpheus," pattern cut
handle, sgd Hawkes **1,250.00**
10″, "Keystone Rose" **135.00**
11″, Harvard, rayed base, double
punty handle, sgd Hawkes **315.00**
11 x 5″, tankard, hobstar and ovals
filled with cane and nailhead dia-
mond, hobstar base **350.00**
12″ jug, champagne, rayed button
Russian, honeycomb handle,
sharply cut **1,500.00**
Jug, SS collar, hobstar base, hobstars
and cross hatching alternating with
prisms, honeycomb handle,
marked Wilcox **650.00**
Milk, hobstars and fans **200.00**
Plate

7″

"Gladys," sgd Hawkes **115.00**
"Grecian," Hawkes **750.00**
"Hindoo," Hoare **115.00**
Hunt, 16 point hobstars, fans,
prisms radiants **100.00**
"Lace," Hawkes **330.00**
10″

"Corinthian," Libbey **285.00**
"Rosaceae," sgd Tuthill **1,000.00**
Thirty two point hobstar center,
hobstar band near rim **160.00**
Powder Jar

4 x 3″, SS Art Nouveau lid **90.00**
5 x 3″, "Harvard" **150.00**
7″ d, sgd Hawkes **165.00**
Punch Bowl

10 x 9″, hobstars and pinwheels, 2 pc **400.00**
12 x 11½″, "Temple," sgd Maple City,
2 pc **1,000.00**
12 x 14″, dental edge, sgd Clark . . . **1,500.00**
14″ d, "Dauntless," Bergen, 1 pc . . . **575.00**
14″ d, hobstar chain, notched prisms,
zipper, mitered panels, sgd Clark,
1 pc **1,210.00**
14 x 7″, fans and cane fields **175.00**
Punch Cup

Set of 6, pedestal, handled, hobstars,
each **75.00**
Set of 10, "Monarch" **300.00**

Set of 11, pedestal, handled, hob-
stars, rayed base, each **60.00**
Punch Set, 16 x 14½″, "Ribbon Star,"
ten cups, 12 pc **3,200.00**
Ramekin Set, ruby cased to clear, clear
button Russian, 2 pc **600.00**
Relish

6″, pinwheel, hobstars, fans, and
prisms **65.00**
7½ x 5½″, flat, oval, "Vintage," hob-
star gallery, sgd Tuthill **275.00**
8 x 3½″, hobstars **35.00**
Rose Bowl

6″ d, Russian **450.00**
6 x 5½″, vesica, fan, and cross-cut
diamond **400.00**
6 x 7″, fan, cane, and prisms **310.00**
7″

Clear button Russian **525.00**
Pedestal, "Bruswick," sgd Hawkes **1,025.00**
9″, "Queens," Hawkes **1,400.00**
Rum Jug, 7½″ h, all over notched prism **325.00**
Salad Set, SP, fork and spoon, cross-
cut diamond glass handles **300.00**
Salt and Pepper Shaker

"Garland," 4″, green, SS lids **55.00**
Notched prism columns **25.00**
Salt Dips

"Feather" **14.00**
Master and 8 individual, notched
prism **100.00**
Notched prism, set of 6 . . . . **65.00**
Spooner

Floral, double handled **135.00**
Hobstars and strawberry diamonds . **160.00**
Stemware

Champagne

Double teardrop stems, strawberry
diamonds and fans, set of 6 . . . **300.00**
Falred bowls, hobstar chain and
bases, set of 9 . . . . **450.00**
"Kalana Lily," Dorflinger **50.00**
"Monarch," saucer shape, set of 12 **1,200.00**
Cordial, cut and engraved, sgd
Hawkes **65.00**
Sherbet

"Chicago," 4″ h, Fry **65.00**
Sgd Egginton, set of 4, each **35.00**
Supremes, 6½″ h, hobstar, strawberry
diamonds, and fans, hobstar
bases, set of 6 . . . . **270.00**
Water

Clear button Russian, facet cut
teardrop stem, rayed base, set of
8, each **125.00**
"Double Lozenge," set of 9 . . . . . **950.00**
Double teardrop stems, 6½ x 3½″,
strawberry diamond, and fans,
wood polished, set of 12 . . . . . **780.00**
Double terdrop stems, hobstar
bases, cane, hobstars, fans,
strawberry diamonds **1,400.00**

Rayed button Russian, 6″ h, teardrop stems, sgd Hawkes, set of 9 .... **1,170.00**

Wine

Amberina bowl, hobstar button Russian, honeycomb stem **650.00**

Cross-cut diamond and fans, 5″ h, set of 8, each **33.00**

Hobstars, fans, and strawberry diamonds, pr, each **30.00**

"Imperial," teardrop stem, sgd Libbey, pr, each **80.00**

Rayed button Russian, knobbed teardrop stem, rayed bases, set of 4 .... **350.00**

Rayed button Russian, teardrop stem, pattern cut base **200.00**

Ruby bowl, rayed button Russian, Dorflinger, teardrop stem, Brooklyn star base **700.00**

Yellow bowl, hobstar and strawberry diamond, teardrop stems, hobstar base **110.00**

String Holder, fancy notched prism, Gorham SS top **125.00**

Sugar Cube Tray, 9″, cane **75.00**

Syrup Pitcher

4″, SP, hinged lid and handle, fancy vertical notched prisms **70.00**

Strawberry diamond and fan, SS top **120.00**

Tantalus, 13″ h, frame, Quadruple plate on copper frame, two 9½ x 3″ sq bottles, honeycomb and engraved florals, sgd Hawkes on frame and glass **250.00**

Toothbrush Holder, cane **140.00**

Toothpick Holder

2½″ h, prism cut **35.00**

3″ h, pedestal, hobstars **90.00**

Floral **25.00**

Tray

11½ x 13½″, oak leaf shape flashed fancy notched prisms, vesicas, cane Pitkins and Brooks **1,025.00**

12″

"Corinthian," sgd Libbery **625.00**

Hobstars, cane, and strawberry diamonds **300.00**

Pinwheels, hobstars, and floral .. **110.00**

13″, "Alhambra" **1,300.00**

13 x 8½″, rect, handled, sunbursts and leaves **250.00**

14″, Kohinoor surrounding intaglio cut medallions, hobstar center, cane, and vesicas **2,000.00**

18″ l, oval, "Carolyn," Hoare, thick heavy blank, well cut **1,600.00**

18 x 10½″, hobstars sharply cut, clear blank **1,700.00**

Tumble Up, handled pitcher with tumbler over top, geometric and floral .. **410.00**

Tumbler, "Hindoo" pattern, sgd "Hoare," $55.00.

Tumbler

"Bristol Rose," Mount Washington, set of 3 .... **210.00**

Champagne, rayed button Russian, Russian bases, set of 6 .... **480.00**

Clear button Russian, set of 8, each **95.00**

"Harvard," rayed base, set of 3 .... **120.00**

Hobstars, set of 5, each **35.00**

Hobstars, strawberry diamonds, fans, hobstar cluster and base, set of 6 **330.00**

Notched prism, hobstar, cane **55.00**

"Panel," sgd Hawkes, rare **400.00**

"Star of David," 4″, set of 4 .... **260.00**

Whiskey, 3½″ h, 2½″ d rim, hobstar chain and cane **125.00**

Umbrella Stand, 24″ h, hobstar chain around top, middle, and base with vertical notched prism bars between **1,600.00**

Vase

4½″ h, bud, trumpet shape, daisy, sgd Sinclaire, pr **165.00**

12″

Corset shape, cosmos and cane . **75.00**

"Russian and pillar" **900.00**

Trumpet, punty, hobstar, and strawberry diamond **75.00**

12 x 4″, cylindrical, "Queens," Hawkes **825.00**

12 x 4½″, chalice, butterflies, and flowers, facet cut knob near base, pattern cut base **375.00**

14″, trumpet, "Queens," sgd Hawkes **825.00**

14 x 5″

"Assyrian," sgd Sinclaire **1,300.00**

"Lotus," Egginton, rayed base ... **395.00**

15″, "Queens," facet cut knob, hobstar base, slight glass tint, sgd Hawkes **1,000.00**

16″, trumpet, "Teutonic," sgd Hawkes **500.00**

Violet Vase

Fancy notched prism bowl, rayed base **190.00**

Hobstars and strawberry diamonds .	**225.00**
Hobstars and zipper	**80.00**
Wall Placket, 9", "Mums," sgd Hawkes Gravic	**150.00**
Water Set	
Floral and butterfly, pitcher and four tumblers	**200.00**
Hobstars, rose hatching, 9" pitcher and six tumblers	**250.00**
Hobstars, sgd Libbey, tankard pitcher and six tumblers	**475.00**
"Poppy," sgd Tuthill, tankard pitcher and six tumblers	**2,000.00**
"Queens," Hawkes, tankard pitcher and six tumblers	**1,800.00**
Whiskey Jug	
8½", swirled bands of strawberry diamond and cane, hobstar chain, fans	**500.00**
"Brunswick," sgd Hawkes	**900.00**
Whiskey Set, strap handle, button jug, six matching pedestal shot glasses, hobstars and "X" split vesicas, fans, all sgd Hoare	**2,300.00**

CUT VELVET

History: Several glass manufacturers made cut velvet during the late Victorian era, c1870–1900. An outer layer of pastel color was applied over a white casing. The piece then was molded or cut in a ribbed or diamond shape in high relief, exposing portions of the casing. The finish had a satin velvety feel, hence the name "cut velvet."

Vase, 6" h, bottle neck, blue, $225.00.

Bowl, 6", butterscotch, tricorn top	175.00
Creamer, 3½", cranberry, DQ, applied multicolored enamel dec	350.00
Ewer, 4¾", deep blue, DQ, applied frosted handle	140.00
Finger Bowl, 4½" d, blue, DQ	125.00
Rose Bowl, 4¼", blue, DQ, crimped top	175.00
Toothpick, 3⅝", yellow, DQ, sq mouth .	180.00
Vase	
5¼", blue, quatrefoil top	100.00

6¼", opaque white, faint pink int., ribbon candy rim	100.00
8¼"	
Blue	185.00
Pink and white	200.00
8⅜", pale blue	250.00
10", rainbow MOP, DQ, blue coralene dec	225.00

CZECHOSLOVAKIAN ITEMS

History: Objects marked "Made in Czechoslovakia" were produced after 1918 when the country claimed its independence from the Austro-Hungarian Empire. The people became more cosmopolitan, liberated, and expanded their scope of life. Their porcelains, pottery, and glassware reflect many influences.

A specific manufacturer's mark may be identified as being much earlier than 1918, but this only indicates the factory existed in the Bohemian or Austro-Hungarian Empire period.

Reference: Ruth A. Forsythe, *Made in Czechoslovakia*, Richardson Printing Corp., 1982.

Vase, 10⅜" h, red ground, black and brown desert oasis and pyramid scene, $45.00.

GLASS

Ashtray, 4" d, malachite green, three rearing horses form legs, heavy circular glass ashtray, Art Deco	150.00
Basket, 6½" h, 5" d, clear with red and yellow spangle, applied clear handle	50.00
Bowl, cased, yellow int., black ext., polished pontil	45.00
Decanter, 15" h, 5½" d, crystal, cobalt steeple stopper, cobalt prunts in elon-	

gated teardrops around body, po-
lished pontil **70.00**
Dish, filigree, frosted, cameo inset, ftd **45.00**
Lamp, mushroom shape, frosted glass
shade, glass base with silhouette of
lady and gentleman, small raised
roses and beading on shade **350.00**
Lamp Shade, beaded, Forsythe "659" **35.00**
Perfume Bottle
5", amber glass, engraved design,
frosted flowers, stopper **25.00**
5¼", cut crystal, yellow with round,
flat, cut dauber **35.00**
Powder Jar, cut crystal, amber **70.00**
Vase
5", fan shape, pink and black, sgd . . **100.00**
9", Jack-in-the-Pulpit, jade green,
black top edge **40.00**
Wine Set, decanter and six glasses,
cranberry and gold, paper label **100.00**

POTTERY AND PORCELAIN

Animal Dish, stylized yellow chick **25.00**
Bookends, Pouter Pigeon, pr **45.00**
Cologne Bottle, 4", glossy blue, bow
front **12.00**
Creamer, 4½", figural, parrot, multico-
lored **35.00**
Pitcher, 4", red black handle **15.00**
Salt Box, Dutch scene **50.00**
Teapot, cov, and underplate, Chelsea
style, delicate florals, marked "E-
mphila Czechoslovakia" **35.00**
Vase, 9¾", orange with silver cranes
and foliage, pr **35.00**

DAVENPORT
LONGPORT
STAFFORDSHIRE

DAVENPORT

History: John Davenport opened a pottery in
Longport, Staffordshire, England in 1793. His ware
was of high quality, light weight, and cream colored
with a beautiful velvety texture.

The firm made soft-paste (Old Blue), lustre
trimmed ware, and pink lustre with black transfer.
There have been pieces of Gaudy Dutch and Spatterware found with the Davenport mark. Later Davenport became a leading maker of ironstone and
early flow blue. His famous "Cyprus" pattern in
mulberry became very popular. His heirs continued
the business until the factory closed in 1886.

Reference: Susan and Al Bagdade, *Warman's*

*English & Continental Pottery & Porcelain, 1st Edi-
tion,* Warman Publishing Co., Inc., 1987.

**Platter, 10⅜ x 13⅝", flow blue, marked
"Amoy Pattern, Davenport," incised
anchor mark, $200.00.**

Breakfast Set, egg cup stand fitted with
six egg cups, four dishes with domed
covers, oval salt, blue and white,
transfer printed, fishermen in river
landscape by a ruin, imp "Davenport,"
anchor mark, c1860 . . . . **400.00**
Charger, 17 1/2", oval, Venetian harbor
scene, light blue transfer **70.00**
Compote, 2 1/2 x 8 1/2", turquoise and
gold band, tiny raised flowers, hp
scene with man fishing, cows at edge
of lake, c1860, pr **175.00**
Creamer, tan, jasperware, basket-
weave, incised anchor mark **50.00**
Cup and Saucer, Amoy pattern, flow
blue, 3 3/4" cup, 6" saucer, incised
anchor mark **65.00**
Cup Plate, teaberry, pink lustre **30.00**
Dish, ftd, tricorn, Belvoir Castle dec . . **85.00**
Ewer, 9", floral dec, multicolored, c1830 **185.00**
Mustard Pot, 3 1/2", hinged SP cov, turquoise, gilt foliage and florals, 1870–
86 . . . . **65.00**
Pitcher, 8"
Cathedral, pink luster, black transfer **200.00**
Country scene, gold wheat and ber-
ries trim **85.00**
Plate
8", octagonal, floral dec, gold rim . . **40.00**
9 1/8", Legend of Montrose, transfer,
1850–70 . . . . **50.00**
10 1/2", blue and white, scenic, imp
anchor mark **25.00**
Platter
18", white, blue border, anchor mark,
c1820 . . . . **200.00**
20" l, rect, blue and white, transfer
printed exotic bird and flower pat-
tern, c1840 . . . . **300.00**

Punch Bowl, 14″ d, int. painted iron-red,
blue, and gilt, chrysanthemum and
rockwork, iron-red trellis border, rim
with flowering foliage on blue ground,
ext. with band of seaweed pattern in
gilt on pale blue ground between
bands of dark blue foliage, puce mark
"Davenport, Manufacturers To Their
Majesties, Long Port, Staffordshire,"
c1830 . . . . **2,200.00**
Sauce Dish, cov, ladle, creamware,
molded leaves, lime green veining,
early **425.00**
Tazza, 9 1/2″, octagonal, ftd, Imari pat-
tern, c1860 . . . . **110.00**
Tea Set, teapot, creamer, and ftd sugar,
blue and white, marked "Davenport,
Godden No. 1194," c1880 . . . . **100.00**
Tureen, 12″, Blue Willow pattern **150.00**
Vase, 9 3/4″, deep blue, gilt trim, butter-
fly handles, c1870–86 . . . . **175.00**

DECOYS

History: Carved wooden decoys, used to lure
ducks and geese to the hunter have become
widely recognized as an indigenous American folk
art form in the past several years.

Many decoys are from the 1880–1930 period
when commercial gunners commonly hunted over
rigs of several hundred decoys. Many fine carvers
also worked through the 1930s and 1940s.

The value of a decoy is based on several factors: (1) fame of the carver, (2) quality of the carving, (3) species of wild fowl—the most desirable
are herons, swans, mergansers, and shorebirds,
and (4) condition of the original paint (o.p.).

The inexperienced collector should be aware of
several facts. The age of a decoy, per se, is usually
of no importance in determining value. Since very
few decoys were ever signed, it will be quite difficult to attribute most decoys to known carvers.
Anyone who has not examined a known carver's
work will be hardpressed to determine if the paint
on one of his decoys is indeed original.

Repainting severely decreases a decoy's value.
In addition, there are many fakes and reproductions on the market and even experienced collectors are occasionally fooled.

Richard A. Bourne Co., Inc., Hyannis, Massachusetts, is one of the leading auctioneers of decoys. At the sale of May 2, 1986, a wood duck
drake carved by Joe Lincoln sold for $205,000.00.
On July 5, 1986, Richard Oliver auctioned a preening pintail drake carved by Elmer Crowell, East
Harwick, MA, 1915, for $319,000.00.

Decoys listed below are of average wear unless
otherwise noted. o.p. indicates original paint.

Reference: Henry A. Fleckenstein, Jr., *American Factory Decoys*, Schiffer Publishing; Carl F.

Luckey, *Collecting Antique Bird Decoys: An Identification & Value Guide*, Books Americana.

Periodicals: *Decoy Hunter Magazine*, 901
North 9th, Clinton, IN 47842, bimonthly. Subscription: $10.00; *Decoy Magazine*, P.O. Box 1900,
Montego Bay Station, Ocean City, MD 21842,
quarterly publication.

Black Breasted Plover, Elisha Burr,
carved, feeding position, o.p. tiny chip
at end of left wing tip **1,800.00**
Black Duck
Lou Rathmell, weight stamped "1941/
LC Rathmell," little wear, o.p. **2,900.00**
Nathan Cobb, hollow carved, carved
signature on bottom, nestled head
position, o.p. **5,500.00**
Bluebill Drake
Elmer Crowell, carved, crossed wing
tips and feather, excellent feather
paint, head is turned slightly to the
left, oval brand on bottom, c1915,
minor crazing, slight age split on
bottom **15,000.00**
Hector Whittington, o.p., shallow chip
on left side of bill, c1935 . . . . **200.00**

**Pintail, Delaware River, Bordentown,
NJ, by Black, $450.00.**

Bluebill Hen, Chauncey Wheeler, o.p.
well preserved **950.00**
Brant, Nathan Cobb, hollow carved, ser-
ified carved signature, head turned to
the left, moderate wear, o.p. **11,000.00**
Bufflehead Drake, A. Elmer Crowell,
miniature, near mint **1,300.00**
Bufflehead Hen, Nate Quillen, branded
"ESH" on bottom, inscribed, moderate flaking and wear, slight age check
in neck **1,000.00**
Canada Goose, Lloyd Parker, excellent
o.p., minor flaking **3,100.00**
Canvasback Drake, John Dilley, full
bodied, feather paint, "Curlew" identification in black, bill replacement by
Kenneth E. DeLong **8,000.00**
Crow, William Bowman, Long Island,
black glass eyes, o.p., age split on
right side of body, reglued chip at end
of tail **2,150.00**

Curlew, Gibian, carved wing tips and feathers, sgd **700.00**
Dowitcher, unknown maker, New Jersey, o.p. little wear, replacement bill **550.00**
Eider Drake, E.F. Brackett, branded "E F Brackett," inlet neck, folkey paint pattern **450.00**
Goldeneye Drake, branded "J W W," carved crossed wing tips, primary feathers, and tail feathers, slight flaking, o.p. **4,750.00**
Goldeneye Hen, Chauncey Wheeler, Alexandria Bay, excellent o.p., minor wear **2,000.00**
Harlequin Duck, unknown maker, Nova Scotia, minor age splitting to body, o.p. **4,500.00**
Mallard Drake, A. Elmer Crowell, rect brand on bottom, carved, raised gesso feet on base, cocked head and turned slightly to right **1,100.00**
Mallard Hen, Stevens Brothers, o.p., flakes areas on body, worn on top of head **3,300.00**
Merganser Drake, branded "A. Shaw," o.p. **2,600.00**
Merganser Hen, Martha's Vineyard, old paint, slight age split in neck, re-glued bill **1,000.00**
Old Squaw Drake, John McGlouchlin, o.p. sgd on bottom **600.00**
Pintail Drake, Ward Brothers, balsa bodied, o.p., minor wear **1,500.00**
Pintail Hen, John Dawson, Delaware River, hollow carved, raised wing tips, o.p., well preserved **16,500.00**
Red Breasted Merganser, Franklin Pierce Wright, Cape Cod, orig horsehair comb, incised wings, maroon feathered breast, o.p. minor flaking and wear, slight age split in neck . . . **15,000.00**
Redhead, unknown maker, full bodied, head turned to the right, oval brand on bottom, o.p. **6,000.00**
Robin Snipe, New Jersey, unknown maker, carved wings, unusual paddle tail, o.p., bill replacement **200.00**
Ruddy Turnstone, John Dilley, feather paint, "Brant Bird" under the tail . . . **7,000.00**
Seagull, Wildfowler, Pt. Pleasant, o.p., excellent **375.00**
Surf Scoter, branded initials "C.M.," oval brand on bottom, small amount of flaking on head **10,500.00**
Swan, New Jersey, carved, preening position, o.p. small chip at end of tail **900.00**
White Winged Scoter, branded "SB" on bottom, two inset lead weights, tack eyes, average flaking and wear, c1850 . . . . **1,000.00**
Widgeon Drake, Ward Brothers, balsa

body, orig paint, sgd Lem and Steve, includes photograph, c1948 . . . . . . **3,600.00**
Willet, Charles Thomas, carved wing tips, slight curve in bill, o.p. **2,700.00**
Yellowlegs, unknown maker, carved, raised wing, open bill with feather in mouth, rect brand on bottom, inscribed on bottom **10,500.00**

DEDHAM POTTERY

History: Alexander W. Robertson established the Chelsea Pottery in Chelsea, Massachusetts, in 1860. In 1872 it was known as the Chelsea Keramic Art Works.

In 1895 the pottery moved to Dedham, and the name was changed to Dedham Pottery. Their principal product was gray crackleware dinnerware with a blue decoration, the rabbit pattern being the most popular. The factory closed in 1943.

The following marks help determine the approximate age of items: (1) Chelsea Keramic Art Works, "Robertson" impressed, 1876–1889; (2) C.P.U.S. impressed in a cloverleaf, 1891–1895; (3) Foreshortened rabbit, 1895–1896; (4) Conventional rabbit with "Dedham Pottery" stamped in blue, 1897; (5) Rabbit mark wtih "Registered", 1929–1943.

Reference: Lloyd E. Hawes, *The Dedham Pottery And The Earlier Robertson's Chelsea Potteries*, Dedham Historical Society, 1968.

Bowl
  4½", Rabbit **120.00**
  7½", Turtle **225.00**
  10", Magnolia, oval **225.00**
  10½ x 2½", Rabbit inside border dec **375.00**
Candlesticks, Rabbit, pr **225.00**
Celery Dish, Rabbit **200.00**
Chocolate Pot, Rabbit **300.00**
Creamer
  3", Magnolia **150.00**
  4", Rabbit **125.00**
Cup and Saucer
  Duck **135.00**
  Elephant **150.00**
  Pond Lily **125.00**
Egg cup, 4", double, Rabbit **150.00**
Mug, Rabbit **148.00**
Pitcher, 8", Rabbit **275.00**
Planter
  6 x 3¼ x 3¼", green, circular mirror dec, marked "JHR, HCR" **250.00**
  8¼ x 5¾ x 3¾", green, zig zag dec, marked **450.00**

8¹¹⁄₁₆ x 4¾ x 4½", pedestal, leaf design, ruffled top, short rabbit mark ... 300.00
8¾ x 5¼ x 3¾", green, blocked mirror, ruffled top, marked "Capt." DPCO in hexagon 350.00

Plate, 6", bread and butter, Azalea pattern, $90.00.

Plate
6"
Grape border, imp rabbit ears mark ... 100.00
Iris 100.00
Polar Bear 200.00
Pond Lily, imp rabbit ears 100.00
Rabbits 75.00
6¼", crab and waves, post 1929 mark ... 325.00
7½"
Azalea 100.00
Grape 100.00
8½"
Fish in center, blue waves, Crackleware, pre 1929 mark 1,100.00
Horse Chestnut, cipher mark of Maude Davenport 250.00
Pond Lily 175.00
Poppy, pre 1929 mark 500.00
Rabbit, 2 ears, pre 1929 mark ... 90.00
Snowtree, pre 1929 mark 125.00
Turkey 150.00
8⅜", Woodcock in flight, pre 1929 mark 1,450.00
10"
Butterfly 300.00
Mushroom, blue mark, imp rabbit ears 125.00
Platter, 12½", Rabbit 225.00
Salt Shaker, Rabbit, light blue, Crackleware 135.00
Sugar, cov, Rabbit 150.00
Tea Cup, 2¼" h, 4" d, Snowtree 100.00
Tile
Horse Chestnut 125.00
Rabbit 120.00
Vase
7¼", Volcanic, orange peel texture,

red dragon's blood glaze, white finger-like runs, marked "Hugh Robertson" 800.00
8"
Crackleware, blue dogwood, emb, rabbit mark 450.00
Glossy shaded lime to dark moss green, marked "Hugh Robertson" 250.00
Volcanic, silver gray and black, light green and blue runs, marked "Hugh Robertson" 300.00
Volcanic, red, orange, and black, yellow rabbit mark 1,000.00
9", Volcanic, shades of chocolate, dark brown, taupe and tan, marked "Hugh Robertson/BW" 400.00

DELFTWARE

History: Delftware is pottery of a soft red clay body with tin enamel glaze. The white, dense, opaque color came from adding tin ash to lead glaze. The first examples had blue designs on a white ground. Polychrome examples followed.

The name originally applied to pottery made in the region around Delft, Holland, beginning in the 16th century and ending in the late 18th century. Tin came from the Cornish mines in England. By the 17th and 18th centuries English potters in London, Bristol, and Liverpool were copying the glaze and designs. Some designs unique to English potters also developed.

In Germany and France, the ware is known as Faience and in Italy as Majolica

Reference: Susan and Al Bagdade, *Warman's English & Continental Pottery & Porcelain, 1st Edition,* Warman Publishing Co., Inc., 1987.

Reproduction Alert: Much souvenir Delft-type material has been produced in the late 19th and 20th centuries to appeal to the foreign traveler. Don't confuse these modern pieces with the older examples.

Apothecary Jar, 9¾", brownish black enameled label 375.00
Bank, 4" l, figural, rabbit, polychrome enameling 250.00
Bird Feeder, 14½", cylindrical, five pierced arches, blue and white swags and florals, line and trellis borders, Bristol, c1760 .... 715.00
Bottle, 10", globular, flared garlic neck, blue and white, stylized baskets of flowers and trailing branches, Liverpool, c1770 .... 500.00
Bowl, 12", blue and white, bird on flowering foliage and insert, int. with flower spray, yellow rim, band of stylized flowerheads, Liverpool, c1740 . 275.00

Miniature Lamp, 10½", Cosmos Brenner stamped on wick turner, $300.00.

Charger
13⅝", broad cavetto with flowers and geometric dec, bird and flowers in center, late 17th C, one faint age crack **600.00**
21", broad cavetto, plain center, scenes of Chinese at tea, shades of blue, mid 18th C **850.00**
Dish, 13½" d, deep, yellow and lavender flowers, green leaves, Lambeth **700.00**
Ewer, 8½", floral dec, zigzag band, blue, purple, and yellow ochre **250.00**
Figure
4", fruit, polychrome enamel, repaired leaf, pr **100.00**
6¾", bird, open base, bright enamel dec, marked "AK," late **100.00**
Flower Brick, 5" l, rect, blue and white

scene, buildings in landscape on long side, figure in boat on short sides, pierced top with blue dot pattern, four ogee feet, English, c1750 . . . . **375.00**
Ink Well
4 x 4 x 2", polychrome flowers, white ground **250.00**
4¼", handle, stylized floral dec, multicolored, Lambeth, English, c1700 **350.00**
Jar
8", ovoid, polychrome floral dec, "Meryland" on front, brass dome lid **875.00**
22", tin glazed, baluster form, piper and dancers, fitted as lamp **425.00**
Mug, 5½", blue and white, bust, "In Memory of Lord Nelson," minor wear **275.00**
Plaque, 16½", portrait of lady, flow blue, urn and letters mark, pierced for hanging **400.00**
Plate, 9", blue and white, floral design, late 18th C **185.00**
Shoe, 6¾", blue and white, high heel, pointed toe, molded buckle, band of trellis pattern ribbon, Bristol, c1760 . **600.00**
Soup Plate, 8¾", blue and white, fisherman on pier, boat, buildings and trees in background, pine cones and foliage border, Bristol, c1760, pr . . . **375.00**
Stein, 7½", blue and white florals, sponged purple dec, pewter lid and base, marked "BP" **450.00**
Tile, manganese, roundels of boats, buildings, and windmills in river scene, stylized floral sprays in corners, Dutch, 18th C, set of 15 . . . . . **550.00**
Tobacco Jar, 11¾", oviform, blue and white, rococo scroll, foliage and florals, "SPANJOLA" in blue, Dutch, c1720 . . . . **1,000.00**

DEPRESSION GLASS

History: Depression glass is a glassware made during the period of 1920–40. It was an inexpensive machine-made glass, produced by several companies in various patterns and colors. The number of pieces within a pattern varied.

Depression glass was sold through variety stores, given as premiums, or packaged with certain products. Movie houses gave it away from 1935 until well into the 1940s.

Like pattern glass, knowing the proper name of a pattern is the key to collecting. Collectors should be prepared to do research.

References: Gene Florence, *The Collector's Encyclopedia of Depression Glass,* Seventh Edition. Collector Books, 1986.; Gene Florence, *Very Rare Glassware Of The Depression Years,* Collector Books, 1987; Carl F. Luckey and Mary Burris, *An Identification & Value Guide to Depression Era Glassware,* Second Edition, Books Americana, 1986, Mark Schliesmann, *Price Survey Second Edition,* Park Avenue Publications, Ltd, 1984, Hazel Marie Weatherman, *1984 Supplement & Price Trends for Colored Glassware Of The Depression Era, Book 1,* published by author, 1984.

Periodical: The Daze, Box 57, Ottisville, MI 48451. Subscription: $15.00.

Collectors' Club: National Depression Glass Association, Inc., P.O. Box 11128, Springfield MO 65808. Dues: $10.00.

Reproduction Alert: Send a self addressed, stamped business envelope to *The Daze* and request a copy of their glass reproduction list. It is one of best bargains in the antiques business.

Additional Listings: See *Warman's Americana & Collectibles* for more examples.

AMERICAN SWEETHEART, Macbeth-Evans Glass Company, 1930–36. Made in blue, cremax, monax, colored rimmed monax, pink, and red.

	Blue	Cremax	Monax	Color Rimmed Monax	Pink	Red
Bowl						
3¾", berry, small	—	—	—	—	25.00	—
4½", soup, cream.	—	—	45.00	—	35.00	—
6", cereal.	—	8.00	10.00	25.00	8.50	—
9", berry, master	—	35.00	40.00	65.00	20.00	—
9½", soup, flat	—	—	35.00	—	27.50	—
11", vegetable, oval	—	—	50.00	—	25.00	—
18", console	700.00	—	275.00	—	—	650.00
Creamer, ftd	90.00	—	8.00	60.00	18.00	75.00
Cup	85.00	—	7.00	55.00	11.00	70.00
Lamp Shade.	—	400.00	375.00	—	—	—
Lazy Susan, 2 tier	—	—	225.00	—	—	—
Pitcher						
7½", 60 oz.	—	—	—	—	375.00	—
8", 80 oz	—	—	—	—	365.00	—
Plate						
6–6½", bread and butter. .	—	—	3.50	14.00	2.25	—
8", salad	60.00	—	6.00	25.00	6.50	50.00
9", luncheon	—	—	7.50	30.00	8.50	—
9¾", dinner	—	—	12.00	45.00	15.00	—
10¼", dinner	—	—	18.00	—	16.00	—
11", chop.	—	—	11.00	—	—	—
12", salver	150.00	—	10.00	—	8.00	125.00
13"	—	—	40.00	90.00	18.50	—
15½", server	225.00	—	165.00	—	—	225.00
Pole Lamp	—	600.00	750.00	—	—	—
Salt and Pepper, single	—	—	100.00	—	125.00	—
Saucer	25.00	—	2.50	14.00	2.50	25.00
Sherbet						
3¾", ftd	—	—	—	30.00	12.00	—
4¼", fdt	—	—	12.50	—	8.50	—
Sugar, open, ftd	90.00	60.00	5.50	60.00	6.50	75.00
Sugar Lid	—	—	130.00	—	—	—
Tidbit, 3 tier	425.00	—	165.00	—	—	425.00
Tumbler						
3½", 5 oz	—	—	—	—	40.00	—
4", 9 oz	—	—	—	—	45.00	—
4½", 10 oz.	—	—	—	—	50.00	—

ANNIVERSARY, Jeannette Glass Co., 1947-49. Made in crystal and pink.

	Crystal	Pink		Crystal	Pink
Bowl			9", dinner	3.50	5.00
4⅞", berry, small	1.50	3.00	12½", sandwich server . . .	4.25	7.00
7⅜", soup, flat	3.50	6.25	Saucer	1.00	1.25
9", fruit	8.00	12.00	Sherbet, ftd.	2.50	4.50
Butter Dish	22.00	28.00	Sugar, cov	5.00	6.50
Compote, 3 legs	3.00	7.50	Vase, 6½".	6.00	8.00
Cup	2.50	4.50	Wall Pocket.	10.00	15.00
Pickle Dish, 9".	3.50	6.50	Wine, 2½ oz	6.00	10.00
Plate					
6¼", sherbet	1.50	2.25			

BEADED BLOCK, Imperial Glass Company, 1927-1930s. Made in amber, crystal, green, ice blue, iridescent, milk glass, pink, red, and vaseline.

	Amber, Green, Pink	Crystal	Other Colors
Bowl			
4½", handled, jelly	6.00	4.00	12.50
5½", square.	6.00	4.00	9.00
6", cereal.	8.50	6.00	15.00
6¼", fruit	6.50	4.50	14.00
6½", handled, pickle.	10.00	8.00	15.00
7¼", round, flared	8.00	6.00	15.00
7½", round, fluted	18.00	12.00	20.00
7½", round, plain	8.00	6.50	14.50
8¼", celery	10.00	8.00	16.00
Creamer.	12.00	10.00	18.50
Pitcher, 5¼"	85.00	—	—
Plate			
7¾", square.	5.00	2.00	8.00
8¾", round	8.00	3.00	15.00
Sugar.	12.00	10.00	18.00
Vase, 6"	10.00	7.50	20.00

BUBBLE, "Bull's eye," "Provincial," Anchor Hocking Glass Company, 1934–65. Made in crystal, dark green, light blue, pink, and red.

	Crystal	Dark Green	Light Blue	Pink	Red
Bowl					
4", berry, small.	2.25	4.00	6.00	—	—
4½", fruit	2.25	6.00	7.50	—	5.00
4½", nappy, handle	8.50	5.50	8.00	—	—
5¼", cereal	3.00	8.75	6.00	—	—
7¾", soup, flat	—	—	7.75	—	—
8⅜", berry, master	6.00	20.00	9.00	8.00	5.00
9", flanged.	—	—	40.00	—	—
Candlesticks, pr	11.00	20.00	—	—	—
Creamer.	7.25	7.50	20.00	—	—
Cup	1.25	4.50	3.25	27.50	—
Lamp	30.00	—	—	—	—
Pitcher, 64 oz, ice lip	40.00	—	—	—	37.50
Plate					
6¾", bread and butter . . .	1.00	1.50	2.25	—	—
9⅜", dinner	2.25	6.00	3.50	—	6.00
9⅜", grill	3.00	6.75	8.50	—	—

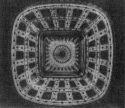
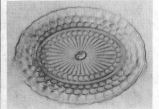

Left, American Sweetheart, soup plate, 9½", pink, $27.50; center, Beaded Block, plate, 7¾", vaseline, $8.00; right, Bubble, platter, 12", pale blue, orig paper label, $12.00.

	Crystal	Dark Green	Light Blue	Pink	Red
Platter, 12″	—	—	12.00	—	—
Saucer	1.50	1.50	1.75	17.50	1.50
Sugar	4.00	6.50	12.50	—	—
Tidbit	—	—	—	—	18.00
Tumbler					
6 oz, juice	5.00	—	—	—	10.00
9 oz, water	10.00	4.75	—	—	5.75
12 oz, iced tea	—	—	—	—	6.00
16 oz, lemonade	—	—	—	—	14.00

CIRCLE, Hocking Glass Company, 1930s. Made in green and pink.

	Green	Pink		Green	Pink
Bowl			8″, luncheon	3.50	3.50
4½″, berry	3.25	3.50	9½″, dinner	7.50	7.50
8″, berry	7.50	8.00	Saucer	1.50	1.50
Creamer	5.00	6.00	Sherbet		
Cup	2.50	2.50	3⅛″	4.00	4.50
Decanter	25.00	28.00	4¾″	5.00	5.25
Goblet			Sugar	4.50	5.00
4½″, wine	15.00	5.00	Tumbler		
8 oz, water	7.50	7.50	4 oz, juice	8.00	8.00
Pitcher, 80 oz	20.00	20.00	8 oz, water	6.00	6.50
Plate			Vase	18.00	20.00
6″, sherbet	2.00	2.00			

COLONIAL BLOCK, Hazel Atlas Glass Company, early 1930s. Made in green and pink, limited production in white, 1950s.

	Green	Pink	White
Bowl			
4″, berry	4.50	4.50	—
7″	12.00	12.00	—
Butter Dish, cov	30.00	32.50	—
Butter Tub	30.00	30.00	—
Candy Dish, cov	20.00	25.00	—
Creamer	8.00	8.50	6.00
Goblet	8.00	8.00	—
Pitcher	25.00	25.00	—
Sugar	8.00	8.00	5.00
Sugar Lid	5.00	5.00	3.00

DAISY, "No. 620," Indiana Glass Co., 1933–44. Made in amber: 1940; crystal: 1933; and green: 1960–81.

	Amber	Crystal	Green
Ashtray	20.00	—	2.75
Bowl			
4⅛″, berry	8.00	3.50	3.50
4¾″, cream soup	6.00	4.50	4.50
6″, cereal	20.00	10.00	10.00
7⅜″, berry	22.00	—	14.50
9″, salad	18.00	5.50	5.50
10″, vegetable, oval	20.00	5.00	5.00
Cake Plate	8.50	5.00	5.00

	Amber	Crystal	Green
Creamer, ftd	6.75	5.00	5.00
Cup	3.50	2.50	2.50
Plate			
6″, sherbet	2.00	1.00	1.00
7⅜″, salad	4.00	2.50	2.50
8⅜″, luncheon	5.00	4.00	4.00
9⅜″, dinner	5.50	3.50	3.50
10⅜″, grill	10.00	5.00	5.00
11½″, sandwich	8.50	5.00	5.00
Platter, 10¾″	12.00	4.50	4.50
Relish, 8⅜″, 3 part	18.00	10.00	10.00
Saucer	1.50	1.00	1.25
Sherbet, ftd	8.50	4.25	4.25
Sugar, ftd	5.75	5.00	5.00
Tumbler			
9 oz, ftd	12.00	9.75	7.50
12 oz, ftd	28.00	15.00	15.00

FLORENTINE NO. 2, "Poppy No. 2," Hazel Atlas Glass Company, 1934–37. Made in crystal, green, ice blue, pink, and yellow. Limited production in cobalt blue and amber.

	Crystal	Green	Ice Blue	Pink	Yellow
Ashtray, 3¼″	12.00	24.50	—	—	15.00
Bowl					
4½″, berry, small	10.00	10.00	—	9.00	13.50
4¾″, soup, cream	7.50	9.00	30.00	12.00	15.00
5½″	25.00	25.00	—	—	35.00
6″, cereal	18.00	18.00	—	14.50	25.00
8″, berry, master	15.00	15.00	—	16.50	19.00
9″, flat	10.00	10.00	—	—	—
Butter Dish	85.00	85.00	—	—	125.00
Candlesticks, pr	40.00	40.00	—	—	45.00
Candy Dish	65.00	65.00	—	95.00	—
Coaster, 3¼″	12.00	12.00	—	14.00	15.00
Compote, ruffled, 3½″	15.00	15.00	45.00	8.00	18.00
Creamer	5.50	7.50	—	—	12.00
Cup	5.00	5.00	—	—	7.00
Custard Cup	45.00	45.00	—	—	65.00
Gravy Boat	—	—	—	—	50.00
Nut Dish, ruffled	—	—	32.00	9.75	—
Pitcher					
6¼″, 24 oz, cone	—	—	—	—	85.00
7½″, 28 oz, cone	35.00	35.00	—	—	22.50
7½″, 48 oz	42.50	42.50	—	100.00	140.00
8″, 76 oz	75.00	75.00	—	200.00	250.00
Plate					
6″, sherbet	2.00	2.50	—	—	4.00
6¼″, indentation	—	—	—	—	22.00
8½″, salad	5.00	5.00	—	6.00	7.00
10″, dinner	6.75	9.00	—	12.00	12.00
10¼″, grill	7.00	7.00	—	—	8.00
11″, oval, gravy	—	—	—	—	42.50
Platter, 11½″	10.00	10.00	—	12.00	30.00
Relish					
10″, 3 part	25.00	25.00	—	14.00	15.00
Plain	—	—	—	—	15.00
Salt and Pepper, pr	35.00	35.00	—	—	40.00

	Crystal	Green	Ice Blue	Pink	Yellow
Saucer	2.50	2.50	—	—	3.00
Sherbet, ftd.	6.00	7.00	—	—	8.50
Sugar, open	5.50	6.50	—	—	9.00
Sugar Lid	18.00	18.00	—	—	23.00
Tray, condiment	—	—	—	—	65.00
Tumbler					
3½", 5 oz, juice	7.50	7.50	—	8.00	18.00
3½", 5 oz, ftd.	6.75	6.75	—	9.00	14.00
4", 5 oz, ftd	7.50	7.75	—	—	16.00
4", 9 oz, water	10.00	10.00	50.00	—	—
4½", 9 oz, ftd.	20.00	20.00	—	12.00	22.00
5", 12 oz, iced tea	20.00	20.00	—	25.00	30.00
Vase or parfait, 6"	40.00	40.00	—	—	55.00

MISS AMERICA, "Diamond Pattern," Hocking Glass Co., 1935–37. Made in crystal and pink, limited production in green, ice blue, and red.

	Crystal	Green	Pink	Red
Bowl				
4½", berry	—	7.50	12.00	—
6¼", cereal	6.00	10.00	12.00	—
8", vegetable	30.00	—	45.00	300.00
8¾", fruit	24.00	—	40.00	—
10", vegetable, oval	10.00	—	14.50	—
Butter Dish, cov	175.00	—	375.00	—
Cake Plate, ftd, 12"	20.00	—	32.00	—
Candy Dish, cov, 11½"	50.00	—	100.00	—
Celery, 10½"	10.00	—	17.50	—
Coaster	14.00	—	20.00	—
Compote, 5"	12.00	—	18.00	—
Creamer, ftd	6.50	—	14.00	125.00
Cup	7.50	10.00	12.00	—
Goblet				
3¾", 3 oz wine	18.00	—	50.00	150.00
4¾", 5 oz, juice	16.00	—	50.00	—
5½", 10 oz, water.	18.00	—	40.00	150.00
Pitcher				
8", 65 oz	50.00	—	85.00	—
8½", 65 oz, ice lip	55.00	—	90.00	—
Plate				
5¾", sherbet	3.00	5.00	4.00	—
6¾", bread & butter	—	6.00	9.50	—
8½", luncheon	5.00	8.00	13.00	—
10", dinner.	9.00	—	17.00	—
10¼", grill	7.00	—	18.00	—
Platter, 12½".	14.00	—	15.00	—
Relish				
8¾", 4 part	8.00	—	16.50	—
11¾", round.	20.00	—	125.00	—
Salt and Pepper	20.00	175.00	40.00	—
Saucer	2.50	—	4.50	—
Sherbet	7.00	—	15.00	—
Sugar.	6.00	—	10.00	125.00
Tumbler				
4", 5 oz, juice.	16.00	—	32.00	—
4½", 10 oz, water.	18.00	15.00	25.00	—
6¾", 14 oz, iced tea	20.00	—	42.50	—

NORMANDIE, "Bouquet and Lattice," Federal Glass Company, 1933–40. Made in amber, iridescent, and pink.

	Amber	Irid	Pink
Bowl			
5", berry, small.	4.00	4.75	4.50
6½", cereal	8.50	6.50	6.75
8½", berry, master	10.50	10.00	14.00
10", veg, oval.	12.00	12.00	20.00
Creamer, ftd	5.50	6.00	6.50
Cup	5.00	5.50	5.00
Pitcher, 8", 80 oz.	50.00	—	70.00
Plate			
6", sherbet.	3.50	2.00	4.00
8", salad	8.50	25.00	9.00
9¼", luncheon	9.00	8.00	9.50
11", dinner.	18.00	12.00	40.00
11", grill.	10.00	14.50	15.00
Platter, 11¼".	15.00	12.00	15.75
Salt and Pepper, pr	35.00	—	56.00
Saucer	2.00	2.50	2.25
Sherbet	7.00	4.50	6.00
Sugar.	5.00	5.75	6.25
Tumbler			
4", 5 oz, juice.	12.00	—	28.00
4¼", 9 oz, water	12.50	—	25.00
5", 12 oz, iced tea	15.00	—	40.00

PINEAPPLE AND FLORAL, "No. 618," Indiana Glass Company, 1932–37. Made in amber, crystal, and red.

	Amber	Crystal	Red
Ashtray, 4½".	16.00	15.00	18.00
Bowl			
4¾", berry, small	22.00	45.00	25.00
5", soup, cream	16.00	14.00	15.00
6", cereal.	18.50	27.00	20.00
7", salad	9.00	3.50	9.00
10", vegetable, oval	15.00	18.00	15.00
Compote	7.00	3.00	7.00
Creamer.	7.00	6.50	7.50

Left, Daisy, creamer and sugar, amber, $12.50; Miss America, candy dish, pink, $100.00; Waterford, goblet, 5¼", crystal, $10.00.

	Amber	Crystal	Red
Cup	5.00	5.00	5.00
Plate			
6″, bread and butter	5.00	2.25	5.00
8⅜″, salad.	8.50	7.50	8.00
9⅜″, dinner	12.00	10.00	12.00
11½″, indentation.	22.00	20.00	22.00
Platter, 11″	14.00	12.00	14.00
Relish, 11½″, divided.	18.00	15.00	18.50
Saucer	3.00	3.00	3.00
Sherbet, ftd.	15.00	15.00	15.00
Sugar.	8.00	6.50	8.00
Tumbler			
4¼″, flat	25.00	22.50	25.00
5″, 12 oz	—	28.00	—
Vase, cone shape	—	25.00	—

ROSEMARY, "Dutch Rose," Federal Glass Company, 1935–37. Made in amber, green, and pink.

	Amber	Green	Pink
Bowl			
5″, berry	4.00	5.00	6.50
5¼″, soup, cream.	8.00	14.00	13.00
6″, cereal.	10.00	12.50	12.50
10″, vegetable, oval	8.00	15.00	12.00
Creamer, ftd	7.00	10.00	10.00
Cup	4.00	7.50	4.50
Plate			
6¾″, salad.	4.50	6.00	4.00
9″, dinner	5.50	10.00	10.00
9½″, grill	6.00	10.00	10.00
Platter, 12″	10.00	15.00	14.00
Saucer	2.00	3.00	2.00
Sugar, ftd	7.00	10.00	8.00
Tumbler, 4¼″, 9 oz	18.00	20.00	24.00

VICTORY, Diamond Glassware Company, 1929–32. Made in amber, green, and pink. Limited production in black and cobalt blue.

	Amber	Green	Pink
Bonbon, 7″	9.00	9.00	9.00
Bowl			
6½″, cereal	8.00	8.25	7.50
8½″, soup, flat	10.00	10.00	10.00
9″, vegetable, oval	25.00	20.00	20.00
12″, console	28.00	20.00	20.00
Candlesticks, pr, 3″	25.00	15.00	15.00
Cheese & Cracker Set.	—	17.50	18.00
Compote, 6″, h	10.00	9.50	9.50
Creamer.	10.00	9.00	9.00
Cup	6.00	5.00	5.00
Goblet, 5″, 7 oz	18.00	12.00	12.00
Gravy Boat, underplate	115.00	115.00	110.00
Mayonnaise Set, underplate, ladle	35.00	28.00	28.00
Plate			
6″, bread & butter.	3.00	2.00	2.00
7″, salad	5.00	3.50	3.50

	Amber	Green	Pink
8", luncheon	5.00	4.00	4.00
9", dinner	12.00	10.00	10.00
Platter, 12"	20.00	15.00	15.00
Sandwich Server	35.00	15.00	18.00
Saucer	4.00	3.50	3.50
Sherbet	10.00	8.00	7.50
Sugar	12.00	12.00	12.00

WATERFORD, "Waffle," Hocking Glass Company, 1938–44. Made in crystal and pink. Limited production in yellow and white. Forest green made in the 1950s.

	Crystal	Forest Green	Pink
Ashtray, 4"	5.00	—	5.75
Bowl			
4¾", berry	4.25	—	6.50
5½", cereal	10.00	—	12.00
8¼", berry	7.00	—	12.50
Butter Dish, cov	24.00	—	175.00
Cake Plate, 10¼", handled	5.00	—	10.00
Coaster, 4"	3.00	—	4.00
Creamer			
Miss America style	18.00	—	—
Oval	2.50	—	7.50
Cup	4.00	—	10.00
Goblet			
5¼"	10.00	—	9.50
5½", Miss America style	25.00	—	40.00
Lamp, 4"	25.00	—	—
Pitcher			
42 oz, tilted juice	18.00	—	—
80 oz, tilted ice lip	24.00	—	100.00
Plate			
6", sherbet	1.50	—	3.50
7⅛", salad	3.75	—	5.00
9⅝", dinner	5.00	—	10.00
13¾", sandwich	8.00	8.00	8.00
Relish, 13¾", 5 part	20.00	—	—
Salad Fork and Spoon, pr	14.00	—	—
Salt and Pepper, pr	4.50	—	—
Saucer	1.50	—	3.50
Sherbet, ftd	2.50	—	7.00
Sugar			
Cov	5.25	—	6.50
Open	2.50	—	10.00
Tray, 14", handled	4.00	30.00	—
Tumbler			
3½", 5 oz, juice	—	—	25.00
4⅞", 10 oz, ftd	8.00	—	10.00

DISNEYANA

History: Walt Disney and the creations of the famous Disney Studios hold a place of fondness and enchantment in the hearts of people throughout the world. The release of "Steamboat Willie" featuring Mickey Mouse in 1928 heralded an entertainment empire.

Walt and his brother, Roy, showed shrewd business acumen. From the beginning they licensed the reproduction of Disney characters in products ranging from wristwatches to clothing. In 1984

Donald Duck celebrated his 50th birthday, and collectors took a renewed interest in material related to him.

The market in Disneyana has been established by a few determined dealers and auction houses. Hake's Americana and Collectibles of York, PA offers several hundred Disneyana items in each of their bimonthly mail and phone bid auctions. Sotheby's collector carousel auctions often include Disney cels, and Lloyd Ralston Toys auctions include Disney toys.

References: Robert Heide & John Gilman, *Cartoon Collectibles*, 1984 (only covers Disney material); Richard Schickel, *The Disney Version: The Life, Times, Art and Commerce of Walt Disney*, Avon Books, 1968; Tom Tumbusch, *Tomart's Illustrated Disneyana Catalog and Price Guide*, Vols. 1, 2, and 3, Tomart Publications, 1985.

Archives: Walt Disney Archives, 500 South Buena Vista Street, Burbank, CA 91521

Collectors' Club: Mouse Club, 2056 Cirone Way, San Jose, CA 95124

Additional Listings: See *Warman's Americana & Collectibles* for more examples.

Advisor: Ted Hake

Alice in Wonderland
  Fan card, full color, caption "Walt Disney's All Cartoon Feature—Alice in Wonderland," 8 x 10" 40.00
  Marionette, composition, blue dress, white apron, yellow hair, black felt hair bow, 14", by Peter Puppet Playthings, 1950s 75.00
Bambi
  Alarm Clock, animated, Flower and Thumper on dial, second hand is butterfly on Bambi's tail, light blue metal case, 2½ x 4½ x 5", orig box, Bayard of France, 1972 . . . . 85.00
  Bowl, cereal, 5" d, Bambi on bottom, butterfly on tail, flowers, Walt Disney Productions, c1940 . . . . 20.00
  Figure, glazed ceramic, turned head looking at butterfly on tail, copyright marked "Walt Disney Productions/ Japan," 2½ x 7 x 6½", c1960 . . . . 30.00
  Picture, framed, "Bambi and Mother," c1940, Courvoisier Galleries sticker, c1940 . . . . 250.00
Davy Crockett, Toy, "Walt Disney's Official Davy Crockett Western Prairie Wagon," red litho tin, full color scene, Mouseketeer symbol on side, orig brown cartoon with red illus, Adco-Liberty Mfg Co, c1950 . . . . 65.00
Donald Duck
  Celluloid, Donald Duck as musketeer on the defense, 9¼ x 6¼" 100.00
  Comic Book Art, orig 8 panel strip, pen and ink by Al Taliaferro, Walt

Disney Comics #55, page 29, 19 x 13" 600.00
  Doll, 16", leatherette, angry Donald, by Richard G. Krueger, c1935 . . . 400.00
  Planter, figural, sitting on top of ABC blocks, 5½", Leeds, c1940 . . . . . 25.00
  Toy, wooden, Donald playing xylophone, paper labels, Fisher Price #177, 6 x 11 x 13", c1940 . . . . . . 50.00
Dumbo
  Figure, 5½" h, Baby Weems, seated, baby bonnet, incised No 41 American Pottery, c1940 . . . . 75.00
  Sketchpad, 24 ink drawings in sequence, stamped Disney Studios, c1940, 13 x 17" 300.00
Fantasia
  Celluloid, satyrs and unicorns dancing in pasture, applied to airbrushed ground, Courvoisier Galleries label, sgd "Walt Disney" in pencil on mat, 1940, 11½ x 8" . . . 1,250.00
  Planter, ceramic, dancing mushrooms, turquiose, high relief on both sides, 12" l x 7" w x 2" d, Vernon Kilns, c1940 . . . . 100.00
  Toy, carousel, unicorns, 25", 1940 . . 225.00
Goofy
  Plate, china, Goofy seated on a crate, brick wall and flowers in back, cameos of Bambi, Thumper, Flower, two butterflies, and bluebird around edge, marked "Beswick, England, 7" 35.00
  Wristwatch, "Backwards," 17 jewels, leather band, MIB 250.00
Mickey Mouse
  Bank, treasure chest, red leatherette, brass trim, emb Mickey and Minnie on top, marked "Zell Products" . . 175.00
  Button, 1¼" celluloid, red, black, white, Good Teeth, Mickey brushing Big Bad Wolf's teeth 65.00

Donald Duck, figure, riding tricycle, bisque, marked "Japan," 3¼" h, $40.00.

Mickey Mouse, figure, 3½" h, hard rubber, black, marked "Walt Disney Copyright, Made in Akron, Ohio," orig tail, $90.00.

Game, Mickey Mouse Coming Home Game, Marx Brothers, 2 x 9 x 20" cardboard box, 16 x 16" board, multicolored **75.00**

Guitar, plastic, 6½ x 21", yellow front, large paper label, six plastic strings, Walt Disney copyright, c1970 .... **15.00**

Handkerchief, 7½" sq, small black figure of Mickey in one corner, 1930s ... **20.00**

Hot Pad, fabric, beige, 6 x 6", 3" center stripe depicts Mickey images in black, white, and red, c1930 .... **25.00**

Painting, Mickey and Minnie on country lane, Mickey pointing to moon, tempera on art, sgd "Walt Disney," c1935, 15½ x 10½" **2,500.00**

Umbrella, two silk screen poses of Mickey, Minnie on satin-like cloth, 20" l, Walt Disney Enterprises, c1930 .... **150.00**

Minnie Mouse

Book, *Minnie Mouse And The Anitque Chair,* Whitman, No 845, hardcover, 5 x 5½", 1948 ...... **20.00**

Figure

3½" bisque, playing accordion, orig label, c1930 .... **40.00**

3½" bisque, carrying first aid kit, c1930 .... **50.00**

Mug, Minnie brushing hair, marked "Salem China" **45.00**

Pinocchio

Celluloid, Jiminy Crickett standing behind the eight ball with fists raised, titled "I'll Teach You," applied to airbrushed ground, 1939, 10½ x 8" . **1,200.00**

Plaque, wood, Jiminy Crickett and Pinocchio seated on Gepetto's sideboard, Blue Fairy holding wand, brown finish, blue dress, yellow hair, white wings, and yellow hat, 4 x 5", c1940 .... **75.00**

Pluto

Celluloid, Sheep Dog, Pluto walking across desert with bone in mouth, 1949, 9 x 27" **100.00**

Mug, glazed china, Pluto on one side, seated Mickey Mouse on other, 3", c1930 .... **30.00**

Planter, glazed china, multicolored, 4 x 8 x 6½", c1940 .... **30.00**

Salt Shaker, glazed china, Disney copyright on base, 4" h, c1960 .. **10.00**

Snow White

Drinking Glasses, 4½" h, full figures, poems on each, set of eight, Libbey, c1930 .... **125.00**

Handkerchief, small image of Snow White, deer, rabbits, and birds, red, white, blue, and brown, 8½" sq, c1938 .... **15.00**

Pin, molded celluloid, multicolored, Snow White surrounded by dwarfs with musical instruments, orig 3½ x 4" white, blue, and yellow card, pin 1¾ x 2" **25.00**

Pitcher, glazed china, raised figures, multicolored, large handle with two bluebirds and squirrel, music box base plays "Whistle While You Work," Wade Heath, England, 7½" h, 6" d, c1938 .... **250.00**

Three Little Pigs

Bisque Set, litho box, 2 x 3½ x 5", top shows wolf puffing at brick house, 3½" figures, c1930 .... **150.00**

Plate, glazed white china, color center scene, Patriot China (Syracuse China Co), 7" **35.00**

Toothbrush Holder, bisque, pigs shown with fife, fiddle, and orange bricks, 2 x 3½ x 4" **75.00**

Zorro

Dominoes, Zorro on horseback on back, 1 4½ x 7½", Halsman, 1950s **35.00**

Lunch Box, litho tin, raised figures, thermos, c1950 .... **25.00**

DOLL HOUSES

History: Doll houses date from the 18th century to modern times. Early doll houses often were handmade, sometimes with only one room. The most common type was made for a young girl to fill with replicas of furniture scaled especially to fit into a doll house. Special sized dolls also were made for doll houses. All types of accessories and styles allowed a doll house to portray any historical period.

References: Flora Bill Jacobs, *Dolls' Houses in America: Historic Preservation in Miniature*, Charles Scribner's Sons, 1974; Donald and Helene Mitchell, *Dollhouses, Past and Present*, Collector Books, 1980; Blair Whitton (ed.), *Bliss Toys And Dollhouses*, Dover, 1979.

Museums: Margaret Woodbury Strong Museum, Rochester, NY; Washington Dolls' House and Toy Museum, Washington, D.C.

R. Bliss, lithograph on board, hinged, two interior rooms, early rural 20th century style, 7½ x 11½ x 16¼", $675.00.

Bliss

Adirondack Cottage, litho on wood, log design, two doors on front, two cut-out windows, balcony, printed windows on side, 18 x 17" **450.00**
House, 2 story, wood, front door opens, litho paper designs, four eisenglass windows, lace curtains, metal porch rail, two chimneys, ext. stair, 20 x 13 x 9" **2,100.00**
Victorian, 2 rooms, 2 story, litho on wood, high steepled roof, dormer windows, spindled porch railing, second floor balcony, 27 x 18 x 11"   **900.00**
Converse
Cottage, red and green litho on redwood, printed bay window, stone base, roof dormer, 15 x 17" **400.00**
Red Robin Farm, double barn doors, six stalls, nine orig animals, cupola on roof, 1912, 19½ x 17" **425.00**
German
English Tudor, 3 rooms, cream, brown trim, yellow recessed section, olive green door, red roof, orig wallpaper, front opens in two sections, c1880, 21 x 12 x 17" **650.00**

Victorian style, 1 room, cardboard, litho, three sided, hinged, wood furniture, marked "Made in Germany," c1880 . . . .   **250.00**
Nita Gearhart, house, 7 rooms, wallpaper covered walls, handmade wood furniture, ten handmade bisque dolls, 10 x 25", c1976 . . . .   **500.00**
McLoughlin, house with garden, 2 story, 2 rooms, c1911, orig box **750.00**
Schoenhut
Bungalow, 1 story, attic, yellow and green, red roof, orig decal, 12¾ x 11 x 9" **350.00**
Mansion, 2 story, 8 rooms, attic, tan brick design, red roof, large dormer, 20 glass windows, orig decal, 1923, 29 x 26 x 30" **1,500.00**
Tootsietoy, Colonial, 2 story, 6 rooms, front opens, double chimneys, 1927   **525.00**

DOLLS

History: Dolls have been children's play toys for centuries. Dolls also have served other functions. During the 14th through 18th century doll making was centered in Europe, mainly in Germany and France. The French dolls produced in this era represented adults and were dressed in the latest couturier designs. They were not children's toys.

During the mid-19th century, child and baby dolls, made in wax, cloth, bisque, and porcelain, were introduced. Facial features were hand painted; wigs were made of mohair and human hair. They were dressed in baby or children's fashions.

Marks from the various manufacturers are found on the back of the head, neck, or back area. These marks are very important in identifying the doll and date of manufacture.

Doll making in the United States began to flourish in the 1900s with names like Effanbee, Madame Alexander, Ideal, and others.

References: Jean Bach, *Collecting German Dolls*, Main Street Press, 1983; Paul Fellows, *Doll Auction Prices*, Wallace-Homestead, 1985; Jan Foulke, *7th Blue Book Dolls and Values*, Hobby House Press Inc. 1986; Wendy Lavitt, *American Folk Dolls*, Alfred Knopf, Inc., 1982; Wendy Lavitt, *Dolls*, Alfred A. Knopf, 1983; Robert W. Miller, *Wallace-Homestead Price Guide To Dolls, 1986–87*, Wallace-Homestead, 1986.

Periodicals: *Doll Reader*, Hobby House Press, Inc., 900 Frederick Street, Cumberland, MD 21502; *Dolls The Collector's Magazine*, Acquire Publishing Co., 170 Fifth Avenue, NY, NY 10010.

Collector's Clubs: Madame Alexander Fan Club, P. O. Box 146, New Lenox, IL 60451; United Federation of Doll Clubs, 2814 Herron Lane, Glenshaw, PA 15116.

Museums: Margaret Woodbury Strong Museum, Rochester, NY; Yesteryears Museum, Sandwich, MA.

Additional Listings: See *Warman's Americana & Collectibles* for more examples.

Ideal, 18″, Deanna Durbin, $180.00.

Alt, Beck, and Gottschalck
  20″, bisque shoulderhead, muslin body, blonde molded hair, painted blue eyes, painted facial features, closed mouth, well costumed, c1885, marks: 890 #8 . . . . **500.00**
  22″, solid domed bisque shoulderhead, kid pin jointed body, bisque forearms, blonde human hair, blue glass inset eyes, closed mouth, well costumed, c1885, marks: 639 Made in Germany **900.00**
Averill, Georgene, 15″, solid domed bisque head, flanged neck, muslin torso, composition lower arms and legs, tinted light brown baby hair and brows, half moon shape blue glass sleep eyes, open mouth, crooked smile, two porcelain lower teeth, well costumed, c1920, marks: Copyright by Georgene Averill/Made in Germany **1,000.00**
Bahr & Proschild
  11″, bisque socket head, composition bent limb baby body, blue glass sleep eyes, open mouth, two upper teeth, well costumed, c1915, marks: BP 585 2.0 . . . . **400.00**
  20″, bisque socket head, composition bent limb baby body, brunette human hair, brown glass sleep eyes,

open mouth, two porcelain upper teeth, c1915, marks: IBP 585 6 . . **700.00**
Bergmann, C. M.
  15″, bisque socket head, composition bent limb baby body, brunette mohair wig, almond shape small gray glass sleep eyes, open mouth, two porcelain upper teeth, well costumed, c1910, marks: Simon and Halbig, C.M. Bergmann 612 6 . . . **900.00**
Borgfeldt, George
  12½″, Hug Me Kiddy, composition face mask, pink felt body, fleecy brunette hair, inset large round glass side glancing googly eyes, pug nose, closed mouth, c1910 . . **425.00**
  26″, bisque socket head, composition bent limb baby body, blonde human hair, brown glass inset eyes, open mouth, two porcelain upper teeth, tongue, well costumed, c1915, marks: G.B. 15 . . . . **1,200.00**
Bru, Casimir, 13″, bisque swivel head, kid-lined bisque shoulderplate, kid gusset jointed body, carved wooden lower legs, bisque forearms, blonde caracul wig, brown glass paperweight inset, accented and shaded lips with small hole in center, c1885, marks: Bru Jne 4 . . . . **3,000.00**
Danel et Cie, 26″, bisque socket head, French composition and wooden jointed body, blonde human hair, amber brown glass paperweight inset eyes, closed mouth, pierced ears, well costumed, c1885, marks: Paris Bebe Depose 11 Eiffel Tower symbol on torso **2,500.00**
Dressel, Cuno and Otto, 7″, bisque socket head, five piece toddler body, almond shape blue glass sleep eyes, open mouth, painted shoes and socks, c1915, marks: 18/0 Jutta 1914 **500.00**
Effanbee, 19″, composition socket head, five piece composition body, molded bent right arm, painted short brown bobbed hair, green sleep eyes, closed mouth, c1935, marks: Effanbee Patsy Ann, Pat. 1285558 . . . . . **200.00**
Falk, Giebeler, 21″, aluminum socket head, composition and wooden ball jointed body, brunette human hair, brown metal sleep eyes, open mouth, four beaded teeth, marks: 20 G, US Pat, six pointed star **275.090**
Fulper, 17″, bisque socket head, composition five piece toddler body, molded short brown curly tousled hair, blue intaglio eyes, closed mouth in "O" expression, two beaded upper teeth, well costumed, c1917, marks: Fulper in scroll, CMU in triangle . . . **2,500.00**

Gaultier, F., 11", bisque swivel head, kid lined bisque shoulderplate, kid fashion body with gusset jointing at hips, brunette human hair, blue glass paperweight inset eyes, closed mouth, pierced ears, well costumed, blue straw bonnet, c1880, marks: 3/0 (head and shoulderplate) F.G. (shoulderplate) **1,500.00**

Gaultier and Gesland, 33", bisque socket head, composition shoulderplate, stockinette cov armature body, composition forearms and legs, blonde human hair over cork pate, dark brown glass paperweight inset eyes, closed mouth, imp dimpled chin, pierced ears, maroon taffeta, brown knit stockings, black leather shoes, c1875, marks: F,14 G, Gesland Bte S.G.D.G. stamp on torso . . **6,250.00**

Greiner, Ludwig, 25", papier mache shoulderhead, muslin body, brown leather arms, stitched fingers, painted hair, painted blue upper glancing eyes, closed mouth, partially exposed ears, well costumed, c1860, marks: Greiner Improved Patent heads, Pat. March 30, '58 . . . . **600.00**

Heinrich Handwerck, 29", bisque head, ball jointed composition body, sleep eyes, pierced ears, open mouth, four teeth, marked Simon & Halbig on head, 1899, $900.00.

Handwerck, Heinrich, 20", bisque socket head, composition and wooden ball jointed body, brunette human hair, brown glass sleep eyes, open mouth, four porcelain teeth,

pierced ears, well costumed, c1900, marks: 109-11 H 21/1 . . . . **500.00**

Hertel, Schwab, and Co, 12", bisque socket head, composition bent limb baby body, blonde mohair wig, blue glass side glancing googly eyes, closed mouth, watermelon smile, well costumed, c1910, marks: 1652/0 . . . **1,800.00**

Heubach, Gebruder

7½", bisque socket head, five pc papier mache body, blonde mohair wig, blue glass side glancing eyes, pug nose, closed mouth, painted shoes and socks, c1915, marks: Beth, inscribed in script, 6/0 Heubach, Germany **750.00**

10", bisque shoulderhead of young baby, muslin body, composition lower arms and legs, blonde forehead curls, blue intaglio eyes, closed mouth, two white beaded teeth, well costumed, c1915 . . . . **400.00**

19", pint tinted bisque shoulderhead, muslin body, composition lower arms and legs, painted light blonde boyish hair, blue intaglio eyes,painted facial features, closed mouth, two beaded upper teeth, well costumed, c1910, marks: 6 Germany 7654, Holz-masse black stamp on leg **900.00**

Horsman, E. I. and Co, 10", solid domed bisque head, flanged neck, muslin body, composition hands, brown painted baby hair, slightly modelled curls, blue glass sleep eyes, closed mouth pouty lips, well costumed, c1925, marks: E.I. Horsman and Co **800.00**

Jumeau, Emile

10", bisque socket head, French composition and wooden jointed body, brunette human hair, blue glass paperweight inset eyes, closed mouth, pierced ears, straight wrists, well costumed, c1880, marks: E. J. 1 Depose, Jumeau Medaille d'or Paris **3,500.00**

14", bisque socket head, French composition and wooden jointed body, brunette human hair over cork plate, blue glass paperweight inset eyes, closed mouth, pierced ears, well costumed, c1880, marks: Bte S.G.D.G.4 Depose Tete Jumeau, artist's checkmarks, Jumeau Medaille d'or Paris, blue stamp on torso **2,500.00**

18", bisque socket head, French eight ball jointed composition and wooden body, straight wrists, blonde mohair wig, blue glass paperweight inset eyes, closed mouth,

pierced ears, well costumed,
c1870, marks: 1 . . . . **4,500.00**
Kammer & Reinhardt
9″, bisque socket head, composition
five piece toddler body with side hip
jointing, star fish hands, brunette
mohair wig, blue glass sleep eyes,
open mouth, two porcelain upper
teeth, well costumed, c1915,
marks: K*R Simon and Halbig 126
Germany 24 . . . . **700.00**
12″, bisque socket head, composition
bent limb baby body, brunette mohair wig, brown glass sleep eyes,
open mouth, two porcelain teeth,
well costumed, c1915, marks: K*R
Simon and Halbig 122 28 . . . . . . **600.00**
17″, bisque socket head, composition
bent limb baby body, brunette mohair wig, dark blue glass sleep
eyes, open mouth, two porcelain
upper teeth, well costumed, c1915,
marks: K*R Simon and Halbig 122
62 . . . . **500.00**
Kestner
10″, bisque swivel head, kid lined bisque torso, blonde mohair wig, blue
glass sleep eyes, closed mouth,
jointed bisque arms and legs, modelled bare feet, cupped hands,
c1885, marks: 4 . . . . **800.00**
16″, bisque socket head, composition
and wooden ball jointed body, one
piece composition legs hinged at
thighs for walking mechanism, brunette human hair, blue glass sleep
eyes, open mouth, six porcelain
teeth, c1895, marks: 289 dep S
(head) D.R.P. Germany Linon
66543 (foot) **700.00**
21″, bisque socket head, composition
and wooden ball jointed body,
blonde mohair wig, blue glass
sleep eyes, open mouth, four porcelain teeth, pierced ears, well costumed, c1910, marks: F½ made in
Germany 10½ 167 . . . . **800.00**
Kley and Hahn, 15″, bisque socket
head, composition bent limb baby
body, brunette mohair wig, almond
shape gray glass sleep eyes, open
mouth, two beaded upper teeth,
tongue, well costumed, c1910, marks:
K&H germany 167-6 . . . . **500.00**
Koppelsdorf, Heubach, 14″, bisque
socket head, composition bent limb
baby body, blonde human hair, blue
glass sleep eyes, open mouth, two
upper teeth, well costumed, c1925,
marks: Heubach Koppelsdorf 300.4 . **400.00**
Kruse, Kathe, 15″, celluloid socket
head, celluloid jointed body, blonde

human hair, blue inset eyes, closed
mouth, well costumed, c1958, marks:
(turtle mark) Modell Kathe Kruse T40
(head and torso) **400.00**
Kuhnlenz, Gebruder, 20″, bisque socket
head, French type composition and
wooden jointed body, straight wrists,
blonde human hair, blue glass paperweight inset eyes, open mouth, four
porcelain teeth, pierced ears, well
costumed, c1895, marks: Bgr. K in
sunburst 44.30 dep **1,000.00**
Lanternier & Cie, 23″, bisque socket
head, French composition and
wooden jointed body, brunette human
hair, almond shape brown glass inset
eyes, open mouth, row of molded
teeth, well costumed, c1900, marks:
depose Fabrication Francaise Favor-
ite No 8 Ed Tasson **650.00**
Lenci, 20″, felt swivel head, masked
pressed and painted features, muslin
torso, felt jointed arms and legs,
blonde mohair wig, blue glass "O"
shape googly eyes, "O" shape
mouth, c1925 . . . . **1,500.00**
Madame Alexander
16″, composition socket head, five
piece composition body, black human hair, brown sleep eyes, real
lashes, closed mouth, c1940,
marks: Princess Elizabeth Madame
Alexander (doll), Snow White, Madame Alexander (cloth tag on cos-
tume) **600.00**
16″, mask felt face, muslin body,
painted facial features, blonde hu-

**Russian, stockinette dolls, 15″, Smo-
lensk peasant costumes, pr, $225.00.**

man hair wig, brown side glancing eyes, closed mouth, mitten hands, orig blue flannel trousers, black felt jacket and hat, white shirt and bowtie, c1933, marks: David Copperfield **525.00**

Marseille, Armand, 20″, bisque socket head, composition and wooden ball jointed body, blonde mohair wig, brown glass sleep eyes, open mouth, well costumed, c1900, marks: made in Germany 390 A5M **400.00**

Mason and Taylor, 12″, wooden, dowel jointed body, sculpted and painted short blonde hair, blue eyes, painted facial features, orig paper band at waist, c1880 .... **300.00**

Ohlhaver, Gebruder, 20″, bisque socket head, composition bent limb baby body, auburn human hair, blue glass sleep eyes, real lashes, open mouth, two molded upper teeth, well costumed in antique christening gown, c1915, marks: Germany Revalo 22-12 .... **600.00**

Pintel et Godchaux, 24″, bisque socket head, French composition and wooden jointed body, brunette human hair over cork pate, large blue glass paperweight inset eyes, closed mouth, pierced ears, c1890, marks: BP.11G **3,000.00**

Putnam, Grace, 11″, Bye-Lo Baby, composition head, flanged neck, muslin body, celluloid hands, painted tan hair, blue glass eyes in half moon shape, closed mouth, c1925, marks: Copyright by Grace S. Putnam Made in USA **1,800.00**

Rabery and Delphieu, 17″, bisque socket head, French composition and wooden jointed body, brunette human hair, amber brown glass paperweight inset eyes, closed mouth, pierced ears, well costumed, c1885, marks: 2/0 R.L.D. **2,000.00**

Recknagel, 13″, bisque socket head, five piece papier mache body, brunette mohair wig, gray glass sleep eyes, open mouth, four teeth, c1920, marks: Dep R 7/0 A **400.00**

Revalo, 12″, bisque socket head, composition and wooden ball jointed body, modeled short brown curly hair, molded blue ribbon and rosette trim, gray eyes, painted facial features, closed mouth, c1915, marks: Revalo dep **450.00**

Schoenau and Hoffmeister, 21″, bisque socket head, composition and wooden ball jointed body, brunette hair, brown glass sleep eyes, real lashes, open mouth, four porcelain teeth, c1920, marks: S*H 1909 Germany **525.00**

Schoenhut, 14″, carved wooden socket head, all wooden spring jointed body, auburn mohair wig, blue intaglio eyes, closed mouth, holes in feet for positioning, c1912, marks: Schoenhut Doll Pat. Jan 17, 1911 USA and Foreign Countries **500.00**

Simon and Halbig, orig gown, turquoise beads and gold trim, sapphire and gold topped walking stick, $5,000.00.

Simon & Halbig

27″, bisque socket head, composition and wooden ball jointed body, brunette mohair wig, blue glass sleep eyes, open mouth, four porcelain teeth, well costumed, c1910, marks: Simon and Halbig K*R 66 .... **500.00**

37″, bisque socket head, composition and wooden ball jointed body, brunette human hair, brown glass sleep eyes, open mouth, four porcelain teeth, pierced ears, c1900, marks: Simon and Halbig 1249 dep Germany 17 .... **2,000.00**

Smith, Ella, 19″, stockinette hardpressed head, muslin body, oil painted arms and legs, painted short brown hair, painted brown eyes, stitched ears, well costumed, c1910, marks: Pat. April, No. 1 Ella Smith's Indestructible Dolls, Roanoke, Alabama **1,700.00**

Societe Francaise de Bebes et Jouets
18″, bisque socket head, French composition and wooden toddler body, side hip jointing, blonde human hair, blue glass sleep eyes, real lashes, closed mouth, pouty downcast expression, well costumed, c1915, marks: S.F.B.J. 252 Paris 8 **2,500.00**
26″, bisque socket head, composition and wooden jointed toddler body, side hip jointing, brunette human hair, blue glass sleep eyes in half moon shape, open mouth, beaded upper teeth, trembel tongue, well costumed, c1910, marks: 21 S.F.B.J. 251 Paris 12, orig paper label on body **3,000.00**

Steiner, Edmund, 13″, bisque socket head, composition and wooden ball jointed body, blonde mohair wig, brown glass inset eyes, open mouth, four teeth, well costumed, c1900, marks: E.U.St. **400.00**

Steiner, Jules Nicholas
15″, Le Petit Parisien Bebe, bisque socket head, French composition and wooden jointed body, straight wrists, blonde human hair, blue glass paperweight eyes, closed mouth, pierced ears, well costumed, c1885, marks: Steiner Paris Fre A 7 (head) Le Petit Parisien Bebe Steiner (stamp on torso) ... **3,500.00**
17″, bisque socket head, French composition and wooden jointed body, straight wrists, brunette human hair, blue glass paperweight inset eyes, closed mouth, tiny molded tongue, pierced ears, well costumed, c1885, marks: J. Steiner Bte S.G.D.G. Fre A 9, Le Petite Parisienne paper label **3,500.00**

Swaine and Company, 14″, solid domed bisque socket head, composition bent limb baby body, lightly tinted blonde baby hair, almond shape blue glass sleep eyes, closed mouth, well costumed, c1915 .... **800.00**

Thuillier, A., 26″, bisque swivel head, kid lined bisque shoulderplate, kid gusset jointed body, bisque forearms, separately sculpted fingers, blonde human hair wig, almond shape blue glass inset eyes, closed mouth, modelled tongue, pierced ears, c1875, marks: A. 11 T. **18,000.00**

DOOR KNOCKERS

History: Before the advent of the mechanical bell or electrical buzzer and chime, a door knocker was considered an essential door ornament to announce the arrival of visitors. Metal was used to cast or forge the various forms; many cast iron examples were painted. Collectors like to find knockers with English registry marks.

Kissing Couple, cast iron, 5½″ h, white ground, flesh color faces, blonde hair on boy, brown hair on girl, heart outlined in pink, $75.00.

BRASS

American eagle on shield, 7½″ h	45.00
Arm and Hammer, adv	40.00
Atlantis, head, dolphin, and seashells .	75.00
Bust of William Shakespeare, 4″	75.00
Devil, head, serpent striker ring	40.00
Lady's hand holding mirror	32.00
Oval, ring knocker, monogrammed ...	25.00
Turtle, marked "China"	40.00
Warrior, head, c1920	35.00

BRONZE

Bust of William Wordsworth, 3¼″ l, 1¼″ w, marked "England"	30.00
Grecian head, 4½″	80.00
Hand, ruffled sleeve, 5″	75.00

CAST IRON

Acanthus leaf, 7″	30.00
Basket of flowers, openwork patterned back plate, painted	45.00
Couple kissing, painted	75.00
Fox, head, knocking ring in mouth, 5½″	75.00
Quaker, head, man wearing wide brimmed hat	50.00
Woody Woodpecker, painted red hair, tree bark back plate	45.00

DOORSTOPS

History: Doorstops became popular in the late 19th century. They can be found flat or three dimensional and were made in cast iron, bronze, wood, and other material. Hubley, a leading toy manufacturer, made many examples.

References: Jeanne Bertoia, *Doorstops: Identification And Values*, Collector Books, 1985; Marilyn Hamburger and Beverly Lloyd, *Collecting Figural Doorstops*, A.S. Barnes and Company, 1978.

Reproduction Alert: Reproductions are proliferating as prices on genuine doorstops continue to rise. There is usually a slight reduction in size in a reproduced piece unless an original mold is used at which time size remains the same. Reproductions have less detail, lack of smoothness to the overall casting, and lack of detail in the paint. If there is any bright orange rusting, this is strongly indicative of a new piece. Beware. If it looks too good to be true, it usually is.

Note: Pieces described below contain at least 80% or more of the original paint and are in very good condition. Repainting drastically reduces price and desirability. Poor original paint is preferred over repaint.

All listings are cast iron and flatback castings unless otherwise noted.

B + H = Bradley and Hubbard.

Advisor: Craig Dinner.

Aunt Jemima, 7½″ h, wedge, white criss cross apron, red kerchief on head, blue dress	225.00
Bear, 15″ h, standing, holding honey pot in both hands, full figure, brown, red lips, some darker coloration	525.00
Bobby Blake, 9½″ h, holding brown teddy bear in right hand, yellow hair, pink socks, dark blue shorts, blue shirt, sgd Hubley #46	315.00
Blow Fish, 8″ h, full figure, standing on two front fins and tail, red and cream, black eyes, Hubley	265.00
Butler, 12½″ h, red vest and bowtie, black tuxedo, white gloves, mustache, short black hair	325.00
Camel, 7″ h, brown, two humps, standing on four feet	245.00
Cat	
13″ l, 4½″ h, full figure, black, sleeping by fireplace	310.00
10¾″ h, white, black patches, seated, licking front paw, tail in front, red tongue, sgd Sculptured Metal Studios	225.00
Church, 8½″ h, white, steeple, gray roof, blue sky, green grass, three red doors	165.00
Clipper Ship, 11¼″ h, three masts, sails, multicolored	35.00
Coach, 6″ h, 11⅜″ l, blue, yellow, and black, red spoke wheels, two brown horses, driver with blue jacket and top	

hat, green and brown base, sgd Hubley #376	85.00
Cottage, 5¾″ h, brown roof, red chimney, Dutch dormer, blue shutters, flowers on sides, sgd Hubley #211	95.00
Dog	
Boston Terrier, 10″ h, full figure, black, white markings	75.00
Dachshund, 8″ h, 12″ l, full figure, sitting on hind legs, leaning against door, front legs erect	315.00
Doberman Pinscher, 8½″ l, 8″ h, black, brown markings, Hubley	255.00
St. Bernard, 10½″ l, 3½″ h, full figure, white, brown markings, laying, head on front paws, Hubley	285.00
Terrier, running, white, black spots, sgd Spencer, Guilford, CT	125.00
Welsh Corgi, 8¼″ h, black, ears extended, tilted head, green grass and base, sgd B & H	185.00
Duck, 7½″ h, figure, 2 sided, yellow, black top hat, white beak, blue pants, black shoes and base	285.00

Lady, 8⅞″ h, cast iron, green turban, yellow dress, green skirt, blue socks, $150.00.

Flower	
Daisies, 17¾″ h, pink and blue flowers, green two tone leaves, cream cosmos vase, sgd Hubley #455	300.00
Gladiolus, 10″ h, yellow, pink, and cream flowers, green two tone leaves, white vase, sgd Hubley #489	110.00
Iris, 10⅝″ h, purple and white flowers, green stems, sgd Hubley # 469	185.00
Marigold, 7½″ h, cream, blue, and yellow flowers, cream vase with horizontal blue stripes, sgd Hubley #315	115.00

Primrose, 7⅜" h, cream flowers with red dots, green leaves, white flower pot and base, sgd Hubley #488 . **135.00**
Roses, 8¾" h, pink and white flowers, green leaves, white urn, sgd Hubley #445 . . . . **125.00**
Tulips, 10½" h, orange and yellow flowers, green leaves, green and mustard pot and base, sgd LACS770 . . . . **165.00**

Footmen, two men side by side, red coats, black pants, and shoes, sgd C Fish, Hubley
9⅛" h **375.00**
12⅛" h **425.00**

Giraffe, 12½", yellow, mustard skin, standing, Hubley **485.00**

Girl
9⅞" h, holding yellow floppy hat on head, blue dress, yellow shoes, green base **295.00**
11¼" h, silhouette, white dress, pink wide brim hat, pink and orange flowers, Albany Foundry **335.00**

Gnome
9½" h, with shovel, figure, red hat, brown apron, blue shirt **245.00**
14½" h, holding barrel on shoulder, figure, pouring grog into cup, red hat and shirt, green pants, black shoes **355.00**

Golfer, 10" h, red jacket, gray pants, socks, and hat, white ball on grass, sgd Hubley #238 . . . . **410.00**

Guitar Player, 11⅞" h, yellow pants, red and green vest, brimmed hat, brown guitar and base **325.00**

House
7½ x 6⅛", yellow and red, brown roof, open door, two chimneys, sgd AM Greenblatt, copyright 1927 #114 . **165.00**
8¾ x 15⅜", two story, gray siding, two red chimneys, tree on right **145.00**

Huckleberry Finn, 12½" h, blue overalls with red trim, yellow floppy hat, brown, staff in right hand, Littco Products label **475.00**

Jungle Boy, 12¾" h, turban, leopard skin, one hand extended **435.00**

Koala, 7¼" h, yellow and black, standing on orange tree stump, orange and black ears, sgd N 5 copyright 1930 Taylor Cook **445.00**

Lighthouse
7¾" h, gray and green rocks, sgd CJO 1290 . . . . **145.00**
11½" h, Gloucester, MA, two houses, green and blue waves, sgd Greenblatt Studios, Boston, MA #8, 1925 **265.00**

Little Red Riding Hood and Wolf, 7½", red cape, basket, yellow hair, green grass, storybook, tan wolf looking sideways with red tongue hanging out, sgd Nuydea **335.00**

Maid of Honor, 8¼" h, cream dress, black hat, yellow hair, holding bouquet in right hand, left hand holding dress out, Hubley **245.00**

Man, 9½" h, holding yellow and red wine bottles, blue apron, green coat and abase **500.00**

Mary Quite Contrary, 15" h, yellow dress, dark green bonnet, holding flower bouquet in right hand, watering can and rake in left **265.00**

Mayflower, 8¼" h, sails, three masts, green and white waves, sgd Mayflower Eastern Spec Mfg Co **40.00**

Monkey on barrel, 8⅜" h, yellow and green, yellow drum with two black stripes, 1930, sgd Taylor Cook #3 . **345.00**

Oxen and wagon, 6¼" h, 10¼" l, tan and white oxen, two people riding covered wagon, red spoke wheels . **75.00**

Pelican, 14⅜" h, 2 sided figure, white, yellow beak and feet, green base, sgd Spencer, Guilford, CT on foot **385.00**

Penguin, 9½" h, black, yellow chest, red and yellow beak, sgd #1 1930 Taylor Cook **575.00**

Pine Trees, 6¾" h, green with white and brown **155.00**

Pirate, 12" h, silver sword, gun in green waistband, red shirt, gray kerchief with red dots, black beard **275.00**

Popeye, 9" h, figure, yellow pipe, red and black shirt, blue pants, sgd 1929 King Features Syn, Made in USA, Hubley **495.00**

Puppy, 7 x 5", figure, yawning, gray and tan, red tongue **215.00**

Rabbit
8" h, white, red sweater, cream pants, holding flowers to nose **295.00**
8⅝" h, grandpa, brown, sitting, red and black tuxedo jacket, white vest, green bowtie **435.00**

Rooster, 13¼", 2 sided, white feathers, red comb, yellow beak and feet, green base, sgd Spencer on leg . . . **400.00**

Salt, 14½" h, figure, yellow pants and coat, black hat and boots, hands in pocket, sgd Eastern Spec Co **245.00**

Senorita, 11¼" h, yellow dress, blue-green shawl, flower in hair, holding basket of flowers in right hand **145.00**

Skunk, 6½" h, 8" l, figure, black with white stripe. curled tail **325.00**

The Patrol, fisherman style figure, kerosene lamp in right hand, black boots and hat, yellow jacket and pants, sgd on front **185.00**

Turkey, 13" h, blue-gray, yellow, and tan

feathers, red head, mustard feet, green grass **435.00**
Uncle Sam, 12″ h, blue and white top hat, white stars on blue vest, red bowtie, white pants with red stripe **535.00**
Woman, 6⅜″ h, figure, holding a flower up to her face with left hand and holding hat in right hand, yellow dress, black hair **135.00**

1727

Dresden
1883-93

N
Dresden
MODERN MARK

DRESDEN/MEISSEN

History: Augustus II, Elector of Saxony and King of Poland, founded the Royal Saxon Porcelain Manufactory in the Albrechtsburg, Meissen, in 1710. Johann Frederick Boettger, an alchemist, and Tschirnhaus, a nobleman, experimented with kaolin clay from the Dresden area to produce porcelain. By 1720 the factory produced a whiter hard paste porcelain than that from the Far East. The factory experienced its golden age in the 1730–50s period under the leadership of Samuel Stolzel, kiln master, and Johann Gregor Herold, enameler.

Many marks were used by the Meissen factory. The first was a pseudo-oriental mark in a square. The famous crossed swords mark was adopted in 1724. A small dot between the hilts was used from 1763–74 and a star between the hilts from 1774 to 1814. Two modern marks are swords with a hammer and sickle and swords with a crown.

The Meissen factory was destroyed and looted by forces of Frederick the Great during the Seven Years' War (1756–1763). It was reopened, but never achieved its former greatness.

In the 19th century, the factory reissued some of its earlier forms. These later wares are called "Dresden" to differentiate them from the earlier examples. Further, there were several other porcelain factories in the Dresden region, and their products also are grouped under the "Dresden" designation of collectors.

Reference: Susan and Al Bagdade, *Warman's English & Continental Pottery & Porcelain, 1st Edition,* Warman Publishing Co., Inc., 1987.

Figures, 4¾″, male holding floral wreath, girl with flowers in apron, blue accented clothing, gold trim, pr, $700.00.

DRESDEN

Candlesticks, 9″ h, encrusted florals, modeled leaves base, multicolored, pr **250.00**
Charger, 14½″, stormy sailing ship scene, gilt floral border, puce, pink, purple and iron-red panels, c1900 .. **725.00**
Clock, 18″, mantel, cartouche form, four putti, floral garlands, underglaze blue crossed swords mark **900.00**
Cup, 3½″, white, relief prunus dec, two handles, attributed to Boettger, unmarked, 1715 .... **250.00**
Demitasse Cup and Saucer, floral reserves, blue ground **250.00**
Dessert Plate, 9″, central female portrait, heavily gilt, green ground, marked, c1910, set of 12 .... **1,000.00**
Figure
4″, boy and girl, multicolored period dress, carrying baskets of flowers, pr **225.00**
10¾″, man with basket of fruit, dog at feet, women with fruit in apron, multicolored period dress, blue crossed swords mark, pr **500.00**
11″, maiden, blindfolding cupid, multicolored, c1900 .... **175.00**
Tea Caddy, 5¼ x 3½″, sq, lacy gold flowers on two panels, scene of courting boy and girl, crossed swords mark, "H" and "Dresden" **175.00**
Vase
8½″, portrait scene, cobalt blue ground, raised gold dec, artist sgd **375.00**

13½", three panels, each with fill figure portrait of young lady, marked "Dresden" **525.00**
Wall Bracket, 14¼", shaped top, floral and putti encrusted base **250.00**

MEISSEN

Basket
10", reticulated, multicolored floral encrusted ext., blue underglaze mark **225.00**
14", reticulated, multicolored floral encrusted ext., blue underglaze mark **250.00**
Beaker, 3¼", bell form, foliate and scrolling pendants, applied acanthus leaves, burnished gold int., overglaze black enamel crossed swords, c1723 **210.00**
Bowl, 10", gold and pink, raised leaf dec, c1920 .... **165.00**
Box, cov, 3½", orange form, blue underglaze crossed swords mark, mid 18th C **1,200.00**
Cake Stand, 16", reticulated, two tiers, underglaze factory mark **875.00**
Candelabra, 26 h, seven lights, six scrolling branch arms, central knop, bulbous standard, tripod base, encrusted pastel florals, three putti holding fruit and flowers, marked, late 19th C, pr **2,000.00**
Clock, 20", mantel, rococo design, young man and woman, encrusted floral case **650.00**
Compote, figural standard **225.00**
Creamer, 4⅝", yellow, two large cartouches with purple sailing vessels, elaborate rococo handle, beak spout, crossed swords mark, c1740 ..... **300.00**
Cup and Stand, cov, 7½" d stand, magenta scale border, spiraling summer flower sprays, gilt, blue underglaze crossed swords mark, mid 18th C .. **700.00**
Dish, 8½", leaf shape, fruit and flowers, molded basketwork border, gilt rim, branch handle, crossed swords and dot mark, c1765 .... **275.00**
Figure
4", monkey band, twenty-two figures, underglaze factory marks **5,250.00**
5", putti, molded with owl and sunflower, underglaze factory mark .. **450.00**
7", malabar, strolling musician, lilac coat, ermine lining, blue underglaze crossed swords mark, mid 18th C **350.00**
8½", wheelwright, blue underglaze crossed swords mark, mid 18th C **1,400.00**
Inkwell, 15", central candle socket, molded putti **2,150.00**
Plate
9", scalloped rim, fluted, green, gold

encircled medallions of flowers, crossed swords mark **165.00**
12", white, gold scalloped edge, four gold quatrefoil panels with gold flowers, crossed swords mark ... **250.00**
Platter, 11¾", hp, central flowers, white ground, cobalt blue border, three oval reserved flower panels, gold trim, late 19th C **375.00**
Salt, 5½" h, double, figural, boy, period dress, seated on basket, foliate work, puce and gilt, blue crossed swords mark, 19th C **415.00**
Soup Plate, floral dec, canceled underglaze factory mark, set of 12 ...... **650.00**
Stand, 7½" d, 6" h, columnar form, polychrome summer flower sprays and woodland birds, pr **750.00**
Sugar Box, cov, 4½ x 3¼ x 3", oval, yellow tiger, brown rim, rabbit finial, crossed swords mark, c1730 ..... **185.00**
Sweetmeat Dish, 7" l, figural, 18th C lady and gentleman, underglaze factory mark, pr **900.00**
Tureen, bellied body, polychrome tulips and spring flowers, oval stepped lid, cabbage finial, blue underglaze crossed swords mark, c1760 .. **1,250.00**
Urn, 10½", cov, floral encrusted dec, coral branch handles, factory marks **275.00**
Vase, 17¼", campana form, cobalt blue glaze, applied coiling serpent handles, gilt, fitted as lamp, pr **625.00**

DUNCAN AND MILLER

History: George Duncan, Harry B. and James B., his sons, and Augustus Heisey, his son-in-law, formed George Duncan & Sons in Pittsburgh, Pennsylvania, in 1865. The factory was located just two blocks from the Monongahela River, providing easy and cheap access by barge for materials needed to produce glass. The men, from Pittsburgh's southside, were descendents of generations of skilled glass makers.

The plant burned to the ground in 1892. James E. Duncan, Sr., selected a site for a new factory in Washington, Pennsylvania, where operations began on February 9, 1893. The plant prospered, producing fine glassware and table services for many years.

John E. Miller, one of the stockholders, was responsible for designing many fine patterns, the most famous being "Three Face." The firm incorporated, using the name The Duncan and Miller Glass Company until its plant closed in 1955. The company's slogan was "The Loveliest Glassware in America." The U. S. Glass Co. purchased the molds, equipment, and machinery in 1956.

References: Gail Krause, *The Encyclopedia Of Duncan Glass*, published by author, 1984, 3rd printing; Gail Krause, *A Pictorial History Of Duncan & Miller Glass*, published by author, 1976; Gail Krause, *The Years Of Duncan*, published by author, 1980.

Collectors' Club: National Duncan Glass Society, P. O. Box 965, Washington, PA 15301. Dues: $10.00. *National Duncan Glass Journal* (quarterly).

Additional Listings: Pattern Glass.

Relish Dish, divided, Sanibel pink, 8¾", $25.00.

Animal	
Goose, fat	250.00
Heron	100.00
Ashtray	
Duck, 4"	22.00
Teardrop, 3", round	4.50
Bonbon, Sylvan, crystal, amber handle, 5½"	15.00
Bowl	
Caribbean, blue, 8½"	35.00
First Love, 5½", handle	32.50
Hobnail, blue opal, 12", crimped	68.00
Passion Flower, 12½"	28.50
Puritan, green, 4¾", ftd	6.50
Sandwich, crystal, 11", flared	40.00
Spiral Flutes, green, 6¾", flange	6.00
Viking Boat	150.00
Cake Plate, Sandwich, crystal, 13", ftd	70.00
Candlesticks, pr	
American Way, blue opal, 2"	28.00
First Love, two tie	100.00
Hobnail, blue opal, 4"	55.00
Candy Box, Canterbury, cov, flat	40.00
Celery	
Sandwich, crystal, 10"	27.00
Sanibel, pink opal, 13", three part	42.00
Center Bowl, Sanibel, blue opal, 14"	70.00
Champagne	
Canterbury, blue	15.00
Remembrance	15.00
Cheese Compote, Canterbury, crystal	18.00

Cigarette Box, crystal	
Duck	50.00
Sandwich	36.00
Claret, Canterbury, blue, 5"	15.00
Cocktail, Caribbean, blue, ftd	35.00
Compote	
Charmaine, rose etching, 7"	35.00
Spiral Flutes, amber, 6"	15.00
Creamer and Sugar, Canterbury, crystal	20.00
Cruet, orig stopper, Sandwich, crystal, 3 oz	25.00
Cup, Sandwich, crystal	6.00
Cup and Saucer	
Hobnail	18.00
Teardrop, crystal	10.00
Demitasse Set, Spiral Flutes, amber	20.00
Deviled Egg Plate, Sandwich, 12"	60.00
Flower Frog, crystal, 5"	16.00
Goblet	
Canterbury, crystal, 6", 9 oz	15.00
First Love	16.50
Sandwich, 5¾", 9 oz	8.00
Terrace, crystal, three ball stem, 10 oz	15.00
Hat, Hobnail, blue opal, 2½"	25.00
Iced Tea Tumbler, Remembrance	16.00
Juice Tumbler, Teardrop	5.00
Mayonnaise, liner, Teardrop	15.00
Mint Tray, Sanibel, blue opal, 7"	24.00
Mustard, cov, Caribbean	28.00
Parfait, Spiral Flutes, green	18.00
Pickle	
Sandwich, crystal, 7"	20.00
Spiral Flutes, green, 8⅝", oval	16.00
Plate	
Indian Tree, etched, 6"	5.00
Nautical, blue, 12"	30.00
Passion Flower, 14½", salad	28.50
Sandwich, crystal, 16"	55.00
Sanibel, pink opal, 8½", salad	27.00
Punch Bowl Set, Caribbean, ruby handles, 15 pcs	225.00
Punch Cup	
Caribbean	6.00
Colonial	5.75
Relish, three part	
First Love, 8½"	24.00
Sandwich, crystal, 10"	22.00
Teardrop, 11"	22.00
Salt and Pepper Shakers, Sandwich, 2½", pr	18.00
Sherbet	
Sandwich, crystal	5.00
Spiral Flutes, green, 4¾"	10.00
Teardrop	4.50
Swan	
3", solid	30.00
5", solid	40.00
7"	20.00
Tumbler	
Canterbury, crystal, 6¼"	10.00
Sandwich, ftd, 3¾", 5 oz	7.00

Urn, 7″, sq handles	**65.00**
Vase	
Caribbean, blue, 7½″, flared	**45.00**
First Love, 8″, cornucopia	**85.00**
Teardrop, 8″	**22.00**

DURAND

History: Victor Durand (1870–1931), born in Baccarat, France, apprenticed at the Baccarat glass works where several generations of his family worked. In 1884 Victor came to America to join his father at the Whitall-Tatum & Co. in New Jersey. In 1897 father and son leased the Vineland Glass Manufacturing Company in Vineland, New Jersey. Products included inexpensive bottles, jars, and glass for scientific and medical purposes. By 1920 four separate companies existed.

When Quezal Art Glass and Decorating Company failed, Victor Durand recruited Martin Bach, Jr., Emil J. Larsen, William Wiedebine, and other Quezal men and opened an art glass shop at Vineland in December, 1924. Quezal style iridescent pieces were made. New innovations included cameo and intaglio designs, geometric Art Deco shapes, Venetian Lace, and oriental style pieces. In 1928 crackled glass, called Moorish Crackle and Egyptian Crackle, was made.

Much of Durand glass is not marked. Some bears a sticker labeled "Durand Art Glass," some has the name "Durand" scratched on the pontil, or "Durand inside a large "V." Etched numbers may be part of the marking.

Durand died in 1931. The Vineland Flint Glass Works was merged with Kimble Glass Company a year later, and the art glass line discontinued.

Bowl, 114½″, irid peacock blue, sgd, NO. 2605	**400.00**
Candlesticks, 10″, blue, sgd, pr	**425.00**

Vase, 14⅜″, irid gold, purple, $975.00.

Compote, 5½″ d, 4½″ h, irid gold and opal, King Tut, sgd	**250.00**
Goblet, 5½″, irid ruby, pale yellow stem and base, sgd	**450.00**
Jar, cov	
7″ d, 9″ h, ruby and amber, opal pull, feather, sgd	**850.00**
8¾″ d, 10¼″ h, irid gold, green, and blue, King Tut, sgd	**1,250.00**
Lamp, 12″ base, 23″ overall, irid blue, gold threading, orig fitting, sgd	**650.00**
Lamp, table, 17″ h base, 31″ h overall, irid gold and ivory, King Tut, sgd . . .	**600.00**
Plate	
7¾″, cobalt blue, opal pulled feather, crosshatch pontil, sgd	**500.00**
8½″, ruby, paneled, 10 sided, hand blown, sgd	**150.00**
Sherbet, 3⅜″, ruby and opal, feather pattern	**150.00**
Vase	
5″, ovoid, irid, blue, inscribed marks	**200.00**
6¼″, mottled orange and opaque white, Cluthra, sgd "K, Du-7, No. 20142–7"	**450.00**
6½″	
Irid blue, stepped, inscribed "Durand/1979-6"	**350.00**
Irid orange luster, bulbous body, thin neck, flared rim, sgd	**300.00**
Opaque green pulled feather, irid gold threading, sgd	**400.00**
6¾″, amethyst, paneled, blue applique on rim and stem, sgd "Emil J. Larson"	**400.00**
8″, int. dec, pale green, middle brown band, sgd in silver	**350.00**
8¼″, irid orange ground, green leaves, sgd, "No. 20281/2–8" . . .	**850.00**
8½″, brilliant irid blue, silvery opaque veining, sgd	**500.00**
11½″, ftd, cobalt blue, opal pulled feather, yellow foot, sgd	**1,000.00**

ENGLISH CHINA AND PORCELAIN (GENERAL)

History: The manufacture of china and porcelain was scattered throughout England, with the majority of the factories located in the Staffordshire district. The number of potteries was over one thousand.

By the 19th century English china and porcelain had achieved a world wide reputation for excellence. American stores imported large amounts for their customers. The special production English pieces of the 18th and early 19th centuries held a position of great importance among early American antiques collectors.

References: Susan and Al Bagdade, *Warman's English & Continental Pottery & Porcelain, 1st Edi-*

tion, Warman Publishing, 1987; Peter Bradshaw, *18th Century English Porcelain Figures, 1745–1795,* Antiques Collectors' Club; Geoffrey A. Godden, *Godden's Guide To Mason's China And The Ironstone Wares,* Antique Collectors' Club; Geoffrey A. Godden, *Lowestoft Porcelain,* Antique Collectors' Club; R. K. Henrywood, *Relief Molded Jugs, 1820–1900,* Antique Collectors' Club.

Additional Listings: Castleford, Chelsea, Coalport, Copeland and Spode, Liverpool, Royal Crown Derby, Royal Doulton, Royal Worcester, Historical Staffordshire, Romantic Staffordshire, Wedgwood, and Whieldon.

BOW

Beaker, 2¾" h, white, applied flowering branches, c1752 . . . . **215.00**
Bowl, 4½", blue trailing vine, white ground, c1770 . . . . **165.00**
Candlesticks, pr
  8⅝", figural, putto wearing wreath and garland, carrying basket, multicolored bocage supporting blue and gold flower form nozzle, pierced scroll edged base, green and gold accents, c1760–65, iron red anchor and dagger mark **715.00**
  9¾", two birds perched on flowering branches, base with dog and sheep, tole peinte stalks candle nozzle, circular grass base **1,045.00**
Cup and Saucer, three molded prunus branches, c1735 . . . . **175.00**
Egg Cup, 2½" h, two half panels of flowers, powder blue ground, c1760, pseudo Oriental mark **845.00**
Figure
  2½" h, seated cat, puce stripes, yellow eyes, oval flower painted base, c1756 . . . . **1,210.00**
  5½", sportsman, seated, gun on arm, tricorn hat, white, sq mound base, c1752 . . . . **310.00**
  8", Mercury leaning on casket and bales, holding bag of gold and caduceus, flowered scroll base, damaged, c1760 . . . . **225.00**
Jug, blue flower, branches, and rockwork, white ground, c1770 . . . . **65.00**
Pickle Dish, 4", leaf shape, molded veins, serrated edge, painted flowers and grapes, c1760 . . . . **140.00**
Plate
  7⅛", octagonal, blue ground, center panel of Oriental island scene reserve, circular and fan shaped panels of landscapes and flowers border, c1765, pseudo Oriental mark **440.00**
  9", octagonal, famille rose dec, rock, peonies, and bamboo **80.00**

Teabowl and Saucer, chrysanthemums and trailing blossoms, famille rose palette, minor damage, iron-red "33," c1755 . . . . **300.00**

CAUGHLEY

Coffeepot, 10½", light brown rural scene transfer, dome top, gooseneck spout, marked "Salopian" **210.00**
Creamer, 5¼", milkmaid and cow scene, marked "Salopian" **180.00**
Custard Cup, cov, 3⅛", blue printed buildings, Oriental river scene **25.00**
Jug, 7¼", cabbage leaf mold, gilt entwined "JPM" in oval gilt and blue cartouche, swags of gilt and blue flowers from pink ribbons, mask spout, c1795 . . . . **285.00**
Tea Caddy, 5¼", blue printed bouquets and butterflies, c1770 . . . . **65.00**
Teapot, cov, 6⅛", blue and white, feather molded body, floral sprays, sprigs, and insect, foliate band on rim, underglaze blue crown mark, minor restoration **600.00**

DERBY

Cup and Saucer, 2¾" h, Japan pattern, octagonal, central mons and alternating panels of prunus and flowering branches, gilt, green, red, and blue, red on speckled green ground, crowned batons mark and "D" in puce and iron-red, c1782–1825 . . . . **300.00**
Figure, 10¼", Andromache weeping over ashes of Hector, leaning on urn, holding floral wreath, purple flowered white gown, gilt leafage, pale puce mantle, chamfered rect base, Greek key molded border, incised "No. 100," c1790 . . . . **725.00**

FLIGHT, BARR AND BARR

Compote, 12", center painted with cluster of summer flowers, gilt satyr's mask handles, gilt rimmed plinth, imp crowned FBB marks, c1820, pr . . **1,875.00**
Pastille Burner, 3½", cottage, four open chimneys, c1815, marked **400.00**
Platter, 20", multicolored center lion surrounded by gray belt, turquoise shaped border, gilt beading, marked **1,200.00**

JACKFIELD

Coffeepot, 7⅝", bulbous, ear shaped handle with orig brass mounts, chain to brass acorn finial on cov **200.00**

Jackfield, teapot, 5¼" h, c1760, Whieldon-type, $500.00.

Creamer

4¼", bulbous, emb design of grapes, leaves, and tendrils, gilt highlights, three paw feet, ear shaped handle ... **150.00**

7½ x 5½", cow, tail arched over back to form handle, raised base, applied gilding to horns and mouth, cov missing ... **175.00**

Pot de Creme, 3⅞", orig cov, ear shaped handle with curled ending, rosette finial ... **100.00**

Sugar, 4½ x 3¾", SS mounted cov and ornate pierced finial, scalloped SS rims ... **225.00**

Teabowl and Saucer, plain ... **95.00**

Teapot, 5¾", emb design of grapes, leaves, and tendrils, gilt highlights, twig shaped spout, three paw feet, ear shaped handle, bird with spread wings finial, three small rim chips ... **165.00**

LONGTON HALL

Bowl, 4¼" d, flared conical shape, blue and white, tall figure walking by pyramid, flower spray int., blue line mark, c1755 ... **750.00**

Coffee Can, cylindrical, blue and white, scenic, c1756 ... **500.00**

Figure, 6¾", abbess and nun, seated, reading gilt edge books, white habit, pale puce lined black veil, rockwork base, c1755, pr ... **700.00**

Vase, 6¾", scroll shape, Rococo, painted floral dec, pr ... **385.00**

LOWESTOFT

Basket, 9½", blue Pine Cone pattern, pierced sides, applied flowerheads, c1780 ... **100.00**

Coffeepot, cov, 9", dark blue, underglaze river scene, Chinese man fishing, trellis diaper border, c1770–75 . **900.00**

Creamboat, 4½", molded figures and shrubs in arcade cartouches, c1780 **145.00**

Pickle Dish, 4", leaf shape, blue fruiting vine, serrated blue border, c1765 .. **200.00**

Sauce Tureen, cov, 7¼", blue painted flowering branches and insects, floral borders, ribbed bodies, c1760–65 .. **1,830.00**

Teapot, cov, 3", child's, underglaze blue, Chinese river scene, house, and trees, husk border, knob finial **425.00**

MASON'S

Bowl, 7¾", Imari style vase of flowers on table, scrolling sprays, red, black, and gold, c1830 ... **125.00**

Creamer, 4", Oriental style shape, marked "Mason's Patent Ironstone" **75.00**

Pitcher, octagonal

4¼", medium transfer of stylized chrysanthemums, pink red, green, deep blue, and gold enamel highlights, polychromed serpent handle, marked "Mason's Patent Ironstone China", minor damage ... **120.00**

5⅛", black transfer

Chinese subject, enamel red, green, pink, and orange-ochre highlights, serpent handle, underglaze black mark "Mason's Patent Ironstone China" ... **100.00**

Chinese temple dogs and stylized flowers, applied orange enamel highlights, serpent handle, underglaze black mark "Mason's Patent Ironstone China," slight 1" hairline ... **100.00**

5¼", smeary medium blue transfer, Blue Pheasants pattern, ornate serpent handle, underglaze blue mark "Mason's Patent Ironstone China," also imp mark ... **75.00**

Platter, oval, floral sprays, iron-red and blue enamel, gilt border, leafy scroll handles, mid 19th C ... **100.00**

NEW HALL

Bowl, 6¼", printed and colored reserved panels of mother and child, dark blue ground, gilt vines, Pattern #1277 .. **100.00**

Creamer, urn, crest design, c1810 ... **50.00**

Dessert Service, two oval dishes, eight plates, bat printed and colored named views, lavender-blue borders, light blue ground, c1815 ... **420.00**

Sugar, cov, multicolored bands of flow-

New Hall, teapot, red and blue floral motif, gold bands, $400.00.

ering foliage, puce rims, two handles,
c1790 . . . . **125.00**
Tea and Coffee Service, cream jug, two
saucer dishes, twelve teacups and
saucers, eight coffee cans, blue, orange, red, green, and gilt, painted elephant near palace dec, Pattern
#876, 35 pcs **1,175.00**
Tray, 8″, oval, white, pink flowers, green
tracery border, c1770 . . . . **250.00**
Waste Bowl, blue, gilt, acorns and oak
leaves, Pattern #562, c1820 . . . . . . **80.00**

ENGLISH SOFTPASTE

History: Between 1820 and 1860 a large number of potteries in England's Staffordshire district
produced decorative wares with a soft earthenware (creamware) base and a plain white or yellow
glazed ground.

Design or "stick" spatterware was created by a
cut-sponge (stamp), hand painting, or transfer.
Blue was the dominant color. The earliest patterns
were carefully arranged geometrics and generally
covered the entire piece. Later pieces had a decorative border with a center motif, usually a tulip.
In the 1850s Elsmore and Foster developed the
Holly Leaf pattern.

King's Rose features a large, cabbage-type rose
in red, pale red, or pink. The pink rose often is
called "Queen's Rose."

Secondary colors are pastels of yellow, pink, and
occasionally green. The borders vary: a solid
band, vined, lined, or sectional. The King's Rose
exists in an oyster motif.

Strawberry China ware comes in three types:
strawberries and strawberry leaves (often called
strawberry lustre), green feather-like leaves with
pink flowers (often called cut-strawberry, primrose,
or old strawberry), and a third type with the decoration in relief. The first two types are character-

ized by rust red moldings. Most pieces have a
creamware ground. Davenport was one of the
many potteries who made this ware.

Yellow-glazed earthenware (canary lustre) has
a canary yellow ground, transfer design which is
usually in black, and occasional lustre decoration.
The earliest pieces date from the 1780s and have
a fine creamware base. A few hand painted pieces
are known. Not every piece has lustre decoration.

Marked pieces are uncommon. Because the
ground is softpaste, the ware is subject to cracking
and chipping. Enamel colors and other types of
decoration do not hold well. It is not unusual to
see a piece with the decoration worn off.

Reference: Susan and Al Bagdade, *Warman's
English & Continental Pottery & Porcelain, 1st Edition,* Warman Publishing Co., Inc., 1987.

Additional Listings: Adams Rose, Gaudy
Dutch, Salopian Ware, Staffordshire Items.

**Design Spatter, plate, 8½″ d, red flow-
ers with light green floral leaves, brown
stem, dark green leaves on vine, lion
and unicorn mark, $65.00.**

DESIGN SPATTERWARE

Bowl
7½ x 4″, polychrome stripes **75.00**
9½″, serrated rim, blue, white, and
black trim **250.00**
10⅝″, star pattern, red, purple, and
shades of green **100.00**
Creamer, 4″, blue and red flower, blue
stick spatter, green stripe on base . . **65.00**
Cup and Saucer, Floral pattern, red,
blue, green, and black **25.00**
Jug, 5½″, Holly Leaf, red and green . . **115.00**
Mug, 4 x 4½″, brown and blue designs **75.00**
Pitcher, 10¾″, red, green, and purple
floral wreaths, red borders **100.00**
Plate
8¾″, blue and white florals **20.00**

8⅞", brown and purple stick spatter,
green stripes . . . . | **25.00**

9", narrow red line border, stars in
center, pinwheels around border . | **65.00**

Platter, 15⅝", Rosebud and Thistle pattern, red stripe and columbine, green
spatter . . . . | **235.00**

Teabowl and Saucer, Holly pattern . . | **40.00**

Teapot, cov, rose dec, pink and blue . | **200.00**

Waste Bowl, floral rim, spatter overlay,
marked "Adams" . . . . | **50.00**

KING'S ROSE

Bowl, 6½", pink rose, solid border . . . | **125.00**

Creamer, helmet shape, brick red rose | **225.00**

Cup and Saucer, handleless
Applied yellow, red, pink, and green
enamel dec . . . . | **75.00**
Line border, minor enamel wear . . . | **100.00**

Gravy Ladle, 6¾", deep purple enamel
dec . . . . | **50.00**

Gravy Tureen, cov, 7⅛ x 4½", pearlware, deep purple enamel dec, shell
like handles, 3" meandering crack on
cov . . . . | **70.00**

Plate
6⅜", emb feather edge border, red,
green, brick-red, and yellow center
flower dec . . . . | **65.00**
7½", blue rim, border design of pink
and red scrolls joined by tiny leaf
King's roses, green leaves, gray
stems, stained . . . . | **25.00**
8⅜", emb feather edge border, red,
green, brick-red, and yellow center
flower dec, imp "Rogers" . . . . . . | **75.00**
9⅝", creamware, polychrome dec,
pink King's Rose border, deep purple thistles and blue-green shamrocks, blue line border, imp "E
Wood and Sons" within circle with
shield of the US in center . . . . . . | **85.00**

Soup Plate, 9¼", broken band border,
puff balls . . . . | **145.00**

Sugar, scalloped rim, ribbed, vine border, pink rose . . . . | **165.00**

Teapot Caddy, 8¼", enameled red,
green, blue, and purple flowers, rust
line border . . . . | **50.00**

Toddy, 5¾", vine border, pink rose . . . | **75.00**

STRAWBERRY CHINA

Bowl, 6¼" d, vine border . . . . | **350.00**

Cup and Saucer, pink border, scalloped
edge . . . . | **220.00**

Plate
5¾", strawberry center, strawberry
and vine border, chipped . . . . | **40.00**
7¼", leaf and strawberry center,
strawberry and vine border . . . . . | **400.00**

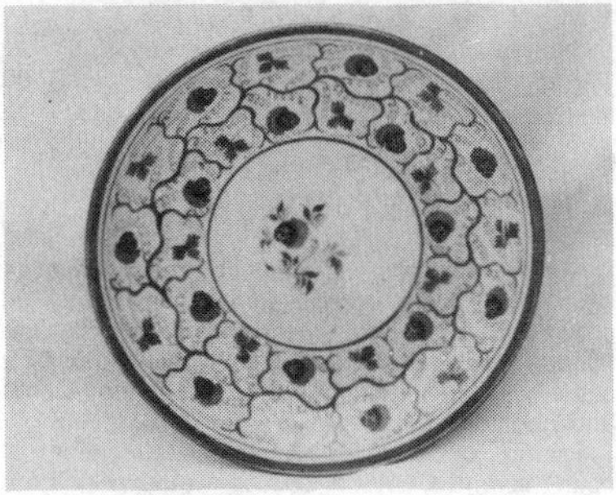

Strawberry China, plate, 8" d, pink luster band, $75.00.

Sugar, cov, raised strawberries, strawberry knob . . . . | **130.00**

Teabowl and Saucer, vine border . . . . | **225.00**

Teapot, raised strawberries and rope
borders . . . . | **300.00**

Waste Bowl, 5¼ x 3½", multicolored
overall strawberry dec, unmarked . . | **115.00**

YELLOW GLAZED EARTHENWARE

Bowl, 6½" d, red flowers, canary ground | **125.00**

Creamer, 4½" h, canary band, white reserves, rust transfers of woman and
child playing badminton and writing,
green and blue enamels, copper luster body . . . . | **45.00**

Jug
4", cylindrical, iron-red transfer of
haymakers, yellow ground, luster
band border, inscribed "Make Hay,"
Staffordshire, c1780 . . . . | **330.00**
5½", black transfer, canary ground,
silver luster banding and roundels
with Hope and Charity, c1810 . . . | **250.00**
6¾", silver luster border, silver resist
vines, olive glazed neck and shoulder, canary ground, c1810 . . . . . . | **360.00**

Mug, 2½", red transfer, children and
beehive, purple luster band, canary
ground . . . . | **95.00**

Pitcher
5½" h, black transfer, Sir Francis Burdett, silver luster roundel, canary
ground, c1835 . . . . | **950.00**
6¾", russet transfer of mother and
child in garden, "Token on Love,"
border molded with animals, early
19th C . . . . | **300.00**

Spill Vase, 5", castle form, seven towers
and clock face, iron-red stepped
base, Staffordshire . . . . | **70.00**

Teabowl and Saucer, gaudy floral dec,
dark red, green, and black, canary
ground **250.00**

FAIRINGS, MATCH-STRIKERS, AND TRINKET BOXES

History: Fairings are small, charming china objects which were purchased or given away as prizes at English fairs in the 19th century. Although fairings are generally identified with England, they actually were manufactured in Germany by Conte and Boehme of Possneck.

Fairings depicted an amusing scene either of courtship and marriage, politics, war, and children or animals behaving as children. Over four hundred varieties have been identified. Most fairings bore a caption. Early examples, 1860–70, were of better quality than later ones. After 1890 the colors became more garish, and gilding was introduced.

The manufacturers of fairings also made matchstrikers and trinket boxes. Some were captioned. The figures on the lids were identical to those of the fairings. The market for the match-strikers and trinket boxes was identical to that for the fairings.

Reference: Susan and Al Bagdade, *Warman's English & Continental Pottery & Porcelain, 1st Edition,* Warman Publishing Co., Inc., 1987.

Advisors: Barbara and Melvin Alpren.

Fairing, Paddling His Own Canoe, white ground, green highlights, gold trim, 2¾ x 2 x 4⅛", $200.00.

FAIRINGS

A Difficult Problem, child with slate . . . **200.00**
Between Two Stools You Fall to the
Ground, two gentlemen assisting lady
to a chair **175.00**
Fast Asleep, baby on Victorian chair . . **200.00**
Kiss Me Quick **175.00**

Landlord In Love, gentleman in dressing
gown peeking through keyhole **250.00**
O Do Leave Me A Drop, two cats drink-
ing out of same bowl **250.00**
Our Best Wishes, hearts dec **150.00**
The Night before Christmas, black faced
figures, children in bed, woman hold-
ing candle **300.00**

MATCH-STRIKERS

Baby, seated with large thimble, striker
at back **200.00**
Dog in doghouse, colorful, striker at
back **200.00**
Girl, picking flowers, holding them in
apron, standing in front of match
holder, corrugated scratch panel . . . **150.00**
Open Your Mouth and Shut Your Eyes **150.00**

TRINKET BOXES

Baby, with cat on a chair, applied flow-
ers **200.00**
Baby and Cat, in bassinet, colorful . . . **250.00**
Basket, oval, two cats on cov **200.00**
Benjamin Franklin, bust on dresser,
American eagle at bottom **250.00**
Cabbage Rose, flower and leaf on
dresser **150.00**
Cavalier, reclining, full color **150.00**
Child's Prayer, young girl in bed **200.00**
Musical Group, two ladies and man,
playing instruments **200.00**

FAIRY LAMPS

History: Fairy lamps, originating in England in the 1840s, are candle burning night lamps. They were used in nurseries, hallways, and dim corners of the home.

Two leading candle manufacturers, the Price Candle Company and the Samuel Clarke Company, promoted fairy lamps as a means to sell candles. Both contracted with other manufacturers of glass, porcelain, and metal to produce the needed shades and cups. For example, Clarke used Worcester Royal Porcelain Company, Stuart & Sons, and Red House Glass Works in England, plus firms in France and Germany. Clarke's trademark was a small fairy with a wand surrounded by the words "Clarke Fairy Pyramid, Trade Mark."

Fittings were produced in a wide variety of styles. Shades ranged from pressed to cut glass, from Burmese to Nailsea. Cups are found in glass, porcelain, brass, nickel, and silver plate.

American firms selling fairy lamps included Diamond Candle Company of Brooklyn, Blue Cross Safety Candle Co., and Hobbs-Brockunier of Wheeling, West Virginia.

Fairy lamps are found in two pieces (cup and shade) and three pieces (cup with matching shade and saucer). Married pieces are common.

Reproduction Alert: Reproductions abound.

Amber, 3¾" h, 3⅛" d, opalescent swirl, clear marked "Clarke " base **100.00**
Baccarat, 5¼ x 4", Rose Tiente, sunburst emb, matching saucer base . . **235.00**
Bisque, 3½" l, owl, shaded gray feathers, blue ribbon at neck, amber and black eyes **150.00**
Burmese
   6 x 4½", large dome shade, acid finish, attributed to Webb, clear cup marked "Clarke" **475.00**
   6 x 6⅛", dome shade, sq folded over base, clear marked "Clarke" insert and candle cup **575.00**
   9½" h, double, sgd "Clarke's Patent" on metal standard and pressed base, center epergne, three vases, pontils with applied strawberries . **1,400.00**
Cranberry, 2⅞ x 2⅞", pyramid shape, frosted, clear marked "Clarke" base **110.00**
Cut Velvet
   4 x 8 x 4¾", deep pink, DQ, white lining, Aladdin cream with gold trim, lamp base, marked "Tunnecliffe Pottery" **375.00**
   5½", pink, raised honeycomb design **225.00**
Nailsea
   2⅞ x 3½", pyramid shape, frosted chartreuse green, opaque white loopings, clear marked "Clarke" base **175.00**
   4 x 4¼", frosted cranberry dome, white loopings, clear marked "Clarke" base **165.00**
   6 x 5⅛", frosted cranberry, large dome shade with ruffled base,

opaque white loopings, clear marked "Clarke" insert cup **425.00**
   7¾ x 6½", chartreuse green, frosted, matching ruffled base, clear marked "Clarke" cup **450.00**
Opalescent
   2⅞ x 3⅞", pyramid shape, blue, emb ribbed, clear marked "Clarke" base **90.00**
   4 x 4½", DQ, clear marked "Clarke" base **110.00**
Overshot
   3 x 4", all-over hobnail pattern, cranberry overshot, clear marked "Clarke" base **100.00**
   3½ x 4", royal blue, crown shape, clear marked "Clarke" base, Victoria's 1884 Jubilee **200.00**
   4⅛ x 3⅛", shell shape, vaseline overshot, clear marked "Clarke" base **135.00**
Pattern Glass
   3½", Diamond Point, cobalt blue, matching base, c1865 . . . . **85.00**
   4 x 4" h, Drape, frosted sapphire blue, clear marked "Clarke" base **135.00**
Pairpoint, 10", grapes and butterflies puffy shade, turned mahogany base **500.00**
Porcelain, 3¼ x 7¾", lighthouse shape, pink, green roof, white and gold trim **175.00**
Satin
   3½ x 2⅞", lemon yellow, DQ, white cased, clear pressed marked "Clarke" base **135.00**
   5½ x 5", shaded pink swirl, MOP, ruffled top of shade, white lining, matching ruffled base, clear insert cup marked "Clarke" **375.00**
Stevens and Williams, 4 x 4½", satin glass, rose, MOP, crimped top shade, cream satin lining, clear marked "Clarke" base **300.00**
Wheeling, 5 x 5½", peachblow, wide ruffled base **750.00**

FAMILLE ROSE

History: Famille Rose is Chinese export enameled porcelain in which the pink color predominates. It was made primarily in the 18th and 19th centuries. Other porcelains in the same group are Famille Jaune (yellow), Famille Noire (black), and Famille Verte (green).

Decorations include courtyard and home scenes, birds, and insects. Secondary colors are yellow, green, blue, aubergine, and black.

Mid to late 19th century Chinese export wares similar to Famille Rose are identified as Rose Canton, Rose Mandarin, and Rose Medallion.

Reference: Sandra Andacht, *Oriental Antiques & Art: An Identification And Value Guide,* Wallace-Homestead, 1987.

Overshot, blue, Clarke base, $200.00.

Snuff Bottle, 2″ w, 2½″ h, $225.00.

Bowl, 10½″, ext. with lady reclining on mat and peony sprays, int. with iron-red peony spray, 18th C 675.00

Brush Washer, 7½″ l, lotus pad shape, int. with ducks, lotus blossoms, and pads, 19th C 620.00

Dish, 10¾″, scalloped rim with birds and flowering plant, int. with peacock and mate, rockwork, flowering, plants, carved wooden frame 125.00

Figurine
   Meiren, 13½″, lady standing on cloud bank, holding basket of flowers, multicolored robes blowing in wind, hair in high knot, early 19th C . . . 500.00
   Peacock, 22¾″, perched on gnarled pine trunk beside bamboo reeds, enameled plumage in delicate tones, black penciled details, re-stored necks, 19th C, pr 2,700.00

Fire Screen, 15¼ x 9¾″, rect plaque in carved rosewood frame, 31¼ x 31″ overall, enameled, figure of Shoulas riding crane, clasping cluster of peaches, scrolling blue clouds, late 19th C 500.00

Garden Seat, 18¾″, hexagonal, animals and cranes beneath ruyi borders with bats and fruit, pierced top and sides 1,800.00

Jardiniere, 16″, ovoid, enameled, two reserves with children in garden, but-terflies and floral cluster ground, band of ruyi heads below rim, wooden stands, 19th C, pr 3,300.00

Jar, 13½″, turquoise, phoenix bird and mate on rockwork, flowering magno-lia, cherry blossoms, and peony, wood cov and stands, 19th C, pr . . . 925.00

Plate, 10½″, butterflies and leafy sprays under openwork beaded lattice band, key fret border, 18th C 360.00

Punch Bowl, 16½″, steeply rounded sides, wide figural band below floral and butterfly boarder, Canton 875.00

Saucer, 5″, center medallion, couple in landscape, gadroon border, 19th C . 100.00

Teapot, 6¾″, couple viewing harbor through spy glass, gilt handles and spout, late 18th C 450.00

Tureen, 11, figural medallions on gilt and floral ground, matching stand, Canton 500.00

Umbrella Stand, 24″, turquoise, ducks in lotus pond, ornate ruyi lappet bor-ders, pr 1,100.00

Vase
   8¼″, double baluster shape, side by side, one turquoise, other yellow, scrolling foliate tendrils, restored . 345.00
   15¾″, bottle, bats and peony blos-soms, lotus blossom borders, collar of upright leaf blades at neck 300.00
   22″, bulbous, long neck, scattered shaped figural medallions, flower ground, pr 1,350.00
   24″, yellow, galleried rim, handled, 2 fluted panels of peonies and leafy branches, stylized lotus motifs, ruyi border on shoulder, gadroon bor-dered base 700.00

Wine Cup, 3⅛″ d, Chinese child watch-ing rooster, hen, and chicks in garden, 1776 dated Zianlong mark, pr 375.00

FENTON GLASS

History: The Fenton Art Glass Company began as a cutting shop in Martins Ferry, Ohio, in 1905. In 1906 Frank L. Fenton started to build a plant in Williamstown, West Virginia, and produced the first piece of glass in 1907. Early production included carnival, chocolate, custard, and pressed plus mold blown opalescent glass. In the 1920s stretch glass, Fenton dolphins, jade green, ruby, and art glass were added.

In the 1930s boudoir lamps, "Dancing Ladies," and various slags were produced. The 1940s saw crests of different colors being added to each piece by hand. Hobnail, opalescent, and two-color over-lay pieces were popular items. Handles were added to different shapes, making the baskets they created as popular today as then.

Through the years Fenton has added beauty to their glass by decorating it with hand painting, acid etching, color staining, and copper wheel cutting. Several different paper labels have been used. In 1970 an oval raised trademark also was adopted.

References: Shirley Griffith, *A Pictorial Review Of Fenton White Hobnail Milk Glass,* published by author, 1984; William Heacock, *Fenton Glass: The First Twenty-Five Years,* O-Val Advertising Corp, 1978; William Heacock, *Fenton Glass: The Sec-ond Twenty-Five Years,* O-Val Advertising Corp, 1980.

Collectors' Club: Fenton Art Glass Collectors Of America, Inc, P. O. Box 2441, Appleton, WI 54911. Dues: $10.00. *Butterfly Net* (bimonthly).

Additional Listings: Carnival Glass.

Advisor: Ferill J. Rice

Basket

Amethyst opalescent, Waterlily & Cattails, berry, 4″	25.00
Burmese, Maple Leaf	35.00
Bowl, Crystal, Viking, 13″ l	160.00
Dot Optic, cranberry opalescent, 7″ d, 3″ h	45.00

Hobnail, opalescent

Cranberry, mayonnaise, 3 pc set	85.00
Turquoise, bowl, 9″	40.00
Silver turquoise, 10″	45.00
#601, shallow, Pekin blue bowl	95.00
#847, Lilac Petal bowl	77.00
#1562, Lilac, banana boat bowl	65.00

Cake Plate

Milk Glass, black crest	50.00
Spanish Lace, green pastel	40.00

Candlesticks, pr

Ivory Crest, cornucopia	65.00
Silver Crest, cornucopia	45.00
Silver Turquoise, short	45.00

Candy Dish

Colonial green, Valencia	15.00
Rosalene, Ogee, 3 pc	85.00
Ruby, irid butterfly, (FAGCA)	65.00

Compote

Ebony, Mikado	125.00
Orange, Roses pattern	8.00
Plum opalescent, hobnail, large, c1962	85.00
Persian Medallion, Rosalene	200.00
Spanish Lace, Violets in Snow, milkglass	17.50

Creamer and Sugar

Colonial blue, thumbprint	25.00

Diamond Optic, #1502

Orchid	40.00
Ruby	60.00
French opalescent, hobnail, mini	15.00

Cruet

Cranberry opalescent

Coin Dot, 6″	75.00
Polka Dot	125.00
Jamestown Blue	32.00

Decanter, hobnail, mulberry, crystal stopper, jug type	250.00

Decanter Service, decanter, tray, six glasses

Georgian, ruby, 8 pc set	125.00
Hobnail, plum opalescent, 8 pc set	125.00

Egg, pedestal

Custard, blue roses	25.00
Ebony, white flowers	50.00
White satin, flowers and butterfly	40.00

Goblet

Colonial

Amber, Empress, sticker	7.50
Pink, thumbprint	11.00

Hat

Black Crest, #1923	55.00
Daisy and Button, topaz opalescent, 4½″	25.00
Peach Crest, 4″, 1924	37.50
Rib Optic, French opalescent, #1922	125.00
Rose Overlay, #1924	35.00
Silver Crest, violets, #1923	65.00
Spiral Optic, cranberry opalescent, 10″, #1927	140.00

Lamp

Boudoir, Coin Dot, blue opalescent	40.00
Courting, Diamond Optic, colonial blue, #7343	70.00
Hurricane, Spiral Optic, snow crest, amber	70.00
Wrisley bottle, Hobnail, cameo opalescent	40.00

Kettle, hobnail

#3979, mustard, blue paste	25.00
#3990, milk glass	7.00

Miscellaneous

Candleholder, three hole, Butterfly, purple carnival	150.00
Decanter, stopper, elephant, crystal	80.00
Jam and Jelly Set, Block and Star, #5603	65.00
Lavabo, Wild Rose, hobnail	300.00

Perfume

Lilac, stopper, #53	45.00
Rose overlay, melon rib	20.00
Silver Crest, melon rib	10.00

Pitcher

Coin Spot, green opalescent, green handle	95.00
Ebony, #1639	60.00
Jacqueline, milk glass, 5″	20.00
Ruby, #1639	80.00

Rose Bowl, 4″ d, 3¼″ h, peachblow coloring, autumn leaf decoration, $50.00.

Rose Bowl
    Heart Optic, cranberry opalescent . .   **60.00**
    Melon ribbed, yellow overlay **30.00**
    Persian Medallion, Persian blue . . .   **27.50**
Salt and Pepper, hobnail
    Cranberry opalescent, #3806, pr . .   **60.00**
    Topaz opalescent, ftd, pr **30.00**
Tumbler
    Colonial blue, thumbprint, ice tea . .   **15.00**
    Ruby, #9133 . . . .   **7.50**
Vase
    Bubble Optic, honey amber, 11″ . . .   **150.00**
    Dolphin, jade, 6″ **18.00**
    Green overlay, beaded, melon, 9″ . .   **45.00**
    Plated, amberina, 9″ **65.00**
    Spiral Optic, emerald snow crest, 8¾″   **90.00**
    Wild Rose and Bow Knot, apple
      green **45.00**
Water Set, pitcher, six tumblers
    Jade green, 6 ring, 7 pc set **195.00**
    Rose, 7 pc set, Ming, Fenton **195.00**

MADE IN
U.S.A.

FIESTA

History: The Homer Laughlin China Company introduced Fiesta dinnerware in January, 1936, at the Pottery and Glass Show in Pittsburgh, Pennsylvania. Fredrick Rhead designed the pattern; Arthur Kraft and Bill Bensford molded it. Dr. A. V. Bleininiger and H. W. Thiemecke developed the glazes.

The original five colors were red, dark blue, light green (with a trace of blue), brilliant yellow, and ivory. A vigorous marketing campaign took place between 1939 and 1943. In 1938 turquoise was added; red was removed in 1943 because of the war effort and did not reappear until 1959. In 1951 light green, dark blue, and ivory were retired and forest green, rose, chartreuse, and gray added to the line. Other color changes took place in the late 1950s, including the addition of a medium green.

Fiesta ware was redesigned in 1969 and discontinued in 1972–73. In 1986 Fiesta was reintroduced by Homer Laughlin China Company. The new china body shrinks more than the old semi-vitreous and ironstone pieces, thus making the new pieces slightly smaller than the earlier pieces. The modern colors are also different in tone or hue. The cobalt blue is darker than the old blue. Other modern colors are black, white, apricot, and rose.

References: Linda D. Farmer, *The Farmer's*

Wife Fiesta Inventory and Price Guide, published by author, 1984; Sharon and Bob Huxford, *The Collectors Encyclopedia of Fiesta,* Collector Books, 1987, 6th Edition.
    Reproduction Alert.
    Additional Listings: See *Warman's Americana & Collectibles* for more examples.

Pitcher, orange, $50.00.

Ashtray, rose **40.00**
Bowl
    4¾″, fruit, medium green **120.00**
    5½″, fruit, turquoise **11.00**
    6″, dessert, rose **18.00**
    7⅜″, salad, ivory **35.00**
    8½″, fruit, red **28.00**
Candleholders, pr
    Bulb, cobalt **40.00**
    Tripod, yellow **100.00**
Carafe, three pint, red **100.00**
Casserole, cov, yellow **48.00**
Coffeepot, yellow **60.00**
Compote, 12″, red **70.00**
Creamer, ring handle, rose **15.00**
Cup and Saucer
    Cobalt **18.00**
    Turquoise **15.00**
Demitasse Cup and Saucer, red **35.00**
Egg Cup, light green **20.00**
Gravy Boat, medium green **50.00**
Jug, two pint, chartreuse **48.00**
Marmalade, cov, yellow **70.00**
Mixing Bowls, nested, set of 3, yellow .   **100.00**
Mustard, cov, yellow **50.00**
Nappy, 8½″, medium green **40.00**
Pie Plate, 8¾″, rose **20.00**
Pitcher
    Juice, disc, rose **100.00**
    Water, yellow, ice lip **35.00**
Plate
    6″, dessert, yellow **3.50**

7", bread and butter, gray	6.50
9", luncheon, light green	8.00
10", dinner, cobalt	10.00
10½", grill, cobalt	6.00
13", chop, ivory	18.00
Platter, 12", oval, turquoise	15.00
Relish Tray, five parts, red	60.00
Salt and Pepper Shakers, chartreuse, pr	16.00
Soup Plate, 6", cream, gray	30.00
Sugar, cov, ivory	20.00
Syrup Pitcher, plastic top, yellow	80.00
Teapot, six cups, ivory	48.00
Tumbler, water, 10 oz, turquoise	22.00
Vase, 8", light green	150.00

FIGURAL BOTTLES

History: Figural Bottles, made of porcelain either in glaze or bisque form, achieved popularity in the late 1800s and remained popular to the 1930s. The majority of figural bottles were made in Germany, with Austria and Japan accounting for the balance. They averaged in size from three to eight inches.

The figural bottles were shipped to the United States empty and filled upon arrival. They were then given away to customers by brothels, dance halls, hotels, liquor stores, and taverns. Some were lettered with the names and addresses of the establishment; others had paper labels. Many were used for holidays, e.g., Christmas and New Year.

Figural bottles also were made in glass and other materials. The glass bottles held perfumes, foods, or beverages.

References: Ralph & Terry Kovel, *The Kovels' Bottle Price List*, Crown Publishers, 1984, 7th ed.; Otha D. Wearin, *Statues That Pour*, Wallace-Homestead, 1965.

Periodicals: Antique Bottle World, 5003 West Berwyn, Chicago, IL 60630; Old Bottle Magazine, P.O. Box 243, Bend, OR 97701.

Additional Listings: See *Warman's Americana & Collectibles* for more examples.

BISQUE

Fireman with hose, woodgrain ground, multicolored, emb "Fire Water," marked "Made in Germany"	35.00
Goat, carrying briefcase and walking stick, emb "You Get My Goat"	40.00
Golfer, yellow suit, emb "Nineteenth Hole," 3⅝"	85.00
Jolly Man, toasting "Your Health," flask style, tree bark back, 4½" h	75.00
Sailor, cartoon type, high gloss front, white pants, blue blouse, hat, marked "Made in Germany," 6½"	100.00

Turkey Trot, bisque, 6⅜" h, tree trunk back, made in Germany, $135.00.

GLASS

Acrobat, lady standing on ball, frosted, pontil	100.00
Birdcage, aqua, c1860, 3½"	80.00
Bunker Hill Monument, white milk glass, 9⅛"	100.00
Cherub holding a medallion, clear, 14"	45.00
Clock, clear glass, paper dial under glass, metal cap, US in relief on back, 5 x 4½"	85.00
Dutchman, milk glass, c1870, 10"	250.00
Elephant, seated, raised trunk, clear, 8½"	30.00
Nude, frosted, French, standing in foliage, 13½"	50.00
Owl, orange, painted face and feet, 8"	65.00
Pineapple, amber, 8⅞"	90.00
Pipe, orig stopper mouthpiece, amber	110.00
Prize Fighter, Bob Fitzsimmons, clear frosted lower torso, opaque flesh color upper torso, 14¾"	250.00
Statue of Liberty, milk glass, cast metal, statue stopper, c1870, 15½"	225.00
Turtle, amber, "Fine Turtle Hair Oil," 5"	100.00

PORCELAIN

Chest of Drawers, Bennington type, Rockingham glaze, c1840, 5½"	350.00
Ma and Pa Carter, pr, multicolored glaze, Germany, c1910, 3⅝"	75.00
Monkey, seated on pot, tan and brown glaze, 5½"	50.00
Pig, green, cream and brown flint enamel, c1840, 8"	300.00

FINDLAY ONYX GLASS

History: Findlay onyx glass, produced by Dalzell, Gilmore & Leighton Company, Findlay, Ohio, was patented in 1889 for the firm by George W. Leighton. Due to high production costs resulting from a complex manufacturing process, the glass was made only for a short time.

Layers of glass were plated to a bulb of opalescent glass through repeated dippings into a glass pot. Each layer was cooled and reheated to develop opalescent qualities. A pattern mold then was used to produce raised decorations of flowers and leaves. A second mold gave the glass bulb its full shape and form.

A platinum lustre paint, producing pieces identified as silver or platinum onyx, was applied to the raised decorations. The color was fixed in a muffle kiln. Other colors such as cinnamon, cranberry, cream, raspberry, and rose were achieved by using an outer glass plating which reacted strongly to reheating. For example, a purple or orchid color came from the addition of manganese and cobalt to the glass mixture.

Mustard Jar, 3⅜″ h, raspberry, $1,400.00.

Bowl, 8″ d, raspberry **200.00**
Butter Dish, cov, 6 x 4½″, platinum . . . **1,250.00**
Celery Vase, 6½″, creamy white, silver **350.00**
Cream Pitcher, soft rose color, Floradine pattern, satin finish, clear handle . . . **945.00**
Mustard, 3⅜″, SP top, raspberry **1,400.00**
Salt Shaker, 5½″, creamy white, silver, nickel plated top **250.00**
Sauce Dish, creamy white, silver **185.00**
Spooner, 4½″, tulip, daisy, and thistle motif, cinnamon **650.00**
Sugar, 3¼ x 4¼″, cranberry **575.00**
Sugar Shaker, creamy white, silver, orig top **375.00**
Toothpick, creamy white, silver **315.00**
Tumbler, 3⅜″, barrel shape, apricot . . **850.00**

FIREARM ACCESSORIES

History: Muzzle loading weapons of the eighteenth and early nineteenth centuries varied in caliber and required the owner to carry a variety of equipment with him, including a powder horn or flask, patches, flints or percussion caps, bullets, and bullet molds. In addition, military personnel were responsible for bayonets, slings, and miscellaneous cleaning equipment and spare parts.

In the mid-19th century, cartridge weapons replaced their black powder ancestors. Collectors seek anything associated with early ammunition from the cartridges themselves to advertising material. Handling old ammunition can be extremely dangerous due to decomposition of compounds. Seek advice from an experienced collector before becoming involved in this area.

Military related firearm accessories generally are worth more than their civilian counterparts. See "Militaria" for additional listings.

Reproduction Alert: The amount of reproduction and fake powder horns is large. Be very cautious!

Bayonet
17⅛″, socket type, 14″ triangular blade deeply stamped "CM," small letter "R," 2⅝″ socket that is ¹³⁄₁₆″ d, orig brown leather scabbard with part of orig buff leather carrying strap **175.00**
21⅛″, 17″ triangular blade stamped "H" with large "US" surcharge, surface with deep age patina, some scaling encrusted rust **100.00**
Trowel Bayonet, for trapdoor Springfield rifle **180.00**
Bullet Mould
Colt, .56 caliber Root rifle or carbine, sprue cutter deeply stamped "COLTS/PATENT," iron body with wooden handles and brass ferrules, 30 to 40% orig blue **225.00**
Colt, Conversion Mould A steel, .36 caliber marking stamped out and remarked "41 CAL," a fitting for seating the primer added to one arm and the cavities enlarged, usual "COLT'S/PATENT" stamping on sprue cutter, 95% orig blue . . . **450.00**
Military .44 Caliber Gang, 12½″, wooden handles with brass ferrules, each side stamped with letter "S," right side stamped "44.H,", casting 6 conical bullets **160.00**
Sharps Rifle Co. Military Gang, iron, 13½″, wooden handles with iron ferrules, casting 6 bullets for the rifle or carbine, one side stamped "SHARP'S RIFLE/MANUFG. CO./ HARTFORD CONN./U.S.," other

side with "W.A.T." inspection mark, sprue cutter moves back and forth in a groove along top of mould . . **950.00**

Smith & Wesson Bullet, 7", casting both a round and conical .44 or .45 bullet, blued steel body, walnut handles, provision for capping shells, over 95% orig blue **175.00**

Carbine Sling, black leather, 2½" wide strap, unmarked, brass fittings and steel swivel and hook **300.00**

Cartridge Belt, Western, approx 28-30 waist, made of doubled-over brown leather 3" wide with single sewn seam and loops for twenty-five .44-.45 cartridges, heavy nickel plated steel buckle, c1900 . . . . **160.00**

Cartridge Board, Union Metallic Cartridge Co., 44 x 31", printed display with attached cartridges, orig oak frame, 55 x 41½", board of frame with applied raised cast panel "TRADE/ U.M.C./MARK" on top and "THE UNION METALLIC CARTRIDGE CO." on bottom, cartridges range from 22 BB cap to one inch Gatling, plus a selection of shotgun shells and a display of various primers in little glazed frame, repainted frame, orig glass cov missing **3,600.00**

Flask, powder, tin, 6½" l, 4" w, Hazard Powder Co., Hazardville, CT, labeled "Indian Rifle Gun Powder," $75.00.

Flask, Powder
Brass
8¼", body emb on one side "RIFLE HORN" within a curved panel surrounded with a toothed design, complete with the original faded green carrying cord, orig lacquer finish **150.00**

8¼", fluted pattern emb on both sides, top stamped "A.M. FLASK & CAP Co.," fitted with orig bright green woven carrying cord, 97% orig gold lacquer finish **125.00**

Copper
6½", Colt Type Navy, emb on both sides with crossed pistols, stars, spread winged eagle clutching a shield and flags over a cannon, with naval anchor, bugle, etc., below, 95% orig lacquer finish, bright blued spring, perfect seams **900.00**

7¾", pear shape, emb on both sides with group of hounds fighting with bear in woods, script initials below, brass top **90.00**

10", Batty Peace Flask, emb pattern on both sides, inspected "A.D.K." at the neck, the top stamped "BATTY" and dated 1853, body retaining over 90% of orig lacquer finish, orig brass carrying rings **350.00**

Horn, German, 13¾", flattened horn body engraved on both sides, back with a series of concentric circles, front with 2 mythological scenes, one with the date 1596, steel mounts with a long belt hook, minor worm damage to body, base loose **500.00**

Iron, military, 10¼" overall, turned wooden plug for spout, body made of moulded or stamped sheet iron with rolled over seam and two steel carrying rings on each side, orig black paint, complete with orig carrying cord, early 19th C **75.00**

Wood, military, German, 9½" h, wood body cov with brown leather and fitted with iron mounts and belt hook, mid-17th C **175.00**

Flask, Shot, leather
7", black pigskin body stamped "SYKES/EXTRA/lb/1," fitted with carrying ring, 2" German silver top with bright steel dispenser stamped "SYKES EXTRA" **70.00**

8½", emb on both sides with a Highland scene showing a Scottish hunter alongside a fallen stag with 2 hounds, brass top . . . . **50.00.**

Grease Pump, brass, 6", for use with an approx .32 caliber bullet, designed for hand use with no provision for attaching to a bench, the grease fitting is not changeable, appears to be simplified version of Pope grease pump **60.00**

Holster, Western
Colt New Service revolver with 7½" barrel, emb or tooled overall with

floral and leaf patterns plus a large scene showing a cowboy on horseback, brown leather, 12½" overall, early 20th C **225.00**

Colt Single Action Holster, tooled decoration along borders on both sides, brown leather **110.00**

Horn, Powder

9½", Franklin Mint Bicentennial Powder Horn, Baccarat crystal horn, SS dec, orig green presentation case **150.00**

10½", orig oak spout plug carved in the shape of an eagle's head, plain wood base fitted with a large brass stud, body with raised carving of a large eagle, an Indian Head, grape vines, a flying pheasant, the American shield, flowers, and the name "Paul/Bohret," late 19th C **300.00**

15¾", US unmarked, turned wooden base and combination screw-off wooden filling plug and post for the carrying strap, 3" brass tip with spring loaded dispenser stamped "US" and large brass carrying ring, c1814–20 .... **1,450.00**

Lithophane, oval, 7 x 5¾", depicts Samuel Colt seated holding a Texas Paterson with loading lever in his right hand, his left arm resting on a desk with papers and holding dividers, mkd "KPM/460/Z" **2,400.00**

Medal

1⅛" d, gold, obv: "SOUTH AFRICA 1900–1" with a lion seated on a crown over thistles and "Q.O.R.G.I.Y.," rev engraved: "1905/C. Squadron/Troop Shooting/Cup/Won by 4th Troop/Sergt. J. D. Eadie" and hallmarks, suspension ring also hallmarked **450.00**

2¾" d, bronze, obv: portrait of Franz Joseph I with titles, rev: 3 figures and "WELTAUSSTELLUNG 1873 WIEN./DEM/MITARBEITER," original maroon leather covered case with green lining **40.00**

Nipple Display Board, cast brass, 4½ x 2", cast lettering and numbers "W & C ELEY LONDON/MANUFACTURERS OF/PERCUSSION CAPS," mounted with 11 dummy steel nipples, each marked with a number or "MILITARY" designating what size cap should be used with each size nipple, late 19th C **250.00**

Powder Measure

6¾" without the 6" powder tube attached (complete with two tubes with knurled middle sections), rect container with two small glass windows to see the powder level,

marked on the wall bracket at the rear "M'L BRASS MFG CO.," body painted lime green with fittings nickel plated **300.00**

9¾", Ideal Universal No. 6, cast address and model number in iron body, complete with original 14 x 8½" instruction sheet printed on both sides, 75% orig black paint, missing screw that holds dispensing tube **175.00**

Rifle Bag, Kentucky, 9 x 7", leather bag, tarred fabric cover, containing some old flints and lead balls, leather carrying strap with handmade 6" wooden leather covered knife scabbared containing old homemade 6½" knife with 3½" blade **175.00**

FIREARMS

History: The 15th century arquebus was the forerunner of the modern firearm. The Germans refined the wheelock firing mechanism during the 16th and 17th centuries. English settlers arrived in America with the smoothbore musket; German settlers had rifled arms. Both used the new flintlock firing mechanism.

A major advance was achieved when Whitney introduced interchangeable parts into the manufacturing of rifles. The warfare of the 19th century brought continued refinements in firearms. The percussion ignition system was developed by the 1840s. Minie, a French military officer, produced a viable projectile. By the end of the 19th century cartridge weapons dominated the field.

Two factors control pricing firearms—condition and rarity. The value of any particular antique firearm covers a very wide range. For instance, a Colt 1849 pocket model revolver with a 5" barrel can be priced from $100.00 to $700.00 depending on whether or not all the component parts are original, whether some are missing, how much of the original finish (bluing) remains on the barrel and frame, how much silver plating remains on the brass trigger guard and back strap, and the condition and finish of the walnut grips. Be careful to note any weapons' negative qualities. A Colt Paterson belt revolver in fair condition will command a much higher price than the Colt pocket model in very fine condition. Know the production run of a firearm before buying it.

References: Norman Flayderman, *Flayderman's Guide To Antique American Firearms. . .And Their Values*, 4th ed., DBI Books, 1987; Joseph Kindig, Jr., *Thoughts On The Kentucky Rifle In Its Golden Age*, 1960, available in reprint; H. Michael Madaus, *American Longarms*, Main Street Press, 1981; Russel and Steve Quetermous, *Modern Guns: Identification & Values*, rev. 5th ed., Collector Books, 1985.

Percussion Pistols - Single Shot, French Naval, 6″ barrel, 11¾″ overall, lock marked "Mre. Rle de Chatellerault," belt hook, $250.00.

FLINTLOCK PISTOLS — SINGLE SHOT

English, military, 7½″ round, steel barrel, lockplate mkd "Tower" and "1772" with British crown, full walnut stock with steel trigger guard and ramrod pipes **700.00**

English, officer's, 7″ round steel barrel mkd "London," lockplate mkd "Sharpe," full oak stock with brass trigger guard and ramrod pipes **500.00**

Kentucky, T. P. Cherington, 12½″ octagonal smoothbore barrel, stamped "T. P. CHERRINGTON" on barrel and lockplate, 45 caliber, brightly polished iron parts, walnut stock **2,500.00**

Kentucky, Daniel Sweltzer & Co, Lancaster, 1807–08, 10½″ round barrel, smoothbore, 54 caliber, walnut stock, only lock may be by Sweitzer with barrel from Guest **6,500.00**

U. S. Model 1805 (Harper's Ferry), 10″ round iron barrel with iron rib underneath holding ramrod pipe, lockplate mkd with spread eagle and shield over "US" and vertically at rear "HARPER'S/FERRY" over "1808," 54 caliber, walnut half stock with brass butt plate and trigger guard (Flayderman 6A-008) **2,750.00**

U.S. Model 1836, Asa Waters, Millbury, MA, 54 caliber, smoothbore, 8½″ round barrel, brass blade front sight, oval shaped rear sight on barrel tang, overall length 14″, swivel type ramrod with button shaped head, all mounting of iron, lockplate mkd "A. H. WATERS & Co/MILLBURY, MASS/ 1844" **1,000.00**

PERCUSSION PISTOLS — SINGLE SHOT

Note: Conversion of flintlock pistols to percussion was common practice. Most English and U.S. military flintlock listed above can be found in percussion. Values for these percussion converted pistols are from 40 to 60% of the flintlock values as given.

Dueling, pair, cased, J. E. Evans, 10″ octagonal barrel, smoothbore barrel, patent breeches stamped "J. E. EVANS/PHILADE," scroll and border engraved patent breeches, trigger guards, and trigger plates, set triggers, 50 caliber, French style brass bound mahogany casing lined in purple velvet containing a powder flash, a can of Eley percussion caps, a screwdriver, a nipple wrench with a screw top containing a nipple-prick, cleaning rod, rammer, mallet head and handle, quantity of bullets, brass plaque on lid inscribed "Mr. Charles Cambos Jr Philadelphia, Pa" **6,000.00**

English, belt, 14½″ overall, 9″ round brass barrel sgd "LONDON" and stamped with Birmingham proofs and a maker's mark, fitted with a round drum for the percussion nipple, "LONDON WARRENTED" lock originally flintlock and converted to percussion with light engraving at rear of the plate and fitted with a plain flat hammer, both tangs of trigger guard shortened, 2 brass ramrod caps but no buttcap, left side fitted with 3″ steel belt hook **300.00**

Tyron, Merrick & Co (partnership between George Tyron and Samuel Merrick, Phila. from 1832–38), 12¾″ overall, 8″ octagonal barrel, smoothbore, 64 caliber, top flat inlaid in gold letters "TYRON, MERRICK & Co," bottom flat stamped with English proofs, walnut half stock with checkered wrist, German silver patch box in butt, barrel keys, and forend tip, steel tailpipe and engraved trigger guard, unsgd back action lock, missing ramrod, break in stock at wrist repaired **400.00**

Unknown Maker, 7½″ overall, 4³/₁₆″ heavy octagonal barrel, 41 caliber, deeply rifled with 8 grooves, stamped with stars on muzzle, silver blade front sight, open rear sight mounted on acute little stylized heart shaped plate, top and upper left flat with scalloped dec at breech, lightly engraved "WARRENTED" lock, tightly grained half stock inlaid with 2 silver stars and a stylized heart, silver star on right, elaborate iron trigger guard with applied silver oval dec on the bow, iron forend tip, iron ramrod with brass tip, silver plated brass oval wrist escutcheon with pointed tips, nipple a modern replacement, ramrod possibly replacement **900.00**

PERCUSSION PISTOLS — MULTI-SHOT

Colt
 1860 Army Model, 8″ round barrel, mkd "ADDRESS COL. SAML COLT, NEW YORK U.S. AMERICA," 44 caliber, 6 shot, cylinder engraved with naval battle scene, walnut grips (Flayderman 5B-092) **850.00**
 Dragoon, Baby Model, 1848, 5″ barrel, mkd "ADDRESS SAML COLT, NEW-YORK CITY," 31 caliber, 5 shot, octagonal barrel, stagecoach holdup cylinder, oval stop slots, varnished walnut one piece grips (Flayderman 5B-039) **1,600.00**
 Dragoon, First Model, c1849, 7½″ part round, part octagonal barrel, mkd "ADDRESS SAML COLT, NEW-YORK CITY -, COLT'S/PATENT," 44 caliber, 6 shot, cylinder engraved with Indian fight scene, square backed trigger guard, walnut grips (Flayderman 5B-023) . . **4,500.00**
 Navy, 1851 Model, 7½″ octagonal barrel, mkd "ADDRESS SAML COLT NEW YORK U.S. AMERICAN," 36 caliber, 6 shot, cylinder engraved with naval battle scene, round trigger guard, walnut grips (Flayderman 5B-124) **750.00**
 Paterson Revolver, No. 5, Holster Model, c1838–40, 9″ octagonal barrel, mkd "Patent Arms M'g Co., Paterson N:J-Colt's Pt.," 36 caliber, 5 shot, cylinder roll scene of stagecoach holdup, hidden trigger, varnished polished walnut grip (Flayderman 5B-007) **10,000.00**
 Sidehammer (Root) Model 1855, 3½″ octagonal barrel mkd "ADDRESS SMAL COLT, HARTFOR, CT," 18 caliber, cylinder engraved with Indian fight scene, hammer mounted on right side of frame, walnut grips (Flayderman 5B-065) **750.00**
Remington
 New Model Police Revolver, 1863–73, 5½″ octagonal barrel, mkd "PATENTED SEPT. 14, 1858, MARCH 17, 1863/E. REMINGTON & SONS, ILION, NEW YORK, U.S.A./NEW MODEL," 36 caliber, 5

Percussion Pistols - Multi-shot, Remington, Army Model, 1861, 8″ octagon barrel, 6 shot, 44 caliber, walnut grips (Flayderman 5E-011), $500.00.

shot, walnut grips (Flayderman 5E-028) **500.00**
 Remington-Beals, 1st Model, 3″ octagonal barrel mkd "F. BEAL'S PATENT" and date, frame mkd "REMINGTONS,ILION,NY," 31 caliber, 5 shot, gutta percha grips, round trigger guard (Flayderman 5E-001) . . **400.00**
Other
 Deringer and Deringer Type
 F. H. Clark & Co., Memphis, TN, c1850s–60s, 41 caliber, 3½″ barrel, mkd "F. H. CLARK & CO./ MEMPHIS," German silver cap on forend, plain unengraved silver mounts, oval shaped barrel wedge escutcheons, wooden ramrod (Flayderman 7D-012) . . **800.00**
 Slotter & Co., Philadelphia, c1860–1869, 41 caliber, 3″ barrel, engraved German silver mountings, varnished walnut stock, checkered handle (Flayderman 7D-026) **575.00**
 Pepperbox
 Thomas K Bacon, Norwich, CT, c1852–58, single action, underhammer, 31 caliber, 6 shot, 4″ ribbed barrel, large curved finger spur for cocking, engraved nipple shield, walnut grips (Flayderman 7B-00a) **375.00**
 Sharps & Hankins, Philadelphia, PA, c1859–74, Model 3A, Serial No. 1759, 32 caliber short rimfire, 4 shot, mkd "ADDRESS SHARPS & HANKINS, PHILADELPHIA, PENN." on top of barrel and "SHARPS PATENT/ JAN.25, 1859" on right side of frame, circular sideplate and button barrel release on left side of frame, gutta percha grips, complete and orig throughout, barrels with 20-30% blue mixed with aged brown, frame with dulled

aged silver color (Flayderman 5F-083) **275.00**

Eben T. Starr, New York, NY, c1860s, Fourth Model, Serial No. 53, 32 caliber rimfire, 4 shot, rounded breech, no visible springs, full Factory engraved with a scroll pattern including the entire barrel (the round sideplate engraved with a toothed pattern), checkered walnut grips, complete and orig, dulled natural steel color with some very very light overall pitting, brass frame with suggestions of the orig silver plate (Flayderman 8A-177) **800.00**

Swedish, "Darling," 30 caliber, 4 shot, 7¾" overall, 3½" barrel, bottom of butt carved with initials "JM," nipple protection shield loose and marred all the way around with deep scuff marks, otherwise complete and orig **250.00**

Revolvers

Hopkins & Allen, Norwich, CT, Dictator Model, late 1860s through early 1870s, 36 caliber, 5 shot round cylinder, roll engraved scene of panel motif, walnut grips (Flayderman 7A-034) **225.00**

C. S. Pettengill, New Haven, CT, Army Model, early 1860s, 44 caliber, 6 shot round cylinder, 7½" octagonal barrel, loading lever assembly standard, double action hammerless type frame, two piece walnut grips, no gov inspector markings (Flayderman 7A-079) **600.00**

REVOLVERS (CARTRIDGE)

Browning, Medallist Automatic, Serial No. 17878T2, 22 caliber, orig Browning case lined with red velvet with weights (one missing) **550.00**

Browning, Nomad, Serial No. 45Pl, 22 caliber, 4½" barrel, orig carton **225.00**

Charter Arms, Pathefinder 22, Serial No. 119194, 22 caliber, 3" barrel, orig carton and papers **950.00**

Colt, Model 1903, Pocket Auto, Serial No. 32955, 38 caliber, spur hammer, hard rubber "COLT" grips, complete and orig, 95% plus bright blue finish, right side of slide with some spotty surface rust (Flayderman 5B-226) . . **500.00**

Hawes Firearms Co., Favorite Target, Serial No. 16937, 22 caliber, 8" barrel, barrel with some spotty rust or acid spots from careless storage **100.00**

Hawes Firearms Co., Western Six-

shooter, Serial No. 66736, 22 caliber, orig carton **80.00**

J. C. Higgins, Model 88, Serial No. 2951, 22 caliber, 6" barrel, orig carton **60.00**

High Standard, Sentennial Mark III, Serial No. H4402, 357 Magnum caliber, 3¾" barrel, orig carton **150.00**

Intercontinental Arms, Dakota, Serial No. 2391, 357 Magnum caliber, 5½" barrel, orig carton **150.00**

Japanese Nambu, Serial No. 80712, 8mm caliber, production code 18.6, mismatched magazine **250.00**

Miroku, Liberty Chief, Serial No. 3040, 38 Special caliber, 3" barrel, orig cardboard carton with yellow satin lining **75.00**

Remington, Model 51, Serial No. PA30819, 380 caliber, 97-98% orig blue **380.00**

Russian Nagant, Serial No. 7271, 7.62mm caliber, left side of frame with Russian markings and "1906," about 50% blue **130.00**

Smith & Wesson, 38 Double Action, Third Model, Serial No. 417855, 38 caliber, 6" barrel, hard rubber checkered "S & W" grips, complete and orig, 95% plus orig bright blue finish, but with some scattered areas of storage pitting on top of the barrel and right side (Flayderman 5G-076) **225.00**

Star, Model PD, presentation, Serial No. 1363196, 45 caliber, plain wood grips with special Toledo work gold damascened medallions, the right the American eagle and shield, the left "John Amber/FROM/YOUR FRIENDS AND STAR" **950.00**

Walther, Manurhin PP, Serial No. 10073A, 9mm caliber, orig carton, missing magazine, bright finished barrel with some slight surface rust discoloration **275.00**

Dan Wesson, Model 15, Serial No. 10245, 357 Magnum caliber, 5¾" barrel, orig carton with spare 5¾" barrel and a pair of finger groove grips . . . **175.00**

FLINTLOCK LONG ARMS

French Model, 1763 Musket, 75 caliber, 44½" round barrel, lockplate mkd "St. Etienne," full length walnut stock with three iron barrel bands, iron trigger guard and butt plate, the major weapon of French infantry troops during the Revolutionary War **1,250.00**

Kentucky, H. Deringer, Philadelphia, 60 caliber, 59⅜" overall, 43⅜" octagonal barrel, brass furniture, patchbox with scalloped edges and stylized eagle head finial, tiger stripped stock **3,000.00**

U.S. Model 1816 Musket, Type II, made at Springfield Armory, 69 caliber, single shot, muzzleloader, 42" round barrel, walnut stock, lockplate mkd "SPRING/FIELD/1829," complete with orig issue bayonet in black leather scabbard, throat mount mkd "R DINGEE/N-YORK" (Flayderman 9A-197 .... **3,000.00**

U.S. Model 1819 Hall Breech-Loading, Second Production Type, made at Harper's Ferry under John H. Hall's patent, 52 caliber, rifling extending to within 1½" of muzzle, single shot, breechloader, 32⅝" round barrel, 3 barrel bands, walnut stock, breech deeply stamped "JH HALL/H. FERRY/US/1838" (Flayderman 9A-249 .... **2,250.00**

PERCUSSION LONG ARMS

Note: Conversion of flintlock long arms to percussion was common practice. Most English, French, and U.S. Military flintlock model long arms listed in the previous section can be found in percussion. Values for these percussion converted long arms are from 40 to 60% of the flintlock values previously noted.

English Infantry Rifle, 577 caliber, 48½" overall, 33" round barrel, stud for a saber bayonet, 900 yard folding sight, lock stamped with a large crown and engraved "John O. Evans 1860," all iron furniture, two clamping barrel ends, lock still retains orig nipple protector and chain **850.00**

Kentucky, 52¼" overall, 36¾" heavy octagonal barrel, top flat engraved with a rope pattern and "L. Biddle" in script (Levi Biddle, Shanesville, OH, c1834–45), lightly engraved percussion lock with indistinct maker's mark, tiger stripped bull stock with brass forend cap, 3 ramrod pipes, trigger guard and butt plate, fancy engraved German silver openwork patch box, long toe plate and stripe along comb, fitted with 15 German silver inlays, missing one inlay, stock with old refinish **1,700.00**

Kentucky, 56" overall, 40½" octagonal barrel, 38 caliber, signed on top flat "FRANCOIS GOME" (No record maker, possibly unknown), lightly engraved "JOSH GOLCHER" lock secured with a large pin with hammered head rather than usual screw, tiger stripped full stock with all German silver mounts including open work patch box with light engraving and 15 inlays including the large oval on the check rest which is engraved with a classic primitive American eagle, old partial break in stock at rear of barrel, otherwise complete and orig **1,200.00**

Remington Model 1863 (Zouave Rifle), Contract Rifle, c1862–65, 58 caliber, single shot, muzzleloader, 33" round barrel, walnut stock, brass patchbox on right side of butt which still retains orig spare nipple and worm, screw fitting for ramrod, 7 groove rifle, lockpate mkd ahead of hammer, American eagle over small "U.S.," two lines under bolster "REMINGTON'S/ILION, N.Y.," horizontally dated at rear "1863" (Flayderman 5E-076) **2,250.00**

U. S. Model 1836 Hall Breech-Loadking Carbine, Harpers Ferry Armory, c1837–40, 64 caliber, smoothbore, single shot, 23" round barrel secured by two barrel bands, walnut stock, breechblock mkd "J. H. HALL/U.S./1839," (Flayderman (A-272) **1,750.00**

U. S. Model 1855, Rifled Musket, made at Harper's Ferry Armory, c1857–61, 58 caliber, single shot, muzzleloader, 33" round barrel, two barrel bands, walnut stock, patchbox on right side of butt, lockplate mkd "U.S./HARPERS FERRY," dated "1858," barrel with same date, complete with orig "U.S." mkd bayonet in black leather brass mounted scabbard (Flayderman 9A-308) **2,750.00**

RIFLES

C. D. Bartley Patent Sporting, Serial No. 3, 38 caliber, 49" overall, 32¼" full octagonal barrel, fitted with Beach's combination front sight and open rear sight, barrel and left side of frame both stamped "THE C.D. BARTLEY'S/PATENT OCT. 5, 1880," checkered walnut butt stock with German silver butt plate, burl walnut forend with pewter nose cap, odd action (when hammer is cocked the breech block moves straight down and stays locked open till the gun is fired; as the hammer drops the breech block moves up) **700.00**

Colt, Model 1855, Military, Serial No. 1396, 56 caliber, 31½" barrel fitted for socket bayonet, full stocked with sling swivels, trap in butt contains brass cleaning rod extension for ramrod, oil finished walnut stock, complete and orig, barrel with 98% blue (Flayderman 5B-079) **5,000.00**

French, Model 1874, bolt action, Serial No. 53912, manufactured at the St. Etienne Arsenal in 1877, barrel and action with 97-98% orig blue **250.00**

German, Model 71/84, bolt action, Serial No. 70430, made at the Amberg Arsenal, 1877, 98% orig blue **350.00**

Sharps, Model 1878, Express, Serial No. 16815, 45 caliber, 27/8" case, straight 30" full octagonal barrel, matted top flat fitted with blade front and folding open rear sights, bottom of barrel slotted for a sling swivel, hole now filled with a key, tang tapped for a sight, holes now filled with tap screws, grained burl walnut checkered forend and buttstock, hard rubber pistol grip cap and butt plate, but with a silver oval plate script engraved "WLE," 95% of orig blue finish, only 31 produced (Flayderman 5F-066) **5,500.00**

Springfield, Model 1903, NRA Sporter, Serial No. 1277238, same number on bolt and Star Gauge barrel **2,300.00**

Springfield, M1 Garand, Serial No. 433182, some slight cuff marks near muzzle **775.00**

Winchester, Low Wall Deluxe, Serial No. 9184, 32 caliber, WCF, 28" half round No. 2 barrel with Beach's combination front sight, open rear sight, tang fitted with orig Winchester peep sight, deluxe pistol grip walnut stocks checkered at the wrist and forend, raised cheek piece on left side, fitted with rifle butt plate, fine to very good cond (Flayderman 5K-116) **2,250.00**

Winchester, Model 1873, Serial No. 72056, 44-40 half round 24" barrel with half magazine, steel shotgun butt plate, fitted with sling swivels, varnished forend and butt stock burl walnut which is usually found only on guns with checkered stocks, barrel with 97-98% blue (Flayderman 5K-041) **1,800.00**

SHOTGUNS

AYA Model 1 Double Barrel, Serial No. 543042, 28 gauge 26" barrels, double triggers, auto ejectors, detachable side lock action fully scroll engraved in English manner, oil finished deluxe walnut stocks with checkered wood butt, orig leather trunk casing with label in lid **3,250.00**

Colt, Model 1878, Serial No. 12346, 10 gauge, 34" barrels, action with border

Shotgun, 10 gauge, pin-fired, French, Lefaucheux, Damascus steel barrel, heavily gold inlayed, cased, $1,500.00.

scroll engraving, grained deluxe varnish stock with hard rubber Rampant Colt butt plate, complete and orig, 97–98% orig Damascus twist finish on barrels (Flayderman 5B-261) ... **4,100.00**

Darne Double Shotgun, Serial No. 5T693, 12 gauge, 27½" barrels, very near new **900.00**

Ferlack Double, Serial No. 1150, 20 gauge, 28" vent rib barrels with beaver tail forend, engraved box lock action with single trigger, built by Bereinigle, butt with a cheek rest on right side, 13½" pull, slight wear of blue at breech **950.00**

Stephen Grant & Sons, Serial No. 17784, 28" barrels with some tight scroll engraving at the breech, gold inlaid with the number "1," the sidelock action fully English scroll engraved and sgd "Stephen Grant & Sons," the opening lever gold inlaid "1," gold inlaid "SAFE," double triggers, auto ejectors, straight English walnut stock with rubber butt pad, 15" pull, orig labeled trunk casing for 2 shotguns with oil bottle, cleaning kit, 2 snap caps and 2 screw drivers ... **7,400.00**

Griffin & Howe Double Barrel, Serial No. 88761, 12 gauge, 29¼" auto ejector barrels sgd "engraved by Josef Fugger" in very small letters, side lock action with scroll engraving and large panels with hunting scenes, left side shooting ruffled grouse in woods, right side shooting quail in fields, bottom shooting ducks in marsh, superbly grained walnut stock with 14¾" pull, double triggers, checkered wood butt plate, belly inlaid with a gold oval engraved "WGR," leg of mutton leather case **4,250.00**

Remington, Model 1100, 150th Anniversary, Serial No. 233790V, 12 gauge, 30" full coke vent rib barrel,

spare 26″ Custom coke barrel and 22″
vent rib barrel with Jetway Coke,
scroll engraved silver oval escutcheon on the butt stock with "JTA" ini-
tials, almost new . . . .　**600.00**
Stevens Model 5100, Serial No. XQ, 20
gauge 28″ barrels, Tenite stocks . . .　**200.00**

FIREHOUSE COLLECTIBLES

History: The volunteer fire company has played
a vital role in the protection and social growth of
many towns and rural areas. Paid professional
firemen usually are found only in large metropolitan areas. Each fire company prided itself on
equipment and uniforms. Conventions and pa-
rades gave the fire companies a chance to show
off their equipment. These events produced a
wealth of firehouse related memorabilia.

Reference: Mary Jane and James Piatti, *Firehouse Collectibles,* The Engine House, 1979.

Museums: Insurance Company of North America (INA) Museum, Philadelphia, PA; Oklahoma
State Fireman's Association Museum, Oklahoma
City, OK; San Francisco Fire Dept. Memorial Museum, San Francisco, CA.

Additional Listings: See *Warman's Americana
& Collectibles* for more examples.

Alarm, SAFA Register, 1″ type, take up
reel . . . .　**225.00**
Axe, nickel plated blade, painted red
handle . . . .　**75.00**
Badge
　Allis-Chalmers Fire Dept . . . .　**30.00**
　Altoona, PA, 6th Ward Hose Co,
　　name imp around early hose cart .　**40.00**
　Fire Commissioner NYFD, 14K solid
　　gold . . . .　**250.00**
　Foreman Pumper 4, Rensselaer, NY,
　　1933, brass, blue enamel . . . . . .　**45.00**
Bell, 11″, brass, iron back . . . .　**100.00**
Belt, parade, white
　Leather, Augusta, ME, No 1, Cushnoe　**75.00**
　Web, stenciled NFD (Nashua, NH) gilt
　　brass shell buckle with eagle, stars
　　and shield . . . .　**175.00**
Bucket, metal, hand forged, red paint,
　brass finial . . . .　**90.00**
Cabinet Card, 4½ x 6½″, fireman in shirt
　and badge, foreman's cap . . . .　**25.00**
Carte de Viste, tintype, seated fireman
　wearing fancy shirt, belt, helmet, belt
　reads Keene . . . .　**75.00**
Catalog, 8½ x 11″, Ahrens Fox Fire En-
　gines, 1927, 32 pgs . . . .　**65.00**
Extinguisher
　Hayward's Hand Fire Grenade, 6¼″,
　　yellow, ground mouth, smooth
　　base, c1870 . . . .　**75.00**

Hazelton's High Pressure Chemical
　Fire Keg, 10½″, metal handle,
　golden amber glass, c1860–90 . .　**100.00**
　Rex, copper and brass, 2½ gal . . . .　**45.00**
Hat, 9 x 11 x 6½″, painted tin, black
　ground, red, blue and black scene of
　early hosecart, "Independence Hose
　Co. 7," gilt, c1850 . . . .　**2,500.00**

**Helmet, "N.F.D.," "1st Asst.," tin, gold
and red trim, white ground, patented
1887–89, $200.00.**

Helmet
　Brass, Barnicoat, Boston, eagle finial　**375.00**
　Leather, Chapman Steamer, Cairns &
　　Bro . . . .　**175.00**
　Metal, painted, parade, medium
　　brown, gold cones and trim, red,
　　gray, and black leather front piece
　　"Phoenix Steam Fire Co 1-JMT,"
　　gilt greyhound dog top piece, 1866
　　on brim . . . .　**800.00**
Lantern, Dietz, King Fire Dept, copper
　bottom . . . .　**130.00**
Lapel Pin, Columbia Firemans Relief
　Assoc . . . .　**20.00**
Mark, lead, 4 x 8½″, Royal Exchange
　Assurance, London, 1835 . . . .　**225.00**
Medal, brass, fireman, trumpet, hydrant,
　and hose, inscribed "Brave, Fearless,
　Generous Hearted" . . . .　**40.00**
Miniature, helmet, 3″, gilded brass,
　"Foreman AWS," c1890 . . . .　**50.00**
Nozzle, hose, 20″, brass, Eastern Cou-
　pling Co, Camden, ME . . . .　**140.00**
Pinback Button, 1¾″, celluloid, black
　and white
　Booth Hose Co, Poughkeepsie, NY,
　　horse drawn apparatus . . . .　**10.00**
　LeRoy Chemical and Hose Co . . . .　**8.00**
Print, 22 x 28″, litho, multicolored, build-
　ing in flames, fireman arriving, title
　"Cut Her Loose Boys," B & L To-
　bacco, 1895 . . . .　**500.00**

Ribbon, 2½ x 5½", silk, black and white, "Voluntary Aid," early wooden hand pumper, c1840	40.00
Ruler, Hartford Fire Insurance, tin, 1885	50.00
Sign, 16" h, 89" l, Firehouse Engine Co, 33, arched masonite, gold letters on black, quarter round wood frame, Back-Bay Fire Station 20th C	750.00
Staff, 49" l, wood, brass end, black ground, gold stenciled letters, "Fire Warden"	400.00
Stereograph, Chicago Fire, after fire scene of court house	8.00
Tintype, 2½ x 3½", two firemen in high hats, initialed shirts, knotted ties, parade belts, sashes, muster badges .	85.00
Trophy	
Axe, 11 x 34", painted red handle and head, yellow trim, silver trumpets and edge, Concord, NH, Fire Dept., marked "Captured by J. J. McNulty, at London, NH, March 13, 1896 . .	250.00
Cup, 12", SS, high relief wreath, inscribed "Presented by F.T. Adams to the Greene County Firemans Assoc, Sept 16th 1907"	500.00
Trumpet, 21" h, SP, presentation, inscribed "Presented to Chas Ostamn, Lieut Engine Co 24, FDNY, by his Harlem Friends, May 11th, 1907," emb geometric and floral dec, emblems of helmet, torch, hook, and ladder	1,850.00
Watch Fob, brass, fire apparatus, beaded edge	15.00

FIREPLACE EQUIPMENT

History: The fireplace was a gathering point in the colonial home for heat, meals, and social interaction. It maintained its dominant position until the introduction of central heating in the mid-19th century.

Because of the continued popularity of the fireplace, accessories still are manufactured, usually in an early American motif.

Reproduction Alert: Modern blacksmiths are reproducing many old iron implements.

Additional Listings: Brass and Iron.

Andirons, pr	
13", brass, double lemon finials, scroll legs, penny feet	275.00
17¾", Federal, brass, spurred feet, ball arch, sgd "Richard Wittingham"	1,800.00
21", brass and wrought iron, brass rosettes, brass lemon top finials, log stops	150.00
25", urn form, faceted standard,	

arched spurred cabriole legs, ball feet, iron log support, NY, c1800 .	3,000.00
Bellows	
18¼", teal blue, gold stenciled basket of fruit, red and white edge stripe, brass nozzle, leather	125.00
20", primitive, curly maple boards, scratch carved compass design, brown stain, tan paint, wrought iron nozzle, releathered	250.00
Bucket, leather, bail handle, tapering cylindrical	
13", leather, two coats of worn green paint, black stenciled label "M. R. E."	150.00
13¼", Mutual Fire Society No 2, Moses Sprague Jun, deep brown rim, gray-green painted body, "1806" above clasped hands, scroll	2,250.00
18½", pr, Perry, J., Perry St., 1846, No 1 and No 2, Newport, RI	1,250.00
Clock Jack, 14" h, iron, spoked wheel, scrolled front plate, 3 gear movement, arched wall bracket	1,250.00
Coal Box, 19 x 20", cast iron, green, floral dec, gold trim, English	175.00
Crane, 31", wrought iron, 18th C	100.00

Fender, 20" l, 6½" h, brass and iron, $150.00.

Fender	
Brass	
35" l, 15" h, reticulated flower sides, paw feet	150.00
54" l, 6¾" h, pierced, bow-front . .	500.00
Wrought iron and wire, 22½" l, 11" d, 7" h	25.00
Fire Board, 34½ x 38¾", pine, orig bird's eye and curly maple imitation grain-	

ing, colored striping, beaded edge
tongue and groove boards, batten
back **100.00**
Fire Mark, cast iron, relief cast design
of four clasped hands and No 906,
7¼ x 10½" **300.00**
Fire Screen
  Brass, tapestry panel of polychrome
  flowers, olive-gold ground, 39¾" h **75.00**
  Maple and mahogany, rect top,
  carved, Federal, NY, c1820 . . . . . **275.00**
  Petit point panel, Dutch scene, walnut
  frame **250.00**
Fireplace, 40¾ x 39¼", brown marble,
shaped shelf and apron, oval central
cartouche, angled fluted stiles, orig
brickwork, Napoleon III, c1870 . . . . **1,320.00**
Grate, 9 x 17½", cast iron, mid 19th C **75.00**
Hearth Brush, 15", turned wooden handle, orig green paint, gilted leaf design highlighted in red and black . . . **700.00**
Jamb Hook, 4½" rect wall plate, brass,
hinged C shaped arm, baluster turned
finial, pr **175.00**
Kettle Shelf, brass, detailed, English re-
gistry mark, 11½ x 14¾ x 12" **245.00**
Peal, 37¾" l, wrought iron, simple well
shaped handle **100.00**
Rotisserie, brass, iron, winding, hanging
hook, brass plaque, emb "John Lin-
wood Warranted" **500.00**
Skimmer, 18¾" l, brass and wrought
iron **125.00**
Spit Toaster, 29", ball shaped finial, cylindrical shaft, adjustable bell shaped
grill, arched tripod legs **250.00**
Tongs, 24", wrought iron, brass finial . **50.00**
Tool Set, brass, three pieces, holder,
mid 19th C **150.00**
Trammel, wrought iron
  27", sawtooth, candle holder **800.00**
  41", scrolled terminals, notched slid-
  ing hook, Chester County, PA . . . **500.00**
  46½", sawtooth pierced hanging hook
  above pot holder **200.00**
Trivet, wrought iron
  8" h, turned wooden handle, penny
  feet **75.00**
  9" h, steel, rect, slats on top, baluster
  and ring turned legs, English, 19th
  C **175.00**
  12" ·h , brass, D shaped surface
  pierced with circular design, engraved ornament, turned wooden
  handle, cabriole legs joined by
  stretcher, English, c1775 . . . . **700.00**
  12½" h, adjustable meat roasting fork,
  wooden handle **450.00**
Utensil Rack, 16¼" l, wrought iron, five
hooks, stylized floral detail, old blue
and green paint **450.00**

FISCHER J. BUDAPEST.

FISCHER CHINA

History: In 1893 Moritz Fischer founded his factory in Herend, Hungary, a center of porcelain production from the 1790s.

Confusion exists about Fischer china because
of its resemblance to the wares of Meissen,
Sevres, and Oriental export. It often was bought
and sold as the product of these firms. Forged
marks of other potteries are found on Herend
pieces. The mark "MF," often joined, is the mark
of Moritz Fischer's pottery.

Fischer's Herend is hard paste ware with lumi-
nosity and exquisite decoration. Pieces are designated by pattern names, the best known being
Chantilly Fruit, Rothschild Bird, Chinese Bouquet,
Victoria Butterfly, and Parsley.

Fischer also made figural birds and animal
groups, Magyar figures (individually and in
groups), and Herend eagles poised for flight.

Reference: Susan and Al Bagdade, *Warman's
English & Continental Pottery & Porcelain, 1st Edition,* Warman Publishing Co., Inc., 1987.

**Vase, 13" h, 8" w, blue, pink, and gold
accents and bands, stamped in blue
"Fischer, J. Budapest," $350.00.**

Bowl, 6 34/", reticulated edge, birds,
butterflies, and flowers, multicolored,
late **48.00**
Cache Pot, 5", Victoria Butterfly pattern,
handled **150.00**
Charger, 13", Chantilly Fruit pattern . . **220.00**
Dish, 4½", triangular, Victoria Butterfly
pattern, gold trim **125.00**
Egg Cup, gilt trim **125.00**

Ewer, 16½" h, handled, reticulated body,
rose, green, blue, and gold **250.00**
Gravy Boat, underplate, ladle, Parsley
pattern **200.00**
Jar, cov, 9½", floral dec, multicolored,
gold trim **250.00**
Pitcher, 12", reticulated, multicolored, all
over dec **300.00**
Plate, 10½", Chantilly Fruit pattern . . .   **100.00**
Tureen, cov, 8½", Victoria Butterfly pat-
tern **250.00**
Vase
3", gold top, cream bottom, hp floral
dec **75.00**
7½", handles, reticulated, multico-
lored floral dec, gold trim **150.00**
10½", reticulated, flowers, pink, blue,
green, and white **175.00**
12", bulbous, extended neck, ochre
ground, multicolored flowers, gold
accents, cobalt blue reticulated
handle with deep rose sides **325.00**
13¾", cornucopia shape, pierced rim,
painted floral dec, four ftd pedestal
base with fish scale dec, orig paper
label, stamped and imp mark, 1913   **275.00**
Vegetable Dish, 9½", Chantilly Fruit pat-
tern **120.00**

FITZHUGH

History: Fitzhugh, one of the most recognized
Chinese Export porcelain patterns, was named for
the Fitzhugh family for whom the first dinner service was made. The peak period of production was
from 1780 to 1850.

Fitzhugh features an oval center medallion or
monogram surrounded by four groups of flowers
or emblems. The border is similar to that on Nanking china. Occasional border variations are found.
Butterfly and honeycomb are among the rarest.

Blue is the common color. Color is a key factor
in pricing with rarity in ascending order of orange,
green, sepia, mulberry, yellow, black, and gold.
Combinations of colors are scarce.

Reference: Sandra Andacht, *Oriental Antiques
& Art: An Identification And Value Guide,* Wallace-
Homestead, 1987.

Reproduction Alert: Spode Porcelain Company, England, currently is producing a copy of the
Fitzhugh pattern in several colors. Oriental copies
also are available.

Hot Water Dish, 19½" l, oval, blue,
c1812 . . . .   **700.00**
Plate
6", rose, c1810 . . . .   **500.00**
9⅝", green, c1875 . . . .   **200.00**
9⅞", green, American eagle dec,
c1810 . . . .   **550.00**

Platter, 15¾", blue, $500.00.

Platter
18½" l, oval, pierced liner, brown,
1810–20 . . . .   **1,400.00**
19¼ x 20⅛", oval, on wood stand,
green, bamboo turned legs and
stretcher **1,100.00**
Pot de Creme, cov, 3½" h, brown, cen-
ter initial "H," Hone service, c1818 .   **500.00**
Soap Dish, cov, pierced drainer, blue
and gold dec, 19th C **200.00**
Soup Plate, 9⅞", orange, c1820 . . . . .   **300.00**
Teapot, cov, 6", orange and brown, 19th
C **850.00**
Vegetable Dish, cov, 9½" l, rect, green,
bud shape knob, mid 19th C **350.00**
Wash Bowl, 16", wide flat rim, blue and
gold birds, roses, and butterflies, 19th
C **800.00**

FLASKS

History: A flask is a container for liquids, usually
having a narrow neck. Early American glass companies frequently formed them in molds which left
a relief design on the front and/or back. Historical
flasks with a portrait, building, scene, or name are
the most desired.

A chestnut is hand blown, small, and has a flattened bulbous body. The pitkin has a blown globular body with vertical ribs with a spiral rib overlay.
Teardrop flasks are generally fiddle shaped and
have a scroll or geometric design.

Dimensions can differ for the same flask because of variations in the molding process. Color
is important, with scarcer colors demanding more
money. Aqua and amber are the most common
colors. Bottles with "sickness," an opalescent scaling which eliminates clarity, are worth much less.

Reference: George L. and Helen McKearin,
American Glass, Crown Publishers, 1941 and
1948.

Chestnut
4¼", clear, checkered diamond, pat-

tern molded, attributed to John Frederick Amelung, ex William J Elsholz collection **1,450.00**

5″, yellow amber, 24 rib mold broken swirled to left, attributed to Zanesville, c1815–25, several pieces of residual slag, blob of glass on bottom, McKearin Plate 235, No. 18, ex William J Elsholz and George McKearin collections **700.00**

5⅛″, greenish-aqua, half pint, blown, 16 ribs, broken swirl, (swirled ribs are bold, vertical ribs faint), Mantua, minor sickness in base, ex Wettlaufer and Jim and Eileen Courtney collections **225.00**

5⅜″, pale blue, blown three mold, McKearin G-III-24, base rayed Type IV, ex William J Elsholz collection **3,750.00**

6½″, pale yellow green, narrow magenta stripe running across middle diagonally, blown three mold, toilet bottle mold blown into plump flask form, McKearin G-I-3, Type II, ex William J Elsholz and George McKearin collections **3,300.00**

7¼″, deep yellow green, blown three mold, McKearin G-I-22, plain base, slight wear and chemical deposit, ex William J Elsholz collection . . . **1,250.00**

8¼″, brilliant amber, expanded vertical ribbing, 24 rib mold, Zanesville **1,200.00**

Gemel

9⅜″, aqua, white loopings, applied base, sheared mouth **100.00**

10″, clear, blown, applied rigaree, quilling and trailing, applied handle, hollow knob containing 1857 US cent, applied six petal tooled foot, handle broken off and missing, McKearin Plate 6, No 5, ex William J Elsholz collection **300.00**

Historical

Anchor/Log Cabin, aquamarine, pint, Spring Garden Glass Works, McKearin G-XIII-58 . . . . **65.00**

Army Dragoon/Dog, citrine, qt, McKearin G-XIII-6 . . . . **150.00**

Clasped Hands/Waterford, aquamarine, McKearin G-XII-2 . . . . **75.00**

Eagle/Masonic, olive-green, half pint, sheared flared mouth, pontil mark, Keene Marlboro Street Glassworks, Keene, NH, McKearin G-IV-24 . . . . **175.00**

Eagle/Willington, amber, pint, double collared mouth, smooth base, Willington Glass Works, Willington, CT, McKearin G-II-64 . . . . **75.00**

Masonic/Eagle, clear, brilliant green, pint, tooled mouth, Keene Marlboro

Scroll with 2 stars, emerald green, bluish tone, pontil, McKearin GIX–11, $125.00.

Street Glassworks, Keene, NH, McKearin G-IV-1 . . . . **250.00**

Pikes Peak/Eagle, aquamarine, pint, McKearin G-X-1-41, type 8, base with dot at center **75.00**

Pine Tree, clear, yellow-green, pint, McKearin G-X-15 . . . . **100.00**

Washington/Taylor, portrait, clear green, qt, sheared mouth, smooth base, Dyottville Glass Works, Philadelphia, PA, McKearin Gfi-37 . . . **135.00**

Pitkin

4½″, olive-green, 36 vertical ribs, New England, early 19th C **375.00**

5″, olive-green, half pint, half post neck, 36 ribs, broken swirl, minor sickness, ex Jim and Eileen Courtney collection **150.00**

6⅝″, yellow, slight olive tone, pint, ribbed and swirled to right, sheared mouth, pontil base, New England . **265.00**

6¾″, green, 32 ribs, broken swirl, Ohio, bubbly glass with small potstones and some tiny surface blisters, ex Baugh and Jim and Eileen Courtney collections **375.00**

Teardrop

7⅜″, opaque white, red, and blue loopings, tooled "three ring" sheared mouth, polished pontil . . **175.00**

9″, rounded, clear, white loopings, double ringed tooled collar, tubular pontil **100.00**

FLOW BLUE

History: Flow blue or flowing blue is the name applied to china of cobalt and white whose color, when fired in a kiln, produced a flowing or smudged effect. The blue varies in color from dark cobalt to a grayish or steel blue. The flow varies from very slight to a heavy blur where the pattern cannot be easily recognized. The blue color does not permeate through the china.

Flow blue was first produced around 1835 in the Staffordshire district of England by a large number of potters including Alcock, Davenport, J. Wedgwood, Grindley, New Wharf, Johnson Brothers, and many others. The early flow blue, 1830s to 1870s, was usually of the ironstone variety. The late patterns, 1880s to 1910s, and modern patterns, after 1910, usually were made of the more delicate semi-porcelain variety. Approximately 95% of the flow blue was made in England, with the remaining 5% made in Germany, Holland, France, and Belgium. A few patterns also were made in the United States by Mercer, Warwick, and Wheeling Pottery companies.

References: Mary F. Gaston, *The Collector's Encyclopedia Of Flow Blue China,* Collector Books, 1983; Veneita Mason, *Popular Patterns of Flow Blue,* Wallace-Homestead, 1983; Petra Williams, *Flow Blue China—An Aid To Identification,* Fountain House East, 1981, revised edition; Petra Williams, *Flow Blue China II,* Fountain House East, 1981, revised edition; Petra Williams, *Flow Blue China and Mulberry Ware—Similarity and Value Guide,* Fountain House East, 1981, revised edition.

Early Pattern, Cashmere, creamer, 5½″ h, $200.00.

EARLY PATTERNS: c1825–1850

Bowl
Cashmere, Ridgway and Morley, c1850, 10½″	140.00
Kin-Shan, Philips & Sons, c1840, 8½″	100.00

Butter Dish, cov
Amoy, Davenport, c1844	125.00
Chusan, Podmore Walker & Co, c1845	120.00

Pelew, E Challinor, c1840	125.00

Creamer
Hong Kong, Charles Meigh, c1845	100.00
Indian Jar, Thomas Ford, c1840	175.00
Sabraon, maker unknown, c1845	200.00
Scinde, J & G Alcock, c1840	200.00
Tonquin, W Adams & Son, c1845	100.00

Cup and Saucer, handleless
Cashmere, Ridgway and Morley, c1850	110.00
Chapoo, Wedgwood, c1850	125.00
Jeddo, Adams & Co, c1840	90.00
Kyber, Adams & Co, c1850	85.00
Oregon, T J & J Mayer, c1845	85.00
Scinde, J & G Alcock, c1840	125.00

Cup Plate
Rhine, Thomas Dimmock, c1844	50.00
Scinde, J & G Alcock, c1840	65.00

Gravy Boat
Daliah, E Challinor, c1850	100.00
Gothic, T J & J Mayer, c1845	200.00
Oregon, T J & J Mayer, c1845	225.00
Scinde, J & G Alcock, c1840	200.00

Plate
California, Podmore Walker & Co, c1849, 7¾″	48.00
Chapoo, Wedgwod, c1850, 8½″	60.00
Jeddo, Adams & Co, c1840, 9″	65.00
Manilla, Podmore & Walker, c1845, 10″	75.00
Oregon, T J & J Mayer, c1845, 9¾″	90.00
Scinde, J & G Alcock, c1840, 9½″	75.00
Troy, Charles Meigh, c1840, 8″	50.00

Platter
Chen-Sei, John Meir, 16 x 12″, octagonal	325.00
Kyber, Adams & Co, c1850, 17″	300.00
Manilla, Podmore & Walker, c1845, 16″	325.00
Scinde, J & G Alcock, c1840, 14″	275.00

Sauce
Amoy, Davenport, c1844	40.00
Shell, Wood & Challinor, c1840	42.00
Tulip & Sprig, Thomas Walker, c1845	38.00

Sauce Tureen, cov, Oregon, T J & J Mayer, c1845, rose knob	300.00
Soap Dish, Scinde, J & G Alcock, c1840, 3 pcs	350.00

Soup Plate
Arabesque, T J & J Mayer, c1845	75.00
Chen-Sei, John Meir, 10¼″ d, flange rim	90.00

Soup Tureen
Chusan, Podmore Walker & Co, c1845	175.00
Scinde, J G Alcock, c1840, cov	600.00

Sugar, cov
Cashmere, Ridgway and Morley, c1850	350.00
Kin-Shan, E Challinor, c1844, pagoda shape, 8½″	225.00
Scinde, J & G Alcock, c1840	250.00

Tea Set, cov teapot, creamer, and cov
sugar
 California, Podmore Walker & Co,
  c1849 .... 300.00
 Oregon, T J & J Mayer, c1845 .... 900.00
Toddy Plate, Tonquin, W Adams & Son,
 c1845 .... 75.00
Vegetable Dish, cov
 Kyber, Adams & Co, c1850, 10½",
  double handles 165.00
 Scinde, J & G Alcock, c1840, oblong 350.00
 Tonquin, W Adams & Son, c1845 .. 375.00
Waste Bowl
 Chen-Sei, John Meir 125.00
 Kyber, Adams & Co, c1850 .... 65.00

MIDDLE PATTERNS: c1850–1870

Coffeepot, Simila, Elsmore & Forster,
 c1860 .... 165.00
Creamer, Genevese, Edge Malkin,
 c1873 .... 100.00
Cup, Shanghae, J Furnival, c1860,
 large 25.00
Dish, Blossom, G L Ashworth & Bros,
 c1865, 9½" d 30.00
Pitcher, milk, Shanghae, J Furnival,
 c1860, 6½ x 7½" 400.00
Plate
 Shanghae, J Furnival, c1860, 9" ... 80.00
Platter
 Hindustan, 12 x 16" 220.00
 Shanghae, J Furnival, c1860, 13½" . 165.00
Saucer, Rock, E Challinor, c1850, 6" .. 42.00
Soup Plate, Blossom, G L Ashworth &
 Bros, 9", flange rim 20.00
Syllaub Cup, Blossom, G L Ashworth &
 Bros 50.00
Vegetable Dish, cov
 Asiatic Pheasants, John Meir & Son,
  c1865 .... 110.00
 Victor, J Maddock & Sons, c1850 .. 115.00

LATE PATTERNS: c1880–1900s

Bone Dish
 Clarence, W H Grindley, c1900 .... 30.00
 La Belle, Wheeling Pottery, c1900 .. 40.00
Boullion Cup and Underplate, Shang-
 hai, c1860, W H Grindley 75.00
Bowl
 Aldine, W H Grindley, c1891, 5" ... 16.00
 Clarence, W H Grindley, c1900, des-
  sert 30.00
 Keele, W H Grindley, c1891, 10" ... 42.50
 Waldorf, New Wharf Pottery, c1892,
  9" 35.00
Butter Dish, cov, Crumlin, Myott, Son &
 Co, c1900, drain insert, 3 pcs 125.00
Butter Pat
 Gironde, W H Grindley, c1891 ..... 15.00
 Osborne, Ridgways, c1905 .... 18.00

Compote, La Belle, Wheeling Pottery,
 c1900, fancy loop handles 155.00
Creamer
 Del Monte, Johnson Bros, c1900 .. 85.00
 Manhattan, Henry Alcock, c1900 ... 60.00
Cup and Saucer
 Argyle, W H Grindley, c1896 ...... 48.00
 Brunswick, Wood & Sons, c1891 ... 42.00
 Chiswick, Ridgways 40.00
 Princeton, Johnson Bros, c1900 ... 45.00
 Regent, Alfred Meakin Ltd, c1897 .. 75.00
 Roseville, John Maddocks, c1891 .. 835.00
Egg Cup, Alaska, W H Grindley, c1891 50.00
Gravy Boat
 Alexandra, S Hancock & Sons,
  c1910, 7½" 30.00
 Argyle, W H Grindley, c1896, at-
  tached underplate 150.00
 Derby, J Furnival, c1902 .... 60.00
 Osborne, Ridgways, c1905 .... 60.00
 Sterling, Johnson Bros, c1910 .... 25.00
Mug, Watteau, Doulton 125.00
Pitcher
 Clarence, W H Grindley, c1900, 8" h 130.00
 Princeton, Johnson Bros, c1900, milk 155.00
Plate
 Alexandra, S Hancock & Sons,
  c1910, 10" 12.00
 Chiswick, Ridways, 9" 100.00
 Dorothy, Johnson Bros, c1900, 9" .. 68.00
 Fairy Villas, W Adams, c1891, 8" .. 35.00
 Idris, W H Grindley, c1900, 10" 25.00
 Normandy, Johnson Bros, c1900, 10" 30.00
 Oxford, Johnson Bros, c1990, 8" ... 35.00
 Roseville, John Maddocks, c1891,
  10" 45.00
 Shanghai, W H Grindley, c1860, 10" 55.00
 Verona, Upper Hanley, c1895, 7½" . 115.00
Platter
 Aldine, W H Grindley, c1891 ...... 75.00
 Alexandra, S Hancock & Sons,
  c1910, 10½ x 8½" 35.00
 Argyle, W H Grindley, c1896, 15" .. 150.00

**Late Pattern, Lancaster, New Wharf
Pottery, cov vegetable dish, raised emb
dec, 12½" w, $140.00.**

Burleigh, Burgess & Leigh, c1903,
12¼" **50.00**
Marie, W H Grindley, c1891, 16 x 11" **135.00**
Tokio, Johnson Bros, c1900, 14" . . . **48.00**
Sauce
Crumlin, Myott, Son & Co, c1900, 5"
d **20.00**
Oxford, Johnson Bros, c1900 . . . . . **20.00**
Sauce Tureen, Regent, Alfred Meakin
Ltd, c1897 . . . . **115.00**
Saucer, Clarence, W H Grindley, c1900 **15.00**
Soup Plate
Chaing, James Gildea, c1885 . . . . . **30.00**
Ladas, Ridgway, c1905, 8" **20.00**
Regent, Johnson Bros, c1897, 10" d,
flange rim **42.00**
Soup Tureen, Roseville, John Mad-
docks, c18891, cov, ladle **450.00**
Sugar, cov
Cambridge, New Wharf Pottery,
c1891 . . . . **65.00**
Del Monte, Johnson Bros, c1900 . . **85.00**
Madison, J & G Meakin, c1910 . . . . **50.00**
St Louis, Johnson Bros, c1900 . . . . **65.00**
Teacup and Saucer, Shanghai, W H
Grindley, c1860 . . . . **55.00**
Teapot, cov, Aldine, W H Grindley,
c1891 . . . . **100.00**
Tureen, cov
Alexandra, S Hancock & Sons, c1910 **70.00**
Leicester, S Hancock & Sons, c1906 **185.00**
Vegetable Dish, cov
Argyle, W H Grindley, c1896, oval . . **165.00**
Clarence, W H Grindley, c1900,
12½", oval **150.00**
Melbourne, oval **200.00**
Osborne, Ridgways, c1905, clover-
leaf shape **185.00**
Waste Bowl, Old Curiosity Shop, Ridg-
way, c1910 . . . . **50.00**

FOOD BOTTLES

History: Food bottles were made in many sizes,
shapes, and colors. Manufacturers tried to make
an attractive bottle that would ship well and allow
the purchaser to see the product, thus assuring
him that the product was as good and as well
made as home preserves.

Reference: Ralph & Terry Kovel, *The Kovels'
Bottle Price List,* Crown Publishers, Inc, 1984, 7th
ed.

Periodicals: *Antique Bottle World,* 5003 West
Berwyn, Chicago, IL 60630; *Old Bottle Magazine,*
P. O. Box 243, Bend, OR 97701.

Additional Listings: See *Warman's Americana
& Collectibles* for more milk bottle listings.

Blueberry Preserve, fluted shoulder,
amber. 11¼" **200.00**

Cocoa, Wan-Eta, Boston, amber, pontil,
4¾" **10.00**
Fruit Extract, California, clear **25.00**
Ginger, F. Brown's Essence Of Jamaica,
aqua **35.00**
Lime Juice, Rose's, 9" **35.00**

**Milk Bottle, Producer's Milk Co., clear,
1 qt, c1915, $15.00.**

Milk
Bedford Dairy, qt **55.00**
Chicago Sterlized Milk Company,
blob top, qt **175.00**
Hoppy's Favorite Milk, pt **30.00**
L. L. Lewis, Brewer, ME, T. Mfg. Co,
tin top, pt **20.00**
Midwest Pasteurized Milk, orange
pyro, round, ½ pt **10.00**
Orchard Farm Dairy Approved Ayr-
shire Milk, cream top, red pyro, qt **30.00**
Price's Dairy Co, El Paso, TX, ribbed
neck, emb, round, qt **20.00**
Sky Royal Dairy, Inc, Royal CA, emb,
round, ½ pt **25.00**
Mustard, Flaccus Mustard Commemo-
rative, U.S.S. Maine Battleship, milk
glass **47.00**
Peanut, Planters, peanut figures on
each corner, glass top, peanut knob,
clear **50.00**
Peanut Butter, Jumbo, hexagonal, fish
bowl, 2 lb **15.00**
Pickle
Cathedral Arches, aqua, 12" **225.00**
H. J. Heinz, gerkins **75.00**
Shaker Pickles, E.D.P & Co, Portland,
ME, emb, aqua, pt **30.00**
Warsaw Pickle Co, aqua, 8¾" **15.00**
Willington, green, pt **350.00**
Syrup
Matewan's Old Time Maple Syrup,
jug **35.00**

Rustle, paper label	**65.00**
Vinegar, H. J. Heinz, barrel	**200.00**

Yogurt

Victoria's, San Bernardino, CA, orange, 8 oz	**6.50**
Yami, Pellissier Dairy Farms, red, round, metal foil lid, 8 oz	**5.00**

FOOD MOLDS

History: Food molds were used both commercially and in the home. For the most part, pewter ice cream molds and candy molds were used on a commercial basis; pottery and copper molds were used in homes. Today, both types are collected largely for decorative purposes.

Pewter ice cream molds were made primarily by two American companies: Eppelsheimer & Co. [molds marked E & Co., N.Y.] and Schall & Co. [molds marked S & Co.]. Both companies used a numbering system for their molds. The Krauss Co. bought out Schall & Co., removed the S & Co. from some, but not all the molds, and added more designs [marked K or Krauss]. The majority of pewter ice cream molds are individual serving molds. When used, one quart of ice cream would make eight to ten pieces. Scarcer, but still available, are banquet molds which used two to four pints of ice cream per example. European pewter molds [CC is a French mold mark] are available.

Chocolate mold makers are more difficult to determine. Unlike the pewter ice cream molds, maker's marks were not always on the mold or were covered by frames. Eppelsheimer & Co. of New York marked many of their molds, either with their name or with a design resembling a child's toy top with "Trade Mark" and "NY." Many chocolate molds were imported from Germany and Holland and were marked with the country of origin and, in some cases, the mold maker's name.

Reference: Judene Divone, *Chocolate Moulds: A History & Encyclopedia,* Oakton Hills Publications, 1987.

Additional Listings: Butter Prints.

CHOCOLATE MOLDS

Clamp type, no hinge, two piece

Cigar, 9¾"	**30.00**
Deer, tin, two piece, 6¼"	**97.50**
Easter Bunny and Chick, sitting on egg, tin, two part, 5¾", marked "Germany"	**75.00**
Hen on basket, marked "E & Co./Toy"	**40.00**
Rabbit, 6"	**35.00**
Stork, marked "E & Co./Toy"	**45.00**

Frame or Book Type [Measurements based on single cavity size]

Basket, 3½ x 6", one cavity	**45.00**
Donkey, pulling car, 7½ x 3", one cavity	**65.00**

Easter Bunny, 4 x 2½", four cavities	**25.00**
Elephants, tin, three cavities	**75.00**
Hearts, dec, 6½ x 6", two cavities . .	**50.00**

Chocolate Mold, Kewpie, 9¾" h, tin, unknown maker, $62.50.

Kewpie Doll, 5 x 3¾", one cavity, marked "Reich"	**65.00**
Mother Hen, bonnet, 5 x 4½"	**45.00**
Owl, 5 x 2½", three cavities	**50.00**
Poodle, 3½ x 3½"	**40.00**
Santa Claus, 4½ x 2", six cavities . .	**70.00**
Turkey, 4½ x 3½", two cavities	**45.00**
Witch, 4½ x 2", four cavities	**55.00**

Tray type [Measurement is overall tray size]

Circus Peanuts, 28 x 13", one hundred and five cavities	**48.00**
Easter Chickens and Rabbits, six different designs, 11 x 17"	**65.00**
Hershey Bar, each section marked "Hershey"	**60.00**
Rabbit, playing saxophone, 14 x 10", six cavities	**40.00**
Turkey, 14 x 10", eight cavities	**45.00**

ICE CREAM MOLDS

Banquet Size

Basket, French flared hinges, marked "Brevete, SGDG, Remarque Fabrique, CC"	**450.00**
Duck, marked "Krauss #44"	**500.00**
Log, 10"	**275.00**
Owl, four pints, marked "S & Co/7" .	**550.00**
Steamship, four pints, marked "E & Co/44"	**625.00**

Individual Size

Acorn, marked "S & Co/135"	**35.00**
Banana, 5¾", marked "E & Co, NY"	**30.00**
Bow, 5¼"	**35.00**
Boy on bicycle, 4½", pewter	**37.00**
Bride, 4¾", marked "E & Co, NY" . .	**37.50**

Ice Cream Mold, Uncle Sam, pewter, E & Co., #1073, $70.00.

Car, 5⅞" l, pewter, marked "N.Y. 623"	**38.00**
Daisy, 4", marked "S & Co"	**35.00**
Eagle, 3¾" d, pewter, "520"	**27.50**
Fig, 2½", French	**28.00**
Fish, 4½" l, pewter, hinged	**20.00**
Lemon, 3¼", marked "C C Brevete" . .	**30.00**
Leprechaun, 5" h, pewter, hinge repair	**35.00**
Lily, three part, marked "S & Co" . .	**42.50**
Orange, 3½"	**25.00**
Pansies, 4¼", three part, marked "E & Co, NY"	**45.00**
Pear, 2¾"	**25.00**
Potato, 3½", marked "E & Co, NY" .	**25.00**
Raspberries, multiple, marked "E & Co, NY"	**37.50**
Rose, 4", marked "S & Co"	**42.50**
Strawberry, 3¼"	**45.00**
Witch, 5⅝", riding broom, marked "E & Co, NY"	**75.00**
Wedding Bell, emb cupid	**35.00**

MISCELLANEOUS

Butter, 4 x 7", rect, two part, "C.W." design, machine cut dovetails	**25.00**
Cheese, 5 x 13", wood, pinned, relief carved design and "Bid," branded "Los," scratch carved date 1893 . . .	**45.00**
Cookie	
Cornucopia, 4¼ x 5¾", cast iron, oval	**25.00**
Six classical heads, 3½ x 6¼", pewter, wood back	**45.00**
Ear of Corn, 6" l, yellowware, oval . . .	**35.00**
Fish, 10⅜" l, redware, green glaze, detail, Shenandoah	**145.00**
Shell, 3", copper	**20.00**
Turk's Head, 9½" d, redware, scalloped rim, clear glaze, brown sponge dec .	**55.00**

POTTERY [Center design indicated]

Crown, large, ironstone, marked "Alcock"	**55.00**

Grape Cluster, 7"	**48.00**
Mermaid, 14¹⁄₁₂", white clay, deep orange glaze int.	**65.00**
Rose, ironstone, marked "Alcock" . . .	**50.00**
Strawberries, 4"	**55.00**

FOSTORIA GLASS   FOSTORIA

History: Fostoria Glass Co. began operations at Fostoria, Ohio, in 1887, and moved to Moundsville, West Virginia, its present location, in 1891. By 1925 Fostoria had five furnances and a variety of special shops. In 1924 a line of colored tableware was introduced. Fostoria was purchased by Lancaster Colony in 1983, and continues to operate under the Fostoria name.

Reference: Hazel M. Weatherman, *Fostoria, Its First Fifty Years*, published by author, c1972.

Collectors' Club: Fostoria Glass Society of America, P.O. Box 826, Moundsville, WV 26041. Dues: $10.00.

Museum: Huntington Galleries, Huntington, WV.

Sandwich Server, Trojan, yellow, $35.00.

Ashtray, Mayfair, red	**18.00**
Basket, Bouquet, #342 etching, 10¼", reed handle	**50.00**
Bonbon, Colony, ftd	**16.00**
Bookends, plume, crystal, pr	**60.00**
Bouillon, Versailles, blue	**45.00**
Bowl	
Meadow Rose, #328 etching, 12", oval	**45.00**
Trojan, #280 etching, 12", flared . . .	**38.00**
Butter Dish, cov, Colony, crystal	**48.00**
Candlesticks, pr	
Baroque, 6¼"	**12.50**
Buttercup, #342 etching	**45.00**
Heirloom, 10", white opal	**45.00**
Candy Dish, cov, Bouquet, #342 etching, 7"	**50.00**

Celery, Arcady, #326 etching, 11½" . . **28.00**
Champagne
  Heather, crystal, 7 oz **12.00**
  Navarre **15.00**
Claret, June, yellow **50.00**
Coaster, Fairfax, blue **6.00**
Cocktail
  Colony, 4" **6.00**
  Mademoiselle, 4¼" **6.00**
  Navarre, 3½ oz **18.00**
Compote, Versailles, pink, high stan-
  dard **45.00**
Creamer, Navarre, 4¼" **15.00**
Creamer and Sugar, Seascape, pink
  opal **45.00**
Cruet, orig stopper
  Century, crystal **40.00**
  Coin, amber **50.00**
Cup and Saucer
  Arcady, #326 etching, ftd **14.00**
  Navarre **16.00**
  Versailles, blue **40.00**
Demitasse Cup and Saucer, Mayfair,
  yellow **20.00**
Goblet
  Corsage, #325 etching, 9 oz **22.00**
  Holly, 7⅞", 10 oz **9.00**
  Jamestown, green, 5⅞", 8 oz **8.00**
  Navarre, 7½" **18.00**
Ice Bucket, Century, 4⅞", tongs **38.00**
Iced Tea, Holly, 6", 12 oz **8.00**
Lunch Tray, Fleur De Lis, 11½", vase-
  line, floral and butterfly cutting, han-
  dles **55.00**
Mayonnaise, Arcady, #326 etching, 2 pt **24.00**
Muffin Tray, Colony, crystal **25.00**
Mustard Jar, cov, American **25.00**
Nappy, Coin, ruby, handle **22.00**
Olive Dish, Coronet, crystal, 6½" **6.75**
Oyster Cocktail, American **10.00**
Plate
  Arcady, #326 etching, 7½" **9.50**
  Colony, crystal, 8½" **8.50**
  Fairfax, blue, 10¼", dinner **45.00**
  Heather Rose, #343 etching, 7½" . . **12.00**
Platter, Fairfax, blue, 15" **85.00**
Relish
  Fairfax, orchid, 8½", two part **10.00**
  Romance, crystal, 10", three part . . **28.00**
Salver, Colony, crystal, 12", ftd **40.00**
Sandwich Server, Chintz **30.00**
Sauce Boat, Fairfax, blue, liner **55.00**
Sherbet
  Baroque **7.50**
  Trojan, topaz, 4½" **12.00**
  Versailles, green, 6" **20.00**
  Vesper, amber, low **15.00**
Sugar, cov, Fairfax, blue **25.00**
Sweetmeat, June, yellow **25.00**
Tidbit Tray, Century, crystal, 3 toes . . . **18.00**
Tray, Heather, crystal, 9", handles . . . **18.00**
Trophy Bowl, American, two handles . **75.00**

Tumbler
  Navarre, 13 oz, ftd **18.00**
  Versailles, blue, 5¼", ftd **22.00**
Urn, Coin, ruby, clear and frosted coins,
  ftd **50.00**
Vase
  American, 8½", cupped **18.00**
  Century, crystal, 6½", handle **38.00**
Vegetable Bowl, American, 10" oval, 2
  pt **30.00**
Wine
  Fascination, crystal, 4 oz **6.00**
  Mademoiselle, 4¾" **6.00**
  Meadow Rose, #328 etching **28.00**

FRAKTUR

History: Fraktur, the calligraphy associated with the Pennsylvania Germans, is named for the elaborate first letter found in many of the hand drawn examples. Throughout its history printed, partially printed-hand drawn, and fully hand drawn works existed side by side. Frakturs often were made by the school teachers or ministers living in rural areas of Pennsylvania, Maryland, and Virginia. Many artists are unknown.

Fraktur exists in several forms—geburts and taufschein (birth and baptismal certificates), vorschrift (writing example, often with alphabet), haus sagen (house blessing), bookplates and marks, rewards of merit, illuminated religious text, valentines, and drawings. Although collected for decoration, the key element in fraktur is the text.

Fraktur prices rise and fall along with the American folk art market. The key market place is Pennsylvania and the Middle Atlantic states.

References: Donald A. Shelley, *The Fraktur-Writings Or Illuminated Manuscripts Of The Pennsylvania Germans,* Pennsylvania German Society, 1961; Frederick S. Weiser and Howell J. Heaney (compilers), *The Pennsylvania German Fraktur Of The Free Library Of Philadelphia,* Pennsylvania German Society, 1976, two volumes.

Museum: The Free Library of Philadelphia, Philadelphia, PA.

HAND DRAWN

Jacob Brenholtz, copy of "Way To Heaven And Hell" broadside, 13 x 16", watercolor on wove paper, dated "August 19th, 1828" . . **5,000.00**
Blowsy (Flying) Angel Artist, birth and baptismal certificate, Northampton County, dated 1800, 9½" x 13½", watercolor, pen, and ink on paper, center text block consumes lower two-thirds of paper, flanked by flowers above which are blowsy angels extending

into center above text block, birth of Magdelena Gunziger **1,500.00**

Crossed Legged Angel Artist, birth and baptismal certificate, Lancaster County, dated 1812, 14 x 17¼", watercolor, pen, and ink on laid paper, block format, floral motif on side borders, crossed legged angel in center of top panel, star burst in center of bottom panel, birth of Michael Klop . **2,500.00**

Heydrich, Baltzer, drawing, Montgomery County, 1845, pen, ink, and watercolor drawing on wove paper, checkerboard border, center with wall (altar) flanked by stylized flowers in a semicirular motif, bird on branch of two of flowers, PA German inscription, "Baltzer Heydrich...1845...in his 83rd year," tones of red, black, green, blue, and yellow, minor stains, tears and damage at fold line, beveled frame with red graining, 16¼ x 20¼" **7,600.00**

Kuster, Friedrich, attributed to, birth certificate, Columbia County, dated 1816, 12¾" x 7¾", pen, ink, and watercolor on laid paper, central text flanked by oversized flowers in green, red, blue, yellow, and black, birth of Siwilla Ana Job, damage at fold lines, penciled additions at bottom edge, tape stains, damage at top edge, old grained frame,12⅜ x 16½" **1,300.00**

Daniel Otto (The Flat Tulip Artist), birth and baptismal certificate, Northumberland County, dated 1788, 11½ x 14¾", watercolor, pen, and ink on paper, central heart text, flanked at bottom by two large parrots with checkered wings facing outward and at top by two smaller parrots with plain wings facing inward, heart with border of attached flowers, red and yellow tones, birth of Catharina Lotz **13,250.00**

Seller, H., birth certificate, Dauphin County, PA, 1807, 16¼ x 19¼", pen, ink, and watercolor on laid paper, central heart flanked at base by large parrots above which is a tulip and peacock, tulip flanked by starburst across top, geometric circles along bottom with "H./Seiler", shades of red, green, blue, brown, yellow, and black, text is primarily in red ink, minor stains, short tears, large tulips have some holes caused by acid ink, bottom edge a bit ragged **12,000.00**

Spanenberg, John, double bookplate for Catharina Haupt, 5¾ x 6¼", pen, ink, and watercolor on laid paper, stylized horizontal floral bands across top and bottom, tones of red, blue, green, yellow, and brown, some stains, fading, and damage on fold line, gilt frame 8½ x 10½" **3,500.00**

Unknown

Bookplate

Southeastern PA, c1820s, 3¾ x 5¾", fly leaf of Martin Luther's *Book of Catechisms,* published by Johann Bar, block motif, central block with heart from which flower radiates, starbursts in corner blocks, stemmed floral motifs in remaining blocks, shades of red, blue, yellow, and green, heart mkd "Salome Beinhauer/ 1828," worn marbleized paper, leather binding for book **2,350.00**

Southeastern PA, c1820–40, 5 x 5⅝", laid paper, central heart with text, face from which radiates two stemmed tulips at top, bottom of heart decorated with fern-like leaves with two star floral motifs, heart contains name "Elizabeth Richter," dark shades of brown, olive, and reddish brown, minor stains, small edge damage, glued to lined paper, frame 10¾ x 11½" **1,650.00**

Southeastern PA, c1840s, 3 x 4¾", watercolor, pen, and ink on paper lining of cardboard book cover, heart with text from which radiates tulips and stems, bird sits on two of lesser tulips, shades of orange, yellow, lavender, and black, for "Georg Reiff," dated 1844, stains, frame 5 x 6¾" . . . **425.00**

Drawing, southeastern PA, c1820–40, laid paper, horizontal dec bands, top with two facing birds surrounded by flowers, block letters "REBECCA SNYDER," birds and flowers, bottom with man and dog flanking central flower, red, yellow, blue, pale green, and brown, stains and small tears, old black frame 8½ x 9¾" **3,700.00**

Reward of Merit, southeastern, PA, c1820–40, wove paper, 8 x 12¾", stylized vining plant with flowers and birds, initials "F/Z," green, brown, blue, and faded red, old damage and repairs, frame 12¾ x 16⅞" **1,600.00**

Song Book, southeastern PA, c1800–10, possibly Bucks County, dated 1804, 6⅜ x 3¾", bookplate has circular text flanked by vertical flower with multi-leaf stem, checkered border, belongs to "Abraham Landes," cover pulled loose from string binding but is not damaged **3,000.00**

HAND DRAWN-PRINTED

Brechall, Martin, birth and baptismal, printed form by Hütter, Easton, 1821, 13 x 16″, central heart, borders hand painted with filigrees and flowers in red, yellow, blue, and green, for Lea Schull 850.00
Dulheur, Henrich, birth and baptismal, 13 x 15¾″ 950.00
Otto, Heinrich, The Great Comet Of 1769, decorated with parrots and shooting stars 2,500.00
Unknown Artist, birth certificate, Northampton County, 1821, 7¾″ x 12″, German calligraphy, inscription within a keystone device, hand painted paired birds and large flowering tulip plants, birth of Maria Margaretha Scherner 750.00

Printed, Birth and Baptismal certificate, printed by A. and W. Blumer, Allentown, PA, confirmation information also included, $125.00.

PRINTED

Adam and Eve
  Bruckman, C. A., Reading 300.00
  Dahlem, M., Philadelphia 400.00
Birth and Baptismal
  Baumann and Ruth, Ephrata 350.00
  Baumann, S., Ephrata 400.00
  Hartman, Joseph, Lebanon 250.00
  Hanesche, J. G., Baltimore 150.00
  Herschberger, Johann, Chambersburg 325.00
  Hütter, C. J., Easton 350.00
  Lepper, Wilhelm, Hanover 300.00
  Lippe, G. Ph., Pottsville 150.00
  Puwelle, A., Reading 125.00

Saeger and Leisenring, Allentown, early form 150.00
Sage, G. A., Allentown 175.00
Scheffer, Theo. F., Harrisburg 75.00
Wiestling, Johann S., Harrisburg 200.00
Note: If signed by a scrivener, increase value by 25% to 40%
Broadside
  Christ Before Pilate, G. S. Peters, Harrisburg, stains and tears, beveled mahogany veneer frame, 16½ x 12½″ 435.00
  "Representation Of The Different Way Leading To Everlasting Life or Eternal Damnation," G. S. Peters, Harrisburg, stains and short tear, cherry on pine frame with corner blocks, 14¼ x 18″ 385.00
Haus Sagen
  Gräter and Blummer, Allentown 175.00
  Palm, Issac, Brecknock Township, Lancaster County 500.00

FRANKART

History: Arthur Von Frankenberg, artist and sculptor, founded Frankart, Inc., in New York City in the mid-1920s. Frankart, Inc., mass produced practical "art objects" in the Art Deco style into the 1930s. Pieces include aquariums, ashtrays, bookends, flower vases, lamps, etc. Although Von Frankenberg used live female models as his subjects, his figures are characterized by their form and style rather than specific features. Nudes are the most collectible; caricatured animals and other human figures were also produced, no doubt, to increase sales.

With few exceptions, pieces were marked Frankart, Inc., with a patent number or "pat. appl. for."

Pieces were cast in a white metal composition in the following finishes: cream—a pale iridescent white; bronzoid—oxidized copper, silver, or gold; french—a medium brown with green in the crevices; gun metal—art iridescent gray; jap—a very dark brown, almost black, with green in the crevices; pearl green—pale iridescent green; and verde—a dull light green. Cream and bronzoid were used primarily in the 1930s.

Note: All pieces listed are all original in very good condition unless otherwise indicated.
Advisor: Walter Glenn.

Ashtray
  5½″ h, gazelle leaps over oval green glass ashtray, stylized 85.00
  10″ h, adv, nude, dancing, one knee up, holds pottery ashtray, match holder on base, "Waugh's Equipment Co, N.Y. 365.00
  10″ h, two nudes, standing back to

back, glass cigarette box on base, supports four 3½" sq ashtrays ... **425.00**

12" h, nude, holds cigarette urn, strides across 4½" sq pottery ashtray **465.00**

Lamp, seated nude relaxes between two 6" crackle glass columns which contain light bulbs, 8½" h, $585.00.

Bookends, pr

5" h, elephants, flared ears, stylized **110.00**

5½" h, angle fish, exaggerated fins, stylized **90.00**

6" h, nudes, seated, legs extended, hands outstretched to knees, backs support books **175.00**

10", nudes, dancing, one knee up, arms back to support books, frog on base **290.00**

Lamp

8" h, nude, kneeling before 4" crystal bubble ball, illuminated base **310.00**

9" h, nude

Sitting atop ribbed column, arms support 3" crackle glass globe on lap **370.00**

Two back to back, kneeling, arms support 8" crackle glass globe . **575.00**

11" h, nude

Coy, stands on geometric base, 3" crackle glass globe at feet **390.00**

Standing, embraces orig 8" candlelight bulb **310.00**

13", nude, peeks around orig 10" candlelight bulb **345.00**

Smoker's Set, 12" h, nude, standing, arched back, arms outstretched to hold green glass cigarette box, 3½" round green glass ashtray on base . **410.00**

Vase, 11" h, nude, standing, embraces 1" diameter frosted glass vase, scalloped top **310.00**

FRANKOMA POTTERY

History: John N. Frank founded a ceramic art department at Oklahoma University in Norman and taught there for several years. In 1933 he established his own business and began making Oklahoma's first commercial pottery. Frankoma moved from Norman to Sapulpa, Oklahoma, in 1938.

A fire completely destroyed the new plant later the same year, but rebuilding began almost immediately. The company remained in Sapulpa and continued to grow. Frankoma is the only American pottery to be permanently exhibited at the International Ceramic Museum of Italy.

In September 1983 a disastrous fire struck once again, destroying 97% of Frankoma's facilities. The rebuilt Frankoma Pottery reopened on July 2, 1984. Production has been limited to 1983 production molds only. All other molds were lost in the fire.

Prior to 1954 all Frankoma pottery was made with a honey-tan colored clay from Ada, Oklahoma. Since 1954 Frankoma has used a brick red clay from Sapulpa. During the early 1970s the clay became lighter and is now pink in color.

There were a number of early marks. One most eagerly sought is the leopard pacing on the FRANKOMA name. Since the 1938 fire, all pieces have carried only the name FRANKOMA.

References: Phyllis and Tom Bess, *Frankoma Treasures*, published by authors, 1983; Susan N. Cox, *Collectors Guide To Frankoma Pottery*, Book I, published by author, 1979, and Book II, published by author, 1982.

Additional Listings: See *Warman's Americana & Collectibles* for more examples.

Advisor: Phyllis Bess.

Ashtray

Advertising **15.00**

Sleeping cocker, Ada Clay **50.00**

Bottle Vase

V-1, 15", 1969, John Frank **50.00**

V-2, 1970, sgd John Frank **50.00**

V-5, 1973, sgd Grace Lee Frank ... **70.00**

V-6, 1974, Grace Lee Frank **70.00**

V-8, 1976, Joniece Frank **65.00**

V-12, 1980, Joniece Frank **45.00**

V-15, 1983, Joniece Frank, finial vase **35.00**

Bust, praying Madonna, 5½" **75.00**

Candleholder, Christ the Light of the World **12.00**

Christmas Card

1948, Franks **85.00**

1952, The Franks **85.00**

1952, Donna Frank **45.00**

1960, Gracetone **75.00**

1960, The Franks **55.00**

1975, Grace Lee & Milton Smith ... **85.00**

Cornucopia, 15" #215 .... **35.00**

Dish, leaf shape, Gracetone **15.00**

Dog Food Spoon **35.00**

Jewelry, earrings, clip, pr **20.00**
Lamp Base, barrel **35.00**
Mask
  Comedy **5.00**
  Tragedy **5.00**
Mug
  American Airlines Eagle **35.00**
  Donkey
    Carter-Mondale, pink and white,
      1977 . . . . **15.00**
    Red and white, 1976 . . . . **18.00**
  Elephant
    Nixon-Agnew, desert gold and
      white, 1973 . . . . **50.00**
    Mountain Haze, 1986 . . . . **5.00**
    White, 1968 . . . . **75.00**
    Woodland moss and white, 1978 . **20.00**

Cider Pitcher, six mugs, green and brown glaze, $60.00.

Pitcher
  Ada Clay **25.00**
  Wagon wheel, 2 qt **20.00**
Plate
  Christmas
    1965 . . . . **225.00**
    1972 . . . . **20.00**
    1979 . . . . **20.00**
    1986 . . . . **12.00**
  Conestoga wagon, 1971 . . . . **30.00**
  Jesus The Carpenter, 1971 . . . . **20.00**
  Liberty, 1986 . . . . **15.00**
  Madonna of Love, 1978 . . . . **15.00**
Salt and Pepper Shaker
  Dutch Shoes, pr **25.00**
  Wagon wheels, pr **10.00**
Sculpture
  Baby Bird **5.00**
  Buffalo **250.00**
  Circus Horse **35.00**
  Colt, prancing, 8" **250.00**
  Fan Dancer
    Ada Clay **200.00**
    Red Clay **150.00**
  Girl, ponytails **25.00**
  Indian, maiden, 12" **10.00**
  Irish, setter, head **55.00**

Mare and Colt, W. Stone **10.00**
Squirrel, 6", W. Stone **5.00**
Toby Mug
  Cowboy, 4½" **8.00**
  Uncle Sam, 4½" **8.00**
Trivet
  Cattle Brands **10.00**
  Lazybone **30.00**
  Wagon Wheel **35.00**
Vase
  Black Foot, #55 . . . . **15.00**
  Fireside
    Pitcher, #77A **50.00**
    Vase, #77 . . . . **50.00**
  Wagon Wheel **15.00**
Wall Pocket
  Acorn, Ada Clay **20.00**
  Boot **15.00**
  Phoebe, bisque, painted features . . **100.00**

FRATERNAL ORGANIZATIONS

History: Benevolent and secret societies played an important part in American society from the late 18th to the mid-20th centuries. Initially the societies were organized to aid members and their families in times of distress or death.

They evolved from this purpose into important social clubs by the late 19th century. In the 1950s, with the arrival of civil rights, an attack occurred on the secretiveness and often discriminatory practices of these societies. The fraternal movement, with the exception of the Masonic organizations, suffered serious membership loss. Many local chapters closed and sold their lodge halls. This resulted in many fraternal items arriving in the antiques market.

Additional Listings: See *Warman's Americana & Collectibles* for more examples.

Masonic, plate, 9¼", maroon border, gold rim, marked "Thomas Maddock & Son's Co., Trenton, NJ," $17.50.

MASONIC

Apron, 11½" h, 14" w, leather, painted,
  gilt, red, and blue, Masonic symbols
  two leather drawstrings, sgd in ink un-
  der flap "De Witt Clinton," on back
  "Gardiner Conklin," New State, early
  19th C **1,450.00**
Ballot Box **40.00**
Blowing Horn **65.00**
Certificate, engraved, Belfast, Ireland,
  c1813 . . . . **150.00**
Gavel, wood, hand carved symbols . . **40.00**
Emblem, gold leaf, deep walnut frame **75.00**
Jug, 11⅜", three color transfers, four
  lines of verse, Liverpool **475.00**
Outfit, ornate, engraved sword, scab-
  bard, belt, sash, and hat **100.00**
Ring, onyx stone, diamond chip, 14K . **90.00**
Shot Glass, 3", cut glass, clear and dec,
  captive enclosed bottom section hold-
  ing three dice, emblem **150.00**
Tankard, 3 x 3", Chapter #5, 1908 . . . **95.00**
Teaspoon, SS, Masonic emblem, Great
  Falls, MT **55.00**
Tobacco Jar, Masonic Concordia Lodge
  #67, 1914 . . . . **110.00**
Tray, 12", mosaic, turquoise, black
  squares, center emblem on round
  white stone, gilt metal base **25.00**

OTHERS

Benevolent & Protective Order of the
  Elks, B.P.O.E.
  Badge, 2 x 3", brass link, purple
    enamel automobile hanger bar,
    raised Indian scene, dark red
    enamel accents, Detroit BPOE
    convention, 1910 . . . . **25.00**
  Beaker, 5" h, cream, black elk head
    design, marked "Mettlach, Velleroy
    & Boch" **100.00**
  Flask, 4½" h, milk glass, elk tooth
    shape, emb elk head, clock, BPOE
    of face, marked "Comp. J.C. Stu-
    bling" **175.00**
  Plaque, 10½" d, Sioux City Lodge
    #112, hp, elk head, BPOE, c1895 **100.00**
  Plate, 9" d, BPOE 22, Brooklyn, NY,
    elk head, multicolored, marked
    "Lamberton" **35.00**
  Shaving Mug, 3½" h, white, colorful
    vining leaves and roses, green elk
    head and BPOE, marked "Ger-
    many" **75.00**
  Stein, 4½" h, purple, brown elk head,
    clock and BPOE, gold rim, marked
    "Buffalo Pottery" **85.00**
Eastern Star
  Hatpin, long shank **30.00**
  Pin, 14K gold, three diamond chips . **60.00**
  Ring, 10K gold, diamond in center . **80.00**

Fraternal Order of Eagles, brass, link,
  upper part symbol and red, white, and
  blue accents, lower segment formed
  like human foot, 1914 convention,
  Charlotte, NC **25.00**
Independent Order of Odd Fellows,
  I.O.O.F.
  Banner, 18 x 30", white silk, metallic
    gold braid border, wood pole at top,
    19th C **75.00**
  Dish, 5¾", pink lusterc1840 . . . . . . **65.00**
  Ribbon, I.O.O.F. Cochise Lodge, #5,
    Tombstone, AZ **45.00**
  Tie Bar, 10K gold **30.00**
  Trivet, 8¼" l, cast iron, insignia and
    heart in hand in laurel wreath . . . **25.00**
Knights of Columbus, sword, dress,
  scabbard, detailed blade, marked
  "The McLilley Co., Columbus, OH" . **45.00**
Knights Templar
  Mug, 4", insignia, amethyst flashed
    design, gold trim **85.00**
  Watch Fob, chain, 32nd degree, Ma-
    sonic **90.00**
Woodsmen of the World
  Belt, cast buckle, "WOW" and
    crossed arc and sledge hammer,
    worn red leather **25.00**
  Tools, seven cast metal tools, fitted 8
    x 9¾" case **45.00**

FRUIT JARS

History: Fruit jars are canning jars used to preserve food. Thomas W. Dyott, one of Philadelphi-
a's earliest and most innovative glass makers, was
promoting his glass canning jars in 1829. John
Landis Mason patented his screw-type canning jar
on November 30, 1858. This date refers to the
patent date, not the age of the jar. There are thousands of types of jars in many colors, types of
closures, sizes, and embossings.

References: Alice M. Creswick, *The Red Book
of Fruit Jars No. 5*, published by author, 1987; Bill
Schroeder, *1000 Fruit Jars: Priced And Illustrated,
Revised 5th Edition*, Collector Books, 1987.

All Right, aqua, qt, handmade, glass lid,
  wire clamp, patent Jan 28th, 1868 . . **100.00**
Alston Jar, clear, qt, handmade, disc lid,
  wire clip, ground lip **75.00**
Atherholt Fisher & Co, clear, qt, hand-
  made, ground glass stopper **175.00**
Atlas Mason, olive, pt, machine made,
  zinc lid **20.00**
Ball
  Deluxe Jar, clear, qt, machine made,
    glass lid, wire bail **5.00**
  Eclipse, clear,½ pt, machine made,
    rounded sq shape, glass lid, wire
    bail **2.00**

Mason's Patent 1858, green, qt, handmade, zinc lid, ground lip . . .	**5.00**
Baltimore Glass Works, aqua, qt, handmade, applied lid	**175.00**
BBGM Co, green, qt, glass lid, wire bail, Patent Nov 30, 1858	**35.00**
Bennett's No 1, clear, qt, machine made, zinc lid	**150.00**
Boldt Mason Jar, blue, pt, machine made, zinc lid	**15.00**
Bosco Double Seal, clear, qt, glass lid	**5.00**
Brighton, clear, qt, handmade, glass lid, toggle	**55.00**

Atlas E-Z Seal, quart, aqua, $5.00.

Cleveland Fruit Juice Co, clear, qt, glass lid, wire bail	**8.00**
Clyde Improved Mason, green, qt, glass lid, metal band	**15.00**
Columbia, aqua, pt, handmade, glass lid, wire clip	**25.00**
Crystal Jar, amethyst, qt, handmade, glass lid	**35.00**
Daisy Jar, clear, qt, handmade, glass lid, metal clip	**125.00**
Dandy, The, amber, qt, handmade, glass lid, wire bail	**80.00**
Drey Ever Seal, clear, ½ pt, machine made, glass lid, wire bail	**4.00**
Dyson's Pure Food Products, Maltese cross, clear, qt, glass lid	**20.00**
Eagle, green, qt, handmade, wax seal	**75.00**
Empress, aqua, qt, handmade, glass lid, zinc band	**125.00**
Everlasting, Improved, clear, pt, machine made, glass lid, toggle	**15.00**
F & S, aqua, qt, glass lid, wire bail, machine made	**10.00**
Faxon, blue, qt, handmade, zinc lid . .	**8.00**
Fruit-Keeper, aqua, qt, zinc lid, handmade	**45.00**

Gem, Wallaceburg, clear, qt, machine made, glass lid, screw band	**8.00**
Halle, green, qt, handmade, wax seal .	**50.00**
Hamilton Glass Works, aqua, qt, metal yoke	**175.00**
Hazel Atlas Lightning Seal, clear, pt, glass lid, wire bail	**10.00**
Improved Crown, clear, pt, handmade, glass lid	**4.00**
Ivanhoe, clear, qt, metal lid, name on bottom	**5.00**
Kerr Glass Top, clear, qt, machine made, glass top, screw band	**2.00**
L'Ideale, green, pt, machine made, glass lid, wire clip	**18.00**
Mallinger, clear, qt, machine made, zinc lid	**4.00**
MG Co, aqua, qt, handmade, wax seal, emb name on base	**20.00**
Mission, bell, trademark, clear, qt, zinc lid	**15.00**
My Choice, aqua, ½ gal, glass lid, clamp, lid and bottom read "Pat Jan 3rd 1888"	**185.00**
Penn, The, green, qt, handmade, glass lid, zinc band	**25.00**
Pint Standard, aqua, pt, wax seal	**50.00**
Potter & Bodine, Philadelphia, aqua, qt, name emb in script	**85.00**
Rau's Improved Grove Ring Jar, aqua, pt, handmade, wax seal	**25.00**
Rose, Imperial, clear, qt, zinc lid	**15.00**
Royal, aqua, qt, glass lid, emb "Royal of 1876"	**80.00**
Sealtite, aqua, qt, machine made, glass lid, wire bail	**2.00**
Stevens, aqua, ½ gal, handmade, wax seal	**75.00**
Sun, green, qt, glass lid, clamp, handmade	**60.00**
Texas Mason, clear, qt, zinc lid	**15.00**
Universal, aqua, qt, zinc lid, name emb upside down	**10.00**
Woodbury Improved, aqua, qt, handmade, glass lid, metal clip	**25.00**

FRY GLASS

History: The H.C. Fry Glass Co. of Rochester, Pennsylvania, began operating in 1901 and continued until 1933. Their first products were brilliant period cut glass. They later produced depression tablewares. In 1922 they patented heat resisting ovenware in an opalescent color. This "Pearl Oven Glass" was produced in a variety of oven and table pieces including casseroles, meat trays, pie and cake pans, etc. Most of these pieces are marked "Fry" with model numbers and sizes.

Fry's beautiful art line, Foval, was produced only in 1926-27. It is pearly opalescent, with jade green or delft blue trim. It is rarely signed, except for occasional silver overlay pieces marked "Rockwell." Foval is always evenly opalescent, never striped like Fenton's opalescent line.

Reproduction Alert: In the 1970's, reproductions of Foval were made in abundance in Murano, Italy. These pieces, including candlesticks, toothpicks, etc., have teal blue transparent trim.

Tumbler, icicle, green handle, 5¼" h, $60.00.

Bowl, 8", pineapple and wheel cutting,
  sgd **100.00**
Candlesticks, 9¾", Foval, Delft blue, pr **275.00**
Compote, 6¾ x 6", Foval, jade green
  stem **100.00**
Creamer, Foval, blue tinted loopings,
  applied Delft blue handle **150.00**
Cruet, Foval, cobalt handle, orig stopper **100.00**
Cup and Saucer, Foval, jade green handle **85.00**
Decanter, 9", ftd, Foval, cobalt handle . **175.00**
Jug, water, Foval, jade green handle,
  foot, SS overlay **325.00**
Lemonade Pitcher, cov, 10½"
  Crackle, clear, glass, jade green handle **100.00**
  Optic, irid, blue handle, polished pontil **125.00**
Plate
  8", luncheon, Foval, jade green rim . **48.00**
  9½", dinner, Foval, Delft blue rim .. **65.00**
Pot, 12", Foval, blue handle and finial . **225.00**
Punch Bowl, 14 x 13" two pc bowl, cut
  glass, Frederick pattern, twelve
  matching cups, sgd **3,000.00**
Punch Cup, clear, Crackle, blue ring
  handle **40.00**
Shot Glass, jade green, opal handle .. **100.00**
Soup Plate
  4¾", cream, Foval, 2 Delft handles,
    matching underplate **75.00**
  7", flat, Foval **40.00**

Teapot, Foval, blue knob, handle, spout **200.00**
Tumbler, lemonade, 12 oz, Foval, jade
  green handle **60.00**
Vase
  7½", Foval, jade green rolled rim and
    foot **200.00**
  8", flared, Foval, jade green ball in
    stem **115.00**
  10", bud, Foval **125.00**
  10¾", narrow neck, Foval, jade applied trim **125.00**
  11", jack-in-the-pulpit, Foval, Delft
    blue spiral twist, crimped rim with
    three rows of blue **175.00**

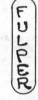

FULPER POTTERY

History: The American Pottery Company of Flemington, New Jersey, made pottery jugs and housewares from the early 1800s. They made Fulper Art Pottery from approximately 1910 to 1930.

Their first line of art pottery was called Vasekraft. The shapes were primarily either rigid and controlled, being influenced by the arts and crafts movement, or of Chinese influence. Equal concern was given to the glazes which showed an incredible diversity.

Pieces made between 1910 and 1920 were of the best quality, because less emphasis was put on production output. Almost all pieces are molded.

Reference: Robert Blassberg, *Fulper Art Pottery: An Aesthetic Appreciation,* Art Lithographers, 1979.

Bookends, figural, books, orig Vasecraft
  label **225.00**
Bowl
  3 x 6", boat shape, green matte ... **40.00**
  4 x 6", leopard skin glaze, two handles, underglaze mark **115.00**
  11", dark blue drip, rose ground ... **95.00**
Candlesticks, 11", yellow and brown
  shading to blue flambe, pr **275.00**
Decanter
  9", musical, gun metal shading to
    green, beige ground, orig stopper **45.00**
  9¾", green glossy glaze, silver highlights, orig stopper **120.00**
Flower Frog, nude, white, gray, and yellow **75.00**
Jar, 8 x 9", pedestal, blue to green ... **400.00**

Vase, 4¾″ h, 4¾″ d, dark olive matte glaze, stamped mark, $125.00.

Jug and Bowl, mottled brown, handthrown, horizontal ribs, vertical ink stamp	180.00
Pitcher, 7 x 4¾″, crystalized blue glaze over mustard, marked "830M"	100.00
Planter, V shape, oval top, crystalized blue glaze over mustard	45.00
Tobacco Jar, cov, 6½″, mirror black	235.00
Vase	
7″, raspberry, three handles, 125th Anniversary sticker	100.00
7½″, round body, pink and red, two handles	110.00
7¾″, green, cucumber textured, orig paper label	200.00
8″, rose flambe shaded to green at top, flat shape, handles at base, sgd	200.00
8½ x 7½″, two handles, green matte	350.00
10″, two handles, cucumber green	225.00
10½″, green-brown shading to sky blue flambe, ink stamp mark	250.00
12″, round base, blue crystalline	260.00
Wall Pocket, Pipes of Pan, matte green	185.00

FURNITURE

History: Two major currents dominate the American furniture marketplace–furniture made in Great Britain and furniture made in the United States. American buyers continue to show a strong prejudice for objects manufactured in the United States. They will pay a premium for such pieces and accept them above technically superior and more aesthetic English examples.

Until the last half of the 19th century formal American styles were dictated by English examples and design books. Regional furniture, such as the Hudson River Valley [Dutch] and the Pennsylvania German styles, did develop. A less formal furniture, often designated as the "country" or vernacular style, developed throughout the 19th and early 20th centuries. These country pieces deviated from the accepted formal styles and have a genre charm that many collectors find irresistible.

America did contribute a number of unique decorative elements to English styles. The American Federal period is a reaction to the English Hepplewhite period. American designers created furniture which influenced, rather than reacted, to world taste in the Gothic Revival style, Arts and Craft Furniture, Art Deco, and Modern International movement.

FURNITURE STYLES [APPROX. DATES]

William and Mary	1690–1730
Queen Anne	1720–1760
Chippendale	1755–1790
Federal [Hepplewhite]	1790–1815
Sheraton	1790–1810
Empire [Classical]	1805–1830
Victorian	
French Restauration	1830–1850
Gothic Revival	1840–1860
Rococo Revival	1845–1870
Elizabethan	1850–1915
Louis XIV	1850–1914
Naturalistic	1850–1914
Renaissance Revival	1850–1880
Neo-Greek	1855–1885
Eastlake	1870–1890
Art Furniture	1880–1914
Arts and Crafts	1895–1915
Art Nouveau	1896–1914
Art Deco	1920–1945
International Movement	**1940–Present**

In the 1986–87 auction season, a Philadelphia Chippendale wing chair sold for over two and one-half million dollars. Many other pieces broke the half million dollar barrier.

Country pieces, with the exception of Windsor chairs, seem to have stabilized and even dropped off slightly in value. The country-designer-look no longer enjoys the popularity it did during the American Bicentennial period.

Furniture is one of the few antiques fields where regional preferences are a factor in pricing. Victorian furniture is popular in New Orleans, and unpopular in New England. Oak is in demand in the Northwest, not so much in the Middle Atlantic states.

Prices vary considerably on furniture. Shop around. Furniture is plentiful unless you are after a truly rare example. Examine all pieces thoroughly. Too many furniture pieces are bought on impulse. Turn furniture upside down; take it apart. The amount of repairs and restoration to a piece has a strong influence on price. Make certain you know about all repairs and changes before buying.

Beware of the large number of reproductions. During the twenty-five years following the American Centennial of 1876, there was a great revival in copying furniture styles and manufacturing techniques of earlier eras. These centennial pieces now are over one hundred years old. They confuse many dealers and collectors.

The prices listed below are "average" prices. They are only a guide. High and low prices are given to show market range.

References: Joseph T. Butler, *Field Guide To American Furniture*, Facts on File Publications, 1985; Rachael Field, *Macdonald Guide To Buying Antique Furniture*, Macdonald & Co Publishers, Ltd, London, England, 1986; Phillipe Garner, *Twentieth-Century Furniture*, Van Nostrand Reinhold, 1980; William C. Ketchum, Jr., *Furniture, Volume 2: Chests, Cupboards, Desks, & Other Pieces*, Alfred A. Knopf Collectors' Guides To American Antiques, 1982; Milo M. Naeve, *Identifying American Furniture: A Pictorial Guide To Styles and Terms, Colonial to Contemporary*, American Association for State and Local History, 1981; Wallace Nutting, *Furniture Treasury*, Macmillan, 3 vols [1928 and 1933], available in reprint; Don & Carol Raycraft, *Collector's Guide To Country Furniture*, Collector Books, 1984; Marvin D. Schwartz, *Furniture: Volume 1: Chairs, Tables, Sofas & Beds*, Alfred A. Knopf Collector's Guides To American Antiques, 1982; Robert W. and Harriett Swedberg, *American Oak Furniture, Style and Prices*, Wallace-Homestead, Book II (1984); —, *Country Furniture and Accessories with Prices*, Wallace-Homestead, Book I (1983), Book II (1984); —, *Country Pine Furniture*, Wallace-Homestead, 1983; —, *Furniture of the Depression Era*, Collector Books, 1987; —, *Victorian Furniture*, Wallace-Homestead, Book I (1976), Book II (1983), Book III (1985); —, *Wicker Furniture*, Wallace-Homestead, 1983; Lyndon C. Viel, *Antique Ethnic Furniture*, Wallace-Homestead, 1983; Dina von Zweck, *The Woman's Day Dictionary Of Furniture*, Citadel Press, 1983.

There are hundreds of specialized books on individual furniture forms and styles. Two examples of note are: Monroe H. Fabian, *The Pennsylvania-German Decorated Chest*, Universe Books, 1978, and Charles Santore, *The Windsor Style In America, 1730–1830*, Vol. 1, 1981, Vol. 2, 1987, Running Press.

Additional Listings: Arts and Craft Movement, Art Deco, Art Nouveau, Children's Nursery Items, Orientalia, Shaker Items, and Stickley.

BEDS

Amish, child's, decorated, pine, orig brown flame graining, light colored ground, sq tapered legs, inset rockers (cut flat), mortised sides, removable round tapering posts, replaced tester frame, 24 x 54 x 55" **600.00**

Bed, Sheraton, mahogany, tester, turned and fluted posts, $6,500.00.

Colonial Revival, Regency style, inlaid rosewood, upholstered head and footboard, shaped framework, brass inlay and mounts, double, 56" h . . . **600.00**
Country, high poster, curly maple, turned posts, chamfered and rope carved detail, paneled pine and poplar headboard with scrolled detail, poplar footboard, orig rails, rope pins missing, 56 x 75 x 86", refinished . . **1,600.00**
Day, country
  Curly maple, turned posts and rails, refinished, minor insect damage, white cotton duck cov and matching cushion, 77" l **1,600.00**
  Maple, Texas, mid 19th C, slat back, molded crest ends, nine slats, painted red, 77" l **1,750.00**
  Pine, molded legs and trim, old red paint with white striping, replaced mattress slats, 27½ x 74½ x 20½" **200.00**
Eastlake, American, c1870, walnut, burl veneer, spoon carving, incised lines, applied roundels, 58 x 63" **1,000.00**
Empire
  American, c1825, tester, mahogany, reeded and acanthus carved posts, 92½" **2,250.00**
  NY, c1820–25, carved maple, baluster and ring turned headposts, carved acanthus, leaves, and swag drapery, double paneled headboard surmounted by carved bowl of fruit, bow shaped scrolled footboard, carved paw feet, 55 x 77" . **2,000.00**
Federal
  American, four poster, maple, shaped ring turned round columns and feet, as found condition, repairs, 54½ x 59½" **500.00**

Massachusetts, c1800, four poster, tester, curly maple, baluster and urn configuration, ring turned headposts and baluster molded and shaped headboard, acorn footposts, gilt metal caps, tapered legs, vase form feet, 512¼ x 78 x 56" . **8,500.00**

New England, c1795–1815, high poster, figured maple, double ring turned posts, tapering column with ebonized bands and bosses, double paneled headboard, ebonized pediment crest, ring turned tapered legs, 59 x 81½ x 94½" **6,000.00**

Georgian, English, c1770–80, four poster, flat tester, mahogany, claw and ball feet, 82" **1,500.00**

Hired Man's, folding, maple, pine headboard, pinned sides to facilitate folding, orig first coat of red paint, 70⅛ x 45¾ x 27⅜" **700.00**

International Movement, American, c1950, mahogany, cane inserts, double, 57" w **100.00**

Jacobean, canopy, carved walnut, deep cove molded cornice, paneled canopy, architectural dec paneled headboard, reeded column supports, bun feet, 60" w, 108" h **2,400.00**

Sheraton

American, birch, plain turned headposts, fluted footposts, 65" **1,200.00**

Country, early 19th C, maple, poster, pine headboard, 57⅕" h headposts, 31" h footposts, pr **1,400.00**

Massachusetts, 1800–10, William Hook, Salem, four poster, mahogany, sq tapered headposts, shaped headboard, carved and fluted footposts, gilt metal caps, 89" **6,500.00**

Suite, American, c1880, maple and bird's eye maple, faux bamboo, bed and bureau, bureau with mirrored superstructure swiveling within bamboo turned frame, spindle gallery, lower section with three long drawers, 75½ x 60 x 62" bed, 48 x 77" bureau . . . **2,500.00**

Victorian

American, c1850, walnut, veneer panels, roundels, applied dec, headboard surmounted by carved head of Columbia, urn finials, 60 x 81 x 92" **2,500.00**

American, late 19th C, brass, straight upright posts with ball finials, cylindrical posts, ball finials, cylindrical support rails for side curtains, vertical and horizontal bars joined with ball details, 87" w **2,000.00**

Louis XVI style, late 19th C, walnut, headboard with arched and molded back, carved giltwood crest, inlaid

brass molding and dec, center quartered panel, turned tapered legs, conforming footboard, label "Schmit, Paris," 48" **350.00**

Bench, 36 x 11½ x 18", single board top, $85.00.

BENCHES

Bin, country, pine, wide single board construction, lid seat, two part bin int., cut out feet, scrolled ends, old dark finish, 62 x 19 x 32" **400.00**

Bucket, pine, single board ends, two shelves, 45¾ x 13 x 42¼" **600.00**

Cobbler, country, pine, top divided shelf, drawers, old nut brown patina, work, old repairs, 44" l **450.00**

Fireside, pine, high back, scalloped top and base, 18 x 59" **750.00**

Garden, country, pine, sq legs, "H" stretcher, chamfered arm supports, slat back, 65¼ x 41" **400.00**

Harness Maker, wooden vise clamp, chamfered legs, wrought iron braces, old red paint, underslung drawer, 63" **200.00**

Kitchen, pine, splayed chamfered legs, holes to attaching sausage stuffer, 6½ x 48 x 22" **175.00**

Mammy, American, shaped crest, half spindle back, repainted, stenciled, 44" **800.00**

Settle, English, 18th C, deal pine, curved paneled back, meat compartment now fitted with shelves, natural finish, 65½ x 26 x 76½" **1,200.00**

Wash, American, late 19th C, pine, 11¾ x 51¾ x 12" **175.00**

Water

American, early 19th C, pine, two shelves, back stretchers, shaped ends, 48" l **400.00**

Country, poplar, one board bootjack ends, two shelves, sq nail construction, 36¼ x 17⅜ x 33½" **350.00**

Window, Regency style, stained wood, carved sides, needlepoint upholstered seat, circular turned legs, 52 x 16 x 30″ **175.00**

BENTWOOD

In 1856, Michael Thonet of Vienna perfected the process of bending wood using steam. Shortly after, Bentwood furniture became popular. Other manufacturers of Bentwood furniture were Jacob and Joseph Kohn; Philip Strobel and Son; Sheboygan Chair Co.; and Tidoute Chair Co. Bentwood furniture is still being produced today by the Thonet firm and others.

Bed, c1900, double, scrolled and carved headboard, conforming footboard, 60″ h **700.00**
Chair
    Arm, Thonet, c1900, scrolled back and arms, cane seat, splayed legs, orig label and stamp **300.00**
    Side, Thonet, c1900, scrolled back, cane seat, orig label **250.00**
Cradle, c1900, oval bentwood basket, shaped cradle, extended ornate scrolled support, 52 x 36″ **750.00**
Easel, artist's **80.00**
Hat and Coat Stand, c1900, 68″ h **125.00**
Rocker, sleigh type, sgd Thonet **850.00**
Screen, Thonet, c1904, three folds, inset with green glass above laminated panels cut with geometric devices, "Spanish Wand" model **3,000.00**
Settee, Kohn, three part scrolled back and arms, cane back and seat, splayed legs, 47″ l **675.00**
Shaving Stand and Mirror, designed by J Hoffman, made by Thonet, c1906, 54″ h **2,250.00**
Table
    Center, Austria, c1900, white marble top, shaped oblong top, narrow frieze on elaborate bentwood cruciform base with interlocking and overlapping scrolls centering on turned standard, 45½ x 28½″ . . . **200.00**
    Writing, Kohn, c1900, rect top, scrolled supports and stretchers, imp mark "J J Kohn," 37 x 21 x 30″ **300.00**

BLANKET CHESTS

Chippendale, New England, c1780, country, maple, molded lift top, case with two simulated and two real thumb molded drawers, bracket feet, old oval brass pulls, refinished, 40½ x 18 x 41½″ **475.00**
Decorated
    Pine, attributed to Daniel Otto, (Flat

Tulip artist), Centre County, PA, 1803, rect hinged top, well with till, front of case painted with two tombstone tablets enclosing vases of tulips and hex signs, center tombstone panel with vase of tulips, pair of rampant lions above inscription AKU 1803, polychrome, brown grained ground, slightly reduced bracket feet, 50½ x 23½ x 23½″ . **30,000.00**
    Pine, attributed to Pennsylvania, Rank or Selzer, orig dark blue paint, two painted arched panels with pots of stylized flowers in red, blue, green, black, and brown on white ground, two white and brown stars on lid, detailed case, till and bracket feet, wrought iron strap hinges and bear trap lock with escutcheon and key, professional molding replacement, 50 x 21¾ x 21″ **2,800.00**
    Pine, orig green paint, red striping, simple red floral dec, sq corner posts, turned feet, two dovetailed drawers, paneled sides and ends, till lid missing, 44¾ x 20 x 33½″ . **850.00**
    Poplar, orig yellow paint, black smoke graining, sq corner posts, turned feet, one board side, ends, and lid, till lid damaged, 43 x 19½ x 23½″ **1,000.00**
    Poplar, OH, paneled, three dovetailed drawers, short turned feet, red graining, blue panels, pots of stylized red, white, and yellow tulips, 48 x 21¼ x 26½″ **1,500.00**
Walnut
    Ohio, dovetailed case, two dovetailed drawers, beaded edges, orig brasses, int. till with secret compartment and dovetailed drawer, orig lock and wrought iron strap hinge, feet and till lid replaced, old refinishing, 46¼ x 19 x 26¼″ **1,000.00**
    Pennsylvania, c1800, two drawers, inlaid line dec, ogee bracket feet, 50½ x 23¼ x 30¾″ **1,750.00**

BOOK CASES

Art Deco, American, early 1900s, polished aluminum, tin plate, pair of leaded glass doors, bird's eye maple back panels, 58 x 17 x 65″ **7,000.00**
Arts and Crafts, Stickley Bros, c1910, oak, rect top, two glazed doors, int. with three adjustable shelves, sq legs, imp mark, 35 x 13 x 56″ **500.00**
Empire, three sections, each with pair doors with Winthrop style glass division, rope twisted columns, paw feet, reeding at top molding **2,750.00**
George III, early 19th C, inlaid mahog-

any, broken pediment centered by lobed urn form finial, pair of glazed doors, shelves, lower section with fitted secretary drawer over three long drawers, inlaid with scrolling foliage, bracket feet, 37¼ x 98¼" **2,750.00**

Georgian, mahogany, breakfront, molded dentil frieze above four glazed doors, lower section with secretary drawer over three long graduated drawers, flanked by two drawers and two cupboards, 72 x 17½ x 81" **750.00**

Queen Anne, walnut and burl walnut veneer, double arch molded cornice dome top, later finials, arched side cornices, pair of glazed doors, three shelves, two candle slides, lower section in two parts, cross banded fall front with fitted interior, base with three long graduated drawers, later bun feet, restorations, 40 x 85" **14,500.00**

Victorian, Boston, mid 19th C, walnut, carved crest, molded cornice over two arched glazed doors, applied burl dec, carved pilasters, two molded drawers, stamped "Blake and Alden, Boston, MA," 54 x 20 x 91" **1,500.00**

BOXES

Ballot
Maple, dovetailed, sliding top, 6 x 8 x 12" **175.00**
Pine, dovetailed, carved wooden handles, c1850, 7 x 7½ x 18¼" **100.00**
Walnut, wide dovetails, brass hardware, 8½ x 11 x 16" **165.00**
Band
New England, printed paper, rural country scene, 10½ x 15" **375.00**
Pennsylvania, white floral pattern on rainbow ground, black beaver hat by C Hickerson, 8" h **150.00**
Bible
American, Colonial, early 18th C, oak, incised compass type dec on front and sides, plain lid **275.00**
Jacobean, carved oak, hinged rect top, plain int., front later carved with scrolled serpent panels, stand with sq legs, 23½ x 21½" **600.00**
Blanket Box, American, early 19th C, painted and decorated imitation rosewood, hinged top, red and black painted graining, 43 x 19½ x 23" . . . **200.00**
Bonnet Box, PA, late 18th C, bentwood, fitted lid, dower chest type dec, green ground, large central stellate device in red, yellow, black, and white, two large sprouting dark green feathered leaf forms, foliage and vines on lid, 21" oval, 11¾" h **5,775.00**

Bride's, oval
Bentwood, fitted lid, painted Biblical scene, sides painted with large red and white tulip buds, black ground, Continental, 18th C **850.00**
Decorated, pine, laced seams, orig red paint, polychrome floral dec on sides, lid scene of two couples, trees and verse, branded mark, 18" l **2,000.00**
Sponged dec, c1840, 27" **375.00**
Candle
Decorated, sliding lid, pine, old red paint, faded floral dec **250.00**
Poplar, sliding lid, sq nail construction, old brown patina, 13¼" l . . . **75.00**
Walnut, sliding lid, dovetailed, 11 x 11 x 3½" **80.00**
Cigar, mahogany, stripe inlay on lid and base, zinc lined, nickel plated hardware, 4 x 7½ x 12" **125.00**
Decorated
Pine, orig red graining, black edge stripe, lined with 1841 New Hampshire newspaper, 12" l **250.00**
Pine, orig salmon paint, black, yellow, red, and green border designs, central flower on each side and top, 13½" l **125.00**
Deed, dome top, tole
Orig brown japanning, stenciled floral dec, 10" l **200.00**
Orig pumpkin colored paint, black striping, band of black and gold stenciled pineapples, minor wear, 9¼" l **200.00**
Desk, table top, poplar, dovetailed case, nailed drawer, lift top lid, dovetailed gallery, int. fitted with pigeonholes, old red paint, repairs, 26 x 26 x 15¾" . . **100.00**
Document
American, flame mahogany veneer, poplar secondary wood, bevel edge lid, divided two part int., orig brass bail handle, 13½" l **200.00**
Pennsylvania, rect, hinged top, multicolored floral and sprig design, 8½ x 3½" **500.00**
Hat
Cardboard, c1880, floral paper cov, 9½ x 12" **65.00**
Pine, domed top, strap handle, 16" sq **185.00**
Knife
Ash or chestnut, scrolled sides, high curved divided, cutout heart shaped handle, 10 x 10½ x 6½" . **165.00**
Inlaid Mahogany, George III, late 18th C, serpentine front, sloping hinged top, central shell in oval reserve, int. lid with six pointed star, fitted int., pr, 9 x 14⅜" **3,000.00**
Mahogany, dovetailed, scalloped di-

vider handle, worn finish, 10¾ x 15¾" **185.00**

Pantry, American
Decorated, mid 19th C, blue and green painted dec, compass star on cov in yellow, black, and putty, 9¼" d **240.00**
Splint Wood, orig dark stain, 14½ x 7" **85.00**

Pipe, cherry, well scalloped top edge with heart cutout in front, circular crest for hanging, dovetailed overlapping drawer, dovetailed base, applied edge molding, refinished, 8 x 22¼" . **4,100.00**

Salt, hanging, oak, dovetailed, cutout opening, 6½ x 7½ x 15" **115.00**

Scouring, hanging, country, walnut and pine, cutout star on front panel, old natural patina, 7¾ x 17" **500.00**

Spice
Grained, American, 19th C, round, locking top, 9¾" **185.00**
Oak, four drawers, brass pulls **125.00**
Pine
Eight drawers, orig green paint .. **225.00**
Nine drawers, wall type, old repaint **150.00**

Trinket, New England, rect, coffered lid
Decorated, red and yellow splotches, dark ground, fitted int., 6¾" h **365.00**
Smoke grained, basket of floral motif on lid, brass feet, 4½" h **600.00**

Cabinet, spool or yarn, oak, 18¾ x 17⅛ x 16", $650.00.

CABINETS

China
Colonial Revival
Chippendale Style, c1940, walnut veneer, breakfront, scrolled broken pediment, center urn finial, pair of glazed doors and panels,

long drawer over two cupboard doors, 44 x 15 x 76" **500.00**
Hepplewhite Style, c1930, mahogany veneer sides, matching veneer drawer fronts, narrow banding, pair glazed doors over three long drawers, brasses, fluted legs, 35 x 17 x 71" **250.00**
Victorian Style, mahogany, rect top, veneer band at top and backboard, carved columns, adjustable shelves, hairy paw feet, 48¾ x 17 x 65¼" **275.00**
Hepplewhite, inlaid mahogany, leaded glass and velvet lined int., 63 x 21 x 75½" **625.00**
Victorian
Oak
Bow Front, leaded glass, amber glass diamonds in top panels, 37½ x 14½ x 61¾" **400.00**
Serpentine Front, carved details, glass front and sides, 38½ x 16 x 62" **550.00**
Swell Front, leaded glass, paw feet, 40½ x 16½ x 59" **675.00**
Tiger Maple, American, late 19th C, select curly and tiger maple, egg and dart molded projecting cornice, two sections, upper with pair of glazed doors, three adjustable shelves, lower with cupboard, three drawers, 49½ x 22¾ x 74" **2,400.00**

Curio, Louis XV, bombe style, serpentine front, typical dec, 32 x 16 x 75" . **1,750.00**

Dye, Diamond Dye Co, oak, litho scene of children playing, 29¾" **300.00**

Hardware, hexagonal, rotating base, eight drawers, two open shelves per side, porcelain pulls **650.00**

Kitchen, Hoosier, oak, glass doors, porcelain work surface, flour bin, etc. .. **450.00**

Liquor, bronze, filigree with knights and other ornamentation, marble top, c1920 .... **950.00**

Medicine, hanging
Oak, corner type, mirrored door, shaped crest, reeded sides, one shelf, refinished **125.00**
Painted pine, glazed door, shaped crest, three shelves, 5½ x 16 x 24½" **180.00**

Side
Art, American, NY, c1875, breakfront outline, stepped rect top, raised central section incised and inlaid with stylized flowerheads, palmettos, fluting and Greek key scrolls, foliate and swag inlaid frieze, central cupboard door below incised and ebonized with central floral sprig medallion flanked by glazed

doors, shelved int., molded plinth
base, 72 x 43½″ **900.00**
George II, third quarter 18th C, mahogany, rect top, two recessed and
graduated shelves, brass column
and lattice form supports, full frieze
drawer, pair of cupboard doors with
oval woven brass grills insets,
straight tapered legs, brass cast-
ered toe caps, 27 x 13 x 52″ **2,800.00**
Smoking, Mission Oak, Charles Rholf,
c1900, plain lines, 30″ h **950.00**
Vitrine, Louis XV, bowed, rouge royal
marble top, tulipwood, 32 x 60½″ . . **3,650.00**
Watchmaker's, single board construc-
tion, ten drawers, six with 42 scooped
out pockets, four undivided, 17 x 31
x 18¾″ **450.00**

CANDLE SHIELDS

Country, cherry. snake feet, turned column, replaced maple scrolled top, refinished, minor repairs, 15 x 15½ x
26½″ **200.00**
George III, mahogany, circular needle-
point panel, pole, tripod base, pr . . . **1,350.00**
Hepplewhite, mahogany, embroidered
floral motif, 53″ **500.00**

**Candlestand, American, mahogany, 18″
d top, 27½″ h, pad feet, $900.00.**

CANDLESTANDS

Classical, attributed to Charles Honore
Lannuier, NY, c1815, cross banded
mahogany, oblong top, cross banded
edge, tilts, vase and drum form standard, down turned acanthus carved
legs, foliate cast brass casters, 23¾
x 18½ x 29½″ **2,750.00**

Federal
American, Cherry, c1820, rect top,
canted corners, spiral carved baluster standard, three arched legs,
18½ x 29½ **625.00**
Massachusetts, 1800–15, inlaid ma-
hogany, elongated octagonal tilt
top, inlaid diamond and banding,
ring turned baluster support, stringing, three arched sq tapering legs,
23 x 30¾″ **2,500.00**
Pennsylvania, Walnut, oval top,
shaped and ring turned round standard, cabriole legs, 16½ x 26 x
28¾″ **250.00**
George III, mahogany, polychrome
grapevine dec, pale blue painted
ground, spiral fluted pedestal, sq tri-
pod legs, 15¾″ w, pr **3,600.00**
Hepplewhite
American, country, cherry, inlay on
top, dovetailed drawer, slender
snake feet with chip carving at base
of turned column, refinished, small
patches in base, 16¼ x 16¾ x 26¾″ **2,600.00**
Eastern Massachusetts, late 18th C,
mahogany, rosewood banded top . **650.00**
Queen Anne, American
Cherry, circular top, snake feet **500.00**
Cherry, sq top, chamfered corners,
snake feet **600.00**
Mahogany, dish top, delicate base,
toe carved snake feet **350.00**
Walnut, circular top, vasiform stem,
snake feet, 27¾″ **450.00**

CHAIRS

Arrowback
Side, decorated, plank seat, orig
brown paint, white and yellow striping, polychrome stenciled crests
with bird, fruit, and foliage, set of 6 **600.00**
Writing Arm, dark green paint, green
and yellow dec **850.00**
Art, American, c1880, parcel gilt and incised walnut, arm, arched crest rail
carved with stylized flowerheads and
floral sprigs, gilt incised frieze dec
with rosettes, inlaid stiles leading to
padded armrests over spindled galleries, flared seat, turned cylindrical
legs, black leather upholstery **600.00**
Art Deco
Arm, tiger's eye maple, brown leather
inserts, red lacquered fretwork . . . **500.00**
Side, walnut, black stain, shaped
back, scrolled side rails, uphol-
stered seat, Viennese **350.00**
Art Nouveau, arm, intricate undercut
carved foliage on arms, legs, and

crest, olive-green crushed velvet upholstery **200.00**

Arts and Crafts, fumed oak, slim, tall lines, cutout design in back panel, shaped wooden seat, 16 x 38" **125.00**

Belter, side, rosewood, pierced, carved grapes and roses, upholstered needlepoint seat and back **3,500.00**

Biedermeier Style, c1850, arm, fruitwood, lyre splat, shaped seat **275.00**

Children's

Arrowback, plank seat **175.00**

Captain's, plank seat, hickory, orig finish **225.00**

High Chair, maple and pine, solid shaped back rail, 8 spindles, c1875 **200.00**

Ladderback, oak, red paint, rush seat **225.00**

Windsor, bow back, 19th C, 5 spindles, black paint, 22¼" **300.00**

Chippendale

Arm, mahogany

Pierced splat, knuckle arms, Philadelphia, c1770 .... **1,750.00**

Wing back, upholstered, yellow floral silk fabric, cabriole legs, claw and ball foot **600.00**

Corner, CT, c1770, cherrywood, shaped crest, carved stylized fan, shaped handholds, pierced vase form splats, turned colonettes, molded seat rail enclosing slip seat, shaped skirt, C scroll carved frontal cabriole leg, claw and ball foot, two paper labels on underside of seat **20,350.00**

Lolling, Martha Washington, mahogany, open tapered and molded arms, sq molded legs, "H" stretcher, reupholstered in rose and ecru damask, refinished **4,250.00**

Side

American, ribbon back, cherry, pierced slats, molded edge seat frame, rushed slip seat, sq legs, molded corners, inside chamfer, orig finish **500.00**

Country, cherry, carved crest and ears, pierced splat, upholstered seat, sq legs, molded corners, "H" stretcher, old refinishing ... **750.00**

Philadelphia, c1765, carved walnut, shaped crest, center carved shell, volute and acanthus carved pierced vase form splat, slip seat, cabriole legs with shell and acanthus carved motifs, claw and ball feet **8,525.00**

Colonial Revival

Country, Indiana, c1900, dining, spindle back, woven seat, thick legs, marked "Old Hickory, Indiana," set of 8 .... **850.00**

Queen Anne style, OH, c1920, walnut

veneer, vase splat, drop in upholstered seat, modified cabriole legs **75.00**

Decorated, country, captain's, worn orig red and black paint, yellow striping . **200.00**

Eastlake, Victorian

Arm, NY, c1876, George Hunzinger, arched crest with spindles, inlay cloth cov woven metal back and seat, marked "Hunzinger NY Pat March 20, 1869, Pat April 18, 1876," 18 x 17½ x 38" **1,200.00**

Side, walnut, small arms, cane seat **225.00**

Empire

Arm chair, barrel back, green watersilk upholstery **675.00**

Side, mahogany and mahogany veneer, fiddleback, serpentine seat, saber leg **185.00**

Federal

Arm, mahogany, cane seat, open back **150.00**

Lolling, MA, c1790, carved mahogany, upholstered back, serpentine crest above shaped arms, molded terminals, down curved supports, flared seat, molded tapering sq legs joined by stretchers, minor repairs **2,000.00**

Side, Haines-Connelly School, Philadelphia, c1810, carved mahogany, sq back, molded crest rail, three reeded and leaf carved uprights, ring turned and reeded stiles, leaf carved seat support, reeded front legs, ring turned and out flaring rear legs, paper label on seat rail inscribed "Charles H Satterthwaite" **2,250.00**

George II, mid 18th C, arm, mahogany, pierced baluster form splat, shaped crest, upswept ears, scrolling arms, drop-in seat, molded frame, angled cabriole legs, ball and claw feet ... **5,000.00**

George III

Arm, tan leather upholstery, tufted seat and back, sq tapering legs ... **1,250.00**

Child's, mahogany, serpentine crest rail, pierced interlaced vertical splat, scrolled arms, flared drop-in seat, molded sq legs joined by stretchers **400.00**

Hall, c1800, inlaid mahogany, shield back, inlaid brass and ebony diamond above shaped seat, turned tapered legs, pr **750.00**

Library, late 18th C, carved mahogany, rect upholstered back, padded arms, down-swept supports carved with flowerheads and foliage, rect seat, sq legs joined by stretchers . **3,150.00**

Side, early 19th C, carved mahogany Central urn form splat carved with beaded pendant, flanked by col-

umnar splats with foliage, flared
seat, sq legs joined by stretchers,
pr **825.00**
Serpentine crest rail carved with
swags, pierced interlaced splat,
rect needlepoint upholstered
drop-in seat, molded sq legs,
stretchers, set of 6 .... **3,300.00**
Gothic Revival, Victorian, side, walnut,
c1850, arched and pierced crest, upholstered back and set, turned legs . **200.00**
Hepplewhite
American, side, cherry, curved crest,
pierced splat with urn detail, slip
seat, sq tapering legs, "H"
stretcher, refinished, pr **1,150.00**
CT, c1780, side, mahogany, pierced
vase splat, urn finial, upholstered
seat, straight tapering legs, replaced rear corner braces **650.00**
Hitchcock, American, 2nd quarter 19th
C, bar back, rush seat, turned legs
and stretchers, black painted ground,
stenciled fruit dec, three side chairs,
matching arm chair **500.00**
International Movement, Heywood-
Wakefield, MA, Lloyd Manufacturing,
tubular metal, backrest and seat upholstered in brown vinyl, c1935 .... **125.00**
Ladderback
American, cherry, rush seat, c1880 . **375.00**
Delaware Valley, c1740–70, 6 arched
graduated slats, rush seat, turned
legs, frontal ring and baluster
stretcher, painted black **2,250.00**
New England, early 18th C, arm
Maple, child's splint seat, mushroom arms **400.00**
Painted, 5 splat back, sausage
turned back posts, replaced rush
seat **1,000.00**
Shaker, Delaware Valley, hard-
wood, splint seat, sgd 1840 ... **1,500.00**
Mission
Arm, Gustav Stickley, c1910, oak, V
back **450.00**
Side, Charles Rohlf, 1900, octagonal
style, butterfly pierced single back
splat, shaped skirt, 37½" **1,500.00**
Wing, L & G Stickley, c1910, oak,
clamp decal mark **900.00**
Morris, oak
Gustav Stickley, c1905, red decal
mark **1,900.00**
Limbert, c1910, pierced wide stretch-
ers, orig paper label **575.00**
Queen Anne
Arm, northern New England, early
18th C, deep frontal skirt, scroll
arms, Spanish feet, worn rush seat **3,250.00**
Side, Boston, MA, c1740, turned ma-
ple, urn form finials above orig

leather upholstered back and seat,
vase and block turned legs, frontal
turned stretcher **12,650.00**
Side, New England
c1720–30, maple, spoon back,
rush seat, oak side stretchers,
Spanish feet, dark walnut finish **900.00**
19th C, burl walnut, inlaid vase
form slat back, needlepoint slip
seat, cabriole legs, pad feet ... **275.00**
c1840–50, cherry, vase form slat
back, needlepoint upholstered
seat, cabriole legs, pad feet, old
repair to crest, refinished **1,400.00**
Side, Philadelphia, c1750, walnut,
shaped crest, vase form splat, slip
seat, lambrequin carved cabriole
legs, shaped stretchers, stockinged
pad feet, repair to left foot and crest **5,500.00**
Side, Rhode Island, c1760, walnut,
shaped crest, vase form splat, slip
balloon seat, cabriole legs, stretchers, pad feet, pr **9,500.00**
Renaissance, Victorian, c1870
Arm, lady's, walnut, upholstered, refinished **500.00**
Side, walnut, maple inlay, upholstered
seat and back **350.00**
Regency, c1815
Arm, inlaid mahogany, curved rect top
rail inlaid with arrow medallion,
scrolled arms, flared drop-in seat,
saber legs, pr **2,250.00**
Desk, fruitwood, swivel, brown
leather, splayed legs, brass casters **375.00**
Rococo, Victorian
Arm, gentleman's, finger molded and
pierced, reupholstered, c1860 ... **700.00**
Side, walnut, balloon back, upholstered seat **200.00**
Sheraton
Arm, balloon seat, scrolled arms,
elaborate back slat, outward curving feet, old rush seat, old refinishing **300.00**
Side, curly maple, scrolled slat, replaced rush seat, detailed turnings,
refinished **625.00**
Victorian
Arm
Bobbin turned frame, c1840, loung-
ing type, reupholstered **600.00**
Upholstered, tufted back, mahogany open arms, scroll feet,
shaped stretcher **150.00**
Corner, carved walnut, lion mask
head carved crest rail, hawk carved
twin back splat, needlework seat,
shaped legs **325.00**
Side, balloon back, shell carved crest
rail, ivory floral fabric cov seat, serpentine legs, set of 6 .... **1,225.00**

William and Mary

English, 17th C, arm, scroll crest, caned and crown carved back flanked by rope twist stiles, 45″, minor restoration **350.00**

English, early 18th C, arm, walnut, pierced leaf crest, molded caned back, acanthus carved rolled arms, block and ring turned legs, 51″ . . **1,150.00**

Chair, arm, Windsor, bow back, maple, New England, c1800, $2,000.00.

Windsor

Bow back, New England, 18th C
Arm, old dark reddish brown alligatored finish, orig bluish gray paint on underside of seat, splayed base, bulbous turned legs and stretchers, oval saddle seat, turned arm supports, knuckle arms, 19″ h seat **6,700.00**

Arm, unrestored, orig condition, several worn coats of paint . . . **4,000.00**

Side, American, hardwoods, sgd "Wallace Nutting" **600.00**

Side, NE or NY, comb, hardwoods, pine seat, bamboo legs **1,300.00**

Brace back, arm, shaped seat, turned arm supports, shaped arms, splayed base with bulbous turn-

ings, "H" stretcher, minor repairs, old refinishing, 18″ h seat **600.00**

Cage back, Pennsylvania, early 19th C, side, pine seats, matched, refinished, set of 6 . . . . **4,000.00**

Comb back, arm, wide saddle seat, turned arm supports, shaped arms, curved crest, scroll carved ears, splayed base, bulbous turnings, "H" stretcher, dark green repair, 17¾″ h seat **3,200.00**

Dove Cote, side, 7 spindles, bamboo turnings, saddle seat **525.00**

Sack back, American, early 19th C, arm, arched crest rail, spindle splats leading to shaped armrests, shaped seat, baluster turned legs joined by stretchers **1,500.00**

Rod back, American, c1830–40, side, green paint and black stencil dec, matched set of 6, as found condition **1,200.00**

Thumb back, side, orig yellow paint, stencil dec, set of 8 . . . . **1,600.00**

Writing, arm, Ebenezer Tracy, CT, comb back, candle slide with lock, small arm drawer, refinished, traces of orig paint **12,000.00**

CHESTS OF DRAWERS

Chippendale

American, c1760, pine and maple, oblong top, molded projecting cornice, six graduated drawers, bracket feet, refinished, orig brasses, 37¼ x 19 x 53¾″ **4,200.00**

Massachusetts, c1775, mahogany, oxbow front, oblong top, thumb molded edge, four graduated long drawers, cockbeaded surrounds, bracket feet, minor repairs to base moldings, 40¼ x 20½ x 30¾″ . . . **8,800.00**

Pennsylvania, c1770
Mahogany, rect top, thumb molded edge, four graduated cockbeaded drawers, flanking fluted quarter columns, ogee bracket feet, replaced feet, 39½ x 22 x 35¼″ **2,650.00**

Walnut, rect top, molded edge, three short drawers over two larger drawers, four graduated long drawers, later claw and ball feet, 41¼ x 59½″ **2,000.00**

Pennsylvania, c1780, cherry, molded projecting cornice, seven long graduated molded drawers, upper faced to simulate two drawers, fluted quarter columns, ogee bracket feet, orig brasses, minor re-

Chest of Drawers, Chippendale, cherry, 37 x 23 x 71½", replaced brasses, $5,500.00.

pairs to feet and upper molding, 41½ x 23¾ x 67¼" **10,500.00**
Pennsylvania, 1793, carved walnut, molded projecting cornice with applied dentil molding, three short drawers with inlaid date and initials DH, five graduated molded drawers, flanking fluted quarter columns, ogee bracket feet, orig brasses, 44 x 23½ x 55½" **35,000.00**
Pennsylvania, late 18th C, walnut, five small drawers at top, four full width drawers, refinished, professionally replaced base, replacement hardware, 41 x 21 x 59¼" . . **2,000.00**
Colonial Revival, Hepplewhite style, c1920, solid mahogany, inlay on drawers and back rail, two small drawers over two long drawers, eagle brasses, 42 x 19 x 38" **350.00**
Empire, New England, c1820, fine crotch grained mahogany veneer, turned maple front legs, paneled sides, cherry top, cornucopia carved panels, orig lacy glass drawer pulls, 46⅝ x 23 x 46½" **600.00**
Federal
American, early 19th C, mahogany, straight front, four graduated drawers, brass bail handles and escutcheons, pin line inlay, French bracket feet, 39 x 21½ x 37¼" . . . **3,000.00**
Massachusetts, c1800, mahogany, bow front, shaped top, brushing slide, three graduated long drawers, splayed feet, 37½ x 35" **1,800.00**
Portsmouth, NH, c1790, inlaid mahogany, bow front, bowed top with inlaid edge, four cockbeaded long drawers, veneered with three flame birch panels within line inlaid borders, flared feet, rear feet replaced, 40½ x 21½ x 36" **21,000.00**
George III, mahogany, straight front, two small over three wide graduated drawers, brass ring pulls, French bracket feet, 41 x 20 x 40½" **950.00**
Georgian, English, c1850, mahogany, pair of small drawers at top, three graduated drawers, restored, refinished, replaced base and hardware, 33 x 19¾ x 35½" **600.00**
Hepplewhite
American, late 18th or early 19th C, cherry, large blanket drawer at top, veneered molding around top, good finish, age splits in top and one side, minor loss to veneer, 43¾ x 19¼ x 43¼" **650.00**
New England, late 18th C, cherry, swell front, fine band of string inlay around top, wider band at top of base, four graduated beaded drawers, French feet, orig brasses, excellent finished condition, 38 x 23¼ x 38½" **2,700.00**
Mission, Gustav Stickley, oak, two doors over eight drawers, red decal, 62" . . **7,000.00**
Queen Anne
Boston, MA, c1760, block front, mahogany, oblong top, molded edge, four graduated blocked drawers, molded base, shaped pendant, bracket feet, minor restoration to feet, 32½ x 21 x 30" **23,000.00**
English, marquetry inlaid walnut, lift lid, vine dec, cabriole legs, large pad feet, minor veneer loss, 48 x 21½ x 35" **500.00**
Sheraton
American, c1800–10, curly cherry, rounded corners, orig hardware, 40 x 21¼ x 41" **2,100.00**
New England, c1800–10, mahogany, swell front, ovolo corners, fluted columns, four cockbeaded drawers, ring turned cut down feet with casters, turned wooden knobs, orig finish, 41½" l **650.00**
William and Mary
Marquetry, inlaid, animal and vine dec, straight front, two small over three wide drawers, bun feet, 37 x 22½ x 37" **1,500.00**
Oak, two parts, rect top, molded edge, four geometrically paneled long drawers, short block feet, 43 x 39½" **2,000.00**
Walnut, oyster veneer, rect top, molded edge, four long drawers, bun feet, 17th C, 36¾ x 37¾" . . . **7,150.00**

CHESTS, OTHER

See also Blanket Chests and Chests of Drawers

Apothecary, mahogany facade, pine secondary wood, dovetailed case, 46 dovetailed drawers, four paneled doors, old finish, old gilt and black labels, plywood back and base molding, orig built-in, 75¾ x 9¾ x 50¼" **1,650.00**

Campaign Chest, English, early to mid 19th C, mahogany, two small drawers over three full width drawers, ball feet and casters, recessed brass handles, 35¾ x 19½ x 41" **850.00**

Chest on Chest

Chippendale, Massachusetts or New Hampshire, c1780–90, curly maple, bonnet top, mahogany plinths, three small drawers top, four graduated drawers over four graduated base drawers, flame finials, refinished, minor repairs, orig hardware, finials and plinths, 39 x 19 x 87½" **18,000.00**

Federal, PA, cherry upper section with molded cornice, three small drawers, four long graduated drawers, base with three long drawers, shaped skirt, flaring bracket feet, 41¾ x 21½ x 75½" **3,600.00**

Georgian, English, 19th C, mahogany, flat top, dentil molding, upper section with two small drawers over three graduated beaded drawers, lower section with three graduated beaded drawers, bracket feet, 40 x 19 x 69⅜" **2,250.00**

Queen Anne, Philadelphia, c1730, walnut, flat top, two sections, upper with molded cornice above three short and three long graduated drawers, fluted canter corners, projecting mid molding above lower section of three graduated long drawers, bracket feet, orig bright cut brasses, 42¾ x 24¾ x 71½" . **18,700.00**

Chest on Frame

Chippendale, PA, c1770, walnut, three parts, removable cornice with scroll carved tympanum, middle section of five short and four long graduated molded drawers, lower section shaped skirt continuing to cabriole legs, claw and ball feet, orig brasses, 41½ x 22¾ x 73½" . **7,500.00**

Queen Anne, PA or NJ, c1765, cherry, two parts, upper section with flat top, projecting molded cornice over five short and three long graduated

molded drawers, lower section with three short molded drawers, cabriole legs, trifid feet, orig brasses, repairs to molding, 42½ x 23½ x 69¼" **12,000.00**

Commode

George III, mahogany, serpentine, four long graduated drawers, inlaid, paneled sides, 58 x 22 x 35½" ... **6,000.00**

Regency, 20th C, gilt bronze, rouge royal marble top, kingwood, two small drawers, two long drawers, channeled sides, 51 x 34" **3,000.00**

Highboy

Chippendale, Salem, MA, c1770, carved walnut, two parts, bonnet top with molded swan's neck pediment centering three spirally turned finials, three short and four long graduated, molded drawers, center drawer fan carved, lower section of three short and one long graduated, molded drawers, center drawer fan carved, volute carved and diamond pierced skirt, angular cabriole legs, claw and ball feet, restoration to base and top of crest, 40 x 21 x 89¼" **22,000.00**

Queen Anne

Connecticut, cherry, pine secondary wood, bonnet top with molded cornice and orig spiral turned finial, concave blocking conforms to carved shell in bottom drawer, upper section with nine drawers, base with four, drawers dovetailed with overlapping lips, orig brasses, carved sunburst in top drawer, bottom drawer with fan edged with relief carved scallops, scalloped apron, cabriole legs, duck feet, orig finish, 34½ x 18¼ x 82¾" . **27,500.00**

Connecticut, c1750–70, carved cherry, flat top, thumb molded cornice above central deep fan carved drawer flanked by four short deep drawers over four long drawers, lower section with long drawer over central deep fan carved drawer flanked by deep drawers, arched apron, cabriole legs, pad feet, orig brasses, 38 x 73" **7,500.00**

Country, curly maple, ten dovetailed overlapping drawers, old brasses, scrolled apron, turned drops, cabriole legs, duck feet, minor repairs and replacements, 19½ x 39½" cornice, 36 x 39½ x 70" **5,000.00**

New England, c1765, maple, flat

top, two sections, upper with molded cornice, four molded graduated drawers, lower with one long and three short drawers, center drawer fan carved, shaped skirt, cabriole legs, pad feet, 37¾ x 20 x 70¾" **30,000.00**

Chests, Other, lowboy, Chippendale, Pennsylvania, walnut, 32½" w, $3,500.00.

Lowboy
  Queen Anne
    Connecticut, c1750, cherry, poplar secondary wood, boldly scalloped top with good overhang, four dovetailed overlapping drawers, carved center fan, scalloped aprons, cabriole legs, slender ankles, well shaped duck feet with pads, orig deep reddish brown finish, excellent patina, pieced repair on front foot, replaced engraved brasses, 20½ x 38 x 32⅛" **145,000.00**
    Connecticut, c1760, carved cherry, rect top, molded edge, long drawer above central shell carved deep drawer flanked by deep drawers, blocked and arched apron, cabriole legs, pad feet, chalk inscription on int. backboard "B.S. Snow," frame slightly reduced, repair to front left leg, 31½ x 30½" **4,000.00**
    Massachusetts, c1755, veneered walnut, rect top, five short molded drawers, shaped skirt hung with turned pendants, cabriole legs, pad feet, orig brasses, remnants of paper label on back, 34½ x 21 x 28¾" **29,700.00**

Mule, Chippendale, country, pine, wide single board construction, rect lift lid, blanket chest top with two fake drawers, two dovetailed overlapping drawers, scrolled feet, turned wood pulls, orig red paint, 38⅜ x 19½ x 41½" . . **1,800.00**
Tea, Federal, American, 1815–25, mahogany, paw feet, eagle carved brackets, inlaid escutcheon, 12 x 7¼ x 8¾" **850.00**

CRADLES

Birch, hooded, dovetailed, cut out rockers, scalloped ends, 41" l **500.00**
Carved hardwoods, four columnar finials and tapering sides, 36" l, 27" h . **175.00**
Mahogany, hooded, shaped sides and end boards, heart hand holds, trestle rockers, flat stretchers, 48" **300.00**
Pine, American, late 18th or early 19th C, pine, hooded, scalloped hood sides, plain bonnet top, orig finish, 45" l **300.00**
Poplar, open, central cut out sides and ends, hand holds, trestle rockers, old dark finish, 41" l **200.00**
Walnut
  Dovetailed, scalloped sides, hand holds, brass knobs, heart cut-out in headboard, large rockers, 43½" . . **350.00**
  Self rocking, patent by Aaron Dodd Crane, Feb 28, 1852, wind-up clockwork mechanism, flat spindles, scroll feet, 44" l **675.00**

CUPBOARDS

Armoire, Victorian
  Louis XV style, late 19th C, rosewood and bird's eye maple, carved crest, mirrored door flanked by two side mirrors, cabriole legs, 62 x 19 x 101" **1,200.00**
  Louis-Phillipe, mid 19th C, inlaid rosewood, arched top, conforming mirrored door, brass molded cross banded frame, base with one long drawer, cabriole legs, ornate brass mounts, 43 x 18 x 89 . . . . **1,500.00**
  Provincial Louis XV/XVI, fruitwood, oblong molded cornice, angled corners, paneled frieze and pair of full doors, dec with sheaves of wheat, cartouche form panels, conforming base, deeply valanced skirt, angled tightly whorled feet, 62 x 19 x 69" **3,500.00**
Chimney, pine, full length overlapping door, seven mortised shelves, wrought iron hinges and slide bolt latch, 12 x 10½ x 91" **2,250.00**

Corner

Carved Pine, Chippendale, PA, c1795, molded projecting cornice, carved frieze, pair of arched glazed doors, red painted shelved int., pair of cupboard doors below, flanking fluted pilasters, restorations to cornice and other minor repairs, 60 x 28½ x 109½" **10,000.00**

Cherry, late Victorian, open, fluted vertical members, floral motifs on drawers, carved rosettes on two lower doors, natural finial, 59 x 31 x 88" **2,000.00**

Curly Maple

One piece, upper pair of glazed doors each with eight panes of wavy glass, lower pair of paneled doors, well scalloped base, minor repairs, refinished, 42¾ x 82¾" **5,800.00**

Two piece, upper section with simple cornice, double doors with six panes of old wavy glass, pie shelf, lower section with three dovetailed drawers, paneled doors, scalloped bracket feet, 55 x 83" **2,800.00**

Mahogany, American, c1820, paneled upper and lower doors, two half drawers in center, carved half columns, 43 x 20 x 84½" ... **1,250.00**

Pine

Chippendale, American, c1760, flat top, board molded cornice, double raised panel doors on both sections, orig blue paint, 50 x 24 x 80" **1,850.00**

Federal, CT River Valley, c1815, flat molded and carved cornice,

Cupboard, corner, Country, pine, 38 x 25 x 61", $3,500.00.

carved rosettes and reeded moldings flanking four raised panel doors, shaped shelves, refinished, 48 x 25 x 78½" **2,500.00**

Colonial Revival, Chippendale style, arched, glazed upper door, two paneled doors below, 29½ x 12 x 70" **350.00**

Pine and Poplar, American, probably PA, early 19th C, 2 pc, upper section with two doors each with six panes of glass, bottom with two paneled doors, small drawer, refinished, 50½ x 21½ x 83⅜" **1,000.00**

Southern Pine, VA, two glazed doors, raised panel doors, wrought iron "H" hinges, bracket feet, 54¾ x 79½" **2,500.00**

Walnut, Ohio, 1 pc, poplar secondary wood, orig worn dark red paint, cove molded cornice, solid panel below six panes in top doors, paneled base doors, orig brass thumb latches, 45 x 82½" **2,800.00**

Hanging

Butternut, base and cornice molding, chamfered corners, drawer, paneled door, orig lock and key, orig red-brown paint, 24 x 14¼ x 27½" **650.00**

Oak, pierced tin door panels, refinished, 45 x 11 x 23¾" **275.00**

Pine, American, 19th C, single plank door, three shelves, orig grained finish, 23½ x 9¼ x 29¾" **600.00**

Jelly

Pine, c1850, two doors, four shelves, gallery top, orig red paint, 15 x 33 x 57½" **750.00**

Poplar, two paneled doors, two overhanging drawers, shaped skirt, red and black graining, orig hardware, 41½ x 21½ x 46" **650.00**

Linen Press, Chippendale, NJ, c1770, carved cherrywood, two parts, upper with molded cornice, two paneled cupboard doors, shelved int., flanking fluted pilasters, lower section of four molded and graduated long drawers, bracket feet, backboards of upper section restored, 50½ x 19 x 89½" . **3,500.00**

Pewter, American, late 18th C, pine, bent back, four shelves, single cupboard door base, refinished, 41¼ x 18¾ x 79⅝" **850.00**

Pie Safe

Maple, American, mid 19th C, refinished, 39¼ x 16 x 43½" **375.00**

Southern Pine, 8 punched tin panels with diamond, stylized tulip, and star, sq leg stand, mortised frame, 42 x 17 x 60" **950.00**

Wall

Oak, curved glass sides, glass door, mirrored back, glass shelves **1,000.00**

Pine

Chippendale, Hackensack, NJ, c1800, two parts, upper section with molded cornice, reeded tympanum, pair of glazed hinged doors, lower section with one long and two short drawers, pair of cupboard doors, bootjack feet, 51 x 18 x 87″ **14,500.00**

Federal, one piece, architectural details, molded cornice, applied moldings, raised panel doors, fluted pilasters, butterfly shelves, orig built-in, repairs, refinished, 40¾ x 21½ x 94″ **1,500.00**

Pine and Poplar, country, decorated, old worn brownish yellow graining over earlier red, two sections, upper section with molded cornice, pair of six pane glazed doors, pie shelf, lower section with three drawers, paneled doors, turned feet, minor repairs, 52 x 19¾ x 83½″ **1,800.00**

Walnut

Chippendale, PA, c1775, upper section molded, dentil carved, two paneled doors, lower section with three drawers, two paneled doors, bracket feet, 62¾ x 19½ x 85″ **2,400.00**

Eastlake, single panel glazed doors, two drawers over blind doors, machine carvings **800.00**

DESKS

Art Nouveau, gilt metal, repousse panels of country scenes, glass top,

Desk, Eastlake, oak, cylinder roll top, $1,000.00.

brocade lining, matching arm chair, Austrian **1,200.00**

Chippendale

Massachusetts, c1789, mahogany, slant front, oxbow front, rect hinged lid, fitted int. of valanced pigeonholes, small drawers, center prospect section of small drawers, upper fan carved, four reverse serpentine front graduated drawers, cockbeaded surrounds, claw and ball feet, incised "EM 1789" on bottom, 42 x 22 x 44″ **12,000.00**

New England, c1785, curly maple, slant front, rect hinged lid, fitted int. with valanced pigeonholes over short drawers, four graduated long drawers, reduced ogee bracket feet, 35½ x 19 x 41½″ **6,325.00**

New England, late 18th C, cherry, slant front, minor restoration, replacement of one inner small drawer, minor wood beetle damage to back edge, orig finish and hardware, 35½″ w **3,500.00**

Pennsylvania, c1770, carved walnut, slant front, rect top, fitted int. with valanced pigeonholes, baluster document drawers and blocked small drawers, four graduated long drawers, later bracket feet, 35¾ x 40¾″ **3,500.00**

Colonial Revival

Chippendale Style, c1930, solid walnut case, walnut veneered slant front lid, block front, fitted int. with secret drawer, paw feet, 32 x 18 x 42″ **425.00**

Governor Winthrop Style, c1920, mahogany veneer, solid mahogany slant front, serpentine front, fitted int. with two document drawers, shell carved center door, four long drawers, brass pulls and escutcheons **400.00**

Queen Anne Style, c1940, walnut veneer top, sides, and front, crotch walnut veneer on two side drawers, shell carved cabriole legs, 44 x 20 x 31″ **400.00**

Spinet Style, c1920, solid mahogany, hinged front, fitted int. with drawers and pigeonholes, cylindrical reeded legs, 39 x 21 x 33″ **250.00**

Federal

Butler's, New York or Phila, c1810, demi-lune, mahogany, oblong top, two convex drawers, center drawer, pull-out writing section with hinged lid opening to three satinwood drawers, two pairs of cupboard drawers below, turned feet, brass bass casters, 47½ x 23 x 43¾" . . **28,600.00**

Cylinder, mid-Atlantic States, c1820, curly maple, three short drawers above retracting cylinder lid opening to short drawers over valanced pigeonholes, center tambour slide, retractable baize lined writing surface, two short drawers and long drawers, turned feet, 40½ x 22 x 50" **5,000.00**

Lady's, writing, Boston, MA, c1800, inlaid mahogany, two parts, upper with molded cornice above two hinged drawers inlaid with satinwood columns, int. with small drawers centering valanced pigeonholes, lower section with hinged baize lined writing flap above two cockbeaded drawers, rect inlaid dies, sq tapering legs ending in shaped angular vase form feet, 39 x 20¼ x 44" **9,000.00**

Tambour, inlaid mahogany and curly maple, two parts, upper section with molded cornice and pair of tambour slides, int. with small drawers and pigeonholes, center prospect door with three small drawers, lower section with baize lined hinged writing flap, two cross banded drawers, inlaid dies, bellflower inlaid sq tapering legs, cross banded cuffs, 36¼ x 19 x 42" . . . **3,850.00**

George I, early 18th C, slant front, walnut, rect cross banded top, canted lid, shaped and stepped int. of small drawers and conforming cubbyholes, center prospect door, rect case with three short, two short and two full cockbeaded and cross banded drawers, bracket feet, 37 x 21 x 40" **6,500.00**

George III, partners, mahogany, rect top, green tooled inset leather top, each side fitted with single drawer over kneehole section flanked by four drawers, brass bail handles, platform base, 60 x 48 x 31" **5,275.00**

Queen Anne, New England, c1760, slant front

Maple, rect hinged lid, stepped int. with valanced pigeonholes, serpentine drawers and center paneled prospect door, arched small drawer, four graduated long drawers, bracket feet, repairs, 37 x 18½ x 43" **2,750.00**

Walnut, shaped top above slant front with central cupboard door flanked by pigeonholes and small drawers, over long drawer, stand with three short drawers, later cabriole legs

carved at the knees with shells, 28 x 37¼" **6,000.00**

Regency, c1815, Davenport, rosewood, sliding sq writing surface, tooled brown leather inset, rect three quarter brass gallery, pull out writing slide on either side fitted with pen and ink drawer, four long drawers, false drawers on other side, turned cylindrical feet, minor losses to molding, 19 x 30" **3,500.00**

Sewing, western PA or Ohio, c1815, painted and dec pine, shaped superstructure, top with hinged lid opening to fitted int. with two drawers and pigeonholes, two hinged doors with polychrome eglomise panels depicting birds, flag, several figures, and cannon, single drawer below, cylindrical feet, painted red, green highlights, 26⅞ x 19 x 36½" **8,250.00**

Sheraton

American, c1820, slant front, maple, bird's eye and tiger maple int., fourteen drawers, rope carved columns, refinished, glass knobs, 41 x 20¼ x 53¼" **1,150.00**

Country, c1845, lady's, pine, turned feet, fluted posts, three dovetailed drawers, fold down writing surface, top upper section with paneled doors, fitted int., 37½ x 18½ x 46½" **1,200.00**

Victorian, black walnut, stencil type free hand painted dec by Ralph Cahoon, mustard yellow ground, 31½ x 21½ x 58½" **800.00**

Wooton, 1875–80, walnut and burl walnut, standard grade, pierced and carved gallery over double panel lifting frieze, maple veneer fitted int., trestle feet, 41" closed, 69½" h **7,500.00**

DOUGH TROUGHS

Cherry, dovetailed, turned feet, white porcelain knobs, name "Hardin" scratched on base **250.00**

Decorated, pine, orig blue paint, early train painted on one side in black, white, and faded red, sq nail construction, curved tin bottom, unpainted inner lid, worn leather hinges, 21 x 31" breadboard top, 15¼ x 25¾ x 28½" **600.00**

Pine, one board top, dovetailed box, later splayed turned legs, old refinishing, 21½ x 40½ x 28¼" **300.00**

Pine and poplar, straight tapering legs, 39¼ x 19¼ x 26½" **500.00**

Poplar, turned cherry legs, chestnut apron and hinged lid, refinished, 19 x 41 x 29½" **300.00**

Walnut, dovetailed, splayed legs, 20 x
27 x 39" **450.00**

DRY SINKS

Cherry, Chippendale, two sections, two
paneled doors on top, rect sink over
two paneled base doors, 46 x 23½ x
77" **900.00**
Curly Maple, 55 x 20¼ x 34½", poplar
door panels, hard wood edge strips,
drawer front replaced, top edge of
well re-cut, refinished **2,250.00**
Maple, PA German, rect top, single
drawer, two doors painted, 30½ x
60½" **850.00**
Pine, American, c19th C, primitive, narrow shelf on splashback, sq legs and
stretchers, old red paint, 40½ x 18½
x 38½" **500.00**
Pine and Poplar
American, crest, paneled doors, one
small nailed drawer, refinished,
62½ x 19¾ x 34" **700.00**
Attributed to PA, c1825, shelf back
with two small drawers, pair of base
cupboard doors, refinished, minor
restoration, 52 x 22½ x 50⅜" **650.00**
Poplar, country, paneled doors, dovetailed drawer, cut out sides, shelf top,
simple cut out feet, old worn refinishing, 48 x 19¾ x 48¾" **1,125.00**
Walnut, rect top, one drawer, two base
doors, 33 x 44" **500.00**

FRAMES

Brass, Art Nouveau style, two oval
openings, easel back, 7 x 12" **125.00**
Curly Maple, refinished, 16¾ x 2 x 20½" **85.00**
Decorated, poplar, orig black paint, gold
stenciled dec, 9¾ x 1¼ x 11¾" **250.00**
Folk Art, leather over wood, birds, ani-
mals in relief, 6 x 6½" **350.00**
Mahogany, gold liner, 35" sq **125.00**
Oak, 19th C, medallions and bull's eyes,
20 x 77" **275.00**
Pine, beveled, worn red flame graining,
varnished, 9⅜ x 1½ x 11⅜" **75.00**
Shadow Box, Victorian, circular, 21½"
deep **100.00**
Veneer
Mahogany
Beveled, varnished, 11¼ x 1½ x
20" **35.00**
Empire, wide molding, 20 x 26" ... **65.00**
Maple, bird's eye, ogee, flat liner, 25
x 3⅝ x 28½" **100.00**
Rosewood, beveled, 7⅝ x 1⅞ x 8¾" **45.00**
Walnut
Chip carved edge, applied hearts at
corners, 16 x 19½" **85.00**

Cross bar corners, 8 x 12" **50.00**
Double liner, 28 x 32" **115.00**
Wood Inlay, intricate design, back la-
beled "This frame was carved and
glued together by hand 1730, Wm
Hall, N.Y. State," worn finish **250.00**

HAT RACKS AND HALL TREES

Art Nouveau
Marquetry, Galle style, c1900, oval
crest plaque with inlaid dec,
shaped mirror, base with inlaid tree
dec, brass bar, scrolled hooks, 26
x 78" **1,000.00**
Walnut, mirror back, framework of hat
hooks, table base with drawer, sq
tapered legs, lower shelf and side
stick stands, 38 x 15 x 80" **275.00**
Colonial Revival
Bronze, emb tin, bust of Washington
flanked by flags, locomotive, ship,
and eagle, mirror in center, 25" .. **100.00**
Cherry, Baroque, c1910, shell carved
crest over cartouche and griffin
carved panel back, lift seat, high
arms, mask carved base, paw feet,
39½ x 21½ x 51" **500.00**
Mahogany, slender circular shaft, four
hanging hooks, quadruple base,
58" **175.00**
Gothic, Victorian, American, c1855,
oak, ornate arched open cut upper
frame, hooks at side, white marble
shelf, ornate open cut base flanked
by umbrella racks **10,000.00**
Mission, American, golden oak, 11 x 11
x 27" **50.00**
Renaissance Revival, Victorian, American, c1870, walnut, ornate carved
cresting, shaped mirror within molded
framework, drop columns at each
side, candle sockets, candle shelves,
and sockets at lower sides, white
marble shelf, single drawer flanked by
umbrella racks, orig brass pans ... **1,450.00**

ICE CREAM PARLOR FURNITURE

Chair
Arm, wood seat **125.00**
Heart back, refinished **75.00**
Spectacle, refinished **85.00**
Child's, table and two chairs, 18" d ta-
ble, 9½" d seat, set **200.00**
Stool
26½" h, refinished **50.00**
30" h, 12" d seat, refinished **60.00**
Table
25" sq, claw and ball feet **225.00**
30" d, oak top **250.00**

Table and four chairs, 30" d table, wood top, 14" d chairs, replaced seats, refinished, set **650.00**

LOVE SEATS

Adams, c1770, triple oval back, bellflower painted satinwood **4,000.00**

Art Nouveau, 62", carved mahogany frame, upholstered **1,000.00**

Chippendale, English, arched upholstered back, rolled arms, two cushion seat, carved foliate apron, 28 x 35 x 30" **900.00**

Colonial Revival, William and Mary style, loose cushion, turned baluster legs, stretcher, 48" **650.00**

Hepplewhite, walnut, spade feet, bellflower inlay, refinished and reupholstered **1,250.00**

Louis XVI, third quarter 18th C, green painted, upholstered back and arms, loose seat cushion, molded rect frame, gently arched crest with two pomegranates above slightly incurvate arms, acanthus terminals, fluted supports, bowed seat rail, straight tapered fluted legs, toupie feet, 50" l . **4,500.00**

Rococo, Victorian, walnut frame, triple crest, rose carving, refinished and reupholstered **750.00**

Wicker, Wakefield Rattan Co, c1890, sunrise motif back, natural finish, 18 x 34" **950.00**

Magazine Rack, Canterbury, American, walnut, single drawer, brass pull, acorn finials, 17¼ x 22¾ x 23¼", $600.00.

MAGAZINE RACKS

George III, mid 19th C, mahogany
Three bays, short turned feet, brass casters, 23 x 17 x 20" **450.00**

Three bays, single drawer, turned handle, elaborate pierced sides flanked by turned posts, 16 x 16 x 22" **425.00**

Eastlake, Victorian, walnut, pierced sides, turned posts, machine carving, 13½ x 26" **150.00**

Mission, Roycroft, c1910, oak, carved emblem, 37" h **475.00**

Regency, early 19th C, mahogany
Typical form, series of four dipped dividers, turned corner supports, one full drawer, turned legs, brass castered feet, 19 x 14 x 19" **1,800.00**

Typical form, two lattice divisions, full basal drawer, turned legs, brass castered feet, 18½ x 12 x 21" . . . **1,500.00**

Victorian, c1875, walnut, pierced and molded sides joined by turned legs and dividers, 24 x 16 x 21" **400.00**

MIRRORS

Adam, English, c1780, giltwood, vase and leaf finial, openwork scroll and leaf dec, oblong mirror plate in upright frame, 28 x 64" **900.00**

Baroque, mid 18th C, parquetry panels, oval plate, shuttle and bead slip molded frame, 26½ x 32½" **950.00**

Centennial, inlaid mahogany, five drawers, large oval mirror, 26¼ x 11 x 26" **150.00**

Chippendale, late 18th C
Inlaid and parcel gilded walnut, swan's neck cresting centering an eagle, two part mirror plate, shaped pendant, eagle finial and fillets restored, 25½ x 63½" **13,200.00**

Mahogany on pine, carved and gilded gesso, emb liner, open foliage side draperies, foliage scrolls capping crest and well detailed Phoenix finial, old finish, 22½ x 51" **4,500.00**

Parcel gilt and mahogany, PA, c1770, scrolled cresting with center fleurde-lis, rect mirror plate, giltwood scalloped inner border, sides hung with gilt foliage and berried vines, scrolled pendant below, minor restorations, 24½ x 48¼" **600.00**

Continental, 18th C, courting, pine, crest with center eglomise basket of flowers panel, marbleized, molded border, mounted in shallow box frame, pr, 11½ x 16¾" **2,000.00**

Eastlake, walnut, incised carving, 25¼ x 56½" **465.00**

Empire, American, giltwood, overhanging cornice, gilt gesso panel, two part mirror plate flanked by heavy baluster and ring turned applied half columns and corner blocks **175.00**

Federal

Convex, wall, American, 1825–50, carved giltwood, convex mirror plate within molded framework gilt spherules and surmounted by spread winged American eagle, flanked by acanthus foliage, chain of spherules hung from beak, pomegranate pendant below, 31 x 54" **4,675.00**

Wall, New York, c1810, giltwood, molded projecting cornice above eglomise panel depicting swan, rect mirror plate, flanked by bundled white colonettes, gilt acanthus leaves highlights, 24 x 47¾" **15,400.00**

George II

Carved Giltwood, late 19th C, Chinaman standing within portico, mirror flanked and separated by frame elaborately carved with pagoda, cresting, C scroll, foliate, icicle, and columnar borders, carved figure of dog with up turned head on base, 58½ x 86" **8,250.00**

Walnut veneer, parcel gilt, scrolled crest centered by pierced gilt foliage, shaped mirror plate flanked by fruit and floral sprig medallions, scrolled pendant below, 21¼ x 39¼" **1,875.00**

George III, third quarter 18th C, oval plate, beaded slip and carved fluted frame, egg and dart border, painted white, parcel gilt, 37¼ x 45" **2,500.00**

Hepplewhite

Shaving, bow front, mahogany, edge inlay, three dovetailed drawers, oval mirror frame, convoluted supports, 14½ x 20" **225.00**

Wall, pine and gesso filigree crests with urn, flowers, wheat, and foliage, wire frame, worn orig gilding and old glass, 19½" l **13,500.00**

Neoclassical, Danish or Swedish, late 18th C, kingwood, rect plate, beaded slip and molded frame, surmounted by arched crest with gilded urns, 14 x 28" **400.00**

Queen Anne, 18th C, walnut

Pier, parcel gilt and verre eglomise, shaped upper section, border of gilt arabesque work with two figures, green ground, triple glass plates, 27½ x 64 .... **4,500.00**

Wall

Figured Veneer, pine secondary wood, applied gilded ornaments on crests and gilded liner, old veneer repairs, discolored mirror, 14¾ x 37" **1,600.00**

Shaped crest above molded slip enclosing mirror plate, 15 x 16" **1,650.00**

Mirror, Queen Anne, walnut, piercing heart and crown, beveled, 2 pc, $6,000.00.

Veneer, ogee frame, gilded liner and detail on low crest, refinished, replaced beveled glass, 13¼ x 22¾" **275.00**

Regency

Girandole, early 19th C, circular convex plate, ebonized slip and molded spherule hung frame, surmounted by seahorse and flowering cornucopia, two scrolling branches above acanthus skirt, 33 x 50" **7,000.00**

Wall, c1815, parcel gilt, cornice with outset corners, ebonized Greek key frieze beneath spheres, rect mirror plate flanked by fluted stiles and ebonized classical busts, 35¼ x 50½" **2,500.00**

Sheraton, architectural, upper panel black, gold, blue, and white reverse painting of George Washington, trophy of flags, arms, marker's name on back, 25¼ x 42¼" **425.00**

Victorian

Cheval, English, c1890, bird's eye maple frame, bamboo style, 33 x 71" **1,320.00**

Pier, mahogany, grape leaf carved molded cornice over rect beveled mirror, spiral column supports with paw feet, 61 x 102½" **625.00**

ROCKERS

Adirondack, American, early 20th C, bent rustic twigs and branches, interwoven latticework back and downswept arms, round seat, curlicue skirt **200.00**

Arrowback, bamboo turnings, scrolled arms, three slat backs, red and black

graining, stenciled floral designs on
slats **125.00**
*Bentwood, sleigh type, signed Thonet **700.00**
*Boston, cane seat **275.00**
Child's, oak, chicken head and gallery
with turned spindles, worn white
paint, red and yellow dec, 36" h ... **200.00**
Eastlake, late 19th C, mahogany platform, incised and pierced cresting
over sq panel back, center, pad arms,
seat upholstered in pink velvet,
reeded arms and supports **200.00**
Ladder Back, arm, four arched back
slats, turned finials, shaped arms,
sausage turnings with bulbous front
stretcher, worn dark brown paint over
old red paint, one rocker replaced .. **400.00**
Mission, L & J G Stickley, arm, c1910,
vertical back and side slats, clamp
decal mark **625.00**
Sewing, lady's, maple, bird's eye,
shaped crest, old caned seat and
back, old refinishing **150.00**
Shaker, Mt Lebanon, NY, c1900, #7,
arms, old brown wash, rush seat,
41½" h **400.00**
Victorian, Grecian influence, c1860,
walnut, caned back and seat, scroll
cut arms, turned legs, refinished and
recaned **350.00**
Wicker, loom woven fiber, padded back,
flattened downswept arms, seat with
loose cushion, turned and fiber
wrapped legs, painted white **150.00**
Windsor
  Bow Back, country, high shaped
  arms, oblong seat, bamboo turnings, splayed base, "H" stretcher,
  added rockers, old refinishing, minor damage **325.00**
  Comb Back, New England, c1800,
  turned, shaped crest, seven spindles back, shaped arms, elliptical
  seat, turned legs, painted **625.00**

SECRETARIES

Colonial Revival, Governor Winthrop,
c1928, mahogany veneer, two sections, broken pediment, center urn finial, molded cornice, pair of glazed
doors, shelves, slant front, fitted int.,
three long drawers, oval brasses, ball
feet, 33 x 80" **500.00**
Federal
  Eastern MA, c1810, mahogany, two
  parts, upper section with shaped
  pediment, turned urn form finials,
  pair of glazed hinged doors, two
  shelves, lower section with hinged
  baize lined writing flag, three cockbeaded graduated drawers, reeded

**Secretary, Country Victorian, c1860,
pine, brass hardware, 24¼ x 45¼ x 87",
$2,000.00.**

legs, C-scroll carved brackets, vase
form feet, 36 x 21 x 81½" **19,800.00**
NY, c1805, lady's, mahogany, two
parts, upper with shaped pediment
centering eagle brass finial and two
urn finials, pair of glazed hinged
doors, adjustable shelves, lower
section with hinged writing flap
opening to divided well, lidded secret well with two drawers, line inlaid frieze, reeded circular legs,
brass ball caps, interior drawers restored, 33 x 20 x 77" **13,200.00**
Salem, MA, c1800, attributed to William Appleton, inlaid mahogany,
two parts, upper with molded
swan's neck crest ending in carved
pomegranates, center orig giltwood
spread wing eagle finial above tympanum inlaid with intersection lines
and diamond, pair of glazed hinged
doors, two shelves, lower projecting section with line inlaid hinged
lid opening to baize lined writing
surface, small drawers over pigeonholes, three graduated cockbeaded drawers, brass bail bracket
feet, orig eagle, glass, baize and
brasses, 43½ x 22 x 96" **36,300.00**
George III, c1760, mahogany, dental
carved molded cornice, twin glazed
lattice doors, lower section fitted with
pull out drawer, fitted int. and writing
surface over three graduated drawers, brass bail handles, bracket feet,
37 x 21 x 80" **2,750.00**
Georgian, late, c1820, mahogany, two
sections, upper with stylized Prince of

Wales crest, pair of glazed doors, arched mullions, adjustable shelves, lower portion with canted lid opening to baize lined writing surface, drawers and cubbyholes, center tambour slide, four full graduated cockbeaded drawers, French bracket feet, 36½ x 20 x 95" **5,000.00**

Hepplewhite, American, c1790–1800, inlaid mahogany, upper cupboard doors, int. with three drawers, four pigeonholes, shelved compartment, rosewood banding, three graduated full width drawers with inlay, 37¼ x 19¼ x 52¼" **6,500.00**

Sheraton, mahogany, two piece, flame veneer facade, upper section with scrolled crest, reeded blocks, and brass rosettes, double doors, three dovetailed int. drawers, fold down writing surface, four dovetailed drawers, applied edge beading, turned feet, refinished, replaced eagle brasses, minor veneer damage, 39 x 17½ x 64" **1,300.00**

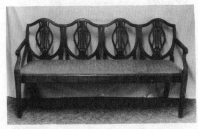

Settee, Hepplewhite, shield back, $1,500.00.

SETTEES

Biedermeier, 2nd quarter 19th C, walnut, chairback, shaped arms, turned supports, sq tapered legs, 64" l **1,200.00**

Classical Style, well shaped crest, plank seat, scrolled arms, turned spindles and legs, refinished, repairs, 80" l .. **450.00**

Decorated, plank seat, half spindle rabbit ear back, turned legs, old blue paint, striping in black, yellow, and gold, 113¾" l **1,475.00**

Federal, American, c1810, blue damask upholstery, inlaid sq tapering legs, brass caster feet, 61" l **3,000.00**

Federal Style, mahogany, molded frame with Fortuny fabric upholstered back and sides, turned and ribbed legs, 53" **500.00**

George III, provincial, early 19th C, oak,

rect top rail, triple chairback, stylized baluster splats, drop-in seat, sq legs joined by stretchers, 50" l **2,125.00**

Jacobean, 17th C, open arm, tapestry cov back, block and ring turned round legs, bulbous shaped stretchers, Spanish feet, 63" l **1,750.00**

Windsor

Bamboo turnings, front corners reshaped, arms replaced, black repaint, 79" l **500.00**

Worn orig brown graining in imitation of curly maple, bamboo turnings, plank seat, three section back with open crests and butterfly medallions, minor repairs, 75½" l, 17½" h seat **3,500.00**

SIDEBOARDS

Classical, NY, c1820, mahogany, rect top, frieze with three inlaid drawers, three hinged cupboard doors, shelves, carved flanking columns, carved animal paw feet, brass casters, 66½ x 24 x 43½" **5,000.00**

Colonial Revival, Queen Anne style, c1920, striped mahogany veneer, two long drawers over pair of drawers flanked by cupboard doors, fiddleback veneer on drawers and doors, burl veneer on oval panels, solid cabriole legs **200.00**

Federal

American, c1820, inlaid mahogany, bow front, single drawer, fan inlay, twin paneled doors, sq tapering legs, bellflower inlay, 71 x 25 x 39" **5,600.00**

Philadelphia, c1800, satinwood inlaid mahogany, oblong top, kidney shaped front, conforming shaped case, two convex drawers, one concave center drawer, pair of cupboard drawers, penwork dec satinwood inlaid dies enclosing ram's head and bellflowers, line inlaid sq tapering legs, cross banded cuffs, orig silver-gilt brasses with grape cluster dec, 72 x 25 x 38¼" **45,100.00**

George III

Faded Mahogany, third quarter 18th C, oblong top, bowed front, rosewood cross banding, satinwood edging, conforming recessed case, center drawer flanked by two bottle drawers, straight tapering line inlaid legs, eagle and shield cartouches, spade feet, 37 x 20 x 34" **8,000.00**

Mahogany, second half 18th C, oblong cross banded top, serpentine front, conforming recessed case, central cockbeaded drawer flanked

by bottle drawer, two short drawers, straight tapered legs, spade feet, 66 x 28½ x 36½" **5,000.00**
George IV, second quarter 19th C, inlaid mahogany, serpentine front, shaped top, central frieze drawer, flanked by one deep drawer and cupboard door, tapering sq legs, spade feet, 57½ x 36¼" **1,500.00**

Sideboard, Renaissance Victorian, walnut, marble top, carved with game birds and fish, $1,000.00.

Hepplewhite, American, 18th C
Cherry, poplar secondary wood, checkerboard banded top, case with dovetailed edge beaded drawers flanked by serpentine doors and drawers, stringing inlay, mahogany cross banding around bottom edge of case, drawers, and doors, inlaid elongated diamonds, almond and circular bead like segments between strings at tops of sq tapered legs, top of posts have inlaid flutes (books), oval emb eagle brasses (two replaced copies), minor age cracks and veneer repairs, old refinishing, 72 x 24⅜ x 39¼" . **11,750.00**
Mahogany, circular inlaid panels on all four doors, 66¼ x 36½ x 39¾" **3,000.00**
Regency, early 19th C, mahogany, D shaped top, single drawer over secret drawer, flanked by deep drawer and bottle drawer, ring turned tapering cylindrical legs, 42½ x 36" **1,600.00**

SOFAS

Chippendale, NY, c1770, mahogany, camel back, shaped crest, outward scrolling arm supports and seat, sq molded legs, flat stretchers, 80" l . . **10,000.00**
Empire, c1830, carved mahogany, shell, fruit, and leaf carved crest rail, seat, back, and shaped arms cov in white fabric upholstery, paw feet, 84" l . . **2,500.00**
Federal
American, c1820, mahogany, rounded back, scroll arms, upholstered seat and pillar cushions, baluster lets, casters, 80" l **950.00**
Northern MA or Portsmouth, NY, c1805, flame birch inlaid mahogany, shaped crest centering oval inlaid flame birch reserve, reeded arm supports, bowed and cross banded seat rail, rect inlaid dies, ring turned and tapering legs, 79" l **38,500.00**
NY, c1805, mahogany, molded crest, fluted rect center reserve, molded arms, turned arm supports, bowed seat, sq tapering legs, spade feet, brass casters, striped upholstery, 77½" l **10,000.00**
NY, c1805, mahogany, reeded crest, rect panel carved with swags, tassels, and bowknots, upholstered back, down curving reeded arms, bowed seat rail, flowerhead inlaid dies, circular reeded tapering legs, brass casters, some repairs to legs, 70" l **6,600.00**
George III, c1800, carved mahogany, arched upholstered back, molded terminals, down curved supports, molded tapering sq legs, 76" l **2,225.00**
Mission, L & J G Stickley, c1910, oak, decal clamp mark, 72" l **1,350.00**
Rococo, NY, c1855, Henry Belter, laminated rosewood, applied floral cresting, 74" l **2,000.00**
Victorian, English, mid 19th C, mahogany veneer, triple back, medium blue upholstery, 60" **425.00**

SPINNING WHEELS

Flax Wheels (Saxony)
Maple, NE, c1830 . . . . **275.00**
Mixed woods, PA, c1810, nice turnings, incised heart dec **450.00**
Mixed woods, PA, c1840, turned . . . **300.00**
Wool Wheels (Walking)
Oak, cast iron parts, 30" d wheel, 45" h **325.00**
Walnut, PA, mid 19th C **450.00**

STANDS

Art Nouveau
Easel, brass, tubular, scrolled and cast dec, 64" **250.00**

Music, walnut **375.00**

Arts and Crafts

Plant, oak, sq top, sq legs, lower platform shelf, 44" **175.00**

Side, fumed oak, cane inserts, cupboard base, 9 x 9 x 25½" **200.00**

Colonial Revival

Chinese, c1900, shaped circular top, marble insert, pierced and carved legs, lower shelf, 18" d, 38" h . . . **200.00**

Martha Washington, c1920, sewing, solid mahogany, three drawers, shaped ends, ring turned legs, 28 x 14 x 29" **100.00**

Country, bed, walnut, turned and sq tapered legs, two dovetailed curly maple drawers, one board walnut top, refinished, 19¾ x 20 x 27¾" **300.00**

Eastlake, American, c1875, walnut, sheet music, carved leaf form crest, warrior head medallion, two hinged holders, scrolled legs, 23 x 42" **250.00**

Federal

Basin, eastern New England, c1805, corner, inlaid mahogany, shaped splashboard, bowed drawer and hinged cupboard door, oval and diamond inlaid dies, inlaid legs, slightly splayed pointed feet, 22 x 16 x 38½" **4,675.00**

Night, northeastern New England, c1805, flame birch and curly maple, inlaid mahogany, rect top, two drawers, rect inlaid dies, shaped medial shelf, ring turned legs, tapering feet, branded "G. W. Seaward" in four places **14,500.00**

George III

Dictionary, walnut **100.00**

Music, c1760–70, mahogany, fluted standard, tripod base, adjustable brass candle arms, 26 x 44" **1,000.00**

Urn, late 18th C, inlaid mahogany, oval top, scalloped gallery above candle slide, tapering sq legs, 16 x 27" **700.00**

Wash, early 19th C, corner, mahogany, arched superstructure above three wells, sq supports joined by platform stretcher fitted with single drawer flanked by false drawers, flared legs, 20 x 45¼" **725.00**

Candle, tilt-top, American, c1790–1800, mahogany, orig condition . . **525.00**

Night, cherry, pine secondary wood, one board top, inlay, banding around apron, and bottom and top edge of dovetailed drawer, slender tapering legs with stringing, refinished, 19¼ x 19⅝ x 25¾" **3,100.00**

Queen Anne, night, walnut, rect top, open shelf, single drawer, brass bail

handle and escutcheons, cabriole legs, pad feet, 20 x 13 x 26" **400.00**

Regency, c1815, music, carved rosewood, rect ratchet support, ring turned and reeded swelling cylindrical standard, shaped triangular plinth, circular feet, 17¼ x 44" **1,200.00**

Sheraton, American, early 19th C

Corner, cherry, drawer and backsplash **525.00**

Country, curly maple turned legs and dovetailed drawer, cherry apron and replaced top, refinished, 19¾ x 22½ x 28¾" **350.00**

Wash, mahogany, pine secondary wood, top with scrolled front apron, cutouts for bowl and accessories, dovetailed gallery, dovetailed lighter burl veneer drawer, applied edge beading, turned and reeded legs and posts, fluted segments at drawer and apron, 17¾ x 16 x 30½" **3,000.00**

Writing, mahogany, poplar secondary wood, lift lid, tilt up writing surface, fitted compartments for pens and ink, two dovetailed drawers with applied beading, fitted dividers in top drawer, pull out shelf on left side, turned legs, ivory escutcheons, ivory pulls, orig finish, 15 x 21 x 30¼" **3,550.00**

Writing, mahogany, pine secondary wood, lift lid, resurfaced tooled green leather tilt up writing surface, biscuit corners, three dovetailed drawers with bird's eye maple veneer, applied mahogany edge bead, inlaid ivory escutcheons, orig emb brass bulls, turned and reeded legs, ring turned posts, old finish, 20⅜ x 17⅜ x 29⅛" **4,600.00**

Victorian, 19th C, stamped "Wheeldon's Patent," music, duet, turned mahogany, pierced rect adjustable rest, turned cylindrical shaft, flared turned cylindrical legs, 16 x 50½" **600.00**

STEPS

Bed

Regency, late, mahogany, each tread with inset tooled leather, turned feet **850.00**

Sheraton, two steps, lift top lids, orig carpet treads **500.00**

Victorian, oak, three steps **275.00**

Library

Georgian, mahogany, leather inserts, 30½ x 16 x 27" **400.00**

Regency

Chair, metamorphic, c1815, mahogany, curved rect top crest rail, horizontal back splat, scrolled

arms, flared caned seat, saber legs, back and seat tilting to form braize lined library steps **4,500.00**
Pole form, leather clad, folding . . **2,200.00**
Victorian, four steps, arm rail support, 76" h **475.00**

STOOLS

Foot
Country, pine, old red paint, high cut out and scalloped feet, solid board top, old carpet covering, 11 x 11 x 12" **150.00**
George III, carved mahogany, umber leather upholstered top, serpentine apron, scrolled toes, 56" l **725.00**
New England, early 19th C, turned birchwood, oval seat upholstered in flame stitch pattern embroidery, vase and ring turned splayed legs, ball feet, pr **900.00**
Provincial, walnut, wrought iron cross stretcher **150.00**
Queen Anne, walnut, rect molded slip seat, four cabriole legs, pad feet . **2,000.00**
Sheraton, English, 14 x 18", mahogany, adjustable top, leather cloth cov **175.00**
Victorian, c1880, mahogany, rect needlepoint top, frieze drawer, short turned legs, casters, 19 x 13 x 11" **125.00**
Windsor, early 19th C, circular, bamboo turned legs and cross stretcher, branded twice "M S Marsh," refinished, faint age split in seat, 10½ to 11" d, 6¾" h **300.00**
Gout
American, c1880, walnut, upholstered, rocking type, 12 x 19 x 21" **175.00**
English, c1890, 12 x 13 x 19" **275.00**
Milking, country, primitive, three legs, heart cut out handle, relief carving of cow, old dark finish **275.00**
Organ, Victorian, circular, three fancy metal legs, ebonized stem, upholstered top **125.00**
Pianoforte, Sheraton, adjustable, mahogany, four splayed fluted legs, screw type mechanism, upholstered seat **250.00**

TABLES

Banquet, Hepplewhite, American, late 18th C, mahogany, later eagle inlay, three part, 99 x 47 x 28 34/4" **3,500.00**
Billiards, B A Stevens, Co, Toledo, OH, 1850–75, inlaid walnut and cast iron, oblong top, geometrically inlaid edge and frieze, joined lions forming "X"

stretcher, twelve cue sticks, orig triangles and cue rack, 110" l **8,000.00**
Card
Chippendale
American, c1770, carved mahogany, hinged rect top, case with frieze drawer, bracketed and reeded sq tapering legs, minor restoration, 38½ x 19¼ x 28¼" . **2,000.00**
Philadelphia, c1770, carved mahogany, rect top, conforming shaped hinged leaf, single drawer frieze, gadrooned skirt, acanthus carved cabriole legs, claw and ball feet, black paint inscription inside swingrail, "G21," 31½ x 14¾ x 28" **24,200.00**
Empire, birch and inlaid burlwood, "D" shape, trestle shaped feet, 30 x 35" **400.00**
Federal
American, flame veneer, inlaid medallion, conforming top, mahogany, slender turned legs, "D" end apron, 17¼ x 35¾ x 29" . . **1,200.00**
Baltimore, c1805, inlaid walnut, D shaped hinged top, oval burl inlay on apron, pinline inlaid sq tapering legs, 35½ x 16½ x 28¼" **4,125.00**
New England, c1805, inlaid mahogany, oblong top, conforming shaped leaf, frieze centering oval inlaid reserve, flanking rect inlaid dies, line inlaid sq tapering legs, tapered feet, 35 x 17 x 29½" . . **5,500.00**
New York, c1805, attributed to Duncan Phyfe, carved mahogany, oblong top, shaped front and conforming shaped hinged leaf swiveling above well, frieze with flowerhead carved dies, center rect reserve carved with swags and tassels and bowknot, brass cockbeaded skirt hung with turned pendants, four ring turned supports, octagonal plinth base with brass moldings, water leaf carved and reeded down curving legs, brass animal paw feet, brass casters, 35¾ x 18 x 28" . **13,200.00**
Georgian, English, late 18th C, mahogany, "D" shaped leaves, tapered legs, refinished, 29⅛" h . . . **415.00**
Hepplewhite, cherry, inlay, shaped apron, conforming top, ovolo corners, flame grain and curly maple veneers, light and dark wood banding, central four petal flower, sq tapering legs with stringing and tulips in light wood, teardrop in dark wood inlay, refinished, 36 x 18 x 28¾" . **3,250.00**
Louis XV, American, c1900, marque-

try, shaped brass beaded top, four shaped drop leaves, floral satinwood inlay, band and string inlay, cabriole legs, 31 x 31 x 30" **425.00**

Queen Anne, English, rect overhanging top, cabriole legs, pad feet, 33 x 17 x 28" **1,000.00**

Regency, English, c1815, satinwood and rosewood, inlaid, 29 x 36" **1,600.00**

Sheraton, MA or NH, inlaid mahogany, serpentine front **2,500.00**

Console, Biedermeier, German, 19th C, fruitwood, rect deep apron, drawer, scroll supports, center wooden backboard and canted base, 21 x 12½ x 33" **600.00**

Dining

Art Deco, maple and ebony, blue rect mirror top, apron, three supports, plinth bases **1,500.00**

Arts and Crafts, L & J G Stickley, oak, sq top, plain apron, sq pedestal, four downswept supports, 50" sq top, 30" h, six extension leaves .. **2,875.00**

Colonial Revival, c1925, extension, rect, walnut veneer top, molded apron, hardwood base, six heavy carved legs, pair of "U" shaped stretchers, 60 x 42 x 31" **125.00**

Empire, mahogany, drop leaf, single drawer, paw feet, 28 x 51" **400.00**

Federal, eastern MA, c1805, inlaid mahogany, two part, rect top, hinged rect leaf, molded edge, frieze centering rect inlaid dies, ring turned and tapering legs, 78 x 35¾ x 29" **23,100.00**

Georgian, late, mid 19th C, mahogany, oval reeded top, twin baluster form standards, downswept tripods, brass castered toe caps, one leaf, 42 x 44 x 29", length extended 63½" **3,600.00**

George III, late 18th C, inlaid mahogany, rect top, rounded corners, frieze with diamond inlaid edge, tapering sq legs, brass casters, 47½ x 29" **3,500.00**

George IV, early 19th C, mahogany, rect top, rounded corners, two baluster turned standards, each with four downswept reeded legs, brass casters, 73 x 27¾" **3,750.00**

Mission, Limbert, c1910, oak, oval top, branded mark, 44¼" **800.00**

Queen Anne, NE, c1765, maple, drop leaf, oblong top, two D-shaped leaves, plain skirt, tapered circular legs, pad feet, minor repair to one foot, 56½ x 27" **5,500.00**

Regency, English, mahogany, extension, circular top with four semi-circular leaves, four downswept legs joined by platform stretcher, brass animal paw feet and casters, 101½ x 29" **5,575.00**

Shaker, early 19th C, stained maple, drop leaf, rect top, two hinged rect leaves, single drawer frieze, sq tapering legs, 34¾ x 35½ x 28" ... **6,600.00**

Victorian, oak, pedestal base, paw feet, 48" d **850.00**

Dressing

George III, c1815, inlaid mahogany, bow front, single drawer over kneehole section, two drawers, circular ring brass pulls and escutcheons, sq tapering legs, 39 x 21½ x 31" . **1,350.00**

Sheraton, selected grain mahogany, single full width drawer, four fluted legs, 31 x 18½ x 30" **625.00**

William and Mary, inlaid oak, rect top, molded edge, single drawer, scalloped apron, trumpet legs, arched stretcher with center ball form finial, bun feet, 30¼ x 28¼" **2,750.00**

Drop Leaf

Chippendale, NH, c1770–90, cherrywood, oblong top, oblong drop leaves, plain apron, molded sq legs, 48½ x 27½" **1,200.00**

Colonial Revival, Hepplewhite style, c1940, mottled mahogany veneer, rect top, hinged leaves, two drawers, 17 x 15 x 26" **200.00**

Empire, country, decorated, pine, worn orig red flame graining, sq tapering pedestal, quatrefoil base, ball feet, 11¾" leaves, 15½ x 41½ x 28" h **350.00**

Hepplewhite, American, c1790, cherry, 47¾ x 24 x 29" **1,500.00**

Queen Anne, cherrywood, single board top, sq legs, turned below apron, duck feet. 41⅞ x 13⅝ x 27" **1,250.00**

Sheraton, American, c1800–10, mahogany, two mid length rounded leaves, turned and fluted legs, orig brass casters, 40 x 26½ x 28¼" . **1,000.00**

Victorian, English, 19th C, mahogany, rect top, two end drawers, vase form turned pedestal, reeded saber legs, 30 x 40 x 28" **950.00**

Game

Colonial Revival, Chippendale style, c1936, figure mahogany veneer top and apron, hardwood pedestal base, three splayed legs, brass paw feet, 32 x 15 x 29" **175.00**

Empire, NY, c1815, flip top, stenciled, acanthus carved legs, caster feet, veneer loss, 35½ x 18 x 28¾" ... **1,800.00**

George I, early 18th C, carved mahogany, hinged rect top, outset rounded corners, brown leather lined playing surface surrounded by wells and candle recesses, frieze drawer, lappet carved cabriole legs, pad feet, 39 x 29″ ... **3,100.00**

Handkerchief, Queen Anne, mahogany, 38¾ x 21 x 28″ **350.00**

Harvest, Sheraton, country, birch, oblong top, oblong drop leaves, turned legs, 85″ **3,000.00**

Hutch, American, late 19th C, hard pine, oval top, 59½ x 43¾ x 29″ **1,500.00**

Kitchen
  Hepplewhite, country, c1790–1800, southern pine, three plank top, six sq tapering legs, refinished, 34½ x 108 x 29″ **1,500.00**
  Pilgrim Century, late 17th or early 18th C, trestle, white pine, hinged top, large compartment beneath, double removable stretchers, hanging drawer or shelf under compartment, shown in Wallace Nutting's *Furniture of the Pilgrim Century*, 49 x 37½ x 30½″ **3,000.00**

Library
  Arts and Crafts
    Gustav Stickley, c1910, oak, oblong top, apron with two short drawers, hammered copper pulls, sq legs joined by medial shelf, branded mark, 42 x 30¾″ **1,870.00**
    Tobey Furniture Co, oak, cross lapped stretchers, key and tenon construction, 17¼ x 23½″ **200.00**
  Colonial Revival, Empire style, c1920, oak, pillar base, scrolled feet, 48 x 28 x 28″ **400.00**
  Federal, late, attributed to Duncan Phyfe NY, c1815, carved and brass inlaid mahogany, rect top, two shaped hinged leaves, single drawer frieze hung with turned pendants, hexagonal supports joined by ring turned and faceted medial stretcher, acanthus carved and reeded down curving feet, animal paw feet, brass casters, 48½ x 42 x 29½″ **12,000.00**
  George III, 19th C, carved mahogany, rect top, gilt dec brown leather writing surface, matching D-shaped flaps, central frieze drawer flanked by banks of double drawers, fluted stiles, tapering sq legs, brass casters, 75 x 30¾″ **4,500.00**
  Louis XVI, carved and gilt walnut, shaped top inset with white leather, leaf carved corner blocks, single drawer, reeded tapering legs, stretcher, 53 x 30 x 30″ **400.00**
  Regency, c1820, attributed to George

Bullock, Pollard oak, rect top, rounded corners, gilt tooled green leather inset writing surface, gadrooned edge, three frieze drawers on either side, lotus and berried sprig carved trestle supports with flowerhead carved terminals, leaftip carved feet on casters, 65 x 29½″ **85,000.00**

Marble Top, Eastlake, c1890, walnut, brown marble top, machine carvings, 15 x 20″ **300.00**

Table, Pembroke, Chippendale, carved mahogany, American, 38″ l, 27½″ h, $3,000.00.

Pembroke
  Colonial Revival, Hepplewhite style, Grand Rapids, c1940, plain cut mahogany veneer top and drop leaves, figured mahogany drawer front, solid base, medallion inlay, sq tapering legs, 15 x 22 x 17″ **75.00**
  Federal
    New England, probably CT, c1815, inlaid cherry, rect top, two shaped leaves, single drawer frieze, sq tapering legs, cross banded cuffs, 39 x 31½ x 23¼″ **2,350.00**
    Newport, RI, c1805, inlaid mahogany, oblong top, two D-shaped leaves, cockbeaded, bowed drawer, reverse faced to simulate working drawer, bookend inlaid dies flanking, line and bellflower inlaid sq tapering legs, cross banded cuffs, 38¼ x 33 x 27½″ **17,600.00**
  George III, late 18th C, mahogany
    Breakfast, hinged rect top, single drawer, lattice panels, platform stretcher, molded sq legs, orig leather-shod casters, 21¼ x 29″c **6,650.00**
    Hinged rect cross banded top, two

rect drop leaves, recessed frieze, full end drawer, straight tapered molded legs, X stretcher, 27 x 19½ x 28½″ **1,500.00**

Hepplewhite, c1790–1800, maple, two shaped hinged drop leaves, straight tapered legs, refinished, 36⅝ x 36¼ x 29″ **750.00**

Sewing

Empire, mahogany, drop leaf, two drawers, pedestal support, sgd "M S Boyer, Boston, MA," descended through family of Marshall Spring Boyer **250.00**

Sheraton, American, c1800, mahogany, drop leaves, two drawers, orig finish **475.00**

Tramp Art, American, late 19th C, "Mother" inscribed on hinged lid, bowlegs, shelf **850.00**

Side, Eastlake, third quarter 19th C, walnut, oval marble top, scrolled pedestal and legs, 19 x 26 x 30″ **250.00**

Table, tavern, Country, New England, 27¼ x 44 x 28½″, $1,500.00.

Tavern

Eastern New England, late 18th C, turned mahogany, oval top, molded skirt, vase turned splayed legs, box stretcher, vase formed feet, 36¼ x 29 x 26¾″ **3,300.00**

Queen Anne

New England, 18th C, porringer corners, splay leg, refinished, 30 x 21½ x 26″ **1,500.00**

Rhode Island, early to mid 18th C, maple, pine top, single large drawer, turned legs, molded stretchers, old refinishing, 34⅞ x 22½ x 26½″ **2,700.00**

Tea

Chippendale

American, c1875, walnut, tilt top, serpentine top, spiral carved urn, shell carved knees, claw and ball feet, 30½″ sq, 27″ h **9,000.00**

Connecticut Valley, mid 18th C, attributed to Eliphalet Chapin, cherry, birdcage supports shaped as miniatures of standard, orig oiled finished, slight restoration to one leg and base of standard, 36½″ d, 29½″h . . . **2,750.00**

New England, c1770, curly maple, tile top, circular top, baluster turned standard, three cabriole legs, snake feet, 31¾″ d, 28″ h . **2,500.00**

Philadelphia, c1770, mahogany, tilt top, circular dished top, tilts and revolves above birdcage support, compressed ball standard, cabriole legs, claw and ball feet, 34″ d, 29″ h **19,800.00**

Georgian, English, mid 19th C

Mahogany, oval tilt top, ring and baluster turned standard, downswept tripod feet, brass casters, 38 x 29 x 26¼″ **1,175.00**

Walnut, well formed, single drawer, 30¾ x 18¾ x 28½″ **2,400.00**

Queen Anne, CT, c1740, maple tray top, rect, orig finish, 29 x 20¼ x 23½″ **6,000.00**

Victorian, tilt top, papier mache, black lacquer, gilt dec, center MOP inlay floral dec, 28″ h **400.00**

Work

Biedermeier, 19th C, mahogany, three drawers **265.00**

Empire, country, curly maple, mahogany cross banding on three dovetailed drawers, stepped back top with two drawers, scrolled crest with carved rosettes on goosenecks, turned legs with relief carved tulips and oval medallions on posts, refinished, 30 x 23 x 43″ **1,300.00**

Federal

American, c1800, inlaid mahogany, oval top, line inlaid edge, well above oval case, line and dot inlaid sq tapering legs, X stretcher, 26 x 18½ x 30½″ **2,325.00**

Pennsylvania, 1790–1815, cherry, astragal end, deep compartment flanked by candle slides, conforming case, short drawer, sq tapering legs, 29¼ x 13 x 28″ . . . **1,250.00**

Hepplewhite

Butternut, removable top, two dovetailed overlapping drawers with int. dividers, mortised and pinned apron, sq tapered legs, old refinishing and repairs, 34 x 36 x 30″ **625.00**

Pine, two board scrubbed top, base with old dark paint, sq tapered legs 26½ x 48 x 28¾″ **300.00**

Shaker, New Lebanon Community,

early 19th C, painted birchwood and pine, rect top, rect splashboard, single molded drawer, circular tapering legs, orig red paint, 37½ x 23 x 25½" **8,900.00**
Sheraton, American, c1800, birch, single drawer, tapering ring turned legs **425.00**

TEA WAGONS

Black lacquer finish, raised Chinese figures, landscape, "D" shaped drop leaves, turned legs, support, two wheels **200.00**
Victorian, brass, glass top and shelf .. **700.00**
Wicker, serpentine edge, scrolled handle, removable glass serving tray top **325.00**

WAGON SEATS

Wagon seats cannot be classified with seats from a wagon. Early wagon seats were usually constructed with a double frame and a basketry-type seat. They served a dual purpose: in the house and in the family wagon for additional seating.

Hickory, spindle back and arms, leather basketweave seat, six legs, 18th C . **750.00**
Ladderback, two slat back, turned stiles, splint seat, red paint, 35" **575.00**
Spindle, two seater, turned arms, open back, five vertical turned spindles, double stretchers, red and green paint, 36" l **800.00**
Windsor
Pine, primitive, shoe feet, 30¾" l ... **500.00**
Walnut, one board seat, trestle feet, natural finish, 33 x 28½" **225.00**

WICKER

Bookcase, four oak shelves, turned wood frame, reed and wood fancy sunburst back, natural finish, c1890 . **500.00**
Carriage, serpentine edges, natural finish, orig velvet upholstery, c1890 ... **450.00**
Chair
Arm, Edwardian style, gentleman's chair, spiderweb caned circular top panel, curved lower back, natural finish, c1880 .... **575.00**
Arm, serpentine arms and back
Inverted triangle design woven in back, Heywood Brothers, painted, c1890 .... **400.00**
Mushroom shaped back splat, painted, c1890 .... **425.00**
Corner, elaborate scrolling, birdcage arms and supports, natural finish . **650.00**
High, shell design back, set in cane

seat, wooden footrest, turned wooden legs, natural finish, c1880 **275.00**
Side
Closely woven back panel with center scalloped design, closely woven shields over legs, Heywood Brothers and Wakefield Co, natural finish, c1890 ..... **350.00**
High back, cane wrapped squares, birdcage design on back and legs, horizontally woven reed seat **200.00**
Foot Stool, upholstered seat, painted, 16 x 11 x 21" **165.00**
Rocker, serpentine edges with braidwork, wooden rockers, painted white, Wakefield Rattan Co **225.00**
Settee, rect back, upholstered section on back and seat, woven arms, scalloped skirt **425.00**
Stand
Lamp, scrolled supports, circular wooden top and mid shelf, 16" d, 30½" h **200.00**
Music, three oak shelves, Wakefield Rattan Co paper label, 19 x 15 x 25", c1883 .... **265.00**
Sewing Basket
Bentwood handle, reed braidwork edges, two baskets, flared legs, natural finish, Wakefield Rattan Co, c1890 .... **250.00**
Hinged circular cov, spiderweb caned top basket, lower shelf open basket, three legs, natural finish, c1870 .... **300.00**
Table
Dining, round, repainted, 20" w, 27¼" h **150.00**
Library, oval, label Karpen Guaranteed Construction Furniture, 46 x 18 x 30" **300.00**

Wicker, stool, painted white, 13½ x 16½ x 12", $175.00.

YARN WINDERS

Floor Type, primitive, oak, mortised frame, two reels, one stationary, other adjustable, 51″ h **100.00**

Niddy Noddy, hickory, turned, mortised and pinned joints, 18″ **85.00**

Spoke Type

4 Spoke

Primitive, counter snap mechanism, 27″ reel, 41″ h **100.00**

Shaker, Sabbathday Lake, combination of hard and soft woods, sq nail construction, geared side counter needle, 26″ reel, 32″ h . **375.00**

Table model, chip carved base, turned standard, geared counter, one spoke folds back, old red paint, 24″ reel **75.00**

6 Spoke

Pine, maple, and bird's eye maple, counter bell, 16″ reel, 40″ h . . . **175.00**

Pine, primitive counter device, old finish, 26″ reel, 37″ h **250.00**

12 Spoke, pine, turned, wooden gear, 45″ h **175.00**

GAME PLATES

History: Game plates, popular between 1870 and 1915, are specially decorated plates used to serve fish and game. Sets originally included a platter, serving plates, and a sauce or gravy boat. Many sets have been divided. Today, individual plates are used for wall hangings.

Reference: Susan and Al Bagdade, *Warman's English & Continental Pottery & Porcelain, 1st Edition,* Warman Publishing Co., Inc., 1987.

BIRDS

Plate

8″, turkey and hunter **25.00**

Plate, 9½″ d, grouse, gilded edge, artist signed "Vitet," Limoges mark on back, $85.00.

8¾″, quail, hp, gilt edge, sgd "L S&S Limoges" **45.00**

9″, grouse, gold trim, Limoges, artist sgd "Comte de Artois" **85.00**

9¼″, wild geese, Buffalo Pottery, 1908 **60.00**

10½″, game bird and two water spaniels, crimped gold rim, sgd "RK Beck" **75.00**

12½″, flying game, hp, heavy gold, rococo border, Limoges, artist sgd "Rogin" **210.00**

13¼″, game bird and pheasant, heavy gold scalloped, emb rococo border, Coronet Limoges, sgd "Brussillon" **245.00**

Platter

14⅛ x 21″, pheasants, scalloped edge, heavy gold handles, pastel ground, artist sgd "Duc," unmarked French Limoges **450.00**

16″, quail, two handles, hp gold trim, Limoges, France **125.00**

Set, 13 pcs, 9″ plates, 12 and platter, each plate with different bird, scalloped gilt rim, white ground, mkd "Limoges" in green, sgd "A.L.," retailers mark in rust, late 19th C **400.00**

DEER

Plate, 9″, buck and doe, forest scene . **50.00**

Set

7 pcs, platter, 6 plates, Buffalo Pottery **300.00**

13 pcs, platter, 12 plates, deer, bear, and game birds, yellow ground, scalloped border, Haviland China, sgd "MC Haywood" **3,000.00**

ELK

Plate, 9″, two elk in natural setting, Buffalo Pottery **45.00**

FISH

Plate

7″, muskie jumping out of water, fluted edge, MZ Austria **40.00**

8″, bass, scalloped edge, gray-green trim, fern on side of fish, Limoges **50.00**

9″, bass, Lenox, sgd "Morley" **65.00**

9½″, trout, flowers, reeds, scalloped rim, heavy gold, blue, and red marks, Limoges, France, artist sgd "Roche" **75.00**

Platter, 14″, bass on lure, sgd "RK Beck" **90.00**

Set

12 pcs, 8¼″ naturalistic fish plates, gilt edge scallop on lower half, ruffled edge on upper, hp, made for

Pres. Rutherford B. Hayes by Haviland & Co, Limoges, c1880 ..... **2,750.00**
13 pcs, trout, gilt dec, Limoges, sgd "G. Saquel" **800.00**
14 pcs, platter, 12 plates, gravy boat, bass, blue beehive mark **250.00**
18 pcs, 9″ plates, each different fish scene, scalloped gilt rim, burgundy border, Rosenthal mark, sgd "Roberts" **800.00**

FOX

Plate, 13″, stalking quail, gold scalloped border, Limoges, artist sgd **350.00**

LION

Plate, 13″, green ground, gold trim, Haviland and Co **125.00**

GAMES, 1840-1940

History: Mass production of board games did not take place until after the Civil War. Firms like McLoughlin Brothers, Milton Bradley, and Selchow and Righter were active in the 1860s, followed by Parker Brothers, who began in 1883. Parker Brothers bought out the rights to the W. & S. B. Ives Co., who had produced some very early games in the 1840s, including the "first" American board game, The Mansion of Happiness. All except McLoughlin Brothers are giants in the game industry today.

McLoughlin Brothers's games are a challenge to find. Not only does the company no longer exist [Milton Bradley bought them out in 1920], but the lithography on their games was the best of its era. Most board games are collected because of the bright, colorful lithography on their box covers. In addition to spectacular covers, the large McLoughlin games often had lead playing pieces and fancy block spinners, thus making them even more desirable.

Common games like Anagrams, Authors, Jackstraws, Lotto, Tiddledy Winks, and Peter Coddles do not command high prices, nor do the games of Flinch, Pit, and Rook, which still are being published.

Games, with the exception of the common ones stated above, generally are rising in price. However, interesting to note is the fact that certain games dealing with good graphics on popular subject matter, e.g. trains, planes, baseball, Christmas and others, often bring higher prices because they are also sought by collectors in those particular fields.

Condition is everything when buying. Do not buy games that have been taped or that have price tags stickered on the face of their covers. Also, beware of buying games at outdoor flea markets

where weather elements can cause fading and warping.

References: R. C. Bell, *The Board Game Book,* The Knapp Press, 1979; Lee Dennis, *Warman's Antique American Games, 1840-1940,* Warman Publishing Co., 1986; Brian Love, *Great Board Games, 1895–1935,* Macmillan Publishing Co., 1979; Brian Love, *Play The Game: Over 40 Games From The Golden Age Of Board Games,* Reed Books, 1978.

Collectors' Club: American Game Collectors Association, P.O. Box 1179, Great Neck, NY 11023.

Museums: The Game Preserve, Peterborough, NH; Washington Dolls' House and Toy Museum, Washington, D.C.

Additional Listings: See *Warman's Americana & Collectibles* for games from the post 1940 period.

Advisors: Lee and Rally Dennis.

American Boys, A Game, Milton Bradley, boxed board game, c1920, 11½ x 16¼″, instructions on back of box cover, 7 round wooden counters ("scouts"), multicolored lithographed board pasted to box bottom, track game **175.00**
An Exciting Motor Boat Race, No. 112, American Toy Manf'g Co, boxed board game, 1925, 11½ x 9¼″, instructions on back of box cover, 4 colored wooden counters, multicolored lithographed board has spinner superimposed, track game **75.00**
A Visit To The Old Homestead, McLoughlin Bros, boxed board game, 1903, wooden box measuring 21½ x 13″, instructions on back of box cover, 19 pcs (spinner, 4 colored wooden tokens, 14 flat round wooden counters), multicolored lithographed board showing beautiful children's figures, track game **300.00**
Bottoms Up, The Embossing Company, © 1934, 6½ x 3″, instructions on back of box cover, pair of dice and 9 round domino-type counters with pigs' bottoms on their backs **15.00**
Cats and Mice, Gantlope, and Lost Diamond, McLoughlin Bros, c1890, 7½ x 14″, wooden "book" board game with slipcase, 3 different multicolored lithographed boards, instruction book, box of playing pieces including block spinner, 32 wooden counters of assorted shapes **120.00**
Colors, Game Of, McLoughlin Bros, boxed board game, c1888, 8 x 15½″, Gem Series, instructions on back of box cover, 23 pcs (spinner, red token, white token, 10 red counters, 10 white

counters), multicolored lithographed board, pooling game **95.00**

Columbia, E. I. Horsman, card game, 1885, 5¼ x 7¼", 52 cards, instruction sheet **35.00**

Comic Conversation Cards, J. Ottmann Lith Co, card game, c1905, 5 x 7", instruction sheet, numerous question and answer cards **40.00**

Glider Racing Game, Milton Bradley, boxed board game, 1930s, 14½ x 8¼", instructions printed on center of board, multicolored lithographed board pasted on box bottom, spinner, 4 round wooden colored counters, track game **40.00**

Glydor, #423, All-Fair, 1931, 15½ x 12½", instructions on back of box cover, multicolored lithographed board with attached spinner and 4 gliders, track game **45.00**

Jack Straws, Crandall (of Montrose, PA), skill game, c1869, covered wooden cylinder 6¼" h, 39 wooden paddle letters, 2 hooks, Anagram game as well **95.00**

Jolly Darkie Target Game, Milton Bradley, skill game, c1905, 8 x 15½", instructions on back of box cover, multicolored lithographed board on platformed box, 3 wooden balls, same picture on board, Black theme **200.00**

Leap For Life Game, Milton Bradley, boxed board game, 1930s, 8¼ x 14", instructions printed in center of board, 4 wooden counters and spinner, multicolored lithographed board **25.00**

Limited Mail And Express Game, Parker Brothers, boxed board game, © 1894, 21 x 14", wooden box, instructions on back of box cover, pack of route cards, 4 wooden colored counters, 4 colored flat metal train tokens, board is multicolored lithographed map of U.S. pasted on box bottom . **300.00**

Merry Goblins, The, Parker Brothers, card game, c1900, 3½ x 4½", instructions on back of box cover, 20 multicolored lithographed cards, played like "Old Maid" **15.00**

Militac, Parker Brothers, card game, 1910, 5½ x 4", 52 cards, instruction card, and advertising card, cards show photographs of pre-WWI NCOs, Officers, and weaponry, red backs state "Tactics-The Military Game" . . **35.00**

Neutral Game of War, Peace And Indemnity, The, Biddle Corp, card game, 1916, 7¼ x 4", 104 cards, instruction card, light green backs depicting swords and cannon **35.00**

New Game Of Red Riding Hood, The,

McLoughlin Bros, card game, c1888, 6¼ x 4½", 42 multicolored lithographed cards, instruction booklet . . **25.00**

New Premium Game of Logomachy, The, McLoughlin Bros, card game, 1887, 8½ x 6", wooden box, 56 multicolored lithographed alphabet cards with bird on backs, instruction booklet, invented by F. A. Wright in 1874 **25.00**

Ocean To Ocean Flight Game, Wilder Mfg Co, boxed board game, c1927, 7½ x 12¼", spinner and 6 counters, multicolored lithographed board of U.S. map, directions in lower left corner of board **65.00**

Owl And The Pussy Cat, The, E. O. Clark, Tokalon Series, boxed board game, c1890, 19¼ x 10½", wooden box, instructions on back of box cover, spinner with 4 wooden counters, multicolored lithographed board with turkey and pig **85.00**

Palmistry, manufacturer unknown, card game, c1910, 6 x 5", numerous pcs including 4 diagrams of human hand, instruction sheet, key sheet **40.00**

Parker Brothers Post Office Game, educational play acting game, c1910, 9 x 12", contains postman's mask, cancel stamp, sheets of stationery, envelopes, postcards, etc. **125.00**

Quartette Union War Game, E. G. Selchow, Civil War card game, 1874, 2½ x 3½", 48 cards, instruction card, cards black on white, involves battles and Union generals **45.00**

Round The World, Milton Bradley, boxed board game, c1912, 21¼ x 14¼", spinner with 4 round wooden counters, multicolored lithographed board with instructions printed on it, track game **195.00**

Rummy, manufacturer unknown, card game, c1910, 5½ x 7½", 48 cards, instruction sheet **12.00**

Setto, Game Of Syllables, Selchow and Righter, © 1882, 6 x 4", 51 black and white cards, 5 illustrated "prize" cards, instruction booklet, invented by Charles P. Goldey **25.00**

Ski-Hi New York To Paris, Cutler & Saleeby Co., #2117, boxed board game, c1927, 12½ x 7½", one die with 4 metal planes, multicolored lithographed board showing ocean, NYC, and Eiffel Tower, track game based on Lindbergh's crossing of the Atlantic **85.00**

Snake Eyes, Selchow & Righter, card game, c1930s, 11 x 7½", 185 pcs (120 cards, dice cup, 2 wooden dice, 62 chips), instructions on back of box cover, multicolored lithographed cards with "craps" expressions printed on them **55.00**

The Popular Game of Tiddledy Winks, Parker Brothers, Salem, MA, Salem Edition, 1897, $25.00.

Teddy Bear's Trip, J. Ottmann Lith Co, card game, c1910, 7¼ x 11¼", storybook, instructions on bottom of box cover together with legend of the storybook, numerous printed cards, played like Peter Coddles **28.00**

Telephone Game, The, J. H. Singer, card game, © 1898, 7½ x 6", numerous question and answer cards, 2 black wooden "receivers" connected to each other by a string **55.00**

Tiny Town Bank, The, Spear, boxed play acting game, c1910, 10½ x 7½", instructions on back of box cover, cardboard bank teller's front, 2 bank books, deposit slips, withdrawal slips, fake paper money and change **85.00**

Uncle Wiggily's New Airplane Game, Milton Bradley, board game with matching box of playing pieces, 1920s, instructions on back of box cover, numerous playing cards and counters, multicolored lithographed board opens to 16" sq, track game . **45.00**

Ups And Downs Of School Life, Spear, boxed board game, c1910, 12½ x 6½", instructions on back of box cover, 10 pcs (folding board, dice cup, 2 dice, 6 wooden counters), multicolored lithographed board featuring amusing pictures of school life **45.00**

When My Ship Comes In, Parker Brothers, card game, © 1888, 5¼ x 4", 84 non-illustrated cards, instruction sheet **25.00**

Wings, Parker Brothers, card game, © 1928, 5½ x 4", 99 cards, instruction booklet, card backs are pink and white picturing air mail planes **20.00**

Witch-ee, Selchow & Righter, boxed board game, c1930s, 6½" sq, instructions on back of box cover, chamois rubbing cloth and Witch-ee fortunes sheet, Halloween decor, multicolored lithographed deck of cards on box bottom with black witch tissue figure, game based on scientific principle of friction by rubbing **60.00**

X-Plor US, All-Fair, board game with matching box of pieces, c1922, 17½" sq, 4 metal airplanes and score pad, orange board has multicolored lithographed map of U.S. with instructions on bottom, track game **45.00**

Young Folks Historical Game, McLoughlin Bros, card game, c1890, 6¼ x 4½", 36 cards, instruction sheet .. **18.00**

Young Traveler, The, Josiah Adams, card game, 1846, 3½ x 2½", 52 cards, instruction card, title card, plain white backs, geographical game ... **75.00**

GAUDY DUTCH

History: Gaudy Dutch is an opaque, soft-paste ware made between 1790 and 1825 in England's Staffordshire district. Most pieces are unmarked; marks of various potters, including the impressed marks of Riley and Wood, have been found on pieces.

The pieces first were hand decorated in an underglaze blue, fired, and then received additional decoration over the glaze. Many pieces today have the over glaze decoration extensively worn. Gaudy Dutch found a ready market within the Pennsylvania German coummunity because it was inexpensive and intense with color. It had little appeal in England.

Reference: Eleanor and Edward Fox, *Gaudy Dutch*, published by author, 1970, out-of-print.

Reproduction Alert: Cup plates, bearing the impressed mark "CYBRIS," have been reproduced and are collectible in their own right. The Henry Ford Museum has issued pieces in the single rose pattern, although they are of porcelain and not soft-paste.

Advisor: John D. Querry.

Butterfly
  Creamer **875.00**
  Cup Plate **750.00**
  Plate, 8" **975.00**
  Tea Bowl and Saucer **800.00**
Carnation
  Coffeepot **1,575.00**
  Cup Plate **550.00**
  Creamer **675.00**
  Plate, 8½" **575.00**

Soup Plate, 8½″ 675.00
Sugar Bowl 775.00
Tea Bowl and Saucer 625.00
Dahlia
  Creamer 850.00
  Plate, 8⅜″ 875.00
  Sugar Bowl 950.00
Double Rose
  Creamer 550.00
  Cup Plate 675.00
  Plate, 8¾″ 675.00
  Tea Bowl and Saucer 475.00
  Toddy Plate 525.00
  Waste Bowl 675.00

Saucer, 5⅝″ d, Dove pattern, $275.00.

Dove
  Creamer 675.00
  Plate, 9¾″ 750.00
  Toddy Plate 675.00
  Tea Bowl and Saucer 650.00
  Teapot 975.00
  Waste Bowl 675.00
Grape
  Creamer 425.00
  Cup Plate 575.00
  Plate
    6⅜″ 350.00
    8½″ 375.00
    9¾″ 425.00
  Platter, 15″ 875.00
  Soup, 8¾″ 425.00
  Teapot 650.00
  Toddy Plate 325.00
  Waste Bowl 375.00
Leaf
  Bowl, 8¾″, unusual shape 975.00
  Tea Bowl and Saucer 775.00
Oyster
  Creamer 375.00
  Plate
    6⅜″ 375.00

8½″ 450.00
9¾″ 475.00
Tea Bowl and Saucer 375.00
Teapot 475.00
Toddy Plate 350.00
Waste Bowl 325.00
Primrose
  Plate, 8¾″, imp Riley 525.00
  Sugar Bowl 850.00
  Tea Bowl and Saucer 675.00
  Waste Bowl 725.00
Single Rose
  Creamer 350.00
  Cup Plate 375.00
  Plate
    6⅜″ 275.00
    8½″ 275.00
    9½″ 325.00
  Soup Plate 350.00
  Sugar, cov 625.00
  Tea Bowl and Saucer 275.00
  Teapot 750.00
  Waste Bowl 275.00
Strawflower
  Plate
    8½″ 625.00
    9¼″ 675.00
  Soup Plate 750.00
Sunflower
  Plate
    6½″ 625.00
    8¼″ 625.00
Urn
  Creamer 325.00
  Cup Plate 400.00
  Plate
    6½″ 325.00
    8¼″ 350.00
    9¾″ 425.00
  Soup Plate, 8⅞″ 475.00
  Tea Bowl and Saucer 350.00
  Teapot 575.00
  Toddy Plate 350.00
  Waste Bowl 375.00
War Bonnet
  Coffeepot, riveted repairs 850.00
  Creamer 575.00
  Cup Plate 625.00
  Plate
    6⅜″ 575.00
    8¼″ 675.00
  Soup Plate 675.00
  Tea Bowl and Saucer 575.00
  Teapot 1,050.00
  Toddy Plate 575.00
  Waste Bowl 650.00
Zinnia
  Plate
    6⅜″ 550.00
    8½″ 575.00
No Name, plate, 8½″ 375.00

GAUDY IRONSTONE

History: Gaudy Ironstone was made in England around 1850. Most pieces are impressed "Ironstone" and bear a registry mark. Ironstone is an opaque, heavy body earthenware which contains large proportions of flint and slag. Gaudy Ironstone is decorated in patterns and colors similar to Gaudy Welsh.

Plate, 8½", impressed mark on back "Pearl White," $75.00.

Biscuit Jar, brass bail handle and lid . .	90.00
Butter Dish, 3¼", octagonal, Seaweed pattern, three color, luster dec, orig insert	85.00
Coffeepot, 10⅜", octagonal, copper luster pinwheel design, minor glaze wear on tip of spout	125.00
Creamer, 5", Morning Glory pattern, underglaze blue and luster	65.00
Cup and Saucer, handleless	
Seaweed, underglaze blue and luster, red and green enamel	48.00
Strawberry, four color, luster dec . . .	65.00
Mug, 3", underglaze blue stripes, luster, and red wavy lines	25.00
Pitcher, 9⅝", Vintage pattern	175.00
Plate	
8½", Seaweed pattern, three color, luster dec	50.00
9⅝", Strawberry, minor stains	35.00
10", floral dec, marked "Davenport, Stone China"	85.00
Platter	
14¼", Berry pattern, Niagara shape, marked "E Walley"	75.00
15", columbine, rosebud, and thistle dec, stick spatter rim	235.00
Soup Bowl, 7⅝", three chrysanthemums, copper luster dec, blue, wide rim	95.00
Sugar, cov, 4⅞", Urn of Flowers pattern, underglaze blue and luster, red and green enamel, emb lion head handles	75.00

Tea Set, Morning Glory, 9¼" cov teapot, 6¼" creamer, 8¼" cov sugar, minor wear	350.00
Waste Bowl, 8¼", Berry pattern	65.00

GAUDY WELSH

History: Gaudy Welsh is a translucent porcelain that was originally made in the Swansea area of England from 1830 to 1845. Although the designs resemble Gaudy Dutch, the body texture and weight differ. One of the characteristics is the gold lustre on top of the glaze.

In 1890, Allerton made a similar ware. These wares are heavier opaque porcelain and usually bear the export mark.

Reference: Howard Y. Williams, *Gaudy Welsh China,* Wallace-Homestead.

Columbine	
Cup and Saucer	35.00
Plate, 8¼"	30.00
Daisy and Chain	
Creamer	75.00
Sugar, cov	125.00
Teapot, cov	165.00
Feather	
Cake Plate	45.00
Cup and Saucer	40.00

Creamer, 5" h, Flower Basket, $85.00.

Flower Basket (also known as Urn or Vase)	
Creamer	85.00
Cup and Saucer, handleless	65.00
Dinner Service, 16 dinner plates, 28 luncheon plates, 8 ovoid salad plates, 4 graduated platters, 56 pcs	1,500.00
Plate, 8½"	45.00
Sugar, cov	85.00

Grape

Creamer, 4″	35.00
Cup and Saucer, handleless	75.00

Morning Glory

Compote, 10¼″ d, 5¼″ h	225.00
Creamer	85.00
Cup and Saucer	50.00
Pitcher, 6½″, Allerton, c1890	75.00
Plate, 8″	70.00
Platter, 14½″	135.00
Tea Set, teapot, creamer, sugar, six cups and saucers	750.00
Vegetable Bowl, round	75.00

Oyster

Bowl, 6¼″	50.00
Creamer, 3½″	45.00
Cup and Saucer	65.00
Jug, 4½″	70.00
Pitcher, 5½″	95.00
Plate, 6″	40.00

Shanghai

Creamer	90.00
Plate, 5½″	75.00

Strawberry

Creamer	90.00
Mug, 4⅛″	125.00
Plate, 8½″	75.00
Spill Holder, 4¾″ h	100.00
Teapot, cov	165.00

Tulip

Condiment Set, England	85.00
Cup and Saucer	50.00
Dish, serving, 9″	40.00
Pitcher, milk	110.00
Plate, 6″	30.00
Teapot, 8½″	135.00
Waste Bowl, 6¾″ d	50.00

Wagon Wheel

Cup and Saucer	65.00
Mug, 2¾″	50.00
Pitcher, 8″	175.00
Plate	
7½″	50.00
8¼″	65.00

GEISHA GIRL PORCELAIN

History: Geisha Girl porcelain is a Japanese export ware whose production commenced during the last quarter of the 19th century and continued heavily until WWII. The ware features kimono-clad Japanese ladies and children amidst Japanese gardens and temples. There are over 125 brightly colored scenes depicting the pre-modern Japanese lifestyle. Over 140 marks and almost 200 patterns and variations have been identified on pieces.

Geisha Girl ware may be totally hand painted, hand painted over a stenciled design, or occasionally decaled. The stenciled underlying design is usually red-orange, but also is found in brown, black, and green (rare).

All Geisha Girl items are bordered by one or a combination of blues, reds, greens, rhubarb, yellow, black, browns, or gold. The most common is red-orange. Borders may be wavy, scalloped, or banded and range from ¹⁄₁₆″ to ¼″. The borders themselves often are further decorated with gold, white or yellow lacings, flowers, dots, or stripes. Some examples even display interior frames of butterflies or flowers.

Geisha Girl is found in many forms including tea, cocoa, lunch, and children's sets, dresser items, vases, serving dishes, etc. Large plates or platters, candlesticks, miniatures, and mugs are hardest to locate. Geisha Girl advertising items add to a collection.

Reference: Elyce Litts, *The Collectors Encyclopedia Of Geisha Girl Porcelain,* Collector Books, 1988.

Periodical: The Geisha Girl Porcelain Newsletter, P.O. Box 394, Morris Plains, NJ 07950. Subscription: $12.00.

Additional Listings: See *Warman's Americana & Collectibles* for more examples.

Reproduction Alert: Geisha Girl porcelain's popularity continued after WWII and it is being reproduced today. Chief reproduction characteristics are a red-orange border, very white and smooth porcelain, and sparse coloring and detail. Reproduced items include dresser, tea and sake sets, toothpick holders, small vases, table plates, and salt and pepper shakers.

Advisor: Elyce D. Litts.

Jug, 5½″, Parasol B, melon ribbed, red-orange with apple green and gold circles, $45.00.

Berry Set, 5 pc, master, four individual, Lady in Rickshaw, blue with gold . . .	65.00
Biscuit Jar, 6½″, Flower Gathering B, red and gold	45.00
Bon Bon Dish, Bamboo Trellis, red and gold	45.00
Bouillon Cup and Saucer, lid, brown and gold, Rivers Edge	38.00

Bowl

6", nut, nine lobed, three feet, Basket A, dark apple green **30.00**

6½", lobed, red, gold lacing, Flag . . **23.00**

9½", octagon shape, Geisha in Sampan E, red-orange, gold buds, Nippon **43.00**

Children's Dishes

Celery Set, child's, 6 pc, master, 5 salts, Flower Gathering A, pine green, Made in Japan **40.00**

Tea Set, teapot, creamer, sugar, Court Lady, hp wholly, red **65.00**

Cup and Saucer

After dinner, Parasol B, red-orange, gold buds, celadon ground, Japan **25.00**

Tea

Geisha in Sampan A, maroon, Made in Japan **9.00**

Kite A, brown and gold **11.00**

Dresser tray, Flower Gathering A, pine green, Made in Japan **35.00**

Hair Receiver

Round, fluted rim, Spider Puppet, blue and gold, marked **40.00**

Square, Geisha in Sampan, red, marked "t't' Japan" **18.00**

Nut Cup, pedestal, fluted, Parasol, red, Made in Japan **11.00**

Olive Dish, 7", oval, Mother and Son C, red-orange, Kutani **25.00**

Pitcher, toy, 3⅜ x 1¾", cylindrical slenderizing towards top, almost indistinguishable pouring lip, Parasol B, red, Japan **15.00**

Plate

6", Chinese Coin **15.00**

8½", Geisha in Sampan A, brown and gold **25.00**

Sake Cup, Garden Bench B, red rim . **6.00**

Salt and Pepper Shaker

Bulbous, Visiting with Baby, individual, blue and gold **20.00**

Square, Pointing, pine green **18.00**

Salt

Fluted, handled, To the Teahouse, red, Kutani **20.00**

Pedestaled, Temple A, floral and turquoise border, marked **25.00**

Stein, 7 12/", Chrysanthemum Garden, red, gold buds, marked "Japan" ... **100.00**

Sugar Bowl, Flower Gathering B, green, gold lacing **15.00**

Vase, 4", Flower Gathering B, money bag shape, feet, red rim **35.00**

GIRANDOLES AND MANTEL LUSTRES

History: A girandole is a highly elaborate branched candleholder, often featuring cut glass prisms surrounding the mountings. A mantel lustre is a glass vase with attached cut glass prisms.

Girandoles and mantel lustres usually are found in pairs. It is not uncommon for girandoles to be part of a large garniture set. Girandoles and mantel lustres achieved their greatest popularity in the last half of the 19th century both in the United States and Europe.

GIRANDOLES, pr

14", SP and cut glass, three tiers hung with faceted drops, scrolled candle arms, c1900 .... **150.00**

15", Victorian, pink, enameled and colored wild flowers, notched prisms .. **275.00**

16", two branch, cut glass, regency ormolu, bell shaped sockets, bobeches hung with beads, stepped oval base **1,000.00**

18", oval base, ormolu mounted, gilt brass foliage, porcelain flowers, maroon parrots, oriental birds as girandoles, electrified **350.00**

27", gilt bronze and cut glass, scrolling candle arms, faceted glass beads and pendant ropes electrified, French, early 20th C **850.00**

35½", bronze, glass, seven light, glass drops suspended from pressed glass stars **500.00**

Mantel Lusters, 14″ h, painted floral dec, pale green ground, gold trim, $400.00.

MANTEL LUSTRES

10", ruby, overlay with white and gilt foliage, faceted cut glass prisms, c1875 **400.00**

10½", green, cut to crystal, ten cut glass prisms **285.00**

12", opalene, green fold over top, white satin glass bodies, gold trim **225.00**

14", double cut overlay, white to emerald green, prisms of alternating lengths **250.00**

15¾″, Bohemian, cobalt blue, gilt scroll-work dec, colored floral sprigs, two rows of clear prisms, late 19th C ... **325.00**

18¾″, white cased, gilted lustres, flaring scalloped rims with line borders, painted figural scenes, overall gilted scrollwork, circular bases **300.00**

GLASS, EARLY AMERICAN

History: Early American glass covers glass made in America from the colonial period through the mid-19th century. As such it includes the early pressed glass and lacy glass made between 1827 and 1840.

Major glass producing centers prior to 1850 were Massachusetts with the New England Glass Company and the Boston and Sandwich Glass Company, South Jersey, Pennsylvania with Stiegel's Manheim factory and Pittsburgh, and Ohio with Kent, Mantua, and Zanesville.

Early American glass was collected heavily during the 1920 to 1950 period. It now is regaining some of its earlier popularity. In April, 1984, Garth's sold the Jim and Eileen Courtney Early American Glass Collection, a major landmark sale. The trend continued with Bourne's three part William J. Elsholz collection in 1987. Leading sources for the sale of early American glass are the mail auctions of David and Linda Arman and the sales of Richard A. Bourne, Early Auction Company, Garth's, and Skinners.

References: William E. Covill, *Ink Bottles and Inkwells*, 1971; Lowell Inness, *Pittsburgh Glass: 1797–1891*, Houghton Mifflin Company, 1976; George and Helen McKearin, *American Glass*, Crown, 1975; George and Helen McKearin, *Two Hundred Years of American Blown Glass*, Doubleday and Company, 1950; Helen McKearin and Kenneth Wilson, *American Bottles And Flasks*, Crown, 1978; Adeline Pepper, *Glass Gaffers Of New Jersey*, Scribners, 1971; Jane S. Spillman, *American And European Pressed Glass*, Corning Museum of Glass, 1981; Kenneth Wilson, *New England Glass And Glassmaking*, Crowell, 1972.

Additional Listings: Blown Three Mold, Cup Plates, Flasks, Sandwich Glass, and Stiegel Type Glass.

Amelung (New Bremen Glass)
Flask, 4¼″, clear, ⅜ pint, checkered diamond, pattern blown molded, ex William J Elsholz collection **1,450.00**
Salt, deep cobalt blue, pattern blown molded and expanded checkered diamond design, applied circular foot, c18th C, McKearin Plate 2, No 6, ex William J Elsholz collection . **2,000.00**
Bakewell
Lamp, fluid, 11¾″ h, clear, blown pear shaped font cut in typical Pittsburgh pattern, large bulbous knops, heavy pressed ftd base, pewter collar, pr, ex William J Elsholz collection **900.00**
Windowpane, 6⅞′ x 4⅞″, clear, church, gothic arch design, sgd "Bakewell" on reverse, Innes Fig 303-2, ex William J Elsholz collection **2,000.00**
Curlings and Robertson, windowpane, 7 x 5″, clear, lacy, Lee Plate 160, ex William J Elsholz and John Grossman collections **9,000.00**

Celery Vase, Boston and Sandwich, $500.00.

Engraved
Celery Vase, 5⅛″ d, 8½″ h; clear, elaborate pattern of festoons, small flowers, and leaf band, twenty gadrooned ribs, applied foot with knob stem, early 19th C, slight crazing . **225.00**
Rummer, 5¼″, clear, blown, engraved designs with fox, chickens, and cattails on rim, spool shaped stem, applied foot, ex Trier collection **90.00**
Wine, 5⅛″ h, clear, blown, Pittsburgh type engraved foliage, tapered stem and bowl, applied foot, ex Trier collection **50.00**
Keene (Marlboro Street) Glass Works
Bottle, 8½″, deep olive green, barrel shape, quart, McKearin GII-7, ex William J Elsholz collection **1,750.00**
Inkwell, 2½″ d, olive-amber, blown three mold, McKearin GIII-29, ex Corning Museum of Glass collection **125.00**
Lockport
Cordial, 2⁹⁄₁₆″, aqua, blown, ex William J Elsholz and George S McKearin collections **650.00**
Creamer, 4⅞″ h, blue, free blown, solid applied handle and foot,

folded rim, wide flaring mouth, pontil **600.00**

Vase, 3½" d, 7⅛" h, blue, free blown, three part vase, flared mouth, round base set onto solid baluster stem, thick solid circular foot, 5¼" d witch ball cov **600.00**

Mantua

Bottle, 8⅜" h, aqua, blown, club shape, 32 ribs, broken swirl, terminal ring, ex Jim and Eileen Courtney collection **350.00**

Flask, 4⅛", chestnut, amber, 16 vertical ribs, terminal ring, attributed to Mantua or Kent, ex Jim and Eileen Courtney collection **300.00**

Pan, 5½" d, 1½" h, brilliant aqua, blown, 15 diamond, folded in rim, ex Jim and Eileen Courtney collection, minor flakes at pontil **3,850.00**

Midwestern

Bowl, 5⅝" d, 3⅞" h, cobalt blue, lacy period, ftd, c1830, one moderate chip under rim, small rim chips and roughage, ex William J Elsholz and James H Rose collections **900.00**

Candlestick

7⅛", clear, free blown sockets, lacy hairpin pattern base, pr, ex William J Elsholz collection **5,250.00**

7½", clear, blown molded, bulbous socket, band of panels around lower half, lacy hairpin pattern base, three bull's eyes chipped **750.00**

Sugar, cov, clear, lacy, Peacock Feather pattern, one foot scallop chipped **500.00**

Mt Vernon Glass Co

Decanter, pint, McKearin GIII-2, Type 1, period diamond pattern stoppers, pr **1,050.00**

Lamp, fluid, 6⁷⁄₁₆", clear, blown three mold, cylindrical font, patterned from half pint decanter mold, mounted with wafer to heavy pressed base of two lion's paws on stepped and scalloped flat oval base, ex William J Elsholz and George S McKearin collections .. **1,200.00**

Pitcher, 7¼", light aquamarine, blown three mold, quart, McKearin GIII-2, Type 1, ex William J Elsholz, George S McKearin, and Crawford Wettlaufer collections **7,500.00**

New Jersey, South

Creamer, 5⅞" h, cobalt blue, applied crimped foot and solid curled handle, tooled rim, ex Gest, Rolfing, and Gotjen collections, int. spall on side of spout **650.00**

Miniature

Candlestick, 2¼" h, light green,

blown, double ball knop stem above flat circular foot, McKearin Plate 28, No 11, ex William J Elsholz and George S McKearin collections **1,000.00**

Compote, 2" d, 1⅞" h, brilliant green, circular, straight sides, hollow knop stem, applied circular foot, McKearin Plate 75, No 20, ex William J Elsholz and George S McKearin collections . **400.00**

Creamer, 1⅜", aquamarine, free blown, baluster shaped bowl, applied circular flat foot, applied solid ear shaped handle, lower end turned back, ex William J Elsholz collection **500.00**

Demijohn, 2³⁄₁₆", aqua, blown, globular body, narrow neck, folded rim, applied ear shaped handle, crimped circular applied foot, folded rim ground flat above handle, ex William J Elsholz and George S McKearin collections . **300.00**

Pitcher, 2⅝", pale aquamarine, threaded neck, applied circular foot, applied handle crimped at base, blown ball cover, McKearin Plate 75, No 10, ex William J Elsholz and George S McKearin collections **1,000.00**

Pitcher

6⅜" h, emerald green, lily pad dec, applied circular foot, tooled, flared mouth, solid handle, attributed to Matt Johnson, ex Gotjen collection, trace of stain in bottom **4,100.00**

7⅝", aquamarine, opaque white loopings, double ribbed applied handle crimped at base, tooled lip, heavy circular applied foot . **650.00**

New York

Compote, 8¼" d, tilted 4 to 4¾" h, bluish-aqua, applied lily pad dec, wide folded rim, heavy applied base, ex McKearin, Wiedeman and Gotjen collections **1,200.00**

Plate, 6⅝" d, ¾" h, cobalt blue, blown, attributed to Lancaster, flake at pontil, ex Jim and Eileen Courtney collection **65.00**

Pittsburgh

Bowl, 5¾" d, 2⁵⁄₁₆" h, sapphire, pattern molded in 12 rib mold, expanded into wide vertical ribbing, outfolded upper rim, circular applied foot, ex William J Elsholz collection **1,900.00**

Candlestick

9", olive green, blown socket with bulbous base, pr, ex William J Elsholz and James H Rose collections **1,700.00**

9³⁄₁₆″, brilliant deep amethyst, hexagonal socket and stem, circular foot, large mold underfill on socket rim **1,000.00**

Compote, cov, 6½″ d, 7″ h, lacy, Hairpin pattern, two large rim chips, two bull's eyes on foot chipped, ex William J Elsholz collection **2,400.00**

Creamer
4½″, deep sapphire blue, applied solid handle, heavy crimped end, McKearin Plate 52, No 3, ex William J Elsholz collection **1,300.00**

5⅛″, opalescent blue, 8 rib pillar molded, short circular stem, circular foot, applied handle, ex William J Elsholz and Crawford Wettlaufer collections **4,500.00**

Inkwell, 5½″, clear, free blown, egg shaped body, two reservoirs, applied rounded well, small cup for seals, short knop stem, circular foot, nine applied rosettes, ex William J Elsholz and George S McKearin collections **1,000.00**

Plate
5¹⁵⁄₁₆″ d, octagonal, clear, lacy, steamboat, Lee 170-3, minute roughage on upper rim, ex William J Elsholz and James H Rose collections **1,800.00**

6⅛″ d, octagonal, clear, lacy, Constitution "Union," Lee 170-4, small rim flakes, light roughage, ex William J Elsholz and James H Rose collections **1,300.00**

Sugar, cov
4¼″ d, 5½″ d cov, 8″ h, moonstone, blown glass pattern, 24 rib broken swirl pattern, Ohio, c1815–25, ex William J Elsholz collection **8,500.00**

7¼″, deep sapphire blue, patterned in 12 rib mold and expanded, foot not pattern molded, McKearin Plate 52, No 2, ex William J Elsholz collection **2,500.00**

Redwood or Redford Glass Works, NY
Bowl, 14″ d, 5⁷⁄₁₆ to 5⅞″ h, brilliant aquamarine, wide flaring rim, heavy out folded edge, applied circular foot, superimposed lily pad dec, similar to McKearin Plate 15, c1831–50, ex William J Elsholz and Crawford Wettlaufer collections . . **4,000.00**

Compote, 9″ d, 4½″ h, brilliant aquamarine, blown, circular bowl flaring to wide out folding rim, short cylindrical stem, circular stepped foot, superimposed gather of lily pad dec, ex William J Elsholz and Crawford Wettlaufer collections . . **9,000.00**

Miniature
Bowl, 2¹¹⁄₁₆″ d, 1⁹⁄₁₆″ h, brilliant bluish-aqua, free blown, curving sides flaring out at top to small torus molding, inward folded rim, applied free blown crimped foot, ex William J Elsholz collection . **450.00**

Pitcher, 1½″, bluish aqua, smoky spirals of green, free blown, barrel shape, high collared neck, tiny folded rim, flat base, applied strong blue ear shaped handle, ex William J Elsholz collection . **400.00**

Pitcher, 10¼″, light aquamarine, free blown, globular body, broad cylindrical neck with fine wide spaced applied threading extending to slightly flaring rim, tiny pinched lip, applied ear shaped aquamarine handle, applied circular foot, superimposed gather tooled swooping lily pad dec, McKearin Plate 20, No 8, ex William J Elsholz and Crawford Wettlaufer collections **19,000.00**

Vase, 4¾″, free blown, brilliant aquamarine, urn form, two applied miniature like handles, ex William J Elsholz and Crawford Wettlaufer collections **700.00**

Saratoga, NY
Creamer, 4″ h, olive-green, yellow tones, applied solid handle and foot, attributed to Morris Holmes . **575.00**

Miniature, pitcher, 1¹³⁄₁₆″, deep green, blown, applied handle crimped at base, McKearin Plate 69, No 3, ex William J Elsholz and George S McKearin collections **700.00**

Sugar, cov, 4½″ d, 3⅛″ h, olive-green, yellow tones, wide folded rim, applied solid foot, attributed to Morris Holmes **550.00**

South Boston
Decanter, 9″, clear, free blown, two bands of chain dec around bodies and two around necks, period stoppers, pr, ex William J Elsholz collection **700.00**

Sugar, cov, 5⅞″ h, clear, free blown, galleried rim, one band of applied chain dec on base and one on cover, ex William J Elsholz collection **3,250.00**

Stourbridge Flint Glass Works, salt, dark blue, lacy, Innes Color Plate 6, tiny flakes, ex William J Elsholz collection **900.00**

Union Glass Works
Cup Plate
Lee-Rose 99, deep amethyst **650.00**
Lee-Rose 227-B, deep green, dark

triangular spot on shoulder, uneven narrow smoky stream around shoulder, small rim nick, light roughage **1,700.00**
Lee-Rose 227-C, deep green, one small rim chip **1,900.00**

Wheeling
Compote, 7¼" d, 4¼" h, octagonal, Oak Leaf pattern, bull's eye rim, Roman Rosette pattern base, two shallow rim flakes, ex William J Elsholz collection **1,000.00**
Windowpane, 7 x 5", clear, portrait of steamboat in center with name "J & C Ritchie" above, c1833, ex William J Elsholz and James H Rose collections **5,000.00**
Whitney Works, Glassboro, NJ, pitcher, 6¹⁵⁄₁₆", medium sapphire blue, free blown, horizontal threading around neck, folded rim, small pinched lip, heavy circular applied foot, solid applied handle crimped at lower end, Joel Duffield, South Jersey c1835–40, McKearin Plate 60, No 6, ex William J Elsholz collection **1,300.00**

Zanesville, OH
Bottle, 6", chestnut, pint, aqua, blown, 24 ribs, broken swirl, ex Jim and Eileen Courtney collection **125.00**
Bowl, 8½" d, 3¾" h, amber, blown, folded rim, minor broken blisters, ex Jim and Eileen Courtney collection **450.00**
Flip, 4⅛" d, 4⅝" h, blue-green, 24 ribs, broken swirl to left **350.00**
Pan, 6⅝" d, light green, blown, faint impression of 24 ribs, folded rim, ex George S McKearin and Jim and Eileen Courtney collections **250.00**
Sugar, cov, 7⁹⁄₁₆", dark amber, patterned in 24 rib mold extended in vertical ribbing and slightly swirled at rim of bowl and lid, attributed White Glass Works, c1815–25, ex William J Elsholz collection **13,500.00**

GONDER POTTERY

History: Lawton Gonder established Gonder Ceramic Arts, Inc., at Zanesville, Ohio, in 1941. He gained experience while working for other factories in the area. Gonder experimented with glazes, including Chinese crackle, gold crackle, and flambe. Lamp bases were manufactured under the name Eglee at a second plant location.

Gonder pieces are clearly marked. The company ceased operation in 1957.

Vase, 6½" h, greenish blue glaze, $6.50.

Basket, 6½" h, ext. turqouise, int. pink coral, leaf pattern, marked "H-39 Gonder USA" **30.00**
Bowl
6½", ribbed, blue and pink **8.50**
7", melon shape, turquoise ext., pink int., imp "E-12/Gonder/USA" **15.00**
Candlestick, pr, 4¾", ext. turquoise, int. pink coral, marked "E-14, Gonder . . **18.00**
Cornucopia, 7¼", brown and pink **15.00**
Creamer and Sugar, dark brown drip and brown spatter **24.00**
Ewer, 13", Shell and Star, green **50.00**
Figure
Elephant, 10½", trunk raised, rose and gray **40.00**
Swan, 7", shaded blue **12.00**
Vase, 9¼", handles, mottled pink and gray-blue, marked "#H5" **10.00**

GOOFUS GLASS

History: Goofus glass, also known as Mexican Ware, Hooligan glass, and Pickle glass, is a pressed glass with relief designs. The back or front was painted. The designs are usually in red and green with a metallic gold ground. It was popular from 1890 to 1920 and was used as a premium at carnivals.

It was produced by several companies: Cresent Glass Company, Wellsburg, West Virginia; Imperial Glass Corporation, Bellaire, Ohio; LaBelle Glass Works, Bridgeport, Ohio; and Northwood Glass Co., Indiana, Pennsylvania, Wheeling, West Virginia, and Bridgeport, Ohio. Northwood marks include "N," "N" in one circle, "N" in two circles, and one or two circles without the "N."

Goofus glass lost its popularity when people found the paint tarnished or scaled off after repeated washings and wear. No record of its manufacture has been found after 1920.

Reference: Carolyn McKinley, *Goofus Glass,* Collector Books, 1984.

Additional Listings: See *Warman's Americana & Collectibles* for more examples.

MARK

W H GOSS

GOSS CHINA AND CRESTED WARE

History: In 1858 William H. Goss opened his Henley factory and produced terra cotta ware. A year later he moved to Stoke-on-Trent and added Parian ware to his line. In 1883 Adolphus, William's son, expanded on his father's idea of decorating small ivory pots and vases, with the coat of arms of schools, hospitals, colleges [especially Oxford and Cambridge], and other motifs to appeal to the souvenir seeking English "day-tripper." The forms used were copied from ancient artifacts in museums.

William died in 1906, his son in 1913. Following business setbacks, the firm was sold in 1929 to Geo. Jones & Sons Ltd., who had previously acquired Arcadian, Swan, and other firms that made crested wares. As late as 1931 the Goss name was still being used. In 1936–37 Cauldon Potteries purchased the Goss assets. Production ceased in 1940. In 1954 Ridgeway and Adderley acquired all Goss assets [molds, patterns, designs, and right to use the Goss name and trademark].

From 1883 to 1931 pieces carry the mark of GOSHAWK, with W. H. Goss beneath, and "England" on later pieces. Many early examples carry an impressed "W. H. Goss," either with or without the printed mark.

Other manufacturers of crested ware in England were: Arcadian, Carlton China, Grafton China, Savoy China, Shelley, and Willow Art. Gemma in Germany also made crested wares.

Crests are of little value unless they match, e.g., Shakespeare's jug with Shakespeare's crest. Collectors tend to collect one form (vase, ewer, jug, etc.), one particular crest, or one type of object (boat, cat, dog, etc.). Price is determined not by crest, but size, condition, and bottom mark.

References: Sandy Andrews, *Crested China: The History of Heraldic Souvenir Ware,* Milestone Publications [England]; John Galpin, *A Handbook Of Goss China,* Milestone Publications; Nicholas Pine, *The 1984 Price Guide To Goss China,* Milestone Publications, 1984; Nicholas Pine and Sandy Andrews, *The 1984 Price Guide To Crested China* (including revisions to *Crested China*), Milestone Publications; Roland Ward, *The Price Guide To The Models Of W. H. Goss,* Antiques Collectors' Club.

Collectors' Clubs: The Goss Collectors Club, 3 Carr Hill Gardens, Barrowford, Nelson, Lanca-

Plate, 8¼", Old Rose Distilling Co., Chicago, $75.00.

Basket, 5", strawberry	45.00
Bowl	
7½", iris, red dec	15.00
9"	
Cherries, red dec, gold ground	20.00
Floral Plumes	18.00
10", pears and apples	30.00
Cake Plate, 11", Dahlia and Fan, red dec, gold ground	32.00
Coaster, 3", Floral, red dec, gold ground	10.00
Compote, 9½", strawberries and leaves, red and green dec, gold ground, ruffled	45.00
Jewel Box, 4 x 2", basketweave, rose	40.00
Lamp, 17", Gone With The Wind, poppies and leaves, red dec, gold ground	165.00
Pitcher, red rose bud, gold leaves	45.00
Plate	
7½", apples, red dec, gold ground	18.00
10½", Floral Star, red dec, gold ground	18.00
Platter, 18", rose, red dec, gold ground	65.00
Powder Jar, basketweave, rose	45.00
Salt and Pepper Shakers, Poppy, 3", pr	32.50
Syrup, Strawberry	32.50
Tumbler, 6", rose, red dec, gold ground	25.00
Vase	
5¾", Cabbage Rose, red flowers, green leaves, gold ground	30.00
7¼", Grapes	25.00
13", flared rim, love birds, flowers and leaves, red and green, gold ground	25.00

shire BB9 6PU; The Crested Circle, 26 Urswick Road, Dagenham, Essex RM9 6EA.
Advisor: Mildred Fishman.

Goss, vase, 2⅝″, No. 382437, model of Roman vase found at Walmar Lodge, $25.00.

GOSS

Bottle
Canterbury, leather	20.00
Sunderland	25.00
Waterlooville Army Water	45.00
Bust, parian, Dickens, 8″	150.00
Creamer, Yarmouth	25.00
Can, Welsh Mills	20.00
Carafe, Goodwin Sands	19.00

Ewer
Chichester, Roman, Beaulieu Abbey	20.00
Japan, Windsor	35.00
Jug, Spanish, Eddyston	30.00
Lamp, Hamworthy, Reigate Poole	30.00
Night Light, Manx Cottage	200.00
Nogen, Irish, wood	22.00

Pitcher
Cambridge	18.00
Leiston, Abbey	22.00
Pot, Roman, Painswick	20.00
Salt, Glastonbury, Wickford	30.00

Urn
Laxey, Huntington	28.00
Tewkesbury Saxon, Lizard	24.00
Vase, pineapple	25.00

OTHER CRESTED WARE MANUFACTURERS

Arcadian
Ewer, Wembley, handled	20.00
Statue, Cinotaph, small	25.00
Toby Jug, Wantage	30.00

Carlton
Bank, bell shape	20.00
Pot, handled, lid	25.00

Coronet
Cottage, Tony Panda	25.00
Pot, Arms of Weymouth, two handles, three legs	15.00

Gemma
Cup, Aberystwyth	18.00
Helmet	30.00

Shelley
Common market Harbarcuth	30.00
Luggage, Portugal, #53	30.00
Rose Bowl, stafford, silver, #147	35.00
Urn, #118, Roman, Chester	25.00
Victoria, Cheshire Cat, matching crest	25.00

Willow Art
Anvil, Saltash	25.00
Shakespeare Cottage	150.00

GOUDA POTTERY

History: Gouda and the surrounding areas of Holland have been one of the principal Dutch pottery centers for centuries. Originally the potteries produced a simple utilitarian Delft type earthenware with a tin glaze and the famous clay smokers' pipes.

When the pipe making portion declined in the early 1900s, the Gouda potteries turned to art pottery. Influenced by the Art Nouveau and Art Deco movements, artists expressed themselves with free form and stylized designs in bold colors.

Reference: Susan and Al Bagdade, *Warman's English & Continental Pottery & Porcelain, 1st Edition,* Warman Publishing Co., Inc., 1987.

Reproduction Alert: With the Art Nouveau and Art Deco revivals of recent years, modern reproductions of Gouda pottery currently are on the market. They are difficult to distinguish from the originals.

Basket, Art Deco, black ext.	100.00

Bowl
6″, cov, floral dec, Anjer mark	65.00
6½″, multicolored floral dec, two handles, Pelta mark	75.00

Candlestick
4⅛ x 7⅛″, Spino pattern, yellow flowers and green leaves, black ground, satin finish, Art Deco, house mark, pr	165.00

Vase, 10½″ h, white Phoenix, black ground, marked "388/IA/Goedewaagen/AB Distel, Gouda, Holland," $300.00.

5 x 2¾″, black, brown, gold, red, and blue Art Deco designs, house mark **85.00**
7¼″, trumpet shaped base, house mark **90.00**
Compote, 6½″, rust, green, blue, and black, house mark **75.00**
Creamer, Verona pattern **35.00**
Decanter, 11″, matching stopper, 13 x 10″ underplate, Art Deco dec, black, matte finish, sgd "Emanuel" **275.00**
Ewer
  4½″, bulbous, handle, black ground, multicolored floral dec **75.00**
  6½″, cobalt, rust, bright yellow design, marked "2960" **115.00**
Inkwell, attached undertray, Kelat house mark **150.00**
Jar
  3¼″ x 4½″, cov, scenic windmills, houses, and boats, multicolored, glossy finish **65.00**
  5¼″, black ground, blue handles, red and light green bands, marked .. **85.00**
Jardiniere, Art Nouveau dec, russet, royal blue, and mustard yellow, black ground **90.00**
Lantern, 6″, Art Nouveau dec, Plazuid House mark **115.00**
Match Holder, 2¼ x 2⅛″, red, blue, gold and black Art Deco designs, satin finish, striker on base **50.00**
Pitcher
  5″, multicolored, Metz Royal mark .. **48.00**
  6½″, Irene pattern, tulip dec **60.00**
Planter, 5 x 7″, Art Nouveau, Royal Zuid mark, 1917 .... **90.00**
Potpourri Jar, 4″, multicolored flowers . **75.00**
Tobacco Jar, cov
  5″, Verona pattern **80.00**

5½″, tan, blue, and green dec, matte finish, house mark **150.00**
Vase
  4″, dahila dec, Royal Soedewahsen mark **42.00**
  6″, multicolored pansies dec, Plazuid house mark **65.00**
  7″, stick type, multicolored, high glaze, Arnhem mark, c1900 ..... **125.00**
  8 x 7¼″, Massa RR, green, cobalt blue, light blue, orange, house mark **135.00**
  8⅛ x 4¾″, Art Deco dec, royal blue, black, gold, red, green, and brown, satin finish, school house mark .. **85.00**
Wall Pocket, 11½″, burnt orange and rust **100.00**

GRANITEWARE

History: Graniteware is the name commonly given to iron or steel kitchenware covered with enamel coating.

The first graniteware was made in Germany in the 1830s. Graniteware was not produced in the United States until the 1860s. At the start of World War I, when European manufacturers turned to the making of war weapons, American producers took over the market.

Colors commonly marketed were white and gray. Each company made their own special color, including shades of blue, green, brown, violet, cream, and red.

Older graniteware is heavier than new graniteware. Pieces with cast iron handles date from 1870 to 1890; wood handles date from 1900 to 1910. Other dating clues are seams, wood knobs, and tin lids.

References: Vernagene Vogelzang and Evelyn Welch, *Granite Ware, Collector's Guide With Prices,* Wallace-Homestead, 1981; Vernagene Vogelzang and Evelyn Welch, *Granite Ware, Book II,* Wallace-Homestead, 1987.

Reproduction Alert: Graniteware still is manufactured in many of the traditional forms and colors.

Additional Listings: See *Warman's Americana & Collectibles* for more examples.

Bean Pot, gray **14.00**
Bed Pan, 14 x 16″, gray, lid **70.00**
Berry Bucket, cov, medium blue **47.50**
Bucket, 9 x 11, gray, iron bail, wood handle **27.50**
Candlestick, gray, mottled **65.00**
Colander, gray mottle **25.00**
Coffee Boiler
  Chuckwagon, 10 qt, white with black, metal bail handle, wood hand grip **18.00**
  Gray **20.00**

Coffeepot, gray, $75.00.

Gray, large	35.00
White	15.00
Coffeepot, white, large	28.00
Cup and Saucer, white, blue trim	14.00
Desk Phone, 1940s	14.00
Flask, gray, no lid	70.00
Funnel, dark blue	25.00
Handkerchief Box, pretty lady on top	8.00
Kettle, 12½″ w, gray, iron bail, wood handle	22.00
Ladle, strainer, light blue	12.00
Lunch Pail, 3 pc, dark blue, white specks, wood bail handle	40.00
Measure	
Pint, gray	25.00
Quart, gray, emb "For Household Use Only"	37.00
Milk Pan	
Crystolite green, swirl	
Large	25.00
Medium	32.00
Small	32.00
Turquoise, swirl	25.00
Miniature Egg Poacher, cov, gray, speckled	90.00
Mold, gray, scalloped	20.00
Muffin Pan	
Eight swirled holes, gray	17.50
Twelve hole, bundt shape, gray	35.50
Mustard Pot, 3½″ h, white, cov, matching 4½″ l ladle	78.00
Percolator, white, ftd, Foval glass dome	32.50
Pie Pan, Crystolite green, swirl	16.00
Plate	
8½″, gray, mottled	12.00
9″, cobalt and white	14.00
Pot, blue swirl	28.00
Roaster	
Cobalt blue, swirl	67.00
Iris blue	87.00
Sugar Shaker, brown, mottled	95.00
Tea Kettle, blue, gooseneck	55.00
Wash Bowl, gray mottle, orig label and price tag	35.00

GREENAWAY, KATE K.G.

History: Kate Greenaway, or "K.G." as she initialed her famous drawings, was born in 1846 in London. Her father was a prominent wood engraver. Kate's natural talent for drawing soon was evident, and she began art classes at the age of 12. In 1868 she had her first public exhibition.

Her talents were used primarily in illustrating. She did cards for Marcus Ward, which are largely unsigned. China and pottery companies soon had her drawings of children appearing on many of their wares. By the 1880s she was one of the foremost children's book illustrators in England.

Reproduction Alert: Some Greenaway buttons have been reproduced in Europe and sold in the United States.

Almanac, 1884, published by George Routledge & Sons, $85.00.

Almanac	
1887, published by George Routledge & Sons	55.00
1925	35.00
Baby Feeding Dish, 4¼″, children playing	70.00
Book	
Little Ann, Kate Greenaway, 1883	75.00
Marigold Garden, illus and ryhmes by Kate Greenaway, Frederick Warne & Co, 56 pgs	30.00
Under The Window, Kate Greenaway, Frederick Warne, London	45.00
Box, 5 x 2 x 3″, boy and girl, Staffordshire	100.00
Button, ¾″, girl with kitten on fence	10.00
Cup and Saucer, girl doing laundry in wooden tub	35.00
Dish, 11″, oval, Jack Sprat and Sunbonnet girl dec	50.00

Figure

    4 x 8½", boy with basket, satin, gold, pink, and blue trim, marked "1893"   **525.00**

    9", girl with tambourine beside tree, marked "Royal Worcester"   **400.00**

Hat, bisque, three girls sitting on brim, flowers **90.00**

Inkwell, bronze, two children, emb ... **200.00**

Jewelry Box, wooden, stenciled children on front **45.00**

Match Safe, pocket, SP, children, emb   **50.00**

Mug, 2½", pink, children playing **60.00**

Napkin Ring, SS

    Boy holding books **165.00**

    Girl feeding yearling **150.00**

Paint Book, 7½ x 9½", "Greenaway Pictures To Paint," sepia tone pictures to paint with instructions **45.00**

Perfume Bottle, 2" l, SS, girls in low relief, orig stopper **200.00**

Pin Tray, children playing seesaw **65.00**

Plate

    5", two girls playing ball **60.00**

    7", boy chasing rabbits **65.00**

Salt and Pepper Shakers, boy and girl in baskets, pr **85.00**

Stickpin, figural, bronze, children playing ring around the rosy, c1900 .... **25.00**

Tape Measure, figural, girl holding muff **45.00**

Teaspoon, SS, figural, girl handle, bowl engraved with Lucy Locket verse .. **50.00**

Toothpick Holder, 4", bisque, boy beside tree stump **60.00**

Vase, 8", children playing with hoops and dancing **125.00**

Whistle, 3", porcelain, girl playing, cream ground **50.00**

GREENTOWN GLASS

History: The Indiana Tumbler and Goblet Co., Greentown, Indiana, produced its first clear, pressed glass table and bar wares in late 1894. Initial success led to a doubling of plant size in 1895 and other subsequent expansions, one in 1897 to allow for the manufacture of colored glass. In 1899 the firm joined the combine known as the National Glass Company.

In 1900, just before arriving in Greentown, Jacob Rosenthal developed an opaque brown glass, called "chocolate," which ranged in color from a dark, rich chocolate to a lighter "cream" coffee hue. Production of chocolate glass saved the financially pressed Indiana Tumbler and Goblet Works. The Cactus and Leaf Bracket patterns were made almost exclusively in chocolate glass. Other popular chocolate patterns are Austrian, Dewey, Shuttle, and Teardrop and Tassel. In 1902 National Glass Company bought Rosenthal's chocolate glass formula so other plants in the combine could use the color.

In 1902 Rosenthal developed the Golden Agate and Rose Agate colors. All work ceased on June 13, 1903, when a fire of suspicious origin destroyed the Indiana Tumbler and Goblet Company Works.

After the fire, other companies, e.g., McKee and Brothers, produced chocolate glass in the same pattern design used in Greentown. Later reproductions also have taken place, with Cactus among the most heavily copied pattern.

References: Brenda Measell and James Measell, *A Guide To Reproductions of Greentown Glass,* 2nd ed., The Printing Press, 1974; James Measell, *Greentown Glass, The Indiana Tumbler & Goblet Co.,* Grand Rapids Public Museum, 1979.

Collectors' Club: National Greentown Glass Association, 1807 West Madison, Kokomo, IN 56901. Dues: $4.00. *N.G.G.A. Newsletter,* quarterly.

Museums: Greentown Glass Museum, Greentown, IN; Grand Rapids Public Museum [Ruth Herrick Greentown Glass Collection], MI.

Additional Listings: Holly Amber and Pattern Glass.

Chocolate, cov sweetmeat, Cactus pattern, $550.00.

Animal Dish, cov

    Hen, Nile green **1,000.00**

    Rabbit, amber **140.00**

Bowl

    Cactus, chocolate, 7¼" **125.00**

    Herringbone Buttress, green, 7¼" .. **130.00**

Butter, cov

    Cactus, chocolate **175.00**

    Cupid, chocolate **575.00**

    Herringbone Buttress, green **200.00**

Celery Vase, Beaded Panel, clear ... **90.00**

Compote

    Geneva, 4½" d, 3½" h, chocolate .. **145.00**

    Robin on Nest, milk glass **200.00**

Cookie Jar, Cactus, chocolate **250.00**

Cordial, Austrian, canary **125.00**

Creamer
Cactus, chocolate	70.00
Cupid, Nile green	400.00
Indian Head, opaque white	450.00
Shuttle, tankard, clear	35.00

Cruet, orig stopper
Beaded Panel	175.00
Dewey, vaseline	135.00
Leaf Bracket, chocolate	200.00

Goblet
Overall Lattice	36.00
Shuttle, chocolate	500.00

Mug
Elf, green	75.00
Herringbone Buttress	65.00
Overall Lattice	40.00

Mustard, cov, Daisy, opaque white	75.00
Nappy, Masonic, chocolate	85.00
Novelty, hairbrush, clear	55.00
Paperweight, buffalo, Nile green	600.00

Pitcher, water
Fleur-De-Lis, clear	80.00
Teardrop and Tassel, cobalt blue	175.00

Plate, Serenade, milk glass	40.00

Punch Cup
Cord Drapery	18.00
Shuttle, chocolate	75.00

Relish, Leaf Bracket, 8 x 5", oval, chocolate	75.00
Salt Shaker, Leaf Bracket	85.00
Sauce, Cactus, chocolate, ftd	48.00

Sugar, cov
Cupid, opaque white	100.00
Dewey, cobalt blue	125.00

Toothpick
Dog's head, clear and frosted	125.00
Sheaf of Wheat, Nile green	315.00

Tumbler
Beehive, chocolate	350.00
Cactus, chocolate	55.00
Dewey, canary	60.00
Indoor Drinking Scene, chocolate	375.00

Vase, 6", Austrian, Nile green	325.00
Water Set, Brazen Shield, pitcher, six tumblers, blue, 7 pcs	450.00

GRUEBY POTTERY

History: William Grueby was active in the ceramic industry for several years before he developed his own method of producing matte glazed pottery and founded the Grueby Faience Company in Boston, Massachusetts, in 1897.

The art pottery was hand thrown in natural shapes, hand molded, and hand tooled. A variety of colored glazes, singly or in combinations, were produced with green being the most prominent. In 1908 the firm was divided into the Grueby Pottery Company and the Grueby Faience and Tile Co., the latter making art pottery until bankruptcy forced closure shortly after 1908.

References: Paul Evans, *Art Pottery of the United States,* Everybodys Press, Inc., 1974; Ralph and Terry Kovel, *The Kovels' Collector's Guide to American Art Pottery,* Crown Publishers, Inc., 1974.

Tile, 6¼ x 6", white horses, green earth, blue ground, $500.00.

Bowl, 4½", blue drip, green ground, rolled rim, c1905	125.00
Paperweight, 2 x 2¾", scarab, blue, imp "Faience Lotus" mark	250.00

Tile
3¾", hexagonal, deer and tree, four colors	125.00
6", cellist, mustard dec, red ground	175.00
6", grape cluster, four colors	175.00

Vase
3", bud, long thin neck, bulbous base, light beige, imp mark, orig label	100.00
5", stick neck, bulbous base, mauve, die mark	275.00
7", teardrop shape, green, imp mark, orig label	175.00
9½", bulbous base, vertical relief leaves, green	550.00
13½", prominent turnings, green glaze, lime green underglaze	600.00

HAIR ORNAMENTS

History: Hair ornaments, one of the first accessories developed by primitive man, were used to remove tangles and keep hair out of one's face. Remnants of early combs have been found in many archeological excavations.

As fashion styles changed through the centuries, hair ornaments kept pace through design and use changes. Hair combs and other hair ornaments are made in a wide variety of materials, e.g., precious metals, ivory, tortoise shell, plastics, and wood.

Combs were first made in America during the Revolution when imports from England were restricted. Early American combs were made of horn and treasured as valued toiletry articles.

Reference: Evelyn Haetig, *Antique Combs and Purses,* Gallery Graphics Press, 1983.

Comb, 5 x 4¼", bakelite, olive with black strips, applied red and blue plastic ovals with center scarab beetle, punched line work on edge of fan, $50.00.

Back Comb, Art Nouveau, tortoise, gilt
  brass and turquoise glass accents . . **125.00**
Barrette, jet glass, cut and faceted,
  c1890 . . . . **25.00**
Comb
  Art Nouveau, French ivory, paste
    stones, decorative, c1910 . . . . . . **45.00**
  Ivory, Oriental, Victorian, c1860 . . . . **145.00**
Hairpin
  Art Nouveau, heavy tortoise shell,
    carved poppy blossom **135.00**
  Tortoise, 14K gold piercework, Vic-
    torain, c1870 . . . . **125.00**
Ornament
  4½", plastic, simulated stones, c1935 **65.00**
  4¾", rhinestones, simulated pearls,
    c1925 . . . . **45.00**

Ornamental Comb, 7¼ x 6", Art Nou-
  veau, plastic piercework, imitation
  blue stones **75.00**
Pompadour Comb
  Art Nouveau, faux tortoise, gilt brass
    and turquoise glass accents, pr . . **75.00**
  Tortoise, English, pique work, paste
    stones, Victorian, c1890 . . . . **135.00**

HALL CHINA COMPANY

History: Robert Hall founded the Hall China Company in 1903 in East Liverpool, Ohio. He died in 1904 and was succeeded by his son, Robert Taggart Hall. After years of experimentation, Robert T. Hall developed a leadless glaze in 1911, opening the way for production of glazed household products.

The Hall China Company made many types of kitchenware, refrigerator sets, and dinnerware in a wide variety of patterns. Some patterns were exclusive, such as Heather Rose for Sears.

One of the most popular patterns was Autumn Leaf, an exclusive premium designed in 1933 for the Jewel Tea Company by Arden Richards. Still a Jewel Tea property, Autumn Leaf has not been listed in catalogs since 1978 but, is produced on a replacement basis with the date stamped on the back.

References: Jo Cunningham, *The Autumn Leaf Story,* Haf-A-Productions, 1976; Jo Cunningham, *The Collectors Encyclopedia of American Dinnerware,* Collector Books, 1982; Jo Cunningham, *Hall China Price Update,* Haf-A-Productions, 1982; Harvey Duke, *Superior Quality Hall China,* published by author, 1977; Harvey Duke, *Hall 2,* published by author, 1985; Margaret and Kenn Whitmyer, *The Collector's Guide To Hall China,* Collector Books, 1985.

Collector's Club: National Autumn Leaf Collectors Club, Box 45, Fowler, IL 62338. Dues: $15.00.

Additional Listings: See *Warman's Americana & Collectibles* for more examples plus a separate section on Autumn Leaf.

Teapot, blue ground, gold trim, $27.50.

MISCELLANEOUS

Bowl, cov, 7" d, blue, Westinghouse ..	25.00
Cookie Jar	20.00
Pitcher, large, lip, red	30.00
Roaster, cov, canary, Westinghouse ..	20.00
Water Server, cov, blue, Westinghouse	45.00

PATTERNS

Autumn Leaf. Premium for Jewel Tea Co. Produced from 1933 until 1978.

Butter, ¼ pound, wings	300.00
Cake Plate	15.00
Clock, electric	345.00
Coffee Server, 8¼"	30.00
Coffeepot, 8½"	55.00
Jug, ball	22.00
Mixing Bowl, 3 pc	38.00
Pitcher, 6"	16.50
Plate, 7¼"	4.00
Platter, 13½"	15.00
Range Shakers and dripping jar, set ..	30.00
Sifter, metal	140.00
Vase	90.00
Vegetable, oval	17.00

Heather Rose. Produced during the 1940s.

Bowl, oval	8.00
Coffeepot, "Terrace"	30.00
Fruit Dish, 5¼"	3.00
Platter, 15½"	14.00
Pitcher	12.00

Orange Poppy. Premium for Great American Tea Co. Produced from 1933 through 1950s.

Bean Pot	55.00
Drip Jar, cov	17.00
Jug, ball	34.00
Salad Bowl	13.00
Teapot, Boston	75.00

Rose Parade. Kitchenware line introduced in the 1940s.

Baker, french	15.00
Bean Pot, tab handle	40.00
Bowl, 7½", straight-sided #4	14.00
Drip Jar, tab handle	18.00
Jug, 7½", "Pert"	25.00

Springtime. Premium for Standard Tea Co. Limited production.

Ball jug, #3	27.00
Batter Bowl, Chinese red	47.00
Bowl	
6", cereal	6.00
9", round	14.00

Casserole, thick rim	25.00
Drip Coffee	75.00
Gravy Boat	18.00
Jug, Radiance, #6	25.00
Plate, 8¼"	4.00
Platter, 14"	9.00
Soup, flat	9.00

TEAPOTS

Aladdin, black and gold	30.00
Birdcage, maroon	40.00
Doughnut, ivory	125.00
Globe, dripless, cadet and gold	175.00
Los Angeles, brown and gold	35.00
Nautilus, yellow, 6 cup	65.00
Philadelphia, pink, gold label	35.00
Plume, pink	20.00
T-Ball, cobalt, made for Bachrach	75.00
Windcrest, yellow	55.00

HAMPSHIRE POTTERY

History: In 1871 James S. Taft founded the Hampshire Pottery Company in Keene, New Hampshire. Production began with redwares and stonewares, followed by majolica decorated wares in 1879. A semi-porcelain, with the recognizable matte glazes plus the Royal Worcester glaze, was introduced in 1883.

Until World War I the factory made an extensive line of utilitarian and art wares including souvenir items. After the war the firm resumed operations, but only made hotel dinnerware and tiles. The company dissolved in 1923.

Reference: Joan Pappas and A. Harold Kendall, *Hampshire Pottery Manufactured by J. S. Taft & Company, Keene, New Hampshire,* published by author, 1971.

Vase, 4¼" h, dark blue glaze, imp mark, $175.00.

Bowl

5 x 2½", green swastika dec 35.00

5½ x 2½", green, molded floral dec,
matte finish 75.00

Chamberstick, 7", hood, handle 60.00

Chocolate Pot, 11", emb floral dec, cobalt glaze, matte finish, marked 135.00

Compote, 13¼", ftd, two handles, Ivy
pattern, cream ground, light green
highlights, red decal mark 140.00

Inkwell, 4⅛ x 2¾", round, large center
hole for ink, three holes for pens,
marked 75.00

Lamp, fluid, 6½", green, marked 60.00

Shaving Mug, scuttle, blue glazed,
molded ferns, gold dec 65.00

Tankard, 8¼", imp abstract floral dec,
green, matte finish, imp "Hampshire" 140.00

Vase

4", figural, avocado, green, matte finish 35.00

6", opalescent green glaze, raised
petal motif, marked "M" in circle . 80.00

6 x 3", squat, leaves, green matte
glaze 70.00

7", tulip buds and broad leaves, green
glaze 75.00

7½", thick textured blue glaze,
marked 180.00

8½", high relief crocus dec, green,
matte finish, marked 150.00

HAND PAINTED CHINA

History: Hand painting on china began in the Victorian era and remained popular through the 1920s. It was considered an accomplished art form for women in the upper and upper middle class households. It developed first in England, but spread rapidly to the Continent and America.

China factories in Europe, America, and the Orient made the blanks. Belleek, Haviland, Limoges, and Rosenthal are among the European firms. American firms include A. H. Hews Co., Cambridge, Massachusetts; Willetts Mfg. Co., Trenton, New Jersey; and Knowles, Taylor and Knowles, East Liverpool, Ohio. Nippon blanks from Japan were used heavily during the early 20th century.

The quality and design of the blank is a key factor in pricing. Some blanks were very elaborate. Many pieces were signed and dated by the artist.

Aesthetics is critical. Value is added to a piece when a decorator goes beyond the standard forms and creates a unique and pleasing design.

Bread and Butter Plate, pink flowers,
gold rim 70.00

Compote, 8⅞" d, 5½" h, shallow, pink
roses, green leaves, artist sgd, dated
1907 .... 125.00

Candlesticks, 8¼" h, white owls, gold stripes, blue ground, painted by M. Hooker in 1914, $95.00.

Cup and Saucer, floral, marked "Clai-
ron" Ohme, Silesia, c1870 ...... 35.00

Demitasse Cup and Saucer, white,
roses and gold, Ahrenfeldt, Limoges 30.00

Egg, 3" l, halved, porcelain 17.50

Jug, 5¾", green and purple grapes,
green leaves, gold trim 90.00

Milk Pitcher, 7" h, white, porcelain, basketweave, yellow flowers, green leaf
handle 17.50

Plate

9⅜" d, cavalier and lady scene,
D.L.R.L. Limoges, France, artist
sgd 100.00

10", light green, peaches, gold border,
Ginori 40.00

Platter, 23½", yellow roses, green
leaves, gold trim, artist sgd, Haviland 240.00

Sugar Shaker, 3½" d, 4½" h, blue and
white, pink roses, green leaves, gold
top and feet 45.00

Teapot, 5", purple violets, green leaves,
gold trim, Lenox 125.00

Tray, 8⅝" l, floral dec, two handles, L.
Haviland, France, sgd 55.00

Trinket Box, 4½ x 3½ x 1½", yellow,
porcelain, couple and woodland setting, marked "JBH #121815, France" 75.00

Vase

Belleek, 11¼", white chrysanthemums, green foliage, yellow and
maroon ground, artist C. Bathurst 400.00

Noritake, flowers, all-over gold, fancy 125.00

HATPINS AND HATPIN HOLDERS

History: When the vogue for oversized hats developed around 1850, hatpins became popular.

Designers used a variety of materials to decorate the pin ends, including china, crystal, enamel, gem stones, precious metals, and shells. Decorative subjects ranged from commemorative designs to insects.

Hatpin holders are porcelain containers which set on a dresser to hold these pins. The holders were produced by major manufacturers, among which were Meissen, Nippon, R. S. Germany, R. S. Prussia, and Wedgwood.

Reference: Lillian Baker, *Handbook for Hatpins & Hatpin Holders,* Collector Books, 1983.

Collector's Club: International Club for Collectors of Hatpins and Hatpin Holders, 15237 Chanera Avenue, Gardena, CA, 90249. Dues: $24.00.

Museum: Los Angeles Art Museum, Costume Dept., Los Angeles, CA

Left: **pear shaped, amber glass, brass filigree base, $7.50; right: bronzed, red stone surrounding imitation diamond center, $8.00.**

HATPINS

Amethyst, SS overlay	45.00
Art Deco, enameled mercury glass sliding shank	75.00
Art Nouveau, SS, plique-a-jour, two baroque pearls	385.00
Carnival Glass, butterfly, green irid	75.00
Crystal, prism shape, 8" steel pin	15.00
Elk's Tooth, gold findings	75.00
Gold Filled, reticulated sides, engraved applied top, 9⅛"	18.00
Mercury Glass, cased elongated teardrop	70.00
Mosaic, 1" d, multicolored flowers on brass button mount	60.00
Quartz, rose, teardrop shape, gold fitting	35.00
Rhinestone studded, 1½" d	25.00
Satsuma, flower, gold trim	60.00
Silver	
Plated, tennis racquet	25.00
Sterling, thistle, hallmarked	85.00
Tortoise Shell, butterfly	90.00

HATPIN HOLDERS

China
Austrian, 5", hp blue forget-me-nots, marked	35.00
Bavarian, portrait of two boys eating fruit, gold ground, marked	50.00
Belleek, gold leaves, tiny blue flowers, red Willets mark	100.00
Germany, pink flowers, green luster, marked	20.00
Handpainted	
4", violets, gold trim and beading	75.00
4½", figure "8" tray, attached hatpin holder, ring tree, purple violets on white ground	50.00
Jasperware, 5¼" h, lilac, Art Nouveau blown out woman's face, elaborate hair style, gold trim	125.00
Nippon, bisque, scenic, large sailing ship	85.00
Royal Bayreuth, rose tapestry, three colored roses, blue mark	350.00
Schlegelmilch, 4¾", scalloped base, roses, luster finish, red mark "R. S. Prussia"	215.00
Schafer & Vater, 5¾", bisque, purple, jewels, raised cameo head	145.00

China, 5" h, violets on blue-green ground, marked "BT Co./Japan," $75.00.

Glass
Bristol, 6½", ftd, multicolored jewels, blue ground, brass fittings	100.00
Carnival, Grape and Cable, purple	175.00
Silver	
Plated, sphinx dec	35.00
Sterling, hockey stick center	75.00

HAVILAND CHINA

History: In 1842, American china importer David Haviland moved to Limoges, France, where he began manufacturing and decorating china specifically for the US market. Haviland is synonymous with fine, white, translucent porcelain although early hand painted patterns were generally larger and darker colored on heavier whiteware blanks than are later ones.

David revolutionized French china factories by both manufacturing the whiteware blank and decorating it at the same site. In addition, Haviland and Company pioneered the use of decals in decorating china.

David's sons, Charles Edward and Theodore split the company in 1892. Theodore opened an American division in 1936 which continues until today. In 1941 Theodore bought out Charles Edward's heirs and recombined both companies under the original name H and Co. The Haviland family sold its interests in 1981.

Charles Field Haviland, cousin of Charles Edward and Theodore, worked for, and then ran, the Casseaux Works after his marriage in 1857 until 1882. Items continued to carry his name as decorator mark until 1941.

Haviland patterns were not consistently named until after 1926. Pattern identification is difficult because of the similarity found in the over 66,000 patterns that have been made. Numbers assigned by Arlene Schleiger and illustrated in her books have become the identification standard for matching.

References: Mary Frank Gaston, *Haviland Collectibles & Art Objects*, Collector Books, 1984; Arlene Schleiger, *Two Hundred Patterns of Haviland China, Books I-V*, published by author, 1950–1977; Serry Wood, *Haviland-Limoges, China Classics II*, Century House, 1951; Harriet Young, *Grandmother's Haviland*, Wallace-Homestead, 1970.

Advisor: Peg Harrison.

Gravy Boat, 8″ l, matching underplate, small pink and blue floral, red "Theodore Haviland, Limoges, France" mark, $42.00.

Bone Dish	
Greek Key, "Albany," H and Co	**20.00**
Pansy, Ragged Robin, gray and pink, 1885 mark	**25.00**
Bouillon Cup and Saucer, blue bows, pink flowers, Theo. Hav.	**27.50**
Bowl	
5″, fruit, "Ranson," white, H and Co .	**10.00**
6″, oatmeal, scalloped edge with gold	**18.00**
7½″, soup, "Troy," blue scroll, pink flower border	**16.00**
Butter Dish	
Silver Anniversary pattern, 3 pc, H and Co	**60.00**
Gold Band, 2 pc, Theo. Hav.	**45.00**
Butter Pat, sq, rounded corners, gold trim	**10.00**
Celery Dish, scalloped edge, green flowers, pale pink scroll	**45.00**
Cream Soup and Saucer, scroll border in cranberry and blue	**30.00**
Creamer and Sugar	
Gold Band, 1930s, Theo. Hav.	**45.00**
Scalloped, small pink flowers, gold trim	**65.00**
Cup and Saucer	
Coffee, scalloped gold edge, deep pink flowers	**30.00**
Tea, small blue flowers, green leaves	**25.00**
Demitasse Cup and Saucer, 1885 ...	**30.00**
Dinner Set	
Gold Band, 77 pcs, service for 12, Theo. Hav.	**1,195.00**
Pink flowered, 55 pcs, service for 8, H and Co	**895.00**
Gravy Boat	
Oval, pink flowers, blue ribbon, H and Co	**45.00**
Round, tray, double handles and lips, navy and rust, Theo. Hav.	**35.00**
Oyster Plate, shell shape indentations, pink edge	**65.00**
Plate	
7½″, bread and butter, gold scalloped edge, pink flowers	**16.00**
8½″, salad	
Blue edge, enameled butterfly and wheat, 1885	**20.00**
Gold band, coupe shape	**18.00**
9″, luncheon	
Frontenac	**18.00**
Whiteware, hp, pink rose, sgd H and Co	**22.00**
9½″, dinner, "Princess," H and Co ..	**22.00**

9¾", dinner, white, scalloped edge .	**20.00**
10" cake, gold handles and border .	**35.00**

Platter

12", turquoise morning glories, gold scalloped edge	**35.00**
16", gold band, scalloped end handles, Theo. Hav.	**55.00**
22", deep pink flowers, two wells, fancy gold edges	**75.00**

Relish Dish, blue and pink flowers . . .	**25.00**
Soup Plate, 9½", olive and rust flowers, 1885 mark	**22.00**

Vegetable Dish

Baker, pattern border, unglazed bottom	**35.00**
Gold edges, small pink roses, cov . .	**65.00**
Moss Rose, blue edges, rope handles, 1885, cov	**65.00**
Scalloped shape, pink roses	**50.00**

HEISEY GLASS

History: The A. H. Heisey Glass Co. began producing glasswares in April, 1896, in Newark, Ohio. Heisey was not a newcomer to the field, having been associated with the craft since his youth. Many blown and molded patterns were produced in crystal, colored, milk (opalescent), and Ivorina Verde (custard) glass. Decorative techniques of cutting, etching, and silver deposit were employed. Glass figurines were introduced in 1933 and continued until 1957 when the factory ceased production. All Heisey glass is notable for its clarity. Not all Heisey glassware is marked with the familiar "H" within a diamond.

References: Neila Bredehoft, *The Collector's Encyclopedia of Heisey Glass, 1925–1938*, Collector Books, 1986; Mary Louise Burns, *Heisey's Glassware of Distinction*, 2nd edition, published by author, 1983; Lyle Conder, *Collector's Guide To Heisey's Glassware for Your Table*, L-W Books, 1984; Tom Felt and Bob O'Grady, *Heisey Candlesticks, Candelabra, and Lamps*, Heisey Collectors of America, Inc, 1984; Sandra Stoudt, *Heisey On Parade*, Wallace-Homestead, 1985.

Collectors' Club: Heisey Collectors of America, P. O. Box 27, Newark, OH, 43055. Dues: $15.00. *Heisey News* monthly.

Museum: National Heisey Glass Museum, Newark, OH.

Reproduction Alert: Some Heisey molds were sold to Imperial Glass of Bellaire, Ohio, and certain items were reissued. These pieces may be mistaken for the original Heisey. Some of the reproductions were produced in colors which were never made by Heisey and have become collectible in their own right.

Examples include: the Colt family in Crystal, Carmel Slag, Ultra Blue, and Horizon Blue: the mallard with wings up in Carmel Slag; Whirlpool

(Provincial) in crystal and colors; and, Waverly, 7" oval footed compote in Carmel Slag.

Almond Dish, Greek Key, crystal, individual size	**35.00**

Animals

Giraffe, head back	**125.00**
Goose, wings down	**285.00**
Pony, standing	**50.00**
Rooster, fighting	**125.00**
Tropical Fish, frosted	**850.00**

Ashtray

Crystolite, Zircon, sgd	**60.00**
Grape Leaf, Moongleam	**65.00**
Orchid, sq	**30.00**
Puritan, sgd	**20.00**

Banana Split Dish, Yeoman, Moongleam, ftd	**35.00**

Basket

Crystolite, 6"	**165.00**
Daisy cutting, 7", sgd	**175.00**

Bonbon

Fern, 6", handle, Zircon	**60.00**
Lariat	**25.00**
Lodestar, 11", Dawn, crimped	**250.00**
Yeoman, 6½", Flamingo	**30.00**

Bowl

Crystal, rolled rim, black and gold trim, star base, 9"	**30.00**
Empress, Moongleam (green,) 6", dolphin ftd	**40.00**
Horn of Plenty, 11", centerpiece, cobalt blue	**350.00**
Orchid, oval, dressing, 2 pt	**45.00**
Queen Anne, 9"	**65.00**
Waverly, 10", crimped	**75.00**

Butter Dish, cov

Cabachon, orchid, etched, ¼ lb, sgd	**225.00**
Rose, crystal	**160.00**

Candelabra

Ridgeleigh, clear, Moongleam base, 3-light, pr	**275.00**
Trident, 2-light, Sahara, 5"	**90.00**

Candleblock, Crystolite, sq	**8.00**

Candlesticks, pr

Cathedral, Moongleam, 9"	**125.00**
Orchid, 5", two light, trident	**110.00**
Queen Anne, crystal, bobeches and prisms	**150.00**

Candy Dish, cov

Pleat and Panel, Flamingo, ftd, sgd .	**50.00**
Rose, crystal, 5¼", flat, round	**150.00**

Celery

Orchid, 11"	**45.00**
Twist pattern, Moongleam	**35.00**

Champagne

Galaxy, green, 5"	**22.00**
Lariat, crystal	**15.00**
Orchid	**30.00**
Rose, crystal	**32.00**

Cigarette Holder

Carcassone, crystal	**12.75**

Kohinoor, sgd 20.00

Claret, Victorian, crystal, 4 oz, two ball
stem 15.00

Coaster
Maple, Flamingo 18.00
Oak Leaf 25.00

Cocktail
Aqua Caliente, Tally Ho etch, crystal
stem 35.00
Creole, Alexandrite, crystal stem ... 120.00
Orchid 40.00
Rooster stem 45.00
Rosalie, crystal, 3 oz 18.00
Seahorse stem 140.00

Cocktail Shaker, Fox Chase etching,
clear 150.00

Cologne Bottle, Victorian, crystal, orig
stopper 32.50

Compote
Pleat and Panel, Flamingo, gold trim,
cov, 7" 65.00
Waverly, orchid etching, 6¼", low
standard 50.00

Condiment Bottle, Orchid 250.00

Cookie Plate, Lariat 20.00

Cordial
Jamestown, Rosalie etching 75.00
Kenilworth 100.00
Oxford, sgd 24.00

Cream Soup, Yeoman, green 15.00

Creamer and Sugar
Lariat, crystal 16.75
Old Colony, crystal, dolphin ftd 50.00
Orchid, individual size 50.00
Prince of Wales, ruby stained 100.00
Victorian, crystal 21.00

Cruet
Colonial, Flamingo, octagonal stop-
per 600.00
Pleat and Panel, Moongleam 95.00
Priscilla 20.00
Saturn 36.00
Yeoman, Flamingo 45.00

Cup and Saucer, Orchid pattern 55.00

Custard Cup, Lariat 10.00

Goblet
Carcassone, Sahara, 11 oz 12.00
Duquesne, clear, 9 oz 10.00
Minuet, crystal 35.00
Narrow Flute, clear 25.00
Orchid pattern 45.00
Renaissance, crystal 35.00
Sussex pattern, Stiegel cobalt blue . 100.00
Trojan, Flamingo, 8 oz 20.00

Ice Bucket
Empress, crystal 55.00
Twist, Moongleam 75.00

Iced Tea Tumbler
Orchid pattern 45.00
Rose 38.00

Ladle, crystal 28.00

Lemon Dish, cov, Empress, 6½", dolphin handles 60.00

Madonna, Zircon, frosted, sgd 1,800.00

Mayonnaise, Plantation, liner, spoon . . 65.00

Mint Dish, Bowtie, green, 4", handles . 40.00

Nut Dish, Empress, Moongleam, individual size, dolphin ftd 32.00

Pitcher, Rose, crystal, ice lip 550.00

Plate
Old Colony, Sahara, 8½", sq 22.00
Rosalie, crystal, 16" 58.00
Rose, 8" 20.00

Relish, three sections
Lariat 45.00
Yeoman, Moongleam, handle 55.00

Rose Bowl, Diamond Optic, Moongleam 48.00

Sauce, Prince of Wales, 5" d, clear . . . 15.00

Sherbet, Victorian, crystal, sgd, $18.00.

Sherbet
Etching #415 .... 15.00
Orchid 25.00
Plantation Ivy, crystal 16.00
Rose, crystal 28.00

Sherry, goose stem 160.00

Sugar Shaker, Plantation, clear 115.00

Toothpick
Prince of Wales, clear, gold trim ... 135.00
Priscilla, clear 65.00

Tumbler
Ambassador, crystal, 8 oz 15.00
Old Colony, Sahara, 5¾", ftd 25.00
Provencal, Zircon, 9 oz, ftd 55.00

Vase
Ridgeleigh, triangle 40.00
Warwick, cornucopia, 9½", pr 75.00

Wine
Locket on Chain 100.00
Old Dominion, Alexandrite 115.00
Orchid 48.00

HOLLY AMBER

History: Holly Amber, originally called Golden Agate, was produced by the Indiana Tumbler and Goblet Works of the National Glass Co., Greentown, Indiana. Jacob Rosenthal created the color in 1902. Holly Amber is a gold colored glass with a marbleized onyx color on raised parts.

A new pattern, Holly [No. 450], was designed by Frank Jackson for Golden Agate. Between January 1903 and June 1903, more than 35 items were made in this pattern; the factory was destroyed by fire in June.

References: Brenda Measell and James Measell, *A Guide To Reproductions of Greentown Glass,* 2nd ed., The Printing Press, 1974; James Measell, *Greentown Glass, The Indiana Tumbler & Goblet Co.,* Grand Rapids Public Museum, 1979.

Collectors' Club: National Greentown Glass Association, P. O. Box 508037, Cicero, IL 60650. *N.G.G.A. Newsletter,* quarterly.

Museums: Greentown Glass Museum, Greentown, IN; Grand Rapids Public Museum [Ruth Herrick Greentown Glass Collection], MI.

Additional Listing: Greentown Glass.

Tumbler, 3⅞″ h, $280.00.

Bowl, berry, 8½″	375.00
Butter, cov	1,000.00
Cake Stand	2,000.00
Compote, jelly, 4¾″ d, open	450.00
Cream	600.00
Cruet, orig stopper	1,350.00
Honey, cov	750.00
Match Holder	400.00
Parfait	575.00
Relish, oval	275.00
Salt and Pepper Shakers, pr	500.00
Sauce	125.00
Sugar, open	400.00
Toothpick, 2½″ h	475.00

HORN

History: For centuries horns from animals have been used for various items, e.g., drinking cups, spoons, powder horns, and small dishes. Some pieces of horn have designs scratched in them. Around 1880 furniture made from the horns of Texas longhorn steers was popular in Texas and the southwestern United States.

Additional Listings: Firearm Accessories.

Chair, steer horns, $900.00.

Beaker, 5¼″ h, George III, SS lined, London maker's mark, 1815, ext. SS rim bordered with rolled band of oak leaves and acorns, contemporary monogram	800.00
Card Case, horn and ivory, floral design	40.00
Chair, arm, horn head rest, back, arms, and legs, upholstered seat	900.00
Comb Case, 7½ x 9″, diamond shape mirror, pocket	35.00
Hat Rack, wall type	25.00
Shoehorn, scratched carved, 1756	65.00
Spoon, 5½″, monogrammed "MBL, 1907," thistle, hallmarked	45.00
Stand, Victorian, four horns form legs, American Southwest, 19th C	275.00

HULL POTTERY

History: In 1905 Addis E. Hull purchased the Acme Pottery Company, Crooksville, Ohio. In 1917 the A. E. Hull Pottery Company began making a line of art pottery, novelties, stoneware, and kitchenware, later including the famous Little Red Riding Hood line. Most items had a matte finish with shades of pink and blue or brown predominating.

After a disasterous flood and fire in 1950, J. Brandon Hull reopened the factory in 1952 as the Hull Pottery Company. New, more modern style molds, mostly with glossy finish, were produced. The company currently produces pieces, e.g. the Regal and Floraline lines, for sale to florists.

Hull pottery molds and patterns are easily identified. Pre-1950 vases are marked "Hull USA" or "Hull Art USA" on the bottom. Many also retain their paper labels. Post-1950 pieces are marked "Hull" in large script or "HULL" in block letters.

Each pattern has a distinctive number, e.g., Wildflower with a "W" and number, Waterlily with an "L" and number, Poppy with 600 numbers, Orchid with 300 numbers, etc. Early stone pieces have an H.

References: Brenda Roberts, *The Collectors Encyclopedia Of Hull Pottery,* Collector Books, 1980.

Additional Listings: See *Warman's Americana & Collectibles* for more examples.

Advisor: Joan Hull.

Vase, 6½″ h, White Lily, cream ground, $35.00.

PRE-1950 (MATTE)

Bowknot
   Candleholders Set, B17-4 . . . . 50.00
   Console Bowl, B16, 13½″ 75.00
   Vase, B4, 6½ 40.00
Calla Lily
   520-33, 10½″ 75.00
   530-33, 5″ 30.00
Camelia
   Ewer, 106, 13½″ 175.00
   123, 6½″ 35.00
   138, 6¼″ 35.00
Dogwood
   Basket, 501, 7½″ 65.00
   Ewer, 516, 11½″ 75.00
   517, 4¾″ 25.00
Iris
   406, 4¾″ 25.00

406, 7″ 35.00
406, 8½″ 45.00
Little Red Riding Hood
   Batter Pitcher, side pour, 7″ 175.00
   Grease Jar, wolf 350.00
   Spice, set of 6 . . . . 2,100.00
Magnolia
   Cornucopia, double, 6, 12″ 65.00
   Ewer, 14, 4¾″ 30.00
   21, 12½″, tassel handle 85.00
Magnolia, pink glossy
   H1, 5½″ 25.00
   H10, 8½″, cornucopia 45.00
   H16, 12½″, winged handle 75.00
Orchid
   304, 10¼″ 85.00
   306, 6¾″ 40.00
   312, 7″ 40.00
Poppy
   602, 6½″, planter 45.00
   606, 10½″ 65.00
Rosella, pink glossy
   Cornucopia, R13, 8½″ 45.00
   Ewer, R9, 6½″ 35.00
   Heart shape, R8, 6½″ 35.00
Stoneware
   Stein, H499, 6½″ 30.00
   Tankard, H492, 8½″ 100.00
   Vase, H32, 8″ 40.00
Thistle, 53 . . . . 40.00
Tulip
   Jardiniere, 115-33, 7″ 65.00
   Vase, 104-33, 6″ 40.00
   107-33, 6″ 335.00
Waterlily
   Ewer, L17, 13½″ 175.00
   Tea Set, L18, 19, 20 . . . . 150.00
   L15, 12½″ 75.00
Wildflower
   Basket, W16, 10½″ 150.00
   W1, 5½″ 25.00
   W18, 12½″ 65.00
Woodland
   Bud Vase, W15, 8½″ 50.00
   Jardiniere, W7, 5½″ 30.00
   Wall Pocket, W13, 7½″, shell 45.00

POST 1950 (GLOSSY)

Blossom Flite
   Basket, T4, 8½″ 50.00
   Honey Jug, T1, 6″ 30.00
   Pitcher, T3, 8½″ 50.00
Butterfly
   B10, 7″ 35.00
   B25, 16″, lavobo set 80.00
Capri
   Dish, C63, leaf 50.00
   Planter, C81, swan, double 50.00
Ebb Tide
   Angel Fish, E6, 7¾″ 45.00
   Planter, E3, mermaid 65.00

Dish, Ebb Tide, E-12, $17.50.

Imperial
Madonna, 7″	35.00
Swan, 69, 8½″	30.00
Urn, F88	20.00

Parchment & Pine
Cornucopia, S6	55.00
Planter, S5, scroll	45.00

Serenade
Candlestick, S16, pr	50.00
Fruit bowl, S15, ftd	75.00
Tea Set, S17, 18, 19	100.00

Sunglow
Basket, 84, 6½″	35.00
Grease Jar, 53, 5¼″	25.00
Salt and Pepper Shaker, 54, 2¾″, pr	15.00

Tokay, Tuscany
Basket, 15, 12″	65.00
2, 6″	30.00

Tropicana
Pitcher, T56, 12½″	65.00
T53, 8½″	45.00

Woodland, glossy
Cornucopia, W2	25.00
Pitcher, W3	30.00
W18	45.00

1935 1950 1957 1964 W by W Goebel W Germany

Goebel Goebel
1972 1979

HUMMEL ITEMS

History: Hummel items are the original creations of Berta Hummel, born in 1909 in Massing,
Bavaria, Germany. At age 18, she was enrolled in the Academy of Fine Arts in Munich to further her mastery of drawing and the palette. Berta entered the Convent of Siessen and became Sister Maria Inconnentia in 1934. In this Franciscan cloister, she continued drawing and painting images of her childhood friends.

In 1935 W. Goebel Co. in Rodental, Germany, began reproducing Sister Berta's sketches into 3 dimensional bisque figurines. The Schmid Brothers of Randolph, Massachusetts, introduced the figurines to America and became Goebel's U.S. distributor.

In 1967 Goebel began distributing Hummel items in the U.S. A controversy developed between the two companies involving the Hummel family and the convent. Law suits and countersuits ensued. The German courts finally effected a compromise. The convent held legal rights to all works produced by Sister Berta from 1934 until her death in 1946 and licensed Goebel to reproduce these works. Schmid was to deal directly with the Hummel family for permission to reproduce any preconvent art.

All authentic Hummels bear both the signature, M.I. Hummel, and a Goebel trademark. Various trademarks were used to identify the year of production. The Crown Mark (CM) was used in 1935, Full Bee (FB) 1940–1959; Small Stylized Bee (SSB) 1960–1972; Large Stylized Bee (LSB) 1960–1963; Three Line Mark (3L) 1964–1972; Last Bee Mark (LB) 1972–1980, Missing Bee Mark (MB) 1979–Present.

References: John F. Hotchkiss, *Hummel Art II*, Wallace-Homestead, 1981; Carl F. Luckey, *Hummel Figurines and Plates, 7th Edition*, Books Americana, 1984; Lawrence L. Wonsch, *Hummel Copycats With Values,* Wallace-Homestead, 1987.

Collectors' Clubs: Goebel Collectors' Club, 105 White Plains Road, Tarrytown, NY 10591. Insight quarterly newsletter. Dues: $17.50; Hummel Collectors Club, 1261 University Drive, Yardley, PA 19067.

Additional Listings: See *Warman's Americana & Collectibles* for more examples.

Ashtray, Joyful, #33, CM, 3½ x 6″	325.00
Bookends, pr	
Apple Tree Boy and Apple Tree Girl, #252A&B, SSB	250.00
Bookworms, #14/A&B, SSB	300.00
Candleholder, Silent Night, #54, LB	175.00
Figurine	
A Stitch In Time, I#255, LB	130.00
Adoration, #23/II, CM	750.00
Auf Widersehen, #153/0, LB	130.00
Baker, #128, LB	85.00
Band Leader, #129, LB	120.00
Bird Duet, #169, 3L	90.00
Boy With Toothache, #217, 3L	110.00
Chick Girl, #57/0, CM	360.00
Chimney Sweep, 12/2/0, LB	70.00

Congratulations, #17/0 (no socks),
FB 225.00
Doll Bath, #319, 3L 130.00
Good Shepherd, #42/0, 3L 90.00
Going To Grandma's, #51/0, FB ... 175.00
Heavenly Angel, #21/0, SSB 75.00
Heavenly Lullaby, #262, LB 110.00
Joyful, #52/0, 3L 135.00
Just Resting, #112/3/0, LB 85.00

Honey Pot, 5″ h, yellow ground, $30.00.

Kiss Me, #311(no socks), 3L 140.00
Knitting Lessons, #256, 3L 350.00
Little Goat Herder, #200/0, SSB ... 120.00
Little Hiker, I#16/2/0, FB 80.00
Little Pharmacist, #322, FB 2,500.00
March Winds, #43, LB 75.00
Mother's Darling, #175, FB 225.00
Not For You, #317, LB 130.00
Playmates, #58/I, SSB 150.00
Postman, #119, FB 145.00
Puppy Love, #1, CM 425.00
School Girls, 177/I, LB 900.00
She Loves Me, She Loves Me Not,
#174, FB 175.00
Surprise, #94/3/0, FB 165.00
The Artist, #304, 3L 350.00
The Builder, #305, 3L 140.00
The Photographer, #178, SSB 140.00
To Market, #49/3/0, FB 195.00
Umbrella Boy, 152/A/II, CM 2,000.00
Wayside Devotion, #28/III, CM 1,300.00
Which Hand?, #258, SSB 350.00
Village Boy, #51/3/0, CM 230.00
Font
Angel Cloud, #206, LB, 2¼ x 4¾″ . 40.00
Child With Flowers, #36/I, SSB ... 100.00
Child Jesus, #26/0, 3L 30.00
Plaque
Ba-Bee Rings, #30/OA&B, FB 250.00
Madonna, #48/0, CM, 3 x 4″ 250.00
Table Lamp
Culprits, #44/A, FB 350.00
Happy Days, #235, LB 280.00
Just Resting, #225/II, 3L 275.00

IMARI

History: Imari derives its name from a Japanese port city. Although Imari ware was manufactured in the 17th century, the wares most commonly encountered are those made between 1770 and 1900.

Early Imari was decorated simply, quite unlike the later heavily decorated brocade pattern commonly associated with Imari. Most of the decorative patterns are an underglaze blue and overglaze "seal wax" red supported by turquoise and yellow.

The Chinese copied Imari ware. Important differences of the Japanese type include grayer clay, thicker glaze, runny and darker blue, and deep red opaque hues.

The pattern and colors of Imari inspired many English and European potteries, such as Derby and Meissen, to adopt a similar style of decoration for their wares.

Reference: Sandra Andacht, *Oriental Antiques & Art: An Identification And Value Guide,* Wallace-Homestead, 1987.

Reproduction Alert: Reproductions abound, and many manufacturers continue to produce pieces in the traditional style.

Bowl, 10″ d, blue, orange, and yellow, c1870, $425.00.

Bottle, 9⅝″, double gourd shape, Tok-kuri, fluted body, gilt, red enamel, and underglaze blue, shaped floral and bird reserves, dense foliate-patterned ground 500.00
Bowl
7½″, polychrome dec, seascape medallion surrounded by landscape and seascape reserves, foliate edge 275.00
8¼″, bell form, painted brocade panels, plum blossoms, shippo-

tsungai bands, bright Imari palette, painted matching int. **100.00**

10⅛″, polychrome dec, landscape medallion encircled by shaped floral reserves, irregular brocade ground **325.00**

14⅞″, high recessed foot, foliate edge, gilt, underglaze blue and colored enamels, central medallion of confronted ho-o biting blossoming sprigs, stylized landscape, alternating large and small reserves of floral and animal motifs, diaper ground, ext. sides with band of shou medallions and butterflies, underglaze lappet band, four character studio mark, "Gyokudo," 19th C **675.00**

Charger

15½″, polychrome and gilt dec, ho-o and kiri medallion, shaped reserves of dragon and birds on branches, brocade ground, imp cartouche "Hizen Yamatoku," pr **800.00**

17⅞″, gilt, underglaze blue and polychrome enamels, central medallion of stylized ho-o in flight, bamboo leaves and floral patterned band, six fan-shaped reserves of six immortal poets, dark blue brocade ground, Meiji period **415.00**

21½″, overall dec of scattered fans, figural and floral dec, brick-red ground, underglaze blue stylized floral band, c1900 . . . . **935.00**

Creamer and Sugar, 5½″ creamer, 5⅞″ cov sugar, ovoid, dragon form handles, gilt and bright enamels, shaped reserves, dragon-like beasts, stylized animal medallions, brocade ground, high dome lid, knob, cipher mark of Mount Fuji and Fukagama Studio marks, Meiji period **500.00**

Jar, 27½″, cov, ovoid, narrow foot, continuous scene of blossoming sakura shrouding pavilion complex, narrow neck band of interlocking foliage spirals, domed lid, shishi finial **715.00**

Jardiniere, 10″, hexagonal, bulbous, short flared foot, alternating bijin figures and immortal symbols, stylized ground **250.00**

Plate

5⅜″, central kirin medallion, nine Chinese sages, scrolling foliate rim band, four character inscription, set of 4 . . . . **250.00**

9″, wide everted rim, central medallion of Chinese scholars seated on garden terrace, blossoming plum tree, gilt highlights, Chinese, early 19th C **300.00**

9½″, pear shape, molded pierced stem form handle, kara shishi amid blossoming peony, wide brocade band, spurious six character Jiajing mark, Meiji period, set of 6 . . . . . **1,000.00**

9⅝″, gilt, multicolored enamels, and underglaze blue, irregular ho-o and floral reserves, blue ground, foliate and cloud design, foliate edge, set of 6 . . . . **500.00**

11½″, scalloped edge, rect dish, recessed ring foot, molded conventional map of Japan, underglaze blue names and borders of provinces, wave ground, base inscribed "Tempo nensei," 19th C **525.00**

12⅛″, floral medallion, alternating floral reserves, brocade ground, Meiji period **150.00**

12½″, scalloped, central medallion, potted plant surrounded by floral reserves, brocade bands, late 19th C **145.00**

Platter, 14″, hexagonal, central reserve of flowers in vase, cavetto with floral reserves, scrolling branches, narrow blue band, Meiji period, pr **1,000.00**

Vase

18⅝″, baluster, waisted neck, flared rim, recessed ring foot, gilt, underglaze blue, and polychrome enamels, two large shaped figural reserves of bijin picking flowers, red enamel cloud collar bands, narrow foliate patterned bands, blue ground at top and bottom, base with four character studio mark . . . **1,430.00**

24″, ovoid, fan shaped reserves of bijin in conversation, floral landscape, reserves of birds and flowers, brocade chrysanthemum ground, pr **1,250.00**

29¾″, trumpet mouth, gilt, underglaze blue, and bright polychrome enamels, continuous scene of Japanese beauties, flowering landscape, large cloud collar bands, shaped floral reserves, blue ground, gilt scrolling tendrils, lower body with large foliate reserves on red enamel ground, int. of wide mouth encircled by two writhing dragons and cloud scrolls over stylized green, gilt, blue, and aubergine wave pattern **1,650.00**

IMPERIAL GLASS

History: Imperial Glass Co., Bellaire, Ohio, was organized in 1901. Its primary product was pattern (pressed) glass. Soon other lines were added including carnival glass, NUART, NUCUT, and NEAR CUT. In 1916 the company introduced "Free-Hand," a lustred art glass line, and "Imperial Jewels," an iridescent stretch glass that carried the Imperial cross trademark. In the 1930s the company was reorganized into the Imperial Glass Corporation and continues to produce a great variety of wares.

Imperial recently has acquired the molds and equipment of several other glass companies—Central, Cambridge and Heisey. Many of the "retired" molds of these companies are once again in use. The resulting reissues are marked to distinguish them from the originals.

Reference: Margaret and Douglas Archer, *Imperial Glass,* Collector Books, 1978.

Collectors' Club: National Imperial Glass Collectors Society, Box 534, Bellaire, OH 43906. Dues: $10.00.

Additional Listings: See Carnival Glass, Pattern Glass, and *Warman's Americana & Collectibles* for more examples of Candlewick.

ENGRAVED OR HAND CUT

Bowl, 9″, berry, Design No. 114, five
  hand cut daisy-like flowers . . . .　**18.00**

Rose Bowl, 5″ d, 3½″ h, $22.50.

Candlesticks, 7″, Amelia, pr . . . .　**32.00**
Nut Dish, 5½″, Design No. 112 . . . . . .　**15.00**
Pitcher, tankard, Design No. 110, flow-
  ers, foliage, and butterfly cutting . . .　**50.00**
Plate, 5½″, Design No. 12 . . . .　**12.00**
Sherbet, ftd, Design No. 300, engraved
  stars . . . .　**10.00**
Syrup, Design No. 112, SP top . . . . .　**32.00**

JEWELS

Bowl, rose luster . . . .　**160.00**
Candy Dish, cov, pink . . . .　**35.00**
Rose Bowl, amethyst, green irid . . . . .　**75.00**
Vase
  6″, irid pearl green and purple luster　**135.00**
  7½″, bulbous, melon shape, wide
    flared mouth, irid red luster . . . . .　**85.00**

LUSTERED (FREE HAND)

Hat, 9″ w, ruffled rim, cobalt blue,
  embedded irid white vines and leaves　**100.00**
Pitcher, 10″ h, applied clear handle, pale
  yellow luster, white pulled loops . . .　**225.00**
Vase
  6″, oyster white, embedded green
    hearts and vines, deep orange lus-
    ter lining . . . .　**250.00**
  7″, cobalt blue, embedded irid white
    vines, heart shaped leaves . . . . .　**200.00**
  8¼″, King Tut, deep irid blue, white
    loops . . . .　**315.00**
  10″, cobalt blue foot, deep ruby bowl,
    blue veining and leaves, irid luster
    finish, bogus Tiffany signature . . .　**175.00**
  10¼″, dark blue, light blue pulled
    loops . . . .　**225.00**
  11¼″, baluster, triangular pull-ups at
    mouth, opal opaque white ground,
    embedded irid blue trailing vines,
    orig paper label . . . .　**325.00**

NUART

Ashtray . . . .　**18.00**
Lamp Shade, marigold . . . .　**50.00**
Vase, 7″, bulbous, irid green . . . .　**125.00**

NUCUT

Bowl, 8½″, berry . . . .　**20.00**
Celery Tray, 11″ . . . .　**15.00**
Compote, jelly, 4½″ . . . .　**12.00**
Fern Dish, 8″‴, brass lining, ftd . . . . . .　**32.00**
Orange Bowl, 12″, Rose Marie . . . . . .　**48.00**
Punch Set, 13″ bowl, base, six cups,
  Rose Marie . . . .　**175.00**
Tumbler, flared rim, molded star . . . . .　**5.00**

PRESSED

Basket, 10½″	30.00
Bonbon, 5¼″, D'Angelo, green, handle	15.00
Bowl, 9″, satin irid, handles	20.00
Butter Dish, cov, Colonial, rose	50.00
Cake Stand, Candlewick pattern, 11″ h	50.00
Cheese Dish, cov, Monticello	35.00
Cordial, Wakefield, amber	10.00
Creamer and Sugar	
Cape Cod, clear	20.00
Flora, rose	15.00
Figure, Terrier, caramel slag	125.00
Goblet, Cape Cod, red	15.00
Mayonnaise, Monaco, amber, underplate, orig spoon	20.00
Salt and Pepper Shakers, Huckabee, aluminum tops, pr	25.00
Sandwich Tray, black handle	25.00
Sweet Pea Vase, 4″	12.00
Wine, Cape Cod, green	20.00

INDIAN ARTIFACTS, AMERICAN

History: During the historic period there were approximately 350 tribes of Indians, grouped into the following regions: Eskimo, Northeast and Woodland, Northwest Coast, Plains, and West and Southwest.

American Indian artifacts are quite popular. Currently the market is in a period of stability following a rapid increase of prices during the 1970s.

References: John W. Barry, *American Indian Pottery*, 2nd ed, Books Americana, 1984; Lar Hothem, *Arrowheads & Projectile Points*, Collector Books, 1983; Lar Hothem, *North American Indian Artifacts*, Books Americana, 1984; *North American Indian Points*, Books Americana, 1984.

Periodical: American Indian Basketry Magazine, P.O. Box 66124, Portland, OR 97266.

Note: American Indian artifacts listed below are objects made on the North American continent during the pre-historic and historic periods.

ESKIMO

Basket, 8½″ d, 9″ h, faded cross design of bear grass	185.00
Figure	
Polar Bear, 2″ h, ivory, carved	95.00
Seal, 2⅛″ l, ½″ h, ivory, carved, detailed face and flippers	100.00
Harpoon, 13″ l, ivory, steel tip, wooden guard for tip	65.00
Mukluks, 11″ l, 16″ h, seal fur, red trade cloth and beads dec, mink fur, red and indigo yarn, sea grass insulate, wolverine fur insole, tassels and binding	500.00
Parka, 46″ l, otter fur, classic style, fur lining, mink trim, wolverine fur hood trim	400.00

NORTHEAST AND WOODLANDS

Bandolier Bag, 41″, beaded, Woodlands	350.00
Jar, 4″, pottery, effigy, Mississippi culture (1200/1600 A.D.)	440.00
Pipe, carved stone, fox, Mississippi culture	900.00
Pouch, 5½ x 6″, polychrome floral beading, black velvet background, flaps, c1890	35.00

NORTHWEST COAST

Bag, 13¼ x 17½″, corn husk, analine polychrome design, trees and flowers on one side, geometric on other, leather strap, Nez Perce	175.00
Canoe Paddle, 33″ l, cedar, carved, red and black painted design, Tlingit . . .	175.00
Hat, 13″ d, 5¾″, woven, double weave	325.00
Snuff Bottle, rawhide, wood stopper, Nez Perce	55.00
Totem Pole, 36½″ h, wood, carved, stylized figure of eagle, spirit with otter, face, snake and raven, patina, concave back, blue, black, gold, and dark ochre paint, adze marks, c1900 . . .	1,050.00

PLAINS

Amulet, 3″ l, turtle form, green, blue, yellow, and white beading, Cheyenne	45.00
Basket, 9″ d, 9½″ h, finely braided rim, soft colors, patina, late 19th C, Jicariloo Apache	235.00
Doll, 13″, dress and high top moccasins, black and white beading with blue and yellow, beaded belt, knife sheath, tin dangles on hem	425.00
Dress	
29 x 50″, tanned buckskin, applied multicolor beaded floral designs, elk centered on front and back, c1910	1,300.00
32 x 50″, white smoked elkhide, red and blue beads around neck and shoulder seam, blue and black cut glass tube beads bands alternating with elk teeth across front and back bodice, beaded fringe, blue and red felt ornaments	725.00
Knife Sheath, 9″, red, blue, and green beading, white ground, Niobrara Sioux, c1880–90	100.00
Moccasins	
5″ l, child's, blue, orange, and white beading, leather at toes worn, Sioux	75.00
10¾″ l, red, white, and blue beading, green vamp, Sioux	125.00
Neckpiece, 23″ l, 5½″ multicolor med-	

allion, 2" loom beaded neck strip, white background, Sioux **85.00**

Pouch

3½" d, circular, spot stitched, multicolor with pink and blue, beaded fringe, Northern **90.00**

6 x 8", green beaded horse, polychrome details, black and yellow stripe borders, handle, Southern . **205.00**

Saddle, wood, rawhide covering, sinew stitched, bird effigy pommel, patina, brass trade bells, early 20th C **105.00**

Tomahawk Club, 15½" l, 8¼" w, blackened head, concave circular design, incised dec on iron blade, Lakota Sioux, c1870 .... **215.00**

Necklace, squash blossom, Navaho, 1940s, turquoise oval from Fox Mine, made from quarters and dimes, $600.00.

WEST AND SOUTHWEST

Basket, 10¾" d, 6" h, yucca and martynia geometric design, cactus plants, Papago **45.00**

Bear, 4½" h, blackware, fine patina, sgd "M. I. Naranjo," Santa Clara **245.00**

Belt, 32½" l, SS stamped link, alternating oval and small butterfly conchos, Navaho **230.00**

Bowl, 10¼" d, 3¾" h, Hopi work, faded central design, c1875, Nampeyo ... **255.00**

Canteen, 7¾", pottery, polychrome, Hopi **600.00**

Doll, 10" h, pottery, polychrome, Yuma **1,500.00**

Jar

7" d, 6" h, redware, black curvelinear design, red slip, buff body, bottle bottom, c1870, San Ildefonse ... **450.00**

9" d, 7½" h, umber design, white slip, red-orange polished slip background, bottle bottom, extensive spalling, Acoma **150.00**

10" d, 8½" h, umber and red ochre design, white slip, red-orange bottle bottom, c1920, Acoma **800.00**

Jewelry, Necklace

16" l, SS, 1500 carats of Morenci blue turquoise, Navaho **650.00**

18" l, nickel silver, Squash Blossom, c1950 .... **375.00**

Plate, 7 x 8", feather design, gun metal sheen, "Blue Corn," San Ildefonso, sgd **500.00**

Pot

7" d, 8" h, parrot effigy, umber and red ochre, buff ground, Casas Grandes **150.00**

11" d, 15" h, umber and red ochre, white slip, buff clay body, Casas Grandes **425.00**

Rug

30 x 45", wool, Ganado design, red, dark brown, and natural, hand carded, Navaho **325.00**

54 x 82", transitional weaving, hand spun wool, analine red, orange, green, black, purple, and natural, corner fringe, c1890, Navaho **1,450.00**

Saddle Blanket, 30 x 59", double, multicolor stripe, fret corners, Navaho .. **150.00**

Tapestry, 43 x 52", sand painted, blue, white, gold and russet, sand color background, attached tag reads: "Type: Sand painting, size: 43 x 52, Weaver: Daisy Buston, Area: Shiprock, N.M. $4,000," Navaho **2,600.00**

Tray, 12¼" d, yucca, martynia (devil's claw) cross design, Papago, c1950 . **105.00**

Vessel, 3½" d, 1" h, squat form, black on black, feather design, gun metal sheet, sgd "Cresencia," Santa Clara **235.00**

INDIAN TREE PATTERN

History: The Indian Tree pattern is a popular pattern of porcelain made from the last half of the 19th century until the present. The pattern consisting of an Oriental crooked tree branch, landscape, exotic flowers, and foliage is found in predominately greens, pinks, blues, and oranges on a white ground. Several English potteries, including Burgess and Leigh, Coalport, and Maddock, made wares with the Indian Tree pattern.

Reference: Susan and Al Bagdade, *Warman's English & Continental Pottery & Porcelain, 1st Edition,* Warman Publishing Co., Inc., 1987.

Bouillon Cup and Underplate, handles **15.00**

Bowl

5⅜", KPM **7.50**

8½ x 11", ftd, Minton **45.00**

Butter, cov, Johnson Bros **40.00**

Platter, oval, 10¾ x 14″, marked "A. & C. Meakin," $65.00.

Cake Plate, 10½″, Coalport	**35.00**
Creamer, Coalport	**25.00**
Cup and Saucer, scalloped, Copeland	**20.00**
Demitasse, Coalport	**25.00**
Egg Cup, 4″, Maddock	**20.00**
Gravy Boat, Brownfield & Son, c1856	**30.00**
Pitcher, 6″, Maddock & Sons	**45.00**
Plate	
6″, KPM	**5.00**
8″, Cauldon	**12.00**
9½″, KPM	**15.00**
10″, Burgess & Leigh	**18.50**
Platter	
8 x 11″, KPM	**25.00**
18½″, Spode	**95.00**
Salt and Pepper, Coalport	**50.00**
Sauce, 5″, Johnson Bros	**8.00**
Soup Plate, 7½″, Caolport	**15.00**
Soup Tureen, 10″, matching cov and ladle, Maddock & Sons	**130.00**
Sugar, Coalport	**25.00**
Teapot, Burgess & Leigh	**50.00**
Vegetable Dish, 10″, oval, Davison & Son	**35.00**

INK BOTTLES

History: Ink was sold in glass or pottery bottles in the early 1700s in England. Retailers mixed their own formula and bottled it. The commercial production of ink did not begin in England until the late 18th century and in America until the early 19th century.

Initially, ink was supplied in pint or quart bottles, often of poor manufacture, from which smaller bottles could be filled. By the mid-19th century when writing implements were improved, emphasis was placed on making an "untippable" bottle. Shapes ranging from umbrella style to turtles were tried. Since ink bottles were displayed, shaped or molded bottles became popular.

The advent of the fountain pen relegated the ink bottle to the back drawer. Bottles lost their decorative design and became merely functionable tems.

References: Ralph & Terry Kovel, *The Kovels' Bottle Price List*, 7th edition, Crown Publishers, 1984; Carlo & Dot Sellari, *The Illustrated Price Guide To Antique Bottles*, Country Beautiful Corp., 1975.

Periodicals: *Antique Bottle World*, 5003 West Berwyn, Chicago, IL 60630; *Old Bottle Magazine*, P.O. Box 243, Bend, OR 97701. Subscription: $10.00.

Additional Listings: See *Warman's Americana & Collectibles* for more examples.

Staffords Ink, 3″ d, 2¼″ h, green glass, $22.50.

Alling's Ink, triangular, green, 1⅞ x 2¼″	**25.00**
Billing & Co, Banker's Writing Ink, "B" in center, aqua, 2 x 1½″	**10.00**
Brickett J. Taylor, cylindrical, flared lip, 4½″	**125.00**
Carter's, cobalt, 6½″	**8.00**
Caw's Black Fluid Ink, light blue, 7¾″	**20.00**
Currier & Hall Ink, Concord, NH, twelve sided, open pontil, aqua, 1840 label, 2½″	**40.00**
David's Turtle Ink, green	**30.00**
Doulton, Lambeth, pouring lip, brown, pottery, 4½″	**10.00**
Hoover, Phila, eight panels, umbrella shape, aqua, 2″	**50.00**
Improved Process Blue Co, aqua, 2⅜″	**4.00**
Irving, sq, aqua, 2½″	**25.00**
Keene Umbrella Ink, eight sided, open pontil, green	**45.00**
Lake's, cone, aqua, 2½″	**15.00**
Mon-Gram Ink, round, clear, 2½″	**6.00**
P. Newman & Co, Gilsum, NH, umbrella type, eight panels, olive green, label, 1½″	**50.00**
Pitkin Ink, Keene, open pontil, dark aqua, 1¾″	**150.00**

Octagon Ink, mushroom shape, pontil,
aqua **20.00**
Signet Ink, screw top, cobalt blue, 7¾" **16.00**
Ward's Ink, pouring spout, round, olive
green, 4¾" **15.00**
Wood's Black Ink, Portland, ME, tapered, ring top, aqua, 2½" **25.00**

INKWELLS

History: The majority of the commonly found inkwells were produced in the United States and Europe from the early 1800s to the 1930s. The most popular materials were glass and pottery because these substances resisted the corrosive effects of ink.

Inkwells were a sign of the office or a wealthy individual. The common man tended to dip his ink directly from the bottle. The period from 1870 to 1920 represented a "golden age," when inkwells in elaborate designs were produced.

References: William E. Covill, Jr., *Inkbottles and Inkwells,* William S. Sullwold Publishing, 1971; Betty and Ted Rivera, *Inkstands and Inkwells: A Collector's Guide,* 2nd edition, Crown Publishers, Inc., 1973.

Collectors' Club: Society of Inkwell Collectors, 5136 Thomas Avenue, Minneapolis, MN 55410. Dues: $24.50.

Additional Listings: See *Warman's Americana & Collectibles* for more examples.

CERAMIC

Bennington, 3½", lion head, Rockingham glaze **275.00**
Delft, 3¾", sq, blue and white, windmills
and boats **75.00**
Dresden, 14" l, porcelain florals, Oriental figures on sides, lacquer base, gilt
bronze standard **500.00**
German, 3½ x 4¾", Buddha, orange
robe, yellow and blue trim, lift off top,
removable ink pot **75.00**
Hand Painted, sq, pink, hinged lid,
matching underplate, thermometer on
front **140.00**
Kauffmann, Angelica, 3½", scenic, gold
trim, hinged lid **100.00**
Martin Bros, 2¼" h, pyramidal, incised
blue, green, and brown waterfall,
bridge, and cottage, marked "Martin,
London, 1881" **50.00**
Moorcroft, green, Flamminian glaze,
marked "Made For Liberty & Co" .. **400.00**
Nidervilles, 3¾" l, hp, pastoral scene
and florals, marked "Nidervilles,
France" **250.00**
Nippon, 4", sq, beige, gold, and black
flowers **125.00**

Quimper, 5", round, scalloped edge,
marked "Henroit Quimper France" . **50.00**
Wedgwood
6" w, Jasperware, oval, blue, white
relief band of anthemion, central
column as taper holder, inkwell and
recess for sander, imp mark, potter's mark, c1790 .... **600.00**
9½" l, Moonstone finish, marked
"Wedgwood" **275.00**

GLASS

Adv, The Block House, Fort Pitt, Pitts-
burgh, PA, figural, amber "Fort Pitt
Steel Casting Co, 1906–1926" **185.00**
Beehive, figural, amber, raised bees .. **165.00**
Blown Three Mold
2" d, 1⅝" h, sapphire blue, smooth
base, short ground neck, possibly
Boston and Sandwich Glass Co,
McKearin GI-7 .... **300.00**
2¾" d, 1½" h, olive amber, smooth
base, pontil, flat collar, McKearin
GII-29 .... **85.00**
Cranberry, 4" d, daisy shape, pewter
hinged cov **225.00**
Cut, 4 x 4 x 3½", sq, paperweight, all
over diamond cutting, cane pattern
base, pen holders on all sides, brass
hinged collar **200.00**
Loetz, 3½ x 3½ x 3", sq, hinged lid,
brass mounts **175.00**

Metal, cast iron, green bronzed finish, pressed glass insert, c1900, $95.00.

METAL

Brass, turned, four part, mounted with
candlestick, late 18th C, 8" h **800.00**

Bronze
　Architectural form, Gothic Revival, fi-
　　gural finial, Victorian . . . .　**145.00**
　Boy chasing geese, Continental, 7″ l　**275.00**
　　Dog, 5¼″ . . . .　**275.00**
　Champleve, 10 x 8″, double, scalloped
　　alabaster base, bronze ball feet, red,
　　blue, and yellow flowers on white,
　　French, c1850 . . . .　**500.00**
　Gilt and Silvered Bronze, neoclassical
　　motif, cupid and griffins, matching pen
　　tray, 9½″ l, 5″ h, Continental, Victorian　**600.00**
　Iron, 5½″ sq, brass plated, high relief of
　　sitting bulldog and terrier waiting at
　　mailbox on tray, mailbox shaped crys-
　　tal insert inkwell, hinged top . . . . . .　**80.00**
　Pewter, 2½ x 4 x 2½″, floral dec on
　　hinged lid, cherubs on pen rest, glass
　　liner, Art Nouveau . . . .　**65.00**
Silver
　6½″, stag's head, rack forms top,
　　heavy silver metal, pen-wide inside
　　lid, 12 sided well . . . .　**100.00**
　9″, rect, pierced gallery, two cubed
　　silver mounted inkwells, pen rest,
　　inlaid wood base, London, 1894　.　**175.00**
　11¼″, rect, reeded borders, ball and
　　claw feet, central seal box, two oc-
　　tagonal wells, pen rests, marked "J.
　　G. & Sons, London," 1905 . . . . . .　**700.00**

MISCELLANEOUS

Jade, 5″, coral and silver dec, marked
　"E I Farmer, NY" . . . .　**200.00**
Marble, 6¼ x 11½″, pink and gray, glass
　inserts . . . .　**100.00**

IRONS

History: Ironing devices have been used for
many centuries, with the earliest references dating
from 1100. Irons from the Medieval, Renaissance,
and early industrial era can be found in Europe,
but are rare. Fine brass engraved irons and hand
wrought irons dominated the period prior to 1850.
After 1850 irons began a series of rapid evolution-
ary changes.

Between 1850 and 1910 irons were heated in
four ways: 1) a hot metal slug was inserted into
the body, 2) a burning solid, e.g., coal or charcoal,
was placed in the body, 3) a liquid or gas, e.g.,
alcohol, gasoline, or natural gas, was fed from an
external tank and burned in the body, and 4) con-
duction heating, usually drawing heat from a stove
top.

Electric irons have not yet found favor among
iron collectors.

References: Esther S. Berney, *A Collectors
Guide To Pressing Irons And Trivets,* Crown Publishers, Inc., 1977; A. H. Glissman, *The Evolution*

Of The Sad Iron, published by author, 1970; Brian
Jewell, *Smoothing Irons, A History And Collector's
Guide,* Wallace-Homestead, 1977.

Collectors' Club: Friends of Ancient Smoothing
Irons, Box 215, Carlsbad, CA 92008; Midwest Sad
Iron Collectors Club, 500 Adventureland Drive, Al-
toon, IA 50009.

Museums: Henry Ford Museum, Dearborn, MI;
Shelburne Museum, Shelburne, VT; Sturbridge
Village, Sturbridge, MA.

Additional Listings: See *Warman's Americana
& Collectibles* for more examples.

Advisors: David and Sue Irons.

**Iron, slug, wood handle, knife gate
door, 5½″ l, 6½″ h, $125.00.**

Box, brass, bullet nose, ox tongue, L
　shape handle, European, c1850 . . .　**150.00**
Charcoal
　Double Spout, "Ne Plus Ultra," side
　　vent, hand heat shield, removable
　　top, 1902 . . . .　**85.00**
　European, chicken or head latch, C
　　handle, scalloped vent, c1860 . . .　**75.00**
Fluter, machine type, brass rolls, circu-
　lar cone base, paint dec, Tucker-New
　Jersey . . . .　**130.00**
Goffering, iron, round base, S center
　post, 4″ barrel, Kenrick . . . .　**85.00**
Liquid Fuel
　Alcohol, iron body, saw grip handle,
　　cylindrical tank, German, c1900 . .　**110.00**
　Natural Gas, "I Want For Comfort Gas
　　Iron," pie shape, wood handle, ex-
　　tension pipe c1910 . . . .　**35.00**
Miniature
　Flat, iron, strap handle, number on
　　top, 2–3″ . . . .　**30.00**
　Streeter, removable handle, various
　　sizes, Sensible, c1880 . . . .　**45.00**
　Swan, iron, paint dec more desirable,
　　various sizes 1¾–5″, c1870 . . . . .　**150.00**
Sad
　Belgium Tear Drop, iron, rect handle,

raised numbers and letters, various
sizes and styles, c1850 . . . . **20.00**
Enterprise, two pointed or straight
back edge, removable C handle . **15.00**
Ober, flat, ribbing on arched handle,
weight number **18.00**
Slug, brass, wood handle, lift trap door,
turned posts, various sizes, c1850–
1900, English **125.00**
Speciality
Hat, flat wood tolliker for crown press-
ing, Cross, c1900 . . . . **45.00**
Polisher, iron, round bottom, Sidons,
England, c1900 . . . . **50.00**
Tailor, cast, narrow, raised weight
number, c1890 . . . . **25.00**

IRONWARE

History: Iron, a metallic element that occurs
abundantly in combined forms, has been known
for centuries. Items made from iron range from the
utilitarian to the decorative. Early hand-forged iron-
wares are of considerable interest to Americana
collectors.

Reference: Kathryn McNerney, *Antique Iron*,
Collector Books, 1984.

Additional Listings: Banks, Boot Jacks, Doorstops, Fireplace Equipment, Food Molds, Irons,
Kitchen Collectibles, Lamps, and Tools.

Andirons, 27¾", wrought, pr **10.00**
Baker, bail, handled lid, self drip bars
inside **35.00**
Bank, 3⅝" h, cast, mechanical, cabin
shape **350.00**
Bed Frame, 67 x 58", black enamel,
brass center rod, lion mask dec . . . **950.00**
Bench, 52" w, wrought, cast bronze
arms, reupholstered, salmon pink vel-
vet seat, floral tapestry back **375.00**
Bookends, farmhouse, trees, and
bridge over stream design, orig
colors, pr **45.00**
Cake Mold, Santa Claus, 2 part, emb
"Hello Kiddies," side rings, Griswold
Mfg Co., Erie, PA **125.00**
Candlestick, 8¼" h, pushup, pitted, hog
scraper, stamped "Bill" **85.00**
Cherry Stoner, four legs, turn handle,
Patent Date Nov. 17, 1863 and May
15, 1866 . . . . **40.00**
Cradle, Victorian style, white **450.00**
Door Stop, 12½" h, cast, Indian with
bow, red paint **225.00**
Doorknocker, 5½" fox head, mouth ring,
expressive eyes, designed ears . . . **65.00**
Fire Back, 22½ x 27", cast, high relief
design, anchors and fleur-de-lis,
arched crest, dated "1788, I.F.C." . . **950.00**

Foot Scraper, 13" h, wrought, faceted
knob finials, set in block of stone . . **150.00**
Fork, 16", wrought, well shape handle **20.00**
Griddle, ftd, flat end handle, dated 1793 **300.00**
Irons
Open handle holes for cooling, emb,
#12 OBER Pat. Pend. **15.00**
Turkish turned-up-toe, beading, han-
dle cast separately **35.00**
Kettle, wire bail, pouring lip, tip bar and
ring, imprinted "Griswold, Erie, PA," . **50.00**
Ladle, 21" l, wrought, wood hand hold
on handle, hook, engraved "D.L." . . **35.00**
Lamp, 26" h, wrought, hanging type,
leaded diamond pane amber glass,
scroll work, 20th C **25.00**

Shoe Scraper, cast iron, 7½" h, $35.00.

Lemon Squeezer, two jointed parts,
emb, "Townsend Lemon Squeezer
Philadephia, Patd. May 30, 1866" . . **50.00**
Light Holder, 15½" h, wrought, twisted
detail, turned wood base **110.00**
Magazine Rack, rococo pattern, crow-
ing cock **135.00**
Muffin Pan, 16 x 11", 12 section, fluted
sides, scalloped top edges, flower-
like shape, handle bars **115.00**
Nut Cracker, emb, "Perfection Nut
Cracker, Malleable Iron Fitting Co.,"
Branford, CT" **30.00**
Planter, 14 x 28 x 14½", cast, rect, acanthus feet, foliage detail, wreath on
each side, black paint, pr **750.00**
Plate, 7¾" d, Gothic design, copper
wash, lightly silvered, blackberry design rim, sq cut edge **85.00**
Scale, 14" l, balance type, red paint,
black and yellow trim, nickel plated
brass pans, marked "Henry Troem-
ner, Phila, No. 5B, Baker's" **100.00**
Sewing Machine, portable, 10½ x 7½ x

7", manual wood handgrip side wheel, claw feet, black japanned finish, gold stenciling, orig label, Empire Co, dated 1860 .... **200.00**

Sign
Cast, 15 x 17", butcher's, gold and silver paint, steer finial **325.00**
Wrought, 21½" h, blacksmith, horseshoe with nails, anvil, and hammer, black paint **350.00**

Skillet, 8½" sq, imprint on bottom, "Griswold Mfg. Co., Erie, PA, U.S.A. #768" **25.00**

Stove Plate, 5", round, emb, wild turkey and tree design **15.00**

Table, 15 x 27", wrought, three legs, brass details **150.00**

Target, 22" w, eagle, cast, white paint, talons **175.00**

Teakettle, 5" h, bar finial, brass bail, marked "Baster Kyle & Co. #8, Louisville, KY, June 28, 1888 .... **125.00**

Tobacco Cutter, 13 x 13 x 5", wrought, mounted on block in sq pine box, sq nail construction **100.00**

Toy, pull, 4⅝" l, cast, blimp shape, "Navy" **85.00**

Tree Holder, 7", cast, tree trunk design, three root shape feet, black paint, gold trim, wood base **25.00**

Trivet
Heart shape, Wilton **25.00**
Jenny Lind, emb **85.00**

Umbrella Stand, 26¼" h, cast, floral detail, light green repaint **100.00**

Windmill Weight, 19" h, cast, rooster, full bodied **625.00**

IVORY

History: Ivory, a yellowish-white organic material, comes from the teeth or tusks of animals and lends itself well to carving. It has been used for centuries by many cultures for artistic and utilitarian items.

Ivory from elephants shows a reticulated crisscross pattern in a cross section. Hippopotamus teeth, walrus tusks, whale teeth, narwhal tusks, and boars tusks also are ivory sources. Vegetable ivory, bone, stag horn, and plastic are ivory substitutes which often confuse collectors.

Note: Dealers and collectors should be familiar with The Endangered Species Act of 1973, amended in 1978, which limits the importation and sale of antique ivory and tortoise shell items.

Bell, 2¼" d, carved zodiac figures, stained details **175.00**

Blotter Holder, 5¾" l, rounded bottom, 19th C **500.00**

Bowl, 2⅛" d, lotus shape, stained deep brown **65.00**

Bracelet, 5", flattened circular shape, stained black int., dark brown ext. .. **190.00**

Brush Holder, 9⅞" h, carved, cylindrical curved tusk, diagonal spiral pattern, scalloped edge collar rim, wood base **880.00**

Buttons, 1¹⁄₁₆", self shank, raised gold dec, birds, insects, and florals, set of 9 .... **800.00**

Calling Card Case, 4⅛", carved figures in garden setting with trees and dwellings, leafy foliate dec on top and bottom edges **140.00**

Candlesticks, 9" h, solid, sq base, pr . **600.00**

Cane Handle, 5½" l, foliate carved, silver mounted, engraved "S. R. Harter/Union/Iowa," 19th C **125.00**

Caulking Mallet, 8⅛" l, wood handle, mid 19th C **150.00**

Cigarette Holder, 6¾", carved **65.00**

Cribbage Board, 16½" l, mounted carved seals, engraved seal hunting scene on bottom **400.00**

Dagger, 10¾" l, spacer turned and scribed, inlaid red sealing wax, mid 19th C **200.00**

Fan Holder, carved openwork, figure of Shoulao flanked by bat and flowering tree **60.00**

Figure
Chinese Maiden, 21" h, carved, holding chrysanthemum bough to face, wearing robes flanked with billowing scarves and rope sash **1,100.00**
Crayfish, 14½" l, carved, joined segmented tail and legs **350.00**
Dog Team, 11" l, drawing burden sled **350.00**
Farmer, 2½" h, 19th C **75.00**
Hand, 4¼" h, carved, clenched fist, 19th C **850.00**
Mouse, mother seated, gnaws a Daikon, four baby mice scamper at her feet and over back, black inlaid eyes, inscribed "Masayoshi" **200.00**
Pheasant, 12½", standing, straw hat tied under chin, short coat over trousers, holding staff and two fish **650.00**
William Shakespeare, 2¼" h, 19th C **75.00**

Frame, 3" h, 3½" w, miniature, easel

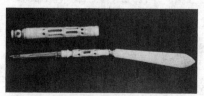

Letter Opener and Pen, 9½" l, top contains Stanhope with map of Atlantic City, $100.00.

back, two small ball feet, carved, scrolling two dragons on sides, artist sgd	100.00
Hair Comb, seven graduated balls, mid 19th C	50.00
Hat Stand, 9″, tripod legs carved in dragon shape, cylindrical centerpiece with incised floral sprigs, 19th C	550.00
Jagging Wheel, 6⅞″, carved walrus handle, whale wheel, mid 19th C	400.00
Letter Opener, 11⅛″, snake coiling over leafy vine, bird on branch	175.00
Napkin Ring, carved, lion stalking prey, Chinese	55.00
Salt and Pepper Shakers, 3³⁄₁₆″ h, 2 pc, painted "S" and "P" in black, mid 19th C	300.00
Seam Rubber, 5⅞″ l, rope carved shaft, turk's head knob, mid 19th C	950.00
Serving Fork and Spoon, mid 19th C	100.00
Sewing Kit Case, 3½″ l, elaborate carved initials, 19th C	40.00
Sword, 44″ l, scabbard carved in four sections, low relief figures, Japanese, Meji Period	880.00
Thermometer, 10½″ h, pagoda shape, raised stepped cylindrical base, three spiral carved columns, Chinese carved stupa, 19th C	1,750.00
Totem, 7¾″ l, 19th C	150.00
Toy, 11½″ h, figure of Liberty on pedestal, red, white, and blue inked flag shield and American flag, holding flag on staff with right hand, "JHTA" on base plaque, side crank revolves figure	1,600.00
Urn, 18″, deity seated on back of mythical beast, her principal hands raised in prayer, sixteen secondary hands holding emblems	925.00
Vase, 9⅝″, domed cov with fu lion knop, medallions with figural scenes reserved on lotus scroll ground, animal mask and loose ring handles, keyfret band on rim, c1900	800.00
Walking Stick, 36″, dragon shape, carved, writhing, scaly, stylized face with curled horns, gaping mouth, 19th C	550.00

JACK-IN-THE-PULPIT VASES

History: Jack-in-the-Pulpit glass vases, made in the trumpet form, were in vogue during the late 19th and early 20th centuries. The vases were made in a wide variety of patterns, colors, and sizes.

Additional Listings: See specific glass categories.

Burmese
3½ x 6¾″, ruffled, yellow, pastel rust

8¼″, crystal to cranberry opalescent, $150.00.

and tan ground, autumn leaves, blue berries, and tendrils dec, Mt Washington	485.00
12⅜″, ribbon candy rim, enamel beading dec, attributed to Webb	975.00
Cased	
4 x 7¼″, creamy opaque ext., white and yellow flowers, green leaves, gold trim, deep rose pink int., amber edge, ormolu leaf feet	125.00
6½ x 6½″, white ext., shaded maroon int., ruffled	115.00
6¾ x 7¼″, white ext., shaded blue hobnail int.	110.00
7 x 15¾″, blue ext., white int., applied clear shell trim and foot	175.00
Cranberry, 4¼ x 6⅜″, DQ, ruffled, applied clear wishbone feet	125.00
Green Overlay, 5¾ x 6¼″, white ext., soft green int., applied clear feet	100.00
Iridescent amethyst and gold lustre, feather veining	200.00
Loetz, 12″, green, silver-blue irid spots, unsigned, c1900	450.00
Nailsea, 3¾ x 7½″, frosted chartreuse green, white loopings, applied frosted feet	135.00
Opalesent, 5¼ x 8½″, chartreuse green, coil stem, five vaseline petal foot	90.00
Spatter	
3¼ x 5″, gold overlay, ruffled pink top	115.00
5 x 8½″, white, green, and cranberry	100.00
6¾ x 7″, mustard, white, and pigeon blood, sapphire blue ground, DQ	100.00

JADE

History: Jade is the generic name for two distinct minerals, nephrite and jadeite. Nephrite, an amphibole mineral from Central Asia and used in pre-18th century pieces, has a waxy surface and ranges in hues from white to almost a black green. Jadeite, a pyroxene mineral found in Burma and used from 1700 to the present, has a glassy appearance and comes in various shades of white, green, yellow-brown, and violet.

Jade cannot be carved because of its hardness. Shapes are achieved through sawing and grinding with wet abrasives, such as quartz, crushed garnets, and carborundum.

Prior to 1800 few pieces are signed or dated. Stylistic considerations are used for dating. The Ch'ien Lung period (1736–95) is considered the "golden age" of Jade.

Reference: Sandra Andacht, *Oriental Antiques & Art: An Identification And Value Guide,* Wallace-Homestead, 1987.

Museum: Avery Brundage Collection, de Young Museum, San Francisco, CA.

Beaker, 3⅝", white, splayed base, large central knop, flared rim, 18th C **1,000.00**
Belt Hook, 4", mottled icy green, dragon shape **125.00**
Bowl, 9" l, greenish white stone, bright green and rust inclusions, carved, quatrefoil form, pendant ring handles, ext. wall lotus scroll, int. with pair of mandarin ducks, Chinese, 19th C, pr **1,300.00**
Brush Pot, 4¼", scrolling cloud pattern dec, Chinese, 19th C **310.00**
Brush Washer, 4⅜" l, translucent olive green, carved, irregular lotus leaf shape, incised vein details, russet inclusions, black mottling **200.00**
Cigarette box, 7", cylindrical, green, SS bottom and collar, hinged cov, surmounted carnelian rooster **300.00**
Cup, 4½", white, boat shape, dragon handles, curved spout, Chinese . . . **350.00**
Dish, domed cov, 4⅝" d, white, compressed globular body, wide flanged

Floral centerpiece, 21½″ w, 12½″ h, $350.00.

rim, carved stylized taotie band dec, bud finial, 19th C **1,800.00**
Ewer, 6", light green, bulbous shape, arched spout, dragon head handles, loose ring **400.00**
Figure
　Boat, 6¾" h, pale gray, setting sail, man pulling on three ropes, standing celestial maiden holding bamboo pole, yellow tones **800.00**
　Female Immortal, 6" h, carved, mirror image, astride prancing steed, playing lute, lavender highlights, pr **5,500.00**
　Maiden, 6" h, carved, tiered robes encircled by billowing scarves, holding chrysanthemum in left hand . . **250.00**
Inkstand, 5", with coral and SS, marked "Edward I, Farmer, New York" **200.00**
Inkstone, 3⅝" l, oval form, incised rim band, oval depression to one side, black and white mottling **175.00**
Lamp, 29" h, Goddess, Kuan Yin, standing, flowing cowl, robes and jewels, child on one upraised arm, rosary and fly whisk in other **1,600.00**
Letter Opener, 6", spinach green **100.00**
Miniature
　Teapot, 3⅞", pale gray green nephrite, bulbous, dragon head and loop handle, short spout, carved single band of double comma motifs, late 19th C **400.00**
　Vase, 4⅞", white, beaker shape, lobed corners, carved, low relief, stylized long tailed birds, bands of stiff leaf design on neck and foot . **250.00**
Pendant, round, creamy, 14K gold mounting, Chinese initials **150.00**
Pitcher, 5⅜" h, band of spirals and whirl circles, rope borders, angular strap handle **520.00**
Planter, 5⅛" h, 7¼" l, rect, dark green, wood base, Chinese, late 18th C . . **450.00**
Plaque, 8¾", carved, archaic bronze vessels, taotie masks, open work handles, Chinese, 18th C, pr **650.00**
Saucer, 4¼", slightly flared rim, short ring foot, deep green, brown mottling **200.00**
Snuff Bottle, greenish-white tone, flattened ovoid shape, sloping shoulders, oval foot, 1800–80, pr **600.00**
Stemcup, 2" h, pale mottled green, two finely carved taotie masks on bowl, hollow foot carved with ring, 18th C . **1,150.00**
Toggle, 1¾" l, white, cluster of peaches, joined by curling lingzhi and leafy stems, small bat to one side **100.00**
Urn, 8" h, flattened ovoid form, incised taotie mask dec, narrow neck, flanking handles, suspending carved chains attached to dome lid, yoke shape hanger **700.00**

JAPANESE AND CHINESE CERAMICS

History: The Chinese pottery tradition has existed for thousands of years. By the sixteenth century, Chinese ceramic wares were being exported to India, Persia, and Egypt. The Ming dynasty (1368-1643) saw the strong development of glazed earthenwares and shapes. During the Ch'ing dynasty, the Ch'ien Lung period (1736-95) marked the golden age of interchange with the west.

Trade between China and the west began in the sixteenth century when the Portuguese established Macao. The Dutch entered the trade early in the seventeenth century. With the establishment of the English East India Company, all of Europe was seeking Chinese-made pottery and porcelain. Styles, shapes, and colors were developed to suit Western tastes. The tradition continued until the late nineteenth century.

Like the Chinese, the Japanese spent centuries developing their ceramic arts. Each region established its own forms, designs, and glazes. Individual artists added to the uniqueness.

Japanese ceramics began to be exported to the west in the mid-19th century. Their beauty quickly made them a favorite of the patrician class.

The ceramic tradition continues into the 20th century. Modern artists enjoy equal fame with older counterparts.

Reference: Sandra Andacht, *Oriental Antiques & Art: An Identification And Value Guide,* Wallace-Homestead, 1987.

Periodical: *The Orientalia Journal,* P. O. Box 94P, Little Neck, NY 11363. Subscription: $12.00.

Additional Listings: Canton, Fitzhugh, Imari, Kutani, Nanking, Rose Medallion, and Satsuma.

CHINESE

Brush Pot, 5½" h, iron-red landscape
dec **425.00**
Charger, 14½", polychrome, flowering
peach branch, laden with fruit, two
diminutive flying wufu **300.00**
Garden Seat, 18½", barrel form, two
water scenes, pink and orange water
plants, suspended interlocking
pierced 'Cash' emblems, diaper and
floral bands, keyfret border **715.00**
Jar, cov, 25" h, two reserves of mythical
phoenix, fanciful landscape, large
pink peony blossoms, two crest
shaped reserves of cranes in flight,
lemon yellow ground, fronted pink lotus, lime green tendrils, ruyi shoulder
band, floral swags, four coral-red applied mock lion mask handles, domed
lid, fu dog finial, 19th C, pr **3,575.00**
Jardiniere
12¼", slender ovoid, everted rim,

finely painted, court women engag-
ing in leisurely pursuits, garden
scene, ruyi head band, flower
sprays, poetic dedication, pr **550.00**
13¾", cylindrical, everted rim, narrow
foot, four horizontal rows of multicolored shou characters, stylized
pale pink and blue lappet bands,
yellow ground, pr **825.00**
Tile, 16¼ x 23", ochre colored rect
plaque, fan shaped waterway scene,
blue and white alternating borders of
confronting dragons and scrolling tendrils, framed **385.00**

CHINESE EXPORT

Candleholder, 5", animal form, crouching lap dog, whimsical face, iron-red
glaze, gilt textured fur, ears, and tail,
bell form urn, 19th C, pr **2,750.00**
Cup, 4½", int. view, figural dragon twin
handles **275.00**
Cup and Saucer, handleless, nude lady
bathing, male attendant pouring
water for her, Ch'ien Lung, c1790 .. **250.00**
Dish
8", carp shape, underglaze blue dec
of scales, fins, and eye on both
sides, three low feet, c1625–50 .. **2,750.00**
11⅝", octafoil, Pseudo Tobacco Leaf
pattern, stylized leaves, cut pomegranates and brocade rings, pink,
deep blue, iron-red and chartreuse,
gold highlights, late 18th C, pr ... **4,675.00**
Figure
5", Blanc-de-Chine, bearded man
wearing visor cap with tassels,
jacket, voluminous breeches,
smoking pipe, seated astride scaly
beast with bushy tail, mane, and
beard, late 17th of early 18th C .. **1,650.00**
6⅝ and 9½"h, cats grinning, ribbon
collars, black painted eyes, one
with turquoise glaze, other with
coral, pr **425.00**
9¼", parrot, green glaze, coral-red
beak and feet, standing on blue
glazed rockwork, pr **1,100.00**
Ginger jar, 9½", ovoid body, continuous
scene of small boats, figures, and pavilions, ruyi head border, cov with
scenes of man and small pagoda, underglaze blue, 19th C **475.00**
Mug, 4½", British Marine dec, iron-red
and black ship flying Union Jacks,
rose and green floral spring on sides,
black edged iron-red chain border,
c1780–90 .... **425.00**
Planter, 4⅜" h, elephant form, pr **750.00**
Plate
7¾", American ship of war, armed .. **1,200.00**

9½", American eagle center, gilt highlights on brown eagle, shield initialed "EHF," salmon rim and gilt border, gilt scallops and blue dots edge, c1795 .... **500.00**

Platter

6¾", oval, scattered pink flowers, gilt spear head band at cavetto, slightly flaring rim with pink and pale turquoise brocade design, ribbon tied 'Cash' emblems, 19th C **1,760.00**

11¾", Pseudo Tobacco Leaf pattern, stylized leaves, cut pomegranates and brocade rings, pink, deep blue, iron-red and chartreuse, gold highlights, late 18th C **3,575.00**

16⅝", octagonal, armorial, arms of Nassau, Earl of Rochfort, motto, Qianlong, c1760, pr **3,850.00**

Punch Bowl, 11½", overall dec of Masonic symbols **900.00**

Sauce Tureen, 12", diamond shape, scalloped edge, Pseudo Tobacco Leaf pattern, stylized leaves, cut pomegranates and brocade rings, pink, deep blue, iron-red and chartreuse, blue and green glazed loop handles, two applied coral-red and yellow floral bloom finial, gold highlights, late 18th C **3,025.00**

Saucer, 6¼" d, iron-red borders, stylized anthemion motif, c1815 .... **50.00**

Teapot, cov, Yixing stoneware, 27⅞" h, squat spherical body, loop handle (repaired), straight spout, rims of pot, spout, cov, knob overlaid with thin layer of brass, incised mengchen mark for Hui Mengchen **400.00**

Vase, 6⅞", cylinder, painted figures and flower vases **180.00**

Warming Dish, 7½", armorial, central well penciled with arms of MacDonald, grassaille and gilt grapevine festoon linked by arms of Forbes and motto, Qianlong, c1795, pr **2,100.00**

JAPANESE

Basket, 5", abstract figures related to tea ceremony, greens, bail handle, Oribe **85.00**

Bowl, 6¾", int. painted in shades of iron-red, green, deep turquoise, black, gray, and gold, spray of chrysanthemums tied with tasseled gilt ribbon, ext. molded around base with border of incised petals, gold highlights, rim highlighted in worn gilting, Arita, 18th C **1,150.00**

Charger, 13¼", two large iron oxide carp, underglaze blue ground, peon-

Banko, teapot, green face, blue-green dragonfly handle, 6" h, 8" w, $190.00.

ies, stylized waves, and flowering branches, Meiji period **165.00**

Ewer, 10½", red and gilt motif, riverscapes and figures, loop handle, dragon finial, Kaga, late 19th C **525.00**

Figure, 3", seated Sumo wrestler, left hand on ground, right raised, Sumida **1,000.00**

Incense Burner, 12", Bijin leaning against lantern, pierced openwork, underglaze blue and white, Hirado, Mikawachi, 19th C **700.00**

Nodder, 5½", Fukujurojin, seated figure, robe with knotted tie cord on chest, extended cylindrical forehead, polychrome dec, Banko **450.00**

Plate, 11¼", hexagonal, kakiemon palette, bird and flowering tree, wide rim of floral reserves on coral diaper ground **145.00**

Sake Bottle, 7¼", rect body, underglaze blue, two pine trees and three pavilions, stylized landscape, sq top with leaf and cloud device, one corner with sq spout, opposite corner pierced with small hole, Arita, late 17th C .. **675.00**

Vase

12", ovoid, cylindrical neck, trumpet mouth, slightly flared foot, two circular painted reserves of ho-o, varying brocade ground, overlaid dragon crawling up the body and around neck, iron-red Fukagama-Sei, Meiji marks **475.00**

20¼", baluster, slender body, short everted rim, turquoise and white chrysanthemums, lappet foot band, gilt highlights **100.00**

44½", ovoid, slightly flared foot, brightly colored enamels, various outdoor scenes of courtiers on elaborate ground, flanked by

Vase, Sumida Guwa, two monkeys wirh dragon costume, red ground, crackle glazed top, 7″ h, sgd cartouche, $375.00.

molded dragon which forms handles grasping tasseled ribbons in claws, surmounted by flaring floriform mouth, extensive gilt overpainting, Kyoto, c1900 . . . . 800.00

JASPERWARE

History: Jasperware is a hard, unglazed porcelain with a colored ground, varying from the most common blues and greens to lavender, yellow, red, or black. The white designs are applied in relief and often reflect a classical motif. Jasperware was first produced at Wedgwood's Etruria Works in 1775. Josiah Wedgwood described it as "a fine Terra Cotta of great beauty and delicacy proper for cameos".

Many other English potters, in addition to Wedgwood, produced jasperware. Two of the leaders were Adams and Copeland and Spode. Several continental potters, e.g., Heubach, also produced the ware.

Reference: Susan and Al Bagdade, *Warman's English & Continental Pottery & Porcelain, 1st Edition,* Warman Publishing Co., Inc., 1987.

Reproduction Alert: Jasperware still is made today, especially by Wedgwood.

Note: This category includes all pieces of jasperware which were made by companies other than Wedgwood. Wedgwood jasperware is found in the Wedgwood listing.

Biscuit Jar, dark blue, white relief of hunt scene, SP bail, cov, and rim, marked "Adams" 175.00
Box, 6″ d, white cameos of cherubs and lovebirds on cov, gray-green ground, ftd, unmarked 175.00

Creamer, 2½″ h, pale pink frolicking Kewpies, sage green ground, sgd "O'Neill" 165.00
Cruet, 6¾″, white relief man and woman toasting each other, small cupid and word "Prosit," sage green ground, matching orig stopper, Germany . . . 100.00
Cup and Saucer, dark blue, white classical figures 100.00
Dish, 4¼″ d, white relief Indian with shield and hatchet, sheaf of wheat border, green ground, sgd "Heubach" 60.00
Hatpin Holder, 4¼″, deep blue, white figures, band of flowers at top, marked "Adams" 50.00
Jar, 3½″ h, white calssical cameos, blue ground, SP lid and handle, marked "Adams, Tunstall, England" 110.00
Jug, 7″, blue, classical figures representing the four seasons, angular handles with foliage motif, silver rim, marked "Adams," late 18th C 225.00

Pitcher, 5⅜″ h, brown ground, Copeland, marked "Football/JMSD&S/1985, Reg. 180288," $300.00.

Pitcher
5″, white cameos of cherubs in roses, green ground, umarked 125.00
8″, blue, white classical figures, marked "Copeland, England," c1885 . . . . 225.00
Planter, large, blue, white relief Apollo and four muses, c1850 . . . . 225.00
Plaque
7½″, white raised semi-nude female figure, green ground, marked "Germany" 110.00
11¼″, white raised figures of children at play, soft green ground, marked "Germany" 125.00

11½", white raised figures of putti, blue ground, marked "Germany" . **175.00**

Spill Vase, deep blue, white relief florals, trees, and muses representing poetry and drama **110.00**

Teapot, 6½", blue, white relief birds and bamboo, pewter top and finial, marked "Copeland-Spode" **150.00**

Tumbler, 4", white classical cameos, brown ground **65.00**

Tureen, cov, 7½" d, blue, white relief bridge scene, floral dec, matching stand, marked "Copeland-Spode," c1820 . . . . **160.00**

Vase

4", white cameos of man with spade, woman under tree, blue ground . . **25.00**

7", white cameo of classic woman, carrying torch, light green ground . **50.00**

Wall Pocket, 7½" h, white classical lady, green ground **30.00**

JEWEL BOXES

History: The evolution of jewelry was paralleled by the development of boxes in which to store it. Jewel box design followed the fashion trends dictated by furniture styles. Many jewel boxes are lined.

Wood, double book shape, 5¼ x 3¼ x 2⅞", hinged cov, Victorian lady motif on top, $17.50.

Art Nouveau, 10 x 8 x 7", ormolu, raised figural and floral dec, plaque dated 1903 . . . . **225.00**

Brass, 2½ x 5½ x 3½", coach shape, glass panels, red velvet lining **125.00**

Glass, 4½ x 2¾", cranberry, enameled floral dec, SP rim **150.00**

Ivory, 8¾ x 5½ x 4¾", rect, hinged lid, delicate engraved and repousse mounts **200.00**

Malachite, 4½ x 2½", veneer, rect, raised feet, satin lining, Russian, 19th C **225.00**

Pewter, 5½ x 9½", engraved brass frame-like ornament on top, oval mosaic work, purple velvet lining, marked "Marshall & Sons, Edinburgh, Scotland" **250.00**

Silver

German, 4¾ x 3 x 3½", ftd, raised figures of man, woman, and animals, pink velvet lining **100.00**

Plated, 8 x 5 x 3", oval, hinged lid, ftd emb cupids, daisy chain and roses, velvet lining, marked "Wilcox" . . . **75.00**

Sterling, 13 x 5 x 4", repousse sides, small petal-like beaded edges, fancy feet, red velvet lining, marked "Meridan" **150.00**

Wave Crest

5¼ x 3", oval, hinged cov, gold emb scroll around edge, blue and white center florals, pink sprays, green leaves, marked **265.00**

6 x 3", pale blue painted flowers, red banner mark **570.00**

JEWELRY

History: Jewelry has been a part of every culture. It was a way of displaying wealth, power, or love of beauty. In the current antique marketplace, it is easiest to find jewelry dating between 1800 to 1950.

Jewelry items were treasured and handed down as heirlooms from generation to generation. In the United States, antique jewelry is defined by law, specifically U.S. Customs laws, as any jewelry one hundred or more years old. The term "heirloom/estate" jewelry, i.e., at least twenty-five years old, property acquired new, used, or through inheritance, is used for old jewelry that does not meet the "antique" definition.

The jewelry found in this listing fits either the antique or "heirloom/estate" definition. The list contains no new reproduction pieces. The jewelry is made of metals and gemstones proven to endure over time. Inexpensive and mass produced costume jewelry is covered in *Warman's Americana & Collectibles.*

Several major auction houses, especially Christie's, Doyle's, and Sotheby's in New York City, hold specialized jewelry auctions several times each year.

Note: The first step in determining the value of a piece of old jewelry is to correctly identify the metal and gemstones. Take into account the current value of the metal and gemstones plus the piece's age, identifying marks, quality, condition, construction, etc.

References: Lillian Baker, *100 Years of Collectible Jewelry,* Collector Books, 1986; Vivienne Becker, *Antique and 20th Century Jewelry,* Van Nostrand Reinhold; Rose L. Goldemberg, *Antique Jewelry: A Practical And Passionate Guide,* Crown Publishers, Inc., 1976; Arthur Guy Kaplan, *The Official Price Guide To Antique Jewelry,* 5th edition, House of Collectibles, 1985.

Advisor: Elaine J. Luartes.

Bar Pin
  Art Deco, platinum, onyx center set
    with diamonds 1,000.00
  Edwardian, platinum, set of half
    pearls and rose diamonds 1,800.00
  Victorian
    SS, "MIZPAH" and ribbon motif,
      English hallmarks 45.00
    YG, 15K, set with three cabochon
      garnets 200.00
Barrette, Edwardian, engraved 14K yg,
  lattice motif set with seed pearls . . . 500.00
Beads
  Art Deco
    Carved ivory, lotus motif, 32" l . . . 450.00
    Crystal rondelles alternating with
      faceted red beads, 44" l 85.00
  Edwardian, seed pearl choker, four-
    teen strands, three gold bars set
    with half pearls 1,900.00
  Victorian
    Coral, graduated beads, 14K yg or-
      nate clasp 225.00
    Opals, forty-three opals alternating
      with faceted crystal rondelles,
      opal bead clasp 1,800.00
Bracelet
  Edwardian, 10K yg, knife edge style,
    two hearts, bow and cluster motif,
    set with seed pearls and diamonds 700.00
  Victorian
    Bangle, gold filled
      Etched band dec 75.00
      Set with garnets 170.00
    Link, 14K rose gold, graduated oval
      cabochon moonstone links 900.00
    Lion head motif, 10K yg, set with
      three diamonds and two garnets 800.00
    Mesh style, 14K yg, clasp set with
      half pearls 1,200.00
Brooch
  Art Nouveau, SS, woman's head, Un-
    ger Bros trademark 350.00
  Art Retro, 14K rose gold, floral spray
    motif set with rubies and diamonds 600.00
  Edwardian, platinum, modified filigree
    style, oval shape, pave set dia-
    monds (approx 3.50 cts TW) and
    one 40 ct sapphire 18,000.00
  Victorian
    Cameo, shell, oval yg frame, wom-
      an's head in profile 400.00

    Eagle motif, 14K yg, mine-cut dia-
      mond suspended from beak . . . 800.00
    Handpainted portrait on porcelain,
      gold filled frame 250.00
Chain
  Art Deco, platinum, fancy links
    spaced with diamonds, (2.5 cts
    TW), 32" l 5,800.00
  Victorian
    Slide Style, 14K yg, curb links,
      fancy shape engraved slide,
      52" l 500.00
    Watch-Vest style, 14K yg, fetter and
      five link style, 12" 350.00
    Woven Hair, repousse gold clasp,
      60" 170.00
Chatelain, Victorian, belt style, silver,
  pierced, sculptured and engraved,
  orig memo case, scissors, sheath,
  and thimble receptacle, English hall-
  marks 800.00
Cuff Links
  Art Deco, platinum, set with mother of
    pearl and half pearls 190.00
  Victorian
    Fancy shamrock motif, SS 80.00
    Plain ball motif, 14K yg 90.00
Earrings, Victorian
  Dangle
    Ram's head motif, ornate, 14k yg . 750.00
    Teardrop circle, 15K yg 475.00
    Urn motif, high carat yellow gold . 675.00
  Diamond Drop style, silver and gold
    circular framed mounts set with
    mine-cut diamonds (approx 1.25
    cts TW) 1,050.00
  Hoop, small, 14K yg 130.00

Locket, Victorian, yellow gold, center is micro mosaic of architectural motif, $250.00.

Lavaliere
Art Nouveau, 14K yg, opal and baroque pearl drop **300.00**
Edwardian, 14K yg, delicate ring-line design set with half pearls **190.00**
Victorian, 14K yg, bell shape, set with diamond and seed pearls **160.00**
Locket
Art Deco, 14K white gold, geometric design **375.00**
Art Nouveau, 14K yg, round swirl motif, set with one diamond **500.00**
Lorgnette, Victorian, silver gilt, oval retractable lenses in ornate cherub motif case **900.00**
Necklace
Art Deco, enamel dec SS links, set with lapis color glass **165.00**
Arts and Crafts, hand made, heavy-link silver chain, mounted with baroque pearl dec with large rect shaped frame set with one polished black opal, two suspended irregular shaped polished black opals **4,500.00**
Victorian, gold chain, set with garnets **500.00**
Pendant
Art Nouveau
Cross, 18K yg, hand made, set with one diamond **750.00**
Dragonfly motif, silver gilt, plique a'jour enamel, set with cabochon opals, baroque pearl, and diamonds **2,000.00**
Victorian
Figural, carved lava, gold fittings . **250.00**
Heart, yg, pave seed pearls **300.00**
Pin
Art Deco
Antelope motif, SS **55.00**
Geometric design, platinum, set with square-cut rubies and round-cut diamonds **2,200.00**
Art Nouveau, gold, sculpture, miniature face set with baroque pearls and cabochon rubies **800.00**
Arts and Crafts, SS, hand hammered floral motif **75.00**
Victorian
Crescent shape, 14 K yg, set with half pearls **100.00**
Scroll motif, 14K yg, set with diamond and seed pearls **400.00**
Starburst motif, pin/pendant combination, 14K yg, set with ruby and seed pearls **185.00**
Ring
Edwardian, platinum, filigree style, three diamonds, straight row setting **2,000.00**
Victorian
9K yg, snakes motif, set with cabochon opal and amethyst, En-

Ring, Victorian, 14K yellow gold, elongated style, turquois straight row set surrounded by rose-cut diamonds, $350.00.

glish hallmarks **450.00**
10K yg, cabochon opal surrounded by six rose-cut diamonds **285.00**
10K yg, set with two mine-cut diamonds, ruby, and emerald **350.00**
14K yg, set with hardstone cameo **500.00**
Seal, Victorian, gold, flower motif, amethyst intaglio **850.00**

Stick Pin, Victorian, scarf, silver gilt, pietra dura (lapis, coral, jade) set in cable-twist frame, $85.00.

Stick Pin, tie
Art Deco, platinum, geometric design, set with diamonds **900.00**
Art Nouveau, 18K yg, miniature Gibson girl enameled portrait, set with diamonds **750.00**
Victorian, 14K yg, gargoyle motif, set with ruby **125.00**
Watch
Art Deco, open face, lapel, SS and marcasite, marked "925" **220.00**

Art Nouveau, open face, lapel, 14K
yg, angel and floral motif **1,200.00**
Art Retro, wristwatch, lady's, 14K yg,
dec with diamonds and sapphires **775.00**
Victorian
Hunting Case, gold filled, Waltham,
three colored gold **400.00**
Pocket, open face, 18 K yg, Ham-
ilton, Arabic numerals **275.00**
Watch Fob, Victorian, 14K yg and
mother of pearl, horn motif **80.00**

JUDAICA

History: As members of the Jewish faith spread
throughout the world, artifacts used in their syn-
agogues and religious celebrations in the home
assumed the artistic attributes of each individual
region. Thus each basic form, whether Hanukah
lamp or Torah breast plate, may come in a wide
variety of styles.

Silver is a favored medium for many objects.
Hence, objects have value both by weight as well
as artistic content. Signed items are the most desired. Sotheby's and Christie's hold at least one
special auction of Judaica each year.

Amulet Case, 5½″, Italian silver, Turin,
master or assayer's mark GB, mid
18th C **5,225.00**
Charger, 23″ d, Continental silver, re-
pousse floral and figural dec, c1780,
48 oz **1,650.00**
Circumcision Cup
3½″, SS, English, marked "Urquart
and Hart, London, 1792" **950.00**
5″, German, double, silver gilt,
marked "Johanna Becker, Augs-
burg," c1755–57 . . . . **13,200.00**
Circumcision Knife, 7″, tortoiseshell, SS,
and steel, Continental, late 18th C . **1,650.00**
Comb, Burial Society, 6″ w, brass, Hun-
garian, 1881 . . . . **5,775.00**
Esther Scroll, 10½″, cased, Austro–
Hungarian silver, Vienna, 1846 . . . . **1,650.00**
Goblet, 4″, presentation, German silver,
c1850 . . . . **660.00**
Hanukah Lamp, 9¾″, Austrian 800 fine
silver, scroll edge backplate surmounted by crown, facing emb with
pair of unengraved tablets flanked by
pair of griffins, cartouche of the Star
of David, rect platform, contiguous
row of eight urn form lamps on wire
frame, four scrolled supports, lacking
servant's lamp, late 19th C, 22 oz 10
dwt **1,800.00**
Kiddush Cup, 5¼″, silver gilt, Polish,
mid 18th C **3,850.00**

Mezuzah Case, 4½″, American silver,
Ludwig Wolpert, NY, stamped "Toby
Pascher Workshop, The Jewish Mu-
seum, NY" **650.00**
Menorah Wall Sconce, 10½″ l, Conti-
nental silver, heraldic repousse back
shield, c1858, 18 oz **2,860.00**

Passover Dish, 15¼″, pewter, German,
maker's initials "D.V.D.," c1768 . . . . **3,750.00**
Passover Plate, 8¾″, ceramic, Conti-
nental, 18th C **500.00**

**Kiddush Cup, 2⅛″ h, engraved dec,
hallmarks, Russian, 1888, $60.00.**

Plaque, 2¾ x 2″, SS, rabbi, inscribed,
after engraving by Boris Schatz,
framed **500.00**
Sabbath Beaker, 3″, silver gilt, German,
Johann Friedrich Schutteler, Lipps-
tadt, c1825 . . . . **1,300.00**
Sabbath Candlesticks, pr, 16¼″, Aaron
Katz, London, 1894, Polish style . . . **1,000.00**
Spice Box
4¾″, SS, Scandinavian, fish form,
blurred marks on tail, articulated
body, hinged head, green jeweled
eyes, 19th C, 1 oz 10 dwt **385.00**
5¼″, SS, filigree, Bohemian, sgd "R.
G., Prague, 1815" **1,200.00**
10″, tower shape, SS, filigree, Polish,
18th C **7,500.00**
Torah Ark Key, 4″, Italian silver, 18th C **4,125.00**
Torah Pointer, 10½″, Polish silver, worn
on index finger, 18th C **825.00**
Urn, 6½″, Bezalel, silver inlaid brass,
c1910 . . . . **1,320.00**
Wine Chalice, 13″ h, Continental silver,
Herman Lang, Augsburg, 17th C, 29
oz **2,325.00**

JUGTOWN POTTERY

History: In 1920 Jacques and Julianna Busbee left their cosmopolitan environs and returned to North Carolina to revive the state's dying craft of pottery making. Jugtown Pottery, a colorful and somewhat off-beat operation, was located in Moore County, miles away from any large city and accessible only "if mud permits."

Ben Owens, a talented young potter, turned the wares. Jacques Busbee did most of the designing and glazing. Julianna handled promotion.

Utilitarian and decorative items were produced. Although many colorful glazes were used, orange predominated. A Chinese blue glaze that ranged from light blue to deep turquoise was a prized glaze reserved for the very finest pieces.

Jacques Busbee died in 1947. Julianna, with the help of Owens, ran the pottery until 1958 when it was closed. After long legal battles, the pottery was reopened in 1960. It now is owned by Country Roads, Inc., a non-profit organization. The pottery still is operating and using the old mark.

Pitcher, 6¼" h, 7"w, tan glaze, incised dec, $90.00.

Bowl
5" d, blue and gray 25.00
5 x 3", frogskin glaze 50.00
Candlesticks, 3" h, Chinese Translation, Chinese blue and deep red, marked, pr 70.00

Cookie Jar, cov, 12" h, ovoid, strap handles 75.00
Creamer, cov, 4¾", yellow, marked ... 45.00
Finger Bowl, Chinese Translation 100.00
Jar
6¼", yellowware, marked 45.00
6¾", cov, bulbous, flaring rim, eared handles, redware, bright orange glaze, minor edge chips 48.00
Mug, brown glaze 25.00
Pie Plate, 9½" d, orange, black concentric circles 65.00
Pitcher, 5", gray and cobalt blue salt glaze 75.00
Rose Jar, cov, 4½" h, blended olive green glaze 48.00
Sugar, cov, 3¾", Tobacco Spit glaze, marked 35.00
Teapot, 5¼", Tobacco Spit glaze, sgd, c1930 .... 40.00
Vase
3¾", Chinese Translation, Chinese blue, marked 100.00
6½", bulbous, open handles, white Chinese glaze 150.00
7", four small handles, salt glaze ... 85.00

KPM *K.P.M*

History: The mark, KPM, has been used separately and in conjunction with other symbols by many German porcelain manufacturers, among whom are the Königliche Porzellan Manufactur in Meissen, 1720s; Königliche Porzellan Manufactur in Berlin, 1832–1847; and Krister Porzellan Manufactur in Waldenburg, mid-19th century.

Collectors now use the term "KPM" to refer to the high quality porcelain produced in the Berlin area in the 18th and 19th centuries.

Reference: Susan and Al Bagdade, *Warman's English & Continental Pottery & Porcelain, 1st Edition,* Warman Publishing Co., Inc., 1987.

Bowl, 10", fruit dec, pastels, marked .. 60.00
Cake Plate, floral dec 20.00
Celery, 6 x 12", floral dec, green mark with sceptre 65.00
Cheese Board, rose and leaf garland border, hole to hang, marked 45.00
Cream Jug, 4¼", cavorting cherubs, orb and scepter mark, c1870 .... 300.00
Cup and Saucer, hunting scene, filigree, 18th C 50.00
Dinner Service, Art Deco style, gilt and jeweled in turquoise and pink, flowering plants on speckled gilt and iron red ground, sea green borders with molded gilt swags, blue scepter, iron red orb, KPM mark, c1880 .... 8,000.00

Plate, 9½″ d, yellow daffodils, pink roses and lilies, white ground, gold rim, red septer and orb mark plus blue mark, $90.00.

Dish, leaf shape, 9½″, painted, birds on flowering branch, burgundy border, gilt drapery, blue scepter, iron red KPM and orb mark, c1860 . . . .   250.00
Fruit Plate, 9″, hp, gold dec, wide scroll reticulated rims, orb mark, set of 4 .   125.00
Lithopane Panel, 4¾ x 5¾″, Scotch boy   150.00
Plaque
  12¼ x 10″, gypsy girl, dark hair, gold earrings and locket, off shoulder bodice, painted by Kietrich after F N Sichel, sgd, imp "KPM" and scepter mark, c1875 . . . .   1,200.00
  25½ x 20¼″, maiden, flowing classical dress, four companions, imp "KPM" and scepter mark, c1875 .   1,200.00
Relish Dish, 9½ x 12″, blue, chrysanthemum, gold trim 125.00
Scent Bottle, molded scrolls, multicolored painted bouquets of flowers, gilt trim, gilt metal C-scroll stopper, marked, mid 19th C 150.00
Urn, cov, cobalt blue and gilt, floral and cherub dec, pr 300.00
Vase, cov, two loop handles, blue, painted floral bouquets with gilt foliage, flared foot, blue scepter and KPM mark, c1860 . . . .   1,150.00

KAUFFMANN, ANGELICA

History: Marie Angelique Catherine Kauffmann was a Swiss artist who lived from 1741 until 1807. Her paintings were copied by many artists who hand decorated porcelain during the 19th century. The majority of the paintings are neo-classical in style.

Reference: Susan and Al Bagdade, *Warman's English & Continental Pottery & Porcelain, 1st Edition,* Warman Publishing Co., Inc., 1987.

Biscuit Jar, deep green, burgundy, heavy gold, classical scene, 3 figures in center reserve with gold beading, sgd A. Kauffmann, Prov. Saxe, E.S. Germany 160.00
Bowl, 10½″, blue, gold dec, 2 ladies . .   255.00
Box, cov, hinged, 2¾ x 1¾″, porcelain, cupid, 2 maidens 40.00
Cake Plate, 10″, ftd, classical scene, 2 maidens and cupid, beehive mark . .   85.00
Compote, 8″, classical scene, beehive mark, sgd 80.00
Cup and Saucer
  Classical scene, heavy gold trim, ftd   90.00
  Portrait, burgundy, gold, Royal Saxe, E.S. Germany 75.00
Inkwell, pink luster, classical lady 75.00
Pitcher, 8½″, garden scene, ladies, children, and flowers sgd 100.00
Plaque, 8¾″, classical scene, 3 maidens dancing 75.00
Plate
  8″, cobalt blue border, reticualted rim, classical scene with 2 figures . . .   55.00
  8¾″, classical scene, 3 maidens dancing 60.00

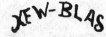

Tobacco Jar, 7½″ h, dark green muted ground with hints of orange and yellow, silver plated rim and lid, $350.00.

Tobacco Humidor, SP top, pipe on top, green ground, ladies and cupid 350.00
Tray, 16½″ d, round, classical figures in reserve, sgd, beehive mark 175.00
Vase, 19″, cobalt blue, classical portrait, sgd 285.00

KEW BLAS

History: Amory and Francis Houghton established the Union Glass Company, Somerville, Massachusetts, in 1851. The company went bankrupt in 1860, but was reorganized. Between 1870 and 1885 the Union Glass Company made pressed glass and blanks for cut glass.

Art glass production began in 1893 under the direction of William S. Blake and Julian de Cordova. Two styles were introduced. A Venetian style consisted of graceful shapes in colored glass, often flecked with gold. An iridescent glass, labeled Kew Blas, was made in plain and decorated forms. The pieces are close in design and form to Quezel products, but lack the subtlety of Tiffany items.

The company ceased production in 1924.

Vase, 10″ h, King Tut variation, white opalescent with gold iridescence, $1,600.00.

Candlesticks, 8½″, irid gold, twisted
  stems, pr 725.00
Compote, 7″ h, twisted stem, ribbed
  bowl, irid gold, pink highlights 375.00
Creamer, 3¼″, irid gold, applied handle   225.00
Finger Bowl and Underplate, 5″ bowl, 6″
  plate, ribbed, scalloped border, metallic luster, gold and platinum highlights 465.00
Goblet, 4¾″, irid gold, curved stem . . .   165.00
Rose Bowl, 3½″, green and gold hooked
  dec, butterscotch ground, gold int. . .   525.00
Sherbet, 5″, irid gold 200.00
Tumbler, 4″, pinched sides, irid gold,
  sgd 185.00
Vase
  5″, spherical, rolled gold rim, green
    and gold pulled feather, white
    ground, early 20th C, sgd 475.00
  6″, dark blue, light blue pulled loops,
    sgd 810.00
  6¼″, cylinder, rolled rim, gold and
    green swags, pale orange, ground,
    early 20th C, sgd, orig paper label   600.00
  7″, bulbous, flared, pulled feather, sgd   1,500.00

7¾″, Zipper, green and gold, sgd . .   850.00
8″, floriform, irid gold, c1910 . . . . . .   175.00
8¼″, baluster, flared rim, gold and yellow pulled feathering, white ground,
  gold int., early 20th C, sgd, orig paper label 500.00

KITCHEN COLLECTIBLES

History: The kitchen was a central focal point in a family's environment until the 1960s. Many early kitchen utensils were handmade and prized by their owners. Next came a period of utilitarian products made of tin and other metals. When the housewife no longer wished to work in a sterile environment, color was added through enamel and plastic and design served both an aesthetic and functional purpose.

The advent of home electricity changed the type and style of kitchen products. Many items went through fads. The high technology field already has made inroads into the kitchen, and another revolution seems at hand.

References: Jane H. Celehar, *Kitchens and Gadgets, 1920 to 1950*, Wallace-Homestead, 1982; Linda Campbell Franklin, *300 Hundred Years of Kitchen Collectibles*, Books Americana, 1982, second edition; Glydon Shirley, *The Miracle in Grandmother's Kitchen*, privately printed, 1983.

Periodical: Kitchen Collectibles News, Box 383, Murray Hill Station, New York, NY 10016.

Additional Listings: Baskets, Brass, Butter Prints, Copper, Fruit Jars, Food Molds, Graniteware, Ironware, Tinware, and Woodenware. See *Warman's Americana & Collectibles* for more examples including electrical appliances.

Lemon Squeezer, Griswold, marked "The Griswold Mfg Co., Erie, PA," $45.00.

Apple Peeler, Keen Kutter, 1898 . . . . .   60.00
Bean Pot, Spongeware, light rust and
  green 85.00
Biscuit Cutter, Rumford 13.00
Bread Board, 9½″, maple, carved and
  shaped border 45.00
Bread Box, metal, brick red 12.00
Butter Churn, Red Wing 95.00
Butter Mold, cow, plunger stick 225.00
Butter Print Roller, six prints, c1850 . .   155.00

Cheese Sieve, 6½" w, 5" h, heart shape, tin, dot and dash type punch design, 3 conical feet 300.00

Coffee Grinder, Pat. July 20, 1886 ... 65.00

Cookie Stamp, 3½" d, flat back, stars and 8 petal flowers, c1820 .... 250.00

Cornstick Pan, glass 15.00

Cherry Pitter, cast iron, table clamp .. 25.00

Danish Pan, Griswold, #32 .... 36.00

Dough Bowl, 38 x 15", handcarved, tapered bottom 235.00

Dough Scraper, copper, 4" handle, half circle steel blade 95.00

Dutch Oven, lid, raised lettering, Griswold, #9 .... 75.00

Egg Beater, tin, iron handle, Peerless #2 .... 25.00

Egg Separator, tin, marked "Watkins 50 Years" 8.00

Food Grinder, Keen Kutter, dated 1907 20.00

Food Mold, ironstone, 9 x 7¾" x 4", Grape Cluster 40.00

Fork, 1¼ x 12", 3 tine, emb, "Rumford the Wholesome Baking Powder" ... 18.00

Funnel 40.00

Griddle Spatula, 1½ x 12½", "Swans Down Cake Flour-Makes Better Cakes" on handle 32.00

Ice Shaver, Griswold 100.00

Lemon Squeezer, wood 55.00

Loaf Pan, Griswold 150.00

Mixing Bowl, apple, Watts #9 ...... 45.00

Muffin Pan, iron, Wagnerware, cut-outs, 1800s 60.00

Nutmeg Grater, tin, marked "Boye" ... 68.00

Pastry Peel, 19" l, ram's head handle . 80.00

Pop-Over Pan, 1890s 42.00

Potato Masher 14.00

Raisin Seeder, turned wood handle, wire grid 55.00

Refrigerator Set, 3 pc, glass, green, crystal knob lids 40.00

Rolling Pin
Stoneware, Yellowware 300.00
Tiger Maple, 1 pc, shaped handles, 17" 95.00

Salt Box, hanging, blue luster, wood lid, Germany 45.00

Skillet, lid, Griswold 125.00

Tea Kettle, tin, black, 2 cup, sgd Kreamer 50.00

Toaster, ceramic base 22.00

Vienna Roll Pan, #5 .... 75.00

Waffle Iron
Griswold, #8, stand 25.00
Keen Kutter 100.00

Washboard, 13½ x 6¾", brown glaze scrub panel, orig label "The Common Sense Washboard," Western Reserve Pottery Co., Warren, OH, c1890–1910 .... 375.00

KUTANI

History: In the mid 1600s Kutani originated in the Kaga province of Japan. Kutani comes in a variety of color patterns, one of the most popular being Ao Kutani, a green glaze with colors such as green, yellow, and purple enclosed in a black outline. Wares made since the 1870s for export are enameled in a wide variety of colors and styles.

Reference: Sandra Andacht, *Oriental Antiques & Art: An Identification And Value Guide*, Wallace-Homestead, 1987.

Vase, 9½" h, $360.00.

Beaker, 4½" h, hp florals and birds, red, orange, and gold, white ground, marked "Ao-Kutani" 85.00

Bowl
6⅝", gilt and bright enamel design, figural, animal, and floral reserves, kinrande ground, base inscribed "Kutani-sei," set of 10 .... 385.00
15¼", bell form body, ring foot, keyfret band, three circular reserves, 36 poets in conversation, gilt diaper ground, Meiji period 445.00

Charger
18⅜", pomegranate tree, chrysanthemums, and two birds on int., birds and flowers between scrolling foliate bands, irregular floral and brocade border, 11 character inscription 525.00
21½", central scene, flock of cranes flying over beach, rocks, and waters, rising sun, floral and brocade borders 375.00

Dish, 10½", central scene, magpies in bamboo forest 250.00

Figure
Bodhidharma, 12", standing, long red robe, flywisk in right hand 175.00

Chinese Sage, 14¼", seated, hands on lamp, overglazed enameled brocade and floral robe **400.00**

Kannon, 14¼", polychrome and gilt dec, standing, dragon mount, high coiffure, wind-swept robe, inscribed "Kutani-sei" **500.00**

Garden Seat, 19" h, barrel shape, two large circular reserves of courtly figures in garden, small reserves with florals and landscape scenes, spiraling brocade ground, top pierced with circular florettes, pr **2,000.00**

Jar, 20½", ovoid, fan shaped reserves of warriors, molded ribbon tied tasseled ring handles, shippo-tsunagi ground, multicolored brocade patterned dome lid, pr **1,350.00**

Mustard Pot, attached saucer, Nishikide diapering, figural raised gold reserves, marked **65.00**

Tea Caddy, 6" h, bulbous, hexagonal, Nishikide diapering, figural raised gold reserves of children, red script mark **75.00**

Tea Service, teapot, creamer, sugar, six cups and saucers, gilt and enamel stylized rakkan dec, cartouche marked "Kintani" **150.00**

Teapot, 4¼ x 6", cov, bulbous, One Thousand Faces **225.00**

Tray, 14", polychrome and gilt, figural scene, red, orange, and gold border **325.00**

Vase
9¾", ovoid, waisted neck, recessed ring foot, upper portion with enameled reddish-brown wave pattern, underglaze blue wide band of archaistic keyfret design, raised borders, lower section with gilt painted stylized lotus blossoms, green enamel scrolling leafy tendrils, bluish-black ground **360.00**

10¾", trumpet, shaped figural and floral reserves, kinrande patterned ground, base inscribed "Kutani 3 'Kuma' zukuri" **250.00**

LALIQUE

History: Rene Lalique (1860–1945) first gained prominence as a jewelry designer. Around 1900 he began experimenting with molded glass brooches and pendants, often embellishing them with semiprecious stones. By 1905 he was devoting himself exclusively to the manufacture of glass articles.

In 1908 Lalique began designing packaging for the French cosmetic houses. He also produced many objects, especially vases, bowls, and figurines, in the Art Noveau style in the 1910s. The full scope of Lalique's genius was seen at the 1925 Paris International Exhibition of Decorative Arts. He later moved to the Art Deco form.

The mark "R. LALIQUE FRANCE" in block letters is found on pressed articles, tableware, vases, paperweights, and mascots. The script signature, with or without "France," is found on hand blown objects. Occasionally a design number is included. The word "France" in any form indicates a piece made after 1926.

The post–1945 mark is "Lalique France" without the "R"; but, there are exceptions to this rule.

Reproduction Alert: Much faking of the Lalique signature occurs, the most common being the addition of an "R" to the post–1945 mark.

Reference: Katherine Morrison McClinton, *Introduction to Lalique Glass*, Wallace-Homestead, 1978.

Ashtray, 5½" d, crystal, ridged top, molded tree pattern on sides **100.00**

Bottle, 12¼", molded, four tapered panel sides frosted stopper, leafage, c1925, inscribed "R. Lalique" **385.00**

Bowl
9" d, molded Pinsons, inscribed marks **125.00**
10" d, Nemours, molded, enamel highlights, inscribed marks **325.00**
14" d, molded base, radiating palm leaves, inscribed and factory stamp **715.00**

Box, cov, 7" d, molded, acid stamp mark **100.00**

Brooch, 1¾", circular, convex surface, molded daisy blossoms, gold foil ground, gilt metal mount, stamped "Lalique," c1925 .... **875.00**

Candlesticks, 7", molded, inscribed marks, pr **375.00**

Centerpiece, 12" h, Deux Poissons, molded **750.00**

Chandelier, 13½" d, bowl shape, Saint Vincent, colorless glass, molded, grape clusters, suspended from silken cord, molded "R. Lalique," inscribed "France," c1925 .... **800.00**

Charger, 10¼", opalescent, molded, parakeets in blossoming branches, marked "R. Lalique" **1,300.00**

Decanter, 13¾", flared base, narrow neck, six female figures and vine panels, rosebud stopper with molded vines, gray wash, molded "R. Lalique," c1925 .... **660.00**

Figure
Buffalo, 4½" h, frosted, inscribed "Lalique France" **180.00**
Cat, 8¼" h, Chat Assis, molded, inscribed marks **325.00**

Cockatoo, 11¾" h, molded, inscribed marks **700.00**
Eagle, molded, clear glass rock formation, inscribed **550.00**
Frog, 4½" l, frosted, inscribed "Lalique France" **180.00**
Pigeon, 10" l, molded, inscribed marks **350.00**
Fingerbowl, 2½" h, 4⅜" d, 7½" d underplate, double row of fish, blue trim, marked "R. Lalique" **200.00**
Goblets, set of 8, 6", Coquelicot, molded rooster stems, black enamel detailing, inscribed "R. Lalique/France," c1928 **275.00**
Hood Ornament, 8¼" h, molded, frosted, dragonfly, inscribed "R. Lalique France" **900.00**
Inkwell, 2¼", three sided, molded, dragonflies **225.00**
Lamp, hanging, 14" h, spherical, molded, frosted, lozenge form blossoms, c1925 .... **650.00**
Lamp Shade, 16" d, hanging, molded, fruit and leaf, opalescent, "R. Lalique/France," c1925 .... **1,100.00**
Mascots, 4½" h, molded, Tete D'Aigle, inscribed marks, pr **550.00**
Menu Holders, set of 12, 2" l, Demi-lune, molded pairs of fruit baskets, inscribed "R. Lalique," c1925 .... **850.00**
Mirror, hand, 6¼", round, two Oiseaux, two firebirds, branches and berries, blue enamel highlights, script sgd "R. Lalique France," c1920 .... **1,300.00**
Necklace, 42" l, Collier Lierre, 18 molded deep aqua-green ivy leaves, green silk cord, inscribed "R. Lalique," c1930 .... **1,200.00**
Nightlight, 15½" h, 19¾" l, molded, frosted, fish on bronze base, amber glass filter, c1925, molded "R. Lalique," inscribed "France" **3,000.00**

Plate, 10¼", swimming trout motif, $380.00.

Pin Tray, swan **100.00**
Pitcher, 8½" h, twelve tumblers, molded, Chene, inscribed marks **1,600.00**
Plate, 14½" d, molded circular form, amber, frosted reverse, high relief, broad border, eleven swirling carp, molded relief block letters, c1925 .... **3,025.00**
Powder Jar, 5¼" d, frosted, circular shape, cover surmounted with two doves, stamped "Lalique made for Nina Ricci Paris" **300.00**
Toothpick Holder, 2", frosted and clear, emb flowers **50.00**
Vase
5¼", molded, Rampillon, opalescent, inscribed "R. Lalique France No. 392" **600.00**
6½", molded, Ferrieres, inscribed "R. Lalique France No 1879," c1925 . **2,000.00**
10" h, molded, bucket shape bowl, supported by a raised circular spreading foot, inscribed "Lalique France," pr **935.00**
13" h, molded, Pierrefonds, inscribed "R. Lalique/France," c1925 ..... **1,350.00**

LAMP SHADES

History: Lamp shades were made to diffuse the harsh light produced by early gas lighting fixtures. These early shades were made by popular Art Nouveau manufacturers including Durand, Quezal, Steuben, Tiffany, and others. Many shades are not marked.

References: Dr. Larry Freeman, *New Lights on Old Lamps*, American Life Foundation, 1984; Jo Ann Thomas, *Early Twentieth Century Lighting Fixtures*, Collector Books, 1980.

American Maker, unmarked, white overlay cut to soft pink, grapes, grapevines, and leaves, 10¼" d **500.00**
Bradley and Hubbard, leaded glass, geometric mottled green pattern, 18" d **350.00**
Burmese, birds, butterflies, and flowers dec, gas fitting, 8¾" **275.00**
Cameo Glass, white leaves, yellow ground
5¼" d, 4" h, 2¼" fitter **150.00**
8⅜" d, 5" h, 3⅞" fitter **225.00**
Cased Glass, shaded rose to pink, mushroom shape, emb swirl design, ruffled top, 6⅞" d, 6⅜" h **225.00**
Custard Glass, brown nutmeg stain, 2" d fitter ring **35.00**
Durand
Gold Egyptian Crackle, blue and white overlay, bulbous, ruffled rim, 9½", sgd **175.00**
Irid gold, candle shade, 3½", sgd .. **125.00**

Opal ground, irid threads, lily, 8″ d, sgd **250.00**
Fenton, blue ground, white opal hobnails, 4″ **85.00**

Carnival Glass, marigold, 2″ fitter, $30.00.

Fostoria
  White luster ground, gold, green leaves, and vines, 5″ d **150.00**
  Zipper pattern, green pulled dec, opal ground, gold lining, 5½″ d **175.00**
Galle, cameo glass, milky sides overlaid with orange and olive, fire polished, floriform, 6½″, sgd **475.00**
Lalique
  Amber, molded shells, 12″, sgd **560.00**
  Crystal, molded ivy, green stain, 13″, sgd **750.00**
Leaded Glass, unmarked
  Mottled green slag, hexagonal, 18″ . **300.00**
  Purple and green grapes, green leaves, greenish amber ground, 22″ **850.00**
Loetz, irid, green oil spotting, ribbon work over white glass int., 8½″ d, c1900 .... **225.00**
Luster Art
  Irid gold, pulled opal feathering, 4¾″ h **100.00**
  Opalescent ground
    Band of gold waves, 5″ h, pr **350.00**
    Blue short hooked feathering, gold borders, gold lining **275.00**
    Irid gold swirls on upper body, green and irid gold base, set of 5 .... **675.00**
Lutz, 7½ to 8″ sq, 6¼″ h, 2½″ fitter, opaque white looping, applied cranberry threading, ribbon edge, sq top **150.00**
Muller Freres, satin frosted white top, cobalt blue base, yellow highlights, 6″ h, set of 3 .... **225.00**
NuArt, irid, Carnival glass, marigold, pr **125.00**

Quezal
  Dark Green, platinum feathering, gold lining, 5½″ **650.00**
  Iridescent gold ground
    Bell form, 5½″ h **150.00**
    King Tut, white pattern, gold lining **165.00**
    Opal fishnet design **175.00**
    Opal snakeskin top, irid gold and green snakeskin base, corset shape, pr **275.00**
  Opalescent Ground
    Irid gold trellis design, gold lining, ruffled rim, 6⅞″ d **765.00**
    Pulled gold feathering, gold lining, 2⅜″ d, 5″ h **165.00**
    Pulled green feathering outlined in gold, irid gold lining, 6½″ d **190.00**
  Rubena, cranberry shading to clear, frosted and clear etched flowers and leaves, ruffled, 7¼″ d, 7⅝″ h, 3⅞″ fitter **175.00**
Steuben
  Aurene
    Irid blue, platinum leaf and vine motif **850.00**
    Irid brown, platinum applied border **425.00**
    Irid gold, tulip shape, 4½″ h **175.00**
  Calcite, etched dec, acorn shape .. **225.00**
  Pale yellow, lime green feathering, gold lining, notched rim, pr **235.00**
Tiffany
  Iridescent blue ground, soft blue, yellow pulled feather dec, scalloped rim, 1⅝″ top d, 1½″ base d, 3″ h . **250.00**
  Iridescent gold ground
    Bell shape, 5¼″, set of 4 ..... **1,000.00**
    Hexagonal, 4⅞″ h, set of 6 ..... **1,500.00**
    Lily shape, set of 3 .... **1,450.00**
Verlys, raised birds and fish dec, 3⅝″ d, 1⅝″ fitter, 5¾″ h **275.00**
Williamson & Co
  Ball, white ground, yellow spots, red pulled feathers, 9″ **175.00**
  Grape cluster, blue, 7½″ **150.00**
  Stalactite, blue and green ground, blue loops, 7″ **135.00**

LAMPS AND LIGHTING

History: Lighting devices have evolved from simple stone age oil lamps to the popular electrified models of today. Aim Argand patented the first oil lamp in 1784. Around 1850 kerosene became a popular lamp burning fluid, replacing whale oil and other fluids. In 1879 Thomas A. Edison invented the electric light bulb, causing fluid lamps to lose favor and creating a new field for lamp manufacturers to develop. Companies like Tiffany and Handel developed skills in the manufacture of electric lamps, having their decorators produce beautiful aesthetic bases and shades.

References: J. W. Courter, *Aladdin, The Magic Name in Lamps*, Wallace-Homestead, 6th Printing, 1980; J. W. Courter, *Collectors Manual & Price Guide Nine, 1983*, privately printed, 1982; Dr. Larry Freeman, *New Light on Old Lamps*, American Life Foundation, 1984; Jo Ann Thomas, *Early Twentieth Century Lighting Fixtures*, Collector Books, 1980; Catherine M. V. Thuro, *Oil Lamps*, Wallace-Homestead, 1976; Catherine M. V. Thuro, *Oil Lamps II*, Thorncliffe House, Inc., 1983.

Collectors' Club: Aladdin Knights, R.D. #1, Simpson, IL 62985, *The Mystic Light of the Aladdin Knights*, (bi-monthly); Historical Lighting Society of Canada, P.O. Box 561, Postal Station R, Toronto, ON M4G 4E1. *The Illuminator.* Dues: $20.00 (American).

Museum: Winchester Center Kerosene Lamp Museum, Winchester Center, CT.

Additional Listings: See specific makers and Pattern Glass.

Early American, pewter, brass cap, 8⅜″ h, single camphene burner, $175.00.

AMERICAN, EARLY

Betty Lamp
 3⅝″, wrought iron, hinged lid, sgd "Montagne" 175.00
 4″, plus hanger, wrought iron, iron wick pick, small bird silhouette on font lid 300.00
 5″ h, wrought iron, wire pick and hanger 175.00
Candle, 23½″, Ambero shades, yellow-gold, horse chestnut and leaves dec, sgd "Pairpoint," pr 600.00
Chandelier, three lights, 23″ h, pierced tin, American, 18th C 950.00
Crusie, 6⅗″ l, 6″ h, 5¾″ l hook, wrought iron, single 125.00
Fat, 3¾″ x 5 x 2″, pottery, boat shaped, wick holes in end and center, PA ... 250.00

Hanging, 15″, aqua, blown bell shaped globe, flared rim, applied knobs in tin crown frame, tooling, cut scallops, punching, traces of red paint 675.00
Kettle
 8⅜″, tin, saucer base, tapered weight stem, cylindrical gimbal font, center wick support 175.00
 10½″, wrought iron, brass feet, spherical font, whale oil burner, twisted stem and pick on chain 190.00
Lacemaker's, 16″, cranberry overshot shade, polished brass base 375.00
Peg
 5½″, brass, acorn shaped, wooden base 100.00
 8″ h, clear blown glass, tin drop burner, new turned wooden base . 115.00
Rushlight Holder, 8″, wrought iron, soapstone base 350.00
Tole, 7″, saucer base, conical font, single spout burner, orig blue japanning 100.00
Whale Oil
 6¼″, tin, saucer base, burner, dark brown japanning 150.00
 7⅜″, pewter, double drop burner, Boston, c1840 .... 225.00

BOUDOIR

Handel, 14″ h, Venetian scenic 7″ shade, ornate base, sgd, #592S ... 600.00
Loetz, 12¼″, white metal base, adjustable irid amber spotted and purple lined shades, pr 1,350.00
Pairpoint, 13″, reverse dec floral mottled shade, marked #C3093 .... 475.00

CHANDELIERS

Brass, 19″, six lights, baluster form standard above scrolled support, molded drip plates, candlecups, faceted pendant, 18th C 2,400.00
Cameo, 23″, etched glass, intaglio sgd "Daum Nancy," c1925 .... 900.00
Gilt Bronze, 26 x 34″, eight lights, scrolling branches, four rams heads above, pendant from ceiling cap, short chain, French, late 19th C 2,500.00
Stickley, 20¼″, hammered copper and glass dome, chain, c1910 .... 6,875.00
Wrought Iron, 24″, wood, six lights, green painted, cylindrical stem, hexagonal swellings joined by six candle arms, crenulated drip pans, Continental 275.00

DESK

Handel, 6½″ d, leaded glass green shade, bronze base, overhanging style, sgd 2,000.00

Louis XVI, 33", silverplated, four light, bouillotte, circular dished stand, ribbed border, hexagonal molded and coved standard, ribbed central knob, sq shaft, four S scroll arms, hexagonal nozzles and drip pans, beaded edges, black tole painted shade ... **3,500.00**

Tiffany Studios, NY, 15", oval frame, two purple-green irid turtleback medallions, sixteen purple irid semiprecious stones embedded in circular bronze base, imp mark **4,500.00**

FLOOR

Aladdin, 60" h, 18" d shade, No. 1250 **325.00**

Handel, 61" h, 20" d, shade, leaded glass, double standard base **3,600.00**

J Kuyken, 69", chromed metal, red glass, c1930 .... **5,775.00**

Michael Taylor, 78", cast plaster, palm tree, painted white, rising leaf molded stem, wide fluted shallow cup, conical base **2,750.00**

Victorian, 68¼", brass, ceramic ornaments, piano type, electrified **425.00**

FLUID

Apollo, 15½", amber hobnail open top, scalloped edge shade **175.00**

Boston and Sandwich, 8", Blackberry pattern **225.00**

New England Glass Co, 9½", Acorn and Drapery pattern, stepped pressed base, three ring knob, free blown font, cut and frosted, pewter collar **250.00**

Ripley

13¾", candle, baptismal font, medium blue with cross and "I.H.S.," marked "Ripley & Co. Pat Pending," pewter connector and sockets, no lid, minor dents **300.00**

14½", marriage, opaque white and blue, double fonts **475.00**

Sandwich Glass

11", Acanthus Leaf pattern, opaque blue and white, whale oil burner, sandy finish **700.00**

13", Onion pattern, opaque white, c1840 .... **650.00**

Satin, 9½" d shade, 16½" h, gold MOP satin base, shade with brass inset and feet, diamonds pattern, stylized flower in each diamond **750.00**

South Jersey, 10¾", blown glass, large pear shaped amethyst font, mounted on clear standard and base, late ... **125.00**

HANGING

Brass, 11½", pierced globular vessel suspended by three chains, 17th C . **365.00**

Handel, 16¼" d, 19" h, gold bronze tassel and foliage emb fixture, satin finished dec shade with foliage dec .. **225.00**

Mount Washington, 15", peachblow, hobnail shade, prisms, brass font and fittings **1,000.00**

Perzel, 40¼", chrome metal and glass **1,225.00**

Victorian, 14½", reticulated brass, umbrella style, jeweled **125.00**

STUDENT

11¾", brass, miniature, green enameled ribbed shade, orig burner, emb Tiny Miller **125.00**

20", brass, double, peachblow shades, rope twist brass wire coil dec, electrified **500.00**

21½", brass, green cased shade, electrified and polished **425.00**

24", tin plated brass, milk glass shade **400.00**

40" l, hanging, double, 10" d green cased glass shades, burnished brass, electrified **1,250.00**

Table, Gone With The Wind style, 31" h, hand painted dec, green ground, artist signed, Fostoria burner, $700.00.

TABLE

Argand, 31½", brass, stepped scalloped base, reeded column and flat spherical font, clear cut and frosted shade, prisms **275.00**

Art Deco, bronze, girl sitting, green art glass shade **165.00**

Art Nouveau, 19" h, 10" sq shade, four large angled mottled green and opaque white glass panels, four panel collar, pewter colored stem, bronze finish base **145.00**

Astral, gold ormolu stem, cut glass globe, marble base, dated 1870 ... **425.00**

Cameo
Daum Nancy, 17″, landscape, yellow glass, mottled red and green, c1900 .... **3,700.00**
Galle, 24″, conical shade of translucent yellow overlaid in sapphire blue, lavender, and brown, etched with azaleas, trumpet shaped base, cameo signature **7,250.00**
Le Verre Francais, mottled gray and dusty rose shade, pumpkin overlay, wrought iron base, embedded Scheider candy cane mark, c1930 **1,000.00**
Muller Les Lundville, 17¾″, dome shade, base overlaid in deep blue, green, peach, and off-white, mountain and lake scene, cameo sgd . **3,600.00**
Durand, 29½″, brass, blue glass standard, opaque white and clear feather pattern **250.00**
Fulper, inlaid slag glass on green pottery shade, green and brown streaked glazed pottery base, c1900 **650.00**
Handel
22″, painted glass shade, tones of green, yellow, orange, and brown, patinated metal, early 20th C **1,450.00**
22½″, frosted, reverse painted sunset landscape 14″ d umbrella shade, bronzed white metal base, sgd .. **500.00**
Jefferson, 21″, reverse painted 16⅛″ shade with florals and leaves, apricot ground, black finished metal base, sgd **650.00**
Jensen, Georg, 27½″, silver, numbered "79" **3,575.00**
Pairpoint, 22¾″ h, 15¾ x 15⅞″ shade, Tivoli shade, old mill and stream landscape, brass base **2,800.00**
Plated Silver Gilt, 35″, banquet, cut glass Daisy and Button onion shaped font, dec white globe, electrified . **150.00**
Rateau, 14½″, gilt bronze, circular shade and dished base, butterflies dec, imp mark, c1925 .... **2,500.00**
Rayo, 21″, brass, jeweled brass umbrella shade, electrified, minor dent in font **75.00**
Tiffany
20¼″, seven light lily, Favrile irid amber glass lily shades, gilt bronze, c1899 .... **4,675.00**
24″, candle, DQ reactive glass, gold feather shade, Queen Anne's lace bronze base, sgd **2,000.00**
26½″, leaded glass, apple blossom design in blue, white, pink and dark green, apple green ground, marked "Tiffany Studios," c1900 ....**13,500.00**
Victorian
19″, yellow globular shade, emb brass font, wrought iron standard . **75.00**

24 x 17 x 29½″, heavily regilded, orig shade and chimney **100.00**
32″
Banquet, mottled amber, green, blue, and opaque white glass globe made of large and small egg shaped and circular pieces, brass standard, electrified **225.00**
Gone with the Wind style, hp floral globe, bronze finished, electrified **150.00**

LANTERNS

History: A lantern is an enclosed, portable light source, hand carried or attached to a bracket or pole to illuminate an area. Many lanterns can be used both indoors and outdoors and have a protected flame. Fuels used in early lanterns included candles, kerosene, whale oil, coal oil, and later gasoline, natural gas, and batteries.

Kerosene, 16½″ h, tin, orig flue, "Ham's Cold Blast," C. T. Ham Co., Rochester, NY, $75.00.

Barn
Brass, kerosene type, emb "US Brass Tubular" **65.00**
Tin, 13¼″, kerosene type, clear globe marked "Dietz D-Lite, No. 2″ **48.00**
Wood, 11″ h, glass on four sides, hinged door **145.00**
Bicycle, nickel plated brass, carbide type, clear bull's eyes lens, red and green faceted glass insert sides, marked "C M Hall Lamp Co., Solar Model, Kenosha, Wis, USA" **50.00**
Candle
Pine, sliding panel, diamond shaped glass panes on sides, pierced, three openings, low strap handle, 10 x 9 x 14¼″ **375.00**
Tin, conical, orig horn glazed sides,

pyramidal vented top, ring handle, bottom stamped "W R," old dark finish, 12" 200.00

Walnut, sq, four glass sides, conical pierced tin top and ring handle, crimped pan and socket, 16" 625.00

Dark room, 17" h, orig black paint, white striping, tin kerosene font and burner, "Carbutt's Dry Plate Lantern, Pa April 25th 1882" label 55.00

Folding, tin, isinglass sides, emb "Stonebridge 1908," 10" 65.00

Kerosene

Brass, 9¾" h, curved lens replaced . 40.00

Tin, 13½" h, clear blown glass globe, star and diamond shape air holes, removable font with replaced kerosene burner, traces of black paint 250.00

Tin, 14¼" h, "Dietz Acme Inspector lamp" 35.00

Tin, 24½" h, orig black paint and kerosene burner, mercury reflector, stenciled label "C.T. Ham Mfg. Co's New No. 8 Tubular Square Lamp, Label Registered 1886" 175.00

Miner's

Tin, coffeepot form, straight spout at side, hook to attach to cap, emb "George Anton, Monohahela City, Washington County, PA" 48.00

Tin, three part, leather fitting for head, adapter with brass plate for pole, two wire loop handles, adjustable reflector, hinged tin door, emb "Ferguson, NY 1878" 150.00

Nautical, masthead, 23" h, 11" d, copper and brass, oil fired, orig burner, label reads "Ellerman, Wilson Line, Hull," mid 19th C 250.00

Political Rally, gilded wrought iron, flat diamond shaped lantern, diamond shaped windows outlined with gilding, amber glass panels, "1842" in gilt, acorn finials, pine carrying staff, mounted on wooden base, 67" h . . . 1,800.00

Railroad, 16", tin, wide reflector, kerosene burner, marked "Buhol No. 100" 75.00

Skater's .

Brass, clear bulbous globe, wire bail handle, 11" 125.00

Cast Iron, lacy base, bulbous clear globe, pierced tin top and wire bail handle, 13½" 225.00

Tin, clear glass pear shaped globe, wire bail handle, 6½" 50.00

Wall, exterior, kerosene type, black painted metal sq frame, glass sides, pyramidal glass sided top, round metal finial, orig burner and mercury reflector, stenciled "C T Ham Mfg Co's New No 8 Tubular Square Lamp," c1886, 24½" 175.00

LEEDS CHINA

History: The Leeds Pottery in Yorkshire, England, began production about 1758. Among its products was creamware that was competitive with that of Wedgwood. The initial factory closed in 1820, but various subsequent owners continued until 1880. They made exceptional cream colored ware, either plain, salt-glazed, or painted with colored enamels, and glazed and unglazed redware.

Early wares are unmarked. Later pieces bear marks of "Leeds Pottery," sometimes followed by "Hartley-Green and Co." or the letters "LP." Reproductions also have these marks.

Reference: Susan and Al Bagdade, *Warman's English & Continental Pottery & Porcelain, 1st Edition,* Warman Publishing Co., Inc., 1987.

Platter, 18th century, $600.00.

Asparagus Dish, 5½" l, creamware, scrolled acanthus shape, England, c1780 .... 100.00

Bowl, 7¼", polychrome dec 175.00

Charger, 15⅝", blue feather edge, five color urn of flowers dec 450.00

Creamer, 4½", gaudy flowers and leaves, creamware 325.00

Cup and Saucer, handleless, multicolored floral design 200.00

Cup Plate, 3¾", gaudy blue and white floral dec 250.00

Egg Cup, 2¾", creamware, reticulated 145.00

Jar, cov, 4¼" h, blue and yellow dec .. 175.00

Jug

5¾" h, sponge dec in shades of gray and blue, entwined strap handle, flower head and foliage terminals . 400.00

8¾", creamware, Mary and Elizabeth/
William and Joseph, floral terminal
on handle 3,500.00
Miniature
Cup and Saucer, handleless, enam-
eled three color flowers 125.00
Pitcher, 2" h, softpaste, three color
dec, emb leaf handle 85.00
Mug, 5", polychrome five color floral dec 240.00
Nut Dish, 4¾", leaf shape, blue Oriental
dec 140.00
Plate
6⅜", five color scene of house,
sponged trees, blue feather edge . 325.00
7½", blue feather edge, five color
strawberry dec 300.00
9½", blue feather edge, floral dec . . 250.00
9¾", blue feather edge, yellow ochre
gaudy floral dec 250.00
Platter, 19¼", blue flowers and leaves,
blue feather edge, minor staining . . 235.00
Sauce Boat, 2⅞" h, blue feather edge 75.00
Soup Plate, blue feather edge 100.00
Sugar
4¼" h, blue and white gaudy floral
dec, open handles 185.00
4¾" h, softpaste, fluted ribs, three
color floral dec 200.00
Teapot, 4⅝", green, yellow, and brown
pineapple dec 570.00
Tray, 8¾", oval, reticulated loop rim,
brown feather edge 150.00
Vegetable Dish, 8¾ x 11", blue feather
edge, four color eagle and shield dec 400.00

LENOX CHINA

History: In 1889 Jonathan Cox and Walter Scott
Lenox established The Ceramic Art Co. at Trenton,
New Jersey. By 1906 Lenox formed his own com-
pany, Lenox, Inc. Using potters lured from Belleek,
Lenox began making an American version of this
famous ware.

Older Lenox china has two marks: a green
wreath and a pallette. The pallette mark appears
on blanks supplied to amateurs who hand painted
china as a hobby. The Lenox Company still exists
and currently uses a gold stamped mark.

Reference: Mary Frank Gaston, *American Belleek*, Collector Books, 1984.

Additional Listings: Belleek.

Ashtray, gold washed SS overlay dec,
cobalt ground 50.00
Bouillon Cup and Saucer, gold band and
handles, monogrammed 25.00

**Vase, 10½", At The Fountain, green top
and bottom, green wreath mark,
c1915–30, $200.00.**

Chocolate Set, chocolate pot, cov, six
cups and saucers, golden wheat dec,
cobalt ground, 13 pcs 275.00
Cigarette Box, white apple blossoms,
green ground, wreath mark 40.00
Cup and Saucer, royal blue, heavy gold
border, wreath and mark "K-22," SS
cup holder marked "Sterling 9403 Na-
varre" 80.00
Honey Pot, 5" h, 6¼" underplate, ivory
beehive, gold bee and trim, marked 75.00
Jug, 4", hp, grapes and leaves, shaded
brown ground, sgd "G Morley" 240.00
Model, Yale Bowl, green mark 100.00
Mug
4¾", cobalt blue, SS overlay, marked
"Ceramic Art Co" 100.00
6¼", monk, smiling, holding up glass
of wine, shaded brown ground, SS
rim 150.00
Perfume Lamp, 9", figural, Marie Anto-
inette, bisque finish, dated 1929 . . . 650.00
Pitcher, lemonade, silver overlay,
marked "Lenox Belleek" 225.00
Plate, 10", hp, orchids 250.00
Salt, 3 x 2 x 1", creamy ivory ground,
molded seashells and coral, green
wreath dec 35.00
Salt and Pepper Shakers, hp, green and
gold bird dec, pr 65.00
Tea Set, teapot, creamer, and sugar,
Hawthorne pattern, silver overlay . . 215.00
Tea Strainer, hp, small roses dec 65.00
Toby Jug, William Penn, ivory, green
mark 150.00
Vase
6", roses dec, sgd "W Morley" 165.00
8", tree stump, robin, glazed white . 125.00
9¼", hp, woodland scene, shaded
brown ground, marked "Ceramic
Art Co" 100.00

LIBBEY GLASS

History: In 1888 Edward Libbey established the Libbey Glass Company in Toledo, Ohio, after the closing of the New England Glass Works of W. L. Libbey and Son in East Cambridge, Massachusetts. The new Libbey company produced quality cut glass for the "Brilliant Period."

In 1930 Libbey's interest in art glass production was renewed. A. Douglas Nash was employed as a designer in 1931.

The factory continues production today as Libbey Glass Co.

Additional Listings: Amberina Glass and Cut Glass.

Candlestick, 6″ h, made by Nash when he worked at Libbey, acid marked "Libbey," $350.00.

Bowl, 8¼″, scalloped rim, turned over ruby border, amberina body, Wave pattern, three applied amber feet, acid stamped "Libbey" in circle, c1900 . . . . **425.00**
Candlestick, 8″, Lightware, twisted stem, engraved pattern #0493, sgd **140.00**
Champagne, opal, squirrel stem **85.00**
Plate, 7″, cut glass, border of strawberry diamonds and fans, sunburst center, sgd **50.00**
Punch Cup, Moravignian pattern, red pulled design, sgd **125.00**
Sugar Shaker, Maize pattern, amber, gold leaf **100.00**
Toothpick, 2½″, pink shading to white, blue flowers, green leaves, sgd **125.00**
Vase
  4⅝ x 6⅜″, wide ruffled top, amberina, sgd "Amberina/Libbey" in circle . . **400.00**
  6″, mushroom flower form, wide flaring rim, amberina, deep shading, sgd, orig label **575.00**

8″, Moravignian, crystal, applied ruby glass dec, sgd **100.00**

LIMITED EDITION COLLECTOR PLATES

History: Bing and Grondahl made the first collector plate in 1895. Royal Copenhagen issued their first Christmas plate in 1908.

In the late 1960s and early 1970s, several potteries, glass factories, mints, and artists began issuing plates commemorating people, animals, events, etc. Christmas plates were supplemented by Mother's Day plates, Easter plates, etc. A sense of speculation swept the field, fostered in part by flamboyant ads in newspapers and flashy direct mail promotions.

Collectors often favor the first plate issued in a series above all others. Condition is a prime factor. Having the original box also increases price.

Limited edition collector plates, more than any other object in this guide, should be collected for design and pleasure and only secondarily for rise in value.

References: Bradford Exchange, Ltd., *The Bradford Book of Collector's Plates,* Charles Winthrope & Sons, 1983; Susan K. Jones, ed., *Collectibles Market Index Guide: To Plates, Figurines, Bells, Graphics, Steins, and Dolls, 1984,* Schiffer Publishing.

Periodicals: Collector Editions, Collector Communications Corp, 170 Fifth Ave, New York, NY 10010. Subscription: $14.00. Collectors Mart, WEB Publications, Inc. 15100 W. Kellogg, Wichita, KS 67235. Subscription: $12.00.

Collectors' Club: International Plate Collectors Guild, P. O. Box 487, Artesia, CA 90701. Dues: $8.50.

Museum: Bradford Museum, Niles, IL.

Additional Listings: See *Warman's Americana & Collectibles* for more examples of collector plates plus many other limited edition collectibles.

BAREUTHER (Germany)

Christmas Plates, Hans Mueller, artist, 8″ d
  1967 Stiftskirche, FE **100.00**
  1969 Christkindlemarkt **20.00**
  1971 Toys for Sale **20.00**
  1973 Christmas Sleigh Ride **20.00**
  1975 Snowman **25.00**
  1977 Story Time (Christmas Story) . **30.00**
  1979 Winter Day **40.00**
  1981 Walk in the Forest **40.00**
  1983 The Night Before Christmas . . **45.00**
  1985 Winter Wonderland **42.50**
  1987 Decorating the Tree **46.50**

Father's Day Series, Hans Mueller, artist, 8″ d
  1969 Castle Neuschwanstein **48.00**

1971 Castle Heidelberg	24.00
1973 Castle Katz	30.00
1975 Castle Lichtenstein	32.50
1977 Castle Eltz	30.00
1979 Castle Rheinstein	30.00
1981 Castle Gutenfels	40.00
1983 Castle Lauenstein	40.00

Mother's Day

1969 Mother & Children	75.00
1971 Mother & Children	20.00
1973 Mother & Children	22.00
1975 Spring Outing	25.00
1977 Noon Feeding	28.00
1979 Mother's Love	38.00
1981 Playtime	40.00

BING AND GRONDAHL (Denmark)

Christmas Plates, various artists, 7″ d

1895 Behind The Frozen Window	3,600.00
1896 New Moon Over Snow Covered Trees	1,475.00
1897 Christmas Meal Of The Sparrows	1,100.00
1898 Christmas Roses And Christmas Star	600.00
1899 The Crows Enjoying Christmas	900.00
1900 Church Bells Chiming In Christmas	800.00
1901 The Three Wise Men From The East	475.00
1902 Interior Of A Gothic Church	275.00
1903 Happy Expectation of Children	150.00
1904 View of Copenhagen From Frederiksberg Hill	125.00
1905 Anxiety Of The Coming Christmas Night	130.00
1906 Sleighing To Church On Christmas Eve	100.00
1907 The Little Match Girl	125.00
1908 St. Petri Church of Copenhagen	85.00
1909 Happiness Over The Yule Tree	100.00
1910 The Old Organist	90.00
1911 First It Was Sung By Angels To Shepherds In The Fields	80.00
1912 Going To Church On Christmas Eve	80.00
1913 Bringing Home The Yule Tree	85.00
1914 Royal Castle of Amalienborg, Copenhagen	75.00
1915 Chained Dog Getting Double Meal On Christmas Eve	125.00
1916 Christmas Prayer of the Sparrows	100.00
1917 Arrival Of The Christmas Boat	75.00
1918 Fishing Boat Returning Home For Christmas	85.00
1919 Outside The Lighted Window	82.00
1920 Hare In The Snow	80.00
1921 Pigeons In The Castle Court	45.00

1922 Star Of Bethlehem	60.00
1923 Royal Hunting Castle, The Hermitage	50.00
1924 Lighthouse In Danish Waters	65.00
1925 The Child's Christmas	60.00
1926 Churchgoers On Christmas Day	60.00
1927 Skating Couple	185.00
1928 Eskimo Looking At Village Church In Greenland	50.00
1929 Fox Outside Farm On Christmas Eve	75.00
1930 Yule Tree In Town Hall Square Of Copenhagen	85.00
1931 Arrival Of The Christmas Train	75.00
1933 The Korsor-Nyborg Ferry	70.00
1935 Lillebelt Bridge Connecting Funen With Jutland	65.00
1937 Arrival Of Christmas Guests	75.00
1939 Ole Lock-Eye, The Sandman	150.00
1941 Horses Enjoying Christmas Meal In Stable	345.00
1943 The Ribe Cathedral	155.00
1945 The Old Water Mill	135.00
1947 Dybbol Mill	65.00
1949 Landsoldaten, 19th Century Danish Soldier	70.00
1951 Jens Bang, New Passenger Boat Running Between Copenhagen And Aalborg	109.00
1953 Royal Boat In Greenland Waters	95.00
1955 Kalundborg Church	115.00
1957 Christmas Candles	155.00
1959 Christmas Eve	120.00
1961 Winter Harmony	115.00
1963 The Christmas Elf	120.00
1965 Bringing Home The Christmas Tree	60.00
1967 Sharing The Joy Of Christmas	45.00
1969 Arrival Of Christmas Guests	30.00
1971 Christmas At Home	20.00
1973 Country Christmas	26.00
1975 The Old Water Mill	24.00
1977 Copenhagen Christmas	25.00
1979 White Christmas	30.00
1981 Christmas Peace	50.00
1983 Christmas in Old Town	55.00
1985 Christmas Eve at the Farmhouse	55.00
1987 The Snowman's Christmas Eve	60.00

Mother's Day Plates, Henry Thelander, artist, 6″ d

1969 Dog And Puppies	400.00
1971 Cat And Kitten	18.00
1973 Duck And Ducklings	20.00
1975 Doe And Fawns	20.00
1977 Squirrel And Young	25.00
1979 Fox And Cubs	30.00
1981 Hare And Young	40.00
1983 Raccoon And Young	45.00
1985 Bear and Cubs	40.00
1987 Sheep with Lambs	42.50

HAVILAND & PARLON (France)

Christmas Series, various artists, 10″ d

1972 Madonna And Child, Raphael, FE	80.00
1974 Cowper Madonna And Child, Raphael	55.00
1976 Madonna And Child, Botticelli	50.00
1978 Madonna And Child, Fra Filippo Lippi	65.00

Lady And The Unicorn Series, artist unknown, 10″ d

1977 To My Only Desire, FE	55.00
1978 Sight	40.00
1980 Touch	110.00
1982 Taste	80.00

Tapestry Series, artist unknown, 10″ d

1971 The Unicorn In Captivity	145.00
1972 Start Of The Hunt	70.00
1974 End Of The Hunt	120.00
1976 The Unicorn Is Brought To The Castle	50.00

LALIQUE (France)

Annual Series, lead crystal, Marie-Claude Lalique, artist, 8½″ d

1965 Deux Oiseaux (Two Birds), FE	200.00
1966 Rose de Songerie (Dream Rose)	210.00
1968 Gazelle Fantaisie (Gazelle Fantasy)	70.00
1970 Paon (Peacock)	50.00
1972 Coquillage (Shell)	55.00
1974 Sous d'Argent (Silver Pennies)	65.00
1976 Aigle (Eagle)	100.00

LENOX (United States)

Boehm Bird Series, Edward Marshall Boehm, artist, 10½″ d

1970 Wood Thrush, FE	225.00
1972 Mountain Bluebird	65.00
1974 Rufous Hummingbird	60.00
1976 Cardinal	58.00
1978 Mockingbirds	60.00
1980 Black-Throated Blue Warblers	75.00

Boehm Woodland Wildlife Series, Edward Marshall Boehm, artist, 10½″ d

1973 Raccoons, FE	80.00
1974 Red Foxes	50.00
1976 Eastern Chipmunks	60.00
1978 Whitetail Deer	60.00
1980 Bobcats	90.00
1982 Otters	100.00

LLARDO (Spain)

Christmas, 8″ d, undisclosed artists

1971 Caroling	30.00
1973 Boy & Girl	50.00
1975 Cherubs	60.00
1977 Nativity	70.00
1979 Snow Dance	80.00

Mother's Day, undisclosed artists

1971 Kiss of the Child	75.00
1973 Mother & Children	35.00
1975 Mother & Child	55.00
1977 Mother & Daughter	60.00
1979 Off to School	90.00

REED & BARTON (United States)

Christmas Series, Damascene silver, 11″ d through 1978, 8″ d 1979 to present

1970 A Partridge In A Pear Tree, FE	200.00
1971 We Three Kings Of Orient Are	65.00

Left: Bing and Grondahl, Christmas plate, 1927, $185.00; Center: Haviland & Parlon Tapestry Series, The Unicorn Is Brought To The Castle, 1976, $50.00; Right: Royal Copenhagen, Christmas plate, 1914, $100.00.

1973 Adoration Of The Kings	75.00
1975 Adoration Of The Kings	65.00
1977 Decorating The Church	60.00
1979 Merry Old Santa Claus	65.00
1981 The Shopkeeper At Christmas	75.00

ROSENTHAL (Germany)

Christmas Plates, various artists, 8½″ d

1910 Winter Peace	550.00
1911 The Three Wise Men	325.00
1912 Shooting Stars	255.00
1913 Christmas Lights	235.00
1915 Walking To Church	180.00
1917 Angel Of Peace	200.00
1919 St. Christopher With The Christ Child	225.00
1921 Christmas In The Mountains	200.00
1923 Children In The Winter Wood	200.00
1925 The Three Wise Men	200.00
1927 Station On The Way	200.00
1929 Christmas In The Alps	225.00
1931 Path Of The Magi	225.00
1933 Through The Night To Light	190.00
1935 Christmas By The Sea	185.00
1937 Berchtesgaden	195.00
1939 Schneekoppe Mountain	195.00
1941 Strassburg Cathedral	250.00
1943 Winter Idyll	300.00
1945 Christmas Peace	400.00
1947 The Dillingen Madonna	975.00
1949 The Holy Family	185.00
1951 Star Of Bethlehem	450.00
1953 The Holy Light	185.00
1955 Christmas In A Village	190.00
1957 Christmas By The Sea	195.00
1959 Midnight Mass	195.00
1961 Solitary Christmas	225.00
1963 Silent Night	185.00
1965 Christmas In Munich	185.00
1967 Christmas In Regensburg	185.00
1969 Christmas In Rothenburg	220.00
1971 Christmas In Garmisch	100.00
1973 Christmas In Lubeck-Holstein	105.00

ROYAL COPENHAGEN (Denmark)

Christmas Plates, various artists, 6″ d 1908, 1909, 1910; 7″ 1911 to present

1908 Madonna And Child	1,750.00
1909 Danish Landscape	140.00
1910 The Magi	120.00
1911 Danish Landscape	125.00
1912 Elderly Couple By Christmas Tree	120.00
1913 Spire Of Frederik's Church, Copenhagen	125.00
1914 Sparrows In Tree At Church Of The Holy Spirit, Copenhagen	100.00

1915 Danish Landscape	150.00
1916 Shepherd In The Field On Christmas Night	85.00
1917 Tower Of Our Savior's Church, Copenhagen	90.00
1918 Sheep and Shepherds	80.00
1919 In The Park	80.00
1920 Mary With The Child Jesus	75.00
1921 Aabenraa Marketplace	75.00
1922 Three Singing Angels	70.00
1923 Danish Landscape	70.00
1924 Christmas Star Over The Sea And Sailing Ship	100.00
1925 Street Scene From Christian-shavn, Copenhagen	85.00
1926 View of Christmas Canal, Copenhagen	75.00
1927 Ship's Boy At The Tiller On Christmas Night	140.00
1928 Vicar's Family On Way To Church	75.00
1929 Grundtvig Church, Copenhagen	100.00
1930 Fishing Boats On The Way To The Harbor	80.00
1931 Mother And Child	90.00
1932 Frederiksberg Gardens With Statue Of Frederik VI	90.00
1933 The Great Belt Ferry	110.00
1934 The Hermitage Castle	115.00
1935 Fishing Boat Off Kronborg Castle	145.00
1936 Roskilde Cathedral	130.00
1937 Christmas Scene In Main Street, Copenhagen	135.00
1938 Round Church In Osterlars On Bornholm	200.00
1939 Expeditional Ship In Pack-Ice Of Greenland	180.00
1940 The Good Shepherd	300.00
1941 Danish Village Church	250.00
1943 Flight Of Holy Family To Egypt	425.00
1945 A Peaceful Motif	325.00
1947 The Good Shepherd	210.00
1949 Our Lady's Cathedral, Copenhagen	165.00
1951 Christmas Angel	300.00
1953 Frederiksborg Castle	120.00
1955 Fano Girl	195.00
1957 The Good Shepherd	115.00
1959 Christmas Night	120.00
1961 Training Ship Danmark	155.00
1963 Hojsager Mill	80.00
1965 Little Skaters	60.00
1967 The Royal Oak	45.00
1969 The Old Farmyard	35.00
1971 Hare In Winter	75.00
1973 Train Homeward Bound For Christmas	75.00
1975 Queen's Palace	75.00
1977 Immervad Bridge	75.00
1979 Choosing The Christmas Tree	60.00
1981 Admiring The Christmas Tree	50.00

1983 Merry Christmas	55.00
1985 Snowman	55.00

Mother's Day Plates, various artists, 6¼″ d

1971 American Mother	125.00
1973 Danish Mother	60.00
1975 Bird In Nest	50.00
1977 The Twins	50.00
1979 A Loving Mother	30.00
1981 Reunion	40.00

SCHIMD (Japan)

Disney Christmas Series, undisclosed artists, 7½″ d

1973 Sleigh Ride, FE	400.00
1975 Caroling	20.00
1977 Down The Chimney	25.00
1979 Santa's Surprise	20.00
1981 Happy Holidays	18.00

Disney Mother's Day Series

1974 Flowers For Mother, FE	80.00
1976 Minnie Mouse And Friends	20.00
1978 Flowers For Bambi	20.00
1980 Minnie's Surprise	20.00
1982 A Dream Come True	20.00

Peanuts Christmas Series, Charles Schulz, artist, 7½″ d

1972 Snoopy Guides The Sleigh, FE	90.00
1974 Christmas Eve At The Fireplace	65.00
1976 Woodstock's Christmas	30.00
1978 Filling The Stocking	20.00
1980 Waiting For Santa	50.00
1982 Perfect Performance	35.00

Peanuts Mother's Day Series, Charles Schulz, artist, 7½″ d

1972 Linus, FE	50.00
1974 Snoopy And Woodstock On Parade	40.00
1976 Linus And Snoopy	35.00
1978 Thoughts That Count	25.00
1980 A Tribute To Mom	20.00
1982 Which Way To Mother?	20.00

WEDGWOOD (Great Britain)

Christmas Series, jasper stoneware, 8″ d

1969 Windsor Castle, FE	225.00
1970 Christmas In Trafalgar Square	30.00
1972 St. Paul's Cathedral	40.00
1974 The Houses Of Parliament	40.00
1976 Hampton Court	46.00
1978 The Horse Guards	55.00
1980 St. James Palace	70.00
1982 Lambeth Palace	80.00
1984 Constitution Hill	80.00
1986 The Albert Memorial	80.00

Mothers Series, jasper stoneware, 6½″ d

1971 Sportive Love, FE	25.00
1972 The Sewing Lesson	20.00
1974 Domestic Employment	30.00
1976 The Spinner	35.00
1978 Swan and Cygnets	35.00
1980 Birds	48.00
1982 Cherubs With Swing	55.00
1984 Musical Cupids	55.00
1986 Anemones	55.00

Queen's Christmas, A. Price, artist

1980 Windsor Castle	30.00
1981 Trafalgar Square	25.00
1982 Piccadilly Circus	35.00
1983 St. Paul's	32.50
1984 Tower of London	35.00
1985 Palace of Westminster	35.00
1986 Tower Bridge	35.00

LIMOGES

History: Limoges porcelain has been produced in Limoges, France, for over a century by numerous factories other than the famed Haviland. One of the most frequently encountered marks is "T. & V. Limoges" which is the ware made by Tressman and Vought. Other identifiable Limoges marks are A. L. (A. Lanternier), J. P. L (J. Pouyat, Limoges), M. R. (M. Reddon), Elite and Coronet.

References: Susan and Al Bagdade, *Warman's English & Continental Pottery & Porcelain, 1st Edition,* Warman Publishing Co., Inc., 1987. Mary Frank Gaston, *The Collector's Encyclopedia Of Limoges Porcelain,* Collector Books, 1980.

Additional Listings: Haviland China.

Basket, berry, 9″, gold border and handle, marked "M Rouget, Limoges, France"	100.00
Berry Set, 9½″ master bowl, eight 8″ serving bowls, hp, purple berries on ext., white blossoms on int., marked "T & V"	250.00
Bowl	
4½″ h, ftd, hp, wild roses and leaves, sgd "J E Dodge, 1892″	75.00
10 x 12″, hp, yellow and brown ducklings, ribbed scallop shell, gilt edge, artist sgd "Jean Pouyat"	100.00
Box, 4¼″ sq, cobalt and white ground, cupids on lid, pate-sur-pate dec	170.00
Cake Plate, 12½″, high quality Royal Worcester-type floral dec	50.00
Candlestick, 6″, satin finish, blue forget-me-nots, cream ground, gold scalloped edges	60.00
Celery Tray, 12½ x 6″, Elite, hp pale green leaves, pink flowers, gold trim, c1912	40.00

Charger, 13½", hp, large red poppies . **65.00**
Chocolate Pot
  7", lavender and green, marked "JPL" **75.00**
  9½", large roses, gold trim, artist sgd **150.00**
Creamer, 3¼", purple flowers, white ground, gold handle and trim **38.00**
Cup and Saucer, hp, flowers and leaves, gold trim, artist sgd **75.00**
Dinner Service, twelve dinner plates, eleven salad plates, eight dessert plates, ten tea cups, eleven saucers, gilt geometric panels, white ground, stamped factory mark "J P,L France," incised numbers, 52 pcs **365.00**
Ewer, 5½", squatty, hp flowers, gold neck and handle **50.00**
Fish Service, twelve sq form plates, six different fishing scenes in center, gilt dec cobalt blue border, matching rect two handled sauce boat, underglaze green mark "CFH/GDM," Gerad Defraissein et Morel, late 19th C, 13 pcs **275.00**
Game Plate, 13½", gold rococo border, artist sgd **200.00**
Hair Receiver, blue flowers and white butterflies, ivory ground, gold trim, marked "JPL" **75.00**
Mug, hp
  Blackberries, pastel foliage, three small pink flowers highlighted with enameled petals, shaded pastel to dark green ground, gold handle and rim, barrel shape, 4" **50.00**
  Iris, marked "JP France," serpent handle **40.00**
  Nasturtiums **45.00**
Mustache Cup and Saucer, roses, green leaves, gold trim **50.00**

Pitcher, 6½" h, gold dec, cobalt ground, red vase mark with green letters, $135.00.

Nappy, 6" d, curved gold handle, gold scalloped edges, soft pink blossoms, blue-green ground **30.00**
Oyster Plate, 8½", scalloped, garlands of pink roses, green leaves, and blue ribbons, white ground, gold trim . . . **50.00**
Perfume Tray, 9½" d, hp, apple blossoms, blue shaded to pink to gray ground, pierced handles **50.00**
Pitcher
  4¾ x 7", milk, hp, pink florals, gold trim **75.00**
  6½", cider, hp, apples, gold trim, artist sgd **120.00**
  8 x 6½", hp, russet yellow apples, multicolored shaded ground, beaded handle, artist sgd "JPL" . **115.00**
  11" h, hp, blackberries dec, artist sgd "JPL" **125.00**
  13½", tankard, green and purple grapes, artist sgd, "Jean Pouyat, 1905" **300.00**
Plaque
  4 x 5½", Jenny Lind, artist sgd, framed **350.00**
  9¾", strutting cockatoo rooster, artist sgd, pierced to hang **70.00**
  13½", gold rococo border, hp, rose and pink roses, green leaves, pastel ground, pierced to hang **250.00**
  18", hp, portrait of young lady, artist sgd "JPL", pierced to hang **475.00**
Plate
  7", hp, columbines **25.00**
  8½", hp, pink roses, leaves, gold trim, scalloped rim **25.00**
  9", hp, pastel florals, Art Nouveau enameled gold dec, ornate gold scalloped rim **30.00**
Platter, 11¾", blue Delft scene **100.00**
Presidential China, 8½" plate, cup, and saucer, William Henry Harrison, made for firm of M W Beveridge, Washington, DC, marked "Harrison 1892," 3 pcs **1,150.00**
Punch Bowl, 13" d, scalloped gold rim, fruit blossom dec, gold band pedestal base **225.00**
Rose Bowl, 8 x 5¾", hp, roses, deep pink ground, ruffled, gold rim and ball feet **75.00**
Shaving Mug, polychrome dec
  Eagle, two flags, shield, scrolls, and roses, marked "Leon Henry Berry" **200.00**
  Hunter, shooting gamebird, dor, gold name **220.00**
Smoking Set, cov jar, pipe rest, tray, hp, artist sgd, dated 1909 . . . . **90.00**
Snuff Box, hp, wildflowers and gold tracery, pink ground, artist sgd, dated 1800 . . . . **200.00**
Tankard Set, 14" tankard, four mugs,

hp, grape dec, gold and green
ground, 5 pcs **300.00**
Tray, 14⅛" d, scenic, thatched cottages,
bridge, and stream, two people on
path, emb leaf border, pink and gold
trim **225.00**
Vase
6 x 20", floral dec, pale green ground,
1½" gold collar **115.00**
12½", beige ground, hp flowers, intricate green and gold handles, gold
trim **230.00**

LINENS

History: The term linen now has become a generic designation for household dressings for table, bed, or bath, whether made of linen, cotton,
lace, or other fabrics.

Linen, as a table cover, is mentioned in the Bible
and other writings of an early age. We see "borde
cloths" in early drawings and paintings with their
creases pressed in sharply. It was a sign of wealth
and social standing to present such elegance.

During the period before the general use of forks
when fingers were the accepted means of dining,
napkins were important. They usually were rectangular and large in size. In the early 18th century,
napkins lost their popularity. The fork had become
the tool of the upper classes who apparently
wished to show off their new found expertise in
the use of the fork. After diners did much damage
to tablecloths, finicky hostesses decided that the
napkin was a necessity. It soon reappeared on the
table.

The Victorian era gave us the greatest variety
of household linens. The lady of the house had
time to sit and sew a fine seam. Sewing became
a social activity. Afternoon callers brought their
handwork with them when they came to gossip
and take tea. Every young girl was expected to fill
her hope chest with fine examples of her prowess.
In the late 19th century these ladies made some
very beautiful "white work," using white embroidery of delicate stitchery, lace insertions, and ruffles on white fabrics. These pieces are highly
sought after today.

The 20th century saw a decline in that type of
fine stitchery. The social pace quickened. Household linens of that period show more bright colors
in the embroidery, the designs become more lighthearted and frivolous, and inexpensive machine
made lace was used. Kitchen towels were decorated with animals or pots and pans. Vanity sets
dominated the bedroom; the Bridge craze put emphasis on tablecloths and napkin sets. To fill the
desire for less expensive lace cloths and bed-
spreads, women of the Depression started cro-
cheting. Many examples of this craft are available.

With the advent of World War II, more women
went to work. The last remanence of fine stitchery

quickly diminished. Technological advances in
production and fibers lessened the interest in hand
made linens.

Collecting And Use Tips: Most old linens are
fragile, some are age stained from being stored
improperly for years. Unless you have a secret for
removing these stains without damaging the fabric,
look for those items in very good or better condition.

Linens which are not used frequently are best
stored unpressed, rolled Boy Scout style, and
tucked away in an old pillowcase out of bright light.
Be sure the linens and pillowcases have been
rinsed several times to remove all residue of de-
tergent.

For laundered pieces which are used often,
wrap in acid free white tissue or muslin folders. If
the tissue is not acid free, it will cause the folded
edges to discolor. If possible, store on rollers to
prevent creasing. Creased areas become weak
and disintegrate in laundering. Acid-free wrapping
material can be purchased from Talas, 104 Fifth
Avenue, New York, NY 10011.

References: Virginia Churchill Bath, *Lace*,
Henry Regnery Co., 1974; Lois Markrich and
Heinz Edgar Kiewe, Victorian Fancywork, Henry
Regnery Co., 1974; *McCall's Needlework Trea-
sury*, Random House, 1963; Francis M. Montgo-
mery, *Textiles In America, 1650–1870*, W. W. Nor-
ton & C. (A Winterthur/Barra Book); Patricia
Esterbrook Roberts, *Table Settings. Entertaining
And Etiquette. A History And Guide*, Viking Press,
1967.

Collectors' Club: International Old Lacers, Box
1029, West Minster, CO 80030. Dues: $8.00.

Museums: Metropolitan Museum of Art, New
York, NY; Museum Of Fine Arts, Boston, MA;
Rockwood Museum, Wilmington, DE; Shelburne
Museum, Shelburne, VT; Smithsonian Institution,
Washington, D.C.

Advisor: Alda Horner.

Bedspread
Appliqued, baby bed size, white muslin, appliqued, animals and flowers,
pastel colors, embroidery, pale blue
appliqued edge, c1935 .... **75.00**
Cotton Knit, double size, flower petal
pattern, three sides fringed, separate pillow sham with four fringed
sides, c1930–40 .... **185.00**
Crochet, double size, small medallion
motif, crocheted together with fine
webbing, pale green, green fringed,
three sides **250.00**
Victorian
60 x 90", white work, muslin, tucking and insertion of machine embroidered eyelet design center
dec, outer three edges eyelet,
c1890 .... **195.00**
104 x 112", white work, bleached

muslin, one third tucking and embroidered eyelet dec, eyelet edges, c1890 .... **225.00**

Bolster Case, white muslin, ends open, appliqued royal blue edging, colorful sprig of flowers, embroidery finish, c1940 .... **45.00**

Bridge Set

Irish Linen, double damask, overall floral and swirl pattern, wide hand hemstitched border, four matching napkins, set **35.00**

Madeira, white linen, drawn and embroidery work, embroidered flower basket corners, scalloped edges, four matching napkins, set **25.00**

Curtain Panel, appliqued linen and re-embroidered floral and scroll pattern, scalloped outer edge and bottom, net background, machine made, each panel 36 x 84", pr **75.00**

Doily

Cotton, 12" sq, white, overall eyelet embroidery, ½" eyelet border **2.50**

Crochet, 24" d, simple design, 3" ruffled edge, white cotton thread ... **12.00**

Filet Net, 14" d, ecru, re-embroidered flowers and leaves **3.50**

Dresser Scarf

Madeira, cut work, hand embroidered satin stitch, pointe lace insets each end, filet lace borders on four sides, c1930 .... **30.00**

Victorian, 122 x 36", white linen, white work, floral design ends, heavy padded satin stitch, scalloped edges, c1890 .... **25.00**

Handkerchief

Batiste, white, 10" sq, 2" w machine made lace border **3.50**

Bride's, 14" sq, linen, narrow hemstitched edge surrounded by four rows of hand applied French lace **45.00**

Chinese silk, natural, open drawn work on one corner, machine hemmed **5.00**

Linen, 9" sq, white

Hand made tatting border **7.50**

Machine made lace border **2.00**

Napkin

Cocktail

Cotton, pale yellow, one corner elephant embroidered, fringed edges, c1930, set of 8 .... **7.50**

Linen, white, one corner reveling men embroidered, fringe edges, c1930, set of 4 .... **3.00**

Dinner, linen

20" sq, cream, rose color scalloped edges, cross-stitched rose motif on one corner, c1950, set of 8 . **16.00**

20" sq, double damask, ½" hand

hemstitched border, wreath motif center, set of 4 .... **22.00**

22" sq, double damask, rose pattern, hand rolled hem, set of 8 . **36.00**

24" sq, double damask, satin stripe border, hand hemstitched, set of 8 .... **40.00**

Ecru, Pointe de Venise lace motif on one corner, hand hemstitched, 1" lace border, set of 12 **150.00**

Luncheon

14" sq, white Swiss linen, one corner flower basket embroidered, c1920, set of 4 .... **12.00**

14" sq, Madeira, Pointe de Venise lace on one corner, surrounded by hand shades of blue embroidery, ½" filet lace border, set of 12 **65.00**

15" sq, ceil blue linen damask, machine hemstitched, set of 8 .... **15.00**

Pillow Case

Boudoir, white

Linen, cut work and embroidery, filet lace showing mythological marine theme in center and filet lace corner, edged in machine made lace, button back, 22 x 15" **65.00**

Percale, scalloped and eyelet border, 19 x 12" **15.00**

Pair

Cotton, embroidered girl with umbrella, bright colors, machine made lace edge, from stamped kit, c1935 .... **15.00**

Madeira, linen, pointe lace surrounded by embroidered cut work, pale blue floral and swirl design, scalloped end opening . **45.00**

Victorian, linen, white, heavy padded satin stitch embroidery, satin stitch scallops on end **45.00**

Pillow Sham

Double bed size, muslin, Victorian white work, narrow machine tucking on border, and embroidered edges, 50 x 35", c1890 .... **65.00**

Single bed size, white muslin, wide border of machine tucking, machine made lace edge, 48 x 34" .. **35.00**

Placemat Set

Cotton, white, Battenberg, lavish corners and edging, napkins to match, c1940, set of 8 .... **75.00**

Linen

Royal blue, white blanket stitch edges, four matching napkins, handmade, c1950, set of 4 .... **12.00**

Woven checks of rose and green, fringed edges, matching fringed napkins, set of 4 .... **15.00**

Runner

Cotton, white, Chinese hand drawn work, 16 x 50", early 20th C **18.00**

Irish linen, white, double damask, allover small flower design, hand rolled ends, 26 x 148", early 20th C **75.00**

Pointe de Venise, cartouche and circle design, hand made, 10½ x 105", early 20th C **275.00**

Sheet

Bridal

Madeira, linen, 18" deep embroidered cut work, filet lace insets, 2" filet lace border top, narrow hemstitching bottom, 86 x 101", pr matching pillow cases, set .. **250.00**

White Linen, 18" satin stitch hand embroidery top, open lily motif cut work, plain scalloping bottom edge **125.00**

White fine linen, floral and spray motif cut work top, scalloped sides down 24", machine hemmed bottom, 44 x 100" **95.00**

Tablecloth, 68 x 100", natural color linen, "Richelieu," all handmade cutwork and embroidery in floral and scroll motif, early 20th century, $575.00.

Tablecloth

54 x 54", tea cloth, Chinese cotton, hand drawn central star motif, deep drawn work borders sides, hand hemstitched border **15.00**

54 x 86", Patchwork, variety of laces, oval central medallion, central paisley motif, satin stitch embroidered voile inserts bordered by 3" net ruching, surrounded by more paisley designs and round motifs, filled with Chantilly lace, net ruching on corners, 3" Chantilly lace border, hand constructed, 1920s **350.00**

60" d, white linen, heavy padded satin stitch, roses and open work, 4" machine made lace border **50.00**

66 x 128", banquet cloth, ecru, allover hand made Pointe de Venise lace, central five medallions motif with floral and foliate design set in panel, bordered swirls of medallion of flowers, interspersed flower vase forms with flowers, floral design outside border, scalloped edge, 12 cream napkins with motif in one corner and 1" matching lace edge, pre 1935, napkins unused **3,500.00**

68" d, linen, scalloped border, ecru merrow stitch edge **15.00**

68 x 98", Irish linen, double damask, Queen Victoria Royal Jubilee 1887, portrait of Queen circular motif center, surrounded by symbols of countries of Realm interspersed with thistles motif, Royal Jubilee and 1887 ribbon motif, fleur-de-lis, maltese crosses, and small bellflowers background border, 19th C **950.00**

68 x 104", white linen, red crossstitched design all four sides, c1940 .... **45.00**

68 x 116", Irish linen, damask, United States Dept of Navy, stars, stripes and rope motif, commercial quality **50.00**

72 x 58", crochet, tobacco string, filet lace sq motifs, c1930–40 .... **50.00**

72 x 90", Irish linen, hand turned ends, central cartouche surrounded by roses **95.00**

72 x 112", ecru linen, allover satin stitch, flower pattern, machine made filet lace inserts with 12" deep filet lace cherubs and urns motifs border, 18" matching motif corners, 12 matching napkins, set **750.00**

92 x 105", cotton, cut work with blue apenzell type cut work and embroidery design center, scalloped edges **75.00**

Towel, hand

20 x 40", linen, damask, 9" Wedding Knots fringe, c1950, Made in Czechoslovakia **25.00**

23 x 15", linen huck, cut work and filet lace inserts on both ends, late 19th C **7.50**

24 x 40", white linen, double damask, gold color woven border leaf pattern, satin stitch monogram "MW", 6" hand tied fringe **18.00**

Tray Cover
   Pale blue linen, embroidered small
     pink flowers, "Good Morning" up-
     per left corner, 2 matching napkins,
     set **12.00**
   Pale yellow organdy, appliqued pale
     yellow linen floral motif, pocket with
     matching napkin, set **15.00**

LITHOPHANES

History: Lithophanes are highly translucent porcelain panels with impressed designs. The design is formed by the difference in thickness of the plaque. Thin parts transmit an abundance of light while thicker parts represent shadows.

Lithophanes were first made by the Royal Berlin Porcelain Works in 1828. Other factories in Germany, France, and England later produced them. The majority of lithophanes on the market today were made between 1850 and 1900.

Collectors' Club: Lithophane Collectors Club, 2032 Robinwood Avenue, Toledo, OH 43620. *Lithophane Collectors Club Bulletin* (bimonthly).

Museum: Blair Museum of Lithophanes and Carved Waxes, Toledo, OH.

Panel, Suitor, 5¼ x 4⅜", impressed "PPM, 1122," c1860, $150.00.

Candlestand, 8¼" h, patterned, 4¾" d
   crystal, cone shaped shade, five dif-
   ferent scenes of Victorian girls **225.00**
Fairy Lamp, 9", four scenic panels, 1 pc
   top **375.00**
Lamp
   Night, 5¼", sq, four scenes, irid green
     porcelain base, gold trim, electrified **600.00**
   Table, 20¾" h, colored umbrella style
     shade, four panels of outdoor Vic-
     torian scenes, bronze and slate
     standard, German **675.00**

Lamp Shade, five panels of children,
   each 5½" w, 5¼" h, sgd "PPM" **500.00**
Panel
   KPM
     2½ x 3¼", view from West Point . **175.00**
     3⅞ x 5¼", lake setting, ship and
       windmill **150.00**
   PPM
     3¼ x 5¼", view of Paterson Falls . **175.00**
     5¼ x 4¼", biblical scene of young
       shepherd bowing to elderly gen-
       tleman and daughter **150.00**
   P.R. Sickle, 4¼ x 5"
     Cupid and girl fishing **150.00**
     Scene of two women in doorway,
       dog, and two pigeons, sgd,
       #1320 .... **115.00**
   Unmarked
     6 x 7½", Madonna and Child **175.00**
     7¾ x 6", Paul and Virginia, scene
       of young man holding bird's nest
       and lemon, young woman, tropi-
       cal setting **100.00**
     8¼ x 6¾", Le Seaux du parc de
       Versailles, numbered **150.00**
Pitcher, puzzle type, Victorian scene,
   nude on bottom **165.00**
Stein, ½ liter
   Floral front, soldier bidding farewell
     on reverse **150.00**
   Negro Boy, 5" **175.00**
   Regimental **190.00**
Tea Warmer
   5⅞" h, 1 pc cylindrical panel, four sea-
     sonal landscapes with children,
     copper frame, finger grip and
     molded base **225.00**
   6" h, four scenic panels, SP holder,
     orig inner oil burner **250.00**

LIVERPOOL CHINA

History: Liverpool is the name given to products made at several potteries in Liverpool, England, between 1750 and 1840. Among the early potters who made tin enameled earthenwares, were Seth and James Pennington and Richard Chaffers.

By the 1780s tin glazed earthenware gave way to cream colored wares decorated with cobalt, enamel colors, and blue or black transfers.

The Liverpool glaze is characterized by bubbles and most often there is clouding under the foot rims. By 1800 about 80 potteries were working in the town producing not only creamware, but soft paste, soapstone, and bone porcelain.

Reference: Susan and Al Bagdade, *Warman's English & Continental Pottery & Porcelain, 1st Edition,* Warman Publishing Co., Inc., 1987.

Jug, 6⅝″ h, Commodore Prebles Squadron Attacking The City of Tripoli, Aug. 3, 1804, $600.00.

Bowl, 8¼″, blue underglaze, iron-red overglaze, green gilting, scene of houses on wooded river islands, c1770 . . . . **450.00**
Jug, 9½″ h, color transfer of American brig, "The Three Sisters," "P. Delano" under spout with Masonic symbols, obverse with black transfer of Masonic symbols and "Lodge No. 25," tan toned ground, two small chips on pouring spout **1,400.00**
Mug, 3¾″, dark brown transfer, Hope, all-over luster trim, c1820–30 . . . . . **125.00**
Pitcher
  5¼″, creamware, brown transfer of two classical women in large oval, brown transfer of flowers on ext. rim, pseudo brown transfer Fitzhugh border on int. rim, floral transfer on handle, highlighted with applied green, red, blue, and magenta, small base chip, minor restoration to spout **100.00**
  6½″, polychromed black transfer of Hope and man waving frantically at two ships, transfer verse "Hope as a Anchor firm and sure. Hold fast the Christian Vessel: And defies the blast," green, yellow, and red highlights **350.00**
  8″, creamware, black transfer
    Man holding bag titled "Tis Comical I Know/To Have All This Rhino," obverse with another man with hand full of coins titled "I'm Lucky I Think/To Have Plenty of Chink," 4″ hairline at rim **150.00**
    Peace, Plenty, and Independence, American flag sailing vessel . . . **1,150.00**
    Washington, chain of fifteen states, banner beneath bust reads "Long Live the President of the United States," marked "F. Morris, Shelton," tiny flake on spout **5,750.00**
    Washington Apotheosis, grieving Liberty and Indian seated in foreground, Father Time raises Washington from his tomb towards rays emanating from heaven, words on tomb "Sacred to the Memory of Washington Ob 14 Dec. A.D., 1977 Ae 68," seal of the United States and ribbon under spout, another transfer of American flag frigate, three pinhead size flakes **3,500.00**
    8⅞″, black transfer oval of Washington, foot on prostrate lion, four soldiers at left, American frigate at right, military symbols, ribbon reads: "By Virtue and Valor, We Have Freed Our Country, Extended Our Commerce, And Laid The Foundation of a Great Empire," obverse with oval formed by chain bearing names of fifteen states enclosing a scene of Liberty and Justice, laurel wreath under spout with "Success to America," tiny flake on spout **3,650.00**

LOETZ

History: Loetz is a type of iridescent art glass made in Austria by J. Loetz Witwe in the late 1890s. Loetz was a contemporary of L. C. Tiffany and worked in the Tiffany factory before establishing his own operation; therefore, much of the wares are similar in appearance to Tiffany. Some pieces are signed "Loetz," "Loetz, Austria," or "Austria." The Loetz factory also produced ware with fine cameos on cased glass.

Bowl
  9½ x 5¼ x 5¼″, oblong, textured ribs, pinched sides, folded rim, heavy rainbow irid, green glass, red spots, ground pontil **300.00**
  10½ x 4″, honeycomb, fluted rim, rainbow spotted irid, green glass, ground pontil **350.00**
  12″ d, ruffled rim, deep cranberry to mottled green to clear irid, sgd . . **400.00**
Bride's Basket, irid blue, silver threading, coin spots, brass holder **375.00**

Inkwell, irid purple and blue, brass lid
and trim **250.00**
Pendant, 1½″, ovoid, irid turquoise, yellow glass **140.00**
Pitcher, 9″, pinched sides, silver irid .. **225.00**
Rose Bowl, 6½″, ruffled, purple irid raindrop dec **200.00**

Vase, 7½″ d, 3⅝″ h, green, purple flowers, $300.00.

Sweetmeat Jar, cov
4¾ x 5¼″, green base, maroon
threading, SS top, sq handle, sgd
"Loetz, Austria" **165.00**
5″ h, irid silver spider web dec, green
ground, sgd **400.00**
Urn, 9¼″, ovoid, two handles, irid, three
color, blue "oil spotting," inscribed
"Loetz, Austria" **1,500.00**
Vase
3¼ x 4″, ruffled rim, green threads,
gold irid, ground pontil **250.00**
5¼″, triple gourd shape, heavy blue
irid waves, salmon cov glass, random platinum raindrops, silver overlay, ground pontil **1,300.00**
5½″, pinched sides, deep blue, snake-
skin dec, lavender irid **350.00**
6⅝″, green irid, tortoise shell dec, sgd
"Loetz, Austria" **185.00**
7″, striped luster ground, silver overlay **375.00**
9½″, gourd form, irid, applied prunts,
blue "oil spotting," unsigned **800.00**
11″, floriform, irid, trefoil lip, amber,
green striations, unsigned **650.00**
11¼″, ruffled, cased, irid, red dec,
goldstones **400.00**
11½″, bud, irid, blue "oil spotting," inscribed "Loetz, Austria" **300.00**

LOTUS WARE CHINA

History: Knowles, Taylor and Knowles Co.,
East Liverpool, Ohio, made a translucent, thinly
potted china between 1891 and 1898. It compared
favorably to Belleek. It first was marked "KTK."
After being exhibited at the 1893 Columbian Exposition in Chicago, Col. John T. Taylor, company
president, changed the marking to Lotus Ware,
because the body resembled the petals of the lotus
blossom.

Blanks also were sold to amateurs who hand
painted them. Most artist-signed pieces fit this category.

Tea Set, pink blossoms in relief on
white, gold trim, marked "KTK,"
$550.00.

Biscuit Jar, 6¾″, ivory panels, red and
blue flowers, heavy gold leaves and
vines, fish net on alternate panels,
pale blue ground, Lotus mark **325.00**
Bowl
5 x 4″, pink flowers, green leaves, and
gilt dec, white ground, marked
"KTK" **525.00**
7½″, boat shape, pink and gold openwork, cherry blossoms, marked
"KTK" **500.00**
Creamer, 3¾″, white ground, undecorated **200.00**
Cup and Saucer, hp violets, white
ground, marked "KTK" **100.00**
Ewer, 7½″, pierced, jeweled, pastel
panels, Lotus mark **500.00**
Pitcher, 7″, bulbous, fish net dec, gold,
marked "KTK" **450.00**
Sugar, 4″, fish net dec, florals, white
ground, handles **350.00**
Teapot, emb flowers, gold trim, white
ground, marked "KTK" **350.00**

Vase
   8 x 5", cylinder, ball feet, green fish
     net pattern, orange flowers **520.00**
   10¼", applied white floral dec, dark
     green ground, Lotus mark, KTK . . **1,000.00**
Wash Bowl and Pitcher, child's, gold
   trim, white ground, mkd KT&K **100.00**

LUSTER WARE

History: Lustering on a piece of pottery creates a metallic, sometimes iridescent, appearance. Josiah Wedgwood experimented with the technique in the 1790s. Between 1805 and 1840 luster earthenware pieces were created in England by makers such as Adams, Bailey and Batkin, Copeland and Garrett, Wedgwood, and Enoch Wood.

Luster decorations often were used in conjunction with enamels and transfers. Transfers used for luster decoration covered a wide range of public and domestic subjects. They frequently were accompanied by pious or sentimental doggerel as well as the humors of everyday life.

Copper luster was created by the addition of a copper compound to the glaze. It was very popular in America during the 19th century and experienced a collecting vogue from the 1920s to the 1950s. Today it has a limited market. The market stagnation can partially be attributed to the large number of reproductions, especially creamers and the "polka" jug, which fool many new buyers. Reproductions are heavier in appearance and weight than the earlier pieces.

Pink luster was made by using a gold mixture. Silver luster was first covered completely with a thin coating of a "steel luster" mixture, containing a small quantity of platinum oxide. An additional coating of platinum, worked in water, was applied before firing.

Sunderland is a coarse type of cream colored earthenware with a marbled or spotted pink luster decoration which shades from pink to purple. A solution of gold compound applied to the white body developed the many shades of pink.

The development of electroplating in 1840 created a sharp decline in the demands for metal-surfaced earthenware.

Reference: Susan and Al Bagdade, *Warman's English & Continental Pottery & Porcelain, 1st Edition,* Warman Publishing Co., Inc., 1987.

Additional Listings: English Softpaste.

COPPER

Beaker, 2¾", blue band **65.00**
Coffeepot, cov, pink luster scenes . . . **250.00**
Creamer
   3⅛" h, two rect panels, Hope trans-
     fers, red, green, blue, and purple
     enamel highlights, pink luster dec
     handle and mouth int. **70.00**

Copper Luster, creamer, 3¾" h, blue band, girl with brown hair and orange dress, white and green dec, girl with rose dress on back, $45.00.

3⅜" h, three bands of copper luster
   alternating with two bands of mustard, round blue flowers **25.00**
4", pink and purple band at neck,
   house dec **50.00**
5½", two bands of pink marble luster   **50.00**
Figure, 8", spaniels, pr **110.00**
Goblet, 4½" h, 3½" d, pink luster band,
   floral resist dec, copper luster int. . .   **45.00**
Jug, 8", three transfers of mother and
   child playing badminton and writing
   letters on canary yellow band **175.00**
Mug
   3⅜", horizontal ribbed base, white
     band with polychrome and luster
     floral design **60.00**
   4", raised green and white flowers on
     tan luster band **50.00**
   4¾", leaves and berries on orange
     luster band **60.00**
Pepper Shaker, 4¼", cream colored
   band **40.00**
Pitcher
   5¼", children with goats, raised grape
     border, c1830 . . . .   **45.00**
   6" h, two narrow white bands with
     pink luster house and trees dec,
     wide copper luster bands **50.00**
   7", green and white flowers raised
     dec on broad blue band **90.00**
   10", wide blue band around body,
     emb greyhound, bull, and urn of
     flowers in polychrome enamel, pink
     and purple luster **200.00**
Plate, 7¾, underglaze green dec, Tea
   Leaf design, copper luster overglaze
   highlight, imp mark "R. Cochran and
   Co" **30.00**
Shaving Mug, 3½" h, 3⅞" d, blue band,

multicolored nymphs in field scenes, scroll handle **65.00**

Teapot, 6", emb ribs, polychrome enameled floral dec **125.00**

PINK

Bowl, 7½", shallow, pink luster border, reddish transfer of grazing sheep .. **30.00**

Child's Mug, 2" h, pink luster band, reddish hunter and dogs transfer, green highlighted foliage transfer **50.00**

Creamer, 4⅜" h, stylized flower band, pink luster highlights and rim, ftd ... **52.00**

Cup and Saucer, magenta transfers, Feith, Hope, and Charity, applied green enamel highlights, pink luster line borders **45.00**

Dish, 12⅝ x 7½", shell shape, impressed "Wedgewood-DUF-I-R," black underglaze "R. PHOLAS EASTATUS" **85.00**

Jug
  5⅜", two huntsmen and hounds, two shades of pink luster, yellow, green, and black, molded pink luster rim, green grapevine border, 1810–20 . **400.00**
  8", church, white toned to tan **150.00**

Mug, 2⅞", overall pink splash luster dec, handled **35.00**

Pitcher
  5½" h, ornate pink luster dec, single and double House **100.00**
  5⅝" h, hunting scenes, deep relief, pink luster, green enamel **55.00**

Plate
  6¼", relief dogs running figures on rim, highlighted with green, red, and pink luster, red, green, and blue stylized floral dec in center .. **50.00**
  7¼", emb daisy border, center pink luster House pattern, pink luster line border **15.00**
  7⅝" d, King's Rose, red, green, and yellow, double pink luster band border **25.00**

Toddy Plate, 5¹/₁₆", pink luster House pattern, emb sprigs of flowers border **40.00**

Toothpick Holder, 2 x 2¾", pink splash luster, white base **65.00**

Waste Bowl, 6", House pattern **125.00**

SILVER

Cake Set, 10" plate, eight 7" plates, wide luster border with pink and purple irises, marked "Bareuther, Bavaria" **125.00**

Creamer, 4¼" h, band of scrolling flowering foliage, iron-red and silver luster, Wedgwood, 19th C **85.00**

Jug, 4½", ribbed, Staffordshire, 19th C **75.00**

Mustard Pot, 3⅞", vertical ribbed design, emb body, matching cov, ftd .. **70.00**

Pepper Pot, 5" h, standing toby form, round hollow base, pouring holes .. **85.00**

Pitcher, 6¼", Sawtooth pattern in canary and silver luster, late 18th C **375.00**

Shaker, 3⅝", ringed circumference, pedestal base **48.00**

Tea Set, pot, dome cov, sugar and creamer, oval, bulbous body, standard handles **135.00**

Vase, 5¼", flared top, painted red and silver luster nasturtium vine, c1810 . **110.00**

Sunderland Luster, jug, 4¼" h, A West View Of The New Bridge, Sunderland, $350.00.

SUNDERLAND

Bowl
  4", pink band **100.00**
  10", House pattern **125.00**

Celery, couple courting, sgd Bucher .. **120.00**

Cup and Saucer, handleless, black transfer, farm scene **85.00**

Dish, pink splash, black transfer, mother playing with son **22.00**

Gravy Boat, House pattern **150.00**

Jug
  5½", black and white transfer of Mariners Arms on front, Cast Iron Bridge on back **140.00**
  9", black transfer, "A Frigate in Full Sail," verse, sailor and maid, French and English coat of arms joined with "Cremea" **200.00**
  17¼", heroic, pink luster inside and out **850.00**

Mug, 5", transfer of The Foresters Arms on front, The Mariner's Compass on back **175.00**

Pitcher
  3¾″, transfer of The Sailor's Farewell on front, six lines of verse on back **75.00**
  9⅛″, black transfer, farmer's arms, "Cast Iron Bridge over the River Wear at Sunderland...," polychrome enameling, marked "Dixon Austin & Co, Sunderland" **475.00**
Plate
  7″, pink splash **15.00**
  8″, floral center, luster border **50.00**
Sugar, House pattern **75.00**
Syrup, cov, 5″ **100.00**
Vase, 7″, trumpet shape **100.00**
Wall Plaque, "Sailor's Farewell" **125.00**
Waste Bowl, pink splash **55.00**

LUTZ TYPE GLASS

History: Lutz type glass is an art glass attributed to Nicholas Lutz. He made this type of glass while at the Boston and Sandwich Glass Co. from 1869 until 1888. Since Lutz type glass was popular, copied by many capable glass makers, and unsigned, it is nearly impossible to distinguish genuine Lutz products.

Lutz is believed to have made two distinct types of glass, striped and threaded glass. This style often is confused with a similar style Venetian glass. The striped glass was made by using threaded glass rods in the Venetian manner. Threaded glass was blown and decorated by winding threads of glass around the piece.

Beverage Set, 7½″ tankard pitcher, four lemonade glasses, four large tumblers, cranberry threading on clear glass, engraved pattern of water plants and great blue heron on pitcher, 9 pcs **400.00**

Bowl, 4¼″ d, 2″ h, blue latticino ribbons, gold stone flakes, $120.00.

Compote, 8⅞ x 6½″, threaded, DQ, amberina, clear hollow stem **500.00**
Finger Bowl, 7″ d, matching underplate, ruffled, amber swirls, amethyst latticino, gold metallic borders **150.00**
Lamp Shade, 8″ sq, 6¼″ h, 2½″ fitter, opaque white loopings, applied cranberry threading, ribbon edge, sq top **175.00**
Punch Cup, 3 x 2⅝″, cranberry threading on clear ground, circular foot, applied clear handle **85.00**
Tumbler, 3¾″, white and amethyst latticino, goldstone highlights **75.00**

MAASTRICHT WARE

History: Maastricht, Holland, is where Petrus Regout founded the De Sphinx pottery, in 1836. The firm specialized in transfer printed earthenwares. Other factories also were established in the area, many employing English workmen and their techniques. Maastricht china was exported to the United States in competition with English products.

Reference: Susan and Al Bagdade, *Warman's English & Continental Pottery & Porcelain, 1st Edition,* Warman Publishing Co., Inc., 1987.

Bowl, 6″ d at top, 3″ h, Vlinder, marked "P. Regout & Co./Maastricht" with seated lion, $35.00.

Bowl
  8″, Oriental scene **40.00**
  9″, stick spatter, gaudy floral dec ... **25.00**
Chocolate Pot, transfer of children, marked **75.00**
Cup and Saucer
  Blue Willow, handleless **25.00**
  Stick spatter and gaudy plychrome floral dec, marked **35.00**

Mug, 3" h, stick spatter and gaudy polychrome floral dec, marked **65.00**
Pitcher, 4½", Oriental scene **65.00**
Plaque, 10", decal of realistic pears,
shaded rust border, back pierced for
hanging **35.00**
Plate
9", gaudy stick spatter dec, polychrome floral enameling **25.00**
9⅛", stick spatter, gaudy red and blue
florals **25.00**
14½", children skating, windmill in
background, blue transfer, sgd . . . **65.00**
Platter, 11½", gaudy polychrome florals
in red, yellow, and green, white
ground **50.00**
Waste Bowl, 5 x 3⅛", multicolored mar-
bleized dec, minor stains **20.00**

**Bone Dish, 7¼ x 4½", green and pink
foliage, tan pig, #8272, $120.00.**

MAJOLICA

History: Majolica, an opaque, tin glazed pottery,
has been produced by many countries for centuries. It originally took its name from the Spanish
Island of Majorca, where figuline (a potter's clay)
is found. Today majolica denotes a type of pottery
which was made during the last half of the 19th
century in Europe and America.

Majolica frequently depicted elements in nature:
leaves, flowers, birds, and fish. Human figures
were rare. Designs were painted on the soft clay
body using vitreous colors and fired under a clear
lead glaze to impart the rich color and brilliance
characteristic of majolica.

Among English majolica manufacturers who
marked their works were: Wedgwood, George
Jones, Holdcroft, and Minton. Most of their pieces
can be identified through the English Registry
mark and/or the potter-designer's mark. Sarreguemines in France and Villeroy and Boch in
Baden, Germany, produced majolica that compared favorably with the finer English majolica.
Most Continental pieces had an incised number
on the base.

Although 600 plus American potteries produced
majolica between 1850 and 1900, only a handful
chose to identify their wares. Among these manufacturers were George Morely, Edwin Bennett,
the Chesapeake Pottery Company, the New Mil-
ford-Wannoppee Pottery Company, and the firm of
Griffen, Smith, and Hill. The others hoped their
unmarked pieces would be taken for English examples.

References: Susan and Al Bagdade, *Warman's
English & Continental Pottery & Porcelain, 1st Edi-
tion,* Warman Publishing Co., Inc., 1987; Mariann
K. Marks, *Majolica Pottery: An Identification And
Value Guide,* Collector Books, 1983; M. Charles
Rebert, *American Majolica 1850–1900,* Wallace-
Homestead, 1981.

Ashtray, figural, snake charmer, seated
on Persian rug **85.00**
Basket, shells, lavender int., rope han-
dle **250.00**
Biscuit Jar, 8⅜ x 7⅝", mottled green,
brown, and aqua int., attached SP ftd
base, hinged SP cov, sphinx finial,
c1875 . . . . **250.00**
Bowl
6", Grape, oval, lavender int., George
Jones **175.00**
9", Shell, figural, blue int., brown ext.,
Holdcroft **150.00**
12", Cabbage Leaf and Floral, lug-
gage strap **300.00**
Bread Plate
Oak Leaf, 13", green and aqua, pink
edge, Etruscan **140.00**
Twin Shells on Wave, 14" **185.00**
Butter Dish, cov, Bamboo, Etruscan . . **225.00**
Butter Pat, Horseshoe, 3", turquoise
and gray **35.00**
Cake Stand, Maple Leaf **135.00**
Cheese Dish, Rope and Fern, 8" **250.00**
Compote, Morning Glory, Etruscan . . . **275.00**
Creamer
Butterfly and Bamboo, 3" **125.00**
Coral, Etruscan **175.00**
Dish, Picket Fence and Morning Glory,
brown mottled center **75.00**
Figure, 18", peasant woman and two
goats, blue, white, brown, and green,
imp numerals **125.00**
Jardiniere, Art Nouveau, pale mottled
blue ground, semi-nude women in
flowing gowns, one standing, two
seated, heavy scroll work, pale pink
int., solid olive green ext., unmarked **175.00**
Match Holder, 2½ x 2¼", drum shape,
yellow and green, striker on base . . **40.00**
Mustache Cup, Shell and Seaweed,
pink and gray **265.00**

Oyster Plate, 10″, five multicolored
  shells **125.00**
Pitcher
  4½″, Corn, straight body, green and
    yellow **50.00**
  7½″, tankard, magenta int., roses and
    olive green ext., mustard handle,
    sgd "Frie Onnaing, France," sun
    over crown over shield mark **115.00**
  8″, Ivy on Tree Bark, brown, English **125.00**
  9″, Dogwood, stem handle, brown
    ground, Holdcroft **175.00**
  9½″, Stork in Marsh, eel figural han-
    dle **250.00**
Plate
  6¾″, rect, Lily of the Valley, leaf center **70.00**
  7½″, Blackberry, basketweave edge,
    mottled center **45.00**
  8″, Fern and Floral **75.00**
  8½″, Strawberries, leaves and blos-
    soms, French **35.00**
  9″, Morning Glory, blue, yellow lobed
    edge **85.00**
  10½″, scalloped rim, shaggy dog and
    house, green, brown, yellow, and
    white **115.00**
Platter, 11¾″, Raspberry, mottled center **100.00**
Relish, Onion and Pickle, cobalt ground **185.00**
Sardine Box, 9½″, Pineapple, fish finial,
  attached underplate **300.00**
Spoon Holder, Fan, 5″ **100.00**
Strawberry Server, 10½ x 6¾″, pale
  green, lavender border, two brown
  baskets, yellow flowers, green leaves,
  English **425.00**
Sugar, cov
  Melon, blue, 4″, Holdcroft **100.00**
  Shell and Seaweed, fish finial **175.00**
Syrup
  Dogwood, 4″ **150.00**
  Sunflower, cobalt ground, Etruscan . **300.00**
Teapot
  Cauliflower, Etruscan **175.00**
  Holly and Berries, blue and green,
    bark handle and spout **160.00**
Tray, 11½ x 14″, oval, shallow, cream
  weave, flowers, leaves, and birds in
  flight, green bamboo border, marked
  "Wedgwood" **350.00**
Urn, 13½ x 10″, bulbous, blown-out
  shoulders, olive green griffin handles,
  double crescent shaped top, four
  panels with lizard entwined in vines,
  pedestal ftd, cream, olive green, dark
  green, brown, and red, imp circle
  mark, Italian **300.00**

MAPS

History: Maps provide one of the best ways to
study the growth of a country or region. From the

16th to the early 20th century, maps were both
informative and decorative. Engravers provided ornamental detailing which often took the form of
bird's eye views, city maps and ornate calligraphy
and scrolling. Many maps were hand colored to
enhance their beauty.

Maps generally were published in plate books.
Many of the maps available today result from these
books being cut apart and sheets sold separately.

In the last quarter of the 19th century, represen-
tatives from firms in Philadelphia, Chicago, and
elsewhere traveled the United States preparing
county atlases, often with a sheet for each township and a sheet for each major city or town. Although mass produced, they are eagerly sought
by collectors. Individual sheets sell for $25 to $75.
The atlases themselves can usually be purchased
in the $200 to $400 range. Individual sheets should
be viewed solely as decorative and not as investment material.

PRINTED

Canada, "British America," Tallis, Lon-
  don/New York, 1851, 12¾ x 9½″, en-
  graved, outline color **75.00**
North America
  "A New And Correct Map Of North
    America, With The West India Is-
    lands, Divided According To The
    Last Treaty Of Peace Concluded At
    Paris 10 February 1763...," Pown-
    all, London, 1777, two sheets, 20½
    x 46½″ at platemarks, full margins,
    from Thomas Jeffreys *American
    Atlas* **750.00**
  "British Possessions in North Amer-
    ica," S Lewis, 1794, 15 x 17″ **50.00**
United States
  "A General Atlas, Improved And En-
    graved Being A Collection Of Maps
    Of The World And Quarters, Their
    Principal Empires, Kingdoms, & c.,"
    Mathew Carey, third edition, Phila-
    delphia, 1814, Maryland, 12½ x
    17¾″ **375.00**
  Boston, town plan showing intrench-
    ments, 1775, 12 x 17″ **1,220.00**
  Florida, US Dept of War, Topograph-
    ical Study of Florida, Washington,
    DC, 1891, 16⅜ x 27¼″, chromolith-
    ograph, three colors **75.00**
  Idaho, "Railroad And County Map Of
    Idaho," Cram, Chicago, 1880, 19¾
    x 16¾″, lithograph, outline color .. **100.00**
  New Hampshire and Vermont, "A
    Map Of The States Of New Hamp-
    shire And Vermont," Denison, Bos-
    ton, 1796, 7½ x 9″ **185.00**
  New York, "A Map of the Province of
    New York...," New Jersey added by
    topographical observation, Claude-

Joseph Sauthier, London, 1776, engraved 29 x 25", framed **700.00**

New York and Brooklyn, ferry routes, hand colored, Mitchell, 1872, 16 x 24" **30.00**

San Diego River, survey to build levee-canal, 1853, 12 x 15" **50.00**

Santa Barbara, US Coast survey, 1857, 18 x 24" **40.00**

South Carolina, "State of South Carolina From The Best Authorities," Samuel Lewis, 15 x 18" **475.00**

"United States...," D Burr, New York, B Davenport, 1842, 17¾ x 21½", engraved, full color, city insets of Albany, Boston, New York, Cincinnati, Philadelphia, Baltimore, and Washington DC **150.00**

World

"A Chart Of The World According To Mercator's Projection Showing The Latest Discoveries Of Capt. Cook," Dilly and Robinson, 1785, 14½ x 19", colored borders and outlines . **100.00**

"A Map Of The World In Three Sections Describing The Polar Regions To The Tropics In Which Are Traced The Tracts Of Lord Mulgrave And Captain Cook, ...," Bell, c1776, 9 x 16½", twin hemisphere, uncolored **125.00**

TEXTILE

England, needlework sampler, polychrome silk and wool threads in cross and chain stitches, detailed map of England and Wales, sgd Rebekah Cole, England, 1793, 17½ x 18¼" . . **600.00**

United States, silk embroidered, state lines, rivers, lakes, and mountain ranges in fine black silk stitches, sgd Ann E. Colson, probably PA, c1809, 25¼ x 27" **4,500.00**

MARBLEHEAD POTTERY

History: This hand thrown pottery had its beginning in 1905 as a therapeutic program introduced by Dr. J. Hall for the patients confined to a sanitarium located in Marblehead, Massachusetts. In 1916 production was removed from the hospital to another site. The factory continued under the directorship of Arthur E. Baggs until it closed in 1936.

Most pieces found today are glazed with a smooth, porous, even finish in a single color. The most desirable pieces are decorated with conventionalized design in one or more subordinate colors.

Creamer, 3¾" h, blue, $80.00.

Bowl

6 x 2¼", sand colored int., matte medium brown ext., marked **85.00**

8½" d, blue-gray int., green matte ext. **100.00**

Bulb Bowl, 6" d, slate gray glaze, c1915 **80.00**

Honey Pot, 3½" h, light yellow-green ground, painted stylized grapevine with clusters of blue grapes, green leaves and vines, marked **465.00**

Rose Bowl, 4⅛ x 3⅛", gray ground, leaf and fruit motif **550.00**

Teapot, 5¾" h, blue matte glaze, modified "C" handle **85.00**

Tile, 4¾" sq, high relief oyster white sailing ship, blue ground, marked **125.00**

Vase

4", bulbous, lavender glaze **125.00**

4½", inverted bell shape, red berries and green leaves on wide neck border, brown tree trunk dec, oatmeal yellow ground, c1915 . . . . **1,000.00**

8⅛", speckled light gray ground, darker gray branches, clusters of nuts and leaves **725.00**

8½", slightly waisted shape, dark green glaze, marked **185.00**

Wall Pocket, acorn shape, light brown matte glaze **85.00**

MARY GREGORY TYPE GLASS

History: The use of enameled decoration on glass, an inexpensive imitation of cameo glass, developed in Bohemia in the late 19th century. The Boston and Sandwich Glass Co. copied this process in the late 1880s.

Mary Gregory (1856–1908) was employed for two years at the Boston and Sandwich Glass Co. factory when the enameled decorated glass was being manufactured. Some collectors argue that Gregory was inspired to paint her white enamel figures on glass by the work of Kate Greenway and a desire to imitate pate-sur-pate. However, evidence for these assertions is very weak. Further, a question can be raised whether or not Mary Gregory even decorated glass as part of her job at Sandwich.

The result is that "Mary Gregory Type" is a better term to describe this glass. Collectors should recognize that most examples are either European or modern reproductions.

Barber Bottle, bulbous shape, slender neck, girl dec, orig stopper	325.00
Box, 3″ h, 5⅜″ d, round, hinged, cobalt blue, girl holding bird, white sprays on sides, ormolu feet	400.00
Carafe, girl, boy on tumbler	400.00
Decanter, 11½″, clear, bulbous stopper, ornate handle, girl with tinted face carrying basket, hand uplifted to birds	135.00
Dresser Set, scalloped tray, two perfume bottles, powder box, ring tree, and pin tray, 6 pcs	1,100.00
Figure, 7″, boy tooting horn, white, enameled	125.00
Jewel Box, 3 x 3½″, cranberry, hinged lid	400.00
Liqueur Glass, stemmed, 3⅜″ h, 1¼″ d, lime green, girl	50.00
Mug, 3⅞″ h, 2¼″ d, amber, applied amber handles, boy on one, girl on other, pr	135.00
Perfume Bottle, 4⅝″ h, 2″ d, cranberry, little girl dec, clear ball stopper	165.00
Pitcher	
5″, ruffled top, electric blue, applied handle, boy in garden	150.00
6⅝″ h, 4¼″ d, lime green, bulbous, optic effect, round mouth, white enamel boy, applied green handle	125.00
Plate, 6¼″ d, cobalt blue, girl with butterfly net	125.00
Rose Bowl, 3′ h, 3¼″ d, 8 crimp top, cranberry, young girl	225.00
Salt Shaker, 5″, blue, paneled, girl in garden, brass top	180.00
Tankard, 2½″ d, 3½″ h, round mouth, emerald green, applied green handle, girl with basket	95.00
Toothpick Holder, cranberry, boy looking at bird	65.00
Tumbler, 5¾″, pedestal, transparent blue, boy, gold bands	135.00

Vase, 9″ h, silver plated stand, 13½″ overall height, $400.00.

Vase	
4¼″ h, 1⅝″ d, cranberry, clear pedestal foot, detailed enamel girl . . .	100.00
7″, cranberry, girl with balloons, foliage	110.00
9″ h, 4″ d, frosted emerald green, girl holds flowers in her apron and hand	150.00
13″ h, 6⅞″ d, scalloped top, applied clear reeded snail handles, cranberry, girl with flowers in her apron	400.00
14″ h, 5¾″ d, cobalt blue, boy with butterflies, pedestal base	225.00
Water Set, fluted pitcher with crimped top, boy with Panama hat, three tumblers, one with girl and two with boys, tinted faces, hands, and hair, enamel, 4 pcs	298.00
Wine Bottle, 9″ h, 3⅛″ d, cranberry, orig clear bubble stopper, girl holding spray	150.00

MATCH HOLDERS

History: After 1850 the friction match achieved popular usage. The early matches were packaged and sold in sliding cardboard boxes. To facilitate storage and to eliminate the clumsiness of using the box, match holders were developed.

The first examples were cast iron or tin, the latter often having advertising on them. A patent for a wall hanging match holder was issued in 1849. By 1880 match holders also were being made from glass and china. Match holders lost popularity in the late 1930s and 1940s with the advent of gas and electric heat and ranges.

Advertising	
Apollinaris Soda Water	25.00
Juicy Fruit, wall	100.00

Advertising, tin, hanging, Hershey's "Happy Home" Bread, multicolored, girl wears pink dress and has blond hair, yellow border, 3⅜ x 1¼ x 5", $225.00.

San Felice Cigars, 1½ x 2¼", brass, hinged lid, raised inscription, logo on lid	25.00
Brass	
Bear chained to post, 3" h, cast, orig fire gilt	225.00
Fire Department, 2 x 2½", copper colored, hinged lid, Reading, PA Fire Hall cello insert in lid, early 1900s	40.00
Owl, glass eyes, cast, 2¾" h	60.00
Bronze, 3", shoe with mouse in toe, 19th C	120.00
Carlsbad, devil	40.00
Cast Iron	
Bird, figural	45.00
Child carrying wood	40.00
Horseshoe shape, antlered stag crest, hanging, cov box at base with knob finial	35.00
Shoe, 5½" h, high button, black paint, c1890	40.00
Glass, 4¼" h, cobalt blue, SP brass trim, cylindrical	40.00
Metal, 2 x 2¼", black enamel paint, hinged lid, inside striking surface, "The Original Teddy" photo in lid, red inscription "Theodore Bear, 149 Market St., Chicago," c1910	75.00
Noritake, 3¾ x 3 x 2½", desert scene, palm trees, purple horizon, orange sky, green wreath mark, marked "Made In Japan"	60.00
Papier Mache, 2¾" h, black lacquer, Oriental dec	15.00
Porcelain, girl, seated, feeding dog on table, sgd Elbogen	125.00
Silver Plated, 3" h, devil's head, brass insert	40.00
Sterling Silver, 1¾ x 2½", hinged lid,	

diecut striking area, cigar cutter on one corner, lid inscription "H. R." and diamond, inside lid inscription "Made For Tiffany & Co/Pat 12, 09/Sterling"	75.00
Tin	
Cigar, ¾ x 1½ x 2¼", wrap around red, white, and blue cello, Davenport Cigars	50.00
Top Hat, 2⅜" h, hinged lid, orig green paint, black band	60.00
White Metal, 2⅝", pig, hinged head . .	35.00
Wood	
Lignum vitae, 3¼"	20.00
Treen, 2¾", black transfer, knob finial	30.00

MATCH SAFES

History: Match safes are small containers used to safely carry matches in one's pocket. They were first used in the 1850s. Match safes are often figural with a hinged lid and striking surface.

Reference: Audrey G. Sullivan, *A History of Match Safes In The United States,* published by author, 1978.

Note: While not all match safes have a striking surface, this is one test, besides size, to distinguish a match safe from a calling card case.

Silver Plated, 1¾ x 2½ x½", rounded body, push up match section, emb on each side, $50.00.

Advertising	
Colemans Mustard, SP, inlaid enamel, brass plaque of Bradfords Victory Over Manchester	100.00
John Trevber Wholesale Liquor & Cigars, Deadwood, SD	32.00
Minnesota State Firemen's Association 1916 Tournament, silvered brass, wrap-around cello, winged nude lady angel illus on button, issued 1915	100.00

National Supply Co, Boston, silvered brass, wrap-around cello, horse head illus, black and white design and text, early 1900 . . . . **45.00**

Sharples Cream Separators, celluloid and metal **85.00**

United Hatters Union, silvered brass, black and white cello insert panels, union text, 1½ x 2¾″, 1900–01 . . **75.00**

Vacuum Oil Co, Rochester, NY, silvered brass, lighthouse with beam and floating barrel of marine oil on one side, 1⅜ x 2¼″ **50.00**

Agate and brass, banded, brown, white, and gray, 2½ x ⅞″ **400.00**

Art Nouveau stylized flowers, loop, 1⅜ x 1⅝″, German (800 silver) **75.00**

Brass

Billiken, watch chain loop, 1908 . . . **275.00**
Dragon, Chinese **175.00**
Metamorphic, skull changes to rooster **275.00**
Milk Pail **185.00**
Walnut **200.00**

Copper and Brass, figural, baby in shirt **150.00**

Gunmetal, three miniature rose diamond horseshoes, 27 diamonds, sapphire, gold button **325.00**

Lapis with brass, cylindrical, hinged top, 2⅝ x ⅞″ **350.00**

Nickel Plated, figural

Cigar **115.00**
Shoe **125.00**

Silver Plated, playing card dec, King of Hearts, two score keeping dials, marked "Gorham" **200.00**

Silvered Pewter, figural, pig **175.00**

Sterling Silver

Five cherubs and angles, wishbone, detailing, dedicated on back, Kerr **350.00**
Woven swirl design, 2¾ x 1½″ **90.00**
Wreath and Ribbon design, 2⅝ x 1¾″ **100.00**

McCOY POTTERY

History: The J. W. McCoy Pottery Co. was established in Roseville, Ohio, in September, 1899. The early McCoy Co. produced both stoneware and some art pottery lines, including Rosewood. In October, 1911, three potteries merged creating the Brush-McCoy Pottery Co. This company continued to produce the original McCoy lines and added several new art lines. Much early pottery is not marked.

In 1910, Nelson McCoy and his father, J. W. McCoy, founded the Nelson McCoy Sanitary Stoneware Co. In 1925, the McCoy family sold their interest in the Brush-McCoy Pottery Co. and started to expand and improve the Nelson McCoy

Co. The new company produced stoneware, earthenware, specialities, and artware. Most of the pottery marked McCoy was made by the Nelson McCoy Co.

Reference: Sharon and Bob Huxford, *The Collectors Encyclopedia of McCoy Pottery,* Collector Books, 1980.

Additional Listings: *See Warman's Americana & Collectibles* for more examples.

Vase, 6″, pink dec, turquoise ground, marked "Brush-McCoy," $75.00.

Basket, Rustic, pinecone dec, 1945 . . **25.00**

Bowl, Mt. Pelee, lava type, charcoal irid, 1902 . . . . **325.00**

Clothes Sprinkler, turtle **10.00**

Cookie Jar

Christmas Tree **350.00**
Frontier Family **30.00**
Have A Happy Day, yellow **6.00**
Kitchen Stove **27.00**
Lollipop **10.00**
Mammie **70.00**
Pineapple **30.00**
Wish I Had A Cookie **22.00**

Creamer and Sugar, Daisy, brown and green **17.50**

Decanter, Pierce Arrow, Sport Phantom **35.00**

Jardiniere

4″, Blossomtime **20.00**
9″, Rosewood, brown glaze, orange streaks **65.00**

Lamp, Arcanture, bird and foliage dec **275.00**

Pitcher, W.C. Fields **25.00**

Planter

Cradle **8.00**
Triple Lily, 1953 . . . . **45.00**

Spittoon, 4½″, pansies, marked "Loy-Nel Art" **100.00**

Tankard, corn, marked "J.W. McCoy" . **80.00**

Tea Set, English Ivy pattern, vine handles, 3 pc **40.00**

Vase
8", onyx, blue, marked "Brush-
McCoy" 18.00
9", iris dec, marked "Loy-Nel-Art" .. 100.00
12", handles, Olympia 175.00
Wall Pocket
Clock 24.00
Orange 15.00
Violin 17.50

McKEE GLASS

History: The McKee Glass Co. was established
in 1843 in Pittsburgh, Pennsylvania. In 1852 they
opened a factory to produce pattern glass. In 1888
the factory was relocated to Jeannette, Pennsylvania, and began to produce many types of glass
kitchenwares, including several patterns of
Depression Glass. The factory continued until
1951 when it was sold to the Thatcher Manufacturing Co.

McKee named its colors Chalaine Blue, Custard,
Seville Yellow, and Skokie Green. McKee glass
may also be found with painted patterns, e.g., dots
and ships. A few items were decaled. Many of the
canisters and shakers were lettered in black to
show the purpose they were intended for.

References: Gene Florence, *Kitchen Glassware of the Depression Years,* 3rd edition, Collec-
for Books, 1988; Lowell Innes and Jane Shadel
Spillman, *M'Kee Victorian Glass,* Dover Publications, 1981.

Additional Listings: See *Warman's Americana
& Collectibles* for more examples.

**Children's Dishes, 10 pcs, custard, red
trim, $85.00.**

Animal Dish, horse 150.00
Birdhouse 85.00
Bowl, 9½", flower band, jade 12.00
Candlesticks, 9", Rock Crystal, pr 130.00
Candy Dish, nude, lid 225.00
Cheese and Cracker Set, red, Rock
Crystal 165.00
Clock, amber, tambour art 300.00
Cookie Jar, Patrician Crystal 80.00

Cruet, stopper, amber, Rock Crystal ... 185.00
Egg Cup, ivory, set of 4 .... 6.00
Ice Bucket, cov, black 55.00
Lamp, nude, green 150.00
Measuring Pitcher, 2 cup, red ships dec 25.00
Punch Bowl Set, bowl, twelve mugs,
Tom and Jerry, red scroll dec 35.00
Reamer, Jadite 20.00
Ring Box, cov, Jadite 15.00
Server, center handle, red, Rock Crystal 125.00
Toothbrush Holder, Jadite 15.00
Vase, 8½", nude, Chalaine 165.00
Water Cooler, 21" h, spigot, vaseline, 2
pc 300.00

MEDICAL AND APOTHECARY ITEMS

History: Medicine and medical instruments are
well documented for the modern period. Some
instruments are virtually unchanged since their invention. Others have changed drastically.

The concept of sterlization phased out decorative handles. Early handles of instruments were
often carved and can be found in mother-of-pearl,
ebony, and ivory. Today's sleekly designed instruments are not as desirable to collectors.

Apothecary items include items commonly found
in an apothecary and pertain to the items used to
store or prepare medications.

References: Bill Carter, Bernard Butterworth,
Joseph Carter, and John Carter, *Dental Collectibles & Antiques,* Dental Folklore Books of K.C.,
1984; Don Fredgant, *Medical, Dental & Pharmaceutical Collectibles,* Books Americana, 1981.

Museums: National Museum of History and
Technology, Smithsonian Institution, Washington,
DC.; Waring Historical Library, Medical University
of South Carolina, Charleston, SC.

**Scale, 10 x 4½ x 5", oak base, drawer
for weights, Springer Torsion Balance
Co., NY, Style E74 #16956, c1890,
$125.00.**

APOTHECARY

Bottle, 5⅞" h, pressed, amber, tole lid .	25.00
Chest, pine, 24 drawers, bracket feet, 49 x 13 x 59", refinished	900.00
Jar, ointment, silver, lid inscribed "O Infirm"	140.00
Mortar and Pestle 4½", brass	75.00
9", turned ash burl, wide turned foot, plain birch pestle	125.00
Pill Roller, 2 pcs, 7 x 14", walnut and brass, makes 24 pills	100.00
Scale, countertop, wooden base, marble top, 2 brass pans, orig weights .	175.00
Sign, 24½ x 54", "F. A. Turner, Druggist...," curved sheet zinc, wooden frame, gold letters and mortar and pestle, black sanded ground	85.00

DENTAL

Account Book and Ledger, 1886—90 .	15.00
Cabinet, oak, door, two rect windows, pull out shelves, ceramic drawer pulls	1,500.00
Catalog, Consolidated Dental Manufacturing Catalog & Price List, New York, 1915	150.00
Chair, mahogany, cast iron, manuf by George Archer, Rochester, NY, c1880	550.00
Instrument Cheek retractor, carved MOP hanlde	75.00
Extracting forceps, SP, design on ahndle, F. Arnold	50.00
Nerve Canal pliers	15.00
Sterilizer, formaldehyde, wall mounted	50.00
Tooth Key, c1950	45.00

MEDICAL

Anesthesia Mask, brass, folding, c1870	75.00
Bleeder, spring loaded, brass, "POL 1842" etched on back, orig box . . .	75.00
Catalog, Dugan Johnson Co. Standard Surgical Instruments, 1920	30.00
Enema Syringe, pewter and ivory, 9" orig mahogany fitted box	155.00
Flems, tortoise shell, orig box	325.00
Hearing Aid, silk tubing	85.00
Lancet, brass, spring, orig case	125.00
Post Mortem Set, cased, c1870	400.00
Saw, amputation, bow blade, ebony handle	120.00
Scalpel, set of 3, ebony, c1860	400.00
Surgical Kit, pocket	275.00

OPTICAL

Book, *Optical Dictionary and Encyclopedia*, 1908	25.00

Eyelid Retractor, ivory handle, marked "Hills King St.," c1853	125.00
Ophthalmoscope, Morton, cased	100.00

MEDICINE BOTTLES

History: The local apothecary and his book of formulas played a major role in early America. In 1796 the first patent for a medicine was issued by the United States Patent Office. Anyone could apply for a patent. As long as the dosage was not poisonous, the patent was granted.

Patent medicines were advertized in newspapers and magazines and sold through the general store and by "medicine" shows. In 1907 the Pure Food and Drug Act, requiring an accurate description of contents of medicine on the label, put an end to the patent medicine industry. Not all medicines were patented.

Most medicines were sold in distinctive bottles, often with the name of the medicine and location in relief. Many early bottles were made in the glass manufacturing area of southern New Jersey. Later companies in western Pennsylvania and Ohio manufactured bottles.

References: Ralph & Terry Kovel, *The Kovels' Bottle Price List*, 7th ed., Crown Publishers, 1984; Carlo & Dot Sellari, *The Illustrated Price Guide To Antique Bottles*, Country Beautiful Corp., 1975.

Periodicals: *Antique Bottle World*, 5003 West Berwyn, Chicago, IL 60630; *Old Bottle Magazine*, P. O. Box 243, Bend, OR 97701. Subscription: $10.00.

Dr. Kilmer's Female Remedy, Binghamton, NY, aqua, 8¾", $20.00.

A. H. Flanders, M.D., NY, amber, 9" . .	65.00
American Drug Store N.O., tapered top, amber, 9¼"	50.00

Barber Medicine Co, Kansas City, MO,
aqua, label, 7½" **20.00**
Chlorate Potassique, pontil, clear,
painted brown, 6½" **20.00**
Dr. E. Bricker's Tonic Mixture For Fever
and Chills, small tapered top, aqua,
6" **40.00**
E. A. Burkhout's Dutch Liniment, Pre-
pared At Mechanicville, Saratoga Co,
NY, pontil, aqua, 5¼" **150.00**
J. A. Gilka, two men with club and
crown, black, 9" **25.00**
Girolamo Pagliano, vertical letters, rect,
beveled corners, apple green, 4⅜" . **25.00**
Gra Car Certosa of Pavia, aqua, 9½" . **20.00**
Granular Citrate of Magnesia, kite with
letter inside, ring top, cobalt, 8" **30.00**
G. W. House Clemens Indian Tonic, ring
top, aqua, 5" **100.00**
Kobole Tonic Med Co, Chicago, IL, milk
glass, 8½" **35.00**
O.K. Plantation, triangular, amber, 11" . **200.00**
Phillips Emulsion, (N backwards), am-
ber, 9½" **30.00**
Pine Tree Tar Cordial, Phila, tree and
patent 1859 on one panel, L.Q.G.
Wisharts on other, blob top, green, 8" **50.00**
Reed & Carnrick, NY, dark blue, 6¼" . **25.00**
Roshton & Aspinwall, New York, Com-
pound Chlorine Tooth Wash on back,
flared top, pontil, golden olive, 6" . . **250.00**
Skoda's Wolefirlle Discovery, aqua, 9" . **30.00**
Teissier Prevos A Paris, graphite pontil,
blue, 7½" **70.00**
USA Hospital Dept, circle, flared top,
oval, cornflower blue, 2½" **80.00**
Warners Safe Remedy, machine made,
amber, 9" **15.00**

MERCURY GLASS

History: Mercury glass is a light bodied, double
walled glass that was "silvered" by applying a solution of silver nitrate to the inside of the object
through a hole in the base of the formed object.

F. Hale Thomas, London, patented the method
in 1849. In 1855 the New England Glass Co. filed
a patent for the same type of process. Other American glass makers soon followed. The glass
reached the height of its popularity in the early
20th century.

Atomizer, dec colored floral bud shaped
glass stopper **48.00**
Bottle, 4¼ x 7½", bulbous, flashed am-
ber panel, cut neck, etched grapes
and leaves, corked metal stopper,
c1840 . . . . **150.00**
Bowl, 4¾", enameled floral dec, gold int. **50.00**
Cake Stand, 8" d, pedestal base, emb
floral dec **75.00**

**Salt, individual, painted floral band,
$20.00.**

Candlesticks
8¼", silver, hp floral dec, green
leaves, white scroll dec **25.00**
12¾", baluster, domed circular foot,
amber, enameled floral sprigs, pr . **300.00**
Compote, 8", circular, baluster stem, circular base, etched grapevines and
berries **150.00**
Creamer, 6½" h, etched ferns, applied
clear handle, Sandwich **125.00**
Garniture, 14", baluster, raised circular
molded foot, everted rim, enameled
foliate motif **215.00**
Goblet, 6⅞" h, silver, etched Vintage
pattern, gold int. **50.00**
Pitcher, 5½ x 9¾", bulbous, panel cut
neck, engraved lacy florals and
leaves, applied clear handle, c1840 . **200.00**
Rose Bowl, 7", ribbed **85.00**
Tiebacks
3", molded, large rosette, pr **75.00**
4", etched budding iris and scrolls, pr **90.00**
Sugar, 4¼ x 6¼", cov, low foot, enameled white foliage dec, knob finial . . **35.00**
Vase
7½", baluster, raised circular molded
base, central enameled panel of
white, green, and red floral buds
and sprigs **85.00**
9¾", cylindrical, raised circular foot,
everted rim, bright enameled yellow, orange, and blue floral sprays
and insects, pr **225.00**
10", cylindrical, raised circular foot,
enameled panel of yellow, blue,
and white floral clusters, pr **300.00**
13", trumpet shape, enameled panel
of orange, yellow, green, and blue
floral clusters and butterflies **220.00**
Wine, engraved Vintage pattern, amber
int. **100.00**

METTLACH

History: In 1809 Jean Francis Boch established a pottery at Mettlach in Germany's Moselle Valley. His father had started a pottery at Septfontaines in 1767. Nicholas Villeroy began his pottery career at Wallerfanger in 1789.

In 1841 these three factories merged. They pioneered in underglaze printing on earthenware, using transfers from copper plates, and in using coal fired kilns. Other factories were developed at Dresden, Wadgassen, and Danischburg.

The castle and Mercury emblems are the two chief marks. Secondary marks are known. The base also contains a shape mark and usually a decor mark. Pieces are found in relief, etched, prints under the glaze, and cameo.

Prices are for print under glaze unless otherwise specified.

References: Susan and Al Bagdade, *Warman's English & Continental Pottery & Porcelain, 1st Edition,* Warman Publishing Co., Inc., 1987; Gary Kirsner, *The Mettlach Book,* published by author, 1984, R. H. Mohr, *Mettlach Steins,* 9th edition, published by author, 1982.

Additional Listings: Villeroy & Boch.
Advisor: Ron Fox.

Beaker
2327, ¼ L, serving girl **85.00**

Vase, 14″ h, Art Deco, blue and gold dec, white ground, marked "Mettlach, Made in Germany, 2913/29/12," $650.00.

2327/1024, ¼ L, PUG, flute player, rim flake	**35.00**
2327/1187, ¼ L, PUG, girl with basket	**65.00**
2366, ½ L, woman and child	**150.00**
2781, ¼ L, cameo, couple, man seated	**230.00**
2816, ¼ L, cameo, dancing couple .	**260.00**
Boot, 225, 1 L, character, folded down top, spur, pointed toe	**500.00**
Coaster, 1032, 5″, dwarfs with drinking horn	**125.00**
Compote, 346, 5½″, relief, grapes and leaves, flake on base	**70.00**
Creamer and Sugar, 3321, etched . . .	**130.00**
Cup and Saucer, relief, cupids, blue gray, and silver	**75.00**
Jar, cov, 1324, 5″, glazed mosaic	**175.00**
Mug, 3287, ½ L, "Sons of the Revolution, Feb. 22, 1910"	**65.00**
Mustard, cov, 3¼″, relief, floral	**85.00**
Pitcher	
2098, 2L, glazed, mosaic	**200.00**
2430, 16½″, pewter cov and thumb piece	**500.00**
Plaque	
1044, 8½″, the different infantry units	**300.00**
1044/102B, 14″, PUG, geese	**100.00**
1044/147, 14″, Lichtenstein castle . .	**375.00**
1044/165, 12″ Meissen/Elbe	**250.00**
1044/190, 12″, Stutgart	**245.00**
1044/1205, 17″, PUG, cavaliers . . .	**385.00**
2112, 16″, etched, dwarf in nest holding wine bottles, sgd "H. Schlitt," rim flake	**1,025.00**
2187/2188, pr, 17½″, knights on horseback, gold ground	**3,600.00**
2322/2322, pr, 14½″, etched soldiers and maidens	**1,300.00**
2323, 14½″, etched, wounded knight and maiden	**900.00**
2625, 7½″, etched, mandolin player .	**300.00**
3038, 10½″, cameo, young angels .	**360.00**
3181, 17″, etched, Hohkonigsburg . .	**1,245.00**
Pokal, 454, ½ L, relief, king fills walking steins, line repair, pr	**350.00**
Pot, 2965, 7½″, Art Nouveau design . .	**350.00**
Punch Bowl, 1888, 6 L, relief, Imperial eagle with state shields	**1,000.00**
Stein	
228, ½ L, relief, cavaliers	**135.00**
1370, ½ L, relief, couple and verse .	**145.00**
1467, ½ L, relief, harvest scene . . .	**225.00**
1508, ½ L, etched, tavern scene, sgd, "Gorig"	**435.00**
1526/598, 1 L, man with rifle scene .	**305.00**
1526/1108, ½ L, ram and dancers scene, sgd "Hein Schlitt"	**265.00**
1733, ½ L, etched, occupational, jockey cap on inlay lid, horseshoe thumb piece, sgd "C. Warth"	**1,20.00**
1909/726, ½ L, comical scene, walking beer stein	**360.00**

Stein, #1132/19/96, man fiddling, crocodile thrashing his tail among the pyramids, high gloss finish, $650.00.

1909/1143, ½ L, Schlitt scene, 4 men in early dress drinking, exceptional relief pewter lid	250.00
1940, 3 L, etched, keeper of the wine, sgd "Warth"	1,500.00
2134, ½ L, etched, dwarf in nest . . .	1,440.00
2184/967, ½ L, dwarf scene, inlay lid	310.00
2530, ½ L, boar hunt	850.00
2772, ½ L, Brown University seal, owl thumb piece	225.00
2893/1197 2L, PUG, Hessen shield .	450.00
2951, ½ L, cameo, crest of Prussian eagle	375.00
Stein Set, 2893/1200, 3L, PUG, six matching 2327/1200, ¼L PUG beakers, state shields, 7 pcs	600.00
Tile, 3¼ x 5¾", blue warrior	225.00
Toothpick Holder, 1461, 2", mosaic . . .	35.00
Tray, 8 x 12", frame and handles, flying geese and large flowers	275.00
Vase	
1836, 5½", brown blue floral relief . .	135.00
2706, 13", Rookwood style	400.00

MILITARIA

History: Wars always have been part of history. Until the mid-19th century, soldiers often had to fill their own needs, including weapons. Even in the 20th century a soldier's uniform and some of his gear are viewed as his personal property, even though issued by a military agency.

Conquering armed forces made a habit of acquiring souvenirs from their vanquished foes. They brought their own uniforms and accessories home as badges of triumph and service.

Saving militaria may be one of the oldest collecting traditions. Militaria collectors tend to have their own special shows and view themselves outside the normal antiques channels. However, they haunt small indoor shows and flea markets in hopes of finding additional materials.

Reproduction Alert: Pay special attention to Civil War and Nazi material.

Collectors' Club: Association of American Military Uniform Collectors, 446 Berkshire Rd, Elyria, OH 44035; Company of Military Historicans, North Main Street, Westbrook, CT 06498; Imperial German Military Collectors Association, Box 38, Keyport, NJ 07735.

Additional Listings: Firearms and Swords. See World War I and World War II in *Warman's Americana & Collectibles* for more examples.

WAR OF 1812

Button, set of 15 buttons, coat and vest, Army, General Service, pewter 1808–30, Infantry, pewter 1812–15, Regiment of Artillerists 1811–13, Artillery 1813–14, Light Artillery 1808–21, Artillery Corps 1814–21	**250.00**

Civil War, belt, Union, state militia, infantry, black leather, brass buckle, c1863, $125.00.

CIVIL WAR

Belt, enlisted man's, black leather, brass retaining clips, oval brass "US" buckle	150.00
Bullet Mold, Confederate, small brass mold, picket pattern bullet	85.00
Button, Confederate, lot of 35 buttons, coat and vest, initials, states	925.00
Canteen	
8", tin, cloth cov, stopper and carrying strap, stamped "Wadden, Porter & Booth, Phila" on pewter spout . . .	150.00
8¼", metal, red-purple wool fabric cov, orig metal mounted cork stopper and chain and cotton strap . .	200.00
Cartridge Box, leather, oval brass plate	

emb "US" outer flap, inner flap marked "H.H. Hartzell/US/Ord Dep'/Sub Inspector," and "E. Metzger, Phila" **275.00**

Drum, 12″ h, 14¾″ d, body painted, 9″ gold and black spread wing eagle clutching red, white, and blue shield, orig label "Russell & Pater/61 Court Street, Boston/Mass," inscription ... **650.00**

Epaulets, officer's, gilded brass, attaching bars with silver stars, emb eagle, shield, olive branches, and arrows button, pr **200.00**

Flag, Grand National Confederate, 5 x 10', used at the 4th Encampment .. **225.00**

Holster, revolver, flap stamped "W Kinsey & Co/Newark NJ" **300.00**

Microscope, Army doctor's, mobile, brass tweezers, mahogany case, 6″ h **35.00**

Pants, light linen, bone buttons **250.00**

Plate, 8½″, tin **35.00**

Slouch Hat, Confederate cavalry **650.00**

Sword, Confederate Cavalry, curved 36″ steel blade, black steel scabbard, brass basket handle, initialed and serial numbered, marked "R" & "S" .. **175.00**

Sword Belt Plate, Union, NY, sq, silver wreath **150.00**

INDIAN WARS

Bayonet, 45/70 Spocket, orig black scabbard, leather frog, with brass US device **25.00**

Belt Buckle, Naval officer, brass, stamped "Horstman, Phila" **100.00**

Hat Insignia, cavalry, brass, crossed sabers, 3″ w **50.00**

Scabbard, large, brass, attached to leather frog, stamped "US" **50.00**

Sleeve Patch, medical, Army, dark blue wool backing, 4 x 4″ **8.00**

Trowel Bayonet, Model 1873, 3½″ w blade **75.00**

FRANCO-PRUSSIAN WARS

Badge, bronze, Emperor Josef under eagle with crown, maker's mark "Wien" **50.00**

Bayonet, black anodized scabbard, 22½″, curved blade, solid brass handle, marked "MRE d'Armes Je St. Etienne, 1873″ **50.00**

Helmet, Prussian General Officer, spiked, silver grade star, enameled black Eagle Order on breast of Heraldic Eagle, gilt chinstrap and rosettes, silk lining **1,500.00**

Medal, "Order of the House of Hohenzollen Knight," badge with swords, silver gilt and enameled breast badge **350.00**

SPANISH AMERICAN WAR

Button, pinback, "Remember The Maine," battleship scene, patent 1896 .... **20.00**

Cartridge Box, US Army **125.00**

Hat Badge, infantry, brass, crossed krag rifles, 2″ l **50.00**

Spy Glass, pocket, Naval, brass, round holder, brown leather grip, 16″ **100.00**

World War I, reverse painting on glass framing U. S. Army discharge and photo, 1919, frame measures 16⅛ x 20⅛″, $60.00.

WORLD WAR I

Bayonet, Erzatz style, Mauser, 12″ steel blade, green painted handle, scabbard, Serial #7979 .... **30.00**

Binoculars, French Officer's, leather carrying case, 8 x 32″, excellent optics **30.00**

Book, *History of the 79th Division, A.E.F.,* 510 pgs, battlefield photos, published 1919 .... **35.00**

Coat, officer's, wool, black scrolls on sleeves, belonged to Capt G. E. Shepherd **30.00**

Compass, British **90.00**

Cup and Saucer, hp, iron cross on cup, Meissen, dated 1914–15 .... **45.00**

Parade Bar, 5 medal, includes EK 2nd Class, nine year service silver medal 3rd class, Hindenburg cross with swords, Leopold Bavarian 1905 medal, and Bavarian reserves medal **75.00**

Pistol, Luger, wood checkered grips, 4″ barrel, proof marks and matching numbers, DWM maker, dated 1915 . **385.00**

Photo Album, Field Artillery Unit #27 under General Hindenburg, 34 photos, dated 1907 .... **135.00**

Propeller, US, wood, four blade **325.00**
Scabbard for bolo knife, canvas and
   leather, 11" l, dated 1918 .... **10.00**
Sword, officer's, German, brass lion
   head handle with ruby eyes, detailed
   mane and mouth holding oak leaf
   guard, helmeted women on back of
   handle, 33" engraved blade, black
   scabbard with brass ring **275.00**
Tachometer, German **120.00**
Tunic, observer's, US Air Service **50.00**
Wound Badge, silver, crossed silver
   swords stickpin **10.00**

WORLD WAR II

Badge Wings, Air Crew Member's, SS,
   snap on back, marked **22.00**
Belt Buckle, German, DAK Luftwaffe
   Em, tan web belt, marked "#85" ... **75.00**
Boots, German, leather, felt wool tops,
   sewn leather reinforcement straps, pr **30.00**
Bracelet, Air Crew Member, SS, curved
   wings **25.00**
Cap, Army Air Force B-2 style, leather,
   wide billed, white lamb's wool lining **12.00**
Coat, Navy, flier's, leather and wool,
   marked "BuAero-US Navy" **50.00**
Combat Boots, light brown, unused .. **10.00**
Desk Stand, prisoners, handmade,
   metal, 6½" h, iron cross, eagle top,
   dated 1940 & 1941, hand scratched
   Air Force Pilot in POW camp from 11/
   44 to 11/45 .... **15.00**
Diver's Knife, deep sea demolition, solid
   brass scabbard, ribbed oak handle
   with brass guard, 8" steel blade ... **120.00**
Flying Cross, ribbons with attached
   bronze oak leaves, cased **50.00**
Helmet, Tanker's, football style, leather
   liner, green, snaps for earphones,
   made by Wilson Ath Goods **65.00**
Leggins, Japanese, straps, hooks,
   brought back from Guam **42.00**
Medal, soldier's, parade ribbon, enameled lapel bar, black leather case .. **20.00**
Pillow Case, soldier's, U.S. Signal
   Corps, 2nd Signal Service Baty, blue
   fringe, 20 x 20" **10.00**
Poster, 29 x 40", "United We Are
   Strong," colorful, allies flags and
   shooting guns, dated 1943 .... **25.00**
Recognition Book, Naval Forces Ship,
   70 pgs, some entries, marked "Re-
   stricted", separate wall chart **10.00**
Swagger Stick, US, officer's, brass shell
   casings, copper bullet tip, 22" l **20.00**
Window Flag, US Merchant Marine, 8½
   x 12" **20.00**

VIETNAM

Ammo Box, steel, M5-20A1, dated ... **10.00**
Helmet, flight, South Vietnam Officer's,
   sun visor, white poly lining, attached
   black muffed earphones, marked
   "Maker Gentax Corp" **65.00**
Leaflet, South Vietnamese Propaganda, 5 x 7", dated 4/69 .... **5.00**
Medal, Air Force Commendation, parade ribbon and lapel bar, case **20.00**
Parachute, cargo, camouflage, nylon
   straps, hooks, etc, American manufacturer **30.00**
Tunic, US Army, Sgt, green gold stripes,
   5th Division red diamonds insignia . **20.00**

MILK GLASS

History: Opaque white glass attained its greatest popularity at the end of the 19th century. American glass manufacturers made opaque white tablewares as a substitute for costly European china
and glass. Other opaque colors, e.g., blue and
green, were made. As the Edwardian era began,
milk glass expanded into the novelty field.

The surge of popularity in milk glass subsided
after World War I. However, milk glass continues
to be made in the 20th century. Some modern
products are reissues and reproductions of early
forms. This presents a significant problem for collectors, although it is partially obviated by patent
dates or company markings on the originals and
by the telltale signs of age.

Collectors favor milk glass from the pre-World
War I era, especially animal covered dishes. The
most prolific manufacturers of these animal covers
were Atterbury, Challinor-Taylor, Flaccus, and
McKee.

References: E. McCamley Belknap, *Milk Glass,*
Crown Publishers, 1949, out-of-print; Regis F. and
Mary F. Ferson, *Yesterday's Milk Glass Today,*
privately printed, 1981; Regis F. and Mary F. Ferson, *Today's Prices For Yesterday's Milk Glass,*
privately printed, 1985; S. T. Millard, *Opaque
Glass,* Wallace-Homestead, 1975, 4th edition.

Periodicals: *Opaque News,* P. O. Box 402,
Northfield, MN 55057. Subscription: $10.00.

Museum: Houston Antique Museum, Chattanooga, TN.

Notes: There are many so-called McKee animal
covered dishes. Caution must be exercised in
evaluating pieces because some authentic covers
were not signed. Further, many factories have
made, and many still are making, split rib bases
with McKee-like animal covers or with different
animal covers. There is also disagreement among
collectors on the issue of flared vs. unflared bases.
The prices for McKee pieces as given are for authentic items with either the cover or base signed.

Pieces for which reproductions are known are marked by an asterisk.

Pieces are cross referenced to the Ferson's and Belknap's books by the (F —-) or (B —-) marking at the end of a listing.

Advisors: Regis and Mary Ferson.

Statuette, Lincoln, 6″ h, satin finish, emb "Centennial Exhibition, Gillinder & Sons," (F563), $300.00.

Animal Dish, cov
Boar's head, 9⅜″ l, detailed molding, red glass eyes, reeded base, horizontal flange, Patent dated May 29, 1886, Atterbury (F332) **700.00**
Fish, 8¾″ l, walking, divided horizontally, five ventral fins support body, detailed scales, red glass eyes (B167b) **175.00**
Hen, 7½″ l, marbleized, head turned to left, lacy base, white and deep blue, Atterbury's (F8) **145.00**
Bottle
Atterbury, duck figural, 11½″ h, vertical bill, head, and neck form flanged opening, rimmed oval for label, no closure (F433) **350.00**
Bob Fitzsimmons, figural, 11½″ h, male nude to waist, pink, arms folded across chest, frosted lower portion clad in boxer trousers (F501) **500.00**
Bowl
Daisy, 8¼·41″ d, all-over leaves and flower pattern, repeated on inner base, open scalloped edge (F165) **80.00**
Lattice Edge, 8″ d, flat base, sharply curving lattice sides, open and closed at rim, fired color flower center (B100c, 106b) **30.00**
Butter
Father, 4⅞″ l, "The Family" table set,

male head, fur hat pinched to form finial (F269) **325.00**
Roman Cross, sq, 4⅞″ l, ftd base, curves outwards toward top, cross pattern, cube shape finial (F240) . **50.00**
Calling Card Receiver, bird, back view, wings extended over fanned tail, head resting on leaf, detailed feather pattern (F669) **130.00**
Candlestick, 7¾″ h, swirl, ribbing twists counter-clockwise form base, column, cup, and wax guard (F522) **35.00**
Candy Container, 4″ l, suitcase, sliding metal base closure, molded straps and clasps, metal handle, molded "Patent Apl'd For" on one side (F566) **57.00**
Celery, 6⅝″ h, blackberry, scalloped rim, plain band above vertical surface, blackberry pattern, low stem rising from circular base, Hobbs Brockunier (F317) **95.00**
Compote
Basketweave, 7⅜″ h, narrow reed woven through double vertical strands, slanting sides, swirled stem, molded "Patd June 30th/74" under base (F343) **90.00**
Chick and Eggs, 11″ h, pedestal, chick emerging from heaped eggs, finial cov, mounted on curved tripod, central support, rounded lacy edge base, emb Atterbury patent date, Aug 6, 1889 inside cov (F362) **175.00**
Condiment Set, Forget-me-not pattern, salt and pepper, 5⅛″ h cruet, trefoil tray, bulbous shape, six lobed, floral pattern, blue, Challinor, Taylor (F164) **190.00**
Creamer
Cobb, 3½″ h, emb, ear of corn, stalks at base and under lip, ftd, Challinor, Taylor (F587) **40.00**
Sunflower, 4⅜″ h, row of paneled sunflowers above row of paneled lilies of the valley, long lip, heavy handle, purple slag, Atterbury (F288 a) . . **60.00**
Door Stop, 9″ l, reclining lion, three stepped oval platform, columned base, chain, "Patent Pending" (F119 A) **175.00**
Egg Cup, 4¼″ h, bird cov, round, fluted, Atterbury (F 130) **130.00**
Inkstand, 4½″ h, high back chair, Daisy and Button pattern, depression in seat for well(F 15A-B) **80.00**
Jar, eagle, 6½″ h, "Old Abe," rests upright, leafy base, "E Pluribus Unum" on encircled banner, gray (F568) . . . **95.00**
Lamp, 11″ h, Goddess of Liberty, bust, three stepped hexagonal base, clear and frosted font, brass screw connector, patent dated, Atterbury (F329) . . **200.00**
Match Safe, 4½″ h, baby in hat, corru-

gated striker, black hat, match design (F534) 310.00

Mustard Jar, 4½" h, bull's head, divided mouth, protruding tongue handle, cold painted, brown, patent data on base, Atterbury (F14) 130.00

Novelty, 7½" l, shoe, 2 pc, ornate, 18th C style, bow at instep, upward curled toe, removable vamp (F178) 125.00

Pepper Shaker, 5¼" h, Johnny Bull Saloon, gentleman in tailcoat, pewter closure, Atterbury (F340) 85.00

Pickle Dish, 9⅝" l, fish, realistic detailed scales, head, and fins, tail handle, Atterbury patent dated June 4, 72 (F360 A) 22.00

Pitcher, 18 x 24", "Here's Happy Days," framed, Vitrolite slab, hunting cabin int., autumn colors, I.W. Harper adv (F Frontispiece) 750.00

Plate
  Bryan-Stevenson campaign, 8¼" d, bust candidates, floral border (F541) 160.00
  Dog and Cat, 6" d, two cats form upper edge, bracketed dog head, open work swirled leaves, emb "He's all right" (B 20 d) 90.00

Platter, 11¼" l, Centennial Liberty Bell, shell handle, scalloped rim, bold John Hancock's signature, patent dated Sept. 28, 1875 (F57 l) 250.00

Salt Box, 6" d, hinged wood lid, "Salt", hanging type, molded on side (F57-A) 45.00

Spooner, 5⅛" h, monkey, cylinder shape, scalloped top, seated monkeys molded around circumference (F275) 105.00

Sugar, Ihmsen Glass Co, nine panel, flared bowl, factory product on low feet panel, cov fits inside base edge (F670) 400.00

Syrup
  Bellflower, 6" h, pressed pattern, single vine, dated, Collins & Wright (F1550) 225.00
  Drape and Tassel, 8⅜" h, china like finish, plain and tasseled netted triangle pattern, pewter closure, Atterbury (F454) 140.00

MILLEFIORI

History: Millefiori (thousand flowers) is an ornamental glass composed of bundles of colored glass rods fused to become canes. The canes were pulled while still ductile to the desired length, sliced, arranged in a pattern and again fused together. The Egyptians developed this technique in the first century B. C.; it was revived in the 1880s.

Reproduction Alert: Millefiori items, such as paperweights, cruets, toothpicks, etc., are being made by many modern companies.

Jewel Box, 2¾" d, 2½" h, dark blue ground, $250.00.

Beads, 30" l, graduated, small green glass beads 75.00

Bowl
  4", applied handles, blue and white canes 80.00
  8 x 2½", tricorn, scalloped, folded sides, amethyst and silver deposit 125.00

Creamer, 3 x 4¼", white and cobalt blue canes, yellow centers, satin finish . . 100.00

Cruet, bulbous, multicolored canes, applied camphor handle, matching stopper 100.00

Cup and Saucer, white and cobalt blue canes, yellow centers, satin finish . . 85.00

Custard Cup, 5", matching underplate, green and orange floral pattern 40.00

Doorknob, 2½", paperweight, center cane dated 1852, New England Glass Co 375.00

Goblet, 7½" h, multicolored canes, clear stem and base 150.00

Pitcher, 6½", multicolored canes, applied candy cane handle 165.00

Rose Bowl, 6", crimped top, cased, white lining 145.00

Slipper, 5", camphor ruffle and heel . . 135.00

Sugar, cov, 4 x 3½", white canes, yellow centers, satin finish 115.00

Vase
  3½", cabinet, waisted, ruffled top, light blue, cobalt blue, medium blue, and white canes, four applied knob handles 35.00
  4", multicolored canes, applied double handles 100.00
  4⅝", multicolored canes, satin finish, three applied clear petal feet 65.00

MINIATURE LAMPS

History: Miniature oil and kerosene lamps, often called "night lamps," are diminutive replicas of larger lamps. Simple and utilitarian in design, miniature lamps found a place in the parlor (as "courting" lamps), hallway, children's rooms, and sickrooms.

Miniature lamps are found in many glass types from amberina to satin glass. Miniature lamps measure 2½ to 12 inches in height with the principal parts being the base, collar, burner, chimney, and shade. In 1877 both L. J. Atwood and L. H. Olmsted patented burners for miniature lamps. Their burners made the lamps into a popular household accessory.

Study a lamp carefully to make certain all parts are original; married pieces are common. Reproductions abound.

References: Ann Gilbert McDonald, *Evolution of the Night Lamp*, Wallace-Homestead, 1979; Frank R. & Ruth E. Smith, *Miniature Lamps*, Schiffer Publishing Ltd., 1981, 6th printing; Ruth E. Smith, *Miniature Lamps - II*, Schiffer Publishing Ltd., 1982.

Note: The numbers given below refer to the figure numbers found in the Smith books.

#9-I, Fire Fly, opaque white, orig dated burner	225.00
#11-I, milk glass pedestal base and shade, clear pressed font, Sandwich, 6¾"	245.00
#25-II, cranberry, Berger Lamp	125.00
#29-I, cobalt blue glass font, emb "Nutmeg," narrow brass band forming handle, nutmeg burner, clear glass chimney, 2¾" base	100.00
#59-II, clear, emb "Vienna"	125.00
#68-I, pewter base, emb rococo design, burner marked "Stellar, E M & Co," 3½"	85.00
#78-I, nickel plated, wall type, emb "Comet," blue glass beehive chimney shade, 7¼"	75.00
#89-I, brass, double student lamp, orig opaque white shades, 9¾"	500.00
#98-II, clear, applied handle	100.00
#100-II, dark blue, emb star	110.00
#109-I, green, Beaded Heart pattern, acorn burner, clear glass chimney, 5½"	190.00
#112-I, amber, Bull's Eye pattern, nutmeg burner, clear glass chimney, 5"	100.00
#116-I, amber, Fishscale pattern, nutmeg burner, clear glass chimney	135.00
#118-I, amber, Buckle pattern, 8½"	125.00
#125-I, red paint, ball shaped shade, emb flowers and designs, acorn burner, clear glass chimney, 7¼"	135.00
#154-II, brass, pedestal, saucer base	80.00

#156-1, milk glass, emb flower and scrolls, 8"	115.00
#184-I, milk glass, beaded and emb design, blue painted highlights on base and globe-chimney shade, hornet burner	200.00
#190-I, milk glass, Block and Dot pattern, 7¾"	135.00
#192-I, clear, Block pattern, hp blue and green flowers, acorn burner, 6½"	60.00
#204-II, blue, camphor shade	100.00
#213-I, red, stain, Chrysanthemum and Swirl pattern base and globe, hornet burner, 9"	425.00
#215-I, milk glass, emb beaded panels and boats, windmill and lighthouse on base, vertical roses of beading on globe-chimney shade, hornet burner, 7¾"	325.00

Smith 230, milk glass, Acanthus pattern, white ground, fired on pink, $175.00.

#230-I, milk glass, Acanthus pattern, fired on yellow dec, base marked "Buc. PA/1898," 8½"	175.00
#231-I, green, satin, Drape pattern, globe shade, nutmeg burner, clear glass chimney, 8½"	315.00
#267-II, Delft blue windmill dec, white opaque base and shade, acorn burner, 8½" h, sgd "Delft" on base, Mt Washington	585.00
#287-I, apricot shaded to clear, overshot glass, tulip molded base and shade, nutmeg burner, clear glass chimney, 8½"	650.00
#289-II, brass, pedestal, handle	100.00
#317-I, milk glass, pink and yellow flowers, shaded green ground	300.00
#369-I, spatter, tortoiseshell, 8¼"	250.00

#393-I, white, satin, emb ribbing, hp
pink, yellow, and green florals, nutmeg burner, clear glass chimney ... **285.00**
#394-I, blue, satin, puffy DQ pattern
base and umbrella shade, nutmeg
burner, clear glass chimney, 8″ **475.00**
#403-I, cranberry opal, Beaded Drape
pattern, 9½″ **350.00**
#409-II, cranberry, threaded base ... **125.00**
#460-I, cranberry, white enamel floral
dec, 11⅝″ **450.00**
#477-I, sapphire blue, hobnail, 7¼″ .. **375.00**
#482-I, clear, Daisy and Cube pattern,
nutmeg burner, 8″ **225.00**
#538-I, amberina, paneled, amber feet,
9¼″ **1,500.00**
#546-I, blue, Swirl pattern, 8½″ **500.00**
#600-I, satin, MOP, Raindrop pattern,
four petal feet, 8¾″ **600.00**

MINIATURES

History: There are three sizes of miniatures:
doll house
scale (ranging from ½ to 1″), sample size, and
child's size. Since most earlier material is in museums or extremely expensive, the most common
examples are 20th century.

Many mediums were used for miniatures: silver,
copper, tin, wood, glass, and ivory. Even books
were printed in miniature. Prices are broad ranged,
depending on scarcity and quality of workmanship.

The collecting of miniatures dates back to the
18th century. It remains one of the world's leading
hobbies.

References: Lillian Baker, *Creative and Collec-
tible Miniatures*, Collector Books, 1984; Flora Gill
Jacobs, *Dolls Houses in America: Historic Pres-
ervation in Miniature*, Charles Scribner's Sons,
1974; Flora Gill Jacobs, *History of Dolls Houses,*
Charles Scribner's Sons; Constance Eileen King,
Dolls and Dolls Houses, Hamlyn; Von Wilckens,
Mansions in Miniature, Tuttle.

Periodicals: Miniature Collector, Collector
Communications Corp., 170 Fifth Ave, New York,
NY 10010; Nutshell News, Clifton House, Clifton,
VA 22024. Subscription: $26.00.

Collectors' Clubs: International Guild Miniature
Artisans, P.O. Box 842, Summit, NJ 07901. Dues:
$25.00. Newsletter (biannual); National Associa-
tion of Miniature Enthusiasts, 123 N. Lemon St.,
Fullerton, CA 92632. Dues: $15.00. *Miniature Ga-
zette* (quarterly).

Museums: Kansas City Doll House Museum,
Kansas City, MO; Margaret Woodbury Strong Mu-
seum, Rochester, NY; Mildred Mahoney Jubilee
Doll House Museum, Fort Erie, Canada; Toy Mu-
seum of Atlanta, Atlanta, GA; Washington Dolls
House and Toy Museum, Washington, DC.

Additional Listings: See Doll House Furnish-

ings in *Warman's Americana & Collectibles* for
more examples.

DOLL HOUSE SIZE

Armoire, tin litho, purple and black ... **18.00**
Bathroom,
Porcelain, toilet, sink, tub, cherry
wood medicine cabinet, Collector's
Miniature Masterpiece **70.00**
Wood, painted white, Strombecker . **35.00**
Bedroom
French Provincial style, antique white,
includes dressing table and bench,
bed, nightstands **150.00**
Stenciled, pair of canopy beds, dressing table with mirror, pair of nightstands and three chests of drawers
with faux marble tops, side chair,
accessories, Biedermeier **1,000.00**
Victorian style, metal, veneer finish,
bed, nightstand and commode with
faux marble tops, armoire and mirror, cradle, Biedermeier clock,
metal washstand **650.00**
Bench, wood, rush seat **20.00**
Buffet, stenciled, three shelves, column
supports, 6½ x 6″, Biedermeier **400.00**
Chair
Golden Oak, center splat, upholstered seats, German, c1875, pr . **70.00**
Ivory, high pointed back, ornately
pierced, 2″ h, 19th C **175.00**
Ormolu, ornate, 3″ h, c1900, pr **75.00**
Chess Table, ivory, ¾″, scale, c1870 . **325.00**

**Chest, Petite Princess, plastic, gold
highlights, marble style top, white
ground, 3″ h, 3⅛″ w, c1960, $22.50.**

Commode, paper hinge broken, Biedermeier **50.00**
Couch, wood frame, floral design seat,
blue painted back, six legs, 6″ h, Tynietoy stamp **70.00**

Curio Cabinet, maple, four graduated
  shelves, fancy carved sides, 7″ **50.00**
Desk
  Chippendale style, slant top, drawers
    open **50.00**
  Roll top, oak, office chair, drawers
    open **75.00**
Dining Room
  Edwardian style, dark red stain, ex-
    tension table, chairs, marble top
    cupboard, grandfather clock, chan-
    delier, candelabra, 5″ bisque head
    and shoulder maid doll, table ser-
    vice for six, Gebruder Schnee-
    grass, Waltershausen, Thuringia,
    c1915 . . . . **1,200.00**
  French style, gilded wood, round ped-
    estal table, six matching chairs, da-
    mask upholstered settee, pier mir-
    ror, fireplace, table with faux marble
    top **800.00**
  Oak, 9 pcs, rug and accessories . . .   **600.00**
Hall Rack, walnut, carved, fretwork,
  arched mirror back shelves, umbrella
  holder **450.00**
Living Room
  Empire style, sofa, fainting couch, two
    side chairs, upholstered tapestry,
    matching drapery **350.00**
  Tudor style, settee, two chairs, foot-
    stool, upholstered, fringe trim, mar-
    ble topped table, candle stand . . .   **250.00**
  Victorian style, upholstered red vel-
    vet, settee, two parlor chairs, foot-
    stool, two plant stands, two gilt fili-
    gree tables, three panel screen,
    Gone with the Wind style lamp . .   **500.00**
Lounge, Victorian style, minor uphol-
  stery wear **100.00**
Parlor Set, 1¼ x 1¾″ couch, four 1¼″ h
  chairs, cut design, painted red, gold
  seats **40.00**
Patio Set, garden tools, lawn accesso-
  ries **50.00**
Piano
  Grand, wood, eight keys, 5″ h **30.00**
  Spinet, wood, cabriole legs, hand-
    made, 3½″ h **25.00**
  Upright, movable keys, bench, 4½″ .   **40.00**
Rocker
  Cast Iron, green and red, 4″ h **40.00**
  Victorian style, faded upholstery . . .   **50.00**
Sewing Table, golden oak, drawer,
  c1880 . . . .   **100.00**
Side Chairs, Victorian, pr **125.00**
Table
  Ivory, ¾″, scale, c1870 . . . .   **275.00**
  Tin, painted brown, white top, floral
    design, 1½″ l, ¾″ h, ornate **20.00**
Trestle Table, golden oak, turned legs
  and stretcher, c1900 . . . .   **30.00**
Vanity, Biedermeier **90.00**

Wing Chair, painted gray and green, flo-
  ral design, 4¾″ h **70.00**

ACCESSORIES

Ashtray, stand, c1910 . . . .   **30.00**
Birdcage, brass, bird, stand, 7″ h **60.00**
Bookends, wood, seated cats, pr **15.00**
Candelabra, metal **150.00**
Carpet Sweeper, gilt, Victorian **65.00**
Cash Register, German **150.00**
Christmas Tree, with accessories **40.00**
Cigar Cutter, metal, c1920 . . . .   **25.00**
Clock, metal **25.00**
Coffeepot, brass **20.00**

**Washer, Kilgore, cast iron, wooden roll-
ers, painted light blue, 1½″ d, 2½″ h,
$45.00.**

Couple
  5″ h, bisque, cloth bodies, 1920–30
    dressed, woman marked #669 . .   **20.00**
  6″ h, bisque heads, hands and feet,
    molded and painted blond hair . . .   **60.00**
Cradle, cat iron, painted green, 2″ l, 2½″
  h **40.00**
Cup and Saucer, china, flower design,
  1″ scale, c1940 . . . .   **8.00**
Decanter, two glasses, Venetian, c1920   **25.00**
Dog House, painted green, gilt design,
  3¼″ l, 3″ h **20.00**
Dust Pan and Broom, pewter, German,
  c1890 . . . .   **30.00**
Fan, table, brass ormolu **350.00**
Fireplace, tin, Brittania metal fretwork,
  draped mantle, carved grate **75.00**
Fireplace Tools, metal, stand, c1930 .   **50.00**
Floor Lamps, brown, ecru shade on
  one, blue shade on other, 2⅗″ h,
  Tootsie Toy, pr **25.00**
Grandfather Clock, rounded top, walnut
  stain door with black and blue, paper
  face, impressed Tynietoy on back . .   **70.00**
Measuring Cup, Pyrex **10.00**

Mirror, wood, Tynietoy, c1930	45.00
Radio, Strombecker, c1930	25.00
Sewing Machine, copper, treadle	50.00
Silhouettes, Tynietoy, c1930, pr	15.00

Stove
Kent, cast iron, painted green, 4½" . **125.00**
Queen, cast metal, cast iron pots and
utensils, 6½" h **175.00**
Tea Set, teapot, cream and sugar, two
cups and saucers, tray, green and
white floral pattern, two handles re-
paired **100.00**
Tea Wagon, gilt, German, c1910 . . . . **160.00**
Teapot, silver, stand, David Clayton,
c1720 . . . . **1,500.00**
Telephone, wall, oak, speaker and bell,
German, c1890 . . . . **30.00**
Towel Stand, golden oak, turned post . **45.00**
Typewriter, steel, black, AM., c1925 . . **70.00**
Umbrella Stand, brass ormolu, sq, emb
palm fronds **50.00**
Urn, silver, handled, ornate **100.00**
Vase, Satsuma, c1900, 1½" h **55.00**

SAMPLE SIZE

Bed, mahogany, poster, canopy top,
turned posts, arched headboard . . . **275.00**
Chest of Drawers
Empire, American, grain painted, tiger striped maple finish, scrolling
splashback, three drawers, boot-
jack sides **300.00**
Federal, American, early 19th C, curly
maple, rect top, four graduated
drawers, bracket feet, 11½ x 7 x
12½" **1,350.00**
Table, game, mahogany, minor veneer
loss, early 19th C, 14¼ x 7⅛ x 10⅜" **600.00**
Plow, pine and steel, splayed handles,
projecting plow support, gilt dec, red
painted ground, inscribed "South
Bend Chilled Plow Co, Pat May 25,
1886, No. 15 trademark," South
Bend, IN, c1886, 23½" l **2,000.00**

CHILD SIZE

Blanket Chest, William and Mary, walnut, dovetailed, turnip feet, inset initials "EB" made with cut-off nails,
green paper lining, 14¾ x 7¼ x 7½" **275.00**
Chest of Drawers
Chippendale, Centennial, mahogany,
four drawers, bracket base, Victorian bail brass, 10⅝ x 6½ x 16¼" **350.00**
Georgian, burl walnut, band inlay,
15½ x 8¼ x 16⅜" **700.00**
Hepplewhite, English, late 19th C, select mahogany with some curl, pair
of small drawers at top, three graduated full width drawers, French

splayed bracket base, brass pulls
with engraved flowers, 11⅞ x 7¾ x
15⅝" **550.00**
Cupboard, country style, pine, two
glazed doors, two drawers and doors
in base, white porcelain knobs, 24½
x 23 x 13" **400.00**
Desk, Chippendale, MA, c1770, painted
and dec maple, slant front, rect
hinged lid, int. of valanced pigeonholes, center two blocked and concave carved drawers, prospect drawers flanking, three graduated long
drawers below, bracket feet, painted
black on reddish-brown ground, 23 x
12½ x 28" **30,000.00**
Dresser, Eastlake style, stenciled de-
sign, mirror panel, one drawer, two
cabinets, 31" h **125.00**
Rocker
Empire style, mahogany, vase
shaped splat, rush seat, scrolled
arms, 22" h **200.00**
Folding, Eastlake style, bamboo turn-
ings, tapestry seat and back, 27" h **125.00**
Side Chair, country style, pine plank
seat, crest rail, turned legs, 22½" h **150.00**
Table, country style, drop leaf, walnut,
turned legs, 24 x 28 x 21" **150.00**
Tea Service, 15 pcs, ridged,white, gold
sprayed on trim, blue flowers, En-
glish, c1900 . . . . **175.00**

MINTON CHINA

History: In 1793 Thomas Minton and others
formed a partnership and built a small pottery at
Stoke-on-Trent, Staffordshire, England. Production began in 1798 with blue printed earthenware,
mostly in the Willow pattern. In 1798 cream colored earthenware and bone china were introduced.

A wide range of styles and wares was produced.
Minton introduced porcelain figures in 1826, Parian wares in 1846, encaustic tiles in the late 1840s,
and Majolica wares in 1850. Many famous designers and artists in the English pottery industry
worked for Minton.

Many early pieces are unmarked or have a
Sevres type marking. The "ermine" mark was

used in the early 19th century. Date codes can be found on tableware and Majolica. Between 1873 and 1911 a small globe signed Minton with a crown on top was used.

In 1883 the modern company was formed and called Mintons Limited. The "s" was dropped in 1968. Minton still produces bone china tablewares and some ornamental pieces.

Reference: Susan and Al Bagdade, *Warman's English & Continental Pottery & Porcelain, 1st Edition,* Warman Publishing Co., Inc., 1987.

Plate, black trim on scalloped edge, green band, basketweave drop, floral center, $6.00.

Bowl, 7½" d, lily pad form, frog on side
   side, dark green glaze, dated 1873 .   **70.00**
Cup and Saucer, Marlow pattern **30.00**
Demitasse Cup and Saucer, Salt Lake
   pattern **35.00**
Dessert Service, Pattern No. G3439,
   fruits, twelve plates, three stands,
   light wear, imp mark, 1880 date code   **825.00**
Dresser Set, pin box, 5½" pitcher, and
   11" d tray, pink roses dec, gold trim,
   incised maker and potter marks,
   c1898 . . . .   **250.00**
Dish, 10¾", earthenware, artist sgd "W
   S Coleman," imp mark, 1869 . . . . .   **685.00**
Ewer, 21¼", majolica, heron and fish,
   after model by J Protat, imp mark,
   1869 date code **2,300.00**
Figure
   8½", facing parrots, blue bodies,
      green highlights on heads, yellow
      beaks, turquoise bases, raised
      mark, pr **90.00**
   12", parian, two nude girls **400.00**
Garden Seat, majolica
   18", "Aesthetic," dark ground, applied
      scrolls and foliage, imp mark, 1881
      date code **2,350.00**
   20¾", streaky turquoise glaze, imp
      "Minton, 1896" **550.00**

Jardiniere, 7" h, molded wooden planks,
   white vines, lilac int., majolica, matching stands, pr **425.00**
Jug
   67½", majolica, green leaves, white
      flowers, lilac rim, imp mark, 1869 .   **600.00**
   9⅞", majolica, bright yellow, green,
      blues, aubergine, and white, imp
      mark "437," and 1873 date code .   **2,345.00**
Oyster Stand, 10", majolica, revolving
   base, glazed green, brown, and
   white, imp mark, 1869 . . . .   **2,225.00**
Plaques, 7⅝ x 7", pate-sur-pate, match-
   ing pr, one with maiden and cupid
   spinning web, other with maiden
   seated on bench with whip in one
   hand, sunflowers stalked with humanistic snail in other, artist sgd "Louis
   Solin," both marked on back, framed   **2,000.00**
Plate
   8½", pink, green, and yellow flowers,
      cream ground, enamel accents . .   **15.00**
   9", portrait panels, multicolored, gilt
      tracery, reticulated border **70.00**
Soup Plate, 10⅜" d, printed and painted
   famille rose style, Orientals, molded
   floral band border, ironstone, c1825 .   **50.00**
Sweetmeat Dish, 8", majolica, blue titmouse on branch, leaf shaped dish,
   imp mark, 1868 . . . .   **665.00**
Tea Service, band of foliage dec,
   painted "Sevres" marks, c1810, 18
   pcs **1,200.00**
Teapot, 5½", majolica, figural, monkey
   wearing blue jerkin grasping large
   fruit, restored spout, c1875 . . . .   **1,240.00**

MOCHA

History: Mocha decoration usually is found on utilitarian creamware and stoneware pieces and is produced through a simple chemical action. A color pigment of brown, blue, green, or black is made acidic by an infusion of tobacco or hops. When the acidic colorant is applied in blobs to an alkaline ground, it reacts by spreading in feathery, seaplant-like designs. This type of decoration usually is supplemented with bands of light colored slip.

Types of decoration vary greatly, from those done in a combination of motifs, such as "Cat's Eye" and "Earthworm," to a plain pink mug decorated with green ribbed bands. Most forms of mocha are hollow, e.g., mugs, jugs, bowls, and shakers.

English potters made the vast majority of the pieces. Marked pieces are extremely rare. Collectors group the ware into three chronological periods: 1780–1820, 1820–1840, and 1840–1880.

Reference: Susan and Al Bagdade, *Warman's English & Continental Pottery & Porcelain, 1st Edition,* Warman Publishing Co., Inc., 1987.

Bowl, 6¼" d, brown, cream, and orange earthworm on tan ground, raised green border, c1790–1820, $600.00.

Bowl
6⅛" d, 3" h, four palm shaped leaves dec, chocolate brown and cream marbleized design, white body, six incised lines highlighted in green, orange-ochre rim, faint 1" rim hairline **2,225.00**
6½" d, 3⅜" h, broad band of deep chocolate brown with six diamond shaped groups of nine cat's eyes, medium blue band around base, minor int. wear, two rim hairlines . **350.00**
Cider Mug, 6⅛" d, 8" h, two wide baby blue bands with flowing black dec, two black lines flank pastel green bands, minor damage **900.00**
Compote, 4⅞" d, 3½", broad purple-gray band, marbleized blue, black, white, and cream, white rim and base **300.00**
Creamer, 3⅝" h, two pairs of triple brown bands flanking broad blue band with white, blue, and brown design, handle with leaf shaped ends . **350.00**
Cup and Saucer, ochre and brown cat's eye dec, brown bands **200.00**
Cup Plate, 3½" d, pale yellow, black seaweed dec **425.00**
Mug, ftd, bold marbled canary, beige, coffee, brown and black earthworm dec, broad shaded leather brown band flanked by canary base and rim, bright canary int. **3,875.00**
Mustard Pot
2¾ x 2¼", wide band of reddish brown with four seaweed dec, design repeated on cov, dark brown line borders, minor damage **175.00**
3⅜", broad blue band beneath underglaze blue geometric dec, blue band on cov, small chip on cov .. **75.00**

3¾", matching cov, orange-ochre ground, dark brown seaweed dec, chocolate brown band around neck, plain white handle **1,150.00**
3⅞", broad tan band with four seaweed dec, two deep brown lines flank several incised lines around neck, highlighted in green, minor damage **85.00**
Pepper Pot, 4½", band of medium tan flanked by parallel deep brown ¼" bands, blue starburst design on top, small chip under top flange **300.00**
Pitcher
5", Liverpool shape, three broad medium blue bands alternating with two incised bands, brown and white checkerboard pattern, handle with leaf shaped ends, applied inverted fleur-de-lis under emb spout **450.00**
6⅛", barrel shape, two parallel thin bands of green arrows flanked by series of wide brown bands which contain white, brown, and baby blue cat's eye and earthworm dec, professional restoration to spout and base of handle **900.00**
8⅜", two wide gray bands with earthworm dec, three sets of two brown lines, separation along side of spout **375.00**
Plate, 8⅜" d, emb design of beads and leaves on rim, highlighted in green, center with swirled marbleized tan, white, cream, and deep brown, bit warped, 2" hairline off rim **225.00**
Porringer, 4⅛ x 2⅞", narrow band of deep chocolate above brick-red band with three palm shaped (tobacco) leaves, deep brown, mocha, and white marbleized design, flared mouth, applied handle **1,450.00**
Salt, 3¼" d, 2¼" h, master, ftd, earthworm dec, blue band, black and white stripes **200.00**
Sugar Shaker, 4½", white, tan, and black cat's eye dec, blue band with tan, white, and black stripes **675.00**
Tankard
3¼" d, 4⅞" h, narrow band of dark powder blue, 4" wide band of marbleized powder blue, brown, white, cream, and brick-red, white int. and handle, faint hairline at rim **725.00**
3¼" d, 5" h, 4⅛" w band of combed and marbleized browns, tan, white, cream, yellow-ochre, brick-red, chocolate brown, and pale green, between two parallel bands of four green incised lines, center medal-

lion with relief bust of military officer, hanging from long ribbon with
emb words "Success to Admiral
Rodney and His Fleet" **3,150.00**
3¾" h, thin blue band flanked by black
and white bands, wide blue-green
band containing four trees, white
emb royal crest imp "1/2 pint" ... **125.00**
4⅝" h, medium blue and tan-ochre
bands with cat's eye dec, handle
with leaf ends **1,000.00**
Waste Bowl
4⅝" d, 2½" h, soft blue band with
white band of geometric arrow
forms, wide band of marbleized
and combed white, rust, soft blue,
brown, and tan **1,200.00**
4⅞" d, 2⅝" h, wide band of orange-
ochre around center with alternating designs of brown seaweed and
groups of four cat's eyes, thin rim
band of brown with green emb
feather edging, minor glaze wear
on rim **625.00**

Vase, 14″ h, blue shaded to pink, gold highlights, $675.00.

16″, green, flecked neck, orange
body, dark inclusions, gold Cluthra
centers **450.00**

MONART GLASS

History: Monart glass is a heavy, simple shaped
art glass in which colored enamels are suspended
in the glass during the glass making process. This
technique was originally develped by the Ysart
family in Spain in 1923. John Moncrief, a Scottish
glassmaker, discovered the glass while vacation-
ing in Spain, recognized the beauty and potential
market, and began production in his Perth glassworks in 1924.

The name "Monart" is derived from the sur-
names Moncrief and Ysart. Two types of Monart
were manufactured: a "commercial" line which incorporated colored enamels and a touch of adventurine in crystal, and the "art" line in which the
suspended enamels formed designs such as
feathers or scrolls. Monart glass, in most instances, is not marked. The factory used paper
labels.

Basket, brown to light tan opal vertical
striations, Cluthra type **585.00**
Bowl, 11½", mottled orange and green **135.00**
Candlestick, two shades of green, goldstone mica, paper label **75.00**
Lamp Shade, 6½" d, white opal **85.00**
Vase
6½", mottled shades of red and blue,
white lining **100.00**
8 x 8½", blue, silver, mica, orange
streaks, small bubbles **150.00**
14½", blue irid, tree bark **145.00**

MONT JOYE GLASS

History: Mont Joye is a type of glass produced
by Saint-Hilaire, Touvier, de Varreaux & Company
at their glassworks in Pantin, France. Most pieces
were lightly acid etched to give them a frosted
appearance and decorated with enameled floral
decorations. All pieces listed are frosted, unless
otherwise noted.

**Vase, 8″, light turquoise Iris, gold high-
lights, acid etched frosting, gold band
around crimped top, $350.00.**

Jar, cov, 7″, cylindrical, clear, etched, enameled iris, gilt leaves, clear knop, gilt factory mark, c1900 . . . . **250.00**
Pitcher, 10″, amethyst, enameled flowers, aqua, blue, pink, and gold, sgd . **250.00**
Vase
  6½″, green, cut poppies, enameled in crimson and gilt, sgd **250.00**
  8½″, cameo, enameled leaves, deep red poppies on icy ground, sgd . . **430.00**
  9″, enameled purple orchids, green leaves **120.00**
  10″, bulbous, narrow neck, clear to opalescent green, thistle dec in natural colors, highlighted in gold . . . **275.00**
  11″, tomato red, lacy gold dec, enameled iris and foliage **200.00**
  13¾″, flattened ovoid shape, cameo, clear, etched, molded and enameled iris, gilt leaves, c1900 . . . . . **325.00**
  18″, green, enameled purple flowers, gold leaves, sgd **250.00**

Ginger Jar, 8″ h with cov, Hibiscus, peach colored flowers, green ground, paper label on inside of lid and base, $500.00.

MOORCROFT

History: William Moorcroft established the Moorcroft pottery in 1913 at Burslem, England. The company initially used an impressed mark, "Moorcroft, Burslem;" a signature mark, "W. Moorcroft," followed.

The majority of the art pottery wares were hand thrown, resulting in a great variation among similarly styled pieces. Color and marks are keys to determining age.

Walker, William's son, continued the business upon his father's death and made the same style wares. Modern pieces are marked simply "Moorcroft" with export pieces also marked "Made in England."

Reference: Susan and Al Bagdade, *Warman's English & Continental Pottery & Porcelain, 1st Edition,* Warman Publishing Co., Inc., 1987.

Beaker, 4½″, ftd, King Edward VIII coronation **200.00**
Bowl
  4½″, hibiscus, blue ground **65.00**
  10″, octagonal, grapes dec **200.00**
  11″, wisteria **185.00**
Box, cov, 4¾ x 3½ x 1½″, orchids, green ground **85.00**
Candlesticks, 10″, tree dec, shades of yellow, cobalt blue ground, script sgd, pr **150.00**
Coffeepot, cov, Sicilian pattern, sgd "Moorcroft-MacIntyre" **250.00**
Compote, 7½″, multicolored cornflowers

dec, green ground, sgd "W Moorcroft" **500.00**
Creamer and Sugar, pansies, cobalt blue ground, pr **85.00**
Ginger Jar, cov, 11¼″, pomegranate dec **515.00**
Jardiniere, 12″, Florian Ware, yellow, green, and white flowers, blue ground, sgd "Moorcroft-MacIntyre" . **500.00**
Loving Cup, 4¼″, three handles, tulips and cornflowers, green, blue, and red, printed and painted signature, c1900 . . . . **340.00**
Marmalade Jar, blue flowers, attached stand, sgd "MacIntyre" **150.00**
Pitcher
  6″, blue flowers, pewter lid, sgd **185.00**
  7″, red poppies, pewter lid, sgd "MacIntyre" **250.00**
Teapot, 8″, orchids, cobalt blue ground **200.00**
Trivet, 5½″, mushrooms, c1922 . . . . . **185.00**
Vase
  7″, pomegranate dec, c1918–29 . . . **285.00**
  10¼″, purple and blue wisteria, cream ground, sgd "Moorcroft Macintyre" **550.00**
  11¾″
    Florian Ware, baluster, poppies and leaves, shades of blue, printed and painted signature, c1900 . . **425.00**
    Hazeldene, cylindrical, green, blue, and yellow trees, printed Liberty mark, c1912 . . . . **1,275.00**
  12″, cylindrical, Florian Ware, poppies and leaves, blue and green, printed and painted signature, c1900 . . . . **465.00**
  12½″, baluster, white slip trail, dark glaze, imp "Burslem," green script sgd, c1920, pr **1,325.00**
  16½″, Hazeldene, blue-gray, green, and blue dec, sgd, c1920 . . . . . . **1,100.00**

MORIAGE, JAPANESE

History: Moriage refers to applied clay (slip) relief motifs and decorations used on certain classes of Japanese pottery and porcelain.

This decorating was done by three methods: 1), handrolling and shaping, which was applied by hand to the biscuit in one or more layers; the design and effect required determined thickness and shape, 2), tubing, or slip trailing, which applied decoration from a tube, like decorating a cake, and 3), hakeme, which is reducing the slip to a liquid and decorating the object with a brush. Color was applied either before or after the process.

Vase, 9½″, violet motif, $300.00.

Biscuit Jar, 6 x 7¼″, maroon band, green ground, maroon shaded flowers, white moriage, gold trim	300.00
Bowl, 7″, orange flowers and leaves, green wreath mark	135.00
Box, 4¾ x 3⅝ x 2¼″, dragon ware, detailed dragon, blue jeweled eyes, scrolled footing, unmarked	38.00
Chocolate Pot, 9″, green ground, four floral medallions, heavy moriage . . .	225.00
Demitasse Set, pot, two ftd cups and saucers, white wisteria flowers, green trim	400.00
Ewer, 3½″, tan, multicolored flowers and panels	65.00
Manicure Set, three tools, buffer, and cov trinket box, heavy dec	175.00
Pitcher	
5″, lavender, berry dec	85.00
6 x 6½″, squatty, panels of roses, sliptrail enamels, fancy handle	250.00
Powder Box, 5″, light green, raised turquoise beading, hp flowers	75.00
Rose Bowl, 5¼ x 4″, green, pink, and blue, brown band at base	225.00

Salt and Pepper Shakers, green ground, blue dots, white tops, gold star dec, pr	35.00
Tea Set, teapot, creamer, cov sugar, five cups and saucers, mauve ground, red roses, delicate white slipwork, unmarked	650.00
Toothpick Holder, 2¼″, light blue, white, green, and purple dec	48.00
Vase	
4½″, handles, violet dec	185.00
5½″, green, tan, and lavender dec . .	110.00
9¼″, pedestal base, green ground, white overall slipwork, floral medallions	250.00
11″, handles, green ground, floral dec and beading	135.00

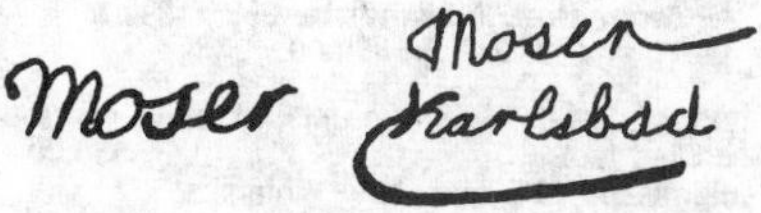

Moser Moser Karlsbad

MOSER GLASS

History: Ludwig Moser (1833–1916) founded his polishing and engraving workshop in 1857 in Karlsbad (Karlovy Vary), Czechoslovakia. He employed many famous glass designers, e.g., Johann Hoffmann, Josef Urban, and Rudolf Miller. In 1900 Moser and his sons, Rudolf and Gustav, incorporated Ludwig Moser & Söhne.

Moser art glass included clear pieces with inserted blobs of colored glass, cut colored glass with classical scenes, cameo glass, and intaglio cut. Many inexpensive enamaled pieces also were made.

In 1922 Leo and Richard Moser bought Meyr's Neffe, their biggest Bohemian rival in art glass. Moser executed many pieces for the Wiener Workstartte in the 1920s. The Moser glass factory continues to produce new items.

Reference: Mural K. Charon and John Mareska, *Ludvik Moser, King of Glass: A Treasure Chest of Photographs And History,* published by author, 1984.

Bowl, 7¼ x 5⅝″, pink opal shaded, multicolored enameled oak leaves and foliage, lustered applied acorns, sgd in gold on base	1,200.00
Box	
3⅜ x 2⅛″, green, multicolored leaves, applied pink berries	265.00
6 x 3¾″, cov, cranberry, white enamel dec of woman carrying cornucopia and grapes, enameled gold vine and berries	650.00
Calling Card Holder, cranberry, tur-	

Powder Box, Alexandrite, 3⅜ x 3⅜ x 4¾″, sgd "Moser," $350.00.

quoise jewels, gold prunts, four scrolled feet 350.00
Centerpiece, 11″, oval bowl, intaglio, emerald green shading to clear, sgd 200.00
Cologne Bottle, 10¾″, cranberry, gold leaves outlined in white, gold and black dots, white dotted blossoms, neck, base, and orig stopper heavily gold encrusted 400.00
Compote, 7 x 6⅝″, purple gilt allegorical figures 225.00
Decanter, 12½″, amber, allover etching 250.00
Ewer, 10¾″, cranberry, gold oak leaves, lacy gold foliage, small applied glass acorns, pedestal foot, ruffled top, applied clear handle, unsigned 750.00
Goblet, 5¾″, deep amethyst, gold figures dec, pr 175.00
Ice Cream Set, master bowl and four serving bowls, mermaid relief, clear and gold, gilt highlights 385.00
Liqueur, 2½″, cranberry, multicolored applied acorns and leaves, sgd 200.00
Mug, 3¼″, green, multicolored oak leaves and bee, applied acorns 300.00
Perfume Bottle, 4¼ x 6½″, malachite, molded bottle and stopper, slab polished sides and top 225.00
Pitcher
 8½″, amber, multicolored floral enamel 200.00
 9½″, sq top, blue and gold, sgd 200.00
Plate, 7⅜″, amberina, gold dec 125.00
Scent Bottle
 3″, purple, prism cutting, orig stopper 200.00
 5″, green, multicolored leaves and berries, ball stopper 165.00
 11″, cranberry, leaves, white and gold dec 400.00
Sweetmeat Dish, round, cranberry, engraved, gold band 225.00

Tumbler
 3½″, octagonal, ruby cut to clear, gold dec 60.00
 3⅞″, thin, delicate crystal, hp, medallion of mischievous cupid teasing bashful maiden 485.00
 4″, lavender, vines, leaves, berries, and floral work, heavy gilting 175.00
Vase
 4⅛″, shaded apricot, opal, multicolored enameled oak leaves, applied lustered glass acorns, sgd 250.00
 7¾″, long green to clear neck, bulbous base, gold and platinum floral dec, diamond point signature 350.00
 8″, chocolate brown ground, jeweled, gold trim 225.00
 8½″, cranberry, lady playing harp, heavy gold dec, handles 250.00
 9½″, emerald green, multicolored florals, applied gold bees, sgd 475.00
 14½″, pigeon blood, enamel dec ... 215.00
Wine, rainbow glass, funnel shape bowl, inverted baby thumbprint pattern, grapes and leaves dec, applied row of gold knobs 325.00

MOSS ROSE PATTERN CHINA

History: Several English potteries manufactured china with a Moss Rose pattern in the mid-1800s. Knowles, Taylor and Knowles, an American firm, began production of a Moss Rose pattern in the 1880s.

The moss rose was a common garden flower grown in English gardens. When American consumers tired of English china with oriental themes, they purchased the Moss Rose pattern as a substitute.

Cup and Saucer, marked "Winterling/Bavaria/Germany," $12.50.

Bowl, 8½", openwork, gold trim, marked
"Rosenthal" 40.00
Box, cov, 6½", oval 24.00
Butter Pat, sq, marked "Meakin" 15.00
Coffee Mug and Saucer, Meakin 40.00
Coffeepot, 9", marked "E. C. & Co" . . 75.00
Cup and Saucer, marked "Edwards" . . 25.00
Dessert Set, eight 7½" plates, eight
cups and saucers, creamer and
sugar, cake plate, 28 pcs, marked "Fr
Haviland" 250.00
Gravy Boat and Underplate, marked
"Green & Co, England" 40.00
Nappy, 4½", marked "Edwards" 10.00
Plate
7½", pink edge, marked "Haviland" . 16.00
8½", marked "KTK" 20.00
9½", marked "Haviland" 12.00
Platter, 10 x 14", rect, marked "Meakin" 26.00
Salt and Pepper Shakers, 5", SS top
and base, marked "Rosenthal," pr . . 50.00
Sauce Dish, 4½", marked "Haviland" . 15.00
Soup Plate, 9", marked "Meakin" 16.00
Sugar, cov 48.00
Syrup, 8½", pewter top, marked "KTK,"
c1872 . . . . 165.00
Tea Service, teapot, 5½" creamer, 6¼"
sugar bowl, marked "Meakin," 3 pcs 200.00
Teapot, 8½", bulbous, gooseneck
spout, basketweave trim, sgd "T & V" 40.00
Tureen, cov, 12", gold trim 70.00
Wash Bowl and Pitcher, 13½" twelve
sided bowl, 11" pitcher 250.00

MOUNT WASHINGTON GLASS COMPANY

History: In 1837 Deming Jarves, founder of the
Boston and Sandwich Glass Company, established for George D. Jarves, his son, the Mount
Washington Glass Company in Boston, Massachusetts. In the following years the leadership and
the name of the company changed several times
as George Jarves formed different associations.

In the 1860s the company was owned and operated by Timothy Howe and William L. Libbey. In
1869 Libbey bought a new factory in New Bedford,
Massachusetts. The Mount Washington Glass
Company began operating again there under its
original name. Henry Libbey became associated
with the company early in 1871. He resigned in
1874 during the general depression, and the glass
works was closed. William Libbey had resigned in
1872 to work for the New England Glass Company.

The Mount Washington Glass Company opened
again in the fall of 1874 under the presidency of
A. H. Seabury and the management of Frederick
S. Shirley. In 1894 the glass works became a part
of the Pairpoint Manufacturing Company.

Throughout its history the Mount Washington
Glass Company made a great variety of glass including: pressed glass, blown glass and art glass,
lava glass, Napoli, cameo, cut glass, Albertine,
and Verona.

References: George C. Avila, *The Pairpoint
Glass Story,* Reynolds-DeWalt Printing, Inc., 1968;
Leonard E. Padgett, *Pairpoint Glass,* Wallace-
Homestead, 1979.

Museum: The New Bedford Glass Museum,
New Bedford, MA.

Additional Listings: Burmese, Crown Milano,
Peachblow, and Royal Flemish.

Biscuit Jar, Albertine, pastel floral dec,
pink leaves, lavender ground 500.00
Box, 7", blown-out floral dec, pink roses,
light to dark green ground 525.00
Bride's Basket, 8¼", sq, cased, deep
rose and white ext., white int., dragon,
floral and leaf dec, ruffled edge . . . 650.00
Candlestick, 12", pink and white, hp florals, ftd Pairpoint holder 200.00
Compote, 6¼" d, 10" h, (¾" d, 7" h
stem,) Napoli, crystal clear body, pastel green chrysanthemum leaves on
wafer base, stem forms pedestal, four
golden yellow chrysanthemum blossoms on underside of flared bowl,
flowers outlined in gold on int. 585.00

Vase, 3½" d, 2⅛" h, opaque to pink floral swirl body, darted floral dec,
$250.00.

Creamer, 3", melon ribbed, enameled
leaf and floral dec, SP handle and
spout 185.00
Cruet, 5¾", amberina, IVT, applied am-
ber handle, period amber stopper . . 325.00
Dresser Jar, 3¼", Burmese color, Timothy Canty pansy and leaf dec, SP
cov, sgd 180.00
Jack-In-The Pulpit Vase, 3½ x 6¾", Bur-
mese, yellow, pastel rust and tan

ground, autmun leaves, blue berries,
and tendrils dec, ruffled, three gold
stripes around base **485.00**
Marmalade Jar, hobnail pattern, amberina **325.00**
Miniature Lamp, 8½" h, Delft blue windmill dec, white opaque base and
shade, Smith #276-II, sgd on base . **585.00**
Perfume, 2¼ x 6", sq, satin, woman in
1890's dress, script on back "Hout's
Milk White March 19, 1894—50th Performance Boston Theatre Boston,"
orig screw atomizer **135.00**
Plate
  7", country scene of stone bridge, cottage, and lack, factory dec, orig paper label **100.00**
  12", twin cupids, leaf and floral border **115.00**
Pitcher, 8", Verona, bulbous, maiden-
hair fern dec, gold highlights, applied
clear reeded handle **225.00**
Rose Bowl, 4", two cupids floating on
cloud, white **185.00**
Salt and Pepper Shakers, pr
  Fig, enameled pansy dec, satin, orig
  prong top **225.00**
  Melon, squatty, enameled daisy dec,
  satin, orig 2 pc top **115.00**
Scent Bottle, white, reserve with couple,
basket of flowers on reverse **100.00**
Sugar Shaker
  3¼ x 4", egg shape, pastel pansies,
  pronged top **585.00**
  5½", IVT, lighthouse shape, bluerina,
  orig metal top **270.00**
Toothpick
  Burmese, enameled yellow and white
  daisies **385.00**
  Satin, opal, soft yellow finish, dotted
  rim, dec **200.00**
Tumbler, peachblow, band of apple
blossom pink shades to soft blue-gray **1,450.00**
Vase
  3¾", classic shape, Lava, shiny jet
  black body, inlaid chips of blue,
  green, and pink, two curl handles,
  gold dec **1,750.00**
  5½", cylindrical, clear, Verona, day lily
  dec, outlined in gold **175.00**
  7⅞", lily shape, Burmese, shiny finish **350.00**
  8¼", lily shape, peachblow, rich color,
  satin finish **1,800.00**
  9⅜", lily shape, Burmese, gilded
  white metal figural holder **200.00**
  9¾", lily shape, Burmese, shiny finish,
  copper lily pad style holder **750.00**
  9⅞", lily shape, Burmese **250.00**
  10", Lava, black, reeded handles, orig
  paper label **2,500.00**
  13⅞", lily shape, Burmese **300.00**
  16", court jester and blossom dec,
  pink ground, sgd **750.00**

18⅜", Napoli, base sgd "Napolia/
841" **1,400.00**

MULBERRY CHINA

History: Mulberry china, made primarily in the
Staffordshire district of England between 1830 and
1850, is porcelain whose transfer pattern is the
color of mulberry juice. The potters that manufactured flow blue also made Mulberry china; the ware
often has a flowing effect similar to flow blue.

References: Susan and Al Bagdade, *Warman's
English & Continental Pottery & Porcelain, 1st Edition,* Warman Publishing Co., Inc., 1987; Petra Williams, *Flow Blue China and Mulberry Ware-Simi-
larity and Value Guide*, Fountain House East,
1981, revised edition.

**Platter, 13½" x 10¼", Cyprus pattern,
Davenport, $100.00.**

Bowl
  4", Rose, E Challinor **60.00**
  9", Vista, Mason, sq **42.00**
Butter Dish, Moss Rose **125.00**
Coffeepot, Jeddo, Adams **175.00**
Creamer
  Corea, Clementson **95.00**
  Jeddo, Adams **100.00**
  Marble, Wedgwood **65.00**
  Tavoy **100.00**
Cup and Saucer, handled cup
  Genoa, Davenport, 1852 .... **40.00**
  Roselle, J M & Son, England **40.00**
Cup and Saucer, handleless cup
  Jeddo **45.00**
  Pelew **48.00**
  Temple, Podmore Walker **40.00**
  Washington Vase, Podmore Walker . **60.00**
Cup Plate, Corean, Podmore Walker . **45.00**
Gravy Boat
  Jeddo, Adams **65.00**
  Pelew **85.00**
Pitcher, 9½", Vincennes, J Alcock **135.00**

Plate

- 7", Genoa 20.00
- 8", Temple 25.00
- 9½"
  - Corea, Clementson 65.00
  - Ning Po 40.00
- 10½"
  - Bochara, Edwards 35.00
  - Cyprus, Davenport 60.00
  - Vincennes 45.00

Platter

- Abbey, 12½ x 9½", Adams, c1900 .. 100.00
- Lucerne, 8 x 10", Parkhurst mark .. 35.00
- Peruvian, 16" 125.00
- Rhone Scenery, 15½" 150.00
- Washington Vase, Podmore Walker, 15¾ x 12¼" 135.00
- Relish, Percy, Morley, shell shape ... 35.00
- Sauce Dish, Corea, Clementson, 5" .. 18.00
- Sauce Tureen, cov, Bochara, Edwards 125.00
- Soup Bowl, Scinde, 10½" 30.00
- Sugar, cov, Jeddo, Adams 75.00
- Teapot, Strawberries 175.00
- Vegetable Bowl, cov, octagonal, pedestal base
  - Cyprus, Davenport 75.00
  - Jeddo 100.00
- Waste Bowl, Jeddo 60.00

MUSIC BOXES

History: Music boxes were invented in Switzerland around 1825. They cover a broad field of automatic musical instruments from a small box to a huge circus calliope.

A cylinder box consists of a comb with teeth which vibrate when stricking a pin in the cylinder and producing music from light tunes to opera and overtures.

The first disc music box was invented by Paul Lochmann of Leipzig, Germany, in 1886. It used an interchangeable steel disc with pierced holes bent to a point which hit the star-wheel as the disc revolved, and thus produced the tune. Discs were easily stamped out of metal, allowing a single music box to play an endless variety of tunes. It reached the height of its popularity from 1890 to 1910. The phonograph replaced it.

Music boxes also were put into many items, e.g., clocks, sewing and jewelry boxes, steins, plates, toys, perfume bottles, and furniture.

Collectors' Club: Musical Box Society, International, Rt. 3, Box 205, Morgantown, IN, 46160. Dues: $20.00.

Museums: Bellms Cars and Music of Yesterday, Sarasota, FL; Lockwood Matthews Mansion, Norwalk, CT.

Additional Listings: See *Warman's Americana & Collectibles* for more examples.

Cylinder-Type, six 6" cylinders, inlaid rosewood case, bells and drum attachments, 17" l, $1,500.00.

CYLINDER-TYPE

- 3½" cylinder, Bremond, 6 tune, inlaid rosewood veneer case, inner glass lid, single comb 300.00
- 4½" cylinder, J. H. Heller, 6 tune, walnut dec, floral motifs, inner glass lid, Bern, Switzerland 600.00
- 5" cylinder, L'Epee, France, 4 tune, simple case 350.00
- 5⅛" cylinder, Junod, 4 tune, inlaid rosewood case, tune indicator, 2 bells, dec figural tune card, inner glass lid ... 1,000.00
- 6" cylinder, Ducommon Girod, 6 tune, case, tune sheet, c1880 .... 750.00
- 7¾" cylinder, 4 tune, key wind, simple case style 750.00
- 8½" cylinder, Imhof and Mukle, spring driven movement, rosewood and ebony case, marquetry dec, trade label, c1880 .... 400.00
- 10¾" cylinder, Paillard, 8 tune, lever wind, rosewood case, floral dec, c1860 .... 800.00
- 12" cylinder, 4 tune, key wind, 20½" plain case 2,500.00
- 13" cylinder, 6 tune, interchangeable cylinders, piccolo attachment, walnut burled case, matching storage table 3,000.00
- 15" cylinder, 12 tune, lever wind, rosewood with floral dec 1,250.00
- 17" cylinder, Baker-Troll, 6 tune, interchangeable cylinders, six bells, bee strikes, walnut case, brass inlay dec, matching storage table 2,500.00

DISC-TYPE

- 6½" disc, Polyphone, 4 bells, spring driven, litho inside cov, wood case, decal 600.00

7½" disc, sq mahogany case, lid int.
shows little girls at play, crank wound,
single comb, Germany, c1900 . . . . . **275.00**

8¾" disc, Criterion, table model, mahog-
any case, figural litho inside lid **750.00**

9" disc, Britannia, simple case, table
model, c1900 . . . . **900.00**

9¼" disc, 6 bells, walnut case, floral inlay lid, figural litho inside cov **950.00**

10½" disc, Perfection, table model, mahogany case, scenic litho inside lid,
zinc discs **1,400.00**

15½" disc, Regina, Style 15, No 23256,
coin operated, double comb, side
crank wind, printed instruction inside
cov, 21" walnut case, leaf tip carved
base, 26 discs, American, c1897 . . . **2,300.00**

17¼" disc, Stella Grand, carved front
panel of base with drawer, oak **2,500.00**

27" disc, Regina Orchestral Corona
Style 33, #46968, automatic disc
changer, mahogany case, spooled
gallery and corner finials, glazed
doors with copper gilt foliate open
spandrels, glazed panel beneath,
35½ x 23½ x 66½", 12 discs
c1905 . . . . **10,450.00**

MISCELLANEOUS

Album, photograph, 2" cylinder, 2 tunes,
Chicago Exposition pictured on cov
with drawings on pages inside, emb
brass clasp closing **250.00**

Bird in Cage, domed cage on sq base,
cast and enameled geometric dec, 9"
h **275.00**

Clock, Musical Longcase Clock, Eroica,
13⅝" disc, highly dec, ornately carved
case **6,500.00**

Roller Organ
Automatic Medlodia, Bates & Co, sliding tremolo stop, 11½ x 9½ x 8½",
gilt stencil dec case, 4 paper rolls **500.00**

Barrel Organ, 6 air, paper roll, 20½ x
11 x 11¼", lid stamped Archibald
Campbell, impressed line border,
scroll spandrels, German **950.00**

Gem, 14¼ x 12 x 8", gilt stenciled
floral case, 23 combs **425.00**

Melodia, Mechanical Organette Co,
12¼ x 10½ x 11½" case, gilt stencil
dec, 4 rolls, late 19th C **520.00**

Whistling Figure, heavily carved man,
elaborate bow tie, bowler hat, hands
in pockets, whistles "How Dry I Am,"
13½" h, c1920 . . . . **525.00**

MUSICAL INSTRUMENTS

History: From the first beat of the prehistoric
drum to the very latest in electronic music makers,

musical instruments have provided popular modes
of communication and relaxation.

The most popular antique instruments are vio-
lins, flutes, oboes, and other instruments associated with the classical music period of 1650 to
1900. Many of the modern instruments, such as
trumpets, guitars, drums, etc., have value on the
"used," rather than antique market.

The collecting of musical instruments is in its
infancy. The field is growing very rapidly. Investors
and speculators have played a role since the
1930s, especially in early string instruments. Sotheby's and Christie's hold annual auctions of fine
musical instruments. Doyle Auctioneers & Appraisers holds two annual absentee auctions covering
the full range of musical instruments.

References: Tom and Mary Anne Evans, *Gui-
tars: From the Renaissance To Rock; The Official
Price Guide To Music Collectibles, Sixth Edition*,
House of Collectibles, 1986.

Collectors' Club: Fretted Instrument Guild of
America, 2344 South Oakley Avenue, Chicago, IL
60608.

Advisor: Glenn M. Kramer.

Accordion, Concertone, 21 pearl keys,
12 basses, four sets of steel reeds,
18 fold bellows, leather cov, rosewood finish frames, marked "Made in
Italy, Nicolo Salanti," early 1920s . . . **300.00**

Bagpipe, Scottish, rosewood chanters,
late 17th C **4,500.00**

Banjo
American, trap door style, snake-
head, straight neck, 1920s **250.00**

Edgemere, nickel shell, wood lined,
17 nickel plated hexagon brackets,
raised frets, birch neck finished in
imitation mahogany, c1900 . . . . . **320.00**

Bugle, American, artillery, brass, c1900 **150.00**

Castanets
Argentinian, early 19th C **170.00**
Spanish, late 18th C **250.00**

Cello, Fonclause, silver mounted, un-
branded, round stick with ivory face,
silver and ebony replacement frog,
French silver and ebony adjuster . . **2,000.00**

Clarinet, Laube, 13 nickel silver keys,
two rings, Grenadilla wood, trimming
cork joints, graduated bore, A, low
pitch, c1920 . . . . **325.00**

Cornet
Artist B-Flat, nickel plated **275.00**
Dupont C, triple SP, satin finish **160.00**
Marceau E-Flat, brass, highly po-
lished, c1905–10 . . . . **110.00**

Flute
French, 22⅜", ivory, one keyed, mid
18th C **6,500.00**
Unmarked, carved, walnut, 16½" l,
c1780 . . . . **625.00**

French Horn, King sgd "USMC,", 1890s **200.00**

Guitar
American, The Kenmore, c1900 . . . **200.00**
The Stanford, hardwood sides and
back, imitation rosewood finish,
spruce top, brass head, rosewood
fingerboard, nickel plated tailpiece **85.00**
Harmonica, Hohner Auto Harmonica,
auto shape, 14 double holes, 28
reeds, metal cov **75.00**
Harp, Italian, rosewood, carved, 62½"
h, third quarter 17th C **3,650.00**
Lute
Flemish, c1470 . . . . **20,000.00**
Swiss, c1750 . . . . **3,150.00**
Mandolin
The Edgemere, English, early 18th C **6,100.00**
Oboe
English, early 18th C **8,000.00**
Italian, c1840 . . . . **700.00**
Piano
Beckwith Cabinet Grand, upright
model, early 1900s **1,400.00**
Kimball Grand, 68", walnut **4,800.00**
Weber Louis XIV Art Grand, New
York, sculptured, gilded case, late
19th C **8,900.00**

**Piccolo, 12″ l, unidentified maker,
$35.00.**

Piccolo
Italian, hardwood, silver trimming, dec
walnut box lined with plush, c1742 **1,100.00**
Meyer, grenadilla wood, ivory head,
six keys, c1900 . . . . **275.00**
Saxophone
Bantone, bell front, tree valves, lac-
quer bore **1,200.00**
Tourville & Co, tenor, silver, satin fin-
ish **350.00**
Tambourine, Brazilian, second quarter
19th C **180.00**
Trombone, Lamoreaux Freres Slide, or-
namented bell, brass, polished,
c1905 . . . . **275.00**
Trumpet, Holton, four valve **1,500.00**
Tuba, Tourville & Co, E-Flat Bass, SP,
satin finish **525.00**

Ukulele, birch body, black rings around
sound hole, white celluloid binding,
c1920 . . . . **50.00**
Violin
Abbati, Giambattista, Modena, 1755–
95 . . . . **7,500.00**
Arthur Bultitude, octagonal stick
mounted with gold and tortoiseshell, tortoiseshell frog, gold flower
ornaments **2,100.00**
Filano, Donato, Naples, 1763–83 . . **3,600.00**
Marcel Lapierre, round stick mounted
with gold and ivory, ivory frog, pearl
dots, gold rings, ivory adjuster . . . **1,200.00**
Zither, Columbia, 19½", maple, c1900 . **150.00**

MUSIC RELATED

Advertising, sign, Poole Pianos, 20 x
13", tin, fancy black lettering **75.00**
Ashtray, 3¼ x 4", Cl, figural, bearded
black man playing banjo, c1920 . . . **65.00**
Book
Anecdotes of Music, Burgh, A, historical and biographical, letters series, 3 volumes, London, 1814 . . . **90.00**
The Violin: How to Master It, Honney-
man, William C, Boston, n.d.c.,
1895 . . . . **65.00**
Mandolin Case, black leather, hand-
sewn, flannel-lined, leather carrying
strap **65.00**
Music Stand, Duet Stand, rosewood,
pierced lyres, brass candleholders,
adjustable baluster support, raised
trefoil base, ball shape feet **1,600.00**
Poster, Metropolitan Opera House, illus,
1920s **125.00**
Violin Chin Rest, Becker's, ebonite and
nickel, pre1900 . . . . **25.00**

MUSTACHE CUPS AND SAUCERS

History: Mustache cups and saucers were popular in the late Victorian era, 1880–1900. They
were made by many companies in porcelain and
silver plate. The cups have a ledge across the top
of the bowl of the cup to protect a gentleman's
mustache from becoming soiled while drinking.

Reference: Susan and Al Bagdade, *Warman's
English & Continental Pottery & Porcelain, 1st Edition,* Warman Publishing Co., Inc., 1987.

PORCELAIN

Austrian, portrait medallion **75.00**
Carlsbad, floral dec, ring handle **35.00**
German, "Papa," florals, pink and
green, gold trim **40.00**

Porcelain, gold decoration, bottom of letters accented in blue, marked "B.S/ C&M," $45.00.

Handpainted, pink and white flowers, green leaves, pale green ground, gold trim	45.00
Haviland, white, gold trim	90.00
Limoges, hp pastel flowers, rococo molded scrolls, allover gold	45.00
Majolica, Bird and Fan pattern	135.00
Onion Meissen, c1890	85.00
Pink Luster, gold leaves, beaded edges	65.00
Royal Worcester, hp, flowers, peach ground	125.00
White Patterned Ironstone, copper luster dec, c1850	250.00

SILVERPLATED

Barbour Bros Co, bright cut floral design	60.00
Derby Silver Co, crimped rim, engraved floral design	45.00
Tufts, 1" band of flowers, strawberries, leaves within border, matching design on saucer, marked	125.00

NAILSEA TYPE GLASS

History: Nailsea type glass is characterized by swirls and loopings, usually white, on a clear or colored ground. One of the first areas where this glass was made was Nailsea, England, 1788–1873, hence the name. Several other glass houses, including American factories, made this type of glass.

Bottle	
10", gemel, clear, white looping, applied rigaree	130.00
10½", bellows, white, rose loopings, applied rigaree, stand	250.00
Candlestick, 10", clear, white looping, folded socket rim, hollow blown	

socket drawn out to a double knop, bulb shaped stem, and two additional knops, inverted cone shaped base, early 19th C	375.00
Drinking Stick, 29" l	100.00
Fairy Lamp, 4" d, 4¼" h, lime green, white looping, pie crust crimped edge	385.00
Finger Bowl, 4¼ x 2¼", ftd, swirled streaks of deep blue and white, clear body, foot drawn from body, applied clear handles imp with cherub's face	50.00
Flask, 8" h, slightly flared, clear, white looping, tooled mouth and pontil	90.00
Mug, 6¾", clear, white looping, attributed to Pittsburgh	250.00
Perfume Bottle, chateline, 3", gold wash stopper	85.00
Pitcher	
4" d, 6½" h, clear, white looping, ftd, solid applied base, triple ribbed solid handle with curled end, flaring formed mouth, attributed to South Jersey, c1840–60	1,125.00
7¾" d, 9¾" h, clear, white and amethyst loopings, applied heavy solid clear handle with gauffered and curled end, applied clear base, flared mouth, attributed to Pittsburgh area	2,750.00
Powder Horn, 13", clear, white loopings and red stripes, stand	250.00
Rolling Pin, 18", clear, pink and white loops	250.00
Sugar, 4½", opaque white, pink and red looping, applied clear foot, attributed to Pittsburgh	125.00
Vase, 5" d, 8" h, cylindrical, flared mouth and base, clear, white looping, plain sheared rim-pontil, attributed to South Jersey	175.00

Fairy Lamp, 4" d base, 4¾" h, rose with white loopings, frosted, clear glass Clarke base, $350.00.

Witch Ball, 5¼″ d, clear, opaque white casing, red looping, attributed to Pittsburgh **250.00**

NANKING

History: Nanking is a type of Chinese porcelain made in Canton, China, from the early 1800s into the 20th century for export to America and England. It often is confused with the Canton pattern.

Three elements help distinguish Nanking from Canton. Nanking has a spear and post border, as opposed to the scalloped line style of Canton. The blues may tend to be darker on the Nanking ware. Second, in the water's edge, Canton usually has no figures. Nanking features a standing figure with open umbrella on the bridge. Finally, Nanking wares often are embellished with gold.

Green and orange variations of Nanking survive, although scarce.

Reference: Sandra Andacht, *Oriental Antiques & Art: An Identification And Value Guide,* Wallace-Homestead, 1987.

Reproduction Alert: Copies of Nanking ware currently are being produced in China. They are of inferior quality and decorated in lighter rather than the darker blues.

Plate, 9½″, water's edge scene, c1780–1800, $95.00.

Cream Pot, cov, 5¼″, scenic, gold dec, late 18th C **215.00**
Cup and Saucer
  Handleless **75.00**
  Loop handle **50.00**
Dish, 7¾″, leaf shape, blue and white, c1795 .... **185.00**
Ewer, 11″, small spout, blue and white, mid 19th C **300.00**
Fruit Bowl, 9″, oval, reticulated, blue and white, matching underplate **700.00**
Jug, 9½″, blue and white, c1800 ..... **450.00**

Platter
  11½ x 14½″, blue and white, pagoda in foreground **400.00**
  14¾″, oval, blue and white, landscape, stylized dragons on cavetto, geometric patterned bands, base inscribed "Da Nihon Tatebayashi-sei," Meiji period **275.00**
Teapot, 5¾ x 4⅜″, scenic, gold dec, matching stand, 18th C **565.00**
Tureen
  9¾ x 11¾″, matching cov, stand, blue and white, Two Birds pattern, large blue rose sprig knob, c1785–95 .. **2,500.00**
  14½ x 10½″, oval, dome cov, flower finial, ftd base, twisted strap handles, early 19th C **1,300.00**
Urn, 5½″, blue, lavender, and green floral, gold handles, pr **325.00**

NAPKIN RINGS, FIGURAL

History: Gracious home dining during the Victorian era meant each household member had their personal napkin ring. Figural napkin rings were first patented in 1869. The remainder of the 19th century saw most plating companies, e.g., Cromwell, Eureka, Meriden, Reed and Barton, etc., manufacturing figural rings, many copying with slight variations the designs of other companies.

Values are determined today by the subject matter of the ring, the quality of the workmanship, and the condition.

Reference: Victor K. Schnadig, *American Victorian Figural Napkin Rings,* Wallace Homestead, 1971, out-of-print.

Reproduction Alert: Quality reproductions do exist.

Additional Listings: See *Warman's Americana & Collectibles* for a listing of non-figural napkin rings.

Advisors: Paul and Paula Brenner.

Baby, crawling, ring on back **170.00**
Barrel, ring on old hickory chair **125.00**
Bird, wings spread over nest of eggs . **145.00**
Boy
  Holding baseball bat, hands clasped behind him **190.00**
  Pulling wheeled cart **245.00**
  Sitting on bench, holding drumstick . **180.00**
Butterfly, perched on pair of fans **95.00**
Cat, glass eyes, ring on back **260.00**
Cherries, stems, leaf base, ball feet .. **70.00**
Cherub, sitting cross legged on base, candleholder and ring combination . **175.00**
Chicken, nesting beside ring **160.00**
Dachshund, supporting ring on back .. **160.00**
Deer, standing next to fence **175.00**
Eagle, one on each side of ring **110.00**

Sheep, Barbour, #13, $200.00.

Fox, standing erect, dressed	225.00
Frog, holding drumstick, pushing drum-like ring	295.00
Goat, pulling wheeled flower cart	245.00
Greenaway, Kate, girl	
Holding stick above begging dog ...	240.00
Pulling wheeled cart	270.00
Horse, standing next to elaborate ring	175.00
Man, walking uphill, ring on shoulders	190.00
Owl, sitting on leafy base, owls perched on upper limbs	250.00
Rabbit, sitting alertly next to ring	175.00
Roman Centurion, stands next to ring, sword drawn	130.00
Sailor Boy, anchor	210.00
Schoolboy with books, feeding begging puppy	225.00
Squirrel, eating nut, log pile base	125.00
Swan, one each side of ring, separate bases	110.00
Turtle, crawling, ornate ring on back ..	200.00

NASH GLASS

History: Nash glass is a type of art glass attributed to Arthur John Nash and his sons, Leslie H. and A. Douglass. Arthur John Nash, originally employed by Webb in Stourbridge, England, came to America and was employed in 1889 by Tiffany Furnaces at its Corona, Long Island plant.

While managing the plant for Tiffany, Nash designed and produced iridescent glass. In 1928 A. Douglas Nash purchased the physical facilities of Tiffany Furnaces. The firm, A. Douglas Nash Corporation, remained in operation until 1931.

Bowl	
7¾ x 2½", Jewel pattern, gold phantom luster	275.00
8¾ x 2", Chintz pattern, light green, sgd	165.00

12 x 3½", irid blue, sgd and numbered	735.00
Candlesticks, 4", ball stem, Chintz pattern, blood red and silver, sgd, pr ..	450.00
Cologne Bottle, Chintz pattern, paperweight stopper	225.00
Compote, 6 x 2", fold over rim, Chintz pattern, green-blue bowl, clear pedestal foot, sgd	175.00
Cordial, 5½", Chintz pattern, green and blue	75.00

Dish, 5⅜ d,½" h, iridescent gold, blue-green ground, etched grape leaves and vines, marked "Nash 569 C-1," $300.00.

Goblet, 6¾", feathered leaf motif, gilt dec, sgd	275.00
Plate	
4½", amber irid, scalloped edge, sgd	325.00
8", Chintz pattern, green and blue ..	175.00
Tumbler, 5", conical, Chintz pattern, blue and silver, low pedestal foot, sgd	115.00
Vase	
4¼", gold irid, marked "Nash/544" ..	350.00
6¼" h, sq top, irid gold, sgd	275.00
9½", green-gold irid, clear irid base, unsigned	275.00
Wine, 6", Chintz pattern, pink and green	110.00

NAUTICAL ITEMS

History: The seas that surround us have fascinated man since time began. The artifacts of sailors have been collected and treasured for years. Because of their environment, merchant and naval items, whether factory or handmade, must be of quality construction and long lasting. Many of these items are aesthetically designed as well.

Richard Bourne, Hyannis, Massachusetts, and Chuck DeLuca, York, Maine, regularly hold auctions of marine items.

References: Alan P. Major, *Maritime Antiques*, A. S. Barnes & Co., 1981; Jean Randier, *Nautical Antiques*, Doubleday and Co., 1977.

Periodical: *Nautical Brass etc.,* Box 744, Montrose, CA 91020. Subscription: $10.00.

Museums: Burgess Mariner's Museum, Newport News, VA; Museum of Science and Industry, Chicago, IL; Mystic Seaport Museum, Mystic, CT; National Maritime Museum, San Francisco, CA.

Advisor: Bill Wheeler.

Account Book, ship "Hope," dated 1857	75.00
Alarm, 13″ h, walnut, brass mounted, 19th C	550.00
Barometer, ebonized fluted sq wood case, orig dolphin and shell-form gimbal, Manzioli, Frieste	1,950.00
Bell, 17″ d, brass, brass mount	550.00
Bench, 46½″ l, used for making ship's dead eyes, early to mid 19th C	2,300.00
Billet Head, 24″ l, orig black and gold paint	3,300.00
Binnacle, 16½″ h, compass, lights, circular mahogany base, orig lamps, marked "E. Miller & Co., Meriden, Conn," 19th C	700.00
Buoy, Breeches, orig	100.00
Bow-Sprit, 44½″ l, eagle's head at front, relief carved foliate work, traces blue and green paint, well preserved	850.00
Candleholder, brass, spring loaded, used as a hanging or standing, weighted bottom, mid 19th C	375.00
Carpenter Chest, 36″ l, tools, five sliding trays, "M. Jobin" on lid, "Eagle" on front	1,000.00

Chronometer

Ship, E. Dent & Co., London, No. 49872, orig box and label, good working order, 7¼″ sq, 7¾″ l case	1,800.00
Yacht, Waltham, case and carrying case, 5 x 5 x 5⅛″	550.00
Clock, 7¼″ d, navigation or engine use, Chelsea	250.00
Deck Seat, 57″ l, 28″ h, carved, polychrome, chest in bottom, originally on *Royal Dutch* yacht, well preserved, 18th C	1,200.00
Ditty Box, 6″ d, 4″ h, pine, pierced baleen, pinwheels, stars, and fretwork, paper backing, Nantucket, 19th C	500.00
Diver's Helmet, copper and brass, Galeazzi	600.00
Diving Suit, helmet, boots, weighted belt and hanger, A. J. Morse & Son, Boston, MA	1,300.00
Figurehead, 51″ l, eagle, carved, early 19th C	4,000.00
Flensing Knife, 56¾″ l, used to separate blanket piece from the carcass, well preserved	500.00
Fog Horn, 30″ l, brass, 19th C	85.00
Gangway Boards, 44″ h, mahogany, relief carved, brass fittings, 19th C, pr	1,700.00
Gradient Indicator, Moss Flower's, 9½″,	

holly wood and brass, level set into top	250.00
Harpoon, 36″ l, incised "B.Y.G." initials on one side, impressed "JD" initials on other, some orig wrapping around cone	475.00
Harpoon Gun, 34″ l barrel, swivel, brass mount, engraved "S. S. Terra Nova. Dundee," well preserved	4,000.00
Jug, 9¼″ h, map of Newburyport Harbour on one side, ship *Massachusetts* transfer on other, early 19th C, repair to spout	2,500.00
Lantern, 18″ h, brass, orig whale oil burner and blown glass globe	550.00
Light, 15″ h, masthead, Whaling Bark *Wanderer,* copper, electrified	150.00
Liquor Chest, 7¼″ sq, 8″ h, mahogany, four gold dec Bristol glass bottles, matching wine glass, early 19th C	300.00
Log Book, Bark *Morning Star,* New Bedford, Saturday, May 14, 1864, thru October 14, 1865, orig boards, back cover worn through at top, spine worn	5,200.00

Model

Masthead, 12⅜″ h, fine detail	450.00

Scale

Bark *Morning Star,* 30″	600.00
Brig, plank on hull frame mounted in case	900.00
Warship, English Prisoner-of-war, bone and ebony, two deck, tortoiseshell mounted base and case, 19 x 9¾ x 18″ case	9,000.00
Whaleboat, cased, harpoons, oars, lines	700.00
Shadowbox, 21″ h, 36½″ l, French boat meeting New York Pilot Boat No. 1, painted sea, clouds, sails, and lighthouse background, 19th C	900.00
Navigation Scale, B. Dodd, early 19th C, 24″ l, boxwood	210.00
Octant, ebony, brass, inlaid ivory scale, James Whythe of Glasgow label	350.00

Painting

Corsini, Raffael, (Italian, Nineteenth Century), *Palmer of Boston M. Powers Master Smyrna January 31st 1832,* 18 x 24¾″, water-color on paper, panoramic view of entire port, three large ships at anchor, American, British, French, Dutch, and Swiss flags in background, framed	15,000.00
Jacobsen, Antonio, (American, 1850–1921), *Portrait of The Fishing Schooner "Anna & Ella,"* 22 x 36″, oil on artist's panel, fishing schooner, dories stacked on deck putting out to sea, bird's-eye maple frame, signed	11,500.00
Russell, Edward J., (American, 1835–	

1906), *American Ship 'Theobald' Comd by A.L. Waterhouse,* 25½ x 38″, water-color on paper, full-rigged ship passing headland, oak frame, signed **2,750.00**

Provision Cask, 13″ h, oak, iron hoops **325.00**

Quarter Board, 90″ l, 8½″ h, Ferryboat *Weehawken* **900.00**

Rudder, 59″ h, small vessel, well preserved, traces of orig white paint, 19th C **50.00**

Sailing Card, *The A1 Extreme Clipper Barque Wm. H. Thorndike,* dated at Boston, February 17, 1874, voyage to Melbourne and Sydney, Australia .. **400.00**

Sea Chest
 Dovetailed, 51 x 21 x 21½″, beckets, lidded compartment inside, provisions for holding four decanters or bottles, orig blue-green paint, "William Bunnell" on front, mid 19th C **700.00**
 Hardwood, 44 x 19 x 18″, orig brown grain painting, dark brown borders, "Capt. F.C. Smith" on front panel . **600.00**

Sextant, double reflecting, cased, 6⅞ x 5¼ x 2⅛″, initialed on top "J.S.," sgd on instrument "Prof. Smith's Etabim i Kolbenhaven," maker "William Petersens Eftenflegen, Lausitz Kickeby," c1820, $1,250.00.

Sewing Box, 9½″ l, multiwood inlays, compass rose, stars, and diamonds, ivory ring handle and escutcheon, mid-19th C **600.00**

Shaving Kit, 8½″ l, mahogany case, hinged lid, mirror inset, two bone handled razors, toothbrush, shaving brush, drill sewing knife, and pewter container **625.00**

Signal Horn, 15″ l, foot operated, "E. A. Gill, Gloucester, MA," 19th C **110.00**

Spyglass, single-draw
 Leather wrapped case, extends to 43¼″, made for W. Desilva, Liverpool, early 19th C **200.00**
 Mahogany tube, Spencer, Browning, and Rust, London, early 19th C .. **175.00**

Steamship Whistle, triple, brass and iron, 19th C **450.00**

Stern Board, carved, polychrome, eagle, orig paint, 27¾″ wingspread, late 19th C **1,500.00**

Strong Box, 27″ l, iron, European-style chest, elaborate locking device, orig key, well preserved, 17th C **1,200.00**

Telegraph, 44″ h, brass, Bendix, Brooklyn, NY **600.00**

Travel Box, 11¾ x 9½ x 4¼″, mahogany, brass escutcheon, handles, and nameplate, engraved "From/Captn Baynes/To John Hunt," mid 19th C . **250.00**

Travel Desk
 17″ l, ebony, three hidden drawers, roller, and pen tray, orig felt cov writing surface **400.00**
 18 x 14 x 28¾″, camphor wood, drawer, fold-out writing lid, raised section containing pigeonholes and compartments, mounted on ebonized base, mid 19th C **1,200.00**

Valentine, sailor's, 8¾″ d, octagon shape, anchor on left side, floral like design on right **1,600.00**

Water Keg, 18″ h, pine, brass hoops and spout **75.00**

Weather Vane
 Galleon, 38″ h, hammered copper .. **200.00**
 Schooner shape, copper sail, early 20th C **150.00**

Wheel, 50″ d, mahogany, brass inset rings, 19th C **600.00**

NAZI ITEMS

History: The National Socialist Party came to power in the 1920s during a period of severe economic depression in Germany. Under the leadership of Adolph Hitler, the party assumed first political control and then social control over Germany. National socialism dominated all aspects of German life. World War II was launched in 1939 to achieve a military conquest of Europe. The Nazi era ended in 1945 when Germany surrendered at the end of World War II.

References: John M. Kaduck, *World War II German Collectibles,* published by author, 1978, 1983 price update; *The Official 1983 Price Guide To Military Collectibles, Fifth Edition,* House of Collectibles, 1985.

Periodicals: *Military Collectors News,* P. O. Box 7582, Tulsa, OK, 74105; *The MX Exchange,* P. O. Box 3, Torrington, CT 06790.

Additional Listings: See *Warman's Americana & Collectibles* for more examples.

Armband, SS Concentration Camp Sonderkomado, large black SS Runes above "Special Command" inscription, white band	250.00
Badge, silver, vertical, Spanish cross, swords	325.00
Banner	
7 x 38", double sided, silver rope hanger	25.00
16 x 21", Artillery Regt #27, black embroidered eagle on wine red field, reverse side white embroidered FR 27 on blue field, three sided white fringe, tie ropes	275.00
Bayonet, police, dress, 13" blade, stag handle, attached police insignia, black leather scabbard, silvered fittings, orig black frog, guard marked "S. MG. 415" and matching numbers	165.00
Belt and Buckle, Railway Officer, brown leather belt, aluminum buckle with gold finish, dated 1940	80.00
Belt Buckle	
Prison official's, round, eagle holding sword and bolts, swastika on breast	50.00
SA, rotated swastika, brass body, SP faceplate, 2 pcs	45.00
Cap Badge, RAD, silver finish, enameled, wreath	25.00
Car Pennant, 8½ x 11½", Teno, printed on both sides, white eagle on blue field, two tie strings	75.00
Cigarette Case, presentation piece, steel, painted, brass plate, emb heads of Mussolini and Hitler, "Vincere," above heads, eagle embracing wreath of swastikas, wreath with Italy's emblem	175.00
Collar Tabs, rank of Zollwachtmeister	10.00
Correspondence Card, 5 x 8", raised gold eagle and Adolf Hitler, Mujnchen, Den address, orig gilt stamped, 2 pcs	45.00
Dagger, orange and yellow celluloid grip, SP fittings and scabbard, marked "E & F Horstaer"	110.00
Document, 6 x 8", "Kriegsurlaubsschein," seal, unissued	10.00
Emblem, 27 x 16", train engine, eagle with swastika	250.00
Fez, SS	175.00
Flag, sport, 58 x 31", double sided, sports eagle and swastika	50.00
Flag Pole Top, 8½", nickel plated, swastika inside round gear	45.00
Hat	
Panzer Officer, cloth, black, eagle and wreath, silver wire bullion, WWII	15.00
Police Officer, back visor, bright eagle and wreath device, green/blue	

wool, silver cord, leather chin strap, pebbled side buttons	150.00
Helmet, Luftwaffe pilot's, summer, throat mikes	250.00
Holster, P-38, black leather, Nazi acceptance mark, pouch for extra clip	50.00
Invitation, 4½ x 7", gold gilt heading, black printed German script, Hitler engraved, orig	35.00
Knife, paratrooper's	100.00

Membership Pins, white metal - Top: NKSOV, World War I Veteran, 1¼" l, $12.50; Bottom: RDB, State Officials Organization, ⅞" l, $10.00.

Lamp, table, 16" h, figural, eagle, Munich party headquarters, plaster, gold leaf, marbleized stand	100.00
Matchbox Holder, celluloid, Stuttgart Panzer headquarters building insert	25.00
Meat Fork, 10" l, SS, Runes engraved in handle	150.00
Mess Kit, steel, large spoon, fork, knife, can opener, steel handle, hallmarked, standing eagle and swastika, 1942	75.00
Painting, oil, 24 x 19½", Hitler, party tunic, in his office, oak leaf frame, orig, sgd	1,200.00
Passbook, D. R. Arbeitsbuch, Weimer eagle, dated 1936, some entries	15.00
Patch, Air Force, 7"	15.00
Postcard, celebrating 700 years of Berlin, seven city and state shields, gold letter inscription, dated 18.8.37, special anniversary cancellation, sent to London	30.00
Shooting Medal, silver finish, "Kreisschiessen Kofstein, 1942"	25.00
Shot Glass, SS, Pioneer Battalion	20.00
Shoulder Boards, police, Wachtmeister Rank, black and silver cord, pink piping, removable style	10.00
Stationery, 8½ x 11½", NSDAP eagle and Der Fuhrer in raised gold, orig single sheet	40.00

Stickpin, SS, NSDAP, swastika	**20.00**
Street Sign, "Juden Gasse," enameled metal, historical piece, orig	**650.00**
Sword	
Dress, eagle and swastika, engraved brass handle, black wire wrapped plastic grip, black painted scabbard	**100.00**
Officer's, dove head, scabbard, NSDAP eagle on guard	**65.00**
Tunic, police, green piping, removable shoulder boards, Bevo collar tabs, Bevo green Police Eagle Arm Shield left sleeve, silver pebbled buttons, tailored cuffs, dark brown trim	**185.00**
Whistle, pewter, concentration camp . .	**25.00**

NETSUKES

History: The traditional Japanese kimono has no pockets. Daily necessities such as money, tobacco supplies, etc., were carried in leather pouches or *inros* which hung from a cord with a netsuke toggle. Netsuke comes from "ne" (to root) and "tsuke" (to fasten).

Netsukes originated in the 14th century and initially were associated with the middle class. By the mid-18th century all levels of Japanese society used them. Some of the most famous artists, e.g., Shuzan and Yamada Hojitsu, worked in the netsuke form.

Netsukes average 1 to 2 inches and are made from wood, ivory, bone, ceramics, metal, horn, nutshells, etc. The subject matter is broad based, but always portrayed in a lighthearted, humorous manner. A netsuke must have no sharp edges and balance so it hangs correctly on the sash.

Value depends on artist, region, material, and skill of craftsmanship. Western collectors favor *katabori*, pieces which represent an identifiable object.

Reference: Sandra Andacht, *Oriental Antiques & Art: An Identification And Value Guide,* Wallace-Homestead, 1987.

Collectors' Club: Netsuke Kenkyukai Society, Box 11248, Torrance, CA 90510.

Reproduction Alert: Recent reproductions are on the market. Many are carved from African ivory.

Chrysanthemum, boxwood, carved, finely etched and curved petal, sgd Kosei, Hideyuki in rect gold plaque .	**1,210.00**
Dancer, carved, circular shape, Shishiabori technique, Okina mask captured in middle of dance, unsigned, 19th C	**385.00**
Dragon, carved openwork technique, captured amidst flaming clouds, unsigned, 19th C	**880.00**
Duck, ivory, carved, sitting, Hakusen . .	**150.00**
Fisherman, ivory, blowing conch horn, sgd	**150.00**

Folk Figure, puckered mouth drawn over to the right side of face, sgd Sangyoku, 19th C	**275.00**
Frogs, stained ivory, two playing on tortoise back, Mitsuyuki	**125.00**
Man, ivory, sgd	
Crawling on bundle of cloth and fan	**100.00**
Seated, 20th C	**125.00**
With walking stick and bundle	**75.00**
Matchlock Gun, iron, movable hammer, lacquered case, brass ring for mounting, 19th C	**330.00**
Monkey	
Boxwood, male, seated, hunched body, fixed gaze to left arm being groomed by right hand, inlaid horn eyes, sgd Ikkan	**1,000.00**
Ceramic, standing, movable head and tongue, wide eyed, orange glaze, red and black accents, translucent blue glazed costume and hat	**225.00**
Quail in Millet, stained ivory, Tadomitsu	**200.00**
Rabbit, boxwood, hunched, feeds on cluster of blossoms held in forepaws, inlaid eyes, sgd Tomokazu, 19th C .	**1,200.00**
Rat, boxwood and ivory, seated, tail curved around body, gnaws at left leg, inlaid eyes, carved partially eaten rice cake, inscribed Kaigyoku, 19th C . .	**800.00**
Seal Form, wood, horse finial, unsigned	**50.00**
Shishi, captured crouching on all fours, gaping mouth, holding small tama, body and paws slightly worn, unsigned, late 18th C	**600.00**
Snail, ivory, mollusk turned head, spiral form shell, overlaid lacquer and aogai beetle, 19th C	**300.00**
Tiger, stained and white striped ivory, snarling showing teeth, Ikko	**300.00**
Turtle, ivory, pouring water from gourd into bowl held by man, Mitsu Hide, late 18th C	**275.00**
Whistle, pottery, bulbous shaft, band of phoenix birds, scrolling foliage,	

Unsigned, ivory, face with popping eyes, $150.00.

green, blue, and purple glaze, yellow glazed ground, deep green bowl and mouth piece, 19th C **470.00**

Woman, boxwood, carved, crouched on one knee, cleans her back with towel, incised and stained features, elaborate coiffure, inscribed Masanao . . . **200.00**

NEWCOMB POTTERY

History: William and Ellsworth Woodward, two brothers, were the founders of a series of businesses which eventually merged into the Newcomb pottery effort. In 1885 Ellsworth Woodward, a proponent of vocational training for women, organized a school from which emerged the Ladies Decorative Art League. In 1886 the brothers founded the New Orleans Art Pottery Company with the ladies of the league serving as decorators. The first two potters were Joseph Meyer and George Ohr. The pottery closed in 1891.

William Woodward was on the faculty at Tulane. Ellsworth taught fine arts at the Sophie Newcomb College, a women's school which eventually merged with Tulane. In 1895 Newcomb College developed a pottery course in which the wares could be sold. Some of the equipment came from the old New Orleans Art Pottery.

Mary G. Sheerer joined the staff to teach decoration. In 1910 Paul E. Cox solved many of the technical problems connected with making pottery in a southern environment. Other leading figures were Sadie Irvine, Professor Lota Lee Troy, and Kathrine Choi. Pottery was made until the early 1950s.

Students painted a quality art pottery with a distinctive high glaze. Designs have a decidedly southern flavor, e.g., myrtle, jasmine, sugar cane, moss, cypress, dogwood, and magnolia motifs. Later matte glazed pieces usually are decorated with carved back floral designs. Pieces depicting murky, bayou scenes are most desirable.

Reference: Jessie Poesch, *Newcomb Pottery: An Enterprise for Southern Women,* Schiffer Publishing, Ltd, 1984.

Collectors' Club: American Art Pottery Association, P.O. Box 714, Silver Spring, MD 20901.

Museum: Newcomb College, Tulane University, New Orleans, LA.

Bowl, 8", pink morning glories, artist sgd . . **500.00**

Chamberstick, 5¼" h, saucer base, candle nozzle, drip pan top, handle, inscribed "Days Turn Is Over–Now Arrives The Night," sgd "M.G.S., 1903" (Mary Sheerer) **2,315.00**

Bowl, 6" d, 2⅝" h, green design, white ground, $750.00.

Mug, 5", high glaze, stylized blue floral dec, beige ground **500.00**

Plaque, 4¾" d, dark blue landscape scene, moss laden oak trees, light blue ground, marked "Henrietta Bailey" **600.00**

Plate, 9⅝", high glaze, incised dec, nasturium blossoms and leaves, shaded cobalt blue, green, and cream, medium blue center, marked "Desiree Roman, 1905" **750.00**

Tile, 3½" sq, oak tree, hanging Spanish moss dec, shaded blue glaze, sgd "A.F.S., 1917" (Anna Frances Simpson) **800.00**

Toothpick, 2⅞", high glaze, carved stylized dec, shaded blue, marked "Sadie Irvine" **350.00**

Vase
   3¼", tree motif, shades of blue, marked **700.00**
   3½", blue, green, and ivory swirls, matte finish, sgd "J. H.," (Julia Hoerner), c1916 . . . . **300.00**
   5½", scenic dec, sgd "Sadie Irvine" . **650.00**
   6", daffodils, mottled turquoise ground, sgd "Sadie Irvine" **700.00**
   6½", cylindrical, wooded landscape, blue-green, sgd "A.F.S." **725.00**
   9⅛", expanding cylinder, incised dogwood blossoms at shoulder, matte blue glaze, artist sgd **1,100.00**

NILOAK POTTERY, MISSION WARE

History: Niloak Pottery was made near Benton, Arkansas. Charles Dean Hyten experimented with native clay, trying to preserve its natural colors. By

1911 he perfected Mission Ware, a marbleized pottery in which the cream and brown colors predominate. The pieces were marked Niloak (kaolin spelled backwards).

After a devastating fire, the pottery was rebuilt and named Eagle Pottery. This factory included the space to add a novelty pottery line which was introduced in 1929. This line usually was marked Hywood-Niloak, until 1934 when the name Hywood was dropped from the mark. Mr. Hyten left the pottery in 1941. In 1946 operations ceased.

Additional Listings: See *Warman's Americana & Collectibles* for more examples, especially the novelty pieces.

Note: Prices listed below are for Mission Ware pieces.

Lamp, electric, base 7¾″ h, $150.00.

Ashtray, marbleized swirls, tan, rouge, cream and gray	**80.00**
Bowl, marbleized swirls	
5 x 1½″, tans and blues	**35.00**
8¼″, brown, tan and rouge	**40.00**
Candlesticks, pr	
8″, marbleized swirls, blue, cream, terra cotta, and brown	**250.00**
9″, marbleized swirls, tans and blues	**350.00**
Toothpick Holder, marbleized swirls, tans and blues	**100.00**
Urn, 4½″, marbleized swirls, brown and blue	**35.00**
Vase	
4½″, marbleized swirls	
Red and brown	**55.00**
Tans and blue	**45.00**
5½″, bulbous, marbleized swirls, rust, blue, and cream	**65.00**
6″, marbleized swirls, cream, turquoise blue, rust, and brown	**70.00**
Wall Pocket, marbleized swirls	**250.00**

NIPPON CHINA, 1891-1921

History: Nippon, Japanese hand painted porcelain, was made for export between 1891 and 1921. In 1891, when the McKinley tariff act proclaimed that all items of foreign manufacture be stamped with their country of origin. Japan chose to use "Nippon." In 1921 the United States decided the word "Nippon" no longer was acceptable and required that all Japanese wares be marked with "Japan." The Nippon era ended.

There are over 220 recorded Nippon backstamps or marks. The three most popular are the wreath, maple leaf, and rising sun marks. Wares with variations of all three marks are being reproduced today. A knowledgeable collector can easily spot the reproductions by the mark variances.

The majority of the marks are found in three different colors: green, blue, and magenta. Colors indicate the quality of the porcelain used: green for first grade porcelain, blue for second grade, and magenta for third grade. Marks were applied by two methods, decal stickers under glaze and imprinting directly on the porcelain.

References: Gene Loendorf, *Nippon Hand Painted China,* McGrew Color Graphics, 1975; Joan Van Patten, *The Collector's Encyclopedia Of Nippon Porcelain, Series One,* Collector Books, 1979; Joan Van Patten, *The Collector's Encyclopedia Of Nippon Porcelain, Series Two,* Collector Books, 1982; Joan Van Patten, *The Collector's Encyclopedia Of Nippon Porcelain, Series Three,* Collector Books, 1986.

Collectors' Clubs: Great Lakes Nippon Collectors Club, Rt 2, Box 81, Peotone, IL 60468; International Nippon Collectors Club, Rt2, Box 81, Peotone, IL 60468. Dues: $20.00; Long Island Nippon Collectors Club, P. O. Box 88, Jericho, NY 11753; New England Nippon Collectors Club, 22 Mill Pond, North Andover, MA 01845.

Additional Listings: See *Warman's Americana & Collectibles.*

Advisor: Kathy Wojciechowski.

Ashtray, 5¾″ d, 2¼″ h, continuous scene, $150.00.

Ashtray
Figural, dachshund, scenic center, moriage trim, match box holder .. **475.00**
Triangular shape, dog's head medallion center, moriage trim, maple leaf mark **225.00**

Basket
8¾" h, pastoral tapestry scene, ducks and pond **790.00**
9" h, moriage sea gull in full flight, slate to dark gray background, maple leaf mark **525.00**

Berry Set, master, five matching smaller bowls, lavender and purple columbines, gold outlining, Wreath, six pcs **95.00**

Bowl
7", red and pink roses, green leaves, gold flowers on edge, gold trim, green M in Wreath mark **65.00**
7½", swans in flight, pond, raised gold beading, crimped top, artist sgd, Leaf **110.00**
8½", sq, Oriental floral dec **50.00**
11¾ x 8¼ x 5", green and purple foliage, gold border, ftd **135.00**
12", bisque, scenic, Egyptian boat, palm trees, city in background, gold bead trim, scroll handles, Maple Leaf mark **200.00**

Bread Tray, gaudy, green and gold, pink asters **225.00**

Calling Card Tray, 7¾ x 6", mythical dragon and bird, blue Maple Leaf mark **45.00**

Candle Lamp, bisque, sailing ships, pastel blue, Wreath, pr **3,200.00**

Candlestick
6" h, Wedgwood and rose nosegay design, Jasperware, Wreath mark, pr **235.00**
10" h, Galle scene, moriage trees, Maple Leaf mark, pr **400.00**

Candy Dish, scalloped edge, pink roses, gold trim, twisted handle **50.00**

Celery Set, 12" l, master, six matching salts, Wreath mark **125.00**

Child's Dishes
Mug, 3¾" h, clowns and rabbit, white, Rising Sun mark **75.00**
Tea Set, teapot, creamer and sugar, four cups, saucers, and plates, gold flowers and beading, white background, Rising Sun **235.00**

Chocolate Set, 9" h pot, five matching cups and saucers, white background, bands of rosebuds and gold top and bottom, Maple Leaf mark **225.00**

Compote, 4¾" h, 8½" d, Wedgwood and rose nosegay dec, Wreath mark .. **200.00**

Cracker Jar, melon ribbed, bisque background, Indian in canoe shooting

moose on river edge, ftd, Wreath mark **425.00**

Decanter, 8" h, blue and pink background, pink and lavender roses, gold overlay designs and trim, Maple Leaf mark **180.00**

Doll
11", boy, bisque head, brown hair and eyes, teeth, composition body, FY mark **275.00**
12", bisque head, sleep eyes, dark brown hair, composition body, Christening gown, FY Nippon mark **175.00**
24", bisque head, hands, and feet, sleep eyes, four teeth, long black hair, leather body, FY mark **435.00**

Dresser Set, woodland scene, tray, hatpin holder, powder box, and hair receiver, Maple Leaf mark **950.00**

Egg Warmer, holds four eggs, stopper, sailboat scene, Rising Sun mark ... **110.00**

Dutch Shoe, 3" l
Bisque scenic design, Wreath mark . **125.00**
Forget-me-nots, multicolored foliage, Wreath mark **100.00**

Ewer, 6" h, multicolored moriage design, enameling technique, floral bouquet medallions front and back, unmarked **90.00**

Ferner
6", floral dec, gold beading, four handles, green M in Wreath mark ... **125.00**
7", man in gondola, bisque **135.00**

Fruit Bowl, 11" w, grapes and vines, gold rim, ftd, Leaf **275.00**

Hair Receiver, 5", yellow and red roses, black ground, blue Maple Leaf mark **60.00**

Hatpin Holder, 5", serpent in relief, mottled ground **165.00**

Humidor
6½", children sitting by tree, M-I-R, Wreath mark **1,750.00**
7¼" h, molded in relief, Indian bust, full headdress, colorful, Wreath mark **2,000.00**

Inkwell, 4", palm trees, boat on lake .. **125.00**
Jam Jar, floral dec, gold trim **45.00**
Jelly Dish, underplate, violet dec, gold design **45.00**

Lazy Susan, 10", floral dec, pastel shades, heavy gold overlay, orig papier mache box **175.00**

Mayonnaise Dish, 4½" d, ladle, multicolored floral dec, gold trim **60.00**

Mug
4¾" h, hunt scene, moriage trim handle, Maple Leaf mark **225.00**
5½" h, gray bisque background, moriage dragon, blue enameled eyes, green M in Wreath mark **225.00**

Napkin Ring, 4" h, figural, owl on tree stump, Wreath mark **375.00**

Nappy, 5", scalloped, cobalt, red flowers, elaborate gold overall design . . **127.50**
Nut Set, 7", master bowl, six cups, relief molded, nut shell shape **225.00**
Pitcher, 7" h, slate gray ground, moriage sea gulls, Leaf mark **250.00**
Planter, 7" d, Egyptian designs, gold outlining, supported by three columns forming Egyptian heads **225.00**
Plaque
10"
    Flying eagle, molded in relief, Wreath mark **4,000.00**
    Three dancing children, rim, animals, Wreath mark **350.00**
    10½", collie and terrier, molded in relief, Wreath mark **950.00**
    12", farmer sowing seeds, molded in relief, Wreath mark . . . **2,100.00**
Plate
    8½", lake, house, and roses scene, cobalt and gold trim, Leaf mark . . **185.00**
    10" w, gold center, cobalt and gold trim, Maple Leaf mark **150.00**
Powder Box, cov
    3½", child's, green, "Happy Face" . . **65.00**
    5¼", portrait on cov, green and white base, heavy gold scrolling, gold feet, blue Maple Leaf mark **125.00**
Punch Bowl and Stand, 12½" d, 6½" h, bisque, bouquet of roses scene, wide rim decorated with gold and jewels, Wreath mark **295.00**
Ring Tree, gold, beading, green M in Wreath mark **40.00**
Salt and Pepper Shaker, cobalt and red roses, gold overlay, beads, Leaf mark **55.00**
Scent Bottle, 4¼", cream, pink and red roses, green raised lattice with white dots **125.00**
Serving Tray, 11" d, gold and burgundy medallions inside gold fluted rim, multicolored roses and leaves center, gold open pierced handles, Royal Kinran mark **195.00**
Shaving Mug, shaded green, floral dec, gold beading, gold handle **225.00**
Spittoon, lady's hand, violets, turquoise beading, green M in Wreath mark . . **150.00**
Stein, relief molded, dog heads, leash handle, green M in Wreath mark . . . **950.00**
Stick Pin Holder, 1½" h, multicolored roses, gold trim, Wreath mark **100.00**
Sugar Shaker, 4¼" h, cobalt, floral, Maple Leaf mark **145.00**
Tankard, 13¼", cobalt, red roses, gold, sgd **250.00**
Tea Set, three pcs, mellon ribbed shape, gold handles and trim, gold overlay design, pink roses, Leaf mark **250.00**
Tea Strainer, pink roses **50.00**
Tea Tile, scenic, cow, pasture **45.00**

Toothpick Holder, 2½", fruit and floral dec, Rising Sun mark **65.00**
Trivet, octagonal, portrait, Egyptian lady, shaded red ground, blue trim . **140.00**
Urn
    9½" h, white flowers, gold outline, fancy handles, dome lid, pedestal base, Royal Kimran **425.00**
    16" h, medallion in center with cow drinking from pond, gold floral overlay, gold stand-up handles, bolted base, Wreath mark **575.00**

Vase, 4½" h, brown beaded deer, tan ground, green base, marked "M" in wreath surrounded by "HP" and "Nippon," $90.00.

Vase
    6", scenic cartouche front, beaded overall, handled, sgd **100.00**
    6¾" h, moriage, floral, hp grapes, ruffled top, three ftd, Royal Moriye mark **265.00**
    7", portrait, gold, handled, ftd **450.00**
    8¼", abstract brown and pink pine cones and needles, olive green ground, gold leaf trim, matte glaze, double scroll handles **275.00**
    8½", red roses, moriage design, loop handles and rim, green M in Wreath mark, pr **400.00**
    9¼", woodland and water scene, shaded ground, gold handles, green M in Wreath mark **150.00**
    11½", scenic, trees, water, etc, lavender accents, neck and base mustard yellow, raised gold flowers, garlands and dots, gold handles, green Wreath mark **235.00**
    12"
        Red flowers, gold neck and base, jeweling, blue Maple Leaf mark **275.00**

Scenic, English countryside and lake, black top and bottom, serpentine handle	**175.00**
13", mums in medallions, gold handles, blue Maple Leaf mark	**225.00**
14", farmer sowing seeds, molded in relief	**2,300.00**
Wall Pocket, 6", molded dog, floral dec	**65.00**
Whiskey Jug, palm trees and lake scene, raised moriage trim	**450.00**
Wine Jug, 9½" h, Monk portrait, bisque background, enamel and moriage work, Wreath mark	**475.00**

NODDERS

History: Nodders are figurines with heads and/or arms attached to the body with wires to enable them to move. They are made in a variety of materials - bisque, celluloid, papier mache, porcelain, and wood.

Most nodders date from the late 19th century with Germany being the principal source of supply. Among the American made nodders, those of Disney and cartoon characters are most eagerly sought.

Boy in Tub, 2 pcs, 3¾ x 2½ x 3¼", marked "PATENT/TT," $25.00.

African Couple, bisque, black man and woman, pr	**575.00**
Baby, 4½", bisque, pink and white gown, pulling off blue sock	**175.00**
Black, 5½", bisque, school boy, seated in chair, white shirt, blue, white, and tan plaid pants, holding slate	**125.00**
Bulldog, 10 x 6½", brown, sanded finish	**60.00**
Buttercup, bisque, German	**175.00**
Colonial Woman, 7½", bisque	**185.00**
Donald Duck, plastic, Louis Marx & Co	**18.00**
Elephant, 8½ x 6½", gray felt, canvas blanket, wood base	**150.00**

Happy Hooligan, 6", papier mache, red jacket, blue pants	**90.00**
Indian Princess, 3¾", bisque, seated, holding fan, pale blue, gold trim . . .	**115.00**
Japanese Boy and Girl, 5½", papier mache, pr	**35.00**
Monk, 5¾", bisque, standing, holding wine pitcher, German	**140.00**
Oriental Couple, 8¾", bisque, pink robes, gilding, seated before keyboard and music book, Continental, 19th C, pr	**500.00**
Orphan Annie, bisque, German	**100.00**
Santa Claus, 10", papier mache, candy container, mica glitter trim, German .	**100.00**
Turkish Girl, 6 x 6", bisque, white beading	**300.00**
Uncle Walt, bisque, German	**100.00**

NORITAKE CHINA

History: Morimura Brothers founded Noritake China in 1904 in Nagoya, Japan. They made high quality chinaware for export to the United States and also produced a line of china blanks for hand painting. In 1910 the company perfected a technique for the production of high quality dinnerware and introduced streamlined production.

During the 1920s Larkin Company, Buffalo, New York, was a prime distributor of Noritake China. Larkin offered Azalea, Briarcliff, Linden, Modjeska, Savory, Sheridan, and Tree In The Meadow patterns as part of their premium line.

The factory was heavily damaged during World War II; production was reduced. Between 1946 and 1948 the company sold their china under the "Rose China" mark, since the quality of production did not match the earlier Noritake China. An 1948 expansion saw the resumption of quality production and the use of the Noritake name once again.

There are close to 100 different marks for Noritake, the careful study of which can determine the date of production. Most pieces are marked "Noritake" and have a wreath, "M," "N," or "Nippon." The use of the letter "N" was registered in 1953.

References: Aimee Neff Alden and Marian Kinney Richardson, *Early Noritake China: An Identification And Value Guide To Tableware Patterns,* Wallace-Homestead, 1987; Lou Ann Donahue, *Noritake Collectibles,* Wallace-Homestead, 1979; Joan Van Patten, *Collector's Encyclopedia of Noritake,* Collector Books, 1984.

Additional Listings: See *Warman's Americana & Collectibles* for price listings of the Azalea pattern.

Ashtray
   4¾"

Circular, figural black and red bird, orange beak, red center, black border and ext., green mark . . .	**100.00**

Cup and Saucer, pink and blue flowers, gold trim, white ground, $25.00.

Triangular, figural pipe in center, shades of brown and tan, green mark	75.00
5″, circular, horses dec, green border, red cigarette rests, red mark	65.00
Bouillon Cup and Saucer, Azalea pattern	24.00
Bowl, 8½″, gold, wood scene border	65.00
Bread Plate, 14 x 6¼″, white, pale green and gold floral border, open handles	24.00
Candy Dish, 6½″, round, black luster, orange flowers, gold trim	135.00
Children's Dishes, white, gold trim, six cups and saucers, plates, teapot, creamer, sugar, cookie plate, platter, cov casserole, orig box, 1922	250.00
Cigarette Holder, 5″ h, bell shaped, floral dec, bird finial, red mark	100.00
Cologne Bottle, 6″, white, floral dec	110.00
Compote, Japanese fisherman by water, houses in background	90.00
Condiment Set, salt and pepper shakers, mustard, and round tray, red ground, blue and yellow birds on perch	75.00
Cup and Saucer, 3″ d cup, 5″ d saucer, white, pink and blue flowers, gold trim	25.00
Demitasse Cup and Saucer, orange and blue florals	18.00
Dresser Doll, figural, gold luster	185.00
Ferner, 6″, triangular	75.00
Hatpin Holder, 4½″, gold luster, black band at top with multicolored flowers	45.00
Lemon Dish, 6″ d, relief molded, lemon, hp blossoms and leaves, M in wreath mark	50.00
Match Holder, 3¾″ h, beehive shape, gold luster finish, green M in wreath mark	48.00
Mustard Jar, underplate, orange luster finish, blueberries finial	45.00

Nut Set, figural, peanut shape, 7¼″ master bowl, six 3″ individual figural dishes	175.00
Perfume, orange luster bottle, blue flower stopper	85.00
Plaque	
8½″ d, silhouette of girl in bouffant dress, looking into hand mirror, green M in wreath mark	100.00
10″, hp, cottage, trees, and pastel flowers, brown rim	65.00
Powder Box, desert scene, Arab on camel, cobalt blue ground, ornate gold beading	300.00
Punch Bowl Set, banquet size, eight matching cups, scenic, swans, cottage, island, and trees, heavy raised gold, green M in wreath mark	675.00
Shaving Mug, 3¾″, hp, scene of stalking tiger, green M in wreath mark	200.00
Tile, hp, scenic, water, willow tree, rushes, and man in boat	38.00
Tobacco Jar, 6½″ h, hp, golfer, red jacket and cap, black and white checkerboard knickers, green M in wreath mark	190.00
Tray, 8″ l, two handles, hp, blue violets, red M in wreath mark	40.00
Vase	
5¼″	
Figural, multicolored bird and beige luster tree trunk, green mark	100.00
Relief Molded, squirrel on berried leafy branch, multicolored, shaded brown ground	150.00
7″, bulbous, figural red birds on rim, orange and pale blue luster, red and black floral dec	150.00
10″, double, figural, parrots on perch	140.00
Vegetable Bowl, Wild Ivy pattern	12.00
Wall Pocket	
6¾ x 5″, bulbous, blue luster, exotic bird dec	60.00
8″, two applied flowers, blue luster finish	36.00
8¼″, cylindrical, floral dec	48.00
9″, octagonal, yellow, peacock dec	85.00

NORITAKE: TREE IN THE MEADOW PATTERN

History: Tree In The Meadow is one of the most popular patterns of Noritake china. Since the design is hand painted, there are numerous variations of the scene. The basic scene features a large tree (usually in the foreground), a meandering stream or lake, and a peasant cottage in the distance. Principal colors are muted tones of brown and yellow.

The pattern is found with a variety of backstamps and appears to have been imported into the United States beginning in the early 1920s. The Larkin Company distributed this pattern through its catalog sales in the 1920–1930 period.

Reference: Joan Van Patten, *Collector's Encyclopedia of Noritake,* Collector Books, 1984.

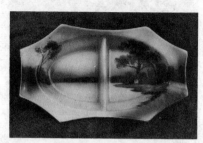

Relish Dish, divided, $45.00.

Ashtray, 5¼", green mark	35.00
Berry Set, large bowl, pierced handles, six small bowls	68.00
Bowl, 6½", green mark	25.00
Cake plate, 10", pierced handles	30.00
Condiment Set, mustard pot, ladle, salt and pepper shakers, tray	40.00
Creamer	25.00
Dish, 6", pierced handles, blue luster border	40.00
Humidor	345.00
Jam Jar, underplate, and spoon	65.00
Lemon Dish, 5½", center ring handle	15.00
Plate	
6½"	10.00
7½"	12.00
8½"	15.00
Platter	
12"	30.00
14"	35.00
Salt and Pepper Shakers, marked "Made In Japan," pr	30.00
Sauce Dish, underplate, and spoon, green mark	50.00
Shaving Mug, 3¾", green mark	85.00
Sugar, cov	25.00
Tea Set, teapot, creamer, and cov sugar, six cups and saucers	135.00
Tea Tile, 5" w, chamfered corners, green mark	25.00
Toothpick Holder	55.00
Vase	
7", fan shape	120.00
8", bulbous	165.00
Vegetable Dish, 9⅜", oval, Noritake mark	30.00
Waffle Set, sugar shaker and syrup jug	70.00
Wall Plaque, 8½", green mark	75.00

NORTH DAKOTA SCHOOL OF MINES

History: The North Dakota School of Mines was established in 1890. Earle J. Babcock, an instructor in chemistry, was impressed with the high purity of North Dakota potter's clay. In 1898 Babcock received funds to develop his finds. He tried to interest commercial potteries in North Dakota clay, but had limited success.

In 1910 Babcock persuaded the school to establish a Ceramics Department. Margaret Cable, who studied under Charles Binns and Frederick H. Rhead, was appointed head. She remained until her retirement in 1949.

Decorative emphasis was placed on native themes, e.g., flowers and animals. Art Nouveau, Art Deco, and fairly plain pieces were made.

The pottery is marked in cobalt blue underglaze with "University of North Dakota/Grand Forks, N.D./Made at School of Mines/N.D. Clay" in a circle. Some earlier pieces only are marked "U.N.D." or "U.N.D./Grand Forks, N.D." Most pieces are numbered (they can be dated with University records) and signed by both the instructor and student. Cable signed pieces are most desirable.

Reference: *University Of North Dakota Pottery, The Cable Years,* Knight Publishing Company, 1977.

Vase, 2¾", dark purple, blue flecks, "U.N.D." stamp, $100.00.

Bowl	
3½ x 4", carved turkeys, green to brown, sgd "Mattson"	275.00
5", dark blue gloss, sgd "JIT"	60.00
5½", carved floral, gray green matte	100.00
Curtain Pull, Indian head, turquoise, marked "Homecoming 1939," orig box	100.00

Paperweight, 3½" d, "Parent's Day, 1938," deep blue **85.00**
Tile, 3½", high relief dec, "R" for Rebekah Assemblies **100.00**
Vase
  4¾", brown and cream glossy, line design **80.00**
  8½", bud, green semi-gloss, sgd "M Cable" **75.00**
  9 x 5¼", hand thrown, green metallic crystalline glaze, marked **165.00**

OCCUPIED JAPAN

History: At the end of World War II, the Japanese economy was devastated. To secure needed hard currency, the Japanese pottery industry produced thousands of figurines and other knickknacks for export. From the beginning of the American occupation until April 28, 1952, these objects were marked "Japan," "Made in Japan," "Occupied Japan," and "Made in Occupied Japan." Only pieces marked with the last two designations are of strong interest to Occupied Japan collectors. The first two marks also were used at other time periods.

The variety of products is endless—ashtrays, dinnerware, lamps, planters, souvenir items, toys, vases, etc. Initially it was the figurines which attracted the largest number of collectors; today many collectors focus on non-figurine material.

References: Gene Florence, *The Collector's Encyclopedia Of Occupied Japan Collectibles,* Collector Books, 1976, 1982 edition; Gene Florence, *The Collector's Encyclopedia Of Occupied Japan Collectibles,* 2nd series, Collector Books, 1979, 1982 revision.

Collectors' Club: Occupied Japan Collectors Club, 18309 Faysmith Avenue, Torrance, CA 90504.

Additional Listings: See *Warman's Americana & Collectibles* for more examples.

Bisque
Ashtray, 2¼", heart shape, hp, floral sprays, white ground **12.00**
Bookends, pr, 5½", Oriental man and woman **35.00**
Creamer, figural cow **20.00**
Figure
  3¹⁄₁₂", frog **15.00**
  6½", boy standing by fence **20.00**
  7 x 5", horse and colt **18.00**
  Miniature, pitcher, multicolored applied floral spray, pink ground ... **8.00**
Planter, 6", figural, peasant girl standing beside leaf covered planter .. **35.00**
Shelf Sitter, 4¾", Oriental girl, green **12.00**
Vase, 7", ftd, emb floral dec **18.00**
Wall Pocket, 5", cuckoo clock, orange luster, pine cone weights **12.00**

Figurine, couple, 4¾", woman wears green dress, man wears maroon coat and blue pants, $15.00.

Celluloid
Doll Carriage, 2¾" h, pink and blue, movable hood, Acme **24.00**
Figure, Betty Boop, 6", blond hair, movable arms **24.00**
Toy, wind-up
  Boy with tin suitcase **45.00**
  Lion **32.00**
Metal
Ashtray, 6¾", chrome plated, pierced floral rim **10.00**
Binoculars, Egyptian figures, emb .. **32.00**
Candy Dish, pedestal base **10.00**
Cigarette Lighter, miniature camera with tripod **40.00**
Harmonica, butterfly shape **20.00**
Jewelry Box, piano shape, silvered . **18.00**
Nut Dish, 6", floral borders **10.00**
Pincushion, figural, shoe, silver finish, red velvet cushion **15.00**
Plate, 4½", pierced scalloped fancy rim, silvered metal **12.00**
Vase, 6", SP, Art Deco style, stylized blossoms, ftd **25.00**
Papier Mache
Nodder, rabbit, sitting **35.00**
Tray, 10½", rect, floral dec **50.00**
Porcelain
Child's Tea Set, 24 pcs, white, floral dec **100.00**
Creamer and Sugar, rose, pink, and white **24.00**
Cup and Saucer, Blue Willow pattern **35.00**
Dish, 5", triangular, handled, gold trim **20.00**
Figure, 3", cherub, playing drum, pierced pedestal base **10.00**
Honey Pot, 4½", black Mammy, head lifts off, spoon as tong, holding spoon and frying pan **35.00**
Humidor, cov with Foo Dog finial, 3 ftd, artist sgd **50.00**

Incense Burner, cobalt blue, floral
   dec, gold trim 18.00
Lamp, figural, Colonial man and
   woman, pr 65.00
Planter, figural, shoe, floral dec 18.00
Plaque, ducks in flight 18.00
Plate, 7½", Ambassador pattern . . . 8.00
Platter, 14", oval, Blue Willow pattern 18.00
Rice bowl, 6", emb dragon 25.00
Salt, master, figural, swan 18.00
Salt and Pepper Shakers, Negro
   chefs, 3½" w, pr 30.00
Sauce, Willow pattern, pink 5.00
Tea Set, cov teapot, four cups and
   saucers, white, small pink roses,
   green leaves 65.00
Wall Pocket, 1½ x 2¾ x 4", Colonial
   woman in balcony 15.00

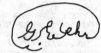

G.E.OHR, BILOXI.

OHR POTTERY

History: Ohr pottery was produced by George
E. Ohr in Biloxi, Mississippi. There is some dis-
crepancy as to when he actually established his
pottery. Some suggest 1878; but, Ohr's autobiog-
raphy indicates 1883. In 1884 Ohr exhibited 600
pieces of his work, indicating that he had been
working for some time.

Ohr's techniques included twisting, crushing,
folding, denting, and crinkling thin walled clay into
odd, grotesque, and sometimes graceful forms.
Much of his early work is signed with an impressed
stamp of his name and location in block letters.
His later work, often marked with the flowing script
designation "G E Ohr," was usually left unglazed.

In 1906, Ohr closed the pottery and stored over
6,000 pieces as his legacy to his family. He hoped
it would be purchased by the U.S. Government,
which never happened. The entire collection remained in storage until it was rediscovered in
1972.

Today Ohr is recognized as one of the leading
potters in the American Art Pottery movement.
Some greedy individuals have taken the later unglazed pieces and covered them with poor quality
glazes, in hopes of making them more valuable.
These pieces, usually with the flowing script mark,
do not have "stilt marks" on the bottom.

Bank, 3¾", acorn shape 90.00
Bowl, 10½ x 2½", three openings, red
   clay, script sgd 150.00
Candlestick
   3⅞", dark and light green mottled
   glaze, marked 175.00

**Puzzle Mug, 4⅝" h, pink and mottled
green glaze, $775.00.**

4½", twisted body, handles, gunmetal
   black 425.00
Inkwell, 4" d, "Merry Xmas 1893 from
   Biloxi" 120.00
Jug, 5", bisque, tapered, script sgd . . . 350.00
Mug
   Single handle, gunmetal gray 350.00
   Three handles, green, brown, and
   gray 700.00
Novelty
   Log Cabin, 3¾ x 2¼", unglazed oys-
   ter white clay 100.00
   Puzzle Mug, 3½", mottled green high
   glaze, pressed rope and leaf han-
   dle, screw under handle, script sgd
   "G E Ohr" 375.00
   Seashell, 4½ x 4", mustard yellow
   glaze, marked 85.00
Pitcher
   5", bulbous, off center handle, brown
   irid, imp mark 415.00
   8¼", black speckled dark mustard,
   handle, imp mark 600.00
Teapot, 4⅛", unglazed bisque, shading
   orange to cream, marked 85.00
Vase
   3", metallic black, leathery bottom,
   concave shoulder 165.00
   3¾", raspberry and brown, wide cylinder, ftd, imp mark 300.00
   4½", dark green speckles, yellow and
   light green ground, imp mark 250.00
   5⅛", thin, unglazed bisque, taupe luster, marked 225.00
   6", deep moss green, narrow vertical
   ridges on one side, metallic black
   smooth surface on other, three
   prong kiln stilt on base, marked . . 400.00
   6¾", bottle shape, green gunmetal
   top to moss speckle 220.00
   7", thick walled, dark blue gloss . . . 250.00

8¾", lightly crimped, light green glaze, brushings of brown and gun-metal, marked **325.00**

OLD IVORY CHINA

History: Old Ivory derives its name from the background color of the china. It was made in Silesia, Germany, during the second half of the 19th century. Marked pieces usually have a pattern number (pattern names are not common) and the crown Silesia mark.

Reference: Susan and Al Bagdade, *Warman's English & Continental Pottery & Porcelain, 1st Edition,* Warman Publishing Co., Inc., 1987.

Plate, 8", marked "VIII," $40.00.

Berry Set, #75, 7 pcs	**225.00**
Bowl	
6½", cereal, #15	**40.00**
9½", #28	**95.00**
Buffet Tray, #200	**80.00**
Cake Plate, #84, open handles	**85.00**
Celery Tray, #84	**80.00**
Chocolate Pot, #11	**350.00**
Creamer, #8	**65.00**
Cup and Saucer, #10	**48.00**
Mustard Pot, #16	**90.00**
Nappy, 6½", #84	**48.00**
Plate	
7½", #11, Clarion	**24.00**
8", #16	**35.00**
9½", #6, Elysee	**100.00**
Platter, #84, 11½"	**150.00**
Relish Tray, #200	**60.00**

Salt and Pepper Shakers, pr	
#15	**100.00**
#28	**110.00**
Soup Plate, #84	**45.00**
Sugar, cov	
#15	**50.00**
#84	**35.00**
Teapot, #84	**285.00**
Toothpick, #10	**135.00**
Vegetable Dish, #84	**60.00**

OLD PARIS CHINA

History: Old Paris china is fine quality porcelain made by various French factories located in and about Paris during the 18th and 19th centuries. Some pieces were marked, but the majority was not. Characteristics of this type of china include fine porcelain, beautiful decorations and gilding. Favorite colors were dark maroon, deep cobalt blue, and a deep green.

Reference: Susan and Al Bagdade, *Warman's English & Continental Pottery & Porcelain, 1st Edition,* Warman Publishing Co., Inc., 1987.

Additional Listing: Continental China and Porcelain (General).

Bowl, basketweave, paw feet, gold floral dec	**200.00**
Cache Pots, 9½", floral scene on one side, courting scene on reverse, gilding, green ground, pr	**1,500.00**
Calling Card Tray, 6", floral dec, maroon ground	**75.00**
Clock Case, 20", surmounted by group of lovers, richly dec clothes, minor damage, c1830	**525.00**
Dessert Service, Royal House of Savoy coat of arms dec, mid 19th C, 43 pcs	**2,400.00**

Compote, 9¼" d at top, 6¾" h, hand painted, gold trim, white ground, $75.00.

Figure, 6" h, recumbent lion, faux lapis
glaze, gilded base, pr **1,800.00**
Jardiniere and Stand, portraits, green
ground, small chips, gilding rubbed,
mid 19th C, pr **1,650.00**
Inkwell, 4¾" h, fountain shape **1,200.00**
Patch Box, scalloped, emb gold dec,
white ground **65.00**
Tea Service, landscape dec, gilding,
c1800, 18 pcs **600.00**
Tray, 13½", sq, mythological, iron-red
Duc d'Angouleme, factory mark,
c1800 . . . . **450.00**
Urn
11½", campana form, scenes of soldiers in landscape, applied handles
and satyr masks, gilding, late 19th
C, pr **350.00**
15" h, landscape panel, gilded field,
stepped base, early 19th C, pr . . . **2,600.00**
Vase
11", campana form, elongated bisque
floral dec neck, everted rim, flower
filled basket dec, gilt C-scroll and
flowerhead borders, sq black slate
plinth, c1850, pr **1,000.00**
14", cov, dec panels on rose pompa-
dour ground, replacement knops,
minor restoration, c1870, pr **775.00**

OLD SLEEPY EYE

History: Sleepy Eye, a Sioux Indian chief who
reportedly had a droopy eye, gave his name to
Sleepy Eye, Minnesota, and one of its leading flour
mills. In the early 1900s Old Sleepy Eye Flour
offered four Flemish gray heavy stoneware premiums, decorated in cobalt blue: a straight-sided
butter crock, curved salt bowl, stein, and vase. The
premiums were made by Weir Pottery Company,
later to become Monmouth Pottery Company, and
finally to emerge as the present-day Western Stoneware Company of Monmouth, Illinois.

Additional pottery and stoneware pieces were
issued. Forms included five sizes of pitchers (4,
5½, 6½, 8, and 9 inches), mugs, steins, sugar
bowls, and tea tiles (hot plates). Most were cobalt
blue on white, but other glaze hues, such as
browns, golds, and greens, were used.

Old Sleepy Eye also issued many other items,
including bakers' caps, lithographed barrel covers,
beanies, fans, multicolored pillow tops, postcards,
trade cards, etc. Production of Old Sleepy Eye
stoneware ended in 1937.

In 1952 Western Stoneware Company made a
22 and 40 ounce stein in chestnut brown glaze
with a redesigned Indianhead. From 1961 to 1972
gift editions, dated and signed with a Maple Leaf
mark, were made for the Board of Directors and
others within the company. Beginning in 1973,
Western Stoneware Company issued an annual

limited edition stein, marked and dated, for collectors.

Reference: Elinor Meugnoit, *Old Sleepy Eye*,
published by author, 1979.

Collectors' Club: Old Sleepy Eye Collectors
Club, Box 12, Monmouth, IL 61462. Dues: $5.00.
Sleepy Eye Newsletter (bimonthly).

Reproduction Alert: Blue and white pitchers,
crazed, weighted, and often with a stamp or the
word "Ironstone" are the most copied. The stein
and salt bowl also have been made. Many reproductions come from Taiwan.

A line of fakes, new items which never existed,
includes an advertising pocket mirror with miniature flour barrel label, small glass plates, fruit jars,
toothpick holders, glass and pottery miniature
pitchers, and salt and pepper shakers. One mill
item has been made, a sack marked as though it
were old but of a size that could not possibly hold
the amount of flour indicated.

Advisors: David and Betty Hallam.

Sign, 13⅝ x 19", lithographed tin, cardboard back, New York Metal Sign
Works, $1,250.00.

MILL ITEMS

Calendar, 1903 . . . . **425.00**
Cookbook, loaf of bread shape **250.00**
Fan, diecut, Indian Chief, c1900 . . . . . **175.00**
Flour Sack, cloth, multicolored indian,
red letters **275.00**
Label, egg crate **20.00**
Match Holder, white **850.00**
Postcard, "Sleepy Eye Monument" . . . **50.00**
Teaspoon, Indian head handle **100.00**
Thimble, aluminum, "Old Sleepy Eye
Flour" **200.00**

OLD SLEEPY EYE CLUB CONVENTION ITEMS

1977 Mug **175.00**
1983 Pitcher **100.00**

POTTERY AND STONEWARE

Butter Crock, Flemish	425.00
Mug, 4¼", blue and white	150.00
Mustache Cup, cobalt blue and white, Western Stoneware Co	2,500.00
Pitcher, blue and white	
#1	125.00
#3	200.00
#5	275.00

Pitcher, 6¼", cobalt on cream, $200.00.

Salt Crock, 6½" d, 4" h, blue on gray	375.00
Stein, 7¾", Western Stoneware Co	
Blue and white	500.00
Brown on gold	675.00
Sugar, 3", blue and white	500.00
Vase	
8½", Indian and cattails, Flemish	350.00
9", blue on gray, Weir Pottery	175.00

ONION MEISSEN

History: The blue onion or bulb pattern is of Chinese origin and depicts peaches and pomegranates, not onions. It was first made in the 18th century by Meissen, hence the name Onion Meissen.

Factories in Europe, Japan, and elsewhere copied the pattern. Many still have the pattern in production, including the Meissen factory now located in East Germany.

Note: Prices given are for pieces produced between 1870 and 1930. Many pieces are marked with a company's logo; after 1891 the country of origin is indicated on imported pieces. Early Meissen examples bring a high premium.

Platter, 25", imp mark, $500.00.

Bone Dish	60.00
Bouillon Cup and Underplate	42.00
Bowl	
6"	40.00
9"	135.00
Butter Dish, cov	40.00
Butter Pat	90.00
Candle Snuffer, 10¼", SP handle	62.00
Cheese Board	45.00
Cheese Dish, cov	150.00
Coffeepot, 9½"	160.00
Compote, 9" h, 9" d, reticulated rim	350.00
Creamer, 3½"	50.00
Cup and Saucer	
Coffee	40.00
Tea	30.00
Darner, wooden handle	75.00
Dipper, wooden handle	100.00
Dish, 10½", round, deep, imp mark	55.00
Egg Cup	225.00
Fish Plate, pierced drain insert	225.00
Fruit Knives, set of 6	85.00
Funnel, 4¾"	85.00
Knife Rest	30.00
Ladle, 4 x 2", wood handle	135.00
Lemon Dish	35.00
Match Holder	35.00
Mustache Cup	85.00
Pastry Wheel	135.00
Pitcher, water, 7", rococo molded, c1860	225.00
Plate	
6"	35.00
9"	48.00
10½"	70.00
Platter	
12", oval, marked	160.00
17"	225.00
19"	250.00
Pot de Creme	50.00
Relish Dish	
6½ x 4¾", oblong, octagonal	45.00
11¾ x 7¼", scalloped edge	85.00
Rolling Pin	150.00
Salt Box	135.00
Sauce Dish, 4¾"	30.00
Soup Bowl, 9"	60.00

Soup Tureen, cov, 10½ x 14″, rose finial	**250.00**
Spill Vase, 5½″, scroll feet	**65.00**
Stein, ½ L, matching conical lid, dwarf	
thumb lift	**500.00**
Sugar, cov, melon ribbed, late 19th C .	**100.00**
Tea Strainer, 5″, l, handle	**65.00**
Teapot, 10″, rose finial, 19th C	**200.00**
Vegetable Dish, cov	
8½″	**90.00**
10″, sq	**130.00**
14″, divided	**225.00**
Vinegar Jar, stopper	**225.00**

OPALESCENT GLASS

History: Opalescent glass is a clear or colored glass with milky white decorations which show a fiery or opalescent quality when held to light. The effect was achieved by applying bone ash chemicals to designated areas while a piece was still hot and then refiring it at tremendous heat.

There are three basic categories of opalescent glass: (1) Blown (or mold blown) patterns, e.g., Daisy & Fern and Spanish Lace; (2) Novelties, pressed glass patterns made in limited pieces which often included unusual shapes such as Corn or Trough; and (3) Pattern (pressed) glass.

Opalescent glass was produced in England in the 1870s. Northwood began the American production in 1897 at its Indiana, Pennsylvania, plant. Jefferson, National Glass, Hobbs, and Fenton soon followed.

Reference: William Heacock, *Encyclopedia of Victorian Colored Pattern Glass: Book II, Opalescent Glass from A to Z*, Antique Publications, 2nd ed., 1977.

Additional Listings: See Pattern Glass for pressed opalescent patterns.

BLOWN

Biscuit Jar, Spanish Lace, vaseline . . .	**275.00**
Bottle, Bull's Eye, blue	**115.00**
Bowl	
Consolidated Criss-Cross, cranberry,	
8″ d	**150.00**
Roman Rosette, lacy, Sandwich, 6¾″	**200.00**
Seaweed, white, 9″	**60.00**
Butter Dish, cov, Spanish Lace, blue . .	**250.00**
Celery Vase	
Consolidated Criss-Cross, Rubena,	
satin finish	**250.00**
Daffodils, blue	**75.00**
Ribbed Coin Spot, cranberry	**150.00**
Creamer, Reverse Swirl, blue	**75.00**
Cruet, Herringbone, orig clear teardrop	
stopper, blue	**115.00**
Curtain Tie Back, 5¾″, fiery, lacy, young	
woman seated holding straw hat,	
Boston & Sandwich Glass Co	**150.00**

Finger Bowl	
Hobb's Hobnail, cranberry	**50.00**
Spanish Lace, blue	**48.00**
Lamp	
Christmas Snowflake, cranberry . . .	**300.00**
Reverse Swirl, cranberry, satin base	**425.00**
Snowflake, cranberry, hand type . . .	**500.00**
Miniature Lamp	
Coin Spot, (Smith #510), 8¾″	**625.00**
Spanish Lace, 4″, blue	**225.00**
Mustard, Reverse Swirl, vaseline	**50.00**

Pitcher, 8¼″ h, light blue spatter design, solid blue handle, Hobbs, Brockunier & Co., $160.00.

Pitcher, water	
Arabian Nights, cranberry	**325.00**
Buttons and Braids, blue	**80.00**
Christmas Snowflake, cranberry . . .	**375.00**
Daffodils, green	**185.00**
Hobb's Hobnail, cranberry, heavy	
opalescent, opal handle	**200.00**
Poinsettia, blue, tankard, 13″	**200.00**
Spanish Lace, ruffled rim, blue	**250.00**
Rose Bowl, Daisy and Fern, blue	**50.00**
Salt Shaker, Consolidated Criss-Cross,	
cranberry, orig top	**85.00**
Spooner	
Consolidated Criss-Cross, cranberry	**125.00**
Spanish Lace, cranberry	**75.00**
Sugar, cov	
Bubble Lattice, cranberry	**125.00**
Reverse Swirl, blue	**125.00**
Stripe, cranberry	**80.00**
Sugar Shaker, orig top	
Bubble Lattice, blue	**135.00**
Poinsettia, blue	**165.00**
Reverse Swirl, cranberry	**150.00**
Syrup Pitcher, orig top	
Bubble Lattice, canary yellow	**150.00**
Coin Spot & Swirl, white	**65.00**
Daisy in Criss-Cross, blue	**250.00**
Poinsettia, blue	**450.00**

Toothpick
  Swirl, blue 100.00
  Windows, cranberry 115.00
Tumbler
  Arabian Nights, blue 60.00
  Consolidated Criss-Cross, white ... 50.00
  Herringbone, cranberry 75.00
  Poinsettia, green 35.00
  Spanish Lace, cranberry 45.00
Water Set, water pitcher and six tum-
  blers, 7 pcs
  Arabian Nights, blue 400.00
  Button and Braids, blue 300.00
  Daffodils, blue 650.00

NOVELTIES

Barber Bottle
  Daisy and Fern, vaseline, 8½″ 75.00
  Stars and Stripes, white 100.00
Bowl
  Beaded Stars, green, 8½″ 40.00
  Jolly Bear, white 75.00
Bushel Basket, blue 75.00
Compote, Dolphin, vaseline 65.00
Epergne, 9½ x 19½″, four lilies, green,
  ruffled base, applied glass spiral trim 325.00
Rose Bowl
  Fancy Fantails, cranberry, four clear
    applied feet 650.00
  Leaf Chalice, green pedestal 50.00
Vase
  4″, melon ribbed body, vaseline, ap-
    plied clear leaf feet, flower petal top 65.00
  10″, Piasa Bird, blue 50.00

OPALINE GLASS

History: Opaline glass was a popular mid to late 19th century European glass. The glass has a certain amount of translucency and often is found decorated in enamel designs and trimmed in gold.

Apothecary Jar, 12¾″, cov, jade green,
  white pedestal 100.00
Basket, deep blue dec, gold enamel .. 150.00
Biscuit Jar, hp, florals and bird dec,
  brass lid and bail handle 150.00
Box, 5½ x 3⅝ x 4¼″, brass fittings ... 125.00
Chalice, white, Diamond Point pattern . 25.00
Cheese Dish, cov, white ground, gold
  enamel dec 180.00
Cologne Bottle, 8¾″, jade green, gold
  ring dec, orig stopper 85.00
Creamer, shaded yellow to white, pink
  roses and blue forget-me-nots, SP
  rim and handle 125.00
Dresser Jar
  5 x 3⅜ x 4⅛″, jade green, cut dia-

Jewel Box, 4″ d, 2½″ h, hinged lid, gold enameling, some cutting, pale green ground, French, $150.00.

  mond designs, gold floral dec, gold
    plated hinge and mounting 200.00
  7½ x 5½ x 5½″, egg shape, blue,
    heavy gold dec 200.00
Ewer, 13¼″, white, Diamond Point pattern 125.00
Finger Bowl, matching underplate, powder blue 125.00
Miniature, wash bowl and pitcher, powder blue, gilt dec 75.00
Perfume Bottle
  2¾″, blue ground, gold flowers and
    leaves, matching stopper 45.00
  4″, blue ground, gold, white, and yel-
    low dec, matching stopper 65.00
  5½″, powder blue ground, gold dec,
    orig stopper 30.00
Pitcher, 4¼″, pink ground, applied white
  handle 70.00
Posy Holder, 8″, blue, figural hand holding small vase, ruffled rim 75.00
Rose Bowl, 4″, opaque green, gilt strawberries, flowers, and leaves dec ... 50.00
Salt, 3¾″, jade green, marked "Turn-
  bridge, England" 75.00
Sugar, cov, shaded yellow to white, pink
  roses and blue forget-me-nots, SP
  cover, rim, and handle 150.00
Toothpick, lavender, small ball feet ... 75.00
Tumble-Up, carafe, tumbler, and underplate, pale green ground, gold beading, black and white jeweled dec, 3
  pcs 300.00
Vase
  4″, blue ground, gold flowers and
    leaves, white beading 50.00
  5½″, Jack-in-the-Pulpit, robin's egg
    blue, applied amber feet 75.00
  8″, jade green, gauffered rim, French 60.00
  13″, urn shape, flared rim, blue
    ground, enameled blue flowers, gilt
    trim, pr 335.00

ORIENTAL RUGS

History: The history of oriental rugs or carpets dates back to 3,000 B.C.; but, it was in the 16th century that they became prevalent. The rugs originated in the regions of Central Asia, Iran (Persia), Caucasus, and Anatolia. Early rugs can be classified into basic categories: Iranian, Caucasian, Turkoman, Turkish, and Chinese. Later India, Pakistan, and Iraq produced rugs in the oriental style.

The pattern name is derived from the tribe which produced the rug, e.g., Iran is the source for Hamadan, Herez, Sarouk, Tabriz, and others.

When evaluating an oriental rug, age, design, color, weave, knots per square inch, and condition determine the final value. Silk rugs and prayer rugs bring higher prices.

References: Linda Kline, *Beginner's Guide To Oriental Rugs*, Ross Books, 1980; Ivan C. Neff and Carol V. Maggs, *Dictionary of Oriental Rugs*, Van Nostrand Reinhold Company, 1979.

Reproduction Alert: Beware! There are repainted rugs on the market.

Anatolia, Turkey, 66 x 44″, double prayer rug, Mirhab border, $1,200.00.

Akstafa, East Caucasus, 6'7″ x 3'2″, prayer, ivory mihrab in overall design of polychrome ascending boteh beneath brick-red prayer arch, black-brown stylized scorpion border, barber pole and reciprocal guard borders, c1900 .... **2,600.00**

Arak, Persia, 17'2″ x 10', red field, all-over symmetry of floral elements, multicolored slant leaf primary border **2,750.00**

Ardebil, Persia, 12'10″ x 9'8″, salmon field, center ivory medallion flanked by two small medallions and geometric motifs within ivory primary border **675.00**

Beshir, Persia, 46½ x 5'11″, silk, compartmented field with geometric floral pattern, madder, indigo, yellow, beige, ivory, and brown, sgd "Noor" **1,750.00**

Chinese
3'2″ x 2'1″, silk, woven in Kashan design, rose field, beige medallion .. **500.00**
11'6″ x 8'4″, white field, floral roundel framed by floral swags **1,000.00**

Fereghan, Kelei, North Persia, 17'1″, x 6', midnight blue field with all-over herati design, ivory angular flowering vine border flanked by brick-red starflower guard borders, c1900 ...... **3,850.00**

Hereke, Turkey, 16'5″ x 10'8″, all-over floral repeat, ivory field framed in red primary border and three pairs of guards **2,000.00**

Heriz, 9'10″ x 13'7″, silk, all-over floral and palmette design, blue, beige, rust, indigo, ivory, and green, some damage **4,675.00**

Isparta, Turkey, 16' x 12', red field, over-all design of detached florals and vases **725.00**

Karadjo, Northwest Persia, 9'3″ x 3'9″, runner, royal blue field, six central star medallions with polychrome geometric, floral, and animal motifs, ivory crab border, saffron and rust guard strips, c1880 .... **1,600.00**

Kashan, 14'9″ x 10'3″, dark blue palmette and flower filled field centering concentric ivory and red medallions anchored with palmettes, red boteh and blossom main border **4,500.00**

Kerman, Persia, 18' x 11'2″, ivory millefleur field with alternating rows of ivory and indigo medallions, ivory primary border, signature cartouche .. **6,650.00**

Kurd, northwest Persia, 7' x 4'3″, brown field, diagonal rows of stepped polychrome flowerheads, rust border, running dog guard border, c1875 ..... **1,200.00**

Lillihan, Persia, 22'2″ x 3', runner, red field, palmettes and flowering branches, reduced size **825.00**

Mahai, 10'3″ x 7'8″, rose herati field, gray waterbug palmette main border **1,300.00**

Nain, Persia, 6'8″ x 4', indigo meander field centering off white and pale blue medallion, ivory spandrels and border **1,000.00**

Pakistani, 9'9″ x 2'8″, runner, woven in Turkoman design, two rows of Tekke guls **300.00**

Saraband, Persia, 19'6″ x 3'4″, runner, abrashed red field, rows of boteh within ivory primary border **700.00**

Sarouk, Persia
6'5″ x 4'3″, ivory field within indigo spandrels, rose herati pattern pole medallion, indigo border **2,750.00**
18' x 11'2″, burgundy field, all-over

floral design, indigo primary border,
yellow and rose guards **5,000.00**
Siraz, Persia, 5'7" x 3'10", rose field,
row of three stepped medallions
within brown spandrels and ivory bor-
der **350.00**
Southpersian Kelim, 6'8" x 4'4", rows of
hexagonal and diamond shaped
medallions **400.00**
Sultanabad, 14'1" x 10'11", brick-red
field centering ivory medallion, dark
and light blue spandrels, red palmette
main guard borders, multiple guard borders **1,800.00**
Tabiz, 6'6" x 4'8", rust arabesque field,
ivory center medallion, green main
border **800.00**
Teheran, 7' x 5", brick-red latticework
field, realistically drawn plants, blue
main border with similar reserve . . . **2,000.00**
Tekke, 9'11" x 6'9", brick-red field with
four rows of Tekke guls flanked by
minor guls, sunburst variation border
with horizontally striped end panels,
c1900 . . . . **2,800.00**
Yomud Torba, 3'7" x 1'7", red-brown
field, two kepse guls framed by half
and quarter guls, ivory main border . **600.00**
Zenjan, Persia, 6'7" x 3'8", diamond
medallion on madder trellis field, dark
brown geometric floral main border . **375.00**

ORIENTALIA

History: Orientalia is a term used to apply to
objects made in the Orient, which encompasses
the Far East, Asia, China, and Japan. The diversity
of cultures produced a variety of objects and
styles.

Reference: Sandra Andacht, *Oriental Antiques
& Art: An Identification And Value Guide,* Wallace-
Homestead, 1987.

Periodical: *The Orientalia Journal, P. O. Box
94, Little Neck, NY 11363. Bimonthly newsletter.*
Subscription: $15.00.

Additional Listings: Canton, Celadon, Cloisonne, Fitzhugh, Nanking, Netsukes, Rose Medallion, Japanese Prints, and other categories.

Basket, Japanese, Ikebana, ovoid,
loosely woven bamboo and reed
body, high loop handle, forked sup-
ports, sgd "Kokosai," 16" h **275.00**
Bowl
Chinese, Ming Dynasty, Longquan,
celadon, scalloped edge, center
with stylized peony, molded petal
form cavetto under flattened
shaped rim, burnt orange foot,
13¼" **500.00**
Japanese, plique a'jour, inverted bell

shape, overall pattern of white blossoming plum branches on apple
green ground, rim and high ring
foot with silver borders, 5" d **900.00**
Korean, Koryo, shallow rounded
sides, int. inlaid with four concentric
bands, crackled gray-green glaze,
7" **200.00**
Box
Chinese, late 19th C, lobed, cloisonne, each face dec with taotie
mask of deep green cloisonnes and
multicolored disintegrated zoom-
orphic tendrils, turquoise ground,
gilt metal stem and branch finial, 12
x 10½" **365.00**
Japanese, metal, enamel and mixed
metal overlay, rect, raised design of
flowering wisteria and peony blossoms, brightly colored translucent
enamel work, silver, shakudo, and
gold metal work, bronze ground,
sgd "Hideyuki," gold inlaid seal, silvered int., 1⅜ x 4¾ x 3¼" **275.00**
Mongolian, sq, ftd, silver covered, fitted with flat corner russet skinned
jade panels flanking principal sides
with turquoise and coral inlay, white
jade panels carved with sage reversed by inscription, alternating
sides with high set loop handles,
loose rings, orange skin nehprite
qilong, cov with circular chaised
corner medallions of demons flanking central inscribed rust colored
jade disk, green stone finial, 5⅞" h **2,000.00**
Brush Pot, Meiji Period, Shibayama
style, ivory, curved tusk, scene of
small birds, butterflies, and pair of
cranes among flowering wisteria
vines, leafy bamboo stalks, blossoming peony, wild pinks and flowers, reverse with long tailed bird beneath
fruiting loquat tree, gold and silver hiramaki-e, takamaki-e, and gold gyobu,
additional inlay of carved and incised
coral, mother of pearl, aogai, tortoise
shell, and semi-precious hardstone,
7⅝" h, pr **2,750.00**
Calligraphy Tablet, Chinese, Qing Dy-
nasty, spinach green made, white
mottling, black flecking, four rows of
Manchurian script, rect, 11⅛ x 4" . . **1,200.00**
Censer, Chinese, late 19th C, cloisonne,
Fang Ding form, deep bodied vessel,
two shaped reserves of scholar's implements on turquoise ground of
scrolling lotus, beige and pink enamels above animal mask legs, tiered
lid, gilt painted metal pierced "Cash"
emblems, 9½" h **225.00**
Charger, Chinese, polychrome enamel,

thick painted "Hundred Antiques" design, ruyi border, 14⅞" **250.00**

Clothing, Chinese
Apron, silk, late 19th C, green, front and back panels with couched gold dragons and phoenix, dragons on narrow pleats, 37¾", pr **800.00**

Robe, 19th C, silk, apricot ground, couched gold dragons, blue satin stitched clouds, Peking knotted emblems, 47" l **1,500.00**

Short jacket and trousers, silk brocade, orchid, wide blue and yellow borders, figural, bird, and floral motifs in satin and couched stitches, red brocade lining, aqua trousers with purple trim, blue embroidered figural and floral bands, blue cotton waist band, mid 18th C **200.00**

Cup and Saucer, Japanese, silver, double walled 2¾" d cup, flared rim, high splayed ring foot, repousse design of blossoming chrysanthemum sprigs, engraved ground of diamond patterned basketweave pattern, triangular faux bamboo handle, matching 4½" d saucer **225.00**

Ewer, Korean, Koryo Dynasty, globular, short shaped spout, double loop handle, short cylindrical neck, brown slip under gray celadon glaze, scroll of stylized flowering branch below wide shoulder petal border **1,250.00**

Fan
Chinese, painted continuous court scene of figures with inlaid textile robes, 10½" l, minor damage **200.00**

Japanese, Gyosai, Battling Frogs, painting of ink and colors on paper, wood fan sticks, sgd, 8½ x 14" ... **400.00**

Figure
Bodhisattva, Edo Period, giltwood, elongated torso, gilt bronze ornaments, face with crystal urna, high chigon, gilt bronze jeweled crown, almond shaped mandorla with low relief carving of cloud scrolls, double lotus base, high galleried hexagonal pedestal, 13" h **500.00**

Buddha, Thai, gilt bronze, standing figure, diaphanous robes, serene face, 12½" **450.00**

Dog, Chinese, 19th C, cloisonne, alert standing figure, gilt painted metal spiral curls along back, raised tail, turquoise ground, stylized fur and multicolored qilong shaped tendrils, face with star shaped cloisonnes below cap of dark green spiral wires, gilt metal ears and feet, 6½" **375.00**

Dragon, Japanese, silver, Meiji period, writhing, scaly body with sharp

jointed projections, flame-like appendages, convoluted posture, raised head, large gold inset eyes, open mouth, long curving whiskers, underside incised "Kunitoko," 16¾" l **6,125.00**

Gamma Sennin, ivory, slender figure stroking frog held on left hand, aged face, long incised beard, brocade patterned robe, wood base, inset plaque sgd "Shozan," 10⅛" h **400.00**

Maiden, Chinese, Tang Dynasty, straw glazed buff colored body, slender figure, high waisted court dress, high chigon, 8⅛" h **250.00**

Chair, arm, carved rosewood, $650.00.

Furniture
Bench, Chinese, Hongmu, late 19th C, rect paneled seat framed by carved backrest, carved row of floral panels set into four rect reserves, carved armrests, scalloped edge apron, high relief carving with Daoist emblems flanking peaches of longevity, scrolled supports, 34½ x 71 x 24" **850.00**

Cabinet, Chinese, rosewood, display type, rect, upper tier of staggered shelves next to single door, above two drawers over double doors, panels heavily carved with flowering lotus and bamboo branches, 72½ x 34½ x 13¼" **300.00**

Chair, Chinese, folding, carved, pierced relief backrest, dragon carved on fretwork **275.00**

Chest
Japanese, Meiji Period, Noh costume type, lacquered, front panel dec with scene of lotus pods and waterlife in gold takamaki-e, hir-

amaki-e, and togidashi shading to silver and black, dense nashiji ground, hinged top fitted with shakudo mounts etched in floral motifs, concave top, back with haga and blossoming iris, int. lined in Edo Period fabric, 24½ x 60 x 24½" **3,350.00**

Korean, storage, 19th C, rect top, two hinged sections, banded with iron bamboo shaped brackets, central hinged lockplate on front, iron U shaped handles, 22¼ x 58½ x 24½" **950.00**

Mizuya, Japanese, Meiji Period, two parts, upper section with four sliding drawers above pair of wire mesh sliding doors fitted with horizontal carved braces, mokko formed poles above group of five drawers, lower section with large compartment fitted with two vertical slatted doors at left flanked by row of two small drawers above four stacked drawers at right, 68¾ x 57½ x 19¾" **1,200.00**

Screen, Korean, c1900, six panel, each painted in ink and color on silk, series of Chinese scholars in mountain landscapes, sgd and sealed, each panel 18" w, 79" h . . **500.00**

Table, Chinese, Huang Huali, D shaped top, inset marble top, shaped frieze, turned legs, D stretcher, scroll feet, 33 x 34½" . . **700.00**

Table Screen, Shibayama, Meiji Period, two panel, rect panels with large reserve of roosters, hens, and chicks, carved and incised inlay of mother of pearl, aogai, tortoise shell, and ivory on ground of gyobu, fundame and nashiji lacquer techniques, inlaid cartouche reading Masayuki, lower horizontal section with blossoming plants, ftd ivory frame carved in low relief with plover and wave designs, silver fittings with floral design, reverse with gold, silver, and red hiramaki-e design of sparrows above leafy plants and butterflies, 12½" h **4,675.00**

Trunk, Chinese, export, red lacquer, gilt dec, scenes of one hundred children, garden landscape reserve bordered by diaper patterns and keyfret bands, front and sides penciled with calligraphy, floral blossoms and foliate tendrils, gilt metal base, 15 x 29 x 21 . . . . **500.00**

Inro, 19th C

Three Case, Shojusai, obverse and reverse dec with woven cane flower basket laden with kiku and ume sprays, gold and silver takamaki-e and hiramaki-e on bright red lacquer ground, turquoise ojime, red lacquer manju netsuke **2,225.00**

Four Case, Shunsho, Noh play rendition of the tale of Dojoji bell, red lacquer ground, bottom lacquered with dense gold nashiji, sgd "Shunsho saku," coral ojime, ivory figure of Noh dancer, sgd "Koma Bunsai" and "Jugyoku" on underside **9,350.00**

Five Case, elegant peacock on branch of blossoming sakura overlooking companion below, leaves overlaid in silver hiramaki-e, tortoise accents, gold highlights, reverse with group of chidori in flight, bright kinji surface **2,500.00**

Jar, dome cov, ovoid, oxblood flambe glaze, knob finial, 13" h, pr **500.00**

Kettle, Japanese, iron, cast with kabucha shape contour, two opposing abstracted animal mask jug handles, textured surface with raised design of live oak leaves, fitted curved lid, pierced jewel finial, 9⅝" l **275.00**

Lantern, Japanese, cast bronze, diamond shaped body, roof form top, 9" **125.00**

Mask, Japanese, Hannya, gilt and polychromed wood, female horned demon, heavy brows, gaping jaw thrust out, revealing fiercesome teeth, black disheveled hair, 10¼" l **600.00**

Pipe Case and Pouch, 19th C, lacquer, carved wooden case, long vertical groves, straw and brown color, overlaid in iroe takamaki-e, green and black leaf sakaki-like plant, linked to brown bead ojime to gray striped linen pouch, miniature blossoming peony, sgd "Issai" **375.00**

Plate, Meiji Period, Shibayama and silver mounts, scalloped edge cavetto with scene of two vases, blossoming peonies, chrysanthemums, fuji bakuma, kikyo, and chidori hovering, overlays of aogai, carnelian, horn, coral, and semi-precious hardstones on bright kinji ground, framed by nine petaled silver openwork border, each with sixteen petal chrysanthemum blossom, sgd "Kogyoku on underside with gilt metal plaque on nashiji ground, 11" d **3,100.00**

Rhinoceros Cup, Chinese, 18th C, blanc de chine, oval wide flaring mouth tapering inward to narrow foot, molded with sky and earth divisions, dragon chasing two flaming pearls above qilong and group of romping tigers, creamy white glazed surface, 6″ l, 3″ h **250.00**

Roof Tile, Chinese, Ming Dynasty, pottery, figural, lead green glaze with yellow and cream, modeled as demon riding fu lion, 22¼″ **3,000.00**

Seal, Chinese, jade, pale green, sq, carved with dragons, horned beasts, pierced, 4¼″ **1,600.00**

Stele, central Indian, 17th C, brown stone, two carved vertical panels, first with four attendant figures fronted by majara, seated female deity, lowest figure holding lotus padma and fly wisk chamara standing on dwarf, second panel with Visnu looking to small figure of earth goddess, small seated figure, 35½ x 9 x 6½″ **1,650.00**

Teapot
Chinese, Famille Verte, fluted, baluster body, straight spout, yellow sq handle, rect panels of blossoming branches, 7″ h **1,250.00**

Japanese, silver, compressed ovoid body, wide band of raised bosses, circular lid with pierced jewel finial bracket, loop handle, S shaped spout, base stamped "jungin (pure silver)," lid inscribed "Club Casbah, Kobe, Dec 14, 1948," 7¼″ h **600.00**

Textile, Chinese
Door Panel, 19th C, counted stitch, cream silk squares with figures of immortals, flowers, and birds, black satin borders, 82½ x 79½″ **1,500.00**

Pillow, Qianlong, Imperial, yellow brocade, central metallic gold dragon, other striding dragons on floral ground, peach, blue, and green, 26½″ **1,250.00**

Urn, Chinese, carved hardstone, baluster, flattened form, lion mask and loose ring at front, dragon heads biting tendrils, domed lid, 9″ **125.00**

Vase
Chinese, 19th C, Nephrite, jade, magnolia blossom, four small buds, curling stems, mottled gray-green and white, 4⅞″ **500.00**

Japanese, 37″ h, cloisonne, baluster, slightly sq sides, bright polychrome enamels with continuous scene of two cranes, large blossoming chrysanthemum plants, mirror black ground, abstract floral patterned bands at rim and foot **1,650.00**

Korean, Silla Dynasty, rounded body, wide cylindrical neck incised with three rows of wavy bands, ribs, olive green glaze, 7½″ h **300.00**

OVERSHOT GLASS

History: Overshot glass was developed in the mid-1800s. A gather of molten glass was rolled over the marver upon which had been placed crushed glass to produce overshot glass. The piece then was blown into the desired shape. The finished effect was a glass that was frosted or iced in appearance.

Early pieces mainly were made in clear. As the demand for colored glass increased, color was added to the base piece and occasionally to the crushed glass.

Pieces of overshot generally are attributed to the Boston and Sandwich Glass Co., although many other companies also made it as it grew in popularity.

Ice Bucket, 5⅛″ d at top, 5⅜″ h to rim, clear, flint glass, silver plated bail and rim, $85.00.

Basket, 4½ x 7″, scalloped, green, applied yellow flower and leaf, applied clear handle **150.00**

Bowl, petal top, blue **150.00**

Compote
8½ x 12¾″, rubina overshot bowl, white metal bronze finished figural standard **125.00**

9 x 8⅞″, applied gold dec cranberry serpent around stem **100.00**

9 x 14″, rubina overshot bowl, white metal bronze finished figural standard **150.00**

Custard Cup, pink, applied clear handle, Sandwich **50.00**

Dish, 6¼″, crimped edge, canary yellow, cranberry overshot **160.00**

Ewer, 13½″, trefoil top, clear, twisted rope handle, Sandwich **250.00**

Mug, 3″, clear, applied clear handle .. **20.00**

Pitcher
　　6″, bulbous, cranberry **115.00**
　　7½″, bulbous, clear **100.00**
　　8″, heavy enamel dec of white roses,
　　　　blue forget-me-nots, and green
　　　　leaves **125.00**
Vase, two handles, metal collar in-
　　scribed "Joseph Barn, Gloucester" . **175.00**

OWENS POTTERY

History: J. B. Owens began making pottery in 1885 near Roseville, Ohio. In 1891 he built a plant in Zanesville and in 1897 began producing art pottery. Not much art pottery was produced by Owens after 1907, when most of their production centered on tiles.

Owens Pottery, employing many of the same artists and designs of its two crosstown rivals, Roseville and Weller, can appear very similar to that of its competitors (i.e. Utopian—brown glaze; Lotus—light glaze; Aqua Verde—green glaze, etc.).

There were a few techniques used exclusively at Owens. These included Red Flame ware (slip decoration under a high red glaze) and Mission (over-glaze, slip decorations in mineral colors) depicting Spanish Mission scenes. Other specialities included Opalesce (semi-gloss designs in lustred gold and orange) and Coralene (small beads affixed to the surface of the decorated vases).

References: Paul Evans, *Art Pottery of the United States,* Everybodys Press, Inc., 1974; Ralph and Terry Kovel, *The Kovels' Collector's Guide to American Art Pottery,* Crown Publishers, Inc., 1974.

Bowl
　　3″, Aborigine, brown Indian designs,
　　　　redware **60.00**
　　4 x 6½″, frogskin, green, dimpled .. **140.00**
Creamer, 3½″, Aqua Verdi, green matte,
　　imp mark **65.00**
Inkwell, 3¾″, Light Weight, lime leaves,
　　brown ground, sgd **100.00**
Jardiniere, 9¼″, orange and cream
　　swirls, green ground, marked "JB
　　Owens/Art Nouveau/1005" **175.00**
Mug, 4½″, Utopian, cherries **75.00**
Pitcher, 12″, tankard, Utopian, goose-
　　berries, artist sgd **275.00**
Tile, 6″, relief foliage dec, matte green,
　　sgd **115.00**

Vase, 6″, Aborigine, $225.00.

Vase
　　5″, Chinese Translation, thick white
　　　　flowing glaze, marked **100.00**
　　6¾″, incised profile of woman's head,
　　　　chocolate brown ground, artist sgd
　　　　"Henri Deux" **200.00**
　　8″, bud, Utopian, floral design, artist
　　　　sgd "Martha Gray" **100.00**
　　11″, Lotus, morning glories dec, artist
　　　　sgd "Charles Fouts" **150.00**
　　14″, two handles, Art Nouveau, frol-
　　　　icking nudes and flowers, green,
　　　　white, and orange, brown ground,
　　　　raised gold base **500.00**

PAIRPOINT

History: The Pairpoint Manufacturing Co. was organized in 1880 as a silverplating firm in New Bedford, Massachusetts. The company merged with Mount Washington Glass Co. in 1894 and became the Pairpoint Corporation. The new company produced speciality glass items, often accented with metal frames.

Pairpoint Corp. was sold in 1938 and Robert Gunderson became manager. He operated it as the Gunderson Glass Works until his death in 1952. From 1952 until the plant closed in 1956, operations were maintained under the name Gunderson-Pairpoint. Robert Bryden reopened the glass manufacturing business in 1970, moving it back to the New Bedford area.

Reference: Leonard E. Padgett, *Pairpoint Glass,* Wallace-Homestead, 1979.

Additional Listings: See *Warman's Americana & Collectibles* for listings of modern Pairpoint Cup Plates.

Biscuit jar, 7 x 6″, hp, daisy dec, apricot
　　ground, molded bulbous base, SP
　　rim, cov, and bail handle, sgd and
　　numbered **300.00**

Centerpiece Set, green and gold, large bowl: 11″ d at top and 7″ h, small bowls: 4″ d at top, 3″ h, $300.00.

Bowl
8 x 6½″, cov, raised gold chrysanthemum blossoms and foliage, eggshell white ground, gold striped handles, fish finial, sgd and numbered 550.00
8½″, peppermint stick, satin, clear, overlay rose rim cut to clear stripes, engraved 125.00
8½ x 3½″, Ambero, heavy, textured ext., int. painted with trailing vines, three pink lotus blossoms, lush green leaves floating on pool of lime green water, sgd "Ambero L"   745.00
Box, 7¼ x 6″, hinged lid, enameled gold and silver iris and foliage, buff ground, sgd 450.00
Candlesticks, pr
4″, amethyst, clear controlled bubble ball connector 100.00
6″, Blue Swirl pattern, clear controlled bubble ball connector 185.00
Calling Card Receiver, 5″ d, engraved floral dec, clear controlled bubble ball connector to saucer base 125.00
Champagne, 5⅛″, Flambo pattern, crystal 50.00
Cologne Bottle, 8″, applied vertical cranberry ribbing, elaborate flower form cranberry and clear stopper 100.00
Compote
6″, amber, engraved florals 75.00
9¼″, cov, ruby, clear controlled bubble ball connector, ruby base, steeple bubble finial 125.00
Decanter, 10″, Old English pattern, quart, matching stopper 1,250.00
Demi-John, 12″, Basket pattern, quart, air-trap stopper 1,250.00
Hat, 4¼″, deep red, white with controlled bubbles, orig paper label . . .   75.00
Inkwell, 4″ d, clear, allover controlled bubbles, SS cap 200.00
Jewelry Box, 10″, hinged, cut, Viscaria pattern, opal flowers, thumbprint base   225.00
Lamp, table, 23⅝″ h, reverse painted

dome shaped shade, autumn village scene, patinated metal baluster form base, sgd and numbered 1,600.00
Napkin Ring, 5¼″, SP, figural, seated Cupid, posy holder, marked 325.00
Perfume Bottle, 5½″, heavy crystal, controlled bubbles 60.00
Punch Cup, cylindrical, flaring rim and low foot, vaseline, engraved grapes   30.00
Rose Bowl, 6½″, egg shape, enameled blue windmill scene, white opaline ground, c1890 . . . .   575.00
Urn, 14″, cov, Vintage pattern, amethyst   225.00
Vase
5½″, bud, amethyst, clear controlled bubble ball connector, orig label . .   100.00
7¾″, jack in the pulpit, ruby, enameled bird on pine bough 165.00
9″, Ambero, int. painted with scene of couple strolling down country lane, textured finish 750.00
15″, winged cherub in flowing pink drape with tray of peonies, reverse with spray of multicolored poppies, gold borders, powder blue rim shading to cobalt blue ground, applied cobalt blue openwork handles   1,250.00
Wine
5⅛″, flambe, red bowl, black stem, Rockwell silver design 150.00
12″, trumpet shape, clear controlled bubble ball connector 150.00

PAPERWEIGHTS

History: Although paperweights had their origin in ancient Egypt, it was in the mid-19th century that this art form reached its zenith. The classic period for paperweights was 1845–55 in France where the Clichy, Baccarat, and Saint Louis factories produced the finest examples of this art. Other weights made in England, Italy, and Bohemia during this period rarely matched the quality of the French weights.

In the early 150s New England Glass Co. in Cambridge, Massachusetts, and the Boston and Sandwich Glass Co. in Sandwich, Massachusetts, became the first American factories to make paperweights.

Popularity peaked during the classic period and faded toward the end of the 19th century. Paperweights were rediscovered nearly a century later in the mid-1900s. Contemporary weights still are made by Baccarat, Saint Louis, Perthshire, and by many studio craftsmen in the U.S. and Europe.

References: Paul Hollister, Jr., *The Encyclopedia of Glass Paperweights*, Paperweight Press, 1969; Leo Kaplan, *Paperweights*, published by author, 1985; George N. Kulles, *Identifying Antique Paperweights-Lampwork*, Paperweight Press, 1987; James Mackay, *Glass Paperweights*,

Facts on File, 1973; Edith Mannoni, *Classic French Paperweights*, Paperweight Press, 1984; L. H. Selman Ltd, *Collector's Paperweights: Price Guide and Catalogue,* Paperweight Press, 1983.

Additional Listings: See *Warman's Americana & Collectibles* for examples of advertising paperweights.

Antique, World's Columbian Exposition, 1892–93, Gillinder, $90.00.

ANTIQUE

Baccarat

Dogrose, 2½″, white petal with blue edge, star cut base, clear 875.00

Millefiori, scattered, 2⅛″, multicolored, one gridel rooster, white lace ground 325.00

Napoleon, Louis, 2½″, sulfide, clear . 160.00

Pansy, 3″, two purple and three lower ochre petals, millefiori center, single bud, ten green leaves and stalk, star cut base 250.00

Pompon, 3″, white flower, single bud, clear, six facets around sides, one on top, star cut base 1,400.00

Wheatflower, 2¼″, white petals spotted with blue, clear, star cut base . 2,000.00

Clichy

Millefiori, 3″, garland around white stardust center, clear 650.00

Pansy, 2⅝″, soft purple upper and lower petals shaded lighter at edges, lower with purple-striped yellow centers, nodding bird, clear 1,400.00

Posy, 3″, surrounded by garland of pastry mold canes, white muslin ground 1,500.00

Sodden Snow, 3″, multicolored pastry mold canes, opaque white ground 950.00

Swirl, 2″, miniature, turquoise and white, predominately red central pastry mold cane 950.00

New England Glass Company

Apple, 3″, molded, deep red shading to yellow, clear 750.00

Clematis, 2⅞″, double pink flowers with striated petals, white center, five green leaves, swirling white latticinio 1,700.00

Fruit, 2¾″ d, harvest of pears and cherries, eight green leaves, white latticinio ground 275.00

Mushroom, concentric circle, 3³⁄₁₆″, faceted with quatrefoils, multicolored, shamrocks, hearts, and millefiori canes, white torsade 325.00

Pear, 3″, russet, molded, clear 1,200.00

Poinsettia, 3⅜″, ten petals, five pale blue dots, and dew drops on petals, pebble ground 325.00

Pantin, Lilies of the Valley, 2⅝″, pink spray, thin pale amber stems, green leaves, clear 6,000.00

Saint Louis

Bouquet, 2⅞″, three blue flowers with yellow centers surrounded by garland of multicolored canes, clear ground 2,500.00

Chrysanthemum, 2¾″, pink with striped petals, four green leaves and stem, swirling white latticinio . 1,850.00

Fruit, 2¾″, peach, ripe and green pears, three cherries, and five green leaves resting on translucent swirling latticinio thread basket . . 500.00

Posy, 2⅝″, five florets, pink, ochre, pale and dark blue, and white, five green leaves, strawberry cut base 490.00

Sandwich

Floral, 2¾″ d, poinsettia type, five soft pink and white petals over five deep blue petals, green stem, three leaves, white latticinio ground . . . 400.00

Floral and Fruit, 3⅞″, red, white, and blue flowers, three pears, and two cherries, twenty green leaves, white latticinio ground 13,000.00

Pansy, 3″ d, clear, bull bloom, two pink, two cobalt, and one white and blue striped petal encircling a blue, pink, and white center cane, three green leaves, single stem 250.00

Poinsettia

2½″ d, blue, ten petal blossom, five jeweled green leaves, white latticinio ground 475.00

2⅞″, pink, twelve petals with green, white and pink center cane, five green leaves, green stem, dewlike air traps 725.00

Wild Rose, 3″ d, white, blue and pink striping, eight leaves on green stem 500.00

Val St. Lambert, cameo, 3¼", French Cameo, cranberry flowers, clear ground **300.00**

Whitefriars, millefiori, close concentric, pale blue, white, olive green, and pink, six facets around sides, one on top, clear **200.00**

MODERN

Ayotee, Rick
Cockatoo, yellow sulfur crest, deep blue translucent ground **350.00**
Snow Owl, perched on pine branch, moon on midnight ground, sgd . . **400.00**

Baccarat
John F. Kennedy, 2⅞" d, sulfide bust, black amethyst ground **90.00**
Mount Rushmore, 4⅛", sulfide, red over white overlay, clear blue base, dated 1976 . . . . **100.00**

Banford, Ray, Iris, 2½", red, white, and blue, green foliage, faceted, sgd Ray Banford **600.00**

Crider, swirls, blue and white, sgd . . . **100.00**

Modern, Charles Kaziun, pink floral center, cobalt blue ground, sgd, $350.00.

Charles Kaziun
1½" d, 2⅛" h, miniature, single rose, green stem, five green leaves, yellow spiral band, light blue ground shot with gold, pedestal base . . . **550.00**
1¾" d, turtle cane center, surrounded by ring of pink and white setup canes, enclosed by a blue spiral ring wrapped in white latticinio, ring ends meet at K signature cane, yellow-green ground shot with gold . **850.00**
1⅞" d, setup canes in center, surrounded by pink and white spiral ring, cobalt ground shot with gold **800.00**

2⅛" d, 3" h, pedestal, deep purple rose, four green leaves, blue and white K signature cane **1,850.00**
2⅜" d, triple cut overlay, blood red to white to clear **4,500.00**
2½" d, faceted, single pink and yellow flowers, star cut base, signature cane in center of three green leaves **1,950.00**
3¼" h, bottle, yellow flowers, long green leaves, mounted on amethyst ground shot with gold, sgd bottle and stopper **900.00**

Perthshire, penguin in hollow bubble, ice blue flash overlay **350.00**

Saint Louis
Faceted, 3" d, bust, Queen Elizabeth encircled in pink and white ring, green and white alternating setup canes, sgd, dated 2/6/53 . . . . **100.00**
Pansy, 3", faceted, white muslin ground, sgd S.L./1980 in red cane on back **250.00**

Stankard, Paul
Cactus, two yellow flowers and buds, stem, translucent dark blue ground **950.00**
Violets, wood, bouquet, purple and white flowers, green leaves and stem, clear ground **1,000.00**

Tarsitano, Debbie, Marsh Marigolds, four yellow flowers, nine deep veined green leaves and stem, clear ground, sgd **750.00**

Whittemore, F. D.
Bottle, miniature
4" h, amethyst and opaque white rose, four green leaves, yellow signature cane **375.00**
4¼" h, white rose resting on four green leaves, yellow signature cane **425.00**
4⅝", single yellow rose resting on four green leaves, yellow signature cane **425.00**
Rose, pedestal base
2½" h, lavender, four green leaves, yellow and black signature cane **100.00**
2¾", pink, four green leaves, yellow and black signature cane **150.00**
2⅞" h, pink, four green leaves, yellow and black signature **125.00**
3⅛" h, powder blue, four green leaves, yellow and black signature cane **175.00**

Paul Ysart
Butterfly, 3", single blue flower with white center, long green stem, eight leaves, mottled pink and white ground **250.00**
Flower
3", yellow and white, brown stem, three green leaves, setup pink

and white canes, deep amethyst
ground 450.00
3½", pink and white, red and white
center, brown stem, eight green
leaves, pink and white setup
canes, mounted on dark blue-
green ground 350.00

PAPIER MACHE

History: Papier Mache is made from a mixture
of wood pulp, glue, resin, and fine sand which is
subject to great pressure and then dried. The finished product is tough, durable, and heat resistant.
Various finishing treatments are used, such as
enameling, japanning, lacquering, mother-of-pearl
inlaying, and painting.

During the Victorian era Papier Mache articles
such as boxes, trays, and tables were in high fashion. Papier Mache also found use in the production
of banks, candy containers, masks, toys, and other
children's articles.

**Cup, 2½" h, floral dec, red band at top,
black on base, gold ground, made in
Russia, $30.00.**

Bank, 2 x 3 x 4¾", red and gold Oriental
dec, black ground 70.00
Candy Container
Angel, 10", fur, wax face, German .. 575.00
Rabbit, 9", glass eyes 45.00
Doll, 7½" h, Charlie Chaplin, head,
hands, and feet with orig polychrome
paint and cloth costume, tin ball and
socket body 235.00
Figure
Boy and dog, 3½" h, polychrome
paint, wood base 175.00
Lion, 4¼" h, orig polychrome paint . 75.00
Santa, 3½" 35.00

Jack-O-Lantern, 7" h, orange, printed
tissue paper screen, electric lamp,
bracket for battery 55.00
Mask, clown head, orig polychrome dec 110.00
Nodder, donkey, glass eyes 25.00
Pip Squeak
Baboon, 6½" h, brown flocked coat
with tan, gray, and white, reglued
to bellow, silent 220.00
Husky, 7" h, orig white paint with
green trim, repaired and reglued
bellow, silent 200.00
Lion, 4¼" h, orig yellow and tan paint,
leather bellow, silent 75.00
Turkey, 3½" h, orig polychrome paint,
bellow cov replaced, silent 275.00
Plate, 12" d, primitive cat painting,
marked "Patented August 8, 1880" . 35.00
Powder Box, lady, bouffant skirt, French 45.00
Roly Poly, clown, 4⅛" h, orig white and
blue paint, polychrome trim, green
ribbon around neck 60.00
Snuff Box
2¾" d, girl in dressing gown holding
mirror painted on lid 150.00
3⅝" d, naval battle on lid, chipped .. 35.00
Tea caddy, 4½" h, 4¾" l, 3" w, oval,
George III, black, turned ivory knop . 125.00
Tobacco Jar, figural, Mandarin 75.00
Toy, Santa, 6¾" h, spring, red felt coat
and white rabbit fur beard 75.00
Tray, 12½" l, shell shape, Victorian, japanned, red, inlaid with radiating
panels of abalone, gilt Oriental figures, c1850 .... 100.00

PARIAN WARE

History: Parian ware is a creamy white, translucent, marble-like porcelain. It originated in England in 1842 and was first known as "Statuary
Porcelain." Minton and Copeland have been credited with its development. Wedgwood also made
it. In America, parian ware was manufactured by
Chistopher Fenton in Bennington, Vermont.

At first parian ware was used only for figures
and figural groups. By the 1850's it became so
popular a vast range of wares were manufactured.

Bowl, 8½" d, crimped edge, roses, high
relief 40.00
Box, 5¾ x 4¼", irregular oval, full figural
sleeping child on lid, Bennington ... 100.00
Bust
Dickens, 8¾" 85.00
Maiden, garland of flowers in hair, late
19th C, 9" h 80.00
Creamer
5"
Tulip relief dec 75.00

Pitcher, Copeland, 4½″ d at top, 4½″ h, grape pattern, twig handle, $50.00.

Wildflower relief dec	**70.00**
Ewer, 10¼″, blue and white, applied grapes and leaves dec, Bennington, c1850	**200.00**
Figure	
Boy	
Colonial dress, sitting on rock, holding bird, dog seated at side, 9½″	**145.00**
Nude, leaning against tree stump, stroking bird, sgd "J & TB," c1865, 8 x 4¾″	**140.00**
Man, cloak and beret, 13½ x 4⅛″ . .	**115.00**
Woman	
Kneeling, hands in front of lamp, palms up, head on ground, 7″ .	**125.00**
Nude, standing, drapery over one arm and down side, round soap bar in hand, turtle at feet, circular base, Bennington, 16″	**165.00**
Loving Cup, 8⅜ x 6⅞″, white relief figures of Bacchus and woman, grapes, and vines, Charles Meigh, c1840 . .	**300.00**
Pastille Burner, 8¼″ sq, relief molded, bird and human figures, raised on turned columns, stepped sq base, pr	**150.00**
Pin Box, oval, white relief cupid, blue ground	**50.00**
Pitcher	
3½″, white grape relief dec, pink ground	**90.00**
6″, lilac bowl, 19th C	**75.00**
6½″, ivy relief dec	**75.00**
7″, lilac and white figural children sleeping dec, English, Victorian . .	**175.00**
7½″, iris relief dec	**75.00**
8″, Philosophers, cameo relief, English	**200.00**
8½″, blue and white, figural relief of "Now I'm Grand Ma Ma and Now I'm Grand Pa Pa," English	**175.00**

10″, figural relief	
Jousting knights, English, 19th C .	**150.00**
Mother and daughter, English, 19th C	**175.00**
Toothpick, 3″, boy kneeling by boat . .	**30.00**
Vase	
6″, bud, relief bird, florals and leaves	**65.00**
10″, applied white monkey type creatures, grape clusters at shoulders, blue ground, c1850, pr	**250.00**

PATE-DE-VERRE

History: Pate-de-Verre can be translated simply as glass paste. It is manufactured by grinding lead glass into a powder or crystal form, making it into a paste by adding a 2 or 3% solution of sodium silicate, molding, firing, and carving. The Egyptians discovered the process as early as 1500 B.C.

In the late 19th century, the process was rediscovered by a group of French glassmakers. Amalric Walter, Henri Cros, Georges Despret, and the Daum brothers were leading manufacturers.

Contemporary sculptors are creating a second renaissance, lead by the technical research of Jacques Daum.

Bowl, 3¾″ d, 2″ h, yellow leaves, purple vines, sgd G Argy-Rousseau, $1,000.00.

Ashtray	
5″, circular, brown beetle surmount, Almeric Walter	**1,200.00**
6¼ x 3½″, center medallion with Egyptian head, reds and purples, small flower buds around edge, raised lattice work on bottom . .	**1,600.00**
Atomizer, 5¾″, red berries, green leaves, sgd "H Berge"	**1,000.00**
Bowl	
2¾″, molded sprays of red berries,	

green-brown branches, body lightly streaked with purple, c1920 ..... 850.00
10¼", ftd, molded with concentric blossoms, long necked birds rim, gray sides streaked with lavender and rose 4,000.00
Clock, 4½", sq, stars within pentagon and tapered sheaves motif, orange and black, molded sgd "G Argy-Rousseau," clock by J E Caldwell .. 2,650.00
Jewelry, pendant, circular, molded green mistletoe leaves encircling purple berried center, amethyst translucent ground trimmed in blue, green knotted silk cord and hanging tassel 600.00
Sculpture
4" h, baby blue jay, dark turquoise, molded sgd "A Walter, Nancy," designed by Henri Berge 1,250.00
12" h, Loie Fuller, dancer, shades of blue, sgd "A Walter" 5,750.00
Tray, 6 x 8", apple green, figural green and yellow duck with orange beak at one end, sgd "Walter, Nancy" 750.00
Vase
7", mottled gray sides molded in low relief with blue Australian bush babies hiding among grasses, molded sgd "G Argy Rousseau-France" .. 6,000.00
9", tapered cylindrical, border of rose faun, satyr, girl among amber waves, framed by purple morning glories, green ground 3,600.00
9¾", baluster shape, aquamarine, purple streaked translucent ground, cobalt and sea-green geometric and stylized floral design, molded sgd "G Argy-Rousseau-France" 2,500.00
10¼", red rosettes, yellow centers, purple tones 6,000.00

PATE-SUR-PATE

History: Pate-sur-Pate, paste on paste, is a 19th century porcelain form featuring relief designs achieved by painting successive layers of thin pottery paste one on top of the other.

About 1880 Marc Solon and other Sevres artists, inspired by a Chinese celadon vase in the Ceramic Museum at Sevres, experimented with this process of porcelain decoration. Solon migrated to England at the outbreak of the Franco-Prussian War and worked at Minton, where he perfected the pate-sur-pate process.

Bowl, 3½ x 7", irid white relief mermaids, green ground, marked "Heubach," c1892 .... 365.00
Box, 4¼ x 4", blue and white, cupids, artist sgd, marked "Limoges" 200.00

Box, 4⅞ x 4⅞ x 2⅛", blue ground, Limoges, $150.00.

Demitasse Cup and Saucer, roses, gold trim, Coalport 350.00
Flask, 8⅞", sunrise, sunset, two white figures floating above horizon, deep olive green parian body, sgd "Frederick Schenk," mounted as table lamps, pr 600.00
Pitcher, 8", mythical figures, bearded mask handle, white and pink 225.00
Plaque
4", white relief pastoral scene with couple courting beneath tree, blue ground, wooden frame, marked "F M Limoges, France" 300.00
7⅝ x 7", pr, one with maiden and cupid spinning web, other with maiden seated on bench with whip in one hand, sunflower stalk with humanistic snail in other, artist sgd "Louis Solin", marked "Mintons" on back, framed 2,000.00
10¼ x 6¼", white relief maiden in gown holding basket in one hand, picking flowers from tree with other, deep blue ground, marked "Limoges," pierced for hanging 250.00
Sardine Dish, 2½ x 5½ x 4½", fish and seaweed dec, deep brown ground, SP cov, sgd "Jones" 500.00
Vase
6", white cupid chasing butterfly, black ground, George Jones 550.00
7", relief of two figures, white and olive, George Jones 500.00
10", pilgrim bottle shape, white relief cupids, one armed with large net, other with arrow, frolicking in tall weeds and flowers, chasing butterflies, gilding on neck, shoulder, and handles, marked "Mintons," c1880 900.00
20¾", amphora shape, handles, eight classical women, black ground, multicolored neck and pedestal

foot, marked "Marc Louis Solin,
Minton," late 19th C **1,000.00**
25⅜", white relief cupid judge and
court of maidens on front, reverse
with cupids surrounding trophies of
justice, polychrome relief flowerheads and foliage on shoulder and
base, deep olive ground, mask
handles, gilt and silvered detailed
on rim and base, marked "Mintons," gilt printed with plume mark
and "Paris Exhibition 1878" **2,000.00**
Wall Pocket, 6¼ x 9", white maid and
cupid with harp, olive green ground . **585.00**

PATTERN GLASS

History: Pattern glass is clear or colored glass
pressed into one of hundreds of patterns. Deming
Jarves of the Boston and Sandwich Glass Co.
invented the first successful pressing machine in
1828. By the 1860s glass pressing machinery had
been improved, and mass production of good
quality matched tableware sets began. The idea
of a matched glassware table service (including
goblets, tumblers, creamers, sugars, compotes,
cruets, etc.) quickly caught on in America. Many
pattern glass table services had numerous accessory pieces among which were banana stands,
molasses cans, water bottles, etc.

Early pattern glass (flint) was made with a lead
formula, giving it a ringing quality. During the Civil
War lead became too valuable to be used in glass
manufacturing. In 1864 Hobbs, Bruckunier & Co.,
West Virginia, developed a soda lime (non-flint)
formula. Pattern glass also was produced in
colors, milk glass, opalescent glass, slag glass,
and custard glass.

The hundreds of companies which produced
pattern glass have involved histories of development, expansions, personnel problems, material
and supply demands, fires, and mergers. In 1899
the National Glass Co. was formed as a combine
of nineteen glass companies in Pennsylvania,
Ohio, Indiana, West Virginia, and Maryland. U. S.
Glass, another consortium, was founded in 1891.
These combines resulted as attempts to save
small companies by pooling talents, resources,
and patterns. Because of this pooling, the same
pattern can be attributed to several companies.

Sometimes the pattern name of a piece was
changed from one company to the next to reflect
current fashion trends. U. S. Glass created the
States series by issuing patterns named for a particular state. Several of these patterns were new
issues, others were former patterns renamed.

References: Richard Carter Barret, *Popular
American Ruby Stained Pattern Glass,* Forward's
Color Productions, Inc., 1968; Bob H. Batty, *A
Complete Guide to Pressed Glass,* Pelican Pub-

lishing Co., Inc., 1978; E. M. Belnap, *Milk Glass,*
Crown Publishers, Inc., 1949; Regis F. and Mary
F. Ferson, *Yesterday's Milk Glass Today,* privately
printed, 1981; William Heacock, *Toothpick Holders from A to Z, Book 1, Encyclopedia of Victorian
Colored Pattern Glass,* Antique Publications,
1981; William Heacock, *Opalescent Glass from A
to Z, Book 2,* Antique Publications, 1981; William
Heacock, *Syrups, Sugar Shakers & Cruets, Book
3,* Antique Publications, 1981; William Heacock,
Custard Glass From A to Z, Book 4, Antique Pub-
lications, 1980; William Heacock, *U. S. Glass
From A to Z, Book 5,* Antique Publications, Inc.
1980; William Heacock, *Oil Cruets From A to Z,
Book 6,* Antique Publications, 1981; William Hea-
cock, *Ruby Stained Glass From A To Z, Book 7*
Antique Publications, Inc., 1986; William Heacock,
More Ruby Stained Glass, Book 8, Antique Pub-
lications, 1987; William Heacock and William
Gamble, *Cranberry Opalescent From A to Z, Book
9* Antique Publications, 1987; William Heacock,
Old Pattern Glass, Antique Publications, 1981;
William Heacock, *1000 Toothpick Holders: A Col-
lector's Guide,* Antique Publications, 1977; William
Heacock, *Rare and Unlisted Toothpick Holders,*
Antique Publications, 1984; William Heacock, *Col-
lecting Glass, Research, Reprint and Reviews,*
Volumes I, II, and III, Antique Publications; William
Heacock and Fred Bickenheuser, *Glass from A to
Z,* Antique Publications, 1981.

Minnie Watson Kamm, *Pattern Glass Pitchers,
Books 1 through 8,* privately printed, 1970, 4th
printing; Ruth Webb Lee, *Early American Pressed
Glass,* Lee Publications, 1966, 36th edition; Ruth
Webb Lee, *Victorian Glass,* Lee Publications,
1944, 13th edition; Bessie M. Lindsey, *American
Historical Glass,* Charles E. Tuttle Co., 1967; Rob-
ert Irwin Lucas, *Tarentum Pattern Glass,* privately
printed, 1981; Mollie H. McCain, *Pattern Glass
Primer,* Lamplighter Books, 1979; Mollie H. Mc-
Cain, *The Collector's Encyclopedia of Pattern
Glass,* Collector Books, 1982; George P. and He-
len McKearin, *American Glass,* Crown Publishers,
1941; James Measell, *Greentown Glass,* Grand
Rapids Public Museum Association, 1979; James
Measell and Don E. Smith, *Findlay Glass: The
Glass Tableware Manufacturers, 1886-1902,* Antique Publications, 1986; Alice Hulett Metz,
Early American Pattern Glass, privately printed,
1958; Alice Hulett Metz, *Much More Early Ameri-
can Pattern Glass,* privately printed, 1965.

Dori Miles, *Wallace-Homestead Price Guide To
Pattern Glass, 11th Edition,* Wallace-Homestead,
1986; S. T. Millard, *Goblets I,* privately printed,
1938, reprinted Wallace- Homestead, 1975; S. T.
Millard, *Goblets II,* privately printed, 1940, reprinted Wallace-Homestead, 1975; Arthur G. Peterson, *Glass Salt Shakers: 1,000 Patterns,* Wallace-Homestead, 1970; Jane Shadel Spillman,
*American and European Pressed Glass in the
Corning Museum of Glass,* Corning Museum of
Glass, 1981; Jane Shadel Spillman, *The Knopf*

Collectors Guides to American Antiques, Glass Volumes 1 and 2, Alfred A. Knopf, Inc., 1982, 1983; Doris and Peter Unitt, *American and Canadian Goblets,* Clock House, 1970; Doris and Peter Unitt, *Treasury of Canadian Glass,* Clock House, 1969, 2nd edition; Peter Unitt and Anne Worrall, *Canadian Handbook, Pressed Glass Tableware,* Clock House Productions, 1983; Dina von Zweck, *The Woman's Day Dictionary of Glass,* The Main Street Press, 1983.

Museums: Corning Museum of Glass, Corning, NY.; National Museum of Man, Ottawa, Ontario, Canada.

Periodical: *Glass Collector's Digest,* Richardson Printing Corp., P. O. Box 663, Marietta, OH 45750. Subscription: $16.00.

Additional Listings: Bread Plates, Children's Toy Dishes, Cruets, Custard Glass, Milk Glass, Sugar Shakers, Toothpicks, and specific companies.

Abbreviations:
GUTDODB—Give Us This Day Our Daily Bread
hs—high standard
ls—low standard
os—original stopper

We continue to be fortunate in assembling a panel of prestigious pattern glass dealers to serve as advisors in reviewing the pattern glass listings found in this edition. Their dedication is symbolic of those dealers and collectors who view price guides as useful market tools and contribute their expertise and time to make them better.

Research in pattern glass is continuing. As in the past, we have tried to present patterns with correct names, histories, and pieces. Catagories have been changed to reflect the most current thinking of all patterns alphabetically. Colored, opalescent, and clear patterns now are included in one listing, avoiding duplication of patterns and colors.

Pattern glass has been widely reproduced. We have listed reproductions with an *. These markings are given only as a guide and clue to the collector that some reproductions may exist in a given pattern.

Advisors: John and Alice Ahlfeld, Mike Anderton, Jerry R. Baker, and Darryl K. Reilly.

ABERDEEN

Non-flint, maker unknown, c1870.

	Clear		Clear
Butter, cov	45.00	Goblet	25.00
Compote		Pitcher, water	60.00
Cov	42.50	Sauce, flat	15.00
Open	25.00	Sugar	
Creamer	40.00	Cov	40.00
Egg Cup	30.00	Open	20.00

ACTRESS (Theatrical)

Made by LaBelle Glass Co., Bridgeport, Ohio, and Crystal Glass Co., c1870. All clear 20% less. Some items have been reproduced in clear and color by Imperial Glass Co.

	Clear and Frosted		Clear and Frosted
Bowl		Celery Vase	
6", ftd	50.00	Actress Head	120.00
8", Miss Neilson	80.00	HMS Pinafore, pedestal	155.00
Bread Plate		Cheese Dish, cov, The Lone	
7 x 12", HMS Pinafore	90.00	Fisherman on cov, Two	
9 x 13", Miss Neilson,		Dromios on base	240.00
motto	80.00	Compote	
Butter, cov	90.00	Cov, hs, 8" d	215.00
Cake Stand, 10"	145.00	Cov, hs, 10" d	225.00
Candlesticks, pr	250.00		

	Clear and Frosted		Clear and Frosted
Cov, hs, 12" d	300.00	5 x 8"	40.00
Open, hs, 10" d	115.00	5½ x 9"	40.00
Open, hs, 12" d	120.00	Pitcher	
Open, ls, 5" d	45.00	Milk, 6½", HMS Pinafore,	
Open, ls, 6" d	50.00	Fanny Davenport and	
Open, ls, 7" d	100.00	Miss Neilson.	275.00
Creamer.	75.00	Water, 9", Romeo & Juliet,	
Dresser Tray.	60.00	balcony scene	250.00
Goblet, Kate Claxton (2		Salt, master	70.00
portraits)	90.00	Salt Shaker, orig pewter top .	50.00
Marmalade Jar, cov	130.00	Sauce	
Mug, HMS Pinafore	50.00	Flat	18.00
Pickle Dish, Love's Request		Footed	25.00
is Pickles.	50.00	Spooner	75.00
Pickle Relish, different		Sugar, cov	90.00
actresses			
4½ x 7"	40.00		

ADONIS (Pleat and Tuck, Washboard)

Pattern made by McKee Bros. of Pittsburgh, Pennsylvania in 1897.

	Canary	Clear	Deep Blue
Bowl, 5", berry	15.00	12.00	20.00
Butter, cov	70.00	60.00	80.00
Cake Plate, 11". . . .	25.00	18.00	32.00
Cake Stand, 10½". .	45.00	30.00	50.00
Celery Vase	35.00	30.00	40.00
Compote,			
Cov, hs	65.00	50.00	75.00
Open, hs, 8"	45.00	40.00	50.00
Open, jelly, 4½" . .	28.00	18.00	32.00
Creamer.	28.00	22.50	32.00
Pitcher, water	55.00	45.00	60.00
Plate, 10"	25.00	18.00	32.00
Relish.	18.00	15.00	20.00
Salt and Pepper pr .	40.00	35.00	45.00
Sauce, flat, 4"	10.00	8.50	12.00
Spooner	35.00	30.00	38.00
Sugar, cov	40.00	35.00	45.00
Syrup	125.00	50.00	125.00
Tumbler	22.00	16.00	24.00

AEGIS (Bead & Bar Medallion, Swiss)

Non-flint pattern made by McKee and Brothers of Pittsburgh, Pennsylvania, in the 1880's. Shards have also been found at the site of the Burlington Glass Works, Hamilton, Ontario.

	Clear		Clear
Bowl, oval.	15.00	Open, hs	25.00
Butter, cov	35.00	Creamer.	30.00
Compote		Egg Cup.	25.00
Cov, hs	40.00	Goblet	30.00

	Clear			Clear
Pickle, 5 x 7"	15.00		Flat	7.50
Pitcher, water	55.00		Footed	10.00
Salt	18.00		Spooner	18.00
Sauce			Sugar, cov	35.00

ALABAMA (Beaded Bull's Eye and Drape)

Made by U. S. Glass Co., c1898. One of the States patterns. Also found in green (rare).

	Clear	Ruby Stained		Clear	Ruby Stained
Bowl berry, master .	45.00	—	Nappy	25.00	—
Butter, cov	60.00	175.00	Pitcher, water	65.00	—
Castor Set, 4 bottles,			Relish	15.00	25.00
glass frame	125.00	—	Salt & Pepper	65.00	—
Celery Vase	35.00	—	Spooner	30.00	—
Compote, open, 5",			Sugar, cov	48.00	—
jelly	65.00	—	Syrup	125.00	175.00
Creamer	45.00	60.00	Toothpick	60.00	135.00
Cruet, os	65.00	—	Tray, water, 10½" . .	40.00	—
Dish, rect	20.00	—	Tumbler	35.00	—
Honey Dish, cov . . .	60.00	—			

ALASKA (Lion's Leg)

Non-flint opalescent made by Northwood Glass Co. from 1897 to 1910. Forms are square except cruet, tumblers, salt and pepper shakers. Some pieces are found with enamel decoration. Sauces can be found in clear ($30.00); the creamer ($110.00) and spooner ($95.00) are known in clear blue.

	Clear Emerald Green	Blue Opal	Vaseline Opal	White Opal
Banana Boat	100.00	275.00	250.00	75.00
Bowl, berry, ftd	55.00	115.00	95.00	45.00
Butter, cov	150.00	280.00	275.00	150.00
Celery Tray	—	130.00	110.00	85.00
Creamer	42.50	85.00	80.00	40.00
Cruet	225.00	250.00	230.00	135.00
Pitcher, water	65.00	385.00	375.00	175.00
Salt Shaker, dec . . .	—	60.00	55.00	45.00
Sauce	42.50	45.00	35.00	25.00
Spooner	55.00	65.00	55.00	50.00
Sugar, cov	65.00	150.00	130.00	100.00
Tumbler	40.00	75.00	65.00	55.00

ALL-OVER DIAMOND (Diamond Splendor, Diamond Block #3)

Made by George Duncan and Sons, Pittsburgh, Pennsylvania, c1891 and continued by U.S. Glass Co. It was occasionally trimmed with gold, and had at least 65 pieces in the pattern. Biscuit jars are found in three sizes; bowls are both crimped and non-crimped; and nappies are also found crimped and non-crimped in fifteen sizes. Also made in ruby stained.

	Clear		Clear
Biscuit Jar, cov	60.00	Ice Tub, handles	35.00
Bitters Bottle	30.00	Lamp, Banquet, tall stem	140.00
Bowl		Nappy	
7″	20.00	4″	15.00
11″	35.00	9″	35.00
Cake Stand	35.00	Plate	
Candelabrum, very ornate, 4		6″	15.00
arm with lusters	175.00	7″	15.00
Celery Tray, crimped or		Pickle Dish, long	15.00
straight	20.00	Pitcher, water, bulbous, 6	
Claret Jug	50.00	sizes	42–60.00
Compote, cov	40.00	Punch Bowl	50.00
Condensed Milk Jar, cov	25.00	Salt Shaker	20.00
Cordial	35.00	Spooner	20.00
Creamer	20.00	Sugar	
Cruet, patterned stopper		Cov	35.00
1 oz	50.00	Open	18.00
2 oz	45.00	Syrup	55.00
4 oz	45.00	Tray	
6 oz	25.00	Ice Cream	30.00
Decanter		Water	30.00
Pint	45.00	Wine	30.00
Quart	45.00	Tumbler	15.00
Egg Cup	20.00	Water Bottle	35.00
Goblet	25.00	Wine	20.00

ALMOND THUMBPRINT (Pointed Thumbprint, Finger Print)

An early flint glass pattern with variants in flint and non-flint. Pattern has been attributed to Bryce, Bakewell, and U. S. Glass. Sometimes found in milk glass.

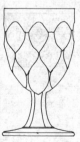

	Flint	Non-Flint		Flint	Non-Flint
Butter, cov	80.00	45.00	Decanter	70.00	—
Celery Vase	50.00	25.00	Egg Cup	45.00	25.00
Champagne	60.00	35.00	Goblet	30.00	12.00
Compote			Salt		
Cov, hs, 4¾″, jelly	60.00	40.00	Flat, large	25.00	15.00
Cov, hs, 10″	80.00	45.00	Ftd, cov	45.00	25.00
Cov, ls, 4¾″	55.00	30.00	Ftd, open	25.00	12.00
Cov, ls, 7″	45.00	25.00	Spooner	20.00	15.00
Open, hs, 10½″	65.00	—	Sugar, cov	60.00	40.00
Cordial	35.00	30.00	Sweetmeat Jar, cov.	75.00	45.00
Creamer	65.00	40.00	Tumbler	40.00	20.00
Cruet, ftd, os	55.00	—	Wine	25.00	12.00

AMAZON (Sawtooth Band)

Non-flint; made by Bryce Brothers, Pittsburgh, Pennsylvania, late 1870s–1880 and also by the U. S. Glass Co., c1890. Mostly found in clear, either etched or plain. Heacock notes pieces in amber, blue, vaseline, and ruby stained. Over 65 pieces made in this pattern, including a toy set. Add 200% for color, e.g., pedestalled amber cruet with maltese cross stopper ($165.00) and pedestalled blue cruet with hand and bar stopper ($200.00). An amethyst cruet with a hand-bar stopper ($275.00) also is known.

	Etched	Plain		Etched	Plain
Banana Stand.....	95.00	65.00	Creamer.........	30.00	28.00
Bowl			Cruet, os	50.00	45.00
4″, scalloped	—	10.00	Egg Cup.........	—	14.00
4½″, scalloped...	—	10.00	Goblet		
5″, scalloped	—	15.00	4½″...........	—	30.00
6″, scalloped	—	25.00	6″............	—	35.00
6½″, cov, oval ...	—	50.00	Nappy, lion head		
7″, scalloped	—	20.00	handle		
8″, scalloped	—	25.00	4½″...........	—	20.00
9″, cov	30.00	25.00	6″............	—	25.00
Butter, cov	65.00	50.00	Pitcher, water	60.00	55.00
Cake Stand			Relish..........	28.00	25.00
Large	—	50.00	Salt & Pepper, pr. ..	50.00	40.00
Small	—	40.00	Salt		
Celery Vase	35.00	30.00	Individual.....	—	15.00
Champagne	—	35.00	Master	—	18.00
Claret.........	35.00	25.00	Sauce, ftd.......	—	10.00
Compote			Spooner	30.00	25.00
Cov, hs. 7″		65.00	Sugar, cov	55.00	45.00
Open, 4½″, jelly..	45.00	35.00	Syrup.........	50.00	42.50
Open, hs, 9½″,			Tumbler	25.00	21.00
sawtooth edge .	—	50.00	Wine	25.00	20.00
Cordial	40.00	25.00			

ANTHEMION (Albany)

Non-flint made by Model Flint Glass Co., Findlay, Ohio, c1890–1900, and by Albany Glass Co. Also found in amber and blue.

	Clear		Clear
Bowl, 7″, sq, turned-in edge .	20.00	Pitcher, water	50.00
Butter, cov	65.00	Plate, 10″..............	25.00
Cake Plate, 9½″	35.00	Sauce	10.00
Cake Stand	40.00	Spooner	25.00
Celery Vase	35.00	Sugar, cov	45.00
Creamer...............	30.00	Tumbler	30.00
Marmalade Jar, cov.......	40.00		

APOLLO

Non-flint, first made by Adams and Co., Pittsburgh, Pennsylvania, c1870, and later by U. S. Glass Co., c1891. Frosted increases price 20%. Also found in ruby stained and engraved.

	Clear		Clear
Bowl		Butter, cov	55.00
4″	10.00	Cake Stand	
5″	10.00	8″	35.00
6″	12.00	9″	40.00
7″	15.00	10″	50.00
8″	20.00	Celery Tray, rect	20.00

	Clear			Clear
Celery Vase	30.00		Salt	20.00
Compote			Salt Shaker	25.00
Cov, hs	50.00		Sauce	
Open, hs	35.00		Flat	10.00
Open, ls, 7″	25.00		Ftd, 5″	15.00
Creamer	35.00		Spooner	25.00
Cruet	65.00		Sugar, cov	40.00
Egg Cup	30.00		Sugar Shaker	45.00
Goblet	35.00		Syrup	110.00
Lamp, 10″	90.00		Tray, water	45.00
Pickle Dish	15.00		Tumbler	30.00
Pitcher, water	65.00		Wine	35.00

ARCHED FLEUR-DE-LIS (Late Fleur-De-Lis)

Made by Bryce, Higbee and Co., in 1897–1898. Also gilded.

	Clear	Ruby Stained		Clear	Ruby Stained
Banana Stand	35.00	135.00	Relish, 8″	15.00	—
Bowl, 9″, oval	18.00	—	Salt Shaker	16.00	40.00
Butter, cov	40.00	135.00	Sauce	8.00	25.00
Cake Stand	35.00	—	Spooner, double		
Compote, jelly, cov	18.00	—	handled	20.00	65.00
Creamer	30.00	70.00	Sugar, cov, double		
Dish, shallow, 7″	12.50	25.00	handled	35.00	100.00
Mug, 3¼″	—	45.00	Toothpick	30.00	225.00 +
Olive, handled	15.00	—	Tumbler	15.00	45.00
Pitcher, water	125.00	300.00	Vase, 10″	35.00	75.00
Plate, 7″, sq	12.00	45.00	Wine	25.00	55.00

ARCHED OVALS

Made by U. S. Glass Co., c1908. Found in gilt, ruby stained, green, and rarely in cobalt blue. Popular pattern for souvenir wares.

	Clear	Cobalt	Green	Ruby Stained
Bowl, berry	12.50	—	18.00	—
Bowl, cov, 7″	40.00	—	—	—
Butter, cov	45.00	—	50.00	80.00
Cake Stand	35.00	—	—	—
Celery Vase	15.00	40.00	20.00	—
Compote				
Cov, hs, 8″, belled	42.00	—	—	—
Open, hs, 8″	30.00	—	—	—
Open, hs, 9″	35.00	—	—	—
Creamer				
Ind	20.00	—	—	—
Regular	30.00	—	—	25.00
Cruet	35.00	—	45.00	—
Goblet	20.00	—	30.00	35.00
Mug	18.00	30.00	20.00	25.00
Pitcher, water	30.00	—	40.00	—
Plate, 9″	20.00	—	25.00	—
Punch Cup	8.00	—	—	—
Relish, oval, 9″	20.00	—	—	—

	Clear	Cobalt	Green	Ruby Stained
Salt & Pepper, pr. . .	45.00	—	50.00	—
Sauce	7.50	—	—	—
Saucer	—	—	—	30.00
Syrup	35.00	—	—	—
Spooner	20.00	—	25.00	35.00
Sugar, cov	35.00	—	40.00	—
Toothpick	18.00	50.00	25.00	35.00
Tumbler	12.00	60.00	18.00	30.00
Wine	25.00	—	30.00	32.00

ARGUS

Flint, thumbprint type pattern made by Bakewell Pears & Co. in Pittsburgh, Pennsylvania, in the early 1870s. Copiously reproduced, some by Fostoria with raised "HFM" trademark for Henry Ford Museum.

	Clear		Clear
Ale Glass	75.00	Lamp, ftd	75.00
Bitters Bottle	60.00	Mug, applied handle	65.00
Bowl, 5½"	50.00	Pitcher, water, applied	
Butter, cov	85.00	handle	200.00
Celery Vase	80.00	Salt, master, open	30.00
Champagne	42.50	Spooner	48.50
Creamer, applied handle . . .	70.00	Sugar, cov	65.00
Decanter, qt	70.00	Tumbler, bar	55.00
Egg Cup	25.00	Whiskey, applied handle . . .	75.00
Goblet	42.50	Wine	45.00

ART (Job's Tears)

Non-flint produced by Adams and Co., Pittsburgh, Pennsylvania, in the 1870s. Reissued by U. S. Glass Co. in the early 1890s.

	Clear	Ruby Stained		Clear	Ruby Stained
Banana Stand	95.00	195.00	Creamer		
Biscuit Jar	85.00	195.00	Hotel, large, round		
Bowl			shape	45.00	55.00
6" d, 3¼" h, ftd . .	30.00	—	Regular	55.00	60.00
7", low, collar			Cruet, os	85.00	225.00
base	30.00	—	Goblet	58.00	—
8", berry, one end			Mug	35.00	—
pointed	50.00	55.00	Pitcher		
Butter, cov	60.00	100.00	Milk	90.00	150.00
Cake Stand			Water, 2½ qt	85.00	—
9"	55.00	—	Plate, 10"	35.00	—
10¼"	65.00	—	Relish	21.00	65.00
Celery Vase	30.00	65.00	Sauce		
Compote			Flat, round, 4" . . .	15.00	—
Cov, hs, 7"	55.00	185.00	Pointed at one		
Open, hs, 9", flar-			end	18.50	—
ed scalloped			Spooner	25.00	55.00
edge	50.00	—	Sugar, cov	45.00	85.00
Open, hs, 9½" d,			Tumbler	35.00	—
9" h	60.00	—	Vinegar Jug, 3 pt . . .	50.00	—
Open, hs, 10" . . .	65.00	—			

ARTICHOKE (Valencia)

Non-flint pattern made by Fostoria Glass Co, Moundsville, WV, January, 1891. Made in clear and frosted (add 50%). Limited production in opalescent and satin glass. Reportedly no goblet was originally produced, but reproductions do exist.

	Clear		Clear
Bobeche...............	35.00	Miniature Lamp..........	250.00
Bowl, 8"...............	32.50	Pitcher, water	90.00
Butter, cov	50.00	Rose Bowl	35.00
Cake Stand	42.50	Sauce, flat	8.50
Celery Vase	35.00	Spooner.................	25.00
Compote, cov, hs	145.00	Sugar, cov	55.00
Creamer...............	35.00	Tray, water	45.00
Finger Bowl, underplate....	40.00	Tumbler	35.00

ASHBURTON

A popular pattern produced by Boston and Sandwich Glass Co. and McKee Brothers from the 1850s to the late 1870s with many variations. Originally made in flint by New England Glass Co. and others and later in non-flint. Prices are for flint. Also reported is an amber handled whiskey mug and a scarce emerald green wine glass ($200.00). Some items known in fiery opalescent.

	Clear		Clear
Ale Glass, 5"............	85.00	Honey Dish.............	15.00
Bar Bottle, qt	75.00	* Jug, qt	90.00
Bitters Bottle............	55.00	Lamp..................	75.00
Bowl, 6½"..............	75.00	* Lemonade Glass.........	55.00
Carafe	175.00	Mug, 7"	110.00
Celery Vase, scalloped top..	125.00	Pitcher, water	450.00
Champagne, cut	75.00	Plate, 6⅝" d	75.00
Claret, 5¼" h	50.00	Sauce	15.00
Compote, open, ls, 7½"....	65.00	Spooner...............	40.00
Cordial, 4¼" h...........	45.00	* Sugar, cov	90.00
Creamer, applied handle ...	175.00	Toddy Jar, cov	300.00
Decanter, qt, cut and pressed		Tumbler, ftd	80.00
os..................	225.00	Whiskey, applied handle ...	75.00
Egg Cup		Water Bottle, tumble up	95.00
Double	95.00	* Wine	
Single	35.00	Cut..................	65.00
Flip Glass, handled	125.00	Pressed	48.00
* Goblet	40.00		

ATLANTA (Square Lion, Clear Lion Head)

Produced by Fostoria Glass Co., Moundsville, West Virginia, c1895. Pieces are usually square in shape. Also found in milk glass, ruby and amber stain.

	Clear	Frosted		Clear	Frosted
Bowl			Compote		
7", scallop rim ...	60.00	—	Cov, hs, 7"......	75.00	110.00
8", low collar			Cov, hs, 8" d, 9½"		
base............	55.00	—	h............	125.00	—
Butter, cov	60.00	110.00	Open, hs, 5", jelly.	55.00	—
Cake Stand, 10" ...	95.00	—	Creamer.........	48.00	60.00
Celery Vase	45.00	75.00	Goblet	50.00	60.00

	Clear	Frosted		Clear	Frosted
Marmalade Jar	65.00	85.00	Sauce, 4″	22.00	—
Pitcher, water	110.00	—	Spooner	50.00	—
Relish, oval.	35.00	—	Sugar, cov	65.00	—
Salt & Pepper, pr. . .	90.00	—	Toothpick	55.00	60.00
Salt			Tumbler	35.00	—
Individual.	30.00	—	Wine	40.00	—
Master	50.00	70.00			

ATLAS

Non-flint glass pattern occasionally ruby stained and etched. Made by Adams and Co., U. S. Glass Co. in 1891, and Bryce Brothers, Mt. Pleasant, Pennsylvania, in 1889.

	Clear	Ruby		Clear	Ruby
Bowl, 9″	20.00	—	Salt & Pepper, pr. . .	20.00	—
Butter, cov, regular .	45.00	75.00	Salt		
Cake Stand			Master	20.00	—
8″	35.00	—	Individual.	20.00	—
9″	40.00	95.00	Sauce		
Celery Vase	28.00	—	Flat.	12.50	—
Champagne, 5½″ h .	40.00	—	Footed	15.00	20.00
Compote			Spooner	30.00	35.00
Cov, hs, 8″	65.00	—	Sugar		
Cov, hs, 5″, jelly .	50.00	65.00	Cov.	38.00	65.00
Open, ls, 7″	40.00	—	Open	20.00	—
Creamer			Syrup (molasses		
Table, applied			can)	65.00	—
handle	30.00	55.00	Toothpick	20.00	45.00
Tankard	25.00	—	Tray, water	75.00	—
Goblet	35.00	—	Tumbler	28.00	—
Marmalade Jar	45.00	—	Whiskey	20.00	45.00
Pitcher, water	45.00	—	Wine	25.00	—

AURORA (Diamond Horseshoe)

Made in 1888 by the Brilliant Glass Works, which only existed for a short time. Taken over by the Greensburg Glass Co. who continued the pattern. Also found etched.

	Clear	Ruby Stained		Clear	Ruby Stained
Bread Plate, 10″,			Relish Scoop,		
round, large star in			handle.	12.00	25.00
center	30.00	35.00	Salt & Pepper, pr. . .	45.00	80.00
Butter, cov	45.00	90.00	Sauce, flat	8.00	18.00
Cake Stand	35.00	85.00	Spooner	25.00	48.00
Celery Vase	30.00	40.00	Sugar, cov	45.00	65.00
Compote, cov, hs . .	65.00	95.00	Tray, water	45.00	60.00
Creamer.	35.00	50.00	Tray, wine.	30.00	50.00
Goblet	30.00	45.00	Tumbler	25.00	45.00
Mug, handle	50.00	65.00	Waste Bowl.	30.00	45.00
Olive, oval	18.00	35.00	Wine	20.00	35.00
Pitcher, water	40.00	100.00	Wine Decanter, os. .	75.00	130.00

AUSTRIAN (Finecut Medallion)

Made by Indiana Tumbler and Goblet Co., Greentown, Indiana, 1897. Experimental pieces were made in cobalt blue, nile green, and opaque colors.

	Amber	Canary	Clear	Emerald Green
Bowl				
8″, round	—	150.00	55.00	—
8¼″, rect	—	145.00	50.00	—
Butter, cov	85.00	250.00	90.00	—
Compote, open, ls . .	—	140.00	75.00	—
Cordial	145.00	100.00	50.00	150.00
Creamer	120.00	80.00	40.00	120.00
Goblet	—	125.00	40.00	—
Nappy, cov	—	135.00	55.00	—
Pitcher, water	—	325.00	100.00	—
Plate, 10″	—	—	40.00	—
Punch Cup	150.00	85.00	18.00	125.00
Rose Bowl	—	150.00	50.00	—
Sauce, 4⅝″ d	—	50.00	20.00	—
Spooner	—	95.00	40.00	—
Sugar, cov	—	135.00	45.00	—
Tumbler	175.00	85.00	25.00	—
Wine	175.00	110.00	30.00	150.00

AZTEC

Made by McKee Glass Co., 1900 to 1910. Late imitation cut pattern, often marked "PRES-CUT" in circle in base; about 75 items in pattern.

	Clear		Clear
Bon Bon, ftd, 7″	15.00	Goblet	35.00
Bowl, berry	15.00	Pitcher, applied handle, ½	
Butter, cov	40.00	gal.	35.00
Cake Plate, trilobed	20.00	Plate	20.00
Cake Stand	30.00	Punch Bowl, stand, and 12	
Carafe, water	40.00	handled cups	125.00
Celery Tray	15.00	Punch Cup	8.00
Celery Vase	18.00	Relish	15.00
Champagne	25.00	Salt & Pepper, pr.	35.00
Compote, open	30.00	Sauce	10.00
Condensed Milk Jar	18.00	Soda Fountain Accessories	
Cordial	20.00	Crushed Fruit Jar	55.00
Cracker Jar, cov	50.00	Straw holder, glass lid . . .	65.00
Creamer		Spooner	15.00
Individual	15.00	Sugar, cov	25.00
Regular	25.00	Syrup	50.00
Cruet	35.00	Toothpick	18.50
Crushed Fruit Bowl, cov,		Tumbler	
8½″	75.00	Iced Tea	22.00
Cup	8.00	Water	20.00
Decanter, cut stopper	32.50	Whiskey	12.00
Finger Bowl, underplate	20.00	Wine	25.00

BABY FACE

Non-flint made by McKee, late 1870s. Some pieces reproduced.

	Clear		Clear
Butter, cov	165.00	Creamer	110.00
Celery Vase	75.00	Goblet	85.00
Champagne	160.00	Pitcher, water	250.00
Compote		Salt	50.00
* Cov, hs, 5¼"	145.00	Spooner	95.00
Cov, hs, 7", scalloped	175.00	Sugar, cov	150.00
Cov, hs, 8", scalloped	250.00	Wine	160.00
Open, hs, 7", scalloped	70.00		
Open, hs, 8", 8" h	60.00		
Open, ls, 8", 4¾" h	85.00		

BALL AND SWIRL

Made by McKee Glass Co, Jeanette, PA, 1894.

	Clear		Clear
Butter, cov	35.00	Pitcher, water	40.00
Cake Stand	35.00	Sauce, ftd	12.50
Compote, open, hs	30.00	Spooner	20.00
Creamer	24.00	Sugar, open	22.50
Goblet	20.00	Syrup	40.00
Mug		Tumbler	15.00
Large	18.00	Wine	28.00
Small	12.00		

BALTIMORE PEAR (Gipsy)

Non-flint, originally made by Adams and Company, Pittsburgh, Pennsylvania, in 1874. Also made by U. S. Glass Company in 1890s. There are 18 different size compotes. Given as premiums by different manufacturers and organizations. Heavily reproduced. Reproduced in cobalt blue.

	Clear		Clear
Bowl		* Pitcher	
6"	30.00	Milk	65.00
9"	40.00	Water	95.00
Bread Plate, 12½"	70.00	Plate	
* Butter, cov	75.00	8½"	30.00
* Cake Stand, 9"	50.00	10"	40.00
* Celery Vase	50.00	Relish	25.00
Compote		* Sauce	
Cov, hs, 7"	80.00	Flat	15.00
Cov, ls, 8½"	45.00	Footed	20.00
Open, hs	30.00	Spooner	42.50
Open, jelly	28.50	* Sugar	
* Creamer	30.00	Cov	50.00
* Goblet	35.00	Open	30.00
Pickle	18.50	Tray, 10½"	35.00

BAMBOO

Made by Pioneer Glass Co of Pittsburgh, PA, in the late 1800s.

	Clear	Ruby Stained		Clear	Ruby Stained
Butter, cov	85.00	160.00	Relish, 8″	20.00	45.00
Celery Vase	30.00	65.00	Salt & Pepper, pr. . .	36.00	75.00
Compote, oval,			Sauce, flat	12.00	—
etched.	45.00	—	Spooner	30.00	65.00
Creamer.	35.00	75.00	Sugar, cov	45.00	90.00
Pitcher, water	75.00	150.00	Tumbler	35.00	70.00

BANDED PORTLAND (Virginia #1, Maiden's Blush)

States pattern, originally named Virginia, by Portland Glass Co. Painted and fired green, yellow, blue, and possibly pink; ruby stained, and rose-flashed (which Lee notes is Maiden's Blush referring to the color, rather than the pattern, as Metz lists it). Double flashed refers to color above and below the band, single flashed refers to color above or below band only.

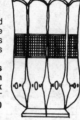

	Clear	Color Flashed	Maiden's Blush Pink
Bowl, 9″	32.00	—	40.00
Butter, cov	50.00	165.00	—
Cake Stand	55.00	—	—
Candlesticks, pr . . .	95.00	—	—
Carafe	80.00	—	90.00
Celery Tray.	30.00	—	—
Celery Vase	25.00	—	45.00
Cologne Bottle	45.00	65.00	75.00
Compote			
Cov, hs, 7″.	85.00	—	—
Cov, jelly, 6″.	40.00	65.00	—
Creamer			
Individual, oval. . .	25.00	35.00	38.00
Regular, 6 oz. . . .	35.00	45.00	50.00
Cruet, os	60.00	90.00	125.00
Decanter, handled. .	50.00	—	—
Dresser Tray.	50.00	—	—
Goblet	40.00	55.00	65.00
Lamp			
Flat.	45.00	—	—
Tall	50.00	—	—
Nappy	18.00	55.00	—
Olive	18.00	—	—
Pin Tray	16.00	—	—
Pitcher, water,			
tankard	75.00	90.00	250.00
Pomade Jar, cov . . .	35.00	45.00	—
Punch Bowl, hs. . . .	110.00	—	300.00
Punch Cup	20.00	—	30.00
Relish			
6½″.	25.00	30.00	20.00
8¼″.	20.00	35.00	—
Ring Holder, gold rim and post, scarce	80.00	—	—

	Clear	Color Flashed	Maiden's Blush Pink
Salt & Pepper, pr. . .	45.00	75.00	75.00
Sardine Box	55.00	—	—
Sauce, round, flat, 4 or 4½"	12.00	—	20.00
Spooner	28.00	—	45.00
Sugar			
Cov, large	45.00	75.00	75.00
Open, individual, oval	20.00	—	35.00
Sugar Shaker, orig top	45.00	—	85.00
Syrup	50.00	—	135.00
Toothpick	35.00	45.00	40.00
Tumbler	25.00	—	45.00
Vase			
6"	20.00	—	38.00
9"	35.00	—	50.00
Wine	35.00	—	75.00

BARBERRY (Berry)

Non-flint made by McKee Glass Co. and the Boston and Sandwich Glass Co. in the 1860s and 1880s. 6" plates are found in amber, canary, pale green, and pale blue; they are considered scarce. Also alleged to have been made at Iowa City. Pattern comes in "9 berry bunch" and "12 berry bunch" varieties.

	Clear		Clear
Bowl		Egg Cup	20.00
6", oval	20.00	Goblet	25.00
7", oval	25.00	Pickle	10.00
8", oval	28.00	Pitcher, water, applied	
8", round, flat.	30.00	handle.	100.00
9", oval	32.00	Plate, 6"	20.00
Butter		Salt, master, ftd	25.00
Cov.	50.00	Sauce	
Cov, flange, pattern on edge	100.00	Flat.	10.00
		Footed	15.00
Cake Stand	150.00	Spooner, ftd	30.00
Celery Vase	40.00	Sugar	
Compote		Cov.	45.00
Cov, hs, 8", shell finial . . .	75.00	Open, buttermilk type	25.00
Cov, ls, 8", shell finial	55.00	Syrup	130.00
Open, hs, 8"	35.00	Tumbler, ftd	25.00
Creamer.	30.00	Wine	30.00
Cup Plate	15.00		

BARLEY

Non-flint, originally made by Campbell, Jones and Co., c1882, in clear; possibly by others in varied quality. Add 100% for color which is hard to find.

	Clear			Clear
Bowl		Pitcher, water		
8″, berry	15.00	Applied handle.		95.00
10″, oval	20.00	Pressed handle		45.00
Bread Tray	30.00	Plate, 6″		35.00
Butter, cov	42.50	Platter, 13″ l, 8″ w		30.00
Cake Stand		Relish		
8″.	25.00	Flat, 8″ l, 6″ w		20.00
10″.	30.00	Wheelbarrow, 8″, pewter		
Celery Vase	25.00	wheels		60.00
Compote		Salt, master, wheelbarrow,		
Cov, hs, 6″.	45.00	pewter wheels		75.00
Cov, hs, 8½″	60.00	Sauce		
Open, hs, 8½″	38.00	Flat.		9.00
Cordial	40.00	Footed		12.00
Creamer.	25.00	Spooner		22.00
Goblet	25.00	Sugar, cov		35.00
Honey, ftd, 3½″	8.00	Vegetable Dish, oval		18.00
Marmalade Jar	55.00	Wine		30.00
Pickle Castor, SP frame and				
tongs	90.00			

BASKETWEAVE

Non-flint, c1880. Some covered pieces have a stippled cat's head finial.

	Amber or Canary	Apple Green	Blue	Clear	Vaseline
Bread Plate, handled, 11″	—	—	25.00	10.00	—
Butter, cov	35.00	60.00	40.00	30.00	40.00
Compote, cov, 7″. . .	—	—	—	35.00	—
Cordial	25.00	40.00	28.00	20.00	30.00
Creamer.	30.00	50.00	35.00	28.00	36.00
Cup & Saucer.	35.00	60.00	35.00	30.00	38.00
Dish, oval	12.00	20.00	15.00	10.00	16.00
Egg Cup.	18.00	30.00	20.00	15.00	25.00
* Goblet	28.00	50.00	35.00	20.00	30.00
Mug	25.00	40.00	25.00	15.00	30.00
Pickle.	18.00	30.00	20.00	15.00	22.00
Pitcher					
Milk.	40.00	60.00	45.00	35.00	50.00
* Water	50.00	75.00	80.00	40.00	65.00
Plate, 11″, handled .	25.00	38.00	25.00	20.00	30.00
Sauce	10.00	10.00	12.00	8.00	12.00
Spooner	30.00	36.00	30.00	20.00	30.00
Sugar, cov	35.00	60.00	35.00	30.00	40.00
Syrup.	50.00	75.00	50.00	45.00	55.00
* Tray, water, scenic center	35.00	45.00	40.00	30.00	55.00
Tumbler, ftd	18.00	30.00	20.00	15.00	20.00
Waste Bowl.	20.00	36.00	25.00	18.00	25.00
Wine	30.00	50.00	30.00	25.00	30.00

BEADED ACORN MEDALLION (Beaded Acorn)

Made by the Boston Silver Glass Co., East Cambridge, Massachusetts, c1869.

	Clear		Clear
Butter, cov, acorn finial.	65.00	Plate, 6″	18.00
Champagne	55.00	Relish.	18.00
Compote, cov, hs	50.00	Salt, master	28.00
Creamer.	40.00	Sauce, flat	15.00
Egg Cup.	20.00	Spooner	28.00
Goblet	30.00	Sugar, cov	45.00
Pitcher, water	90.00	Wine	30.00

BEADED BAND

Attributed to Burlington Glass Co., Hamilton, Ontario, Canada, c1884. Limited production and scarce pattern. May have been made in light amber and other colors.

	Clear		Clear
Butter, cov	45.00	Relish	
Cake Stand, 7⅝″.	28.00	Double	30.00
Compote, cov, hs, 8″	55.00	Single	15.00
Creamer.	28.50	Sauce, ftd.	10.00
Goblet	28.00	Spooner	25.00
Pickle, cov	45.00	Sugar, cov	40.00
Pitcher, water, applied strap		Syrup.	85.00
handle.	100.00	Wine	30.00

BEADED GRAPE MEDALLION

Non-flint made by Boston Silver Glass Co., Cambridge, Massachusetts, c1868. Also found in flint; add 40%.

	Clear		Clear
Bowl, 7″	25.00	Pitcher, water, applied	
Butter, cov, acorn finial.	48.00	handle.	125.00
Cake Stand, 11″	150.00	Plate, 6″	20.00
Celery Vase	50.00	Relish	
Castor Set, 4 bottles	110.00	Cov.	140.00
Compote		Open, mkd "Mould Pat'd	
Cov, collared base	80.00	May 11, 1868	40.00
Cov, hs	75.00	Salt	
Open, hs, 8″	35.00	Individual, flat	20.00
Creamer, applied handle . . .	45.00	Master, ftd.	20.00
Egg Cup.	25.00	Spooner	30.00
Goblet		Sugar, cov, acorn finial.	60.00
Buttermilk	30.00	Vegetable, cov, ftd.	75.00
Lady's.	30.00	Wine	55.00
Honey Dish, 3½″.	10.00		

BEADED MIRROR (Beaded Medallion)

Flint pattern made by Boston Silver-Glass Co, Sandwich, Massachusetts, patented May 11, 1869. Finials are acorn shaped. Also found in non-flint. Values are about the same.

	Clear		Clear
Butter, cov	40.00	Goblet	28.50
Castor Bottle		Pitcher, water	85.00
Mustard	15.00	Plate, 6″	20.00
Oil	25.00	Relish	18.50
Set, 5 pcs, metal frame	100.00	Salt, ftd	18.00
Celery	35.00	Sauce, flat	8.00
Compote, cov, hs	50.00	Spooner	25.00
Creamer	42.00	Sugar, cov	45.00
Egg Cup	18.50		

BEADED SWAG (Bead Yoke)

Made by Heisey Glass Co., c1900. Made in emerald green, ruby stained, custard glass and milk glass (called "opal" by Heisey). Prices listed are for clear glass, ruby stained 25% more, custard and milk 25% more, emerald green 40% more.

	Clear		Clear
Bonbon	25.00	Custard Cup, handled	15.00
Bowl		Finger Bowl	25.00
4″	20.00	Finger Bowl Underplate	20.00
4½″	20.00	Goblet	25.00
5″	20.00	Molasses Jar, metal lid	75.00
7″	25.00	Mug, souvenir type	30.00
8″	35.00	Pickle Tray, rect, deep	30.00
9″	45.00	Pitcher, water, half gallon	
10″	50.00	Bulbous	75.00
Butter, cov	45.00	Tankard	85.00
Cake Stand		Salt Shaker	20.00
9″	65.00	Sauce	10.00
10″	65.00	Spooner	30.00
Celery Vase	45.00	Sugar, cov	35.00
Compote, open	50.00	Toothpick	38.00
Creamer	35.00	Tumbler	25.00
Cruet	48.00		

BEADED SWIRL (Swirled Column)

Made by George Duncan & Sons, c1890. The dual names are for the two forms of the pattern. Beaded Swirl stands on flat bases and is solid in shape. Swirled Column stands on scrolled (sometimes gilded) feet, and the shape tapered towards the base. Some pieces trimmed in gold and also in milk white.

	Clear	Emerald Green		Clear	Emerald Green
Bowl			Creamer		
Berry, 7″	12.00	20.00	Flat	25.00	35.00
Flat	18.00	25.00	Footed	30.00	40.00
Footed, oval	18.00	24.00	Dish	12.00	18.00
Footed, round	18.00	24.00	Egg Cup	14.00	15.00
Butter, cov	35.00	45.00	Goblet	35.00	40.00
Cake Stand	35.00	45.00	Mug	10.00	12.00
Celery Vase	30.00	55.00	Pitcher, water	40.00	85.00
Compote			Sauce		
Cov, hs	42.00	52.00	Flat	8.00	12.00
Open, hs	38.00	45.00	Footed	10.00	14.00

	Clear	Emerald Green		Clear	Emerald Green
Spooner			Sugar Shaker	35.00	60.00
Flat	25.00	40.00	Footed	35.00	45.00
Footed	30.00	45.00	Syrup	48.00	100.00
Sugar, cov			Tumbler	20.00	30.00
Flat	35.00	45.00	Wine	28.00	35.00

BEADED TULIP (Andes)

Non-flint made by McKee Brothers, Pittsburgh, Pennsylvania, c1894.

	Clear	Emerald Green		Clear	Emerald Green
Bowl, 9½", oval	20.00	—	Relish	20.00	—
Butter, cov	50.00	125.00	Sauce		
Cake Stand	50.00	—	Flat, leaf shape		
Compote, cov, hs . .	55.00	—	edges	10.00	—
Creamer	35.00	75.00	Footed	12.00	—
Goblet	35.00	—	Spooner	30.00	—
Marmalade Jar	40.00	—	Sugar, cov	45.00	80.00
Pickle, oval	18.00	—	Tray		
Pitcher			Water	50.00	—
Milk	—	65.00	Wine	50.00	—
Water	65.00	—	Wine	30.00	—
Plate, 6"	25.00	—			

BEATTY HONEYCOMB (Beatty Waffle)

Non-flint made by Beatty Glass Co., Tiffin, Ohio, c1888. Reproduced by Fenton Glass in green opalescent (basket, rose bowl, and vases) and milk glass.

	Blue Opal	White Opal		Blue Opal	White Opal
Bowl, berry	100.00	50.00	Pitcher, water	200.00	150.00
Butter, cov	115.00	90.00	Salt & Pepper, pr. . .	65.00	45.00
Celery Vase	85.00	65.00	Sauce	20.00	20.00
Creamer			Spooner	40.00	30.00
Individual	35.00	20.00	Sugar, cov		
Regular	30.00	25.00	Individual	65.00	55.00
Cruet, os	250.00	185.00	Regular	70.00	65.00
Mug	35.00	25.00	Toothpick	50.00	45.00
Mustard	60.00	45.00	Tumbler	50.00	40.00

BEAUTIFUL LADY

Made by Bryce, Higbee and Co. in 1905.

	Clear		Clear
Banana stand, hs	30.00	Cake Stand, hs	35.00
Bowl		Compote	
8", low collared base	15.00	Cov, hs	35.00
9", flat	18.00	Open, hs	25.00
Bread Plate	15.00	Open, jelly	15.00
Cake Plate, 9"	25.00	Creamer	25.00

	Clear		Clear
Cruet	30.00	Salt and Pepper	40.00
Goblet	35.00	Spooner	15.00
Pitcher, water	45.00	Sugar, cov	25.00
Plate		Tumbler	12.00
7″, sq	15.00	Vase, 6½″.	15.00
8″.	15.00	Wine	20.00
9″.	25.00		
11″.	25.00		

BELLFLOWER

A fine flint glass pattern first made in the 1830s and attributed to Boston and Sandwich. Later produced by McKee Glass Co. and other firms for many years. There are many variations of this pattern - single vine and double vine, fine and coarse rib, knob and plain stems, and rayed and plain bases. Type and quality must be considered when evaluating. Very rare in color. Prices are for high quality flint. Reproductions has been made by the Metropolitan Museum of Art.
   Abbreviations: DV - double vine; SV - single vine; FR - fine rib; CR - coarse rib.

	Clear		Clear
Bowl		Hat, SV-FR, made from tum-	
6″ d, 1¾″ h, SV	75.00	bler mold, rare	350.00
8″, all types	75.00	Honey Dish, SV-FR, 3″	35.00
Butter, cov, SV-FR.	80.00	Lamp, whale oil, SV-FR,	
Castor Set, 5 bottle, pewter		brass stem, marble base .	175.00
stand	225.00	Mug, SV-FR	200.00
Celery Vase, SV-FR	175.00	Pitcher	
Champagne		Milk, DV-FR.	500.00
DV-FR, cut bellflowers . . .	250.00	Milk, DV, pint	125.00
SV-FR, knob stem, rayed		Milk, SV-CR, quart.	125.00
base, barrel shape	100.00	Water, DV-CR	350.00
Compote		*Water, SV-FR	250.00
Cov, hs, 8″ d, SV-FR	375.00	Plate, 6″, SV-FR	100.00
Cov, ls, 7″ d, SV	200.00	Salt, master,	
Cov, ls, 8″ d, SV	225.00	SV-FR, ftd.	65.00
Open, hs, 8″, SV	225.00	DV-FR	20.00
Open, ls, 7″, DV-FR, scal-		Sauce, flat, SV-FR	15.00
loped top	150.00	Spooner	
Open, ls, 7″.	125.00	DV	45.00
Open, ls, 8″, SV.	150.00	SV-FR.	35.00
Open, ls, 9″, SV-CR	125.00	Sugar	
Cordial, SV-FR, knob stem,		Cov, DV	100.00
rayed base, barrel shape .	115.00	Cov, SV-CR.	95.00
Creamer, DV-FR	135.00	Open, DV-CR	68.00
Decanter, qt, SV-FR, bar		Sweetmeat, cov, hs, 6″, SV .	300.00
top	185.00	Syrup, SV-FR, applied han-	
Dish, SV-FR, 8″, round, flat,		dle	400.00+
scalloped top.	65.00	Tumbler	
Egg Cup		DV-CR	95.00
CR	35.00	SV-FR, ftd.	90.00
SV-FR.	40.00	* SV-FR, cut bellflowers . . .	250.00
Goblet		Whiskey, 3½″, SV-FR	150.00
DV-FR, cut bellflowers . . .	230.00	Wine	
SV-CR, barrel shape	45.00	DV-FR, cut bellflowers,	
SV-CR, straight sides	40.00	barrel shape.	250.00
SV-FR, knob stem, barrel		SV-FR, knob stem, rayed	
shape	55.00	base, barrel shape	90.00
* SV-FR, plain stem, rayed		SV-FR, plain stem, rayed	
base. barrel shape	30.00	base, straight sides. . . .	75.00

BETHLEHEM STAR (Star Burst; Bright Star)

Made by Indiana Glass Co., Dunkirk, IN, c1907.

	Clear		Clear
Butter, cov	35.00	Goblet	30.00
Celery Vase	25.00	Pitcher, water	50.00
Compote		Relish	15.00
Cov, hs, 8"	55.00	Sauce, flat	10.00
Cov, hs, 4½"	45.00	Spooner	25.00
Creamer	30.00	Sugar, cov	40.00
Cruet, os	35.00	Wine	25.00

BIGLER

Flint, made by Boston and Sandwich Glass Co. and by other early factories. A scarce pattern in which goblets are most common and vary in height, shape and flare.

	Clear		Clear
Bar Bottle, qt	80.00	Lamp, whale oil, monument	
Bowl, 10" d	40.00	base	155.00
Butter, cov	125.00	Mug, applied handle	60.00
Celery Vase	100.00	Plate, 6"	32.00
Champagne	75.00	Salt, master	20.00
Cordial	50.00	Tumbler, water	55.00
Creamer	75.00	Whiskey, handled	100.00
Cup Plate	30.00	Wine	45.00
Egg Cup, double	50.00		
Goblet			
Regular	45.00		
Short Stem	50.00		

BIRD AND STRAWBERRY (Bluebird)

Non-flint, c1890. Made by Beatty and Indiana Glass Co., Dunkirk, IN. Pieces occasionally highlighted by the coloring of birds blue, strawberries pink, and leaves green, plus the addition of gilding.

	Clear	Colors		Clear	Colors
Bowl			Creamer	45.00	135.00
5"	25.00	45.00	Cup	25.00	—
9½"	45.00	85.00	Goblet	100.00	150.00+
10½"	55.00	95.00	Nappy	40.00	—
Butter, cov	100.00	200.00	Pitcher, water	225.00	285.00
Cake Stand	65.00	125.00	Plate, 12"	110.00	—
Celery Vase	45.00	—	Spooner	45.00	100.00
Compote			Sugar, cov	65.00	125.00
Cov, hs	125.00	200.00	Tumbler	45.00	75.00
Open, ls, ruffled	65.00	125.00	Wine	50.00	—

BLEEDING HEART

Non-flint, originally made by King & Son, Pittsburgh, PA, c1870, and by U. S. Glass Co., c1898. Also found in milk glass. Goblets are found in six variations. Note: A goblet with a tin lid, containing a condiment (mustard, jelly, or baking powder) was made. It is of inferior quality compared to the original goblet.

	Clear		Clear
Bowl		Egg Cup.	40.00
7¼", oval.	20.00	Goblet, knob stem.	35.00
8".	35.00	Honey Dish.	18.00
9¼", oval, cov	65.00	Mug, 3¼".	55.00
Butter, cov	65.00	Pickle, 8¾" l, 5" w, pear	
Cake Stand		shape	35.00
9".	60.00	Pitcher, water, applied	
10".	85.00	handle.	150.00
11".	90.00	Plate	75.00
Dessert slots	125.00	Platter, oval.	65.00
Compote		Relish, oval, 5½ x 3⅝".	35.00
Cov, hs, 8".	75.00	Salt, master, ftd.	45.00
Cov, hs, 9".	95.00	Salt, oval, flat	20.00
Cov, ls, 7".	60.00	Sauce, flat	10.00
Cov, ls, 7½".	60.00	Spooner	30.00
Cov, ls, 8".	75.00	Sugar	
Open, ls, 8½"	30.00	Cov.	60.00
Creamer, applied handle . . .	65.00	Open	25.00
Creamer, molded handle . . .	35.00	Tumbler, ftd	75.00
Dish, cov, 7"	48.00	Wine	150.00+

BLOCK AND FAN

Non-flint made by Richard and Hartley Glass Co., Tarentum, PA, late 1880s. Continued by U. S. Glass Co. after 1891.

	Clear	Ruby Stained		Clear	Ruby Stained
Biscuit Jar, cov	65.00	100.00	Regular.	25.00	45.00
Bowl			Large	30.00	100.00
4", flat.	15.00	—	Small	35.00	75.00
8", flat.	25.00	—	Cruet, os	40.00	—
8", ftd	20.00	—	Dish, large, rect. . . .	25.00	—
10 x 6", rect.	50.00	—	Finger Bowl	55.00	—
Butter, cov	45.00	65.00	Goblet	45.00	85.00
Cake Stand			Ice Tub.	45.00	50.00
9".	32.50	—	Orange Bowl.	50.00	—
10".	35.00	—	Pickle Dish	20.00	—
Carafe	40.00	95.00	Pitcher		
Celery Tray.	25.00	—	Milk.	35.00	—
Celery Vase	30.00	75.00	Water	45.00	125.00
Compote			Plate		
Open, hs, 8". . . .	40.00	165.00	6".	20.00	—
Open, ls, 4". . . .	10.00	—	10".	22.00	—
Open, ls, 7". . . .	25.00	—	Relish, rect.	25.00	—
Open, ls, 8".	30.00	—	Rose Bowl	25.00	—
Condiment Set, salt,			Salt & Pepper	30.00	—
pepper & cruet on			Sauce		
tray	75.00	—	Flat, 5.	8.00	—
Creamer			Ftd, 3¾"	12.00	25.00
Individual.	—	35.00	Spooner	25.00	—

	Clear	Ruby Stained		Clear	Ruby Stained
Sugar, cov	45.00	—	Tumbler	30.00	—
Sugar Shaker	40.00	—	Waste Bowl	30.00	—
Syrup	65.00	95.00	Wine	45.00	65.00
Tray, Ice Cream, rect	75.00	—			

BOSWORTH (Star Band)

Non-flint, Indiana Glass Co., c1907.

	Clear		Clear
Bowl, berry	12.00	Pitcher, water	30.00
Butter, cov	25.00	Relish	12.00
Celery Vase, handles	18.00	Spooner	15.00
Compote, jelly	15.00	Sugar, cov	30.00
Creamer	20.00	Tumbler	15.00
Goblet	25.00	Wine	20.00

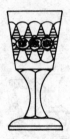

BOW TIE

Non-flint made by Thompson Glass Co., Uniontown, PA, c1889.

	Clear		Clear
Bowl		Pitcher	
8"	35.00	Milk	85.00
10¼ d, 5" h	65.00	Water	75.00
Butter, cov	65.00	Punch Bowl	100.00
Butter Pat	25.00	Relish, rect	25.00
Cake Stand, large, 9" d	60.00	Salt	
Compote, open		Individual	20.00
hs, 5½"	60.00	Master	45.00
hs, 9¼"	65.00	Salt Shaker	40.00
ls, 6½"	45.00	Sauce, flat	18.00
ls, 8"	55.00	Spooner	35.00
Creamer	45.00	Sugar	
Goblet	60.00	Cov	55.00
Honey, cov	55.00	Open	40.00
Marmalade Jar	75.00	Tumbler	45.00
Orange Bowl, ftd, hs, 10"	75.00		

BRITTANIC

Non-flint, made by McKee & Bros, c1902, and McKee-Jeanette Glass Works, c1903. Also made in emerald green in a finger or waste bowl. Also made in amber stain, valued at 80% of ruby stained prices.

	Clear	Ruby Stained		Clear	Ruby Stained
Banana Stand	75.00	100.00	Compote, cov	55.00	75.00
Bowl, berry	20.00	30.00	Creamer	30.00	50.00
Butter, cov	40.00	90.00	Custard Cup	15.00	—
Cake Stand	45.00	—	Cruet, os	35.00	150.00
Castor Set, 4 bottles	65.00	175.00	Goblet	30.00	55.00

	Clear	Ruby Stained		Clear	Ruby Stained
Honey Dish, cov, sq	50.00	—	Salt and Pepper ...	45.00	85.00
Lamp			Spooner	25.00	45.00
7½"	65.00	—	Sugar, cov	40.00	85.00
8½"	75.00	—	Toothpick	25.00	150.00
Mug, 3¾"	15.00	25.00	Tumbler	20.00	45.00
Pitcher, water	50.00	100.00	Wine	22.00	48.00
Rose Bowl	20.00	75.00			

BROKEN COLUMN (Irish Column, Notched Rib, Rattan)

Made in Findlay, Ohio, c1891, by Columbia Glass Co., c1892, and later made by U. S. Glass Co. May also have been made at Portland, ME. Notches may be ruby stained. A cobalt blue cup is known. The square covered compote has been reproduced. Some items have been reproduced for the Metropolitan Museum of Art. Some items are reproduced by the Smithsonian Institution with a raised "SI" trademark.

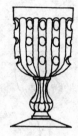

	Clear	Ruby Stained		Clear	Ruby Stained
Banana Stand.....	110.00	—	Creamer.........	42.50	125.00
Basket, applied han-			Cruet, os	85.00	150.00
dle, 12" h, 15" l ..	125.00	—	Decanter	95.00	—
Biscuit Jar	85.00	165.00	Finger Bowl	30.00	—
Bowl			* Goblet	48.00	100.00
4", berry	—	20.00	Marmalade Jar	85.00	—
6", berry	20.00	45.00	Pickle Castor, sp		
8"	35.00	—	frame	95.00	400.00
9"	40.00	—	Pitcher, water	90.00	215.00
Bread Plate	60.00	125.00	Plate		
Butter, cov	85.00	175.00	4"	—	20.00
Cake Stand			5"	35.00	—
9"	70.00	225.00	7½"	40.00	95.00
10"	80.00	245.00	Relish		
Carafe, water	65.00	150.00	Oval, 7½ x 4" ...	20.00	—
Celery Tray, oval...	35.00	—	Oval, 11 x 5"...	22.00	—
Celery Vase	50.00	135.00	Rect, 7½ x 5" ...	25.00	—
Claret...........	45.00	—	Salt Shaker.......	30.00	65.00
Compote			* Sauce, flat	15.00	30.00
Cov, hs, 5¼" d,			* Spooner	35.00	85.00
10½" h.......	65.00	200.00	Sugar, cov	75.00	140.00
Cov, hs, 7" d, 12"			Sugar Shaker	60.00	200.00
h	85.00	—	Syrup..........	130.00	400.00
Cov, hs, 10".....	70.00	350.00	Toothpick	250.00	—
Open, hs, 7" d ...	—	150.00	Tumbler	42.00	55.00
Open, hs, 8" d ...	75.00	175.00	Vegetable, cov	90.00	—
Open, ls, 5" d, 6"			Wine	50.00	125.00
h, flared......	65.00	135.00			

BUCKLE

Flint and non-flint pattern. Sandwich Glass Co. in Massachusetts is attributed to the flint production. The non-flint production was made by Gillinder and Sons in Philadelphia, PA, in the late 1870s.

	Flint	Non-Flint
Bowl		
8", berry, orig had wire basket frame.	60.00	50.00
10"	60.00	50.00
Butter, cov	65.00	60.00
Cake Stand, 9¾".	—	30.00
Compote		
Cov, hs, 6" d	95.00	40.00
Open, hs, 8½", fluted	45.00	40.00
Open, ls	40.00	35.00
Creamer, applied handle	110.00	40.00

	Flint	Non-Flint
Egg Cup	35.00	28.00
Goblet	45.00	30.00
Pickle	40.00	15.00
Pitcher, water, applied handle	425.00	85.00
Salt, flat, oval	30.00	15.00
Salt, footed	24.00	18.00
Sauce, flat	10.00	8.00
Spooner	40.00	35.00
Sugar		
Cov	75.00	55.00
Open	45.00	28.00
Tumbler	55.00	30.00
Wine	90.00	45.00

BUCKLE WITH STAR (Orient)

Non-flint made by Bryce, Walker and Co. in 1875, U. S. Glass Co. in 1891. Finials are shaped like Maltese crosses.

	Clear
Bowl	
6", cov	25.00
7", oval	15.00
8", oval	15.00
9", oval	15.00
10", oval	18.00
Butter, cov	50.00
Cake Stand	30.00
Celery Vase	30.00
Compote	
Cov, hs, 7"	60.00
Open, hs, 9½"	30.00
Creamer	35.00
Goblet	30.00
Mug	60.00
Mustard, cov	75.00
Pickle	15.00
Pitcher, water, applied handle	70.00

	Clear
Relish	15.00
Salt, master, ftd	20.00
Sauce	
Flat	8.00
Footed	10.00
Spooner	20.00
Sugar	
Cov	40.00
Open	20.00
Syrup	
Applied handle, pewter or Brittania top, man's head finial	80.00
Molded handle, plain tin top	60.00
Tumbler	55.00
Wine	35.00

BUDDED IVY

Non-flint, c1870. Contemporary of Stippled Ivy. Pieces have applied handles and ivy leaf finials.

	Clear
Butter, cov	45.00
Compote	
Cov, hs	60.00
Cov, ls	45.00
Open, hs	25.00
Creamer	38.00
Egg Cup	30.00
Goblet	28.50
Pitcher, water	50.00

	Clear
Relish	17.50
Salt, ftd	25.00
Sauce, ftd	7.50
Spooner	24.00
Sugar	
Covered	45.00
Open	25.00
Syrup	45.00
Wine	28.50

BULL'S EYE

Flint made by the New England Glass Co. in the 1850s. Also found in colors and milk glass, which doubles the price.

	Clear		Clear
Butter, cov	150.00	Lamp	100.00
Carafe	45.00	Mug, 3½", applied handle	110.00
Castor Bottle	35.00	Pitcher, water	285.00
Celery Vase	85.00	Relish, oval	25.00
Champagne	95.00	Salt	
Cologne Bottle	85.00	Individual	38.50
Cordial	75.00	Master, ftd	100.00
Creamer	125.00	Spooner	40.00
Cruet	85.00	Sugar, cov	125.00
Decanter, qt, bar lip	120.00	Tumbler	85.00
Egg Cup		Water Bottle, tumble up	100.00
Cov	165.00	Whiskey	70.00
Open	48.00	Wine	50.00
Goblet	65.00		

BULL'S EYE AND DAISY

Made by U. S. Glass Co., 1909. Also made with amethyst, blue, green, and pink stains in eyes. Prices close to ruby stained pieces.

	Clear	Emerald Green	Ruby Stained
Bowl	12.00	16.00	25.00
Butter, cov	25.00	28.00	90.00
Celery Vase	18.00	25.00	40.00
Creamer	20.00	22.00	50.00
Decanter	—	110.00	—
Goblet	20.00	22.00	50.00
Pitcher, water	35.00	40.00	95.00
Salt Shaker	20.00	20.00	35.00
Sauce	7.00	10.00	20.00
Spooner	15.00	20.00	40.00
Sugar, open	20.00	30.00	45.00
Tumbler	14.00	16.00	35.00
Wine	24.00	32.50	42.50

BULL'S EYE AND FAN (Daisies in Oval Panels)

Made by U.S. Glass, c1910.

	Amethyst Stain	Clear	Emerald Green	Pink Stain	Sapphire Blue Stain
Bowl					
5", pinched ends	—	—	18.00	—	—
8", berry	—	15.00	20.00	—	30.00
Butter, cov	—	45.00	65.00	—	—
Cake Stand	—	25.00	—	—	—
Creamer					
Individual	—	14.00	—	—	—
Regular	—	25.00	30.00	—	35.00
Custard Cup	—	10.00	—	—	—
Goblet	25.00	24.00	45.00	25.00	45.00

	Amethyst Stain	Clear	Emerald Green	Pink Stain	Sapphire Blue Stain
Lemonade Mug. 5" .	—	20.00	—	—	—
Pitcher					
Lemonade, ftd . . .	—	55.00	—	—	—
Water, tankard . . .	55.00	40.00	100.00	50.00	100.00
Relish.	20.00	18.00	35.00	20.00	35.00
Sauce	25.00	16.00	20.00	25.00	30.00
Spooner	25.00	21.50	45.00	25.00	45.00
Sugar, cov	40.00	35.00	60.00	30.00	35.00
Toothpick	—	35.00	45.00	65.00	—
Tumbler	55.00	15.00	45.00	40.00	35.00
Wine	22.00	20.00	40.00	40.00	25.00

BULL'S EYE WITH DIAMOND POINT (Union)

Made in flint by New England Glass Co., c1869.

	Clear		Clear
Butter, cov	225.00	Pitcher, water, 10¼", tankard	275.00
Celery Vase	165.00	Salt, master, cov	100.00
Champagne	145.00	Sauce	20.00
Cologne Bottle, os.	90.00	Spooner	100.00
Creamer.	200.00	Sugar, cov	175.00
Cruet, os	80.00	Syrup.	155.00
Decanter, qt, os.	200.00	Tumbler	125.00
Egg Cup.	90.00	Tumble-Up	165.00
Goblet	120.00	Whiskey	150.00
Honey Dish, flat	25.00	Wine	135.00
Lamp, finger, applied handle	150.00		

BULL'S EYE WITH FLEUR-DE-LIS

Flint, c1850.

	Clear		Clear
Bar Bottle, qt	110.00	Lamp, marble base	175.00
Bowl, fruit.	85.00	Mug, handle	100.00
Butter, cov	175.00	Pitcher, water	375.00
Celery Vase	85.00	Salt, master	55.00
Creamer.	250.00	Spooner.	50.00
Egg Cup.	50.00	Sugar, cov	115.00
Goblet	80.00	Wine	50.00

BUTTERFLY & FAN (Grace, Japanese)

Non-flint pattern made by Duncan, Pittsburgh, PA, c1880.

	Clear		Clear
Bread Plate	40.00	Cov, hs, 7" d	95.00
Butter, cov, ftd.	50.00	Open, hs.	30.00
Celery Vase	35.00	Creamer, ftd	30.00
Compote		Goblet	30.00
Cov, hs, 8" d	95.00	Marmalade Jar	50.00

	Clear			Clear
Sauce, ftd	15.00	Open		26.00
Spooner	30.00	Tumbler		15.00
Sugar, ftd				
Covered	40.00			

BUTTON ARCHES

Non-flint, made by Duncan and Miller Glass Co. in 1885. Pieces have frosted band. Some pieces, known as "Koral," usually souvenir type, are also seen in clambroth, trimmed in gold. In the early 1970s souvenir ruby stained pieces, including a goblet and table set, were reproduced.

	Clambroth	Clear	Ruby Stained
Bowl, 8″	—	20.00	50.00
Butter, cov	—	48.00	100.00
Cake Stand, 9″	—	35.00	180.00
Compote, jelly	—	48.00	50.00
Creamer	25.00	20.00	45.00
Cruet, os	—	55.00	175.00
* Goblet	40.00	25.00	40.00
Mug	30.00	25.00	30.00
Mustrd, cov, underplate	—	—	100.00
Pitcher			
Milk	—	35.00	80.00
Water, tankard	—	75.00	125.00
Plate, 7″	—	10.00	25.00
Punch Cup	—	15.00	25.00
Salt, ind	—	15.00	
Salt Shaker, three types	—	15.00	30.00
Sauce, flat	—	12.50	22.00
Spooner	—	25.00	40.00
Sugar, cov	—	35.00	75.00
Syrup	—	—	175.00
Toothpick	30.00	24.00	35.00
Tumbler	20.00	24.00	35.00
Wine	25.00	15.00	35.00

BUTTON BAND (Umbilicated Hobnail, Wyandotte)

Non-flint made by Ripley and Co. in 1880s and U. S. Glass Co. in 1890s. Can often be found engraved, priced the same.

	Clear			Clear
Bowl, 10″	30.00	Goblet		30.00
Butter, cov	45.00	Pitcher		
Cake Stand, 10″	60.00	Milk		40.00
Castor Set, 5 bottles in glass stand	135.00	Water, tankard		50.00
Compote		Spooner		20.00
Cov, hs, 9″	95.00	Sugar, cov		30.00
Open, 1s	45.00	Tray, water		40.00
Cordial	25.00	Tumbler		20.00
Creamer	30.00	Wine		35.00

CABBAGE ROSE

Non-flint made by Central Glass Co, Wheeling, WV, c1870. Reproduced in colors.

	Clear		Clear
Basket, handled, 12″	100.00	Cov, ls, 8½″...........	110.00
Bitters Bottle, 6½″ h	100.00	Open, hs, 7½″.........	75.00
Bowl, Oval		Open, hs, 9½″.........	100.00
7½″..................	32.50	Creamer, applied handle ...	55.00
8½″..................	38.00	Egg Cup..............	35.00
9½″..................	40.00	* Goblet	40.00
Bowl, Round		Mug..................	60.00
6″...................	25.00	Pitcher	
7½″, cov	65.00	Milk.................	150.00
7½″, open	35.00	Water	125.00
Butter, cov	60.00	Relish, 8½″ l, 5″ w, rose-filled	
Cake Stand		horn of plenty center	38.00
11″.................	40.00	Salt, master, ftd.........	28.00
12½″................	50.00	Sauces, six sizes	10–20.00
Celery Vase	48.00	Spooner...............	25.00
Champagne	50.00	Sugar	
Compote		Cov.................	55.00
Cov, hs, 7½″	110.00	Open, buttermilk type....	40.00
Cov, hs, 8½″	120.00	Tumbler	40.00
Cov, ls, 6″	95.00	Wine	35.00
Cov, ls, 7½″..........	100.00		

CABLE

Flint, c1850. Made by Boston and Sandwich Glass Co. to commemorate the laying of Atlantic Cable. Also found with amber stained panels and in opaque colors (rare).

	Clear		Clear
Bowl		Goblet	75.00
8″, ftd	45.00	Honey Dish............	15.00
9″..................	70.00	Lamp, 8¾″	
Butter, cov	100.00	Glass Base	135.00
Cake Stand, 9″	55.00	Marble Base	100.00
Celery Vase	75.00	Pitcher, water, rare	425.00
Champagne	250.00	Plate, 6″..............	75.00
Compote, open		Salt, ind, flat	35.00
hs, 5½″	65.00	Salt, master, cov	45.00
ls, 7″................	50.00	Sauce, flat	20.00
ls, 9″................	55.00	Spooner...............	40.00
ls, 11″	75.00	Sugar, cov	95.00
Creamer...............	400.00	Syrup	145.00
Decanter, qt, ground stopper.	155.00	Tumbler, ftd	175.00
Egg Cup		Wine	125.00
Cov.................	225.00		
Open	60.00		

CACTUS

Non-flint made by Indiana Tumbler and Goblet Co. c1895. Made in clear and chocolate. Pattern made in opalescent vaseline by Fenton Art Glass in 1950.
Additional Listings: Greentown Glass (chocolate pieces).

Bowl	Clear
7¼" d	50.00
8¼"	70.00
Butter, cov	125.00
Cake stand	165.00
Celery Vase	80.00
Compote, cov, hs, 8¼"	125.00
Creamer, cov	80.00
Cruet, os	100.00
Mug	50.00
Nappy	50.00

	Clear
Pitcher, water	175.00
Plate, 7½"	80.00
Sauce	
Flat, 5¼"	32.50
Footed	45.00
Spooner	50.00
Sugar, cov	80.00
Syrup	65.00
* Toothpick	50.00
Tumbler	45.00
Vase, 6"	60.00

CALIFORNIA (Beaded Grape)

Non-flint made by U. S. Glass Co., Pittsburgh, PA, c1890. Also with gold trim.

Bowl	Clear	Emerald Green
5½", sq	18.00	20.00
5½ x 8"	—	30.00
6" sq	—	25.00
7½", sq	25.00	35.00
8", round	28.00	30.00
Bread Plate, 10¼ x 7¼"	25.00	45.00
Butter, cov	65.00	100.00
Cake Stand, 9"	65.00	85.00
Celery Tray	30.00	45.00
Celery Vase	45.00	65.00
Compote		
Cov, hs, 6½"	65.00	95.00
Open, hs, 5", sq.	55.00	75.00
Open, hs, 7"	45.00	80.00
Open, hs, jelly	55.00	75.00

	Clear	Emerald Green
Creamer	40.00	50.00
Cruet, orig swirled stopper	65.00	125.00
* Goblet	35.00	50.00
Olive, handle	20.00	35.00
Pickle	20.00	30.00
Pitcher, water	85.00	120.00
* Plate, 8¼", sq.	28.00	40.00
Salt & Pepper	45.00	65.00
* Sauce, 4"	15.00	18.00
Spooner	30.00	45.00
Sugar, cov	45.00	55.00
Sugar Shaker	75.00	85.00
Toothpick	35.00	65.00
* Tumbler	32.50	45.00
* Wine	35.00	65.00

CANADIAN

Non-flint, made by Burlington Glass Works, Hamilton, Ontario, Canada, c1870.

	Clear
Bowl, 7" d, 4½" h, ftd	75.00
Bread Plate, 10"	45.00
Butter, cov	85.00
Cake Stand, 9¼"	95.00
Celery Vase	55.00
Compote	
Cov, hs, 6"	50.00
Cov, hs, 7"	95.00
Cov, hs, 8"	110.00
Cov, ls, 6"	50.00
Open, ls, 7"	35.00
Creamer	55.00

	Clear
Goblet	50.00
Mug, small	40.00
Pitcher	
Milk	75.00
Water	90.00
Plate, 6", handles	30.00
Sauce	
Flat	15.00
Footed	18.00
Spooner	45.00
Sugar, cov	80.00
Wine	35.00

CANE

Non-flint made by Gillinder Glass Co. and McKee Glass Co., c1885. Goblets and toddy plates with inverted "buttons" known.

	Amber	Apple Green	Blue	Clear	Vaseline
Bowl, 9½", oval....	15.00	—	—	—	—
Butter, cov	45.00	60.00	75.00	40.00	60.00
Celery Vase	38.00	40.00	50.00	32.50	40.00
Compote, open, ls, 5¾"..........	28.00	30.00	35.00	25.00	35.00
Creamer.........	35.00	40.00	50.00	25.00	30.00
Finger Bowl	20.00	30.00	35.00	15.00	30.00
Goblet	28.50	40.00	35.00	20.00	35.00
Honey Dish.......	—	—	—	15.00	—
Match holder, kettle.	18.00	—	35.00	30.00	35.00
Pickle...........	25.00	20.00	25.00	15.00	20.00
Pitcher, milk	60.00	55.00	65.00	40.00	55.00
Pitcher, water	60.00	55.00	65.00	40.00	55.00
Plate, toddy, 4½"...	20.00	25.00	30.00	14.00	18.00
Salt & Pepper.....	60.00	50.00	80.00	30.00	70.00
Sauce, flat	—	9.50	—	7.00	—
Slipper	30.00	—	25.00	15.00	30.00
Spooner.........	42.00	35.00	30.00	20.00	30.00
Sugar, cov	45.00	45.00	45.00	25.00	45.00
Tray, water	35.00	35.00	45.00	30.00	40.00
Tumbler	24.00	30.00	35.00	20.00	25.00
Waste Bowl, 7½"...	35.00	30.00	35.00	20.00	30.00
Wine	35.00	40.00	35.00	20.00	35.00

CANE HORSESHOE (Paragon)

Made by U. S. Glass Co., 1909. Prices are for pieces with gold trim.

	Clear		Clear
Bowl, 8"	15.00	Cruet, os	30.00
Butter, cov	25.00	Goblet	20.00
Cake Stand	30.00	Pitcher, water	40.00
Celery Tray...........	20.00	Relish.................	15.00
Celery Vase	25.00	Sauce	10.00
Compote		Spooner..............	20.00
Cov, hs.............	45.00	Sugar, cov	30.00
Open, hs............	35.00	Syrup	35.00
Open, ls	35.00	Tumbler	15.00
Creamer.............	30.00	Wine	20.00

CAPE COD

Non-flint, attributed to Boston and Sandwich Glass Co., c1870.

	Clear		Clear
Bowl, 6", handled	30.00	Compote	
Bread Plate	45.00	Cov, hs, 6" d	50.00
Butter, cov	55.00	Cov, hs, 8"...........	100.00
Celery Vase	45.00	Cov, hs, 12"..........	175.00

	Clear		Clear
Cov, ls, 6″	50.00	Plate	
Open, hs, 7″	50.00	5″, handles	30.00
Creamer	45.00	10″	45.00
Decanter	160.00	Platter, open handles	45.00
Goblet	45.00	Sauce, ftd	20.00
Marmalade Jar, cov	65.00	Spooner	35.00
Pitcher		Sugar, cov	55.00
Milk	65.00	Wine	35.00
Water	75.00		

CARDINAL

Non-flint, c1875, attributed to Ohio Flint Glass Co., Lancaster, OH. There were two butter dishes made, one in the regular pattern and one with three birds in the base - labeled in script Red Bird (cardinal), Pewit, and Titmouse. The latter is less common. Goblet and creamer reproduced.

	Clear		Clear
Butter, cov		Pitcher, water	125.00
Regular	65.00	Sauce	
Three birds in base	75.00	Flat, 4″	10.00
Cake Stand	75.00	Footed, 4½″ or 5½″	20.00
* Creamer	35.00	Spooner	35.00
* Goblet	35.00	Sugar	
Honey Dish, 3½″		Cov	65.00
Cov	45.00	Open	35.00
Open	20.00		

CAROLINA (Inverness)

Made by Bryce Brothers and later by U. S. Glass Co., as part of the States series, c1903. Ruby stained pieces often are souvenir marked. Some clear pieces found with gilt or purple stain.

	Clear	Ruby Stained		Clear	Ruby Stained
Bowl, berry	18.00	—	Pitcher, milk	55.00	—
Butter, cov	50.00	—	Plate, 7½″	12.00	—
Cake Stand	35.00	—	Relish	12.00	—
Compote			Salt Shaker	15.00	35.00
Open, hs, 8″, beaded	50.00	—	Sauce		
Open, hs, 9½″	24.00	—	Flat	10.00	—
Open, jelly	12.00	—	Footed	15.00	—
Creamer	20.00	—	Spooner	25.00	—
Goblet	35.00	45.00	Sugar, cov	30.00	—
Mug	30.00	35.00	Tumbler	20.00	—
			Wine	22.50	35.00

CATHEDRAL (Orion)

Non-flint pattern made by Bryce Bros., Pittsburgh, PA., in the 1880s and by U. S. Glass Co. in 1891. Also found in ruby stained, add 50% to clear prices.

	Amber	Amethyst	Blue	Clear	Vaseline
Bowl, berry, 8″	35.00	50.00	40.00	25.00	40.00
Butter, cov	60.00	110.00	62.00	45.00	60.00
Cake Stand	50.00	75.00	60.00	40.00	68.00
Celery Vase	35.00	60.00	40.00	30.00	38.00
Compote					
Cov, hs, 8″	80.00	125.00	100.00	70.00	90.00
Open, hs, 9½″ . . .	50.00	85.00	65.00	40.00	—
Open, ls, 7″	45.00	80.00	35.00	25.00	48.00
Open, jelly	—	—	—	25.00	—
Creamer					
Flat, sq	50.00	82.00	—	35.00	48.00
Tall	45.00	80.00	50.00	30.00	45.00
Cruet, os	80.00	—	—	45.00	—
Goblet	48.00	70.00	50.00	30.00	55.00
Lamp, 12¾″ h	—	—	185.00	—	—
Pitcher, water	75.00	110.00	75.00	60.00	100.00
Relish, fish shape . .	40.00	50.00	50.00	—	45.00
Salt, boat shape . . .	15.00	30.00	20.00	10.00	20.00
Sauce					
Flat	16.00	30.00	20.00	12.00	16.00
Footed	18.00	35.00	22.00	15.00	20.00
Spooner	40.00	65.00	50.00	35.00	45.00
Sugar, cov	70.00	100.00	60.00	50.00	60.00
Tumbler	32.50	40.00	35.00	25.00	40.00
Wine	40.00	60.00	55.00	28.00	50.00

CHAIN WITH STAR

Non-flint, made by Portland Glass Co, Portland, ME, and U. S. Glass Co., c1890.

	Clear		Clear
Bread Plate, 11″, handles . .	30.00	Pitcher, water	50.00
Butter, cov	35.00	Plate, 7″	25.00
Cake Stand		Relish	12.50
8¾″	30.00	Salt Shaker	20.00
10½″	35.00	Sauce	
Compote		Flat	12.50
Cov, hs	55.00	Footed	14.00
Cov, ls	45.00	Spooner	20.00
Open, ls	30.00	Sugar, cov	35.00
Creamer	25.00	Syrup	45.00
Goblet	25.00	Wine	20.00
Pickle, oval	12.00		

CHAMPION (Greentown #11)

Made by McKee Bros. and Indiana Tumbler and Goblet Co., 1894–1917. Pieces are often found with gold trim.

	Amber Stained	Clear	Emerald Green	Ruby Stained
Bowl, sq or round				
Berry, master	55.00	—	—	65.00
Berry, individual . .	—		—	
Butter, cov	100.00	45.00	—	100.00
Cake Stand	100.00	35.00	—	90.00

	Amber Stained	Clear	Emerald Green	Ruby Stained
Celery Vase	—	—	—	100.00
Compote				
Cov.	—	55.00	—	—
Open, fluted top. .	150.00	40.00	—	225.00
Creamer.	—	25.00	—	60.00
Cruet, os	150.00	30.00	—	195.00
Cup	—	—	—	25.00
Goblet	65.00	25.00	—	65.00
Ice Bucket	125.00	40.00	—	—
Marmalade Jar	—	25.00	—	—
Pickle Dish, 8″.	—	15.00	—	—
Pitcher, water	150.00	70.00	—	175.00
Plate, 8″ or 10″	—	25.00	—	—
Rose Bowl	—	25.00	45.00	—
Salt Dip	—	10.00	—	65.00
Salt Shaker.	35.00	15.00	—	35.00
Spooner	40.00	20.00	—	45.00
Sugar, cov	75.00	40.00	—	85.00
Syrup	150.00	75.00	—	—
Toothpick	65.00	20.00	40.00	70.00
Tray, water	—	45.00	—	—
Tumbler	40.00	15.00	—	45.00
Wine	—	20.00	—	—

CHANDELIER (Crown Jewel)

Non-flint, O'Hara Glass Co., Pittsburgh, PA, c1880, continued by U. S. Glass Co. Also attributed to Canadian manufacturer. Sauce bowls made in amber, $35.00.

	Etched	Plain		Etched	Plain
Banana Stand.	—	85.00	Pitcher, water	80.00	80.00
Bowl, 8″ d, 3¼″ h . .	35.00	37.50	Salt, Master	—	35.00
Butter, cov	85.00	65.00	Salt & Pepper	75.00	50.00
Cake Stand, 10″ . . .	85.00	70.00	Sauce, flat	—	16.50
Celery Vase	40.00	40.00	Sponge Dish.	—	30.00
Compote			Spooner.	35.00	30.00
Cov, hs	80.00	75.00	Sugar, cov	70.00	60.00
Open, hs, 9½″ . . .	70.00	68.00	Sugar Shaker	75.00	60.00
Creamer.	60.00	50.00	Tray, water	70.00	50.00
Finger Bowl	40.00	30.00	Tumbler	40.00	38.50
Goblet	45.00	40.00	Violet Bowl	—	40.00
Inkwell, dated hard					
rubber top	—	85.00			

CHECKERBOARD (Bridle Rosette)

Made by Westmoreland Glass Co., early 1900s. Reproduced earlier in milk glass and in recent years with pink stain. The Cambridge "Ribbon" pattern, usually marked Nearcut, is similar.

	Clear		Clear
Bowl, 9″, shallow.	20.00	Compote, open, ls, 8″	25.00
Butter, cov	35.00	Creamer.	25.00
Celery Tray.	15.00	Cruet, os	40.00
Celery Vase	30.00	Cup	10.00

	Clear			Clear
Goblet	30.00	Salt and Pepper		40.00
Honey, cov, sq, pedestal	45.00	Sauce, flat		8.00
Pitcher		Spooner		24.00
Milk	40.00	Sugar, cov		35.00
Water	35.00	Tumbler		
Plate		Iced Tea		15.00
7"	22.00	Water		18.00
10"	25.00	Wine		12.00
Punch Cup	5.00			

CHERRY THUMBPRINT (Cherry & Cable, Paneled Cherry)

Non-flint pattern made by Northwood Glass Co. in the late 1880s. Some pieces are decorated with colored cherries and the cable is gold. Some items have been reproduced.

	Clear	Decorated		Clear	Decorated
Bowl, berry	15.00	30.00	Sauce, ftd	15.00	20.00
Butter, cov	45.00	95.00	Spooner	35.00	50.00
Creamer	35.00	60.00	Sugar, cov	65.00	85.00
Cup, pedestal	15.00	30.00	Tumbler	30.00	45.00
Pitcher, water	80.00	110.00			

CLASSIC

Clear and frosted non-flint produced by Gillinder and Sons, Philadelphia, PA, in the late 1870s. Pieces with log feet instead of a flat or collared base are worth more.

	Clear		Clear
Bowl, 7", cov, log feet	125.00	Plate	
Butter, cov, log feet	200.00	Jas G. Blaine	185.00
Celery Vase		Pres. Cleveland	180.00
Collared	100.00	Thomas H. Hendricks	170.00
Log feet	125.00	John A. Logan	225.00
Compote		Warrior	160.00
Cov, 6½", collared	150.00	Sauce	
Cov, 6½", log feet	240.00	Flat	30.00
Cov, 7½"d, log feet	220.00	Log Feet	45.00
Cov, 8½", collared	175.00	Spooner	
Cov, 12½", collared	325.00	Collared	95.00
Open, 7¾", log feet	100.00	Log feet	125.00
Creamer	150.00	Sugar, cov	
Goblet	210.00	Collared	150.00
Marmalade Jar, cov	350.00	Log feet	175.00
Pitcher, water		Sweetmeat Jar	175.00
Collared	200.00		
Log feet	250.00		

CLASSIC MEDALLION (Cameo #1)

A pattern of 1870–1880, maker unknown.

	Clear		Clear
Bowl		Creamer	35.00
6¾″, ftd	38.00	Pitcher, water	80.00
8″, straight sides	30.00	Sauce, ftd	15.00
Butter, cov	40.00	Spooner	25.00
Celery Vase	30.00	Sugar, cov	40.00
Compote			
Cov, hs	50.00		
Open, 7″d, 3¾″h	30.00		

CLEAR DIAGONAL BAND

Non-flint, c1880. Also has been found in light amber.

	Clear		Clear
Bread Plate, Eureka	40.00	Marmalade Jar	35.00
Butter, cov	40.00	Pitcher, water	40.00
Cake Stand	40.00	Plate	15.00
Celery Vase	25.00	Relish, oval	8.00
Compote		Salt & Pepper	30.00
Cov, hs	45.00	Sauce, flat	7.50
Cov, ls	30.00	Spooner	20.00
Creamer	' 25.00	Sugar, cov	40.00
Dish, oval	10.00	Wine	20.00
Goblet	18.00		

COIN—COLUMBIAN

Non-flint, c1890. Prices listed for clear, frosted 50% higher.

	Clear		Clear
Butter, cov	125.00	Salt & Pepper Shakers, pr . .	50.00
Cake Stand	40.00	Sauce	12.00
Celery	75.00	Spooner	45.00
Compote		Sugar	
Cov, 8″	75.00	Covered	60.00
Open, 7″	60.00	Open	35.00
Creamer	65.00	Syrup, gold coins	225.00
Cruet	65.00	* Toothpick	25.00
* Goblet	55.00	Tray, water	125.00
Lamp, oil, 9½″	125.00	* Tumbler	25.00
Pitcher		Wine	70.00
Milk, gilt	175.00		
Water	75.00		

COLORADO (Lacy Medallion)

Non-flint States pattern made by U. S. Glass Co. in 1898. Made in amethyst stained, ruby stained, and opaque white with enamel floral trim, all of which are scarce. Some pieces found with ornate silver frames or feet. Purists consider these two are separate patterns, with the Lacy Medallion restricted to souvenir pieces. Reproductions have been made.

	Blue	Clear	Green
Banana Stand	45.00	25.00	40.00
Bowl			
6"	35.00	20.00	30.00
7½", ftd	40.00	25.00	35.00
8½", ftd	65.00	45.00	60.00
Butter, cov	200.00	60.00	125.00
Cake Stand	70.00	55.00	65.00
Celery Vase	65.00	35.00	48.00
Compote			
Open, ls, 6"	45.00	20.00	42.00
Open, ls, 9¼" . . .	95.00	35.00	65.00
Creamer			
Individual.	45.00	24.00	40.00
Regular.	95.00	45.00	70.00
Mug	40.00	20.00	30.00
Nappy	40.00	18.00	35.00
Pitcher			
Milk.	145.00	—	100.00
Water	375.00	125.00	185.00
Plate			
6"	50.00	18.00	45.00
8"	65.00	20.00	60.00
Punch Cup	30.00	20.00	25.00
Salt Shaker.	65.00	30.00	40.00
Sauce, ruffled	35.00	15.00	25.00
Sherbet	50.00	15.00	45.00
Spooner	75.00	40.00	60.00
Sugar			
Cov, regular.	80.00	65.00	75.00
Open, individual. .	35.00	24.00	30.00
Toothpick	60.00	35.00	45.00
Tray, Calling Card . .	45.00	25.00	35.00
Tumbler	35.00	18.00	30.00
Vase, 12"	85.00	35.00	60.00
Violet Bowl	60.00	—	—
Wine	—	25.00	40.00

COMET

Flint made by Boston and Sandwich Glass Co in the late 1840s and early 1850s.

	Clear		Clear
Butter, cov	200.00	Pitcher, water	575.00
Compote, open, ls	140.00	Spooner	85.00
Creamer.	175.00	Tumbler	110.00
Goblet	90.00	Whiskey	110.00
Mug.	135.00		

CONNECTICUT

Non-flint. One of the States patterns made by U. S. Glass Co., c1900. Found in plain and engraved. Two varieties of ruby stained toothpicks ($90.00) have been identified.

	Clear		Clear
Biscuit Jar	25.00	Dish, 8", oblong.	20.00
Bowl		Lemonade, handled.	20.00
4"	10.00	Pitcher, water	40.00
8"	15.00	Relish.	12.00
Butter, cov	35.00	Salt & Pepper	35.00
Cake Stand	40.00	Spooner	25.00
Celery Tray.	20.00	Sugar, cov	35.00
Celery Vase	25.00	Sugar Shaker	35.00
Compote		Toothpick	40.00
Cov, hs	40.00	Tumbler, water	15.00
Open, hs, 7"	25.00	Wine	35.00
Creamer.	28.00		

CORD AND TASSEL

Non-flint, made by La Belle Glass C., Bridgeport, OH, and patented by Andrew Baggs in 1872. Also made by Central Glass Co. and other companies. Heavily reproduced.

	Clear		Clear
Bowl, oval.	25.00	Lamp, applied handle,	
Butter, cov	65.00	pedestal	100.00
Cake Stand, 10"	65.00	Mug, applied handle	55.00
Castor Bottle	25.00	Mustard Jar, cov	45.00
Celery Vase	35.00	Pitcher, water, applied han-	
Compote		dle	95.00
Cov, hs,.	90.00	Salt & Pepper	45.00
Open, ls	35.00	Sauce	10.00
Cordial	40.00	Spooner	25.00
Creamer.	25.00	Sugar, cov	55.00
Egg Cup.	35.00	Syrup.	125.00
Dish, oval, vegetable	25.00	Tumbler, water	45.00
* Goblet	40.00	* Wine	40.00

CORD DRAPERY

Made by National Glass Co., Greentown, IN, from 1899 to 1903; later by Indiana Glass at Dunkirk, IN, after 1907.

	Amber	Blue	Clear	Emerald Green
Bowl, 7½".	25.00	25.00	20.00	30.00
Butter, cov	75.00	75.00	60.00	150.00
Cake Stand	50.00	55.00	45.00	75.00
Compote				
Open, 6"	45.00	60.00	48.00	85.00
Open, 7"	75.00	75.00	60.00	95.00
Open, jelly	—	55.00	45.00	—
Creamer.	45.00	50.00	40.00	60.00
Cruet, os	265.00	100.00	90.00	125.00

	Amber	Blue	Clear	Emerald Green
Cup	18.00	18.00	15.00	25.00
Goblet	50.00	50.00	55.00	65.00
Jelly, cov	85.00	95.00	65.00	115.00
Pickle, 9¼″, oval . . .	40.00	—	25.00	—
Pitcher, water	175.00	75.00	60.00	75.00
Plate	35.00	40.00	25.00	40.00
Relish.	25.00	25.00	22.00	30.00
Sauce, flat	15.00	15.00	10.00	15.00
Spooner	40.00	40.00	35.00	45.00
Sugar, cov	125.00	60.00	45.00	75.00
Syrup	295.00	—	90.00	—
Sweetmeat, cov, 6½″ d, 5¼″ h	165.00	—	—	—
Tumbler	30.00	30.00	32.00	45.00
Wine	45.00	45.00	40.00	60.00

CORDOVA

Non-flint made by the O'Hara Glass Co., Pittsburgh, Pa. It was exhibited for the first time at the Pittsburgh Glass Show, December 16, 1890. Toothpick has been found in ruby stained, valued at $35.00.

	Clear	Emerald Green		Clear	Emerald Green
Bowl, Berry, cov . . .	30.00	—	Punch Bowl	87.50	—
Butter, cov, handled .	50.00	—	Punch Cup	15.00	30.00
Cake Stand	70.00	—	Nappy, handled, 6″d	12.00	—
Celery Vase	45.00	—	Salt Shaker.	20.00	—
Cologne Bottle	20.00	—	Spooner	35.00	45.00
Compote			Sugar, cov	40.00	80.00
Cov, hs	40.00	—	Syrup	125.00	40.00
Open, hs	35.00	—	Toothpick	18.00	—
Creamer.	35.00	45.00	Tumbler	18.00	—
Finger Bowl	16.00	—	Vase	15.00	—
Inkwell, metal lid . . .	80.00	—			
Mug, handled	15.00	30.00			
Pitcher					
Milk.	30.00	—			
Water	45.00	—			

COTTAGE (Dinner Bell)

Non-flint made by Adams and Co., Pittsburgh, PA, in the late 1870s and U. S. Glass Co. in the 1890s. Known to have been made in emerald green, amber, light blue, and amethyst. Add 50% for amber, 75% for other colors.

	Clear	Ruby Stained		Clear	Ruby Stained
Banana Stand.	55.00	—	Cake Stand		
Bowl			9″	40.00	—
7 ½, oval.	15.00	—	10″	45.00	—
9½, oval	20.00	—	Celery Vase	35.00	—
Butter, cov			Champagne	35.00	50.00
Flat.	45.00	—	Compote		
Footed	45.00	—	Cov, hs 6″	60.00	

	Clear	Ruby Stained		Clear	Ruby Stained
Cov, hs 7"	65.00	—	6"	12.50	—
Cov, hs hs, 8" . . .	60.00	—	7"	16.50	—
Cov, hs, 8¼"	80.00	—	8"	22.00	—
Open, hs, 8¼"d . .	65.00	—	9"	32.50	—
Jelly	35.00	45.00	Relish.	10.00	—
Creamer.	25.00	50.00	Salt Shaker.	25.00	—
Cruet, os	45.00	—	Saucer.	15.00	40.00
Cup and Saucer . . .	35.00	—	Spooner	20.00	—
Dish, oval, deep . . .	22.00	—	Sugar, cov	45.00	—
Finger Bowl	18.00	—	Syrup	65.00	—
Goblet	30.00	—	Tray, water	35.00	—
Pitcher			Tumbler	25.00	—
Milk.	28.00	—	Waste Bowl.	20.00	—
Water	50.00	—	Wine	35.00	—
Plate					
5"	5.00	—			

CROESUS

Made in clear by Riverside Glass Works, Wheeling, WV, in 1897. Produced in amethyst and green by McKee Glass in 1899. Pieces trimmed in gold; prices are for examples with gold in very good condition. Reproduced.

	Amethyst	Clear	Green
Bowl			
4", ftd	45.00	10.00	30.00
6¼", ftd	200.00	65.00	115.00
8", flat	165.00	—	120.00
8", ftd	115.00	25.00	115.00
8", ftd, cov.	145.00	35.00	115.00
10", ftd	165.00	—	120.00
* Butter, cov	185.00	85.00	165.00
Cake Stand, 10" . . .	175.00	40.00	140.00
Celery Vase	300.00	55.00	115.00
Compote			
Cov, hs, 5".	115.00	28.00	115.00
Cov, hs, 6".	115.00	28.00	115.00
Cov, hs, 7".	135.00	30.00	125.00
Open, hs, 5"	65.00	18.00	60.00
Open, hs, 6"	75.00	18.00	60.00
Open, hs, 7"	80.00	20.00	75.00
Compote, jelly.	225.00	20.00	185.00
Condiment Set (cruet, salt & pepper on small tray). . . .	225.00	185.00	185.00
Creamer			
Individual.	100.00	—	185.00
Regular	150.00	55.00	65.00
Cruet, os	325.00	135.00	185.00
Pitcher, water	350.00	80.00	235.00
Plate, 8", ftd	75.00	20.00	65.00
Relish, boat shaped.	70.00	30.00	60.00
Salt & Pepper	135.00	40.00	125.00
Sauce			
Flat.	40.00	15.00	32.00
Footed	45.00	18.00	40.00
Spooner	80.00	60.00	70.00

	Amethyst	Clear	Green
Sugar, cov	185.00	85.00	125.00
*Toothpick	100.00	25.00	85.00
Tray, condiment . . .	75.00	25.00	30.00
*Tumbler	65.00	20.00	40.00

CRYSTAL WEDDING

Non-flint made by Adams Glass Co., Pittsburgh, PA, in the late 1880s and U. S. Glass Co. in 1891. Also found in frosted, amber stained, and cobalt blue (rare). Heavily reproduced in clear, ruby stained, and milk with enamel trim.

	Clear	Ruby Stained		Clear	Ruby Stained
Banana Stand	85.00	—	Milk, sq	125.00	—
Bowl			Water, round	110.00	195.00
4½″, ind berry . . .	15.00	—	Water, sq.	165.00	—
6″, sq, cov	50.00	—	Plate, 10″	25.00	40.00
7″, sq, cov	55.00	—	Relish	20.00	—
8″, sq, master			Salt		
berry	50.00	—	Individual	20.00	—
8″, sq, cov	60.00	—	Master	35.00	—
Butter, cov	50.00	125.00	Salt Shaker	35.00	—
Cake Plate, sq	45.00	85.00	Sauce	10.00	20.00
Cake Stand, 10″	60.00	—	Spooner	30.00	60.00
Celery Vase	40.00	125.00	Sugar, cov	70.00	85.00
Compote			Syrup	85.00	200.00
Open, hs, 7″, sq. .	60.00	—	Toothpick	50.00	—
Open, ls, 5″, sq . .	50.00	—	Tumbler	35.00	45.00
Creamer	50.00	75.00	Vase		
Cruet	95.00	—	Footed, twisted . .	25.00	—
Goblet	45.00	55.00	Swung	25.00	—
Pickle	25.00		Wine	45.00	—
Pitcher					
Milk, round	110.00	—			

CUPID AND VENUS

Non-flint made by Richards and Hartley Glass Co., Tarentum, PA, in the late 1870s. Also made in vaseline, rare.

	Amber	Clear		Amber	Clear
Bowl			Compote		
8″, cov, ftd	—	28.00	Cov, hs, 8″	—	100.00
9″, oval	—	32.00	Cov, ls, 7″	—	55.00
Bread Plate	75.00	40.00	Cov, ls, 9″	—	95.00
Butter, cov	—	55.00	Open, ls, 8½″,		
Cake Plate	—	45.00	scalloped	135.00	35.00
Cake Stand	—	45.00	Open, hs, 9¼″	—	45.00
Celery Vase	—	40.00	Cordial, 3½″	—	55.00
Champagne	—	90.00	Creamer	—	36.50

	Amber	Clear
Cruet, os	—	85.00
Goblet	—	65.00
Marmalade Jar, cov.	—	65.00
Mug		
Miniature	—	40.00
Medium, 2½"	—	35.00
Large, 3½"	—	40.00
Pitcher		
Milk	190.00	75.00
Water	215.00	65.00

	Amber	Clear
Plate, 10", round	75.00	40.00
Sauce		
Flat	—	10.00
Footed, 3½", 4" and 4½"	—	15.00
Spooner	—	35.00
Sugar, cov	—	65.00
Wine, 3¾"	—	75.00

CURRANT

Non-flint, made by Campbell, Jones and Co., and patented in 1871.

	Clear
Bowl, 7", vegetable	18.00
Butter, cov	75.00
Cake Stand	
9¼"	60.00
11"	85.00
Celery Vase	4500
Compote	
Cov, hs, 8"	65.00
Cov, hs, 9"	135.00
Cov, ls, 8"	45.00
Cordial	45.00
Creamer, applied handle	40.00
Egg Cup	25.00
Goblet	28.50
Pitcher	
Milk, applied handle	125.00

	Clear
Water, applied handle	85.00
Plate, oval	
5" x 7"	25.00
6" x 9"	30.00
Salt, ftd	30.00
Sauce, ftd, 4"	12.00
Spooner	25.00
Sugar	
Cov	55.00
Open, buttermilk type	30.00
Tumbler, ftd	30.00
Wine	25.00

CURRIER AND IVES

Non-flint made by Bellaire Glass Co. in Findlay, OH, in 1890. Known to have been made in colors, but rarely found. A decanter is known in ruby stained.

	Clear
Bowl, oval, 10", canoe shaped	30.00
Butter, cov	50.00
Compote	
Cov, hs, 7½"	95.00
Open, hs, 7½", scalloped	50.00
Creamer	30.00
Cup and saucer	35.00
Dish, oval, boat shaped, 8"	27.50
Goblet, knob stem	30.00
Lamp, 9½", hs	75.00
Pitcher	
Milk	60.00
Water	70.00

	Clear
Plate, 10"	20.00
Relish	18.00
Salt Shaker	30.00
Sauce, oval	12.00
Spooner	30.00
Sugar, cov	45.00
Syrup	50.00
Tray	
Water, Balky Mule	65.00
Wine, Balky Mule	50.00
Water Bottle, 12"h, os	55.00
Wine, 3¼"	18.00

CURTAIN (Sultan)

Clear non-flint pattern made by Bryce Brothers, Pittsburgh, Pennsylvania, late 1870s.

	Clear		Clear
Bowl		Finger Bowl	30.00
7½″	30.00	Goblet	30.00
8″	45.00	Mug	25.00
Butter, cov	55.00	Pickle	15.00
Cake Stand		Pitcher, water	75.00
8″	40.00	Plate, 7″, sq	20.00
9½″	45.00	Salt Shaker	25.00
Castor Set, salt, pepper, and		Sauce, 4¾″	8.00
mustard, stand	115.00	Spooner	25.00
Celery Tray	30.00	Sugar	
Celery Vase	30.00	Covered	38.00
Compote, open, hs, 10″	48.00	Open	20.00
Creamer	25.00	Tray, water	35.00
Cruet, os	45.00	Tumbler	20.00

CURTAIN TIE BACK

Clear non-flint pattern made in the mid 1880s.

	Clear		Clear
Bowl, 7½″, sq	18.00	Salt & Pepper, pr.	35.00
Bread Plate	35.00	Sauce	
Butter, cov	40.00	Flat	12.00
Celery Vase	36.00	Footed	14.00
Compote, cov, hs	40.00	Spooner	30.00
Creamer	28.00	Sugar	
Goblet		Covered	32.00
Fancy base	30.00	Open	18.00
Flat base	20.00	Tray, water	30.00
Pickle	12.00	Tumbler	18.00
Pitcher, water	45.00	Wine	20.00
Relish	12.00		

DAHLIA

Non-flint, made by Portland Glass Co, Portland, ME, c1865, and Canton Glass Co., c1880. Also attributed to a Canadian manufacturer.

	Amber	Apple Green	Blue	Clear	Vaseline
Bowl	30.00	25.00	25.00	18.00	30.00
Bread Plate	55.00	50.00	50.00	45.00	55.00
Butter, cov	80.00	70.00	70.00	40.00	80.00
Cake Plate	60.00	45.00	45.00	24.00	60.00
Cake Stand, 9″	72.50	50.00	50.00	25.00	72.50
Champagne	80.00	65.00	65.00	55.00	80.00
Compote					
Cov, hs, 7″	100.00	85.00	85.00	55.00	80.00
Open, hs, 8″	60.00	45.00	45.00	30.00	60.00
Cordial	55.00	50.00	50.00	35.00	55.00
Creamer	40.00	35.00	35.00	25.00	40.00

	Amber	Apple Green	Blue	Clear	Vaseline
Egg Cup					
Double	80.00	65.00	65.00	50.00	80.00
Single	55.00	40.00	40.00	25.00	55.00
Goblet	65.00	55.00	55.00	35.00	65.00
Mug					
Large	55.00	55.00	55.00	35.00	55.00
Small	50.00	45.00	40.00	30.00	50.00
Pickle...........	35.00	30.00	30.00	20.00	35.00
Pitcher					
Milk...........	70.00	55.00	55.00	40.00	70.00
Water	100.00	90.00	90.00	55.00	90.00
Water, applied					
handle	—	—	—	125.00	—
Plate					
7"	45.00	40.00	40.00	20.00	45.00
9", handles	35.00	45.00	50.00	18.00	50.00
Platter	50.00	45.00	45.00	30.00	50.00
Relish, 9½" l	20.00	20.00	20.00	15.00	25.00
Salt, ind, ftd	35.00	30.00	30.00	5.00	35.00
Sauce					
Flat...........	15.00	12.00	15.00	10.00	15.00
Footed	20.00	15.00	15.00	10.00	20.00
Spooner	50.00	45.00	50.00	35.00	50.00
Sugar, cov	75.00	60.00	60.00	40.00	75.00
Syrup	75.00	—	—	55.00	—
Wine	45.00	40.00	45.00	25.00	45.00

DAISY AND BUTTON

Non-flint pattern made in the 1870s by several companies in many different forms. In continuous production since inception.

	Amber	Apple Green	Blue	Clear	Vaseline
Bowl, triangular	40.00	45.00	45.00	25.00	65.00
Bread Plate, 13" ...	35.00	60.00	35.00	20.00	40.00
Butter Chip	10.00	24.00	15.00	8.00	25.00
Butter, cov					
Round.........	70.00	90.00	70.00	65.00	95.00
Square	110.00	115.00	110.00	100.00	120.00
Butter Pat........	30.00	40.00	35.00	25.00	35.00
Canoe					
4"	12.00	24.00	15.00	10.00	24.00
8½"	30.00	35.00	30.00	25.00	35.00
12"	60.00	35.00	28.00	20.00	40.00
14"	30.00	40.00	35.00	25.00	40.00
Castor Set					
4 bottle, glass std.	90.00	85.00	95.00	80.00	75.00
5 bottle, metal std	105.00	100.00	110.00	100.00	95.00
Celery Vase	45.00	50.00	40.00	30.00	48.00
Compote					
Cov, hs, 6".	35.00	50.00	45.00	25.00	50.00
Open, hs, 8"	75.00	65.00	60.00	40.00	65.00
Creamer.........	35.00	40.00	40.00	18.00	35.00
Cruet, os	100.00	60.00	55.00	45.00	60.00
Egg Cup.........	20.00	30.00	25.00	15.00	30.00
Finger Bowl	30.00	50.00	35.00	30.00	42.00

	Amber	Apple Green	Blue	Clear	Vaseline
Goblet	40.00	50.00	40.00	25.00	40.00
Hat, 2½"	30.00	35.00	40.00	20.00	40.00
Ice Tub	—	—	—	—	75.00
Inkwell	40.00	50.00	45.00	30.00	45.00
Parfait	25.00	35.00	30.00	20.00	35.00
Pickle Castor	125.00	90.00	150.00	75.00	150.00
Pitcher, water					
Bulbous, reed handle	125.00	95.00	90.00	75.00	90.00
Tankard	62.00	65.00	62.00	60.00	65.00
Plate					
5", leaf shape	20.00	24.00	16.00	18.00	25.00
6", round	10.00	22.00	15.00	6.50	24.00
7", square	24.00	35.00	25.00	15.00	35.00
Punch Bowl, stand	90.00	100.00	95.00	85.00	100.00
Salt & Pepper	30.00	40.00	30.00	20.00	35.00
Sauce, 4"	18.00	25.00	18.00	15.00	25.00
Slipper					
5"	45.00	48.00	50.00	45.00	50.00
11½"	40.00	50.00	30.00	35.00	50.00
Spooner	40.00	40.00	45.00	35.00	45.00
Sugar, cov	45.00	50.00	45.00	35.00	50.00
Syrup	45.00	50.00	45.00	30.00	45.00
Toothpick					
Round	40.00	55.00	25.00	40.00	45.00
Urn	20.00	25.00	20.00	10.00	35.00
Tray	65.00	65.00	60.00	35.00	60.00
Tumbler	18.00	30.00	35.00	15.00	25.00
Vase, wall pocket	125.00	—	—	—	—
Wine	15.00	25.00	20.00	10.00	45.00

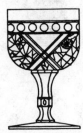

DAISY AND BUTTON WITH CROSSBARS (Mikado)

Non-flint pattern made by Richards and Hartley, Tarentum, PA, c1888.

	Amber	Blue	Clear	Vaseline
Bowl				
6"	26.00	30.00	20.00	28.00
9"	40.00	40.00	25.00	35.00
Bread Plate	30.00	45.00	25.00	35.00
Butter, cov				
Flat	55.00	55.00	45.00	55.00
Footed	—	75.00	25.00	60.00
Celery Vase	36.00	40.00	30.00	50.00
Compote				
Cov, hs, 8"	55.00	65.00	45.00	55.00
Open, hs, 8"	45.00	50.00	30.00	45.00
Open, ls, 7"	30.00	—	—	—
Creamer				
Individual	25.00	30.00	18.00	30.00
Regular	42.50	45.00	35.00	40.00
Cruet, os	75.00	55.00	35.00	100.00
Goblet	42.50	40.00	25.00	40.00
Mug, 3"h	15.00	18.00	12.50	20.00
Pitcher				
Milk	45.00	50.00	35.00	50.00
Water	85.00	70.00	45.00	65.00

	Amber	Blue	Clear	Vaseline
Salt & Pepper	40.00	45.00	30.00	40.00
Sauce				
Flat	15.00	18.00	10.00	15.00
Footed	18.00	25.00	15.00	24.00
Spooner	35.00	35.00	25.00	35.00
Sugar, cov				
Individual.	25.00	35.00	10.00	25.00
Regular	50.00	60.00	25.00	55.00
Syrup	50.00	60.00	35.00	50.00
Toothpick	40.00	40.00	28.00	35.00
Tumbler	20.00	25.00	18.00	25.00
Wine	28.50	32.50	25.00	30.00

DAISY AND BUTTON WITH NARCISSUS (Daisy and Button with Clear Lily)

Non-flint made in late 1890s. Later made by Indiana Glass Co. Dunkirk, IN, into 1920s. Sometimes found with flowers flashed with cranberry flashing and pieces trimmed in gold. Many pieces have been reproduced.

	Clear	Flashed Color		Clear	Flashed Color
Bowl, 6″ w, 9¼″ l,			Salt Shaker	18.00	—
oval, ftd	45.00	—	Sauce		
Butter, cov	50.00	—	Flat	10.00	—
Celery Vase	20.00	—	Footed, 4″	15.00	—
Compote, open, ls . .	35.00	—	Spooner	30.00	—
Creamer	25.00	—	Sugar, cov	38.00	42.50
Decanter, os	40.00	62.50	Tray, water or wine,		
Goblet	25.00	—	10″	30.00	40.00
Pitcher, water	50.00	70.00	Tumbler	18.00	20.00
Punch Cup	10.00	18.00	Wine	22.00	25.00

DAISY AND BUTTON WITH V ORNAMENT (Van Dyke)

Made by A. J. Beatty & Co., 1886–1887.

	Amber	Blue	Clear	Vaseline
Bowl				
9″	35.00	42.00	45.00	55.00
10″	40.00	45.00	40.00	45.00
Butter, cov	85.00	80.00	65.00	90.00
Celery Vase	50.00	55.00	30.00	55.00
Creamer	30.00	50.00	30.00	50.00
Finger Bowl	28.50	45.00	22.50	55.00
Goblet	35.00	45.00	25.00	50.00
Mug	20.00	30.00	20.00	35.00
Pickle Castor	120.00	120.00	85.00	100.00
Pitcher, water	65.00	90.00	48.00	60.00
Punch Cup	12.00	20.00	12.50	25.00
Sauce, flat	20.00	20.00	12.00	30.00
Spooner	40.00	38.50	35.00	45.00
Sugar, cov	60.00	50.00	40.00	75.00
Toothpick	32.50	40.00	28.50	35.00
Tray, water	55.00	65.00	35.00	55.00
Tumbler	25.00	28.00	15.00	35.00

DAKOTA (Baby Thumbprint, Thumbprint Band)

Non-flint made by Ripley and Co., Pittsburgh, PA, in the late 1880s and early 1890s. Later reissued by U. S. Glass Co. as one of the States patterns. Prices listed are for etched fern and berry pattern; also found with fern and no berry, and oak leaf etching, and scarcer grape etching. Other etchings known include fish, swan, peacock, bird and insect, bird and flowers, ivy and berry, stag, spider and insect in web, buzzard on dead tree, and crane catching fish. Sometimes ruby stained with or without souvenir markings. There is a four piece table set available in a "hotel" variant, prices are about 20% more than the regular type.

	Clear Etched	Clear Plain	Ruby Stained
Basket, 10 x 2", metal bail	150.00	90.00	165.00
Bowl, berry	45.00	30.00	—
Butter, cov	65.00	60.00	125.00
Cake Cover, 8"	200.00	150.00	—
Cake Stand			
9½"	58.00	35.00	—
10½"	60.00	45.00	—
Celery Tray	35.00	25.00	—
Celery Vase	40.00	30.00	—
Compote			
Cov, hs, 5"	60.00	—	—
Cov, hs, 7"	65.00	—	—
Cov, hs, 8"	75.00	—	—
Cov, hs, 9"	75.00	—	—
Cov, hs, 12"	95.00	75.00	—
Cov, 6", jelly	65.00	50.00	—
Open, hs, 7"	55.00	40.00	—
Condiment Tray, metal handles	—	75.00	—
Creamer	50.00	28.50	65.00
Cruet	75.00	55.00	—
Goblet	35.00	28.00	75.00
Pitcher			
Milk	100.00	80.00	200.00
Tankard	125.00	95.00	225.00
Water	95.00	75.00	190.00
Plate, 10"	85.00	—	—
Salt Shaker	65.00	50.00	125.00
Sauce			
Flat	20.00	18.00	—
Footed	25.00	20.00	—
Spooner	30.00	25.00	65.00
Sugar, cov	65.00	55.00	85.00
Tray, water	100.00	75.00	—
Tumbler	35.00	30.00	40.00
Waste Bowl	65.00	45.00	—
Wine	38.00	25.00	45.00

DART

Clear non-flint pattern made in Ohio in the 1880s.

	Clear		Clear
Bowl	12.00	Butter, cov	25.00

	Clear			Clear
Compote			Pitcher, water	35.00
Cov, hs, 8½″ d, 12½″ h. . .	60.00		Sauce, ftd.	12.50
Open, jelly.	18.00		Spooner	20.00
Creamer.	25.00		Sugar, cov	35.00
Goblet	24.00		Tumbler	15.00

DEER AND PINE TREE (Deer and Doe)

Non-flint pattern, made by Belmont Glass Co., and McKee Glass Co. 1883. Souvenir mugs with gilt found in clear and olive green. Also made in canary (vaseline). The goblet has been reproduced.

	Amber	Apple Green	Blue	Clear
Bread Plate	90.00	80.00	100.00	70.00
Butter, cov	125.00	110.00	115.00	95.00
Cake Stand	—	—	—	75.00
Celery Vase	—	—	—	50.00
Compote				
Cov, hs, 8″, sq. . .	—	—	—	68.00
Open, hs, 7″	—	—	—	45.00
Open, hs, 9″	—	—	—	55.00
Creamer.	95.00	85.00	90.00	65.00
Finger Bowl	—	—	—	55.00
*Goblet	—	—	—	55.00
Marmalade Jar	—	—	—	75.00
Mug	40.00	45.00	50.00	40.00
Pickle.	—	—	—	24.00
Pitcher				
Milk.	—	—	—	70.00
Water	125.00	110.00	115.00	100.00
Platter, 8 x 13″	—	—	80.00	60.00
Sauce				
Flat.	—	—	—	20.00
Footed	—	—	—	28.00
Spooner	—	—	—	40.00
Sugar				
Covered	—	—	—	60.00
Open	—	—	—	25.00
Tray, water	100.00		90.00	60.00

DELAWARE (Four Petal Flower)

Non-flint pattern made by U. S. Glass Co. c1899. Also found in amethyst (scarce), clear with rose trim, custard, and milk glass.

	Clear	Green With Gold	Rose With Gold
Banana Bowl	50.00	55.00	65.00
Bowl			
8″.	30.00	35.00	50.00
9″.	25.00	60.00	55.00
Bride's Basket, SP			
frame	—	115.00	165.00
Butter, cov	60.00	125.00	145.00

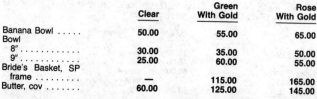

	Clear	Green With Gold	Rose With Gold
Claret Jug, tankard shape	110.00	195.00	200.00
Celery Vase, flat . . .	75.00	90.00	95.00
Creamer.	45.00	65.00	70.00
Cruet, os	90.00	145.00	150.00
Finger Bowl	25.00	50.00	45.00
Lamp Shade, round.	—	—	75.00
Pin Tray	30.00	55.00	65.00
Pitcher, water	50.00	150.00	125.00
Pomade Box, jeweled	—	200.00	325.00
Puff Box, bulbous, jeweled	—	175.00	315.00
Punch Cup	15.00	40.00	40.00
Sauce, 5½", boat . .	15.00	35.00	30.00
Spooner	45.00	60.00	55.00
Sugar, cov	65.00	85.00	100.00
Toothpick	45.00	85.00	100.00
Tumbler	20.00	45.00	48.50
Vase			
6"	—	45.00	70.00
8"	—	55.00	75.00
9½"	—	80.00	85.00

DEW AND RAINDROP

Non-flint made in the 1880s by Kokomo Glass Co, Kokomo, IN. After 1900, Federal Glass and others made this pattern using a lesser quality glass, and without the tiny dewdrops on stems. Prices listed are for the earlier, more brilliant, 1880 pattern. A ruby stained creamer and water pitcher are documented.

	Clear		Clear
Bowl, 8"	40.00	Sauce, flat	15.00
Butter, cov	65.00	Spooner	35.00
Cordial	45.00	Sugar	
Creamer.	35.00	Cov.	35.00
Goblet	30.00	Open	25.00
Pitcher, water	65.00	Wine	20.00
Salt and Pepper	40.00		

DEWDROP IN POINTS

Non-flint made by Brilliant Glass Works, Brilliant, OH, in the late 1870s and Greensburg Glass Co, Greensburg, PA, after 1889.

	Clear		Clear
Bread Plate	24.00	Open, hs.	25.00
Butter, cov	40.00	Open, ls	22.50
Cake Stand	40.00	Creamer.	38.00
Compote		Goblet	25.00
Cov, hs	60.00	Pickle.	20.00

	Clear		Clear
Pitcher, water	35.00	Spooner	24.00
Plate, 12″	24.00	Sugar	
Platter, 9 x 11¾″	24.00	Cov.	40.00
Sauce		Open	24.00
Flat	12.00	Wine	25.00
Footed	15.00		

DEWDROP WITH STAR

Non-flint made by Campbell, Jones and Co., Pittsburgh, PA, in 1877. There was no goblet made in this pattern.

	Clear		Clear
Bowl		Honey, underplate	75.00
6″	8.00	Lamp, patented 1876.	85.00
7″	20.00	Pitcher, water, applied	
9″, ftd	24.00	handle.	125.00
Bread Plate, sheaf of wheat		*Plate	
center	35.00	5″	12.00
Butter, cov, dome lid	50.00	7″	15.00
Cake Stand	40.00	9″	20.00
Celery Vase	40.00	Relish.	15.00
Cheese Dish, cov, dome lid .	110.00	*Salt, ftd	20.00
Compote		Sauce	
Cov, hs, dome lid	75.00	Flat.	10.00
Cov, ls, 5″	60.00	Footed	12.00
Open, hs	45.00	Spooner	35.00
Creamer, applied handle . . .	35.00	Sugar, cov, domed lid	50.00

DEWEY (Flower Flange)

Made by Indiana Tumbler & Goblet Co., Greentown, IN, 1894. Later by U. S. Glass Co. until 1904. Some experimental colors were made including a nile green opaque mug ($75.00).

	Amber	Caramel	Clear	Green	Vaseline
Bowl, 8″, ftd	65.00	175.00	50.00	65.00	70.00
Butter, cov	75.00	160.00	45.00	65.00	95.00
Creamer.	45.00	150.00	30.00	50.00	55.00
Cruet, os	125.00	180.00	75.00	145.00	125.00
Mug	55.00	155.00	35.00	55.00	58.00
Parfait	35.00	—	—	—	—
Pitcher, water	90.00	175.00	55.00	175.00	175.00
Plate, 7½″, ftd	35.00	130.00	30.00	40.00	65.00
Relish.	42.00	145.00	20.00	42.00	45.00
Sauce, flat	25.00	—	5.00	25.00	30.00
Spooner	40.00	130.00	25.00	40.00	50.00
Sugar, cov					
Individual.	45.00	—	25.00	45.00	65.00
Regular.	50.00	150.00	35.00	55.00	75.00
Tumbler	55.00	150.00	40.00	45.00	65.00

DIAGONAL BAND

Made in c1875-1885, maker unknown.

	Amber	Apple Green	Clear
Bread Plate	30.00	35.00	24.00
Butter, cov	60.00	80.00	35.00
Cake Stand	40.00	55.00	30.00
Celery Vase	45.00	50.00	25.00
Compote			
Cov, hs, 7".	65.00	80.00	55.00
Cov, ls, 8"	62.50	70.00	45.00
Open, hs, 7½" . . .	45.00	50.00	20.00
Creamer.	40.00	50.00	30.00
Goblet	30.00	45.00	28.00
Pitcher			
Milk.	—	—	32.00
Water.	65.00	95.00	40.00
Plate, 6".	—	—	12.50
Relish, 6⅞" oval . . .	14.00	18.00	10.00
Sauce			
Flat.	—	—	6.00
Footed	—	15.00	12.50
Spooner.	24.00	40.00	20.00
Sugar			
Cov.	40.00	50.00	30.00
Open	22.00	28.00	15.00
Wine	35.00	45.00	20.00

DIAMOND AND SUNBURST

Non-Flint made by Bryce, Walker and Co, 1894.

	Clear		Clear
Butter, cov	40.00	Goblet	25.00
Butter Pat.	10.00	Relish.	10.00
Cake Stand	35.00	Salt, ftd	18.00
Celery Vase	25.00	Spooner.	16.00
Compote		Sugar	
Cov, hs	50.00	Cov.	40.00
Open, hs.	28.50	Open	20.00
Creamer.	35.00	Syrup	45.00
Decanter, os	45.00	Tumbler	25.00
Egg Cup.	25.00	Wine	28.50

DIAMOND POINT

Flint, originally made by Boston and Sandwich Glass Co., in the 1830-1840 period, and by the New England Glass Co. Many other companies manufactured this pattern throughout the 19th century.

	Flint	Non-Flint		Flint	Non-Flint
Bowl			8", cov	60.00	20.00
7", cov	60.00	20.00	8", open	45.00	15.00

	Flint	Non-Flint		Flint	Non-Flint
Butter, cov	95.00	50.00	Pitcher		
Cake Stand, 14"	185.00	—	Pint	160.00	—
Candlesticks, pr	145.00	—	Quart	280.00	—
Celery Vase	68.00	30.00	Plate		
Champagne	70.00	—	6"	30.00	—
Claret	65.00	—	8"	50.00	—
Compote			Salt, master, cov	75.00	—
Cov, hs, 8"	135.00	—	Salt & Pepper	45.00	—
Open, hs 10½", flared	100.00	—	Sauce, flat	14.00	—
			Spillholder	45.00	—
Open, ls, 7½"	50.00	40.00	Spooner	40.00	25.00
Creamer, applied handle	115.00	—	Sugar, cov	65.00	—
			Syrup	95.00	—
Decanter, qt, os	165.00	—	Tumbler, bar	65.00	35.00
Egg Cup	42.00	20.00	Whiskey, applied handle	70.00	—
Goblet	45.00	35.00			
Honey	15.00	—	Wine	75.00	28.00
Mustard, Brittania cov	25.00	—			

DIAMOND QUILTED

Non-flint, c1880. Heavily reproduced.

	Amber	Amethyst	Blue	Clear	Vaseline
Bowl					
6"	10.00	20.00	—	—	—
7"	18.00	—	—	—	25.00
Butter, cov	50.00	100.00	100.00	40.00	75.00
Celery Vase	35.00	60.00	50.00	40.00	40.00
Champagne	—	36.00	—	21.00	38.00
Compote					
Cov, hs, 8"	140.00	120.00	120.00	45.00	90.00
Open, ls, 9"	—	—	—	15.00	35.00
Creamer	45.00	40.00	70.00	25.00	55.00
*Goblet	40.00	40.00	40.00	30.00	35.00
Mug	—	30.00	40.00	—	—
Pitcher, water	75.00	85.00	80.00	50.00	75.00
Sauce					
Flat	12.00	—	16.50	8.00	18.00
Footed	16.00	18.00	18.00	12.00	22.00
Spooner	35.00	40.00	40.00	30.00	50.00
Sugar, cov	50.00	75.00	55.00	40.00	60.00
Tray	55.00	70.00	75.00	30.00	65.00
*Tumbler	45.00	40.00	40.00	25.00	32.50
Vase, 9"	—	—	—	48.00	—
* Wine	20.00	40.00	35.00	15.00	20.00

DIAMOND SPEARHEAD

Made by Northwood-Dugan Glass Co., Indiana, PA, around 1900. No cruet reported. A cake stand has been found, but it was not listed in early catalogues. Also made in canary opalescent, prices same as blue opalescent. A cake stand, 10", $65.00, and a carafe, $180.00 are known in canary opalescent.

	Clear	Cobalt Blue Opal	Green Opal	Sapphire Blue Opal	White Opal
Bowl, berry	20.00	—	40.00	40.00	35.00
Butter, cov	40.00	150.00	85.00	75.00	—
Carafe	—	—	180.00	—	—
Celery Vase	20.00	—	45.00	40.00	35.00
Compote					
Cov, hs	—	—	35.00	30.00	32.00
Cov, ls, jelly	—	—	60.00	50.00	—
Creamer	20.00	70.00	35.00	30.00	32.00
Cup and Saucer . . .	—	—	60.00	60.00	—
Goblet	—	—	90.00	50.00	—
Mug	20.00	—	55.00	50.00	—
Pitcher, water	50.00	200.00	85.00	75.00	—
Plate, 10"	—	—	80.00	—	—
Relish.	—	—	25.00	20.00	—
Sauce	—	—	15.00	10.00	—
Spooner	20.00	—	50.00	40.00	—
Sugar, cov	30.00	—	50.00	45.00	—
Syrup	—	230.00	75.00	65.00	—
Toothpick	—	125.00	80.00	90.00	—

DIAMOND THUMBPRINT

Flint, attributed to Boston and Sandwich Glass Co., and other factories from 1840 to 1850s.

	Clear		Clear
Bitters Bottle, orig pewter pourer, applied lip, polished pontil	475.00	Finger Bowl	85.00
		*Goblet	325.00
Butter, cov	200.00	Honey Dish.	25.00
Celery Vase, scalloped top. .	185.00	Pitcher, water	400.00
Champagne	265.00	Sauce, flat	25.00
Compote		* Spooner	85.00
Cov, hs, 8".	150.00	Sugar, cov	150.00
Open, ls, scalloped, 8" . . .	50.00	Tumbler, bar	135.00
Creamer	250.00	Whiskey, applied handle . . .	300.00
Decanter		Wine	250.00
Pint, ns	175.00		
Quart, os	225.00		

DOLLY MADISON (Jefferson's #271)

Non-flint pattern made by Jefferson Glass Co., Follansbee, WV, c1907.

	Blue Clear	Blue Opal	Clear	Clear Opal	Green Opal
Bowl, berry, 9¼" . . .	35.00	50.00	30.00	35.00	45.00
Butter, cov	40.00	110.00	25.00	65.00	120.00
Creamer	35.00	65.00	30.00	80.00	90.00
Pitcher, water	45.00	150.00	45.00	125.00	140.00
Sauce	20.00	45.00	15.00	45.00	50.00
Spooner	30.00	75.00	25.00	75.00	85.00
Sugar, cov	45.00	65.00	55.00	45.00	100.00
Tumbler	30.00	40.00	30.00	40.00	60.00

DRAPERY (Lace)

Non-flint made by Doyle and Co., Pittsburgh, PA, in the 1870s. Reportedly made by Sandwich Glass Co. at an earlier period. Pieces with fine stippling have applied handles; pieces with coarse stippling have pressed handles.

	Clear		Clear
Butter, cov	45.00	Plate, 6″	30.00
Compote, ls	55.00	Sauce, flat	10.00
Creamer, applied handle	35.00	Spooner	40.00
Egg Cup	25.00	Sugar, cov	30.00
Goblet	40.00	Tumbler	28.00
Pitcher, water, applied handle	65.00		

EGG IN SAND (Bean)

Non-flint, c1880. Has been reported in colors, but rare.

	Clear		Clear
Bread Plate, octagonal	28.00	Salt and Pepper	65.00
Butter, cov	48.00	Sauce	12.00
Compote, cov, jelly	35.00	Spooner, flat rim	25.00
Creamer	30.00	Sugar, cov	35.00
Dish, swan center	40.00	Tray, water	40.00
Goblet	35.00	Tumbler	30.00
Pitcher, water	45.00	Wine	35.00
Relish	12.00		

EGYPTIAN

Non-flint, attributed to Boston and Sandwich Glass Co., c1870.

	Clear		Clear
Bowl, 8½″	50.00	Goblet	45.00
Bread Plate		Honey	14.00
Cleopatra	50.00	Pickle, oval	20.00
Mormon Temple	300.00	Pitcher, water	185.00
Butter, cov	75.00	Plate, 12″, handles,	
Celery Vase	90.00	Pyramids	75.00
Compote		Relish	20.00
Cov, hs, 7″, Sphinx base	225.00	Sauce, ftd, 4½″	15.00
Open, hs, 7½″, Sphinx base	75.00	Spooner	40.00
Creamer	50.00	Sugar, cov	70.00

EMPRESS (Double Arch #2)

Made by Riverside Glass Works, Wellsburg, WV, c1898. Also found in amethyst (rare). Clear and emerald green pieces trimmed in gold; prices are for pieces with gold in very good condition.

	Clear	Emerald Green		Clear	Emerald Green
Bowl, 8½"	—	45.00	Pitcher, water	65.00	150.00
Breakfast Set, ind creamer and			Salt Shaker.	30.00	50.00
			Spooner	30.00	45.00
sugar	40.00	—	Sugar, cov	45.00	125.00
Butter, cov	50.00	100.00	Sugar Shaker	55.00	110.00
Celery Vase	55.00	—	Syrup	60.00	—
Creamer.	35.00	75.00	Toothpick	—	125.00
Cruet	50.00	150.00	Tumbler	32.50	55.00
Oil Lamp, atypical . .	60.00	—			

ESTHER (Tooth and Claw)

Non-flint made by Riverside Glass Works, Wellsburg, WV, c1896. The green has gold trim. Also found in ruby stained and amber stained with enamel decoration.

	Clear	Green	Ruby Stained
Bowl, 8"	35.00	50.00	—
Butter, cov	65.00	100.00	150.00
Cake Stand, 10½". .	60.00	80.00	—
Celery Vase	40.00	90.00	—
Compote, jelly, hs . .	—	75.00	—
Cracker Jar.	—	—	200.00
Creamer.	45.00	70.00	75.00
Cruet, os	45.00	245.00	—
Goblet	40.00	95.00	75.00
Pitcher, water	65.00	165.00	250.00
Plate, 10"	—	60.00	—
Relish.	20.00	25.00	40.00
Salt & Pepper.	50.00	100.00	—
Spooner	35.00	50.00	60.00
Sugar, cov	55.00	70.00	100.00
Syrup.	—	175.00	—
Toothpick	45.00	75.00	—
Tumbler	25.00	48.50	55.00
Wine	35.00	—	—

EUREKA

Flint made by Mckee & Bros in Pittsburgh, PA, in the late 1860s. Pieces have applied handles and bud finials. Made in flint and non-flint.

	Clear		Clear
Bowl		Egg Cup.	30.00
6", round	25.00	Goblet	30.00
7", oval	30.00	Pitcher, water	95.00
8", oval	40.00	Salt, ftd	30.00
Butter, cov	60.00	Sauce, flat	12.50
Champagne	40.00	Spooner	40.00
Compote		Sugar	
Cov, hs	85.00	Cov.	50.00
Open, hs	50.00	Open	25.00
Cordial	40.00	Tumbler, ftd	25.00
Creamer.	45.00	Wine	30.00

EXCELSIOR

Flint made by several firms, including Sandwich and McKee, from 1850s-1860s. Quality and design vary. Prices are for high quality flint.

	Clear		Clear
Bar Bottle	50.00	Goblet, Maltese Cross	50.00
Bowl, 10″, open	125.00	Lamp, hand	95.00
Bitters bottle	75.00	Mug	30.00
Butter, cov	100.00	Pickle Jar, cov.	45.00
Candlestick	125.00	Pitcher, water	325.00
Celery Vase, scalloped top	75.00	Salt, master	30.00
Claret	45.00	Spillholder	75.00
Compote		Spooner	60.00
Cov, ls	125.00	Sugar	
Open, hs	85.00	Cov.	90.00
Cordial	40.00	Open	50.00
Creamer	85.00	Syrup	110.00
Egg Cup		Tumbler, bar	60.00
Double	55.00	Whiskey, Maltese Cross	65.00
Single	40.00	Wine	55.00

EYEWINKER

Non-flint made in Findlay, OH, in 1889. Reportedly made by Dalzell, Gilmore and Leighton Glass Co., who were organized in 1883 in West Virginia, moved to Findlay in 1888. Made only in clear glass; colors have been reproduced. A goblet and toothpick originally were not originally made in this pattern.

	Clear		Clear
Banana Dish	85.00	Lamp, Kerosene	125.00
Bowl, 9″, cov	75.00	Nappy, folded sides, 7¼″	30.00
* Butter, cov	70.00	Pitcher, water	75.00
Cake Stand, 8″	55.00	Plate	
Celery Vase	45.00	7″	30.00
Compote		9″, sq, upturned sides	65.00
Cov, hs, 6½″	60.00	10″, upturned sides	85.00
Cov, hs, 9½″	90.00	Salt Shaker	35.00
Open, 7¼″, with fluted edge	65.00	Spooner	35.00
Open, 4½″, jelly	45.00	Sugar, cov	55.00
Creamer	65.00	Syrup, pewter top	110.00
Cruet	65.00	Tumbler	35.00

FEATHER (Doric)

Non-flint made in Indiana in 1896 and by McKee Glass. Later the pattern was reissued with variations and quality differences. Also found in amber stain (rare).

	Clear	Emerald Green		Clear	Emerald Green
Banana Dish	45.00	175.00	7″	25.00	—
Bowl, oval 9¼″	18.00	75.00	8″	30.00	—
Bowl, round			Bowl, sq		
4″	15.00	—	4½″	15.00	—
4½″	15.00	—	8″	30.00	—
6″	20.00	—	Butter, cov	65.00	125.00

	Clear	Emerald Green		Clear	Emerald Green
Cake Plate	30.00	—	Goblet	58.00	150.00
Cake Stand			Honey Dish	15.00	—
8″	40.00	125.00	Marmalade Jar	60.00	—
9½″	50.00	125.00	Pickle Castor	145.00	—
11″	65.00	175.00	Pitcher		
Celery Vase	35.00	85.00	Milk	50.00	165.00
Champagne	65.00	—	Water	58.00	225.00
Compote			Plate, 10″	35.00	—
Cov, hs, 8½″	125.00	250.00	Relish	18.00	—
Cov, ls, 4¼″, jelly	40.00	100.00	Salt Shaker, pr	35.00	70.00
Cov, ls, 8¼″	85.00	—	Sauce	12.00	—
Open, ls, 4″	15.00	—	Spooner	25.00	60.00
Open, ls, 6″	20.00	—	Sugar, cov	45.00	80.00
Open, ls, 7″	30.00	—	Syrup	125.00	275.00
Open, ls, 8″	35.00	—	Toothpick	65.00	125.00
Cordial	100.00	—	Tumbler	45.00	85.00
Creamer	40.00	65.00	Wine		
Cruet, os	45.00	250.00	Scalloped border	40.00	—
Dishes, nest of 3: 7″, 8″, and 9″	40.00	—	Straight border	30.00	—

FESTOON

Non-flint, 1890-1894. No goblet or wine was made in this pattern.

	Clear		Clear
Bowl		Plate, 7, 8, 9″	35.00
7 x 4½″, rect	25.00	Relish, 9 x 5½″	40.00
8″, Berry	25.00	Sauce, flat	7.50
9″, rect	30.00	Spooner	35.00
Butter, cov	55.00	Sugar	
Cake Stand, 10″	42.00	Cov	45.00
Compote, open, hs	65.00	Open	20.00
Creamer	38.00	Tray, water, 10″	35.00
Marmalade Jar, cov	60.00	Tumbler	22.00
Pickle Castor, cov	110.00	Waste Bowl	30.00
Pitcher, water	65.00		

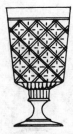

FINECUT

Non-flint made by Bryce Bros., Pittsburgh, PA, c1879, and by U. S. Glass Co. in 1891.

	Amber	Blue	Clear	Vaseline
Bowl, 8¼″	15.00	20.00	12.00	15.00
Bread Plate	50.00	60.00	25.00	50.00
Butter, cov	55.00	75.00	45.00	60.00
Cake Stand	—	—	30.00	—
Celery Tray	—	45.00	25.00	40.00
Celery Vase, SP holder	—	—	—	115.00
Creamer	35.00	40.00	20.00	75.00
Goblet	45.00	55.00	22.00	42.00
Pitcher, water	95.00	95.00	95.00	75.00

	Amber	Blue	Clear	Vaseline
Plate				
6″	—	20.00	8.00	—
7″	25.00	40.00	15.00	20.00
10″	30.00	50.00	21.00	45.00
Relish	35.00	40.00	18.00	35.00
Sauce, flat	14.00	15.00	10.00	14.00
Spooner	30.00	45.00	18.00	40.00
Sugar				
Covered	45.00	55.00	35.00	45.00
Open	40.00	45.00	25.00	40.00
Tray, water	50.00	55.00	25.00	50.00
Tumbler	—	—	18.00	28.00
Wine	—	—	24.00	30.00

FINECUT AND BLOCK

Made by King Glass Co., Crystal Glass Co. in c1890, and by McKee Glass Co. c1894. Also attributed to Portland Glass Co. Made in clear, solid colors of amber, blue, and yellow (all comparable in price), and in clear with color blocks.

	Clear	Solid Colored Pieces	Colored Block: Amber	Colored Block: Blue	Colored Block: Yellow or Pink
Bowl, 9″	35.00	—	—	—	—
Butter, cov					
Flat	65.00	—	—	—	—
Footed	75.00	165.00	—	—	—
Cake Stand					
Large	40.00	—	—	—	—
Small	35.00	—	—	—	—
Celery Tray	30.00	45.00	50.00	45.00	60.00
Compote					
Cov, ls	35.00	—	—	—	—
Open, ls, 8½″ . . .	30.00	—	45.00	40.00	45.00
Open jelly	18.00	50.00	75.00	75.00	75.00
Creamer	45.00	65.00	70.00	60.00	70.00
Goblet					
Buttermilk	30.00	—	—	55.00	85.00
Lady's	45.00	—	—	50.00	—
Regular	32.00	65.00	60.00	65.00	60.00
Pitcher					
Milk	45.00	85.00	95.00	95.00	125.00
Water	45.00	85.00	95.00	95.00	125.00
Plate, 5¾″	12.50	—	—	—	—
Punch Cup	12.00	—	—	20.00	—
Relish, rect	12.00	—	55.00	50.00	55.00
Salt, individual	12.00	—	—	—	—
Sauce					
Flat	10.00	16.00	16.00	12.00	16.00
Footed	12.00	18.50	18.00	14.50	—
Spooner	30.00	20.00	55.00	65.00	50.00
Sugar, cov	45.00	—	120.00	130.00	120.00
Tray					
Ice Cream	55.00	—	—	—	—
Water	60.00	—	—	—	—
Tumbler	20.00	50.00	50.00	45.00	45.00
Wine	30.00	—	45.00	45.00	45.00

FINECUT AND PANEL

Non-flint pattern made by many Pittsburgh factories in the 1880s. Reissued in the early 1890s by U. S. Glass Co. An aqua wine is known.

	Amber	Blue	Clear	Vaseline
Bowl				
7"	28.00	35.00	15.00	25.00
8", oval	55.00	—	18.00	30.00
Bread Plate	50.00	45.00	30.00	—
Butter, cov	45.00	75.00	40.00	60.00
Cake Stand, 10"	50.00	55.00	30.00	50.00
Compote				
Cov, hs	125.00	135.00	50.00	130.00
Open, hs	65.00	65.00	35.00	60.00
Creamer	35.00	50.00	25.00	40.00
Goblet	40.00	48.00	20.00	30.00
Pitcher				
Milk	65.00	—	—	50.00
Water	85.00	85.00	40.00	45.00
Plate, 7¼"	25.00	30.00	15.00	25.00
Platter	30.00	50.00	25.00	30.00
Relish	20.00	30.00	16.00	18.00
Sauce, ftd	14.00	25.00	8.00	15.00
Spooner	35.00	45.00	20.00	30.00
Sugar, cov	37.50	42.50	30.00	32.50
Tray, water	60.00	55.00	50.00	60.00
Tumbler	25.00	30.00	20.00	38.00
Waste Bowl	30.00	35.00	20.00	35.00
Wine	30.00	35.00	20.00	35.00

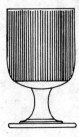

FINE RIB

Flint made by New England Glass Co. in the 1860s. Later made in non-flint, which has limited collecting interest and priced at ⅓ the value of flint.

	Clear Flint		Clear Flint
Bitters Bottle	50.00	* Honey Dish, 3½"d	16.00
Bowl, 7", cov	85.00	Lamp	150.00
Butter, cov	75.00	Mug	45.00
Castor Set	200.00	Pitcher, water, applied handle	350.00
Celery Vase	50.00		
Champagne	65.00	Plate, 6" or 7"	20.00
Compote		Salt	
Cov, hs, 8"	65.00	Cov, ftd	85.00
Open, hs, 7¾"	50.00	Individual	35.00
Open, ls, 9"	60.00	Spooner	65.00
Cordial	45.00	Sugar, cov	75.00
Creamer, applied handle	125.00	Tumbler, bar	65.00
Decanter, quart bar lip	75.00	Tumble-up	125.00
Egg Cup	48.00	Whiskey, handled	75.00
* Goblet	60.00	Wine	45.00

FISHSCALE (Coral)

Non-flint made by Bryce Brothers, Pittsburgh, PA, in the mid-1880s and by U. S. Glass Co. in 1891.

	Clear		Clear
Bowl		Mug, large	35.00
Cov, 7″	55.00	Pitcher	
Cov, 9½″	45.00	Milk	35.00
Open, 8″	20.00	Water	55.00
Bread Plate	28.00	Plate	
Butter, cov	45.00	7″, round	20.00
Cake Plate	55.00	9″, square	30.00
Cake Stand		Relish	15.00
9″	32.50	Salt Shaker	35.00
10½″	35.00	Sauce	
Celery Vase	30.00	Flat	7.50
Compote		Footed	15.00
Open, hs, 8″	30.00	Spooner	25.00
Open, hs, 9″	40.00	Sugar, cov	50.00
Open, jelly	20.00	Tray, condiment, rect	35.00
Creamer	30.00	Tumbler	55.00
Goblet	30.00	Waste Bowl	25.00
Lamp, Finger	75.00		

FLAMINGO HABITAT

Maker unknown, etched pattern.

	Clear		Clear
Bowl, 10″, oval	40.00	Creamer	48.00
Celery Vase	45.00	Goblet	38.00
Champagne	40.00	Sauce, ftd	15.00
Cheese Dish, blown, folded		Spooner	25.00
rim, dome lid	95.00	Sugar, cov	50.00
Compote		Tumbler	30.00
Cov, 4½″	75.00	Wine	42.00
Cov, 6½″	95.00		
Open, 5″, jelly	35.00		
Open, 6″	40.00		

FLEUR-DE-LIS AND DRAPE (Fleur-de-Lis and Tassel)

Non-flint made by U. S. Glass Co., c1892. Clear and emerald green pieces often trimmed with gilt. Also made in milk glass (rare).

	Clear	Emerald Green		Clear	Emerald Green
Bowl	15.00	30.00	Open, hs		
Butter, cov	45.00	55.00	5″	25.00	30.00
Cake Stand	35.00	55.00	6″	25.00	30.00
Claret	35.00	50.00	7″	30.00	35.00
Compote			8″	30.00	40.00
Cov, ls			Creamer	25.00	40.00
5″	30.00	40.00	Cruet, os	45.00	85.00
6″	35.00	40.00	Cup	20.00	30.00
7″	35.00	45.00	Cup and Saucer	25.00	35.00
8″	45.00	60.00	Goblet	35.00	45.00

	Clear	Emerald Green		Clear	Emerald Green
Honey Dish, cov . . .	40.00	55.00	Spooner	25.00	40.00
Mustard Jar, cov . . .	35.00	50.00	Sugar, cov	30.00	55.00
Pitcher			Syrup, metal top . . .	50.00	125.00
Milk.	40.00	60.00	Tumbler	20.00	30.00
Water	50.00	65.00	Waste Bowl.	30.00	40.00
Plate, 8″	20.00	35.00	Water Tray, 11½″ . .	24.00	50.00
Salt Shaker.	20.00	35.00	Wine	25.00	45.00

FLORIDA (Emerald Green Herringbone, Paneled Herringbone)

Non-flint made by U. S. Glass Co., late 1880s-1890s. One of States patterns. Reproduced in green and other colors.

	Clear	Emerald Green		Clear	Emerald Green
Bowl			Plate		
7¾″	20.00	25.00	7½″	10.00	18.00
9″	20.00	25.00	9¼″	15.00	28.00
Butter, cov	40.00	55.00	Relish		
Cake Stand			6″, sq	10.00	15.00
Large	60.00	68.00	8½″, sq	15.00	22.00
Small	28.00	38.00	Salt Shaker.	25.00	50.00
Celery Vase	30.00	35.00	Sauce	8.00	15.00
Compote, open, hs,			Spooner	20.00	35.00
6½″, sq	—	40.00	Sugar		
Creamer.	30.00	45.00	Cov.	32.00	50.00
Cruet, os	40.00	125.00	Open	18.00	25.00
* Goblet	25.00	40.00	Syrup.	60.00	175.00
Mustard Pot, attach-			Tumbler	20.00	30.00
ed underplate, cov	25.00	45.00	Wine	25.00	50.00
Nappy	15.00	25.00			
Pitcher, water	50.00	75.00			

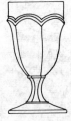

FLUTE

More than 15 Flute variants were produced in flint and non-flint glass from the 1850s through the 1880s. Some of the flint variants are Beaded Flute, Bessimer Flute, New England Flute, etc., all with comparable prices. Prices listed are for flint.

	Clear		Clear
Ale Glass	50.00	Goblet	35.00
Bitters Bottle.	75.00	Honey	18.00
Butter, cov, ls	60.00	Lamp	75.00
Candlestick, 4″	42.00	Mug	35.00
Claret.	45.00	Pitcher, water	75.00
Compote		Sauce, flat	18.00
Open, ls, 8½″	40.00	Sugar	
Open, ls, 9½″	45.00	Covered	50.00
Creamer.	45.00	Open	30.00
Decanter, bar lip	100.00	Tumbler	18.00
Egg Cup		Whiskey, handled	30.00
Double	50.00	Wine	30.00
Single	40.00		

FRANCES WARE

Made by Hobbs, Brockunier & Co., Wheeling, West Virginia, c1880. A clear frosted hobnail or swirl pattern glass with amber stained top rims. It may be pressed or mold blown. Swirl pieces are noted, otherwise they are hobnail.

	Clear	Frosted/Amber Stain		Clear	Frosted/Amber Stain
Bowl, 7½"	50.00	75.00	Spooner	45.00	50.00
Box, 5¼", round, cov	45.00	65.00	Sugar		
			Cov.	60.00	85.00
Butter, cov	80.00	110.00	Open	40.00	60.00
Creamer.	50.00	85.00	Sugar Shaker, swirl .	65.00	70.00
Finger Bowl, 4"	40.00	50.00	Syrup, swirl.	85.00	145.00
Mustard, cov, swirl. .	—	135.00	Toothpick	75.00	95.00
Pitcher			Tray		
8½"	90.00	150.00	Leaf shape, 12".	75.00	125.00
11"	150.00	185.00	Rect, rounded		
Salt & Pepper			edges, 14 x 9½" .	—	150.00
Hobnail	50.00	65.00	Water, oval	—	150.00
Swirl	60.00	—	Tumbler	35.00	45.00
Sauce, 4", sq	18.00	32.00			

FROSTED CIRCLE

Produced by Bryce Bros., Pittsburgh, Pennsylvania, from 1876 to c1885. Later by U. S. Glass Co. in the late 1890s. Reproduced.

	Clear Circle	Frosted Circle		Clear Circle	Frosted Circle
Bowl, cov			Cup and Saucer . . .	25.00	35.00
7"	20.00	25.00	* Goblet	35.00	45.00
8"	25.00	30.00	Pitcher, water	55.00	60.00
Butter, cov	55.00	65.00	Plate		
Cake Stand			4"	10.00	22.00
8"	30.00	35.00	9"	22.00	17.00
9½"	40.00	50.00	Punch Cup	15.00	20.00
Champagne	35.00	65.00	Salt & Pepper	35.00	65.00
Compote			Sauce	8.50	12.00
Cov, 7", hs.	30.00	45.00	Spooner	35.00	40.00
Cov, 8", hs.	45.00	65.00	* Sugar, cov	42.50	50.00
Open, 7", hs	20.00	30.00	Sugar Shaker	40.00	65.00
Open, 10", hs	45.00	55.00	Syrup	85.00	125.00
Creamer.	30.00	40.00	Tumbler	25.00	35.00
Cruet, os	45.00	65.00	Wine	35.00	45.00

FROSTED LEAF

Flint, c1850. Listed as also being produced by Portland Glass Co. between 1873 and 1874 in non-flint. Non-flint pieces valued at 50% of flint prices.

	Flint		Flint
Butter, cov	135.00	Creamer.	375.00
Celery Vase	130.00	Decanter, os	250.00
Champagne	160.00	Egg Cup.	120.00
Compote, cov	250.00	Goblet	125.00

	Flint
Pitcher, water	400.00
Salt, ind	40.00
Sauce, flat	20.00
Spooner	80.00
Sugar	
Cov	175.00
Open, buttermilk type	75.00

Tumbler	Flint
Footed	125.00
Regular	185.00
Wine	185.00

FROSTED STORK

Non-flint made by Crystal Glass Co, Bridgeport, OH, c1880. Now reproduced.
Details of the stork's activities differ from scene to scene on the same piece.

	Clear
Bowl, 9″	50.00
Bread Plate, oval	50.00
Butter, cov	85.00
Creamer	45.00
Finger Bowl	50.00
* Goblet	70.00
Jam Jar, cov	100.00
Pickle, cov	100.00
Pitcher, water	150.00

	Clear
Platter, 11½ x 8″	
101 border	70.00
Scenic border	90.00
Relish	45.00
Sauce, flat	20.00
Spooner	40.00
Sugar, cov	95.00
Tray, water	100.00
Waste Bowl	50.00

GALLOWAY

Non-flint made by U. S. Glass Co., 1904. Clear glass with and without gold trim;
also known with rose stain and ruby stain.

	Clear w/ Gold	Rose Stained
Basket, no gold	75.00	
Bowl		
6½″	25.00	—
8½″, oval	25.00	—
8½″, round	25.00	—
9¾″	35.00	50.00
11″ d, 3″ h	45.00	—
Butter, cov	65.00	125.00
Cake Stand	60.00	
Carafe, water	55.00	75.00
Celery Vase	35.00	75.00
Champagne	45.00	—
Compote		
Open, hs, 4¼″	30.00	—
Open, hs, 10″, scalloped	85.00	—
Creamer		
Individual	15.00	—
Regular	30.00	50.00
Cruet	45.00	—
Egg Cup	25.00	—
Finger Bowl	38.00	—
Goblet	55.00	—
Lemonade	35.00	—
Mug	35.00	50.00
Olive, 6″	20.00	30.00

	Clear w/gold	Rose Stained
Pitcher		
Milk	40.00	—
Tankard	75.00	—
Water, ice lip	65.00	125.00
Plate, 8″, round	20.00	30.00
Punch Bowl	160.00	—
Punch Bowl Plate,		
20″	65.00	—
Punch Cup	10.00	15.00
Relish	20.00	30.00
Rose Bowl	25.00	—
Salt Dip	15.00	—
Salt & Pepper, pr.	35.00	—
Sauce, flat	10.00	—
Sherbet	25.00	—
Spooner	30.00	—
Sugar, cov	55.00	75.00
Sugar Shaker	40.00	—
Syrup	65.00	—
Toothpick	30.00	—
Tumbler	25.00	—
Vase, swung	30.00	—
Waste Bowl	38.00	—
Water Bottle	40.00	—
Wine	40.00	—

GARFIELD DRAPE

Non-flint pattern issued in 1881 by Adams & Co., Pittsburgh, Pennsylvania, after the assassination of President Garfield.

	Clear		Clear
Bread Plate		Honey Dish............	15.00
Memorial, portrait of		Goblet	40.00
Garfield	65.00	Pitcher	
"We Mourn Our Nation's		Milk................	70.00
Loss", portrait........	75.00	Water, applied strap	
Butter, cov..............	60.00	handle	100.00
Cake Stand, 9½".........	75.00	Relish, oval.............	18.00
Celery Vase	40.00	Sauce	
Compote		Flat................	8.50
Cov, hs, 8"..........	100.00	Footed	12.00
Cov, ls, 6"	60.00	Spooner..............	30.00
Open, hs, 8½"	40.00	Sugar, cov	60.00
Creamer..............	45.00	Tumbler	35.00

GEORGIA (Peacock Feather)

Probably Richards and Hartley, but reissued by several glass companies, including U. S. Glass Co. in 1902 as part of their States series. Rare in blue. (Chamber lamp, pedestal base, $275.00). No goblet known in pattern.

	Clear		Clear
Bowl, 8"	30.00	Lamp	
Butter, cov	45.00	Chamber, pedestal......	65.00
Cake Stand, 11"	40.00	Hand, oil, 7"	80.00
Compote		Pitcher, water	70.00
Cov, hs, 8"...........	50.00	Plate, 5¼".............	18.00
Open, hs, 7"	30.00	Relish................	10.00
Open, jelly...........	20.00	Salt & Pepper...........	60.00
Condiment Set, tray, oil cruet,		Sauce	12.50
salt and pepper	75.00	Spooner..............	35.00
Creamer.............	35.00	Sugar, cov	45.00
Cruet, os	55.00	Syrup, metal lid.........	55.00
Decanter	70.00	Tumbler	20.00

GIANT BULL'S EYE (Bull's Eye and Spearhead)

Made by Bellaire Glass Co., Findlay, Ohio, and continued by U. S. Glass Co. after 1891.

	Clear		Clear
Brandy bottle, os, tall,		Goblet	35.00
narrow	55.00	Lamp, handled	125.00
Butter, cov	45.00	Pitcher, water	75.00
Claret Jug, tankard shape ..	60.00	Tray, wine, 7¼"..........	45.00
Compote, cov	75.00	Tumbler	30.00
Creamer..............	30.00	Vase	35.00
Cruet, os	60.00	Wine	30.00
Decanter, os...........	50.00		

GIBSON GIRL

Non-flint. Made by Kokomo Glass Co., c1904.

	Clear		Clear
Butter, cov	75.00	Salt Shaker	50.00
Creamer	85.00	Spooner	50.00
Pitcher, water	175.00	Sugar, cov	75.00
Plate, 10"	75.00	Tumbler	65.00

GOOSEBERRY

Non-flint of the 1880s. Made by Boston and Sandwich Glass Co. and others in clear and milk glass. Reproduced in milk glass.

	Clear	Milk Glass		Clear	Milk Glass
Butter, cov	50.00	60.00	Pitcher, water, applied handle	165.00	100.00
Compote			Sauce	10.00	15.00
Cov, hs, 6"	45.00	65.00	Spooner	25.00	30.00
Cov, hs, 7"	55.00	75.00	Sugar, cov	45.00	55.00
Cov, hs, 8"	65.00	90.00	Syrup, applied handle	75.00	90.00
Creamer	30.00	50.00	Tumbler	35.00	40.00
Goblet	35.00	45.00			
Mug	30.00	40.00			

GOTHIC

Flint made by Boston and Sandwich Glass Co., c1860s.

	Clear		Clear
Bowl, 7"	70.00	Creamer	75.00
Butter, cov	85.00	Egg Cup	50.00
Castor Set	100.00	Goblet	50.00
Celery Vase	85.00	Sauce, flat	18.00
Champagne	125.00	Spooner	40.00
Compote		Sugar, cov	85.00
Cov, hs, 8"	110.00	Tumbler	95.00
Open, ls, 7"	65.00	Wine	95.00

GRAND (Diamond Medallion)

Non-flint, made by Bryce, Higbee and Co. 1885. Stemware comes in plain and ringed stems.

	Clear		Clear
Bowl, 6", cov	30.00	Compote	
Bread Plate, 10"	25.00	Cov, hs, 5½"	60.00
Butter, cov		Cov, hs, 7½"	75.00
Flat	35.00	Open, hs, 9"	65.00
Footed	45.00	Cordial	35.00
Cake Stand		Creamer	25.00
8"	30.00	Goblet	30.00
10"	35.00	Pitcher, water	40.00
Celery Vase, pedestal	25.00	Plate, 10"	25.00

	Clear		Clear
Relish, 7½″, oval	10.00	Spooner	20.00
Salt & Pepper	45.00	Sugar, cov	35.00
Sauce		Syrup, metal top	75.00
Flat	7.50	Waste Bowl, collared	30.00
Footed	10.00	Wine	30.00

GRAPE BAND

Issued in flint by Bryce, Walker and Co. in the late 1850s; non-flint in 1869.

	Flint	Non-Flint		Flint	Non-Flint
Butter, cov	75.00	50.00	Plate, 6″	—	18.00
Compote			Salt Dip	—	20.00
Cov, hs	—	50.00	Spooner	—	30.00
Open, hs	—	25.00	Sugar		
Creamer, applied			Cov	—	45.00
handle	—	48.00	Open, buttermilk		
Egg Cup	—	20.00	type	—	35.00
Goblet	40.00	25.00	Tumbler	35.00	20.00
Pickle	—	15.00	Wine	35.00	25.00
Pitcher, water	—	85.00			

GRASSHOPPER (Long Spear)

Maker unknown; over 40 pieces documented. Pieces without the grasshopper bring 40–50% less. Creamer and sugar known in vaseline and blue. Goblet is modern.

	Amber	Clear		Amber	Clear
Bowl			Pickle	—	20.00
Covered	55.00	35.00	Pitcher, water	125.00	75.00
Open, ftd	—	25.00	Plate, 8½″, ftd	—	25.00
Butter, cov	—	65.00	Salt Dip	—	40.00
Celery Vase	90.00	80.00	Sauce		
Compote			Flat	—	10.00
Cov, hs, 7″	—	50.00	Footed	—	15.00
Cov, hs, 8½″	—	65.00	Spooner	75.00	65.00
Creamer	—	45.00	Sugar		
Marmalade Jar, cov,			Cov	—	65.00
insert	—	125.00	Open	—	45.00

HAIRPIN (Sandwich Loop)

Flint pattern made in the Sandwich factory c1850. Finials are acorn shaped, handles are applied.

	Clear		Clear
Celery Vase	40.00	Sauce, flat	15.00
Champagne	50.00	Spooner	40.00
Compote, cov hs	225.00	Sugar	
Creamer	45.00	Covered	95.00
Decanter, os, qt	65.00	Open	50.00
Egg Cup	30.00	Tumbler	30.00
Goblet	40.00	Whiskey, handled	48.00
Salt, cov, ftd	85.00	Wine	35.00

HALLEY'S COMET (Etruria)

Clear non-flint pattern made by Model Flint Glass Co, c1880. The tail of the comet forms continuous loops. A ruby stained wine is known.

	Clear		Clear
Bowl		Goblet	**45.00**
4", cov, 3 ftd	**40.00**	Pitcher, water	**85.00**
8"	**25.00**	Punch Cup	**35.00**
9"	**28.00**	Relish.	**25.00**
Butter, cov	**80.00**	Salt & Pepper, pr.	**45.00**
Cake Stand	**75.00**	Spooner	**35.00**
Celery Vase	**48.00**	Sugar	
Compote		Covered	**65.00**
Cov, hs, 10".	**60.00**	Open	**35.00**
Open, hs, 8"	**40.00**	Syrup	**48.00**
Creamer.	**35.00**	Tumbler	**25.00**
Cruet, os	**60.00**	Wine	**30.00**

HAMILTON

Flint, 1860. Some attribute pattern to Boston and Sandwich Glass Co. Other companies also may have made it.

	Clear		Clear
Butter, cov	**75.00**	Pitcher, water	**175.00**
Celery Vase	**60.00**	Plate, 6"	**45.00**
Compote		Salt, ftd	**30.00**
Cov, hs	**95.00**	Spooner	**36.00**
Open, ls, 6", scallop rim . .	**80.00**	Sweetmeat Dish, hs, cov . . .	**95.00**
Creamer, applied handle . . .	**75.00**	Sugar, cov	**75.00**
Egg Cup, frosted leaf.	**50.00**	Tumbler, water or bar	**85.00**
Goblet	**45.00**	Whiskey, applied handle . . .	**95.00**
Lamp, hand	**85.00**	Wine	**90.00**

HAND (Pennsylvania #2)

Made by O'Hara Glass Co., Pittsburgh, Pennsylvania, c1880. Covered pieces have a hand holding bar finial, hence the name.

	Clear		Clear
Bowl		Creamer.	**40.00**
9"	**24.00**	Goblet	**45.00**
10"	**38.00**	Marmalade Jar, cov	**50.00**
Butter, cov	**75.00**	Pickle	**20.00**
Cake Stand	**55.00**	Pitcher, water	**75.00**
Celery Vase	**42.50**	Sauce	
Compote		Flat.	**8.00**
Cov, hs, 7".	**60.00**	Footed	**15.00**
Cov, hs, 8".	**95.00**	Spooner	**30.00**
Open, hs, 7¾"	**45.00**	Sugar, cov	**75.00**
Open, ls, 9"	**20.00**	Syrup.	**45.00**
Cordial, 3½"	**75.00**	Wine	**50.00**

HANOVER (Block With Stars #2, Blockhouse)

Originally made by Richards and Hartley, of Tarentum, Pennsylvania, in 1888 and possibly earlier. Made in many pieces. Also made in blue.

	Clear	Dark Amber		Clear	Dark Amber
Bowl, 10", berry....	20.00	40.00	Ketchup Bottles, pr .	50.00	75.00
Bread Plate, 10" ...	20.00	30.00	Mug		
Butter, cov	40.00	80.00	Large	22.00	48.00
Cake Stand, 10" ...	42.00	62.00	Small	18.00	40.00
Celery Vase	27.00	38.00	Pitcher, water	50.00	85.00
Cheese Dish, cov,			Plate		
10"	50.00	95.00	4"	25.00	40.00
Compote			6"	25.00	40.00
Cov, hs	45.00	90.00	10"	18.00	45.00
Open, hs	40.00	—	Puff Box, glass lid .	45.00	—
Open, ls	40.00	45.00	Sauce, ftd	10.00	15.00
Creamer.........	30.00	45.00	Spooner	25.00	37.00
Cruet, os	20.00	—	Sugar, cov	45.00	55.00
Goblet	25.00	55.00	Tumbler	25.00	30.00

HARP (Lyre)

Flint glass made by Bryce Bros., Pittsburgh, Pennsylvania, in the late 1840s and early 1850s. Also found in McKee catalog of 1859.

	Clear		Clear
Butter, cov	150.00	Nappy	100.00
Compote, cov, ls, 6"	200.00	Salt, master	75.00
Goblet, rare	1,000.00	Spill holder	85.00
Lamp		Spooner	95.00
Hand...............	200.00	Sweetmeat Jar, cov	200.00
Stand	225.00		

HARTLEY (Paneled Diamond Cut With Fan)

Non-flint pattern made by Richards and Hartley in 1880s, and by U. S. Glass Co in 1891. Trilobed form has either plain or engraved panels. Twenty-three pieces documented.

	Amber	Blue & Vaseline	Clear
Bowl, berry			
7", ftd	35.00	40.00	18.00
9"	30.00	40.00	20.00
Bread Plate, trilobed	30.00	40.00	20.00
Butter, cov	50.00	60.00	40.00
Cake Stand, 10" ...	45.00	50.00	40.00
Celery Vase	32.00	40.00	25.00
Compote			
Cov, ls, 7¾"....	68.00	75.00	45.00
Open, 7" and 8"..	30.00	40.00	18.00
Creamer..........	30.00	35.00	28.00
Dish, centerpiece ..	40.00	45.00	20.00
Goblet	35.00	40.00	25.00

	Amber	Blue & Vaseline	Clear
Pitcher			
Milk, qt	80.00	85.00	75.00
Water, ½ gal	90.00	90.00	85.00
Plate	45.00	50.00	30.00
Relish	18.00	20.00	15.00
Spooner	28.00	30.00	18.00
Sugar, cov	40.00	50.00	30.00
Tumbler	30.00	35.00	20.00
Wine	40.00	45.00	28.00

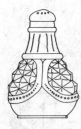

HARVARD YARD (Harvard #1)

Made by Tarentum Glass Co., 1896. Also found in clear with gold, emerald green, pink, and ruby stained.

	Clear		Clear
Butter, cov	30.00	Plate, 10″	15.00
Cake Stand	30.00	Salt Dip	15.00
Cordial	25.00	Spooner	18.00
Creamer	18.00	Sugar, cov	25.00
Egg Cup	15.00	Toothpick	18.00
Goblet	25.00	Tumbler	20.00
Pitcher, water	40.00	Wine	18.00

HEART WITH THUMBPRINT (Bull's Eye in Heart)

Non-flint, made by Tarentum Glass Co. 1898. Some emerald green pieces have gold trim. Made experimentally in custard, blue custard, opaque nile green and cobalt. Some pieces are found with ruby stain. (Goblet $85.00)

	Clear	Emerald Green		Clear	Emerald Green
Banana Boat	75.00	—	Cruet	75.00	—
Barber Bottle	100.00	—	Finger Bowl	45.00	—
Bowl			Goblet	58.00	120.00
7″ sq	35.00	—	Hair Receiver, metal		
9″	42.00	—	lid	65.00	—
9½″ sq	32.50	—	Ice Bucket	60.00	—
10″ scalloped	35.00	—	Lamp		
Butter, cov	75.00	125.00	Finger	65.00	115.00
Cake Stand, 9″	125.00	—	Oil, 8″	50.00	160.00
Carafe, water	100.00	—	Mustard, SP cov . . .	95.00	100.00
Card Tray	20.00	—	Nappy, turned up		
Celery Vase	65.00	—	edges	32.50	—
Compote			Pitcher, water	90.00	—
Open, hs, 7½″,			Plate		
scalloped	90.00	—	6″	25.00	75.00
Open, hs, 8½″ . . .	100.00	—	10″	35.00	—
Cordial, 3″ h	125.00	—	Powder Jar, SP cov.	65.00	—
Creamer			Punch Cup	22.00	45.00
Ind	22.50	45.00	Rose Bowl	30.00	—
Regular	60.00	90.00	Salt & Pepper	95.00	—

	Clear	Emerald Green		Clear	Emerald Green
Sauce, 5″	18.00	35.00	Tray, 8¼″ l, 4¼″ w . .	35.00	—
Spooner	50.00	—	Tumbler	60.00	—
Sugar			Vase		
Ind	25.00	35.00	6″	35.00	65.00
Regular, cov	85.00	90.00	10″	60.00	—
Syrup	75.00	—	Wine	45.00	—

HICKMAN (La Clede)

Non-flint pattern made by McKee Glass Co., Pittsburgh, Pennsylvania, c1897. Also made in ruby stain (rare).

	Clear	Emerald Green		Clear	Emerald Green
Banana Stand, ftd . .	65.00	—	Cup		
Bon bon, 9″, sq. . . .	15.00	—	Custard	12.00	—
Bottle, Pepper	25.00	—	Lemonade	12.00	—
Bowl			Dish, 4″ sq	16.00	—
Round, or with			Goblet	35.00	50.00
scalloped top			Ice Bucket	60.00	—
4″	12.00	—	Mustard Jar, under-		
4½″	12.00	—	plate, cov	45.00	—
5″	14.00	—	Nappy, 5″	10.00	—
6″	15.00	—	Olive, 4″, handle . . .	10.00	20.00
7″	15.00	—	Pickle	15.00	20.00
8″	18.00	—	Pitcher, water	55.00	—
Square, 7″	15.00	18.00	Plate, 9¼″	15.00	—
Butter, cov	35.00	58.00	Punch Bowl	175.00	375.00
Cake Stand			Punch Cup	10.00	15.00
8½″	30.00	—	Punch Glass, ftd . . .	30.00	—
9½″	32.50	—	Relish	18.00	15.00
Celery Vase	28.00	—	Rose Bowl	25.00	—
Champagne	25.00	—	Salt, individual, flat,		
Cologne Bottle, fac-			sloping sides	10.00	—
eted stopper	30.00	—	Salt Shaker, single		
Compote			Round, long cut		
Cov, hs, 7″	55.00	—	neck	15.00	—
Open, hs, 8″	45.00	—	Round, squat	20.00	30.00
Open, ls, 4½″,			Square	20.00	—
jelly	40.00	45.00	Spooner	27.00	—
Condiment Set, han-			Sugar, cov	42.00	50.00
died tray, cruet,			Sugar Shaker	45.00	—
pepper bottle,			Toothpick	45.00	75.00
open salt	85.00	—	Tumbler	30.00	—
Cordial	24.00	—	Vase, 10¼″	12.00	45.00
Creamer	25.00	35.00	Wine	30.00	—
Cruet, os	45.00	—			

HIDALGO (Frosted Waffle)

Non-flint made by Adams and Co., Pittsburgh, Pennsylvania, in the early 1880s and U S Glass Co in 1891. This pattern comes etched and clear, and also with part of pattern frosted. Add 20% for frosted.

	Amber Stained	Clear		Amber Stained	Clear
Bowl, 10", sq	35.00	20.00	Pitcher		
Bread Plate, cupped,			Milk.	—	40.00
sq, 10"	75.00	60.00	Water	—	45.00
Butter, cov	—	50.00	Plate, 10"	—	35.00
Celery Vase	35.00	20.00	Salt, master, sq.	—	25.00
Compote			Salt & Pepper	—	40.00
Cov, hs, 7½"	85.00	65.00	Sauce, handled. . . .	—	10.00
Cov, ls, 6"	—	50.00	Spooner	—	20.00
Open, hs, 10" . . .	—	45.00	Sugar, cov	—	48.00
Open, hs, 1l"	—	50.00	Sugar Shaker	—	45.00
Cruet	—	65.00	Syrup	—	60.00
Cup and Saucer . . .	—	40.00	Tray, water	—	55.00
Goblet	40.00	20.00	Tumbler	—	25.00
Nappy, handled, sq .	—	18.00	Waste Bowl.	—	25.00
Pickle, boat shaped.	18.00	12.00			

HINOTO (Diamond Point With Panels)

Flint made by Boston and Sandwich Co in the late 1850s.

	Clear		Clear
Butter, cov	85.00	Salt	35.00
Celery Vase	65.00	Spooner	35.00
Champagne	60.00	Sugar, cov	75.00
Creamer.	75.00	Tumbler	45.00
Egg Cup.	35.00	Whiskey	50.00
Goblet	60.00	Wine	60.00

HOBNAIL, OPALESCENT

Made by several companies with variations in forms of pieces, c1880–1900. Pieces are found round in shape, with frilled tops, pieces on three feet, pieces on four feet, square in shape or octagonal in shape. Highly reproduced. Fenton Glass still makes this pattern.

	Blue Opal	Opal	Vaseline Opal	White Opal
Butter, cov				
Flat.	100.00	110.00	105.00	85.00
Four Feet	110.00	115.00	110.00	90.00
* Celery Vase	85.00	120.00	100.00	65.00
* Creamer				
Flat.	95.00	115.00	110.00	85.00
Four Feet	100.00	120.00	115.00	95.00
Cruet, os	—	—	125.00	50.00
Mug	35.00	55.00	50.00	30.00
Pitcher, water	100.00	125.00	120.00	95.00
Sauce, flat	25.00	35.00	30.00	20.00
Spooner				
Flat.	25.00	40.00	30.00	20.00
Four Feet	35.00	40.00	30.00	25.00
Sugar, cov				
Flat.	40.00	60.00	55.00	30.00
Four Feet	45.00	65.00	60.00	35.00
Syrup.	85.00	125.00	110.00	75.00

	Blue Opal	Opal	Vaseline Opal	White Opal
Toothpick	30.00	50.00	50.00	30.00
Tumbler	40.00	55.00	50.00	30.00
Spooner	25.00	30.00	20.00	
*Sugar, open	20.00	25.00	15.00	
Tray, water, 11½" . .	35.00	40.00	30.00	
*Wine	24.00	28.00	17.50	

HOLLY

Non-flint made by Boston and Sandwich Glass Co., late 1860s, early 1870s.

	Clear		Clear
Butter, cov	150.00	Salt	
Cake Stand, 11"	125.00	Flat, oval	65.00
Celery Vase	60.00	Ftd	60.00
Compote, cov, hs	165.00	Sauce, flat	20.00
Creamer, applied handle . . .	125.00	Spooner	60.00
Egg Cup	65.00	Sugar	
Goblet	100.00	Cov.	125.00
Pitcher, water applied handle	185.00	Open, buttermilk	60.00
		Tumbler	125.00
		Wine	100.00

HONEYCOMB

A popular pattern made in flint and non-flint glass by numerous firms, c1850–1900, resulting in many minor pattern variations. Rare in color.

	Flint	Non-Flint		Flint	Non-Flint
Ale Glass	50.00	25.00	8 x 6¼"h	65.00	—
Barber Bottle	45.00	25.00	11 x 8"h	135.00	—
Bowl			Compote, open, ls,		
7¼", oval, base mkd "Mould pat'd May 11, 1869," acorn finial on cov	90.00	40.00	7½", scalloped . . .	40.00	—
			Cordial, 3½"	25.00	—
			Creamer, applied handle	35.00	20.00
10"	—	40.00	Decanter		
Butter, cov	65.00	45.00	Pint	55.00	18.50
Cake Stand	55.00	35.00	Quart, os	70.00	65.00
Castor Bottle	25.00	18.00	Egg Cup	18.00	20.00
Celery Vase	45.00	25.00	Finger Bowl	48.00	—
Champagne	65.00	—	Goblet	25.00	15.00
Claret	35.00	—	Honey, cov	—	25.00
Compote, cov, hs			Lamp		
6½" x 8½"h	100.00	50.00	All Glass	—	45.00
9¼ x 11½"h	110.00	65.00	Marble base	—	40.00
Compote, open, hs			Lemonade	40.00	20.00
7 x 5"h	35.00	25.00	Mug, half pint	25.00	15.00
7 x 7"h	60.00	40.00	Pitcher, water, applied handle	100.00	60.00

	Flint	Non-Flint		Flint	Non-Flint
Plate, 6″	—	12.50	Tumbler		
Pomade Jar, cov	48.00	20.00	Bar	25.00	—
Relish	30.00	—	Flat	—	12.50
Salt, master, cov, ftd	35.00	40.00	Footed	—	15.00
Salt & Pepper	—	40.00	Lemonade	40.00	—
Sauce	12.00	7.50	Vase		
Spillholder	24.00	—	7½″	45.00	—
Spooner	35.00	20.00	10½″	75.00	—
Sugar			Whiskey, handled	125.00	—
Cov	75.00	45.00	Wine	35.00	18.00
Open	30.00	25.00			

HORN OF PLENTY

A fine flint glass pattern reputed to have been first made by Boston and Sandwich Glass Co. in the 1850s. Later made in flint and non-flint by other firms.

	Clear Flint		Clear Flint
Bowl, 8½″	145.00	Egg Cup	45.00
Butter, cov		* Goblet	75.00
Conventional finial	125.00	* Lamp	200.00
Head of Washington	400.00	Mug, small, applied handle	150.00
Shape of Acorn	130.00	Pepper Sauce Bottle, pewter top	200.00
Butter Pat	20.00	Pitcher, water	575.00
Cake Stand	350.00	Plate, 6″	100.00
Celery Vase	160.00	Relish, 7″ l, 5″ w	45.00
Champagne	125.00	Salt, master, oval, flat	75.00
Compote		Sauce, 5¼″	25.00
Cov, hs, 6¼″	175.00	Spillholder	65.00
Open, hs, 7″	125.00	Spooner	45.00
Open, hs, 8″	115.00	Sugar	
Open, hs, 9¼″	200.00	Cov	125.00
Open, hs, 10½″	140.00	Open	65.00
Open, ls, 8″	55.00	Tumbler	
Open, ls, 9″	85.00	Bar	85.00
Cordial	100.00	Water	75.00
Creamer, applied handle		Whiskey	
5½″h	235.00	Applied handle	235.00
7″h	175.00	Shot glass, 3″	100.00
Decanter		Wine	125.00
Pint	150.00		
Quart, os	100.00		

HORSESHOE (Good Luck, Prayer Rug)

Non-flint made by Adams & Co. and others in the 1880s.

	Clear		Clear
Bowl, cov, oval		Bread Plate, 14 x 10″	
7″	150.00	Double horseshoe handles	65.00
8″	195.00		

	Clear			Clear
Single horseshoe handles.	40.00	Marmalade Jar, cov.		98.00
Butter, cov	85.00	Pitcher		
Cake Plate	40.00	Milk.		110.00
Cake Stand		Water		75.00
9".	75.00	Plate		
10"	85.00	7".		45.00
Celery Vase, knob stem. . . .	40.00	10"		48.00
Cheese, cov, woman		Relish, 5 x 7"		18.00
churning	275.00	Salt		
Compote		Individual, horseshoe		
Cov, hs, 7", horseshoe		shape		20.00
finial	65.00	Master, horseshoe shape.		90.00
Cov, hs, 8".	70.00	Sauce		
Cov, hs, 11".	85.00	Flat.		12.50
Creamer, 6½"	95.00	Footed		20.00
Doughnut Stand	75.00	Spooner.		35.00
Finger Bowl	55.00	Sugar, cov		55.00
Goblet		Vegetable Dish, oblong		35.00
Knob Stem	40.00	Wine		150.00
Plain Stem	38.00			

HUMMINGBIRD (Flying Robin)

Non-flint, c1880. A clear water pitcher is known in a mold variant.

	Amber	Blue	Canary	Clear
Butter, cov	110.00	110.00	85.00	60.00
Celery Vase	90.00	90.00	65.00	45.00
Compote, hs, open .	95.00	95.00	65.00	48.00
Creamer.	75.00	75.00	60.00	40.00
Goblet	55.00	70.00	50.00	35.00
Pitcher				
Milk.	65.00	95.00	—	50.00
Water	125.00	150.00	100.00	85.00
Sauce, ftd.	25.00	30.00	30.00	18.00
Spooner.	40.00	75.00	45.00	30.00
Sugar, cov	100.00	100.00	65.00	55.00
Tray, water	150.00	120.00	80.00	60.00
Tumbler, bar	75.00	75.00	45.00	30.00
Waste Bowl, 5¼". . .	—	—	—	35.00
Wine	—	—	—	48.00

ILLINOIS

Non-flint. One of the States patterns made by U. S. Glass Co., c1897. Most forms are square. A few items are known in ruby stained, including a salt, $50.00, and a lidless straw holder with the stain in the inside, $95.00.

	Clear	Emerald Green		Clear	Emerald Clear
Basket, applied han-			Celery Tray, 11" . . .	40.00	—
dle, 11½".	100.00	—	Cheese, cov	50.00	—
Bowl, 8"	35.00	—	Creamer		
Butter, cov	60.00	—	Ind	30.00	—
Candlesticks, pr . . .	100.00	—	Regular.	40.00	—

	Clear	Emerald Green		Clear	Emerald Green
Cruet	55.00	—	Sauce	15.00	—
Lamp, tall, banquet, matching shade . .	500.00+	—	Spooner . . . . Straw Holder	35.00	—
Marmalade Jar	135.00	—	Glass cov	175.00	225.00
Olive	12.00	—	Open	180.00	—
Pitcher, water			Sugar		
Square	65.00	—	Ind	30.00	—
Tankard, round, SP rim	75.00	135.00	Regular, cov . . . . Sugar Shaker	55.00 65.00	— —
Plate, 7″, sq	24.00	—	Syrup, pewter top . .	95.00	—
Relish			Toothpick		
7½″ x 4″	18.00	—	Adv emb in base .	45.00	—
8½ x 3″	18.00	—	Plain	30.00	—
Salt			Tray, 12 x 8″, turned		
Ind	15.00	—	up sides	50.00	—
Master	25.00	—	Tumbler	25.00	40.00
Salt and Pepper, pr	35.00	—	Vase, 6″, sq	35.00	45.00

INTAGLIO (Flower Spray with Scroll)

Made by Northwood Co., Indiana, Pennsylvania, c1899. Also reported in custard trimmed in green and gold. Creamers in blue opalescent were used as premiums in 1901 by Arbuckle Coffee.

	Blue Opal	Custard	Vaseline Opal	White Opal
Bowl, berry	50.00	50.00	60.00	45.00
Butter, cov	165.00	175.00	170.00	150.00
Compote, jelly	45.00	100.00	60.00	35.00
Creamer	60.00	100.00	50.00	40.00
Cruet, os	100.00	250.00	110.00	95.00
Pitcher, water	200.00	—	225.00	125.00
Sauce	35.00	90.00	42.00	25.00
Spooner	75.00	115.00	80.00	50.00
Sugar, cov	150.00	100.00	100.00	85.00
Tumbler	50.00	70.00	58.00	45.00
Wine	—	—	—	20.00

INVERTED FAN AND FEATHER

Made by Northwood Co., Wheeling, West Virginia, c1900. Also known in carnival and canary opalescent. See Pink Slag.

	Blue Opal	Clear Opal	Custard	Green With Gold
Bowl, berry				
Individual	40.00	—	—	—
Master	125.00	100.00	225.00	110.00
Butter, cov	275.00	195.00	245.00	200.00
Compote, jelly	200.00	195.00	175.00	195.00
Creamer	80.00	65.00	175.00	85.00
Cruet	200.00	195.00	575.00	195.00
Pitcher, water	325.00	200.00	500.00	215.00
Rose Bowl, ftd	150.00	—	—	—
Salt Shaker, single .	—	—	95.00	

	Blue Opal	Clear Opal	Custard	Green With Gold
Spooner	100.00	75.00	100.00	75.00
*Sugar, cov	145.00	95.00	125.00	100.00
*Tumbler	80.00	25.00	80.00	35.00

INVERTED FERN

Flint, c1860. Attributed to Boston and Sandwich Glass Co. Goblets reproduced in color.

	Clear		Clear
Butter, cov	95.00	Pitcher, water	200.00
Champagne	115.00	Salt, master, ftd.	35.00
Compote, open, hs, 8"	55.00	Sauce, flat	10.00
Creamer, applied handle . . .	125.00	Spooner	65.00
Egg Cup	30.00	Sugar, cov	75.00
Goblet, rayed base	40.00	Tumbler	95.00
Honey Dish	15.50	Wine	60.00
Plate, 6"	100.00		

INVERTED STRAWBERRY

Non-flint, made by Cambridge Glass Co., c1908. Ruby stained also found in souvenir types. No original toothpick made. Reproduced in carnival glass, amethyst, and green.

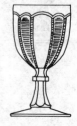

	Clear	Ruby Stained		Clear	Ruby Stained
Basket, applied handle	65.00	—	Nappy	15.00	—
Bowl, 9"	25.00	—	*Pitcher, water	45.00	—
Butter, cov	65.00	—	Plate, 10"	24.00	40.00
Celery Tray, handled	30.00	—	Punch Cup	12.00	—
			Relish, 7"	12.00	—
Compote, open, hs, 5"	38.00	—	Rose Bowl	30.00	—
			Salt, individual	20.00	—
Cremaer	25.00	—	Sauce, flat, 4"	18.00	—
Cruet	45.00	—	Spooner	25.00	—
Goblet	25.00	—	Sugar, cov	45.00	—
Mug	20.00	30.00	*Toothpick	25.00	—
			Tumbler	—	45.00

IOWA (Paneled Zipper)

Non-flint made by U. S. Glass Co. c1902. Part of the States pattern series. Available in clear glass with gold trim (add 20%) and pink or cranberry stained. Also found in amber (goblet $65.00), green, canary, and blue. Add 50% to 100% for color and amber stained.

	Clear		Clear
Bowl, berry	12.00	Compote, cov, 8"	40.00
Bread Plate, motto	80.00	Creamer	30.00
Butter, cov	40.00	Cruet, os	30.00
Cake Stand	35.00	Cup	18.00
Carafe	35.00	Goblet	28.00

	Clear		Clear
Lamp	125.00	Spooner	30.00
Olive	18.00	Sugar, cov	35.00
Pitcher, water	50.00	Table Set, 4 pc	125.00
Punch Cup	18.00	Toothpick	22.00
Salt Shaker, single	24.00	Tumbler	25.00
Sauce, 4½"	6.50	Wine	36.00

IRIS WITH MEANDER (Iris)

Made by Jefferson Glass Co., Steuberville, Ohio, c1903. Available in gold trim in clear, apple green, amethyst (toothpick $50.00; water pitcher $115.00), and blue. Also found in amber, opalescent (rare) and green opalescent (usually found in berry sets and toothpicks).

	Blue Opal	Canary Opal	White Opal
Bowl, berry	95.00	80.00	50.00
Butter, cov	310.00	195.00	125.00
Compote, jelly, 5"	85.00	75.00	50.00
Creamer	145.00	100.00	60.00
Cruet, os	200.00	150.00	100.00
Pickle	30.00	30.00	20.00
Pitcher, water	225.00	200.00	125.00
Plate, 7"	50.00	60.00	35.00
Salt & Pepper	100.00	100.00	85.00
Sauce	30.00	30.00	30.00
Spooner	75.00	65.00	50.00
Sugar, cov	150.00	100.00	80.00
*Toothpick	85.00	60.00	50.00
Tumbler	60.00	45.00	30.00
Vase, 11"	60.00	35.00	25.00

IVY IN SNOW (Ivy in Snow-Red Leaves, Forrest Ware)

Non-flint pattern made by Co-operative Flint Glass Co., Beaver Falls, Pennsylvania, in the 1880s. Phoenix Glass of Monaco, Pennsylvainia, also produced this pattern from 1937 to 1942 and was called Forrest Ware. Ivy In Snow-Red Leaves is the name used for pieces where the leaves are ruby stained. Some pieces have a ruby stained band. Also known in amber stained. Widely reproduced pattern.

	Clear	Ruby Stained		Clear	Ruby Stained
Bowl, 8 x 5½"	30.00	—	Goblet	32.00	65.00
Butter, cov	55.00	—	Marmalade Jar	35.00	—
Cake Stand, 8"	45.00	—	Mug	25.00	40.00
Celery Vase	25.00	75.00	Pitcher		
Compote			Milk	—	195.00
Cov, hs, 8"	75.00	—	Water	55.00	—
Open, jelly	30.00	—	Plate		
Creamer			6"	20.00	—
Regular	28.00	75.00	7"	25.00	—
Tankard	35.00	135.00	10"	30.00	—
Finger Bowl	25.00	—	Relish	18.00	—

	Clear	Ruby Stained		Clear	Ruby Stained
Spooner	35.00	60.00	Syrup	70.00	275.00
Sugar			Tumbler	25.00	45.00
Covered	50.00	75.00	Wine	32.00	55.00
Open	35.00	50.00			

JACOB'S COAT

Non-flint, c1880. Colors are rare, add 50%.

	Clear		Clear
Bowl, 8"	20.00	Pitcher	
Butter, cov	48.00	Milk	45.00
Celery	25.00	Water	45.00
Creamer	24.00	Spooner	30.00
Goblet	30.00	Sugar, cov	48.00

JACOB'S LADDER (Maltese)

Non-flint made by Portland Glass Co, Portland, ME, and Bryce Bros, Pittsburgh, PA, in 1876, and U. S. Glass Co in 1891. A few pieces found in amber, yellow, and blue. A salt dip is known in pale green.

	Clear		Clear
Bowl		Creamer	40.00
6" x 8¾"	20.00	Cruet, os, ftd	85.00
6¾" x 9¾"	25.00	Goblet	55.00
7½" x 10¾"	25.00	Honey, 3½"	12.00
9", berry, ornate SP holder, ftd	125.00	Marmalade Jar	75.00
		Mug	50.00
Butter, cov	75.00	Pitcher, water	150.00
Cake Stand		Plate, 6¼"	20.00
8" or 9"	50.00	Relish	
11" or 12"	75.00	7¾ x 5½"	15.00
Castor Bottle	18.00	9½ x 5½"	15.00
Castor Set, 4 bottles	100.00	Salt, master, ftd	30.00
Celery Vase	40.00	Sauce	
Cologne Bottle, Maltese cross stopper, ftd	85.00	Flat, 4", and 5"	8.00
		Footed, 4"	12.00
Compote		Spooner	35.00
Cov, hs, 6"	60.00	Sugar	
Cov, hs 7½"	60.00	Cov	55.00
Cov, hs 9½"	125.00	Open	30.00
Cov, hs, 13½ x 9"	75.00	Syrup	
Open, hs, 7½"	35.00	Knight's Head finial	125.00
Open, hs, 8½", scalloped	30.00	Plain top	70.00
Open, hs, 9½", scalloped	38.00	Tumbler, bar	75.00
Open, hs, 10"	65.00	Wine	35.00

JERSEY SWIRL (Swirl)

Non-flint pattern made by Windsor Glass Co., Pittsburgh, Pennsylvania, c1887. Heavily reproduced in color. The clear goblet also reproduced.

	Amber	Blue	Canary	Clear
Bowl, 9¼"	55.00	55.00	45.00	35.00
Butter, cov	55.00	55.00	50.00	40.00
Cake Stand, 9"	75.00	70.00	45.00	30.00
* Celery Vase	42.00	42.00	35.00	30.00
* Compote, hs, 8" . . .	50.00	50.00	45.00	35.00
Creamer	45.00	45.00	40.00	30.00
Cruet, os	—	—	—	25.00
* Goblet				
Buttermilk	40.00	40.00	35.00	30.00
Water	40.00	40.00	35.00	30.00
Marmalade Jar	—	—	—	50.00
Pickle Castor, SP frame and lid	—	—	—	125.00
Pitcher, water	50.00	50.00	45.00	35.00
Plate, round				
6"	25.00	25.00	20.00	18.00
8"	30.00	30.00	25.00	20.00
10"	38.00	38.00	35.00	30.00
Salt, Ind	20.00	20.00	18.00	15.00
Sauce, 4½", flat . . .	20.00	20.00	15.00	10.00
Spooner	30.00	30.00	25.00	20.00
Sugar, cov	40.00	40.00	35.00	30.00
Tumbler	30.00	30.00	25.00	20.00
Wine	50.00	50.00	40.00	18.00

JEWELED HEART

Made by Northwood Glass Co., Indiana, Pennsylvania, and others, 1898–1910. Also made in clear, blue, and apple green. A clear creamer is valued at $25.00, 6" plate $18.00, and a clear with gold water pitcher is $75.00. A clear green toothpick is $45.00. No goblet or wine were originally made. Heavily reproduced.

	Green Opal	Sapphire Blue Opal	White Opal
Bowl, berry, ruffled edge	100.00	115.00	50.00
Butter, cov	130.00	135.00	100.00
* Creamer	90.00	100.00	50.00
Cruet	200.00	175.00	85.00
Pitcher, water	135.00	150.00	100.00
Salt Shaker	40.00	50.00	35.00
Sauce	25.00	30.00	20.00
Spooner	75.00	80.00	45.00
* Sugar, cov	100.00	85.00	55.00
Sugar Shaker	100.00	110.00	75.00
Syrup	125.00	140.00	125.00
* Toothpick	35.00	35.00	30.00
Tumbler	25.00	35.00	25.00

JUMBO

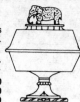

A non-flint novelty pattern made by Canton Glass Co., Canton, Ohio in the 1870s and by Aetna Glass in 1883. The unique motif was used to commemorate P. T. Barnum's famous elephant, "Jumbo."

	Clear		Clear
Butter, cov		Creamer, plain Jumbo	225.00
Oblong, plain Jumbo	250.00	Goblet	350.00
Round, Barnum's head	325.00	Spoon Rack	350.00
Castor Set, elephant's head		Spooner, Barnum's head	100.00
holder with bottles	550.00	Sugar	
Compote		Covered, Barnum's head	400.00
Cov, 7"	400.00	Open, plain Jumbo	100.00
Cov, 8"	500.00	Toothpick, box on back	100.00
Cov, 10"	750.00		
Cov, 12"	800.00		

KANSAS (Jewel With Dewdrop)

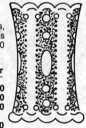

Non-flint originally produced by Co-Operative Flint Glass Co., Beaver Falls, Pennsylvania. Later produced as part of the States pattern series by U. S. Glass Co. in 1901. Also known with jewels stained in pink or gold. Mugs, valued at $50 are known in vaseline and blue.

	Clear		Clear
Banana Stand	50.00	Creamer	40.00
Bowl		Goblet	45.00
7", oval	25.00	Mug, regular	45.00
8½"	42.00	Pitcher	
Bread Plate, ODB	60.00	Milk	50.00
Butter, cov	55.00	Water	60.00
Cake Plate	45.00	Relish, 8½", oval	20.00
Cake Stand		Salt Shaker	50.00
7⅝"	45.00	Sauce, flat, 4"	15.00
9"	50.00	Sugar, cov	50.00
10"	85.00	Syrup	125.00
Celery Vase	35.00	Toothpick	55.00
Compote		Tumbler	40.00
Open, hs, 6½", jelly	50.00	Whiskey	15.00
Open, hs, 9½"	60.00	Wine	50.00
Open, ls, 6½"	45.00		

KENTUCKY

Non-flint made by U. S. Glass Co., c1897, as part of the States pattern series. The goblet is found in ruby stained ($50.00). A footed, square sauce ($30.00) is known in cobalt blue with gold. A toothpick holder is also known in ruby stained, $150.00.

	Clear	Emerald Green		Clear	Emerald Green
Butter, cov	50.00	—	Punch Cup	10.00	30.00
Cake Stand, 9½"	40.00	—	Salt & Pepper	25.00	—
Creamer	25.00	—	Sauce, ftd, sq	8.00	16.00
Cruet, os	45.00	—	Sugar, cov	30.00	—
Cup	10.00	30.00	Toothpick, sq	35.00	60.00
Goblet	20.00	50.00	Tumbler	20.00	30.00
Nappy	8.50	18.50	Wine	25.00	35.00
Pitcher, water	55.00	—			

KING'S CROWN (Ruby Thumbprint; X.L.C.R.)

Known as Ruby Thumbprint when pieces are ruby stained. A non-flint pattern made by Adams and Co., Pittsburgh, Pennsylvania, in the 1890s and later. Made in clear and with the thumbprints stained amethyst, gold, green, and yellow, and in clear with etching and trimmed in gold. It became very popular after 1891 as ruby stained souvenir ware. Cobalt blue pieces reported as very rare. Approximately 87 pieces documented. NOTE: Pattern has been copiously reproduced for the gift-trade market. New pieces are easily distinguished: in the case of Ruby Thumbprint, the color is a very pale pinkish red; green and blue pieces have an off-color. Reproduced in milk glass. Available in amethyst stained in goblet ($30.00) and wine ($10.00) and in green stained in goblet ($25.00) and wine ($15.00). Add 30% for engraved pieces.

	Clear	Ruby Stained		Clear	Ruby Stained
Banana Stand, ftd . .	85.00	135.00	Creamer		
Bowl			Ind	25.00	35.00
9¼", pointed	35.00	90.00	Regular	50.00	65.00
10", scalloped . . .	45.00	95.00	Cup & Saucer	50.00	70.00
Butter, cov	50.00	90.00	Goblet	30.00	45.00
Cake Stand			Mustard, cov	40.00	75.00
9"	65.00	125.00	Pickle, lobed	18.00	40.00
10"	75.00	125.00	Pitcher		
Castor Bottle	45.00	70.00	Milk, tankard	75.00	100.00
Castor Set, glass			Water, bulbous . . .	95.00	225.00
stand, 4 bottles . .	175.00	325.00	Water, tankard . . .	110.00	200.00
Celery Vase	40.00	60.00	Punch Cup	25.00	—
Claret	35.00	50.00	Salt, master, sq	25.00	60.00
Compote			Salt, ind, oblong . . .	16.00	30.00
Cov, hs, 6"	85.00	—	Salt & Pepper	40.00	70.00
Cov, hs, 7"	45.00	195.00	Sauce, 4"	15.00	20.00
Cov, hs, 8"	55.00	245.00	Spooner	40.00	50.00
Cov, ls, 12"	90.00	225.00	Sugar, cov	50.00	85.00
Open, hs, 5½"	55.00	65.00	Toothpick	30.00	40.00
Open, hs, 8¼" . . .	75.00	95.00	Tumbler	18.00	38.00
Open, ls, 5¼" . . .	30.00	45.00	Wine	25.00	40.00

KING'S #500

Made by King Glass Co. of Pittsburgh, Pennsylvania in 1899. It was made in clear, frosted, and a rich, deep blue, known as Dewey Blue, both trimmed in gold. Continued by U. S. Glass Co. in 1891 and made in a great number of pieces. A clear goblet with frosted stem ($50.00) is known. Also known in dark green and a ruby stained sugar is reported ($95.00).

	Clear w/Gold	Dewey Blue w/Gold		Clear w/Gold	Dewey Blue w/Gold
Bowl			Celery Vase	20.00	—
7"	10.00	30.00	Compote		
8"	12.00	35.00	Covered	45.00	—
9"	14.00	95.00	Open	30.00	—
Butter, cov	50.00	125.00	Creamer	30.00	50.00
Cake Stand	40.00	60.00	Cruet	45.00	135.00

	Clear w/Gold	Dewey Blue w/Gold		Clear w/Gold	Dewey Blue w/Gold
Cup	15.00	35.00	Rose Bowl	20.00	45.00
Decanter, locking top	100.00	—	Salt Shaker, single	15.00	40.00
			Sauce	15.00	35.00
Lamp			Spooner	30.00	70.00
Hand	45.00	—	Sugar, cov	45.00	75.00
Stand	65.00	—	Syrup	55.00	175.00
Pitcher, water	55.00	200.00	Tumbler	20.00	45.00
Relish	20.00	30.00			

KLONDIKE (Amberette, English Hobnail Cross)

This pattern reported to have been made originally by A. J. Beatty And Co., c1885. It was also made by Hobbs, Brockunier Co., and Dalzell, Gilmore and Leighton Co. Made in colors other than clear and amber stained, which are the original colors. Made to commemmorate the Alaskan Gold Rush. The frosted panels depict snow; the amber bands, gold. Found clear and frosted, with or without scrolls, depending on the maker. Prices are listed for frosted; clear panels, approximately 30% less.

	Frosted Amber Stain		Frosted Amber Stain
Bowl, berry, 8"	175.00	Sauce, flat	75.00
Butter, cov	365.00	Spooner	175.00
Cake Stand, 8", sq	500.00	Sugar	
Celery Vase	225.00	Cov	250.00
Condiment Set, cruet and		Open	200.00
shaker on tray	1,000.00	Syrup, pewter lid	650.00
Creamer	250.00	Toothpick	375.00
Cruet, os	550.00	Tray, 5½", sq	200.00
Goblet	350.00	Tumbler	130.00
Pitcher, water	525.00	Vase, trumpet shape	
Punch Cup	125.00	8"	275.00
Salt Shaker, single	100.00	10"	265.00

KOKOMO (Bar and Diamond, R and H Swirl Band)

Made in clear glass by Richards & Hartley, Tarentum, Pennsylvania in the late 1880s to 1891. Found in ruby stained and etched. About 54 pieces manufactured.

	Clear	Ruby Stained		Clear	Ruby Stained
Bowl, 8½", ftd	20.00	—	Open, hs, 8"	35.00	—
Bread Tray	30.00	45.00	Open, ls, 7½"	20.00	—
Butter, cov	35.00	—	Condiment Set, ob-		
Cake stand	45.00	165.00	long tray, shakers,		
Celery Vase	15.00	45.00	cruet	80.00	195.00
Compote			Creamer	30.00	50.00
Cov, hs, 7½"	35.00	165.00	Cruet	65.00	—
Open, hs, 5"	20.00	—	Decanter, 9¾", wine	55.00	95.00
Open, hs, 6"	25.00	—	Finger Bowl	25.00	35.00
Open, hs, 7"	30.00	—	Goblet	30.00	45.00

	Clear	Ruby Stained		Clear	Ruby Stained
Lamp, hand, atypical—has no diamonds	50.00	100.00	Spooner	25.00	45.00
			Sugar, cov	45.00	65.00
			Sugar Shaker	35.00	75.00
Pitcher, water, tankard	55.00	85.00	Syrup	45.00	130.00
Salt & Pepper in holder	45.00	—	Tray, water	35.00	90.00
			Tumbler	20.00	35.00
Sauce, ftd, 5"	8.00	10.00	Wine	20.00	35.00

LEAF AND DART (Pride)

Made by Boston and Sandwich Glass Co., Sandwich, Massachusetts, and Richards and Hartley Flint Glass, Pittsburgh, Pennsylvania, c1860. Shards have been found at Burlington Glass Works, Hamilton, Ontario.

	Clear		Clear
Bowl, 8¼", ftd	25.00	Relish	15.00
Butter, cov	85.00	Salt, master, ftd	
Celery Vase	42.00	Cov	65.00
Creamer, applied handle	40.00	Open	30.00
Cruet, pedestal, applied handle	100.00	Sauce, 4", flat	8.50
Egg Cup	22.00	Spooner	35.00
Goblet	35.00	Sugar, cov	45.50
Honey Dish	5.00	Tumbler, ftd	25.00
Pitcher, water, applied handle	80.00	Wine	40.00

LIBERTY BELL (Centennial)

Made by Gillinder and Co., Philadelphia, Pennsylvania for the Centennial Exposition, 1876. Some items also made in milk glass. Reproduced.

	Clear		Clear
Bowl, 8", ftd	100.00	Plate	
Bread Plate, 13⅜ x 9½"		6", dated	75.00
Clear, no signatures	85.00	8"	55.00
Milk glass, sgd John Hancock	200.00	10"	80.00
		Platter, 13 x 8", twig handles, 13 states	75.00
Butter, cov	100.00	Relish, oval	45.00
Creamer		Salt Dip, ind, oval	35.00
Applied handle	75.00	Salt Shaker	95.00
Reed handle	85.00	Sauce, ftd	25.00
Goblet	35.00	Spooner	45.00
Mug, snake handle	335.00	Sugar, cov	90.00
Pickle	45.00		
Pitcher, water, applied reeded handle	400.00		

LILY OF THE VALLEY

Non-flint pattern made by Boston & Sandwich, Sandwich, Massachusetts, in the 1870s. Shards have also been found at Burlington Glass Works, Hamilton, Ontario. Lily of the Valley on Legs is a name frequently given to those pieces having three tall legs. Legged pieces include a covered butter, covered sugar, creamer and spooner. Add 25% for this type.

	Clear		Clear
Butter, cov	65.00	Relish	22.50
Cake Stand	65.00	Salt, master	
Celery Tray	40.00	Cov	125.00
Celery Vase	45.00	Open	50.00
Compote		Sauce, flat	12.00
Cov, hs, 8½"	85.00	Spooner	35.00
Open, hs	50.00	Sugar	
Creamer, applied handle	65.00	Covered	65.00
Cruet,os	95.00	Open, buttermilk type	50.00
Egg Cup	25.00	Tumbler	
Goblet	35.00	Flat	20.00
Nappy, 4"	20.00	Footed	30.00
Pickle, scoop shape	20.00	Vegetable Dish, oval	30.00
Pitcher		Wine	100.00
Milk	75.00		
Water	135.00		

LINCOLN DRAPE WITH TASSEL

Flint pattern made originally by Boston & Sandwich Glass Co., probably continued by other companies, c1865. Commemorative of Lincoln's death. Items without tassels are valued at 20% less. Some very rare pieces in cobalt blue are 200% more.

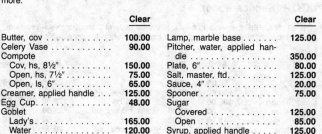

	Clear		Clear
Butter, cov	100.00	Lamp, marble base	125.00
Celery Vase	90.00	Pitcher, water, applied han-	
Compote		dle	350.00
Cov, hs, 8½"	150.00	Plate, 6"	80.00
Open, hs, 7½"	75.00	Salt, master, ftd	125.00
Open, ls, 6"	65.00	Sauce, 4"	20.00
Creamer, applied handle	125.00	Spooner	75.00
Egg Cup	48.00	Sugar	
Goblet		Covered	125.00
Lady's	165.00	Open	85.00
Water	120.00	Syrup, applied handle	125.00
Honey	20.00	Wine	135.00

LION

Made by Gillinder and Sons, Philadelphia, Pennsylvania, in 1876. Available in clear (20% less). Many reproductions.

	Frosted		Frosted
Bread Plate, 12" including lion handles, GUTDODB	125.00	Cake Stand	85.00
Butter, cov		Celery Vase	85.00
Lion's head finial	90.00	Champagne	175.00
Rampant finial	125.00	Cheese, cov, rampant lion finial	400.00

	Frosted		Frosted
Compote		Paperweight, lion head	125.00
Cov, hs, 7″, rampant finial .	150.00	Pitcher	
* Cov, hs, 9″, rampant finial,		Milk	375.00
oval, collared base	150.00	Water	250.00
Cov, 9″, hs	185.00	Relish, lion handles	40.00
Open, ls, 8″	75.00	Salt, master, rect lid	250.00
Cordial	175.00	* Sauce, 4″, ftd	25.00
* Creamer	70.00	* Spooner	70.00
Egg Cup, 3½″ h	65.00	Sugar, cov	
* Goblet	75.00	Lion head finial	85.00
Lamp	350.00	Rampant finial	95.00
Marmalade Jar, rampant		Syrup, orig top	350.00
finial	85.00	Wine	165.00

LOG CABIN

Non-flint made by Central Glass Co. Wheeling, West Virginia, c1875. Also available in color, but rare. Creamer, spooner, and covered sugar reproduced in clear and cobalt blue.

	Clear		Clear
Bowl, cov, 8 x 5¼ x 3⅝″ . . .	225.00	Pitcher, water	300.00
Butter, cov	250.00	Sauce, flat	75.00
Compote, hs, 10½″	275.00	* Spooner	120.00
* Creamer	115.00	* Sugar, cov	275.00
Marmalade Jar	275.00		

LOOP (Seneca Loop)

Flint, c1850s–1860s; later in non-flint. Made by several firms. Sandwich produced fiery opalescent pieces. Yuma Loop is a contemporary with comparable values.

	Flint	Non-Flint		Flint	Non-Flint
Bowl, 9″	50.00	25.00	Goblet	20.00	18.00
Butter, cov	60.00	40.00	Pitcher, water, applied handle	170.00	60.00
Cake Stand	100.00	—	Salt, master, ftd	25.00	18.00
Celery Vase	75.00	20.00	Spooner	30.00	24.00
Champagne	45.00	24.00	Sugar, cov	70.00	30.00
Compote			Syrup	95.00	—
Cov, hs, 9½″	135.00	—	Tumbler		
Open, hs, 9″	115.00	40.00	Footed	25.00	15.00
Cordial, 2¾″ h	40.00	20.00	Water	40.00	20.00
Creamer, applied handle	70.00	35.00	Wine	30.00	12.00
Egg Cup	30.00	20.00			

LOOP AND DART

Clear and stippled non-flint pattern of the late 1860s and early 1870s. Made by Boston & Sandwich, Sandwich, Massachusetts, and Richards & Hartley, Tarentum, Pennsylvania. Pattern related to Loop and Dart with Diamond Ornament and Loop and Dart with Round Ornament. Flint add 25%.

	Clear		Clear
Bowl, 9", oval	25.00	Pitcher, water	75.00
Butter, cov	45.00	Plate, 6"	35.00
Cake Stand, 10"	40.00	Relish	18.00
Celery Vase	35.00	Salt, master	50.00
Compote		Spooner	30.00
Cov, hs, 8"	85.00	Sugar, cov	50.00
Cov, ls, 8"	65.00	Tumbler	
Creamer	38.00	Footed	30.00
Cruet, os	75.00	Water	25.00
Egg Cup	25.00	Wine	40.00
Goblet	30.00		

LOOP AND DART WITH DIAMOND ORNAMENT

Clear and stippled non-flint pattern of the late 1860s and early 1870s. Made by Boston & Sandwich, and Richards & Hartley. Pattern related to Loop and Dart and Loop and Dart with Round Ornament. Flint add 25%.

	Clear		Clear
Bowl, 9", oval	20.00	Spooner	25.00
Butter, cov	45.00	Sugar	
Celery Vase	30.00	Covered	40.00
Creamer	35.00	Open	20.00
Egg Cup	24.00	Tumbler	
Goblet	28.00	Footed	35.00
Relish	15.00	Water	40.00
Salt, master	18.00	Wine	35.00
Sauce, flat	4.50		

LOOP AND DART WITH ROUND ORNAMENT

Clear and stippled non-flint pattern of the late 1860s and early 1870s. Made by Boston & Sandwich, and Richards & Hartley, also attributed to Portland Glass Co, Portland, ME. Pattern related to Loop and Dart and Loop and Dart with Diamond Ornaments. Flint add 25%.

	Clear		Clear
Bowl, 9", oval	28.00	Pitcher, water	90.00
Butter, cov	80.00	Plate, 6"	35.00
Butter Pat	15.00	Relish	25.00
Celery Vase	35.00	Salt, master	28.00
Champagne	80.00	Sauce, flat	8.00
Compote		Spooner	26.00
Cov, hs, 8"	85.00	Sugar, cov	60.00
Cov, ls, 8"	65.00	Tumbler	
Open, hs, 8"	45.00	Footed	30.00
Creamer	45.00	Water	35.00
Egg Cup	30.00	Wine	35.00
Goblet			
Buttermilk	35.00		
Water	32.00		

LOOP AND JEWEL (Jewel and Festoon; Venus)

Non-flint made by Beatty Glass and National Glass Co. then continued by Indiana Glass Co. Made until 1915. About 40 pieces known. A few rare pieces available in milk white.

	Clear		Clear
Bowl, 8"	15.00	Relish, 8"	22.00
Butter, cov	55.00	Salt & Pepper	32.00
Compote, 6½"	20.00	Sauce, flat, 4"	5.00
Creamer	25.00	Sherbet	45.00
Dish, 5" sq	15.00	Spooner	25.00
Goblet	18.00	Sugar, cov	40.00
Pickle, 8", rect.	18.00	Syrup	55.00
Pitcher, water	45.00	Vase, 8¾"	40.00
Plate, sq.	15.00	Wine	30.00

LOUISIANA (Sharp Oval and Diamond, Granby)

Made by Bryce Bros., Pittsburgh, Pennsylvania in 1870s, continued later (about 1892) by U. S. Glass Co. as one of the States patterns. Also available with gold and also comes frosted.

	Clear		Clear
Bowl, 9", berry	20.00	Mug, handled, gold top	25.00
Butter, cov	70.00	Nappy, 4", cov.	30.00
Cake Stand	45.00	Pitcher, water	65.00
Celery Vase	30.00	Relish	15.00
Compote		Spooner	25.00
Cov, hs, 8"	50.00	Sugar, cov	45.00
Open, hs, 5", jelly	40.00	Tumbler	22.00
Creamer	32.50	Wine	35.00
Goblet	30.00		
Matchholder, attached			
saucer	30.00		

MAGNET AND GRAPE (Magnet and Grape with Stippled Leaf)

Flint first made by Boston and Sandwich Glass Co., c1860. Later non-flint versions have grape leaf in either clear or stippled. Reproduced by Metropolitan Museum, New York with frosted leaf.

	Flint Frosted Leaf	Non-Flint Stippled or Clear Leaf		Flint Frosted Leaf	Non-Flint Stippled or Clear Leaf
Bowl, cov, 8"	—	75.00	Celery Vase	175.00	25.00
Butter, cov	185.00	40.00	Champagne	125.00	35.00

	Flint Frosted Leaf Leaf	Non-Flint Stippled or Clear Leaf		Flint Frosted Leaf	Non-Flint Stippled or Clear Leaf
Compote, open, hs, 7½″	110.00	65.00	Water, applied handle	350.00	75.00
* Creamer	175.00	40.00	Relish, oval	35.00	15.00
Decanter, os			Salt, ftd	60.00	25.00
Pint	150.00	75.00	Sauce, 4″	24.00	8.00
Quart	200.00	85.00	Spooner	95.00	30.00
Egg Cup	100.00	25.00	* Sugar, cov	150.00	80.00
* Goblet			Syrup	125.00	55.00
American Shield	300.00	—	* Tumbler, water	110.00	30.00
Low Stem	75.00	—	Whiskey	140.00	25.00
Regular stem	70.00	30.00	* Wine	85.00	40.00
Pitcher					
Milk, applied handle	—	75.00			

MAINE (Paneled Stippled Flower)

Non-flint made by U. S. Glass Co., Pittsburgh, Pennsylvania c1890. Researchers dispute if goblet was made originally. Sometimes found with enamel trim.

	Clear	Emerald Green		Clear	Emerald Green
Bowl, 8″	30.00	40.00	Pitcher		
Bread, oval, 10 x 7¾″	30.00	—	Milk	—	85.00
Butter, cov	48.00	—	Water	50.00	125.00
Cake Stand	40.00	60.00	Relish	15.00	—
Compote,			Salt Shaker, single	30.00	—
Cov, jelly	—	65.00	Sauce	15.00	—
Open, hs, 7″	20.00	30.00	Sugar, cov	45.00	75.00
Open, ls, 9″	30.00	35.00	Syrup	60.00	225.00
Creamer	30.00	—	Tumbler	20.00	45.00
Mug	35.00		Wine	40.00	62.50

MANHATTAN

Non-flint with gold, made by U. S. Glass Co., c1902. A depression glass pattern also has the "Manhattan" name. A table sized creamer and covered sugar are known in true ruby stained, and a goblet in known in old marigold carnival glass. Heavily reproduced.

	Clear	Rose Stained		Clear	Rose Stained
Basket,	80.00	—	Carafe, water	40.00	—
Biscuit Jar, cov	60.00	85.00	Celery Vase	25.00	—
Bowl			Cheese, cov, 8⅜″ d.	—	115.00
6″	18.00	—	Compote, cov, hs, 9½″	45.00	—
8¼″, scalloped	20.00	—	Creamer		
10″	22.00	—	Individual	25.00	—
12½″	25.00	—	Regular	30.00	60.00
Butter, cov	55.00	—			
Cake Stand, 10″	40.00	50.00			

	Clear	Rose Stained		Clear	Rose Stained
Cruet			Salt Shaker, single .	20.00	35.00
Large	65.00	115.00	Sauce	14.00	20.00
Small	50.00	—	Spooner	20.00	—
Goblet	25.00		Straw Holder, cov . .	65.00	—
Ice Bucket	—	65.00	Sugar		
Olive, Gainsborough	30.00	—	Individual, open . .	12.00	—
Pitcher, water, tank-			Regular, cov	40.00	65.00
ard, ½ gal	60.00	—	Syrup	48.00	125.00
Plate			Toothpick	30.00	—
6″	6.50	30.00	Tumblers		
8″	15.00	—	Ice Tea	30.00	—
10¾″.	20.00	—	Water	20.00	—
Punch Bowl	125.00	—	Vase, 6″	18.00	—
Punch Cup	10.00	—	Water Bottle	40.00	—
Relish, 6″	12.00	—	Wine	20.00	—

MARDI GRAS (Duncan and Miller #42, Paneled English Hobnail with Prisms)

Made by Duncan and Miller Glass Co., c1898. Available in gold trim and ruby stained.

	Clear	Ruby Stained		Clear	Ruby Stained
Bowl, 8″, berry	18.00	—	Punch Cup	10.00	—
Butter, cov	65.00	145.00	Relish.	12.50	—
Cake Stand, 10″ . . .	65.00		Sherry, flared or		
Celery Tray, curled			straight	20.00	—
edges.	25.00	—	Spooner	25.00	—
Champagne, saucer	32.00	—	Sugar, cov	35.00	65.00
Claret.	35.00	—	Syrup, metal lid. . . .	65.00	—
Compote Cov, hs .	55.00	—	Toothpick	45.00	80.00
Open, jelly, 4½″ . .	30.00	55.00	Tumbler		
Cordial	35.00	—	Bar	25.00	—
Creamer Ind, oval .	20.00	—	Champagne.	20.00	—
Regular.	35.00	60.00	Water	30.00	40.00
Finger Bowl	20.00	—	Vase, trumpet shape,		
Goblet	37.50	—	3 sizes	20.00	—
Lamp Shade.	35.00	—	Wine	30.00	—
Pitcher Milk	50.00	—			
Water	100.00	200.00			

MARYLAND (Inverted Loop and Fan; Loop and Diamond)

Made originally by Bryce Brothers, Pittsburgh, Pennsylvania. Continued by U. S. Glass Co. as one of their States patterns.

	Clear w/gold	Ruby Stained		Clear w/gold	Ruby Stained
Banana Dish.	30.00	—	Celery Vase	25.00	—
Bowl, berry	15.00	—	Compote		
Bread Plate	25.00	—	Cov, hs	65.00	85.00
Butter, cov	65.00	—	Open, hs, 7½″ . . .	40.00	—
Cake Stand, 8″	40.00	—	Open, jelly	25.00	—
Celery Tray.	20.00	—	Creamer.	30.00	55.00

	Clear w/gold	Ruby Stained		Clear w/gold	Ruby Stained
Goblet	30.00	48.00	Salt Shaker, single	30.00	—
Olive, handled	12.00	—	Sauce, flat	14.00	25.00
Pitcher			Spooner	30.00	—
Milk	40.00	—	Sugar, cov	45.00	60.00
Water	50.00	85.00	Toothpick	45.00	65.00
Plate, 7″, round	25.00	—	Tumbler	25.00	50.00
Relish, oval	18.00	—	Wine	40.00	60.00

MASCOTTE (Minor Block)

Non-flint made by Ripley and Co., Pittsburgh, Pennsylvania, in the 1870s. Reissued by U. S. Glass Co. in 1898. The butter dish shown on Plate 77 of Ruth Webb Lee's *Victorian Glass* is said to go with this pattern. It has a horseshoe finial and was named for the famous "Maude S," "Queen of the Turf" trotting horse during the 1880s. Apothecary jar and pyramid jars made by Tiffin Glass Co.

	Clear	Etched		Clear	Etched
Bowl			Open, hs, 9″	—	35.00
Cov, 5″	—	35.00	Open, ls, 8″	30.00	45.00
Cov, 6″	—	35.00	Creamer	40.00	45.00
Cov, 7″	—	45.00	Goblet	40.00	45.00
Cov, 8″	—	50.00	Pitcher, water	55.00	65.00
Cov, 9″	—	55.00	Plate, turned in		
Open 9″	35.00	40.00	sides	38.00	—
Butter Pat	8.00	12.00	Pyramid Jar, 7″ d,		
Butter, cov			one fits into other		
"Maude S"	100.00	—	and forms tall jar-		
Regular	50.00	65.00	type container with		
Cake Basket, handle	80.00	65.00	lid, three sizes		
Celery Vase	35.00	40.00	with flat sepa-		
Cheese, cov	70.00	80.00	rators	40.00	—
Compote			Salt Dip	25.00	—
Cov, hs, 5″	—	40.00	Salt Shaker, single	15.00	25.00
Cov, hs, 6″	—	45.00	Sauce		
Cov, hs, 7″	—	55.00	Flat	8.00	15.00
Cov, hs, 8″	75.00	85.00	Footed	12.00	16.00
Cov, hs, 9″	—	90.00	Spooner	30.00	35.00
Open, hs, 5″	—	25.00	Sugar, cov	45.00	48.00
Open, hs, 6″	—	25.00	Tray, water	40.00	55.00
Open, hs, 7″	—	30.00	Tumbler	20.00	30.00
Open, hs, 8″	—	35.00	Wine	25.00	30.00

MASONIC (Inverted Prism)

Non-flint made by McKee Glass Co., Jeannette, Pennsylvania, c1894-1920. Rare pieces are found in emerald green (add 50%) and in ruby stained (100%)

	Clear		Clear
Bowl, sq or round		6″ (round only)	20.00
4″	20.00	7″	25.00
4½″	20.00	8″	30.00
5″	20.00	9″, salad, silver frame	45.00

	Clear		Clear
Butter, cov		Nappy, heart shape	30.00
Flat.	45.00	Pitcher, water, tankard	60.00
Footed	60.00	Relish, serpentine shape . . .	15.00
Cake Stand		Salt Dip	
9"	36.00	Round.	15.00
10"	40.00	Square	15.00
Celery	20.00	Salt Shaker	
Compote		Round.	15.00
Cov, 8"	45.00	Square	25.00
Open, 8½"	35.00	Sardine Box, rect, flat	25.00
Creamer.	25.00	Spooner.	25.00
Cruet	35.00	Syrup Jug.	75.00
Custard Cup	15.00	Sugar, cov	40.00
Goblet	25.00	Toothpick	30.00
Handle, salad fork	20.00	Tumbler	15.00
Honey Dish, cov, flat, sq . . .	40.00	Wine	28.00

MASSACHUSETTS (Geneva #2, M2-131)

Made in 1880s, maker unknown, and continued in 1898 by U. S. Glass Co. as one of the States series. The vase ($45.00) and wine ($45.00) are known in emerald green. Some pieces reported in cobalt blue and marigold carnival glass. Reproduced in clear and colors.

	Clear		Clear
Bar Bottle, metal shot glass		Olive	8.50
for cover	75.00	Pitcher, water	75.00
Bowl		Plate, 8"	32.00
6", sq	17.50	Punch Cup	15.00
9", sq	20.00	Relish, 8½"	25.00
Butter, cov	75.00	Rum Jug	90.00
Celery Tray.	28.00	Spooner.	22.00
Cologne Bottle, os.	37.50	Sugar, cov	40.00
Compote, open	35.00	Toothpick	40.00
Cordial	55.00	Tumbler	
Creamer.	28.00	Champagne or Juice	25.00
Cruet, os		Water	30.00
Regular.	40.00	Whiskey (shot).	15.00
2 oz	55.00	Vase, 7"	25.00
Goblet	45.00	Wine	40.00
Mug	24.00		

MELROSE

Non-flint pattern made by Greensburg Glass Co., Greensburg, Pennsylvania, in 1887 in clear, etched, and ruby stained. Add 20% for etching.

	Clear		Clear
Bowl, berry	25.00	Creamer.	25.00
Butter, cov	45.00	Goblet	20.00
Cake Plate	30.00	Pitcher, water	45.00
Cake Stand	32.00	Plate, 8"	10.00
Celery Vase	25.00	Salt, individual	6.00
Compote		Salt Shaker.	18.00
Cov, hs, 8"	90.00	Sauce, flat	8.00
Open, hs, 7"	25.00	Spooner.	30.00
Open, jelly.	18.00	Sugar, cov	35.00

	Clear			Clear
Tray, water 11½″	45.00	Waste Bowl		20.00
Tumbler	18.00	Wine		18.00

MICHIGAN (Loop & Pillar)

Non-flint made by U. S. Glass Co., c1893. One of the States pattern series. The 10¼″ bowl ($42.00) and punch cup ($12.00) are found with yellow or blue stain. Also found with painted carnations. Other colors include "Sunrise," gold, and ruby stained.

	Clear	Rose Stained		Clear	Rose Stained
Bowl			Olive, two handles . .	—	35.00
7½″	12.50	—	Pickle	12.00	—
9″	55.00	60.00	Pitcher		
10¼″	25.00	62.00	8″	50.00	—
Butter, cov	60.00	110.00	12″	70.00	150.00
Celery Vase	35.00	85.00	Salt Shaker, single, 3		
Compote			types	20.00	30.00
Jelly, 4½″	25.00	—	Sauce	14.00	20.00
Open, hs, 9¼″ . . .	65.00	—	Sherbet, cup,		
Creamer			handled	7.00	15.00
Ind, 602 tankard . .	20.00	65.00	Spooner	40.00	50.00
Regular	30.00	50.00	Sugar, cov	50.00	65.00
Cruet, os	60.00	100.00	Syrup	75.00	—
Crushed Fruit Bowl .	75.00	—	* Toothpick	45.00	100.00
Finger Bowl	15.00	—	Tumbler	30.00	40.00
Goblet	38.00	50.00	Vase, bud	35.00	35.00
Honey Dish	10.00	—	Wine	35.00	50.00
Lemonade Mug	—	33.00			
Nappy, Gainsborough handle	35.00	—			

MINERVA

Non-flint made in the United States and probably in Canada in the 1870s. There are two forms.

	Clear			Clear
Bowl			Creamer	40.00
Footed	40.00	Goblet	80.00
Rectangular			Marmalade Jar, cov	165.00
7″	25.00	Pickle	30.00
8 x 5″	30.00	Pitcher, water	165.00
9″	45.00	Plate		
Butter, cov	85.00	8″	55.00
Cake Stand			10″, handled	60.00
8″	95.00	Platter, oval, 13″	70.00
9 x 6½″	100.00	Sauce		
10½″	120.00	Flat	20.00
13″	145.00	Footed, 4″	25.00
Compote			Spooner	55.00
Cov, hs, 7″	90.00	Sugar		
Cov, ls, 8″	80.00	Cov	65.00
Open, hs, 10″	55.00	Open	35.00
Open, hs, octagonal ftd . .	95.00			

MINNESOTA

Non-flint made by U. S. Glass Co., late 1890s. One of the States patterns. A two-piece flower frog has been found in emerald green ($46.00).

	Clear	Ruby Stained		Clear	Ruby Stained
Basket	65.00	—	Mug	25.00	—
Biscuit Jar, cov	55.00	150.00	Olive	15.00	25.00
Bowl, 8½", flared. . .	30.00	—	Pitcher, water, tank-		
Butter, cov	55.00	—	ard	85.00	200.00
Carafe	35.00	—	Plate		
Celery Tray, 13" . . .	25.00	—	5", turned up		
Compote			edges	25.00	—
Open, hs, 10",			7⅜" d	15.00	—
flared.	60.00	—	Relish.	20.00	—
Open, ls, 9", sq . .	55.00	—	Sauce, boat shape .	15.00	35.00
Creamer			Spooner	25.00	—
Individual.	20.00	—	Sugar, cov	40.00	—
Regular.	30.00	—	Syrup	55.00	—
Cruet	35.00	—	Toothpick, 3 handles	35.00	—
Cup	18.00	—	Tumbler	18.00	—
Goblet	28.00	50.00	Wine	40.00	—
Hair Receiver	30.00	—			

MISSOURI (Palm and Scroll)

Non-flint made by U. S. Glass Co. c1899, one of the States pattern series. Also made in amethyst and canary.

	Clear	Emerald Green		Clear	Emerald Green
Bowl, berry, 8".	18.00	35.00	Pitcher		
Butter, cov	65.00	65.00	Milk.	40.00	85.00
Cake Stand, 9"	50.00	—	Water	75.00	85.00
Celery Vase	30.00	—	Salt Shaker, single .	25.00	40.00
Cordial	35.00	—	Sauce, flat, 4".	14.00	16.00
Creamer.	25.00	40.00	Spooner	25.00	48.00
Cruet	55.00	125.00	Sugar, cov	50.00	65.00
Dish, cov 6"	65.00	—	Syrup	65.00	—
Doughnut stand, 6".	40.00	—	Tumbler	—	38.00
Goblet	50.00	60.00	Wine	38.00	50.00
Mug	35.00	45.00			
Pickle Dish, rectan-					
gular	18.00	27.50			

MOON AND STAR (Palace)

Non-flint and frosted (add 30%). First made by Adams & Co., Pittsburgh, Pennsylvania, in 1874 and later by several manufacturers, including Pioneer Glass who probably decorated ruby stained examples. Six different compotes documented. Heavily reproduced in clear and color.

	Clear		Clear
Bowls		Bread Plate [Tray], rectan-	
6".	36.50	gular	45.00
8", Berry	30.00	Butter, cov	65.00
12½", Round	42.00	Cake Stand, 10"	48.00

	Clear		**Clear**
Carafe	40.00	Pickle, oval	20.00
Celery Vase	70.00	Pitcher, water, applied	
Champagne	40.00	handle	140.00
Claret	47.50	Relish	20.00
Compote		Salt, ind	12.00
Cov, hs, 8″	75.00	Salt & Pepper, pr.	65.00
Cov, hs, 10″	68.00	Sauce	
Cov, ls, 6½″	55.00	Flat	8.00
Cov, ls, 10″	68.00	Footed	12.00
Open, hs, 9″	40.00	Spooner	45.00
Open, ls, 7½″	25.00	Sugar, cov	65.00
Creamer, applied handle	55.00	Syrup	100.00
Cruet	100.00	Tray, water	65.00
Egg Cup	35.00	Tumbler, ftd	60.00
Goblet	45.00	Wine	50.00
Lamp	140.00		

NAILHEAD (Gem)

Non-flint, made by Bryce, Higbee, and Co., in 1880s. Also found in ruby stained (goblet at $30.00, pitcher at $65.00).

	Clear		**Clear**
Bowl, 6″	18.00	Creamer	25.00
Butter, cov	48.00	Goblet	25.00
Cake Stand		Pitcher, water	35.00
9½″	32.00	Plate	
10½″	35.00	Round, 9″	20.00
Celery	45.00	Square, 7″	16.50
Compote		Sauce, flat	12.00
Cov, 8″, hs	48.00	Spooner	24.00
Cov, ls, 7″	45.00	Sugar, cov	40.00
Open, hs, 6½″	25.00	Tumbler	35.00
Open, 9½″, hs	40.00	Wine	20.00

NEVADA

Non-flint made by U. S. Glass Co. as a States Pattern. Pieces are sometimes partly frosted and have enamel decoration. Add 20% for frosted.

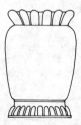

	Clear		**Clear**
Biscuit Jar	45.00	Salt	
Butter, cov	68.00	Ind	8.00
Cake Stand, 10″	35.00	Master	14.00
Celery	27.50	Salt Shaker, single, two	
Compote, cov, 8″, hs	45.00	types	15.00
Creamer	32.00	Sauce	10.00
Cruet	35.00	Spooner	35.00
Cup, custard	12.00	Sugar, cov	35.00
Pickle, oval	10.00	Syrup, tin top	45.00
Pitcher, water, tankard, ½		Toothpick	38.00
gal	40.00	Tumbler	15.00

NEW ENGLAND PINEAPPLE

Flint made by Boston and Sandwich Glass Co. in early 1860s. Rare in color. The goblet has been reproduced in clear and color.

	Flint	Non-Flint		Flint	Non-Flint
Bowl, 8", scalloped	85.00	—	Mug	95.00	—
Castor Bottle	50.00	—	Pitcher, water	350.00	—
Castor Set, 4 bottles, complete	300.00	—	Plate, 6"	90.00	—
Champagne	175.00	—	Salt		
Compote			Ind	24.00	—
Cov, hs, 5"	150.00	—	Master	45.00	40.00
Cov, hs, 8"	175.00	—	Sauce, flat	15.00	10.00
Open, hs, 7"	90.00	—	Spooner	50.00	35.00
Open, hs, 8½"	125.00	—	Sugar, cov	125.00	55.00
Creamer, applied handle, 2 sizes	185.00	70.00	Sweetmeat, cov	225.00	—
Decanter, qt, os	225.00	—	Tumbler		
Egg Cup	50.00	35.00	Bar	110.00	—
Goblet			Water	85.00	—
Lady's	70.00	—	Whiskey, handled	145.00	—
Regular	65.00	—	* Wine	150.00	—

NEW HAMPSHIRE (Bent Buckle, Modiste)

Non-flint made by U. S. Glass Co. in the States Pattern series. There is a large ruby mug ($50.00), 5½" bowl ($25.00), syrup ($48.00), toothpick ($40.00), and tumbler ($40.00). A vase is known in green stain ($30.00).

	Clear w/gold	Rose Stained		Clear w/gold	Rose Stained
Bowl			Mug, large	15.00	45.00
Flared, 8½"	15.00	25.00	Pitcher, water, tankard	70.00	70.00
Round, 8½"	18.00	30.00	Relish	18.00	—
Square, 8½"	25.00	35.00	Sugar		
Butter, cov	70.00	70.00	Cov	45.00	60.00
Cake Stand, 8¼"	30.00	—	Ind, open	20.00	25.00
Carafe	60.00	—	Toothpick	25.00	40.00
Celery Vase	35.00	50.00	Tumbler	18.50	32.00
Compote, open	38.00	42.00	Vase	20.00	35.00
Creamer			Wine	28.00	35.00
Ind	30.00	30.00			
Regular	30.00	45.00			
Cruet	55.00	75.00			
Goblet	25.00	50.00			

NEW JERSEY (Loops and Drops)

Non-flint made by U. S. Glass Co. in States Pattern Series. Items with perfect gold are worth more than those with worn gold. An emerald green 11" vase is known, value $75.00.

	Clear w/gold	Ruby Stained		Clear w/gold	Ruby Stained
Bowl			Pitcher, water		
8", flared	25.00	50.00	Applied handle	80.00	210.00
9"	32.50	65.00	Pressed handle	50.00	185.00
10", oval	30.00	—	Plate		
Bread Plate	30.00	—	8"		
Butter, cov	75.00	100.00	Flat	12.00	—
Cake Stand, 8"	65.00	—	Footed	22.00	—
Celery Tray, rectangular	25.00	—	12"	30.00	—
Compote			Salt & Pepper		
Cov, hs, 5", jelly	45.00	55.00	Hotel	50.00	—
Cov, hs, 8"	75.00	—	Small	35.00	40.00
Open, hs, 6¾"	30.00	—	Sauce	14.00	30.00
Open, hs, 8"	60.00	—	Spooner	27.00	75.00
Creamer	35.00	60.00	Sugar, cov	60.00	80.00
Cruet	48.00	—	Sweetmeat, 8", open, ftd	40.00	—
Goblet	40.00	—	Syrup, no gold	90.00	—
Olive, pointed, flared	18.00	—	Toothpick	55.00	—
Pickle, rectangular	15.00	—	Tumbler	28.00	45.00
Pitcher, milk, applied handle	75.00	—	Wine, straight or flared	42.00	45.00

O'HARA DIAMOND (Sawtooth and Star)

Non-flint, made by O'Hara Glass Co. in 1928 and by U. S. Glass Co. in 1898.

	Clear	Ruby Stained		Clear	Ruby Stained
Bowl, berry			Lamp, Oil	50.00	—
Individual	—	25.00	Pitcher, water,		
Master	25.00	75.00	tankard	—	165.00
Butter, cov, ruffled base	45.00	125.00	Plate		
Compote			7"	20.00	—
Cov, hs	40.00	185.00	8"	30.00	—
Open, hs, jelly	48.00	145.00	10"	40.00	—
Condiment Set, pr salt and pepper, sugar shaker, tray	—	250.00	Salt, master	15.00	35.00
			Salt Shaker	—	35.00
			Spooner	20.00	55.00
Creamer	30.00	60.00	Sugar, cov	35.00	90.00
Cruet	55.00	150.00	Sugar Shaker	55.00	150.00
Cup and Saucer	40.00	60.00	Syrup	55.00	200.00
Goblet	25.00	50.00	Tumbler	30.00	45.00

ONE HUNDRED ONE

Non-flint made by the Bellaire Goblet Co., Findlay, Ohio, in the late 1870s.

	Clear		Clear
Bread Plate, 101 border, Farm implement center, 11"	75.00	Celery Vase	50.00
		Compote	
Butter, cov	60.00	Cov, hs, 7"	60.00
Cake Stand, 9"	65.00	Cov, ls	60.00
		Creamer	45.00

	Clear		Clear
Goblet	48.00	Sauce	
Lamp, hand, oil, 10″	80.00	Flat	10.00
Pitcher, water, applied		Footed	15.00
handle	120.00	Spooner	25.00
Plate		Sugar	
6″	15.00	Cov	45.00
7″	25.00	Open	15.00
8″	30.00	Wine	60.00
Relish	20.00		

OPEN ROSE

Non-flint, c1870. Attributed to Boston and Sandwich Glass Co.

	Clear		Clear
Bowl, oval, 9″ x 6″	25.00	Pitcher, water, applied han-	
Butter, cov	55.00	dle	165.00
Compote		Relish	15.00
Cov, hs, 8″	60.00	Salt, ind, ftd	30.00
Cov, hs, 9″	60.00	Sauce	10.00
Open, ls, 7½″	35.00	Spooner	40.00
Creamer	40.00	Sugar	
Egg Cup	25.00	Cov	50.00
Goblet		Open	30.00
Lady's	32.00	Tumbler	50.00
Regular	30.00		

OREGON #1 (Beaded Loop)

Non-flint. First made in the 1880s. Reissued in 1907 as one of the States series. Reproduced in clear and color by Imperial.

	Clear		Clear
Bowl		Mug	35.00
7″	15.00	Pickle Dish, boat shape	15.00
8″	18.50	Pitcher	
9″, berry, cov	25.00	Milk	40.00
Bread Plate	35.00	Water	60.00
Butter, cov	35.00	Relish	15.00
English	65.00	Salt, master	18.00
Flanged	50.00	Sauce	
Flat	40.00	Flat, 3½ to 4″	10.00
Cake Stand	35.00	Footed, 3½″	15.00
Carafe, water	35.00	Spooner	
Celery Vase	30.00	Flat	24.00
Compote		Footed	26.00
Open, hs, 8″	50.00	Sugar, cov	
Open, ls, 9″	40.00	Flat	25.00
Creamer		Footed	30.00
Flat	30.00	Syrup	55.00
Footed	35.00	Toothpick	35.00
Cruet	45.00	Tumbler	25.00
Goblet	32.50	Wine	40.00
Honey Dish	10.00		

PALM BEACH

Attributed to U. S. Glass Co., Pittsburgh, Pennsylvania, c1905. Made in clear with fired-on colors, opalescent white, blue, and canary. Also made in carnival glass. Clear with color decoration is valued at 50% of blue opalescent prices. White opalescent is valued at 80% of blue opalescent prices. Carnival glass generally is higher than blue opalescent.

	Blue Opal	Canary Opal		Blue Opal	Canary Opal
Bowl, berry	90.00	100.00	Pitcher, water	200.00	215.00
Butter, cov	140.00	135.00	Sauce	25.00	25.00
Compote, jelly	60.00	60.00	Spooner	65.00	75.00
Creamer	50.00	50.00	Sugar, cov	70.00	75.00
Finger Bowl	45.00	45.00	Tumbler	45.00	50.00

PALMETTE

Non-flint, late 1870s. Syrup known in milk glass.

	Clear		Clear
Bowl		Egg Cup	30.00
8″	25.00	Goblet	35.00
9″	15.00	Lamp, 8½″, all glass	80.00
Bread Plate, handled, 9″	30.00	Pickle, scoop shape	18.00
Butter, cov	65.00	Pitcher, water	95.00
Cake Stand	65.00	Relish	18.00
Castor Bottle	20.00	Salt, master, ftd	22.00
Castor Set, 5 bottles	125.00	Salt Shaker	55.00
Celery Vase	40.00	Sauce, flat, 6″	10.00
Champagne	70.00	Shaker, saloon, oversize	60.00
Compote		Spooner	35.00
Cov, hs, 7″	65.00	Sugar, cov	55.00
Cov, hs, 8½″	75.00	Syrup, applied handle	100.00
Cov, hs, 9¾″	85.00	Tumbler	
Open, ls, 5½″	25.00	Bar	60.00
Open, ls, 7″	30.00	Water, ftd	35.00
Creamer, applied handle	50.00	Wine	40.00

PANELED FORGET-ME-NOT (Regal)

Non-flint, made by Bryce Bros., Pittsburgh, Pennsylvania, c1870. Made in limited production in amethyst and green.

	Amber	Blue	Clear
Bread Plate	—	—	25.00
Butter, cov	45.00	60.00	30.00
Cake Stand, 10″	70.00	90.00	45.00
Celery Vase	45.00	70.00	36.00
Compote			
Cov, hs, 7″	—	—	65.00
Cov, hs, 8″	80.00	100.00	68.00
Open, hs, 8½″, scalloped rim	—	—	55.00
Open, hs, 10″	—	—	40.00
Creamer	45.00	60.00	35.00
Cruet, os	—	—	45.00

	Amber	Blue	Clear
Goblet	55.00	70.00	40.00
Marmalade Jar, cov.	60.00	80.00	40.00
Pickle, boat shape. .	25.00	35.00	15.00
Pitcher			
Milk.	—	—	50.00
Water	90.00	110.00	75.00
Relish, scoop shape	—	—	65.00
Salt & Pepper, pr. . .	—	—	65.00
Sauce, ftd.	18.00	25.00	15.00
Spooner	40.00	50.00	25.00
Sugar, cov	60.00	80.00	40.00
Wine	55.00	70.00	55.00

PANELED "44" (Athenia, Reverse "44")

Non-flint made by U. S. Glass Co., c1912. Most pieces bear intertwined U. S. Glass Co. mark in base. Forms include pedestals and handles. Comes trimmed in gold and untarnishable platinum. Lemonade set (six piece set $150.00), goblet, and covered butter ($95.00) in rose or green staining. Some pieces in plain blue.

	Clear w/ platinum		Clear w/ platinum
Bon Bon, trifid ftd, cov	35.00	Olive, flat, handless.	30.00
Bowl, 8″, flat	50.00	Pitcher, water	
Butter, cov, flat	55.00	Flat, bulbous, ½ gal	90.00
Candlestick, 7″	50.00	Footed, tankard	95.00
Cruet	65.00	Salt & Pepper, pr.	75.00
Creamer		Sugar, cov, flat, handled. . . .	60.00
Flat.	45.00	Sugar, powdered, flat, no	
Footed	55.00	handles.	55.00
Finger Bowl	30.00	Toothpick	45.00
Goblet	45.00	Tumbler, water	30.00
Lemonade Set, pitcher, 6		Vase, loving cup shape	40.00
tumblers	200.00	Wine	50.00

PANELED GRAPE, LATE

Non-flint made by D. C. Jenkins Glass Co, Arcadia and Kokomo, IN, c1913 to 1932.

	Clear		Clear
Bowl, 8″, cov.	35.00	Pitcher	
Butter, cov	40.00	Milk.	35.00
Celery Vase	38.50	Water	45.00
Compote, cov, 6½″ d, 9″ h . .	35.00	Spooner	20.00
Creamer.	25.00	Sugar, cov	40.00
Goblet	30.00	Syrup, glass lid	40.00

PANELED THISTLE (Delta)

Non-flint made by J. P. Higbee Glass Co., Bridgeville, Pennsylvania, in the early 1900s. The Higbee Glass Co. often used a bee as a trademark. This pattern has been heavily reproduced with a similar mark. Occasionally found with gilt. A covered sugar in ruby stained is known.

	Clear		Clear
Basket, small size	50.00	Plate	
Bowl		7"	20.00
8", bee mark	25.00	10", bee mark	30.00
9", bee mark	35.00	Punch Cup, bee mark	25.00
Butter, cov, ...	60.00	Relish, bee mark.	15.00
Cake Stand, 9"	35.00	Rose Bowl, 5"	50.00
Celery Tray.	20.00	Salt, ind	20.00
Celery Vase	30.00	Sauce	
Compote		Flared, bee mark	14.00
Open, hs, 8"	30.00	Footed	20.00
Open, hs, 9"	35.00	Spooner	25.00
Open, ls, 5", jelly	30.00	Sugar, cov	45.00
Creamer, bee mark	40.00	Toothpick, bee mark	45.00
Cruet, os	50.00	Tumbler	25.00
Doughnut Stand, 6"	25.00	Vase, 5"	25.00
Goblet	35.00	Wine, bee mark.	40.00
Honey, cov, sq, bee mark. . .	75.00		
Pitcher			
Milk.	60.00		
Water	70.00		

PAVONIA (Pineapple Stem)

Non-flint made by Ripley and Co. in 1885 and by U. S. Glass Co. in 1891. This pattern comes plain and etched.

	Clear	Ruby Stained		Clear	Ruby Stained
Bowl, 9"	20.00	—	Plate, 6½", etched. .	17.50	—
Butter, cov, flat	75.00	125.00	Salt		
Cake Stand, large,			Ind	15.00	50.00
etched.	55.00	—	Master	28.00	50.00
Celery Vase, etched	45.00	75.00	Sauce, ftd, 3½" or		
Compote			4"	15.00	—
Cov, hs, 6".	45.00	—	Spooner, pedestal . .	45.00	50.00
Cov, hs, 8".	55.00	—	Sugar, cov, flat	55.00	75.00
Open, jelly, etched.	38.00	—	Tray, water, etched .	75.00	—
Creamer, etched . . .	48.00	65.00	Tumbler, etched		
Finger Bowl, ruffled			bellflowers	30.00	45.00
underplate.	48.00	110.00	Wine, etched	35.00	40.00
Goblet, etched	35.00	60.00			
Mug	—	50.00			
Pitcher					
Lemonade.	125.00	135.00			
Water	75.00	125.00			

PENNSYLVANIA (Balder)

Non-flint issued by U. S. Glass Co., 1898. Also known in ruby stained. A ruffled jelly compote documented in orange carnival.

	Clear w/gold	Emerald Green		Clear w/gold	Emerald Green
Biscuit Jar, cov	65.00	100.00	8", sq	20.00	40.00
Bowl			Butter, cov	55.00	85.00
8", berry	25.00	35.00	Carafe	45.00	—

	Clear w/gold	Emerald Green		Clear w/gold	Emerald Green
Celery Vase	45.00	—	Punch Bowl	175.00	—
Compote, hs, ruffled,			Punch Cup	10.00	—
jelly	50.00	—	Sauce	10.00	—
Creamer			Spooner	24.00	35.00
Ind	18.00	35.00	Sugar, cov	40.00	55.00
Regular	35.00	50.00	Syrup	50.00	—
Cruet, os	45.00	—	Toothpick	45.00	85.00
Decanter, handle,			Tumbler	28.00	40.00
os	100.00	—	Whiskey	15.00	—
Goblet	28.00	—	Wine	20.00	45.00
Pitcher, water	60.00	—			

PEQUOT

Made by Portland Glass Co., Portland, Maine, between 1863 and 1873. Shards found at Burlington Glass Works, Hamilton, Ontario. Some items are known in blue and amber. Add 100% for colors.

	Clear		Clear
Bowl, 6", pedestal	20.00	Goblet	45.00
Butter, cov	48.00	Marmalade Jar	50.00
Celery Vase	45.00	Pitcher, water, applied hollow	
Champagne	45.00	reeded handle	150.00
Compote		Spooner	40.00
Cov, hs, 7½"	55.00	Sugar, cov	55.00
Open, hs, 7½"	35.00	Wine	35.00
Creamer	48.00		

PICKET

Non-flint made by the King Glass Co., Pittsburgh, Pennsylvania in the 1870s. Pattern has five different size compotes. Toothpick holders are known in apple green, vaseline, and purple slag.

	Clear		Clear
Bowl, 9½", sq	30.00	Goblet	40.00
Bread Plate	70.00	Pitcher, water	90.00
Butter, cov	50.00	Salt	
Celery Vase	40.00	Ind	10.00
Compote		Master	35.00
Cov, hs, 6"	65.00	Sauce	
Cov, hs, 8"	100.00	Flat	18.00
Cov, ls, 8"	125.00	Footed	20.00
Open, hs, 6"	30.00	Spooner	35.00
Open, hs, 7", sq	35.00	Sugar, cov	45.00
Open, hs, 8"	35.00	Toothpick	35.00
Open, hs, 10", sq	70.00	Tray, water	50.00
Open, ls, 7"	50.00	Waste Bowl	30.00
Creamer	40.00	Wine	50.00

PINEAPPLE AND FAN #1 (Heisey's #1255)

Made by A. H. Heisey and Co., Newark, Ohio, c1897, before the Heisey trademark was used. Came in about 70 pieces. Pieces often trimmed in gold. Also known in custard and ruby stained (toothpick at $125.00).

	Clear	Emerald Green		Clear	Emerald Green
Banana Stand....	20.00	—	Goblet	15.00	—
Biscuit Jar, cov	55.00	85.00	Mug............	30.00	45.00
Bowl, 5½".......	12.00	30.00	Pitcher, water	60.00	225.00
Butter, cov	50.00	175.00	Rose Bowl	35.00	75.00
Cake Stand	45.00	75.00	Salt, ind	25.00	—
Celery Tray, flat....	25.00	—	Salt Shaker.......	20.00	—
Compote			Spooner	30.00	65.00
Open, hs, 8"......	30.00	225.00	Sugar, cov		
Open, jelly, 5".....	32.00	—	Individual.	25.00	50.00
Creamer			Regular........	45.00	125.00
Individual.......	25.00	50.00	Syrup	60.00	175.00
Regular........	35.00	95.00	Toothpick	75.00	125.00
Cruet	60.00	285.00	Tumbler	25.00	60.00
Custard Cup	12.00	30.00	Vase, 10", trumpet..	25.00	45.00

PLEAT AND PANEL (Derby)

Non-flint made by Bryce Bros., Pittsburgh, Pennsylvania, c1870–80 and by U. S. Glass Co., in 1891. Found in square and rectangular forms. Rare in blue, canary, amber, and amethyst. Colored items valued at 50% to 75% higher. Do not confuse with the Depression era Heisey pattern of the same name.

	Clear		Clear
Bowl, 8", cov............	35.00	Lamp	65.00
Bread Plate	35.00	Marmalade Jar, cov.......	50.00
Butter, cov	48.00	Pitcher, water	50.00
Butter Pat..............	25.00	* Plate	
Cake Stand		6"	20.00
8"	32.00	8"	24.00
10"	40.00	Relish, 8½".............	18.00
Celery Vase	35.00	Salt, master	20.00
Compote		Spooner..............	30.00
Cov, hs, 8"............	48.00	Sugar, cov	40.00
Open, hs, 8"	35.00	Tray, water, 14 x 9¼"......	50.00
Creamer...............	35.00	Wine	50.00
* Goblet	30.00		

PLUME

Non-flint made by Adams Glass Co., Pittsburgh, Pennsylvania, c1874 and by U. S. Glass Co. in 1891. Has both horizontal and vertical plumes. Also found etched. Pattern contains 46 pieces. Some items are frosted.

	Clear	Ruby Stained		Clear	Ruby Stained
Bowl			Berry, master....	35.00	—
8", scalloped rim .	25.00	—	Butter, cov	50.00	135.00
8", sq	20.00	—	Cake Stand, 10" ...	40.00	—

	Clear	Ruby Stained		Clear	Ruby Stained
Celery Vase	30.00	65.00	6 tumblers, 12½" tray	200.00	—
Compote			Pitcher, water, applied handle	50.00	140.00
Open, hs, 7"	24.50	—	Sauce, flat, 4"	15.00	—
Open, hs, 9", crimped	38.00	—	Spooner	25.00	40.00
Creamer	35.00	50.00	Sugar, cov	45.00	60.00
Goblet	35.00	55.00	Syrup	65.00	—
Lemonade Set, engraved vertical plumes on pitcher,			Tumbler	25.00	35.00

PORTLAND

Non-flint pattern made by several companies c1880–1900. An oval pintray in ruby souvenir ($20.00) is known, and a flat sauce ($25.00).

	Clear w/gold		Clear w/gold
Basket, handled	85.00	Goblet	38.00
Biscuit Jar	50.00	Lamp base, 9"	75.00
Bowl		Pitcher, water, straight sides.	55.00
Berry	20.00	Pomade Jar, SP top	30.00
Small, flat, cov	30.00	Puff Box, glass lid	35.00
Butter, cov	50.00	Punch Cup	18.00
Cake Stand, 10½"	45.00	Relish	15.00
Carafe, water	45.00	Sauce	8.00
Celery Tray	25.00	Spooner	35.00
Compote		Sugar, cov	45.00
Cov, hs, 6"	60.00	Sugar Shaker	40.00
Open, hs, 8¼"	40.00	Syrup	50.00
Open, hs, 9½"	45.00	Toothpick	30.00
Open, ls, 7"	45.00	Tumbler	22.00
Creamer	30.00	Vase	25.00
Cruet, os	48.00	Water Bottle	40.00
Decanter, qt, handled	50.00	Wine	25.00

PRIMROSE

Non-flint made by Canton Glass Co., Canton, Ohio, c1880. Also made in milk glass. Apple green is scarce.

	Amber and Yellow	Blue and Green	Clear
Bowl, 8"	32.00	35.00	24.00
Butter, cov	50.00	60.00	35.00
Cake Stand, 10" . . .	50.00	65.00	40.00
Celery Vase	35.00	40.00	25.00
Compote, cov, ls, 6"	40.00	45.00	30.00
Creamer	35.00	48.00	30.00
Egg Cup	30.00	35.00	20.00
Goblet			
Knob Stem	40.00	45.00	30.00
Plain Stem	35.00	40.00	25.00
Lamp, finger	—	—	195.00

	Amber and Yellow	Blue and Green	Clear
Pickle...........	18.00	20.00	14.00
Pitcher			
Milk..........	45.00	55.00	35.00
Water	55.00	50.00	45.00
Plate			
4½"...........	15.00	20.00	12.00
9", handled	30.00	35.00	20.00
Platter, 12 x 8"	35.00	45.00	30.00
Relish...........	18.00	20.00	14.00
Sauce, ftd........	18.00	25.00	15.00
Spooner.........	25.00	30.00	20.00
Sugar, cov	40.00	55.00	35.00
Tray, water.......	50.00	60.00	35.00
Waste Bowl.......	30.00	35.00	20.00
Wine	40.00	45.00	28.00

PRINCESS FEATHER (Rochelle)

Non-flint made by Bakewell, Pears & Co. in the late 1870s. Occasional pieces made in flint. Later by U. S. Glass Co. in the 1890s. Also made in milk glass. A rare blue opaque tumbler has been reported.

	Clear		Clear
Bowl		Goblet	38.00
7", cov, pedestal	35.00	Pitcher, water	65.00
7", oval	20.00	Plate	
8", oval	25.00	6"..................	30.00
9", oval	30.00	7"..................	35.00
Butter, cov	50.00	8"..................	40.00
Cake Plate, handled	35.00	9"..................	45.00
Celery Vase	40.00	Relish...............	20.00
Compote		Sauce	8.00
Cov, hs, 7"............	50.00	Spooner..............	30.00
Cov, hs, 8"............	50.00	Sugar	
Open, ls, 8"	35.00	Cov.................	55.00
Creamer, applied handle ...	55.00	Open	25.00
Dish, oval	20.00	Wine	45.00
Egg Cup..............	40.00		

PRISCILLA #1 (Findlay)

Non-flint made by Dalzell, Gilmore & Leighton, Findlay, Ohio, in the late 1890s and continued by National Glass Co. Fenton reproduced pattern in clear, colors, and opalescent in 1951. Also introduced many forms different from the original such as 12½" plate, goblet, wine, 6" handled bonbon, and sugar and creamer.

	Clear		Clear
Banana Stand...........	80.00	Open, hs, 7"	45.00
Bowl, 10¼", straight sides ..	50.00	Open, hs, 10", scalloped..	60.00
Butter, cov	65.00	Creamer...............	25.00
Cake Stand, 9½".........	60.00	Cruet, os	65.00
Celery Vase	55.00	Doughnut Stand	60.00
Compote		Goblet	45.00
Cov, hs, 9"............	75.00	Mug.................	20.00

	Clear		Clear
Pitcher, water		Sugar, open	20.00
Bulbous.	70.00	Syrup	75.00
Tankard	75.00	Toothpick	50.00
Plate	25.00	Tumbler	25.00
Sauce	8.00	Wine	35.00
Spooner	30.00		

PRISCILLA #2 (Fostoria's 676)

Made by Fostoria Glass Co., Moundsville, West Virginia, in 1898. Also made in custard with green or gold trim and white milk glass.

	Clear	Emerald Green		Clear	Emerald Green
Bowl, 8½", berry	15.00	35.00	Pickle	15.00	25.00
Butter, cov	65.00	95.00	Pitcher, water	30.00	65.00
Cake Stand	35.00	70.00	Salt Shaker		
Carafe, water	40.00	65.00	Large	12.00	30.00
Celery Vase	35.00	60.00	Small	12.00	30.00
Compote			Sauce, flat, 4½"	10.00	15.00
Cov.	55.00	75.00	Sherbet	8.00	15.00
Open	40.00	55.00	Spooner	30.00	50.00
Creamer	35.00	70.00	Sugar, cov	45.00	80.00
Cruet, os	65.00	250.00	Syrup, nickel top	55.00	150.00
Egg Cup	20.00	35.00	Toothpick, 4½"	35.00	65.00
Finger Bowl	15.00	20.00	Tumbler	25.00	35.00
Marmalade Jar, cov.	45.00	115.00	Water Bottle	—	95.00

PRISM WITH DIAMOND POINTS

Flint made by Bryce Brothers and also attributed to Boston and Sandwich Glass Co. A flint milk glass spooner is known.

	Clear		Clear
Butter, cov	65.00	Pitcher, water	100.00
Compote, cov, hs, 6"	90.00	Salt, master	30.00
Creamer	75.00	Spooner	45.00
Egg Cup		Sugar, cov	50.00
Double	55.00	Tumbler	40.00
Single	35.00	Wine	50.00
Goblet	45.00		

QUARTERED BLOCK (Duncan & Miller #24)

Made by Duncan & Miller Co. c1903.

	Clear	Ruby Stained		Clear	Ruby Stained
Bowl	25.00	60.00	Lamp	75.00	—
Butter, cov	45.00	125.00	Pitcher, water	45.00	150.00
Celery Vase	30.00	—	Sauce	7.50	—
Compote, open, hs	35.00	—	Spooner	20.00	45.00
Creamer	30.00	55.00	Sugar, cov	40.00	45.00
Goblet	38.00		Syrup	50.00	—

	Clear	Ruby Stained		Clear	Ruby Stained
Toothpick	35.00	100.00	Water Bottle	35.00	—
Tumbler	20.00	40.00	Wine	30.00	—
Vase	15.00	—			

QUEEN ANNE (Bearded Man)

Non-flint made by LaBelle Glass Co., Bridgeport, Ohio, c1879. Finials are Maltese cross. At least 28 pieces documented. A table set and water pitcher are known in amber.

	Clear		Clear
Bowl, cov		Egg Cup	45.00
8", oval	45.00	Pitcher	
9", oval	55.00	Milk	45.00
Bread Plate	50.00	Water	80.00
Butter, cov	65.00	Spooner	40.00
Celery Vase	35.00	Sugar, cov	55.00
Compote, cov, ls, 9"	75.00	Syrup	90.00
Creamer	38.00		

QUESTION MARK (Oval Loop)

Made by Richards and Hartley in 1895 and later by U. S. Glass Co., 1891. An 1888 catalog lists 32 pieces. Scarce in ruby stained.

	Clear		Clear
Bowl		Creamer	30.00
4", round, ftd	15.00	Goblet	20.00
7", oblong	18.00	Nappy, ftd	20.00
7", round, ftd	20.00	Pitcher	
8", oblong	25.00	Milk, bulbous	40.00
8", round, ftd	25.00	Milk, tankard	40.00
9", oblong	30.00	Water, bulbous	45.00
10", oblong	25.00	Water, tankard	45.00
Butter, cov	30.00	Salt Shaker	15.00
Candlestick, chamber, finger		Sauce, 4", collared	10.00
loop	45.00	Spooner	20.00
Celery Vase	28.00	Sugar Shaker	35.00
Compote		Sugar, cov	25.00
Cov, hs, 7"	50.00	Tumbler	15.00
Cov, hs, 8"	65.00	Wine	20.00
Open, hs, 7"	25.00		
Open, ls	15.00		

RED BLOCK (Late Block)

Non-flint with red stain made by Doyle and Co.; later made by five companies plus U. S. Glass Co. in 1892. Prices for clear 50% less.

	Ruby Stained		Ruby Stained
Bowl, 8"	75.00	Creamer	
Butter, cov	110.00	Individual	45.00
Celery Vase, 6½"	85.00	Regular	70.00

	Ruby Stained		Ruby Stained
Decanter, 12", os, variant...	175.00	Salt Dip, ind	50.00
*Goblet	45.00	Salt Shaker, single	60.00
Mug	40.00	Spooner	45.00
Pitcher, water, 8" h	175.00	Sugar, cov	75.00
Rose Bowl	75.00	Tumbler	35.00
Sauce, flat, 4½"	30.00	*Wine	40.00

REVERSE TORPEDO (Bull's Eye Band, Bull's Eye with Diamond Point #2, Pointed Bull's Eye)

Made by Dalzell, Gilmore & Leighton Glass Co., Findlay, Ohio, c18881890. Also attributed to Canadian factories.

	Clear		Clear
Banana Stand, 9¾"	135.00	Open, hs, 7"	65.00
Biscuit Jar, cov	165.00	Open, hs, 8⅜" d	45.00
Bowl		Open, hs, jelly	50.00
8½", shallow	30.00	Open, ls, 9¼", ruffled	
9", fruit, pie crust rim	68.00	edge	90.00
10½", pie crust rim......	75.00	Goblet	85.00
Butter, cov	75.00	Honey Dish, sq	145.00
Cake Stand	85.00	Pitcher, water, tankard,	
Celery Vase	55.00	10¼"..............	140.00
Compote		Sauce, flat, 3¾"	24.00
Cov, hs, 7"..........	80.00	Spooner..............	30.00
Cov, hs, 10"...........	125.00	Sugar, cov	85.00
Cov, hs, 6"...........	80.00	Syrup...............	165.00
Open, hs, 10½" d, V shape bowl	90.00	Tumbler	35.00

RIBBED IVY

Flint, late 1850s. Attributed to Boston and Sandwich Glass Co.

	Clear		Clear
Bowl, 6"	15.00	Salt, master	
Butter, cov	100.00	Cov.................	115.00
Castor Bottle...........	35.00	Open, scalloped rim.....	40.00
Celery Vase	350.00	Sauce	12.00
Champagne	110.00	Spooner..............	40.00
Compote		Sugar, cov	85.00
Cov, hs, 6", jelly........	125.00	Sweetmeat, cov, on stand ..	165.00
Open, hs, 9", scalloped		Tumbler	
edge	85.00	Bar	75.00
Creamer................	125.00	Water	75.00
Decanter, quart, os	150.00	Whiskey	
Egg Cup...............	30.00	Handled	100.00
Goblet	45.00	Plain...............	70.00
Hat...................	385.00	Wine	75.00

RIBBON

Non-flint, usually frosted, made by Bakewell, Pears, Pittsburgh, Pennsylvania, in the late 1860s. It has been erroneously called "Frosted Ribbon" at times, which can be confusing. Other Ribbon patterns are Clear Ribbon, Frosted Ribbon, Double Ribbon, Fluted Ribbon, and Grated Ribbon.

	Frosted		Frosted
Butter, cov	70.00	*Goblet	35.00
Cake Stand, 8½"	40.00	Pitcher, water	75.00
Celery Vase	40.00	Platter, 9" x 13", oblong, cut	
Cheese, cov	85.00	corners	62.50
Cologne Bottle, os.	65.00	Sauce	
Compote		Footed	18.00
Cov, hs, 8"	75.00	Tab-handled	18.00
Cov, ls, 7"	45.00	Spooner	35.00
Open, hs, 10½", SP, Dol-		Sugar, cov	65.00
phin stand	225.00	Tray, water, 15"	100.00
Open, ls, 7"	35.00	Waste Bowl.	35.00
Creamer.	30.00	Wine	110.00

RIBBON CANDY (Bryce)

Non-flint, made by Bryce Brothers, Pittsburgh, Pennsylvania, 1880s. Reissued by U. S. Glass Co. in 1890s. Bowls come in a variety of sizes: open or with lids; flat or with a low collared foot. Also known in emerald green.

	Clear		Clear
Bowl		Cordial	45.00
3½", round	10.00	Creamer.	25.00
4", round	10.00	Cruet, os	65.00
8", oval	25.00	Cup and Saucer	40.00
8", round	25.00	Goblet	40.00
Butter, cov, 2 types	45.00	Honey, cov, sq	75.00
Cake Stand		Lamp, oil	75.00
8"	30.00	Pitcher	
10½"	45.00	Milk.	35.00
Claret.	40.00	Water	75.00
Compote		Plate	
Cov, ls, 5"	30.00	6"	18.00
Cov, ls, 6"	30.00	8"	25.00
Cov, ls, 7"	40.00	11"	35.00
Cov, ls, 8"	40.00	Relish.	16.00
Open, hs, 5"	15.00	Salt & Pepper.	50.00
Open, hs, 6"	20.00	Sauce, flat, 4"	10.00
Open, hs, 7"	25.00	Spooner	25.00
Open, hs, 8"	30.00	Sugar	
Open, ls, 3"	10.00	Cov.	45.00
Open, ls, 4"	10.00	Open	20.00
Open, ls, 5"	10.00	Syrup.	90.00
Open, ls, 6"	15.00	Tumbler	25.00
Open, ls, 7"	20.00	Wine	45.00
Open, ls, 8"	25.00		

RISING SUN (Sunshine)

Made by Ripley and Co., then continued by U. S. Glass Co. in 1908 at Glassport, Pennsylvania. Also found in carnival and scarce in ruby stained. A sugar cube dispenser in a silver plated holder was made for the Alaska-Yukon Pacific Exposition in 1909 ($150.00).

	Clear w/gold	Rose or Green Decorated		Clear w/gold	Rose or Green Decorated
Bowl, berry	12.00	—	Pitcher, water	95.00	—
Butter, cov	32.50	45.00	Relish	15.00	—
Cake Plate, 10½"	22.50	—	Sauce, flat	8.00	—
Cake Stand	35.00	—	Spooner	18.00	—
Celery Vase	25.00	30.00	Sugar, cov		
Compote			Regular or Hotel, three-handled	40.00	—
Cov, hs	45.00	—	Tall, ftd, no handle	35.00	—
Open, hs	30.00	35.00	Toothpick, triple-handled	18.00	35.00
Creamer			Tumbler	15.00	25.00
Regular or Hotel	25.00	—	Whiskey (shot)	12.00	16.00
Tall, ftd	22.50	—	Wine	25.00	30.00
Cruet, os	40.00	—			
Dish, ruffled edge	15.00	—			
Goblet	20.00	25.00			

ROMAN KEY (Frosted Roman Key)

Flint glass pattern of the 1860s made Union Glass Co. and by others in several variants. Available in clear but not as popular. Sometimes erroneously called "Greek Key."

	Flint Frosted		Flint Frosted
Bowl		Decanter, os	160.00
8"	45.00	Egg Cup	45.00
10"	50.00	Goblet	50.00
Butter, cov	80.00	Pitcher, water	225.00
Celery Vase, ftd	80.00	Salt, ftd	45.00
Champagne	75.00	Sauce, 4"	18.00
Compote		Spooner	45.00
Open, hs, 8", cable rim	60.00	Sugar, cov	90.00
Open, ls, 7"	95.00	Tumbler, bar	45.00
Creamer, applied handle	125.00	Wine	85.00

ROMAN ROSETTE

Non-flint made by Bryce, Walker and Co. 1875-1885. Reissued by U. S. Glass Co. in 1892 and 1898. Attributed to Portland Glass Co. Also seen with English registry mark. Also known in amber stained.

	Clear	Ruby Stained		Clear	Ruby Stained
Bowl			Bread Plate	30.00	75.00
6"	12.00	—	Butter, cov	50.00	125.00
8½"	22.00	50.00	Cake Stand, 9"	45.00	—

	Clear	Ruby Stained		Clear	Ruby Stained
Celery Vase	30.00	95.00	Plate, 7½".	35.00	65.00
Compote			Relish, oval, 9"	20.00	40.00
Cov, hs, 4½", jelly	50.00	—	Salt & Pepper, glass		
Cov, hs, 6".	65.00	—	tray.	55.00	100.00
Creamer.	32.00	45.00	Sauce	15.00	20.00
Cordial	30.00	—	Spooner	25.00	45.00
*Goblet	40.00	—	Sugar, cov	45.00	95.00
Lemonade Mug. . . .	18.00	—	Syrup	65.00	125.00
Pitcher			Wine	35.00	55.00
Milk.	45.00				
Water	50.00	140.00			

ROSE-IN-SNOW

Non-flint made by Bryce Bros., Pittsburgh, Pennsylvania in the square form, c1880. Also made in the more common round form by Ohio Flint Glass Co. and after 1891 by U. S. Glass Co.

	Amber and Canary	Blue	Clear
Butter, cov			
Round.	50.00	125.00	45.00
Square	60.00	150.00	50.00
Cake Stand, 9"	—	—	90.00
Compote			
Cov, hs, 8".	85.00	175.00	80.00
Cov, ls, 7"	80.00	150.00	75.00
Open, ls, 5¾" . . .	40.00	120.00	35.00
Creamer			
Round.	60.00	100.00	45.00
Square	65.00	120.00	45.00
* Goblet	40.00	100.00	35.00
* Mug, "In Fond Remembrance" . .	45.00	110.00	32.00
* Pickle Dish			
Double, 8½" x 7" .	45.00	110.00	100.00
Single, oval, handles at end. . . .	25.00	95.00	20.00
Pitcher, water, applied handle.	175.00	200.00	125.00
Plate			
5"	—	—	35.00
6"	20.00	80.00	18.00
7"	22.00	82.00	20.00
Platter, oval.	—	—	125.00
Sauce			
Flat.	15.00	20.00	12.00
Footed	8.00	48.00	18.00
Spooner			
Round.	30.00	80.00	25.00
Square	38.50	100.00	35.00
Sugar, cov			
Round.	55.00	120.00	50.00
Square	48.00	140.00	45.00
Tumbler, bar	55.00	100.00	50.00

ROSE SPRIG

Non-flint made by Campbell, Jones & Co., Pittsburgh, Pennsylvania 1888.

	Amber and Canary	Blue	Clear
Biscuit Jar, dome lid	—	—	100.00
Cake Stand, 9″	75.00	90.00	70.00
Celery Vase	50.00	60.00	40.00
Compote			
Cov, hs..........	—	—	75.00
Open, hs, 7″	70.00	—	60.00
Open, hs, 8″, oval	72.00	—	—
Creamer.........	65.00	55.00	45.00
Goblet	55.00	70.00	42.50
Mug............	—	—	40.00
Nappy, 6″	30.00	35.00	25.00
Pitcher			
Milk...........	65.00	70.00	50.00
Water	65.00	70.00	50.00
Plate, 8″.........	38.00	45.00	30.00
Relish, boat shape .	30.00	35.00	25.00
* Salt			
Patent Date 1888.	62.50	75.00	50.00
Sleigh	30.00	40.00	25.00
Sauce, ftd........	25.00	—	—
Spooner.........	30.00	35.00	25.00
Sugar, cov	54.00	70.00	45.00
Tray, water	55.00	70.00	45.00
Tumbler	40.00	45.00	35.00
Wine	55.00	72.00	50.00

ROSETTE (Magic)

Non-flint made by Bryce Bros., Pittsburgh, Pennsylvania, in the late 1870s. Continued by the U. S. Glass Co. Later made in Ohio in 1898.

	Clear		Clear
Bowl, 7¼″, cov	30.00	Pickle.................	12.00
Bread Plate, 9″, handles ...	25.00	Pitcher	
Butter, cov	35.00	Milk, qt	48.00
Cake Stand		Water, ½ gal	65.00
7″..................	24.00	Plate, 7″..............	12.00
10″..................	26.00	Relish, fish shape	15.00
11″..................	35.00	Salt Shaker.............	25.00
Celery, 8″	20.00	Sauce, flat, handled.......	8.00
Compote		Spooner...............	25.00
Cov, hs, 6″............	40.00	Sugar, cov	35.00
Cov, hs, 8″............	70.00	Sugar Shaker	35.00
Cov, hs, 11½″	50.00	Tray, 10¼″	35.00
Open, hs, 7″	30.00	Tumbler, 5″.............	16.00
Open, hs, 4½″, jelly	25.00	Waste Bowl.............	25.00
Creamer..............	25.00	Wine	20.00
Goblet	30.00		

ROYAL IVY ("New" Jewel)

Non-flint made by Northwood Glass Co. in 1889. Made in cased spatter, clear and frosted rainbow cracquelle, clear with amber, stained ivy, and clambroth opaline. These last mentioned were experimental pieces, not made in sets.

	Clear Frosted	Rubena Clear	Rubena Frosted
Bowl, berry, small . .	30.00	—	45.00
Butter, cov	100.00	175.00	275.00
Creamer, applied handle. .	60.00	150.00	200.00
Cruet	90.00	—	325.00
Marmalade Jar, SP cov.	125.00	—	—
Pickle Castor, SP frame	—	—	375.00
Pitcher, water, applied handle.	100.00	175.00	275.00
Rose Bowl	55.00	70.00	85.00
Spooner	45.00	70.00	95.00
Sugar, cov	150.00	165.00	180.00
Sugar Shaker	65.00	135.00	150.00
Syrup	120.00	225.00	300.00
Toothpick	—	—	125.00
Tumbler	35.00	50.00	75.00

ROYAL OAK (Acorn)

Non-flint made by Northwood Glass Co., Martins Ferry, Ohio, c1899. In early 1900s, it was made in opaque, white with colored tops and colored acorns and leaves. Milk-white pieces are rare.

	Clear Frosted	Rubena Clear	Rubena Frosted
Butter, cov	175.00	—	225.00
Creamer.	150.00	—	150.00
Cruet, os	215.00	425.00	480.00
Mustard Jar, cov . . .	90.00	—	—
Pickle Castor Insert.	—	—	245.00
Pitcher, water	100.00	400.00	350.00
Salt Shaker, single .	40.00	—	—
Spooner	75.00	—	100.00
Sugar, cov, acorn finial	125.00	—	180.00
Sugar Shaker	75.00	—	165.00
Syrup.	135.00	—	—
Tumbler	65.00	—	85.00

SAWTOOTH (Mitre Diamond)

An early clear flint-glass pattern made in the late 1850s by the New England Glass Co., Boston and Sandwich Glass Co., and others. Later made in non-flint by Bryce Brothers and U. S. Glass Co. Also known in milk glass and clear deep blue.

	Flint	Non-Flint
Butter, cov	75.00	45.00
Cake Stand, 10"	85.00	55.00
Celery Vase, 10"	60.00	30.00
Champagne	55.00	32.00
Compote		
Cov, hs, 9½"	85.00	48.00
Open, ls, 8", sawtooth edge	50.00	30.00
Creamer		
Applied handle	75.00	40.00
Pressed handle	—	30.00
Cruet, acorn stopper	100.00	—
Egg Cup	45.00	25.00
Goblet		
Knob Stem	45.00	25.00
Plain Stem	—	20.00

	Flint	Non-Flint
Pitcher, water		
Applied handle	125.00	—
Pressed handle	—	55.00
Plate, 6½"	45.00	30.00
Pomade Jar, cov	50.00	35.00
Salt		
Cov, ftd	65.00	40.00
Open, smooth edge	25.00	20.00
Spooner	65.00	25.00
Sugar, cov	65.00	35.00
Tumbler, bar	50.00	25.00
Wine, knob stem	35.00	25.00

SCALLOPED DIAMOND POINT (Late Diamond Point Band, Panel with Diamond Point, Diamond Point With Flute)

Non-flint pattern. Not to be confused with early flint Diamond Point. Made by Central Glass Co., Wheeling, West Virginia. Also made by U. S. Glass Co. after 1891. A wine ($75.00) is known in electric blue, and in amber ($50.00).

	Clear
Bowl, oval, 9"	20.00
Butter Dish, cov	35.00
Cake Stand	
8"	30.00
12"	60.00
Cheese Dish, cov, 8"	50.00
Compote, cov, hs, 8"	75.00
Cov, 5", jelly	35.00
Creamer	60.00
Goblet	30.00

	Clear
Mustard Jar, cov	30.00
Pickle Dish, oval	20.00
Pickle Jar, cov	45.00
Plate	
5"	12.00
9"	25.00
Sauce, ftd, 4"	12.00
Spooner	25.00
Sugar, cov	35.00
Wine	35.00

SCALLOPED TAPE (Jewel Band)

Non-flint, c1880. Maker unknown. Occasionally found in amber, blue, canary, and light green.

	Clear
Bread Plate, oval, "Bread Is The Staff of Life"	45.00
Butter, cov	35.00
Cake Stand	35.00
Celery Vase	35.00
Compote	
Cov, hs, 8"	55.00
Open, hs	40.00
Creamer	30.00
Dish, rect, cov, 8"	45.00
Egg Cup	25.00
Goblet	30.00

	Clear
Pitcher	
Milk	35.00
Water	50.00
Plate, 6"	15.00
Sauce	
Flat, 4"	8.50
Ftd	12.00
Spooner	20.00
Sugar, cov	35.00
Tray, 6 x 7"	25.00
Wine	25.00

SCROLL (Stippled Scroll)

Non-flint, made by Duncan Glass Co., c1870s. Also made in milk glass. Some items reproduced by Imperial.

	Clear		Clear
Butter, cov	50.00	Salt, ftd	
Celery	32.00	Individual	25.00
Compote		Master	25.00
Cov, hs	65.00	Spooner	30.00
Open, hs	35.00	Sugar	
Creamer, applied handle	40.00	Cov	45.00
Goblet	35.00	Open, buttermilk	30.00
Pitcher, water, applied handle	75.00	Tumbler, ftd	25.00
		Wine	30.00

SCROLL WITH FLOWERS

Non-flint. Attributed to Central Glass Co. in the 1870s and Canton Glass Co. Occasionally found in amber, apple green, and blue.

	Clear		Clear
Butter, cov	40.00	Pickle, handled	18.00
Cake Plate, 10½″, handled	25.00	Pitcher, water	45.00
Compote, cov	45.00	Plate, double-handled, 10½″	40.00
Cordial	35.00	Sauce, double-handled	10.00
Creamer	40.00	Spooner	28.50
Egg Cup, handled	18.00	Sugar, cov	45.00
Goblet	25.00	Wine	30.00
Mustard Jar, cov	50.00		

SEDAN (Paneled Star and Button)

Clear non-flint pattern made in the 1870s.

	Clear		Clear
Bowl	20.00	Relish	10.00
Butter, cov	38.50	Salt Shaker	20.00
Celery Tray	18.00	Sauce, flat	5.00
Celery Vase	25.00	Spooner	18.00
Compote		Sugar	
Cov, hs, 8½″	35.00	Covered	35.00
Open, hs	20.00	Open	15.00
Creamer	24.00	Tumbler	20.00
Goblet	20.00	Wine	18.00
Pitcher, water	35.00		

SHRINE (Jewel with Moon and Star)

Non-flint made by Beatty & Indiana Glass Co., Dunkirk, Indiana, c. late 1880s.

	Clear		Clear
Bowl		6½″	25.00
4″	15.00	9½″	30.00

	Clear		Clear
Butter, cov	50.00	Platter	40.00
Cake Stand, 8½"	40.00	Relish	15.00
Celery	45.00	Salt Shaker	30.00
Creamer	40.00	Sauce	25.00
Goblet	45.00	Spooner	30.00
Pickle	20.00	Sugar,cov	50.00
Pitcher, water		Tumbler	
Normal Size	50.00	Lemonade	36.00
Jumbo Size	100.00	Water	35.00

SHUTTLE (Hearts of Loch Haven)

Made by Indiana Tumbler and Goblet Co., Greentown, Indiana, between 1894 and 1903. Some items reproduced.

	Clear	Cara-mel		Clear	Cara-mel
Bowl, berry	25.00	—	Mug	25.00	95.00
Butter, cov	50.00	150.00	Pitcher, water	50.00	—
Celery Vase	30.00	—	Spooner	20.00	—
Cordial	32.00	—	Sugar, cov	40.00	—
Creamer	30.00	—	Tumbler	25.00	80.00
Cruet, os	75.00	—	Wine	24.00	50.00

SKILTON (Oregon #2)

Made by Richards & Hartley of Tarentum, Pennsylvania in 1888 and by U. S. Glass after 1891. This is not one of the U. S. Glass States pattern series and should not be confused with Beaded Loop, which is Oregon #1, named by U. S. Glass Co. It is better known as Skilton (named by Millard) to avoid confusion with Beaded Loop.

	Clear	Ruby Stained		Clear	Ruby Stained
Bowl			Creamer	30.00	55.00
4", round	10.00	—	Dish, oblong, sq	25.00	—
5", round	15.00	—	Goblet	35.00	50.00
6", round	20.00	—	Olive, handled	20.00	—
7", rect	20.00	—	Pickle	15.00	—
8", rect	25.00	—	Pitcher		
9", rect	30.00	—	Milk	45.00	125.00
Butter, cov	45.00	110.00	Water	50.00	125.00
Cake Stand	35.00	—	Salt & Pepper, pr	45.00	—
Celery Vase	35.00	95.00	Sauce, ftd	12.00	20.00
Compote			Spooner, flat	25.00	55.00
Cov, hs, 7"	45.00	—	Sugar, cov	35.00	85.00
Cov, hs, 8"	45.00	—	Tray, water	45.00	—
Open, ls, 4"	10.00	—	Tumbler	25.00	40.00
Open, ls, 7"	25.00	—	Wine	35.00	45.00
Open, ls, 8"	30.00	75.00			

SMOCKING

Flint pattern made c1850.

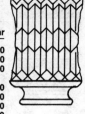

	Clear			Clear
Bar Bottle, blob top	100.00	Pitcher, water		100.00
Bowl, 9"	75.00	Spillholder		75.00
Compote, cov, ls, 7"	90.00	Spooner		40.00
Creamer	90.00	Sugar		
Egg Cup	50.00	Cov		85.00
Goblet	85.00	Open		50.00
Lamp		Vase, 10"		75.00
Hand	225.00	Whiskey		75.00
Stand	175.00	Wine		40.00

SNAIL (Compact, Idaho, Double Snail)

Non-flint made by George Duncan & Sons, Pittsburgh, Pennsylvania, c1880, and by U. S. Glass Co. in the States Pattern series. Ruby stained pieces date after 1891. Add 30% for engraved pieces.

	Clear	Ruby Stained		Clear	Ruby Stained
Banana Stand	145.00	225.00	Cruet, os	75.00	275.00
Basket, cake or fruit			Finger Bowl	30.00	—
9"	85.00	—	Goblet	50.00	80.00
10"	95.00	—	Pitcher		
Bowl			Milk, tankard	85.00	—
4"	20.00	45.00	Water, bulbous	100.00	—
4½"	20.00	—	Water, tankard	135.00	250.00
7", cov	60.00	45.00	Plate		
7", oval	28.00	45.00	5"	35.00	—
7", round	28.00	45.00	6"	35.00	—
8", cov	60.00	45.00	7"	40.00	—
8", oval	28.00	45.00	Punch Cup	35.00	—
8", round	28.00	45.00	Relish, 7", oval	25.00	—
9", oval	30.00	—	Rose Bowl		
9", round	30.00	—	3"	50.00	—
10"	35.00	45.00	5"	45.00	—
Butter, cov	75.00	160.00	6"	45.00	—
Cake Stand			7"	50.00	—
9"	75.00	—	Salt		
10"	85.00	—	Ind	35.00	—
Celery Vase	40.00	85.00	Master	35.00	75.00
Cheese, cov	95.00	—	Salt & Pepper		
Compote			Bulbous	65.00	100.00
Cov, hs, 6"	50.00	—	Straight sides	45.00	100.00
Cov, hs, 7"	50.00	—	Sauce	—	45.00
Cov, hs, 8"	8.00	—	Spooner	35.00	75.00
Cov, hs, 10"	125.00	—	Sugar		
Open, hs, 6"	30.00	—	Ind, cov	35.00	—
Open, hs, 7"	45.00	—	Regular, cov	60.00	100.00
Open, hs, 8"	35.00	—	Sugar Shaker	85.00	200.00
Open, hs, 9", twisted stem, scalloped	75.00	—	Syrup	100.00	225.00
			Tumbler	40.00	62.00
Creamer	55.00	75.00	Vase	50.00	—
Cup, Custard	20.00	—	Violet Bowl, 3"	50.00	—
			Wine	65.00	—

SPIREA BAND

Non-flint made by Bryce, Higbee & Co., Pittsburgh, Pennsylvania, c1885.

	Amber	Blue	Clear	Vaseline
Bowl, 8″	25.00	40.00	22.00	30.00
Butter, cov	50.00	55.00	35.00	45.00
Cake Stand, 11″ . . .	45.00	55.00	40.00	45.00
Celery Vase	40.00	50.00	25.00	40.00
Compote, cov, hs, 7″	44.00	65.00	40.00	44.00
Cordial	38.00	42.00	20.00	38.00
Creamer.	37.50	44.00	35.00	35.00
Goblet	35.00	44.00	25.00	35.00
Pitcher, water	65.00	80.00	35.00	60.00
Platter, 10½″.	32.00	42.00	20.00	32.00
Relish.	30.00	35.00	18.00	30.00
Sauce				
Flat.	10.00	12.00	5.00	9.00
Ftd	15.00	18.00	8.00	14.00
Spooner	30.00	35.00	20.00	35.00
Sugar, open	32.00	40.00	25.00	32.00
Tumbler	24.00	35.00	20.00	30.00
Wine	30.00	35.00	20.00	30.00

SPRIG

Non-flint made by Bryce, Higbee & Co., Pittsburgh, Pennsylvania, mid-1880s.

	Clear		Clear
Bowl, 10″, scalloped	45.00	Goblet	38.00
Bread Plate	40.00	Pitcher, water	50.00
Butter, cov	65.00	Relish.	12.00
Cake Stand, 8″	35.00	Sauce	
Celery Vase	40.00	Flat.	14.00
Compote		Ftd	18.00
Cov, hs	60.00	Spooner	25.00
Open, hs.	45.00	Sugar, cov	50.00
Creamer.	30.00	Wine	35.00

STAR ROSETTED

Non-flint made by McKee Brothers, Pittsburgh, PA, c1875.

	Clear		Clear
Bread Plate	40.00	Pitcher, water	50.00
Butter, cov	48.00	Plate, 7″.	20.00
Compote		Relish, 9″	14.00
Cov, hs, 8½″	60.00	Sauce	
Cov, jelly	55.00	Flat.	7.00
Cov, sweetmeat	55.00	Footed	14.00
Open, hs, 8½″	35.00	Spooner	25.00
Creamer.	35.00	Sugar	
Goblet	28.00	Cov.	48.00
Pickle.	14.00	Open	24.00

STARS AND STRIPES (Brilliant)

Made by Jenkins Glass Co., Kokomo, Indiana, in 1899. Appeared in 1899 Montgomery Ward catalog as "Brilliant."

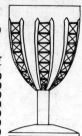

	Clear		Clear
Bowl, berry	15.00	Pitcher, water	40.00
Butter, cov	20.00	Salt Shaker	15.00
Celery Vase	15.00	Sauce	6.00
Cordial	15.00	Spooner	15.00
Creamer	18.00	Sugar, cov	20.00
Cruet Set	35.00	Tumbler	15.00
Cup, sherbert, handled	8.00	Wine	15.00
Goblet	20.00		

STATES, THE (Cane and Star Medallion)

Non-flint made by the U. S. Glass Co. in 1908. Also found in emerald green; add 50%.

	Clear w/ gold		Clear w/gold
Bowl		Punch Cup	12.50
7", round, 3 handles	30.00	Relish, diamond shape	25.00
9¼", round	30.00	Salt & Pepper	40.00
Butter, cov	65.00	Sauce, flat, 4", tub shape	15.00
Celery Tray	20.00	Spooner	25.00
Cocktail	25.00	Sugar	
Compote		Covered	40.00
Open, hs, 7"	35.00	Open, ind	15.00
Open, hs, 9"	50.00	Open, table	20.00
Creamer		Syrup	65.00
Ind, oval	18.00	Toothpick, flat, rectangular,	
Regular, round	30.00	curled lip	45.00
Goblet	35.00	Tray, 7¼" l, 5½" w	18.00
Pitcher, water	45.00	Tumbler	25.00
Plate, 10"	35.00	Wine	30.00
Punch Bowl, 8 cups	120.00		

STIPPLED CHAIN

Clear non-flint pattern made by Gillinder and Sons, Philadelphia, Pennsylvania, c1870.

	Clear		Clear
Bowl	25.00	Pitcher, water	65.00
Butter, cov	50.00	Relish	18.00
Cake Stand	45.00	Salt, ftd	25.00
Celery Vase	40.00	Sauce, flat	15.00
Creamer	35.00	Spooner	28.00
Egg Cup	28.00	Sugar, cov	40.00
Goblet	28.00	Tumbler	20.00
Pickle	18.00		

STIPPLED DOUBLE LOOP

Clear and stippled non-flint pattern of the 1880s.

	Clear		Clear
Butter, cov	50.00	Salt Shaker	20.00
Cake Stand	40.00	Spooner	20.00
Celery Vase	40.00	Sugar, cov	25.00
Creamer	35.00	Tumbler	30.00
Goblet	60.00	Wine	25.00
Pitcher, water	55.00		

STIPPLED FORGET-ME-NOT

Non-flint made by Findlay Glass Co. Findlay, Ohio in the 1880s. Also found in amber, blue, and white.

	Clear		Clear
Butter, cov	50.00	7", Star center	30.00
Cake Stand		9", Kitten center, handles	55.00
9"	35.00	9", Star center	35.00
10"	75.00	Relish, oval	15.00
12"	80.00	Salt, master, oval	35.00
Celery	30.00	Sauce, ftd	15.00
Compote		Spooner	25.00
Cov, hs, 8"	50.00	Sugar, cov	35.00
Cov, ls, 6"	45.00	Toothpick, hat shaped	100.00
Open, hs	45.00	Tray, water, aquatic scene	50.00
Creamer	30.00	Tumbler	30.00
Goblet	45.00	Wine	35.00
Mug	30.00		
Pitcher, water	50.00		
Plate			
7", Baby in Tub reaching for ball	55.00		

STIPPLED GRAPE AND FESTOON

Non-flint made by Doyle and Co, Pittsburgh, PA, c1870. Pieces have applied handles and acorn finials.

	Clear		Clear
Butter, cov		Pickle	30.00
Flange	60.00	Pitcher	
Regular	45.00	Milk	75.00
Celery Vase	35.00	Water	90.00
Compote		Relish	30.00
Cov, hs, 8"	45.00	Sauce, flat	12.00
Cov, ls, 8"	35.00	Spooner	30.00
Cov, ls, 9"	55.00	Sugar	
Open, ls	35.00	Cov	60.00
Creamer	50.00	Open	40.00
Egg Cup	35.00	Wine	45.00
Goblet	32.50		

STRAWBERRY (Fairfax)

Non-flint pattern first made in 1870 and patented by John Bryce. Attributed to Boston and Sandwich Glass Co. by Lee. Later made by Bryce, Walker & Co.

	Clear	Milk		Clear	Milk
Bowl, oval, 9¼" x 6"	30.00	—	Sauce, flat	14.00	—
Butter, cov	55.00	50.00	Spooner	40.00	40.00
Compote			Sugar		
Cov, hs, 8"	75.00	—	Cov.	65.00	65.00
Cov, ls, 8"	65.00	—	Open, buttermilk .	40.00	45.00
Creamer, applied			Syrup, applied han-		
handle.	65.00	75.00	dle	95.00	—
*Egg Cup	37.50	32.00	Tumbler, bar	45.00	—
*Goblet	40.00	60.00	Wine	95.00	—
Pitcher, water, ap-plied handle.	125.00	135.00			

STRAWBERRY AND CURRANT (Multiple Fruits)

One of a non-flint series of fruit patterns which has become known as Multiple Fruits (Cherry and Fig, Loganberry and Grape, Blackberry and Grape, and Cornucopia with Sprig of Cherries). They were made by Dalzell, Gilmore, and Leighton in Findlay, Ohio. A Loganberry and Grape jelly goblet, with "U" shaped bowl; is of inferior quality and not part of the pattern.

There are matching pieces in all forms, although whether or not all forms were made in all four patterns is not known. Reproduction goblets found in clear, opalescent, and colors.

	Clear		Clear
Butter, cov	50.00	Sauce, ftd	12.00
Celery Vase	35.00	Spooner	30.00
Cheese, cov	50.00	Sugar, cov	40.00
Compote, open, hs	35.00	Syrup	80.00
Creamer	40.00	Tumbler	25.00
* Goblet	30.00		
Mug	38.50		
Pitcher			
Milk	40.00		
Water	50.00		

STRIGIL

Non-flint pattern made in the 1880s by Tarentum Glass Co, Tarentum, PA. May be gilded.

	Clear		Clear
Bowl, 8"	20.00	Punch Cup	10.00
Butter, cov	35.00	Sauce, flat	5.00
Celery Tray	15.00	Spooner	18.00
Celery Vase	25.00	Sugar, cov	32.00
Creamer	15.00	Tumbler	18.00
Cruet, os	25.00	Wine	25.00
Egg Cup	20.00		
Goblet	40.00		
Pitcher			
Milk	30.00		
Water	35.00		

SWAG WITH BRACKETS

Made by Jefferson Glass Co., Steubenville, Ohio, c1904. Also found in non-opalescent, gold trimmed, amethyst, blue, and vaseline.

	Blue and Canary Opal	Green Opal	White Opal
Butter, cov	175.00	150.00	—
Compote, Jelly	45.00	55.00	30.00
Creamer	80.00	75.00	55.00
Cruet, os	150.00	110.00	—
Pitcher, water	250.00	200.00	130.00
Salt Shaker, single	50.00	40.00	35.00
Spooner	75.00	65.00	40.00
Sugar, cov	150.00	85.00	50.00
Toothpick	135.00	85.00	40.00
Tumbler	75.00	50.00	35.00

TEARDROP AND TASSEL (Sampson)

Non-flint made by the Indiana Tumbler & Goblet Co., Greentown, Indiana, c1890, to celebrate Admiral Sampson's victory in the Spanish-American War.

	Clear	Cobalt Blue	Emerald Green	Nile Green Opaque
Bowl, 7½"	40.00	55.00	50.00	75.00
Butter, cov	55.00	95.00	155.00	325.00
Celery Vase	40.00	—	—	—
Compote				
Cov, hs, 7"	75.00	90.00	80.00	125.00
Cov, jelly	65.00	—	—	—
Open, ls, 5"	20.00	—	—	—
Open, ls, 8"	30.00	45.00	35.00	65.00
Creamer	45.00	100.00	45.00	90.00
Goblet	110.00	125.00	175.00	95.00
Pickle	20.00	55.00	40.00	55.00
Pitcher, water	50.00	150.00	150.00	900.00
Salt Shaker, single	50.00	75.00	60.00	70.00
Sauce	15.00	20.00	—	—
Spooner	30.00	45.00	35.00	65.00
Sugar, cov	60.00	135.00	70.00	90.00
Tumbler	40.00	50.00	45.00	65.00
Wine	65.00	80.00	70.00	110.00

TENNESSEE (Jewel and Crescent; Jeweled Rosette)

Made by King Glass Co., Pittsburgh, Pennsylvania, and continued by U. S. Glass Co., in 1899, as part of the States series.

	Clear	Colored Jewels		Clear	Colored Jewels
Bowl, berry	20.00	45.00	Cake Stand		
Bread Plate	40.00	75.00	9½"	35.00	—
Butter, cov	55.00	—	10½"	45.00	—

	Clear	Colored Jewels		Clear	Colored Jewels
Celery Vase	25.00	—	Pitcher		
Compote			Milk	55.00	—
Cov, 5", jelly	40.00	55.00	Water	65.00	—
Open, hs, 8"	45.00	—	Relish	20.00	—
Open, hs, 9"	45.00	—	Spooner	35.00	—
Open, hs, 10"	45.00	—	Sugar, cov	45.00	—
Open, ls, 7"	35.00	—	Syrup	50.00	—
Creamer	25.00	—	Toothpick	45.00	50.00
Goblet	30.00	—	Tumbler	25.00	—
Mug	35.00	—	Wine	35.00	—

TEPEE (Arizona, Duncan #28)

Non-flint pattern made by George A. Duncan and Sons in 1894, Pittsburgh, PA. A ruby stained cakestand is known.

	Clear		Clear
Bowl, berry	18.00	Pitcher, water	40.00
Butter, cov	40.00	Salt Shaker	16.00
Carafe, water	40.00	Sauce	8.00
Celery Vase	30.00	Spooner	25.00
Champagne	35.00	Sugar, cov	36.00
Compote, jelly	22.00	Syrup	45.00
Creamer	32.00	Toothpick	28.00
Cup	8.00	Tumbler	18.00
Goblet	35.00	Wine	30.00

TEXAS (Loop with Stippled Panels)

Non-flint made by U. S. Glass Co., c1900, in the States Pattern series. Occasionally pieces found in ruby stained. Reproduced in solid colors.

	Clear w/gold	Rose Stained		Clear w/gold	Rose Stained
Bowl			Pickle, 8½"	25.00	—
7"	24.00	40.00	Pitcher, water	75.00	—
9", scalloped	35.00	50.00	Plate, 9"	35.00	60.00
Butter, cov	75.00	125.00	Sauce		
Cake Stand, 9½"	60.00	80.00	Flat	12.00	15.00
Celery Tray	30.00	—	Footed	15.00	—
Celery Vase	40.00	—	Spooner	35.00	—
Compote			Sugar		
Cov, hs, 6"	60.00	—	Individual, cov	45.00	—
Cov, hs, 8"	75.00	—	Regular, cov	65.00	—
Open, hs, 5"	40.00	—	Toothpick	35.00	95.00
Creamer			Tumbler	25.00	—
Individual	20.00	—	Vase		
Regular	40.00	—	6½"	25.00	—
Cruet, os	60.00	165.00	9"	35.00	—
Goblet	65.00	95.00	Wine	50.00	100.00

TEXAS BULL'S EYE (Filley, Bull's Eye Variant)

Originated by Bryce Bros., Pittsburgh, Pennsylvania, and continued by Findlay Glass, Findlay, Ohio. Also made in Canada. Originally made in semi-flint (no bell tone, but some lead content).

	Clear		Clear
Butter, cov	55.00	Sugar	
Creamer	35.00	Cov	45.00
Egg Cup	30.00	Open	40.00
Goblet	30.00	Tumbler	50.00
Pitcher, water	55.00	Wine	32.00
Spooner	25.00		

THISTLE (Early Thistle)

Non-flint, made by Bryce, Walker & Co. in 1872.

	Clear		Clear
Bowl, 8″	30.00	Relish	25.00
Butter, cov	55.00	Salt, ftd	35.00
Cake Stand, large	75.00	Sauce, flat	12.00
Compote		Spooner	35.00
Cov, hs	85.00	Sugar	
Cov, ls	50.00	Cov	65.00
Cordial	60.00	Open, buttermilk type	40.00
Creamer, applied handle	65.00	Syrup	100.00
Egg Cup	40.00	Tumbler	40.00
Goblet	50.00	Wine	50.00
Pitcher, water, applied handle	100.00		

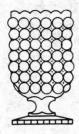

THOUSAND EYE

The original pattern was non-flint made by Adams Glass Co, Tarentum, PA, 1875, and by Richards and Hartley, 1888. (Their Pattern No. 103). It was made in two forms: Adams with a three knob stem finial, and Richards and Hartley with a plain stem with a scalloped bottom. Several glass companies made variations of the original pattern and reproductions were made as late as 1981. Crystal Opalescent was produced by Richards and Hartley only in the original pattern. (Opalescent celery vase $70.00; open compote, 8″, $115.00; 6″ creamer, $85.00; ¼ gallon water pitcher, $140.00; ½ gallon water pitcher, $180.00; 4″ footed sauce, $40.00; spooner, $60.00; and 5″ covered sugar, $80.00). Covered compotes are rare and would command 40% more than open compotes. A 2″ mug in blue is known.

	Amber	Apple Green	Blue	Clear	Vaseline
ABC Plate, 6″, clock center	50.00	55.00	52.00	45.00	52.00
Butter, cov					
6¼″	65.00	75.00	70.00	45.00	90.00
7½″	65.00	75.00	70.00	45.00	90.00
Cake Stand					
10″	50.00	78.00	55.00	30.00	84.00
11″	50.00	78.00	55.00	30.00	84.00

	Amber	Apple Green	Blue	Clear	Vaseline
Celery, hat shape ..	50.00	65.00	60.00	35.00	55.00
Celery Vase, 7"....	50.00	60.00	52.00	45.00	55.00
Christmas Light....	27.00	45.00	35.00	25.00	40.00
Cologne Bottle	25.00	45.00	35.00	20.00	45.00
Compote, cov, ls, 8", sq............	—	100.00	100.00	—	—
Compote, open					
6".............	35.00	40.00	38.00	25.00	38.00
7".............	38.00	44.00	40.00	30.00	40.00
8", round.......	40.00	50.00	44.00	35.00	48.00
8", sq, hs.......	39.00	50.00	48.00	38.00	55.00
9".............	48.00	56.00	52.00	40.00	52.00
10"............	55.00	65.00	60.00	45.00	60.00
Cordial..........	35.00	52.00	40.00	25.00	58.00
Creamer					
4".............	32.00	40.00	36.00	25.00	38.00
6".............	38.00	75.00	55.00	35.00	72.00
Creamer & Sugar Set..........	—	—	—	100.00	—
*Cruet, 6".........	40.00	58.00	47.00	35.00	60.00
Egg Cup..........	65.00	85.00	70.00	45.00	90.00
*Goblet	37.00	42.00	38.00	35.00	45.00
Honey Dish, cov, 6 × 7¼".......	85.00	95.00	90.00	70.00	92.00
Inkwell	45.00	—	75.00	35.00	80.00
Jelly Glass	20.00	25.00	22.00	15.00	23.00
Lamp, Kerosene					
hs, 12"	120.00	150.00	130.00	100.00	140.00
hs, 15"	125.00	155.00	135.00	110.00	150.00
ls, handled	110.00	115.00	110.00	90.00	120.00
Mug					
2½"............	23.00	30.00	25.00	20.00	32.00
3½"............	23.00	30.00	25.00	20.00	32.00
Nappy					
5".............	34.00	—	39.00	30.00	45.00
6".............	39.00	—	44.00	35.00	52.00
8".............	45.00	—	50.00	42.00	60.00
Pickle...........	25.00	30.00	27.00	20.00	29.00
Pitcher					
Milk, cov, 7".....	85.00	110.00	105.00	70.00	105.00
Water, ¼ gal	70.00	85.00	80.00	55.00	80.00
Water, ½ gal	80.00	92.00	84.00	65.00	85.00
Water, 1 gal.....	90.00	100.00	95.00	85.00	95.00
*Plate, sq, folded corners					
6".............	24.00	28.00	26.00	20.00	26.00
8".............	26.00	30.00	28.00	22.00	30.00
10"............	34.00	50.00	36.00	25.00	34.00
Platter					
8 × 11", oblong..	40.00	48.00	42.00	38.00	45.00
11", oval	75.00	80.00	55.00	40.00	75.00
Salt Shaker, pr					
Banded........	60.00	66.00	62.00	58.00	62.00
Plain..........	50.00	60.00	55.00	40.00	56.00
Salt, ind	80.00	95.00	90.00	50.00	90.00
Sauce					
Flat, 4"	10.00	22.00	12.00	8.00	15.00
Footed, 4"......	12.00	25.00	15.00	10.00	20.00
Spooner.........	32.00	48.00	40.00	27.00	45.00

	Amber	Apple Green	Blue	Clear	Vaseline
*String Holder	35.00	60.00	45.00	29.00	40.00
Sugar, cov, 5"	52.00	70.00	54.00	45.00	55.00
Syrup, pewter top . .	80.00	100.00	70.00	55.00	70.00
Toothpick					
Hat	35.00	52.00	58.00	30.00	45.00
Plain	35.00	50.00	55.00	25.00	40.00
Tray, water					
12½ ", round	64.00	78.00	65.00	55.00	60.00
14", oval	65.00	80.00	75.00	60.00	74.00
*Tumbler	26.00	62.00	34.00	21.00	30.00
*Wine	35.00	50.00	40.00	20.00	40.00

THREE-FACE

Non-flint made by George E. Duncan & Son, Pittsburgh, Pennsylvania, c1872. Designed by John E. Miller, a designer with Duncan, who later became a member of the firm. Companies in the Pittsburgh area produced many patterns in expectation of the 1876 Philadelphia Centennial Exposition. It has been heavily reproduced.

	Clear		Clear
Biscuit Jar, cov	300.00	Cov, ls, 4"	150.00
Butter, cov	140.00	Open, hs, 7"	75.00
Cake Stand		Open, hs, 8"	75.00
9"	165.00	Open, hs, 9"	135.00
10"	170.00	Open, ls, 6"	75.00
11"	175.00	Open, jelly, paneled	
Celery Vase		"Huber" top	85.00
Plain	95.00	Creamer	135.00
Scalloped	95.00	Goblet	85.00
Champagne		Lamp, Oil	140.00
Hollow stem	250.00	Marmalade Jar	200.00
Saucer type	150.00	Pitcher, water	295.00
Claret	85.00	Salt Dip	35.00
Compote		Salt & Pepper	75.00
Cov, hs, 7"	165.00	Sauce, ftd	25.00
Cov, hs, 8"	175.00	Spooner	80.00
Cov, hs, 9"	190.00	Sugar, cov	110.00
Cov, hs, 10"	225.00	Wine	50.00
Cov, ls, 6"	160.00		

THREE PANEL

Non-flint made by Richards & Hartley Co., Tarentum, Pennsylvania, c1888, and by U. S. Glass Co. in 1891.

	Amber	Blue	Clear	Vaseline
Bowl				
7"	25.00	40.00	20.00	45.00
8½"	25.00	40.00	20.00	45.00
10"	40.00	50.00	35.00	48.00
Butter, cov	45.00	50.00	40.00	50.00

	Amber	Blue	Clear	Vaseline
Celery Vase, ruffled top	—	40.00	35.00	—
Compote, open, ls, 7"	35.00	55.00	25.00	40.00
Creamer	40.00	45.00	38.00	40.00
Cruet	250.00	—	—	—
Goblet	32.00	42.00	28.00	38.00
Mug	35.00	45.00	25.00	35.00
Pitcher, water	95.00	65.00	40.00	60.00
Sauce, ftd	20.00	12.00	10.00	18.00
Spooner	40.00	45.00	30.00	42.00
Sugar, cov	55.00	60.00	48.00	70.00
Tumbler	35.00	40.00	20.00	30.00

THUMBPRINT, EARLY (Argus, Giant Baby Thumbprint)

Flint originally produced by Bakewell, Pears and Co, Pittsburgh, PA, c1850-60. Made by several factories in various forms. Reproduced in color by Fenton.

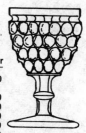

	Clear		Clear
Ale Glass	40.00	Creamer	60.00
Banana Boat	150.00	Decanter, qt, os	
Berry Set, 7 pcs	195.00	Pattern base	125.00
Bitters Bottle	140.00	Plain base	85.00
Cake Stand	50.00	Egg Cup	40.00
Celery Vase		Goblet	50.00
Patterned base	100.00	Honey Dish	10.00
Plain base	90.00	Plate, 8"	50.00
Champagne	100.00	Salt, master, ftd	35.00
Claret	70.00	Spooner	48.50
Compote		Sugar, cov	65.00
* Cov, 4"	80.00	Tumbler	45.00
* Cov, ls, 7"	100.00	Wine	75.00
Open, 8", scalloped top, flared	125.00		

TOKYO

Made by Jefferson Glass Co., Steubenville, Ohio, c1905. Also found in clear, blue, and apple green—all with gold trim. Some reproductions made by and signed Fenton.

	Blue Opal	Green Opal	White Opal
Bowl, berry	55.00	45.00	35.00
Butter, cov	135.00	100.00	70.00
Compote, jelly	40.00	45.00	35.00
Creamer	80.00	60.00	50.00
Cruet	185.00	140.00	90.00
Dish, 6½"	40.00	45.00	40.00
Pitcher, water	185.00	150.00	100.00
Salt Shaker, single	50.00	40.00	30.00

	Blue Opal	Green Opal	White Opal
Sauce	30.00	25.00	20.00
Spooner	45.00	40.00	30.00
Sugar, cov	85.00	75.00	60.00
Toothpick	110.00	80.00	50.00
Tumbler	50.00	45.00	35.00
Vase	60.00	60.00	45.00

TORPEDO (Pigmy)

Non-flint made by Thompson Glass Co., Uniontown, Pennsylvania, c1889. A black amethyst master salt ($150.00) also known.

	Clear	Ruby Stained		Clear	Ruby Stained
Banana Stand.....	75.00	—	Marmalade Jar, cov .	55.00	—
Bowl			Pickle Castor, sp		
Cov, 8″	40.00	—	holder	125.00	—
Open, 4″	—	20.00	Pitcher		
Open, 7″	18.00	—	Milk, 8½″	75.00	150.00
Open, 8″	20.00	—	Water, 10½″.....	85.00	175.00
Open, 9″	20.00	45.00	Punch Cup	25.00	—
Open, 9½″, flared			Salt		
rim.	38.00	—	Ind	20.00	—
Butter, cov	85.00	—	Master	30.00	—
Cake Stand, 10″ ...	55.00	—	Salt Shaker, single, 2		
Celery Vase, scal-			types.	50.00	—
loped top	42.00	—	Sauce, 4½″, collared		
Compote			base	15.00	—
Cov, hs, 13¾″ ...	165.00	—	Spooner, scalloped		
Cov, hs, 4″, jelly..	65.00	—	top	45.00	—
Open, hs, 8½″ ...	60.00	—	Sugar		
Creamer.........	50.00	—	Cov...........	65.00	—
Cruet, os, applied			Open	30.00	—
handle.	80.00	—	Syrup...........	95.00	175.00
Cup and Saucer ...	65.00	—	Tray, water		
Decanter, os, 8″ ...	85.00	—	10″, round	85.00	—
Finger Bowl	48.00	—	11¾″, clover		
Goblet	55.00	85.00	shaped	75.00	—
Lamp			Tumbler	36.00	50.00
3″, handled	75.00	—	Wine	75.00	—
8″, plain base, pat-					
tern on bowl ...	85.00	—			

TREE OF LIFE (Portland's)

Flint and non-flint pattern made by Portland Glass Co., 1864–74. Originally made in green, purple, yellow, amber, and light and dark blue. Color is rare today. A blue finger bowl in a SP holder is valued at $175.00.

	Flint		Flint
Bowl, berry, oval	30.00	Cologne Bottle, facetted	
Butter, cov	55.00	stopper	48.00
Celery Vase, SP frame	55.00	Champagne	55.00

	Flint
Compote	
Open, hs, 8½"	125.00
Open, hs, 10"	110.00
Open, ls, 10"	50.00
Creamer	
Applied handle	70.00
Molded handle	50.00
Silverplated holder	75.00
Egg Cup	30.00
Epergne, sgd "P.G. Co. Patd"	125.00
Finger Bowl, underplate	60.00
Fruit Dish, SP holder	90.00
Goblet	
Clear shield on side	50.00
Plain	35.00
Regular, sgd "P.G. Flint"	65.00
Ice Cream Tray	50.00

	Flint
Lemonade	25.00
Pitcher	
Milk	
Applied handle	95.00
Molded handle	65.00
Water	
Applied handle	95.00
Molded handle	65.00
Plate, 6"	25.00
Sauce	
3¾"	12.00
Leaf shape	15.00
Spooner	35.00
Sugar	
Covered	70.00
Silverplated holder	75.00
Tray, water	90.00

TRIPLE TRIANGLE

Made by Doyle and Co. of Pittsburgh, Pennsylvania, in 1890. Continued by U. S. Glass Co. after 1891. Also found in clear (50% less).

	Ruby Stained
Butter, cov, handled	80.00
Celery Tray	45.00
Creamer	55.00
Cup	30.00
* Goblet	45.00
Mug	35.00
Pitcher, water	135.00

	Ruby Stained
Sauce, flat	20.00
Spooner, handled	55.00
Sugar, handled, cov	75.00
Table Set, 4 pc	265.00
Tumbler	38.50
*Wine	45.00

TRUNCATED CUBE (Thompson's #77)

Non-flint made by Thompson Glass Co., Uniontown, Pennsylvania, c1892. Also found with engraving.

	Clear	Ruby Stained
Bowl		
4", berry	—	15.00
8"	—	40.00
Butter, cov	50.00	90.00
Celery Vase	40.00	55.00
Creamer		
Ind	20.00	35.00
Regular	35.00	75.00
Decanter, os, 12" h	60.00	150.00
Goblet	30.00	50.00

	Clear	Ruby Stained
Pitcher, water, tankard	50.00	110.00
Spooner	30.00	50.00
Salt Shaker, single	15.00	30.00
Sugar, cov	30.00	70.00
Syrup	40.00	100.00
Toothpick	30.00	40.00
Tumbler	22.50	35.00
Wine	35.00	40.00

TULIP WITH SAWTOOTH

Originally made in flint glass by Bryce Bros., Pittsburgh, Pennsylvania, c1860. Later made in non-flint.

	Flint	Non-Flint		Flint	Non-Flint
Bottle, bar	70.00	—	Egg Cup	40.00	—
Bottle, pint	—	45.00	Goblet	65.00	30.00
Butter, cov	125.00	82.00	Mug	80.00	—
Celery Vase	85.00	24.00	Pitcher, water	150.00	—
Champagne	75.00	35.00	Plate, 6"	60.00	—
Compote			Pomade Jar	45.00	—
Cov, hs, 6"	90.00	—	Salt, master, plain		
Cov, hs, 8½"	95.00	—	edge	28.00	15.00
Cov, ls, 8½"	85.00	—	Spooner	35.00	—
Open, hs, 8"	—	60.00	Sugar, cov	95.00	—
Open, ls, 9"	60.00	—	Tumbler		
Creamer	85.00	—	Bar	85.00	28.00
Cruet			Footed	50.00	—
Applied handle	60.00	—	* Wine	60.00	20.00
Pressed handle	—	40.00			
Decanter, os, handled	150.00	—			

TWO PANEL

Non-flint in oval forms made by Richards and Hartley Glass Co., Tarentum, Pennsylvania, 1880–1886, and by U. S. Glass Co. in 1891.

	Amber	Apple Green	Blue	Clear	Vaseline
Bowl					
5½"	35.00	40.00	40.00	15.00	25.00
8"	35.00	40.00	40.00	20.00	35.00
10 x 8½ x 3"	—	50.00	—	—	—
Butter, cov	50.00	55.00	55.00	30.00	40.00
Celery Vase	45.00	50.00	50.00	25.00	40.00
Compote					
Cov, hs, 6½", oval	55.00	—	—	35.00	75.00
Cov, hs, 8"	85.00	85.00	95.00	35.00	95.00
Creamer	40.00	45.00	45.00	20.00	35.00
* Goblet	30.00	35.00	45.00	28.00	40.00
Lamp, high standard	85.00	125.00	100.00	45.00	115.00
Mug, 2 sizes	30.00	35.00	40.00	20.00	30.00
Pitcher, water	60.00	60.00	65.00	35.00	50.00
Platter	25.00	—	—	—	—
Salt					
Ind	18.00	15.00	18.00	5.00	15.00
Master	20.00	25.00	20.00	10.00	12.00
Salt Shaker	40.00	45.00	40.00	25.00	30.00
Sauce					
Flat, oval	10.00	12.00	10.00	8.00	10.00
Footed	12.00	14.00	15.00	10.00	12.00
Spooner	45.00	50.00	45.00	25.00	35.00
Sugar, cov	50.00	55.00	55.00	30.00	40.00
Tray, water	50.00	55.00	55.00	45.00	50.00
Tumbler	35.00	42.50	35.00	15.00	40.00
Waste Bowl	40.00	45.00	40.00	20.00	30.00
*Wine	40.00	45.00	40.00	20.00	30.00

U. S. COIN

Non-flint frosted, clear, and gilted pattern made by U. S. Glass Co. in 1892 for three or four months. Production was stopped by U. S. Treasury because real coins, dated as early as 1878, were used in the molds. 1892 coin date is the most common.

	Clear	Frosted		Clear	Frosted
Bowl			Goblet	250.00	400.00
6″	170.00	220.00	Goblet, dimes	—	550.00
9″	215.00	325.00	Lamp		
Bread Plate	175.00	275.00	Round font	275.00	450.00
Butter, cov, dollars			Square font	300.00	—
and halves	250.00	500.00	Mug, handled	185.00	300.00
Cake Stand, 10″ . . .	225.00	400.00	Pickle	200.00	—
Celery			Pitcher, water, dol-		
Tray	200.00	—	lars	400.00	800.00
Vase, quarters . . .	135.00	350.00	Sauce, ftd, 4″, quar-		
Champagne	—	400.00	ters	100.00	185.00
Compote			Spooner, quarters . .	225.00	325.00
Cov, hs, 7″	300.00	500.00	Sugar, cov	225.00	350.00
Open, hs, 7″, quar-			Syrup, dated pewter		
ters and dimes . .	200.00	300.00	lid	—	525.00
Open, hs, 7″, quar-			*Toothpick	180.00	275.00
ters and halves.	225.00	350.00	Tray, water, 8″, rect .	275.00	—
Creamer	350.00	500.00	Tumbler	135.00	235.00
Cruet, os	375.00	500.00	Waste Bowl.	225.00	—
Epergne	500.00	1,000.00	Wine	225.00	375.00

U. S. SHERATON

Made by U. S. Glass Co in 1912. This pattern was made only in clear, but can be found trimmed with gold or platinum. Some pieces are marked with the intertwined U. S. Glass trademark

	Clear		Clear
Bon Bon, 6″, ftd.	15.00	Squat, medium	30.00
Bowl		Tankard	35.00
6″, ftd, sq	15.00	Plate, sq	
8″, flat.	12.00	4½″	8.00
8″, ftd, sq	14.00	9″	12.00
Bureau Tray	30.00	Pomade Jar	14.00
Butter, cov.	35.00	Puff Box	14.00
Celery Tray	30.00	Punch Bowl, cov, 14″	90.00
Compote		Ring Tree	25.00
Open, 4″, jelly	12.00	Salt Shaker	
Open, 6″	14.00	Squat	12.00
Creamer		Tall	15.00
After dinner, tall, sq ft	12.00	Salt, ind	14.00
Berry, bulbous, sq ft	15.00	Sardine Box	35.00
Large	18.00	Spooner	
Cruet, os	25.00	Handled	15.00
Finger Bowl, underplate. . . .	24.00	Tray	12.00
Goblet	18.00	Sugar, cov	
Lamp, miniature	50.00	Individual.	15.00
Marmalade Jar	30.00	Regular.	20.00
Mug	15.00	Sundae Dish.	8.50
Mustard Jar, cov	25.00	Syrup, glass lid	35.00
Pickle.	10.00	Tumbler	
Pin Tray	9.00	Iced Tea	12.00
Pitcher, water		Water	10.00
One half gallon	30.00		

UTAH (Frost Flower, Twinkle Star)

Non-flint made by U. S. Glass Co. in 1901 in the States Pattern series. Add 25% for frosting.

	Clear		Clear
Bowl		Creamer	30.00
Cov, 6″	20.00	Goblet	25.00
Open, 8″	18.00	Pickle	12.00
Butter, cov	35.00	Pitcher, water	48.00
Cake Plate, 9″	20.00	Salt & Pepper, pr.	40.00
Cake Stand		Salt & Pepper, in holder	45.00
8″	20.00	Sauce, 4″	9.00
10″	30.00	Spooner	15.00
Celery Vase	20.00	Sugar, cov	35.00
Compote		Tumbler	15.00
Cov, ls, 6″, jelly	25.00	Wine	45.00
Open, ls, 6″, jelly	18.00		

VALENCIA WAFFLE (Block and Star #1)

Made by Adams & Co., c1885–1895; continued by U. S. Glass after 1891.

	Amber	Apple Green	Blue	Clear	Vaseline
Bowl, berry	15.00	25.00	20.00	12.00	15.00
Bread Plate	30.00	—	30.00	25.00	35.00
Butter, cov	55.00	65.00	45.00	40.00	42.50
Cake Stand, 10″	60.00	40.00	45.00	38.00	40.00
Celery Vase	40.00	48.00	45.00	35.00	40.00
Castor set, complete	60.00	—	65.00	50.00	60.00
Compote					
Cov, hs, 7″ d	60.00	75.00	75.00	50.00	70.00
Cov, ls	40.00	50.00	65.00	30.00	40.00
Creamer	35.00	—	45.00	30.00	32.50
Dish	20.00	—	25.00	10.00	20.00
Goblet	40.00	—	40.00	30.00	35.00
Pitcher					
Milk	40.00	50.00	45.00	35.00	40.00
Water	65.00	50.00	50.00	40.00	45.00
Relish or Pickle	20.00	20.00	25.00	15.00	20.00
Salt Dip	35.00	—	—	—	—
Sauce, ftd, 4″, sq.	12.00	—	18.00	10.00	15.00
Spooner	30.00	—	35.00	20.00	35.00
Sugar, cov	40.00	—	50.00	35.00	45.00
Syrup	95.00	80.00	95.00	—	—
Tray, 10½ x 8″	—	35.00	—	—	—
Tumbler	25.00	—	30.00	18.00	25.00

VERMONT (Honeycomb with Flower Rim; Inverted Thumbprint with Daisy Band)

Non-flint made by U. S. Glass Co., 1899–1903. Also made in custard (usually decorated), chocolate, caramel, and novelty slag, milk glass, and blue. Toothpick has been reproduced in clear and opaque colors.

	Clear w/gold	Green w/gold		Clear w/gold	Green w/gold
Basket, handle	30.00	45.00	Pitcher, water	40.00	100.00
Bowl, berry	25.00	45.00	Sauce	15.00	25.00
Butter, cov	40.00	75.00	Spooner	25.00	75.00
Celery Tray	30.00	35.00	Sugar, cov	35.00	80.00
Creamer	30.00	55.00	*Toothpick	35.00	60.00
Goblet	40.00	60.00	Tumbler	20.00	40.00

VIKING (Bearded Head)

Non-flint, made by Hobbs, Brockunier, and Co. in 1876 as their centennial pattern. No tumbler or goblet originally made.

	Clear		Clear
Apothecary Jar, cov	45.00	Creamer, 2 types	50.00
Bowl		Egg Cup	40.00
Cov, 8", oval	45.00	Marmalade Jar	100.00
Cov, 9", oval	55.00	Mug, applied handle	50.00
Bread Plate	70.00	Pitcher, water	110.00
Butter, cov	75.00	Relish	25.00
Celery Vase	45.00	Salt, master	40.00
Compote		Sauce	15.00
Cov, hs, 9"	95.00	Spooner	35.00
Cov, ls, 8", oval	75.00	Sugar, cov	65.00
Open, hs	60.00		

WAFFLE AND THUMBPRINT

Flint made by the New England Glass Co. and Boston & Sandwich Glass Co., c1850. Later by Bryce, Walker & Co., Pittsburgh, Pennsylvania.

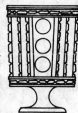

	Clear		Clear
Bowl, 5 x 7"	30.00	Lamp	
Butter, cov	95.00	9½"	115.00
Celery Vase	105.00	11", whale oil	175.00
Champagne	70.00	Pitcher, water	400.00
Claret	100.00	Salt, master	45.00
Compote, cov, hs	150.00	Spooner	45.00
Creamer	125.00	Sugar, cov	125.00
Decanter, os		Sweetmeat, cov, hs, 6"	150.00
Pint	100.00	Tumbler	
Quart	145.00	Flip Glass	125.00
Egg Cup	45.00	Water, ftd	75.00
Goblet, knob stem	65.00	Whiskey	95.00
		Wine	60.00

WASHINGTON (Early)

Flint made by New England Glass Co., c1869.

	Clear		Clear
Ale Glass	125.00	Butter, cov	175.00
Bowl, 6 x 9", oval	45.00	Celery Vase	95.00
Bottle, bitters	85.00	Champagne	125.00

	Clear		Clear
Compote		Lamp	145.00
Cov, hs, 6″	125.00	Pitcher, water	250.00
Cov, hs, 10″	175.00	Plate, 6″	60.00
Cordial	150.00	Salt, master	55.00
Creamer	200.00	Sauce	25.00
Decanter, os	150.00	Spooner	65.00
Egg Cup	75.00	Sugar, cov	125.00
Goblet	95.00	Tumbler	85.00
Honey Dish, 3½″	30.00	Wine	100.00

WASHINGTON CENTENNIAL (Chain with Diamonds)

Non-flint made by Gillinder & Co., Philadelphia, Pennsylvania, for centennial celebration.

	Clear		Clear
Bread Plates		Creamer, applied handle	90.00
"Carpenter's Hall"	100.00	Egg Cup	45.00
"George Washington"	100.00	Goblet	48.00
"Independence Hall"	100.00	Pitcher, applied handle	
Butter, cov	80.00	Milk	85.00
Cake Stand		Water	100.00
8½″	45.00	Relish, claw handle, dated	48.00
10″	65.00	Salt, master, oval, flat	35.00
Celery Vase	60.00	Sauce, flat	15.00
Champagne	65.00	Spooner	35.00
Compote		Sugar, cov	70.00
Cov, hs, 9″	75.00	Syrup, metal lid	150.00
Open, hs, 8″	45.00	Wine	50.00

WEDDING RING (Double Wedding Ring)

Flint, c1860; non-flint, c1870s. Toothpick, frequently seen in muddy purple, not originally made. Reproduced in various colors.

	Flint		Flint
Butter, cov	100.00	Pitcher, water	165.00
Celery Vase	80.00	Relish	60.00
Champagne	95.00	Sauce	30.00
Cordial	75.00	Spooner	80.00
Creamer	85.00	Sugar, cov	100.00
Decanter, os	125.00	Tumbler	85.00
Goblet	85.00	Wine	95.00

WESTWARD HO! (Pioneer)

Non-flint, usually frosted, made by Gillinder & Sons, Philadelphia, Pennsylvania, late 1870s. Molds made by Jacobus who also made Classic. Has been reproduced.

	Clear		Clear
Bread Plate	180.00	Compote	
Butter, cov	185.00	Cov, hs, 5″	225.00
Celery Vase	125.00	Cov, hs, 9″	235.00

	Clear			Clear
Cov, ls, 5"	150.00	Pitcher, water		200.00
Open, hs, 8"	125.00	Sauce, ftd, 4½"		35.00
Creamer	95.00	Spooner		85.00
Goblet	80.00	Sugar, cov		175.00
Marmalade Jar, cov	175.00	Wine		200.00
Mug				
2"	225.00			
3½"	150.00			

WHEAT AND BARLEY (Duquesne)

Non-flint made by Bryce Bros., Pittsburgh, Pennsylvania, in the late 1870s. Later made by U. S. Glass Co., 1891.

	Amber	Blue	Clear	Vaseline
Bowl, 8", cov.	35.00	40.00	25.00	35.00
Butter, cov	45.00	60.00	35.00	55.00
Cake Stand				
8"	30.00	45.00	20.00	30.00
10"	40.00	50.00	30.00	40.00
Compote				
Cov, hs, 7"	45.00	55.00	40.00	45.00
Cov, hs, 8"	50.00	55.00	45.00	50.00
Open, hs, jelly	32.50	40.00	30.00	35.00
Creamer	30.00	40.00	28.00	35.00
Goblet	35.00	47.50	25.00	40.00
Mug	30.00	40.00	20.00	35.00
Pitcher				
Milk	45.00	65.00	30.00	55.00
Water	55.00	70.00	45.00	65.00
Plate				
7"	20.00	30.00	15.00	25.00
9", closed handles	25.00	35.00	20.00	40.00
Salt & Pepper	45.00	55.00	35.00	45.00
Sauce				
Flat, handle	12.00	15.00	10.00	15.00
Footed	15.00	15.00	10.00	15.00
Spooner	30.00	40.00	24.00	30.00
Sugar, cov	40.00	50.00	35.00	40.00
Syrup	175.00	195.00	45.00	—
Tumbler	38.50	35.00	18.00	30.00

WILDFLOWER

Non-flint made by Adams & Co., Pittsburgh, Pennsylvania, c1874, and by U. S. Glass Co., c1898. This pattern has been heavily reproduced.

	Amber	Apple Green	Blue	Clear	Vaseline
Bowl, 8", sq	25.00	35.00	35.00	18.00	25.00
Butter, cov					
Collared base	40.00	50.00	50.00	35.00	45.00
Flat	35.00	45.00	45.00	30.00	40.00
Cake Stand, 10½"	50.00	80.00	75.00	45.00	50.00
Champagne	40.00	55.00	50.00	32.00	45.00

	Amber	Apple Green	Blue	Clear	Vaseline
Celery Vase	55.00	60.00	55.00	35.00	55.00
Compote					
Cov, hs, 8", oblong	80.00	85.00	85.00	50.00	75.00
Cov, ls, 7"	—	—	70.00	—	—
Open, hs	80.00	—	—	—	—
Creamer	32.50	50.00	35.00	40.00	45.00
* Goblet	36.00	40.00	40.00	30.00	40.00
Pitcher, water	55.00	75.00	50.00	40.00	65.00
Plate, 10", sq	30.00	30.00	45.00	25.00	30.00
Platter					
10", oblong	40.00	45.00	40.00	30.00	30.00
11 x 8", deep scalloped edges . . .	—	—	45.00	—	—
Relish	20.00	22.00	20.00	18.00	20.00
*Salt, turtle	45.00	50.00	50.00	30.00	40.00
Salt Shaker	25.00	55.00	35.00	20.00	45.00
Sauce, ftd, 4", round	17.50	18.00	18.00	15.00	17.50
Spooner	30.00	35.00	30.00	20.00	40.00
Sugar, cov	45.00	45.00	50.00	30.00	45.00
Syrup	125.00	150.00	140.00	65.00	150.00
Tray, water, oval . . .	50.00	60.00	60.00	40.00	55.00
Tumbler	40.00	35.00	35.00	25.00	35.00
Wine	45.00	45.00	45.00	32.00	40.00

WILLOW OAK (Wreath)

Non-flint made by Bryce Bros. Pittsburgh, Pennsylvania, c1880, and by U. S. Glass Company in 1891.

	Amber	Blue	Canary	Clear
Bowl, 8"	25.00	40.00	48.00	20.00
Butter, cov	55.00	65.00	80.00	40.00
Cake Stand, 8½" . . .	60.00	65.00	70.00	45.00
Celery Vase	45.00	60.00	75.00	35.00
Compote				
Cov, hs, 7½"	50.00	65.00	80.00	40.00
Open, 7"	30.00	40.00	48.00	25.00
Creamer	40.00	50.00	60.00	35.00
Goblet	40.00	50.00	60.00	35.00
Mug	35.00	45.00	54.00	30.00
Pitcher				
Milk	50.00	60.00	72.00	45.00
Water	55.00	60.00	72.00	50.00
Plate				
7"	35.00	45.00	54.00	30.00
9", closed handles	32.50	35.00	42.00	30.00
Salt Shaker	25.00	40.00	48.00	20.00
Sauce				
Flat, handle, sq . .	15.00	20.00	24.00	10.00
Footed, 4"	20.00	25.00	30.00	15.00
Spooner	35.00	40.00	48.00	30.00
Sugar, cov	68.50	70.00	75.00	40.00

	Amber	Blue	Canary	Clear
Tray, water, 10½″ ..	35.00	50.00	60.00	30.00
Tumbler	30.00	35.00	42.00	25.00
Waste Bowl.	35.00	40.00	48.00	30.00

WINDFLOWER

Non-flint, made by McKee Glass Co, in the late 1870s.

	Clear		Clear
Bowl, 8″, oval	30.00	Pitcher, water, applied handle	65.00
Butter, cov	50.00	Salt, master, ftd.	25.00
Celery Vase	40.00	Sauce	15.00
Compote		Spooner	30.00
Cov, hs	65.00	Sugar	
Cov, ls, 8″	75.00	Cov.	60.00
Open, ls, 7″	35.00	Open	35.00
Creamer, applied handle . . .	40.00	Tumbler	40.00
Egg Cup.	35.00	Wine	45.00
Goblet	38.00		

WISCONSIN (Beaded Dewdrop)

Non-flint made in Pittsburgh, Pennsylvania, in the 1880s. Later made by U. S. Glass Co. in Indiana, 1903. One of States patterns. Toothpick reproduced in colors.

	Clear		Clear
Banana Stand.	75.00	Cup & Saucer.	50.00
Bowl		Goblet	50.00
4½ x 6½″	28.00	Marmalade Jar, straight sides, glass lid.	125.00
6″, oval, handled, cov. . . .	25.00	Mug.	35.00
7″, round	30.00	Pitcher	
8″, oblong, preserve	35.00	Milk.	55.00
Butter, flat flange.	75.00	Water	70.00
Cake Stand, 9½″.	55.00	Plate, 6¾″.	25.00
Celery Tray.	45.00	Punch Cup	12.00
Celery Vase	45.00	Relish.	25.00
Compote		Salt Shaker, single	30.00
Cov, hs, 6″.	45.00	Spooner	30.00
Cov, hs, 7″.	45.00	Sugar, cov	55.00
Cov, hs, 8″.	50.00	Sugar Shaker	60.00
Open, hs, 9½″	35.00	Sweetmeat, 5″, ftd, cov	35.00
Open, hs, 10½″	35.00	Syrup.	75.00
Open, jelly	20.00	* Toothpick	55.00
Condiment Set, SP, horse-radish on tray	100.00	Tumbler	40.00
Creamer.	50.00	Wine	50.00
Cruet, os	55.00		

WYOMING (Enigma)

Made by U. S. Glass Co., in the States Pattern series, 1903.

	Clear		Clear
Bowl, 8″	15.00	Goblet	55.00
Butter, cov	50.00	Mug	40.00
Cake Plate	55.00	Pitcher, water	75.00
Cake Stand	70.00	Relish	12.00
Compote, cov, hs, 8″ d	85.00	Spooner	30.00
Creamer		Sugar, cov	45.00
Covered	50.00	Wine	60.00
Open	35.00		

X-RAY

Non-flint made by Riverside Glass Works, Wellsburgh, West Virginia, 1896 to 1898. Prices are for pieces with gold trim. A toothpick holder is known in amethyst ($125.00). Also, a toothpick holder with marigold iridescence is known ($35.00).

	Clear	Emerald Green		Clear	Emerald Green
Bowl, berry, 8″, beaded rim	25.00	45.00	Salt & Pepper, pr	25.00	45.00
Butter, cov	40.00	75.00	Sauce, flat	8.00	15.00
Celery Vase	—	50.00	Spooner	25.00	40.00
Compote, cov, hs	40.00	65.00	Sugar		
Creamer			Cov, regular	35.00	50.00
Individual	15.00	30.00	Open, individual	18.00	30.00
Regular	30.00	60.00	Syrup	—	185.00
Cruet	—	125.00	Toothpick	30.00	60.00
Pitcher, water	40.00	75.00	Tumbler	12.00	25.00

YALE (Crow-foot, Turkey Track)

Non-flint made by McKee and Brothers Glass Co., Jeannette, Pennsylvania, patented, 1887.

	Clear		Clear
Butter, cov	45.00	Pitcher, water	55.00
Cake Stand	50.00	Syrup	65.00
Celery Vase	35.00	Salt Shaker, single	30.00
Compote		Sauce, flat	10.00
Cov, hs	48.00	Spooner	25.00
Open, scalloped rim	25.00	Sugar, cov	35.00
Creamer	30.00	Tumbler	20.00
Goblet	35.00		

ZIPPER (Cobb)

Non-flint made by Richards & Hartley, Tarentum, Pennsylvania, c1880.

	Clear		Clear
Bowl, 7″	15.00	Celery Vase	25.00
Butter, cov	40.00	Cheese, cov	55.00

	Clear			Clear
Compote, cov, ls, 8″	45.00		Salt Dip	5.00
Creamer.	35.00		Sauce	
Cruet, os	42.00		Flat.	5.00
Goblet	20.00		Footed	10.00
Pitcher, water, ½ gal	40.00		Spooner	25.00
Relish, 10″	15.00		Sugar, cov	35.00

ZIPPERED BLOCK (Cryptic, Nova Scotia Ribbon & Star, Duncan #90)

Non-flint made by George A. Duncan & Sons, Pittsburgh, Pennsylvania, in the late 1870s and later by U. S. Glass. Also made in Canada. Comes frosted and frosted with cut stars. Add 20% for frosting.

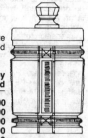

	Clear	Ruby Stained			Clear	Ruby Stained
Butter, cov	75.00	150.00		Pitcher, water	125.00	185.00
Celery	40.00	—		Salt Shaker.	50.00	80.00
Compote, cov, hs . .	125.00	—		Sauce	15.00	25.00
Creamer.	45.00	100.00		Spooner	30.00	60.00
Goblet	40.00	60.00		Sugar, cov	60.00	115.00
Lamp	85.00	—		Tumbler	30.00	45.00
Pickle, oblong	25.00	40.00				

MISCELLANEOUS

Alaska, table set, 4 pcs, vaseline opalescent	600.00
Argus Variant, wooden master mold for tumbler, 5½″, dark mellowed hardwood	80.00
Ashburton, wooden master mold for goblet, 8⅜″, dark mellowed hardwood, probably Sandwich	375.00
Bellflower, cologne bottle, 9¼″, coarse rib, clambroth, matching faceted stopper, mkd Eau de Cologne	300.00
Bird and Strawberry, goblet, colored, gilded	400.00
Bull's Eye with Fans, celery vase, 8½″, flint, bull's eye pattern on base	50.00
Chilson, goblet, 6⅝″	120.00
Duchess, toothpick, green, gold trim . .	140.00
Four Petal, creamer, 6⅞″, flint, applied handle	135.00
Frosted Classic, vase, ftd, non-flint . . .	75.00
Heart, creamer, 4½″	80.00
Lacy Medallion, toothpick, clambroth, hp floral dec	45.00
Palace, perfume bottle, 5¾″, polished pontil	120.00
Panama, sweet pea bowl, flaring edges	20.00
Sandwich Star, spillholder, electric blue	565.00
Swag With Brackets, table set, 3 pc, blue opalescent	250.00
Tape Measure/Shield, creamer, 6¼″, flint, applied handle	60.00

Thumbprint/Argus, compote, cov, hs, 18¾ x 10⅛″, flint, solid applied finial, thick scalloped patterned base, minor shallow chips	1,200.00
U. S. Coin, compote, open, hs, 8 x 7⅞″, frosted half dollars	375.00
U. S. Regal, basket, wide handle	40.00

S.E.G.

PAUL REVERE POTTERY

History: Paul Revere Pottery, Boston, Massachusetts, was an outgrowth of a club known as "The Saturday Evening Girls." The S.E.G. was a group of young female immigrants who met on Saturday nights for reading and crafts such as ceramics.

Regular production began in 1908. The name Paul Revere was adopted because the pottery was located near the Old North Church. In 1915 the firm moved to Brighton, Massachusetts. Known as the "Bowl Shop," the pottery grew steadily. In spite of popular acceptance and technical advancements, the pottery required continual subsidies. It finally closed in January, 1942.

Items produced ranged from plain and decorated vases to tablewares to illustrated tiles. Many decorated wares were incised and glazed either in an Art Nouveau matte finish or an ocasional high glaze.

In addition to the impressed mark, paper "Bowl Shop" labels were used prior to 1915. Pieces also can be found dated with P.R.P. or S.E.G. painted on the base.

References: Paul Evans, *Art Pottery of the United States,* Everybodys Press, inc., 1974, Ralph and Terry Kovel, *The Kovels' Collector's guide to American Art Pottery,* Crown Publishers, Inc., 1974.

Bowl, child's, blue tones, yellow and green center design, 5½" d, 2¼" h, $175.00.

Bookends, pr, 5 x 3¾", rect, owls on branch, turquoise ground, marked "S.E.G."	385.00
Bowl, 5", blue, marked "S.E.G., 1921"	75.00
Creamer	
2", blue bands and squirrel dec	150.00
3½", mountains, trees, and sky, beige ground, marked "S.E.G."	260.00
Egg Cup, underplate, yellow chick dec, blue ground, marked "S.E.G."	165.00
Hatpin Holder, incised daisy motif, blue ground, gold trim, marked "S.E.G."	165.00
Jug, 4½", rabbit dec, yellow ground, border marked "David-His Jug"	175.00
Plate	
6", green spatter, dark blue ground	32.00
8", dancing yellow chicks, blue band dec, marked "S.E.G."	325.00

8½", floral border, three color dec, marked "S.E.G."	45.00
Tile, 4 x 6", incised scene of Paul Revere on horse, dog at his side, inscription "A Glimmer & then a Gleam of Light," shades of blue, green, brown, and white, artist sgd "Rose Buchini, 1911"	500.00
Trivet, 5½" sq, stylized mustard yellow crocus, green leaves in corners, darker green ground, artist sgd "Albina Mangini, 1911," partial paper label	900.00
Vase, cylindrical, incised stylized cypress trees, blue and green landscape, marked "S.E.G., 1913"	3,850.00
Wall Pocket, 6"	
Mottled blue glaze, orig paper label	115.00
Turquoise	70.00

PEACHBLOW

History: Peachblow, an art glass which derives its name from a fine Chinese glazed porcelain, resembles a peach or crushed strawberries in color. Three American glass manufacturers and two English firms produced peachblow glass in the late 1880s. A fourth American firm renewed the process in the 1950s. The glass from each firm has its own identifying characteristics.

Hobbs, Brockunier & Co., Wheeling peachblow: Opalescent glass, plated or cased with a transparent amber glass; shading from yellow at the base to a deep red at top; glossy or satin finish.

Mt. Washington "Peach Blow": A homogeneous glass, shading from a pale gray-blue to a soft rose color. Pieces may be enhanced with glass appliques, enameling, and gilting.

New England Glass Works, New England peachblow [advertised as "Wild Rose," but called "Peach Blow" at the plant]: Translucent, shading from rose to white; acid or glossy finish. Some pieces enameled and gilted.

Thomas Webb & Sons and Stevens and Williams, England: Around 1888 these two firms made a peachblow style art glass marked "Peach Blow" or "Peach Bloom." A cased glass, shading from yellow to red. Occasionally found with cameo-type designs in relief.

Gunderson Glass Co.: About 1950 produced peachblow type art glass to order; shades from an opaque faint tint of pink, which is almost white, to a deep rose.

Note: All pieces listed below are satin finish unless otherwise noted.

GUNDERSON

Butter Dish, cov, 8⅞ x 4¾", scroll finial, dome cov, scalloped edge	175.00

Compote, 7⅛" d, 6⅞" h, swirled knob,
widely scalloped rim 175.00
Creamer, ftd 65.00
Cruet, 6½" 175.00
Sugar, ftd, open 65.00
Tumbler, 4" 125.00
Vase, 9½", lily form, deep color 150.00

MT. WASHINGTON

Perfume Bottle, ribbed, hp, apple blos-
som dec, orig stopper 1,850.00
Pitcher, 6⅞", bulbous, sq handle 3,700.00
Vase, 8¼", lily form, satin finish 1,800.00

NEW ENGLAND

Darner, 6" l 150.00
Celery Vase, 6¼", crimped top, glossy 800.00
Finger Bowl, 5¼ x 2½", wide ruffled top 335.00
Pitcher, hobnail, applied frosted ribbed
handle 700.00
Punch Cup, applied white opaque
reeded handle 125.00
Salt and Pepper Shakers, metal holder,
orig tops, pr 850.00
Spooner, 4", ribbon candy rim 100.00
Toothpick, sq top, shiny finish 385.00
Tumbler, 3⅞", shiny, faint traces of
agata type black mottling and gold
tracery 385.00
Vase
5", bulbous, satin finish, ruffled rim . 75.00
6½", satin finish, applied clear handles, ruffled rim 125.00
7⅞", lily form, shiny finish 850.00
8½", gourd form, wide cup shaped
top, shiny finish 600.00
8⅞", lily form, satin finish 1,000.00
Whimsey, pear shape, 4¾" h, Sandwich 120.00

WEBB

Bowl, 8", sq, shiny finish 225.00
Celery Vase, 6½", acid finish 175.00
Punch Cup, shiny finish, cream lining . 115.00
Rose Bowl, 4", ribbed, acid finish, white
lining 425.00
Vase
7", stick, bulbous base, glossy, gold
prunus branches, flowers, and butterflies, cream lining 225.00
10½", gold and black dec, shiny fin-
ish, marked "VII" on bottom 275.00

WHEELING

Creamer, 4", shiny finish, applied amber
handle 400.00
Decanter, 9" h, applied twisted amber
handle, amber stopper, slight anneal-
ing imperfection 550.00

Wheeling, vase, 10" h, $1,050.00.

Fairy Lamp, 5½" d, 5" h, wide ruffled
base 650.00
Pitcher, 4½", Drape Pattern, pinched sq
neck, squat bulbous shape, applied
clear ribbed handle 325.00
Salt Shaker, bulbous, orig SP top 200.00
Sugar Shaker, 5½", orig SP top 60.00
Tumbler
3³⁄₁₆", shiny finish 425.00
3¾", cylindrical, magenta shading to
yellow 250.00
Vase
6" d, 6½" h, bulbous 600.00
7", cylindrical, flared, gently ruffled
top, Drape pattern, narrow amber
border 650.00
8", stick, excellent color 565.00
8½", stick, ring of amber rigaree
around base of neck 350.00
10", Morgan, orig amber glass stand,
satin finish 3,100.00
10½", stick neck, bulbous base, minor
annealing imperfections on neck . 1,250.00

PEKING GLASS

History: Peking glass is a type of cameo glass
of Chinese origin. Its production began in the
1700s and continued well into the 19th century.
The background color of Peking glass may be a
delicate shade of yellow, green, or white. One style
of white background is so delicate and transparent
that it often is referred to as the "snowflake"
ground. The overlay colors include a rich garnet
red, deep blue, and emerald green.

Bowl
4", molded and incised as open
flower, yellow, cracked and re-
stored 125.00

Box, cov, turquoise, 4⅝″ d, $275.00.

6″
    Bell form, everted rim, flowering branch and bird, orange overlay, pr **250.00**
    Table dec type, long stemmed flower below flying bird, green overlay, pr **275.00**
6¼″, bell form, inset ring foot, deeply carved with chrysanthemum branch and long tailed bird, prunus branch and two song birds on reverse, yellow, pr **4,125.00**
Cup, 3″ d, flaring, everted rim, engraved, dragon and cloud motif, blue, silver holder, 19th C **225.00**
Jar, 5⅛″, cov, globular, four shaped medallions containing flower springs, ruyi band on shoulders, opaque white, red overlay, floriform knops, late 19th C, pr **800.00**
Snuff Bottle
    2½″, flattened ovoid body, horses dec, camphor ground, blue overlay, blue glass stopper with aventurine **175.00**
    3″, floral form, camphor ground, six color overlay floral dec, green glass stopper, late 19th C **200.00**
Vase
    8″, bird and floral motif, white ground, dark green overlay **350.00**
    8½″, baluster, meandering morning glory vines and butterfly, green overlay, pr **300.00**
    9¼″, stick neck, raised design of blossoming lotus plants, yellow **175.00**
    10″, bottle form, carved birds in flight, orchid plants, yellow **400.00**

PELOTON

History: Wilhelm Kralik of Bohemia patented Peloton art glass in 1880. Later it also was patented later in America and England.

Peloton glass is found with both transparent and opaque grounds with opaque being more common. Opaque colored glass filaments (strings) are applied by dipping or rolling the hot glass. Generally, the filaments (threads) are pink, blue, yellow, and white (rainbow colors) or a single color. Items also may have a satin finish and enamel decorations.

Biscuit Jar
    5¾ x 5½″, emb ribbed opaque white cased glass, all-over pink, blue, yellow, and white applied filaments, SP rim, cover and handle **565.00**
    6¾″, ribbed body, pale blue ground, multicolored filaments, white lining, SP rim, cover, and bail handle ... **500.00**
Bowl, 3½ x 2½″, pinched top, ribbed sides, clear ground, white, pink, blue, and olive green filaments, fiery opal pastel orchid lining **175.00**

Cruet, clear, light blue, muticolored filaments, clear stopper, 7″ to top of stopper, $300.00.

Finger Bowl, clear, multicolored filaments **65.00**
Rose Bowl, 2½ x 2¼″, crimped top, opaque white ground, pink, yellow, blue, and white filament **250.00**
Toothpick
    2½″, clear ground, green filaments . **100.00**
    3″, clear, white filaments **125.00**
Tumbler, 3¾″, clear ground, yellow, pink, red, light blue, and white filaments **125.00**
Vase
    3 x 3¼″, ball shape, flared ruffled top, orchid pink ground, blue, pink, yellow and white filaments **175.00**
    3 x 6¾″, stick, yellow ground, white, rose, blue, and yellow filaments, white lining **225.00**

4¾ x 4¼", squat, ribbed, tricorn folded down rim, clear ground, rose, yellow, blue and white filaments, white lining **300.00**

PERFUME, COLOGNE, AND SCENT BOTTLES

History: Decorative bottles to hold scents have been made in various shapes and sizes. They reached a "golden age" during the second half of the 19th century.

An atomizer is a perfume bottle with a spray mechanism. Cologne bottles usually are larger and have stoppers which also may be used as applicators. A perfume bottle has a stopper that often is elongated and designed as an applicator.

Scent bottles are small bottles used to hold a scent or smelling salts. A vinaigrette is an ornamental box or bottle with a perforated top used to hold aromatic vinegars or smelling salts. Fashionable women of the late 18th and 19th centuries carried them in purses or slipped them into gloves in case of a sudden fainting spell.

Reference: Hazel Martin, *A Collection Of Figural Perfume & Scent Bottles*, published by author, 1982; Jacquelyne North, *Commercial Perfume Bottles*, Schiffer Publishing, 1987; Jacquelyne North, *Perfume, Cologne, and Scent Bottles*, Schiffer Publishing, 1987.

ATOMIZERS

Bohemian, ruby etched, Deer and Castle pattern **85.00**
Czechoslovakian, 8", cobalt blue glass, large enameled and faceted crystal stopper finial, c1930 .... **85.00**
DeVilbiss, black amethyst art glass, goldstone spiderweb dec, bulb missing **80.00**
Moser, 4½", sapphire blue melon ribbed glass body, tiny gold florals, leaves, and swirls, orig gold top and bulb .. **250.00**
Steuben, 7", Aurene, gold **360.00**

COLOGNES

Amethyst, 4", etched animals and buildings **75.00**
Apple Green, 5¼", hexagonal, cut bull's eyes and punty dec, ground stopper **525.00**
Aurene, blue irid, three lug feet, unsigned Steuben **800.00**
Cameo Glass, English
   2½ x 3⅜", round body, white florals and butterfly, frosted vaseline ground, hallmarked silver hinged cap **800.00**

Cologne, glass, clear, 6½" h, $40.00.

5¾", white florals and butterfly, raisin ground, hallmarked silver hinged cap **1,350.00**
Cranberry Glass, floral dec, gold trim, clear stopper **200.00**
Cut Glass, 3½" d, 7" h, slim cut neck, bulbous body, Cane pattern, pointed stopper **100.00**
Malachite, 6½", sgd "Moser" **240.00**
Paperweight Type
   5½", clear, pink, blue, yellow, and white flowers with bubble centers, green ground, marked "St Clair Glass Works, Elwood, IN" **65.00**
   7½", clear glass, brass filigree ftd frame, brass cap, crystal stopper . **125.00**

PERFUMES

Cased Glass, 2½ x 4⅛", pink, gold bands, enameled gold florals and flower garlands, orig clear ball stopper **100.00**
China, figural
   1¼ x 2 x 3⅜", lady and parrot, blue, white, black, yellow, green, and orange, metal and cork stopper ... **70.00**
   2 x 4¼", child, seated in yellow bag, purple collar and black hat, metal and cork stopper, Germany **40.00**
Cranberry Glass
   2 x 5¼", gold bands, small blue and white florals, gold ball stopper ... **120.00**
   2⅛ x 4⅛", lavender and gold branches, foliage, and stylized multicolored flowers, orig clear ball stopper with gold trim **165.00**
   2⅜ x 3¾", bulbous, enameled blue and gray flowers, blue, orange, and white leaves, clear flattened ball stopper **90.00**

Cut Glass

6½″, Button and Star pattern, faceted stopper, rayed base, Brilliant period, American	100.00
8½″, amber, cut panels and designs, matching stopper	180.00
Czechoslavakian, 1¾ x 2½″, overall filigree florals and mesh, white enameled florals, blue mirrored faceted stones, jeweled screw on cap and dauber	50.00
German, figural, miniature, blown glass	
Cat, clear body, blue head	40.00
Rabbit	30.00
Umbrella	27.50
Pairpoint, 5½″, heavy crystal, controlled bubbles	60.00
Satin Glass, MOP, DQ, shading yellow to white, lay down horn shape, 6″ l .	400.00

Scent, ceramic, multicolored, Samson, 5″ h, $750.00.

SCENTS

Cameo, lay down, aqua and white	400.00
Czechoslovakian, lay down, multicolored jewels, enameled top	100.00
Enameled flowers, 3″, pale blue body, hinged metal cap, finger ring, c1900	65.00
Ruby Glass, cylindrical, SS cap dated 1884	90.00
Sterling Silver, 1¼″ d, head of bearded man, wearing helmet, head of classical woman on reverse, hallmarked, chain handle	60.00
Webb, 7″, opaque white body, covered with stylized bamboo plant dec, burnished gold, lush tropical foliage of palm trees, ferns and cacti, long neck with gold bamboo like dec on dark green ground, hallmarked "JG & S" SS top, SS chain	485.00

VINAIGRETTES

Cut Glass, 3⅞″, SS overlay, cobalt glass, yellow flashing, emb SS cap	125.00
Gold	
1⅛″, rect, hinged cov, florals, engraved grill, scrolling foliage, marked "A J Strachan, London, 1800"	1,3200.00
2½″, flattened cartouche shape, putto playing lute, another playing with hound, carnelian intaglio base with two lovebirds and chaplet, inscribed "Vivons Fidelle," English, mid 18th C	650.00
Silver	
1″, purse shape, florals at clasp, engraved basketwork body, hallmarks for John Lawrence & Co, Birmingham, England, 1819	450.00
1¾″, Victorian, rect, emb view of Windsor Castle on cov, leaf tip emb sides, marked "Gervaise Wheeler, 1839"	725.00

PETERS AND REED POTTERY

History: J. D. Peters and Adam Reed founded their pottery company in South Zanesville, Ohio, in 1900. Common flowerpots, jardinieres, and cooking wares comprised their early major output. Occasionally art pottery was attempted, but it was not until 1912 that their Moss Aztec line was introduced and widely accepted. Other art wares included Chromal, Landsun, Montene, Pereco, and Persian.

Peters retired in 1921 and Reed changed the name of the firm to Zane Pottery Company. Marked pieces of Peters and Reed Pottery are unknown.

Vase, Moss Aztec, designed by Frank Ferrel, 7⅞″ h, $47.50.

Bowl
- 6½", Pereco, matte green glaze, butterfly dec **40.00**
- 8½", Landsun, blue, yellow, and green **36.00**

Candlesticks, pr, Pereco, green, semi-matte finish **30.00**

Jardiniere, 6½ x 7½", green lion's head dec, beige ground **75.00**

Jug, bulbous, grape clusters and vine dec, standard glossy brown glaze, single handle **50.00**

Mug, 5½", grape clusters and vine dec, standard glossy brown glaze **35.00**

Pitcher, 4", man with banjo, standard glossy brown glaze **35.00**

Rose Bowl, wreath and vine dec, standard glossy brown glaze, three small feet **40.00**

Vase
- 6 x 4", hexagonal, pinched sides, floral medallion dec, standard brown glaze **60.00**
- 8", chromal scene, blue and brown, glazed **200.00**
- 8½", Shadow Ware, blue and cream drip glaze, olive green ground ... **40.00**
- 9¾", pine cones and needles, green wash glaze, terra cotta ground ... **65.00**

Wall Pocket
- 7½", Moss Aztec, grapes dec, sgd "Ferrell" **48.00**
- 7¾", Pereco, Egyptian dec **70.00**

Window Box, 13", Moss Aztec, depicting Homer and two nudes, sgd "Ferrell" **150.00**

PEWTER

History: Pewter is a metal alloy, consisting mostly of tin with small amounts of lead, copper, antimony, and bismuth added to improve formability and hardness. The metal can be cast, formed around a mold, spun, easily cut, and soldered to form a wide variety of utilitarian articles.

Pewter ware was known to the ancient Chinese, Egyptians, and Romans. English pewter supplied the major portion of the needs of the American colonies for nearly 150 years before the American Revolution. The Revolution ended the embargo on raw tin and allowed the small American pewter industry to flourish. This period lasted until the Civil War.

The listing concentrates on the American and English pewter forms most often encountered by the collector.

Reference: Donald L. Fennimore, *The Knopf Collectors' Guides to American Antiques, Silver & Pewter*, Alfred A. Knopf, Inc., 1984.

Collectors' Club: Pewter Collector's Club of America, 15 Indian Trail, Woodbridge, CT 06515.

Basin
- Compton, Thomas, London, 1802–17, 10⅜", pitted center **200.00**
- Ellis, Samuel, London, 1721–64, 8" . **250.00**
- Graham & Wardrop, Glasgow, Scotland, 10", int. pitted **150.00**
- Hamlin, Samuel, Providence, RI, 1769–1810, 5¾" **700.00**
- Jones, Gershom, Providence, RI, 1774–1809, 7¾" **850.00**
- Townsend & Compton, London, 1785–1801, 11½", hammered booge **300.00**
- Unmarked, American, 7⅞", rampant lion touch mark of Thomas Danforth II **250.00**

Beaker
- Boardman and Hart, NY, c1830, 5¼" **850.00**
- Flagg, Asa F, and Henry Homan, Cincinnati, OH, whiskey size **225.00**
- Yale, Hiram, Wallingford, CT, 1820–30, 3", sgd "Yale" and "Britannia" **300.00**

Bedpan, Samuel Hamlin, Sr and Jr, Providence, RI, 10½" d **250.00**

Bowl, Baptismal, Trask, Oliver, Beverly, MA, 10¾", broad scooped rim, domed feet **2,750.00**

Candlestick
- Hopper, Henry, New York, 1842–47, 9⅞", trumpet shape, straight line touch **350.00**
- Unmarked
  - American, 9⅜", orig insets, pr ... **325.00**
  - Dutch, c1700, 6½", provision for snuffer, weighted base **225.00**
  - English, 1800–25, 8¾", push up ejectors, pr **375.00**

Chalice, unmarked, American, attributed to T D Boardman, 19th C, 7¼", pr **450.00**

Coffeepot, Savage, Middletown, CT, 10" h, $300.00.

Charger

Badger, Thomas, Boston, MA, c1790, 12¼" **500.00**

Dimcomb, Samuel, Birmingham, England, 1740–75, 18", smooth brim **350.00**

Giddings, Joseph, West County, England, c1710, 20⅜" **650.00**

Hamlin, Samuel, Providence, RI, 1767–1801, 15" **700.00**

Unknown maker, English, c1750, 12", smooth brim, minor knife marks .. **75.00**

Coffeepot

Cellew & Co, Cincinnati, OH, 1830–60, 11½" **400.00**

Dunham, Rufus, Westbrook, ME, 1837–61, 10¾", lighthouse shape **350.00**

Gleason, Roswell, Dorchester, MA, 1822–71, 10¼", lighthouse shape **450.00**

Porter, Allen, Westbrook, ME, 1830–40, 11¾", bulbous, bold straight line "A. Porter" touch in rect on bottom **600.00**

Simpson, Samuel, Yalesville, CT, 1835–52, 11¼", minor pitting in foot ring **500.00**

Commode Inset, unmarked, American, 11" d, 7" h **100.00**

Communion Chalice, Reed & Barton, Taunton, MA, 1840–50, 6¾", pr ... **350.00**

Communion Service, Boardman, Thomas Danforth, New York City and Hartford, CT, 11" h flagon, two 10⅛" d plates **650.00**

Cream Pitcher, H Joseph, 3¾", pyriform **1,750.00**

Cuspidor, William H Savage, Middletown, CT, 8⅜" d **350.00**

Dish, Deep

Boyd, Parks, Phila, PA, 1795–1819, 12", large eagle touch **800.00**

Griswold, Ashbil, Meriden, CT, 1802–42, 11⅛", double struck with large eagle touch **250.00**

Townsend, John and Thomas Giffin, London, 1777–1801, 12", hammered booge, numerous knife marks **250.00**

Flagon

Boardman & Co, New York, c1825, lighthouse shape **900.00**

Calder, William, Providence, RI, 1817–56, 11" **850.00**

Trask, Oliver, Boston, MA, c1830, 10⅞" **550.00**

Funnel, unmarked, English, c1800, 3½" d, 4½" l **175.00**

Goblet, unmarked, American, attributed to Israel Trask, early 19th C, 5⅛" .. **200.00**

Inkwell, unmarked, c1800, 3¼" d, circular, ironstone china inset with slight blue discoloration, lid, age and glaze cracks **100.00**

Ladle

Hall & Cotton, Middlefield, CT, c1840, 12¾", straight line rect touch **300.00**

Kruiger, Lewis, Phila, PA, c1830, 14", turned wood handle **250.00**

Yates, John, England, mid 19th C, 14¼", soup, fiddle handle **200.00**

Lamp

Chamber, unmarked, American, attributed to Meriden Brittania Co, c1840, 5¾", whale oil burners, pr . **350.00**

Fluid, unmarked, American, 6½", acorn shaped font, ring handle attached to font, double divergent brass camphene burner **400.00**

Gimball, unmarked, American, 8", double camphene burner and ring handle, one cap missing **300.00**

Hand, Capen & Molineaux, c1850, 2¾", single camphene burner, saucer base **125.00**

Spout, unmarked

4" h, English or Continental, 18th C, molded spouts, pr **500.00**

13½", Continental, 19th C, glass font, pan type burner, saucer base **400.00**

Whale Oil

Capen & Molineaux, New York City and Dorchester, MA, 1844–54, 9¼", brass camphene burners . **400.00**

Dunham, Rufus, Westbrook, ME, 1837–61, 9", cylindrical font, double drop whale oil burners . **375.00**

Smith & Co, Boston, 1850, 6½" .. **250.00**

Smith, Eben, Beverly, MA, 1813–56, 6", acorn type font **300.00**

Unmarked, American

4½", single drop burner **200.00**

6¼", onion shaped font, brass camphene burner, pedestal base, gadroon molding **325.00**

Loving Cup, James Dixon & Sons, England, 7" h, two handles **125.00**

Measure, unmarked, English

Half Pint, c1700, baluster, cov **350.00**

Set, bellied, c1830–50, ten measures ranging from ½₄ of pint to ½ gallon, Type IV, assembled **2,200.00**

Mug

Austin, Nathaniel, Charlestown, MA, 6" h, late 18th C **1,350.00**

Bassett, Frederick, NY, c1780, 4½" h **1,600.00**

Kilbourn, Samuel, Baltimore, MD, early 19th C, 4" h **750.00**

Unmarked, American

Attributed to Thomas Danforth Boardman, Hartford, CT, c1820, 2¹¹⁄₁₆", one gill **325.00**

Attributed to Samuel Danforth, Hartford, CT, 1795–1816, 4½", pint **650.00**

Unmarked, English, mid 19th C, owner's name inscribed on front, quart **100.00**

Pitcher

Boardman, Thomas Danforth, CT, 1840, 6¼", two quarts, cider type, "X" quality mark, minor denting and resoldering **500.00**

Curtis, Daniel, Albany, NY, c1830, 8" h **725.00**

McQuilkin, William, Phila, PA, 10", baluster shape, scrolled handle .. **950.00**

Plate, Blakslee Barns, Phila, 8" d, c1810, $175.00.

Plate

Austin, Richard, Boston, MA, 1792–1817, 8½" **200.00**

Badger, Thomas, Boston, MA, 1787–1815

7⅞", name touch and Boston scroll touch **225.00**

8½" **350.00**

Barns, Blakslee, Phila, PA, 1812–17, 7⅞", second touch of straight line touch "B Barnes/Philad'a," stamped "DM" in rim **225.00**

Belcher, Newport, RI, 1769–84, 8" ... **350.00**

Billings, William, Providence, RI, c1800, 11½" **775.00**

Calder, William, Providence, RI, 1817–56, 7⅞", eagle touch **350.00**

Curtis, Daniel, Albany, NY, 1822–40, 7⅞", "X" quality mark, faint touch, pitted, ... **150.00**

Melville, David or Thomas, Newport, RI, 1790–95, 8¼" **200.00**

Pierce, Samuel, Sr, Greenfield, MA, 8", earliest eagle touch **250.00**

Whitmore, Jacob, Middletown, CT, 1758–90, 7⅞", two small areas of pitting **200.00**

Will, Henry, NY, late 18th C, 15" ... **1,450.00**

Platter, Thomas Compton, London, 20 x 15⅜", oval **500.00**

Porringer

Boardman, Thomas D and Sherman, Hartford, CT, 1830, 4", old English style handle, straight line touch .. **550.00**

Danforth, Samuel, Hartford, CT, 1795–1816, 3⅝", basin type, old English style handle **850.00**

Green, Samuel, Boston, 1790–1810, 5⁷⁄₁₆", crown handle, reverse "SG" signature **200.00**

Hamlin, Samuel E, Providence, RI, 1790–1810, 5¼" **600.00**

Hamlin, Samuel E, Jr, Providence, RI, 1801–56

5¼", flower handle, bold touch on top of handle **550.00**

5⅜", flower handle, strong eagle touch on top of handle **700.00**

Lee, Richard, New England, 1770–1820

2⅞" **650.00**

5", flower handle **325.00**

Melville, David, Newport, RI, 1755–93, 5", geometric handle, Newport style bracket **500.00**

Unmarked, American

Attributed to Boston, c1775–1800, 4¼", "IC" signature on reverse of crown handle **125.00**

Attributed to CT, c1780–1800, 3⅜", English style handle **150.00**

Attributed to New England, c1800–25, 3⁷⁄₁₆", heart and crescent handle **275.00**

Salt, English, 3⅜" d, pedestal, octagonal base, candlestick standard **185.00**

Snuff or Spice Box, George Coldwell, NY, 4¾", bright cut engraving, straight line touch **400.00**

Shaving Dish, Griswold, Ashbil, Meriden, CT, 1802–42, 4⅜", circular, cov **250.00**

Sugar Bowl

Boardman, Thomas Danforth, Hartford, CT, 5¾", baluster shape, scrolled handles **500.00**

Will, William, 4¾", double bellied, beaded rim and foot **3,500.00**

Unmarked, New England, c1825–40, 6¾" h, cov, strap handles **100.00**

Syrup Pitcher, unmarked, American, 5⅞", lighthouse shape, reversed "C" handle, old resoldering on spout .. **75.00**

Tankard

Griffin, Thomas, London, late 18th C, 7½" h **475.00**

Redhead, Anthony, English, Stuart, 6½", flat lid, wriggle work engraving **485.00**

Young, Peter, 6¾", cylindrical, molded base, flat top **4,500.00**

Teapot

Boardman & Hart, New York, 1830–40, 8¼", "X" quality mark **225.00**

Calder, William, Providence, RI, 1817–56, 7¾", lighthouse shape, squatty **550.00**
Waste Bowl, unmarked, New England, c1825–40, 4¾" **175.00**
Wine Taster (or toy porringer), unmarked, attributed to Richard Lee, c1800–20, 2½" d **175.00**

PHOENIX BIRD CHINA

History: Phoenix Bird pattern is a blue and white china exported from Japan during the 1920s to 1940s. A limited amount was made during the "Occupied Japan" period.

Initially it was available at Woolworth's 5 & 10, through two wholesale catalog companies, or by selling subscriptions to needlecraft magazines. Myott Son & Co., England, also produced this pattern under the name "Satsuma," c1936. These earthenware items were for export only.

Once known as "Blue Howo Bird China," the Phoenix Bird pattern is the most sought after of seven similar patterns in the Hō-ō bird series. Other patterns are: Flying Turkey (head faces forward with heart-like border); Howo (only pattern with name on base); and, Twin Phoenix (border pattern only, center white). The Howo and Twin Phoenix patterns are by Noritake and are occasionally marked "Noritake." Flying Dragon (bird-like), an earlier pattern, comes in green and white as well as the traditional blue and white and is marked with six oriental characters. A variation of Phoenix Bird pattern has a heart-like border and is called Hō-ō.

Phoenix Bird pattern has over 500 different shapes and sizes. Also varying is the quality found in the execution of design, shades of blue, and shape of the ware itself. All these factors must be considered in pricing. The maker's mark tends to add value; over 90 marks have been cataloged.

Post 1970 pieces were produced in limited shapes with precise detail, but are on a milk white ground and usually don't have a maker's mark. When a mark does appear on a modern piece, it appears stamped in place.

Reference: Joan Collett Oates, *Phoenix Bird Chinaware,* privately printed, *Book One,* 1984, *Book Two (A Through M),* 1985, *Book Three (N through Z and Post 1970),* 1986.

Collectors' Club: Phoenix Bird Collectors of America, 5912 Kingsfield Drive, West Bloomfield, MI 48233. Dues: $10.00 *Phoenix Bird Discoveries.*

Additional Listings: See *Warman's Americana & Collectibles* for more examples.

Advisor: Joan Oates.

Cake Tray, #3	**45.00**
Child's Tea Set, #4, 3 pc	**65.00**
Child's Tureen, #2	**45.00**
Chocolate Pot, scalloped, tall	**125.00**

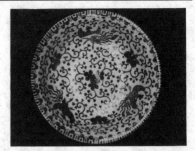

Bowl, marked "Japan" and "T" in flower, 10" d, 2⅝" h, $45.00.

Coffeepot, post 1970	**35.00**
Condensed Milk Holder	**75.00**
Creamer and Sugar, #20	**50.00**
Custard Cup	**15.00**
Egg Cup, double	**18.00**
Fruit Dish, 5½" d, scalloped, wide border	**10.00**
Gravy Boat, attached plate	**60.00**
Hair Receiver	**65.00**
Pitcher, buttermilk	**55.00**
Plate	
9¼" d, breakfast	**30.00**
9¾" d, dinner	**45.00**
Platter	
7¾ x 5", scalloped	**25.00**
12¼ x 9"	**45.00**
15 x 9¾"	**60.00**
Rice Bowl, "A"	**10.00**
Rice Tureen, #3-A	**85.00**
Salt and Pepper Shakers, pr	**25.00**
Sauce Boat, #2	**45.00**
Sauce Boat Underplate, #2	**20.00**
Soup Bowl, 7¼ x 1½" h	**20.00**
Syrup, #1	**35.00**
Teapot	
Pre 1970	**45.00**
Post 1970, rattan handle	**25.00**
Tile, 6" d	**25.00**

PHOENIX GLASS

History: Phoenix Glass Company, Beaver, Pennsylvania, was established in 1880. Known primarily for commercial glassware, the firm also produced a molded, sculptured, cameo-type line from the 1930s until the 1950s.

Basket, 4½", dogwood dec, pink ground	**48.00**
Bowl	
9½ x 5½", bittersweet, white ground	**150.00**
13½", canoe shape, sculptured blue lovebirds, opal ground	**325.00**

Candlesticks, pr
3¼", blue, bubbles and swirls	**48.00**
4", blue, frosted	**37.50**

Centerpiece, 14", sculptured diving
nudes, three colors **200.00**

Compote, 8½", dragonflies and water
lilies dec, butterscotch ground **80.00**

Lamp, table
17½", green peacock feather pattern,
irid blue, sgd "Phoenix Studios,
Tom Arnold, #197" **185.00**

20", red cardinals on tree branches,
green berries, ivory ground **225.00**

Plate
6¾", dancing nudes, frosted and clear	**38.00**
8½", cherries, frosted and clear	**55.00**
14", white daffodils, blue ground . . .	**85.00**

Powder Box, cov
6¾ x 3¾", sculptured roses, humming
bird, amethyst **125.00**

7¼ x 4½", sculptured white violets,
pale lavender ground **100.00**

PHONOGRAPHS

History: Early phonographs were commonly called "talking machines." Thomas A. Edison invented the first successful phonograph in 1877. Other manufacturers followed with their variations.

Collectors' Club: Antique Phonograph Collectors Club, 502 E. 17th Street, Brooklyn, NY 11226. Dues: $10.00 *The Antique Phonograph Monthly* (10 issues).

RCA Victor, Victrola, mahogany, two doors in back, castors, 22½ x 24½ x 48½", $300.00.

Amberola Model 75, diamond reproducer	**375.00**
Baltiphone, console, 38" h, 78 rpm . . .	**250.00**
Berliner Trade-Mark Gramophone . . .	**2,000.00**
Britannia, key wind, open mechanism, c1910, Germany	**200.00**
Busy Bee, disc model	**400.00**
Columbia Eagle, orig, reproducer, lid .	**300.00**

Edison
Amberola Model 30, table model, four
minute cylinder, oak case, 11 x
12½ x 14¼" **300.00**

Fireside Model, oak case, bentwood
cover, oak cygnet horn, 9¾" w . . . **800.00**

Gem, orig horn, oak case **450.00**

Standard Model B, Model C reproducer, nickel plated winding handle,
oak case, one cylinder, 13" l **275.00**

Triumph Model, brass bell horn,
chromed crane **475.00**

Heywood Wakefield, wicker **1,750.00**

Reginaphone, Style 155, oak serpentine cabinet, double comb, oak horn **4,500.00**

Regina Reginaphone Disc Musical Box
and Phonograph, five 15½" discs, 12"
turntable, oak case, MOP inlay, c1904 **2,000.00**

Robeyphone, disc type, large horn, English **500.00**

Vase, pale green, frosted, 9½" h, $130.00.

Vase
6", pink owls, cream color ground . . **75.00**

6½", red flashed lovebirds, flowers,
clear ground **65.00**

8⅜", fan shape, sculptured praying
mantis, foliage, pearlized and
frosted, pale blue-gray ground . . . **150.00**

9½", heavily gilted roses, white
ground **125.00**

10", dogwood, blue, white ground,
partial paper label **80.00**

10¼", Madonna, blue ground, sculptured head, white irid **240.00**

11", sculptured, coral, green, and
brown dogwoods, white ground . . **275.00**

12", white foliage, sepia ground . . . **100.00**

| Standard X Talking Machine, large blue horn | 425.00 |

Thorens, portable, brown leather case, Switzerland ... 125.00

Victor
Monarch Senior, brass bell horn, ornate oak case ... 850.00
Schoolhouse, oak case ... 1,400.00
Type MS Disc, 10″ d, turntable, carved oak cabinet, brass bell, 25½″ h ... 725.00

PICKARD CHINA

History: The Pickard China Company was founded by Wilder Pickard in Chicago, Illinois, in 1897. Originally the company imported European china blanks, principally from the Havilands at Limoges, which they then hand painted. The firm presently is located in Antioch, Illinois.

Plate, blues, greens, and rose, marked "Hutschenreuther," 8½″ d, $275.00.

Biscuit Jar, 6½″, hp chrysanthemums, cream ground, gold trim, SP bail and cov ... 85.00
Bowl, 10½″, ruffled, poppies and leaves, gold trim, artist sgd, 1905 ... 175.00
Cake Plate, 10¾″, sq, Oriental birds, sgd "Nichols," c1919 ... 180.00
Coffee Set, cov coffeepot, creamer, and sugar, artist sgd, 3 pcs ... 300.00
Compote, 10½″, fruit and flower dec, gold border, handle, and pedestal base, artist sgd ... 175.00

Creamer and Sugar, birds, butterflies, and flowers, artist sgd ... 140.00
Cup and Saucer, enamel beading, artist sgd ... 80.00
Hatpin Holder, allover gold design of etched flowers, c1925 ... 45.00
Lemonade Set, tankard pitcher, five tumblers, bluebells and foliage, lemon colored ground ... 100.00
Marmalade Jar, 6″, matching cov and underplate, hp, dogwoods and leaves, gold trim, artist sgd ... 85.00
Mug, 5½″, berries, gold handle and rim, artist sgd ... 150.00
Perfume Bottle, yellow primroses, shaded ground, artist sgd and dated 1905, Limoges blank, gold stopper ... 200.00
Pitcher
7¼″, cherry clusters, gold trim, artist sgd ... 200.00
8½″, bulbous, hexagonal, colored fruit, blossoms, and foliage, silver bands, gold trim, artist sgd, c1912 ... 285.00
10″, tulips, artist sgd ... 265.00
Plate
7½″, hp, currants, 1898 ... 75.00
8⅜″, handles, Art Nouveau dec, gold and light turquoise ... 50.00
8 1″, poppies, gold tracery and rim, sgd "Challinor" ... 150.00
8½″, violets, green leaves, shaded purple ground, scalloped gold rim, 1905 mark ... 90.00
Platter, 12″ d, hp, landscape, sgd "Marker" ... 225.00
Powder Box, 4″ d, roses, artist sgd ... 100.00
Punch Bowl, 14″, artist sgd "Schoner," Limoges blank ... 665.00
Relish Dish, 9½ x 4¼″, pink and green leaves, open handles, maple leaf mark ... 70.00
Salt and Pepper Shakers, pr
Allover gold etched design ... 30.00
Pink rosebuds, blue forget-me-nots, gold scrolls, 1905 mark ... 40.00
Stein, 7″, large bunches of grapes and leaves, black ground, gold handle, rim, and base, artist sgd, c1898 ... 275.00
Tea Set, ftd cov teapot with dolphin's head spout, tankard creamer, cov sugar, 11″ d tray, pearlized ground, turquoise blue, pink, and rose tulips, gold tracery and trim on rims and handles, artist sgd ... 650.00
Tray, 11″ d, circular, bisque, teal blue, gold grapes and leaves, engraved, sgd "Coufall," 1905 mark ... 200.00
Urn, 11½″, allover gold, 3″ band of grapes and strawberries, artist sgd, Belleek blank ... 500.00
Vase
6″, Spring scene, handles, matte fin-

ish, sgd "Challinor," maple leaf mark **300.00**

9", large golden yellow, pink, and deep rose chrysanthemums and green leaves, soft turquoise blue shaded to green ground, gold trim, artist sgd, 1898 .... **300.00**

15", multicolored peonies, pastel ground, gold scalloped rim and base, artist sgd **300.00**

PICKLE CASTORS

History: A pickle castor is a table accessory used to serve pickles. It generally consists of a silver plated frame fitted with a glass insert, matching silver plated lid, and matching tongs. Pickle castors were very popular during the Victorian era. Inserts are found in pattern glass and colored art glass.

Cranberry
Egg Shape, enameled white flowers and leaves, orig SS cov and frame, attributed to Webb **275.00**

Thumbprint, 13", enameled daisies, twig feet, elaborate floral cut-out sides, top and tongs **325.00**

Crown Milano, 9" h, creamy white body, swags of pastel pink and white blossoms, resilvered floral emb lid and holder, 3¾ x 4½" h DQ glass insert, sgd on base "Pairpoint Mfg Co, New Bedford Quadruple Plate 661" **845.00**

Northwood, Netted Apple Blossom insert, ornate SP ftd frame **275.00**

Clear, castle scene in medallions, silver plated frame, $125.00.

Pattern Glass
Beaded Dart, sapphire blue insert, resilvered ftd Meriden frame and tongs **250.00**

Cane, topaz insert, dec SP frame .. **145.00**

Cupid and Venus, clear insert, ftd Pairpoint frame, stylized swan head tongs **85.00**

Daisy and Button, blue insert, SP Wilcox frame, lid and tongs **235.00**

Pigeon Blood, Beaded Drape insert, Consolidated Glass Co, orig cov and frame **425.00**

Rubena, vertical optic pattern insert, Pairpoint, ornate ftd fretwork frame and bail handle **225.00**

Vaseline, white opal design, polished pontil, orig ruffled cov shaped as emb flower, stem finial, ornate ftd frame . **450.00**

PIGEON BLOOD GLASS

History: Pigeon blood refers to the deep orangish-red colored glass ware produced around the turn of the century. Do not confuse it with the many other red glass wares of that period. Pigeon blood has a very definite orange glow.

Salt and Pepper Shakers, pr, metal tops, 2¾" h, $100.00.

Biscuit Jar, Torquay, SP rim, cover, and handles **275.00**

Bowl, 9", master berry, Torquay, SP rim **110.00**

Butter Dish, cov, Venecia, enameled dec **350.00**

Creamer, Venecia, enameled dec **125.00**

Decanter, 9½", orig stopper **75.00**

Pickle Castor, Beaded Drape insert, SP cov and frame, Consolidated Glass Co **425.00**

Pitcher, water
Diamond Quilted, 10½", tankard shape **185.00**

Torquay, SP trim **325.00**

Sugar Shaker, Bulging Loops, orig top **150.00**

Syrup, Beaded Drape, Consolidated Glass Co., orig hinged lid **245.00**

Toothpick, Bulging Loops **125.00**

Tumbler, 3¼", alternating panel and rib **75.00**

Vase
6", gourd shape, cased, gold leaf dec, applied elephant head handles, Webb, pr **375.00**
11½", applied clear foot and rigaree **150.00**

PINK SLAG

History: True pink slag is found only in the molded Inverted Fan and Feather pattern. Quality pieces shade from pink at the top to white at the bottom.

Reproduction Alert: Recently pieces of pink slag, made from molds of the now defunct Cambridge Glass Company, have been found in the Inverted Strawberry and Inverted Thistle pattern. This is not considered "true" pink slag and brings only a fraction of the Inverted Fan and Feather pattern prices.

Tumbler, 4" h, $450.00.

Bowl, 9" d, ftd	500.00
Butter, cov	650.00
Compote, jelly	375.00
Creamer	450.00
Cruet, 6¾" h	1,500.00
Jam Jar	875.00
Pitcher, water	750.00
Punch Cup, 2½" h, ftd	275.00
Salt Shaker	300.00
Sauce Dish, 4½" w, 2½" h, four ball feet	285.00
Sugar, cov	550.00
Toothpick	400.00
Tumbler	450.00

PIPES

History: The history of pipe making dates as early as 1575. Almost all types of natural and man-made materials, some which retained smoke and some that did not, were used to make pipes.

Among the materials were amber, base metals, clay, cloisonné, glass, horn, ivory, jade, meerschaum, parian, porcelain, pottery, precious metals, precious stones, semi-precious stones, assorted woods, *inter alia*. Chronologically the four most popular materials and their generally accepted introduction dates are: c1575, clay; c1700, woods; c1710, porcelain; and, c1725, meerschaum.

National pipe styles exist around the globe, wherever tobacco smoking is custom or habit. Pipes reflect a broad range of themes and messages, e.g., figurals, important personages, commemoration of historical events, mythological characters, erotica and pornographica, the bucolic, the bizarre, the grotesque, and the graceful.

Pipe collecting began in the mid-1880s; William Bragge, F.S.A., Birmingham, England, was an early collector. Although firmly established through the efforts of free-lance writers, auction houses, and museums (but not the tobacco industry), the collecting of antique pipes is an amorphous, maligned, and misunderstood hobby. It is amorphous because there are no defined collecting bounds; maligned because it is conceived as an extension of pipe smoking, now socially unacceptable [many pipe collectors are avid non-smokers]; and, misunderstood because of its association with the "collectibles" field.

References: R. Fresco-Corbu, *European Pipes*, Lutterworth Press, 1982; E. Ramazzotti and B. Mamy, *Pipes et Fumeurs des Pipes. Un Art, des Collections, Sous le Vent*, 1981; Benjamin Rapaport, *A Complete Guide To Collecting Antique Pipes*, Schiffer Publishing, 1979.

Collectors' Club: Pipe Collectors International, Inc., P. O. Box 22085, 6172 Airways Boulevard, Chattanooga, TN 37422. *Pipe Smoker*. Dues: $15.00.

Museums: Museum of Tobacco Art and History, Nashville, TN; National Tobacco-Textile Museum, Danville, VA; U.S. Tobacco Museum, Greenwich, CT.

Cheroot holder, amber stem, 3¹³/₁₆" l, $175.00.

PIPES

Briar
Man, 7″ l, bearded, tasseled hat and
pipe, carved, marked "G.B.D." ... 55.00
Queen Victoria, head, 6¼″, carved,
silver trim, case, hallmarked 75.00
Clay, 18″ l, figural, young man with curly
hair, wooden slim stem, french, Gam-
bier 65.00
Glass, large ovoid bowl, long shaped
stem, red and ivory dec 75.00
Meershum
Boy with mandolin, 12″, carved 200.00
Carved man lid, 6″ 50.00
Negro, 8″, figural, cream, bust bowl 900.00
Wild Animal, 17″, carved, dated 1800 150.00
Opium, 7¾″, cranes, reed stem, brass
fittings, Oriental, c1800 .... 85.00
Porcelain
Character, 10″, man under barrel .. 60.00
Family Crest 1847, 30″, marked
"Made by Cmielow Factory, Po-
land" 75.00
Floral, 12″, relief 125.00
Graf Zeppelin, 9″, P.O.G. 125.00
Hunter, 24″, sleeping 125.00
Occupational, 12″, machine, stem
chips 75.00
Stag, 12″, marked "P.O.G." 75.00
Pottery
Man with pipe, set on lid, post war . 60.00
Monk, post war 45.00
Ram, post war 65.00
Regimental
4 Field Art. Regt. Magdellburg 1896–
98, 36″ l 260.00
149 Inft. regt. 1881, blacksmith tools
in rear, 10″ l 85.00
Soapstone, Eskimo man, 9″, skinning
animal, late 19th C 140.00

TAMPS

Boot, 1½″, wood 35.00
Column, 2¾″, ivory 15.00
Man, 1⅝″, bending at waist, SP, marked
"E.P.N.S." 25.00
Napoleon, 2⅜″, brass 25.00
Robin Hood, 2¼″, brass, marked "Eng-
land" 35.00

POCKET KNIVES

History: Alcas, Case, Colonial, Ka-Bar, Queen,
and Schrade are the best of the modern pocket
knife manufacturers, with top positions enjoyed by
Case and Ka-Bar. Knives by Remington and Winchester, firms no longer in production, are eagerly
sought.

Form is a critical collecting element. The most
desirable forms are folding hunters (1 and 2
blades), trappers, peanuts, Barlows, elephant
toes, canoes, Texas toothpicks, Coke bottles, gun
stocks, and Daddy Barlows. The decorative aspect
also heavily influences prices. Values are for
pocket knives in mint condition.

References: James F. Parker, *The Official Price
Guide to Collector Pocket Knives, 9th Edition,*
House of Collectibles, 1987; Jim Sargent, *Sar-
gent's American Premium Guide To Pocket
Knives: Identification and Values,* Books Ameri-
cana, 1986; Ron Stewart and Roy Ritchie, *The
Standard Knife Collector's Guide,* Collector
Books, 1986.

Periodical: *Knife World,* P. O. Box 3395, Knox-
ville, TN 37917.

Collectors' Clubs: American Blade Collectors,
P.O. Box 22007, Chattanooga, TN 37422; Canadian Knife Collectors Club, 3141 Jessuca Court,
Mississauga, ON L5C1X7; The National Knife Collectors Association, 7201 Shallowford Road, Chattanooga, TN 37421.

Museum: National Knife Museum, Chattanooga, TN.

Additional Listings: See *Warman's Americana
& Collectibles* for more examples.

CASE

Case uses a numbering code for its knives. The
first number (1–9) is the handle material; the second number (1–5) designates the number of
blades; the third and fourth number (0–99) the
knife pattern. Stage (5), pearl (8 or 9), and bone
(6) are most sought in handle materials. The most
desirable patterns are 5165—folding hunters,
6185—doctors, 6445—scout, muskrat—marked
muskrat with no number, and 6254—trappers.

In the Case XX series a symbol and dot code is
used to designate a year.

1920-40
5254, stag handle, 4⅛″, stamped
"Tested XX" 1,350.00
6111½, green bone, long pull,
stamped "Tested XX" 400.00
6265, green bone, 5¼″, flat blade,
stamped "Tested XX" 300.00
6465, green bone, 5¼″, saber balde,
bail in handle stamped "Teste XX" 1,750.00
9265, imitation pearl, 5¼″, flat blade,
stamped "Tested XX" 400.00
1940-65
3254, yellow composition 4⅛″,
stamped "XX" 125.00
42057, white composition, 3⅜″ mkd
on handle "OFFICE KNIFE" 90.00
6246R, green bone, 4⅜″, bail in handle, stamped "Tested XX," rigger's
knife 150.00

6265, red bone, 5¼", flat blade,
stamped "XX" 250.00
8271, genuine pearl, 3¼", long pull
stamped "XX" 220.00
Fly Fisherman 150.00
1965-70
4200, white composition, 5½", serrated master blade, stamped
"USA," melon tester 125.00
5265, stag, 5¼", saber ground, bolsters drilled stamped "USA" 85.00
62009, bone, 3⁵⁄₁₆", master blade in
front, stamped "USA," Barlow ... 35.00
6265, red bone, 5¼", flat blade,
stamped "XX" 225.00
Muskrat, bone 3⅞", 10 dot 50.00
1970-80 (Number of dots indicate year)
5111½, genuine stag, 4⁷⁄₁₆", lockback,
Cheetah, large stamp 175.00
62009, bone stag, 3⁵⁄₁₆", Barlow ... 35.00
6265, stag, 5¼", saber ground, bolsters drilled, 10 dot 75.00
Fly Fisherman 100.00
Muskrat bone, 3⅞", 10 dot 40.00

KA-BAR (Union Cut. Co., Olean, New York)

The company was founded by Wallace Brown
at Tidioute, PA in 1892. It was relocated in Olean,
NY, in 1912. The products have many stampings
including Union [inside shield]; U-R Co. Tidioute
[variations]; Union Cutlery Co. Olean, NY; Alcut
Olean, NY; Keenwell, Olean, NY; and Ka-Bar. The
larger knives with a profile of a dog's head on the
handle are the most desirable. Pattern numbers
rarely appear on a knife prior to the 1940s.

22156 .... 500.00
24107 .... 1,000.00
31187, 2 blades 150.00
61161, light celluloid handle 100.00
61126L, dog's head 850.00
61187, Daddy Barlow 150.00
6191L 600.00
6260KF 100.00

KEEN KUTTER (Simons Hardware, St. Louis, MO)

K02220, office knife 50.00
K1881, Barlow 70.00
K1920 .... 300.00
6354, Scout 100.00

REMINGTON, last made in 1940

R293, Field and Stream Bullet, bone,
long pull, 5¼" 1,750.00
R953, toothpick, bone, 5" 225.00
R3273, Cattle, brown bone, equal end,
3¾" 235.00

**Remington, Baby Bullet, $2,000.00.
(Note: A special collectors' edition was
issued and should not be confused
with the original.)**

R4233, Junior Scout, brown bone, scout
shield, pinched bolsters, 3⅜" 200.00

RUSSELL, Turner Fall, MA

60, 1 blade 100.00
55, 2 blades 125.00
600, Daddy Barlow 200.00

WINCHESTER

1051, Texas Jack, celluloid, 4¼" 300.00
1621, Budding, ebony, 4¾" 130.00
1920, Folding Hunter, bone, 5⅜" 1,000.00
2337, Senator, pearl, 3¼" 100.00
2703, Barlow, brown bone, 3½" 140.00
3944, Whittler, bone, 3¼" 225.00
4961, Premium Stockman, bone, 4" .. 285.00

OTHER MANUFACTURERS

Elephant Toe
Ibberson, pearl work back 300.00
Kutwell, Olean, NY 200.00
Primble, John 250.00
Folding Hunter
Case, Nantucket Sleigh Ride 125.00
Marble Arms Co 350.00
Neft Saftey 220.00
New York Knife Co. 400.00
Novelty Cutlery Co., pictured handle 125.00
Queen Cutlery Co. Titusville, PA, buf-
falo horn 200.00
Robeson 175.00
Russell 150.00
Schrade, Trail of Tears 150.00
Union Cutlery Co., Tidioute, PA 100.00
Valley Forge Cutlery Co., NJ 200.00

POISON BOTTLES

History: Poison bottles were designed to warn
and prevent accidental intake or misuse of their
poisonous substances, especially in the dark. Poison bottles generally were made of colored glass,
embossed with "Poison" or a skull and cross-
bones, and sometimes were coffin-shaped.

John H. B. Howell of Newton, New Jersey, designed the first safety closure in 1866. The idea did not become popular until the 1930s when bottle designs became simpler and the user had to read the label to identify the contents.

References: Ralph and Terry Kovel, *The Kovels' Bottle Price List, 7th Edition,* Crown Publishers, Inc., 1984; Carlo & Dot Sellari, *The Illustrated Price Guide to Antique Bottles,* Country Beautiful Corp., 1975.

Periodicals: *Antique Bottle World,* 5003 West Berwyn, Chicago, IL 60630; *Old Bottle Magazine,* P. O. Box 243, Bend, OR 97701. Subscription: $10.00.

English, aqua, diamond on front, rectangle on back, impressed "70" on bottom, 3⁵⁄₁₆" h, $35.00.

Baker, Chester, A, Boston, cobalt blue, emb	45.00
Carbolic Acid, ring top, cobalt, poison crosses all around, 5"	15.00
Durfee Embalming Fluid Co, amethyst, 8¾"	25.00
Extrait FL: De Quinquina, amber, 6½"	20.00
Ikey Einstein Poison, rect, ring top, clear, 3¾"	25.00
JTM & Co, three cornered, "Poison" on one side, ring top, amber, 10"	80.00
Lin Saponis, green, 6¾"	20.00
Liq Morph Hydrochl Poison, cobalt, label, 4½"	40.00
Melvin & Badger Apothecaries, Boston, MA, irregular hexagon, cobalt blue, 6"	30.00
Norwich, IGA, cobalt blue, 8"	75.00
Owl Poison Ammonia, three cornered, cobalt, label, 5¼"	25.00
Spirits, silver, milk glass, 9"	20.00
Syr:Fer:Iodid, cobalt, 7"	75.00
Tinct Opii, poison on base, cobalt, 7"	40.00
Victory Chemical Co, Quick Death Insecticide, 148 Fairmount Ave, Phila, PA, 8 oz, clear, 7"	12.00

POLITICAL ITEMS

History: Since 1800 the American presidency always has been a contest between two or more candidates. Initially souvenirs were issued to celebrate victories. Items issued during a campaign to show support for a candidate were actively being distributed in the William Henry Harrison election of 1840.

Campaign items cover a wide variety of materials—buttons, bandannas, tokens, pins, etc. The only limiting factor has been the promoter's imagination. The advent of television campaigning has reduced the emphasis on individual items. Modern campaigns do not seem to have the variety of materials which were issued earlier.

References: Herbert Collins, *Threads of History,* Smithsonian Institution Press, 1979; Theodore L. Hake, *Encyclopedia of Political Buttons, United States, 1896–1972,* Americana & Collectibles Press, 1985; Theodore L. Hake, *Political Buttons, Book II, 1920–1976,* Americana & Collectibles Press, 1977; Theodore L. Hake, *Political Buttons, Book III, 1789–1916,* Americana & Collectibles Press, 1978; Edmund B. Sullivan, *American Political Badges and Medalets, 1789–1892,* Quarterman Publications, Inc., 1981. (Note: Theodore L. Hake issued a revised set of prices for his three books in 1984.)

Collectors' Club: American Political Items Collectors, P.O. Box 340339, San Antonio, TX 78234.

Museum: Smithsonian Museum, Washington, D.C.

Note: The abbreviation "h/s" is used to identify a head and shoulder photo or etching of a person.

Additional Listings: See *Warman's Americana & Collectibles* for more examples.

Advisor: Theodore L. Hake.

Alarm Clock, Spiro Agnew, wind-up, die-cut hands, orange case, red, white, and blue dial, orig box, unused, Made in West Germany, c1960	30.00
Ashtray, 5" d, china, white, gold band, "Vote Republican In '52" inscription, man hitchhiking next to exhausted Democratic donkey with GOP elephant lumbering down road cartoon, "My Ass Is Tired" caption	15.00
Badge	
1896, McKinley-Hobart, ribbon, celluloid jugate attached, "Sound Money/No Repudiation/Republican/Traveling Men's/Club/Peoria, Ill," 8 x 2½"	50.00
1910, Taft, Wisconsin Republican Convention, Badge, inscribed on black ribbon "We oppose men who are Republicans for office and Democrats in office," Taft medal on bottom, delegate label on top, 5 x 2"	45.00

1949, Truman, Truman-Barkley inauguration jugate, gray ribbon attached, "Democrats/from/Cambria-
Indiana/Armstrong-Somerset/
Counties/Johnstown, PA," 4 x 2" . **175.00**

Bandanna

1896, Bryan, cotton, 17¾ x 18¼",
black and white, jugate of Bryan
and Sewall, eagle and shield at top,
coin and rooster in center, White
House at bottom, numerous slo-
gans **80.00**

1928, Hoover, 17 x 18", linen, white
ground, blue oval bust portrait in
center, "Our President," surrounded by state seals in red ... **60.00**

29" sq, red, white, and blue, "I Like
Ike" slogan repeated four times,
white stars on red and white elephants on blue border **35.00**

**Booklet, Vol. 1, No. 1, 45 pgs, 8⅜ x
10½", $25.00.**

Bank, 1½ x 3½ x 2½", cast iron, still,
"Teddy" on one side, orig gold paint,
c1908 .... **80.00**

Bottle Stopper, figural, LB Johnson, 2½
x 3 x 4", three dimensional head, red
foil "Japan" sticker, c1964 .... **20.00**

Bumper Sticker, 4 x 7", orange and
black, license plate design, inscribed
"Elect JFK-60 President" **8.00**

Button

1896, 1¾", sepia portrait of Bryan, St
Louis Button Company **30.00**

1900, 1¼", McKinley and Roosevelt,
blue and gold **25.00**

1904, Parker-Davis, jugate, multicolor, ribbon center, 1¼" **50.00**

1912, Progressive, head of moose,
"Progressive," white and gold on
light blue **15.00**

1916, Wilson, ⅞", black and white
portrait, blue rim with "Progressive
Policies Become Law Under Wilson" **15.00**

1920, Coolidge-Dawes, jugate, ⅞",
black and white, text above and below oval portrait **45.00**

1924, Hoover, oval, red, white, and
blue, "100%/HOOVER/AMERI-
CAN" **10.00**

1932, Roosevelt-Garner, jugate,
black and white, "Return our country to the People" **200.00**

1940, ⅞", "I'M FOR WILLKIE AND
McNARY," jugate, black and white,
lettering on right is lighter **55.00**

1948, Dewey-Warren, jugate, ⅞" ... **20.00**

1968, 1⅝" Goldwater, black, white,
and blue, bust portrait, "I'll Back
Barry" **6.00**

Coolidge, ¾", litho, white on blue **15.00**

Car Attachment, 2½" d, silvered metal
holder, tin plate with black and white
portrait and slogan "Keep Coolidge",
threaded shaft **250.00**

Cigar, 1928, Al Smith, 8½", black, white,
gold, red, and green label picturing
Smith, orig box **22.50**

Gearshift Knob, 2" d, Woodrow Wilson,
solid amber celluloid, metal ring surrounds rubber disk with Wilson's portrait, c1916 .... **50.00**

Glass

1896, McKinley-Hobart, clear, tumbler, 3¾", etched pictures in
wreath, names below **45.00**

1902, Roosevelt, clear, punch cup,
2¾", etched "President Roosevelt/
1902/Oyster Bay," on bottom
"Bloomingdales New York" **35.00**

Inaugural Item

Invitation, 1885, Cleveland-Hen-
dricks, ball, 7 x 9¾" **45.00**

Program

1881, Garfield-Arthur, 16 pgs **35.00**

1957, Eisenhower, Rockwell cov,
50 pgs **15.00**

Letter Opener, 1¾ x 8", plastic, white,
blue image and red lettering, "Vote
Demo! Hubert Humphrey For President!", 1968 .... **7.00**

License Plate

1940, Willkie, white key on composi-
tion, "Good/Will-kie/to White
House/1940," made by Kuleness
Co, Paulding, OH, 5½ x 10" **30.00**

1964, Wallace, "Johnson for King/
Wallace for President," red, white,
and blue, 6 x 12" **12.00**

Match Holder, 1½ x 2¼", Jefferson portrait, "National Democratic Club April

13, 1907" slogan, ART Mfg Co New
York, 1904 patent date **20.00**

Medal, copper, 1⅞", Buchanan, buck
leaping over cannon and "Ann/Breck-
inridge," rev with portrait of Washington and slogan **150.00**

Megaphone, 7½" l, cone shape, plastic,
white, blue inscription "President
Nixon. Now More Than Ever," 1972 . **10.00**

Mirror, Taft, 2¼" d, black and white, bust
of Taft, "Its Up To The Man On The
Other Side To Put This Tried & Safe
Man At The Head Of The Government" **125.00**

Mug
　1928, Hoover, 7" toby, face with seat-
　ing posture base, cream color, fac-
　simile signature on side **50.00**

Note Pad, 2 x 2¾", Cleveland picture
on front with wife, Baldwin & Gleason
1886 copyright **10.00**

Pen, 5½" l, dark blue, silver inscription
"Businessmen For Humphrey/Thank
You/Hubert H. Humphrey" **8.00**

Pencil, mechanical, 5½" l, light gray
point end, transparent plastic covering JFK portrait clip end, diecut "109"
PT boat that floats back and forth,
skyline background scene **20.00**

Pennant
　1948, Truman, oval with Truman h/s
　and name on left "For President"
　in center, white, red ground, 4½ x
　12" **25.00**

Pin
　1896, McKinley, Nose Thumber, gold
　color, push heels to reveal Mc-
　Kinely thumbing nose, on reverse
　"McKinley to Democrats and Pop-
　ulists, 1⅞" **200.00**
　1928, Smith, enamel, donkey with
　derby **15.00**
　1936, Landon, brass, sunflower,
　"Landon/Knox" in pedals **12.00**
　1956, Eisenhower, bar, "IKE" above,
　"volunteer" inscribed, and "56" in
　relief **7.50**

Plate
　1884, Blaine, china, 9", black on
　white, floral motif beneath **35.00**
　1948, Dewey, 6½", white, glazed, por-
　trait and "New York State Fair-
　Chamber of Commerce-Farm Din-
　ner-Syracuse-1949" **12.00**

Platter, 9 x 11½", oval, china, jugate
portraits of W. H. Taft and J.S. Sherman, surrounded by red, white and
blue flags, and purple roses, eagle
with shield below, gold floral design
border **35.00**

Postcard
　1908, Hopefuls, "Watching the Pres-

**Plate, 1956 National Convention, San
Francisco, CA, Eisenhower/Nixon,
marked "Vernon Kilns," 12¾" d, $65.00.**

idential Game," Hughes, Foraker,
Cannon, Taft, and Fairbanks on
one side of fence, T. Roosevelt on
other, cartoon, multicolored **20.00**
　1908, Taft, mechanical, black, white,
　and yellow elephant with rope tail,
　black and white portrait slides out
　when pulled by tail, , October 24,
　1908 postmark, brief message ... **25.00**
　1940, "No More Fireside Chats," red,
　white, and blue **5.00**

Ribbon
　1880, Hancock and English, 2¾ x 6",
　jugate, black and white, beige
　cloth, marked "Junior/Hancock/
　Club/of Chambersburg" **125.00**

Salt and Pepper Shakers, pr, ceramic,
beige and tan, Ike's head lifts off for
one shaker, body serves as other,
c1952 .... **15.00**

Soap, 1964, Goldwater, bath size, wrap-
per with black, silver, and white on
gold **7.50**

Stereocard, McKinley And His Eight
Chosen Advisors-Cabinet Room, Executive Mansion, 1900 .... **5.00**

Stickpin
　Blaine, 1884, cardboard photo **30.00**
　Coolidge, 1920, green and silver li-
　cense plate logo, "Cal/24/Cool-
　idge," ¼ x 1" **15.00**
　Benjamin Harrison, 2" l, brass **15.00**
　McKinley, 2", 1" d gold and silver en-
　graved dish, mounted, c1896 .... **20.00**

Stud, 1896, "How The Farmer Loves
Gold Bugs," lapel, three insects im-
paled on points of pitchfork, black
ground **100.00**

Tab
　1928, "HOOVER-CURTIS,"White let-
　ters on blue metal tab **7.00**

1936, Landon-Knox, diecut elephant ... **10.00**
Tape Measure, 1¾" d, gold glass case, metal measure, red, white, and blue inscription "President Nixon Now More Than Ever," orig plain gold box ... **5.00**
Tapestry, 19½ x 38", JF Kennedy with American flag and US Capitol, inscribed back "Made In Italy" **20.00**
Tie, 1936, Landon, "For President/h/s/ Alfred M. Landon," brown ground, white lettering, round picture **25.00**
Tie Clip, brass, hat shape, "LBJ" in black lettering, orig dark blue card .. **5.00**
Token
  1838, Hard Times Token, copper, front tortoise and safe, black donkey, 28mm **8.00**
  1893, Grover Cleveland, brass, luster, inscription "United States Mint Exhibit/World's Columbian Exposition Chicago/1893, 1" **12.00**
  1845, James Garfield, brass, White House and canal boat, inscription "Canal Boy 1845/President 1881" inauguration souvenir, 1" **10.00**
Watch Fob
  William J Bryan, 1¼" black and white celluloid, mounted, black leather fob with strap **30.00**
  Taft, silvered brass, red and blue enamel pennant design, 1908 patent date on back **25.00**
Window Sticker
  4½ x 12", "Coolidge and Dawes," red, white. and blue, paper, 1924 .... **5.00**
  6" d, jugate, red, white, and blue portraits of Roosevelt and Garner ... **40.00**

POMONA GLASS

History: Pomona glass, produced only by the New England Glass Works and named for the Roman goddess of fruit and trees, was patented in 1885 by Joseph Locke. It is a delicate lead, blown art glass which has a pale, soft beige ground and a top one inch band of honey amber.

There are two distinct types of backgrounds. First ground, made only from late 1884 to June 1886, was produced by fine cuttings through a wax coating followed by an acid bath. Second ground was made by rolling the piece in acid resisting particles and acid etching. Second ground was made in Cambridge until 1888 and until the early 1900s in Toledo where Libbey moved the firm after purchasing New England Glass works. Both methods produced a soft ground appearance, with fine curlicue lines more visible on first ground pieces. Designs are used on some pieces, which were etched and then stained in color. The most familiar design is blue cornflowers.

Do not confuse Pomona with "Midwestern Pomona," a pressed glass with a frosted body and amber band.

Reference: Joseph and Jane Locke, *Locke Art Glass: A Guide For Collectors,* Dover Publications, 1987.

Mustard, Midwestern, Flower and Pleat pattern of U.S. Glass, frosted, washed color, silver plated top, 3⅛" h, $40.00.

Beverage Set, 8½" tankard pitcher, six glasses, second grind, Cornflower, DQ **600.00**
Bowl, ruffled, first grind, amber edge . **65.00**
Carafe, second grind, Cornflower **200.00**
Celery, first grind, Cornflower **300.00**
Creamer, second grind, Daisy and Butterfly, applied clear handle, three applied clear feet **275.00**
Cruet, 5½", first grind, Blueberry, gold leaves, applied clear handle, clear ball stopper **285.00**
Lemonade Mug, 5¾", first grind
  Cornflower, blue flowers **275.00**
  Optic Diamond Quilt pattern, irid, clear handle and upper border ... **165.00**
Pitcher, milk, second grind
  Blueberry **200.00**
  Cornflower, sq top **225.00**
Punch Cup, first grind, Cornflower, blue flowers **100.00**
Toothpick, first grind, Cornflower **245.00**
Tumbler, 3⅝", first grind, Cornflower, blue flowers **200.00**
Vase
  2½", fan top, first grind, amber stain, 4" pie crust crimped top **185.00**
  10⅞", lily form, second grind **400.00**

PORTRAIT WARE

History: Plates, vases, and other articles with portraits on them were popular in the second half of the 19th century. Although male subjects, such as Napoleon or Louis XVI, were used, the ware usually depicted a beautiful woman, often unidentified.

A large number of English and Continental China manufacturers made portrait ware. Because most ware was hand painted, an artist's signature often is found.

Additional Listings: KPM and Royal Vienna.

Bowl, 15″ l, 10¾″ h, reclining maiden, draped white cloth, pastoral landscape, marsh scene on reverse, waisted oval stand, foliage scrolls and gilt dec on copper luster ground, three scrolled feet, red "Germany, Gestezlich Geschutzt," blue pseudo Vienna shield mark, artist sgd "Donath" . . . **3,000.00**

Ewer, oval portrait of maiden, one with diaphanous red gown, floral sash, standing before classical architecture, flowing brown hair, titled "Sehnsucht," other with red dress, holding white shawl, dark hair, entitled "Echo," elaborate palmette and Greek key gilt tooled reserves, shaded brown to copper luster ground, three large foliate scroll and spray registers, molded scrolled handle and leaf tip spout, socle base, circular plinth, scrolled feet, obscured factory mark, blue pseudo Vienna shield mark, black titles, artist sgd "Wagner," pr . **4,125.00**

Plate, 12½″ d, marked "Bonaparte," Haviland blank, $75.00.

Plate

7″, young woman, long hair, shaded green ground, wide lacy gold border, marked "R. C. Bavaria" **30.00**

8½″, maidens and cherub frolicking in garden, magenta border **75.00**

9½″

La Rose, white dress, crimson robe, brown eyes, upswept hair, pale brown ribbon, shaded blue border, silver and gilt scrolling floral sprigs, Vienna shield mark in blue, title and "DEC 29 DEPOSE" in black, numbered in red, artist sgd "Wagner," c1900 **1,000.00**

Woman, gold trim, artist sgd "Roi de Rome," marked "Sevres" . . **160.00**

9⅝″, Carl Magnus Hutschenreuther, c1900

Duchess of Devonshire, pale red dress, white shawl, curled blond hair, red and blue hat, gray plumes, green scrolled border, gilt scaled scrolls, floral sprays, and flower filled urns, imp factory mark, "Lamb Dresden 135.K" in blue, title in green, artist sgd "A. Lamm" **800.00**

Mme. Recamier, white dress, blue ribbon sash, red cloak, brown eyes, upswept black hair, gray ground, green scrolled border, gilt scaled scrolls, floral sprays, and flower filled urns, imp blue factory mark "Lamb Dresden 135.K," title in black, artist sgd "A. Lormin" **825.00**

10″

Cherubs pulling wheel cart in garden, etched gold border, marked "Hutschenreuther, Bavaria" . . . **110.00**

Dutch children playing windmills, "Bavaria" and beehive mark . . . **100.00**

Urn, cov, 30″ h, elongated waisted cylindrical neck painted in reserve with bust portrait of Marie Antoinonette on one, Louis XVI on other, gilt border with foliage scrollwork, drum form body painted with continuous landscape frieze depicting aristocratic ladies and gentlemen in 18th C costumes, waisted lobed base and foot, gilt highlights and rims, pierced dome cov with gilded pineapple knob, bleu celeste ground, marked "Sevres," pr **1,250.00**

Vase

6⅜″, bud, cylindrical, oval self portrait, after Vigee Librun, flanked by molded gilt scrolls, green ground, gilt vertical banding, floral sprigs, and foliate scrolls, gilded asymmetrical rim and foot, crowned Dresden mark, "34927" in black, c1900 . . . . **250.00**

8¼″, young woman, pale red dress, white shawl and gloves, upswept blond hair, holding large lilac spray, gilt and silver tooled stylized floral sprig and scroll borders, copper luster ground, obscured factory mark, underglaze blue pseudo Vienna mark, underglaze blue pseudo title "Flieder (Lilac)" and "DEC .786 Depose" in black, gilt numerals, artist sgd "Wagner" 935.00

8¾", young woman, white dress, pink shawl, gilt tooled floral spray borders, copper luster ground, reserve with gilt foliage medallion, laurel sprigs in upswept brown hair, obscured factory mark, pseudo Vienna shield mark in blue, red title "Laurel, Germany," artist sgd "Wagner" 725.00

11", classical maiden, bleu-du-roi ground, gilt and jeweled highlights, underglaze blue pseudo shield mark, Vienna, c1900 . . . . 425.00

POSTERS

History: The poster was an extremely effective and critical means of mass communication, especially in the period before 1920. Enormous quantities were produced, helped in part by the propaganda role played by posters in World War I.

Print runs of two million were not unknown. Posters were not meant to be saved. Once they served their purpose, they tended to be destroyed. The paradox of high production and low survival is one of the fascinating aspects of poster history.

The posters of the late 19th century and early 20th century represent the pinnacle of American lithography printing. The advertising posters of firms such as Strobridge or Courier are true classics. Philadelphia was one center for the poster industry.

Europe pioneered in posters with high artistic and aesthetic content. Many major artists of the 20th century designed posters. Poster art still plays a key role throughout Europe today.

References: John Barnicoat, *A Concise History of Posters*, Harry Abrams, Inc., 1976; George Theofiles, *American Posters of World War I: A Price and Collector's Guide*, Dafram House Publishers, Inc.

Additional Listings: See *Warman's Americana & Collectibles* for more examples.

Advisor: George Theofiles.

ADVERTISING

"Arrow Shirts," J. C. Leyendecker, 11 x 21", c1915, man in smoking jacket and tie reading book 125.00

"Big Ben Smoking Tobacco/Delaine Hours," 14 x 20", red, blue, and green, black horses 65.00
"Ivory Soap," 11 x 21", Art Deco, two women inspecting garment 90.00
"Lippincott's," March 1895, J. J. Gould, 12 x 18", woman in Victorian winter attire 200.00
"R. R. Donnelley & Sons, Printers and Binders, Chicago," Ostertag, 13 x 21", three women posing like Art Nouveau "Three Kings," floral motif dec, metallic gold background, beautifully printed, 1894 . . . . 150.00

Entertainment, Texas Guinan, c1935, 27 x 41", $225.00.

CIRCUS, SHOWS, AND ACTS

Barnum and Bailey, combined shows, "Presenting 150 Horses In The Fete Of Garlands," 30 x 40", c1919–20 . . 175.00
Hagenbeck-Wallace Circus, "The Great Angelo Troup," 28 x 41", Angelos shown, females jumping through the air, landing on shoulders of tuxedoed males, c1935 . . . . 165.00
Kay Bros, "Saijiro Kitchie-The Greatest Of All Japanese Head Balancers," 28 x 40", yellow and blue, Kitchie in litho, vignettes of acts all around, photo at left side, c1935 . . . . 135.00
Ringling Bros Barnum & Bailey, "Rudy Rudynoff, Peerless Equestrian," 28 x 41", Rudynoff in Cossack-like uniform, close-up of steed on one side, Great Dane on other 200.00

MOVIE

One Sheet, Silent
"Chase Me," Otis litho, Fox Sunshine

Comedy, Arbuckle at beach with two ladies 300.00
"Dawn Of Revenge," 1922, 41 x 27", Richard Travers, Otis litho, linen backed 150.00
"Second Hand Line," Charles Jones, c1915, man in boat wooing girl . . 135.00
One sheet, 27 x 41"
"A Hard Days Night," 1964, The Beatles 200.00
"Doomed Caravan," 1940, William Boyd, western design, orig Paramount 80.00
"Guilty Bystander," 1950, Zachary Scott, Faye Emerson, Moody Filmnoir design 40.00
"Partners In Time," 1946, Lum and Abner, pastel designs 60.00
"The Glass Webb," 1955, Edward G. Robinson 70.00
"The Last Time I Saw Paris," 1954, Elizabeth Taylor, Van Johnson, bust portraits 50.00
Three Sheets
"Butterfield 8, 1960, The Sandpiper, 1965, Suddenly, Last Summer, 1960," 41 x 27", Elizabeth Taylor . 80.00
"Leave It To Me," 42 x 80", c1916, William Russell and woman 175.00
"The Stowaway," 40 x 80", 1936, Shirley Temple, close-up 450.00

THEATRICAL

"Bunco In Arizona," 30 x 40", 1907, saloon scene, man shooting pistol from hand of another 200.00
"Child Slaves Of New York," 20 x 30", Strobridge Litho, Arab holding man in front pointing Kaldah The Mystic, frightened victorian beauty, bottom "He Is The Detective—You Know What To Do!", 1903 . . . . 165.00
"Fogg's Ferry, Don't Kill Me Mammy," c1905, woman at beach hitting black child 100.00
"Life's Shop Window," 40 x 80", litho, perplexed woman looking to baby, handed her by Indian woman in field, c1900 . . . . 210.00
"Nip and Tuck, Detectives Out Of The Window Into The Water," 28 x 21", JM Jones Co, man falling from upended rain barrel into jaw's of ferocious mastiff, c1880 . . . . 225.00
"The Beautiful Indian Maidens," 20 x 27", Enquirer Co, fourteen Victorian ladies dressed in tights and head dresses, catching duck dressed in tuxedo, lobster with smiling man's' face, 1898 . . . . 200.00
"The Gambler Of The West," Strob-

ridge, 20 x 30", 1906, comedic bad man 190.00

TRANSPORTATION

"Air France Nordafrika," 25 x 40", airliner swoops over exotic North African setting, brilliant color, c1946 . . . . . . 250.00
"Automobiles," Bayard A Clement, 75 x 51", Bayard tears past viewer, aerodynamic wood speedboats background, c1909 . . . . 975.00
"Fisk Tires, Easy To Ride. Safe To Buy," 16 x 22", c1900, Art Nouveau, woman on cycle 125.00
"Orix Bicycles," Fillipo Romoli, 28 x 39", beautiful blonde woman in green bathing suit, leaning against her Orix cycle, 1940 . . . . 300.00
"Take The Union Pacific Railway To Denver and San Francisco," Omaha Republican Print, 9 x 24", two huge letters U and P with names of towns serviced, 1883 . . . . 135.00

WORLD WAR I

"All Together. Enlist In The Navy," 40 x 29", sailors of all nations beckon, standing beside each other 165.00
"Be A US Marine," 29 x 40", marine image, no-nonsense pose, looming stars and stripes 375.00
"First Call-I Need You In The Navy This Minute!" 10 x 11", Uncle Sam, full color, Navy recruiting use 275.00
"I Want Your For The US Navy," 27 x 41", appealing blonde in Navy jacket looks seductively to viewer, 1917 . . 500.00
"Join Us! Coast Artillery Corps USA," 25 x 19", railway gun and crew image 135.00
"Over There! Skilled Workers On The Ground Behind The Lines In The Air Service," 30 x 38", three color lithograph, American Doughboy with hand in air beckoning to silhouette of biplane near hanger, 3" black and gray bottom border, rebuilt 375.00
"You-Help My Boy Win The War, Buy A Liberty Bond," 21 x 11", close-up of mother in front young Doughboy . . . 100.00

WORLD WAR II

"Buy War Bonds," N. C. Wyeth, 22 x 14", patriotic image, Uncle Sam holding billowing flag in one hand, pointing sternly toward unseen enemy with other 150.00
"Enlist In The Waves/Release A Man To Fight At Sea," 42 x 28", recruiting image 100.00

"Every Child Needs A Good School Lunch," 1944, 27 x 19", promoting nation's school lunch program, blue, brown, green, yellow, black, photo image 70.00

"Our Fighters/Deserve Our Best," 1942, 40 x 29", US Army Ordinance, defiant soldier helping wounded buddy, flaming and devastated landscape 85.00

"Remember Dec 7th!" 40 x 28", tattered American flag flies at half mast, fire and smoke background 180.00

"Strong In The Strength Of The Lord," 1942, 28 x 22", three strong arms lift weapons in support of people's cause 75.00

"The United Nations Fight For Freedom," 28 x 20", colorful image, flags of Allied Nations surrounding Statue of Liberty 120.00

POT LIDS

History: Pot lids are the lids from pots or small containers which originally held ointments, pomades, or soap. Although a complete set of pot and lid is desirable to some collectors, lids are the most collectible. The lids frequently were decorated with multicolored underglaze transfers of rural and domestic scenes, portraits, florals, and landmarks.

The majority of the containers with lids were made between 1845–1920 by F. & R. Pratt, Fenton, Staffordshire, England. In 1920, F. & R. Pratt merged with Cauldon Ltd. Several lids were reissued by the firm using the original copper engraving plates. They were used for decoration and never served as actual lids. Reissues by Kirkhams Pottery, England, generally have two holes for hanging and often are marked as reissues. Cauldon, Coalport, and Wedgwood were other firms making reissues.

References: Susan and Al Bagdade, *Warman's English & Continental Pottery & Porcelain, 1st Edition*, Warman Publishing Co., Inc., 1987; A. Ball, *The Price Guide to Pot-Lids And Other Underglaze Multicolor Prints On Ware*, Antique Collectors' Club, 1980.

Note: Sizes are given for actual pot lids; size of any framing not included.

Albert Memorial, multicolored, 4" **25.00**

Anchovy Paste, black label, white ironstone, 3½", marked "England" **25.00**

Arctic Expedition, multicolored, T J & J Mayer, 3", rim chip **320.00**

Bloater Paste, black label, white ironstone, 4½" d, marked "England" ... **25.00**

Deer Drinking, multicolored, 4" **25.00**

Dr. Johnson, multicolored, 4" **125.00**

Dublin Industrial Exhibition, multicolored, 3¾" **50.00**

Embarking For The East, multicolored, Pratt, 4⅛", orig jar **100.00**

Farriers At Work, sgd "Wouvermann Pinx," Pratt, 4¾" **65.00**

I See You My Boy, multicolored, 4½" . **20.00**

Lady Brushing Hair, multicolored, 3" .. **220.00**

Landing The Catch, Pratt type, 4⅛" .. **100.00**

Napirima, Trinidad, T J & J Mayer, c1853, medium **165.00**

"Shakespeare's House Henley St. Stratford on Avon," 4⅛" d, $150.00.

No By Heaven I Exclaimed..., multicolored, 4½" **175.00**

Peace, multicolored, 5½", rect, lobed corners **25.00**

Persuasion, multicolored, 4⅛" **150.00**

Philadelphia Exposition, 1876, multicolored, 4" **65.00**

Picnic On The Banks Of The River, Gothic Ruins, Pratt, 4¾" **90.00**

Residence of Anne Hathaway, 4" **100.00**

Residence of the Late Sir Robert Peel, Pratt **150.00**

Trysting Place, The, small **165.00**

Queen Victoria on Balcony, T J & J Mayer, large **265.00**

View of Windsor Castle, Pratt, 6½" ... **150.00**

Village Wedding, The, multicolored, Pratt, 4¼" **50.00**

Ville De Strasbourg, Pratt type **75.00**

Walmer Castle, Kent, Tatnell & Son, 4½" **200.00**

Washington Crossing the Delaware, Pratt, orig jar **225.00**

Wellington, T J & J Mayer, c1850, medium **100.00**

Windsor Castle, 6" **100.00**

Woman With Lamb, multicolored, William Wood, 4", orig jar **135.00**

PRATT

PRATT
FENTON

PRATT WARE

History: The earliest Pratt earthenware was made in the late 18th century by William Pratt, Lane Delph, Staffordshire, England. In 1810–1818, Felix and Robert Pratt, William's sons, established their own firm, F. & R. Pratt, in Fenton in the Staffordshire district. Potters in Yorkshire, Liverpool, Sunderland, Tyneside, and Scotland copied the ware.

The wares consisted of relief molded jugs, commercial pots and tablewares with transfer decoration, commemorative pieces, and figure and animal groups.

Much of the early ware is unmarked. The mid-19th century wares bear several different marks in conjunction with the name Pratt, including "& Co."

References: Susan and Al Bagdade, *Warman's English & Continental Pottery & Porcelain, 1st Edition,* Warman Publishing Co., Inc., 1987; John and Griselda Lewis, *Pratt Ware 1780–1840,* Antique Collectors' Club, 1984.

Additional Listing: Pot Lids

Bowl
  7" d, painted stylized flowerheads, multicolored **130.00**
  9⅞" d, 3½" h, dark brown int., green transfer of Dr Syntax Drawing After Nature, polychrome **100.00**
Compote, 56¼ x 9½", Spanish dancer scene, gold border **250.00**
Cup Plate, 3⅛", white Dalmatian, black spots **65.00**
Figure
  Deer, 4½", recumbent, hollow, c1820 **525.00**
  Faith, c1800 .... **120.00**
  Hope, 7", c1800 .... **125.00**
  St George Slaying The Dragon, 9", two women at side, multicolored, c1780 .... **2,750.00**
Flask, 7¾", The Late Duke of Wellington on front, Rt Hon Sir Robt Peel on reverse, multicolored print, reserved on malachite ground, gilt borders, c1865 .... **400.00**
Jar
  4¾", relief of gentleman with mug, white and blue, raised trim, c1820 **350.00**
  7¾", molded oval panels of peacocks in landscapes, blue, brown, green, and ochre, lower section with vertical leaves, band of foliage on rim, c1790 .... **600.00**

Jug, 11", figural, Bacchus and Pan, sea lion handle, 1800 .... **685.00**
Mug, 4¼", multicolored scenes, maroon ground **135.00**
Mustard Jar, dark blue hunt scene, tan ground **55.00**
Pipe, 8", neatly coiled in concentric circles, 1800 .... **1,100.00**

Plaque, "Christ In The Wheat Field," sgd "J. Austin," multicolored, c1850s, 13" d, $100.00.

Plaque, pierced for hanging
  5¾" d, relief of bird with insect perched on cherry branch, brown, ochre, and green, c1775 .... **350.00**
  11" l, oval, relief of two recumbent lions, yellow ochre, brown, and green, blue border, c1800 ...... **570.00**
Plate
  5½", fishing scene, multicolored, rust border, gold trim **85.00**
  9", Haddon Hall, classical figure border **100.00**
Tea Caddy, 4¾", relief bust of King George III, polychrome **175.00**
Toby Jug
  9⅜", Martha Gunn, blue, yellow, brown, and ochre, c1770–80 .... **3,400.00**
  10¾", Hearty Goodfellow, blue jacket, yellow-green vest, blue and yellow striped pants, blue and ochre sponged base and handle, stopper missing, slight glaze wear, c1770–80 .... **1,500.00**

PRINTS

History: Prints serve many purposes. They can be a reproduction of an artist's paintings, drawings, or designs. Prints themselves often are an original art form. Finally, prints can be developed for mass appeal as opposed to aesthetic statement. Much of the production of Currier & Ives fits this latter category. Currier & Ives concentrated on genre, urban, patriotic, and nostalgia scenes.

Prints are beginning to attract a wide following. This is partially because prices have not matched the rapid rise in oil and other paintings.

References: Frederic A. Conningham and Colin Simkin, *Currier & Ives Prints*, Crown Publishers, Inc., 1970, revised edition; Michael Ivankovich, *A Price Guide to Wallace Nutting Pictures*, Cheetah Prints, 1984; Denis C. Jackson, *The Price & Identification Guide to J. C. Leyendecker & F. X. Leyendecker*, published by author, 1983; Carl F. Luckey, *Collector Prints Old and New*, Books Americana, 1982; Craig McClain, *Currier & Ives: An Illustrated Value Guide*, Wallace-Homestead, 1987; Wallace Nutting, *The Wallace Nutting Expansible Catalog* (reprint of 1915 catalog), Diamond Press, 1987; Ruth M. Pollard, *The Official Price Guide To Collector Prints, 7th Edition*, House Of Collectibles, 1986; Marian S. Sweeney, *Maxfield Parrish Prints*, published by author, 1974.

Collectors' Clubs: American Historical Print Collectors Society, Inc., 25 West 43rd St., Suite 711, New York, NY 10036. *Imprint*; Prang-Mark Society, Century House, Old Irelandville, Watkins Glen, NY 14891. *Prang-Mark Society Newsletter*.

Reproduction Alert: Reproductions are a problem, especially Currier & Ives prints. Check the dimensions before buying any print.

Albers, Anni, Fox I, color print, 1972, sgd, dated, numbered 100/150, 14¾ x 13⅜″	175.00
Appian, The Road to the Village, etching, 4⅞ x 8⅛″, good impression, margins, sandwiched between mat and backing	15.00
Arms, John Taylor	
In Memoriam, etching, 1939, sgd, dated, 14⅝ x 12″, fine impression, framed	2,100.00
Sunlight on Stone, Caudebec en Caux, etching, 1931, sgd, dated, and numbered Ed 100 II, 14⅜ x 7⅝″, fine impression, margins, pen inscription on verso	575.00
Audubon, J J	
Cedar Bird, Plate 43, 1833, 12¼ x 19¼″	3,600.00
Gold Winged Woodpecker, Plate XXXVII, hand colored etching, engraving, and aquatint, by R Havell, J Whatman Turkey Mill, 1828 watermark, 25¾ x 20¾″, framed	1,450.00
Tufted Auk, Plate 249, 1835, 19⅜ x 14¼″	1,000.00
Baille, J, The Landing of Columbus, 18436	100.00
Beal, Gifford, Circus Bare-Back Riders, litho, sgd, 6⅜ x 5⅝″, good condition, framed	175.00
Benton, Thomas Hart	
Down The River, litho, 1939, sgd, 12½ x 9⅞″, from edition of 250 published by Associated American Artists, margins	850.00
Frisky Day, litho, 1929, sgd, 7⅞ x 12″, from edition of 250 published by Associated American Artists, margins, light staining	700.00
Braque, Georges, Three Birds, color litho, sgd in pencil, tear in upper edge of print, stain in right margin, framed	150.00
Calder, Alexander, White Circles and Elipse, color litho, 1976, sgd and numbered 79/175, 22 x 30″, printed by Mourlot, Paris, full sheet, minor handling creases	400.00
Cezanne, Paul, Paysage a Auvers, etching, 1873, 5¼ x 4⅜″, good impression, large margins, lightly discolored	200.00
Chagall, Marc, Bay of Angels, color litho and poster, sgd and dated 1962, 30¾ x 22⅞″, good printing, margins, bottom title folded under, framed	850.00
Currier and Ives	
American Choice Fruits, 1868, large	900.00
American Railroad, Snowbound, small	950.00
Autumn in New England, Cider Making, large	2,500.00
Clipper Ship, "Flying Cloud," 1852, large	2,500.00
John Quincy Adams-Sixth President of the United States, small	150.00
Kiss Me Quick!, small	250.00
Noah's Ark, small	150.00
Prairie Hunter, One Rubbed Out, 1852, large	2,400.00
Three Jolly Kittens, After The Feast, 1871, small	275.00
Through To The Pacific, 1870, 8 x 12½″	800.00
Woodcock Shooting, small	415.00
Dali, Salvador (After)	
Christ of Gala, two color prints in portfolio case, one with pencil signature, other with emb signature, numbered E222/325, 16⅞ x 17″, both in good condition, margins	200.00
Hawaiian Fisherman, color print, sgd and numbered CXCIV/CCCL, 11¾ x 23⅜″, margins, framed	225.00
Davies, Arthur B.	
Orchard of Bounties, litho, sgd, 15¼ x 10¾″, good printing, chine applique, margins	250.00
Dehn, Adolf, Golden Gate, litho, sgd, 9¼ x 13⅝″, from edition published by Associated American Artists, margins, framed	150.00

Eby, Kerr, Cornwall, drypoint, 1927, sgd, 5⅜ x 9⅜″, good impression, margins, some discoloration, paper tape on upper corners **60.00**

Filmus, Tully

Festive Dance, litho, sgd, titled, and numbered 20/100, 15½ x 20½″ .. **100.00**

Klezmer, litho, sgd, titled, and numbered 67/100, 19⅛ x 15½″ **125.00**

Flint, William Russell, Preparing Their Meal, drypoint, sgd and numbered XLIII, 6¾ x 8⅞″, good impression, margins, laid down around edges .. **125.00**

Foujita, Tsuguharu, Mother with Children, color litho, 1964, sgd and inscribed "E. A.," 19⅛ x 13½″, good printing, margins, light staining, framed **850.00**

Froelich, Paul, Circus Horses in Rehearsal, etching, sgd in pencil twice, 8 x 9⅝″, good impression on chine applique, trimmed margins, mat stained, old tape stains, framed ... **50.00**

Girardet, P, after H Sebron, New York-Winter Scene in Broadway, color engraving, 28 x 38⅞″, good printing, published by M Knoedler, Oct 1, 1859, margins, verso discolored, mat burn, framed **2,000.00**

Gorsline, Douglas, Woman with Newspaper on a Subway Platform, etching, sgd, 8¼ x 6¾″, good impression, margins, good condition, piece of masking tap at upper edge, framed . **375.00**

Grant, Gordon, Dock Side Politics, litho, sgd in pencil, 9⅛ x 12″, from edition published by Associated American Artists, good printing on board, glued to mat window, lightly discolored, framed **75.00**

Gropper, William, Three Jurists, etching, sgd and numbered 29/100, 3⅞ x 5⅝″, good impression, brown ink, wide margins, good condition, framed ... **125.00**

Haden, Francis Seymour, A River in Ireland, etching with drypoint, 1864, sgd, 9¼ x 13⅝″, good impression on laid paper, trimmed margins, lightly discolored **2,000.00**

Hassam, Childe, drypoint, sgd with monogram

Calvary Church in Snow, 1915, inscribed title, 7 x 4⅞″, trimmed margins, slight mat burn, framed **750.00**

Rainy Day St Marks, 1915, 7 x 4⅜″, slight mat burn, pin holes in corners, framed **850.00**

Hirsch, Joseph, Lovers, color litho, sgd and numbered 80/100, 7⅛ x 16⅛″, good printing, one pinhole in right, another in left margin, framed **65.00**

Horlor, E, Louis Sherry, etching, 9⅛ x 7¾″, good impression, margins, sandwiched between mat and backing **70.00**

Hutson, Victoria, Petunias and Butterfly, litho, sgd and dated 1935 in pencil, 8 x 6″, good printing, margins, paper tape, mat stain, framed **30.00**

Louis Icart, Venetian Nights, $950.00.

Icart, Louis, color etching and aquatint, good impression, margins, good condition

Black Lace, sgd, oval, 19½ x 14½″, one scratch in print below woman's toe, old tape and glue in margins, framed **950.00**

Charmes de Montmartre, sgd, inscribed with titled, numbered 144, 21¼ x 14¼″ **1,000.00**

Farewell, sgd and inscribed "Epreuve d'artiste," oval, 15 x 19½″ **950.00**

Little Prisoner, sgd, 15½ x 19¾″, some discoloration, mounted on board, framed **900.00**

Orange Seller, The, sgd and numbered 291/500, oval, 19⅛ x 13¾″, framed **800.00**

Puppies, sgd and inscribed "Ep. d'artiste," 16½ x 20⅞″, margins trimmed, paper loss at edges, laid down **750.00**

Sur les Quais, sgd, titled, and numbered 135, 13¾ x 6⅜″ **1,100.00**

Kellogg

Emma **45.00**

Prodigal Son Returned To His Father **75.00**

Kollwitz, Kathe, Weberzug, etching, 1897, inscribed with artist's name and title, 8½ x 11⅝″, good late printing, margins, taped to backing, framed . **125.00**

Kuhn, Walt, Clown and Girl, drypoint, sgd and titled, 7⅛ x 5¾″, framed .. **175.00**

Landeck, Armin, Streetlight and Coliseum, etching, sgd and dedicated "To Sal and Joe," 18½ x 13⅜", good impression, margins, framed 250.00

Lepere, Auguste, View of Notre Dame from the right bank of the Seine, etching, 1917, sgd in pencil, numbered 27/150, 12¾ x 18⅝", good impression, full margins, on Japan, framed 275.00

Levine, Jack, Adam and Eve, sgd, pencil on paper, 13¾ x 10⅞", framed .. 450.00

Lewis, Martin, drypoint
Derrick, sgd and inscribed "imp," 8 x 11⅞", good impression, margins, top left corner missing, framed ... 1,200.00
Rain on Murray Hill, 1928, sgd, 8 x 11⅞", fine impression, margins, slightly discolored, taped to mat window, framed 2,900.00
Suburban Evening, 1925, sgd, collection mark on verso, 9⅞ x 8", good impression, margins, signature strengthened, framed 1,000.00

Lichtenstein, Roy, Man and Woman, After Leger, color silkscreen, 42 x 35½", framed 175.00

May Ray, Personage, color litho, 1975, sgd with initials and numbered 13/175, 23¼ x 18½", blindstamp of publisher Transworld Art, NY, printed by Mourlot, Paris, margins, minor handling creases 300.00

Marsh, Reginald, Tug in New York Harbor, color serigraph, 15½ x 19⅛", framed 450.00

Matisse, Henri, Odalisque Couchee a Mi-Corps, litho, 1923, sgd in pencil and numbered 47/50, 9⅛ x 12¼", sheet laid down, edges torn, missing pieces, old glue along margins, mat window glued to print, framed 3,200.00

Meyron, Charles, Le Galerie Notre-Dame, etching, 1853, 11⅛ x 6¾", good impression in dark brown, black ink, margins, discolored, several small tears around and into image . 450.00

Miro, Joan
Grans Rupestres Nr. 24, color aquatint and woodcut, 1979, sgd and numbered 29/30, good printing, printed to edges 300.00
Translunaire, color litho, aquatint, and embossing, sgd and numbered 40/50, 24 x 18½", fine impression, margins, minor creases at top and bottom of image, framed 2,000.00

Moore, Henry
Head of a Girl, etching, sgd and numbered⁵/50, 10 x 7¼", good impression, large margins, good condition, framed 650.00
Stonehedge II, color litho, 1973, sgd

and numbered P1.2 60/60, 11¼ x 17¾" 225.00

Poole, Burnell, With Stunsails Alow and Aloft, etching, sgd in pencil, titled, and numbered 39/100, 11⅞ x 14⅞", good impression, full margins, foxing and mat burn, laid down, framed 75.00

Nutting, Wallace, framed, matted, 8 x 10"
Chimney Corner, The 85.00
Coming Out of Rosa, The 50.00
Farm Borders 25.00
Grace of Elms, The 75.00
New England Uplands 45.00
Sip of Tea 75.00
Stepping Stones At Bolton Abbey .. 70.00
Wayside Inn Corner 70.00
Weaver, The 65.00

Parrish, Maxfield
Air Castles, 12 x 16" 125.00
Book Lover, The, 10 x 8" 75.00
Dinkey Bird, 10¼ x 15½" 75.00
Errant Pan, The, 6 x 8" 35.00
Garden of Allah, The, 18 x 9" 100.00
Old King Cole 200.00
Walls of Jasper, youth and castle, 12 x 14" 85.00

Rembrandt Van Rijn
The Death of the Virgin, etching and drypoint, 1639, 15½ x 12⅜", good impression, margins trimmed, some rippling of paper and small losses, spots of foxing 2,000.00

Rivera, Diego, Flower Market, litho with color, 1930, sgd, dated, and numbered B-25-39, 11 x 15¾", good printing, margins, discolored, some foxing in margins 300.00

Rodin, Auguste, Buste de Bellone, drypoint, c1883, sgd, 5⅞ x 4", good impression, heavy laid paper, large margins, discolored in margins and verso, spots of old glue and tape, framed 2,225.00

Ryder, Chauncey F, A Meadow Brook, etching and drypoint, sgd, titled in pencil, 6 x 7⅞", good impression, margins, mat burn, light foxing, framed 75.00

Schreiber, Georges, From Arkansas, litho, sgd in pencil, 14½ x 11½", from edition published by Associated American Artists, margins, faint light staining, taped to mat, framed 100.00

Soyer, Rachel
Protected, litho, sgd in pencil, 13½ x 6¼", from edition published by Associated American Artists, margins, faint light staining, taped to mat, framed 350.00
Young Model, litho, sgd and titled, 12 x 9⅝", from edition published by

Associated American Artists, margins, framed 450.00

Verner, Elizabeth O'Neill, Live Oak, Middleton Place, etching, sgd, titled, and numbered 8, 10 x 9⅞, good impression, margins, laid down, framed ... 90.00

Wengenroth, Stow, The Coast Road, litho, sgd and numbered Ed/24, 10⅝ x 15⅞", good printing, margins, mat burn, discoloration along left edge .. 275.00

Whistler, James Abbott McNeill, etching Courtyard, Brussels, sgd with butterfly, inscribed with title in margin, 8⅜ x 4⅞", good impression, on Japan, irregular margins, lightly discolored in margins, framed 2,300.00

Seymour, 5⅜ x 3⅞", good impression, on Japan, margins, spots of foxing and traces of old tape 700.00

PURPLE SLAG (MARBLE GLASS)

History: Challinor, Taylor & Co., Tarantum, Pennsylvania, c1870s–80s, was the largest producer of purple slag in the United States. Since the quality of pieces varies considerably, there is no doubt other American firms made it as well.

Purple slag also was made in England. English pieces are marked with British Registry marks.

Other color combinations, such as blue, green, or orange, were made, but are rarely found.

Additional Listings: Greentown Glass (chocolate slag) and Pink Slag.

Reproduction Alert: Purple slag has been heavily reproduced over the years and still is reproduced at present.

Bowl, 10¾", scalloped, hp orange and gold flowers 50.00

Cake Stand 75.00

Celery Vase, Fluted Rib, Challinor, 8¼" h, 4¼" d at top, $90.00.

Celery Tray, 12 x 4⅛ x 2½" h, rowboat shape, Daisy Block 135.00

Compote, 4½", crimped top 65.00

Creamer, Flower and Panel 85.00

Cruet, 7", Imperial Glass 45.00

Goblet, Flute 40.00

Match Holder, Daisy and Button 40.00

Mug, rabbit 65.00

Plate, 10½", closed lattice edge 100.00

Salt, 2½ x 4" 50.00

Spooner, Scroll with Acanthus 65.00

Sugar, cov, Flute 200.00

Tumbler, 3¼" 48.00

Quezal

QUEZAL

History: The Quezal Art Glass Decorating Company, named for the "quetzal," a bird with brilliant colored feathers, was organized in 1901 in Brooklyn, New York, by two disgruntled Tiffany workers, Martin Bach and Thomas Johnson. They soon hired two more Tiffany workers, Percy Britton and William Wiedebine.

The first products, unmarked, were exact Tiffany imitations. In 1902 the "Quezal" trademark was first used. Quezal pieces differ from Tiffany pieces in that they are more defined and the decorations more visible and brightly colored. No new techniques came from Quezal.

Johnson left in 1905. T. Conrad Vahlsing, Bach's son-in-law, joined the firm in 1918, but left with Paul Frank in 1920 to form Lustre Art Glass Company which copied Quezal pieces. Martin Bach died in 1924; and, by 1925 Quezal ceased operations.

Wares are signed "Quezal" on the base of vases and bowls and rims of shades. The acid-etched or engraved letters vary in size and may be found in amber, black, or gold. A printed label of a quetzal bird was used briefly in 1907.

Bowl, 4⅞ x 3", irid white and gold body, gold pulled feather design, gold int., sgd "Quezal B122" 300.00

Candlesticks, 7¾", blue irid, sgd, pr .. 550.00

Cruet, white opal ground, green pulled feather design, clear yellow stopper and applied handle 2,300.00

Lamp Shade, gold ribbed, sgd, matched set of 3 .... 225.00

Perfume Bottle, 5", flattened teardrop shape, bulbous stopper, Gorham SS monogrammed foliate mounts 585.00

Salt, 2¾", irid gold, ribbed 175.00

Toothpick, 2¼", melon ribbed, pinched sides, irid blue, green, purple, and gold, sgd 185.00

Vase, green feathers, gold border, opal ground, highly iridescent gold stretched interior, sgd "Quezal/J/860," 6½" h, $1,500.00.

Vase

6⅜", squatty, irid gold neck, white body, irid gold feather pulled dec, green zigzag band around shoulder, sgd "Quezal 861"	**900.00**
6⅝", ivory and green, platinum pulled feather design, sgd "Quezal 739"	**1,100.00**
6⅞", irid blue, abstract gold threading, opaque white hearts, sgd	**500.00**
10", jack in the pulpit, irid gold, opaque white and green pulled feather design, sgd "Quezal G471"	**1,900.00**
Wall Sconce, 14", irid floriform shade, white ground, gold pulled feather design, gold int., molded brass sconce, foliage and mirror dec, sgd at base of shade	**175.00**

QUILTS

History: Quilts have been passed down as family heirlooms for many generations. Each is an individual expression. The same pattern may have hundreds of variations in both color and design.

The advent of the sewing machine increased, not decreased the number of quilts which were made. Quilts still are being sewn today.

The key considerations for price are age, condition, aesthetic beauty, and design. Prices are now at a level position. The exception is the very finest examples which continue to bring record prices.

References: John Finley, *Kentucky Quilts, 1800–1900,* Phantheon Books, 1982; Cathy Florence, *Collecting Quilts: Investments In America's Heritage,* Collector Books, 1985; William C. Ketchum, Jr., *The Knopf Collectors' Guides to American Antiques: Quilts,* Alfred A. Knopf, Inc., 1982; Rachel and Kenneth Pellman, *The World of Amish Quilts,* Good Books, 1984.

Album

Pieced and appliqued, child's, brightly colored blue, green, yellow, pink, white, and brown printed and solid calico patches, appliqued birds, peacocks, wood grouse, doves, butterflies, flowers, fruit, and flowering branches, center block appliqued "Flora" above date 1874, NJ, 48 x 50"	**5,000.00**
Pieced, calico, red and various shades of yellow, blue field, each white center sq with pen and ink signature and date 1858, white homespun backing, minor age stains, 76 x 89"	**500.00**

Amish

Appliqued, crib, cotton, four geometric cross motifs in pale gray, black ground, pale gray primary border, subsidiary large black border, pale gray edge, chain, foliate vine, and vertical bar quilting, Ohio, c1930, 45 x 37"	**350.00**
Pieced, cotton, central large six pointed star, lavender and pale lavender, black ground, lavender and black borders, concentric feathered wreath, leaf, potted plant, and chain quilting, Lancaster County, PA, late 19th C, 77 x 84"	**3,850.00**
Bear Paw, pieced, cotton, white geometric and printed orange and blue squares, chintz floral patterned border with blue piping, diagonal bar quilting, 85 x 76"	**1,150.00**
Bowtie, pieced, turquoise, beige, and slate blue, minor fading, rebound, 76 x 86"	**125.00**
Carolina Lily, applique, red and blue calico, white field, machine applique, hand quilted, minor stains, 73 x 73" .	**350.00**
Crazy, pieced, random patches of velvet, satin, cotton, and calico, shades of yellow, blue, green, brown, red, purple, white, and black, fifty-six squares joined by turkeywork stitching, embroidered floral sprigs, flowerheads, and foliage, brown border, Victorian, 75 x 69"	**425.00**
Crown of Thorns, pieced, cotton, six rows of blue triangular patches alternating with white patches, embroidered with stylized foliate motifs within blue and white band borders, blue and white scalloped edges, midwestern, c1920, 80 x 69"	**650.00**

Double Irish Chain, pink and green, white field, c1920 . . . . **185.00**

Feathered Star, pieced olive green and yellow calico, white cotton field, tulips, hearts, wreaths, and meandering vines quilting, American, 19th C, 96" sq **2,650.00**

Grandma's Fan, multicolored prints, 1930 . . . . **170.00**

Honeycomb, spruce green, gold, indigo, c1880, Amish **175.00**

Lightning Bar, pieced, red and yellow calico, 82 x 84" **325.00**

Log Cabin, 82″ square, $225.00.

Monkey Wrench, pieced, cotton, yellow stylized pinwheel motif, white ground, square, stylized floral sprig and berry, and triangular quilting, yellow edge, Missouri, 1930, 78 X 59" **675.00**

Ocean Waves, pieced, multicolored triangular calico patches, printed red and white borders, Missouri, early 20th C **500.00**

Optical Star, pieced, white, yellow, and purple, lavender machine sewn binding, 72 x 82" **200.00**

Our Village Green, pieced, brown, pink, and navy blue calico, machine stitched binding, minor wear and stains, 70 x 78" **100.00**

Pinwheel, applique, four large pinwheels and vining border, red and yellow-green, 96 x 96" **600.00**

Polka Dot, pieced, bright pink and green calico, 72 x 80" **165.00**

Postage Stamp, pieced, cotton and calico, green, black, blue, brown, and gray diamond patches, diamond quilting, Iowa, third quarter 19th C, 81 x 67" **850.00**

Princess Feather, pieced and appliqued, bright green and orange patches, white field, wreath, flowerhead, and blossom quilting, swag leaf border, PA, 19th C, 84" sq **1,500.00**

Rosebuds, applique, vining border, red and green calico, stains, minor wear, corner embroidered "Pauline Devon, Farmington, 1857," 86 x 88" **225.00**

Sampler, pieced, pink, yellow, gray, green, brown, purple, blue, and black calico, five rows of four random patterns, including log cabin, diamond within square, monkey wrench, and star, printed yellow bar border and subsidiary red printed border, chain square and diamond quilting, PA, c1920, 84 x 72" **1,200.00**

Schoolhouse, pieced, cotton, four rows of pink schoolhouse squares, white trim, blue band borders, white intersecting squares, concentric semi-circle quilting, minor wear, late 19th C, 65 x 74" **725.00**

Star, stars in blocks, deep pink ground, c1925 . . . . **225.00**

Star Flower, applique, vining floral border, red, blue, and goldenrod, red and goldenrod puffed berries and circles, machine stitched vine on border, red binding very worn, 68 x 78" **500.00**

Star Medallion, pieced
Nine large stars in red, green, and yellow calico, white field, five color diamond border, minor fabric wear and loss, 82 x 86" **200.00**

Twelve stars in solid green and goldenrod, pink calico, white field, feather wreath and meandering vine quilting, minor wear, 84 x 85" **475.00**

Star of Bethlehem, pieced and appliqued cotton and chintz, red, yellow, beige, rose, and green printed calico and chintz patches, white cotton ground appliqued with chintz paisley, floral, and butterfly cut-outs, cube and herringbone quilting, broad and deep colored rosebud and blossom border, Charles County, MD, mid 19th C, 97 x 90" **6,500.00**

Tree of Life, pieced, cotton, five rows of four green, brown, and white stylized diagonal tree motifs within red bar borders, green intersection squares, triangular, bar, and band quilting, minor fading and patches, c1875, 81 x 69" **500.00**

Wrench, pieced, multicolored prints, pink calico field, 64 x 72" **250.00**

QUIMPER

History: Quimper faience, dating back to the 17th century, is named for Quimper, a French town where numerous potteries were located. Several mergers resulted in the evolution of two major houses - the Jules Henriot and Hubaudire-Bousquet factories.

The peasant design first appeared in the 1860s, and many variations exist. Florals and geometrics, equally popular, also were produced in large quantities. During the 1920s the Hubaudire-Bousquet factory introduced the Odetta line which utilized a stone body and Art Deco decorations.

The two major houses merged in 1968, each retaining its individual characteristics and marks. The concern suffered from labor problems in the 1980s and recently was purchased by an American group.

Marks: The HR and HR Quimper marks are found on Henriot pieces prior to 1922. The HenRoit Quimper mark was used after 1922. The HB mark covers a long span of time. The addition of numbers or dots refers to inventory numbers and are found on later pieces. Most marks are in blue or black. Pieces ordered by department stores, such as Macy's and Carson Pirie Scott, carry the store mark along with the factory mark, making them less desirable to collectors. A comprehensive list of marks is found in Bondhus's book.

References: Susan and Al Bagdade, *Warman's English & Continental Porcelain & Porcelain, 1st Edition,* Warman Publishing Co., Inc., 1987; Sandra V. Bondhus, *Quimper Pottery: A French Folk Art Faience,* published by author, 1981; Millicent Mali, *Quimper Faience,* Airon, Inc., 1979; Marjatta Taburet, *La Faience de Quimper,* Editions Sous le Vent, 1979, French text.

Museums: Musee des Faiences de Quimper, Quimper, France; Victoria and Albert Museum, French Ceramic Dept., London, England.

Advisors: Susan and Al Bagdade.

Bookends, pr
  Baby, seated, multicolored, #823, sgd "SAVIGNY" **1,000.00**
  Young boy, young girl, seated, multicolored, #833, sgd "SAVIGNY" .. **1,200.00**
Bowl
  4⅛" d, 2" h, sq male peasant in center, scattered florals, marked "Marshall Field Quimper France" **45.00**
  6¼", H-H, cov, floral, male peasant

Bone Dish, pr, rims outlined in blue, pierced for hanging, marked "Henriot Quimper France," 9⅛" l, 5¾" w, pr, $270.00.

  and florals on cov, blue sponged handles, marked "Henriot Quimper France" **150.00**
  6⅜" d, female peasant, floral band, ruffled rim outlined in blue, pierced for hanging, marked "Henriot Quimper France" **75.00**
Butter Dish, cov, 6⅜" d, floral band, blue scallops and fleur-de-lis border on base, male peasant on cov, shell knob, repaired inner rim, marked "HR Quimper" **125.00**
Cache Pot, 4" d, 3¾" h, seated male peasant with horn, floral band, blue ruffled rim, marked "Henriot Quimper France" **125.00**
Cake Stand, 9" d, 4½" h, peasant man with flute, marked "Henriot Quimper France" **185.00**
Children's Dishes, 3⅞" d, male on one, female on other, floral and four dot border, outlined rim, marked "Henriot Quimper France," pr **90.00**
Creamer, 3½" h, female peasant, floral sprays, blue ground, marked "Henriot Quimper France" **50.00**
Cup, 3" d, 2¼" h, rust, yellow, and green floral band, handleless, marked "Henriot Quimper France" **45.00**
Cup and Saucer, seated male peasant with horn in gold medallion, blue and rust cross hatched circles, marked "Henriot Quimper France" **75.00**
Cup Plate, 4⅜" d, female peasant, red dash and blue dot border, marked "Henriot Quimper France" **45.00**
Egg Cup, 4" h, female peasant and florals, gold dash attached base, marked "HB Quimper France" **75.00**
Figure
  5" h, male and female peasant, marked "Henriot Quimper," pr ... **450.00**

9″ h, young peasant girl in yellow dress, sgd "B SAVIGNY" 295.00
10″ h, girl carrying umbrella, multicolored 295.00

Hatpin Holder, 4½″ h, man on front, yellow ground, marked "HB Quimper France" 110.00

Inkstand, 7½″ l, 6⅜″ w, male peasant, orange and blue cross hatch border, floral depression between double wells, marked "Henriot Quimper France" 185.00

Cruets, blue sponging, marked "Henriot Quimper France," 5⅜″ h, 8″ w handle to handle, pr, $150.00.

Jardiniere, 9½″ H-H, 2⅝″ h, seated female with egg basket facing seated male on rock, florals on reverse, green sponged rim, ftd, marked "Henriot Quimper France 72" 225.00

Mayonnaise Set, 4″ sq bowl, 6″ sq underplate, matching ladle, marked "HR Quimper France" 85.00

Pitcher
4⅝″ h, male peasant, floral, side and top handle, spout, marked "Henriot Quimper" under handle 85.00
5″ h, figural, bust of man lighting pipe, royal blue jacket, black handle, marked "Henriot Quimper" 210.00
7⅜″ h, female peasant, florals, blue dash handle, pinched spout, marked "Henriot Quimper" under handle 135.00

Plaque, 4½″ d, rooster in center, blue streaked border, hanger on top, marked "Henriot Quimper France," pr 60.00

Plate
5¾″ d, bread and butter, male or female peasant, red, green, and blue floral border, blue rim, marked "HB Quimper France," set of 6 . . . . . . 120.00
6¾″ d, octagon, male peasant, single stroke floral rim, marked "Henriot Quimper" 110.00
7⅜″ d, floral center, green sponged border, marked "HB Quimper France" 50.00
7⅞″ d, octagon, male on one, female on other, floral band borders, marked "Henriot Quimper France," pr 190.00
8″ d
Floral center, blue sponged borders, marked "Henriot Quimper France," pr 95.00
Rooster and florals, marked "HR Quimper" 65.00
8⅜″ d, octagon, male peasant, ermine tail corners, floral band rim, marked "HR quimper France" . . . 135.00
8⅚″ d, blue, green, red, and yellow geometrics, cross hatches and feathers, yellow and blue band border, marked "Henriot Quimper" . . 135.00
9¼″ d, crest supported by lion rampants, multicolored interlaced border, marked "HR Quimper" 250.00
9½″ d, male and female peasant, front view, floral band border, shaped rims, marked "Henriot Quimper France," pr 290.00
10″ sq, octagon, male peasant, red cross hatching and blue dividing lines on border, marked "HB Quimper France" 65.00
10½″ l, modeled fish head and tail, female peasant, pierced for hanging, marked "Henriot Quimper France" 95.00

Platter, 11½″ l, 7⅛″ w, male on one, female on other, yellow and blue striped border, pierced for hanging, marked "Henriot Quimper France," pr 190.00

Porringer, 6¾″ H-H, Rouen border with fleur-de-lis, orange rim, marked "HB Quimper" 75.00

Relish Dish, 7½″ l, male peasant with folded arms, green and blue flowers, pale blue glaze, dark blue scalloped rim, pierced for hanging, marked "HR Quimper" on front 275.00

Sign, 8″ sq, black ermine tails at clipped corners, marked "Brittany Ware From Old France, Henriot Quimper" in dark blue on front 125.00

Teabag Holder, 3⅝″ l, bagpipe shape, female peasant, orange and blue rim, marked "Henriot Quimper France" . 35.00

Trivet, 6″ sq, female peasant, yellow ground, marked "HB Quimper France" 110.00

Tumbler, 4½″ h, male peasant, yellow and blue band border, blue sponge handle, marked "Henriot Quimper France" 65.00

Wall Pocket
    5″ l, bellow shape, peasant woman
        on front, HB mark 65.00
    5½″ l, 3⅜″ w, molded bagpipe shape,
        ribbons top and bottom, florals,
        hole for hanging, marked "HB
        Quimper France" 95.00
    9¾″ l, modeled as double wrapped
        cones, male on one side, female
        on other, loop for hanging, marked
        "HB Quimper" 150.00

RADIOS

History: The radio was invented 100 years ago. Marconi was the first to assemble and employ the transmission and reception instruments that permitted sending electric messages without the use of direct connections. Between 1905 and the end of World War I many technical advances were made to the "wireless,"including the invention of the vacuum tube by DeForest. By 1920 technology progressed. Radios filled the entertainment needs of the average family.

Changes in design, style, and technology brought the radio from the black boxes of the 1920s to the styled furniture pieces and console models of the 1930s and 1940s, to midget models of the 1950s, and finally to the high-tech radios of the 1980s.

References: Philip Collins, *Radios: The Golden Age,* Chronicle Books, 1987; Grinder & Fathauger, *Radio Collectors Directory And Price Guide,* Ironwood Publishing; David and Betty Johnson, *Antique Radios: Restoration and Price Guide,* Wallace-Homestead, 1982.

Periodical: *Radio Age,* 636 Cambridge Road, Augusta, GA 30909.

Collectors' Clubs: Antique Wireless Association, 17 Sheridan Street, Auburn, NY 13021; Antique Radio Club of America, 81 Steeplechase Road, Devon, PA 19333.

Museums: Antique Wireless Museum, East Bloomfield, NY; Caperton's Radio Museum, Louisville, KY; Muchow's Historical Radio Museum, Elgin, IL; Museum of Wonderful Miracles, Minneapolis, MN; New England Museum of Wireless and Steam, East Greenwich, RI; Voice of the Twenties, Orient, NY.

Additional Listings: See *Warman's Americana & Collectibles* for more examples.

American Bosch, Model 28, Ambotone
    cone speaker 130.00
Atwater Kent, Model 20, speaker horn   125.00
Columbia, table model, oak 135.00
Crosley
    Model 4-29, battery operated, 1926 .   110.00
    Model 10-135 . . . .   45.00
Fada, 5½ x 10½ x 6″, Art Deco style
    yellow case, red trim 200.00

Westinghouse, Jukebox Model 1, Model 34X475, white case, gold center band, purple fabric across speaker, carrying handle, 6 x 5½ x 9″, $95.00.

General Electric, Model 81, 8 tube,
    1934 . . . .   195.00
Metrodyne Super 7, 1925 . . . .   250.00
Philco
    Model 37-84, Cathedral, schematic
        design, 1937 . . . .   85.00
    Model 551, 1928 . . . .   125.00
RCA, Radiola 20, 1925 . . . .   135.00
Spartan, Model 5218 . . . .   85.00
Stromberg Carlson, Model 636A, console, 1928 . . . .   120.00
Westinghouse, Model WR-602 . . . . . .   45.00

RAILROAD ITEMS

History: Railroad collectors have existed for decades. The merger of the rail systems and the end of passenger service made many objects available to private collections. The Pennsylvania Railroad sold its archives at public sale.

Railroad enthusiasts have organized into regional and local clubs. Join one if interested. Your local hobby store can probably point you to the right person. The best pieces pass between collectors and rarely enter the general market place.

References: Stanley L. Baker, *Railroad Collectibles: An Illustrated Value Guide, 3rd Edition,* Collector Books, 1985; Richard Luckin, *Dining On Rails,* published by author, 1983.

Museums: Baltimore and Ohio Railroad, Baltimore, MD; Museum of Transportation, Boston, MA; New York Museum of Transportation, Albany, NY; California State Railroad Museum, Sacramento, CA.

Collectors' Clubs: Railroad Enthusiasts, 456 Main Street, West Townsend, MA 01474; Railroadiana Collectors Association, P.O. Box 365, St. Ignatius, MT 59865; Railway and Locomotive Historical Society, 3363 Riviera West Drive, Kelsey-ville, CA 95451.

Periodicals: Key, Lock and Lantern, P.O. Box 15, Spencerport, NY 14559. Subscription: $12.00.

Additional Listings: See *Warman's Americana & Collectibles* for more examples.

Advisor: Alan H. Altman.

Baggage Checks, brass
    Baltimore & Ohio Southwestern Rail-road, 4¾ x 2¼", reads "B&OSWRR CINCINNATI, O.," manufactured by American Railway Supply **65.00**
    Missouri Kansas & Texas Railway, 4¾ x 2¼", reads MISSOURI KAN & TEX RY COMPANY" **70.00**
Bell, brass, steam type **425.00**
Business Document, ALS, Pennsylva-nia Railroad stationery, Office of Su-perintendent, 1860, orig envelope .. **40.00**
China
    Ashtray, Norfolk & Western, Dog-wood, 3¾", no backstamp, Syra-cuse China **65.00**
    Butter Pat, Atchison, Topeka & Santa Fe, Black Chain, 3¼" d, no back-stamp, Sterling China **20.00**

Ticket Case, oak cabinet, tin ticket holders, 16 x 8½ x 17½", $150.00.

Celery Tray, Chicago, Burlington & Quincy, Violet & Daisies, 10¾ x 4¾", no backstamp, Syracuse China **75.00**
Cup and Saucer
    Baltimore and Ohio, Capital, both pieces have top logo, no back-stamp, Shenango China **225.00**
    Southern Pacific, Prairie Mountain Wildflower, backstamp, Syracuse China **75.00**

Plate
    6¼", Chesapeake and Ohio, Greenbrier, no backstamp, Shen-ango China **25.00**
    9", Baltimore and Ohio, Derby, no backstamp, Shenango China .. **65.00**
Platter, oval, Missouri Pacific, Eagle, 10½ x 7¼", top logo, backstamp, Syracuse China **65.00**
Sauce Dish, Great Northern, Moun-tain & Flowers, 5", backstamp, Syr-acuse China **35.00**
Soup
    Reading, Bound Brook, 8", back-stamp, Lamberton China **350.00**
    Southern, Pelican, 9", top marked, no backstamp, Lamberton China **100.00**
Glassware
    Cordial, 4½" h, stemmed, gold NEW YORK CENTRAL" in oval logo ... **50.00**
    Water, New York Central, 4½" h, 2¾" d, black and gold diesel engine and cars, "NEW YORK CENTRAL SYSTEM" in black log, "ROUTE TO THE WORLD'S FAIR NEW YORK WORLD'S FAIR 1964– 1965" in black and gold **25.00**
    Wine, Baltimore & Ohio, 4" h, stemmed, gold line around top, se-ries of train cars running around glass, "B &O" on side of one gold and one white train car **35.00**
Hats with Cap Badges
    Delaware & Hudson, old style hat with two gold bands running around out-side, enameled badge with circle at top with "the D&H" "CONDUC-TOR" in gold at bottom **175.00**
    Louisville & Nashville, old style hat with two gold buttons marked "L&N" with cord running between buttons, domed style badge with red "L&N" in rect box and black enamel "CONDUCTOR" at bottom **95.00**
    Seaboard Airline, old style hat with two "SEABOARD" buttons and sil-ver band running between buttons, cap badge with silver "SEABOARD AIRLINE" at top and "FLAGMAN" at bottom **75.00**
Lantern, Tall Globe
    Colorado & Southern Railway, Adams & Westlake Company "The Ad-ams," last patent date Nov. 30, 1897, framed marked in large let-ters "C&S Ry," double horizontal wire guards, twist-off pot and burner, 5⅜" unmarked cobalt blue globe **250.00**
    Lehigh Valley Railroad, Keystone Lantern Co. "The Casey," last pat-ent date June 2, 1903, frame

marked in large letters "L.V.R.R.,"
single horizontal wire guard, 5⅜"
L.V.R.R. extended base globe ... **350.00**

Lantern Globes
Canadian National Railroad, 5⅜",
clear cast, extended base, globe
has cast "CNR" in serifs **85.00**
Louisville & Nashville, 5⅜", amber,
etched "L&N RR," globe is ex-
tended base, manufactured by
MacBeth Pearl Glass 220 ...... **210.00**
Northern Pacific, 5⅜", amber, etched
"N.P.R.R.," globe also etched on
backside "SAFETY ALWAYS" ... **150.00**
Union Pacific, 5⅜", amber, etched
"Southern Ry" **65.00**

Pocket Mirror, Frisco **90.00**

Silver, Flatware
Fork, dinner, Missouri Pacific, top and
bottom marked with logo, Century,
International Silver **12.00**
Knife
Dinner, Northern Pacific, top and
bottom marked with logo, Em-
bassy, Reed & Barton **18.00**
Steak, Soo Line, bottom marked
with logo, Vassar, Reed & Barton **28.00**
Spoon
Grapefruit, California Zephyr, bot-
tom marked with logo, Century,
International Silver **15.00**
Teaspoon, Union Pacific, bottom
marked "U.P.R.R.," Zephyr, Inter-
national Silver **8.00**
Serving, Rock Island Lines, top
marked, Empire, Gorham **18.00**

Silver, Holloware
Bouillion Cup Holder, Lehigh Valley,
4", hammered mounts, side logo is
raised "LVRR" in diamond, Barth . **135.00**
Creamer, Great Northern, 4 oz,
#05082, side logo is incised over
"G" and "N," International Silver . **50.00**
Gravy Boat, Pullman, 2 oz, #SL0688,
backstamped with name of rail-
road, International Silver **65.00**
Ice Bucket, double handled, Southern, 7½", #1833-S, side logo incised "Southern," Reed & Barton . **400.00**
Tip Tray, Western Pacific, 6½",
#05090, backstamped with name
of railroad, International Silver ... **65.00**

Switch Keys
BELT, Adlake, 3756 .... **20.00**
MK&TRY, Slaymaker, 28928, fat bar-
rel **35.00**
SANTA FE ROUTE, A & W, football
hallmark **28.00**
WP&BRR, C, tapered barrel **175.00**
Tablecloth, Baltimore & Ohio **20.00**
Ticket and envelope, Milwaukee Road,
1930 .... **5.00**

RAZORS

History: Razors date back several thousand
years. Early man used sharpened stones. The
Egyptians, Greeks, and Romans had metal razors.

Razors made prior to 1800 generally were
crudely stamped WARRANTED or CAST STEEL,
with the maker's mark on the tang. Until 1870
almost all razors for the American market were
manufactured in Sheffield, England. Most blades
were wedge shaped; many were etched with slo-
gans or scenes. Handles were made of natural
materials: various horns, tortoise shell, bone, ivory,
stag, silver, and pearl. All razors were handmade.

After 1870 razors were machine made with hollow ground blades and synthetic handle materials.
Razors of this period usually were manufactured
in Germany (Solingen) or in American cutlery factories. Hundreds of molded celluloid handle patterns were produced.

Cutlery firms produced boxed sets of two, four,
and seven razors. Complete and undamaged sets
are very desirable. Most popular are the 7-Day
sets with each razor etched with a day of the week.

The fancier the handle or more intricately etched
the blade, the higher the price. Rarest handle materials are pearl, stag, sterling silver, pressed horn,
and carved ivory. Rarest blades are those with
scenes etched across the entire front. Value is
increased by certain manufacturer's names, e.g.,
H. Boker, Case, M. Price, Joseph Rogers, Simmons Hardware, Will & Finck, Winchester, and
George Wostenholm.

hgb = hollow ground blade
wb = wedge blade

Reference: Robert A. Doyle, *Straight Razor
Collecting, An Illustrated Price Guide*, Collector
Books, 1980, out-of-print.

Periodical: *Blade Magazine*, P.O. Box 22007,
Chattanooga, TN 37422. Subscription: $15.95

Additional Listings: See *Warman's Americana
& Collectibles* for more examples.

Advisor: Robert A. Doyle.

AMERICAN BLADES

American Knife Co, Plymouth Hollow,
Conn, wb, stamped "A Real American," black horn handle **55.00**
Case Brothers, Little Valley, NY, blade
stamped "Tested XX," yellow
wrapped rope pattern handle **30.00**
Golden Rule Cutlery Co, Chicago USA,
blade ground slightly out of shape,
four beautiful woman in bathing suits
on handle **65.00**
Ontario Cutlery Co, Geneva, NY, blade
etched with two crossed American
flags, crown above and "The Mighty"
below, black and white striped handle **25.00**
Schrade Cutlery Co, Walden, NY, hgb,

McKinley and Roosevelt, political, labeled "1900, F. J. Elwell/Rockdale, NY," $225.00.

etched "Everlasting Sharp," green swirl handle with German silver ends, gray and green orig box with model number 158-R **135.00**

Waterville Cutlery Co, Waterville, Conn, blade "Waterville Hand Forged," black celluloid handle with raised floral pattern, oak leaf and acorn scroll **65.00**

ENGLISH BLADES, SHEFFIELD

Joseph Allen, medium hgb, ivory handle with inlaid escutcheon plate of German silver **30.00**

Chris Johnson, wide hgb, plated brass handle **55.00**

Joseph Rodgers & Sons, wb, stag handle with inlaid rect escutcheon plate **125.00**

Wade & Butcher, hgb, etched in ribbon "Wade & Butcher," Art Nouveau handle stamped "Sterling," raised scroll across front and back, monogrammed **320.00**

Geo Wostenholme, blade etched with adv, ivory handle emb **30.00**

GERMAN BLADES

Cosmos Mfg Co, hgb, ivory handle, raised nude picking purple grapes, green leaves **95.00**

Imperial Razor, blade etched with battleship *US Oregon* scene, dark blue celluloid handle **40.00**

F. A. Koch & Co, Made In Germany, ivory handle, colored scene of branches, oak leaves, and deer dec **45.00**

Lewis Razor Co, hgb, celluloid handle, stork eating fish and standing in cattails **50.00**

Chas T. Scott, hgb, marbleized green celluloid handle **12.00**

Wadsworth Razor Co, semi wb, carved bone handle, c1870 . . . . **55.00**

Zartina Cutlery Works, hgb, floral SS handle **275.00**

SWISS BLADES

Joh. Engstrom, frameback, seven interchangeable "wafer" blades, black horn handle, c1880 . . . . **65.00**

Tornablom, hgb, ivory handle **27.00**

SETS OF RAZORS

Pair, G. W. Ruff's Peerless, hgb, ivory handles, leather over wood case with "Gentlemen's Companion Containing 2 Razors Special Hollow Ground," red lining **55.00**

7-Day Set, Crown and Sword, blades etched "The Crown & Sword Razor Extra Hollow Ground," black handles with raised "Crown and Sword," homemade felt lined wood case, plaque with "RAZORS emb on top . **45.00**

RED WING POTTERY

History: The Red Wing pottery category covers several potteries from Red Wing, Minnesota. In 1868 David Hallem started Red Wing Stoneware Co., the first pottery, with stoneware as its primary product and with a red wing stamped under the glaze as its mark. The Minnesota Stoneware Co. started in 1883. The North Star Stoneware Co., 1892–1896, used a raised star and the words Red Wing as its mark.

The Red Wing Stoneware Co. and the Minnesota Stoneware Co. merged in 1892. The new company, the Red Wing Union Stoneware Co., made stoneware until 1920 when it introduced a pottery line which it continued until the 1940s. In 1936 the name was changed to Red Wing Potteries, Inc. During the 1930s it introduced several popular lines of hand painted pattern dinnerware which were distributed through department stores, Sears, and gift stamp centers. Dinnerware declined in the 1950s, being replaced with hotel and restaurant china in the early 1960s.The plant closed in 1967.

References: David A. Newkirk, *A Guide To Red Wing Markings*, Monticello Printing, 1979; Dolores Simon, *Red Wing Pottery With Rumrill*, Collector Books, 1980; Lyndon C. Viel, *The Clay Giants*,

The Stoneware of Red Wing, Goodhue County, Minnesota, Book 2, Wallace-Homestead, 1980.

Additional Listings: See *Warman's Americana & Collectibles* for more examples.

Vase, green-blue, marked "Red Wing, USA," 10″ h, $25.00.

Ashtray, "1953 Anniversary," wing shape, red, three markings	35.00
Bean Pot, lid, Saffron	75.00
Bowl, crockery, spatter, blue, rust, cream, "Geneva Iowa"	80.00
Saffron #6	90.00
Bowl and Pitcher, blue and white, lily .	350.00
Butter Jar, deep blue lettering, 20 lb . .	200.00
Canteen, stoneware, 1900–08	350.00
Casserole, all-over sponge dec, lid . . .	150.00
Churn, molded blue elephant ear leaves, 3 gal, sgd "Minnesota" oval on bottom	400.00
Clock, figural, wall, electric, marked "Tik-Tok Baker"	40.00
Crockery, quart, white, marked "Minnesota"	95.00
Cuspidor, mold seam, brown and white, unsigned	100.00
Jar, ball lock, self-sealing, 3 gal	75.00
Jug	
Beehive, 5 gal, large wing	135.00
Funnel top, salt glaze, 1 gal, marked "Minnesota"	70.00
Shoulder, birchleaf, molded, 4 gal, sgd	125.00
Measure, Convention Commemorative, acid proof	65.00
Nappy, white, marked "Minnesota" . . .	60.00
Pitcher, cherry band, medium size	30.00
Salt Box, spongeband, lid, hanging . . .	450.00
Snuff Jar, white glaze, 1 quart, marked "RW"	75.00
Spittoon, salt glaze, "Red Wing Stoneware Company" stamped on side . .	275.00

Umbrella Stand, blue sponge dec, unsigned	500.00
Vase	
6½″ h, Art Pottery, paper label, pr . .	35.00
9¾″, four relief panels with brown semi-glaze trees, gray matte ground, marked	45.00
Water Cooler, "Ice Water," lid, #4, orig cork	265.00
Water Pitcher, Saffronware adv	125.00

REDWARE

History: The availability of clay, the same used to make bricks and roof tiles, accounted for the great production of red earthenware pottery in the American colonies. Redware pieces are mainly utilitarian—bowls, crocks, jugs, etc.

Lead glazed redware retained its reddish color, but a variety of colored glazes were obtained by the addition of metals to the basic glaze. Streaks and mottled splotches resulted in redware items resulted from impurities in the clay and/or uneven firing temperatures.

"Slipware" is a term used to describe redwares decorated by the application of slip, a semi-liquid paste made of clay. Slipwares were made in England, Germany, and elsewhere in Europe for decades before becoming popular in the Pennsylvania German region and elsewhere in colonial America.

Plate, four slip cup, yellow on reddish brown, 9½″ d, $200.00.

Apple Butter Jar	
4¾″, tooled lines at shoulder, strap handle, and flared lip, glaze wear and flaking	55.00
7¼″, strap handle, mottled green glaze, amber spots, hairlines and old flakes	120.00

Bank
3⅜", knob finial, reddish matte glaze, small chips 65.00
5", knob finial, purplish brown glaze, small edge chips 55.00
5¼" h, ovoid, tooled lines at shoulder, knob finial, slightly amber glaze with brown flecks, minor wear ... 125.00
Bottle, 5½" l, keg shaped, bung hole, gray glaze, brown and green spots, hairlines and minor chips 250.00

Bowl
4⅜ x 2", protruding foot, int. with brown cross and dots, ext. with dots, brown fleck glaze, old rim repair, minor wear, small flakes 175.00
5¼ x 3⅛", crown like molded handles, mottled brownish black glaze, minor wear and small edge flakes .. 375.00
15½ x 2½", coggled edge, three and four line yellow slip dec, minor wear and old flakes 1,800.00

Charger
11½", yellow slip crossed wavy lines, worn and chipped 475.00
12", coggled rim, yellow slip scroll design, wear, chips, and hairlines .. 350.00
Creamer, 3¾", strap handle, running black splotches, clear glaze, minor wear, small flakes, close fitting mismatched lid 175.00
Cup, 3¾", flared lip, applied handle, clear glaze with mottled amber, minor wear and glaze flakes 85.00
Cup and Saucer, dark brown glaze, small flakes, handle glued 50.00
Cuspidor, 8 x 4¼", tooled bands, brown and green running glaze with brown dashes, some wear and edge chips 250.00
Dish, oval, 10¾ x 14 x 2", coggled edge, yellow slip dec of wavy lines, rim hairline, edge chipped 350.00

Figure
1½" h, bird, simple molded detail, white slip, amber glaze, edge wear 75.00
9¼" l, 6½" h, dog, reclining, gold dec, attributed to John Bell, ex-McKearin collection 250.00
Flask, 6½" h, tooled lines and brown splotched glaze, old hairline in side, chip on lip 220.00

Flower Pot
4⅝", tooled lines, crimped lip, brown flecked glaze, brown sponging, attached saucer, wear and edge chips 155.00
5¾", well tooled rim, black fleck glaze, brown sponging, mismatched saucer 85.00
8½" h, edge tooling on rim and attached saucer base, yellow slip int., ext. with yellow slip and splotches of brown and green, clear shiny glaze, Shenandoah, some wear and chips 500.00

Jar
4⅝", ovoid, protruding lip, amber glaze, brown sponging, minor flakes 355.00
5⅝"
Applied handle, tooled lines at shoulder, mottled brown glaze with black flecks, minor wear and edge chips 85.00
Well shaped, tooled lines, flaring lip, mottled greenish glaze, brown sponging, rim chips 200.00
6¼", ovoid, tooled lines at shoulder, flared lip, mottled brown glaze, minor wear and chip on base 225.00
7¾", ovoid, tooled lines and applied handles, shiny glaze with amber highlights, dark brown splotches, wear and edge chips 400.00
8¼ x 6¾", imp label "John W. Bell, Waynesboro, Pa.," brown int. glaze, unglazed ext. with good patina, minor wear, small flakes 80.00
9½", flared lip, yellow slip stripes, green highlights, brown wavy lines, rim hairline and small rim chips, two old chips on base 1,350.00

Jug
6⅝" h, ovoid, wide ribbed strap handle, black shiny glaze, minor wear, small edge flakes 200.00
6¾", tooled line at shoulder, strap handle, shiny glaze with few brown splashes, hairline in shoulder 125.00

Loaf Pan
9½ x 13½", coggled edge, four line yellow slip dec, old surface and edge flakes 825.00
11½ x 15½ x 3", coggled edge, three line yellow slip dec, old edge flakes, good wear, minor flakes in slip ... 950.00
Milk Bowl, 7 x 3¼", tooled dot line and bulbous lip, brown sponged glaze, minor wear 225.00

Mug
3⅝", medium brown glaze, one splash of darker brown, attributed to John Bell, minor glaze wear ... 120.00
4½", rich brown sponging, imp "John Bell" 775.00
5¼", butter print-like applied star design, strap handle and tooled lip, clear glaze with greenish highlights, good patina, minor glaze flakes and wear 125.00

Pie Plate
6½", coggled edge, yellow slip stylized tulip design, hint of green, old chips 950.00

6⅞", yellow slip X and O design, brown spots, old edge chips 675.00

7⅝", coggled edge, yellow slip double tulip, highlighted in rich green, old chips 1,625.00

8", coggled edge, three line yellow slip dec, small old surface flakes . 260.00

9⅞", coggled edge, three line yellow slip dec, wavy lines and dots, worn, center slip chipped, small old edge chips 150.00

Pipe Bowl, 5¼", greenish amber glaze, brown flecks 100.00

Pitcher

4½ x 5⅛", yellow slip int., ext. with three deep rim scallops in brown glaze bordered and dec with yellow slip designs on rim and handle, hairlines, chips and glaze flakes, some old rim flakes colored in ... 55.00

5⅞", ribbed strap handle, tooled dot line, black sponged glaze, chips, replaced lid 175.00

8 x 4⅝", cup shape, tooled dotted line, ribbed strap handle, brown sponging on rim, four vertical bands, hairlines and glued break out on bottom 150.00

Plate, 7" d, coggled edge, yellow slip dec 650.00

Preserving Jar

6", tooled lines just below shoulder, protruding lip, black fleck glaze, three vertical bands of brown sponging, wear and small chips .. 150.00

7", tooled lines, wide vertical brushed brown bands, some wear, small chips 200.00

10¾", tooled lines at shoulder and flared lip, brown splotches, hairlines in base and lip chips 150.00

Salt

2 x 1⅜", mottled greenish amber glaze, brown circles and sponging, edge chips 165.00

3" l, scroddle ware, marbleized yellow slip with brown and green, cast from lacy salt 325.00

Slip Cup, 1⅞" h, single hole for quill, int. glazed 115.00

Turk's Head Mold

7¼", scalloped rim, brown sponged glaze, minor edge flakes 55.00

8 x 2¼", scalloped rim, greenish amber glaze, brown sponging, wear and small flakes 115.00

8⅞", scalloped rim, black sponged glaze, old chips 65.00

9¼", scalloped rim and black sponged glaze, some filled in rim chips and small flakes 65.00

Watch Holder, 4" h, dark brown glaze,

scalloped rims, ex-McKearin collection 200.00

RELIGIOUS ITEMS

History: Objects for the worshipping or expression of man's belief in a superhuman power are collected by many people for many reasons.

Icons are included since they are religious mementos, usually paintings with a brass encasement. Collecting icons dates from the earliest period of Christianity. Most available today were made in the late 19th century.

Painting and embroidery, possibly European, 20¾ x 27", $400.00.

Altar Coffer, 31¼ x 63 x 19", Chinese, 19th C, rect top, multicolored lacquer dec, black lacquered ground, central five-clawed dragon with pair of flaming chasing dragons, stylized waves, three small drawers painted with lotus and keyfret panels above two stacks of three drawers flanking double doors dec with confronting dragons and stylized florals 1,550.00

Bible, English, 1801, Philadelphia, published by Carey, full leather binding, color bookplate of Christian Hoober . 100.00

Bible Box, carved oak, dated 1613 ... 300.00

Diorama, 16½ x 22", painted wax, wedding of the Virgin after Raphael, late Renaissance style 5,000.00

Figure, Italian

19" h, Christ crucified, carved ivory, crown of green thorns on brown painted hair, nailed to later ebonized crucifix with sp caps, late 18th C 1,000.00

30¾", saint, parcel gilt and polychrome, standing, wavy brown hair, red and gilt foliate patterned robe tied at waist, cloak at hips, circular base, 19th C **1,325.00**

Icon

Greek, 7¼″ h, Virgin and Child, carved gilt wood border, 17th C . . **1,350.00**

Russian

13¼ x 11″, Mother of God with St Dimitry and St Evdokin on left, St Aviv on right, c1800 . . . . **800.00**

18½ x 15¾″, Resurrection, 12 holy days surrounding central scene, painted on silver and gold leaf ground, c1800 . . . . **750.00**

Madonna, 28″, wooden, polychrome, heavily robed standing figure, hands clasped, red and brown robes, gilt foliate scrollwork, circular plinth, Spanish, 18th C **750.00**

Panel

6 x 8″, oval, composition, Holy family, mirrored bordered frames, Baroque, pr **300.00**

38 x 41½″, carved and polychromed wood, high relief carving of Christ and Apostles at Last Supper, large inverted gilt shell, later parcel gilt, ebonized frame, Spanish Baroque, early 18th C **2,250.00**

Prayer Book, ivory and silver inlaid case **150.00**

Reliquary, 21½ x 10½ x 32″, fruitwood, parquetry, molded frame, inlaid bands and columns, molded cornice, projecting base with three drawers, contemporary mirrored plate back, Italian Baroque, 19th C **800.00**

Reliquary Figure, 17¼″, St Jerome, parcel gilt and polychromed wood, three quarter length frontal bust, wearing robe cape, cowl, and wide brimmed tasseled hat, oval reliquary recess, carved rect plinth base, Spanish, 18th C **800.00**

Reliquary Panel, 12 x 15¾″, shaped rect form, large embroidered silk blossoms and foliage, pair of silver threaded cornucopia and bone relic, gold and colored thread ornaments, mounted on glazed and carved giltwood frame, Continental, 18th C . . . **175.00**

REVERSE PAINTING ON GLASS

History: The earliest examples of reverse painting on glass were produced in the 13th century Italy. By the 17th century the technique had spread to Central and Eastern Europe. It spread westward as the glass industry center moved to Germany in the late 17th century.

The Alsace and Black Forest region developed a unique portraiture style. The half and three-quarter portraits often were titled below the portrait. Women tend to have general names. Most males are of famous men.

The English used a mezzotint method, rather than free-style, to create their reverse paintings. Landscapes and allegorical figures were popular. The Chinese began working in the medium in the 17th century, eventually favoring marine and patriotic scenes.

Reverse painting was done in America. Most were by folk artists, unsigned, who favored portraits, patriotic and mourning scenes, floral compositions, landscapes, and buildings. Known American artists include Benjamin Greenleaf, A. Cranfield, and Rowley Jacobs.

In the late 19th century commercially produced reverse paintings, often decorated with mother-of-pearl, became popular. Themes included the Statue of Liberty, the capitol in Washington, D.C., and various world fairs and expositions.

PORTRAITS

Chinese Export, Beauty seated in rootwood chair, pheasant perched at feet, 19 x 21″ **3,125.00**

Chinese Export, Mandarin, seated, smoking, attendant standing, 19 x 21″ **3,200.00**

George and Martha Washington, bust portrait, white wig, white shawl, shaded brown ground, 19th C, 28 x 24″, pr **350.00**

Nikolaus, Kaizer Aller Russina, green uniform, blue sash, gold highlights, brown ground, 9½ x 12″ orig frame . **225.00**

Oslreicherin, bust of young woman, ornately coifed hair, necklace, low-cut dress, titled, orig frame, 12 x 9½″ . . **335.00**

Cottage Scene, MOP highlights on house, green frame with gild plaster end pieces, 12 x 24″, $85.00.

SCENES

A Visit To The Grandmother, scene of three generations of women and cat, black border, title on back, orig gilt frame, 21¾ x 27¾″ **225.00**

Chinese Export, pair of Chinese maidens, long robes, landscape visible through window opening, early 19th C, giltwood frame, 27¼ x 19½", pr . **3,850.00**

Church and trees, bright colors, beveled frame, 9⅜ x 11⅜" **300.00**

Country scene, house, lake, and boat, ornate frame **85.00**

Floral wreath, multicolored foil backing, black ground, giltwood frame, 18½ x 16½" **50.00**

Naval Battle, "Perry's Lake Erie Victory, Sept 10th, 1813," multicolored, 7 x 9" **250.00**

Spring and Summer, personification, 11¾ x 15¾", framed **375.00**

RIDGWAY

History: Throughout the 19th century the Ridgway family, through a series of partnerships, held a position of importance in Shelton and Hanley, Staffordshire, England. The connection began with Job and George, two brothers, and Job's two sons, John and William. In 1830 John and William separated with John retaining the Cauldon Place factory and William the Bell Works. By 1862 the porcelain division of Cauldon was carried on by Coalport China Ltd. William and his heirs continued at the Bell Works and the Church [Hanley] and Bedford [Shelton] works until the end of the 19th century.

Many early pieces are unmarked. Later marks include the initials of the many partnerships.

References: Susan and Al Bagdade, *Warman's English & Continental Pottery & Porcelain, 1st Edition,* Warman Publishing Co., Inc., 1987; G. A. Godden, *The Illustrated Guide To Ridgway Porcelains*, Barrie & Jenkins, 1972.

Additional Listings: Staffordshire, Historical, and Staffordshire, Romantic.

Bowl, 10" d, Coaching Days, Eloped, silver rim **65.00**

Cup and Saucer, green transfer, children at play **85.00**

Dinner Service, underglaze blue, enamels, and gilding, printed coat of arms, marked "Imperial Stone China," 54 pcs, minor damage and staining . . . **950.00**

Dish, 10¼" d, Oriental scenes, blue ground **25.00**

Jug, 5" h, soft paste, white griffins and cherubs, brown body, mask spout . . **150.00**

Pitcher

6" h, tavern scene, mustard ground, c1835 . . . . **65.00**

10" h, salt glaze, raised scenes of Burns poems, marked "Ridgway & Company, design published Oct 1, 1835" **225.00**

Mug, silver luster rim, black coaching scenes, caramel-mustard ground, marked "Scenes from Coaching Days, Coaching Ways by Special Permission of MacMillan & Co., Ltd," 3¼" top d, 4¼" h, $45.00.

Plate, 7½", gray transfer, Columbian Star pattern, imp "John Ridgway" . . **25.00**

Platter, 17", Asiatic Places, dark blue, two people on mound in foreground scene, vase with flowers to left, temple background, cartouche enclosing label "Ridgways Asiatic Palaces" . . **155.00**

Saucer, 5¼", blue, small child petting lamb, imp "Ridgway" on back **90.00**

Soup Tureen, 13½", black transfer, Indus pattern, marked "Ridgway, Sparks & Ridgway" **135.00**

Teapot, 4¾" h, molded formal and fluted borders, mid 19th C **30.00**

Tray, 12½" d, Pickwick Series, "Mr. Pickwick at the Election," black transfer, caramel ground, silver scalloped edge **100.00**

Vase

9⅞" h, scroll panel, printed Oriental emblems, green ground, double handles **60.00**

10" h, gold bands, open blue iris on bottom **75.00**

RING TREES

History: A ring tree is a small, generally saucer shaped object made of glass, porcelain, metal, or wood with a center post in the shape of a hand, branches, or cylinder for hanging or storing finger rings.

GLASS

Cranberry, floral dec, gold trim **115.00**

Fenton, turtle **20.00**

| Opaline, blue, hp gold, blue, and white floral dec, ftd, 4½″ | 70.00 |
| Spatter, yellow, white, and clear, 3¾″h | 65.00 |

PORCELAIN

Child's hand, fingers extended, 4″, Parian Ware	45.00
German, hand on saucer, dec	22.50
Limoges, multicolored blossoms, white ground, marked "T & V. Limoges"	40.00
Minton, 3″ h, pastel flowers on top, gold edge and knob, marked "Minton, England"	40.00
Nippon, gold hand, rim dec	35.00
RS Poland, violets, pearlized finish	100.00

Sterling Silver, marked "RW&S," base 3″ d, 2″ h, $175.00.

POTTERY

| Irid gold, 3½″, Zsolnay | 75.00 |
| Pink and green flowers, gold, hp, marked "M Z Austria" | 65.00 |

ROCKINGHAM AND ROCKINGHAM BROWN GLAZED WARES

History: Rockingham ware can be divided into two categories. The first consists of the fine china and porcelain pieces made between 1826 and 1842 by the Rockingham Company of Swinton, Yorkshire, England, and its predecessor firms:

Swinton, Bingley, Don, Leeds, and Brameld. The Bramelds developed the cadogan, a lidless teapot. Between 1826 and 1842 a quality soft paste body with a warm, silken feel was developed by the Bramelds. Elaborate specialty pieces were made. By 1830 the company employed 600 workers and listed 400 designs for dessert sets and 1,000 designs for tea and coffee services in their catalog. Unable to meet its payroll, the company closed in 1842.

The second category of Rockingham ware is pieces produced in the famous Rockingham brown glaze, which was intense and vivid purple-brown when fired. It had a dark, tortoise shell mottled appearance. The glaze was copied by many English and American potteries. American manufacturers who used Rockingham glaze include D. & J. Henderson of Jersey City, New Jersey, United States Pottery in Bennington, Vermont, potteries in East Liverpool, Ohio, and several potteries in Indiana and Illinois.

Reference: Susan and Al Bagdade, *Warman's English & Continental Pottery & Porcelain, 1st Edition,* Warman Publishing Co., Inc., 1987.

Additional Listings: Bennington and Bennington-Type.

Salt, 4½″ h, $125.00.

Baker, 11½ x 8½″, mottled	175.00
Bowl	
6½″ d, 3½″ h, emb, diamond quilted band near base	60.00
9½″ d, 3⅛″ h, emb reeding	70.00
Creamer, 6¼″, cow shape, brown glaze	100.00
Dish	
8¼ x 9⅛″, rect, emb rim dec	105.00
12″ l, oval	90.00
Foot Warmer, brown glaze	65.00
Pie Plate, 10¼″ d	105.00
Pitcher	
6″ h, emb floral rim	40.00
8⅜″ h, emb scene of cranes, acorns, and oak leaves, serpent handle, animal head spout	70.00

9¼" h, emb hunter, dog, and game .	75.00
9¾" h, emb animals, hound handle .	50.00
Plate, 8¾", octagonal, pr	130.00
Platter, 15" l, emb scalloped rim	350.00
Salt Container, 6" d, crest, emb peacocks, hanging hole	45.00
Teapot	
8¼" h, Rebecca at well	65.00
9¾" l, figural, duck, emb detail, rect lid	195.00
Tobacco Jar	
5¼" h, 6½" d, emb design, peacocks, lid	125.00
9" h, cov, emb gothic arches	225.00
Tray, 8½ x 11", scalloped rim	95.00

ROCKWELL, NORMAN

History: Norman Rockwell (February 3, 1894–November, 1978) was a famous American artist. During the time he painted, from age 18 until his death, he created over 2,000 works.

His first professional efforts were illustrations for a children's book. He next worked for *Boy's Life,* the Boy Scout magazine. His most famous works were used by *Saturday Evening Post* for their cover illustrations.

Norman Rockwell painted everyday people in everyday situations, mixing a little humor with sentiment. His paintings and illustrations are treasured because of this sensitive approach. Rockwell painted people he knew and places with which he was familiar. New England landscapes are found in many of his illustrations.

References: Denis C. Jackson, *The Norman Rockwell Identification And Value Guide To: Magazines, Posters, Calendars, Books, 2nd Edition,* published by author, 1985; Carl F. Lucky, *Norman Rockwell Art and Collectibles,* Books Americana, Inc., 1981; Mary Moline, *Norman Rockwell Collectibles, 5th Edition,* Rumbleseat Press, 1984.

Museums: Corner House, Stockbridge, MA; Norman Rockwell Museum, Northbrook, IL.

Reproduction Alert: Because of the popularity of his works, they have been reproduced on many objects. These new collectibles should not be confused with original artwork and illustrations. However, they do allow a collector more range in collecting interests and prices.

Additional Listings: See *Warman's Americana & Collectibles* for more examples.

HISTORIC

Book, Mark Twain, *The Adventures of Tom Sawyer,* 1936	50.00
Calendar, 1922, Warren National Bank, Music Master	300.00
Poster, The Saturday Evening Post 100th Year of Baseball, 22 x 28", 1939	175.00

MODERN

Bell, Royal Devon, Butter Girl, 1976 . .	40.00
Coin, Ford Motor Co, 50th Anniversary	35.00

Poster, "Save Freedom of Speech," World War II, distributed by Office of War Information, 20 x 28", $100.00.

Figure	
Gorham Fine China	
Batter Up	50.00
Four Seasons, Childhood, 1973, set of four	500.00
Pride of Parenthood	60.00
Grossman Designs, Inc.	
Barbershop Quartet, 1975	125.00
Tom Sawyer, Series No. 1, 1976 .	100.00
Ingot, Franklin Mint, tribute to Robert Frost, 1974	275.00
Plate	
Ages of Love, Gorham Fine China, 1973, Four Seasons series, set of 4	300.00
Doctor and Doll, Royal Devon, 1975, Mother's Day	90.00
Scotty Gets His Tree, Rockwell Society of America, 1974, Christmas	175.00
Under The Mistletoe, Franklin Mint, SS, 1971	175.00
Print	
Circle Fine Arts, limited edition, sgd and numbered	
Dressing Up, pencil sgd	2,800.00
Ichabod Crane	5,000.00
Music Hath Charms	3,000.00
Wet Paint, 24 x 30", collotype . . .	1,550.00
Eleanor Ettinger, Inc.	
After The Prom, 24 x 26¾", litho .	4,500.00
Gilding The Eagle, 21 x 25½", litho	3,225.00
The Swing, 20 x 21", litho	4,750.00

ROGERS & SIMILAR STATUARY

History: John Rogers, born in America in 1829, studied sculpturing in Europe and produced the first plaster-of-paris statue, "The Checker Players," in 1859. It was followed by "The Slave Auction" in 1860.

His works were popular parlor pieces of the Victorian era. He produced at least 80 different subjects and the total number of groups made from the originals is estimated to be over 100,000.

Casper Hennecke, one of Rogers' contemporaries, operated C. Hennecke & Company from 1881 until 1896 in Milwaukee, Wisconsin. His statuary often is confused with Rogers' work since both are very similiar.

It is difficult to find a statue in undamaged condition and with original paint. Use the following conversions: 10% minor flaking; 10% chips; 10–20% piece or pieces broken and reglued; 20% flaking; 50% repainting.

References: Paul and Meta Bieier, *John Rogers' Groups of Statuary*, published by author, 1971; Betty C. Haverly, *Hennecke's Florentine Statuary*, published by author, 1972; David H. Wallace, John Rogers: The People's Sculptor, Wesleyan Univ., 1976.

ROGERS

Balcony, The, 32½" h, 11/4/1879, orig paint, some flaking, violin repaired	600.00
Council of War	
Type A, 24½" h, 3/31/1868	875.00
Type B, 3/31/1868, orig paint, flaked, chair cov chipped, document cracked	500.00
Type C, 24" h, minor flaking	475.00
Faust & Marguerite–Leaving The Garden, 25½" h, 1890	400.00
Fugitive's Story, 16" h, 1891	600.00

Hennecke's Florentine Statuary, Conquering Jealousy, 13" h, $200.00.

Mail Day, 16" h, 1864	650.00
One More Shot, 24" h, 1865	425.00
Referee, The, 22" h, 1880, repainted	350.00
School Days, 21½" h, 1877	700.00
Union Refugees, spelter, 1864, one of seven known, hammer of rifle chipped	1,200.00

ROGERS TYPE

After The Case, 20" h	110.00
By Jingo, 17" h, orig paint, minor chipping	125.00
Can't You Talk, 10½" h	135.00
First Love, 13" h, repainted	165.00
Holy Family, 18" h	225.00
Romeo & Juliet, 16" h	150.00
Wellers, The, 11½" h	300.00

ROOKWOOD POTTERY

History: Mrs. Marie Longworth Nicholas Storer, Cincinnati, Ohio, founded Rookwood Pottery in 1880. The name of this outstanding American art pottery came from her family estate "Rookwood," named for the rooks (crows) which inhabited the wooded grounds.

There are five elements to the Rookwood marking system—the clay or body mark, the size mark, the decorator mark, the date mark, and the factory mark. Rookwood art pottery can best be dated from factory marks.

In 1880–1882 the factory mark was the name "Rookwood" incised or painted on the base. Between 1881 and 1886 the firm name, address, and year appeared in an oval frame. Beginning in 1886, the impressed "RP" monogram appeared and a flame-mark was added for each year until 1900. After 1900 a Roman numeral, indicating the last two digits of the year of production, was added at the bottom of the "RP" flame-mark monogram. This last mark is the one most often found on Rookwood pottery today.

Though the Rookwood pottery filed for bankruptcy in 1941, it was soon reorganized under new management. Efforts at maintaining the pottery proved futile, and it again was sold in 1956 and in 1959. The pottery was moved to Starkville, Mississippi, in conjunction with the Herschede Clock Co. It finally ceased operation in 1967.

Rookwood wares changed with the times. The variety is endless, in part because of the great variations in glazes and designs due to the creativity of the many talented artists.

References: Herbert Peck, *The Book of Rookwood Pottery*, Crown Publishers, Inc., 1968; Herbert Peck, *The Second Book of Rookwood Pottery*, published by author, 1985.

Collectors' Club: American Art Pottery Association, P.O. Box 714, Silver Spring, MD 20901.

Ashtray, MacGregor Goldsmith, medium blue, 1949, 5¾″ d, $87.50.

Ashtray, oblong, celadon green, high glaze, 1953 . . . . 25.00
Basket, 7 x 4 x 4″, two handles, four feet, upfolded sides, underglaze slip painted flowers, standard brown glaze, artist sgd "Edith Regina Felton, 1887" 400.00
Bookends, pr
   Colonial Girls, 6½″, white glaze, 1924 150.00
   Dachshund, brown, tan highlights, 1927, artist sgd "Louise Abel" . . . 200.00
   Elephant, walking, white glaze, 1921 175.00
   Rook, chocolate brown glaze, artist sgd "William McDonald" 165.00
Bowl, 5½ x 6″, yellow and green flowers, standard reddish-brown glaze, marked with "U" and "7" on bottom 50.00
Candleholder, figural, pond lily, ivory glaze, 1927 . . . . 25.00
Creamer, 3″, underglaze slip painted leaf and berries, standard glaze, shape #655, artist sgd "Sallie E. Coyne, 1903" 250.00
Cup and Saucer, 2½ x 4½″, holly leaves and berries, standard glaze, artist sgd "Sara Sax, 1897" 300.00
Desk Set, Arts and Crafts style double inkwell, matching letter holder, high glaze, 1926 . . . . 300.00
Ewer
   8″, nasturtiums, standard glaze, artist sgd "Sallie E. Coyne, 1892" 375.00

10″, trefoil top, underglaze slip painted maple leaves and buds, standard glaze, artist sgd "Constance A. Baker, 1897" 475.00
Figure
   3¾″ h, seated monkey, tan glazed, 1936, various marks 100.00
   4″ l
      Cat, medium blue, matte finish, 1929, various marks 80.00
      Elephant, ivory glaze, matte finish, artist sgd "William McDonald, 1926" 75.00
   5¼″, rooster, green, yellow, brown, and red matte finish, artist sgd "Charles T. McLaughlin, 1928" with various other marks 225.00
Flower Frog, 6″ h, figural, raven, black glaze, 1923 . . . . 200.00
Jug
   4⅝″, shades of brown, white, and gold, bird, pine boughs, and clouds, artist sgd "Martin Rettig, 1884" with various other marks 300.00
   4¾″, blue, turquoise, black, green, brown, ivory, and gold spiders and webs dec, artist sgd "William P. McDonald, 1883," with various other marks 250.00
Mug
   4¾″, pint, dark and light brown, yellows, and flesh tones, elderly Flemish lady dec, artist sgd "Grace Young, 1897" with various other marks 1,000.00
   5″, dog portrait, standard glaze, artist sgd "MAD, 1897" 1,000.00
Plaque
   5 x 8″, rect, titled "The Bay," artist sgd "Lenore Asbury, 1920," framed 750.00
   7¼ x 9¼″, scenic vellum, winter landscape, artist sgd "Sara Sax, 1917" 1,200.00
Plate, 7⅛″, yellow, pansies and swirl dec, standard glaze, artist sgd "Laura A. Fry, 1887" 240.00
Tea Tile, 5¾″, ftd, parrot perched in flowering tree, four pastel colors, 1920 . . . . 80.00
Teapot, 7¼″, thistle dec, standard glaze, artist sgd "OGR, 1892" 575.00
Tile
   4½ x 4¼″, blue-green, emblem of Packard Motor Co, 1910 . . . . 75.00
   5¾″, circular, seagulls in flight, two colors, 1943 . . . . 60.00
   12 x 12″, architectural, standing cherubs 300.00
Vase
   4½″, medium and dark brown, yellow-brown nasturtiums, sgd "Laura E. Lindeman, 1907" with various other marks 200.00

5¼", yellow and green blossoms, wax matte glaze, artist sgd "Margaret Helen McDonald, 1930" with various other marks 200.00

6", bud, floral, standard glaze, artist sgd "CCN, 1897" 200.00

6¼", wisteria, standard glaze, artist sgd "BH, 1893" 375.00

6⅝", background shaded from green to soft peach, blue at top, violet flowers, wax matte glaze, unidentified signature, miscellaneous other marks, 1938 . . . . 450.00

6¾", Art Deco motif, wax matte, artist sgd "LA, 1923" 300.00

7", flowers in shades of blue and lavender, vellum, artist sgd "HEW, 1907" 375.00

Vase, wax resist ducks, blue tones, #1659E, 1910, artist signed "Kath-Van Horne," 7⅜" h, $1,250.00.

8", stylized blue peacock feathers, green ground, vellum, artist sgd "Sara Sax, 1910" 800.00

8¼", Iris, berries and leaves, shaded gray to orchid to black ground, artist sgd "Sara Sax," shape #909C 1,000.00

9", slightly raised yellow flowers and green leaves, various black, dark green, and yellowish-brown backgrounds, artist sgd "Albert R. Valentien, 1894" with various other marks 400.00

9½", shaded blues and tans landscape dec, vellum glaze, artist sgd "Edward Diers, 1921," faint age cracks in bottom 300.00

10½", black, brown, and yellow, nasturtiums, dark green glaze, handle 75.00

10¾", scenic, blue and dark river landscape, vellum, artist sgd "ETH, 1939" 850.00

ROSE BOWLS

History: A rose bowl, a decorative open bowl with a crimped, pinched, or petal top, held fragrant rose petals or potpourri which served as an air freshener in the late Victorian period. Practically every glass manufacturer made rose bowls in a variety of patterns and glass types, including fine art glass.

Additional Listings: See specific glass categories.

Satin Glass, yellow, white casing, 4½" d, 4" h, $75.00.

Amberina, 6", Hobnail 250.00

Cameo, 3¼", enameled three petal top, mottled gold, river landscape cutting, acid cut, sgd "Daum Nancy" 625.00

Cranberry, 6", opalescent, hobnail . . . 60.00

Cut Velvet, 3¾", rose, DQ, white lining 175.00

Opalescent, Swirl, blue 75.00

Peachblow, 4", six crimps 125.00

Rubena Overshot, 3¾", eight crimps . . 70.00

Satin Glass

4", yellow, shell pattern 75.00

6", blue, shaded, crimped top 65.00

Spangled, 6", cased, lavender, silver veining, attributed to Cape Cod Glass Works 80.00

Stevens and Williams, 3", satin glass, DQ, MOP, rainbow, alternating stripes of pastel yellow, pink, and blue, imp sgd "Stevens & Williams, Stourbridge Glass" 1,045.00

Vaseline, 3", "World's Fair 1893," banners and foliage dec, polished pontil 125.00

ROSE CANTON, ROSE MANDARIN, ROSE MEDALLION

History: The pink rose color has given its name to three related groups of Chinese export porcelain. Rose Mandarin was produced from the late 18th century to approximately 1840. Rose Canton began somewhat later extending through the first half of the 19th century. Rose Medallion originated in the early 19th century and was made through the early 20th century.

Rose Mandarin derives its name from the Mandarin figure(s) found in garden scenes with women and children. The women often feature gold decorations in their hair. Polychrome enamels and birds separate the scenes.

Rose Medallion has alternating panels of figures and birds and flowers. The elements are four in number, separated evenly around the center medallion. Peonies and foliage fill voids.

Rose Canton is similar to Rose Medallion except the figure panels are replaced by flowers. People are present only if the medallion partitions are absent. Some patterns have been named—Butterfly and Cabbage, Rooster, etc. The category actually is a catchall for all pink enamel ware not fitting into the first two groups.

Reference: Sandra Andacht, *Oriental Antiques & Art: An Identification And Value Guide*, Wallace-Homestead, 1987.

Reproduction Alert: Rose Medallion is still made, although the quality does not match the earlier examples.

ROSE CANTON

Bowl, 11½″, green, alternating sections of florals and figures	285.00
Brush Pot, 4½″, scenic, ladies, reticulated, gilt trim	265.00
Charger, 13″, floral panels, 19th C	200.00
Compote, flower and butterfly medallions, pedestal base	300.00
Plate, 8½″, floral dec	75.00
Soup Tureen, cov, lozenge shape, gilt floral ground, figural scenes	300.00
Sugar, cov, handle	100.00
Teapot, 5″, flowers and butterflies	135.00

Rose Mandarin, plate, unmarked, 9⅞″ d, $90.00.

ROSE MANDARIN

Cup and Saucer, scenic panels, butterfly and floral border	140.00
Garden Seat, 18½″, early 19th C	2,500.00
Plate, 12″, scenic center, garden setting, border reserved with panels of bats	300.00
Teapot, 7½″, enamel, orange, pink, green, lavender, and yellow, mandarin panels, gilding	675.00
Vegetable Dish, scalloped cov, flowers, butterflies, and bird panels and borders, boating scene on cov	650.00

ROSE MEDALLION

Bouillon Cup and Saucer, cov, handle	65.00
Bowl, 9¼″, lobed rim, c1850	375.00
Condiment Set, creamer, sugar, salt and pepper shakers, and tray	950.00
Creamer, 3½″, c1800	115.00
Cup and Saucer, scalloped rim	75.00
Flower Pot, 3¼″, three small feet	175.00
Mug, 4⅝″, interwoven strap handle, c1880	175.00
Plate, 7½″, quatrefoil shape, reserves of figures and birds, c1860	65.00
Pomade Jar, 2½ x 2¼″, cylindrical, scenic lid, man and woman at window	125.00
Sauce Boat, 4¼″, int. border with rose and butterfly dec, ext. with household scenes, orange glaze	150.00
Shrimp Dish, 10¼″, c1850	250.00
Sugar, cov, 5½″, dome lid, bud finial, shaped body, c1890	250.00
Teapot, 9¾″, high dome lid, "S" handle	650.00
Vase, 15½″, celadon ground, Ku-form, c1850	475.00

MARKE

ROSENTHAL

History: Rosenthal Porcelain Manufactory began operating at Selb, Bavaria in 1880. Specialties were tablewares and figurines. The firm is still in operation.

Reference: Susan and Al Bagdade, *Warman's English & Continental Pottery & Porcelain, 1st Edition*, Warman Publishing Co., Inc., 1987.

Bowl, 9″, hp, clusters of cherries, green ext., gold trim, double handles, artist sgd	85.00
Cake Plate, 11″, Rembrandt bust portrait center, light and dark blue	55.00

Hat Pin Holder, white ground, gold band on neck, gold top, 4⅞″ h, $90.00.

Chocolate Set, chocolate pot, cov, 10″ d plate with handle, four cups and saucers, transitional Art Deco–Art Nouveau dec, brown shaded to beige, cream ground, gold trim, artist sgd, 1922, 10 pcs	**135.00**
Compote, 13 x 8¾″, oblong, blue Delft dec, ornately scrolled blank, marked "Rosenthal, Delft, Savoy, Germany"	**150.00**
Cup and Saucer	
Donatello pattern, light green, dark green, and gold, white ground . . .	**10.00**
Empress Flower pattern, relief design	**25.00**
Portrait, woman, gold trim, artist sgd	**50.00**
Demitasse Cup and Saucer, medallion portrait	**45.00**
Figure	
6″, young boy frolicking with lamb, artist sgd	**200.00**
10½″, group of birds, bright blue, green, orange, yellow and brown, underglaze green factory mark, imp "J Feldtmann," numbered	**425.00**
15¾″, Oriental dancer, right leg raised, ornate yellow, blue, mauve, green, black, and gilt costume, Oriental man seated at base	**1,215.00**
Gravy Boat and Underplate, Aida pattern, gold trim, c1920	**30.00**
Model	
6″ h, Dachshund, seated	**150.00**
8 x 6″, Pointer dog, black and white	**125.00**
8 x 8″, Poodle, standing, white, green collar, artist sgd	**235.00**
10 x 6 x 5″, reclining deer	**350.00**
Mug, grapes dec, artist sgd, dated . . .	**35.00**
Plate	
4″, white glaze, SS rim	**10.00**
8¾″, bearded Dutch fisherman, lavender trousers and cap, pale blue ground	**38.00**
9″, Versailles pattern	**25.00**

Urn, cov, 10½″, portrait of woman, garden setting, multicolored	**240.00**
Vase	
7″, shaded tan and rust foliage, crackle glaze, artist sgd, 1946	**90.00**
8″, blue and white Dutch scene	**80.00**
10¼″, Copenhagen series, SS overlay, marked, c1890	**385.00**

ROSEVILLE POTTERY

History: In the late 1880s a group of investors purchased the J. B. Owens Pottery in Roseville, Ohio, and made utilitarian stoneware items. In 1892 the firm was incorporated and joined by George F. Young who became general manager. Four generations of Youngs controlled Roseville until the early 1950s.

A series of acquisitions began: Midland Pottery of Roseville in 1898, Clark Stoneware Plant in Zanesville (formerly used by Peters and Reed), and Muskingum Stoneware (Mosaic Tile Company) in Zanesville. In 1898 the offices also moved from Roseville to Zanesville.

In 1900 Roseville introduced its art pottery—Rozane. Rozane became a trade name to cover a large series of lines. The art lines were made in limited amounts after 1919.

The success of Roseville depended on its commercial lines, first developed by John J. Herald and Frederick Rhead in the first decades of the 1900s. In 1918 Frank Ferrell became art director and developed over 80 lines of pottery. The economic depression of the 1930s brought more lines, including Pine Cone.

In the 1940s a series of high gloss glazes were tried to revive certain lines. In 1952 Raymor dinnerware was produced. None of these changes brought economic success. In November 1954 Roseville was bought by the Mosaic Tile Company.

References: Sharon and Bob Huxford, *The Collectors Encyclopedia Of Roseville Pottery*, Collector Books, 1976; Sharon and Bob Huxford, *The Collectors Encyclopedia Of Roseville Pottery, Second Series*, Collector Books, 1980.

Collectors' Club: American Art Pottery Association, P. O. Box 714, Silver Spring, MD 20901.

Additional Listings: See *Warman's Americana & Collectibles* for more examples.

Ashtray, Donatello, 3″, unmarked	**50.00**
Bank, monkey, 5½″	**125.00**
Basket	
Imperial, 6″	**42.00**
Pine Cone, blue	**300.00**

Children's Dish, yellow ground, 7½" d, $45.00.

Rozane, 3", two handles	50.00
Waterlily, green, 8"	50.00
Bookends, White Rose, 6½", pr	75.00
Bowl	
Ferrella, 12", brown	200.00
Magnolia, green	35.00
Pine Cone, 6", brown	45.00
Snowberry, green and brown	35.00
Candlestick	
Baneda, pr	200.00
Donatello, 6½"	65.00
Luster, 12", pr	85.00
Rozane, pr	75.00
Children's Dishes	
Creamer, 3", chicks dec	45.00
Feeding Dish, 5", rolled rim, five chicks	135.00
Mush Set, bowl and pitcher, chicks dec	75.00
Compote, Donatello, 9"	110.00
Console Bowl, Sunflower	75.00
Ewer	
Bushberry, 10", blue	100.00
Magnolia, 10"	70.00
Water Lily, brown	75.00
Flower Frog, Magnolia, blue and gray, handle	30.00
Flower Pot, Cherry, 4"	100.00
Hanging Basket	
Apple Blossom, pink, orig chains	85.00
Cherry	300.00
Jardiniere	
Blackberry	250.00
Donatello, 6½"	45.00
Futura, 6", gray and pink	100.00
Jardiniere and Pedestal	
Jonquil, 29"	550.00
Normandy	750.00
Jug	
Blackberry, 5"	100.00
Cherry, 4½"	90.00
Lamp, Vista, 10" base	225.00

Mug	
Dutch, 4½"	45.00
Rozane, cherries dec, artist sgd "L"	125.00
Pitcher, Freesia, blue	55.00
Planter, Pine Cone, green, 4½ x 4½"	40.00
Powder Box, Donatello	260.00
Rose Bowl, Tourmaline, 4"	22.00
Sand Jar, Pine Cone, green	525.00
Tea Set, Apple Blossom, green	125.00
Umbrella Stand, blended majolica	170.00
Urn	
Monticello, double handles, blue	125.00
Sunflower, 6½"	130.00

Vase, Pauleo pattern, gray-purple mottled effect, paper label, 6", $395.00.

Vase	
Blackberry	
4"	85.00
8"	180.00
Bushberry, green	85.00
Cherry Blossom, 7", pink	120.00
Cosmos, 10", green	90.00
Foxglove, pink	65.00
Fuchsia, 10", blue, double handles	110.00
Futura, 7", pink	300.00
Imperial II, 5½"	75.00
Jonquil, 6½", double handles	70.00
Monticello, 5 x 7", double handles	100.00
Morning Glory	135.00
Orian, 10½", blue	70.00
Pine Cone, 12", blue	175.00
Tourmaline, 6", blue, silvery streaks	50.00
Zephyr Lily, blue	50.00
Wall Pocket	
Apple Blossom	35.00
Carnelian II	75.00
Corinthian	
8"	65.00
12"	110.00
Dogwood I	75.00
Donatello, 10"	85.00
Floran	65.00

Imperial II	225.00
White Rose, blue	90.00
Window Box, Rosecraft, green	125.00

ROYAL BAYREUTH

History: In 1794 the Royal Bayreuth factory was founded in Tettau, Bavaria. Royal Bayreuth introduced their figural patterns in 1885. Designs of animals, people, fruits, and vegetables decorated a wide array of tablewares and inexpensive souvenir items.

Tapestry ware, rose and other patterns, were made in the late 19th century. The surface of the ware feels and looks like woven cloth. Tapestry ware was made by covering the porcelain with a piece of fabric tightly stretched over the surface, decorating the fabric, glazing the piece, and firing.

The Royal Bayreuth crest mark varied in design and color. Many wares were unmarked. It is difficult to verify the chronological years of production due to the lack of records.

Royal Bayreuth still manufactures dinnerware. It has not maintained production of earlier wares, particularly the figural items.

Reference: Susan and Al Bagdade, *Warman's English & Continental Pottery & Porcelain, 1st Edition,* Warman Publishing Co., Inc., 1987.

Additional Listings: Sunbonnet Babies.

Corinthian
Chamberstick, serpent handle, green	115.00
Humidor, cov	200.00
Pitcher, 6", classical figures, black ground, yellow bands, leaf dec around neck and base	125.00
Toothpick Holder, three handles	75.00

Devil and Cards
Ashtray	125.00
Creamer, 4"	120.00
Demitasse Cup and Saucer	135.00
Dresser Tray	500.00
Humidor, 7¾" h, winged finial	675.00
Match Holder, wall type	200.00
Pitcher	
5"	2356.00
7½", figural red handle	500.00
Wall Pocket, figural	200.00

Grape Cluster
Creamer, white MOP, marked "Germany"	85.00
Mustard, pink MOP, Tettau mark	100.00
Relish, white MOP	80.00

Lobster
Ashtray, 6¼" l	50.00
Celery Tray, 12½" l	65.00
Pitcher, 4¼"	100.00
Sugar, cov	115.00

Miscellaneous Patterns
Ashtray
Pine Cones, figural, black and gold	60.00
Swan scene, twisted handle	45.00
Bread Plate, figural, oak leaf, white satin finish	175.00
Candleholder, farm scene, ring handle	80.00
Candy Dish, oval, Bavarian women and horses	60.00
Chocolate Pot, dome shaped lid, ornate handle, floral and fruit dec	175.00
Cigarette Set, box and matching holder, musicians dec	150.00

Lobster, creamer, 4", $50.00.

Creamer, figural
Bear	300.00
Bo Peep	55.00
Crow, black	120.00
Dachshund	140.00
Duck	100.00
Geranium	130.00
Goat, head	100.00
Hound Dog, brown	85.00
Iris, unmarked	290.00
Lamplighter	165.00
Parakeet	140
Robin	115.00
Seal	225.00
Strawberry	70.00
Marmalade Jar, cov, figural, strawberry	175.00

Match Holder, hanging, shell, MOP,
green and gold 60.00
Mug, long horned steer dec 75.00
Mustard, Lemon, cov, orig spoon ... 75.00
Pitcher, figural
  Clown, 4½", red 250.00
  Elk, blue mark 115.00
  Parrot, 4¼" 150.00
Plate, Lettuce, 7" d, yellow flowers,
  ring handle 40.00
Powder Dish, cov, figural, elk 85.00
Relish, figural, poinsettia, 7½" l 100.00
Toothpick
  Brittany woman dec, three gold feet 125.00
  Colonial dining room scene, three
    handles, blue mark 125.00
  Elk, figural, blue mark 125.00
Vase
  3⅜", two handles, Dutch girl and
    boats scene, silver top rim, hall-
    marks 45.00
  4½", floral 45.00
Wall Pocket, figural, strawberry 225.00
Murex Shell
  Cigarette Vase 90.00
  Creamer 50.00
  Milk Pitcher, marked "Atlantic City" . 75.00
  Salt Shaker, marked "Bavaria" 30.00
  Sherbet 70.00
Nursery Rhyme
  Creamer, Little Jack Horner 55.00
  Jug, 6½", Babes in Woods, two little
    girls talking to troll 300.00
  Match Holder, girl and dog 200.00
  Vase, 3¼", girl with candle, silver rim,
    green mark 50.00
Poppy
  Bowl, 6" 85.00
  Demitasse Creamer and Sugar, red . 150.00
  Gravy Boat, red, green lettuce leaf
    underplate 75.00
  Match Holder, wall, red 115.00
  Mustard, spoon, Deponiert and green
    mark 100.00
  Plate, 5¾" 50.00
  Teapot, ... 175.00
Sand Babies
  Dresser Tray 150.00
  Planter, 3" h, two handles 100.00
  Sugar 75.00
  Wall Pocket 175.00
Snow Babies
  Cereal Set, sledding 150.00
  Creamer and Sugar 185.00
  Plaque, pierced, 9" 175.00
  Plate, babies on ice 75.00
Sunbonnet Babies
  Candlesticks, pr
    Fishing 325.00
    Sewing 325.00
    Washing 325.00

Cereal Set, bowl, 7" underplate,
  washing and ironing 385.00
Creamer and Sugar, boat shape,
  cleaning 300.00
Cup and Saucer, sewing 145.00
Dish
  Diamond shape, sewing 155.00
  Heart shape, farming 165.00
  Spade shape, sweeping 155.00

Sunbonnet, plate, marked "Royal Bayreuth" in blue, $150.00.

Nappy, cleaning 155.00
Pitcher, milk, washing, pinch nose .. 235.00
Plate
  7", cleaning 100.00
  8", washing 100.00
Relish, 8", open handle, fishing 175.00
Wall Pocket, cleaning 500.00
Tomato
  Biscuit Jar 265.00
  Box, cov, 4½ x 3¾" 50.00
  Mustard, 2½ x 4" 45.00
  Pitcher, water 275.00
  Plate, 8¾" 30.00
  Tea Set, leaf base 185.00

ROSE TAPESTRY

Basket, 4¼ x 4", three color roses, single rope handle 275.00
Bowl, 6", three color roses 150.00
Box, cov, 4 x 1¾", pink and yellow roses 285.00
Cake Plate, 10½", pink roses 200.00
Creamer and Sugar, three color roses,
  gold handles 350.00
Dresser Set, hair receiver, powder jar,
  hatpin holder, oval box, and tray,
  three color roses 950.00
Fernery, flared, three color roses, pink,
  white, and yellow, tiny gold handles,
  orig insert, blue mark 245.00
Hair Receiver, three color roses, ftd .. 200.00

Hatpin Holder

Pink roses, pale green ground, gold trim, marked 400.00
Three color roses, blue mark 350.00
Mustard Jar, spoon, pink and white roses 225.00
Pitcher, 3½", gold trim 165.00
Plate, 6" d, three colored roses, gold rim 150.00
Ring Tree, saucer base 425.00
Sauce Dish, 6" d, pink roses 135.00
Shoe, lady's, blue mark 350.00
Vase, 5½", four color roses, soft green ground, apricot, yellow, pink, and white roses, narrow base, bulbous center, narrow top 300.00

TAPESTRY, MISCELLANOUS

Basket

Cavalier scene 285.00
Violets pattern 200.00
Box, cov, 2½", five sheep 185.00
Chocolate Pot, mountain goats, pastoral scene 415.00
Clock, Christmas Cactus pattern, dresser type, blue mark 400.00
Hair Receiver, colonial couple 165.00
Humidor, 6¾", scenic, gold trim, mushroom finial 350.00
Powder Box, 4", scenic, brown, green, and aqua 365.00
Vase

4", chrysanthemums 350.00
6¼", portrait of lady, wearing bonnet 275.00

ROYAL BONN

History: In 1836 Franz Anton Mehlem founded a Rhineland factory that produced earthenware and porcelain, including household, decorative, technical, and sanitary items. In 1890 the name Royal was added to the mark. All items made after 1890 include the name "Royal Bonn." The firm reproduced Hochst figures between 1887 and 1903. These figures, produced in both porcelain and earthenware, were made from the original molds from the defunct Prince-Electoral Mayence Manufactory in Hochst. The factory was purchased by Villeroy and Boch in 1921 and closed in 1931.

References: Susan and Al Bagdade, *Warman's English & Continental Pottery & Porcelain, 1st Edition,* Warman Publishing Co., Inc., 1987.

Biscuit Jar, pink and lavender flowers, green leaves, beige ground, raised gold trim, matte finish, SP cover, rim, and handle 100.00

Oyster Plate, white ground, impressed "Franz Art Mehlem," $100.00.

Bone Dish, Apple Blossom pattern . . . 12.00
Bowl, 7", multicolored chrysanthemum dec, blue ground, pedestal base . . . 45.00
Cake Plate, 10¼", dark blue floral transfer 20.00
Celery Tray, floral dec, gilt trim 80.00
Ewer, 12", pink, yellow, and blue flowers, cream ground, gold trim 175.00
Jardiniere, 15 x 12", hp, multicolored flowers 365.00
Plate

8½", sq, chrysanthemums, hp, gold outlines, pr 70.00
9", floral dec, gilt tracery 60.00
Portrait Ware

Plate, 8½", Mme Le Brum and child, shades of green, scalloped edge . 25.00
Vase, 6", young woman, framed in gold, dark red ground, sgd "Bouck" 200.00
Teapot, 3½ x 9¼ x 4½", red, black, and light blue, gilding, marked "1755" in cartouche with crown 75.00
Urn, cov, 14½", multicolored flowers, dark green glaze, two gold handles, gold dec foot, artist sgd "Jos Roden" 250.00
Vase

7½", pastel flowers, cream ground, gilt tracery, collar, and side ring handles 225.00
8½ x 8", tapestry, scenic 425.00
9", stick type neck, bulbous base, sq sloping shoulders, gold C-scroll handle, hp, floral dec 75.00
10", gold handles, hp, bluebird, autumn flowers, c1895 . . . . 125.00
11", orchids dec, gold trim, scalloped edge, double handles, crown mark 150.00

ROYAL COPENHAGEN

History: Franz Mueller established a porcelain factory at Copenhagen in 1775. When bankruptcy threatened in 1779, the Danish king acquired ownership, appointing Mueller manager and adopting the name "Royal Copenhagen." The crown sold its interest in 1867; the company remains privately owned today.

Blue Fluted, Royal Copenhagen's most famous pattern, was created in 1780. It is of Chinese origin and comes in three styles: smooth edge, closed lace edge, and perforated lace edge (full lace). Many other factories copied it. Flora Danica, named for a famous botanical work was introduced in 1789 and remained exclusive to Royal Copenhagen. Botanical illustrations were done free hand; all edges and perforations were cut by hand.

Royal Copenhagen porcelain is marked with three wavy lines which signify ancient waterways and a crown, the latter added in 1889. Stoneware does not have the crown mark.

Reference: Susan and Al Bagdade, *Warman's English & Continental Pottery & Porcelain, 1st Edition,* Warman Publishing Co., Inc., 1987.

Additional Listings: Limited Edition Collectors' Plates.

Butter Pat, Symphony pattern, set of 6	20.00
Candle Bobeches, 3½" d, Full Lace pattern, blue, pr	65.00
Candlesticks, 7" h, white and gilt, circular columns molded with foliate swags suspended from tied ribbons enriched in gilding, lower and upper parts with shallow grooves, bases with stylized foliage, matched set of four	1,000.00
Cup and Saucer, Half Lace pattern, blue, fluted	25.00
Dinnerware, Flora Danica pattern, pink and green, botanical specimen, gilt dentil rim, underglaze blue triple wave mark, numbered, printed mark, green painter's mark, black botanical inscription	
Compote, 6", pink and gold molded beadwork border, pr	1,250.00
Creamer and Sugar, branch handles	900.00
Fish Plates, 10⅛", various fish species in aquatic setting, green and	

gold molded beadwork border, set of 12	4,500.00
Pickle Dish, 6" l, shaped, everted rect handle	300.00
Plate, set of 12	
5⅝", bread and butter	2,200.00
7⅝", salad	3,575.00
10⅛", dinner	4,125.00
Platter	
14", round	825.00
16⅛", oval	1,125.00
17¼", oval	1,650.00
Salad Bowl, 9½"	900.00
Wine Cooler, 7¼", twig handle, flowerhead and leaf sprig terminals, pr	3,350.00

Figurine, Chimney Sweep and Lady, #1276, 9¾" h, $750.00.

Figure	
5½", cat, sitting, gray and white, green eyes	125.00
7¼", boy with teddy bear	200.00
8½", faun, perched on half columns, holding pipes, rabbit at base, No. 433	125.00
11", polar bear, hunting	250.00
Inkwell, 6 x 8½", Blue Fluted pattern, matching undertray	125.00
Jar, 16½", flat sided circular shape, rocky seascape dec, bronze cov, oval bronze base, knop feet	450.00
Pitcher, 4", cobalt blue ground, floral dec	50.00
Plate, 8", hp, fruit center	35.00
Tureen, cov, 18" l, Blue Fluted pattern, c1897	275.00
Vase	
6", bulbous, celadon green, molded leaves, applied frog, 19th C	200.00
7¾", floral and dragonfly dec, c1890	175.00

ROYAL CROWN DERBY

History: Derby Crown Porcelain Co., established in 1875 in Derby, England, had no connection with earlier Derby factories which operated in the late 18th and early 19th centuries. In 1890 the company was appointed "Manufacturers of Porcelain to Her Majesty" (Queen Victoria) and from that date has been known as "Royal Crown Derby."

Derby porcelains from 1878 to 1890 carry only the standard crown printed mark. After 1891 the mark carries the "Royal Crown Derby" wording; and, in the 20th century "Made in England" and "English Bone China" were added to the mark.

A majority of these porcelains, both tableware and figures, were hand decorated. A variety of printing processes were used for additional adornment. Today, Royal Crown Derby is a part of Royal Doulton Tableware, Ltd.

Reference: Susan and Al Bagdade, *Warman's English & Continental Pottery & Porcelain, 1st Edition,* Warman Publishing Co., Inc., 1987.

Ewer, Chinese red ground, gold dec, 9¾″ h, $265.00.

Ashtray	8.00
Bowl, 11″ d, hp floral dec, cobalt blue rim	90.00
Cake Basket, 12″ h, rect, meandering roses, polychrome and gilt, ftd, marked, c1830	150.00

Creamer, 1⅛″, miniature, cobalt, orange, and white floral dec, marked	110.00
Cup and Saucer	
Blue, Mikado	15.00
Roses, Pinxton	18.00
Dessert Set, Imari type dec, 35 pcs	450.00
Dinner Set, Japanese pattern, Imari palette, marked, c1870, 30 pcs	1,400.00
Dish, 9″, scattered rose sprays, floral border, late 18th C	150.00
Plate	
8″	10.00
8½″, #2451 pattern	60.00
8¾″	15.00
10¾″, Imari pattern	95.00
Toothpick Holder, 3½″, green, hp floral reserve	135.00
Urn	
7″ h, apple green, scenic reserve, figures, landscape, handles terminating at masks, sq pedestal base, c1880	300.00
11½″ h, cobalt blue, red, and gold floral pattern, painted red crown mark	400.00
Vase	
4¼″, pink, gold floral, two gold handles	200.00
7″, dark red and gold, two handles, c1884	185.00
8½″, broad baluster shape, yellow, painted Oriental florals, iron-red, green, and gilt, Japanese style, 1892	370.00
10½″, swan neck, Imari pattern	125.00

ROYAL DOULTON FLAMBE

ROYAL DOULTON

History: Doulton pottery began in 1815 under the direction of John Doulton at the Doulton & Watts pottery in Lambeth, England. Early output was limited to salt-glazed industrial stoneware. John Watts retired in 1854. The firm became Doulton and Company, and production was expanded to include hand decorated stoneware such as figurines, vases, dinnerware, and flasks. In 1872 the firm began marking their ware "Royal Doulton."

In 1878, John's son, Sir Henry Doulton, purchased Pinder Bourne & Co. in Burslem and the companies became Doulton & Co., Ltd. in 1882. Decorated porcelain was added to Doulton's earthenware production in 1884. The Royal Doulton mark was used on both wares.

Most Doulton figurines were produced at the Burslem plants from 1890 until 1978, when they were discontinued. A new line of Doulton figurines was introduced in 1979.

Beginning in 1913, an "HN" number was assigned to each new Doulton figurine design. The "HN" numbers refers to Harry Nixon, a Doulton artist. "HN" numbers were chronological until 1940, after which blocks of numbers were assigned to each modeler. From 1928 until 1954, a small number appeared to the right of the crown mark; this number added to 1927 gives the year of manufacture of the figurines.

Dickens ware, in earthenware and porcelain, was introduced in 1908. The ware was decorated with characters from Dickens' novels. The line was withdrawn in the 1940s, except for plates which continued until 1974.

Character jugs, a 20th century revival of early Toby models, were designed by Charles J. Noke for Doulton in the 1930s. They come in 4 major sizes and feature fictional characters from Dickens, Shakespeare and other English and American novelists, and historical heroes.

Doulton's Rouge Flambee (also Veined Sung) is a highly glazed, strong colored ware noted most for the fine modeling and exquisite colorings, especially in the animal items. The process used to produce the vibrant colors in this ware is a Doulton secret.

Production of stoneware at Lambeth ceased in 1956; production of porcelain continues today at Burslem.

References: Susan and Al Bagdade, *Warman's English & Continental Pottery & Porcelain, 1st Edition*, Warman Publishing Co., Inc., 1987; Ralph and Terry Kovel, *The Kovels' Illustrated Price Guide to Royal Doulton*, Crown, 1980; Jocelyn Lukins, *Collecting Royal Doulton Character & Toby Jugs*, Venta Books, 1985; Kevin Pearson, *The Character Jug Collectors Handbook, 3rd Edition*, Kevin Francis Publishing Ltd, 1986; Kevin Pearson, *The Doulton Figure Collectors Handbook*, Kevin Francis Publishing Ltd, 1986; Ruth M. Pollard, *The Official Price Guide To Royal Doulton, 4th Edition*, House of Collectibles, 1985.

Doulton Lambeth, candlesticks, pr, earth tones of green, brown, and blue, signed "Parkington," 5¾" d base, 11½" h, $425.00.

Animal Mold
Kitten, 2581	30.00
Mallard, HN 807	45.00
Setter with Pheasant, HN 2529, sgd "JB"	325.00
Terrier, reclining, front paws crossed, HN 1101	65.00

Ashpot, Farmer John ... 65.00
Ashtray, Barleycorn ... 90.00
Child's Feeding Dish, boy pushing wheelbarrow at beach, c1908 ... 60.00
Beaker, Edward VII Coronation, brown transfer ... 75.00
Biscuit Jar, 6½ x 5½", SP cov, rim and handle, Coaching Days Series ... 225.00

Bowl
3½, 8" d, Oasis in the desert	100.00
9¼" d, 2¼" h, marked "Rosalind"	70.00

Busts, mini
Sairey Gamp	65.00
Tony Weller	65.00

Candleholder, rural scene ... 65.00
Candlestick, silicon, tan and brown, pr ... 135.00
Chamberstick, rural scene ... 50.00

Character Jug, tiny, 1¼"
Auld Mac	210.00
Fat Boy	100.00
John Peel	250.00
Mr. Micawber	85.00
Sairey Gamp	75.00

Character Jug, miniature, 2¼ to 2½"
Dick Turpin, masked	20.00
Gondolier	350.00
John Barleycorn	65.00
Mad Hatter	25.00
Mikado	275.00
Mr. Pickwick	55.00
Pied Piper	20.00
Sancho Panzo	25.00
Viking	115.00
Walrus	40.00

Character Jug, small, 3½ to 4"
Captain Hook	320.00
Falstaff	25.00
Fortune Teller	350.00
Gardener	40.00
Guardsman	35.00
Mikado	275.00
Punch and Judy	375.00
Scaramouche	350.00
Robin Hood, feather handle	60.00
Sgt Buz Fuz	120.00
Simon the Cellarer	65.00
Trapper	40.00

Character Jug, large, 5¼ to 7"
Aramis	50.00

Baccus 50.00
Capt Hook 275.00
Cavalier 125.00
Clown, white hair 850.00
Don Quixote 50.00
Gondolier 475.00
Granny 50.00
Parson Brown, A mark 135.00
Vicar of Bray 165.00
Creamer and Sugar, florals, gold outline 45.00
Cup and Saucer, hp, c1892 .... 80.00
Demitasse Cup and Saucer, hp, c1880 80.00
Dickens Ware
Ashtray, Sairey Gamp, A mark 90.00
Bowl, 7¾″ d, 3⅞″ h, three characters, marked 145.00
Demitasse Cup and Saucer, Mr. Pickwick on 2⅛″ cup, Sam Weller on 4″ d saucer 55.00
Jug, Bill Sykes, 3″, miniature 95.00
Mug, Cap'n Cuttle, 4″ d, 4¼″ h, two handles, marked 145.00
Pitcher, pottery, sq shape
5¾″ h, 2⅞″ d, Mr. Micawber 95.00
6⅝″ h, 3¼″ d, Trotty Veck 115.00
7⅜″ h, 3½″ d, Alfred Jingle 125.00
Plate, Head Rack 85.00
Sandwich Tray, 5⅝ x 11″, rect shape, Bill Sykes 85.00
Sauce Dish, Fat Boy, 5¼″ 45.00
Vase
Alfred Jingle, 7⅝″, 5″ d, sq flattened shape, two handles 135.00
Old Peggoty, 5¼″ h, 4⅛″ d, pottery, two handles 75.00
Sydney Carton, 7 x 3¾″, handle 135.00
Disc, Wee Willie Winkie 185.00
Ewer
7 x 3¾″, cream, pansies, maroon, yellow with green leaves, gold handle, pink collar 195.00

Figurine, Bon Appetit, matte finish, #HN2444, 6½″ h, $225.00.

Figurine
A Courting 400.00
Autumn Breezes, 1913 .... 185.00
Bachelor 225.00
Bedtime, A mark 30.00
Clockmaker 170.00
Cobbler 225.00
Darby 175.00
Delight, #1772 .... 155.00
Dorcas #1558 .... 250.00
Favorite, #2249 .... 120.00
First Waltz, #2862 .... 145.00
Foaming Quart, #2162 .... 100.00
Johnny Appleseed 305.00
Lunch Time, #2485 .... 150.00
Mary Had A Little Lamb, #2048 ... 75.00
Orange Lady, #1953 .... 175.00
Paisley Shawl, 9″ 175.00
Pensive Moments, #2704 .... 125.00
Potter, #1493 .... 250.00
Queen of the Ice, 2435 .... 110.00
Sweet Susie, #1918 .... 475.00
Votes For Women, #2816 .... 150.00
Flambe
Animal Mold, fish, 12½″ 800.00
Bowl, 9¾ x 3″, Oriental style, handled 225.00
Jardiniere, blue and white, woman playing guitar scene 210.00
Plate, 6″, landscape scene 45.00
Jardiniere, 7⅛″ h, 7¼″ d, Welsh ladies and children walking toward church, marked "Welsh Ladies Series Ware" 325.00
Jug
Golfer 250.00
Gondolier, large 400.00
Quaker Oats 495.00
Rip Van Winkle 250.00
Simple Simon 475.00
Mug
Captain Ahab 55.00
Captain Hook 400.00
Parson Brown 120.00
Santa, 1st edition 100.00
Pitcher
5½″, Coaching Days 85.00
8″, Old Bob Ye Gvard, pinch-in type 95.00
12″ h, 6″ d, country scene 180.00
Plate
Jester 40.00
Maypole Parade 30.00
Rochester Castle, old mark 45.00
Romeo, 10″ 65.00
Shakespeare Plays, 10″ 45.00
The Coachman, 10″ 60.00
The Gleaners, 9½″, reticulated border 35.00
Tony Weller, 13½″ 125.00
Tankard, 12″ h, 6″ d, rural scene 170.00
Tea Caddy, 4 x 3″, old woman drinking tea, SS lid, Kingsware 350.00
Teapot, cov 60.00
Teapot, creamer and sugar, Burslem, set 145.00

Toby Jug

Beefeater, D6233 . . . . 45.00

Bacchus, wreath of grapes and leaves on head, twisted vine handle, 7" h 80.00

Stoneware, 6½" h, blue coat, double XX, Harry Simeon 375.00

Tray, 5 x 11", Robin Hood Series 85.00

Tumbler, 4", Jackdaw of Rheims Series 125.00

Vase

4", Disraeli Commemorative, relief portrait head, primroses, incised green banner reads "1804, His Favorite Flower 1881," Lambeth . . . 250.00

9 x 3¾", goats, incised in black on beige center, green and brown borders top and bottom, sgd "Hannah Barlow" 495.00

10⅜ x 4⅛", Pastoral sunset scene, artist sgd "H Morrey" 325.00

11", stoneware, cobalt, gold enameled panel, hp flowers, #7010 . . . 145.00

11 x 11½", beige, maiden overlooking pool 525.00

Figure

7¾", woman getting dressed, #3396, sgd "Eli Straback" 125.00

11½ x 4" d, boy and girl, peasant dress, pink, green, and gold, satin finish, pink raised triangle mark, pr 550.00

14¾ x 4½" d, shepherdess, rose toga, beige sheepskin robe, green turban, two white and tan goats on green grass, semi-gloss finish, marked "Royal Dux Bohemia" . . . 575.00

ROYAL DUX

History: Royal Dux porcelain was made in Dux, Bohemia (Czechoslovakia) by E. Eichler at the Duxer Porzellan-Manufaktur, established in 1860. Many items were exported to the United States. By the turn of the century Royal Dux figurines, vases, and accessories were captivating consumers, especially Art Nouveau designs.

A raised triangle with an acorn and the letter "E" plus Dux, Bohemia was used as a mark between 1900 and 1914.

Reference: Susan and Al Bagdade, *Warman's English & Continental Pottery & Porcelain, 1st Edition,* Warman Publishing Co., Inc., 1987.

Figurine, brown dress with pink trim and gold highlights, marked with pink triangle and "#448," 9" h, $400.00.

17", camel with rider, pink triangle mark 395.00

18", fisherman, carrying net, over the knee boots and hat, green and brown, pink triangle mark 635.00

19", lady reading book 750.00

21" h, harvester and wife, cobalt blue and white, gold trim, both holding sheath of wheat, man with sickle, pink triangle mark, paper label, pr 725.00

23" h, hunter with dog 475.00

Jug, 9½", woman at fountain 175.00

Mantle Set, 12½" d double handled bowl, two 12½" vases, applied pink roses, yellow and green ground . . . 145.00

Tray, figural, irid blue, center maiden holding basket on her back 300.00

Vase

5", dark peach coloring, applied peaches and leaves 100.00

8" h, orange and green, flowers and cherries, pr 85.00

11", green, rose, and ivory, maiden holding conch shell 300.00

Basket, 2¼ x 4 x 4½", brown, weave pattern, applied cherries 125.00

Bowl, shell shape, reclining woman int., earthtone colors, pink triangle mark . 275.00

Candleholder, lady in pants suit, pink triangle mark 250.00

Centerpiece

7¾ x 4¼ x 11", Art Deco, off white, two nudes kneeling by center vase, cobalt blue and gold trim, raised pink triangle, marked "Royal Dux Bohemia" 475.00

14", blue, blown out body of woman
in white, pink triangle mark **300.00**

GERMANY

RW

RUDOLSTADT

ROYAL FLEMISH

History: Royal Flemish was produced by the
Mount Washington Glass Co., New Bedford, Mas-
sachusetts. The process was patented by Albert
Steffin in 1894.

Royal Flemish has heavy raised gold enamel
lines on frosted transparent glass that separates
areas into sections, often colored in russet tones.
It gives the appearance of stained glass windows
with elaborate floral or coin medallions in the design.

Advisors: Clarence and Betty Maier.

**Biscuit Jar, orange tones, silver plated
top, 8" h, $1,450.00.**

Ewer, 13" h, gold and brown panels dec
with gold shields bearing rampant
lions, gold tracery forms an intricate
floral dec at base and top, unsigned   **2,000.00**
Jar, cov, 9½" h, olive green and gold
sections, Roman motif medallions,
gold scrolls and leaves, fancy pointed
swirled finial, unsigned **2,250.00**
Vase
  8½" h, sq, rounded corners, two del-
    icate applied handles, raised gold
    borders separate mauve and olive
    green panels, Roman coin motif
    dec, unsigned **1,300.00**
  11" h, bulbous stick shape, gold and
    green panels, dragon and floral
    medallions, unsigned **1,600.00**
  12½" h, bulbous stick shape, raised
    gold enamel lines and circles,
    winged creatures and multicolored
    shadow floral design outlined in
    gold, unsigned **1,400.00**

ROYAL RUDOLSTADT

History: Johann Fredrich von Schwarzburg-Ru-
dolstadt was the patron of a faience factory located
in Rudolstadt, Thuringen, East Germany, from
1720 to c1790. The pottery's mark was a hayfork
and later crossed two-prong hayforks in imitation
of the Meissen mark.

In 1854 Ernst Bohne established a factory in
Rudolstadt. His pieces are marked "EB."

The "Royal Rudolstadt" designation originated
with wares imported by Lewis Straus and Sons
(later Nathan Straus and Sons) of New York from
the New York and Rudolstadt Pottery between
1887 and 1918. The factory's mark was a diamond
enclosing the initials "RW" and which was surmounted by a crown. The factory manufactured
several of the Rose O'Neill (Kewpie) items.

Reference: Susan and Al Bagdade, *Warman's
English & Continental Pottery & Porcelain, 1st Edition,* Warman Publishing Co., Inc., 1987.

**Sugar and Creamer, cream ground, tur-
quoise, pink, and gold leaves, gold
handles and finial, marked "R.W." in
crown, $75.00.**

Bowl, 9½", ivory, purple flower, gold trim   **55.00**
Cake Plate, 12", pink, white roses, gold
  handles and trim **75.00**
Candlesticks, 7", ivory, emb acanthus
  leaves, petal shape cups, marked on
  base "Crown Mark," pr **50.00**
Celery Dish, 13", hp yellow rose, gold
  trim, handled, artist sgd **80.00**
Child Set, teapot, creamer and sugar
  with lid, four cups, saucers, and
  plates **275.00**
Dresser Set, tray, hatpin holder, hair re-

ceiver, ring tree, cov jar, rose dec, 6
pcs **250.00**
Ewer, 10″, ivory, floral dec, gold handle
and trim **100.00**
Hair Receiver, 4¼″ d, shaded yellow
ground, yellow roses, green leaves,
gold trim **75.00**
Hatpin Holder, lavender and roses . . . **25.00**
Inkwell, 6 x 3½″, cream, multicolored
flowers, attached saucer, sgd **60.00**
Nut Set, master bowl, six small bowls,
white and green roses, fluted, ftd, B
under crown mark, set **250.00**
Pin Tray, 5″, clover dec **25.00**
Pitcher
8″ h, 5″ d, cream, gray and gold birds,
coral and pink leaves, raised mark **75.00**
11″, bulbous, floral dec, gold handle **125.00**
Plate
8½″, pink, yellow, and white roses,
gold pie crust molded rim **30.00**
8⅞″, white ground, gold trim, marked
"Germany/RW/Rudolstadt" **40.00**
Relish Dish, 8¾″, hp floral dec **25.00**
Teapot, cov, 5½″, ivory, pink, lavender,
and green hp floral dec **95.00**
Urn on stand, cov, 10″, mythological
scene, Hector and Andro crowning
maiden, gold handled, cobalt blue
ground, artist sgd **125.00**
Vase
4″ h, floral dec, elephant handles . . **90.00**
6½″, enameled florals, gold beading,
elaborate gold handles, flower form
opening, cobalt ground **155.00**
13½″, green, orange and pink flow-
ers, brown leaves, gold details,
ivory ground, blue mark #6230 on
base **125.00**

ROYAL VIENNA

History: Production of hard paste procelain in
Vienna began in 1720 with Claude Innocentius du
Paquier, a runaway employee of the Meissen factory. In 1744 Empress Maria Theresa brought the
factory under royal patronage; subsequently the
ware became known as Royal Vienna. The firm
went through many administrative changes until it
closed in 1864. The quality of its workmanship
always was maintained.

Many other Austrian and German firms copied
the Royal Vienna products, including the use of
the "Beehive" mark. Many of the pieces on today's
market are from these firms.

Reference: Susan and Al Bagdade, *Warman's
English & Continental Pottery & Porcelain, 1st Edition,* Warman Publishing Co., Inc., 1987.

**Box, cov, hand painted, signed inside
"Wagner," 2½″ h, $750.00.**

Bowl
4½″ d, cov, flower spray, gilt cartouches, pierced cov, rose bud finial, blue beehive mark, c1900 . . **50.00**
5″, portrait, blue, gold trim, handled . **140.00**
Charger,13⅜″ d, octagonal, gilding,
center scene of maiden and companion being crowned, paneled ground,
blue shield mark, c1900 . . . . **660.00**
Chocolate Pot, burgundy and gold, bust
of lady, beehive mark **185.00**
Demitasse Cup and Saucer, portrait,
lady and dog, scalloped green border
with gold design, blue beehive mark **75.00**
Dish, 8″, shell shape, flower sprigs, gilt
zig-zag on blue border, c1773 . . . . . **360.00**
Ewer, 6¼″ h, maiden and cupid in reverse, gold, maroon, and dark green,
sgd "Kauffmann," beehive mark . . . **195.00**
Figure, 7″ h, young boy, period dress,
enameled colors, imp beehive mark **285.00**
Jug, 8½″, portrait, mother and small
child, mask shape lip, sgd "LCF,"
c1920 . . . . **275.00**
Pitcher, 4½″, cherub dec, cobalt blue
ground, red crown mark **300.00**
Plaque, 12″, portrait, woman with child,
gilt tracery, raised gold and jewels,
pink ground, artist sgd, beehive and
"Flora" mark **425.00**
Plate
9″, maiden draped in white center,
band of flowers in hair, serenaded
by angel playing lute, cobalt border
with gold dec, artist sgd, under-
glaze beehive mark **350.00**
10″, hp, four Dutch children waiting at
shore, dark green border, gold tra-
cery, beehive mark **45.00**
Platter, portraits in medallions, beehive
mark, c1850 . . . . **750.00**
Tray, 8¼ x 12″, pale green, hp violet
dec, gold trim **175.00**

Urn
  5¼", crimson and green, gold bordered cartouche on front, handles, beehive mark 265.00
  13" h, cov, man and woman in classic garden setting, cupid on reverse, multicolored, sgd "Wagner" 550.00
Vase
  4½", urn shape, double handles, Flora figural dec, lavender irid, Tiffany finish, red crown mark 300.00
  7", bottle shape, gold, brown, and blue, Terra Sita portrait, sgd "Wagner," beehive mark 500.00
  10½", portrait, title "Prussia's Peace Brings Plenty," burgundy and gold, two "Royal Vienna" marks 250.00

ROYAL WORCESTER

History: In 1751 the Worcester Porcelain Company, led by Dr. John Wall and William Davis, acquired the Bristol pottery of Benjamin Lund and moved it to Worcester. The first wares were painted blue under the glaze, followed closely by painting on the glaze in enamel colors. Among the most famous 18th century decorators were James Giles and Jefferys Hamet O'Neale. Transfer-print decoration was developed by the 1760s.

A series of partnerships took over upon Davis's death in 1783: Flight (1783–93), Flight & Barr (1793–1807), Barr, Flight & Barr (1807–13), and Flight, Barr & Barr (1813–40). In 1840 the factory was moved to Chamberlain & Co. in Diglis. Decorative wares were discontinued. In 1852 W. H. Kerr and R. W. Binns formed a new company and revived the ornamental wares.

In 1862 the firm became the Royal Worcester Porcelain Co. Among the key modelers of the late 19th century were James Hadley and his three sons and George Owen, expert at pierced clay pieces. Royal Worcester absorbed the Grainger factory in 1889 and the James Hadley factory in 1905. Modern designers include Dorothy Boughty and Doris Lindner.

Reference: Susan and Al Bagdade, *Warman's English & Continental Pottery & Porcelain, 1st Edition,* Warman Publishing Co., Inc., 1987.

Museum: Charles William Dyson Perrins Museum, Worcester, England.

Basket
  3½", light body, gold trim, green mark 120.00
  5¾" h, cane weave base, twisted reed handle, tan, gold highlights, purple mark, Reg #26402/1080, c1891 . 450.00
Biscuit Jar, 6" h, cov, underplate, flowers, beige ground 325.00
Bone Dish, 5¾", cream, blue floral dec 55.00

Bowl
  5¾", scalloped rim, matte ext., glazed int., hp floral, ivory ground, wide gold bands on rim and base, c1890 120.00
Candle Snuffer, white, pink plume ... 60.00
Candlesticks, 11⅜" h, 3¾" d, figural, classic lady wears gold laurel wreath, semi-gloss, cream, gold trim, 1862, pr 900.00
Chocolate Pot, 9" h, hp yellow thistles, purple mark 65.00
Cologne, 3¾", pansies, lavender, rust, and pale yellow, green leaves, SP cap, sgd, 1887 .... 220.00
Creamer and Sugar, cov, blue, pink, and yellow floral, green and rust leaves, gold outlining, sgd, c1888 .... 275.00
Cup and Saucer, polychrome Imari dec, matching 8¾" plate, imp "FBB" with crown 115.00
Demitasse Cup and Saucer, blue and white, crescent mark 95.00
Dish, 5½", shell, blue and white, bird on rockwork, flowering plants and insects, foliage border, c1755 ...... 350.00
Ewer
  6½" h, flowers, gold trim, horn handle, white ground 180.00
  17½" h, cream, flowers and butterflies, gold handle, spout, and rim . 750.00

Jug, Melon Ice, cantelope body, gold handle and leaves, purple mark, c1890, 7¾" h, $350.00.

Figurine
  April, modeled by Dougty 95.00
  Boy and girl getting water from cistern, 6½" w, 7½" h, Hadley, dated 1882 .... 350.00
  Irishman, 2⅝ x 2⅞", 6⅞" h, Countries

of the World Series, beige, satin finish, marked 1891 .... 395.00
John Bull, 2⅝ x 2⅞″, 6⅞″ h, beige, satin finish, marked, 1891 ...... 400.00
Sweet Anne #3630 .... 150.00
Wednesday's Child 85.00
Jug, 10″, mask spout, floral dec, gold trim 375.00
Lamp, figural, 13″ Elizabethan era woman playing lute, 18″ tree base, supports 14″ brass arm that holds two Clarke Cricklites, orig inserts and shades, dated 1898, marked "Clarke and Worcester" 2,475.00
Mug, 3¼″, white, holly dec, gold trim, purple mark, 1892 .... 75.00
Pitcher
  8″, fluted top, gold handle, florals, artist sgd, 1889 .... 200.00
  8½″ h, 7″ w, tobacco leaf shape,cream, gold outlining, curled leaf handle, green mark, purple importers mark "French & Co, Boston," c1885 .... 175.00
Plate
  9½″, man fishing in pond, trees, and castled mountain top scene 250.00
  10½″, eagle, gold trim, Bicentennial, Ltd Edition 85.00
Rose Jar, 4⅜″ h, cov, pink, gold outline, purple mark 125.00
Serving Dish, 11″ l, oval, Imari dec, gilt, unmarked 175.00
Soup Bowl, cov, 6″ d, pink leaf and berry design, cream ground, gold handles and knob 150.00
Spill Vase, 5¼″, emb full figures of girls, sunflowers and cattails, pr, 1908 ... 450.00
Sugar Bowl, 5¼″ h, porcelain, swirled ribs, purple and green enameled foliage with gilt, imp "BFB" with crown 75.00
Tankard, 10″, gold mask face under spout, gold handle, floral dec 350.00
Teapot, 5″ h, pastel floral sprays, gold leaves, purple mark 265.00
Urn, 12″ h, hp bird, white ground, reticulated handle and top 965.00
Vase
  3¼″ h, butterflies on front and back, gilt foliage, double handles, green mark, c1883 .... 95.00
  7½″, double walled top, reticulated pink top and base with blue and ivory enameled dots, reserved with gilt birds, butterflies, and ducks, allover gold gilt dots, sgd, c1890 ... 950.00
  10¼″, robin's egg, blue, raised gilt daisies, slender ivory neck, mask handles, marked, c1902 .... 375.00
  12″ h, Water Carrier, cream and gold 80.00
  15¼″, sheep in mountainous landscape, gilt foliage, handles termi-

nating in lotus flowers, pierced cov, crown finial, green mark, early 20th C 900.00

ROYCROFT

History: Elbert Hubbard, founder of the Roycrofters in East Aurora, New York, during the turn of the 19th and 20th centuries, was considered a genius in his day. He was an author, lecturer, manufacturer, salesman, and philosopher.

Hubbard established a campus which included a printing plant where he published "The Philistine," "The Fra," and "The Roycrofter." His most famous book was "A Message to Garcia," published in 1899. His "community" also included a furniture manufacturing plant, a metal shop, and a leather shop.

References: Nancy Hubbard Brady, The Book of The Roycrofters, House of Hubbard, 1977; Nancy Hubbard Brady, Roycroft Handmade Furniture, House of Hubbard, 1973; Charles F. Hamilton, Roycroft Collectibles, A. S. Barnes & Company, Inc., 1980; Paul McKenna, A New Pricing Guide For Materials Produced by The Roycroft Printing Shop, Tona Graphics, 2nd edition, 1982.

Additional Listing: Arts and Crafts Movement and Copper.

Bookends, copper, #305, 1919, 5⅜″ h, $125.00.

Ashtray, 6 x 4″, copper, brass finish, attached match holder, pedestal 85.00
Bookends, pr
  6 x 6″, leather, tooled design, marked with orb on back 150.00
  7 x 6″, wood, carved orb mark on front 200.00

10 x 5″, copper, fleur-de-lis design, large orb mark **100.00**

Candlesticks, 20½″, hammered copper, twisted standard with two applied candleholders, orb mark, pr **300.00**

Cigarette Box, hinged cov **60.00**

Furniture
Desk, oak, four drawers on left, 30 x 60 x 30″ **650.00**
Hall Chair, 46″ h, oak, wood seat, carved orb mark **475.00**
Rocker, 38″ h, mahogany, leather seat, orb mark **275.00**
Table, library, oak, two drawers, 52 x 33 x 30″ **750.00**

Lamp, 18″, hammered copper, round base, helmet shade **465.00**

Letter Opener, hammered copper **30.00**

Platter, 22″, oval, handles **175.00**

Vase
7½″, bud, pyramid base, Steuben Aurene glass insert **265.00**
19″, American Beauty, hammered copper **450.00**

RUBENA GLASS

History: Rubena crystal is a transparent blown glass which shades from clear to red. It also is found as the background for frosted and overshot glass. It was made in the late 1800s by several glass companies, including Northwood and Hobbs, Brockunier & Co. of Wheeling, West Virginia.

Rubena was used for several patterns of pattern glass including Royal Ivy and Royal Oak.

Beverage Set
Emb floral design, gold outlines, 13¼″ tankard pitcher, base with rough satin finish, ornate white enamel scrollwork, applied clear handle, six 5″ matching tumblers **880.00**
Hobnail, opalescent, pitcher, applied clear handle, six matching tumblers **750.00**
Swirl, opalescent, pitcher, sq ruffled mouth, four matching tumblers . . . **350.00**

Bowl, 4½″, Daisy and Scroll **60.00**

Celery Vase, threaded, Northwood . . . **72.00**

Compote
8½ x 12¾″, rubena overshot bowl, white metal bronze finished figural standard **125.00**
9 x 14″, rubena overshot bowl, white metal bronze finished figural standard **150.00**

Creamer, Medallion Sprig, applied clear handle **160.00**

Decanter, 9″, bulbous base, narrow neck, applied clear handle **140.00**

Marmalade Jar, cov, enamel dec, sgd "Moser" **315.00**

Perfume, 3¼″ h, SP top rim, cranberry cut stopper **125.00**

Pickle Castor, vertical optic insert, fancy fretwork on ftd Pairpoint SP frame . . **225.00**

Sugar, cov, Royal Ivy, frosted **135.00**

Sugar Shaker, 6½″, sq, cut diagonal stripes, Georgian style SP top **140.00**

Tumbler, Royal Ivy, 3¾″ h **48.00**

Vase, coralene dec, gold trim, 5″ h, $275.00.

Vase
6″, bud, bank of cut diamonds, enameled floral dec **60.00**
9½″, six crimp gold trim top, chrysanthemum dec, gold foliage, pr **265.00**

RUBENA VERDE GLASS

History: Rubena Verde, a transparent glass that shades from red in the upper section to yellow-green in the lower, was made by Hobbs, Brockunier & Co., Wheeling, West Virginia, in the late 1880s. It often is found in the inverted thumbprint (IVT) pattern, termed "Polka Dot" by Hobbs.

Bride's Bowl, 9½″ d, ruffled, red rim shading to green center, bronzed cast white metal holder **175.00**

Butter Dish, cov, Daisy and Button base, Thumbprint cov **225.00**

Celery Vase, 6¼″, IVT **225.00**

Compote, 6″, Honeycomb **125.00**

Creamer, IVT, bulbous, reeded handle **265.00**

Cruet, 6″, Hobnail, clear faceted stopper **250.00**

Pitcher
Hobnail, 7½″ h, bulbous base, sq mouth, Hobbs, Brockunier & Co . . **400.00**
Reverse Thumbprint, sq top, applied vaseline handle, Hobbs, Brockunier & Co **250.00**

Bride's Basket, miniature, 6½″ handle to handle, 4½″ h, $100.00.

Salt and Pepper Shakers, orig tops, pr	200.00
Sugar Shaker, enameled floral dec . . .	185.00
Syrup, 6¾″, IVT, orig hinged pewter cov	300.00
Tumbler, 3¾″, paneled	95.00
Vase	
4″, threaded dec	225.00
7″, bulbous, scalloped rim, enameled floral dec	225.00
10″, heavy enameled gold foliage . .	150.00

RUBY STAINED GLASS, SOUVENIR TYPE

History: Ruby stained glass was produced in the late 1880s and 1890s by several glass manufacturers, primarily in the area of Pittsburgh, Pennsylvania.

Ruby stained items were made from pressed clear glass which was stained with a ruby red material. Pieces often were etched with the name of a person, place, date, or event and sold as souvenirs at fairs and expositions.

In many cases one company produced the pressed glass blanks; a second company stained and etched them. Many patterns were used, but the three most popular were Button Arches, Heart Band, and Thumbprint.

Reference: William Heacock, *Encyclopedia of Victorian Colored Pattern Glass, Book 7: Ruby-Stained Glass From A to Z*, Antique Publications, Inc., 1986.

Bread Tray, Triple Triangle, Cape Cod	65.00
Butter Dish, Button Arches, Atlantic City, 1919	75.00
Candy Dish, cov, Columbia Expo, 1893	65.00
Goblet	
Ruby Thumbprint, Mother	30.00
Triple Triangle, 1906	30.00
Mug	
Button Arches, Charles Bray	25.00
Heart, World's Fair, 1904	20.00
Napkin Ring, Diamond with Peg, 1907	85.00

Pitcher, Button Arches, tankard, Pittsburgh	125.00
Punch Cup, Button Arches, Chicago . .	20.00
Sauce Dish, Cathedral, Niagara Falls .	18.00
Spooner, York Herringbone, World's Fair, 1893	45.00
Toothpick Holder	
King's Crown, Atlantic City, 1899 . . .	25.00
Ruby Thumbprint, 1899	25.00
Shamrock, Coney Island	30.00

Mug, souvenir, Blairsville, PA, 2⅝″ top d, 3¼″ h, $25.00.

Tumbler	
Inverted Strawberry pattern, engraved "Deshler, OH"	30.00
Red Block, World's Fair, 1893	35.00
Whiskey Glass, Thumbprint, 1907 . . .	25.00
Wine	
Bull's Eye Band, PA	18.00
Button Arches, World's Fair	25.00
Campanula, Mother	30.00
Triple Triangle, Christmas	35.00

RUSSIAN ITEMS

History: During the late 19th and early 20th centuries Russia contained skilled craftsmen in lacquer, silver, and enamel wares. Located mainly in Moscow during the Czarist era, 1880–1917, were a group of master craftsmen, led by Faberge, who created exquisite enamel pieces. Faberge also had an establishment in St. Petersburg and enjoyed the patronage of the Russian Imperial family and the royalty and nobility from throughout Europe.

Almost all enameling was done on silver. Pieces are signed by the artist and the government assayer.

The Russian Revolution in 1917 brought an abrupt end to the century of Russian craftsmanship. The modern Soviet government has exported some inferior enamel and lacquer work, usually lacking in artistic merit. Modern pieces are not collectible.

Advisors: Melvin and Barbara Alpren.

Spoon, 4¾″, red, blue, green, pink, navy, and white, made by Nikolai Alekseev, Moscow, 1890, orig box, 5¾ x 2 x 1″, $525.00.

ENAMEL

Bell Push, 1½″, nephrite sq, white guilloche enameling and moon stone, IGK, Moscow, 1895 . . . . **1,400.00**
Bonbonniere, 1¾″ d, shaded, pastel colors en suite, 11th Masters Artel, Moscow, 1900 . . . . **1,500.00**
Box, cov, 2″ d, Pan Slavic style, slip-on lid, Anton Kuzmichev, Moscow, 1900 **1,000.00**
Caviar Bowl, 3¼″ d, Pan Slavic style enameling, geometric and floral patterns, A E, Moscow, 1900 . . . . **1,250.00**
Cigarette Case, 4 x 3″ w, shaded enamel en suite, pastel floral pattern, Pavel Ovchinnikov, Moscow, 1899 . . **3,500.00**
Creamer and Sugar and Tongs, Pan Slavic enameling, geometric and floral patterns, swing handle on sugar bowl, Nikolai Zverev, Moscow, 1900, 3 pcs **3,000.00**
Demitasse Spoon, 4½″ l, shaded enamel, geometric pattern, twisted knop handle, Ivan Saltykov, Moscow, 1900 . . . . **200.00**
Kovsh, 5″ l, Art Nouveau style, enameled flowers on gilded silver, Pavel Ovchinnikov, Moscow, 1890 . . . . . . **2,500.00**
Salt
  Champleve enamel, 2″ l, gilded silver, Anton Kuzmichev, Moscow, 1894 . **800.00**
  Shaded enamel on gilded silver, circular, three ball feet, Maria Semenova, Moscow, 1908 . . . . **800.00**
Scent Flask, 1¾″ d, Atomizer, En Plein floral, shaded on reverse side, gilded silver, C.B., Moscow, 1890 . . . . **2,500.00**
Serving Spoon, 7¾″ l, Pan Slavic style, Anton Kuzmichev, Moscow, 1889 . . **800.00**

Sugar Shovel, 4½″ l, all-over shaded enamel pastel floral pattern, Ivan Khlebnikov, Moscow, 1899 . . . . **1,000.00**
Tea Holder, glass, shaded enamel, gilded silver, reticulated edges, pastel colors, Maria Semenova, Moscow, 1895 . . . . **2,900.00**

MISCELLANEOUS

Dessert Cup, liner, handled, c1893 . . . **35.00**
Figure, Troika with Driver, 10″, brass, two passengers, sgd "Gratchen" and foundry marks **2,900.00**
Plate, 10″, Imperial Russian Porcelain, gilt on cobalt blue ground, four hp floral panels, Alexander III, dated 1893 **200.00**
Vase, 12″ h, cut glass, 5″ base flares out to 10″ d **900.00**

SILVER

Basket, cake, 9¼″, chased cornucopia border, swing handle, gilt int., Moscow, c1910 . . . . **525.00**
Candleholder, figure, flared shell shape saucer, molded flower at handle, attached matchbox, marked "84" and artist initials **125.00**
Dessert Spoon, 6⅝″, vermeil bowl, floral engraving, reverse side gold, marked "84" **30.00**
Goblet, 3″, mid 19th C **75.00**
Soup Ladle, Fiddle pattern, Moscow, 1891–96 . . . . **150.00**
Tray, 7⅝″ d, circular, engraved floral spray dec, Moscow, 1894 . . . . **150.00**

SABINO GLASS

History: Sabino glass, named for its creator Ernest Marius Sabino, originated in France in the 1920s and is an art glass which was produced in a wide range of decorative glassware: frosted, clear, opalescent, and colored glass. Both blown and pressed moldings were used. Hand sculpted wooden molds that were cast in iron were used and are still in use at the present time.

In 1960 the company introduced a line of figurines, one to eight inches high, plus other items in a fiery opalescent glass in the Art Deco style. Gold was added to the batch to attain the fiery glow. These pieces are the Sabino that is most commonly found today. Sabino is marked with the name in the mold, an etched signature, or both.

Ashtray
  Shell, 3½ x 5½″ **30.00**
  Violet, 4½″ **40.00**
Bird
  Cluster, two **150.00**

Scent Bottle, six nudes, inscribed "Sabino, France," 5" h, $100.00.

Mocking, 4½ x 6"	100.00
Teasing, 2½ x 3", wings up	75.00
Blotter, rocker type, 6 x 3", crossed American and French flags	275.00
Bowl, berry, large	150.00
Butterfly, large, 6"	25.00
Candlestick, double, grapes	135.00
Cat, 2"	20.00
Cherub	20.00
Chick, drinking	45.00
Dog, Collie, 2"	50.00
Dove, head down, small	20.00
Elephant	25.00
Fox	22.00
Hand, left	200.00
Hen	30.00
Knife Rest, Duck	20.00
Mockingbird, 6"	80.00
Mouse, 3"	50.00
Napkin Ring, birds, opal	45.00
Owl, 4½"	65.00
Powder Box, small	40.00
Rabbit, 2"	20.00
Rooster, large	400.00
Scent Bottle, Petalia	50.00
Statue, Venus de Milo, large	65.00
Tray, butterfly, round	85.00
Vase, Art Deco, topaz, 12"	500.00

ℂ S SALOPIAN

SALOPIAN WARE

History: Salopian ware was made at Caughley Pot Works, Salop, Stropshire, England, in the 18th century by Thomas Turner. The ware is polychrome on transfer. One time classified as Polychrome Transfer, it retains the more popular name of Salopian. Wares are marked with an "S" or "Salopian" impressed or painted under the glaze. Much of it was sold through Turner's Salopian warehouse in London.

Bowl, 6¼", milkmaid and cow, multicolored	125.00
Charger, 11", bird on branch, blue transfer	400.00
Coffeepot, 9½" h, multicolored stag scene, woodland setting	1,000.00
Creamer, 5¼" h, milkmaid and cow scene	180.00
Cup and Saucer, handleless, 3⅝" d cup, 5⅞" d saucer, cottage scene	120.00
Cup Plate, 4½", double deer	350.00

Cup and Saucer, cup: 1¾" top d and 2⅞" h, saucer: 4¾" d, $175.00.

Dish, 10", oval, milkmaid and cow, scalloped edge, blue transfer	200.00
Mug, 2½", double deer, five colors	400.00
Plate, 8⅝" d, fishermen on bank, painted centers, dark blue and gold borders, palmettes, scrolls and loops, imp "Salopian"	120.00
Punch Bowl, 9⅝" d, 4¼" h, brown monochrome, wide border of flowers and leaves on int. and ext., Willow pattern, applied blue enamel rim	175.00
Sauce Dish, 4⅝", polychromed scene of woman and two children, manor house in background, brown transfer with yellow, blue, pink, and green applied highlights	150.00
Sugar Bowl, 5" h, cov, yellow bird, blue, yellow, and orange dec	325.00
Teapot, Oriental scene	200.00

SALT AND PEPPER SHAKERS

History: Collecting salt and pepper shakers, whether late 19th century glass forms or the contemporary figural and souvenir types, is becoming more and more popular. The supply and variety is practically unlimited; the price for most sets is within the budget of cost conscious, young collectors. Finally, their size offers an opportunity to assemble a large collection in a small amount of space.

One can specialize in types, forms, or makers. Great art glass artisans such as Joseph Locke and Nicholas Kopp, designed salt and pepper shakers in the normal course of their work. Arthur Goodwin Peterson is the leading research scholar in the field. His *Glass Salt Shakers: 1,000 Patterns* provide the reference numbers given below. Peterson made a beginning; there are hundreds, perhaps thousands of patterns still to be cataloged.

The clear colored and colored opaque sets command the highest prices, clear and white sets the lowest. Although some shakers, e.g., the tomato or fig, have a special patented top and need it to hold value, it is not detrimental to the price to replace the top of a shaker.

The figural and souvenir type is often looked down upon by collectors. Sentiment and whimsy are prime collecting motivations. The large variety and current low prices indicate a potential for long term price growth.

Generally older shakers are priced by the piece, figural and souvenir types by the set. The pricing method is indicated at each division. All shakers are assumed to have original tops unless noted. Identification numbers are from Peterson's book.

References: Melva Davern, *The Collectors' Encyclopedia of Salt & Pepper Shakers: Figural And Novelty,* Collector Books, 1985; Helene Guarnaccia, *Salt & Pepper Shakers*, Collector Books, 1984; Mildred and Ralph Lechner, *The World of Salt Shakers*, Collector Books, 1976; Arthur G. Peterson, *Glass Salt Shakers: 1000 Patterns*, Wallace-Homestead, 1970.

Additional Listings: See *Warman's Americana & Collectibles* for more examples.

ART GLASS (PRICED INDIVIDUALLY)

Acorn, 3", blue satin, SS ornate top, 21-A	45.00
Bulging Loop, Rib #8, 3", pigeon blood, orig brass top, 37-C	65.00
Fig, enameled pansy dec, satin, orig prong top, Mt Washington	110.00
Knobby, heavy opaque white, hp pastel flowers, shading to pale yellow, orig pewter top	42.50
Lob #5, satin, hp, orange floral spray, pewter top with finial, Mt. Washington, 33-C	62.50
Melon, squatty, enameled daisy dec, satin, orig two piece top, Mt Washington	55.00
Medallion Sprig, 3¼", shaded cobalt blue to white, orig brass top, 33-S . .	67.50

FIGURAL AND SOUVENIR TYPES (PRICED BY SET)

Ducks, 2½", sitting, glass, clear bodies, blue heads, sgd "Czechoslovakia" .	35.00
Lobsters, 3", marked "Made in Japan"	15.00
Mickey and Minnie Mouse, white, gold trim, chipped	35.00
Nipper, RCA Dog, marked "Lenox" . . .	35.00
Refrigerator, 2⅞", old G.E. refrigerator shape, white opaque glass, black trim, chrome plated top, 36-N	30.00
Squirrels, 3½", standing, metal, SP top	37.50

Opalescent, Reversed Twist, blue with opal stripes, orig top, $45.00.

OPALESCENT GLASS (PRICED INDIVIDUALLY)

Chrysanthemum Base, 2¾", blue, 24-U	55.00
Fluted Scrolls, vaseline, Northwood . .	40.00
Jewel and Flower, blue, 164-J, Northwood, replaced top	35.00
Ribbed, 3", white, brass top, 36-W . . .	42.50
Seaweed, cranberry	45.00
Windows, blue, pewter top	45.00

OPAQUE GLASS (PRICED INDIVIDUALLY UNLESS OTHERWISE NOTED)

Acorn, white, floral dec, Mt. Washington, pr	75.00
Apple Blossom, milk glass	25.00
Brownie, 2¾" h. rounded cube, four vertical sides, Palmer-Cox Brownies in different postures on each (F448) . .	75.00
Creased Waist, yellow, milk glass	30.00
Diamond Point and Leaf, 2¾" h, blue, diamond point ground broken by compound leaf extending up side of shaker (F489)	35.00
Everglades, Northwood, purple slag, white, gold highlights, pewter top, 160-K	70.00
Melon Ribbed, red, floral dec, pewter top	72.50

Muranese, 3½″, New Martinsville, pr . .	48.00
Punty Band, Custard	42.50
Winged Scroll, Custard	87.50

PATTERN GLASS (PRICED INDIVIDUALLY)

Beautiful Lady, clear, Bryce, Higbee and Co, 1905	20.00
Block and Fan, clear, non-flint, US Glass Co, 1891	15.00
Cane, apple green, non-flint, Gillinder Glass Co, c1885	25.00
Crown Jewel, etched, O'Hara Glass Co, c1880	35.00
Croesus, amethyst, gold trim, McKee Glass, 1899	75.00
Diamond Horseshoe, ruby stained, Brilliant Glass Works, 1888	40.00
Diamond Point, flint, Boston and Sandwich Glass Co, 1830–40	22.00
Francesware, hobnail, frosted, amber stained, Hobbs, Brockunier & Co, c1880	30.00
Mikado, vaseline, non-flint, Richards and Hartley, c1888	20.00
Tooth and Claw, green, gold trim, non-flint, Riverside Glass Works, c1896 .	50.00

SALTGLAZED WARES

History: Saltglazed wares have a distinctive "pitted" surface texture, made by throwing salt into the hot kiln during the final firing process. The salt vapors produce sodium oxide and hydrochloric acid which react on the glaze.

Many Staffordshire potters produced large quantities of this type of ware during the 18th and 19th centuries. A relatively small quantity was produced in the United States. Saltglazed wares still are made today.

Reference: Susan and Al Bagdade, *Warman's English & Continental Pottery & Porcelain, 1st Edition*, Warman Publishing Co., Inc., 1987.

Basket	
7¹⁵⁄₁₆″, reticulated sides, c1770	3,500.00
12½″, relief molded grapes and leaves, open twig handles, English, c1750–60, faint age crack	1,400.00
Cream Jug, 3⅜″ h	275.00
Cream Pitcher, 5″ h, cov, loop handle, three paw feet, applied grape and leaf design, Chinese lion finial, English, c1730–40	3,200.00
Dessert Plate, 8⅜″, basketweave border, center relief band of pears, English, c1755	950.00
Dish	
7″ w, 9⅝″ l, leaf shape, pressed, molded, ftd, raised dec of bird on branch, English, c1740–50	3,000.00

Syrup, celadon hue, classical dec, pewter lid, 7″ h, $175.00.

9⅛″ d, molded, gadroon rim, polychrome enamel and gilt, scene of fisherman and wife, multicolored floral sprays border, English, c1760	4,500.00
10″ d, molded scroll and basketweave design in high and low relief, blue, yellow, and iron-red enamels, English, c1760–70, two hairline cracks, two minute rim nicks	5,000.00
Figure, sheep, Rockingham, c1830, pr	400.00
Fruit Dish, 9″ l, oval, molded, reticulated, yellow, turquoise, and strawberry, English, c1760–65, chip on foot ring . .	5,200.00
Jar, cov, 2¼″ d, handle	250.00
Jug, 7″, pyriform, strainer spout, polychrome enamels and gilding, bird, butterfly, and floral dec, floral dec handle, English, c1760, lid missing, two hairline cracks in rim	3,000.00
Mug, tavern, stoneware, strap handle, applied raised deer hunt dec, inscribed "Jno Coldre at Whiteham, 1716," English, attributed to Vauxhall area of London	4,600.00
Pitcher, 9″, dog form, pouring spout at nose, brown glaze, Continental, 19th C	250.00
Sauceboat, 4″ h, three mask and paw feet, scrolls, shells, and trellis relief dec, English, c1750–60, age crack at bottom, one toe chipped	1,150.00
Tea Strainer, professionally repaired . .	150.00
Vase, 12″, orange, mottled royal blue, puffy ribbed body, symmetric design on heavy royal blue base	275.00

SALTS, OPEN

History: When salt was first mined, the supply was limited and expensive. The necessity for a receptacle in which to serve the salt resulted in the first open salt, a crude, hand-carved, wooden trencher.

As time passed salt receptacles were refined in style and materials. In the 1500s both master and individual salts existed. By the 1700s firms such as Meissen, Waterford, and Wedgwood were making glass, china, and porcelain salts. Leading manufacturers in the 1800s included Libbey Glass Co., Mount Washington, New England Glass Company, Smith Bros., Vallerysthal, Wavecrest, Webb, and many outstanding silversmiths in England, France, and Germany.

Open salts were used as the only means of serving salt until the appearance of the shaker in the late 1800s. The ease of procuring salt from a shaker greatly reduced the use and need for the open salts.

References: L. W. and D. B. Neal, *Pressed Glass Dishes Of The Lacy Period 1825–1850*, published by the author, 1962; Allan B. and Helen B. Smith have authored and published ten books on open salts beginning with *One Thousand Individual Open Salts Illustrated* (1972) and ending with *1,334 Open Salts Illustrated: The Tenth Book* (1984). Daniel Snyder did the master salt sections in Volumes 8 and 9. In 1987 Mimi Rudnick compiled a revised price list for the ten Smith Books.

Note: The numbers in parenthesis refer to plate numbers in the Smith's publications.

Advisor: Daniel M. Snyder.

CONDIMENT SETS WITH OPEN SALTS

China, Viking Ship, gold dec, "Czecho-
slovakian" (461) **35.00**
Metal, collie pulling rickshaw, contains
salt, pepper, and mustard dishes,
blown glass liners, Oriental (461) . . **350.00**
Porcelain, Limoges, double salt and
mustard, sgd "JM Limoges" (388) . . **65.00**
Pottery, Quimper, double salt and mustard, white with blue and green floral
dec, sgd "Quimper" (388) **95.00**

Individual, china, Limoges, white ground, gold dec, green interior, marked "D & C, France," 1⅝ d, 1¾ h, $10.00.

INDIVIDUALS

China
  Austria, tub shape, floral dec, sgd
    "Brothers" and "O&EG Royal Aus-
    tria" (441) **38.00**
  Chinese Export, celadon type,
    c1750–70 (434) **250.00**
  Noritake, oval, int. dec in blue and
    gold (382) **35.00**
  Royal Bayreuth, lobster claw, unsgd
    (87) **65.00**
  Staffordshire, Toby (96) **225.00**
Colored Glass
  Amber, pedestal, Decagon, Cam-
    bridge (468) **32.50**
  Blue, basketweave, colorless rigaree
    (378) **250.00**
  Cobalt Blue, pedestal, gold bands,
    applied flowers, sgd "Moser" (380) **55.00**
  Cameo Glass, E. Galle, green ped-
    estal, enamel dec, sgd, early (205) **275.00**
  Cranberry, ruffled salt held by rigaree
    in wire holder, unmarked (373) . . **185.00**
  Ruby, dolphin in center (451) **85.00**
  Wavecrest
    Marked, red banner mark, metal
      base (45) **175.00**
    Unmarked, stain glass, blown out
      petals (91) **175.00**
Cut Glass
  Eight curved sides, polished cut bot-
    tom (470) **18.00**
  Hexagonal, 12 point star in bottom,
    sgd "Libbey" (464) **45.00**
  Pedestal, Hawkes, sgd with trefoil
    emblem (86) **55.00**
  Tub, tab handles, Diamond and Fan
    (361) **55.00**
Double Salts
  China
    Bowls, boat shaped, anchor handle
      of floral dec (392) **195.00**
    Shells, maiden sitting between
      them, French (392) **225.00**
  Glass
    Baccarat, pedestal, paneled sides,
      one salt frosted panels, sgd
      (395) **125.00**
    Clear, octagonal, Thumbprint, at-
      tributed to Sandwich (394) **75.00**
  Pottery, blue with pink and white flow-
    ers around bowls, French, Longwy,
    c1900 (392) **65.00**
In Metal Frames
  Amber intaglio, Webb butterfly, brass
    stone-studded frame (248) **85.00**
  Clear, 4 ftd SS holder with 4 peacocks
    around outside, mkd "Sterling"
    (411) **42.00**
  Cobalt blue liner, round SS, hall-

marked, mkd "Made in Dublin, Ireland 1795" (412) **215.00**
Cranberry, dark, blown glass in Baroque gold washed frame, mkd "Whiting 3582" and "Gorham G" (412) **95.00**

Metals
German Silver, dolphin feet, German, c1890–1910 (353) **95.00**
Silver plated, pot, hallmarked "Wilcox Silver Plate Co" (414) **35.00**

Sterling
Georg Jensen, Denmark, porringer (238) **195.00**
Tiffany, ball feet, 1879 (232) **55.00**

Pressed Glass
Acorn Band, Portland (53) **42.50**
American, Fostoria, round, gold rim, rayed bottom (465) **47.50**
Fancy Loop, Heisey, unmkd (83) ... **22.50**
Hawaiian Lei, Higbee (477) **22.50**
Mt. Vernon, Cambridge (80) **27.50**
Vernon, rounded rim, 12 panels on lower sides above ring of indented diamonds which merge with rayed bottom (477) **22.50**
Wood, bucket, white porcelain int. (232) **45.00**

FIGURALS

Goat, hauling green milk glass cart, sgd "Baccarat," 6" l (458) **135.00**
Peacock, glass, amethyst wings, green base (462) **55.00**
Seahorse, brilliant turquoise, white base, supports shell salt, mkd with first Belleek black mark (458) **350.00**

INTAGLIOS

Scene of Niagara Falls (368) **65.00**
Tree, 6 intaglios showing Venus and Cupid (423) **110.00**

Master, copper luster, 3″ d, 2¼″ h, $55.00.

MASTERS

China
Belleek, shell shaped (314) **42.50**
Germany, pedestal, girl sitting on grass, mkd "Printemps, Monbijou, Germany" (387) **55.00**
Moss Rose, white (320) **45.00**

Colored Glass
Amberina, hexagonal, cased (316) . **65.00**
Blue, opalescent, silver rim, Registry number "176566" (384) **110.00**
Blue, Millefiori, "Made In China" (318) **95.00**
Cranberry, geometrically cut to clear (384) **120.00**
Green, light, dark green ruffled top, open pontil (449) **75.00**
Purple Slag, leaf and flower print (313) **60.00**
Raspberry, heavy, sq, Pairpoint (444) **65.00**
Satin Glass, tulip shaped, silver leaf holder (312) **80.00**

Cut Glass, heart shape, alternating diamond and fan pattern (404) **65.00**

Lacy
Clear
Double, beaded rim and handles (329) **60.00**
Eagle (EE7b:327) **180.00**
Lafayette Boat (BT6:329) **260.00**
Oblong Double (OG12:326) **70.00**
Staghorn (SN1:328) **100.00**
Colored
Lyre, green (LE1:324) **225.00**
Mount Vernon, light citron (MV1a:324) **375.00**
Round, blue green, pedestal (RP20:322) **270.00**
Strawberry Diamond, yellow green (SD7:324) **280.00**

Metal
Gold, pedestal, mkd "1880" (349) .. **80.00**
Pewter, pedestal, cobalt blue liner (349) **60.00**
Silver, plated, applied legs, triple plate, Simpson Hall Miller & Co (312) **47.50**

Sterling Silver
Boy with bow and arrow holding salt on head, blue glass insert, mkd "800" Germany (355) **400.00**
Pedestal, 4 medallion profiles, monogrammed "S.C.W.," made in 1865, mkd with Gorham hallmark and number 520 (358) ... **95.00**
Perforated beaded holder, ruby liner, mkd "Sterling" and "8322" (411) **55.00**

Pressed Glass
Arched Panel, octagonal, round rim (410) **25.00**
Basketweave, sleigh (397) **110.00**

Chandelier (409)	**45.00**
Snail (348)	**30.00**
Toboggan (397)	**175.00**
Pressed Glass, Pedestal	
Barberry (344)	**35.00**
Eyewinker (346)	**82.50**
Paneled Diamond (331)	**47.50**
Sunflower (346)	**35.00**

SAMPLERS

History: Samplers served many purposes. For a young child they were a practice exercise and permanent reminder of stitches and patterns. For a young woman they demonstrated her skills in a "gentle" art and preserved key elements of family genealogy. For the mature woman they were a useful occupation and functioned as gifts or remembrances, e.g., mourning pieces.

Schools for young ladies of the early 19th century prided themselves on the needlework skills they taught. The Westtown School in Chester County, Pennsylvania, and the Young Ladies Seminary in Bethlehem, Pennsylvania, are two examples. These schools changed their teaching as styles changed. Berlin work was introduced by the mid-19th century.

Examples of samplers date back to the 1700s. The earliest ones were long and narrow, usually done only with the alphabet and numerals. Later examples were square. At the end of the 19th century, the shape tended to be rectangular.

The same motifs were used throughout the country. The name is a key element in determining the region. Samplers are assumed to be on linen unless otherwise indicated.

References: Glee Krueger, *A Gallery of American Samplers: The Theodore H. Kapnek Collection*, Bonanza Books, 1984 edition; Anne Sebba, *Samplers: Five Centuries of a Gentle Craft*, Thames and Hudson, 1979.

1862, Lillie S. A. Beddall, cross stitch on homespun linen, 16 x 30½", $600.00.

1701, 21 x 8⅝", Mary Smith, possibly English, vivid yellow, blue, beige, brown, and green threads on finely woven rect brown crash ground, bands of alphabets, numerals, leafy sprig panels, birds and flowering vines above "Mary Smith is my name and with my needle I wrought the same the sixth year of my age 1701," losses and staining, framed	**450.00**
1776, 27½ x 9½", American, Mrs. Cook, lengthy record in green, black, and brown threads on brown crash linen ground, inscribed "Mrs. Cook the wife Mr...Cook of Foxborough who died...1775....," bottom worked by numerals and name Molly Cook, losses to needlework, framed	**500.00**
1784, 16¾ x 18½", American, bands of double alphabets and numerals above two houses, flowering shrubs, dogs, and central floral sprig, inscribed "May 7, 1784," within blue chain borders, some fading and staining, framed	**400.00**
1812	
10½ x 19", Lydia Bates, Dec 26, green, black, beige, blue, yellow, and white silk and wool stitches, spans of alphabets and numerals above two memorial dates over elaborate yellow silk two story house, green roof and windows, two gentlemen, two ladies, and child, leafy tree, flanked by floral sprigs and birds, diamond border, ebonized frame	**2,500.00**
14¼ x 15½", Emma Rousby Thompson, small delicate black and white stitches on homespun, alphabets, crowns, trees, verse, and name, damage along fold lines, modern frame	**300.00**
1818	
19½ x 25½", Elizabeth Cooke Crittenton, aged 12 years, July 24, 1818, shades of blue, green brown, and gold on homespun, needlework scene of harbor with houses, church, and trees, floral garland and alphabets with verse, some fading, framed	**1,850.00**
26½ x 17", Susan Stone, Groton, CT, Sept 24, pink, yellow, blue, green, and white silk stitches, linen ground, bands of alphabets above pious verse, below landscape of large weeping willow tree, large yellow basket of rose blossoms, two yellow birds kissing, sgd, meandering berry and leaf border outlined with sawtooths	**2,000.00**

1824, Mary Peck, Providence, RI, April 27, brown, beige, green, tan, black, and blue threads on brown crash linen ground, bands of alphabets and numerals above pious verses, memorial markers inscribed "R.A." and "S.B.," beneath flowering willow tree and hearts, framed **1,000.00**

1827, 19¾ x 16½", Regina Rayton, Chester Co, PA, green, blue, yellow, pale pink, and gold silk stitches, loosely woven linen ground, pious verse entitled "Emblem of Innocence" above scene of young girl with decoupage face and arms, seated in blue chair, checkerboard house, large leafy tree with large green parrot, small yellow bird and butterfly with gilt threaded wings hovering above, wide borders of tulips and carnations, green silk ribbon banding, indistinctly signed and dated, orig frame and wood backing **8,250.00**

1828, Elizabeth M. Konkle, PA, 18 x 22", green, pale pink, white, beige, and brown silk stitches on loosely woven linen ground, central pious verse enclosed within undulating floral line, heavily embroidered flowers, butterflies and baskets of fruit, hillcock with brown and white rabbits, ducks, foxes, and birds, inscribed "To My Parents, Henry and Margaret Konkle," sgd **2,000.00**

1831
15 x 15", Martha Nash, verse, vining border, stylized flowers, and houses, silk and cotton threads on homespun, green has bled a little, other colors faded, old frame **250.00**

16¾ x 15⅜", Emma Collins, age 11, fine linen ground worked with inscription "To the memory of William Scott who departed this life the 17th of April 1830 aged 68 years. Also Ann, his wife, the 26th of December aged 53 years in the same year of our Lord," followed by lengthy pious verse, and "By this my friends may see What care my Parents took of Me Emma Collins, aged 11 years 1831," floral sprigs within diamonds flanked by large tree, foliate scroll border, stains, losses to time, framed **600.00**

1833, 16¼ x 18¼", Julia Spencer, age 10, black, brown, beige, green, and yellow threads on dark brown crash linen ground, bands of alphabets and numerals, inscription above landscape scene with two story house, green windows, brown roof, white

picket fence flanked on one side by church with steeple, large trees, zig-zag floral sprig borders, framed **1,250.00**

1837, 19⅛ x 17⅛", Sarah P. Carr, age 9, black, green, beige, yellow, green, and brown threads on sq crash brown linen ground, bands of alphabets and numerals above verse "this fading Record of my hands Reminds me that another stands I inscribed against my name Of all this mortal part was wrought Of all thinking soul has thought For glory or for shame, Of fall river December 16, 1837 wrought by Sarah P. Carr aged nine years, above large flower basket and foliate sprigs, chain borders, scrolling stylized floral sprig border, minor staining, framed . **1,450.00**

1841, 20 x 20¾", homespun, cross stitch and needlepoint, alphabets, vining border, house, butterflies, and stylized flowers and animals, good color, stains, and small holes, framed **700.00**

1844, 15¾ x 19½", H. Millar, Millar's School, homespun, alphabets, crowns, stylized trees, flowers, dogs, rabbits, and peacock, wear, stains, and damage, old walnut frame **300.00**

1929, 14½ x 19¼", Susan Hathaway, age 12, black, faded blue, and brown on golden colored homespun, alphabets and name, one small hole in homespun, matted and framed **250.00**

SANDWICH GLASS

History: In 1818 Deming Jarves was listed in the Boston Directory as a glass factor. The same year he was appointed general manager of the newly formed New England Glass Company. In 1824 Jarves toured the glass-making factories in Pittsburgh, left New England Glass Company, and founded a glass factory in Sandwich.

Originally called the Sandwich Manufacturing Company, it was incorporated in April 1826 as the Boston & Sandwich Glass Company. From 1826 to 1858 Jarves served as general manager. The Boston & Sandwich Glass Company produced a wide variety and quality of wares. The factory used the free-blown, blown three-mold, and pressed glass manufacturing techniques. Clear and colored glass both were used.

Competition in the American glass industry in the mid-1850s forced a lowering of quality of the glass wares. Jarves left in 1858, founded the Cape Cod Glass Company, and tried to maintain the high quality of the earlier glass. At the Boston & Sandwich Glass Company emphasis was placed on mass production. The development of a lime glass (non-flint) led to lower costs for pressed glass. Some free-blown and blown-and-molded pieces, mostly in color, were made. Most of this Victorian era glass was enameled, painted, or acid etched.

By the 1880s the Boston & Sandwich Glass Company was operating at a loss. Labor difficulties finally resulted in the factory closing on January 1, 1888.

References: Raymond E. Barlow and Joan E. Kaiser, *The Glass Industry In Sandwich*, Vol. 4, published by author, 1983; George S. and Helen McKearin, *American Glass*, Crown Publishers, Inc., 1941 and 1948; Ruth Webb Lee, *Sandwich Glass. The History Of The Sandwich Glass Company*, Charles E. Tuttle, 1966; Ruth Webb Lee, *Sandwich Glass Handbook*, Charles E. Tuttle, 1966; L. W. and D. B. Neal, *Pressed Glass Dishes Of The Lacy Period 1825–1850*, published by author, 1962; Catherine M. V. Thuro, *Oil Lamps II: Glass Kerosene Lamps*, Wallace-Homestead, 1983.

Periodical: *The Sandwich Collector*, McCue Publications, P. O. Box 340, East Sandwich, MA 02537. Subscription: $12.00.

Museum: Sandwich Glass Museum, Sandwich, MA.

Additional Listings: Blown Three Mold and Cup Plates.

Toilet Bottle, clear, c1820, 5¼″, $65.00.

Bowl
9¼″, Gothic Arches, clear, lacy, Lee 129	150.00
10″, Princess Feather, clear, lacy, Lee 119	450.00

Candlestick, 9″ h, dolphin, clear, dolphins and shells on socket, McKearin 204-65 ... 800.00

Compote
6¼ x 4¾ x 3¼″, oblong, clear, lacy, relish dish standard	200.00
12 x 9″, Sandwich Star, electric blue	5,000.00

Creamer, Gothic Arch, deep purple-blue, lacy ... 800.00

Cup Plate, Lee-Rose 440-B, deep blue, heart ... 325.00

Custard Cup, overshot, pink, applied clear handle	50.00
Decanter, 12″ h, 1½–2 pint capacity, Sandwich Star, canary yellow, period stopper, pr	3,300.00
Dish, 12 x 9 x 1¾″, oblong, Peacock Eye	800.00
Jewel Casket, cov, 6½″ l, oblong, clear, lacy, Lee 162	1,100.00
Lamp, 10⅝″, whale oil, free blown teardrop shape font, triangular scrolled base, paw feet	700.00

Miniature
Bowl, cov, 1⅝″ d, pattern around base	100.00
Cup and Saucer, handleless, lacy, Lee 80-7	250.00
Flat Iron, blue-green	600.00
Plate, opal, lacy, Lee 81-5	150.00
Tray, 2¾ x 2″, oval, paneled	100.00
Wash Bowl and Pitcher, clear, Lee 80-3	350.00

Ointment Jar, opaque white, orig pewter lid, oval, concave panels, 3″ d ... 125.00

Plate, 7⅛″, Peacock Eye, translucent moonstone, lacy, Lee 108-2 ... 150.00

Scent Bottle
Deep emerald green, violin shape, orig pewter screw top, McKearin 241-31	225.00
Deep purple-blue, waisted, orig pewter top, McKearin 241-28	225.00
Medium purple-blue, McKearin 241-55	130.00

Sugar, cov, Gothic Arch, fiery opal, Lee-158-4 ... 500.00

Tray, 10″ l, Butterfly, clear, lacy, Lee 95-3 ... 300.00

Vase
7¼″, Bull's Eye and Ellipse, dark emerald green, gauffered rims, pr	3,000.00
9¾″, tulip shape, honey amber, flint, Lee 198-2, pr	1,800.00

Vegetable Dish, cov, 10½″, clear, lacy, grape border, Lee 151-1 ... 5,500.00

Whiskey Glass
1⅞″, octagonal, amber	200.00
2⅜″, hexagonal, deep cobalt blue, flint	225.00

SARREGUEMINES

SARREGUEMINES CHINA

History: Sarreguemines ware is a faience porcelain, i.e., tin-glazed earthenware. The factory was established in Lorraine, France, in 1770, under the supervision of Utzcheider and Fabry. The factory was regarded as one of the three most prominent manufacturers of French Faience. Most of the wares found today were made in the 19th century. Later wares are impressed Sarreguemines and Germany due to a change of boundaries and location of the factory.

Reference: Susan and Al Bagdade, *Warman's English & Continental Pottery & Porcelain, 1st Edition,* Warman Publishing Co., Inc., 1987.

Lamp, crystalline glaze, tan, ground, impressed mark, 11¼" h vase, 21½" h to top of harp, $200.00.

Bouillon Cup, 8" underplate, copper luster finish	40.00
Bowl, basketweave, relief tomatoes, handles	30.00
Box, 6" d, multicolored dec of children in Kate Greenaway type dress	60.00
Compote, 9½", majolica, series of five different raised fruits, natural colors	65.00
Creamer, 5", row of ducks, frog, flower border	48.00
Dish, cov, 8½", majolica, basketweave, white egg lid finial	175.00
Pitcher	
7½", majolica, figural, face, bushy eyebrows, collar base	85.00
8", shoemaker scenes	145.00
8¾", smiling face reverses to frowning face	75.00
Plate	
7½", multicolored French comic scene	20.00
8½", multicolored, boy and girl in doorway	35.00
12", majolica, strawberries, plums, and grapes	85.00
Vase	
6½", green ground, oil drop finish, imp "Sarreguemines 115 227," stamped "ETNA"	140.00
8½", majolica, relief gargoyles and lizards, avocado, sgd	125.00
9", Sang de Bouef, high glaze, imp mark	125.00

SARSAPARILLA BOTTLES

History: Sarsaparilla refers to a number of tropical American, spiny, woody vines of the lily family whose roots are fragrant. An extract was obtained from these dried roots and used for medicinal purposes. The first appearance in bottle form dates from the 1840s. The earliest bottles were stoneware, later followed by glass.

Carbonated water often was added to sarsaparilla to make a soft drink or to make consuming it more pleasurable. For this reason, sarsaparilla and soda became synonymous even though they were two different entities.

References: Ralph & Terry Kovel, *The Kovels' Bottle Price List, 7th Edition,*, Crown Publishers, 1984; Carlo & Dot Sellari, *The Illustrated Price Guide to Antique Bottles.* Country Beautiful Corp., 1975.

Periodicals: *Antique Bottle World*, 5003 West Berwyn Chicago, IL 60630; *Old Bottle Magazine*, .P. O. Box 243, Bend, OR 97701. Subscription: $10.00.

Additional Listings: See *Warman's Americana & Collectibles* for a list of soda bottles.

Andries, Dr E, rect, golden amber	375.00
Ayer's Sarsaparilla, deeply whittled, pontil	50.00
Belding's, Dr Ira, Honduras Sarsaparilla, clear, 10½"	20.00
Bull's Extract Of Sarsaparilla, beveled corner, 7 x 2"	385.00
Compound Extract Of Sarsaparilla, amber, gallon	125.00
Foley's Sarsaparilla	15.00
Green's, Dr	15.00
Guysott's Yellow dock & Sarsaparilla	35.00
Lancaster Glassworks, barrel, golden amber	120.00
Murray's, Burnham, ME, aqua	20.00
Riker's Compound Sarsaparilla, rect, beveled corners, aqua	30.00
Skoda's Sarsaparilla, amber	20.00
Townsend's, Dr, Sarsaparilla, olive green, pontil	80.00
Warren Allen's Sarsaparilla Beer, tan, pottery	125.00
Yager's Sarsaparilla, clear	25.00

SATIN GLASS

History: Satin glass, produced in the late 19th century, is an opaque art glass with a velvety matte (satin) finish, achieved through treatment with hydrofluoric acid. A large majority of the pieces were cased or had a white lining.

While working at the Phoenix Glass Company, Beaver, Pennsylvania, Joseph Webb perfected

Mother-of-Pearl (MOP) satin glass in 1885. Similar to plain satin glass in respect to casing, MOP satin glass has a distinctive surface finish and an integral or indented design, the most common being diamond quilted (DQ).

The most common colors are yellow, rose, or blue. Rainbow coloring is considered choice. Satin glass, both plain and MOP, has been widely reproduced.

Additional Listings: Cruets, Fairy Lamps, Miniature Lamps, and Rose Bowls.

Tumbler, Baby Raindrop, MOP, white on white, 3¾" h, $175.00.

Basket, 8½ x 9½", herringbone, MOP, pink-salmon ext., tightly crimped edge, frosted clear twisted thorn handle	635.00
Bowl, 6½ x 4", DQ, MOP, rainbow, soft pink, yellow, and blue shading to white center, ruffled, four applied clear feet, clear berry pontil, marked "Patent"	1,000.00
Bride's Basket, 11 x 15½", deep rose, enamel swan and floral dec, heavy bronze holder with birds perched at top	400.00
Cologne Bottle, 5½", globular, peach, SS top	250.00
Cruet, 7" h, DQ, MOP, blue, matching satin stopper, applied clear reeded handle	630.00
Dish, 5¾", raspberry, ivory ruffled rim .	50.00
Ewer, 9½", DQ, MOP, deep apricot shading to light, thorn handle	255.00
Jar, cov, 6¼", DQ, MOP, salmon, applied clear flower finial	325.00
Perfume Bottle, 4", globular, ivory, SS top, gold dec	115.00
Pitcher, 8¼", coin spot, MOP, blue, applied frosted handle	150.00
Rose Bowl, 7", swirled pink and opalescent, three camphor glass feet	225.00
Toothpick, 2½", DQ, MOP, yellow	150.00
Tumbler, DQ, MOP, deep blue to pearly	

white, heavy enameled, pink blossoms, multicolored foliage	285.00
Vase	
5½", broken egg shape, colorless satin feet, DQ, MOP, blue	200.00
6", MOP, brown and pearl, Federzeichnung design, patent date	1,400.00
6¾", raindrop, MOP, amber, ruffled rim, pr	200.00
8", herringbone, MOP, light blue, two thorn handles	175.00

SATSUMA

History: Satsuma, named for a war lord who brought skilled Korean potters to Japan in the early 1600s, was a hand-crafted Japanese faience glazed pottery. It is finely crackled, has a cream, yellow-cream, or gray-cream color, and is decorated with raised enamels in floral geometric and figural motifs.

Figural satsuma was made specifically for export in the 19th century. Later satsuma, referred to as satsuma-style ware, is Japanese porcelain also hand decorated in raised enamels. From 1912 to the present, satsuma-style ware has been mass produced. Much of the ware on today's market is of this later period.

References: Sandra Andacht, *Oriental Antiques & Art: An Identification And Value Guide*, Wallace-Homestead, 1987; Sandra Andacht, *Treasury of Satsuma*, Wallace-Homestead, 1981.

Basket, 8", children and old man, c1850	975.00
Berry Set, 10" bowl, four nappy dishes, diapered border, figures, and florals .	135.00
Bowl, 4¾ x 2", overall floral motif, early 19th C	300.00
Box, cov, 3½", circular, three ball feet, ladies and children by river on cov, landscape sides, int. with sprigs of flowering plum, sgd "Kinkozan," late 19th C	250.00
Brooch, 1½", flower shape, floral and bamboo design, wide cobalt border, sgd "Mon"	65.00
Brush Holder, 5", cream, flowers and butterflies	50.00
Button, Daikoku dec	100.00
Cache Pots, 10½", hexagonal, scenic, earth tones, figural handles, 19th C, pr	1,350.00
Charger, 12½", Thousand Warriors pattern, diaper border of dragons, multicolored, c1850	1,500.00
Condiment Dish, 8¾", circular, multicolored enamels, herons dec, 3 pcs . .	75.00
Figure, Kannon, 7½", diety molded in royal ease posture, holding rosary, serene face, jet black coiffure, floral diadem, gilt patterned cowl flowing	

Jar, cov, maroon ground, white flowers, and gold handles and feet, c1830, 8½" h, $125.00.

over shoulders and back, partially opened robes scattered with gilt and pastel floral patterns, base inscribed "Satsuma 'Iwaida'" 175.00

Ginger Jar, 8¾ x 7¼", bulbous, melon ribbed, diaper pattern, encrusted gold, enameled mums, mythical bird with enameled wings, c1890 . . . . . . 200.00

Incense Container (Kogo)

3¾", compressed circular body, flat lid with gilt and bright polychrome enameled figural arhats scene, backdrop of celestial mansions, straight ext., sides painted with brocade band of scalloped edge roundels, scattered Satsuma mon, black ground, gilt spirals and granulation, base cartouche reading "Satsuma-yaki 'Kotoen'" 475.00

5" d, compressed circular body, convex lid, inset high ring foot, top with minute gilt and polychrome enamels, sq reserve of country cottage, abstract patterned roundel, wide band of millefleur, gilt granulated ground, gilt edged border, int. painted with overall pattern of scattered brocade patterned maple leaves and stylized waves, base cartouche inscribed "Kinkozan-zukuri," Meiji period 700.00

Match Holder, hanging, figural, butterfly 65.00

Plate

8¾", fan shape, colored enamels of large phoenix in flight, cloud scrolls, multicolored and gilt ribs, monogrammed "EGS," set of 16 . . . . . 400.00

9⅝", cream crackle glaze, brush fence, chrysanthemums, bamboo, stylized foliate rim, sgd, late 19th C 385.00

Tea Caddy, cov, 4½", green to beige, foliage dec, orig insert 100.00

Tea Set, teapot, creamer, cov sugar,

Thousand Flowers pattern, c1900, 3 pcs 200.00

Urn, 6¼", rect, two molded elephant head handles, bright polychrome enamels, gilt, rect reserve of spring scene with mother and children, blossoming landscape reserves, gilt keyfret band, gilt painted baskets of ferns, dark blue ground, recessed dome shaped lid, gilt knob finial, base imp "Kinkozan-zukui," Meiji period . . 900.00

Vase

6½", ovoid, two figural reserves, brocade ground, two high-relief figures seated on shoulder, Satsuma mon and mark 200.00

9¾", baluster, high waisted neck, rolled rim, high flared foot, polychrome enamels and gilt, continuous frieze of blossoming wisteria vines, flowering iris plants, gilt geometric patterned bands, base cartouche "Ryuzan," Meiji period . . . 250.00

15¼", hexagonal, rolled rim with keyfret band, recessed high circular foot, bright polychrome enamels, large rect reserves, family on spring excursion, two samurai watched by maiden alternating with gilt painted panels of blossoming plants on dark blue ground, gilt shippo-tsunagi bands, base inscribed "Takarayama" 1,650.00

60", earthenware, high shouldered ovoid body, trumpet mouth, flared foot, reserves of Heian court figures, garden landscapes, shippo-tsunagi gilt ground, applied handles, c1900 . . . . 2,750.00

SCALES

History: Prior to 1900 the simple balance scale commonly was used for measuring weights. Since then scales have become more sophisticated in design and more accurate. A variety of styles and types include beam, platform, postal, and pharmaceutical.

Collectors' Club: International Society of Antique Scale Collectors, 20 N. Wacker Drive, Chicago, IL 60606.

Apothecary Scale, marble top 100.00
Baby, wicker 45.00
Balance

Cast Iron, 14" l, nickel plated brass pans, orig red paint with black and yellow trim, marked "Henry Troemner, Phila, No 5B, Baker's" 100.00

Butter, 27" w, wood, carved handle, worn black paint 75.00

Egg, Farm Master, red ground, black, yellow, and red letters, $30.00.

Wrought Iron, 22″ h, cast iron base, tin pans 60.00
Candy
  Dayton, brass pan, metallic orange . 300.00
  National Store Co, tin pan, c1910 . . 85.00
Coin Operated, 69″ h, floor model, porcelain top and bottom, mirrored front, wood back, marked "National Weighing Machine, NY" 175.00
Counter, blue and chrome with tan, marked "Toledo" 165.00
Grain, brass 235.00
Hand Held, wide side gauge, unusual cylinder, marked "Chatillon, NY" . . . 20.00
Postal, 4¼″ h, desk, SS, cased, monogram, marked "Shreve & Co," c1900–22 . . . . 250.00
Steelyard, wood, weighted bulbous end, turned shaft, 18th C 200.00
Store
  Hanson Weighmaster, 6 x 14 x 10″, cast iron case with ground, black lettering and indicator 25.00
  Howe, cast iron, red base, gold highlights, brass pan, five weights, patent June 18, 1867 . . . . 80.00
  National Store Specialty Co, green base 175.00
  Toledo Computing Scale Co, 26 x 28 x 11″, gold paint, pan, patent Sept 11, 1906 . . . . 35.00

SCHLEGELMILCH PORCELAINS

History: Erdmann Schlegelmilch founded his porcelain factory in Suhl in the Thuringia region in 1861. Reinhold, his brother, established a porcelain factory at Tillowitz in Upper Silesia in 1869. In the 1860s Prussia controlled Thuringia and Upper Silesia, both rich in the natural ingredients needed for porcelain.

By the late 19th century an active export business was conducted with the United States and Canada due to a large supply of porcelain at reasonable costs achieved through industrialization and cheap labor. Both brothers marked their pieces with the RSP mark, a designation honoring Rudolph Schlegelmilch, their father. Over 30 mark variations have been discovered.

The Suhl factory ceased production in 1920, unable to recover from the effects of World War I. The Tillowitz plant, located in an area of changing international boundaries, finally came under Polish socialist government control in 1956.

References: Susan and Al Bagdade, *Warman's English & Continental Pottery & Porcelain, 1st Edition,* Warman Publishing Co., Inc., 1987; Mary Frank Gaston, *The Collector's Encyclopedia Of R.S. Prussia and Other R.S. and E.S. Porcelain,* Collector Books, 1982; George W. Terrell, Jr., *Collecting R.S. Prussia Identification and Values,* Books Americana, 1982; Clifford S. Schlegelmilch, *Handbook Of Erdmann And Reinhold Schlegelmilch, Prussia-Germany And Oscar Schlegelmilch, Germany, 3rd Edition,* published by author, 1973.

Reproduction Alert: Many "fake" Schlegelmilch pieces are appearing on the market. These reproductions have new decal marks, transfers, or recently hand painted animals on old, authentic R.S. Prussia pieces.

R. S. Germany, bowl, 10″ d, hexagonal, relief petal border with gray tones, four red roses, buds, and foliage, gold edge, light green mark, $50.00.

R. S. GERMANY

Biscuit Jar, 6½″ h, 6″ d, white flowers, green leaves, gold trim, two handles, cream and green ground, marked . . 115.00
Bonbon Dish, 7¾″ l, 4½″ w, pink carnations, gold dec, silver-gray ground, looped inside handle 30.00
Bowl
  5¼″ d, pinkish white and blue tulips, gold dec, wide flat rim, green ground, blue mark, set of 6 . . . . . 95.00

10½", Lily mold, pink and yellow
roses 200.00
Bread Plate, Iris variant edge mold, blue
and white, gold outlined petal and rim,
multicolored center flowers, steeple
mark 115.00
Brides Bowl, ornate, floral center, ftd . . 45.00
Cake Plate, deep yellow, two parrots on
hanging leaf vine, open handle, green
mark 225.00
Candy Dish, 7", sq, gray-green, orange
roses, wide scalloped rim, pierced
handles 35.00
Celery Tray, 11" l, 5¾" w, lily dec, gold
rim, open handles, blue label 100.00
Chocolate Pot, demitasse, white rose
florals, blue mark 85.00
Creamer and Sugar, pedestal, sheep-
herder scene, overall dec, red mark 650.00
Cup and Saucer, plain mold, swan, blue
water, mountain and brown castle
background, red mark 235.00
Demitasse Cup and Saucer, 3", pink
roses, gold stenciled design, satin fin-
ish, blue mark 55.00
Gravy Boat, white, blue flowers, gold
rim, handle, blue mark 30.00
Hatpin Holder 75.00
Inkwell, 3", pink roses, gold scroll, hp,
artist sgd, blue mark 70.00
Mustard Pot, cov
Floral, green, handled 30.00
Roses 20.00
Napkin Ring, green, pink roses, white
snowballs 45.00
Nut Bowl, 5¼" d, 2¾" h, cream, yellow
roses, green scalloped edge 55.00
Pin Box, 2" h, orange poppy on cov,
green mark 35.00
Pitcher, 5¾", light blue, chrysanthe-
mums, pink roses, gold trim 65.00
Planter, green, white tulips, blue mark . 125.00
Plate
6½" d, dessert, yellow and cream
roses, green and rich brown
shades, set of 6 . . . . 125.00
9¾", white flowers, gold leaves,
gilded edge, green ground, marked
"RS Germany" in dark green, script
sgd "Reinhold Schlegelmilch/Til-
lowitz/Germany" in red 40.00
10", hp flowers 40.00
Powder Box, cov, green poppies, green
mark 45.00
Salt and Pepper Shakers, shaded
green, peach floral dec, gold trim, pr 45.00
Sauce Dish and Underplate, green, yellow roses, blue mark 40.00
Syrup, cov, 6", bluebells 65.00
Tea Tile, peach and tan, greenish white
snowballs, red mark over faint blue
mark 150.00

Tray, 11½ x 7¼", sheepherder and mill
scene 255.00
Vase
4", bottle shape, shaded green to
cream, cottage scene, marked . . . 65.00
6", bud, green, floral dec 30.00

R. S. Poland, vases, pr, cream and
brown background tones, white and
yellow flowers, 12" h, $575.00.

R. S. POLAND

Candleholder, floral dec, marked 115.00
Creamer, soft green, chain of violets,
applied fleur-de-lis feet, red mark . . 100.00
Flower Holder, pheasants, brass frog in-
sert 675.00
Vase
8¾" h, 4" d, pink and white roses, gold
band top with garlands of gold
roses and leaves, cream ground,
marked 165.00
12", floral, pr 575.00

R. S. PRUSSIA

Berry Bowl, 10", Iris mold, blown-out,
pink roses and daisies, red mark . . . 285.00
Berry Set, poppies, iris mold, 5 pc . . . 300.00
Biscuit Jar, Sunflower mold, red mark . 400.00
Bowl
10 x 2½", red, gold, and black border,
marked "Mme Recamier" 575.00
10 x 3", blown out iris mold, red mark 225.00
10½ x 3", blown out irises, pink and
red roses, gold tracery 200.00
10¾ x 3", satin finish, pink roses,
green leaves, white ground, gold
trim, mold #213 . . . . 430.00
11", yellow roses, red mark 130.00
Bun Tray
Medallion, 14", hanging basket and
rose dec, wide cobalt trim, un-

signed 125.00
Melon boy, brown, red mark 650.00

R. S. Prussia, pitcher, poppies, blown out base, red mark, 10¼" h, $800.00.

Butter Dish, porcelain insert, cream, gold shading, pink roses, raised enamel, red mark 700.00
Cake Plate
  9½", floral dec, turquoise ground, iris mold, open handle, unsigned 40.00
  10½", floral dec, red mark 85.00
Celery Tray
  12", flowers in bowl dec 125.00
  12½", pink and yellow roses, green shadows, Lily mold, unmarked . . . 75.00
Chocolate Pot, cobalt blue, white flowers, hp, transfer, applied gold, gold handle 1,000.00
Chocolate Set
  10 pcs, chocolate pot, four cups and saucers, dark green, pink Bachelor Button type flowers, fancy handles, red mark 800.00
  17 pcs, fluted pot with lid, cov sugar and creamer, six cups and saucers, pink roses, yellow daisies, light blue and peach ground, gold trim, ftd 3,000.00
Compote, 4", green florals 85.00
Cookie Jar 120.00
Creamer, green, cottage scene 185.00
Creamer and Sugar
  Gaston mold 604, pink roses, cov . . 275.00
  Icicle mold, reflecting water lilies, ftd, red mark 275.00
Cup, roses, ftd, ornate, red mark 25.00
Demitasse Cup and Saucer, dainty flowers 100.00
Demitasse Set, surreal dogwood and leaf dec, red mark 950.00
Dresser Tray
  Pale blue, Tiffany dec rim 650.00
  Poppies, Carnation mold, satin finish, blown out, red mark 330.00

Ewer, 8¼", small roses, gold leaves, pedestal base, red mark, satin finish 400.00
Hair Receiver, green Lilies of the Valley, white ground, red mark 110.00
Hatpin Holder, 4¾", scalloped base, roses, luster finish, red mark 215.00
Plate, 8½", Gibson girl "Evelyne," sgd Prussia 350.00
Nut Set, Calla Lily pattern, 5 pc 165.00
Relish Dish, 9", blown-out mold, lavender and pink gloss finish, pink and white roses, two handles, red mark . 80.00
Shaving Mug, mirrored, green shadows, pink poppies, red mark 275.00
Spoon Holder, 14" l, pink and white roses 200.00
Sugar Shaker, 5", scalloped base, pearl finish, roses, red mark 235.00
Tankard, 11", drapery mold, Rose and Snowball 425.00
Tea Strainer and Undercup, 6", pink flowers, unmarked 150.00
Tea Set, cov, teapot, sugar, and creamer, raised gold, pink, and yellow roses, Tiffany glaze band, pedestal foot, ornate handles, unsigned 450.00
Toothpick Holder, green shadows, pink and white roses, six ftd jeweled, red mark 250.00
Tray, 10¼ x 7", blownout iris mold, hidden image, woman's head, floral center 300.00
Vase
  5¼", cobalt, flowers and leaves 225.00
  6", pearl jeweled, satin finish, pink and white roses, purple bottom, shadow leaves at top, solid gold handles, red mark 325.00
  9½", six sheepherders, pink flowering trees, red mark 700.00
  10", fall season dec, green tints, red mark 650.00

R. S. Suhl, bowl, 10", yellow rose dec, $75.00.

R. S. SUHL

Box, cov, Nightwatch	650.00
Jar, cov, 7", tapestry dec	135.00
Pin Tray, 4½", round, Nightwatch	375.00
Plate, 8½", windmill scene and water, green mark	100.00
Vase, 8", four pheasants, green mark	265.00

R. S. Tillowitz, relish dish, oval, 9¼" w, $20.00.

R. S. TILLOWITZ

Berry Set, 10" master bowl, six 5" bowls, pink and white roses dec, blue mark, 7 pcs	160.00
Creamer and Sugar, soft yellow and salmon roses	45.00
Plate, 6½", mixed floral spray, gold beading, emb rim, brown wing mark	100.00
Relish Tray, 8" l, oval, hp, shaded green, white roses, green leaves, center handle, blue mark	35.00
Syrup, pastel pink snowballs, blue mark	35.00
Teapot, creamer and sugar, stacking, yellow, rust, blue flowers, gold trim, ivory ground, marked "Royal Silesia," and green mark in wreath	75.00

SCHNEIDER GLASS

Schneider

History: Brothers Ernest and Charles Schneider, founded a glassworks at Epiney-sur-Seine, France, in 1913. Charles, the artistic designer, previously had worked for Daum and Galle.

Although Schneider art glass is best known, the firm also made table glass, stained glass, and lighting fixtures. The art glass exhibits simplicity of design; bubbles and streaking often are found in larger pieces. Other wares include cameo cut and hydrofluoric acid etched designs.

Schneider signed their pieces with a variety of script and block signatures, "Le Verre Francais," or "Charder." Robert, son of Charles, assumed art direction in 1948. Schneider moved to Loris in 1962.

Vase, light amber, signed, 7" d, 7½" h, $150.00.

Bowl		
9¼", mottled, red and purple, marked		175.00
10 x 4", red rim, mottled yellow ftd center, wrought iron handled holder with roses and leaves, sgd		225.00
Charger, 29¼", bowl shape, satin finish, opaque, rust-reds and browns, sgd "Schneider France, Ovington, NY"		625.00
Compote		
8¼", deep amethyst, knobbed stem and pedestal, marked		115.00
15 x 5", purple and red, sgd		275.00
Dish, 13½ x 5½", mottled orange and dark blue, amethyst with white ribbing pedestal base		260.00
Ewer, 6½", mottled blue and gray, applied black amethyst handle		225.00
Pitcher		
6", raspberry body, mottled handle and spout		350.00
7½", maroon, white, and pink, marked		325.00
Plate, 4", mottled, deep pink		75.00
Vase		
5½", cased, blue, black, and clear, orange lining, wrought iron ftd base, c1925, sgd		250.00
9½", round, handles, orange with lavender and lemon pulls at raised neck, marked		325.00
17", trumpet, ftd, clear with streaks of pink and raspberry, controlled bubbles, marked		325.00

SCHOENHUT TOYS

History: Albert Schoenhut, son of a toymaker, was born in Germany in 1849. In 1866 he ventured to America to work as a repairman of toy pianos for Wanamaker's, Philadelphia, Pennsylvania. Finding the glass sounding bars inadequate, he perfected a toy piano with metal sounding bars.

His piano was an instant success, and the A. Schoenhut Company had its beginning.

From that point, toys seemed to flow out of the factory. Each of his six sons entered the business. The business prospered until 1934 when misfortune forced the company into bankruptcy. In 1935 Otto and George Schoenhut contracted to produce the Pinn Family Dolls.

At the same time, the Schoenhut Manufacturing Company was formed by two other Schoenhuts. Both companies operated under a partnership agreement that eventually led to O. Schoenhut, Inc., which continues today.

Some dates of interest: 1872-toy piano invented; 1903-Humpty and Dumpty and Circus patented; 1911–1924-wooden doll production; 1928–1934-composition dolls.

Reference: Richard O'Brien, *Collecting Toys*, 4th Edition, Books Americana, 1985.

Spark Plug, wood, felt, leather, and rope, painted body, copyright 1922 by King Features, $250.00.

Animals

Alligator, glass eyes	225.00
Bear, brown painted eyes	125.00
Buffalo, painted eyes	150.00
Bulldog, brown painted eyes	225.00
Camel, painted eyes, two humps, 8″	175.00
Cat, glass eyes, leather ears, 7″	215.00
Donkey, small, painted eyes	50.00
Giraffe, painted eyes, 11″	245.00
Hippopotamus, glass eyes	250.00
Lion, glass eyes, 9″	165.00
Ostrich, painted eyes	250.00
Tiger, glass eyes	185.00
Zebra, glass eyes	225.00
Building Blocks, orig box	175.00
Building Toy, Little Village Builder, orig box	75.00

Circus, Humpty Dumpty
Accessories

Barrel	18.00
Chair	18.00
Platform	15.00
Tent, 25 x 35″	350.00

Performers

Acrobat, lady	125.00
Bare back rider on white horse, 6½″	200.00
Lion Tamer, wooden head	175.00
Ringmaster, wooden head, 8½″	150.00
Complete Set, animals with glass eyes, tent, 52 pcs	5,575.00

Doll, carved wooden socket head and painted facial features, wooden spring jointed body, marked "Schoenhut Doll Pat. Jan 17, 1911, USA"

13″, Nature Baby, domed head, bent limb baby body, painted baby hair, almond shaped green eyes, c1915	375.00
15″, carved brown boyish hair, intaglio eyes, closed somber mouth, blue cotton sailor suit	1,125.00
19″, blonde mohair wig, blue painted intaglio eyes, closed pouty mouth, 2 pc linen suit, c1915	325.00

Farm Characters

Farmer	135.00
Goat, painted eyes	150.00
Goose, painted eyes	200.00
Horse, painted eyes, 10″	150.00
Lamb, painted eyes	150.00
Milkmaid	75.00
Pig, glass eyes	160.00

Personalities

Barney Google	175.00
Felix, 7 pc ball jointed body, Patent 1925, 4″	200.00
Hobo	125.00
Jiggs and Maggie, pr	750.00
Teddy Roosevelt, 8″	450.00
Piano, 8½ x 9½ x 16″, 15 keys	125.00
Trinity Chimes	150.00

SCIENTIFIC INSTRUMENTS

History: Chemists, doctors, geologists, navigators, and surveyors used precision instruments as tools of their trade. Such objects are well designed and beautifully crafted. The principal medium is brass. Fancy hardwood cases also are common.

Reference: Crystal Payton, *Scientific Collectibles Identification & Price Guide*, published by author, 1978; Anthony Turner, *Early Scientific Instruments, Europe 1400–1780*, Sotheby's Publications, 1987.

Barometer, rosewood veneer, thermometer, marked "Rochester, NY"	800.00

Chronometer

Ship, orig case, 5″ d, Hamilton, dated 1941, not working	350.00
Yacht, 6″ sq case, Hamilton	300.00

Microscope, barrel type, unidentified maker, orig box with orig fittings, $600.00.

Compass, mahogany, boxed, orig lamp, marked "John Bliss & Co"	**425.00**
Heeling Error Instrument, orig case, marked "Pratt No. 5"	**100.00**
Inclinometer, cased, French, marked "Made by H Bellieni of Nancy," dated 1900	**125.00**
Measuring Device, compensated, measures in meters, marked "Made by Troughton & Simms, London," 19th C	**25.00**
Quadrant, ebony, case label "Frederic W Lincoln, Jr, Boston"	**500.00**
Sextant, brass, pr binoculars, case with certificate of Examination from "National Physical Laboratory at Surrey, dated October, 1905," marked "Heath & Co Ltd, Crayford, London"	**650.00**
Stadimeter, cased	**50.00**
Surveyor's Compass, 4¾" sq case, removable handle, 19th C	**225.00**
Telegraph, 45¼" h, brass, marked "Made by J W Ray & Co"	**550.00**
Telescope	
Floor Model, brass, orig tripod, sighting scope, tripod marked "Stanley," English, early 19th C	**2,400.00**
Table Model, tapered wood tube, brass tripod, Dollond, London, late 18th to early 19th C	**1,300.00**

SCRIMSHAW

History: Norman Flayderman defined scrimshaw as "the art of carving or otherwise fashioning useful or decorative articles as practiced primarily by whalemen, sailors, or others associated with nautical pursuits." Many collectors expand this to include the work of Eskimos and War of 1812 French POWs.

Collecting scrimshaw was popularized during the presidency of John F. Kennedy.

References: E. Norman Flayderman, *Scrimshaw, Scrimshanders, Whales And Whalemen,* N. Flayderman & Co., 1972, out-of-print; Richard C. Malley, *Graven By The Fishermen Themselves,* Mystic Seaport Museum, Inc., 1983.

Museums: Cold Spring Harbor Museum, Long Island, NY; Kendall Whaling Museum, Sharon, MA; Mystic Seaport Museum, Mystic, CT; National Maritime Museum, San Francisco, CA; Old Dartmouth Historical Society, New Bedford, MA; Whaling Museum, Nantucket, MA.

Reproduction Alert: The biggest problem in the field is fakes. A very hot needle will penetrate the common plastics used in reproductions. Ivory will not generate static electricity when rubbed, plastic will. Patina is not a good indicator; it has been faked with tea, tobacco juice, burying in raw rabbit hide, and other ingenious ways. Usually an old design will not be of consistant depth of cut as the ship rocked and tools dulled; however, skilled forgers have even copied this.

Advisor: Bill Wheeler.

Pipe Tamp, figural, serrated tamp end, 2½", $175.00.

Basket, 8⅛" l, oval, reticulated whalebone, wood bottom, swing whalebone handle, handmade coin silver rivets, early to mid 19th C	**2,750.00**
Bodkin	
3" l, clenched hand at one end, multisided cuff, abalone inlays, early to mid 19th C	**275.00**
4⅛" l, walrus ivory, carved and turned, mid 19th C	**100.00**
Cane	
32⅝" l, whalebone shaft, ivory handle in claw hammer form, mid 19th C	**450.00**

36″ l, rope carved whalebone shaft, walrus ivory and rubber top and bottom, handle fits deeply into shaft and pinned with two whale ivory pins, American, mid 19th C **1,300.00**

36½″, whalebone shaft, L shape handle, separated from shaft by teak and whale ivory rings, mid 19th C **250.00**

Coat Rack

23⅞″, panbone mounted on pine, three sperm whale teeth hangers, early to mid 19th C **900.00**

31¾″ l, molded hardwood, four large sperm whale teeth hangers, early to mid 19th C **600.00**

Corset Busk

12¾″ l, engraved, two plant studies, heart at bottom filled with geometric engraving, third quarter 19th C . . **300.00**

13½″ l, reddish-brown inked, unusual engraving **800.00**

Cribbage Board, 17½″ l, walrus tusk, engraved, game animals, hunting scenes, and map, late 19th C **450.00**

Cup, 4⅝″ h, animal leg bone, engraved with seminude female figure, European, early 19th C **175.00**

Ditty box, 7″ l, engraved, baleen, landscape of buildings, willow trees and figure of man with walking stick detail, orig mahogany cov with whalebone and wood finial, second quarter 19th C **600.00**

Egg Cup, 3⅝″, turned, mid 19th C, one minor age crack **125.00**

Jackknife, 5½″ l open, whalebone handle, pinned blade, early to mid 19th C **170.00**

Jagging Wheel, 5″ l, whale ivory, comma shape handle, baleen ring and inlays, American, second quarter 19th C . . **450.00**

Knitting Needles, 12″ l, whalebone, alternating whale ivory and island wood rigs, carved clenched hands at top, second quarter 19th C, pr **2,600.00**

Letter Opener, 7½″, whale shape, whale and gaff rigged schooner on one side, "18 E.C. 37" on other, good patina . **250.00**

Mantle Ornament, 10½″ l, 7½″ h, two carved and engraved teeth, eagle's head form engraved with ship, mounted on wood base with whalebone black splash, simulated whalebone drawer, turned whalebone feet, two whale ivory and baleen star inlays, rope carved circular frame, mid 19th C **1,100.00**

Panbone, 10½ x 9 x 6″, engraved, whaling scene, William Perry, New Bedford, c1920–30 . . . . **1,200.00**

Pincushion, 6¾″ d, octagon shape, mounted on walnut, ebony, whalebone, and mother-of-pearl inlay base, mid 19th C **175.00**

Rolling Pin, 20″, turned mahogany cylinder, acorn shape, whale ivory handles, c1825–40 . . . . **1,100.00**

Scribe, 9″ l, whalebone, American, second quarter 19th C **400.00**

Sewing box, 12″ l, 9″ w, exotic woods, whale ivory and wood inlays, ebony and whale ivory drawer pulls, third quarter 19th C **550.00**

Sewing Knife, lady's, bone, walking sailor's figure **70.00**

Spoon, 10⅜″ l, tortoiseshell bowl, whalebone handle, handle riveted to bowl, early to mid 19th C **150.00**

Sewing Stand, 7 x 5¼ x 7″, turned bone finials, single drawer, third quarter 19th C **200.00**

Swift

15¾″ h, double, whalebone and whale ivory, abalone shell heart inlay on upper clamp, mid 19th C . . **1,350.00**

23¼″ h, whalebone and whale ivory, cup at top supported by standard with pewter band, mid 19th C . . . **1,100.00**

Table, 17¾ x 18¼ x 26″, tapered turned legs, cherry wood, 29 individual whale ivory, baleen, and abalone inlays, orig hand written label on bottom **1,500.00**

Tongue Depressor, 7¼″ l, 1″ w, ivory, eagle under words "Union Forever" on one side, wreath and "BP to LB 1841 AD" on other **250.00**

Walking Stick, 34¾″ l, lady's, tapered whalebone shaft, turned whale ivory knob, circular dark wood set in top, mid 19th C **200.00**

Walrus Tusk, 14½″ l, cribbage board and engravings of game and bird on one side, Eskimo hunting seal on other side **225.00**

Watch Holder, 9 x 6⅜ x 10″, dovetailed, whale ivory and baleen inlays, engraved flowers, curved scrolled supports, single drawer, other whale ivory and abalone shell inlays, American Waltham railroad watch with name "Nicholas Eisboa" **3,250.00**

Whale Tooth

3¼″ l, pinpoint and regular engraving, half figure portraits, stylishly dressed ladies, mid 19th C, pr . . . **500.00**

4¾″, carved, deep relief nude, third quarter 19th C **550.00**

5″ l, engraved, full figure portrait of young couple on one side, full rigged ship and sun ray bearing a face on other, second quarter 19th C **1,100.00**

6½″ l, relief carved, female figure reading book, third quarter 19th C **550.00**

SEBASTIAN MINIATURES

History: Sebastians are hand painted, lightly glazed figurines of characters from literature and history. They range in size from 3 to 4 inches. Each figurine is made in limited numbers. Other series include children and scenes from family life.

Prescott W. Baston, the originator and designer of Sebastian figures, began production in 1938 in Marblehead, Massachusetts. Sebastian Studios are located in Hudson, Massachusetts. Prescott Baston died on May 25, 1984.

Each year a Sebastian Auction is held in Boxborough, Massachusetts, at the Sebastian Collector's Society meeting. Prices are determined from this source plus the work of the Sebastian Exchange Board which develops a price list that is the standard reference for the field.

Reference: Dr. Glenn S. Johnson, *Sebastian Miniature Collectors Guide,* published by author, 1982.

Periodical: *The Sebastian Exchange,* P. O. Box 4905, Lancaster, PA 17604.

Collectors' Club: Sebastian Collector's Society, 321 Central Street, Hudson, MA 01749. Dues: $10.00. *Sebastian Miniature News* (quarterly).

Cleopatra, Queen of Egypt, version 1, #359, marked "Des. by Prescot W. Baston, Marblehead," 3″ h, $200.00.

Amish Folk	100.00
Baby Buggy of 1850	85.00
Colonial Carriage	75.00
Crockett, Davy, #249	225.00
Evangeline, #12	125.00
Family Sing, #371	200.00
Gabriel, #11	135.00
Gibson Girl, #316-A	85.00
House of Seven Gables, #111	100.00
Hudson, Henry, #311	175.00
Jackson, Andrew, #159-A	250.00
Jefferson, Thomas, #124	85.00
Kennel Fresh, ashtray, #239	300.00
Lincoln, Abraham, seated	125.00

Mary Had A Little Lamb, #137	100.00
Parade Rest, #216	100.00
Peggotty, #52-A	85.00
Ross, Betsy, #129	85.00
Santa Claus, #123	100.00
Shaker Man, #1	150.00
St Joan of Arc, bronzed	275.00
Twain, Mark, #315	100.00
Van Winkle, R., #144	75.00
Victorian Couple, #89-B	85.00
Washington, George, pen holder, sgd "PW Baston, 1961"	22.50

SEVRES

History: The principal patron of the French porcelain industry in early 18th century France was Jeanne Antonette Poisson, Marquise de Pompadour. She supported the Vincennes factory of Gilles and Robert Dubois and their successors in its attempt to make soft paste porcelain in the 1740s. In 1753 she moved the porcelain operations to Sevres near her home, Chateau de Bellevue.

The Sevres soft paste formula used sand from Fontainbleau, salt and saltpeter, soda of alicante, powdered alabaster, clay, and soap. Louis XV allowed the firm to use the "double L's." Many famous colors were developed, including a cobalt blue. The great scenic designs on the ware were painted by such famous decorators as Watteau, La Tour, and Boucher. In the 18th century Sevres porcelain was the world's foremost diplomatic gift.

In 1769 kaolin was discovered in France, and a hard paste formula developed. The baroque gave way to rococo, a style favored by Jeanne du Barry, Louis XV's next mistress. Louis XVI took little interest in Sevres. Many factories began to turn out counterfeit copies. In 1876 the factory was moved to St. Cloud and was eventually nationalized.

Reference: Susan and Al Bagdade, *Warman's English & Continental Pottery & Porcelain Co.,* Inc., 1987.

Box, cov, 7¾″ l, scroll molded cartouche shaped cov, painted floral swags, wreath suspending flower filled basket, gilt, foliate scrolled borders, pink ground, int. with scattered floral sprays, gilt metal mounts, pseudo interlaced L's mark, c1900	350.00

Urns, pr, cobalt blue ground, gold scrolls, center medallion of pair of rustic lovers fishing, reverse with spray of full blown summer flowers, gilt bronze chamfered square base, 14″ h, $1,800.00.

Clock, mantel, 22″ h, Louis XVI style, black Roman and Arabic numerals, porcelain case with gilt and foliate scrolls, bleu celeste ground, shaped panel painted with large floral spray, white ground, gilt borders, gilt bronze laurel branch mounts, seated putto grotesque mask, shell and berry pendant, gilt bronze foliate and reed cast chapter rings, foliate scroll feet, 18th C dial and movement inscribed "Jn Baptiste, Baillon," late 19th C 3,200.00

Cup and Saucer, swan shape, white, gilded neck and head form handle, saucer with stylized leaf tip border, interlaced L's and blue J, c1830 ... 60.00

Dish, 6¼″ round, blue, openwork rim, center scene of pastoral lovers, scrolled tripod feet, sgd "A Max" ... 225.00

Ewer, cov, 12″, urn shape, courting scene, reverse with couple walking, pastels, gilt metal rim, ftd, and pedestal base, artist sgd 285.00

Figure, white biscuit
  7 x 6″, modeled by Falconet after Boucher, Marchand de Plaisir, young girl and two boys in 18th C dress, sundial, dog on leash, naturalistic base, imp "T" and shield mark, c1757 .... 900.00
  8″, modeled by Blondeau after Boucher
    La Petite Fille Au Tablier, young girl, wearing scarf and jacket, grapes and fruit in outstretched apron, standing barefoot by tree stump, shaped oval base, c1760 ..... 800.00
    Le Jeune Suppliant, young boy, clasped hands, short sleeve jacket and breeches, standing barefoot by basket of flowers, rockwork base 800.00
  8 x 9¼″, allegorical group, Charity, two infants in arms and lap, kissing hand of standing woman offering small bag, broken ewer and basin on ground, raised oval plinth base, incised "13," late 18th C 900.00
  16 x 21″, modeled by Biozot, Apollo and Daphne, nymph transforming into laurel tree, Apollo to one side, flaring cape, River God Peneus seated on overturned vase, naturalistic base, modern gilded stand, imp "Sevres," c1790 .... 3,000.00

Jardiniere
  7¼ x 8″, rounded cylindrical body, central scene of 18th C lovers in wooded or garden setting, jeweled gilt borders, gilt foliate scrolls, jeweled medallions, bleu du roi ground, pierced foliate gilt bronze rim and lion head ring handles, gilt bronze drapery swag and foliate scroll base, scrolled feet, late 19th C, pr 2,225.00
  15½ x 5½″, elongated oval form, two young girls and boy seated in rowboat moored in marsh, reverse painted with wo young boys dressed as hunters approaching a seated girl, octagonal musical trophies on sides, gilt tooled foliate scrollwork, bleu celeste ground, diapered borders, base inscribed in black "Jacquel 3 rue de la Paix-Paris," artist sgd "E. Apoil," late 19th C 1,550.00

Letter Box, 9⅝ x 6½″, narrow rect top and shaped triangular sides, large floral sprays, white ground, gilt and bleu celeste borders, rect slanted lid with scene of two 18th C dressed maidens and gallant, wooded landscape, divided int., two inkwells, engraved brass panel on back, lockplate sgd "Ch Olliver, 11 Blvd. de la Madeleine," third quarter 19th C 1,200.00

Portrait Plate, 9½″, Mme Lavalliere, gold scalloped rim, artist sgd, double L under crown mark 125.00

Salt, master, swan shape, incised feathers, 6″ oval liner, gold trim, First Imperial Period , 1804–09 .... 500.00

Vase, 15⅜″, seated maiden, pearls in hair, red dress, three cupids in clouds, gilt bronze socle base, bleu celeste lobed porcelain circular base, ribbon tied laurel wreath cartouches, foliate scroll handles suspending rings, fol-

iate scroll feet, Louis XVI style, artist
sgd "Felix Bellanger," c1900 . . . . . . **1,650.00**

SEWING ITEMS

History: As late as 50 years ago, a wide variety
of sewing items were found in almost every home
in America. Women of every economic and social
status were skilled in sewing and dress making.

Even the most elegant ladies practiced the art
of embroidery with the aid of jeweled gold and
silver thimbles. Sewing birds, an interesting con-
venience item, were used to hold cloth (in the
bird's beak) while sewing. Made of iron or brass,
they could be attached to table or shelf with a
screw-type fixture. Later models featured a pincushion.

References: Joyce Clement, *The Official Price
Guide To Sewing Collectibles,* House of Collecti-
bles, 1987; Victor Houart, *Sewing Accessories: An
Illustrated History,* Souvenir Press (London), 1984;
Gay Ann Rogers, *An Illustrated History of Needle-
work Tools,* John Murray (London), 1983.

Museums: Fabric Hall, Historic Deerfield, Deerfield, MA; Museum of American History, Smithsonian Institution, Washington, D.C.; Shelburne Museum, Shelburne, VT.

Additional Listings: See *Warman's Americana
& Collectibles* for more examples.

**Sewing Box, Tea Trade, 1st quarter
19th C, black lacquer, gold Oriental
scenes and foliage, orig ivory tools, including bodkins, birds, needles,
spools, hooks, etc., orig key, 14½ x 10
x 6⅛", $785.00.**

Advertising Trade Card, Singer Sewing
Machine Co, birds, dated 1899 . . . . 20.00
Box, 4½" l, straw work, abstract design
on sides, cottage on cov, English,
19th C 150.00

Darning Egg, 5¾" l, ebony egg, SS han-
dle with raised floral and Scroll dec . 45.00
Embroidery Hoop, 5¼" d, SS 35.00
Hem Gauge, cast iron, marked "Pe-
louze," c1894 . . . . 30.00
Needle and Pin Case
Leather, 2 x 1⅞", black, emb gold . . 45.00
Tin, Boyd adv, slide top, 1912 . . . . . 8.00
Wood, 2½", carved, silk-lined, c1870 55.00
Needle Case
Ivory, ornate, marked "Stanhope" . . 90.00
Nipper and phonograph, 2½ x 1½",
RCA Victor 30.00
Prisoner-of-war, bone, 4½" l, reticu-
lated, early 19th C 150.00
Needle Threader, metal, Champion Oil
adv 10.00
Pin Cushion
Beaded, 4½ x 5 x 8", figural, red,
beaded, "bird" on tail, two straw-
berries, thimble pocket 150.00
Doll, porcelain head, 4", flapper . . . 75.00
Scissors
Embroidery, 3", SP, emb floral dec on
handles, patent 1864 . . . . 20.00
Tailor's, 10", steel, japanned handles,
bent trimmers 15.00
Sewing Bird
Iron, one pincushion, bird with long
sweeping curved tail which turns
under 290.00
Silver Plated, double pincushion, emb
bird and clamp 165.00
Sewing Kit, 3" h, "Ladies Companion,"
leather, stainless steel thimble, scis-
sors, needle case, and punch, stain-
less steel hinges on oval box, late
1700s 110.00
Spool Cabinet
Brooks, two drawer, reversed glass
insert 265.00
Clark's Christmas, six drawer 650.00
Tape Measure
Advertising, Lydia Pinkham Medi-
cines 30.00
Brass, pig, tail turns to pull out tape 95.00
Porcelain, girl with mandolin 35.00
Thimble
Brass, applied butterfly with rhine-
stone insets, fret band, amethyst
top 45.00
China, floral dec, hp, artist sgd 15.00
Gold, engraved leaf border, 14K . . . 85.00
Sterling Silver, cherubs and garlands,
engraved design on band, Simons
Bros 30.00
Tortoise Shell, inset band 80.00
Thimble Case
Crochet, basket shape, handle and
cov 20.00
Mother-of-Pearl, hinged top 65.00

Papier Mache, floral design, gilded hinged top	40.00
Tracing Wheel, 6¼″, steel wheel, brass shaft, wood handle	12.00

SHAKER

History: The Shakers, so named because of a dance used in worship, are one of the oldest communal organizations in the United States. This religious group was founded by Mother Ann Lee who emigrated from England and established the first Shaker community near Albany, New York, in 1784. The Shakers reached their peak in 1850 with 6,000 members.

Shakers lived celibate and self-sufficient lives. Their philosophy stressed cleanliness, order, simplicity, and economy. Highly inventive and motivated, the Shakers created many utilitarian household forms and objects. Their furniture reflected a striving for quality and purity in design.

In the early 19th century, the Shakers produced many items for commercial purposes. Chairmaking and the packaged herb and seed business thrived. In every endeavor and enterprise, the members followed Mother Ann's advice: "Put your hands to work and give your heart to God."

Reference: Don and Carol Raycraft, *Shaker, A Collector's Source Book II,* Wallace-Homestead, 1985.

Periodical: *The Shaker Messenger,* P.O. Box 45, Holland, MI 49423.

Butter Churn, strap hinges, old red paint, $400.00.

Basket, 3¼ x 3½″, miniature, berry, woven splint, circular rim tapering to sq base, simple bent splint handle, midwestern, 19th C	150.00
Bottle, 9″, aqua, emb "Shaker Pickles," base labeled "Portland, Maine, E. D. P. & Co"	90.00

Box, cov, utility	
7½ x 3½″, painted chrome yellow, oval bentwood form, lid, printed paper label inscribed "Isaac N. Youngs," first half 19th C	6,600.00
10¾ x 4½″, painted green, oval bentwood form, 19th C	2,000.00
Brush, 10¾″, horsehair, turned wooden handle	85.00
Carpet Beater, 41½″ l, bent willow, turned beech handle	85.00
Clothing	
Dress, homespun linen, pale brown, wide double collar, twelve later buttons, late 19th C	200.00
Sunbonnet, 11″, brown and white gingham check, machine stitched, Hancock	40.00
Dough Scraper, 4½″, wrought iron . . .	40.00
Dry Measure, 14½″ d, 7¾″ h, pine, cylindrical bentwood body, nailed end, metal band rim, cast iron semi-circular handles, int. with stenciled Shaker label, late 19th C	175.00
Furniture	
Apothecary Cabinet, stained wood, rect, front fitted with twelve small drawers, molded white glazed porcelain handles, identification labels, drawer sides inscribed with various content titles, New England, 19th C, 66 x 13″	400.00
Blanket Chest, red painted wood, hinged rect top with molded edge, int. till, paneled front and sides raised on tapering cylindrical legs, lid int. inscribed in pencil "Bloomsburg, C B Hutton, Box 105, Orangevill," midwestern, 19th C, 37 x 24¾″	1,000.00
Chair	
Counter, painted and dec, single arched slat back, rush seat, turned legs, turned stretchers, ochre dec, stamped "FW" on top right front leg, Freegift Wells, Watervliet, NY, c1845	8,800.00
Deacon's, stained birchwood, removable elongated finials, four arched back slats, shaped arms, flattened mushroom caps, rush seat, turned legs, turned stretchers, orig black paint, ink inscription "Chair was made by Sister Sarah Collins, 1863, Mt. Lebanon, NY Geo. H. Wells, 1931, Dora Pierce, 1931, Sister A. Wilson 1868, Mt. Lebanon, NY Shaker Colony," and two orig sales tags inscribed "George H. Wells"	7,150.00
Clothes Rack, red painted wood,	

three horizontal bars, top bar mounted on either side with three hooks, rect uprights continuing to form arched feet, New England, late 19th C, 36½″ w, 72″ h **2,500.00**
Rocker, curly maple, lemon form finials, four arched graduated back slats, mushroom capped arms, rush seat, turned legs and stretchers, rockers, Enfield, CT, first half 19th C **14,300.00**
Table
Dining, maple, drop leaf, rect top, hinged rect leaves, single drawer, sq tapering legs, first half 19th C, 34¾ x 35½ x 28″ **6,600.00**
Side
Birchwood, rect top, frieze with molded drawer, slightly turned circular tapering legs, New Lebanon Community, c1830, painted red, 42 x 23 x 28″ ... **6,600.00**
Cherry, red stained, two board scrubbed rect top, single drawer, turned wood pull, tapering sq legs, 19th C, 36 x 28⅞″ **1,250.00**
Work, painted birchwood and pine, rect top and splashboard, single molded drawer, circular tapering legs, orig red paint, New Lebanon Community, first half 19th C, 37½ x 23 x 25½″ **8,800.00**
Hanger, 24″, bentwood, chestnut **65.00**
Pantry Box, bentwood, oval, lappet construction
Blue painted, single lappet on rim and body, off-white painted int., 6 x 2¼″ **325.00**
Matched set of four, sgd "S. Marmouth Kegsilk, August 1848," New England, 4⅝″, 7⅞″, 11½″, and 13½″ **3,575.00**
Sewing Box, pink cotton lining and pin cushion, stamped "Shaker Goods, Alfred, Maine" **100.00**
Sock Stretcher, 26″ l, wood **20.00**
Whisk, 14¼″ l, wood, primitive **45.00**
Yarn Winder, 18″ l, 20¼″ h, movable winder with rect bars joined by block and cylindrical shaft, slightly arched trestle base joined by stretchers, dark green paint, late 19th C **350.00**

SHAVING MUGS

History: Shaving mugs hold the soap, brush, and hot water used to prepare a beard for shaving. They come in a variety of materials including tin, silver, glass, and pottery. One style is the scuttle, so called because of its "coal scuttle" shape, with separate compartments for water and soap.

Shaving mugs were popular between 1880 and 1925, the period of the great immigration to the United States. At first barber shops used a common mug for all customers. This led to an epidemic of a type of eczema, known as barber itch.

Laws were passed requiring each individual to have his own mug. Initially names and numbers were used. This did not work well for those who could not read. The occupational mug developed because illiterate workers could identify a picture of their trade or an emblem of its tools. Fraternal emblems also were used and were the most popular of the decorative forms. Immigrants especially liked the heraldry of the fraternal emblems since it reminded them of what they knew in Europe.

European porcelain blanks were decorated by American barber supply houses. Prices ranged from fifty cents for a gold name mug to two dollars and fifty cents for an elaborate occupational design. Most of the art work was done by German artists who had immigrated to America.

The invention of the safety razor by King C. Gillette, that was issued to three and one-half million servicemen during World War I, brought an end to the shaving mug era.

References: Susan and Al Bagdade, *Warman's English & Continental Pottery & Porcelain, 1st Edition,* Warman Publishing Co., Inc., 1987; Robert Blake Powell, *Occupational & Fraternal Shaving Mugs of The United States,* published by author, 1978.

Advisor: Edward W. Leach.

BARBER SHOP: FRATERNAL

Ancient Order Of Foresters, deer head, crossed American flags, shield, lodge #7995 .... **275.00**
B.L.E.E., Brotherhood of Locomotive Eng., "BLE" monogram **90.00**
Elks, B.P.O.E., double emblem, Dr. title **300.00**
Fraternal Order of Eagles, eagle holding F.O.E. plaque **250.00**
International Brotherhood of Paper Makers, paper making machine, clasped hands, IB of PM **265.00**
International Order of Mechanics, ark ladder, I.O.M. **250.00**
Jr. Order United American Mechanics, arm, hammer, compass, square, and crossed flags **275.00**
Loyal Knights of America, eagle, flags, and six pointed star **275.00**
Retail Clerks Union, red star, clasped hands, initials, ARCIP **175.00**
United Mine Workers of America, picks and shovels, hand clasp **350.00**

Occupational, carpenter, block plane, brown dec, gold name and trim, $300.00.

BARBER SHOP: OCCUPATIONAL

Brewery, man pulling dolly, vaulted ceiling, row of kegs	400.00
Butcher, man standing with prize steer	500.00
Caboose, B.R.R.T.	400.00
Cavalry, Lt. 6th, eagle, crossed flags and sabers	750.00
Chicken Farmer, rooster crowning	225.00
Coal Miner, man in mine shoveling coal into cart	350.00
Coke Kiln, man with poker pulling coke chunks out of kiln	375.00
Cooper, man working on wooden barrel	400.00
Dentist, upper false teeth	350.00
Hand Car Operator on track, two men pumping	350.00
Hotel Clerk, clerk at desk, guest signing register	375.00
Hotel Owner, picture of hotel, owner's name	575.00
Ice Cream Parlor, metal dish of strawberry ice cream with spoon, worn gold trim	250.00
Livery Stable, horse drawn wagon with driver in front of stable	275.00
Marksman, crossed rifles, target eagle wreath	225.00
Musical, banjo, owner's name	350.00
Oysterman, open oyster shell	450.00
Painter, two men on scaffold painting house	385.00
Phonograph, outside horn phono	350.00
Photographic	
Dog trainer, man showing pit bull dog	375.00
Man with beard	250.00
Poultry Farmer, rooster, hen, and chicks, worn gold trim	100.00
Shepherd, sheep standing in field	350.00
Soldier, 22nd Inf. Div., crossed rifles, bayonets	400.00

Theater Owner, movie entrance scene, patrons on sidewalk, hand bills	750.00
Trolley, overhead lines	400.00
Trolley Repair Wagon, horse drawn, scaffolding	1,250.00
Truck, chain driven, early	375.00
Tugboat in water, crew and captain, title	750.00

BARBER SHOP: OTHER

Bluebird, holding ribbon, owner's name	65.00
Drape and Flowers, purple drape, pot of flowers, gold name	85.00
Flowers, purple, wheatheads, gold name	65.00
Horses In Storm, white and black horses, copied from painting	100.00
Pansies, blue and gold flowers on either side of name	95.00

GOLDEN SPORTSMAN MUGS

Father in top hat, Victorian ice skating scene	65.00
The Bartender, three customers, saloon scene	75.00
The Dentist, pulling teeth, patient in chair	100.00
The Engineer, locomotive tender	75.00
The Iceman, horse drawn ice wagon, driver, man on back	85.00

Scuttle, pearlized shell motif, marked "Made In Germany," $55.00.

SCUTTLES

Character	
Fish shape, green and brown	45.00
Skull shape	75.00
Rose Decorated, mirror, R.S. Prussia	175.00
Scuttle	
Moss and rose, green leaves, gold dec	50.00

Ribbed, multicolored flowers, gold dec	65.00
Silver Plated	150.00

SHAWNEE POTTERY

History: The Shawnee Pottery Co. was founded in 1937 in Zanesville, Ohio. The company acquired a 650,000 square foot plant that formerly housed the American Encaustic Tiling Company and where it produced as many as 100,000 pieces of pottery per day until 1961, when the plant closed.

Shawnee limited its chief production to kitchenware, decorative art pottery, and dinnerware. Distribution was primarily through jobbers and chainstores.

Shawnee can be marked "Shawnee," "Shawnee U.S.A." "USA #—," "Kenwood," or with character names, e.g., "Pat. Smiley," "Pat. Winnie," etc.

Reference: Mark Supnick, *Collecting Shawnee Pottery: A Pictorial Reference And Price Guide*, published by author, 1983.

Advisor: Mark Supnick.

Planter, Wishing Well, green, marked "710," 8½ x 5¼, $15.00.

Butter Dish, Corn King, marked "Shawnee #72"	35.00
Casserole, Corn King	
Large, marked "Shawnee #74"	43.00
Small, marked "Shawnee #73"	35.00
Creamer	
Elephant, marked "Pat. USA"	15.00
Puss 'n Boots, gold trim, decals marked "Pat. Puss 'n Boots"	110.00
Cookie Jar	
Clown, seal	75.00
Corn King	65.00
Winnie The Pig, marked "Pat. Winnie USA or USA"	75.00
Pitcher	
Bo Peep, marked "Pat. Bo Peep"	35.00

Chanticleer (chicken)	
Gold trim hand dec, decals	**145.00**
Marked "Pat. Chanticleer	**45.00**
Pig, marked "Pat. Smiley"	**45.00**
Planter	
Canopy Bed, marked "Shawnee #734"	**32.00**
Doe, seated next to log, #766	**19.00**
Dutch boy and girl at well	**12.00**
Teapot, Tom Tom the Piper's Son, marked "Tom the Piper's Son #44"	**35.00**
Vase	
Doves, marked "USA #829," pr	**20.00**
Swan, marked "USA #806"	**12.00**

SILHOUETTES

History: Silhouettes (shades) are shadow profiles, produced by hollow cutting, mechanical tracing, or painting. They were popular in the 18th and 19th centuries.

The name came from Etienne de Silhouette, a French Minister of Finance, who tended to be tight with money and cut "shades" as a pastime. In America the Peale family was one of the leading silhouette makers. An impressed stamp marked "PEALE" or "Peale Museum" identifies their work.

Silhouette portraiture lost popularity with the introduction of daguerreotype prior to the Civil War. In the 1920s and 30s a brief revival occurred when tourists to Atlantic City and Paris had their profiles cut as souvenirs.

Woman, 6 x 5", hollow cut, signed "Elizabeth Baker, Boston, 1824," $225.00.

Children	
3¼ x 3¾", primitive hollow cut, black cloth baking, emb brass on wood frame, gold repaint	50.00
6½ x 10¼", pair of full length children, gilded detail, simple ink wash ground, labeled "Master Hubbard," framed	200.00

10 x 13¾", full length of girl in garden, bird in one hand, flower in other, ink wash ground, pen and ink inscription "Annabelle Wallace, Aug. Edouart fecit 1842," walnut shadow box frame, gilded liner 675.00

Gentleman, 8¼ x 11½", Sea Captain, black backing, white litho ground showing window, ship, black cut paper ink set and cap on floor, highlighted in pencil, red, and gold on spyglass, sgd "Sam'l Metford, Newport, RI," identified on back in pencil as Charles Procter, framed 2,350.00

Group

3½ x 2¾", oval, watercolor and cut paper mounted on black fabric, inscribed on reverse: "Samuel Fish and Mrs. Elvira Fish, Gov Wentworth's family, NH," repousse brass frames, c1825 . . . . 4,000.00

13½ x 15½", family, brushed white highlights on each, black backing, white ink wash ground of room int., fireplace, entitled "The Lesson 1840," printed paper label "Clay Turner, Profiles From Life," inscription "George Walters and his family, Jan 7th, 1840" on back of paper visible through window in backing, birdseye veneer ogee frame 900.00

Women

3⅞ x 2⅜", young woman, emb signature of Peales Museum, framed 75.00

4¾ x 4", Susan, labeled "daughter of Anthony Sidon and Wife of John Torbert, Born July 28, 1760," ebonized frame 300.00

4⅞ x 5⅞", young woman, hollow cut, black cloth backing, eglomise glass with worn gilded frame 75.00

15¼ x 18¼", hollow cut, black cloth backing, mounted in multicolored floral wreath reverse painted tinsel picture, black ground, molded frame with gilded liner 100.00

SILVER

History: The natural beauty of silver lends itself to the designs of artists and craftsmen. It has been mined and worked into an endless variety of useful and decorative items. Pure silver is too soft to be fashioned into strong, durable, and serviceable utensils. Therefore, a way was found to give silver the required degree of hardness by adding alloys of copper and nickel.

Silversmithing in America goes back to the early 17th century in Boston and New York. It began in the early 18th century in Philadelphia. Boston was influenced by the English styles, New York by the Dutch.

References Frederick Bradbury, *Bradbury's Book of Hallmarks*, J. W. Northend, Ltd, 1987; Louise Bilden, *Marks Of American Silversmiths In the Ineson-Bissell Collection*, Univ. of VA Press, 1980; Donald L. Fennimore, *Silver & Pewter*, Alfred A. Knopf [Knopf Collector's Guides To American Antiques], 1984; House of Collectibles, *The Official Price Guide To American Silver and Silver Plate*, 5th Edition, House of Collectibles, 1986; Dorothy T. Rainwater, *Encyclopedia of American Silver Manufacturers, 3rd Edition;* Schiffer, 1986; Seymour B. Wyler, *The Book Of Old Silver, English, American, Foreign*, Crown Publishers, Inc., 1937 (available in reprint).

Periodical: *Silver*, P. O. Box 1243, Whittier, CA 90609. Subscription: $18.00.

Additional Listings: See Silver Flatware in *Warman's Americana & Collectibles* for more examples in this area.

American, coin, teaspoons, J. M. Mitksch, Bethlehem, PA, two of matching set of 6, 6" l, $175.00.

AMERICAN, 1790–1840
Mostly Coin

Coin silver is slightly less pure than sterling silver. Coin silver has 900 parts silver to 100 parts alloy. Sterling silver has 925 parts silver. American silversmiths followed the coin standards. Coin silver also is called Pure Coin, Dollar, Standard, or Premium.

Beaker, 3⅜" h, tapered cylindrical form, molded borders, base engraved "W. P. to Nannie," stamped on base, John Adam, Alexandria, VA, c1820, 4 ozs 825.00

Bowl, 6¼" d, circular, pedestal base, beaded borders, marked on base twice, Christian Wittberger, Philadelphia, c1795 . . . . 1,500.00

Cann, good clear mark, Jacob Hurd, Boston, MA, 1740–50, 12½ oz 3,900.00

Caster, 5½" h, baluster, domed lid, spiral turned flame finial, engraved and pierced drum, body inverted pyriform, spreading circular foot, lid and body with three gadrooned moldings, initial punch on one side, mark illegible, few bruises **500.00**

Coffeepot, 15½", vase form, incurved neck, pedestal base, beaded borders, swan neck leaf capped spout, reel shaped cov with vase finial, wood scroll handle, marked on base, Christian Wittberger, Philadelphia, c1795, split in cov, 42 ozs **4,500.00**

Creamer, spheroid body, scrolled handle, flaring open concave spout, conforming circular stepped base, monogrammed, Bailey & Kitchen, Philadelphia, 1833–46 .... **250.00**

Cup, 4¼", beaker form, two S scroll handles, monogrammed, Ebenezer Moulton, Newburyport, MA, c1810, 5 ozs **475.00**

Fish Server, reticulated panel of acorns and leaves, incised monogram "H," orig ivory handle, Joseph Lownes, Philadelphia, PA, c1780, 4½ oz, needs minor repair where handle joins silver **300.00**

Ladle
    Sauce, feather edge stem, bright cut, terminal monogrammed, spirally fluted bowl, marked twice on lower back of stem, William Hollingshead, Philadelphia, c1775 .... **800.00**
    Soup, 13¼" l, circular bow, curved flaring handle, pointed oval grip, handle engraved with bright cut border forming oval reserves, one with pendant bellflower, other with monogrammed, rouletttework border, marked Christian Wittberger, Philadelphia, c1790, 5 ozs **1,000.00**

Lemon Strainer, 3⅝" d, hemispherical bowl pierced in flowerhead pattern below border of lozenges, single incised line rim, side applied with scrolled strap clip for attachment to rim of bowl, marked, Adrian Bancker, NY, c17620, 2 ozs **1,650.00**

Mug, engraved initials "MAA," William Carrington, 6 oz **200.00**

Pepper Box, 3" h, cylindrical form, molded borders, domed foot, fluted scroll strap handle, domed cov pierced in flowerhead pattern, domed finial, marked on base three times, Miles Beach, Litchfield and Hartford, CT, c1780, 20 ozs, 5 dwts **1,250.00**

Porringer
    5", engraved with initials "WL" on the handle, straight line mark with ea-

gle in circle, Abel Moulton, Newburyport, MA, c1800, 6½ oz **2,600.00**

7½", pierced unornamented handle, deep bowl, John & Peter Targee, NY, 1811–25, 9 ozs, 2 dwts **1,450.00**

Spoon
Tablespoon
    Boelin, Joseph, NY, upturned midrib handle, fluted rattail bowl, terminal engraved with initials, marked on back of stem, c1720, 2 ozs **375.00**
    Brasher, Ephraim, NY, mid 19th C, strong marks, single drop, 2 ozs **225.00**
    Frederick Curtis & Co, Burlington, VT, c1786, engraved "Badgley," set of four, 5 ozs **100.00**
    Sargeant, Jacob, Hartford, CT, c1761, raised sheaf of wheat on handle, appears unused, 2 oz . **150.00**
    Teaspoon, Myer Myers, NY, 1723–95, engraved initials on handle **225.00**

Sugar Nippers, 4¼" l, scissor form, spurred ring grips, shaped arms, shell tips, circular hinge engraved on each side with initials, marked on inside of each tip, Jacob Hurd, Boston, c1750, 10 dwts **3,150.00**

Teapot
    10" h, spheroid body, stepped domed top, acorn finial, scrolled handle, leaf capped swan-like spout, conforming circular stepped base, Bailey & Kitchen, Philadelphia, 1833–46 .... **600.00**
    12" l, Federal style, oval body, banded design engraved on shoulder, hinged lid, urn finial, wood handle, maker's mark, R & H Farnam, Boston, post 1807, 18 ozs **500.00**

Tongs, engraved "PK," Matthew Petit, New York, NY, c1790, 2 oz **100.00**

Waste Bowl, 7½", globular body, lobed sides, concave paw and ball feet terminating in acanthus leaves, ring handles attached over lion mask roundels, William Thomson, NY, 1811–25, 23 ozs, 14 dwts **350.00**

SILVER, AMERICAN, 1840–1920
Mostly Sterling

There are two possible sources for the origin of the word sterling. The first is that it is a corruption of the name Easterling. Easterlings were German silversmiths who came to England in the Middle Ages. The second is that it is named for the starling (little star) used to mark much of the early English silver.

Sterling silver has 925/1000 parts pure silver. Copper comprises most of the remaining alloy.

Sterling, American, c1900, engraved "Gertrude/1902/From Charles, Jr., 7" l, $45.00.

American manufacturers began to swith to the sterling standard about the time of the Civil War.

Alvin Corp., Providence, RI, salts, 3⅜", set of four, oval, pierced sides, ball and claw feet, cobalt blue glass liners, 4 ozs **200.00**

Bailey, Banks and Biddle Co., basket, 9½", Art Nouveau, oval, pierced, flared sides, swing handle, monogrammed, 11 ozs, 10 dwts **350.00**

Baltimore Silversmiths Mfg Co., Baltimore, 1903–05, soup cup frames and liners, set of twelve, 3½" d, 1¾" h, double handles, threaded rims, engraved with scrolls suspending medallions, monogrammed, set of twelve porcelain Lenox liners, gilt trim, 30 ozs, 6 dwts **500.00**

Barbour Silver Co., Hartford, CT, box, cov, 7¼", sq, Rococo style rose and foliate sections, handle set with green stone, raised on four thread edged feet, gilt int., monogrammed, 19 ozs **350.00**

Cartier, basket, 6" sq, 7¼" h, hand made, woven with silver strips, strap handle, 12 ozs, 16 dwts **600.00**

Dominick & Haff, Newark, NJ
  Cake Plate, 13¾", plain face, emb rim with basket of flowers motif, 31 ozs, 6 dwts **450.00**
  Compote, 8" h, shaped and chamfered sq top pierced and chased in floral designs, inverted trumpet form stand, pierced rim at bottom, monogrammed, 11 ozs, 8 dwts . . **385.00**
  Flatware, seventy-three pcs, Renaissance pattern, monogrammed, orig filled oak case, 114 ozs, 10 dwts . **1,450.00**
  Service Plates, 11", set of twelve, plain, rolled edges and rims pierced with Greek key design spaced with

medallions of hanging leaves and bell flowers, monogrammed, 151 ozs, 18 dwts **2,200.00**

Duhme Co, Cincinnati, OH, 1898–1907, punch bowl, 14" d, chased and pierced with floral border at rim and feet, 76 ozs **2,750.00**

Wm. B. Durgin Co., Concord, NH, center bowl, 15½ x 7¾", flaring pierced sides, pedestal stem, domed base, spreading circular foot, rims of bowl and base with applied frieze of chased scrolling leafage, central face monogrammed and dated 1913, 50 ozs, 18 dwts **1,430.00**

Gorham Mfg Co., Providence, RI
  Bread and Butter Plates, 6½", set of ten, Florenz pattern, monogrammed, 1929, 59 ozs, dwts . . . **950.00**
  Cheese Dish, cov, 11¼", Maintenon pattern, 1924, retailed by Spaulding & Co., Chicago, 34 ozs, 12 dwts **475.00**
  Coffee Set, four pcs, 12" h Turkish form coffeepot, creamer, open sugar, and 14¾" tray, Iris pattern, wavy strapwork leaves and iris blossoms chased and worked on repoussé, lobed wavy feet, hollow ware pcs monogrammed, tray with worked border, plain face, Martelé silver, 950 standard, retailed by Theodore B. Starr, NY, 81 ozs, 8 dwts **9,350.00**
  Dressing Table Set, lady's, twenty pcs, two salve jars, two scent bottles, two powder jars, two cov puff jars, cov jewelry box, cov hatpin tray, engraved with swags of cloth and flowers, matte ground, center circular reserve with monogram on each pc, orig fitted case, retailed by Anderson & Randolph, San Francisco, 1877, 42 ozs, 10 dwts **2,575.00**
  Epergne, 23¼ x 23¼", Rococo style, four multiple scrolled feet, connecting aprons of scrolling foliage centering leafy spray, supporting platform with collet base for large glass bowl (cut with scrolling foliage), four leaf capped scrolling arms supporting smaller matching glass bowls, 85 ozs **4,125.00**
  Fruit Bowl, 11 x 3½", spreading circular form, ringed foot, monogrammed, 27 ozs, 18 dwts **275.00**
  Meat Platter, 16½ x 22½", Plymouth pattern, well at both ends, groove at sides, monogrammed, 80 ozs, 8 dwts **935.00**
  Salver, 14¼", circular, quatrefoil form, emb and flat chased border, plain face, 35 ozs, 6 dwts **300.00**

Tea and Coffee Set, six pcs, Maintenon pattern, 14" hot water kettle (1929) on stand (1930), 11" coffeepot (1926), teapot, cov sugar, creamer, and waste bowl, 164 ozs, 18 dwts **5,000.00**

Tea Tray, 25¼", Maintenon pattern, 1930, 162 ozs **2,750.00**

Vase, 9", pierced lap-over mouth, threaded rim, ovoid body, circular domed pedestal base, pierced foot, plated gilt frog, 26 ozs, 6 dwts . . . **360.00**

Graff, Washbourne & Dunn, NY

Center Bowl, 14¾", French border, hand chased, shaped circular form, fold-over pierced skirt rim, pierced frog cover,inscription on underside, for J. E. Caldwell & Co., 39 ozs . . **650.00**

Service Plates, 11½", set of eleven, French border, hand chased, retailed by Theodore B. Starr, Inc., NY, 221 ozs, 12 dwts **6,000.00**

Samuel Kirk & Son, Inc., Baltimore. flatware, service for twelve, Florentine pattern, 72 pcs **900.00**

Matthews Co, Newark, NJ, 1907–30, child's set, three pcs, 5½" d plate, mug, and brush, acid etched with scenes and names of nursery rhymes, 5 ozs, 10 dwts **250.00**

Meriden Brittania Co., Meriden, CT

Dessert Plate, 10½" d, shaped circular form, wide applied cast reticulated border with winged masks, foliate scrolls, and flowers, 19 ozs **200.00**

Flower Basket, 14½", cylindrical body, wavy open mouth, threaded rim, swelling shoulder, swinging strap handle, pierced with flat chased floral design, monogrammed, 62 ozs **1,650.00**

Pratt, 20th C, pitcher, water, 6" d, 8½" h, hand hammered, plain melon form body, curved handle, helmet form lip, rolled over edge, ring foot, monogram, 29 ozs, 10 dwts **825.00**

Reed & Barton, Taunton, MA, garniture, 11" trumpet shaped vase with fluted rim, three 6½" vases attached by chains, fourth vase and chain lacking monogram, weighted bases **220.00**

Shreve & Co, San Francisco

Bread and Butter Plates, 7⅛", set of sixteen, German Iris pattern, chased borders in heavy relief, monogrammed, 80 ozs, 8 dwts . . **1,650.00**

Cocktail Shaker, 10½" h, cylindrical body, peened surface, fish tail removable pourer, side set with gilt and enameled medallion, bell mark, 20 ozs, 4 dwts **500.00**

Presentation Tray, 16¾", unadorned peened surface with inscription and date 1915, bell mark, 52 ozs **365.00**

Sandwich Plate, 11¼", flat, chased, scrolling flower and tendril design, monogrammed, bell mark, 19 ozs, 18 dwts **225.00**

Teapot, 9½", Art Nouveau style, undulating vines, 19 ozs, 10 dwts . . **385.00**

Vase

9½", SS collar with chased German bearded iris on neck, modified Art Nouveau pierced border at lip, faceted polygonal glass base **1,000.00**

13", champagne bucket shape, fold-over lip pierced and engraved with scrolling flowers, matching underplate, bell mark, 92 ozs **1,870.00**

Spaulding & Co., Chicago, 1888–1920, dish, 11", grape leaf form, tendril and leaf handle, 25 ozs **400.00**

Tiffany & Co, NY, pitcher, water, 11¾", ovoid body, tapering neck, diagonally shaped spout joining strap handle, ring foot, inscribed on underside, dated 1958, 50 ozs, 8 dwts . . **1,210.00**

R. Wallace & Sons Mfg Co., Wallingford, CT, roast carving set, La Reine pattern, 3 pcs **100.00**

Wood & Hughes, NY, c1870

Hot Water Urn, 20" h, Renaissance Revival style, trumpet shaped body ending in pressed band of leaves and berries, lid engraved with scrolling design on matted surface, twisted post finial, handles with foliate ends and capped with figure of putto on each side, spigot handle topped with bust of female beauty, legs of attached stand cast openwork foliage, orig burner, 82 ozs, 10 dwts **935.00**

Soup Ladle, 15" l, Medallion pattern, silver-gilt bowl, scalloped edge, fitted leather case with purple velvet lining, 9 ozs, 18 dwts **660.00**

SILVER, CONTINENTAL

Continental silver does not have a strong following in the United States. The strong feeling of German silver cannot compete with the lightness of the English examples. In Canada, Russian silver finds a strong market.

Austrian

Centerpiece, 22½ x 16½", diamond shaped bowl on four feet, one foot on each side with heart shaped leaf flowing to reeded supports, ends with figures of Venus and Cupid, four straps issuing from ends and sides joining by four angled stalks and robed figure of Flora, holding clusters of grapes, marked AB, 800 standard, 116 ozs, 10 dwts **7,150.00**

Hot Water Kettle, 10¾", inverted pyriform kettle, scrolling handle, hinged lid with ivory finial, matching stand with heating pan, ivory handle, and three extra ivory knobs, M & K, Vienna, 1862, 66 ozs, 10 dwts **1,210.00**

Danish

Coffee Set, three pcs, 7" coffeepot with ivory handle, creamer with ivory handle, cov sugar, Blossom pattern, Georg Jensen, 26 ozs, 10 dwts **2,750.00**

Compote, 12½" h, bowl applied with threaded band alternating with leaves, bulbous pedestal engraved with band of foliage, cushion foot with circular medallions in repousse encircled with strapwork and foliage, Michelsen, Copenhagen, 1851, assayer's mark for P. R. Hinnerup, zodiac marks for Libra and Scorpio, 39 ozs **800.00**

Dutch

Creamer, 6", pyriform body, three inverted cabriole legs, branch form scrolling handle, neck engraved and bright cut foliage dec, HB, Amsterdam, 1793, 6 ozs **250.00**

Marrow Scoop, 9¼", plain design, double ends, Amsterdam, 18th C, 1 oz **360.00**

Salad Fork and Spoon, bowl of spoon with crowned double lion crest, fork with basket of fruit flanked by birds, spoon marked Amsterdam, import mark, and rubbed assay mark, fork marked Embden, assay mark for Leeuwarden, both handles marked 833 standard, 1909, 9 ozs, 8 dwts **250.00**

Wedding Cup, 13", silver-gilt, goblet shape, repousse with trellis supporting foliage and flowers on matte ground, ship finial on inverted goblet, body made from seashell, silver deck, mast sail, tiller, and anchor, 14 ozs **500.00**

French

Asparagus Tongs, 10", engine turned dec, 950 standard, J. G., late 19th C **200.00**

Bowl, 17½ x 4⅜", shell shape, fluted sides, four scroll feet with fluted palmette terminals, rim applied with alternating ball and bead pattern within a meander, A. Aucol, 950 standard, 49 ozs **1,450.00**

Dessert Bowls, 4¼ x 2¾", plain, threaded bands at rim and circular

ftd base, monogrammed, Paris, post 1879, 950 standard, 82 ozs, 6 dwts, set of 12 . . . . **1,650.00**

Dish Stands, 6 x 3", ring form, four scroll feet terminating in leafage, suspending floral garlands, 950 standard mark post 1879, return mark post 1888, 31 ozs, pr **425.00**

German

Bread Basket, 15", oval, pierced openwork and repoussé ornaments, floral garland borders entwining flower filled baskets at ends holding agricultural implements, draped over ribbons tied in French knots, alternating with cartouche at either side with scene of kneeling suitor and intended in Alpine landscape, each scene spaced with facing pair of birds and flowers, base with medallion of two infants playing with baby ducks, 19th C, 800 standard, 15 ozs **525.00**

Ewer, 10¼", Baroque taste, silver-gilt, emb and chased bird and floral garlands, scrolling foliage and bands of strapwork on pricked ground, domed circular foot, double C scroll handles, marked B & Z, post 1888, 800 standard, 26 oz, 10 dwts . . . **1,210.00**

Table Ornament, owl, 9¼" h, chased plumage, glass eyes, marked sterling, retailed by I. F. and Son, Ltd, 30 ozs, 4 dwts **1,100.00**

Tea and Coffee Service, silver gilt, pyriform bodies and domed tops, elaborately chased all-over with panels of scrolling foliage and flowers, pricked ground, floral swags centering cartouche on either side, scrolling finial, domed spreading feet, 14½" h hot water kettle on stand with burner, 12" h coffeepot, teapot, two handled sugar and creamer, marked W. W. H., post 1888, 160 ozs, 14 dwts, coffeepot handle loose **5,500.00**

Norwegian

Coffee Set, 3 pcs, engine turned, cobalt blue enamel, gilt int., ivory handle on 7" coffeepot, David Andersen **800.00**

Liqueur Goblets, 3¾" h, set of twelve, engine turned and enameled, stems and feet of plain silver, gilt bowl ints. **465.00**

Unmarked

Caster, 7½" h, Baroque style, bulging globular body, cylindrical neck and stem, domed circular foot and cap, dolphin finial, applied relief and chased flowers, scrolling leaves

and armorial, 19th C, pseudo hall-
marks, 9 ozs, 18 ozs, pr **365.00**
Table Ornament, pair of pheasants,
hinged wings, 19″ l, 31 ozs, 10 dwts **1,450.00**
Vase, 16½″, inverted pyriform shape,
scalloped trumpet motifs, domed
circular foot, all-over scrolling foliage and floral sprays, pricked
ground, cartouche on either side,
one in reserve, other with genre
scene of peasants outside tavern,
late 19th C, English import marks
of I. F. & Son, Ltd., London, 1928,
pr **4,500.00**

SILVER, ENGLISH

From the 17th century to the mid-19th century,
English silversmiths set the styles which American
silversmiths copied. The work from the period exhibits the highest degrees of craftsmanship. Active
collection of English silver takes place in the American antiques marketplace.

Charles II, tumbler, 3″ d, hammered
sides, slightly convex bottom, marks
rubbed, 2 ozs **250.00**
George I, caudle cup, 5″ h, plain lip, cast
S scroll handles, reeded and gadrooned body, socle base, maker's
mark rubbed, London, c1725, 9 ozs **200.00**
George II
  Candlesticks, pr, segmented shafts
  on circular convex shaped feet,
  maker's mark stamped twice,
  Thomas England, London, c1725–
  39, 27 ozs, 4 dwts, lacking nozzles **900.00**
  Inkstand, 8″ l, oblong tray, gadrooned
  edge, baluster form inkwell and
  pounce pot, tapered stand of differing origin, raised on ball and claw
  feet, Magdeline Feline, London,
  c1758, 14½ ozs **900.00**
  Sauce Boat, boat form, flying double
  C scroll leaf capped handles, tripod
  shell feet, shell terminals, repousse
  sides with flowers, lip edge with
  gadrooning, armorial under spout,
  marks partially rubbed off, William
  Grundy, London, 1759, 16 ozs, 6
  dwts, pr **2,750.00**
  Tankard, 4¾″, plain baluster form,
  double scroll handle, William Kidney, London, 1742, 14 ozs, 6 dwts **715.00**
George III
  Basket, 14½ x 3½″, oval, threaded
  swing handle, scalloped rim,
  threaded with pierced border, oval
  pierced foot, bright cut armorial and
  monogram on face, Peter and
  Anne Bateman, London, 1795, 22
  ozs, 18 dwts **1,320.00**

Candlesticks, pr
  4¾″, detachable nozzles, segmented shafts, shaped sq base,
  fluted acanthus leaf corners,
  Richard Rugg, London, 1776, 9
  ozs, 4 dwts, plug in socket of one
  stick **715.00**
  5½″, Rococo style, detachable noz-
  zles, segmented shafts, spreading shaped sq base, William
  Cripps, London, 1768, 11 ozs, 6
  dwts **3,575.00**
Calling Card Tray, 6¾″ d, shell and S
  scroll molded border enclosing
  plain surface, raised on double C
  scroll legs, pad feet, attributed to
  Edward Capper, London, c1768, 7
  ozs **175.00**
Center Bowl, 8½ x 3½″, shallow, ap-
  plied rim with branches and flowers, Victorian dec on sides in repousse of flowers and foliage,
  monogram in central cartouche,
  domed ring foot, caryatid handles,
  Paul Storr, London, 1805, 18 ozs,
  10 dwts **665.00**
Chocolate Pot, 11½″ h, pyriform, leaf
  capped scroll handle, hinged lid,
  foliate finial, circular foot, body engraved with cartouches centered
  by scrolling foliate medallions, one
  inscribed 1847, Robert Gray & Son,
  Glasgow, Edinburgh mark, 1804,
  23 ozs, 4 dwts, foot repaired **800.00**
Cup, 8″ h, urn form, plain scrolling S
  handles, socle base, John Lang-
  lands, Newcastle, 29 ozs **600.00**
Epergne, 22″ h, triple tiered frame
  supported by four multiple foliate
  scrolled feet linked by side aprons
  of floral sprays, center of lowest tier
  open with four foliage scrolling
  strap-form stretchers supporting
  pineapple, enclosed by four reserve swelling leaf-capped arms on
  second oval tier, central detachable
  boat shaped pierced basket, six detachable circular paterae form shallow armorial engraved baskets,
  leaf-capped scrolling branches
  ending in beaded circular supports,
  Thomas Powell, London, 1771, 194
  ozs, 14 dwts **11,000.00**
Marrow Scoop, 9″ l, feather edge,
  Thomas Chawner, London, 1774, 1
  oz **250.00**
Pepper Caster, 6″, baluster form,
  beaded edge, one cov bright cov,
  other plain, Hester Bateman, London, 1781 and 1783, 8 ozs, 6 dwts,
  pr **935.00**
Salt Cellars, 2¼ x 1¼″, plain circular

bowl, three hoot feet, rope twist rim, traces of gilt int., Hester Bateman, London, 1776, 2 ozs, 10 dwts, pr . **385.00**

Salver, 10″, shaped piecrust top, beaded border, three claw and ball feet, chased armorial of later date, Hester Bateman, London, 1781, 18 ozs **1,540.00**

Snuff Box, 3½″ l, oblong lid, cast floral rim, engraved turned surface above conforming case, band of scrolling floral engraving, Joseph Willmore, Birmingham, c1818, 3½ ozs **285.00**

Spoon, berry, gilt, repousse chased bowl, handles chased with flowers and strapwork, Hester Bateman, London, 1786, set of six, 11 ozs, 14 dwts **525.00**

Teapot, 5½″, flattened scrolling pyriform, gadrooned base, angular treen handle, plain collar, R. and S. Hennell, London, c1807, 20 ozs .. **275.00**

Toast Rack, 6¾ x 5¾″, oval frame and rack, beaded border, four claw and ball feet, pierced bright cut base, Hester Bateman, London, 1783, 8 ozs **825.00**

Tray, 18¾″, circular S scroll and shell cast border, plain surface, figural armorial and motto, raised on shell cast legs, Peter and Anne Bateman, c1813–4, 85 ozs **2,000.00**

George IV

Fruit Basket, 14¾″, pierced basket with applied border chased with scrolls and fluted garlands, sides of fluted swirls terminating in acanthus leaves, swing openwork handle, pierced band of flowers and scrolls base, central face engraved with rampant cat, inscribed below "Touch Not The Cat Bot A Glove," Robert Hennell, London, 1820, 45 ozs, 16 dwts **5,000.00**

Grape Shears, 6″ l, gilt handles, shells, flowers, and fruit on matte ground, Jonathan Hayne, London, 1822, 3 oz, 10 dwts **500.00**

Salt, 3¾″ d, double border of scrolls and flowers, tripod hoof feet, gilt int., Charles Price, London, 1822, 15 ozs, set of 4 .... **375.00**

Victorian

Creamer, 4″, pyriform, shaped flaring lip, C scroll handle, incurvate legs ending in pad feet, J. Whipple and Co., Exeter, c1878, 2 ozs **75.00**

Cruet Stand, 7½ x 10″, boat shaped bulging body, spiral gadrooned border, four scrolled leafy feet, segmented columnar handle with heart

shaped handle, cut plate to hold bottles, wooden platform below, monogram on body, six glass bottles, diaper cut band, James Edwards, London, 1845 .... **900.00**

Dressing Spoon, Fiddle, Thread, and Shell pattern, Samuel Hayne & Dudley Cater, London, 1844, 6 oz, 10 dwts **350.00**

Tea and Coffee Service, teapot, 10″ coffeepot, creamer, and cov sugar, Rococo style, pyriform bodies, leafy reserved cartouches, fluted quatrefoil sections, handles of double leafy S curves, tea and coffee spouts of matte work still leaves, acanthus feet, J. W. & J. W., Edinburgh, 1850, 86 ozs **3,125.00**

Tea Kettle, 14″ h, indented ovoid shape, highly worked emb, chased, and engraved surface, Elizabethan figures in village dec, hinged lid with male sitting on keg, leaf capped spout terminating in bearded mask, matching stand applied with cast and reticulated floral swags headed by female masks, three cabriole legs, leafy feet, strut branching from each leg to support fuel container, I. Foligno, London, 1867, 80 ozs, 10 dwts **1,450.00**

Wine Coaster, 5½ x 6¾″, bulging boat shaped body, repousse and chased with scrolls and flowers, four tab feet emb with anthemia, monogrammed, William K. Read, London, 1856 .... **300.00**

Wine Cooler, 9½ x 11½″, Greek vase shape, bulging lobed body with acanthus leaves, emb and chased border of English rose, Scotch thistle, and Irish shamrock at top, overhanging lip with alternating leaves, squat stem with border of tongues and leaves, circular foot chased with acanthus on matted ground, S curved handles ending in acanthus leaf terminals, Edward, Edward Jr, John, and W. Barnard, London, date letter rubbed, c1840s, 74 ozs **3,850.00**

Edward VII

Asparagus Tongs, 9″ l, crested Fiddle, Thread, and Shell pattern, W. W. BT. London, 1903, 6 oz **175.00**

Cup, cov, 5″ h, lid fitted with feet to act as stand, cylindrical cup, flared lip, scrolling handles, dec at base with geometric anthemion, maker's mark rubbed, London, c1901–2, 16 ozs **200.00**

George V, kettle on lampstand, 12¾″ h,

pyriform body, faceted leaf capped swan neck spout, domed hinged cov, knob finial, turned wood and C scroll handle, stand of four scrolled and pad supports, threaded skirt, detachable burner, EJG, London, 1931, 54 ozs . **625.00**

English, Sheffield, vase, 8½″ h, opalescent fluted glass top, $175.00.

SILVER, ENGLISH, SHEFFIELD

Sheffield Silver, or Old Sheffield Plate, was made by a fusion method of silver plating used from the mid-18th century until the mid-1880s when the silver electroplating process was introduced.

Sheffield plate was discovered in 1743 when Thomas Boulsover of Sheffield, England, accidentally fused silver and copper. The process consisted of sandwiching a heavy sheet of copper between two thin sheets of silver. The result was a plated sheet of silver which chould be pressed or rolled to a desired thickness. All Sheffield plate articles were worked from these plated sheets.

Most of the silver plated items found today marked "Sheffield" are not early Sheffield plate. They are later wares made in Sheffield, England.

Biscuit Box, 6½″ h, sq, hinged lid, lion mask and loose ring handles, faux tray base with paw supports, gadroon borders, unmarked, English, 19th C, replated **250.00**
Candelabra, pr, 19½″, tapering turned column form, heavily gadrooned banding, surmounted by twin scrolling candle arms **900.00**
Casserole, cov, 6½ x 5½″, Baroque style, oval body standing on four scroll feet terminating in shell flanked leaves, leaf capped handles terminating in leaves, covs with leaf capped entwined branch handles, armorial on sides and cov, unmarked, early 19th C, pr, copper showing . . . **825.00**

Entree Dish, cov, 12½ x 9″, gadrooned borders, shells and flowers at corners, covs with fluted borders and conforming borders, detachable handle with double bound branch terminating on calyx of acanthus leaves, armorial engraved on side, unmarked, first or second quarter, 19th C, pr **1,320.00**
Inkstand, 9″, rect tray, twin pen channels, faceted crystal pounce pot and inkwell, central chamberstick, 19th C **425.00**
Plateau, 17½″, Rococo style, mirror plate in shell and scroll border, conforming spreading border, spreading shell form sides, mask, and scroll feet, possibly T. J. Creswick, mid 19th C, feet cut down **625.00**
Sauce Dish, cov, 5½ x 6½″, form of cov calyx craters, disc shaped lids with gadrooned handles, spoon openings on rim, bowl with spiral gadrooned border, hot water reservoir, pair of double threaded handles, lobed sides, conforming circular foot with spiral gadrooned ring, early 19th C, pr **715.00**
Tea Urn, 15½″, urn finial cov, ring handles with lion masks, lion paw feet attached to underplate, engraved English coat of arms, first half 19th C, copper showing **250.00**
Tray, 28½″, oval, beaded bracket handles, applied egg and dart border, face with wide hand chased band of foliage dec, four bead feet, James Dixon & Sons, c1835–50, one foot missing **475.00**
Tureen, cov
13½ x 11″, Rococo taste, elongated lobed oval body, four scrolling foliage feet, pair of reeded bracket handles terminating in leaves, lip gadrooned and spaced with shells and leaves, fitted cov rising to chased foliage handle terminating with spreading foliate, marked GD **2,100.00**
14 x 20″, turtle shape, detachable hinged lid, unmarked **1,760.00**
Wine Cooler, campana urn form, applied vintage motif on lip and neck, bracket handles joined to waist with acorn and oak leaf motif, continuing in a band, circular foot with continuous frieze of leaf and tongue, lead liner, maker's mark JW, c1830–40, pr **3,300.00**

SILVER, PLATED

Plated silver production by an electrolytic method is credited to G. R. and H. Ekington, England, in 1838.

In electroplating silver, the article is completely shaped and formed from a base metal and then coated with a thin layer of silver. In the late 19th century, the base metal was Britannia, an alloy of tin, copper, and antimony. Other bases are copper and brass. Today the base is nickel silver.

In 1847 the electroplating process was introduced in America by Rogers Bros., Hartford, Connecticut. By 1855, a number of firms were using the method to mass produce silver plated items in large quantities.

The quality of the plating is important. Extensive use or polishing can cause the base metal to show through. The prices for plated silver items are low, making it a popular item with younger collectors.

Plated, American, Camille, International Silver Co, 6¼ x 9¼″ tray, $35.00.

Bowl, 17¾ x 6¾″, Neoclassical style, plain body, four paw feet with acanthus terminals, lion mask ring handles, band of spiral gadrooning, unmarked **600.00**

Butler's Tray, 18½ x 28″, crescent shape, threaded edge, solid galleried sides imp with repeating rect band of flowers and leaves, face bright cup in Egyptianizing floral motif, large circular medallion with traces of acid etched design of Athena drawn in chariot in reserve at center, large bracket handles with lotus terminals, unmarked, late 19th C **665.00**

Butter Dish, three pcs, base, lid, insert, delicate tiny double rows of beading around base, on edges, and dome lid, cut glass drip tray, Meriden Silver Plate Co **50.00**

Candelabrum, 10¾″, Rococo taste, beaded scrolling foliage, twisted threaded arms, central shaft with four individual screw-in arms, stick convertible from squat single to high single light or high quintuple light, one flame finial, made from orig Sheffield plate dies **150.00**

Champagne Bucket, 9″, cylindrical, bracket handles, applied scroll border band, monogrammed, Simpson, Hall, Miller & Co **250.00**

Cheese Ball Frame, 5″ d, mechanical, vitriculture border, E. G. Webster & Sons **75.00**

Cigar Holder, 10½″ h, champagne bottle with beaded trim, engraved "CIGARS," marked Graham Silver **75.00**

Desk Set, four pcs, inkstand, letter holder, letter opening, and half moon blotter, raised design of Rococo flowers, scrolls, trellis, and stork, marked J. B. **75.00**

Egg Caddy, emb floral platform holding six egg cups, dec prongs, feet with raised lion's masks, heart shaped bail handle, six egg spoons with shell shaped bowls, marked Simpson Hall Miller **225.00**

Epergne, 17½″, etched trumpet form glass vase centering emb flat circular plate with pierced handles, domed pedestal base with beaded border, shaped sq base **350.00**

Flatware, After Dinner, four berry spoons, two nutcrackers, and grape shears, gilt bowls, emb and chased berries, English, H. H. & Co., retailed by Marshall and Sons, 87 George St., Edinburgh, orig fitted presentation case **300.00**

Frame, 9¾ x 17½″, 2″ wide border with raised figures, dancing and seated peasants, trees, houses, and fences in village scene, rough textured finish **90.00**

Fruit Stand, 16″ d, slightly dished shaped circular bowl, emb with vitricultural dec, four ftd base, International **200.00**

Ice Bucket, cov, Baroque pattern, thermos lined, Wallace **225.00**

Jardiniere, 25½″, Baroque style, oblong, pair of leaf capped scroll handles, body emb with broad band of acanthus leaves and foliate scrollwork, supported by pair of griffins, stepped oval platform base, metal liner **1,200.00**

Meat Cover, 18 x 10½″, domed body, bright cup with panel of foliage swags and roses, beaded base edge, twisted branch handle, monogrammed, maker's marks, Victorian . **225.00**

Mustard Pot, 3½″, SP holder, reticulated sides, cranberry glass insert **50.00**

Pitcher, 12″, cov, ice water, tankard form, branch handle terminating in leaves, figural thumbpiece, hinged lid surmounted by swan, body with bright cut dec of diamond panels, dogwood blossoms in reverse, inscription on center panel, Reed & Barton **275.00**

Punch Bowl Set, 20¼ x 8″ punch bowl, twelve cups, circular waiter, Harvest pattern, Wallace 250.00

Sardine Box, small Greek key border on box, lid with figural fish finial, fancy feet, monogrammed, glass liner . . . 75.00

Syrup, 8″, geometric and floral strap work body, figural lady's head on lid and handle, Meriden, 1865, replated 85.00

Tea and Coffee Service, five pcs, 10¾″ h coffeepot, teapot, cov sugar, creamer, and waste bowl, King George pattern, plain pyriform shape, four hoof feet terminating in a shell, International 250.00

Tea Urn, 19¼″, Neoclassical style, plain urn form, domed cov, urn finial, lion masks supporting ring handles, stepped base, four ball feet, John Taylor, London, c1780–1810 . . . . . . 450.00

Tray, 25¼″, Winthrop pattern, shaped rect, Rococo form, flat chased surface, bracket handles, Reed & Barton 200.00

Umbrella Stand, 20½″, elongated trumpet shape, interlaced flowering branches, H. Wilkinson & Co., copper showing 225.00

Watch Holder, 6″, cherub holds bird aloft, stands on raised base, emb trim around edge, Meriden Co 125.00

Wine Coasters, pr, 5¾″, sides emb with repeating repousse frieze of female mask crowned with grapes, scrolling grape vines and leaves on pricked ground, base of wood, engraved armorial central plug, English 550.00

SILVER DEPOSIT GLASS

History: Silver deposit glass, consisting of a thin coating of silver actually deposited on the glass by an electrical process, was popular at the turn of the century. The process was simple. The glass and a piece of silver were placed in a solution. An electric current was introduced which caused the silver to decompose, pass through the solution, and remain on those parts of the glass on which a pattern had been outlined.

Ashtray, 8″, mallards 25.00
Bowl, 10½″, cobalt blue, flowers and foliage, silver scalloped edge 85.00
Cake Plate, 10″, swirled edge, Heisey mark 65.00
Compote, 7 x 7″, clear, floral dec 75.00
Cruet, 8″, clear, floral dec, orig stopper 65.00
Decanter, 13¼″, crystal, Continental silver mounts, grape clusters and leaves dec, orig stopper 80.00
Ice Tub, closed tab handles, floral and foliage dec, matching SS ice tongs . 125.00

Creamer, clear glass, 2¾″ h, $32.50.

Perfume Bottle, 4½″, clear, vine and grape leaf dec 40.00
Plate, 12″, crystal, floral dec 75.00
Sherbet and Underplate, cobalt blue, vine and grape leaf dec 30.00
Sugar Shaker, vine and grape leaf dec, SP top 60.00
Tray, 11″, cobalt blue, vine and grape leaf dec 100.00

SILVER OVERLAY

History: Silver overlay is silver applied directly to a finished glass or porcelain object. The overlay is cut and decorated, usually by engraving, prior to being molded around the object.

Glass usually is of high quality, either crystal or colored. Lenox used silver overlay on some porcelain pieces. The majority of design motifs are from the Art Nouveau and Art Deco periods.

Candy Dish, black, handled, Rockwell . 75.00
Cologne Bottle, 5½″, clear, lattice pattern 100.00

Compote (Tazza), black amethyst glass, marked "Rockwell," 5½″ d, 3¼″ h, $130.00.

Creamer and Sugar, floral overlay ... **35.00**
Cruet, 7½", amber, Art Nouveau flowers
and leaves **135.00**
Jardiniere, 7", ftd, white over pale magenta glaze, silver blossoming vine border, silver rim, imp factory mark . **175.00**
Loving Cup, 3½", three handles, cranberry ground **500.00**
Perfume, 5", bulbous, green glass, elaborate silver dec **375.00**
Pitcher, lemonade, marked "Lenox Belleek" **225.00**
Vase
3 x 6½", DQ, MOP, green satin glass, stylized Art Nouveau design, sgd . **735.00**
3½", emerald green ground **125.00**
7¼", plum ground, marked "T & V" . **325.00**
8", trumpet shape, green glass, floral dec, name shield, marked **275.00**
Wine, 4", clear, cherry dec **38.00**

with vine border and sprigs, seven holes, urn knob, 1810 .... **350.00**
Cup and Saucer, flower and vine dec . **85.00**
Goblet, 4" h, floral vine borders, Staffordshire, c1810, pr **165.00**
Jug, 4⅜", shield shape, painted florals, blue ground, c1820 .... **260.00**
Mug, child's, girl reading, floral dec ... **100.00**
Pitcher
4⅝", shield shape, vertical ribbing, medallions with stylized flowerheads, rose vine border, c1820 .. **165.00**
7", hunting scene, dog handle, imp "Wedgwood" **185.00**
Teapot, 5½", flower and vine dec **285.00**
Vase, 7½", Leeds, ovoid, flared rim, flowering vines and foliage, rect base, c1810 .... **300.00**

SMITH BROS. GLASS

History: After establishing a decorating department at the Mount Washington Glass Works in 1871, Alfred and Harry Smith struck out on their own in 1875. Their New Bedford, Massachusetts, firm soon became known worldwide for its fine opalescent decorated wares, similar in style to those of Mt. Washington.

Their glass often is marked on the base with a red shield enclosing a rampant lion and the word "Trademark."

Reproduction Alert: Beware of examples marked "Smith Bros."

Rose Bowl, Shasta Daisy, gold rim, white beads, 3⅛" d, 4" h, $165.00.

SILVER RESIST

History: Silver resist ware was first produced about 1805. It is similar to silver luster in respect to the silvering process and differs in that the pattern appears on the surface.

The outline of the pattern was drawn or stenciled on the ware's body. A glue or sugar-glycern adhesive was brushed over the part not to be lustered, causing it to "resist" the lustering solution which was applied and allowed to dry. The glue or adhesive was washed off. When fired in the kiln, the luster glaze covered the entire surface except for the pattern.

Pitcher, pine and pine cone dec, marked "Wedgwood and Barlston," 5" h, $80.00.

Bough Pot, cov, 8½", Leeds, "D" shaped body, three arched panels with grapes and gooseberries, cov

Bowl, 4¼", melon ribbed, yellow daisies dec, cream white satin ground **235.00**
Creamer and Sugar, individual size, 2¾" h creamer, 3¼ x 3½" cov sugar, slightly ribbed satin glass, tiny yellow and orange flowers, SP trim, sugar marked **410.00**
Mustard jar, 2", ribbed, gold prunus dec, white ground **300.00**

Potpourri Vase, 10″, enameled chrysanthemums and leaves, gold outlines,
satin ground, sgd 950.00
Powder Box, 5½ x 3½″, melon ribbed,
blue and gold florals, cream ground 450.00
Rose Bowl, 2½″, beaded rim, pink and
rose pansies, green leaves, creamy
white ground, sgd 200.00
Salt Shaker, melon ribbed, ring neck,
floral dec, white satin ground, orig
pewter top 115.00
Toothpick, columned ribs, pansies dec,
blue enameled dots around rim, white
ground 115.00
Vase
6¾″, Swirl pattern, blue flowers,
gilded leaf dec 425.00
7¼″ h, 8″ w, double, pilgrim, lavender
wisteria, traced in gold, gold beading on top 1,215.00
7¼″ h, 8″ w, double, canteen, hp,
enamel dec of spray of single petaled pink wild roses, butter yellow
dec, orig paper label 785.00

SNOW BABIES

History: Snow babies, small bisque figurines
spattered with glitter sand, were made originally in
Germany and marketed in the early 1900s. There
are several theories about their origin. One is that
German doll makers copied the designs from the
traditional Christmas candies. Another theory, the
most accepted, is that they were made to honor
Admiral Peary's daughter who was born in Green-
land in 1893 and was called the "Snow Baby" by
the Eskimos.

Reference: Ray and Eilene Early, *Snow Babies*, Collector Books, 1985.

Babies
Flying propeller airplane, 1½ x 2½″ 125.00
Holding camera, one arm extended,
1½″ 85.00

Bear, standing on skis, 2″ h, $75.00.

Ice Skating, boy and girl, 2″, pr 250.00
Playing musical instruments, 7 ba-
bies, 2″ 315.00
Riding bear, 2⅞″, red, blue, and ma-
roon 150.00
Seated
1″, arm extended 40.00
2″, one leg tucked under 30.00
Sledding, 2¾″, pulled by huskies ... 75.00
Christmas Tree Ornament, snow angel,
1¾″ 200.00
Figure
Elf, 1½″ 50.00
Kitten, 1½″ 48.00
Snow Man 50.00
Sheep, 2″ 45.00
Match Holder, 3½″ 125.00
Planter, 8″ 175.00

SNUFF BOTTLES

History: Tobacco usage spread from America
to Europe to China during the 17th century. Europeans and Chinese preferred to grind the dried
leaves into a powder and sniff it into their nostrils.
The elegant Europeans carried their snuff in boxes
and took a pinch with their finger tips. The Chinese
upper class, because of their lengthy fingernails,
found this inconvenient and devised a bottle with
a fitted stopper and attached spoon.

In the Chinese manner, these utilitarian objects
soon became objects d'art. Snuff bottles were
fashioned from precious and semi-precious
stones, glass, porcelain and pottery, wood, metals,
and ivory. Glass and transparent stone bottles often were enhanced further with delicate hand
paintings, some done on the interior of the bottle.

Reference: Sandra Andacht, *Oriental Antiques
& Art, An Identification and Value Guide*, Wallace-
Homestead, 1987.

Collectors' Club: International Chinese Snuff
Bottle Society, 2601 North Charles Street, Baltimore, MD 21218.

Agate, 2⅜″, banded, turquoise stopper,
late 19th C 125.00
Amber, 2⅝″, carved, Buddha's hand, citron fruit, turquoise stopper 300.00
Amethyst, 2¼″, pear shape, carved,
matching stopper, flat foot 175.00
Aquamarine, 1¾″, carved leaves, butterfly, rose tourmaline stopper, wood
stand, 20th C 1,750.00
Chalcedony, 3″, butterscotch, medium
high relief, Shou symbol, early 19th C 100.00
Cinnabar, 2¾″, deep blood red, carving
of figures, scenic design, matching
stopper, apocryphal seal of Chien
Lung, 20th C 100.00

Chinese, porcelain, jade stopper, tapered cylinder form, c1825–50, 3¹¹/₁₆″ h, $275.00.

Enamel on Metal, 2⅜″, prunus blossoms, flowers, mid 20th C	100.00
Interior Painted Glass, 3¼″, four children playing under a tree, sgd Yung Shao-t'ien, c1898	175.00
Jade, 2″, brown, peacock carved in white coloration of stone, 20th C	225.00
Lapis Lazuli, 2″, carved foo dog holding coral ball stopper in mouth, 20th C	350.00
Peking Glass, 3⅛″, five color overlay, fish and aquatic plants, early 19th C	350.00
Porcelain, 2⅜″, Famille Rose enamels, silver mounted jade stopper, late 18th C	150.00
Quartz, 3″, rose, relief carving of two birds, blossoms, carved foot, matching carved stopper, late 18th C	325.00
Tourmaline, 2⅝″, rose, Kuan Yin carving, matching stopper, 20th C	350.00
Turquoise, 2⅞″, highly polished, 20th C	115.00
Wood, black lacquered finish, MOP inlay	65.00

SOAPSTONE

History: The mineral steatite, known as soapstone because of its greasy feel, has been utilized for carved figural groups and other designs by the Chinese and others. Utilitarian pieces also were made. Soapstone pieces were very popular during the Victorian era.

Bookends, vase with trailing vines and flowers, pr	55.00
Bowl, 11½″, irregular oval, flat bottom, carved figure ext., carved teak stand, Chinese, 19th C	225.00
Candlesticks, 5⅛″ h, red tones, flowers and foliage, pr	90.00

Figure	
Geisha, 3½ x 3¼″, kneeling, Chinese, c1880	125.00
Oriental, 11¾″, dog and basket of flowers slung over shoulder, brown finish, carved wood stand	75.00
Jardiniere, 8 x 6″, carved, bird and foliage, shaded gray-green to brown	85.00
Plaque, 9½″ h, birds, trees, flowers, and rocks. stand	115.00
Teapot, 5 x 3″, carved, figures, vines, and flowers	350.00
Toothpick Holder, two containers with carved birds, animals, and leaves	80.00

Vase, chyrsanthemum, foliage, and bird carving, 9½″ h, $225.00.

Vase	
6½″, carved animals, flowers, foliage, marked "China"	80.00
8½″, double, carved monkey, pig, and bird, dark mahogany brown, Chinese, 19th C	150.00

SOUVENIR AND COMMEMORATIVE CHINA AND GLASS

History: Souvenir, commemorative, and historical china and glass includes those items produced to celebrate special events, places, and people.

Among the china plates, those by Rowland and Marcellus and Wedgwood are most eagerly sought. Rowland and Marcellus, Staffordshire, England, made a series of blue and white historic plates with a wide rolled edge depicting scenes beginning with the Philadelphia Centennial in 1876 and continuing to the 1939 New York World's Fair. Wedgwood collaborated in 1910 with Jones, McDuffee and Stratton to produce a series of historic dessert-sized plates depicting scenes throughout the United States.

Many localities issued plates, mugs, glasses, etc., for anniversary celebrations or to honor a local historical event. These items seem to have greater value when sold in the region from which they originated.

Commemorative glass includes several patterns of pressed glass which celebrate persons or events. Historical glass includes campaign and memorial items.

References: Bessie M. Lindsey, *American Historical Glass,* Charles E. Tuttle Company, Inc., 1967; Frank Stefano, Jr.; *Wedgwood Old Blue Historical Plates And Other Views Of The United States Produced For JONES, McDUFFEE & STRATTON Co., Boston, Importer; A Check-List with Illustrations,* published by author, 1975.

Additional Listings: Cup Plates, Pressed Glass, Political Items, and Staffordshire, Historical. Also see *Warman's Americana & Collectibles* for more examples.

Plate, blue, Niagara Falls, history of falls on back, impressed and marked "Wedgwood," 1905, 9⅛" d, $75.00.

CHINA

Creamer, 3⅛", bulbous base, straight neck, black basalt, hp enamel crest of Ontario, Canada, green maple leaf, side trim, orange Ontario banner underneath, green enamel rim and handle trim, marked "Wedgwood, England" and painters no.	250.00
Pitcher	
Masonic Hall, Chester, PA, blue and white transfer, tankard shape	225.00
William Penn, coral Indian handle, Lenox	150.00
Plate	
Rowland and Marcellus, 10½" d	
Atlantic City, NJ	45.00
Garfield Memorial	40.00
Williamsport, PA, city hall	40.00

Staffordshire, 10" d, Lewis & Clark Centennial Expo 1905, flow blue, marked	50.00
Wedgwood, 7½" d, blue	
King Edward VII Coronation, dated June 26, 1902	50.00
Marietta College 125th Anniversary, 1960	20.00
Signing of the Declaration of Independence, blue	45.00
Vase, 6½" h, scrolled enameled panel of Niagara Falls with scenic background, all-over enameled pink apple blossoms, purple highlights, brass base	425.00

GLASS

Bottle, General Douglas MacArthur, aqua, one-half pint, 1942	35.00
Butter Dish, Liberty Bell	140.00
Cup, World's Columbian Exposition, figural, leaf, Libbey	65.00
Goblet, G. A. R., 1887, 21st Encampment	100.00
Mug, Columbus	40.00
Paperweight	
Plymouth Rock, clear	65.00
Washington Monument, deep blue, sq base, bust of Washington on oval medallion sq and compass medallion on opposite corner, top inscribed "Cornerstone, July 4th–48, Dedicated Feb 21, '85," 5½" h	165.00
Plate, Niagara Falls, Lindsey 490	60.00
Platter, clear and frosted, three presidents, remembrance center	55.00
Tile, 4" d, Detroit Women's League, multicolored irid	130.00
Trinket Box, satin, pink, Martha Washington, New Martinsville	95.00

SOUVENIR AND COMMEMORATIVE SPOONS

History: Souvenir and commemorative spoons have been issued for hundreds of years. Early American silversmiths engraved presentation spoons to honor historical personages or mark key events.

In 1881 Myron Kinsley patented a Niagara Falls spoon; and, in 1884 Michael Gibney patented a new flatware design. M. W. Galt, Washington, D.C., issued commemorative spoons for George and Martha Washington in 1889. From these beginnings a collecting craze for souvenir and commemorative spoons developed in the late 19th and first quarter of the 20th century.

References: Dorothy T. Rainwater and Donna H. Fegler, *American Spoons, Souvenir and His-*

torical, Everybodys Press, Inc., 1977; Dorothy T. Rainwater and Donna H. Fegler, _A Collector's Guide To Spoons Around The World,_ Everybodys Press, Inc., 1976.

Collectors' Club: American Spoon Collectors, Box 260, Warrensburg, MO 64093. Dues: $12.50.

Additional Listings: See _Warman's Americana & Collectibles_ for more examples.

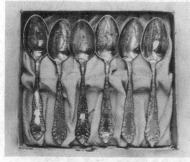

Great White Fleet, set of 6, silver plate, marked "Standard," orig box, spoons 4¼" l, $80.00.

Atlantic City, NJ, Steel Pier, chased floral handle, demitasse	32.00
Boulder, CO, name in bowl, Indian head handle	34.00
Canada, SS	25.00
Cripple Creek, CO, SS	45.00
Decatur, IL, SS	40.00
Denver, mule handle, SS	15.00
Grand Army of Republic, engraved bowl	65.00
Huron, SD, Ralph Voorhees Hall	35.00
Jamestown Expo	35.00
Keokuk, IA, SS	52.00
King Cotton	30.00
Lake Okajobi, cut-out Indian head handle	45.00
Memorial Arch, Brooklyn, round oak stove	30.00
Mission Inn, California	35.00
Mt. Vernon	45.00
New Orleans, SS	35.00
Palm Springs Aerial Tramway, SP, John Brown, marked "Antico"	100.00
Pasadena, Golden Gate, diecut bear finial	40.00
Philadelphia, SS	35.00
Portland, Oregon, SS	25.00
Prophet, veiled	135.00
Queen Elizabeth, 1953 Coronation	15.00
Rabbit's Foot	15.00
Richmond, MO, SS	25.00
Rip Van Winkle	30.00
Rushville, IL, SS	30.00
Salem, witch	40.00
San Antonio, TX, SS	35.00
San Francisco, CA, SS	35.00
Silverton, CO, SS	25.00
Statue of Liberty, NY	40.00
Teddy Roosevelt, riding horse, full figure handle	85.00
Towle's Log Cabin	25.00
Williamsport, emb shield, knight's head on handle, teaspoon	35.00
Winona Hotel, IN, SS	35.00
World's Fair, Chicago 1893, SS	50.00

SPANGLED GLASS

History: Spangled glass is a blown or blown molded variegated art glass, similar to spatter glass, with the addition of flakes of mica or metallic aventurine. Many pieces are cased with a white or clear layer of glass. Spangled glass was developed in the late 19th century and still is being manufactured.

Originally spangled glass was attributed only to the Vasa Murrhina Art Glass Company of Hartford, Connecticut, which distributed the glass for Dr. Flower of the Cape Cod Glassworks, Sandwich, Massachusetts. However, research has shown that many companies in Europe, England, and the United States made spangled glass, and attributing a piece to a specific source is very difficult.

Basket, white cased base, pink, yellow, orange, and white, clear thorn handle, 6 x 5½ x 5½", $200.00.

Basket, 6½ x 4¾", pink and white, silver mica, white casing, looped thorn handle	165.00
Beverage Set, bulbous pitcher, six matching tumblers, rubena, opales-	

cent mottling, silver flecks, attributed to Sandwich, c1850–60 . . . . 250.00

Bride's Bowl, 10⅜", multicolored, ruby, cranberry, and green, ivory-yellow ground, silver flecks 100.00

Condiment Set, cranberry, green flecks, SP holder, 3 pcs 200.00

Creamer and Sugar, cov, blue, gold mica flecks 225.00

Cruet, Leaf mold pattern, cranberry, mica flecks, white casing, Northwood 450.00

Fairy Lamp, 6⅜", multicolored, gold mica flecks, Clarke insert 200.00

Finger Bowl, 4¼ x 2½", ftd, swirled streaks of white, gold, and emerald green, clear body, foot drawn from body, applied clear handles imp with cherub's face 75.00

Pitcher, 7½", bulbous, four sided top, apricot, gold mica flecks form diamond pattern, white casing, pontil . . 165.00

Rose Bowl, 6" d, lavender, silver veining, attributed to Cape Cod Glass Works 80.00

Sugar Shaker, cranberry, mica flecks, white casing, Northwood 115.00

Tumbler, 4", pink, white, orange, red, yellow, and silver spangles 75.00

Vase
  5¾", shades of pink, ftd, mica chips 80.00
  6⅛", green, red, chartreuse, blue, yellow, white, and adventurine, applied striped handles, pontil 85.00
  6½", bulbous, melon ribbed, blue, silver flecks, white casing 90.00
  7⅛", ruffled mouth, pale blue, silver flecks, fiery opal casing, pontil . . . 50.00

SPATTER GLASS

History: Spatter glass is a variegated blown or blown molded art glass. It originally was called "End-of-Day" glass, based on the assumption that it was made from leftover batches of glass at the end of the day. However, spatter glass was found to be a standard production item for many glass factories.

Spatter glass was developed at the end of the 19th century and still is being produced. It was made in the United States and Europe.

Reproduction Alert: Many modern examples come from Czechoslovakia.

Basket
  5" w, 6½" h, aqua, brown, and white spatter, swirled ribbed body, ruffled edge, applied clear thorn handle . 240.00
  6 x 5½", blue, white casing, applied clear thorn handle 185.00

Quill Holders, pr, cranberry, cased, brass tops, c1880, 4" d, 5" h, $120.00.

Box, 7½ x 4½", egg shaped, hinged, white casing, yellow and blue flowers, gold and white leaves, three applied clear feet 275.00

Candlestick, 7½", yellow, red, and white streaks, clear overlay, vertical swirled molding, smooth base, flanged socket 50.00

Creamer, 4¾", pink and white, applied clear handle, Northwood 45.00

Cologne Bottle, 8½", etched adv "Rich Secker Sweet Cologne, New York," applied clear handles 60.00

Darning Egg, multicolored, attributed to Sandwich Glass 125.00

Fairy Lamp, 3¼ x 2⅞", pyramid shape, pink, yellow, and white, white casing, clear base marked "Clarke" 100.00

Jar, cov, 6½ x 3¼", gold, maroon, white, and green, yellow casing, leaf finial . 75.00

Pitcher
  8½", Swirl pattern, pink, brown, and cranberry, applied rococo handle . 85.00
  10¾", tankard shape, pink and white, clear casing, applied clear handle 110.00

Rose Bowl, 4½", pink and blue, pontil . 40.00

Salt, master, 3 x 3¼", white, maroon, green, blue, and yellow, white casing, applied crystal rigaree and leaf dec . 65.00

Tumbler, 3¾", royal blue and white . . . 35.00

Vase
  7½", bulbous, ruffled rim, ruby, white spatter, gold butterflies, flowers, and foliage, etched mark, pr 450.00
  9¼", jack in the pulpit, ruffled, DQ, white and peach spatter top, green base 100.00

SPATTERWARE

History: Spatterware is made of common earthenware, although occasionally creamware was used. The earliest English examples were made about 1780. The peak period of production was

1810–1840. Marked pieces are rare. Firms known to have made spatterware are Adams, Barlow, and Harvey and Cotton.

The amount of spatter decoration varies from piece to piece. Some objects simply have decorated borders. These often are decorated with a brush, requiring several hundred touches per square inch to achieve the spatter effect. Other pieces have the entire surface covered with spatter. Aesthetics of the final product is a key to value.

Collectors today focus on the patterns—Cannon, Castle, Fort, Peafowl, Rainbow, Rose, Thistle, Schoolhouse, etc. On flat ware the decoration is in the center. On hollow pieces it occurs on both sides.

Color of spatter is another price key. Blue and red are most common. Green, purple, and brown are in a middle group. Black and yellow are scarce.

Like any soft paste, spatterware was easily broken or chipped. Prices are for pieces in very good to mint condition.

References: Susan and Al Bagdade, *Warman's English & Continental Pottery & Porcelain, 1st Edition,* Warman Publishing Co., Inc., 1987; Carl and Ada Robacker, *Spatterware and Sponge,* A. S. Barnes & Co., 1978.

Reproduction Alert: "Cybris" spatter is an increasing collectible ware made by Boleslow Cybris of Poland. The design utilizes the Adams type peafowl and was made in the 1940s. Many contemporary craftsmen also are reproducing spatterware.

Saucer, multicolored, 6½" d, $30.00.

Beaker, 2½" h, blue, brown, and yellow rainbow spatter	275.00
Bowl	
5⅞", Peafowl, blue spatter	275.00
18¾", Tulip, blue spatter	300.00
Chamber Pot, 8½ x 6", rose dec in red, green, and black, blue spatter	250.00
Creamer	
Peafowl, blue spatter	400.00
Rainbow, blue and red spatter	150.00
Cup and Saucer	
Acorn, blue spatter	250.00
Castle, purple spatter	185.00
Peafowl, green spatter	350.00
Schoolhouse, five colors	550.00
Thistle, purple spatter	245.00
Honey Pot, Schoolhouse, red, yellow, and blue	3,000.00
Mustard Pot, Peafowl, green spatter	785.00
Pitcher, Rainbow, green and red spatter	475.00
Plate	
American Eagle, underglaze blue, eagle clasping arrows in talons, perched before shield with 13 stars, purple spatter border rim, 3⅞", c1840	375.00
Dahlia, red, blue, and green, blue spatter, 8⅜"	275.00
Fort, blue spatter, 5⅛"	175.00
Peafowl, blue spatter, 8¼"	300.00
Rainbow, blue and red spatter, 5⅛"	200.00
Tulip, purple spatter, 6¼"	275.00
Platter, Rainbow, red and blue spatter	500.00
Sugar, cov, Peafowl, blue spatter	450.00
Teabowl and Saucer, Coxcomb, red, blue spatter	235.00
Teapot, Peafowl, blue, green, yellow, and black, red spatter, 7"	135.00
Toddy Plate, Acorn, brown, and black, green and purple spatter, 5⅛"	375.00
Wash Bowl and Pitcher, Peafowl, red, blue, green, yellow, and black, 14½ x 13¼"	1,000.00

SPONGEWARE

History: Spongeware is a specific type of decoration, not a type of pottery or glaze.

Spongeware decoration is found on many types of pottery bodies—ironstone, redware, stoneware, yellow ware, etc. It was made in both England and the United States. Marked pieces indicate a starting date of 1815, with manufacturing extending to the 1880s.

Decoration is varied. In some pieces the sponging is minimal with the white underglaze dominant. Other pieces appear to be sponged solidly on both sides. Pieces from 1840–1860 have sponging which appears in either a circular movement or a streaked horizontal technique.

Examples are found in blue and white, the most common colors. Other prevalent colors are browns, greens, ochres, and greenish-blue. The greenish-blue results from blue sponging which has been overglazed in a pale yellow. A red overglaze produces a black or navy color.

Other colors are blue and red (found on English creamware and American earthenware of the

1880s), gray, grayish-green, red, dark green on stark white, dark green on mellow yellow, and purple.

References: Susan and Al Bagdade, *Warman's English & Continental Pottery & Porcelain, 1st Edition,* Warman Publishing Co., Inc., 1987; Earl F. and Ada Robacker, *Spatterware and Sponge,* A. S. Barnes & Co., 1978.

Pitcher, cobalt blue and tan, 8″ h, $200.00.

Bank, 6″, pig, blue and brown sponging,
   cream ground **165.00**
Batter Bowl, 7½ x 4¼″, pour spout, blue
   sponging, yellowware ground, re-
   placed wire bail handle **120.00**
Bean Pot, cov, green, brown, and ochre
   sponging **150.00**
Bowl
   6″, blue sponging, white ground . . . **55.00**
   6½, blue and rust sponging, cream
     ground, Iowa adv **50.00**
   6¾ x 3″, brown and green sponging,
     cream ground **40.00**
   10¾ x 4⅛″, light blue sponging, tan
     ground, arch molded sides **210.00**
Creamer, 4″, green, corset shape **65.00**
Cup and Saucer, blue and white,
   straight sides **110.00**
Cuspidor, blue sponging, white ground,
   molded basketweave dec **150.00**
Inkwell, green **180.00**
Jar, cov, 6″, blue sponging, cream
   ground, wire handle **215.00**
Jug
   3″, green, brown, and ochre sponging **125.00**
   7¼″, flared top, blue sponged bands,
     cream ground, applied handle . . . **125.00**
Mug, 1¾″, red sponging, cream ground **125.00**
Nappy, 8½″, rect, blue sponging, white
   ground, only int. sponged **175.00**
Pie Plate, 10¼″, blue sponging, white
   ground **165.00**

Pitcher, 5″, brown, blue, red, and white
   sponging, cream ground **125.00**
Plate, 10¼″, blue sponging, white
   ground, scalloped rim **120.00**
Sugar, blue and red sponging, cream
   ground **175.00**
Wash Bowl and Pitcher, 11⅝ x 8½″,
   blue and olive green sponging, blue
   bands, white ground **325.00**

STAFFORDSHIRE ITEMS

History: A wide variety of ornamental pottery items originated in England's Staffordshire district, beginning in the 17th century and extending to the present. The height of production was from 1820 to 1890.

These naive pieces are considered folk art by many collectors. Most items were not made carefully; some were even made and decorated by children.

The types of objects are varied, e.g., animals, cottages, and figurines (chimney ornaments). The key to price is age and condition. The older the piece, the higher the price is a general rule.

References: Susan and Al Bagdade, *Warman's English & Continental Pottery & Porcelain, 1st Edition,* Warman Publishing Co., Inc., 1987; P. D. Gordon Pugh, *Staffordshire Portrait Figures Of The Victorian Era,* Antique Collectors' Club Ltd.

Figure, The Vicar and Moses, 9½″, $215.00.

Chimney Ornaments
   Cats, 5½″, black spotted white bod-
     ies, orange cushions, green collars,
     mid 19th C, pr **1,200.00**
   Dogs, 8″, King Charles Spaniels,
     black and brownish-gray, c1820–
     30, pr **450.00**

Commemorative Cup, 4⅜", Admiral
Hood, blackish-gray, green, and flesh
tones, brown eyes, c1780–90 . . . . . 550.00
Cow Creamer, 5½", spotted ochre and
indigo glazes, hobbled back legs,
green milkmaid on base, orig cov,
c1785–1800 . . . . 1,500.00
Figure
   Cat, 5¾", enamel sponged yellow and
   brown, oval blue banded base,
   c1775–85 . . . . 1,800.00
   Deer, 6", bocage, naturalistic colors,
   stag missing antlers, c1820–35, pr   225.00
   Ewe, 3⅞", reclining, relief textured,
   pale blue eyes, green glazed base,
   c1780–90 . . . . 300.00
   Female Fish Peddler, 8¾", glazed
   enamel gaudy dec, carries basket
   with sign "Haddies," c1800 . . . . . 275.00
   Group, 7", bocage, man and woman
   in front of tree, titled "Tenderness,"
   naturalistic colors, sgd "John Walton," c1820, repairs 325.00
   Owl, 7¾", cream ware, raised wings,
   molded relief feathers, sponged
   manganese dec, possibly by
   Thomas Whieldon, c1770–80 . . . 13,000.00
   Ram and Ewe, 5 x 4", relief textured,
   sponged blue manganese and yellow, green glazed bases, c1780–
   90, pr 3,200.00
Inkstand
   3½" h, swan, coleslaw dec, wings
   with pink highlights 175.00
   4½" l, dog, reddish-brown whippet,
   blue base 200.00
Mantel Vase, 8", pearl ware, cov, dia-
pered pattern with medallions of
Chinese scenes, polychrome enam-
els, c1790–1810 . . . . 950.00
Mug
   3½", pearl ware, underglaze blue dec
   "Beer," and floral sprays, c1800 . . 500.00
   5½", cream ware, hand colored transfer printed dec of gentry on outing,
   c1790–1810 . . . . 300.00
Pastile Burner, 4½", two part, porcelain,
four gilt edge windows and door in
front, heavily encrusted multicolored
blossoms, multi-petaled pink roses,
single leaf painted inside base,
c1835, repairs to flowers 2,000.00
Sauce Tureen, 8 x 4", cov, pearl ware,
duck, relief textured, feathers, green,
yellow, blue, and brown, c1770–80 . 1,300.00
Tea Service, strawberry luster, cov teapot, creamer, spill bowl, large dish,
eight cups and saucers, c1820–40,
20 pcs 475.00
Teapot, 5", cream ware, matching cov,
floral finial, blue, green, yellow, and
rose stylized leaves, splattered iron-

red ground, chinoiserie scenes,
c1780–1800 . . . . 500.00
Toy Figure
   Cat, 2½" h, agate ware, c1740–50 . 450.00
   Lion, 2½" h, pink, iron-red, and black,
   green base, c1800 . . . . 325.00
Watch Holder, 8¼" h, pearl ware, monument, two children wearing classical
dress, blue, brown, yellow, green, and
ochre, c1785–1800 . . . . 1,000.00

STAFFORDSHIRE, HISTORICAL

History: The Staffordshire district of England is
the center of the English pottery industry. There
were eighty different potteries operating there in
1786, with the number increasing to 179 by 1802.
The district includes Burslem, Cobridge, Eturia,
Fenton, Foley, Hanley, Lane Delph, Lane End,
Longport, Shelton, Stoke, and Tunstall. Among the
many famous potters were Adams, Davenport,
Spode, Stevenson, Wedgwood, and Wood.

In historical Staffordshire the view is the most
critical element. American collectors pay much
less for non-American views. Dark blue pieces are
favored. Light views have lost popularity during
the past five years and, in many cases, have
dropped in value. Among the forms, soup tureens
have shown the highest price increases.

A recent development in historical Staffordshire
is the mail auctions of David Arman of Woodstock,
Connecticut, who is following a marketing trend
which he and other dealers have established for
a number of specific antiques categories.

References: David and Linda Arman, *Historical
Staffordshire: An Illustrated Check List,* published
by author, 1974, out-of-print; David and Linda Arman, *First Supplement, Historical Staffordshire:
An Illustrated Check List,* published by author,
1977, out-of-print; Susan and Al Bagdade, *Warman's English & Continental Pottery & Porcelain,
1st Edition,* Warman Publishing Co., Inc., 1987;
Ada Walker Camehl, *The Blue China Book,* Tudor
Publishing Co., 1946, (Dover, reprint); A.W. Coysh
and R. K. Henrywood, *The Dictionary Of Blue And
White Printed Pottery, 1780–1880,* Antique Collectors' Club, 1982; Ellouise Larsen, *American Historical Views On Staffordshire China,* 3rd Edition,
Dover Publications, 1975.

Notes: Prices are for proof examples. Adjust
prices by 20% for an unseen chip, a faint hairline,
or an unseen professional repair; by 35% for knife
marks through the glaze and a visible professional
repair; by 50% for worn glaze and major repairs.

The numbers in parenthesis refer to items in the
books by Linda and David Arman, which constitute
the most detailed list of American historical views
and their forms.

Advisors: David and Linda Arman.

W. ADAMS & SONS ADAMS

ADAMS

The Adams family has been associated with ceramics from the mid 17th century. In 1802 William Adams of Stoke-upon-Trent produced American views.

In 1819 a fourth William Adams, son of William of Stoke, became a partner with his father and was later joined by his three brothers. The firm became William Adams & Sons. The father died in 1829 and William, the eldest son, became manager.

The company operated four potteries at Stoke and one at Tunstall. American views were produced at Tunstall in black, light blue, sepia, pink, and green in the 1830–40 period. William Adams died in 1865. All operations were moved to Tunstall. The firm continues today under the name of Wm. Adams & Sons, Ltd.

Adams, plate, 10″ d, Mitchell & Freeman's China & Glass Warehouse, Chatham Street, Boston, dark blue, c1804–40, (444), $400.00.

Hudson River Series
View Near Sandy Hill, Hudson River, pink, 4″ cup plate (461) 70.00
Log Cabin, medallions of Gen. Harrison on border, teapot, pink (458) 275.00
Seal of United States, dark blue, pitcher, 7½″ (443) 1,000.00
U.S. Views
Lake George, U.S., brown, vegetable dish (448) 225.00
Shannondale Springs, Virginia, U.S., pink, 8″ plate (451) 60.00

CLEWS

From sketchy historical accounts that are available, James Clews took over the closed plant of A. Stevenson in 1819. His brother Ralph entered the business later. The firm continued until about 1836 when James Clews came to America to enter the pottery business at Troy, Indiana. The venture was a failure because of the lack of skilled workmen and the proper type of clay. He returned to England but did not re-enter the pottery business.

Cities Series, dark and medium blue
Albany, 10″ plate (16) 275.00
Chillicothe, 10½″ platter (20) 3,200.00
Washington, 7¾″ plate (30) 275.00
Doctor Syntax, dark blue
Doctor Syntax setting out on his first tour, 12″ covered dish (35) 1,750.00
Doctor Syntax and the gypsies, soup tureen (51) 3,000.00
Doctor Syntax turned nurse, 7¾″ plate (56) 165.00
Don Quixote Series, dark blue
Don Quixote's Library, vegetable dish (68) 600.00
Sancho Panza's debate with Teresa, 9″ plate (78) 150.00
Landing of Lafayette at Castle Garden, dark blue (1)
Cup Plate, 3½″, oval medallion 400.00
Pitcher, 5½″ 800.00
Plate, 7½″ 275.00
Platter, 21¾″, well and tree 1,200.00
Teapot 700.00
Peace and Plenty, dark blue (34)
Cup Plate, 4½″ 900.00
Platter, 17″ 500.00
Picturesque Views Series
Bakers Falls, Hudson River, pink, 9″ plate (101) 60.00
Fort Edward, Hudson River, light blue, 4⅛″ cup plate (102) 75.00
Hudson, Hudson River
Gravy Tureen, black (107) 250.00
Penitentiary in Allegheny, near Pittsburgh, pink, 15½″ tray (117) 275.00
Troy From Mount Ida, light blue, 6″ pitcher (120) 200.00
Pittsfield Elm, dark blue, soup, 10½″ (33) 250.00

Clewes, plate, 10¼" d, Picturesque Views Series, Near Fishkill, Hudson River, brown, (111), $175.00.

States or America and Independence Series, dark blue

Building, Deer on Lawn, 10½" plate (2)	250.00
Dock, large building and ships, 19½" platter (4)	1,500.00
Mansion, small boat with flag in foreground, 13½" bowl (12)	1,500.00

J & J. JACKSON

J. & J. JACKSON

Job and John Jackson began operations at the Churchyard Works, Burslem, about 1830. The works formerly were owned by the Wedgwood family. The firm produced transfer scenes in a variety of colors, such as black, light blue, pink, sepia, green, maroon and mulberry. Over 40 different American views of Connecticut, Massachusetts, Pennsylvania, New York, and Ohio were issued. The firm is believed to have closed about 1844.

J & J Jackson, plate, American Scenery Series, The Race Bridge, Philadelphia, (486), $60.00.

American Scenery Series, all colors

Albany, NY, 20" platter (462)	275.00
At Richmond, VA, 7" plate (465)	60.00
Bunker Hill Monument, 6½" plate (468)	150.00
Hartford, CT, 10" soup (476)	60.00
Iron Works at Saugerties, 12" platter (478)	250.00
Water Works, Phila, 9" plate (487)	60.00
Yale College, deep dish (493)	125.00

THOMAS MAYER

In 1829, Thomas Mayer and his brothers, John and Joshua, purchased Stubbs' Dale Hall Works of Burslem. They continued to produce a superior grade of ceramics.

Arms of the American States, dark blue

CT, gravy tureen (498)	4,500.00
DE, 17" platter (499)	3,000.00
PA, 21" platter (506)	12,000.00
Lafayette at Franklin's Tomb, dark blue, sugar bowl (510)	700.00

CHARLES MEIGH

Job Meigh began the Meigh pottery in the Old Hall Pottery, in 1780. Later his sons and grandsons entered the business. The firm's name is recorded as Job Meigh & Sons, 1823; J. Meigh & Sons, 1829; Charles Meigh, 1843.

The American Cities and Scenery series was produced by Charles Meigh between 1840 and 1850. The colors are light blue, brown, gray, and purple. Sometimes the colors appear in combination.

Albany, 7½" pitcher (544)	200.00
Baltimore, washbowl (546)	225.00
Capitol at Washington, tureen, round, cover (550)	500.00
City Hall, New York, 10¼" plate (551)	65.00
Hudson City, 10¼" soup (552)	60.00
Utica, cup plate (556)	90.00
Village of Little Falls, 8¼" plate (558)	60.00
Yale College, New Haven, 9½" plate (560)	60.00

MELLOR, VENEABLES & CO.

Little information is recorded on Mellor, Veneables & Co. except that they were listed as potters in Burslem in 1843. Their Scenic Views series with the Arms of the States Border does include the arms for New Hampshire. This state is missing from the Mayer series. However, the view was known in England and collectors search for a Mayer example.

Arms of States, white body, light color
 transfers (529)
  MD, teapot 250.00
  PA, sugar bowl 200.00
Scenic Views, Arms of States Border,
 light blue, pink, brown, purple
  Albany, 15″ platter (516) 275.00
  The President's House from the
   River, 14″ pitcher (520) 250.00
  Tomb of Washington, Mt. Vernon,
   7½″ plate 85.00
  View of Capitol at Washington, 11″,
   vegetable dish (526) 225.00

J.W.R.

Stone China

W. RIDGWAY

J. & W. RIDGWAY AND WILLIAM RIDGWAY & CO.

John and William Ridgway, sons of Job Ridgway and nephews of George Ridgway who owned Bell Bank Works and Couldon Place Works, produced the popular Beauties of America series at the Couldon plant. The partnership between the two brothers was dissolved in 1830. John remained at Couldon.

William managed the Bell Bank works until 1854. Two additional series were produced based upon the etchings of Bartlett's American Scenery. The first series had various borders including narrow lace. The second series is known as Catskill Moss.

Beauties of America is in dark blue. The other series are found in the light transfer colors of light blue, pink, brown, black, and green.

American Scenery
  Albany, washbowl (279) 275.00
  Columbia Bridge on the Susque-
   hanna, soup tureen (281) 450.00
  Peekskill Landing, Hudson River, tea-
   pot (287) 200.00
  Valley of the Shenandoah from Jef-
   ferson's Rock, 7″ plate (289) 60.00

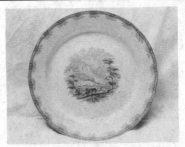

John & William Ridgway, plate, 9¼″, American Scenery Series, Harper's Ferry from the Potomac Side, light blue, (284), $60.00.

  Wilkes-Barre, Vale of Wyoming, cof-
   feepot (294) 275.00
Beauties of America, dark blue
  Almshouse, Boston, soup tureen
   (254) 2,500.00
  Bank, Savannah, gravy tureen (257) 1,200.00
  City Hall, New York, 10″ plate (260) . 125.00
  Exchange, Charleston, vegetable
   dish (265) 900.00
  Octagon Church, Boston, 10″ soup
   (271) 175.00
Catskill Moss
  Anthony's Nose, 6″ plate (295) 60.00
  Caldwell, Lake George, 5″ sauce dish
   (298) 60.00
  Kosciusko's Tomb, 10″ plate (305) . 75.00
  Valley of Wyoming, cup (317) 35.00
Columbia Star, Harrison's Log Cabin
  End View, plate (276) 90.00
  Side View, cup with handles (277) .. 65.00

ROGERS

ROGERS

John Rogers and his brother George established a pottery near Longport in 1782. After George's death in 1815, John's son Spencer became a partner and the firm operated under the name of John Rogers & Sons. John died in 1816. His son continued the use of the name until he dissolved the pottery in 1842.

Boston Harbor, dark blue (441)
  Cup Plate 1.000.00
  Cup and Saucer 375.00
  Waste Bowl 600.00
Boston State House, dark blue (442)
  Creamer 450.00
  Platter, 19″ 550.00
  Soup Tureen 3,000.00

R.S.W.

STEVENSON

As early as the 17th century the name Stevenson has been associated with the pottery industry. Andrew Stevenson of Cobridge introduced American scenes with the flower and scroll border. Ralph Stevenson, also of Cobridge, used a vine and leaf border on his dark blue historical views and a lace border on his series in light transfers.

The initials R. S. & W. indicate Ralph Stevenson and Williams are associated with the acorn and leaf border. It has been reported that Williams was Ralph's New York agent and the wares were produced by Ralph alone.

Ralph Stevenson and Williams, plate, 10″ d, Park Theater, New York, acorn and leaf border, medium blue, (357), $425.00.

Acorn and Oak Leaves Border, dark
blue
  Columbia College, New York, 7½″
    plate (350) **450.00**
  State House, Boston, 5″ plate (360)   **500.00**
  Water Works, Phila, 10″ soup (363) .   **375.00**
Floral and Scroll Border, dark blue
  Almshouse, New York, 10″ plate (394)   **750.00**
  Catholic Cathedral, New York, 7½″
    plate (395) **1,400.00**
  Troy from Mt. Ida, 9¾″ platter (402) . **1,750.00**
  View of New York From Weehawk,
    soup tureen (404) **10,000.00**
Lace Border
  Erie Canal at Buffalo, 10″ soup (386)   **150.00**
  New Orleans, Sugar Bowl (387) . . .   **225.00**
  Riceborough, GA, washbowl (388) .   **450.00**

Stevensons, platter, 12½ x 16¼″, Alms House, Boston, vine border, dark blue, (365), $1,250.00.

Vine Border
  Almshouse, New York, 7″ pitcher
    (366) **900.00**
  Battery, New York, 7¾″ plate (367) .   **550.00**
  Columbia College, New York, 8″ plate
    (372) **475.00**
  Hospital, Boston, 9″ plate (378) **225.00**
  Pennsylvania Hospital, Phila, soup
    tureen (383) **8,500.00**

STUBBS

In 1790 Stubbs established a pottery works at Burslem, England. He operated it until 1829 when he retired and sold the pottery to the Mayer brothers. He probably produced his American views about 1825. Many of his scenes were from Boston, New York, New Jersey and Philadelphia.

Rose Border, dark blue
  Boston State House, 7″ pitcher (335)   **600.00**
  City Hall, New York, plate, 6″ (336) .   **350.00**
Spread Eagle Border, dark and medium
blue
  City Hall, New York, 6½″ plate (323)   **325.00**

Fair Mount Near Phila, platter, 22"
(324) **1,200.00**
Highlands, North River, 10" plate
(325) **1,500.00**
Hoboken in New Jersey, salt shaker
(326) **600.00**
State House, Boston, 14½" platter
(331) **700.00**
Upper Ferry Bridge over the River
Schuylkill (332)
Dish, round **500.00**
Platter, 19" **750.00**
Vegetable Dish **650.00**
Wash Pitcher **600.00**

S. TAMS & CO.

The firm operated at Longton, England. The exact date of its beginning is not known, but believed to be about 1810–15. The company produced several dark blue American views. About 1830 the name became Tams, Anderson, and Tams.

Capitol, Washington
Bowl, deep (514) **1,500.00**
Wash Pitcher (514) **1,700.00**
United States Hotel, Phila, soup, 10"
(515) **750.00**

WOOD

Enoch Wood, sometimes referred to as the Father of English Pottery, began operating a pottery at Fountain Place, Burslem, in 1783. A cousin Ralph Wood was associated with him. In 1790 James Caldwell became a partner and the firm was known as Wood and Caldwell. In 1819 Wood and his sons took full control.

Enoch died in 1840. His sons continued under the name of Enoch Wood & Sons. The American views were first made in the mid 1820s and continued through the 1840s.

It is reported that the pottery produced more signed historical views that any other Staffordshire firm. Many of the views attributed to unknown makers probably came from the Woods.

Marks vary, although always with the name Wood. The establishment was sold to Messrs. Pinder, Bourne & Hope in 1846.

Celtic China, light transfer colors
Columbus, GA, 3⅞" cup plate (238) **350.00**

Shipping Port on the Ohio, KY, 12"
platter (249) **450.00**
Transylvania University, Lexington,
KY, 10" soup (250) **100.00**
West Point, Military Academy, open-
work dish (252) **350.00**
Floral Border, irregular, dark blue
Commodore MacDonnough's Victory
(154)
Coffeepot **1,750.00**
Cup and Saucer **325.00**
Entrance of the Erie Canal into the
Hudson at Albany (156)
Plate, 6" **750.00**
Soup, 10" **825.00**
Erie Canal, Aqueduct Bridge at Roch-
ester, pitcher, with first canal view,
5½" (157) **1,200.00**
Wadsworth Tower, sugar bowl (155) **450.00**
Four Medallion, Floral Border Series,
light transfers
Castle Garden, 8" plate (225) **60.00**
Race Bridge, Phila, gravy tureen
(233) **275.00**
General Jackson (224)
Cup Plate **500.00**
Pitcher, luster, 4" **1,500.00**
Plate, 7" **750.00**

Wood, Enoch, plate, 7½", Catskill Mountains, shell border, dark blue, (162), $350.00.

Shell Border, circular center, dark blue
Belleville on the Passaic River, soup
tureen (159) **6,000.00**
Castle Garden Battery, New York,
18½" platter (160) **1,500.00**
City of Albany, State of New York, 10"
plate (163) **375.00**
Highland, Hudson River, vegetable
dish (167) **1,000.00**
Mount Vernon, 5¾" plate (173) **600.00**
Railroad, Baltimore and Ohio, incline,
9" plate (182) **600.00**

West Point Military Academy, 12″ platter (188) **1,200.00**
White House, Washington, cup plate (189) **1,750.00**
Shell Border, irregular center, dark blue Cadmus, 10″ soup (125) **375.00**
Commodore MacDonnough's Victory, coffeepot (130) **1,500.00**
Constitution and Guerriere, 10″ plate (131) **1,000.00**
Erith on the Thames, vegetable dish (136) **750.00**
Union Line, 10″ soup (144) **375.00**
Wadsworth Tower (147)
Coffeepot **1,500.00**
Cup and Saucer **275.00**
Waste Bowl **450.00**
Washington's Tomb, dark blue (190B)
Creamer **550.00**
Soup, 10″ **750.00**
Sugar Bowl **650.00**
Teapot **750.00**

UNKNOWN MAKERS

Anti-slavery, light blue, 9¼″ plate (608) **150.00**
Erie Canal inscription (597)
Cup Plate, 3¾″ **1,750.00**
Pitcher, 5¼″ **1,500.00**
Famous Naval Heroes
Pitcher, 7″ (604) **750.00**
Washbowl (604) **1,000.00**
Franklin Flying a Kite, light blue, 3¾″ platter, miniature (603) **95.00**
Great Fire, City of New York, series, plates, each (605-607) **125.00**
Mount Vernon, Washington's Seat, 8″ pitcher (600) **1,000.00**

STAFFORDSHIRE, ROMANTIC

History: The Staffordshire district of England produced dinnerware with romantic scenes between 1830 and 1860. A large number of potters were involved and over 800 patterns have been identified.

The dinner services came in a variety of colors with light blue and pink perhaps the most popular. Usually the pattern is identified on the back of the piece. It was not uncommon for two potters to issue pieces with the same design. Therefore, check the pattern name as well as the maker's name.

It would be impossible to list all patterns. A representative selection follows. Some price ranges to keep in mind are: cups and saucers (handleless) $35–50; cup plates $40–75; plates, 9–10″, $10–50; platters $25–75.00.

Reference: Petra Williams, *Staffordshire: Romantic Transfer Patterns,* Fountain House East,

1978; Petra Williams, *Staffordshire II,* Fountain House East, 1986.

Plate, Parisian Chateau, R. Hall, 10¼″ d, $50.00.

Asiatic Plants, maker unknown
Bowl **75.00**
Cup and Saucer **65.00**
Plate, 10½″ **85.00**
Vegetable Bowl, cov, ornate handles, finial, light blue, 12 x 9½″ **135.00**
Canova, Thomas Mayer, c1834–1848
Cup and Saucer **45.00**
Cup Plate, green **30.00**
Plate, 7½″, pink **20.00**
Platter, 18 x 11½″ **85.00**
Soup Plate **35.00**
Vegetable Bowl, 8½″, blue, cov with floral finial **120.00**
Waste Bowl, 4″ **40.00**
Friburg, Davenport, c1844
Bowl **45.00**
Cup and Saucer, handleless **60.00**
Plate, 10½″ **55.00**
Platter **100.00**
Teapot, tall, paneled, fruit finial **200.00**
Tureen, matching underplate **150.00**
Medici, Mellor, Veneables & Co., 1834–1851
Bowl **30.00**
Cup and Saucer **40.00**
Gravy Boat **80.00**
Plate, 12 sided **37.50**
Platter **75.00**
Sugar Bowl, tab handles **80.00**
Palestine, John Ridgway, c1830–1855
Bowl **27.00**
Creamer **55.00**
Cup and Saucer, handleless **50.00**
Plate **45.00**
Platter, 16½ x 10″ **65.00**
Sugar, cov **80.00**
Vegetable Bowl, open, matching underplate **130.00**

Rhone Scenery, T. J. & J. Mayer, c1850

Dish, 5½″, oblong	40.00
Plate	
8½″	48.00
9¼″, 12 sided, brown	35.00
Platter, 7 x 5″	45.00
Toothbrush holder	50.00

Siam, J. Clementson, c1839–1864

Bowl	35.00
Creamer	55.00
Cup and Saucer	35.00
Gravy Boat	60.00
Plate, 9″	45.00
Sauce Dish, 4″	27.00
Sugar, cov	75.00
Tureen with matching underplate, cov	125.00

Stained

23¾ x 27½″, vibrant fiery blues, greens, amethyst, amber, caramel, red, and various slag colors, arch and geometric pattern	300.00
48 x 22″, panel, birds, pond with lotus blossoms, attributed to Duffner-Kimberly	1,500.00
51 x 32½″, stained and leaded, morning glory border, large open peony with foliage center, attributed to John Lafarge	2,800.00
65 x 21″, window, Prairie School, linear design, orig frame	725.00
78 x 22″, door, arched frame, stylized poppies and leaves	375.00

STAINED AND/OR LEADED GLASS PANELS

History: American architects in the second half of the 19th century and the early 20th century used stained and leaded glass panels as a chief decorative element. Skilled glass craftsmen assembled the designs, the best known being Louis C. Tiffany.

The panels are held together with soft lead cames or copper wraps. When purchasing a panel, check the lead and have any repairs made to protect your investment.

Collectors' Club: Stained Glass Association of America, 1221 Locust St, Suite 405, St. Louis, MO 63103. *Stained Glass Magazine* (quarterly).

Leaded, window, semi-circular, orig frame, 42 x 22″, $300.00.

Leaded

16 x 60″, double motif, diamond divided into four sections, elongated drop ending in point, beveled, side panels frosted, orig frame, 16 x 60″	300.00
30¼ x 13¼″, Gothic interlocking arch motif, etched design inside arched sections, beveled orig frame	200.00
46¼ x 16¾″, triple sq motif, diamond divided into four sections, short drop, beveled, orig frame	225.00

STANGL POTTERY BIRDS

History: Stangl ceramic birds were produced from 1940 until the Stangl factory closed in 1972. The birds were produced at Stangl's Trenton plant and shipped to their Flemington, New Jersey, plant for hand painting.

During World War II the demand for these birds and Stangl pottery was so great that 40 to 60 decorators could not keep up with the demand. Orders were contracted out to private homes. These orders then were returned for firing and finishing. Colors used to decorate these birds varied according to the artist.

As many as ten different trademarks were used. Almost every bird is numbered; many are artist signed. However, the signatures are used only for dating purposes and add very little to the value of the birds.

Several birds were reissued between 1972 and 1977. These reissues are dated on the bottom and valued at approximately one half of the older birds.

References: Joan Dworkin and Martha Horman, *A Guide To Stangl Pottery Birds*, Willow Pond Books, Inc., 1973; Norma Rehl, *The Collectors Handbook of Stangl Pottery*, Democrat Press, 1982.

Additional Listings: See Stangl pottery in the American Dinnerware category in *Warman's Americana & Collectibles* for more examples.

3276 Bluebird	65.00
3402D Orioles	85.00
3404 Lovebirds, pr	95.00
3405 Cockatoo, 6¼″	45.00
3406 Kingfisher	60.00
3408 Bird of Paradise	80.00
3443 Duck, blue and gray	210.00
3444 Cardinal, pink	70.00
3447 Prothonotary Warbler	60.00
3448 Blue Headed Vireo	40.00
3450 Passenger Pigeon, 19″ l, professionally repaired wing	450.00

Cockatoo, #3580, 8⅞″ h, $125.00.

3453 Key West Quail Dove	225.00
3583 Parula Warbler	38.00
3589 Indigo Bunting	36.00
3595 Bobolink	125.00
3598 Kentucky Warbler	40.00
3629 Broadtail Hummingbird	85.00
3635 Goldfinches, 4 x 11″	185.00
3634 Allen Hummingbird	48.00
3810 Blackpoll Warbler	100.00
3811 Chestnut Backed Chickadee	80.00
3813 Evening Grosbeak	120.00
3852 Cliff Swallow	60.00

STATUES

History: Beginning with primitive cultures, man produced statues in the shape of people and animals. During the Middle Ages most works were religious and symbolic in character and form. The Renaissance rediscovered the human and secular forms.

During the 18th and 19th centuries it was fashionable to have statues in the home. Many famous works were copied for popular consumption.

Statuette or figurine denotes smaller statues, one-fourth life size or smaller.

Reference: Anita Jacobsen (ed.), *Jacobsen's Painting and Bronze Price Guide*, published by author.

Additional Listings: Bronzes and Busts.

Bronze
  8″, egret, neck held close, frog clasped in beak, standing on rocky marsh, inscribed "Ghingre," brown rubbed patina, black patina circular molded base 150.00
  44½″, Sophocles Celebrating the Victory at Salamis, nude, holding tortoiseshell and horn lyre, rect plinth base inscribed in Greek, after J

Donoghue, also inscribed "F. Barbedienne Fondeur, Paris," brown patina, c1900 .... 44,000.00
Cast Iron, 27″, Victory, winged figure wearing swirling tunic, resting on marble sphere, sienna marble plinth, French, early 19th C 850.00
Gilt, silvered, patinated bronze, and carved marble, 24½″, girl, carved white marble face and hands, ruffled bonnet, laced bodice beneath shawl, lifting skirt as she steps across stream, oval base, inscribed "Monginot," French, c1900 .... 2,250.00
Ivory and gilt bronze, 14½″, fashionable woman, carved ivory head and forearms, lace and ribbon dec bodice and wide skirt with train, hat with wide, undulating brim, incised "Armand Quenard," mounted on shaped sq black and white striated marble plinth, c1900 .... 725.00

Venus, white powdered marble, metal base, unmarked, 10″ h, $90.00.

Marble
  39″, Venus after her bath, resting on her right leg, circular base, neck restored, weathered 1,200.00
  45″, young maiden, partially draped figure resting on rocky base, floral garland in her hair, circular base, weathered 2,250.00
Porcelain, 7⅜″, blacksmith, pale green vest under brown apron, Meissen, attributed by J. J. Kaendler, incised "99," c1750, hammer and sword repaired 1,200.00
Silvered Bronze, 32½″, Cupid and Psyche, cloth draped around naked figure, winged Cupid gazing over her shoulder, circular base 3,000.00

Wood, 26½", pair of angels, striding forward with one hand at side, other outstretched, flowing knee length robes, polychrome, Spanish, 19th C   **725.00**

STEIFF

History: Margarete Steiff, GmbH, established in Germany in 1880, is known for very fine quality stuffed animals and dolls as well as other beautifully made collectible toys. It is still in business, and its products are highly respected.

The company's first products were wool-felt elephants made by Margaret Steiff. In a few years the elephant line was expanded to include a donkey, horse, pig, and camel.

By 1903 the company also was producing a jointed mohair Teddy Bear, whose production dramatically increased to over 970,000 units in 1907. Margarete's nephews took over the company at this point. The bear's head became the symbol for its label, and the famous "Button in the Ear" round, metal trademark was added.

Newly designed animals were added: Molly and Bully, the dogs, and Fluffy, the cat. Pull toys and kites also were produced, as well as larger animals on which children could ride or play.

Become familiar with genuine Steiff products before purchasing an antique stuffed animal. Plush in old Steiff animals was mohair; trimmings usually were felt or velvet. Unscrupulous individuals have attached the familiar Steiff metal button to animals that are not Steiff.

References: Peggy and Alan Bialosky, *The Teddy Bear Catalog*, Workman Publishing, 1984, revised edition; Shirley Conway and Jean Wilson, *100 Years of Steiff, 1880–1980*, Berlin Printing, 1980; Shirley Conway and Jean Wilson, *Steiff Teddy Bears, Dolls, and Toys With Prices*, Wallace-Homestead, 1984; Margaret Fox Mandel, *Teddy Bears And Steiff Animals*, Collector Books, 1984.

Collectors' Club: Hobby Center Toys Steiff Club, 7856 Hill Avenue, Holland, OH 43528. Dues: $6.00.

Additional Listings: Teddy Bears. See Stuffed Toys in *Warman's Americana & Collectibles* for more examples.

Bison, 10", pull toy, brown mohair and felt, metal wheels, 1914 . . . .   **275.00**
Cat, 5", Tom, black velvet body, mohair tail, glass eyes, sewn nose and mouth, c1960 . . . .   **85.00**
Dog
  Cocker Spaniel, 6½", long and short mohair, jointed head, black sewn nose, felt mouth, squeaker **65.00**
  Collie, 20½ x 10", long and short mohair, glass eyes, sewn nose, felt mouth **125.00**

Teddy Bear, light brown mohair, jointed, hump, long nose, blue and white checkered apron, 12", $300.00.

Poodle, 8", Snobby, long and short mohair, jointed glass eyes, c1960   **90.00**
Duck, Mallard, 8", pull toy, felt and velvet, metal wheels **275.00**
Goat, 5 x 6", mountain, gray mohair, glass eyes, felt horns, c1950 . . . . .   **50.00**
Monkey, 19", white mohair, felt face, hands, and feet, green glass eyes, c1905 . . . .   **700.00**
Pony, 5½", white and brown mohair, felt ears, red vinyl saddle and bridle, c1950 . . . .   **85.00**
Seal, 6", Floppy Robby, buff Dralon, soft stuffing, sewn eyes, c1950 . . . .   **65.00**
Teddy Bear, 11", Zotty, tan curly mohair, jointed body, glass eyes, sewn nose, felt mouth, c1950 . . . .   **150.00**
Turtle, 5", mohair body, vinyl shell, glass eyes, c1950 . . . .   **65.00**
Zebra, 5", black and white felt, c1950 .   **40.00**

STEINS

History: A stein is a mug especially made to hold beer or ale, ranging in size from the smaller ³⁄₁₀ liters and ¼ liters to the larger 1, 1½, 2, 3, 4, and 5 liters, and in rare cases to 8 liters. (A liter is 1.05 liquid quarts.)

Master steins or pouring steins hold 3 to 5 liters and are called krugs. Most steins are fitted with a metal hinged lid with thumblift. The earthenware character-type steins usually are German in origin.

References: Susan and Al Bagdade, *Warman's English & Continental Pottery & Porcelain, 1st Edition,* Warman Publishing Co., Inc., 1987; Major John L. Hairell, Ret, *Regimental Steins*, published by author, 1984; Gary Kirsner and Jim Gruhl, *The Stein Book*, Glentiques, Ltd., 1984; Dr. Eugene

Manusov, *Encyclopedia of Character Steins*, Wallace-Homestead, 1976; Mike Wald, *HR Steins*, SCI Publications, 1980.

Collectors' Club: Stein Collectors International, P.O. Box 463, Kingston, NJ 08528. Dues: $20.00 *Prosit* (quarterly).

Additional Listings: See Mettlach.

Advisor: Ron Fox

11″ h, raised relief dwarf motif in blue, green, and pink, beige pebbled ground, pewter top, marked "DRGM," $200.00.

Brass, 17½″, relief, coins and faces, fancy figural handle, rampant lion finial **1,150.00**
Faience
  ¾ L, verse between trees, Hannoverisch Munden Factory, 1810 . . . . **440.00**
  1 L, violin player, Bayrueth factory, 1780 . . . . **1,650.00**
Glass
  Blown
    ½ L, enameled floral and verse, c1850 . . . . **275.00**
    1 L, cut circle design, stag under prism lid, pewter base rim **320.00**
  Blown with pewter, ½ L, amber glass, elaborate pewter faces, serpent handle **575.00**
  Mold Blown, ½ L, flashed cranberry panels, porcelain inlay, turquoise inset thumblift **210.00**
  Glass and Pewter, relief, ½ L, Alpine scene **275.00**
  Ivory, 9½″, hand carved, three scenes, reattached finial, sgd "B. Rudolph Stuttgart" **2,475.00**
  Lithophane, ½ L, clown **350.00**
  Mettlach, etched, 1 L, knight on white horse, #2765, sgd "Schlitt" **2,640.00**
  Pewter, ½ L, relief, eagles and angels faces, eagle finial **155.00**

Porcelain
  Bohne, ½ L, bisque, indian **275.00**
  Regimental, 1 L, Naval S.M.S. Von Der Tann 1909–12, four naval scenes, bolt hinge, naval litho, rear roster **1,290.00**
  Schierholz, ½ L, rabbit E.C.S. #62 . **2,255.00**
Pottery
  Relief, 1 L
    Cavaliers drinking **115.00**
    Fox hunt scene, fox family on lid . **100.00**
    Man with two women, man as lid, sgd "KB" **75.00**
  Russian Enamel, 6½″, on silver, turquoise, light and dark blue, violet, white, and red enamel, gold wash, silver marks on base and lid, Silversmith Gustau Klingert, Moscow, 1889 **6,000.00**
Stoneware
  Character, ½ L, monk, E.C.S. #357 **115.00**
  Dreihausen, 13″, red metallic glaze, minor rim chips, thumblift missing **600.00**
  Print over glaze, ½ L, Munich child and city side scenes **175.00**
  Relief
    21½″, cobalt and purple glaze dec, handle repaired **130.00**
    ½ L, Occupational, fireman, strap repair **80.00**
    1 L, Enameled Apostle, worn **165.00**
  Westerwald, ½ L, impressed tool work, cobalt dec **150.00**

STEUBEN GLASS

History: Frederic Carder, an Englishman, and Thomas G. Hawkes of Corning, New York, established the Steuben Glass Works in 1904. In 1918 the Corning Glass Co. purchased the Steuben Company. Carder remained with the firm and designed many of the pieces bearing the Steuben mark. Probably the most widely recognized wares are "Aurene," "Verre De Soie," and "Rosaline," but many other types were produced.

The firm continues operating, producing glass of exceptional quality.

References: Paul Gardner, *The Glass of Frederick Carder*, Crown Publishers, 1971; Paul Perrot, Paul Gardner, and James S. Plaut, *Steuben: Seventy Years Of American Glassmaking*, Praeger Publishers, 1974.

Museum: The Corning Museum of Glass, Corning, NY.

Candlestick, Celeste, amber cup, cobalt blue stem, etched floral design, amber base, 10″ h, $100.00.

ACID CUT BACK

Bowl, 8 x 7¼″, green jade, cut chrysanthemums and leaves dec	600.00
Candlesticks, pr, 14″, black cut to clear, Poussin pattern, flowers and leaves	2,250.00
Jar, cov, 5½″, apple green leaves and flowers, white ground	800.00

Vase
9½″, urn shape, chartreuse, cased with green, scroll, fern, and classic medallion motif, sgd	1,300.00
10″, green jade and alabaster, cut flowers and birds	700.00

ANIMALS

Dinosaur, 12¾″ l, modeled by James Houston	600.00
Elephant, 8½″	350.00
Penguin, 6½″, numbered	175.00
Rabbit, numbered	125.00
Rooster, 10″ h, modeled by Donald Pollard, inscribed "Steuben"	600.00
Sea Horse, 9¼″ h, modeled by Lloyd Atkins, numbered	265.00
Songbird, 4½″, numbered	185.00
Squirrel, 5″ h, modeled by Lloyd Atkins, inscribed "Steuben"	250.00

AURENE

AURENE

Atomizer, 7″, gold	360.00
Basket, 6″ h, gold, mirror finish, sgd, #455	825.00
Bowl, 7¾″, gold, irid, low amber glass foot, inscribed "Aurene/2852"	200.00

Candlesticks, 5¼″, gold, sgd "Aurene 6637," pr	1,000.00
Champagne, gold, sgd	100.00
Finger Bowl and Underplate, millefiori, irid gold, green vines and leaves, applied white flowers, sgd "Aurene/Haviland & Co"	1,150.00
Flower Frog, 4¾″, irid blue, sgd "Aurene 2775"	300.00
Jar, cov, 4¼″, blue, sgd "Steuben 1458 Aurene"	650.00
Plate, 8½″, gold, sgd and numbered 3059	220.00

Vase
4″, millefiori, green luster, silver veining, sgd "Aurene/650"	2,100.00
5½ x 5⅞″, red, irid gold and opaque white feather design, sgd "Aurene/548"	3,900.00
8½″, fan, blue, silvery gold veining, sgd "Steuben Aurene 6297"	1,400.00

CALCITE

Centerpiece Bowl, 12″, blue, sgd	500.00
Goblet, 6″, gold	250.00
Rose Bowl, 6½″ x 4″, calcite ext., gold Aurene int., shape no. 2687	350.00
Sherbet and Underplate, blue Aurene lining	500.00

GROTESQUE

Bowl
8″, cobalt blue shaded to clear, sgd	175.00
9½ x 5¾″, ivory	375.00

Vase
8″, marine blue, sgd	250.00
11″, red shaded to clear	300.00

IVORINE

Candlestick, 4 x 3″, foliate form, ftd	125.00
Lamp Shade, 5″ h	75.00

Vase
3″, green edge trim	175.00
4⅜″, flaring, sgd "Steuben"	220.00
12″, triple, two lily form with center trumpet vase, sgd "Steuben"	900.00

MISCELLANEOUS

Bottle, crystal, teardrop stopper	85.00
Candlesticks, 4½″, mushroom shape, green, sgd, pr	135.00
Champagne, 4⅝″, opal striped pink bowl and stem	100.00
Decanter, 11″ h, engraved Thistle pattern, ring stopper	175.00
Goblet, 8¼″ h, opal striped pink bowl, green stem and foot, sgd	300.00
Sherbet, amethyst, clear stem	50.00

Table Service, green, swirl molded, pr
6" h candlesticks, 12½" d circular ftd
center bowl, eleven goblets, eleven
champagnes, eleven sherbets, twelve
plates, c1920 . . . . **3,850.00**
Vase
6¼", three tree trunks, clear green,
sgd **225.00**
6½", spiral, modeled by Donald Pol-
lard **275.00**

ORIENTAL POPPY

Champagne, green stem **375.00**
Compote, 7", twisted green stem **700.00**
Cordial, green stem and foot, sgd **300.00**
Perfume Bottle, 10½", opal, rose, c1925

. . . . **1,150.00**
Sherbet, 4½" **250.00**

VERRE DE SOIE

Basket, 9½ x 4½", engraved **225.00**
Cocktail Shaker, 10", turquoise prunts . **300.00**
Compote, 10 x 6", ruffled edge, twisted
stem **375.00**
Nut Dish, 4", green rim **35.00**
Plate, 8½", sgd "F Carder" **125.00**
Sherbet and Underplate, engraved flo-
rals **250.00**
Tumbler, 5", sgd **75.00**
Vase
4", flared, ruffled rim, shape no. 162 **85.00**
7", aquamarine, turquoise band on
rim, shape #938 . . . . **225.00**

STEVENGRAPHS

History: Thomas Stevens of Coventry, England,
first manufactured woven silk designs in 1854. His
first bookmark was produced in 1862, followed by
the first Stevengraphs, perhaps in 1874, but defi-
nitely in 1879 at the York Exhibition. The first "portrait" Stevengraphs (of Disraeli and Gladstone)
were produced in 1886, and the first postcards
incorporating the silk woven panels in 1903. Stevens offered many other items with silk panels,
including valentines, fans, pin cushions, needle
cases, etc.

Stevengraphs are miniature silk pictures, matted
in cardboard, and usually having a trade an-
nouncement, or "label," affixed to the reverse.
Thomas Stevens' name appears on the mat of the
early Stevengraphs directly under the silk panel.
Many of the later "portraits" and the larger silks
(produced initially for calendars) have no identification on the front of the mat other than the phrase
"woven in pure silk" and have no label on the back.
Other companies, notably W. H. Grant of Coventry,
copied this technique. Their efforts should not be
confused with Stevengraphs.

American collectors favor the Stevengraphs of
American interest, such as "Signing of the Declaration of Independence," "Columbus Leaving
Spain," "Landing of Columbus." Sports related
Stevengraphs such as "The First Innings" (baseball), and "The First Set" (tennis) are also popular,
as well as portraits of Buffalo Bill, President and
Mrs. Cleveland, George Washington, and President Harrison.

The bookmarks are longer than they are wide,
have mitred corners at the bottom, and are finished
with a tassel. Originally, Stevens' name was woven
into the fold-over at the top of the silk, but soon
the identification was woven into the fold-under
mitred corners. Almost every Stevens bookmark
has such identification, except the ones woven at
the World's Columbian Exposition in Chicago,
1892–93.

Postcards with very fancy embossing around the
aperture in the mount almost always have Stevens' name printed on them. Embossed cards
from the "Ships" and "Hands Across The Sea"
series generally are not printed with Stevens'
name. The most popular postcard series in the
United States are "Ships" and "Hands Across the
Sea," the latter incorporating two crossed flags
and two hands shaking. Seventeen flag combinations have been found, but only seven are common. Stevens produced silks that were used in the
"Alpha" Publishing Co. cards. Many times the silks
were the top or bottom half of regular bookmarks.

References: Geoffrey A. Godden, *Stevengraphs and Other Victorian Silk Pictures*, Associated University Presses, Inc., 1971; Chris Radley,
The Woven Silk Postcard, privately printed, 1978;
Austin Sprake, *The Price Guide to Stevengraphs,*
The Antique Collectors' Club, Baron Publishing,
1972.

Collectors' Club: Stevengraph Collectors' Association, 20B Curtis Ave, Camden, ME 04843.
Dues: $10.00. Newsletter (quarterly).

Museum: Coventry, England.

Note: Prices are based on pieces in mint or
close to mint condition.

Advisor: John High.

BOOKMARK

A Birthday Blessing Wishing You Many
Happy Returns **35.00**
Assassinated At Washington, President
Lincoln **150.00**
For A Good Boy, I had a little doggy . . **60.00**
For A Good Girl, Sweet Maggie had a
little bird **60.00**
Little Bo-Peep **50.00**
Little Jack Horner **50.00**
Little Red Riding Hood **50.00**
The Late Earl Of Beaconsfield, Peace
With Honour **25.00**

Postcard, Hands Across The Sea, *R. M. S. Lusitania,* American and Swedish flags, $60.00.

POST CARD

Anne Hathaway's Cottage	40.00
Hands Across The Sea, man and woman's hands	
R.M.S. Carmania, GB and USA flags	40.00
U.S.M.S. Philadelphia, USA and Norway flags	100.00
Houses Of Parliament	60.00
Princes Street, Edinburgh	60.00
R.M.S. Hilary	125.00
R.M.S. Ivernia	40.00
R.M.S. Lusitania	70.00
R.M.S. Saxonia	40.00
Shakespeare's Birthplace	40.00

STEVENGRAPH

A Gentleman in Kharki	300.00
Are Your Ready?	150.00
John L. Sullivan, story label	100.00
Rt. Hon. Joseph Chamberlain, M.P.	150.00
Rt. Hon. J. Chamberlain, M.P., flower spray	125.00
The Final Spurt	175.00
The First Innings	300.00
The First Over	250.00
The First Set	250.00
The First Touch	150.00

STEVENS AND WILLIAMS

History: In 1824 Joseph Silvers and Joseph Stevens leased the Moor Lane Glass House at "Briar Lea Hill" (Brierly Hill), England, from the Honey-borne family. In 1847 William Stevens and Samuel Cox Williams took over, giving the firm its present name. In 1870 the firm moved to its Stourbridge plant. In the 1880s the firm employed such renowned glass artisans as Frederick C. Carder, John Northwood, other Northwood family members, James Hill, and Joshua Hodgetts.

Stevens and Williams made cameo glass. Hodgets developed a more commercial version using thinner-walled blanks, acid etching, and the engraving wheel. Hodgetts, an amateur botantist, was noted for his brilliant floral designs.

Other glass products and designs manufactured by Stevens and Williams include intaglio ware, Peach Bloom (a form of peachblow), moss agate, threaded ware, "jewell" ware, tapestry ware, and Silveria. Stevens and Williams made glass pieces covering the full range of late Victorian fashion.

After WWI the firm concentrated on refining the production of lead crystal and achieving new glass colors. In 1932 Keith Murray came to Stevens and Williams as a designer. His work stressed the pure nature of the glass form. Murray stayed with Stevens and Williams until WWII and later followed a career in architecture.

Reference: R.S. Williams-Thomas. *The Crystal Years,* Stevens and Williams Limited, England, Boerum Hill Books, 1983.

Additional Listings: Cameo Glass.

Vase, ruby red throat, top deep gold shading to peach to buff, multicolored dec, 8" h, $400.00.

Basket, 5 x 9", creamy opaque, applied green and amber ruffled leaves, rose pink lining, amber edge, applied amber handle and feet	350.00
Bonbon, 5½ x 2¾", flared, threaded rose and clear, c1890	65.00
Bowl, 6¾ x 3¼", box pleated top, pink MOP satin, Swirl pattern, cream lining	500.00

Cruet, 3½″ d, 9½″ h, amber, opaque Arboresque pattern, applied amber handle, amber pedestal foot, orig flattened amber stopper 150.00

Pitcher, 10½″, applied green handle forms leaves and yellow flower, cranberry overlay, blue int., applied amber rim and feet 600.00

Plate, 4¾″ d, ruffled shell shape, shaded pink to green, MOP satin, Swirl pattern 175.00

Rose Bowl, 3″, DQ, MOP, rainbow, alternating stripes of pastel yellow, pink, and blue, imp "Stevens & Williams, Stourbridge Glass," crown logo, patent 1,045.00

Vase

5″, pink MOP satin, Swirl pattern . . . 85.00

5¾″, egg shape, opal and cranberry vertical stripes, gold and black floral dec, applied clear rigaree extends to three feet, pr 125.00

6¼″, fluted, shaded white to pink, applied gold and green flowers and leaves, sgd 215.00

8¼″, shaded pink, white lining, applied amber and green leaves and branches, applied soft blue and cream flowers, amber centers, applied amber loop feet 300.00

10″, slender refined shape, six medallions of applied clear glass, trailing stems swirling to base, engraved ornate stylized petals and foliage, sgd in pontil "Frederick Carder," Stevens and Williams logo 745.00

11½″, gourd shape, pink MOP satin, applied Matso-No-Ke trim, ftd . . . 650.00

STICKLEYS

History: There were several Stickley brothers: Albert, Gustav, Leopold, George, and John George. Gustav often is credited with creating the Mission style, a variant of the Arts and Crafts style. Gustav headed Craftsman Furniture, a New York firm, much of whose actual production took place near Syracuse. A characteristic of Gustav's furniture is exposed tenon ends. Gustav published *The Craftsman*, a magazine supporting his anti-machine points of view.

Originally Leopold and Gustav worked together. In 1902 Leopold and John George formed the L. and J. G. Stickley Furniture Company. This firm made Mission style furniture and cherry and maple early American style pieces.

George and Albert organized the Stickley Brothers Company, located in Grand Rapids, Michigan.

Reference: David M. Cathers, *Furniture Of The American Arts and Crafts Movement*, New American Library, 1981.

Book, *Craftsman Homes,* 1909, orig buckram cov, 11 x 8¼″ 175.00

Catalog, Stickley Bros. Furniture, 1930 35.00

Chandelier, 20¼″, hammered copper and glass dome, hanging chain, c1910 . . . . 6,875.00

Furniture

Bed, child's, 55½ x 35½ x 42¾″, oak, four sides insert with spindles, head and foot crest rails, headboard with rod to hold shirred fabric, 1½″ red decal 2,250.00

Bookcase, 13½ x 35 x 55″, fumed oak, one door, mortise and tenon, 2½″ red decal 2,500.00

Chair, Morris, oak, orig cushions, label "The Work of L. & J. G. Stickley" 450.00

Rocker, oak, upholstered seat and back, label "The Work of L. & J. G. Stickley" 500.00

Table, library, 36 x 30 x 30″, oak, 1½″ red decal 600.00

Lamp, table, 15″ h, copper standard, conical wicker shade, marked "G. Stickley" 375.00

Sconce, 10 x 15″, copper, brass accents, separate bobeches for candles, marked "342, Stickley Bros." . . 425.00

STIEGEL TYPE GLASS

History: Baron Henry Stiegel founded America's first flint glass factory at Manheim, Pennsylvania, in the 1760s. Although clear glass was the most common color made, amethyst, blue (cobalt), and fiery opalescent are found. Products included bottles, creamers, flasks, flips, perfumes, salts, tumblers, and whiskeys. Prosperity was short lived. Stiegel's extravagant living forced the factory to close.

It is very difficult to identify a Stiegel-made item. As a result the term "Stiegel type" is used to identify glass made at that time period in the same shapes and colors.

Enamel decorated ware also is attributed to Stiegel. True Stiegel pieces are rare. An overwhelming majority is of European origin.

Reference: Frederick W. Hunter, *Stiegel Glass*, 1950, available in Dover reprint.

Reproduction Alert: Beware of modern reproductions, especially in enamel wares.

ENAMELED

Bride's Bottle, clear, enameled dec

5¾″, sprays of flowers, red, yellow, white, green, and baby blue 250.00

6″, long neck, rolled mouth, Carpenter's Arms, reverse inscribed "Vivat

der Schreiner 1825," red, white, yellow, and blue **200.00**
6½", single white dove on floral branch, white, red, baby blue, yellow, and black, orig pewter collar . **350.00**
6⅞", large spray of flowers, white, red, yellow, blue, and black, slight haze on bottom **275.00**
Flip, 6½", basket of flowers and leaves **375.00**
Whiskey, man on prancing horse **265.00**

ENGRAVED

Flip, clear
6 x 7¾", clear, Phoenix bird between two tulips **150.00**
6⅜ x 7¼", lovebirds in sunburst, frosted **400.00**
Mug, cov, floral motif, strap handle . . . **400.00**
Vase, 9¾", clear, hollyhocks and ferns dec, hollow base, hollow stem, pontil **100.00**

Salt, cobalt blue, twelve heavy vertical ribs, swirled to the right, 2½" h, $325.00.

OTHER

Bowl, amethyst, fifteen expanded diamond pattern, miniature **425.00**
Christmas Light, 4", yellow-green, expanded diamond, metal fixture **125.00**
Creamer, 4⅛", cobalt blue, twenty expanded diamonds **300.00**
Perfume Bottle, daisy in hexagon pattern, flake on neck **4,000.00**
Salt, blue, checkered diamond **750.00**
Sugar, cov, deep sapphire blue, eleven expanded diamond pattern **2,500.00**

STONEWARE

History: Made from dense kaolin clay and commonly salt-glazed, stonewares were hand-thrown and high-fired to produce a simple, bold vitreous pottery. Stoneware crocks, jugs, and jars were produced for storage and utility purposes. This use dictated shape and design—solid, thick-walled forms with heavy rims, necks, and handles with little or no embellishment. When decorated, the designs were simple: brushed cobalt oxide, incised, slip trailed, stamped, or tooled.

Stoneware has been made for centuries. Early American settlers imported stoneware items at first. As English and European potteries refined their earthenware, colonists began to produce their own wares. Two major North American traditions emerged based only on the location or type of clay. North Jersey and parts of New York comprise the first area; the second was eastern Pennsylvania spreading westward and into Maryland, Virginia, and West Virginia. These two distinct locations, style of decoration, and shape are discernible factors in classifying and dating early stoneware.

By the late 18th century, stoneware was manufactured in all sections of the country. During the 19th century, this vigorous industry flourished until glass "fruit jars" appeared and the widespread use of refrigeration. By 1910, commercial production of salt-glazed stoneware came to an end.

Reference: Don and Carol Raycraft, *Country Stoneware And Pottery*, Collector Books, 1985.

Preserving Jar, Hamilton, Greensboro, PA, cobalt blue dec, $325.00.

Batter Jug, W J & E O Schror, cov, handle, Albany slip, sgraffito birds, imp label, incised 1873 . . . . **450.00**
Bowl
Hermann, P, Baltimore, 10", milk, cobalt blue leaf motif **200.00**
Hickerson, J H, Strasburg, VA, 8¼", cobalt blue foliage dec on rim, floral sides **225.00**
Butter Churn
Ballard, A K, 6 gal, cobalt blue, floral and leaf motif **245.00**

Unidentified Maker, 19½″, 6 gal, slightly ovoid, molded rim, eared handles, brushed cobalt blue stylized florals and "6" 250.00

Butter Crock

Bell, Samuel and Solomon, Strasburg, VA, 6″, applied handles, brown slip floral motif, imp mark on shoulder, c1834–82 .... 250.00

Ratcliff, D L, & Co, Wheeling, WV, 5¾″, straight sides, stenciled cobalt blue label 120.00

Unidentified Maker, 10″, feather motif, matching lid 300.00

Canning Jar

Clark, N & Co, Mount Morris, NY, cobalt blue leaf dec 165.00

Rouston, Wooster, OH, 8″, narrow mouth, Albany slip, three brushed white flowers 125.00

Weymon & Bros, Pittsburgh, PA, 9¾″, stenciled label, leaf motif 100.00

Crock

Burger & Long, Rochester, NY, 3 gal cobalt tulip and leaves 125.00

Donaghho, A P, stenciled cobalt blue label, 1 gal 60.00

Fort Edward Pottery Co, Fort Edward, NY, 19th C, 5 gal, straight sided, standing stag flanked by pine and elm tree, flattened eared handles, some rim chips, 12⅝ x 12″ 5,775.00

Hamliton & Jones, Greensboro, PA, 7″, stenciled cobalt label, straight sides 160.00

Irvine, S, Newville, 4 gal, ovoid, three flowers 425.00

Lewis & Cady, Fairfax, VT, 9 x 9½″, 2 gal, ovoid, brushed cobalt blue design 285.00

Maquoid & Co., Wm A, Little West 12th St. 3, 10″, 3 gal, cylindrical, projecting rim, applied handles, cobalt blue figure of farmer, wide brim hat, holding rake and sickle, imp label, c1860 .... 7,150.00

Unidentified Maker, 13½″, ovoid, double tulips 300.00

West Troy Pottery, 3 gal, cobalt blue chicken pecking corn 375.00

Flask, 5½″, flattened ovoid 85.00

Jar

Bouchner, A & W, 12¼″, 4 gal, eared handles, cobalt blue tulips and foliage, imp label 725.00

Crolius, C, Manhattan-Wells, NY, 7½″, ovoid, eared handles, imp swags and single flower, cobalt blue wash 1,100.00

Reppert, T F, Eagle Pottery, Greensboro, PA, 14½″, 4 gal, eared handles, stenciled cobalt label and spread winged eagle, brushed "4" and wavy lines 625.00

Jug

Cowden & Wilcox, 4 gal, large cluster of grapes 500.00

Farrar & Co, W H, Geddes, NY, 11″, 1 gal, cobalt blue bird, sprouted flower to left, continuous curving line with dots to right, imp label, c1841 .... 4,620.00

Heilbronner, H, Schenectady, NY, 2 gal, bird on leafy branch 475.00

Norton & Co, Bennington, VT, 1 gal, bird 300.00

Ottman Bros & Co, Fort Edward, NY, 2 gal, flower 100.00

Unidentified Maker, 14½″, script inscription "Industry must prosper most glorious news for the bee hive," bands of cobalt blue filled flowers at neck, center with beehive and buzzing bees, drawn handle, cracked 3,000.00

Webster & Berge, 13¼″, 2 gal, cobalt blue stenciled griffins, imp label .. 135.00

Pitcher, H Prudy, 4 gal, cobalt blue double flower 500.00

Preserving Jar

McCarthey & Hayless, Louisville, KY, 8″, stenciled cobalt blue label ... 200.00

Janson Bros, "Pure French Mustard, Cinti, OH," 9½″, stenciled cobalt blue label 150.00

Spittoon, 8″, cobalt blue leaf and floral motif 175.00

Water Cooler, Cyrus Fenton, 24½″, domed cov, ovoid, applied loop handles, incised florals, cobalt blue highlights 650.00

STONEWARE, BLUE AND WHITE

History: Blue and white stoneware refers to molded, salt glazed, domestic, utilitarian earthenware with a blue glaze produced in the late 19th and early 20th centuries. Earlier stoneware was usually handthrown and either undecorated, hand decorated in Spencerian script floral and other motifs, or stenciled. The stoneware of the blue and white period is molded with a design impressed, embossed, stenciled, or printed.

Although known as blue and white, the base color is generally grayish in tone. The blue cobalt glaze may coat the entire piece, appear as a series of bands, or accent the decorative elements.

All types of household products were available in blue and white stoneware. Bowls, crocks, jars, pitchers, mugs, and salts are just a few examples. The ware reached its height between 1870 and 1890. The advent of glass jars, tin containers, and chilled transportation brought its end. The last blue and white stoneware was manufactured in the 1920s.

Reference: Kathryn McNerney, *Blue & White Stoneware*, Collector Books, 1981.

Collectors' Club: Blue & White Pottery Club, P. O. Box 297, Center Point, IA 52213. Dues: $10.00

Reproduction Alert: A vast majority of the blue and white stoneware found in antiques shops and flea markets is unmarked reproductions from Rushville Pottery, Rushville, OH.

Berry Bowl, 4½" d, 2½" h, diffused blues	50.00
Bowl	
9½" d, 5" h, currants and diamonds dec	75.00
10½" d, 5½" h, feather dec	100.00
Butter Crock, blue dec, ear handle, orig lid, PA	475.00
Cake Crock, four blue bands, "cake" stencil, replaced tin lid	325.00
Chamberpot, Beaded Rose Cluster and Spear Points	100.00
Coffeepot, 11½" h, 6" d, swirl, blue tipped finial knob, spurs handle, iron base cap	350.00
Cookie Jar, 8" h, 7¼" d, grooved blue, orig lid	125.00
Cup, 2½" d, 4½" h, Wildflower, emb ribbon and bow	60.00
Ice Crock, 6" d, 4½" h, Rope Bands, ice tongs, and ice block dec, late 1800s	125.00
Pickle Crock, blue band, barrel shape, bail handle	60.00
Pie Plate, 10½", blue walled, brick edge base, imp star shaped mark	100.00

Pitcher, swan pattern, 8¼" h, $175.00.

Pitcher

7¾", Peacock, emb spout	250.00
8", Indian Chief, feather headdress medallion on waffle ground	200.00
9", large butterfly surrounded by raised rope medallion, diffused	

blues, small butterflies between raised rope bands top and bottom	150.00
10", Old Fashioned Garden Rose	125.00
Rolling Pin, 13" l, swirl design, orig wood handles	200.00
Salt, fern leaf design	135.00
Soap Dish	
Cat's Head	125.00
Indian War Bonnet	140.00
Spittoon, emb, sponged blue earthworm pattern	120.00
Toothbrush Holder, blue band, rolled rim	35.00
Toothpick Holder, Swan	55.00
Washbowl and Pitcher, Feather and Swirl	250.00

STRETCH GLASS

History: Stretch glass was produced by many glass manufacturers in the United States between the early 1900s and the 1920s. The most prominent makers were Cambridge, Fenton (who probably manufactured more stretch glass than any of the others), Imperial, Northwood, and Steuben. Stretch glass can be identified by its iridescent, onionskin-like effect. Look for mold marks. Imported pieces are blown and show a pontil mark.

Compote, amber and green iridescent bowl, clear stem and base, 7⅝" top d, 4½" h, $65.00.

Basket, 10½", white	100.00
Bobeches, scalloped, vaseline, pr	40.00
Bowl, 10 x 4½", yellow irid, Imperial	85.00
Candlesticks, 10½", vaseline, pr	50.00
Candy Dish, topaz, Fenton	60.00
Compote, 7⅝ x 4½", green irid, clear stem, amber base	65.00
Creamer and Sugar, Rings pattern, tangerine	75.00
Nappy, 7", vaseline, Fenton	32.00
Pitcher, lemonade, celeste blue, cobalt handle	200.00
Plate	
6", red, paneled, Imperial	50.00
9¾", vaseline	48.00

Rose Bowl, 3½ x 5″, pink, melon ribbed	50.00
Sherbet, 4″, red, melon ribbed	50.00
Vase	
5½″, pink, Imperial	75.00
11¾″, bud, slender neck, pink	40.00

STRING HOLDERS

History: The string holder developed as a utilitarian tool to assist the merchant or manufacturer who needed tangle-free string or twine to tie packages. The early holders were made of cast iron, some patents dating to the 1860s.

When the string holder moved to the household, lighter and more attractive forms developed, many made of chalkware. The string holder remained a key kitchen element until the early 1950s.

Plaster, boy with top hat and pipe, 8¾″ h, $35.00.

Brass, desk, emb roses and scrollwork, 3″ h, 2″ d, ornate, marked "The DM Read Company Fair Week 1909"	15.00
Cast Iron	
Advertising, "Use Higgins German Laundry Soap. It is the Best," black, four wall or counter mounts, 6″ h	60.00
Girl ice skating, polychrome paint, 7″ h	375.00
Woman, string comes out of mouth, repainted	350.00
Ceramic, bear	10.00
Chalkware	
Baby	35.00
Mexican Man	25.00
Scotty Dog	45.00
Spanish Senor and Senorita, pr	50.00
Glass	
Beehive, 4¾″, tin enclosure	38.00
Cut, notched prisms, Gorham SS top	185.00
Plaster, cat, cream, red ball	20.00
Porcelain, rooster, Royal Bayreuth	220.00

Pottery, figural, dog, Bennington	165.00
Silver Plated, 3⅝″ h, 3¾″ d, dome shape, repousse wreath around body, Pairpoint	65.00
Stoneware, bird	30.00

SUGAR SHAKERS

History: Sugar shakers, sugar castors, or muffineers all served the same purpose: to "sugar" muffins, scones, or toast. They are larger than salt and pepper shakers, were produced in a variety of materials, and were in vogue in the late Victorian era.

CHINA

Austrian, 4½″, border of delicate pink roses, shaded blue ground, marked "MZ Austria"	55.00
Nippon, 3⅛ x 4⅞″, panels of pink and red roses, cream ground, gold dec handle	65.00
Schlegelmilch, RS Prussia, 5″, scalloped base, pearl finish, roses, red mark	235.00

Milk Glass, 4½″ h, blue, melon ribbed, metal top, $80.00.

GLASS

Milk Glass	
Apple Blossom	85.00
Bulbous, three Palmer Cox Brownies dec, pale blue ground	175.00
Challinor's Forget-Me-Not, white, opaque, orig top	100.00
Mt Washington	
Egg shape	
Daisies dec, yellow shading to brown ground	150.00
Pansies dec, peach shading to yellow ground	250.00
Lighthouse shape, 5½″, IVT, bluerina, orig metal top	270.00

Melon ribbed, blue and white forget-me-nots, yellow ground	200.00
Opalescent Glass	
Reverse Swirl, cranberry, 6"	125.00
Ribbed Lattice, blue	75.00
Pattern Glass	
Acorn, opaque pink	165.00
Coin Spot, cranberry, SP top	75.00
Inverted Thumbprint, vaseline, orig top	60.00
Leaf Umbrella, cranberry spatter, white casing	225.00
Medallion Sprig, rubena	165.00
Royal Oak, rubena, frosted	225.00
Wisconsin, orig top	65.00
Satin	
Diamond Quilted, MOP, blue	225.00
Fleurette pattern, 3¼", pink, orig brass top	125.00

SWANSEA

History: This superb pottery and porcelain was made at Swansea (Glamorganshire, Wales) as early as the 1760s with production continuing until 1870.

Marks on Swansea vary. The earliest marks were SWANSEA impressed under glaze and DILL-WAN under glaze after 1805. CAMBRIAN POT-TERY was stamped in red under glaze from 1803-1805. Many fine examples, including the Botanical series in pearlware, are not marked, but may have the botanical name stamped under glaze.

Fine examples of Swansea often may show imperfections, such as firing cracks. These pieces are considered mint because they left the factory in this condition.

Reference: Susan and Al Bagdade, *Warman's English & Continental Pottery & Porcelain, 1st Edition,* Warman Publishing Co., Inc., 1987.

Reproduction Alert: Swansea porcelain has been copied for many decades in Europe and England. Marks should be studied carefully.

Cake Plate, 12½", painted florals, gilt rim and handles, c1813	375.00
Creamer, 6½", cow, cov, pink splash luster, rect base, c1825	425.00
Cup and Saucer, 4¼", pink roses, turquoise and gilt ground, printed mark, c1820	375.00
Goblet, 5", copper luster, three polychrome rose sprigs, green band with black edge, c1830	65.00
Pitcher, 6½", Chinese pattern, multicolored	300.00
Plate	
8¼", floral dec, printed mark, artist sgd "William Pollard," c1820	600.00

Plate, floral dec, marked "Swansea" underglaze, 8½" d, $150.00.

9⅝", blue transfer, scattered bouquets, c1820	135.00
Serving Dish, 10¼", oval, center floral bouquet, full blown roses on rim, gilt dentil, imp mark	465.00

SWORDS

History: The first swords in America came from Europe. The chief cities for sword manufacturing were Solingen in Germany, Klingenthal in France, and Hounslow and Shotley Bridge in England. Among the American importers of these foreign blades was "Horstmann" whose mark is found on many military weapons.

New England and Philadelphia were the early centers for American sword manufacturing. By the Franco-Prussian War, the Ames Manufacturing Company of Chicopee, Massachusetts, was exporting American swords to Europe.

Sword collectors concentrate on a variety of styles: commission vs. non-commission officers' swords, presentation swords, naval weapons, and swords from a specific military branch such as cavalry or infantry. The type of sword helped identify a person's military rank and, depending on how he had it customized, his personality as well.

Following the invention of repeating firearms in the mid-19th century, the sword lost its functional importance as a combat weapon and became a military dress accessory. Condition is a key criterion determining value.

Reference: Harold L. Peterson, *The American Sword 1775–1945,* Ray Riling Arms Books Co, 1965.

AMERICAN

Artillery, Saber, Model 1860, stamped at obverse ricasso "U.S./L.D" and on reverse with ribbon "MADE BY/AMES MFG Co./CHICOPEE/MASS.," almost perfect grip on hilt, scabbard with some spotty age staining **800.00**

Artillery, Light, Saber, Model 1840, stamped at obverse ricasso "U.S./ C.E.W./1864," reverse with faint "AMES" etc. markings, orig scabbard **350.00**

Cavalry, Saber, Model 1840, stamped on obverse ricasso "US JH" and on reverse "N.P. AMES CABOTVILLE 1846," crisp brass hilt, steel scabbard with some polishing marks **800.00**

Cavalry, Saber, Model 1840, stamped "US/WD" on obverse, reverse with "AMES MFG. CO./CABOTVILLE/ 1849," scabbard with moderate uniform age patina **525.00**

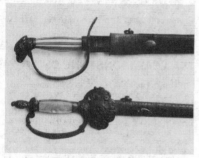

Top: Foot Officer's saber, non-regulation, 1810, $350.00; bottom: Artillery Officer's, Indian head pommel, 1821–50, $250.00.

Cavalry, Sword, Model 1913, blade stamped "S flaming bomb A/1914" and "US/16327," orig khaki webbing cov scabbard with steel mounts, right side of hilt bent slightly inward **175.00**

Confederate, Officer's, 83½" overall, 33¼" unmarked blade with unstopped fuller, brass basket guard with large "CS" in counterguard surrounded by floral patterns, leather grip wound with twisted brass wire, complete with part of orig scabbard, brass throat mount Serial No. 47 and engraved "MADE BY/James Coning/Mobile/ Ala," brass middle mount unmarked, drag missing **5,000.00**

Fraternal, Ames, deluxe, 27" blade, etched against gilt ground for 18½", obverse with profuse scrolls, a standing knight in armor and "Wilson Dan-

iel Rau," reverse with scrolls, a panel showing knights jousting with a castle at the side, a trophy of flags, and "AMES/Sword Co/CHICOPEE/ MASS," fancy cast and silvered hilt with black painted grips, silvered scabbard with fancy openwork mounts with enameled crown and cross, Maltese cross **100.00**

Halberd, Colonial, steel head, 17" overall, 12" leaf shaped blade, 29½" straps for attachment to shaft, deep age patina, small areas of light cleaning, scattered pitting, fitted to restoration 87½" oak shaft **125.00**

Naval Cutlass, Model 1860, dated 1862, stamped with Ames markings, brass guard with issue markings "6M/514," complete with orig copper riveted black leather scabbard with issue marks "10M/556," missing wire wrapping on grip **700.00**

Non-commissioned Officer, Model 1840, obverse stamped "US/DFM/ 1860," reverse "EMERSON/&/SIL-VER/TRENTON, N.J.," orig brass mounted black leather scabbard . . . **300.00**

Polearm, military
97" overall, 6" iron tip, heavy 4½" point square in cross-section, forged one piece with 17" straps, butt a 2½" iron cone with 8½" straps, again forged as one piece, straps all attached to heavy oak shaft with screws, shaft mkd "U.S." and "T.H." **500.00**

98½" overall, 14¼" forged iron tip, 8½" spear point blade, 11¾" attaching straps, all forged as one piece, forged iron butt 9½" overall made of two iron straps attached to a 3" cone, all forged in one piece, orig heavy wood shaft with period black painted surface, first half of 19th C **225.00**

EUROPEAN

Continental
Halberd Head, 21¼" head, 47" overall including orig straps for attaching to pole, pole cut off just before end of straps, pierced blade unmarked **500.00**

Sword, Officers, 36" overall, 30½" deeply etched blade with scrolls, trophies of flags, and torch, cast brass hilt with grapeleaf openwork pattern guard, fancy relief casting of stirrup and pommel, white sharkskin cov grip wound with 3 strands of wire, steel scabbard with relief cast brass mounts **350.00**

Sword, Presentation, German silver scabbard with high raised cast brass mounts in oak leaf and acorn pattern, orig script inscription between throat and middle mount, "Presented to/Lt. H. H. Dumont,/By Co. F 189th O.V.I./1865," sword 40" overall, 34" curved "W.CLAUBERG/ SOLINGEN" blade, deeply etched for 15½" on each side with trophies of arms, scrolls, etc., hollow silver plate casting grip in dot and leaf pattern **2,100.00**

MIDDLE EAST

Eastern, 30⅝" overall, 25½" blade engraved overall with large figures of various animals, iron hilt with gold damascened dec and ivory scales that are mellowed old replacements, engraved animals with considerable traces of gold dec **125.00**
Persian, Saber, 36" overall, 31" curved blade, damascened panel containing Farsi writing, iron hilt with stylized lion head pommel dec with gold damascening, orig black leather cov wood scabbard with iron drag **375.00**

TEA CADDIES

History: Tea once was a precious commodity. Special boxes or caddies were used as containers to accomodate different teas, including a special cup for blending.

Around 1700 silver caddies appeared in England. Other materials, such as Sheffield plate, tin, wood, china, and pottery, also were used. Some tea caddies became very ornate.

Pewter, Japanese, 5" h, $175.00.

Porcelain
4¾" h, blue Fence pattern, barrel shape **50.00**
5¼" h, two panels of boy and girl courting and multicolored flowers, gold tracery, Dresden **130.00**
5½" h, Chinese Export, polychrome floral enameled crest, fruit finial .. **125.00**
Tin, 4", oval, red, yellow, and green floral dec, orig black paint **125.00**
Wood
Burl Walnut, 4⅜ x 7½ x 4¾", two compartments, string inlay, ivory escutcheon, chamfered corners, brass hinges **575.00**
Mahogany, 10" l, stringing and cross landing, fitted int. with lidded compartment, SP handle, Hepplewhite **145.00**
Rosewood Veneer, 8⅞" l, inlaid pearl escutcheon, decorative molding on lid, divided int., shell shape silver tea scoop with Birmington hallmark **175.00**

TEA LEAF IRONSTONE CHINA

History: Tea Leaf Ironstone china flowed into America from England in great quantities in the 1860 to 1910 period and graced the tables of working class America. It traveled to California and Texas in wagons and by boat down the Mississippi River to Kentucky and Missouri. It was too plain for the rich homes; its simplicity and strength appealed to wives forced to watch pennies. Tea Leaf found its way into the kitchen of Lincoln's Springfield home; sailors ate from it aboard the *Star of India*, now moored in San Diego and still displaying Tea Leaf.

Tea Leaf was not manufactured exclusively by English potters in Staffordshire, contrary to popular opinion. Although there were more than 30 English potters producing Tea Leaf, at least 21 American potters helped satisfy the demand. However, American potters perpetuated the myth by using backstamps bearing the English coat-of-arms and the marking "Warrented." The American housewife favored imported ware to that made by Americans.

Anthony Shaw (1850–1900) first registered the pattern in 1856 as Luster Band and Sprig. Edward Walley (1845–56) already was decorating ironstone with luster trefoil leaf, a detached bud, and trailing green vine. Walley's products are designated Pre-Tea Leaf and are sought by eclectic collectors. Other early variants include "Morning Glory" and "Pepper" by Elsmore & Forster(Foster) (1853–57) and "Teaberry" by Clementson Bros. (1832–1916). Clover leaf, cinquefoil, and pinwheel all may be found in a collection specializing in early ware.

The most prolific Tea Leaf makers were Anthony

Shaw and Alfred Meakin (1875–). Johnson Bros. (1883–), Henry Burgess (1864–92) and Arthur J. Wilkinson (1897–), all of whom shipped much of their ware to America and followed close behind Shaw and Meakin.

Although most of the English Tea Leaf is copper luster, Powell & Bishop (1868–78) and their successors, Bishop & Stonier (1891–1936), worked exclusively in gold luster. Beautiful examples of gold luster by H. Burgess still are being found. Mellor, Taylor & Co. (1880–1904) used gold luster on their children's tea sets.

J. & E. Mayer, Beaver Falls, Pennsylvania, were English potters who immigrated to America and produced a large amount of copper luster Tea Leaf. The majority of the American potters decorated with gold luster, with no brown underglaze like that found under the copper luster.

East Liverpool, Ohio, potters such as Cartwright Bros. (1864–1924), East End Pottery (1894–1909), Knowles, Taylor & Knowles (1870–1934), and others decorated only in gold luster. Since no underglazing was used with the gold, much of it has been washed away.

By the 1900s Tea Leaf's popularity had waned. The sturdy ironstone did not disappear. It was stored in barns and relegated to attics and basements. Much of it was disposed in dumps, where one enterprising collector has dug up some beautiful pieces.

A frequent myth about Tea Leaf is that pieces marked "Wedgwood" are THE Wedgwood, Josiah. This is not true! Dealers and collectors who perpetuate this myth should be confronted. Enoch Wedgwood was the only potter of that name to produce Tea Leaf. Enoch Wedgwood's product is beautiful with large showy leaves. He deserves full credit for his work.

Reference: Annise Doring Heaivilin, *Grandma's Tea Leaf Ironstone*, Wallace-Homestead, 1981.

Collectors' Club: Tea Leaf Club International, P. O. Box 904, Mount Prospect, IL 60056. Dues: $20.00. *Tea Leaf Reading* (bimonthly).

Museums: Lincoln Home, Springfield, IL; Sherman Davidson House, Newark OH; Ox Barn Museum, Aurora, OR.

Reproduction Alert: There are reproductions that are collectible, and there are *reproductions*! Avoid the latter. Collectible reproductions were made by Cumbow China Decorating Co. of Abington, Virginia, from 1932 to 1980. Wm. Adams & Sons, an old English firm, made reproduction Tea Leaf from 1960 to 1972. Red Cliff, who decorated Hall China blanks with Tea Leaf and clearly marked them, worked in the late 1960s and early 1970s.

Ruth Sayer started making Tea Leaf reproductions in 1981. Although her early pieces were not marked, all of it now is marked with a leaf and the initials "RS" on the bottom. In 1968 Blakeney Pottery, a Staffordshire firm, manufactured a poor quality reproduction of Meakin's Bamboo pattern

and marked it "Victoria." It was distributed through a Pennsylvania antiques reproduction outlet.

Advisor: Julie Rich.

Bakers, open	
Pepper Leaf variant, Elsmore & Foster, 9 x 7"	60.00
Pinwheel variant, unmarked, 9½ x 7⅜"	20.00
Tea Leaf	
Meakin, individual, 5½ x 3⅝"	22.00
Shaw, 10" d, ribbed, small chip	40.00
Bone Dish, Tea Leaf	
Grindley, leaf shaped, chip	35.00
J & E Mayer, impressed stem pattern	65.00
Meakin, scalloped edge	40.00
Butter Dish, 3pcs (base, lid, liner), Tea Leaf	
J & E Mayer	70.00
Meakin, Bamboo, chip in base	60.00
Shaw, Lily Of The Valley	190.00
Wedgwood	115.00
Butter Pats	
Clover Leaf variant, 3" d	7.00
Tea Leaf	
Meakin, 3⅛" d	9.00
Wilkinson, 2¹⁵⁄₁₆" d	8.00
Cake Plate, Tea Leaf	
J & E Mayer, emb	60.00
Meakin, Bamboo, small chip	32.50
Shaw, Daisy	90.00
Chamber Pot, Tea Leaf, Meakin, Bamboo, cov	150.00
Children's Ware, Tea Leaf	
Mug, unmarked, 2¾" h	225.00
Set, 15pcs, Knowles, Taylor, Knowles	1,200.00
Sugar Bowl, Mellor Taylor	250.00
Coffee/Teapot	
Cinquefoil variant, unmarked, emb wheat, repairs	110.00
Pepper Leaf variant, unmarked, 9¼" h, two cracks	95.00
Tea Leaf	
J & E Mayer, 9" h	145.00
Meakin, Fish Hook, 8¾" h	120.00
Shaw, Chinese shape, 9⅝" h	245.00
Creamer, Tea Leaf	
Edge, Malkin	85.00
J & E Mayer	65.00
Meakin, Fish Hook, 5⅛" h	110.00
Cup and Saucer	
Pepper Leaf variant, unmarked, 3" d handled cup	60.00
Teaberry, unmarked, 3" d handled cup	65.00
Tea Leaf	
W & E Corn, gold luster, 3" d handled cup	55.00
Grindley, 3¾" d handled cup	57.50
Shaw, Chinese shape, 3½" d handleless cup	80.00

Cup Plate, Tea Leaf
  Meakin 35.00
  Royal Burslem Pottery 30.00
Doughnut Stand, Tea Leaf
  Meakin 255.00
  Red Cliff, modern 95.00
Plates
  Pinwheel variant, 10" d 12.00
  Pre-Tea Leaf variant, 10" d 12.50
  Tea Leaf
    Meakin, 9" d 9.00
    Shaw, Lily Of The Valley, emb, 9¾"
      d 16.00
    Teaberry, Clementson, 4½" d 27.50
Pitcher, wash, Tea Leaf, Davenport,
  pink luster 850.00
Shaving Mug, Tea Leaf
  Grindley 100.00
  Shaw 130.00
  Shaw, Lily Of The Valley 155.00
Soap Dish, Tea Leaf
  Powell & Bishop, gold luster, no liner 35.00
  Shaw, Lily Of The Valley, liner 220.00
  Wilkinson, open 50.00
Sugar Bowl, Tea Leaf, J & E Mayer . . 65.00

Clementson Brothers, Teaberry, Prairie shape: sugar bowl, $85.00; teapot, $150.00; and creamer, $235.00.

Toothbrush Holders, Tea Leaf
  Meakin, Chelsea 210.00
  Powell & Bishop, gold luster, 5" h . . 45.00
  Shaw, round 115.00
  Wedgwood 45.00
Tureens, Tea Leaf
  Sauce
    Mellor Taylor, Lionhead, 3 pcs
      (base, lid, underplate) 295.00
    Shaw, Cable, 4 pcs (base, lid, un-
      derplate, ladle) 500.00
    Shaw, Lily Of The Valley, 3pcs
      (base, lid, underplate) 480.00
    Wedgwood, 4 pcs (base, lid, un-
      derplate, ladle) 325.00
  Soup, Shaw, Cable, 3 pcs (base, lid,
    ladle) 550.00
Vegetable Dish, cov
  Tea Leaf
    Meakin, Fish Hook 80.00

Shaw, hexagon shape 120.00
  Wilkinson 50.00
  Teaberry, Clementson 140.00
Wash Bowl and Pitcher, Tea Leaf
  J & E Mayer 350.00
  Meakin, Fish Hook 110.00
  Mellor Taylor, ribbed 300.00

TEDDY BEARS

History: Originally thought of as "Teddy's Bears," the name comes from President Theodore Roosevelt. These stuffed toys are believed to have originated in Germany and in the United States during the 1902–03 period.

Most of the earliest Teddy Bears had humps on their backs, elongated muzzles, and jointed limbs. The fabric used was usually mohair; the eyes were either glass with pin backs or black shoe buttons. The stuffing was generally excelsior. Kapok (for softer bears) and wood-wool (for firmer bears) also were used as stuffing materials.

Quality older bears often had elongated limbs, sometimes with curved arms, oversized feet, and felt paws. Noses and mouths were black and embroidered onto fabric.

The earliest Teddy Bears are believed to have been made by the original Ideal Toy Corporation in America and a German company, Margarete Steiff, GmbH. Bears made in the early 1900s by other companies can be difficult to identify because they had a strong similarity in appearance and because most tags or labels were lost through childhood play.

Teddy Bears are rapidly increasing as collectibles and their prices are increasing proportionately. As in other fields, desirability should depend upon appeal, quality, uniqueness, and condition. One modern bear already has been firmly accepted as a valuable collectible among its antique counterparts: the Steiff Teddy put out in 1980 for the company's 100th anniversary. This is a reproduction of that company's first Teddy and has a special box, signed certificate, and numbered ear tag. Eleven thousand of these were sold worldwide.

References: Peggy and Alan Bialosky, *The Teddy Bear Catalog*, Workman Publishing, 1984, revised edition; Shirley Conway and Jean Wilson, *100 Years Of Steiff, 1880–1980*, Berlin Printing, 1980; Shirley Conway and Jean Wilson, *Steiff Teddy Bears, Dolls, and Toys With Prices*, Wallace-Homestead, 1984; Margaret Fox Mandel, *Teddy Bears And Steiff Animals*, Collector Books, 1984; Ted Menten, *The Teddy Bear Lovers Catalog*, Delilah Communications, Ltd., 1983; Susan Brown Nicholson, *Teddy Bears on Paper*, Taylor Publishing Co., 1985; Patricia N. Schoolmaker, *A Collector's History Of the Teddy Bear*, Hobby House Press, Inc., 1981; Helen Sieverling (comp.) and Albert C. Revi (ed.), *The Teddy Bear And*

Friends Price Guide, Hobby House Press, Inc., 1983.

Periodicals: *The Teddy Bear And Friends*, Hobby House Press, Inc., 900 Frederick Street, Cumberland, MD 21502; *The Teddy Bear News*, P. O. Box 8361, Prairie Village, KS 66208.

Collectors' Clubs: Good Bears Of The World, P. O. Box 8236, Honolulu, HI 96815. Dues: $8.00. *Bear Tracks* (quarterly); Teddy Bear Boosters Club, P. O. Box 520, Stanton, CA 90680; Teddy Bear Collectors Club, P. O. Box 601, Harbor City, CA 90710.

BEARS

7", gold mohair, squeaker, hump, shoe button eyes, jointed at hips and shoulders, swivel head, long upturned nose, elongated torso, thin limbs, black sewn nose and mouth, straw stuffed	85.00
8", mohair, squeaker, glass eyes, hump, jointed at hips and shoulders, swivel head with long nose, felt paws, brown sewn nose	110.00
12", mohair, squeakers, shoe button eyes, humps, jointed at hips and shoulders, swivel head, felt paw, straw stuffed, Steiff, early 1900s . . .	165.00
13", dark brown plush, jointed at hips and shoulders, long nose, high set ears, felt paws, black sewn nose and mouth, solidly stuffed	25.00
14" l, articulated limbs and head, yellow haircloth, recovered paw pads, replaced button eyes, embroidered features, repairs	75.00
17", brown plush, cream paws, squeaker in tail, plastic eyes, molded nose and mouth, soft stuffed, label "Ideal"	40.00
20", light mohair, squeaker, glass eyes, jointed at hips and shoulders, swivel head, felt paws, brown sewn nose and mouth, straw stuffed, Steiff, 1920s	150.00
21", gold mohair, glass stick pin eyes, pear shape torso, jointed at hips and shoulders, swivel head, felt paws, brown sewn nose and mouth, straw stuffed, 1930s	100.00

BEAR RELATED ITEMS

Jack-in-the-Box, 8", tin, teddy bear with parasol, wood handle, plays music, bear bobs up and down	150.00
Paper Doll, 10½", cardboard tab for stand-up, four color outfits and hats, orig printed envelope, c1910	350.00
Perfume Bottle, 3¾", mohair, black button eyes, jointed at hips and shoul-	

Cup and Saucer, 2¼" cup with bears playing soccer, 4⅜" d saucer with bears golfing, unmarked, $125.00.

ders, head removes to show glass bottle	65.00

TELEPHONES

History: The deregulation of the nation's telephone industry and increasing interest in antique telephones has led to increasing values for old telephones and equipment.

Lovers' telegraphs and other crude sound operated and unpatented telephones existed prior to Alexander Graham Bell's 1876 patent. However, it is generally accepted that Bell invented the telephone powered by electricity.

The most valuable antique telephones come from the pre-1895 period and must be marked, dated, or easily documented. Instruments also must be unaltered and have all major original parts. Telephones marked Charles Williams, Jr., a Boston manufacturer whose factory was the "birthplace" of the infant Bell Telephone Company, are among the most valued.

Post 1895 telephones have value if modified or converted to be compatible with today's modern phone network. Conversions should be done by an expert who will supply additional parts without removing any of the major components to accomplish conversion.

Refinishing also requires expert skills. Do not remove original circuitry. Restoring nickel and black baked enamel finishes is most desirous. Buffing original parts to expose the brass beneath will make it difficult to distinguish those parts from the many dated and old fashioned marked, solid brass fake parts and whole telephones which have been flooding the market for a decade. No mass produced telephone made in the United States prior to 1950 was offered with a shiny brass finish!

Reference: R.H. Knappen, *History And Identification Of Old Telephones,* 2 volumes, published by author, 1978; R.H. Knappen, *Old Telephones Price Guide And Picture-Index To History Of Old Telephones,* published by author, 1981.

Collectors' Club: Telephone Collectors International, P.O. Box 700165, San Antonio, TX 78270. Membership: $18.00.
Advisor: Dan Golden.

Automatic, Dialing Telephones
Couch, S.H., Autophone	250.00
Globe Automatic, wall model	950.00
Lorimer Automatic, all models	1,500.00
Monson Automatic, wall model	1,200.00
National Automatic, wall model	1,500.00
Ness Automatic, wall model	700.00
Select-O-Phone	200.00

Strowger Patent
Automatic Electric, candlestick model	1,200.00
Pre-1898 models	2,500.00
Wall Model, large	1,500.00
Wall Model, small	650.00

Double Box Telephones
48″ l, tandem, any manufacturer	550.00
49 to 60″ l, tandem two boxes	750.00
60 to 70″ l, tandem two boxes	1,200.00
71″ and longer	1,500.00
Oak, plain, Stromberg-Carlson type, c1899	350.00
Unusual in any way, any manufacturer	450.00

Fiddleback Telephones
Gilliand, American Bell, Blake or Charles Williams transmitter	1,000.00
Vought Berger, Kellogg, Western Electric, Stromberg Carlson, Dean, Diamond, etc	275.00

Pay Phones
Common 1950s style	195.00

Gray Pay Station
Desk Model, wood, slots for coins up to dollar, marked	3,000.00
Wall Phone, wood	2,500.00
Wall Phone, 72″	3,000.00
1920s style (Known as Laurel & Hardy style)	400.00
Pay Box, cast iron, small, c1910	150.00

Single Box Wall Telephones, wood
Picture Frame Front
Cathedral Top, lightning arrestors at top	300.00–400.00
1910–15	225.00
Plain Front, 1915–20	200.00
Unusual style	450.00–600.00

Stands
Gossip Benches, approx	70.00
Ornate, carvings	600.00
Plain, 1920s style	150.00

Switchboards
Hotel Annunciators	50.00–400.00
Mansion Annunciators, depending on size and ornateness	75.00–450.00
Pre-1894, wall mount, marked American Bell-Blake, Gilliand, Edison, National Bell, or Charles Williams	2,000.00

Single Box Tandem, William Abbott, 1901, $1,200.00.

Pre-1910, wall mount	500.00

Pre-1935
Light Bulbs	250.00
Transmitter broom	400.00
1935 to present	Surplus Value

Telephone Booths
1890s, leaded glass	2,000–3,500.00
1910 to 1912, single door	2,000.00

1914 to 1940, folding door
Oak	1,200.00
Walnut	1,100.00

Triple Box
American Bell, Edison, Blake, Berliner on transmitter	1,700.00
American Electric, Kokomo	1,200.00
Bell Telephone	1,200.00
Chicago	950.00
Elliott	1,200.00
Gilliand	2,000.00
Keystone	900.00
Mianus	900.00
Molecular	1,400.00

Note: If any of these sets are missing the 7″ long exposed terminal receiver, subtract $150.00.

Upright Desk Stands (Candlestick Phones)
Hour Glass or Potbelly shape	750.00
Oil Can shape	500.00

Straight Pipe, regular style
Dial type	185.00
No dial	95.00
With magneto box	160.00

Notes: Extremely unusual candlestick phones made of wood or in an outrageous style may be worth in excess of $1,000.00. All phones mass produced from the WWI to 1950 were made in black. The Western Electric model is now being reproduced in solid shiny brass.

TEPLITZ CHINA

History: Around 1900 twenty-six ceramic manufacturers were located in Teplitz, a town in the Bohemian province of Czechoslovakia. Other potteries were located in the nearby town of Turn. Wares from these factories were molded, cast, and hand decorated. Most are in the Art Nouveau and Art Deco styles. Most pieces do not carry a specific manufacturer's mark. They are simply marked "Teplitz," "Turn-Teplitz," and "Turn."

Reference: Susan and Al Bagdade, *Warman's English & Continental Pottery & Porcelain, 1st Edition,* Warman Publishing Co., Inc., 1987.

Vase, turquoise and tan, base marked "Crownoakware," artist signed, 14½", $200.00.

Bowl
　3″, enameled boy and dog, gray
　　ground, marked "Stellmacher" ... 　75.00
　6¾″, ecru, enameled flowers, c1912 　175.00
Box, cov, 6¼ x 9 x 5½″, figural, turtle,
　two multicolored children kneeling on
　back, deep green shell, gray features,
　gold trim, satin finish, marked "Turn
　Vienna Teplitz" .... 　365.00
Candlestick, 5¼″, figural, woman in
　flowing gown, c1905 .... 　135.00
Ewer
　6½, hp, pink and gold flowers, light
　　green ground, light pink neck, gold
　　twig handle .... 　85.00
　9½″, cream, red roses, gold trim,
　　marked "Royal Teplitz" .... 　60.00

Figure
　12½″, young girl, peasant clothes,
　　basket resting on tree stump .... 　350.00
　15″, man and woman, court clothes,
　　multicolored, pr .... 　250.00
Jug, 8″, classical man, smoking pipe,
　bronze ground, marked "Stellmacher,
　Teplitz" .... 　175.00
Pitcher, 9½″, lily pad dec, green and
　pink, c1895 .... 　185.00
Vase
　5″, bud, relief rooster head in medal-
　　lion, multicolored geometric dec .. 　90.00
　5½″, reticulated top, two handles, por-
　　trait of girl .... 　135.00
　7″, blue and lavender poppies, raised
　　gold beading, four handles, red
　　crown mark, pr .... 　180.00
　12″, raised raspberries, applied rib-
　　bons, green irid finish, double han-
　　dles .... 　375.00
Window Box, 12 x 3 x 4, boat shape,
　rose dec, spider web ground, orig
　liner .... 　125.00

TERRA COTTA WARE

History: Terra cotta is ware made of a hard, semi-fired ceramic clay. The color of the pottery ranges from a light orange-brown to a deep brownish red. It is usually unglazed, but some pieces can be found partially glazed or decorated with slip designs, incised, or carved. Examples include utilitarian objects as well as statuettes and large architectural pieces. Fine early Chinese terra cotta pieces recently have brought substantial prices.

Bean Pot, round, ten cup size, unglazed
　cov, incised "For Baked Beans" ... 　40.00

Syrup, enameled center band of phoenix birds, pewter top, 6½″ h, $115.00.

Cup and Saucer 85.00
Figure, 16", gypsy couple, man with
  base fiddle at side, woman with tam-
  bourine, pr 225.00
Jug, 7½" h, marked "Cambridge Ale" . 150.00
Pipe Holder, 5 x 9", Chinese boy, black
  glaze 80.00
Tobacco Jar, 11", figural, Bismark, sit-
  ting in easy chair 250.00
Vase, 6" h, 4½" d, raised daisy dec,
  green glazed int. 35.00
Wall Plaque, 8½", sgd "C Conrad, Salz-
  burg" 25.00

TEXTILES

History: Textiles are cloth or fabric items, especially anything woven or knitted. Those that survive usually represent the best since these were
the objects that were used carefully and stored by
the housewife.

Textiles are collected for many reasons—to
study fabrics, understand the elegance of an historical period, and for decorative and modern use.
The renewed interest in clothing has sparked a
revived interest in textiles of all forms.

Reference: William C. Ketchum, Jr., *The Knopf
Collectors' Guides to American Antiques, Quilts,*
Alfred A. Knopf, Inc., 1982; Betty Ring, *Needlework: An Historical Survey,* Main Street Press,
1984 (revised edition); Helene Von Rosenstiel,
*American Rugs And Carpets: From The Seven-
teenth Century To Modern Times,* William Morrow
And Company, 1978; Carleton L. Safford and Robert Bishop, *America's Quilts And Coverlets,* Bonanza Books, 1985.

Collectors' Club: Costume Society of America,
330 West 42nd Street, Suite 1702, New York, NY
10036.

Additional Listings: Clothing, Linens, Quilts,
and Samplers.

Coverlet, geometric, center seam, red,
white, and blue, 72 x 94", applied 3¾"
fringe, $350.00.

Bedspread, cotton, white, candlewick
  pot of flowers and meandering floral
  border, tied fringe, 80 x 92" 135.00
Blanket
  Homespun, wool, white, blue stitched
    chenille-like star and pine trees,
    20th C, 70 x 108" 75.00
  Wool, embroidered, attributed to
    Chester County, PA, panels of linen
    homespun, central floral circle en-
    closing small bird, borders with ran-
    dom design of birds, hearts, leaves,
    pineapples, flowerheads, candle-
    stand with vase of flowers, houses,
    inscribed "Remember Me, Forget
    Me Not, S. R., Sarah, 1852," 100 x
    84" 725.00
Bolster Cover
  Homespun, navy blue and white
    plaid, white back, hand sewn, 20 x
    60" 150.00
  Trapunto, basket of flowers with vin-
    tage and floral designs, finely
    quilted ground, lace trim, worn ball
    fringe on three sides, stains, wear,
    and small holes, 23 x 42" 200.00
Comforter, crib, pieced, black, green,
  and beige checkerboard design, red
  sawtooth border, Berks County, PA,
  26½ x 45" 50.00
Coverlet
  Bride's, trapunto, all white, cotton
    American, early 19th C, field with
      luxuriant pendant blossoms and
      meandering vines, oval reserve
      of urn with climbing floral vines,
      heightened with seed stitching,
      white cotton fringe, 88 x 90" . . . 2,450.00
    Baltimore, early 19th C, center area
      with elegant urn mounted on
      pedestal, topped with pineapple,
      feathered tassels pendant from
      floral chains, borders with undu-
      lating grapevines, daisy sprigs,
      and clover leaves, 100 x 104" . . 1,200.00
  Embroidered, Eunice Freeman,
    Dutchess County, NY, 1808, red,
    yellow, pink, and blue wool crewel
    stitches on dark brown wool twill
    panels, central field embroidered
    with large oven woven basket with
    large stylized blossoms, floral bou-
    quets, berries, and vines, corners
    with sprays of large scale blos-
    soms, checkerboard vase flanked
    by peacocks above open heart and
    initials "EF 70" and "1808" at base,
    chain swag with flowers, berries,
    and stars border, 92 x 94" 17,600.00
Jacquard
  One piece, double weave, Centen-
    nial design, Capitol building, flo-

ral border with birds, light green, lavender, dark brown, and natural, minor overall and edge wear, bottom fringe loose, 75 x 78" .. **175.00**

One piece, double weave, stylized floral design, purple and green, sgd "1902 K. M. M.," 56 x 84" . **250.00**

One piece, single weave, floral design, corners sgd "Manufactored (sic) by Fehr & Keck, Emaus, 1845," red, green, and natural, 78 x 90" **525.00**

Two piece, double weave, blue and white, eagle corners, dated 1848, 80 x 88" **700.00**

Two piece, double weave, blue and white snowflake and circle design, sewn on fringe, minor age stains, 78 x 86" **350.00**

Two piece, single weave, compotes of flowers and floral border with corners sgd "Susanna Zech," red, blue, green, and natural, minor age stains, bit of edge wear, 80 x 90" **375.00**

Two piece, single weave, floral medallions, pot of flowers border, corners sgd "Jacob Snyder, Dekalb County, Indiana, 1856," two shades of blue, salmon, and natural white, overall wear, top border rebound, 67 x 82" **325.00**

Two piece, single weave, medallions, birds and floral border, red, olive green, and natural, corners sgd "Jacob Stephen Springvil, Seneca County, Ohio, 1853," 78 x 88" **500.00**

Overshot, two piece, Optical pattern, tomato red and natural, minor wear and age stains, 66 x 90" **175.00**

Drawstring Bag, embroidered, Catherine Lee, MA, c1790, sq white silk bag embroidered on obverse with spread winged American eagle beneath rose and pink stars, stylized cloud like banderole, delicate meandering floral border, reverse with basket of blossoms and foliage, two butterflies, initialed "CL" in gilt metallic threads, yellow silk cord drawstring, 7 x 7½" ... **4,450.00**

Mattress Cover, blue and white homespun, one seam, white homespun backing, 60 x 104", very minor wear and age stains **115.00**

Paisley Shawl, multicolored red woven design, olive green central field, minor wear, 68 x 70" **120.00**

Picture, embroidered

Hartford, CT, early 19th C, biblical scene in New England setting, moss green, gold, vermilion, beige, and brown silk and silk chenille, gilt metal thread highlights, gold sequins, figures of King in rich robes offering feather, Queen richly dressed, hand maiden, posed on patterned rug, townscape painted in distance, attributed to Miss Patten's school, 17 x 20½" **700.00**

PA, early 19th C, blue, green, gold, beige, silver, white, and yellow silk threads on silk ground, blue coat shepherd playing flute, small white lamb climbing onto lap of shepherdess, flock surrounding them under two large leafy trees, several perched birds, spotted brown and white dog, 15½ x 17½", paper label on reverse with names and dates **4,675.00**

Rug

Hooked

11 x 39", yarn, pictorial, scene of red barn, purple house, green tree, pond in foreground with ducks and chicks, birds in flight in distance, PA, early 20th C .. **275.00**

24 x 46", yarn, sheared, all-over triangular motifs, shades of gray, blue, red, black, and purple, American, late 19th C **285.00**

26 x 47½", yarn, eight point stars in green, orange and blue, green trellis border with orange intersection points, American, c1900 .... **250.00**

31 x 86", yarn, fiery sunburst design, minor edge wear **200.00**

34 x 56", rag, black dog, beige and gray ground, tan grid and light blue dots **750.00**

41 x 60", rag, multicolored floral checkerboard design, minor wear **275.00**

Penny, felt, overlapping tan and brown petals, embroidered blue and red edges, center with applied oval brown panel embroidered with vase filled with three red and green floral sprigs, American, early 20th C, 28 x 34½" **475.00**

Rug

Braided, 52 x 78", alternating gray and blue squares, border of red and black squares **85.00**

Woven, 65 x 33", pink, blue, and green squares, American **85.00**

Show Towel

Homespun, cross stitch and cut work, tied fringe, gray and several shades of brown embroidery floss, 10 x 10" plus fringe, framed, 12¾ x 16¾" **475.00**

Homespun, linen and cotton cut work,

floral embroidery with "C. L.," minor
stains, 13½ x 51" **100.00**
Linen, embroidered in pink threads
with numerous stars, flowerheads,
birds, reindeer, dogs, potted flowering shrubs, zig-zag crochet panel
with fringe below, sgd "Anna Marie
Nies, 1816," 15 x 60" **350.00**
Tablecloth
Homespun cotton, white on white
woven design, one seam, hand
sewn hems, red embroidered cor-
ner initials "T. W. 15," 50 x 53" . . . **25.00**
Homespun linen, white on white de-
sign, three stripes, minor wear and
stains, 38 x 63" **10.00**
Towel
Homespun cotton, brown and white,
machine sewn hems, soft color, minor wear, small holes, 19½ x 24" . **35.00**
Homespun linen, natural color, natural and white embroidery, 11½ x
32" **20.00**
Tapestry, Brussels, second half 17th C,
silk, wool, and silver thread, depicting
departure of Meleager for the Hunt of
the Calydonian Boar, central field
filled with equestrians, attendants and
hunting dogs, foliate border woven
with flower filled urns, fruits, arrow-
filled quivers, and masks in rust, burgundy, gold, green, olive, ivory, um-
ber, blue, and pink, 16'3" x 11'10" . . **21,000.00**
Uncut Printed Cloth Doll, "Kellogg's
Johnny Bear," copyright 1925, minor
stains on edge, 11½ x 13¼" **125.00**

**Bowl, pink glass, darker pink threads,
5" d, 2" h, $35.00.**

Lemonade Mug, 5⅜", clear glass, cranberry threading, Sandwich **125.00**
Mayonnaise, underplate, cranberry,
ground pontil **70.00**
Perfume Bottle, 5½", clear, pink thread-
ing **175.00**
Pitcher, 6", clear, red and clear applied
threading over entire body and neck,
applied clear ruffles around base of
neck, applied clear solid handle, polished pontil, attributed to Sandwich **150.00**
Rose Bowl, 5 x 6", clear, pink threading **48.00**
Vase
8", petal top, cranberry, white threading, sgd "Stevens and Williams" . **130.00**
9⅛", gold luster, Art Nouveau style,
applied dec and feather design, bogus Tiffany signature, possibly by
Durand or Carder **1,200.00**

THREADED GLASS

History: Threaded glass is glass decorated with
applied threads of glass. Before the English invention of a glass threading machine in 1876, threads
were applied by hand. After this invention,
threaded glass was produced in quantity by practically every major glass factory.

Threaded glass was revived by the art glass
manufacturers, such as Durand and Steuben, and
continues to be made today.

Bowl, 16", clear, topaz threaded edge,
controlled air bubbles, Steuben **125.00**
Candlestick, 9⅞", clear, cut,flared base,
bell nozzle with frosted floral and
beaded dec, amethyst rim and
threading in stem **175.00**
Finger Bowl, matching underplate, yel-
low green opal, pr **75.00**
Epergne, four purple lilies, white trim . **375.00**
Goblet, pink, threaded bowl, clear base
and stem, Steuben **80.00**

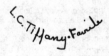

TIFFANY

History: Louis Comfort Tiffany (1849–1934) established a glass house in 1878 primarily to make
stained glass windows. There he developed a
unique type of colored iridescent glass called Favrile. His Favrile glass differed from other art glass
in manufacture as it was a composition of colored
glass worked together while hot. The essential
characteristic is that ornamentation is found within
the glass. Favrile was never further decorated.
Different effects were achieved by varying the
amount and position of colors which project movement in form and shape.

In 1890, in order to utilize surplus materials at
the plant, Tiffany began to design and produce
"small glass" such as iridescent glass lamp
shades, vases and stemware in the Art Nouveau manner.

Commercial production began in 1896. Most Tiffany wares are signed with the name L. C. Tiffany or the initials L.C.T. Some pieces also carry the word "Favrile" as well as a number. A number of other marks can be found, e.g., Tiffany Studios and Louis C. Tiffany Furnaces.

Louis Tiffany and the artists in his studio also are well known for the fine work in other areas—bronzes, pottery, jewelry, silver and enamels.

References: Victor Arwas, *Glass, Art Nouveau and Art Deco,* Rizzoli International Publications, Inc., 1977; Robert Koch, *Louis C. Tiffany, Rebel In Glass,* Crown Publishers, Inc., 1966.

Note: All glass is of the Favrile type unless otherwise noted.

Bronze, compote, 6¼″ top d, 4″ h, $275.00.

BRONZE

Blotter, rocker type, caramel slag glass inserts, marked "Tiffany Studios"	150.00
Box, gilt bronze and Favrile glass, 6½″ l, rect, hinged cov, Pine Needle pattern, amber and white opaque marbleized glass, imp "Tiffany Studios/New York/809," c1900–28	150.00
Desk Blotter, intricate spider web dec, pr	135.00
Inkwell, dore	
Octagon, shape #864	300.00
Relief shell shapes on top, laurel leaf garland sides	235.00
Letter Clip, Adam pattern, sgd	165.00
Paperweight, spaniel, marked "Tiffany Studios"	150.00
Salt, 3⅛″, irid gold liner, sgd "Tiffany Furnaces"	300.00
Stamp Box, Zodiac pattern, dore finish, sgd	125.00

GLASS

Barber Bottle, 7″, irid gold, irid purple linear dec, bronze hinged lid, sgd "10157"	700.00
Bottle, 5½″, irid gold, sgd "L. C. Tiffany Favrile"	500.00
Bowl	
4¼″, irid gold, millefiori, green vines and leaves, white flowers, sgd "L. C. T. R8810"	650.00
4¾″, opal yellow, leaf design, ftd, sgd at pontil	275.00
Butter Pat, gold irid, deeply scalloped rim, orig paper label	175.00
Cologne Bottle, 5″ h, irid gold luster, applied dec, orig stopper, sgd	850.00
Compote, 11¾″ d, 4⅜″ h, pastel, pink and opal, irid, engraved near rim with figure of butterfly, sgd "L. C. Tiffany Favrile 1848Y"	800.00
Cup Plate, 3″, irid gold, sgd "L.C.T. Favrile"	150.00
Decanter, 9½″, irid gold, intaglio cut panels, sgd "L. C. Tiffany Favrile"	1,100.00
Finger Bowl, underplate, ruffled edge, irid	350.00
Nappy, 5″ l, irid gold, sgd "L. C. Tiffany Favrile 2361E"	250.00
Rose Bowl, 3⅜ x 2⅜″, irid gold, green vines and leaves, sgd "L. C. Tiffany Favrile 638E"	500.00
Parfait Glass, 6¼″, opal striped green pastel, ftd	275.00
Salt, 2¾″, irid blue, paneled, sgd "L.C.T. Favrile"	300.00
Sauce, 4⅜″, irid blue, intaglio cut leaf band, scalloped rim, sgd "L. C. T. Favrile 1254"	350.00
Seal, irid gold, unsigned	225.00
Sherbet, 5½ x 4½″, irid gold, opal with green feather pattern, sgd "L. C. Tiffany Favrile 9595C"	600.00
Tumbler, 6⅜″, ftd, pastel, blue-green, vertical opal ribbing, sgd "L. C. Tiffany Favrile"	275.00
Vase	
3½″, Favrile, gold, delicate pulled handles, classic shape, sgd and numbered	475.00
4½ x 4¾″, butterscotch irid, stretched, onion skin, flared, ftd, full signature, numbered	525.00
4⅝″, red, wide neck tapering to bulbous base, sgd "L. C. Tiffany Favrile 1125 3323K"	2,150.00
5¼″, clear, heavy floral green, white, and yellow paperweight base, sgd "L. C. Tiffany Favrile 626V"	4,750.00
7″, cameo, frosted white body, orange poppies and green leaves, sgd "L. C. Tiffany Favrile 4530C"	5,500.00
9⅛″, Art Nouveau, gold luster, applied dec, threading, and feather design, bogus Tiffany signature, attributed to Durand or Carder	1,200.00

11", floriform, opal and green, sgd "L. C. T. W2603" **1,800.00**
12½", floriform, irid gold, green, and opal, sgd "L. C. T. Favrile Y7443" **3,500.00**
Whiskey, 2½", irid gold, tooled dec, labeled "Whiskey," sgd "L.C.T." **225.00**

LAMPS

Candle Lamp, 17" h, gold dec German china columnar candlesticks, set with Tiffany lamp, irid white and green feather design, irid gold luster chimney, matching shade, fixtures labeled "The Twilight," 1894 patent, set of 4 **1,400.00**
Desk, 7¼" d lemon yellow cased shade, counterbalance, inscribed "L. C. T. Favrile" and imp "Tiffany Studios, NY" **1,500.00**
Table
20½", ten slender cylindrical stems curving at top, pendant calyx form sockets, assembled irid amber lily form shades, inscribed "L.C.T. Favrile," gilt bronze circular base with spreading overlapping lily pads and buds, etched finished, base imp "Tiffany Studios/New York/381," c1899–1900 .... **12,100.00**
31½", 10½" d spherical leaded glass shade dec with network of intertwined branches and overlapping leaves, shades of green, amber, and claret, six alternating long and short prongs, tapering slender cylindrical artichoke leaf molded stem spreading circular foot, base with green and brown patination, imp "Tiffany Studios/New York/4243/438" **35,750.00**

SILVER

Bowl, 8½", Japanese style, overlaid with copper and gold, c1880, marked ... **1,225.00**
Coffee and Tea Service, five pcs, floral band at shoulders, slightly ribbed, monogrammed, c1891–1907, 93 oz **2,860.00**
Service Plates, 9¾", set of fourteen, raised edge, c1930, marked "Tiffany & Co, New York" **4,500.00**
Soup Tureen, cov, 12", oval, Wave pattern, 1891 .... **3,200.00**
Table Service, King's pattern, c1900, 275 pcs **10,175.00**
Tray, 28½", oval, rim with relief of lions among vines, six paw feet, c1900, monogrammed **4,125.00**

TIFFIN GLASS

History: A. J. Beatty & Sons built a glass manufacturing plant in Tiffin, Ohio, in 1888. On January 1, 1892, the firm joined the U. S. Glass Co. and was known as factory "R". Quality and production at this factory were very high and resulted in fine depression era glass. Beginning in 1916 wares were marked with a paper label. From 1923 to 1936, Tiffin produced a line of black glassware, called Black Satin. The company discontinued operation in 1980.

References: Fred Bickenheuser, *Tiffin Glassmasters, Book I,* Glassmasters Publications, 1979; *Tiffin Glassmasters, Book II,* Glassmasters Publications, 1981; Fred W. Bickenheuser, *Tiffin Glassmasters, Book III,* Glassmasters Publications, 1985.

Vase, 5" h, bulbous, black ground, painted red poppies and green leaves, $45.00.

Basket, orange	20.00
Cake Plate, Shaggy Rose	15.00
Candy Jar, cov, vaseline, frosted stripes	36.00
Champagne	
Classic Shawl Dancer, crystal, puffed stem	18.00
Flanders, topaz	18.00
Persian Pheasant	20.00
Claret, Persian Pheasant	30.00
Cocktail	
June Night	22.00
Persian Pheasant	18.00
Creamer, Fontaine, blue, tall	45.00
Creamer and Sugar, Flanders, crystal .	30.00
Cup and Saucer, Primo, green	6.00
Goblet	
Cherokee Rose	22.00
Classic, pink, reed stem	20.00
Classic Shawl Dancer, crystal, puffed stem	20.00

June Night 22.00
Persian Pheasant 24.00
Iced Tea Tumbler
Byzantine, crystal, black base 15.00
Flanders, topaz, ftd 22.50
Jug, Classic Shawl Dancer, crystal 175.00
Marmalade Jar, cov, Jungle pattern, green satin, painted parrots dec and floral sprays, handles 100.00
Pitcher, La Fleur, topaz 225.00
Plate
Flanders, crystal, 6″, ruffled 6.00
Othello Ebony, 10¾″, dinner 25.00
Tray, Birch Tree, Deerwood pink, center handle 45.00
Tumbler, Flanders, topaz, 9 oz, ftd 15.00
Vase
Dahlia, 10½″, green satin 35.00
Heliotrope, 7¼″ 30.00
Poppy, pink 45.00
Whiskey, La Fleur, topaz, ftd 12.50
Wine, Persian Pheasant 25.00

TILES

History: The use of decorated tiles peaked during the latter part of the 19th century. Over one hundred companies in England alone were producing tiles by 1880. By 1890 companies had opened in Belgium, France, Australia, Germany, and the United States.

Tiles were not limited to adorning fireplaces. Many were installed into furniture, such as washstands, hall stands, and folding screens. Since tiles were easily cleaned and, hence, hygienic, they readily were used on the floors and walls of entry halls, hospitals, butcher shops, or any place where sanitation was a concern. Many public buildings and subways also employed tiles to add interest and beauty.

Condition is an important fact in determining price. A cracked, badly scuffed and scratched, or heavily chipped tile has very little value. Slight chipping around the outer edges of a tile is, at times, considered acceptable by collectors, especially if these chips can be covered by a frame.

It is not uncommon for the highly glazed surface of some tiles to have become crazed. Crazing is not considered a deterent as long as it does not detract from the overall appearance of the tile.

References: J. & B. Austwick, *The Decorated Tile,* Pitman House Ltd., 1980; Susan and Al Bagdade, *Warman's English & Continental Pottery & Porcelain, 1st Edition,* Warman Publishing Co., Inc., 1987; Julian Barnard, *Victorian Ceramic Tiles,* N. Y. Graphic Society Ltd., 1972; Terence A. Lockett, *Collecting Victorian Tiles,* Antique Collectors Club, 1979; Hans Van Lemmen, *Tiles: A Collectors' Guide,* Seven Hills Books, 1985.

Collectors' Club: Tile & Architectural Ceramics Society, Ironbridge Gorge Museum, Ironbridge, Telford, Shropshire, England TF8 7AW.

Claycraft, CA, brown, blue, and green, imp "Claycraft from CA, Aztec design," 1920, 8 x 6″, $60.00.

American Encaustic Tiling Co, Zanesville, OH
3″ sq, President McKinley, orig label with biography, slight glaze crazing 50.00
4¼″ sq, white, black design of horseman riding through brush 30.00
California Art
5¾″, landscape, tan and green 50.00
7½ x 11½″, peacock and grapes, multicolored 120.00
Cambridge Art Tile, Covington, KY, 6 x 18″
Goddess and Cherub, amber, pr 200.00
Night and Morning, pr 475.00
J. & J. G. Low, Chelsea, MA
4¼″ sq
Blue, putti carrying grapes, pr 60.00
Teal Blue, swirled foliate 50.00
Yellow-green, floral 25.00
6″ d, circular, yellow, minor edge nicks and glaze wear 30.00
6″ sq, yellow-green, geometric design 25.00
6⅛ x 4½″, rect, blue-green, picture of woman, titled "Autumn" 75.00
7⅜ x 5⅜″, rect, blue-green, portrait of stylish lady, small chip on corner 75.00
Kensington, 6″, sq, classic female head, brown 40.00
KPM, 5¾ x 3⅜″, portrait of monk, titled "Hieronymous of Ferrara sends this image of the prophet to God," small nicks to corners 225.00
Marblehead, 4⅝″ sq, ships, blue and white, pr 100.00

Minton China Works
　6", Aesops Fables, Fox and Crow,
　　black and white . . . . 　60.00
　6 x 12", Wild Roses, polychrome slip
　　dec . . . . 　48.00
　8" sq, teal blue, titled "Autumnus" . . 　50.00
Minton Hollins & Co
　6", urn and floral relief, green ground 　30.00
　8", Morning, blue and white . . . . . . 　100.00
Mosaic Tile Co, Zanesville, OH
　6", Fortune and the Boy, polychrome 　75.00
　8", Delft windmill, blue and white,
　　framed . . . . 　45.00
Pardee, C.
　4¼", chick and griffin, blue-green
　　matte . . . . 　175.00
　4½", white rabbit, light green ground,
　　sgd . . . . 　100.00
　6" sq, portrait of Grover Cleveland,
　　gray-lavender . . . . 　120.00
Paul Revere Pottery
　3⅞" sq, green trees and landscape,
　　circular mark, part of orig label . . 　150.00
　4⅜" d, circular
　　Paul Revere Trademark, blue,
　　　green, black, yellow, and brown
　　　on white . . . . 　200.00
　　Swan, yellow, brown, green, and
　　　white, slight age crack . . . . 　125.00
Providential Tile Works, Trenton, NJ
　Round, stove type, hole in center,
　　flowered . . . . 　10.00
　Square, 6", raspberries . . . . 　20.00
Rookwood
　4½ x 4¼", blue-green, emblem of
　　Packard Motor Co, 1910 . . . . 　75.00
　5¾" d, circular, seagulls in flight, two
　　colors, 1943 . . . . 　60.00
Sherwin & Cotton
　6" sq, dog head, brown, artist sgd . . 　100.00
　6 x 9", Abraham Lincoln, brown . . . 　135.00
　6 x 12", Quiltmaker and Ledger, or-
　　ange, pr . . . . 　250.00
Trenton Tile Co, Trenton, NJ, 6" sq
　Blue glaze, man's head, wearing gar-
　　land of leaves, modern frame . . . 　25.00
　Yellow-green, portrait of U. S. Grant 　110.00
U. S. Encaustic Tile Works, Indianapo-
　lis, IN
　6" sq
　　Boy with umbrella, amber . . . . . . 　75.00
　　Wreath, flowered, light green . . . . 　15.00
　6 x 18", panel, Dawn, green, framed 　150.00
Wedgwood, England
　6" sq
　　Low relief white daisies, speckled
　　　green ground . . . . 　20.00
　8"
　　Shakespeare's　　　Mid-Summer
　　　Night's Dream, moth . . . . 　100.00
　　Tally Ho, man riding horse, blue
　　　and white . . . . 　75.00

TINWARE

History: Beginning in the 1700s many utilitarian household objects were made of tin. Tin is non-toxic, rust resistant, and fairly durable, so it can be used for storing food. It often was plated to iron to provide strength. Because it was cheap, tinware and tin plated wares were in the price range of most people.

An early center of tinware manufacture in the United States was Berlin, Connecticut. Almost every small town and hamlet had its own tinsmith, tinner, or whitesmith. Tinsmiths used patterns from which to make items. They cut out the pieces, hammered and shaped them, and soldered the parts. If a piece was used with heat, a copper bottom was added because of the low melting point of tin. The Industrial Revolution brought about machine made, mass produced tinware pieces. The hand made era ended by the late 19th century.

This category is a catchall for tin objects which do not fit into other categories in our book.

Additional Listings: Advertising, Kitchen Collectibles, Lanterns, Lamps and Lighting, and Tinware: Decorated.

Fish Pan, oval, 13 x 11⅞ x 2½", $12.00.

Baker's Horn, 57" l, slightly battered,
　mouth piece missing . . . . 　45.00
Butter Churn, 13½ x 16", drum . . . . . . 　115.00
Cake Mold, 2 pc, domed . . . . 　35.00
Candle Mold, 11" h, twelve tube . . . . . 　65.00
Candle Sconce, 8" h, oval reflector,
　crimped edges, worn black paint . . 　75.00
Candlestick, 7¾" h, side pushup, brass
　trim . . . . 　90.00
Chocolate Mold
　3½", cherub on rocking horse,
　　marked "Ringers" . . . . 　65.00
　4⅛", story book, lovers and castle . . 　55.00
　4⅝", baby, soccer player, folding . . . 　75.00
　5", rabbit . . . . 　55.00
Cookie Cutter
　Boot, 3½" h . . . . 　35.00
　Pony, 4½" l . . . . 　38.00
　Rooster, 6¼", crimped tail . . . . 　150.00

Food Mold, 9" l, fish, oval 55.00
Grater, 7¼ x 11¾" 35.00
Lamp, 7½" h, double spout, saucer
base, brass plated 55.00
Lantern
  Candle, 11" h, hexagonal, conical top,
  scalloped vents, black repaint, ring
  handle 85.00
  Folding, 7" h, mica lights, brass hook
  fasteners, storage case 60.00
Pie Crimper, 7¾" l 40.00
Quilt Pattern, 12¾" h, punched detail . 85.00
Spatula, 6½ x 13¾", pierced design in
  blade, sgd 35.00
Teapot, 6¾" h, well shape, cast pewter
  handle, pewter finial 50.00

TINWARE: DECORATED

History: Decorating sheet iron, tin, and tin coated sheet iron sheet dates back to the mid-18th century. The Welsh called the practice pontipool, the French To'le Peinte. In America the center for tin decorated ware in the late 1700s was Berlin, Connecticut.

Several styles of decorating techniques were used: painting, japanning, and stenciling. Designs were done by both professionals and itinerants. English and Oriental motifs strongly influenced both form and design.

A special type of decoration was the punch work on unpainted tin practiced by the Pennsylvania tinsmiths. Forms included coffeepots, spice boxes, and grease lamps.

ABC Plate, 7¾" d, Who Killed Cock Robin 60.00

Milk Can, black ground, orig stenciling, red and gold stylized flowers, 8½" h, $175.00

Bank, Uncle Sam, hat shape, red, white,
  and blue 35.00
Bowl, 10½", black, gilt floral dec 100.00
Candle Sconce, 14" h, scalloped crest
  dec, emb sunburst design, removable
  reflector 425.00
Candle Snuffer, 2½" h, conical shape,
  brown, yellow floral dec 40.00
Creamer, 4" h, red flowers, yellow
  swirls, black ground 200.00
Decoy, shorebirds, folding, orig paint,
  mounted on driftwood base, 11¾" h,
  label "Patent Oct 27, 1874," pr 225.00
Document Box, 6¼" l, 4½" h, two large
  fruit, red, white, yellow, and green,
  sprouting tendrils with dark green
  heart shape leaves, black ground,
  rect domed hinged lid 625.00
Dust Pan, 8" l, miniature, orig white
  paint, blue striping 38.00
Foot Warmer, 7¾ x 9 x 5⅞", punched
  heart design, brown patina, mortised
  wood frame with turned corner posts 225.00
Teapot, 8¾", red, yellow, and green florals, brown ground, tapering cylinder,
  slightly domed cov, straight spout,
  strap handle 300.00
Tray, 32", oval, black, stenciled foliate
  scrolls, flowers, leaves, mid 19th C . 220.00
Tree Stand, Santa with reindeer 25.00
Urn, pr, 10¾", shaped, brown, floral dec,
  scroll handlers, cov with pineapple finials, 19th C 250.00

TOBACCO CUTTERS

History: Before pre-packaging, tobacco was delivered to merchants in bulk form. Tobacco cutters were used to cut the tobacco into desired sizes.

Cast iron, marked "Brighton," $45.00.

Brown's Mule, iron, counter top 55.00
Climax, 17" l 50.00
Cupples Arrow & Superb 50.00
Drummond Tobacco Co 65.00
John Finzer & Brothers, Louisville, KY 45.00
Griswold Tobacco Cutter, Erie, PA ... 55.00
E C Simmons Keen Kutter 225.00

Sprague Warner & Co **75.00**
Unmarked, graduated 6¼ to 7¼″ w,
  10½″ l, cast iron cutter, wood base . **45.00**

TOBACCO JARS

History: A tobacco jar is a container for storing tobacco. Tobacco humidors were made of various materials and in many shapes, including figurals. The earliest jars date to the early 17th century. However, most examples in today's market were made in the late 19th or early 20th centuries.

Head, Moor, brown tinted turban, black face, green color, high glaze, marked "1368" and "83," 7¹/₁₆″ h, $140.00.

Bisque
  3¾ x 5″, bust of black woman, green, pink, and white turban and scarf, gold earrings **90.00**
  4⅝ x 6″, figural, monkey's head, light brown, glossy gray cap, eye-glasses, white collar and bowtie, yellow and brown bee finial **175.00**
Brass, 5½″, int. tin case, early 19th C . **40.00**
Jasper Ware, raised white Indian chief on cov, Indian regalia on front, green ground **185.00**
Majolica, figural
  American Indian, bust, 5″ **135.00**
  Bear, smoking pipe, 6″ **125.00**
Milk Glass, hp, hunting dogs, green and maroon ground, metal top, Handel Ware **525.00**
Porcelain, figural
  Arab Head **100.00**
  Humpty Dumpty **115.00**
  Skull, marked "Carlsbad, Austria" . . **150.00**
Pottery
  4½ x 5½″, Oriental man, black mus-tache and goatee, hat cov **120.00**
  4⅝ x 5⅝″, bust of black man, straw hat, gold earrings, blue shirt **130.00**

TOBY JUGS

History: A toby jug is a drinking vessel usually depicting a full-figured, robust, genial drinking man. They originated in England in the late 18th century. The term "Toby" probably related to the character Uncle Toby from *Tristam Shandy* by Laurence Sterne.

References: Susan and Al Bagdade, *Warman's English & Continental Pottery & Porcelain, 1st Edition,* Warman Publishing Co., Inc., 1987; Vic Schuler, *British Toby Jugs,* Kevin Francis Publishing Ltd. (London), 1986.

Additional Listings: Royal Doulton.

Reproduction Alert: Within the last 100 years or more, tobies have been reproduced copiously by many potteries in the United States and England.

Cream Ware, 10½″, man seated on bar-rel, yellow, black, green and rasp-berry, orig cracked hat lid, possibly Scottish, 19th C **200.00**
Delft, 11¼″, man seated on barrel, green hat, green and black sponged coat, blue and yellow pants, old cork stopper, c19th C **350.00**
Pearl Ware, Yorkshire, 10″, satyr han-dle, small toby jug resting on gentle-man's left knee, goblet in right hand, grotesque dwarf standing between knees, underglaze dec of blue jacket, yellow neckpiece, brown trousers, black shoes, black and white sponged hair, inner rim of hat and base sponged blue, ochre, and rasp-berry **3,750.00**
Pratt, 10¾″, Hearty Good Fellow, blue jacket, yellow-green vest, blue and yellow striped pants, blue and ochre

Hearty Good Fellow, red coat, yellow breeches, 11½″ h, $275.00.

sponged base and handle, stopper missing, slight glaze wear, c1770–80 **1,500.00**

Staffordshire

9", pearl ware, seated figure, sponged blue jacket, ochre buttons, ochre and lavender speckled vest and trousers, brown hair and hat, green glazed base, shallow flake inside hat rim, attributed to Ralph Wood, c1770–80 . . . . **1,900.00**

9¼", Thin Man, full chair, green, blue, and brown, holding pipe and foaming mug, attributed to Ralph Wood, c1765–75 . . . . **5,000.00**

9¾", Doctor Johnson, black and white clothes, missing hat stopper, attributed to Enoch Wood, c1790–1810 **700.00**

11", Martha Gunn, attributed to Ralph Wood, lid missing, c1765–75 . . . . **4,500.00**

11¾", Rodney's Sailor, black hat, green coat, white trousers with blue stripes, imp "65" on base, Ralph Wood, lid missing, c1765–75 . . . . **5,700.00**

Whieldon, 9½", pearl ware, seated figure, yellow greatcoat, green vest, blue trousers, holding brown jug in left hand, raises foaming glass of ale towards mouth, lid missing, c1770–80 **1,500.00**

Wilkinson, 11¾'", Winston Churchill, multicolored, designed by Clarice Cliff, black printed marks, number, and facisimile signature, c1940 . . . . **765.00**

Yorkshire, 10", seated, holding jug and goblet, blue coat, copper luster on hat, waistcoat, and breeches, c1830 **375.00**

TOOLS

History: Before the advent of assembly line and mass production, practically everything required for living was handmade at home or by a local tradesman or craftsmen. The cooper, the blacksmith, the cabinet maker, and the carpenter all had their special tools.

Early examples of these hand tools are collected for their workmanship, ingenuity, place of manufacture, or design. Modern day craftsman often search out old hand tools for use to authentically recreate the manufacture of an object.

References: Ronald S. Barlow, *The Antique Tool Collector's Guide to Value,* Windmill Publishing Company, 1985, (1987 reprint with current prices); Kathryn McNerney, *Antique Tools, Our American Heritage,* Collector Books, 1979; R. A. Salaman, *Dictionary of Tools,* Charles Scribner's Sons, 1974.

Collectors' Club: Early American Industries Association, P. O. Box 2128, Empire State Plaza Station, Albany, NY 12220. *The Chronicle* (monthly).

Museum: Shelburne Museum, Shelburne, VT.

Broad Axe, marked "Wm Beatty & Son, Cast Steel, Chester," 23½" I, $65.00.

Barn Beam Drill	50.00
Clamp, wood, 13½" jaws, pr	110.00
Chisel, 22½" I, blade stamped "E Connor"	45.00
Claw Hammer, Winchester	55.00
Hay Rake	
62" I, wood	190.00
67" I, branded "M B Young" .	200.00
Level, wood and brass, patent Dec 1886, marked "Davis & Cook"	40.00
Mallet, 34" I, burl, hickory handle	200.00
Mitre Box, laminated maple, birch, and oak, graduated quadrant, Stanley . .	25.00
Plane	
Chaplin No. 1210	60.00
Keen Kutter K110	20.00
Stanley, No. 10½	100.00
Ruler, 24", folding, brass trim, Stanley No. 54	10.00
Saw	
Band, 76" h, mortised and pinned wood frame, orig red paint with blue and white striping, blade and blade guides, laminated cherry and maple top	300.00
Buck, 30", wood, worn varnish finial, marked "W T Barnes"	35.00
Keyhole, 9", well shaped wood handle	25.00
Scribe	
7½" I, hewn wood handle	35.00
21" I, curly maple, adjustable fence and arm	65.00
Square, cherry, iron, brass bound blade, marked "Set Try"	45.00
Trammel, 29¾" I, wrought iron, sawtooth	65.00
Wheel Measure, 14½" I, wrought iron .	40.00
Wrench, alligator, hand forged	12.00

TOOTHPICK HOLDERS

History: Toothpick holders, indispensible table accessories of the Victorian era, are small containers used to hold toothpicks.

They were made in a wide range of materials: china (bisque and porcelain), glass (art, blown, cut, opalescent, pattern, etc.), and metals, especially silver plate. Makers include both American and European firms.

Toothpick holders were used as souvenir items by applying decals or transfers. The same blank may contain several different location labels.

References: William Heacock, *Encyclopedia Of Victorian Colored Pattern Glass, Book I, Toothpick Holders From A To Z*, Antique Publications, 1981; William Heacock, *1,000 Toothpick Holders: A Collector's Guide*, Antique Publications, 1977; William Heacock, *Rare & Unlisted Toothpick Holders*, Antique Publications, 1984.

Collectors' Club: National Toothpick Collector's Society, P. O. Box 246, Sawyer, MI 49125. Subscription: $10.00.

Additional Listings: See *Warman's Americana & Collectibles* for more examples.

Advisor: Judy Knauer.

Pomona Glass, Flower and Pleat, yellow stain, 2¼", $150.00.

China
  Bisque
    Bear with umbrella, unmarked ... 85.00
    Skull, blue anchor shape mark ... 55.00
  Meissen, clown 55.00
  Royal Bayreuth, elk 100.00
  Royal Doulton, Santa scene, green
    handles 65.00
  Schlegelmilch, R. S. Germany, mop
    luster 35.00
  Unmarked
    Flower form mold 30.00
    Raised beaded dec, Moriage 35.00
Glass
  Cut Glass
    Pedestal, chain of hobstars 135.00
    Star, clear, Federal Glass, c1910–
    14 .... 45.00
  Figural
    Baby Bootie, amber, c1890–95 .. 38.00

  Elephant, amber, c1890 .... 65.00
  Pig, pink 75.00
Milk Glass
  Alligator, c1885 .... 50.00
  Parrot and Top Hat, c1895 ..... 28.00
  Rose Urn, dec, two handles, Fostoria Glass Co, c1905 .... 38.00
  Scroll, claw ftd, light pink and blue
    dec, c1900 .... 40.00
Opalescent, Swirl pattern, blue 65.00
Pattern Glass
  Arched Fleur-de-lis, clear 30.00
  California, (Beaded Grape,) green
    with gold 60.00
  Intaglio Sunflower, clear 25.00
  Michigan, clear, yellow stain 175.00
  Monkey, clear, 3¾" h 45.00
  Teardrop and Cracked Ice, c1900–
    03 .... 75.00
  Texas, gold 27.00
  Wisconsin (Beaded Dewdrop) ... 40.00
Ruby Stained Glass
  Button Arches, souvenir Battleview,
    NJ 30.00
  Gold Swinger 35.00
  Truncated Cube 35.00

TORTOISE SHELL ITEMS

History: For many years amber and mottled colored tortoise shell has been used in the manufacture of small items such as boxes, combs, dresser sets, and trinkets.

Note: Anyone dealing in the sale of tortoise shell objects should be familiar with the Endangered Species Act and Amendment in its entirety. As of November, 1978, antique tortoise shell objects can be legally imported and sold with some restrictions.

Cigarette Case, brass clasps, 3½ x 2⅞", $40.00.

Box
  1½ x 3½", hinged cov 135.00
  11 x 7½ x 4", rect, fitted int. 150.00
Cigarette Box, SS mounts, hallmarked
  "Birmingham," c1925 .... 275.00

Hair Comb, carved crest, five oval cameo relief medallions with pierced borders, 19th C 375.00

Inkwell, SS mounts, marked "V C Vickerey, 179-81-3 Regent St W, London," c1900 . . . . 275.00

Ladle, 10", tortoise shell bowl, agate, coral, and amber mounted handle, 19th C 200.00

Razor, straight, faux tortoise shell handle, Landers 30.00

Salt and orig spoon, SS rivets 20.00

Stickpin, carved fly perched on coral branch, gold filled pin 75.00

Tea Caddy
6½" w, slightly domed panel, rect hinged lid, central plaque, two lidded compartments 990.00
6¾", rounded, rect hinged lid, fitted int., metal plaque and escutcheon 880.00

TOYS

History: In America the first cast iron toys began to appear shortly after the Civil War. Leading 19th century manufacturers include Hubley, Dent, Kenton, and Schoenhut. In the first decades of the 20th century, Arcade, Buddy L, Marx, and Tootsie Toy joined the earlier firms. Wooden toys were made by George Brown and other manufacturers who did not sign or label their work.

In Europe, N:auurnberg, Germany, was the center for the toy industry from the late 18th through the mid 20th century. Companies such as Lehman and Marklin produced high quality toys.

Several auction houses, including Lloyd Ralston Toys and Phillips, have specialty auctions consisting entirely of toys.

Every toy is collectible. The key is the condition and working order if mechanical. Examples listed are considered to be in good to very good condition to mint condition unless otherwise specified.

References: Linda Baker, *Modern Toys, American Toys, 1930–1980*, Collector Books, 1985; Jurgen and Marianne Cieslik, *Lehmann Toys*, New Cavendish Books, 1982; Fred and Marilyn Fintel, *Yesterday's Toys With Today's Prices*, Wallace-Homestead, 1985; Gordon Gardiner and Alistair Morris, *The Illustrated Encyclopedia of Metal Toys*, Harmony Books, 1984; Ernest & Ida Long, *Dictionary of Toys Sold in America*, 2 vols, published by author; David Longest, *Character Toys and Collectibles*, Collector Books, 1984; David Longest, *Character Toys and Collectibles, Second Series*, Collector Books, 1987; Albert W. McCollough, *The Complete Book of Buddy "L" Toys: A Greenberg Guide*, I. Greenberg Publishing Co., 1982; Brian Moran, *Battery Toys*, Schiffer Publishing, 1984; Richard O'Brien, *Collecting Toys: A Collectors Identification and Value Guide*, 4th Edition, Books Americana, 1985; Martyn L.

Schorr, *The Guide To Mechanical Toy Collecting*, Performance Media, 1979; Peter Viemeister, *Micro Cars*, Hamilton's, 1982; James Wieland and Dr. Edward Force, *Tootsie Toys, World's First Die Cast Models*, Motorbooks International, 1980; Blair Whitton, *The Knopf Collector's Guide to Amerian Toys*, Alfred A. Knopf, 1984.

Periodicals: *The Antique Toy World*, 4419 Irving Park Road, Chicago, IL 60618; *Professor Pug Frog's Newsletter*, 3 Hillside Avenue, Peabody, MA 01960.

Museums: American Museum of Automobile Miniatures, Andover, MA; Museum of the City of New York, New York, NY; Perelman Antique Toy Museum, Philadelphia, PA; Smithsonian Institution, Washington, D.C.; Margaret Woodbury Strong Museum, Rochester, NY; Toy Museum of Atlanta, Atlanta, GA.

Additional Listings: Disneyana and Schoenhut. Also see *Warman's Americana & Collectibles* for more examples.

Arcade, Freeport, IL, 1893–1946
Bus, Greyhound Lines GMC, cast iron, 1933, 10" l 125.00
Chester Gump Cart, painted cast iron, 7½" l 225.00
Coupe, two side windows, c1920, 6¾" 100.00
Gas Pump, painted cast iron, mechanical, 6¼" h 115.00
Yellow Cab Taxi, cast iron, orig black and orange paint, 5" 200.00
Auburn Rubber, Auburn, IN, 1913–1968
Bulldozer and Earthmover, 8" l bulldozer, 8" l earthmover, orig 18 x 5" box 40.00
Early American Frontier Set, 44 pcs of Indians, Frontiersmen, wild animals, cabins, and accessories, orig box, 17 x 12" 115.00
Public Service Set, 17 pcs, soft rubber, seven vehicles, ten figures, c1950, orig box 75.00
Bing, German
Airplane and Tower, painted and litho tin, 7½" 250.00
Automobile, litho tin windup, 5" 125.00
Combination Railroad Coach, litho and hp tin 100.00
Postcard Projector, painted tin, 9" h, smokestack missing 50.00
Yacht, painted tin, canopy, live steam attachment, 16" 1,750.00
Buddy L, American, 1921–Present, painted pressed steel
Aerial Towers Tramway, orig labels rough, incomplete 7,500.00
Baggage Line, orig labels 1,500.00
Bus, orig labels 2,000.00
Coal Hopper, doors open, coal chutes missing, black rubber tires 3,600.00

Coal Truck, labels and paint restored 900.00
Dump Truck, Robotoy, mechanical, orig labels, electrical hookup, orig box 1,400.00

Fire Truck
Aerial 700.00
Hook and Ladder, hose reel, orig labels 1,300.00
Steam Pumper, nickel plated, orig labels 850.00
Water Tower, nickel plated hose tower, incomplete 2,300.00

Hanger, two BL12 mono-airplanes, motors missing, orig labels incomplete 650.00
Ice Delivery Truck, orig canvas top . 900.00
International Harverster Truck, red, spoked wheels, orig labels 2,500.00
Overhead Crane 1,900.00
Wrecker, orig labels, 1 gear broken, hook missing 2,000.00

Carette, German, battleship, lithographed tin, red, light green, paint flaked, dented, 9", $400.00.

Chein, J., Harrison, NJ, c1930
Army Truck, tin, cannon, 8½" 30.00
Clown in Barrel, litho tin windup, 7½" 150.00
Organ, Cathedral Player, litho tin windup, multicolored, hand crank . 65.00
Roadster, litho tin windup, c1925, 8½" 65.00
Walking Popeye, litho tin windup, 6" h 125.00

Dent
Bus, Public Service, painted cast iron, 13½" l, 2nd series 375.00
Coupe, painted cast iron, 9½" l, 2nd series 450.00
Zeppelin, painted cast iron, 12½" l, 2nd series 275.00

Fisher Price, East Aurora, NY, 1930–Present
Donald Duck Choo Choo, pull top, 4 x 8 x 7", c1940 .... 75.00
Hot Diggety, windup, Black boy, colorful cloth outfit, painted wooden head, cardboard body, black metal ski-like feet, feet shuffle back and forth, 6" h, c1934, orig box 700.00

Puffy Train, pull toy, paper on wood, plastic arms, multicolored, 6" l, c1950, orig box 90.00
Woodsy-Wee Circus, nine paper litho on wood animals, one clown and circus wagon, 1931, orig 16 x 12" box, unplayed with condition 600.00

Gong Bell Toy Co, Keene, NY, cat and dog bell toy, $1,250.00.

Gong Bell Toy
Black Boy Baiting Alligator, painted cast iron, mechanical, 8" l 1,600.00
Trix, pull toy, litho paper on wood, mechanical, 16¼" 150.00

Gunthermann, Martin, German
Clown and Acrobatic Dog, litho and hp tin windup, working, clown missing one leg 200.00
Musicians, litho and painted tin, windup, cloth dressed, paper accordion, 8½" base 2,000.00
Playing Boy, hp tin windup, vibrating movement, side to side body action swings celluloid ball in circular motion, c1910, 7½" 200.00

Horsman, E. I., Golden ABC Cubes, block set litho paper on wood, c1883, orig wood framed 14½ x 9½ x 2" box, 40 pcs 340.00

Hubley, Lancaster, PA, 1894–1965
Circus Chariot, painted cast iron, three horses, Kenton clown figure, 10" l 300.00
Elephant, painted cast iron, howdah 350.00
Life Saver Truck, holds pack in back, c1930 .... 80.00
Limousine, c1920, 7" 65.00
Motorcycle, cast iron, red, policeman, black rubber tires, 4" l 80.00
Sedan, painted cast iron, nickel plated grill and bumper, white rubber tires, red hubcaps, 7" l 175.00

Street Sweeper, cast iron, 8″ 675.00

Ives, Bridgeport, CT
Cannon, painted cast iron, Hotchkiss,
firecracker, 9½″ l 175.00
Fire Engine, pumper, painted cast
iron, 23″ 2,150.00
Magic Snake Toy, japanned and
painted cast iron, 4″ h 400.00

Katz, Red Arrow Airplane, litho tin, copy
of Spirit of St. Louis, framed box lid,
missing tin tab 250.00

Kenton, Kenton, OH
Cabriolet, painted cast iron, rubber
tires under horse, 16″ l, 2nd series,
orig box 275.00
Carriage, painted cast iron, silver
wheels and shafts, cream body,
black trim, orig lady rider, 17″ l . .   900.00
Log Wagon, painted cast iron, 15″ l .   375.00
Overland Cage Wagon, painted cast
iron and tin, orig white bear and
reins, 14″ l 300.00
Overland Calliope, painted cast iron,
iron wheels under horse, 1 wheel
and outriders missing, 14″ l 400.00
Sulky, painted cast iron, 7½″ l 100.00

Keystone, painted pressed steel,
marked "Packard"
American Railway Express, screen
sides, orig labels, rubber tires . . .   2,300.00
Dump Truck, scissors action, coal
chute, orig labels, all metal wheels   450.00
Fire Truck
Aerial Ladder, rubber tires, ladders
missing, old repaint 325.00
Chemical Pump Engine, incom-
plete 800.00
Water Tower, rubber tires and
hoses 1,200.00
Koaster Truck, orig labels, rubber
tires 1,000.00
Moving Van, rubber tires, orig labels
rough 300.00
Steam Roller, orig string for bell, la-
bels, orig box 1,100.00
Wrecker, rubber tires, orig labels, mechanical, 1 brace and hook missing   350.00

Kilgore, roadster, painted and nickel
plated cast iron, 6″ l 400.00

Kingsbury, Keene, NH, painted pressed
steep, windup
Biplane, white rubber tires, 16″ l, 12″
wingspan 375.00
Bus, Greyhound, white rubber tires,
18″ l, restored 125.00
Fire Truck
Aerial Ladder, airflow design, black
rubber tires, 24″ l 60.00
Ladder, red and yellow, ladder ex-
tends to 37″, 18″ 100.00
Pumper, cast iron and wood details,
not working, 10″ l 100.00

Sunbeam Racer, yellow, driver, black
rubber tires, plastic windshield, rubber bumper, c1930 . . . .   340.00

**Lehmann, Nürnberg, Germany, 1881–
Present**
Balky Mule, litho tin windup, cloth
dressed 160.00
Going To The Fair, painted and litho
tin, momentum 600.00
Mandarin, painted and litho tin
windup, orig braids, 7½″ l 1,000.00
Mars Captive Balloon, 1896 . . . . . .   2,225.00
Oh My Alabama Coon Jigger, litho tin
windup, 4½ x 3 x 2″ litho tin base,
10″ h 375.00

Linemar
Campus Express, litho tin, multicolored, working crank sound, 4½″ l   65.00
Disneyland Roadster, litho tin friction,
1½″ celluloid Nephew Duck driver,
plastic windshield, c1950, 4½″ . . .   160.00
Dockyard Crane, litho tin windup, 8 x
3″ base, c1950 . . . .   50.00
Donald Duck In His Convertible, litho
tin friction, celluloid Donald at
wheel, orig cartoon box, c1950 . .   275.00
Figuro, litho tin friction, multicolored,
3″ l, c1950 . . . .   90.00
Jalopy Car, litho tin, graffiti filled, siren
sound, 4½″ l 60.00
Jam-Licking Bear, mechanical, plush
body, tin base, reaches into litho tin
strawberry jam can and then licks
paw, c1950, orig box 100.00
Mickey Mouse Crazy Car, litho tin
windup, orig tin ears and arms, not
working 150.00
Sam The City Gardener, litho tin
windup, red, white, and brown plastic figure pushes litho tin cart with
seven plastic garden tools, red
pressed steel base, c1950, orig box   115.00

Marklin, German
Armored Car, hp tin, clockwork, 14½″
l, c1930 . . . .   975.00
Ocean Liner, painted tin, red, black,
and white deck, clockwork, marked
on rudder, c1910, 15″ l 1,750.00

Marx, American, 1921–Present
Airplane, WWII, US Army, litho tin
windup, 8″ w 60.00
Dick Tracy Police Car, litho tin, plas-
tic, windup, electric, rubber tires,
10″ l 225.00
G-Man Pursuit Car, litho tin windup,
no key, 14″ l 375.00
Home Town Set, 2 x 5 x 3″ litho tin,
c1930, orig box
Butcher Shop 100.00
Home Town Police Station 240.00
Liberty Bus, litho tin friction, black and

Marx, Popeye Express, lithographed tin, wind-up, $275.00.

red, green metal wheels, c1930, 5″ l 100.00
Moon Mullins & Kayo Dynamite Handcar, litho tin windup, not working 300.00
Pinocchio, litho tin windup, blinking eyes, nose glued, 8½″ h 200.00
Police Motorcycle with Sidecar, litho tin windup, celluloid pieces, 8½″ l . 175.00
Racer, litho tin windup, red, yellow, and black, black tin tires, c1930, 5″ l 100.00
Rocket Racer, litho tin windup, rubber front bumper 225.00
Touring Auto, green and yellow tin, emb side louvers and doors, red tin tires, grill marked "103," red and black litho tin uniformed figure, 10″ l, c1920 .... 275.00
Schieble, c1920, car, Hillclimber Roadster Coupe, pressed steel, friction, black, 17″ l 375.00
Schuco, marked "U.S. Zone Germany,"
    Car, 3000, cream colored tin, chrome grill and five gears, 4″ l 65.00
    Fox 1111, windup, dark orange tin body, chrome grill, tin litho name plate 115.00
    Microracer 1043, windup, gray cast body, red int., gray rubber tires, white grill marked "Schuco," orig box, 4″ l 100.00
    Old Timer Ford Coupe, 1917 T, tin and plastic, windup, 6″ l, orig box . 50.00
Steelcraft
    Fire Truck, painted pressed steel, rubber tires, orig labels
        Combination Hook and Ladder and Hose Reel 900.00
        Mack Chemical Wagon 2,000.00
Strauss, Ferdinand, New York City, 20th C
    Tip-Top Porter, litho tin windup, porter pushing blue and yellow cart, 6″ l, c1930 .... 165.00

Tombo-The Alabama Coon Jigger, litho tin windup, multicolored, 5 x 3 x 2″ base 400.00
Trikauto-The Circus Wonder, litho tin windup, bright yellow and red, orig 7½″ box with circus motif artwork, c1920 .... 425.00
Unidentified Maker
    American
        Tricycle, painted and stenciled wood, cast iron hardware, 34″ l, c1860 .... 1,200.00
        Velocipede, painted and stenciled wood, cast iron, 40″ l, c1870 .. 1,000.00
    German
        Balloonist, painted tin, clockwork, straw basket, 15″ h 1,750.00
        Ferris Wheel, painted tin, live steam attachment, 15″ h 1,600.00
        Minstrel Drummer, painted tin windup, 8½″ 700.00
        Pool Player, penny-toy, litho tin man hits metal cue ball, spring operated pool stick, c1920, 2½ x 4″ 200.00
Unique Art
    Dogpatch Band, litho tin windup ... 400.00
    GI Joe and K9 Pups, litho tin windup, 9½″ h 175.00
    Kiddy Cyclist, litho tin windup 100.00
    Police Motorcycle, litho tin windup, multicolored, uniformed officer, 8½″ l 150.00
    Rodeo Joe, litho tin windup 150.00
Wolverine
    Merry-Go-Round, litho tin, spring action, horses and airplanes, 12″ h . 160.00
    Zilotone, litho tin windup, working, faded, one disk 200.00
Wyandotte
    Hoky Poky, litho tin windup, multicolored, 6″ red pressed steel base, two clowns, c1930 .... 200.00
    Truck Line
        Open Van & Trailer, 10″ l red plastic cab, 17″ l pressed steel trailer, litho tin int., black plastic tires, c1950, orig box 100.00
        Rack Truck, painted pressed steel, litho grill 50.00
        Tow Truck, painted pressed steel, black rubber tires, litho grill 125.00

TRAINS, TOY

History: Railroading has always been an important part of childhood, largely because of the romance associated with the railroad and the emphasis on toy trains.

The first toy trains were cast iron and tin; windup motors added movement. The Golden Age of toy trains was 1920–1955 when electric powered units were available and names such as Ives, American Flyer, and Lionel were household words. The construction of the rolling stock was of high quality. The advent of plastic in the late 1950s lessened this quality considerably.

Toy trains were designated by a model scale or gauge. The most popular are HO, N, O and standard. Narrow gauge was a response to the modern capacity to miniaturize. Its popularity has lessened in the last few years.

Condition of trains is critical. Items in fair condition (scratched, chipped, dented, rusted or warped) and below generally have little value to a collector. Restoration is accepted, provided it is done accurately. It may enhance the price one or two grades. Prices listed below are for very good to mint condition unless noted.

References: John O. Bradshaw, *Greenberg's Guide To Kusan Trains*, Greenberg Publishing Co, 1987; Bruce C. Greenberg and James Patterson, *Greenberg's Guide To American Flyer S Gauge*, 2nd Edition, Greenberg Publishing Co, 1984; Bruce Greenberg, *Greenberg's Price Guide To Lionel Trains: 1901–1942*, 3rd Edition, Greenberg Publishing Co., 1983; Bruce Greenberg, *Greenberg's Price Guide To Lionel Trains: 1945–1983*, Greenberg Publishing Co., 1982; Bruce C. and Linda F. Greenberg, *Greenberg's Price Guide To Lionel Trains, Prewar and Postwar, 1901–42 & 1945–83, Pocket Edition*, Greenberg Publishing Co., 1983; Bruce Greenberg, *Greenberg's Price Guide to Lionel Trains, Postwar O and O-27 Trains*, 3rd Edition, Greenberg Publishing Co., 1982; Ron Hollander, *All Aboard!*, Workman Publishing Co, 1981; Al McDuffie, et. al., *Greenberg Guide to Ives Trains*, 1901-1932, Greenberg Publishing Co, 1984; John Hubbard, *The Story of Williams Electric Trains*, Greenberg Publishing Co., 1987; Dallas J. Mallerich, III, *Greenberg's Guide to Athern Trains*, Greenberg Publishing Co., 1987. Note: Greenberg Publishing Company (7543 Main Street, Sykesville, MD 21784) is the leading publisher of toy train literature. Anyone interested in the subject should write for their catalog and ask to be put on their mailing list.

Collectors' Clubs: Lionel Collector's Club, P.O. Box 11851, Lexington, KY 40578; The National Model Railroad Association, P.O. Box 2186, Indianapolis, IN 46206; The Toy Train Operating Society, Inc., 25 West Walnut Street, Suite 305, Pasadena, CA 91103; The Train Collector's Association, P.O. Box 248, Strasburg, PA 17579.

Additional Listings: See *Warman's Americana & Collectibles* for more examples.

AMERICAN FLYER

Car
631, T & P, gondola, red **95.00**
962, Vista Dome, Silver Rocket, green stripe **55.00**

4041, American, pullman, light green, standard gauge **75.00**

IVES

Car
51, Newark, coach, O gauge, yellow litho, gray roof **75.00**
67, Caboose, four wheels **50.00**
184, Club Car, std gauge, olive, c1927 . . . . **100.00**
Locomotive
3241, electric, std gauge, dark green, c1925 . . . . **750.00**
3251, electric, O gauge, orange with brown trim **100.00**
4637, electric, std gauge, restored, new wheels **550.00**
Set, American, cast iron, black and red locomotive, tender, 1182 passenger car, 1193 royal blue line passenger cars, finished in blue and red roofs, c1895 . . . . **950.00**

Lionel, electric, No. 233 "O" gauge, engine #262, hopper car #803, gondola #902, cattle car #806, caboose #802, orig box, $165.00.

LIONEL

Car
514, Ventilated Refrigerator Car, white with green, orig box, paint flaking **100.00**
0708, Penn, baggage, HO gauge . . **40.00**
0807, HO gauge, flat car with bulldozer **135.00**
6457, O gauge, caboose, lighted . . . **45.00**
Shell Tank, O gauge, painted diecast, decals **225.00**
Locomotive
5, B & O gauge, Tunnel, maroon finish, c1904 . . . . **3,700.00**

150, O gauge, maroon, green windows **160.00**
251E, O gauge, red with cream trim, brass plates **120.00**
252, O gauge, peacock **90.00**

Set

Locomotive #262, 262T, 602, 600, and 601, O gauge, diecast and pressed steel, rusting **175.00**
Locomotive #408E, 419, 431, 418, 490, standard gauge, locomotive wheels cracked **1,600.00**

TRAMP ART

History: Tramp art was prevalent in the United States from 1875 to the 1930s. Items were made by itinerant artists who left no record of their identity. They used old cigar boxes and fruit and vegetable crates. The edges of items were chip-carved and layered, creating the "Tramp Art" effect. Finished items usually were given an overall stain. Today they are collected primarily as folk art.

Reference: Helaine Fendelman, *Tramp Art: An Itinerant's Folk Art Guide,* E. P. Dutton & Co., 1975.

Picture Frame, 26 x 20″, $200.00.

Basket, handle **12.00**
Box

7 x 8 x 5¼″, yellow and orange alternating layers **85.00**
13″ l, two drawers, hinged lid, applied diamond and triangle dec **100.00**
Christmas Tree Holder, 8¼″ h, 32 x 32″, solid fence and arched gate, worn green and white paint, gold trim ... **175.00**
Watch Holder, 14 x 14½″, hutch shape **165.00**
Frame, 16¼ x 21¼″, cross corner, natural finish **25.00**

Miniature, 9″ h, chest of drawers, varnish finish **125.00**
Model, 25 x 25″, galleon, fully rigged, canvas sails, polychrome paint **275.00**
Sewing Box, pin cushion and spool holders on top, one drawer, chip carved trim around edges **65.00**

TRUNKS

History: Trunks are portable containers that clasp shut for the storage or transportation of personal possessions. Normally "trunk" means the ribbed flat, or dome top models of the second half of the 19th century. Unrestored they sell between $50 and $150. Refinished and relined the price rises to $200 to $400, with decorators being a principal market.

Early trunks frequently were painted, stenciled, grained, or covered with wallpaper. These are collected for their folk art qualities and as such experience high prices.

Reference: Martin and Maryann Labuda, *Price & Identification Guide to Antique Trunks,* published by author, 1980.

Leather covered, initialed with nail heads, iron hardware and rivets, 26½ x 15 x 12½″, $225.00.

DOME TOP

Leather covered wood, 16″ l, brass studding dec, bail handle **30.00**
Oak, immigrant type, 46¾″ l, dovetail, wrought iron strap hinges, banding, end handles and lock, dark finish .. **270.00**
Pine, 25″ l, orig dark green paint with orange striping and yellow dots, orig iron hinges and end handles, replaced lock **65.00**

FLAT TOP

Camphor wood, 39⅓ x 19¼″, rect, dovetail, brass bound corners, shaped hasp, escutcheon and carrying handles, fitted int. **550.00**

Pigskin, 14 x 8", red, painted Oriental maidens and landscapes within quatrefoils on front and sides, brass loop handles and lock, Chinese, 19th C . **125.00**

VAL SAINT-LAMBERT

History: Val Saint-Lambert, a twelfth century Cistercian abbey, was located during different historical periods in France, Netherlands, and Belgium (1930 to present). In 1822 Francois Kemlin and Auguste Lelievre, along with a group of financiers, bought the abbey and opened a glassworks. In 1846 Val Saint-Lambert merged with the Société Anonyme des Manufactures de Glaces, Verres à Vitre, Cristaux et Gobeletaries. The company bought many other glassworks.

Val Saint-Lambert developed a reputation for technological progress in the glass industry. In 1879 Val Saint-Lambert became an independent company employing 4,000 workers. Val Saint-Lambert concentrated on the export market making table glass, cut, engraved, etched, and molded pieces, and chandeliers. Some pieces were finished in other countries, e.g., silver mounts added in the United States.

Val Saint-Lambert executed many special commissions for the artists of the Art Nouveau and Art Deco periods. The tradition continues. The company also made cameo-etched vases, covered boxes, and bowls. The firm celebrated its 150th anniversary in 1975.

Atomizer, Art Deco motif, cut glass, clear, green, marked "Val St. Lambert for Saks," bulb missing, 6" h, $140.00.

Ashtray, 5⅛" d, round, spiraling points, acid etched signature, pr **150.00**

Bowl, 8 x 4", 2" applied handles, smoky green, slightly scalloped, frosted feather pattern sides, molded signature **185.00**

Chest Set, crystal, clear crystal half, green and clear crystal remaining half, each pc labeled and sgd, 6½" h tallest pc **300.00**

Dresser Jar, cov, 4¾", double cut, ruby cut to clear, sgd **100.00**

Pitcher, clear, paneled, diamond shaped cuttings, sgd **85.00**

Vase, 23¾", slender neck, wide sloping foot, cameo, clear glass overlaid with white, brown, and green, c1900 . . . **5,000.00**

Wine Glass, intaglio cut, ribbons, bows, and cranberry cameos, gold trimmed stems, set of 12 . . . . **480.00**

VALENTINES

History: Early cards were handmade, often containing both handwritten verses and hand drawn pictures. Many cards also were hand colored and contained cutwork.

Mass production of machine-made cards featuring chromolithography began after 1840. In 1847 Esther Howland of Worcester, Massachusetts, established a company to make valentines which were hand decorated with paper lace and other materials imported from England. They had a small "H" stamped in red in the top left corner. Howland's company eventually became the New England Valentine Company (N.E.V. Co.).

George C. Whitney and his brother founded a company after the Civil War which dominated the market from the 1870's through the first decades of the 20th century. They bought out several competitors, one of which was the New England Valentine Company.

Lace paper was invented in 1834. The 1835 to 1860 period is known as the "golden age" of lacy cards.

Embossed paper was used in England after 1800. Embossed lithographs and woodcuts developed between 1825–40, with early examples being hand colored.

References: Ruth Webb Lee, *A History of Valentines*, available from the National Valentine Collectors Association; Frank Staff, *The Valentine And Its Origins*, out-of-print.

Collectors' Club: National Valentine Collectors Association, Box 1404, Santa Ana, CA 92702. Dues: $8.00. *Newsletter* (quarterly).

Additional Listings: See *Warman's Americana & Collectibles* for more examples.

Advisor: Evalene Pulati.

Aquatint, English, 8 x 10", 1840 . . . . . **75.00**

German, foldout, diecut, four line verse, marked "Schanaer," $40.00.

Cameo, Berlin & Jones, 5 x 7", 1860 .	35.00
Cobweb, Dobbs, 8 x 10", hand colored, 1860	35.00
Comic, English, 5 x 7", lithographed center with verse, 1860	18.00
Cutwork, Pennsylvania German, 16" sq, handcolored, 1820	350.00
Easel Back, 6 x 9", fancy cutwork border, 1900	10.00
Lacy Folder, 3 x 5"	
Hand assembled, emb, 1850	15.00
Howland, signed, 1855	25.00
N.E.V. Co., layered, 1875	18.00
Mechanical, R. Tuck, large paper doll, 1900	25.00
Pulldown, German	
5 x 10", five layers, 1920	20.00
8 x 12", large ship, 1910	75.00

VALLERYSTAHL GLASS

History: Vallerystahl (Lorraine), France, has been a glass producing center for centuries. In 1872 two major factories, Vallerystahl glassworks and Portieux glassworks, merged and produced art glass until 1898. Later, pressed glass covered animal dishes were introduced. The factory continues operation today.

Animal Dish, cov
  Dog, patterned quilt top, raised flowers on base, milk white, sgd **165.00**

Snail, figural strawberry base, milk white, sgd	90.00
Swan, blue milk glass	90.00
Breakfast Set, hen cov dish, six egg cups, basket form master salt, and tray, milk white, 9 pcs	450.00
Butter Dish, cov, turtle, snail finial, milk white	100.00
Candlesticks, Baroque pattern, amber, pr	75.00

Animal Dish, cov, blue milk glass, squirrel finial, $75.00.

Dish, cov, figural, lemon, milk white, sgd	65.00
Plate, 6", Thistle pattern, green	65.00
Salt, cov, hen on nest, white opal	35.00
Sugar, cov, 5" h, Strawberry pattern, salamander finial, milk white, gold trim .	75.00
Tumbler, 4", blue	40.00
Vase, 8", cylindrical, Optic Diamond pattern, green, painted rose thistles, sgd	150.00

VAN BRIGGLE POTTERY

History: Artus Van Briggle, born in 1869, was a talented Ohio artist who studied in Paris for three years while working at Rookwood. In 1899 he moved to Colorado for his health and established his own pottery in Colorado Springs in 1901.

Van Briggle's work was influenced heavily by the Art Nouveau "school" he saw in France. He produced a great variety of matte glazed wares in this style. Colors varied.

The "AA" mark, a date, and "Van Briggle" were incised on all pieces prior to 1907 and sometimes into the 1910s and 20s. Dated pieces are the most desirable.

Artus died in 1904. Anne Van Briggle continued the pottery until 1912.

References: Barbara Arnest (ed.), *Van Briggle Pottery: The Early Years*, The Colorado Springs Fine Art Center, 1975; Scott N. Nelson, *Collector's Guide To Van Briggle Pottery*, published by author, 1987.

Collectors' Club: American Art Pottery Association, 270 Spangler Mill Road, New Cumberland, PA 17070.

Museum: Pioneer Museum, Colorado Springs, CO.

Reproduction Alert: Van Briggle pottery still is made today. These modern pieces often are confused for older examples. Among the glazes used are Moonglo (off white), Turquoise Ming, Russet, and Midnight (black).

1901–1920

Bookends, pr, 7¼ x 7″, figural, bears standing against tree trunks, dark blue-green glaze, pre 1920	200.00
Bowl	
3″, dragonfly design, deep plum, 1917	100.00
5¾ x 2″, buff colored clay body, flowers in panels, shaded light blue glaze, Pattern 322, 1906	300.00
Candlesticks, pr, 9¼″, figural, facing children, light green, medium blue glaze, late teens	90.00
Figure	
Elephant, raised trunk, turquoise, AA mark	90.00
Rabbit, early	45.00

Vase, Lorelei, matte glaze, slight greenish cast to outside, darker green on face and bust, marked "A. Van Briggle, 1898" in rust underglaze, 7⅜″ h, $1,000.00.

Vase	
3¾″, robin's egg blue wash, buff colored clay, 1908–11	120.00
4¼′, olive green, rose brushed around bottom, Pattern 549, 1907	225.00

4½″, poppy seed pods, matte moss green curdled to yellowish green, some smooth areas, Shape 452, 1907	275.00
5″, copper clad, shape #696, c1907	1,000.00
6¼″, dark green long slender leaves, deep dark blue, matte glaze on leathery texture, Shape 636, 1908–11	275.00
7¼″, brown glaze, shape #296, 1906	475.00
7½″, medium blue, cream colored clay body, thistle-like flowers, 1918	225.00
Wall Pocket, 7½″, turquoise matte, relief, AA mark	75.00

1921–1968

Ashtray, 6½ x 6½″, Hopi Indian maiden kneeling, grinding corn, turquoise Ming glaze	75.00
Boot, 2½″	35.00
Bust, 6½″, child reading book	45.00
Indian Maiden, 4 x 6″, bent over rock, ear of corn in hands, blue-green . . .	50.00
Lamp Base, 17″ h, colonial lady shape, turquoise Ming glaze, brushed blue accents, late 1940s	75.00
Paperweight, 3″, rabbit, maroon	60.00
Pitcher, conical, plain, blue, Pattern 435	100.00
Vase, 13″, honey brown, green butterflies	225.00
Wall Pocket, 12″, stylized flowers, magenta, Pattern 720	130.00

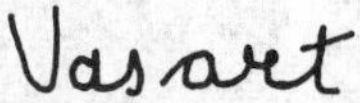

VASART

Vasart

History: Vasart is a contemporary art glass made in Scotland by the Streathearn Glass Co. The colors are mottled, and sometimes shade from one hue to another. It is readily identified by and engraved signature on the base.

Ashtray, mottled light blue, 4½″ d, $50.00.

Ashtray, 4½" d, mottled blue to pink, sgd	50.00
Basket, 8¼ x 5", green shading to pink	85.00

Bowl

6½", pierced handle, pink and green	30.00
8", green-gray, gold stone flecks . . .	75.00
Hat, sgd	25.00
Mug, mottled white and lavender	35.00
Plate, 8", green-gray, gold stone flakes	75.00
Rose Bowl, mottled white and green . .	40.00

Vase

8½", mottled blue shading to pink . .	100.00
9", ftd, jade green, sgd	75.00

VENETIAN GLASS

History: Venetian glass has been made on the island of Morano, near Venice, since the 13th century. Most of the wares are thin walled. Many types of decoration have been used: embedded gold dust, lace work, and applied fruits or flowers.

Reproduction Alert

Wine, set of 6, c1880–90, $175.00.

Ashtray, curled edges, blue, silver flecks	30.00
Barber Bottle, green overlay, cut to clear	125.00
Bowl, cranberry, pie crust edge	55.00
Candleholders, 3¾", flower form, aqua, opalescent, and clear, gold dec, pr .	80.00

Candlesticks, pr

12", clear, gold dust	135.00
15¾", pink, clear glass shot with gold, dolphin standard	125.00
Centerpiece, 13 x 9", figural, swan, blue, flower frog	35.00
Chalice, 11", blue, gold Biblical figures, pr	200.00
Cologne Bottle, 10¾", pink, flower form stopper with long applicator, pr	125.00
Compote, 6⅜ x 7½", pink, clear glass, gold dec, dolphin standard	100.00

Cruet, lavender, double swirled, orig stopper	100.00
Flower Frog, 13 x 9", swan, blue	35.00
Goblet, 6¼", green, pink rigaree	40.00
Plate, 7", pink and white alternating latticino stripes	60.00
Rose Bowl, ruffled, ftd, pink, gold flecks	100.00
Salt, swan shape, pink, gold trim	35.00

Vase

6", Art Nouveau woman on side . . .	30.00
10½", ftd, goblet shape, quilted pattern, petals, stem, and applied berries, pale green, gold trim	48.00

VERLYS GLASS

History: Verlys glass is an art glass originally made in France after 1930. For a period of a few months, Heisey Glass Co., Newark, Ohio, produced the identical glass, having obtained the rights and formula from the French factory.

The French-produced glass can be distinguished from the American product by the signature. The French is mold marked; the American is etched script signed.

Ashtray, oval, 6" w, $45.00.

Animal Cov Dish, duck, frosted	65.00
Ashtray, 4½", frosted doves, floral border, script mark	50.00

Bowl

6", Pinecone, French blue	100.00
13½", Poppy, frosted	125.00
14", Dragonfly, etched mark	150.00
Box, 6½", butterflies, script mark	100.00
Candy Dish, 7", sculptured florals on cov, opal	375.00
Charger, 13", Waterlily	145.00

Plate, 11¾", bird dec	**165.00**
Powder Box, lovebirds, frosted	**65.00**
Vase	
6½ x 4½", sculptured lovebirds at base, frosted	**75.00**
10", Thistle, clear and frosted	**240.00**

VILLEROY & BOCH

History: Pierre Joseph Boch established a pottery near Luxemburg, Germany, in 1767. Jean Francis, his son, introduced the first coal-fired kiln in Europe and perfected a water-power-driven potter's wheel. Pierre's grandson, Eugene Boch, managed a pottery at Mettlach; Nicholas Villeroy also had a pottery nearby.

In 1841 the three potteries were merged into the firm of Villeroy & Boch. Early production included a hard paste earthenware comparable to English ironstone. The factory continues to use this hard paste formula for its modern tablewares.

Reference: Susan and Al Bagdade, *Warman's English & Continental Pottery & Porcelain, 1st Edition*, Warman Publishing Co., Inc., 1987.

Additional Listings: Mettlach.

Plate, green mark, imp "8670," 6½" d, $17.50.

Bowl, 8⅛", stick spatter, gaudy polychrome floral dec	**40.00**
Child's Plate, blue and white, incised	**40.00**
Coffeepot, 8", Virginia pattern	**85.00**
Creamer, "Aragon," unused	**15.00**
Chop Plate	**20.00**

Jug, 14¼", brown earthenware, peasants in field, white relief, pewter mounts, 19th C	**175.00**
Mug, elk dec, sgd	**40.00**
Plaque, 17", scene of castle on rock, gold trim, #1108, Mettlach	**350.00**
Plate	
9", gaudy stick spatter, polychrome floral design	**20.00**
10", gaudy stick spatter, polychrome floral design	**25.00**
Punch Bowl, cov, underplate, 3 quart, blue, scene of dancing figures, #2087	**750.00**
Salt Box, 9½", wood lid, blue dec	**150.00**
Stein, 6" h, #1180, chocolate brown, applied creamware dec on sides and lid, pewter handle, Mettlach, hairline int.	**40.00**
Tile, blue and white Dutch scene with windmills	**50.00**
Tumbler, ¼ L, Prosit, child with hammer, # 1014, Geschutz	**85.00**
Vase	
6¼", Art Deco, green and brown, gold outlining, white ground, pr	**185.00**
12", gray and white relief design, flowering vines, molded cherub handles, c1842	**110.00**

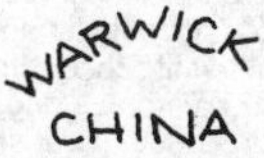

WARWICK

History: Warwick China Manufacturing Co., Wheeling, West Virginia, was incorporated in 1887 and continued until 1951. The company was one of the first manufacturers of vitreous glazed wares in the United States. Production was extensive and included tableware, garden ornaments, and decorative and utilitarian items.

Pieces were hand painted or decorated by decals. Collectors seek portrait items and fraternal pieces for groups such as the Elks, Eagles, and Knights of Pythias.

Some experimental, eggshell-type porcelain was made before 1887. A few examples are in the market.

Bowl, 9½ x 3¼", insert and underplate, black ground	**60.00**
Egg Cup, large, Tudor Rose	**15.00**
Gravy Boat, red currants, green leaves, gold trim	**50.00**
Marmalade Jar, cov, handles, pale yellow florals, brown ground	**100.00**
Mug, 4½", singing monk, brown ground	**45.00**
Plate	
9½", monk drinking wine, brown ground	**75.00**

Pitcher, monk playing fiddle, brown tones, standard glaze, marked "IOGA," 4¼" h, $75.00.

10", herons, green ground	135.00
Portrait Plate, 10", gypsy lady, multicolored, white ground	65.00

Vase
10½"
Bouquet shape, portrait, girl, flamingo shaded ground, twig handles ... **275.00**
Urn shape, gypsy girl portrait, blue blouse and hair ribbon, brown shaded ground, twig handles .. **150.00**
11", red hibiscus, brown ground ... **75.00**
11½", bouquet shape, portrait, lady with white rose, brown ground ... **170.00**
11¾", Verona, ring handles, pine cones dec, coral shading to yellow to brown ... **115.00**
12", bouquet shape, portrait, lady with red roses, brown ground ... **170.00**

WATCHES

History: The market in all types of watches is brisk. They can be found from flea markets to the specialized jewelry sales at Butterfield's, Phillip's, and Sotheby's. Condition of movement is first priority; design and detailing of case is second.

In pocket watches, listing aids are size (18/0 to 20), number of jewels in movement, open or closed (hunter) face, and whether the case is gold, gold filled, or some other metal. The movement is the critical element since cases often were switched. However, an elaborate case, especially of gold, adds significantly to value.

Pocket watches designed to railroad specifications are desirable. They are 16 to 18 in size, have a minimum of 17 jewels, adjust to at least five positions, and conform to many other specifications. All are openfaced.

Study the field thoroughly before buying. The literature is vast including books and newsletters from clubs and collectors. Abbreviations: S = size; gf = gold filled; yg = yellow gold; j = jewels.

References: Howard Brenner, *Collecting Comic Character Clocks and Watches*, Books Americana, 1987; Roy Ehrhardt, *Foreign and American Pocket Watch: Identification and Price Guide, Book 3*, Heart of America Press, 1976; Cooksey Shugart and Tom Engle, *The Complete Guide To American Pocket Watches: 1986*, Overstreet Publications, 1986.

Collectors' Club: National Association of Watch & Clock Collectors, 514 Poplar Street, Box 33, Columbia, PA 17512. Dues: $20.00. *Bulletin* (bi-monthly) and *Mart* (bi-monthly).

Museums: American Clock & Watch Museum, Bristol, CT; Hoffman Clock Museum, Newark, NY; National Association of Watch and Clock Collectors Museum, Columbia, PA; The Time Museum, Rockford, IL.

Character
Babe Ruth, wrist	**165.00**
Big Bad Wolf, pocket, slogan on reverse, Ingersoll, Disney, c1930 ..	**400.00**
Donald Duck, wrist, rect face, 1940s	**90.00**
Richard Nixon, wrist, Nixon on dial .	**45.00**

Pendant
Belforte, 18K gold, oval shaped case, white enamel and gold key motif border, oblong shaped link chain with applied translucent peach colored enamel over quilloche ground, pendant loop and bow set with small diamond, c1910 ... **1,250.00**
Swiss, 30 S, 15j, 12¾ Ligne brass cylinder escapement, 14K yg enameled (black) hunter ... **450.00**

Pocket
Railroad
Bunn (Illinois), 16 S, 23j, 10K gf case ... **325.00**

Elgin, ladies, 6 S, 7 jewel, gold filled, demi-hunting, engraved "Miss Sally to Mary, 1896," case marked "Fahats 10K", $175.00.

Hampden, 18 S, 23j, gold jewel setting, adjusted to heat, cold, isochronism, and five positions, nickel plate case, double roller, two tone **275.00**

Seth Thomas, 18 S, 15j, locomotive engraved on silveroid case **65.00**

Waltham Watch Co, 18 S, 17j, M#1883 .... **260.00**

Regular

Elgin, 8 S, hunter, 14K, #1141341, lever set, machine turned case . **465.00**

Howard, 18 S, 19j movement, orig case **375.00**

Howard, open face, 16 S, 17j, gf . **135.00**

Illinois, 16 S, hunter, 17j, nickel lever movement #1923165, yg filled case #537918 .... **250.00**

Movado, 17j, open face, movement #1617359, 14K yg case **500.00**

New York Standard, yellow playing card dial **650.00**

Patek Philippe, 18j, open face, circular dial, raised gold bar nos., subsidiary second dial, nickel lever movement, 18K plain case, sgd, #882371 .... **950.00**

Waltham, 18 S, 17j, silveroid case, lever set, 1903 .... **85.00**

Wristwatch, Lady's

Bucherer, 18K, white gold, 12 diamonds with brick work solid band and cov over dial **2,200.00**

Bulova, 14K, 23j, yg, surrounded by 24 diamonds **665.00**

Girod, 14K **150.00**

Le Roy & Fils, London, platinum and diamond, rect, strap set at intervals with six old European cut diamonds, each .65 carat, numerous rose cut diamonds **2,000.00**

Longines, 14K **200.00**

Nicolet, 17j, flexible band, cabochon crystal, small diamond on each side of ½ sq face **85.00**

Wristwatch, Man's

Baylor, 14K, yg, rect fancy case, small diamond set in white gold on dial . **185.00**

Corum, 18K, rect, heavy case **600.00**

Elgin, 14K, automatic, c1960 ..... **250.00**

Patek Philippe, 18K, 18j, nickel lever movement, optionally adjusted to heat cold, and isochronism, and five positions, sgd, #794679 .... **850.00**

WATERFORD

History: Waterford crystal is quality flint glass commonly decorated with cuttings. The original factory was established at Waterford, Ireland, in

1729. Glass made before 1830 is darker than the brilliantly clear glass of later production. The factory closed in 1852. After 100 years it reopened and continues in production.

Compote, 4⅞" d, 4¼" h, $150.00.

Bowl, 9", leaf cut border over trelliswork sides **100.00**

Creamer and Sugar, diamond cut **50.00**

Cruet, 5", waisted body, short fluted neck, fluted rim, strawberry leaves and fan cutting, faceted stopper ... **100.00**

Decanter, 10", deep cut Sawtooth Rib pattern, double rope ring neck, orig stopper **250.00**

Jar, cov, 6", diamond cut body, triple sprig chain bordering thumb cut rim and star cut lid, faceted knob finial . **100.00**

Salt, 3", cut, star base **30.00**

Vase, 7", fluted neck, flared rim, hobnail cut, triple sprig chains, star cut centered base **85.00**

Water Set, 6" pitcher, six tumblers, diamond cut **600.00**

Wine Glass, diamond and flute cut, star base **25.00**

Wine Glass Rinser, grape and vine border, honeycomb base, c1870 ..... **100.00**

WAVE CREST WARE

WAVE CREST

History: The C. F. Monroe Company of Meriden, Connecticut, produced the opal glassware known as wave crest from 1898 until World War I. The company bought the opaque, blown molded glass blanks for decoration from the Pairpoint Manufacturing Co. of New Bedford, Massachusetts, and other glass makers including European factories. Florals were the most common decorative motif. Trade names used were "Wave Crest Ware," "Kelva," and "Nakara."

Reference: Elsa H. Grimmer, *Wave Crest Ware*, Wallace-Homestead, 1979.

Biscuit Jar, 5½ x 9", Helmschmied Swirls molded multicolored ground, long stemmed yellow roses, incised floral and leaf dec on lid, marked "Quadruple Plate" **385.00**

Bowl, 5¼", Emb Rococo mold hp cherubs and enameled florals, ormolu rim and foot, sgd **315.00**

Box, Helmschmied Swirl, blue forget-me-nots, 4½" d, 3" h, $250.00.

Box, hinged lid
4 x 3", octagonal, mottled sage green, hp orange and white flowers, ormolu fittings, orig lime green lining, sgd "Kelva" **335.00**
5¼ x 3", Emb Rococo mold, creamy white ground, cupids and flowers, sgd **535.00**
5½", Bishop's hat mold, hp lid scene of girl picking flowers, ftd **275.00**
7¼", round, Emb Rococo mold, pink ground, hp flowers **400.00**
8", Queen Louise, marked "Nakara" **800.00**

Calling Card Tray, 4½ x 2½", Emb Rococo mold, white ground, pastel flower dec, brass rim **150.00**

Cigarette Box, 4" h, Emb Rococo mold, creamy white ground, enameled flowers, ornate ormolu ftd base and rim, tab handles **325.00**

Collars and Cuff Box, 7" sq, hinged lid, egg crate mold, pastel blue ground, hp pastel flowers and "Collars and Cuffs," sgd **725.00**

Ferner, 8 x 4½", octagonal, blue and cream panels, hp flowers, sgd **300.00**

Finger Bowl, matching underplate **300.00**

Fork, hp blue forget-me-nots, silver ferrule **110.00**

Jardiniere, 7¼ x 8½", Emb Rococo mold, pink ground, yellow and pink flowers, plain ormolu rim and base, cupid's masks at feet **700.00**

Jewelry Box
5", puffy egg crate mold, creamy white ground, pink roses, hinged lid, ormolu rims and feet, orig lining **500.00**
5½ x 6", petticoat mold, creamy white ground, enameled cobalt blue and pink flowers, ormolu rims, lock closure, and feet, orig lining, sgd . . . **1,125.00**
7 x 6½", puffy egg crate mold, ftd, satin finish, hp lid, child with bow and arrow, orig lining **1,200.00**

Mirror Tray, 3 x 2¼" oval mirror, 6¼" h overall, pink flowers, blue ground, marked "Kelva" **500.00**

Powder Jar, cov, 3 x 3", blown mold full relief rose on lid, sgd "Kelva" **300.00**

Salt and Pepper Shakers, swirled necks, bulbous bottom, bust of cat surrounded by wreath of green foliage, pr **110.00**

WEATHER VANES

History: A weather vane indicates wind direction. The earliest known examples were found on late 17th century structures in the Boston area. The vanes were handcrafted of wood, copper, or tin. By the last half of the 19th century, weather vanes adorned farms and houses throughout the nation. Mass produced vanes of cast iron, copper, and sheet metal were sold through mail order catalogs or at country stores.

The champion vane is the rooster. In fact, the name weathercock is synonymous with weather vane. The styles and patterns are endless. Weathering can affect the same vane differently. For this reason, patina is a critical element in collecting vanes.

Whirligigs are a variation of the weather vane. Constructed of wood and metal, often by unskilled craftsmen, whirligigs not only indicate the direction of the wind and its velocity, but their unique movements served as entertainment for children, neighbors, and passersby.

Reproduction Alert: Reproduction of early models exist, are being aged, and sold as originals.

Arrow
10½" h, 14¼" d, cast iron, emb rooster counter balance, painted black **150.00**
71¼" h, gilded copper, zinc point, cast aluminum directionals, turned wood finial **100.00**

Horse, Blackhawk, marked "Harris & Co," 26" w, $2,500.00.

Cow, 16" l, 15" h, sheet metal, weathered brown, white, and green repaint, wood base 460.00

Eagle
  24" w, 19" h, full bodied, copper, detailed and dark patina 275.00
  38½" h, cast aluminum, black and gold paint, added wood base ... 70.00

Horse and Driver, 36" l, cast zinc, green patina, wood base, soldered repairs 6,000.00

Pig, orig lightning rod 135.00

Rooster, hand forged 175.00

Running Horse, orig lightning rod 135.00

Ship, 31" l, wood, four masts, zinc sails, wire rigging, weathered gray finish . 270.00

WEBB, THOMAS & SONS

History: Thomas Webb & Sons was established in 1837 in Stourbridge, England. The company probably is best known for its very beautiful English cameo glass. However, many other types of colored glass were produced including enameled glass, iridescent glass, pieces with heavy glass ornamentation, cased glass, and other art glass besides cameo.

Additional Listings: Burmese, Cameo, and Peachblow.

Bowl
  5¼", ivory satin, pinpoint floral dec, sgd in base 250.00
  10", butterscotch, gold floral dec, two handles 165.00

Bride's Basket, 10", pink satin, DQ, MOP, ruffled edge, metal base, sgd . 300.00

Claret Jug, opaque white body, brilliant gold palm trees and bamboo stalks, rust and dark green ferns and tropical foliage, SP flip top lid, collar, and handle, hallmarked and numbered 335.00

Cologne Bottle, 5½" h, globular, peach satin, SS screw top 250.00

Flower Holder, 12 1 2 x 8¾", gold irid glass foot, brass leaves and branches, four irid gold ribbed flower shaped vases 500.00

Jar, 5" d, DQ, MOP, blue, berries dec, SP hallmarked collar, lid, and bail handle 450.00

Perfume Bottle, 3½", globular, carved white blossoms, blue satin ground, SS screw on cap 875.00

Rose Bowl
  3⅛ x 2⅞", crimped top, gold prunus blossoms and butterfly, shaded brown satin ground, cream lining . 365.00
  3¾", blue swirled MOP satin glass bowl, green satin glass leaf shaped base 220.00

Salt, master, frosted, Adam and Eve, butterfly signature 65.00

Scent Bottle
  1¼ x 4¼", lay down, gold prunus blossoms, green shaded to yellow satin ground, hallmarked SS domed monogrammed cap 400.00
  3½", black satin, white floral dec, small label reads "Lily of the Valley" 80.00

Toothpick, Alexandrite, ruffled edge .. 1,000.00

Vase, ruby ext., white lining, two color gold dec, 8½" h, $450.00.

Vase
  3½ x 4½", cameo, deep frosted red ground, opaque white flowers and clover, butterfly on back, sgd "Thos. Webb & Sons" 1,250.00
  5¼", stick top, bulbous, blue satin glass 115.00
  6⅞", peach blow, acid finish, deep cream lining, shaded rose to cream, heavy gold daisies and leaves, large gold dragonfly on back 650.00

8¾", brown satin, fluted, elaborate gold filigree dec, blue and white enamel highlights, pr 600.00

9", butterscotch satin, DQ pattern, pr 400.00

12⅜", jack in the pulpit, Burmese, ribbon candy rim, fine dec, enamel beading around foot 975.00

WEDGWOOD

WEDGWOOD

History: In 1754 Josiah Wedgwood entered into a partnership with Thomas Whieldon of Fenton Vivian, Staffordshire, England. Products included marbled, agate, tortoise shell, green glaze, and Egyptian black wares. In 1759 Wedgwood opened his own pottery at the Ivy House works, Burslem. In 1764 he moved to the Brick House (Bell Works) at Burslem. The pottery concentrated on utilitarian pieces.

Between 1766 and 1769 Wedgwood built the famous works at Etruria. Among the most renowned products of this plant were the Empress Catherina of Russia dinner service (1774) and the Portland Vase (1790s). Product lines were caneware, unglazed earthenwares (drabwares), piecrust wares, variegated and marbled wares, black basalt (developed in 1768), Queen's or creamware, Jasperware (perfected in 1774), and others.

Bone china was produced under the direction of Josiah Wedgwood II between 1812 and 1822 and revived in 1878. Moonlight lustre was made from 1805 to 1815. Fairyland lustre began in 1920. All lustre production ended in 1932.

A museum was established at the Etruria pottery in 1906. When Wedgwood moved to its modern plant at Barlaston, North Staffordshire, the museum was continued and expanded.

References: Susan and Al Bagdade, *Warman's English & Continental Pottery & Porcelain, 1st Edition,* Warman Publishing Co., Inc., 1987; Harry M. Buten, *Wedgwood ABC, But Not Middle E,* Buten Museum of Wedgwood, 1964, available in reprint; David Buten and Jane Clancy, *Eighteenth-Century Wedgwood: A Guide For Collectors And Connoisseurs,* Main Street Press, 1980; Robin Reilly, *Dictionary Of Wedgwood,* Antique Collectors Club, 1980.

Collectors' Club: The Wedgwood Society, 246 N. Bowman Avenue, Merion, PA 19066; The Wedgwood Society, The Roman Villa, Rockbourne, Fordingbridge, Hents, England, SP 6 3PG.

Museum: Buten Museum, Merion, PA.

BASALT

Beaker, 5⅛", black, imp mark, 19th C . 80.00

Bust

2⅛" d, 4¼" h, Aristophanes, marked "Wedgwood" 400.00

18½", Mercury, sgd "Wedgwood" on bust and plinth 125.00

Coffeepot, 9¼", basketweave, Widow Warburton finial, unmarked 325.00

Creamer

2¾ x 2", black, one side classic figural scene of old man with serpent and young man with dish in his hand, reverse side classical figure of old woman washing young woman's feet 130.00

3⅛", bulbous base, straight neck, black, hp enamel crest of Ontario, green maple leaf, side trim, orange Ontario banner underneath, green enamel rim and handle trim, marked "Wedgwood, England" and painters no. 250.00

Figure

4¾" bulldog, standing, amber glass eyes, black, modeled by Hubert Light, imp "Wedgwood," c1914 .. 300.00

5⅞ x 9⅜", Cleopatra, nude, sitting, asp on her wrist, marked "Wedgwood" 650.00

Pendant, oval, black, lion chasing horse, beaded SS frame and chain . 75.00

Pitcher

4¾", tankard shape, black, classical women and children scene, grape and vine border, large mark with "8" in circle 155.00

Tea Set, 5¾" teapot, 4¼" sugar, 4½" creamer, Strawberry pattern 450.00

Urn, cov, 11", pedestal, sq base, swags, acanthus leaves at base and cov, c1860 .... 1,700.00

Vase, 7¾", urn shape, cov, high relief floral swags suspended from rams' heads enclosing flower head motifs, knob finial, scroll handles with foliage motif, sq pedestal, imp mark, c1770 875.00

Wine Ewer, 16" h, figural models by John Flaxman on shoulders, swags of vine and water reeds, stiff leaves, bands of overlapping foliage, gadrooned stems, sq bases, imp mark, c1860, pr 900.00

CANEWARE

Dish, 9¾", rect, molded with overlapping leaves, imp mark, letter "L", c1790 .... 250.00

Fruit Stand, 12⅜", foliate scroll handles,

rect flaring foot, imp "Wedgwood," early 19th C **200.00**
Sugar, cov 6", smear glaze, prunus blossoms, c1800 .... **300.00**
Teapot, c1820, smear glaze Arabesque scene, dog finial **225.00**
Vase, 8¾", sq, pierced domed lid, concave sides, relief brown classical figures, brown foliage caryatid corner supports suspending swags, four brown paw feet, stepped shaped sq base, imp mark, c1800 .... **1,200.00**
Waste Bowl, 5½" d, Wicker pattern, imp mark, c1820 .... **100.00**

CREAMWARE

Basket, 9"d, round, reticulated, c1790 . **200.00**
Compote, 8¼" d, 4¾" h, basketweave, reticulated foliate scroll, rope twist rim handles **175.00**
Cup and Saucer, daisies, enameled dec **65.00**
Dish, 10¼", oval, clusters of fruit, green printed rim transfer, scrolling flowering branches, gilt rims, artist sgd "F. H. Cox," imp mark, Pat #G4744, c1880 .... **150.00**
Plate, 9½", black printed transfer, green enamel crustacean, shaped rim with green line, imp mark, c1780 ...... **95.00**
Sauce Dish, cov, attached underplate, oval, two handles, glazed **250.00**
Soup Tureen, cov, 17" w, blue and green bands of flowering foliage between black lines, handles with foliage terminals, flower head finial, imp mark, Pattern #313, c1810 ...... **360.00**
Sugar, cov, 8", stand, painted iron-red, green, blue, and yellow bands of flowering foliage, disc finial and flower head motif cov, imp mark, iron-red mark "Pat #1173," c1860 .... **235.00**
Tray, 6¼" w, diamond shape, transfer printed and painted, embracing cupids among clouds, sgd "EL," imp mark, letters "C," "AVO," c1865 ... **250.00**
Urn, 6", mottled blue and brown, glazed, mounted on basalt plinth, marked "Wedgwood and Bentley," c1768–80 **475.00**
Water Set, 4 pcs, pitcher, two tumblers, and tray, dog handles, gilt, Victorian **850.00**

DRABWARE

Child's Tea Set, 3½" teapot, cov sugar bowl, milk jug, waste bowl, basketweave, button knobs, imp mark, early 19th C **275.00**
Cup and Saucer, applied blue bands of flowering foliage **100.00**
Jug, 8", classical women emb on

panels, loop handle, Wedgwood mark, c1820 .... **2,250.00**
Teapot, 8½", Gothic dec, bearded man faces on lower section, imp "Wedgwood" **225.00**
Vase, 10", blue and white, three sections, figural swan handles **400.00**

Jasperware, pitcher, blue ground, white classical figures, marked "Wedgwood," c1940, 14" h, $100.00.

JASPERWARE

Ashtray, 4½", spade shape, dark blue, cupids dec, marked "Made in England" **30.00**
Biscuit Jar, 5¼ x 7¾", white floral dec, lavender ground, acorn finial, artist sgd "Barnard" **710.00**
Box, cov, 4" sq, dark blue, white classical figures, flower heads on corners of lid, vine border, marked, c1860 .. **165.00**
Cake Plate, 9", black, raised white classical ladies border, orig box **48.00**
Candlesticks, pr, 6¼", blue, white coat of arms of St. Andrews, inscribed name and motto, scrolling foliage, circular column, flaring feet, imp marks **325.00**
Comb Tray, 9 x 6½", dark blue, classical scenes, floral border, marked "Wedgwood, England" **185.00**
Cup and Saucer, tri-color, green ground, white relief rams' heads suspending floral swags enclosing oval medallions of classical figures on lilac ground, imp marks, 19th C **250.00**
Dish, 4½", heart shape, dark blue, classical dec, marked "Made in England" **130.00**
Hair Receiver, cov, heart shape, medium blue, large white angel dec, numbered only **250.00**
Jardiniere, 7", oval, blue, white trailing vine and circles, scrolling vine rim band, flower head handles **900.00**
Loving Cup, 4 x 4½", three handles, olive green, white cameo medallions of

Washington, Franklin, and Lafayette, marked "Wedgwood, England" **450.00**

Mug, 4⅞", dark blue, white classical figures and medallion, SS rim, marked "Wedgwood, Elkington & Co, Ltd" . . **140.00**

Mustard Jar, 3½", yellow, black grape swags and lion's heads, two white bands around base, SP lid, marked Wedgwood only **250.00**

Pin Tray, 2½ x 6", dark blue, classical dec, marked "Wedgwood, England" **40.00**

Pitcher
6", blue ground, white classical dec . **100.00**
7¾", sage green, classical figures, cupid, and cherubs, marked "Wedgwood, England" **85.00**

Plaque, 9 x 7", oval, white Virgin Mary cameo medallion, flowers and vine border, lilac, marked "Made in England" **135.00**

Plate, 9", Shell, solid white **200.00**

Preserve Jar, 6", cov, dark blue, matching underplate, four classical Muses in cartouches, marked "Wedgwood, England" **200.00**

Ring Tree, dark blue, rose border, classical scenes, unmarked **175.00**

Sweetmeat, cov, 3¼", cylindrical, dark blue, white horses and figures, knob finial, marked "Wedgwood" **185.00**

Tablet, 2 x 5", black and white **225.00**

Tea Set, teapot, creamer, cov sugar, sage green, straight sided Brewster shape, cameo medallions of Washington and Franklin, marked "Wedgwood, England" **575.00**

Toothpick Holder, 2¼", dark blue, white bust of Josiah Wedgwood, marked "Wedgwood, Made In England" . . . **75.00**

Urn, cov, 7½", tri-color, white ground, green swags and acanthus leaves, lilac rams' masks, two green medallions with white classical figures on lilac ground, floral lilac shoulder band, flared foot, ball finial, scroll handles, imp mark, mid 19th C **900.00**

Vase, 8¼", light blue, white classical figures cameos, white handles, bolted pedestal base with white scrolling vine dec, marked **375.00**

LUSTERS

Butterfly
Bowl, 2¾ x 1¾", octagonal, gold outlined multicolored butterflies, gold trim, mottled MOP luster ext., mottled flame int., Portland vase mark **115.00**
Mug, 2", three handles, blue, tan, and pink, gold butterflies, coral int., marked "Wedgwood Lustre" **200.00**

Dragon
Box, cov, 5¾ x 4⅞", mottled green luster ext., gold dragons, ornate gold bands, MOP luster int., three jewels on base, maroon luster widow finial, Portland vase mark . **450.00**
Garniture Set, 11" center vase, two 8" sq vases, flying cranes and dragon breathing flames, 3 pcs **900.00**
Salt, 2¼", orange dog's head in bowl, blue ext. **130.00**
Vase, 4¾ x 9¾", gold outlined dragon breathing flames, ornate gold designs at top, base, and rim int., mottled powder blue luster ext. **450.00**

Fairyland
Bowl, 6⅜ x 3", gold outlined green eyed Firbolgs, ruby ext., green luster int., center scene of Thumbelina, Portland vase mark **1,000.00**
Melba Cup, 4¼ x 3¼", elves on branch in int., leapfrogging elves on ext., stars in sky **750.00**
Plate, 10¾", elves on bridge, gold center, lacy gold fairies and florals on gold border, mottled blue back **1,700.00**
Vase, 8⅜ x 4¼", "Candlemas," multicolored, gold details, Portland vase mark and "Z5157, Wedgwood" **1,275.00**

Hummingbird
Jar, cov, 9", gold outlined multicolored hummingbirds, mottled green ext., gold trim, marked "Wedgwood" . . **725.00**
Vase, 2½ x 5⅛", gold outlined multicolored hummingbirds, mottled blue luster ground, mottled flame luster int. **200.00**

Moonlight
Goblet, 3¼", pink with yellow and green splashes, gilt rim, imp mark, c1810 . . . . **300.00**
Plate, 9¾", purple luster splotches, c1810 . . . . **200.00**
Vase, 3¼ x 8⅛", "Boys on Bridge" dec, Portland vase mark **1,150.00**

MAJOLICA

Bowl, 9 x 4⅛", white and brown, emb white seashells, rose and gold seaweed, turquoise int., SP rim band, imp mark **125.00**

Creamer, 3", Strawberry pattern, turquoise int., imp mark **160.00**

Match Holder, 4¾ x 3½", green and brown, striker on base, imp mark . . **90.00**

Pitcher, 8½", jug shape, jeweled design, turquoise int., c1860 . . . . **350.00**

Plate, 6½", butterflies, florals, and fans dec **65.00**

Platter, 12½", basketweave center, bamboo edge 100.00

Sugar, 7", Fan pattern, flowering prunus, gray-green, yellow, and pink, turquoise int., two branch handles, imp mark, 1878 .... 165.00

Teapot, cov, 6¼", Bamboo pattern, imp mark, 1871 .... 625.00

Water Bottle, 10", multicolored florals, horizontal blue stripes, cream ground, 1879 .... 300.00

Capri Ware, inkwell, 2⅝" d, $625.00.

MISCELLANEOUS

Bulb Pot, 9½", figural, hedgehog, light blue, glazed, imp mark 475.00

Calendar Tile, 1910, The Mayflower Approaching Land, brown and white .. 65.00

Compote, 5⅝ x 4", green luster scrollwork, copper luster trim, yellow luster ext., two handles, pedestal base, c1920 .... 100.00

Honey Pot, cov, 3¾", stoneware, beehive shape, translucent smear glaze, c1820 .... 225.00

Pepper Pot, 3½", bulbous, relief grapes and leaves, white, imp mark 100.00

Pitcher, brown transfer, ivory ground, 1878 .... 85.00

Tray, 15¾", oval, smear glaze, rim relief molded, band of scrolling flowering foliage, imp mark, early 19th C 280.00

Vase, 4¾", flaring, bands of brown ovals below band of flower heads, yellow glazed brown ground, imp mark, mid 19th C 165.00

PEARLWARE

Bough Pot, 9", pierced cov, D-shape, speckled, molded floral swags, still foliage border, gilt, imp mark, c1810, pr 1,200.00

Compote, 10¾ x 6¼", Havelock pattern, floral border, imp mark, c1840–68 .. 265.00

Jug, 4½ x 5¾", blue, scenic transfer,

gold wreath with initials under spout, gold grim, imp mark, c1820 ...... 275.00

Plate, 8½", shell shape, ribbon handle, 1882 .... 75.00

Soup Tureen, cov, ladle, blue dahlias, green foliage, black rope edge, imp mark 400.00

Vase, cov, 6⅝", tan slip, engine turned gadroons, relief beadwork and swags, imp mark, late 18th C 425.00

QUEEN'S WARE

Box, 4 x 5", powder blue, relief berries, marked "Wedgwood England" 100.00

Crocus Pot, 6", rect, bombe shape, classical motifs in oval medallion 115.00

Cup and Saucer, relief vintage rim border, #2223 .... 25.00

Tea Set, Edward VIII Coronation, blue, c1937, 3 pcs 400.00

ROSSO ANTICO

Creamer, 6", applied center black band of scrolling flowering foliage, imp mark, mid 19th C 225.00

Inkwell, 4⅛", pavilion shape 125.00

Jug, 6", pinched spout, applied black formal foliage and bellflowers, c1820 200.00

Teapot, cov, 10½", squatty, band of hieroglyphs at shoulder, crocodile finial, 1810 .... 420.00

TERRA COTTA WARE

Ashtray, 4½", classical dec, marked "Made in England" 35.00

Box, heart shape 100.00

Compote, jasper 125.00

Pin Dish, 4", oval, cupids playing, marked "Made in England" 30.00

Vase, 5¼", Portland shape, black relief lilies and foliage, flaring rim, band of grass, angular handles, applied mask terminals, imp mark, mid 19th C ... 300.00

WELLER POTTERY

History: In 1872 Samuel A. Weller opened a small factory in Fultonham, near Zanesville, Ohio, to produce utilitarian stoneware, such as milk pans and sewer tile. In 1882 he moved his facilities to Zanesville. In 1890 Weller built a new plant in the Putnam section of Zanesville along the tracks of the Cincinnati and Miskingum Railway. Additions followed in 1892 and 1894.

In 1894 Weller entered into an agreement with William A. Long to purchase the Lonhuda Faience Company, which had developed an art pottery line under the guidance of Laura A. Fry, formerly of Rookwood. Long left in 1895, but Weller continued to produce Lonhuda under a new name, Louwelsa. Replacing Long as art director was Charles Babcock Upjohn. He, along with Jacques Sicard, Frederick Hurten Rhead, and Gazo Fudji, developed Weller's art pottery lines.

At the end of World War I, many prestige lines were discontinued and Weller concentrated on commercial wares. Rudolph Lorber joined the staff and designed lines such as Roma, Forest, and Knifewood. In 1920 Weller purchased the plant of the Zanesville Art Pottery and claimed to be the largest pottery in the country.

Art pottery enjoyed a revival when the Hudson Line was introduced in the early 1920s. The 1930s saw Coppertone and Graystone Garden ware added. However, the Depression forced the closing of the Putnam plant and one on Marietta Street in Zanesville. After World War II, cheap Japanese imports took over Weller's market. In 1947 Essex Wire Company of Detroit bought the controlling stock. Early in 1948 operations ceased.

Reference: Sharon and Bob Huxford, *The Collectors Encyclopedia Of Weller Pottery*, Collector Books, 1979.

Collectors' Club: American Art Pottery Association, P. O. Box 714, Silver Spring, MD 20901.

Additional Listings: See *Warman's Americana & Collectibles* for more examples.

Vase, Eocean, gray ground, pink flowers, 7⅝" h, $160.00.

Basket
Cameo, 7½", white relief florals, matte coral ground 28.00
Eocean, 6½", florals, glossy gray to black ground 150.00
Bowl
Ardsley, 5", sword shaped green leaves forming handles, water lily form 55.00
Blue Drapery, 5½", clusters of roses, vertical folded blue matte ground . 20.00
Coppertone, 10½ x 2", lilypads, applied frog on edge 135.00
Glendale, 16", birds and nests, flower frog 275.00
Malvern, 10", matching flower frog . 55.00
Candlesticks, pr
Blue Drapery, 9", double gourd form, clusters of roses 85.00
Roma, 9", triple candelabra, pink flowers, cream ground 160.00
Chalice, Rosemont, 10", robins, butterflies, flowers, and branches, black ground 240.00
Ewer
Dickensware, 2nd line, 11½", incised fish, matte green ground, sgd "E. L. Pickens" 565.00
Louwelsa, green 350.00
Figure
Canaries, two on branch, textured Brighton base 160.00
Cocker Spaniel, 10½ x 14", ink stamp mark 800.00
Hanging Basket
Cameo 30.00
Souevo, 6½" 175.00
Jardiniere
Aurelian, pedestal base, slip painted florals, glossy brown glaze, artist sgd 1,250.00
Blueware, 8½ x 7" 150.00
Cameo Jewel, 8", applied jewels and female heads, light gray shading to dark ground, imp block lettered mark 200.00
Dickensware, Line I, portrait of cavalier, caramel ground 500.00
Woodcraft, 9½", figural squirrel and woodpecker, tree trunk ground . . . 275.00
Lamp, oil, Turada, blue 650.00
Mug, Louwelsa, blue, cherries dec ... 275.00
Pitcher
Aurelian, 12", tankard, slip painted berries, glossy brown glaze, artist sgd 350.00
Dickensware, 3rd line, 12½", molded full figure of man, long coat and hat, gray, marked "Weller" by hand, sgd "LM" 350.00
Zona, 8", kingfisher, half kiln ink stamp mark 175.00

Tobacco Jar, Louwelsa, brass lid **175.00**
Umbrella Stand, Flemish, 12½″, panels
of vines and pink morning glories,
blended brown and green ground,
imp block lettered mark **350.00**
Vase
Aurelian, 12 x 10″, pillow shape, slip
painted blackberries, glossy brown
glaze, artist sgd **350.00**
Dickensware, 11″, gourd shape, deep
brown ground, autumn colored
leaves and berries on branch, artist
sgd "A. G." **245.00**
Silvertone, 6¾″, bud **35.00**
Wild Rose, 9½″ **35.00**
Wall Pocket
Blue Drapery, 9″, clusters of roses,
blue ground **50.00**
Glendale, 7½″, multicolored molded
bird and nest, ink stamp mark . . . **200.00**
L'Art Nouveau, 6½″, blown-out floral,
matte green and yellow glaze . . . **165.00**
Sydonia, 9½″, four fluted spouts, mot-
tled blue glaze **100.00**

WHALING

History: Whaling items are a specialized part of
nautical collecting. Provenance is of prime importance since whaling collectors want assurances
that their pieces are from a whaling voyage. Since
ship's equipment seldom carries the ship's identification, some individuals have falsely attributed a
whaling provenance to general nautical items.
Know the dealer, auction house, or collector from
whom you buy.

Special tools, e.g., knives, harpoons, lances,
spades, etc., do not overlap the general nautical
line. Makers' marks and condition determine value
for these items.

Richard Bourne, Hyannis, Massachusetts, and
Chuck DeLuca, York, Maine, regularly hold auctions featuring whaling material.

Reference: Thomas G. Lytle, *Harpoons And
Other Whalecraft*, Old Dartmouth Historical Society, 1984.

Museums: Cold Spring Harbor Museum, Long
Island, NY; Kendall Whaling Museum, Sharon,
MA; Mystic Seaport Museum, Mystic, CT; National
Maritime Museum, San Francisco, CA; Old Dart-
mouth Historical Society, New Bedford, MA; Whal-
ing Museum, Nantucket, MA.

Additional Listings: Nautical Items and Scrimshaw.

Advisor: Bill Wheeler.

Blubber Spade, initial "K" carved in stub
of handle **200.00**
Carpenter's Chest, 36″ l, five sliding
trays, tools, name "M Jobin" on lid,
whaleship *Eagle* on front **1,200.00**

Cooper's Scribe, 8″ l, wood, brass
keeper screw, c1850, Greenport, NY **75.00**
Fid, 9½″ l, bone **200.00**
Harpoon, 23″, wrought iron, double tog-
gle, split column mount, John Hill
style **275.00**
Journal, *Obed Mitchel*, Nantucket, Pa-
cific Ocean voyage, Sept 4, 1841 to
May 9, 1845, kept daily by Eihu Cof-
fin, ship's master, 293 pgs, folio,
suede binding, leather label **2,000.00**
Line Throwing Rocket, "Schermuly
Speedline International," yellow
waterproof case, trigger, and safety
pin **75.00**
Sailor's Valentine, 16″, octagonal
shape, mounted in orig frame, anchor
design center, 19th C **750.00**
Seam Rubber, wooden, 5″ l, 2″ w, deep
relief carvings on knob and handle . **300.00**
Sewing Box, 10¼″ l, scrimshaw and
wood, made at sea on board *Alaska*
for Mrs. Parnell Fisher, substantial
amount memorabilia from trip within
box **800.00**
Whalebone Products
Match Safe, 1 x 1½″, ivory, friction
scratch carved striker on side,
spring loaded top **140.00**
Swift, 20¾″, whalebone ivory clamp
and cup with inlaid piece abalone,
slats fastened by two rows silver
pins, mid 19th C **1,200.00**
Toy
Doll, 9½″ h, jigger, male, top hat,
scribed clothes **1,200.00**
Gambling, 1″ d,¾″ h, stained red
numbers cut into 8 sides **90.00**
Sailor's Puzzle, bottle with primitive
model of bark *Annie*, anchor
forms stopper **120.00**
Whistle, 2″ w, 1″ l, rigged for lanyard,
shrill police type sound **110.00**

WHIELDON   WHIELDON

History: The Staffordshire potter, Thomas
Whieldon, established his shop in 1740. He is best
known for his mottled ware, molded in forms of
vegetables, fruits, and leaves. Josiah Spode and
Josiah Wedgwood, in different capacities, had connections with Whieldon.

Whieldon ware is a generic term. His wares
were never marked and other potters made similar
items. Whieldon ware is agate-tortoise shell earthenware, in limited shades of green, brown, blue
and yellow. Most pieces are utilitarian items, e.g.,
dinner ware and plates, but figurines and other
decorative pieces are found.

Reference: Susan and Al Bagdade, *Warman's English & Continental Pottery & Porcelain, 1st Edition*, Warman Publishing Co., Inc., 1987.

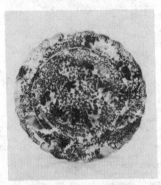

Plate, feather edge, 9½" d, $450.00.

Charger, 13⅞", rim molded with bands of stars and dots, leaf form cartouches, mottled gray and green glaze, yellow and brown sponging, two rim firing cracks, c17660–70 . . . **1,200.00**

Dish, leaf, 5½" l, gray and brown mottling, splashes of green and yellow on white, three small feet, c1770 . . . . . **400.00**

Pitcher, cov, 8¾", green, brown, and gray-blue glaze, applied flower and scroll design, three mask and paw feet, matching cov with bird finial, c1755–60, finial repaired **8,000.00**

Plate
8½", octagonal, splashed manganese, raised rope twist rim, c1755, pr **1,000.00**
9½", splashed manganese, blue, green, and ochre, feather molded edge, pr **900.00**

Spill Bowl, 5¾" d, mottled brown and white glaze, vertical yellow, green, and blue stripes, c1770 . . . . **450.00**

Tea Caddy, 5½" h, rect, canted corners, flat shoulder, splashed brown glaze, c1755 . . . . **425.00**

Tray, 6 x 9¾", rect, gadrooned rim, sq handles, mottled gray-green glaze, yellow and brown all-over sponging, brown sponged reverse, c1760–70 . **2,000.00**

WHISKEY BOTTLES, EARLY

History: The earliest whiskey bottles made in America were blown by pioneer glass makers in the 18th century. The Biningers (1820–1880s) were the first bottles specifically designed for whiskey. After the 1860s distillers favored the cylindrical 'fifth' form.

The first embossed brand name bottle was the amber E. G. Booz Old Cabin Whiskey bottle which was issued in 1860. Many stories have been told about this classic bottle. Unfortunately, most are not true. Research has proved that "booze" was a corruption of the words "bouse" and "boosy" from the 16th and 17th centuries. It was only a coincidence that the Philadelphia distributor also was named Booz. This bottle has been reproduced extensively.

Prohibition (1920–1933) brought the legal whiskey industry to a standstill. Whiskey was marked "medicinal purposes only" and distributed by private distillers in unmarked or paper label bottles.

The size and shape of whiskey bottles are standard. Colors are limited to amber, amethyst, clear, green, and cobalt blue (rare). Corks were the common closure in the early period, with the inside screw top being used in the 1880–1910 period.

Bottles made prior to 1880 are the most desirable. In purchasing a bottle with a label, condition is a critical factor. In the 1950s distillers began to issue collectors' special edition bottles to help increase sales.

References: Ralph & Terry Kovel, *The Kovels' Bottle Price List, 7th Edition*, Crown Publishers, 1984; Carlo & Dot Sellari, *The Illustrated Price Guide To Antique Bottles*, Country Beautiful Corp., 1975.

Periodicals: *Antique Bottle World*, 5003 West Berwin, Chicago, IL 60630; *Old Bottle Magazine*, P. O. Box 243, Bend, OR 97701. Subsription: $19.00.

Additional Listings: See *Warman's Americana & Collectibles* for a listing of Collectors' Special Editions Whiskey Bottles.

Spruance Stanley & Co, San Francisco, CA, 1869, amber, 11½", $30.00.

Backbar
  Atherton, Julius Kessler & Co., Distillers, indented, gold paint 35.00
  G. & B, Whiskey, decanter, bulbous shape, gold letters 35.00
  Booth & Sedgewicks Cordial Gin, iron pontil, sq, green, 10″ 95.00
  Casper's, round, paneled shoulder, cobalt blue, 12″ 210.00
  Chestnut Grove, jug, pontil, amber, applied seal, 8¾″ 90.00
  Cutter, J. F., star and shield, olive green, whittled 150.00
  Davis Rye, pinch bottle, gold paint . . . 55.00
  Eagle Liqueur Distilleries, olive 50.00
  Hotaling, A. P., light amber, whittled, four pcs 50.00
  Imperial, aqua, ½ pint 20.00
  Lacey, W. A. Whiskey, stenciled, two tone, threaded stopper, 4½″ 50.00
  Ludlow, green, pint 975.00
  Macy & Jenkins, NY, handled, amber . 18.00
  Melchers Finest Canadian, Geneva, dark green 28.00
  Moonshine, cylinder, smiling moon face, amber 300.00
  Old Club Whiskey, Mach & Jenkins, NY, applied handle, amber 15.00
  Peacock, Honolulu, monogram, cylinder, light amber 65.00
  Pharazyn, H., figural, Indian warrior, yellow amber, 12¼″ 625.00
  Turner Brothers, sq, barrel, golden amber, collared mouth 100.00
  Weltys Private Stock Rye Whiskey, heavily emb, amber 25.00
  Wharton's Whiskey, Witter Glass Work Glassboro NJ, amber, 10″ 250.00

WHITE PATTERNED IRONSTONE

History: White patterned ironstone is a heavy earthenware, first patented in 1813 by Charles Mason, Staffordshire, England, using the name "Patent Ironstone China." Other English potters soon began copying this opaque, feldspathic, white china.

All white ironstone dishes first became available in the American market in the early 1840s. The first patterns had simple Gothic lines similar to the shapes used in transfer wares. Pattern shapes were named New York, Union, and Atlantic, designed to appeal to the American housewife. Motifs, such as wheat, corn, oats, and poppies, were embossed on the forms as the American western prairie influenced design. Eventually over 200 shapes and patterns, with variations of finials and handles, were made.

White patterned ironstone is identified by shape names and pattern names. Many potters only named the shape in their catalogs. Pattern names usually refer to the decoration motif.

References: Jean Wetherbee, *A Look At White Ironstone*, Wallace-Homestead, 1980; Jean Wetherbee, *A Second Look At White Ironstone*, Wallace-Homestead, 1985.

Vegetable Tureen, Wheat and Leaf, marked "Stone China, W. Taylor Hanley," 11½″ w, $75.00.

Bowl, cov, 10½″, President, Edwards, 1856 . . . . 125.00
Butter, cov, Athens, Podmore Walker, 1857 . . . . 80.00
Chamber Pot, Wheat & Blackberry, Meakin 35.00
Coffeepot, Washington Shape, John Meir 125.00
Creamer
  Fig, Davenport 60.00
  Wheat in the Meadow, Powell & Bishop, 1870 . . . . 40.00
Cup and Saucer, Oak Leaf, Pankhurst, 1863, handleless 50.00
Ewer, Scalloped Decagon, Wedgwood 140.00
Gravy, Wheat & Blackberry, Meakin . . 25.00
Pitcher, Ceres, Elsmore & Forster 115.00
Plate
  Ceres, Elsmore & Forster, 8½″ 12.00
  Gothic, Adams, 9½″ 18.00
Platter
  Columbia, 20 x 15″, octagonal 125.00
  Wheat, Meakin, 20¾ x 15⅜″ 50.00
Punch Bowl, Adriatic, scalloped edge . 335.00
Relish, Ceres, Elsmore & Forster, 1860 40.00
Soup Tureen, cov, Lily of the Valley, Shaw 225.00
Sugar, cov, Hyacinth, Wedgwood 40.00
Teapot
  Hyacinth, Wedgwood 85.00
  Niagara, Walley 110.00

Vegetable, cov

Prairie Flowers, Livesley & Powell ..	**85.00**
Ribbed Bud, J W Pankhurst	**80.00**
Wheat & Blackberry, Meakin	**80.00**

WILLOW PATTERN CHINA

History: Josiah Spode developed the first "traditional" willow pattern in 1810. The components, all motifs taken from Chinese export china, are: a willow tree, "apple" tree, two pagodas, fence, two birds, and a three figures crossing a bridge. The legend, in its many versions, is an English invention based on the design components.

By 1830, there were over 200-plus makers of willow pattern china in England. The pattern has remained in continuous production. Some of the English firms that still produce willow pattern china are: Burleigh, Johnson Bros. (Wedgwood Group), Royal Doulton's continuation of the Booths pattern, and Wedgwood.

By the end of the 19th century, pattern production spread to France, Germany, Holland, Ireland, Sweden, and the United States. In the United States, Buffalo Pottery made the first willow pattern beginning in 1902. Many other companies followed, developing willow variants using rubber-stamp simplified patterns as well as overglaze decals. The largest American manufacturers of the traditional willow pattern were Royal China and Homer Laughlin, usually preferred because it is dated. Shenango pieces are most desired among restaurant quality ware.

Japan began producing large quantities of willow pattern china in the early 20th century. Noritake began about 1902. Its early pieces used a Nippon "Royal Sometuke" mark. Most Japanese pieces are porous earthenware with dark blue pattern using the tradition willow design, usually with no inner border. Noritake did put the pattern on china bodies. Unusual forms include salt and pepper shakers, ¼ lb. butter dishes, and canisters. "Occupied Japan" may add a small percentage to the value of common table wares. Maruta and Moriyama marked pieces are especially valued. The most sought after Japanese willow is the fine quality NKT Co. ironstone with a copy of the old Booths pattern. Recent Japanese willow is a paler shade of blue on a porcelain body.

The most common dinnerware color is blue. However, pieces can also be found in black (with clear glaze or mustard-color glaze by Royal Doulton), brown, green, mulberry, pink (red), and polychrome. Although colors other than blue are hard to find, there is less demand; thus, prices may not necessarily be higher.

The popularity of the willow design has resulted in a large variety of willow-decorated products: candles, fabric, glass, graniteware, linens, needlepoint, plastic, tinware, stationery, watches, and wall coverings. All this material has collectible value.

References: Mary Frank Gaston, *Blue Willow: An Identification & Value Guide*, Collector Books, 1983 (revised prices, 1986); Veryl Marie Worth and Louise M. Loehr, *Willow Pattern China: Collector's Guide, 3rd Edition*, H. S. Worth Co, 1986.

Periodicals: *American Willow Report*, 1733 Chase Street, Cincinnati, OH 45223. Subscription: $10.00; *Willow Transfer Quarterly*, 39 Medhurst Road, Toronto, Canada M4B 1B2. Subscription: $15.00.

Reproduction Alert: The Scio Pottery, Scio, Ohio, currently manufactures a willow pattern set sold in variety stores. The pieces have no marks or back stamps, and the transfer is of poor quality. The plates are flatter in shape than those of other manufacturers.

Additional Listings: Buffalo Pottery. See *Warman's Americana & Collectibles* for more examples.

Advisor: Connie Rogers.

Egg Cup, marked "Allertons, Made in England," 4¼" h, **$25.00.**

Cake Stand, porcelain, Royal Worcester	**225.00**
Child's Set, Japanese, 15 pcs	**150.00**
Cup and Saucer	
Booths	**25.00**
Homer Laughlin	**6.00**
Japanese, NKT Co., Booths copy ..	**16.00**
Shenango	**12.00**
Pepper Pot, 19th C	**115.00**
Pitcher, English, 1 qt	**55.00**
Plate, 10"	
Johnson Bros	**15.00**
Royal China	**8.00**
Royal Doulton, gold trim	**55.00**
Platter	
Allerton, 9 x 12"	**45.00**
Homer Laughlin, 13" d	**15.00**
Syrup Jug, pewter lid, Royal Doulton .	**125.00**

Teapot
Homer Laughlin	35.00
Johnson Bros	55.00

Tumbler, glass, frosted 10.00

WOODENWARE

History: Many utilitarian household objects and farm implements were made of wood. Although they were used heavily, these implements were made of the strongest woods and well taken care of by their owners.

This category serves as a catch-all for wood objects which do not fit into other categories.

Additional Listings: See *Warman's Americana & Collectibles* for more examples.

**Bowl, burl, early 19th C, 16¾ x 5¾",
$600.00.**

Apple Box, 8½" octagonal, poplar, dark finish 85.00
Ashtray, 32" h, silhouette, bellboy, orig polychrome paint, emb tin ashtray .. 85.00
Baker's Peal, 56½" l, dark brown patina 115.00
Bible Box, 17¼ x 21", 8" h, pine, dovetailed, lid molding, orig wrought iron strap hinges, almond shaped escutcheon, refinished 75.00
Bowl, 6" d, 1⅝" h, patina 40.00
Box, 11" w, hanging, scalloped rim and crest, divided int., worn orig red paint, black edge striping 190.00
Bucket, metal bands, wire bail handle, worn yellow paint 50.00
Butter Print, 4" d, deeply carved fleur-de-lis design, cased 55.00
Candle Box, 16" l, walnut, dovetailed, dark brown finish, sliding lid 100.00
Cookie Board, 5½ x 9½", two circular flower designs on one side, recessed polka dots in rect on other 135.00
Cranberry Scoop, 16¾" l, fish tail handle, natural patina 120.00
Dough Box, 34½" l, pine and poplar, dovetailed, worn red paint 200.00

Grain Measure, 15¼" d, 8¼" h, bent-wood, natural patina 55.00
Hobby Horse, 40" l, two cut out silhouettes, dapple gray paint, red rockers, harness detail, 20th C 155.00
Inkwell, 4⅝" d, turned, orig brown sponging, stenciled gilt dec, two glass inserts 45.00
Jar, 5¾" h, turned, scrubbed white finish, Pease 140.00
Knife Box, 9¼ x 14¼", mahogany, dovetailed, orig brass handle 120.00
Kraut Cutter, 14½ x 51", dovetailed hopper, pine and poplar, worn scrubbed finish 100.00
Lamp
Kerosene, turned foot, stem, and font, brass collar 85.00
Table, 19" h, barrel shaped canteen, blue, turned wood base, red, white, and blue striped wool homespun shade 275.00
Nut Cracker, 8½" l, carved, ram with glass eyes 65.00
Reel, 28" d, 39" l, curly maple, oak, and other wood, worn patina 115.00
Salt Box, 12½ x 20", hanging, pine, shaped crest with cross hatched design, concentric circles in top ears, wrought iron nail construction, dark finish 145.00
Spice Box, 8½" l, dovetailed, six section int., shaped sliding lid, initials "H.P." 200.00
Toby Jug, 6⅛" h, carved, orig polychrome paint 500.00
Wash Board, 13½ x 7", sewer pipe tile insert 175.00

WORLD'S FAIRS AND EXPOSITIONS

History: The Great Exhibition of 1851 in London marked the beginning of the World's Fair and Exposition movement. The fairs generally feature exhibitions from nations around the world displaying the best of their industrial and scientific achievements.

Many important technological advances have been introduced at world's fairs. Examples include the airplane, telephone, and electric lights. The ice cream cone, hot dog, and iced tea were products of vendors at fairs. Art movements often were closely connected to fairs with the Paris Exhibition of 1900 generally considered to have assembled the best of the works of the Art Nouveau artists.

References: Kurt Krueger, *Meet Me In St. Louis—The Exonumia Of The 1904 World's Fair*, Krause Publications, 1979; Howard Rossen and John Kaduck, *Columbia World's Fair Collectibles*, Wallace-Homestead, 1976, revised price list 1982.

Collectors' Clubs: Expo Collectors–Historians Organizations, 1436 Killarney Avenue, Los Angeles, CA 90065; World's Fair Collectors Society, Inc., P. O. Box 20806, Sarasota, FL 34238.

1876, Philadelphia, Centennial
Bell, hand, brass replica of Liberty Bell, undated, adv inscription "Chew Liberty Bell Tobacco Mfg By Rucker, Witten And Morris," orig brass clapper, 2½" d at bottom, 3½" h 65.00
Pin, 1 x 1¼", emb brass, picture of Washington in center of Liberty Bell, inscription "1776 Centennial 1876" 30.00
Worker's Passbook, 3 x 4", stiff paper, 4 pgs, black and white photo of employee 65.00

1893, Columbian Exposition, change purse, white metal (tin) top, roll bars to allow change to enter, leather base, 2¾ x 1⅞", $50.00.

1893, Chicago, Columbian Exposition
Advertising Trade Card, oversized, Clark's O.N.T. Thread, Electrical Building 8.00
Badge, 1½ x 2½", emb brass link badge, Columbus on U.S. shore with Indians, "400th Anniversary/ Discovery Of America/Oct. 1892" . 60.00
Fan, 12¼" h, 23" w opened, full color illus of fairgrounds, mounted on flat wood swivel pieces 55.00
Paperweight, 3", domed, Art Building illus 30.00
Sheet Music, *Columbus or World's Fair Grand March*, Frank Drayton, National Music Co, Chicago, 1892 15.00
1901, Buffalo, Pan-American Exposition
Pin, pan shape, 2¼" l, diecut litho tin, "C Klinck's Daisy Leaf Lard," red,

white, and blue, full color lard pail in center 27.50
Matchsafe, 1½ x 2½", silvered brass, ladies outstreached arms as crest of Niagara Falls, Manufacturers & Liberal Arts Building on back 70.00
1904, St. Louis, Louisiana Purchase Exposition
Paperweight, 3", domed, sepia photo of Cascades Building and lagoon . 35.00
Pin, Heinz Pickle, 1¼" l, composition, "Heinz" in raised letters on one side, "St. Louis '04" on other, brass hanging loop 17.50
Vase, 5" h, irid blue and purple, double handles, Electricity Bldg picture, numbered 45.00
1915, San Francisco, Panama-Pacific International Exposition
Fob, 1½", dark-finish silvered brass, inscribed "Completion Of The Panama Canal 1915," title, and date of Exposition 35.00
Thermos, 14", Panama Pacific Expo, engraved 120.00
1933, Chicago, Century of Progress
Bottle Opener, 5" h, figural, copper-colored metal, mythological Egyptian lady and American Legion logo, Fort Dearborn exhibit and "Chicago 1933" on back 25.00
Marble Bag, 5" h, "Master Marbles," tan and dark suede leather bag, red, blue, and green, tinted illus, white lettering, Grenadier soldier and marble player on each side of small building composed of marbles, bag nearly filled with glass marbles 65.00
Puzzle, jigsaw, 11 x 16", "H. M. Pettit Approved Bird's Eye View Of A Century Of Progress," 8½ x 8½ x 1" box 20.00
Tie Clip, 1 x 2", silvered metal, diecut, silver and black enamel of fair building 20.00
Watch Box, 2¼ x 2½ x ¾", for "Chicago World's Fair Watch #9531," black and white illus of early fort on lid 60.00
1939, New York, New York World's Fair
Compact, 3" d, light colored wood, hinged lid with brass border, full color celluloid scene of Hall of Communications 25.00
Flashlight, 3½" d, 2" silvered steel circular shape, foldup 3½" d ball, rev with blue-enameled design of Trylon and Perisphere, official "NYWF copyright" license, two "C" batteries 125.00
Jewelry Box, wood, 7½ x 9½ x 3",

heavily textured black finish, textured Art Deco design of Trylon and Perisphere on lid, floral paper-lined int. 75.00

Pencil, mechanical, 10½" l, ¾" d, gold colored wood barrel, cartoon illus of person with camera clinging to Trylon and lady sitting on Perisphere, marked "N.Y.W.F. Eagle Pencil Co.," rubber eraser 30.00

1939, San Francisco, Golden Gate International Exposition

Guide Book, 5½ x 8", soft cover, 118 pgs, 16 x 19" foldout map, diecut tab index, Junket Dessert adv on back cov 20.00

Scarf, 27½ x 29", linen-like, light blue and brown illus, off-white ground .   40.00

1964, New York, New York World's Fair

Jewelry Box, 3½ x 5½ x 2½", pirate's treasure chest, metal, medium gloss black enamel, silver-brass plate on lid with title of fair and illus of Heliport, Swiss Sky Ride, U.S. Pavilion, Monorail, and Unisphere   12.00

Record, *The Triumph Of Man*, 33⅓ rpm, 7" sq cardboard jacket, Traveler's Insurance Companies giveaway 8.00

YELLOW WARE

History: Yellow ware is a heavy earthenware of differing weight and strength which varies in color from a rich pumpkin to lighter shades which are more tan than yellow. Although plates, nappies, and custard cups are found, kitchen bowls and other cooking utensils are most prevalent.

The first American yellow ware was produced at Bennington, Vermont. English yellow ware has additional ingredients which make its body much harder. Derbyshire and Sharp's were foremost among the English manufacturers.

Bank, 5" l, pig, green and amber 45.00
Bowl
  8⅜" d, 4¼" h, blue and brown sponge

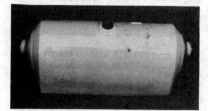

Foot Warmer, 14" l, $175.00.

spatter with a touch of red, minor wear 45.00

12¼" d, 6½" h, mixing, emb ext., brown bands, faint label on bottom   35.00

Creamer, 4½" h, green and brown sponging 75.00

Crock, 5⅞" d, 4¼" h, emb "Butter," oval splotches of brown 165.00

Cuspidor, 5 x 7½", green, blue, and tan sponge glaze 60.00

Figure, lamb, 16" l, worn white paint, ears missing 500.00

Jar
  6" h, 7" d, white band, dark brown stripes, blue seaweed dec 700.00
  8¾" h, brown slip dec 525.00
  12¼" h, brown running glaze, chipped lid 85.00

Mug
  3¼", brown polka dots 675.00
  3⅞", white band with brown stripes .   115.00
  4", white band with brown stripes and blue seaweed dec, Liverpool, OH   325.00

Pitcher
  4½" h, emb ribs, rect area with transfer label "Equity Elev. & Trading Co...Whitman, ND," green and brown sponging 45.00
  7⅜" h, keg shape, emb staves, green and brown sponging 35.00

Salt Box, 6" d, emb peacocks, brown sponged glaze 150.00

ZANE WARE
MADE IN U.S.A.

ZANE POTTERY

History: In 1921 Adam Reed and Harry McClelland bought the Peters and Reed Pottery in Zanesville, Ohio. The firm continued production of garden wares and introduced several new art lines: "Sheen," "Powder Blue," "Crystalline," and "Drip." The factory was sold in 1941 to Lawton Gonder.

Additonal Listings: Gonder and Peters and Reed.

Bowl
  5¼", Wilse Blue, dragonfly dec 50.00
  6½", blue, marked "Zanesware" . . .   25.00

Jardiniere, 34" h, green matte glaze, artist sgd "Frank Ferreu" 300.00

Vase
  5", green, cobalt blue drip glaze . . .   25.00

Wall Pocket, Moss Aztec, 8¼″ l, $45.00.

8⅝″, Landsun Drip, light yellow-
green, taupe drip dec **50.00**

LA MORO
ZANESVILLE POTTERY

History: Zanesville Art Pottery, one of several
potteries located in Zanesville, Ohio, began production in 1900. A line of utilitarian products was
first produced. Art pottery was introduced shortly
thereafter. The major line was La Moro which was
hand painted and decorated under glaze. The impressed block print mark La Moro appears on the
high glazed and matte glazed decorated ware. The
firm was bought by S. A. Weller in 1920 and became known as Weller Plant No. 3.

References: Louise and Evan Purviance and
Norris F. Schneider, *Zanesville Art Pottery In Color*,
Mid-America Book Company, 1968; Evan and
Louise Purviance, *Zanesville Art Tile In Color*, Wal-
lace-Homestead Book Co., 1972.

**Teapot, souvenir type, dark green,
marked "TYCES Pottery, Zanesville,
Ohio," 2¾″ h, $40.00.**

Jardiniere, 8¼″ h, cream to light amber peony blossoms, ruffled rim, shaded brown ground	**75.00**
Plate, 4½″, applied floral dec	**25.00**
Teapot, 2¾″ h, souvenir, dark green, marked "Tyces Pottery/Zanesville/ Ohio"	**40.00**
Tile, 6 x 18″, woman, blowing horn, cream ground	**275.00**
Vase, 7″, pansy dec, olive to brown glaze, marked "La Moro"	**125.00**

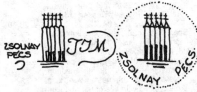

ZSOLNAY POTTERY

History: Vilmos Zsolnay (1828–1900) assumed
control of his brother's factory in Pécs, Hungary,
in the mid-19th century. In 1899 Miklos, Vilmos's
son, became manager. The firm still produces ceramic ware.

The early wares are highly ornamental, glazed,
and have a cream color ground. "Eosin" glaze, a
deep rich play of colors reminiscent of Tiffany's
iridescent wares, received a gold medal at the
1900 Paris exhibition. Zsolnay Art Nouveau pieces
show great creativity.

Originally no trademark was used. Beginning in
1878 a blue mark depicting the five towers of the
cathedral at Pécs was used. The initials "TJM"
represent the names of Miklos's three children.

Zsolnay's recent series of iridescent glazed figurines, which initially were inexpensive, now are
being sought by collectors and show a steady increase in value.

Reference: Susan and Al Bagdade, *Warman's
English & Continental Pottery & Porcelain, 1st Edition*, Warman Publishing Co., Inc., 1987.

Bowl	
4½ x 3″, multicolored, filigree, ftd ..	**75.00**
10″ d, carved, cherubs dec, curved leaf handles	**500.00**
Centerpiece, 16 x 4 x 5″, crescent shape, double walled, reticulated, irid florals, gold trim	**285.00**
Dish, 8½″, fan shape, rolled over edge, reticulated	**175.00**
Figure	
4″, kitten, irid green	**75.00**
5″, German Shepherd, irid	**50.00**

Pitcher, 9″ h, pink cherub design, c1870   **100.00**
Plate
   8½″ d, shell shape, reticulated, red
     and gold flowers, beige ground,
     steeple mark **180.00**
   10¾″, Persian type design, red, blue,
     and silver luster **300.00**
Ring Tree, 3½″, irid gold **75.00**
Vase
   5½″ h, applied simulated stone with
     thumbprints, irid red glaze **155.00**
   6″, double walled, reticulated, pastels,
     marked **135.00**
   9¾″, square shape, reticulated, blue,
     orchid, tan, and cream glaze flow-
     ers and leaves, two upright han-
     dles, four claw feet **550.00**

**Coffeepot, yellow ground, multico-
lored, Zsolnay castle mark, 9½″ h,
$300.00.**

PHOTO CREDITS

We wish to thank those who permitted us to photograph objects in their possession. Unfortunately, we are unable to identify the sources for all of our pictures; nevertheless, we are deeply appreciative for all who contributed to this and past editions, and to the editions of *Warman's Americana & Collectibles*.

California: Carlsbad, Dan Golden; Moor Park, Tony and Jackie Anello; Oceanside, Lois Misiewicz; San Francisco, Butterfields; Santa Ana, Evalene Pulati. **Connecticut**: New Canaan, Mildred Fishman; Sandy Hook, Bea Morgan; Stamford, Donna Schilero, West Hartford, Arnold Chase; Westport, Tom Gallagher; Woodbury, Daria of Woodbury; Woodstock, David and Linda Arman. **Delaware**: Lewes, The Price's, Sea Gert Antiques. **Florida**: Cape Coral, The Calico Cat, Elizabeth Clancey, The Collector's Den, Sandra Martz, Country Closet Antiques; Clearwater Beach, Bill Wheeler, The Oar House; Ft. Myers, Ft. Myers Antique Mall, Mina Tinsley, Things Unlimited; Hollywood, Cynthia and Joseph Klein; Miami Beach, Estelle Zalkin; Orlando, Peg Harrison, Harrison's Antiques. **Georgia**: Atlanta, Walter Glenn, Geode Ltd., Jim Marin, Art Deco Atlanta. **Illinois**: Arlington Heights, T. Johnson; Chicago, Dick and Bindy Bitterman, Eureka! Antiques and Collectibles; Lislie, Susan Nicholson; Mapleton, White's Antiques and Furniture Finishing; Monmouth, David and Betty Hallam; Northbrook, Al and Susan Bagdade, Norman Rockwell Museum; Peotone, Kathy Wojciechowski.

Iowa: Spencer, Paul and Paula Brenner; Spirit Lake, Gaylord and Margaret Franken. **Maine**: Kennebunk, Richard W. Oliver Auction & Art Gallery; Oxford, Oxford Common; Topsham, Allan and Helen Smith, The Country House. **Maryland**: Laurel, Ken Cohen, Julie Rich; Temple Hills, John Rosenberg; **Massachusetts**: Cambridge, Stan Tillotson; Hyannis Port, Richard A. Bourne, Inc.; Winchester, Lorry and Bruce Hanes, Dad's Follies; Worcester, Ralph R. Saarinen. **Michigan**: Monroe, Herb and Joyce Krueger, Mostly Majolica; Utica, Virgil Rogers and David Graves, Avant-Garde; West Bloomfield, Joan Collett Oates. **Missouri**: Sedalia, Crystal and Leyland Payton.

New Hampshire: Peterborough, Lee and Rally Dennis; Salem, Bea and Bill Laycock, B & B Antiques & Collectibles. **New Jersey**: Bellmawr, Angie Ricciaardi Antiques; Demarest, Mimi Rudnick, The Salt Lady Antiques; Hackensack, Roz Albert; Madison, Don Fiore, The Toy Man; Magnolia, Carol Pollock, Custom Covers; Montclair, Susan Morse; Moorestown, Cindy and James Townes, Ladybug's Cupboard; Morris Plains, Elyce Litts; New Egypt, Red Barn Antiques; Old Bridge, Sue Theurich, Respectable Collectables; Paterson, Edward W. Leach; Short Hills, Cynthia Klein, Joseph Klein, C. J. K. Kollectibles; Stewartsville, Marcia and Bob Weissman, Neat Olde Things; Toms River, Shelley, Norman and Phyllis Galinkin; West Orange, Barbara and Melvin Alpren; Woodcliff Lake, Joan Raines Antiques.

New York: Auburn, Lower Lake Collectibles; Carmel, Bob Cahn, The Primitive Man; Elmsford, Gerald and Carol Newman; Fishkill, Robert A. Doyle, Livingston, Langes Steinworld; New Paltz, Charlotte and Larry Settle; New York, John High; Queens, Flamingoes; Valley Stream, Craig Dinner; Webster, Richard and Joan Randles, From The Cutter's Wheel. **North Carolina**: Chapel Hill, Alda Horner, Whitehall Shop. **Ohio**: Akron, Betty Franks; Beachwood, Rita Orons; Canton, Lewis Bettinger; Cincinnati, Connie Rogers; Newton Falls, Bob and Kathy Wujcik; Novelty, Peggy Bialosky; Urbana, Parker's Antiques. **Oklahoma**: Tulsa, Phyllis Bess.

Pennsylvania: Adamstown, Dottie Freeman and Allan Teal; Allentown, The Borgmans, Wanamaker R.R. Depot Antiques, LeFevre's Antiques, Jim Lo Antiques, Phyllis and Alvin Kahn, The Pen Man's Antiques, Arlene Rabin, Edna Stauffer, Today & Yesterday; Bath, Roy Repsher; Bethlehem, Doris M. Squyres; Cabot, Clair Bargerstock; Coatesville, Chet Ramsay Antiques; Cogan Station, Roan Bros. Auction Gallery; Coopersburg, Neil and Clodogh Wotring; Danville, Lissa L. Bryan-Smith, Dick Smith, Holiday Antiques; Eagleville, Tyler's Antiques; Easton, Harold Mellor, Coach and Four Antiques; Elkins Park, Rose Sill, The Window Sill; Emmaus, Anna M. Benner; Glen Rock, Ron Lieberman; Johnstown, Precious Metals Co; Lampeter, James S. Maxwell, Jr.; Leola, R. C. Lauchnor's Collectables; Lititz, Doug Flynn and Al Bolton, Holloway House; Montgomeryville, Clarence and Betty Maier, Burmese

Cruet; Montoursville, M. Jeanne Foust, Jeanne's Glass House; New Freedom, George Theofiles, Miscellaneous Man; New Hope, Debby Bogdan, Ferry Hill, Ted and Linda Freed; Northampton, David and Sue Irons, Irons Antiques; Oley, Mrs. Lena Eyrich; Orefield, Gloria Burkos, Gloria's Collectibles; Philadelphia, Shelly Hoffman, Ed Kelberg, Marcy Kula, Ed Volkrecht, Ed's Antiques, Inc., Murray and Selma Petersons; Pittsburgh, Regis and Mary Ferson, Edward Grzybowski; Pottsville, George and Tedi Hahn, Doorway To Glass; Quakertown, Doris Castellon, Brick House Antiques, Mary Webber, Webber's Antiques; Schnecksville, David Koch; Whitehall, Herb and Nancy Hallman, The Churn Antiques; Wilkes-Barre, Al Sallitt Antiques, Golden Webb Antiques; Williamsport, Michael Rath; Yardley, Ellie Archer; York, Lookenbill's Antiques.

South Dakota: Huron, Joan Hull. **Tennessee**: Elaine J. Luartes, Athena Antiques. **Texas**: Dallas, Ted Birbilis; Euless, The Stevensons. **Vermont**: Cavendish, Henry and Doris Sigourney, Sigourney's Antiques. **Virginia**: Portsmouth, Whitney LeCompte. **Virginia**: Arlington, Carolyn Smith; Crozet, Betty L. Loba, Rose Valley Antiques; Hopewell, Carolyn R. Morris, Yestermorrow's Collectibles and More; Portsmouth, Whitney Le Compte; Radford, Roy M. Collins. **Wisconsin**: Kaukauna, Ferill J. Rice.

INDEX

Year After Year Collectors Ask:
"What does Warman's say?"

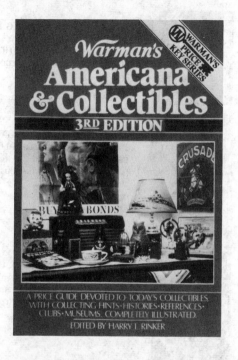

REMEMBER WHEN

. . . you traded bubble
gum cards

. . . sent away for a
radio premium

. . . bought your first
'Batman and Robin'
comic book.

All of these items and
thousands more are part
of the antiques market's
most thriving new field
—collectibles.

Warman's Americana & Collectibles documents under one cover the broad
aspects of this key antiques field. But it is more than a price guide:
- Collecting Hints for every category
- Histories
- References, periodicals and collectors clubs
- 27,000 items, 250 categories and 500 photographs

Available in leading book stores or use the convenient order form
in this book.

Warman price guides are available from leading book stores and antiques booksellers, or they can be ordered directly from the publisher.

☐ **WARMAN'S ANTIQUES AND THEIR PRICES, 22nd Ed.,** edited by Harry L. Rinker. The standard price reference for the general antiques field. 50,000 items, 1,000 photos and illustrations, histories, references, 100's of American Pattern Glass designs, fully indexed. April 1988.   Paperback **$11.95**

☐ **WARMAN'S ENGLISH & CONTINENTAL POTTERY & PORCELAIN** by Susan and Al Bagdade. A price and reference guide to the entire field. 200 makers, 1,000's of items, 600 + photos and factory marks, plus histories, references and collecting hints..   Paperback **$18.95**

☐ **WARMAN'S AMERICANA & COLLECTIBLES, 3rd Ed.,** edited by Harry L. Rinker. An all new edition of the best-selling price guide and reference in the collectibles field. 560 pages, 600 photos, 25,000 prices, histories, references, clubs. Fully indexed. January 1988.   Paperback **$13.95**

☐ **WARMAN'S ANTIQUE AMERICAN GAMES: 1840-1940, 1st Ed.** By Lee Dennis. A new comprehensive record and price guide of 800 games, 100 companies; 725 photos, fully indexed. The only book to cover this field so extensively.   Paperback **$14.95**